Effective
Fund-Raising Management

Effective
Fund-Raising Management

Kathleen S. Kelly
University of Southwestern Louisiana

IEA **LAWRENCE ERLBAUM ASSOCIATES, PUBLISHERS**
1998 Mahwah, New Jersey **London**

For George, Too

Lawrence Erlbaum Associates, Inc., Publishers
10 Industrial Avenue
Mahwah, New Jersey 07430

Library of Congress Cataloging-in-Publication-Data

Kelly, Kathleen S.
Effective fund-raising management / Kathleen S. Kelly.
     p. cm.
    Includes bibliographical references and index.
    ISBN 0-8058-1321-7 (alk. paper). — ISBN 0-8058-
2010-8 (alk. paper)
      1. Fund raising—United States—Management.
    2. Charities—United States—Finance—Management.
    3. Nonprofit organizations—United States—Finance—
Management.   I. Title.
    HV41.9.U5K44   1998
    361.7'068'1—dc20   96-8095
                                          CIP

Books published by Lawrence Erlbaum Associates are printed
on acid-free paper, and their bindings are chosen for strength
and durability.

Printed in the United States of America
10 9 8 7 6 5 4 3 2 1

Contents

Foreword   **xi**

Series Editor's Preface   **xiii**

Preface   **xv**

1   The Function of Fund Raising: Introduction and Overview   **1**
of the Book

     Integrating Practice and Theory: A Text   2

     Definitions and Presuppositions   5

     Overview of the Book   15

     Missing: Women, Minorities, and an International
     Perspective   34

     Suggested Readings   36

Part I: The Practice:
Parameters, Practitioners, and Professionalism

2   Parameters of Fund Raising   **39**

     America's Philanthropic Tradition   39

     Donor Motivations   43

     The Nonprofit Sector   52

     The Charitable Subsector   58

     Suggested Readings   68

3   Fund-Raising Practitioners   **69**

     Number and Scope   69

Job Titles 70
Types of Organizational Employers 72
Characteristics 80
Feminization of Fund Raising 89
Suggested Readings 102

4 Professionalism of Fund Raising   103
Criteria of a Profession 103
Public Relations: An Alternate Route 124
Long-Standing Linkages 129
Suggested Readings 131

Part II: The Principles:
Historical, Organizational, Legal, Ethical, and Theoretical

5 Historical Context of Fund Raising   135
One Good Book 135
Evolution of the Fund-Raising Function 138
Four Models of Fund Raising 155
Suggested Readings 173

6 Organizational Context of Fund Raising   174
Practice of the Older Models 174
Empirical Test of the Models 179
Explanatory Study of the Models 184
Organizational Roles of Fund Raisers 192
Fund Raisers as Staff Managers 200
Fund Raisers as Department Managers 209
Suggested Readings 218

7 Legal Context of Fund Raising   219
Call For Action 219
Privileged Status 224
Key Concepts and Actors 226
Forces Driving Fund-Raising Regulation 244
Overview of IRS Compliance 259
Suggested Readings 270

8   Ethical Context of Fund Raising   **271**
        Organizations and Ethics   272
        Crisis of Credibility   274
        Solicitation Firms   276
        Joint Ventures   294
        Presuppositions and Ethics   304
        United Way and Press Agentry Fund Raising   308
        Suggested Readings   323

9   Theoretical Context of Fund Raising   **324**
        Systems Theory   324
        Definitions and Philanthropy Theories   327
        Stakeholders and Boundary Spanners   336
        Autonomy and Accountability   340
        Theory of Magic Buttons   350
        Coorientation Theory   357
        Situational Theory of Publics   362
        Fund-Raising Effects   369
        Integrated Relationship Management   380
        Suggested Readings   387

                Part III: The Process, Programs, and Publics

10 The Fund-Raising Process   **391**
        ROPES and Practitioner Descriptions   392
        Strategic Planning   394
        Research   402
        Objectives   412
        Programming   416
        Evaluation   427
        Stewardship   432
        Testing ROPES   442
        Suggesting Readings   443

11 Fund-Raising Programs: Annual Giving   **444**
        Role of Volunteers   444
        Principle of Proportionate Giving   450

Different Forms of Gifts 453
Annual Giving 455
Suggested Readings 474

12 Fund-Raising Programs: Major Gifts   **475**
Largest Gifts 476
Largest Returned Gift 479
Endowments 482
Negotiation 487
Process 491
Sexual Harassment 495
Suggested Readings 501

13 Fund-Raising Programs: Planned Giving   **502**
Unprecedented Opportunity 504
Threshold of Knowledge 505
Commensurate Scope 512
Protection, Not Exploitation 517
Charitable Bequests 521
Life Income Agreements 524
Other Vehicles 531
ROPES Process 535
Learning and Research Opportunities 541
Suggested Readings 542

14 Fund-Raising Programs: Capital Campaigns   **544**
Evolving Purpose 544
Underlying Motivations 548
Effectiveness 558
Replacing the Campaign 567
Suggested Readings 569

15 Donor Publics: Individuals, Corporations, and Foundations   **570**
Foundation Donors 570
Corporate Donors 590
Individual Donors 611
Suggested Readings 621

CONTENTS

References   **622**

Author Index   **649**

Subject Index   **657**

Foreword

With this volume, Kathleen Kelly, who long ago staked out fund raising as her scholarly niche, brings definition and substance to this century-old but still amorphous vocation. The first textbook designed to support academic courses on fund raising—now taught in some 60 colleges and universities—*Effective Fund-Raising Management* will do much to advance the ethics and expertise of tomorrow's army of fund raisers. It will be equally valuable for today's professionals who, for the most part, have risen to their positions by serving an apprenticeship under others who came up the same way.

It is somewhat of a puzzle that it has taken this long to develop a sound guide to the management of fund raising. Although Kelly's book represents a great deal of original research, its extensive references and the suggested readings demonstrate that scholarship and commentary on philanthropy and fund raising have ballooned since historian Merle Curti's pioneering Philanthropy Project of the early 1960s. Curti and his colleagues rescued this field from the limbo of scholarly neglect. My history of U.S. fund raising was one of the results of that project, financed by the Ford Foundation.

Kelly's text is a successful blend of practical "know how" and the theory that undergirds it. Divided into three parts—the Practice, the Principles, and the Process, Programs, and Publics—it is an all-encompassing work. Some students are likely to question the strong emphasis on theory in a textbook, but we older hands know that theory is the most practical contribution an author can make to any field.

A major contribution of the text is to define and delineate the fund-raising process. Using the acronym ROPES, Kelly sees the process as starting with Research, defining Objectives, outlining Programming from this base, Evaluating the work done, and finally assessing the Stewardship of the funds raised. In time, I predict that this will become the standard operating procedure of fund raising.

Two other major contributions of this volume are the timely chapters on the legal and ethical contexts of fund raising. Underscore timely because 1997 brought us an unceasing parade of headlines and endless investigations of alleged illegal, improper, or at the least, unethical fund raising. The accumulation of scandals and the abuses of paid solicitors have long created a certain amount of mistrust of this vocation and of the organizations it supports. This is not new. I devoted a chapter to "The Cheats in Fund Raising" in my 1965 history. The situation has only grown worse in recent years.

In 1993, a Gallup national poll found 74% of respondents thought that mandatory regulation of charitable organizations was needed.

Kelly candidly details many recent scandals and illegalities that have spawned this public demand for more regulation and fewer tax benefits in the philanthropy of our nation. Among the cases she cites are United Way of America, Covenant House, and the Foundation for New Era Philanthropy. Another source of public distrust is the millions of dollars fleeced from a generous but gullible American public in fund drives conducted by paid solicitors. In these scams, the donors' dollars go not to a good cause, but to line the pockets of shrewd, unscrupulous promoters. Honesty cannot be legislated, nor can laws fully protect citizens against schemers. The U.S. Supreme Court has repeatedly ruled that fund raising is free speech, and thus is protected by the Constitution. The burden, as Kelly argues, rests with fund raisers and other managers of charitable organizations. They must accept and act on the premise that loss in public support ultimately leads to demands for governmental action.

This brings us to the author's excellent chapter on the laws and regulations that govern fund raising. Practitioners, especially, will find this chapter helpful because most professionals are not lawyers or accountants, yet they cannot carry on their jobs without knowledge of a maze of laws and regulations—federal, state, and local. In fact, almost all aspects of fund raising must deal with these complexities. Kelly describes the regulatory environment as "stormy," a climate created in part by continuing scams. Indeed, many of the laws are directed at the flock of paid solicitors who hurt legitimate organizations, which ties the subject of ethics to legal concerns. As regulations multiply and the demands for removal of tax benefits become more strident, current and future fund raisers need the careful schooling that this author provides.

Organized fund raising dates from the early 1900s. The work of such pioneers as Bishop William Lawrence, Charles Sumner Ward, and Lyman Pierce has evolved into a vocation that raises more than $150 billion annually to support the nation's voluntary agencies. And well that it has. These agencies, made possible by fund raising, are essential to the well-being of our democratic, pluralistic society—meeting needs that government cannot or will not meet. Therefore, it is crucial that fund raisers be better equipped to exercise more precision and professionalism in their work. Kelly's book provides today's and tomorrow's fund raisers with the competence and ethical standards they require to meet the challenges of the 21st century.

This text represents a giant leap forward, and I believe that it will define the field much in the same way that its elderly cousin, *Effective Public Relations*, defined the principles and practices of public relations in this century. *Effective Fund-Raising Management* is a seminal book that will bring welcomed professionalism, competence, and ethical behavior to this vital democratic calling. I am pleased to launch it on this laudable mission.

—Scott M. Cutlip
University of Georgia

Series Editor's Preface

Kathleen Kelly's second contribution to the Lawrence Erlbaum Associates Public Relations Subseries is a major contribution to the literature on public relations and to fund raising as a specialization in public relations. Her first book, *Fund Raising and Public Relations: A Critical Analysis*, traced the historical roots of fund raising and developed a critical-ethical theory centered on the effects of fund raising for the autonomy of an organization. *Effective Fund-Raising Management* moves Kelly's work forward into the normative domain, of *how to* practice and manage fund raising both effectively and ethically.

Kelly clearly establishes fund raising as a public relations function, because non-profit organizations use fund-raising procedures and techniques to build relationships with a strategic set of stakeholder publics: their donors. She also establishes a scholarly and theoretical framework for the professional practice of fund raising—the major purpose of and the integrating thread for the Public Relations Subseries. True professions base practice on an intellectual body of knowledge, and—for the first time—Kelly has written a textbook on how to practice fund raising that is based on such a body of knowledge.

I believe that *Effective Fund-Raising Management* makes available an outstanding textbook for existing courses on fund raising. In addition, I hope that it will stimulate the development of new courses in fund raising in universities that have doubted the intellectual content of the discipline. At the same time, professional fund raisers will learn a great deal from reading the book. The techniques should be familiar to them, but the theoretical grounding for these techniques should provide a framework both for understanding why their own work sometimes is more effective and ethical than at other times and for explaining their work to administrators and critics who question the appropriateness of what fund raisers do.

I welcome this book to the subseries and look forward eagerly to the impact I believe it will have on the discipline of fund raising and its family discipline of public relations.

—*James E. Grunig*
University of Maryland

Preface

Among the hardest questions scholars ask themselves is whether their work has "yielded knowledge that is in any sense usable; if so, to whom and how?" (Boris, Fox, & Hall, 1993, p. 219). P. D. Hall framed the questions for those studying philanthropy and nonprofit management by asking what contributions, if any, their research has made "to scholarship (by enriching the viewpoints of mainstream disciplines), to practice (by adding to the competence and self-awareness of nonprofit managers), and to public policy (by leading legislators, regulators, and jurists to understand the role of nonprofit enterprise)" (p. 219). The critical issue of *usable knowledge* guided the writing of this first textbook on fund raising.

Throughout my academic career, I have purposefully integrated my work in the mainstream discipline of communication, specifically, in public relations. Illustrating, articles I wrote on fund raising were published in two of the leading communication journals in 1995. My placement of fund raising in the public relations domain has broadened the discipline's scope and influenced the work of other scholars. *Effective Fund-Raising Management* continues this tradition.

I also have purposefully maintained close ties to the "real" world of practice. For example, in 1996, I was recertified by the National Society of Fund Raising Executives and earned senior accreditation from the Public Relations Society of America. My 17 years of professional experience informs my research and writing. I only am comfortable generating knowledge when I can "test" it periodically on practitioners. During the 5 years it took to write this text, I made a total of 10 practitioner presentations, from Boston to Seattle, which allowed me to discuss my ideas with those who *do* what I was attempting to explain. Such interaction helped ensure the usefulness of *Effective Fund-Raising Management*.

Special care was taken in the book to highlight public policy issues affecting fund raising. Indeed, the emphasis given to law and ethics is intended to improve relationships between government and the charitable subsector. Whereas some may argue that my condemnation of certain practices supplies critics with damaging ammunition, I believe ignorance is a poor defense to more regulation. The primary purpose of *Effective Fund-Raising Management* is to increase knowledge about and thereby promote understanding of this function so vital to our democratic society. My fervent hope is that it succeeds.

Writing the first textbook on any subject is difficult; writing one on a subject lacking in theory and research often seemed impossible—particularly for a sole author.

Textbooks, in almost all cases, rely heavily on previous studies by multiple scholars. Because fund raising has not accumulated a body of knowledge, I frequently had to stop to research and support concepts presented in this book. As compared to its counterparts then, *Effective Fund-Raising Management* is more accurately defined as a scholarly work than as a text.

The volatile regulatory environment in which fund raising is practiced added to my difficulties. While writing the book, laws changed and new initiatives were introduced, which required seemingly unending revisions. The need for constant updating likely will remain. For example, in August 1997, the federal government enacted new laws that lowered the set tax rate on capital gains to 20% for most gifts of appreciated property and increased the lifetime exemption on gift and estate taxes to $1 million over the next 10 years. As recommended in chapter 7, current and future fund raisers must use environmental scanning to keep up with regulatory changes.

ACKNOWLEDGMENTS

This textbook could not have been written without the theoretical base provided by my public relations colleagues. I am indebted to Scott Cutlip, Jim and Lauri Grunig, Glen Broom, David Dozier, and Bob Heath, among others. Likewise, I thank the scholars who have invested in researching and building theory on philanthropy and nonprofit management, including but not limited to Peter Hall, Joe Galaskiewicz, Kristen Grønbjerg, Roger Lohmann, Susan Ostrander, Bob Payton, Rich Steinberg, and Jon Van Til. I also extend my appreciation to practitioner authors whose thoughtful efforts stimulated and validated my ideas, in particular, Marianne Briscoe, Dave Dunlop, Peg Duronio, Jim Greenfield, Peg Hall, Jim Lord, Joe Mixer, Vicki Steele, Gene Tempel, and Mike Worth.

Another group contributed significantly to this text—staff members of *The Chronicle of Philanthropy*. Just 10 years ago, the biweekly newspaper emerged as the first objective source of timely information on the nonprofit sector. My reliance on its invaluable coverage is demonstrated by the Author Index, which lists numerous citations for such editors and reporters as Elizabeth Greene, Stephen Greene, Holly Hall, Jennifer Moore, and Grant Williams.

Acknowledgments would be incomplete without mentioning family and friends who provided a necessary infrastructure of love and support. Those who find this book of value owe much of their gratitude to my husband George, daughter Jodie, mother Idun Mehrman, sister Julie, brother Russ, neighbors Gil and Sweets Lastrapes, and my steadfast friends in Minnesota, Maryland, and Louisiana. A whispered kiss goes to Jennifer.

Finally, I am grateful to Lily Endowment Inc. for a grant that supported the initial research and writing of this book. There were times I might have chosen a less demanding course of inquiry except for my desire to produce a text worthy of the foundation's vote of confidence.

Although many people contributed to the book, any and all errors it contains are mine. I look forward to subsequent dialogues that will improve fund-raising practice.

—*Kathleen S. Kelly*

1

The Function of Fund
Raising: Introduction
and Overview of the Book

Fund raising is an organizational function unique to that sector of our democratic society alternatively referred to as nonprofit, voluntary, or independent. Its practitioners are important actors in what many distinguish as the *third* sector, as opposed to the first two societal sectors of business and government, and the fourth and most fundamental sector of family. Although organizations in this third sector have been raising funds throughout most of our nation's history, it has been only since the early 1900s that systematic efforts have been employed to bring about desired outcomes. Now, as we approach the end of this century, it is appropriate that we move beyond the *organization* of fund-raising activities to their *management*—specifically, toward managing the fund-raising function effectively so that it contributes to the overall success of those nonprofit organizations that are charitable.

In doing so, we face a number of obstacles. The nonprofit sector is the smallest and least studied of the four. It generally is defined by what it is not, rather than by what it is. Americans give generously; a philanthropic tradition pervades our society, yet we have little understanding of why or of the interdependencies involved in gift giving and receiving. Unresolved definitional issues, such as the difference between philanthropy and charity, create confusion and deny us common terminology on which to build knowledge. Unlike other major concepts in philanthropy, fund raising developed outside the formal structures of scholarship and study. In other words, practitioners, without a disciplinary or scientific framework, have conceived what fund raising is and how it is practiced. Rarely have their applied principles been tested or questions raised as to how the function *should* be practiced.

These and other barriers—although difficult to overcome—are not insurmountable (otherwise this book could not have been written). Ground-breaking work by scholars in philanthropy, fund raising, and public relations during the early 1990s finally has provided us with the conceptual tools needed to define fund raising as a social and behavioral science. Equally important, the sociopolitical and economic context in which contemporary fund raising is practiced demands a managerial, or theory-based, approach that moves this critical function from the shadows of intuition and handed-down hunches into the light of scientific explanation. It is the overarching

1

premise of this book that unless such efforts are made now, the very survival of the nonprofit sector will be endangered.

Underscoring this sense of urgency, attorney Bruce Hopkins (1990) warned in an essay on legal issues in fund raising and philanthropy:

> All that has been achieved, that is cherished, that has been taken for granted by the philanthropic community is under examination, challenge, and threat. There are many, in and out of government, who believe that nonprofit organizations are largely anachronisms and that features such as tax exemptions and the charitable deduction should yield to the dictates of a flatter tax system. (p. 205)

Proponents of the nonprofit sector would extend this book's premise to include the well-being of our entire society as we know it. In its report on innovative approaches to nonprofit funding, for example, the Institute for Public Policy and Administration (1988) stated:

> A deeper assessment of the role of the nonprofit sector, however, must recognize nonprofits as a key feature of our democratic, pluralistic society; they are important even beyond the services they provide. The independent, nonprofit sector embodies the American tradition of encouraging any person or group to take the initiative to speak, act, or organize for the public good. (p. 2)

Robert Payton, Henry Rosso, and Eugene Tempel (1991) declared, "We believe that fund raising is an essential part of American philanthropy; in turn, philanthropy—as voluntary action for the public good—is essential to American democracy" (p. 4). These well-known fund-raising practitioners and authors used the following syllogism to demonstrate this underlying argument:

1. Major premise: Philanthropy is necessary in a democratic society.
2. Minor premise: Fund raising is necessary to philanthropy.
3. Conclusion: Fund raising is necessary to a democratic society. (p. 5)

Eugene Dorsey (1991), former president of the Gannett Foundation and former chair of Independent Sector (a coalition of foundations, nonprofits, and corporations recognized as the sector's leading voice on national issues), used the human heart as a metaphor for the collection of organizations that "keeps pumping the lifeblood of our republic" (p. xx). He then offered the following benediction, which this book adopts as a guiding norm for fund-raising practice: "May the raisers of funds always be conscious of their responsibilities to preserve and strengthen this organ so vital to sustaining American life" (p. xx).

INTEGRATING PRACTICE AND THEORY: A TEXT

The purpose of this book is to teach students about fund raising—a growing occupation that currently employs tens of thousands of men and women in the United States. Until recently, almost all fund raisers were trained "on the job," through an apprenticeship tradition of senior practitioners mentoring newcomers. Maturing of the occupation and dramatic increases since the 1980s in the number of charitable organizations and their demand for fund raisers have broken down the earlier system and moved fund-raising education into the formal classroom.

To the best of my knowledge and as confirmed by researchers, *Effective Fund-Raising Management* is the first book written for the primary purpose of teaching fund raising for academic credit. As such, it is not a "how-to" manual nor a "motivational" book, which constitute almost all of the existing literature. Although many of its chapters deal with practical application, the book's objective is to integrate fund-raising practice with theory. Payton et al. (1991) justified this endeavor: "There has been an over-emphasis on the 'how-to' to the neglect of the 'why'" (p. 279). The book relies on authoritative sources from the practitioner literature, as well as my own 17 years of full-time experience, to present information on the process of raising gifts, programs used to do so, and the donor publics with whom fund raisers are concerned—the *how* of fund raising. To provide the theoretical framework, the *how come* of fund raising, it draws on theories and research from the social and behavioral sciences—particularly public relations—that help us understand and evaluate this organizational function. Much of the material represents original research undertaken to produce a first-time text that is as comprehensive as possible.

Specifically, this book is designed for graduate and upperdivision undergraduate courses dealing with fund raising that are offered by colleges and universities. Such courses currently are taught in diverse academic areas, including management, public administration, arts and humanities, education, history, law, social work, and in the social sciences of economics, sociology, and psychology. Fund raising is also incorporated in public relations education (Kelly, 1991c). According to Independent Sector's *Compendium of Resources for Teaching About the Nonprofit Sector, Voluntarism and Philanthropy* (Crowder & Hodgkinson, 1991a), about 57 colleges and universities offer more than 150 courses related to fund raising. Most observers agree that those numbers will increase sharply during the last part of the 1990s as the demand for fund raisers continues to outstrip the supply. Yet the absence of textbooks to support such courses has not been addressed until now.

Illustrating this gap, Crowder and Hodgkinson (1991b) found in their survey of faculty who teach courses about philanthropy and the nonprofit sector that only one book was used by more than one instructor to teach fund raising: practitioner Thomas Broce's (1986) nontheoretical guide, *Fund Raising*, which Dannelley (1986) described as "an interesting mix of practical advice and romantic social concepts" (p. 39). Respondents consistently included textbooks among their greatest resource needs and recommended that the survey's sponsor, Independent Sector, "promote the publication of a college text on the basic concepts of fund-raising [*sic*]" (p. 9).[1]

Most of the literature on fund raising has been written for practitioners, primarily by other practitioners. Little theory has been used to ground the many time-proven principles that have evolved. Payton (1991) commended practitioner-authored books as examples "of what the Greeks called *phronesis*, 'practical wisdom'" (p. xiii). He added, however, "Increasingly, the study of fund raising will benefit from the constructive criticism of the academy as well as from a wider and deeper empirical knowledge base" (p. xiv). Van Til (1990) concluded his book, *Critical Issues in*

---

[1]As explained shortly, the correct spelling of *fund raising* is in the form of two unhyphenated words.

American Philanthropy, by offering 11 guidelines for effective practice. The first of the 11 was: "A sophisticated understanding of the theory and practice of philanthropy is required if effective professional practice is to be sustained" (p. 276).

As emphasized by Carbone (1986) and others, fund raising has an enormous body of lore and experience but limited theoretical knowledge. Elizabeth Boris (Boris, Fox, & Hall, 1993), former director of the Nonprofit Sector Research Fund at the Aspen Institute and now director of the Center on Nonprofits and Philanthropy at the Urban Institute, complained, "Courses on everything from fundraising [*sic*] to dealing with board-staff relationships are still based on anecdotes—how I did it and how you can do it, too" (pp. 224–225). Boris' informed observation reminds us that the role of education is to teach not only *how* something is practiced, but how it *should* be practiced.

Effective Fund-Raising Management was written to address this resource need. Unlike existing books, it moves beyond anecdotal evidence to present practical knowledge within a framework of theory and research. It explores territory previously uncharted in the literature, such as the historical and organizational contexts of contemporary practice. It raises difficult and unresolved questions and attempts to answer them. A deliberate feature of the text is to point out, in every chapter, rich opportunities for research—specifically, problems and theories appropriate for master's theses and doctoral dissertations. Furthermore, it anchors fund raising to standards of ethical and socially responsible behavior, advocating a normative model of how fund raising should be practiced, as opposed to simply describing how it predominantly is practiced today.

The text is intended to build on my earlier work, *Fund Raising and Public Relations: A Critical Analysis* (Kelly, 1991a), which theoretically grounded fund raising in systems theory, defined it as a specialization of public relations, and conceptualized the beginnings of a theory of donor relations. This book is not intended to replace that scholarly work, nor to duplicate information found in its 500-plus pages. The first book can be used as a companion volume to this text when added explanation is desired, and special care has been taken to cite appropriate topics. Likewise, various how-to books on the mechanics of fund raising are referenced to avoid needless duplication. Each chapter ends with a list of suggested readings, which were selected as the best and most recent sources—along with references—for enhancing understanding of both details and abstract ideas. The reading lists are cumulative in that a work suggested in an early chapter is not repeated in subsequent chapters, regardless of its relevance to multiple areas. Utilization of supplementary literature allows *Effective Fund-Raising Management* to devote necessary space to subjects not covered in existing works—subjects that cannot be ignored in any book claiming to be a text.

Its public relations orientation should not deter those who teach and study fund raising within other academic disciplines. The theories used draw heavily from such older disciplines as sociology, psychology, and organizational behavior. The basic concepts are generic to sound management practice. Although some may disagree with the choice of domain in which fund raising is placed, they still will find the bulk of the book relevant to their needs. Its contents should be of value to current practitioners seeking continuing education; however, its target audience consists of those who will lead charitable organizations in the future. Because it links practice to scholarship and research within each chapter, it is expected that additional audiences who have had difficulty finding serious literature on the subject, such as scholars of philanthropy and nonprofit management, will also find it of value.

The book is organized into three parts with alliterative titles starting with the letter *P*, which provides both a system for organizing the major concepts of fund raising and new terminology for facilitating discussion of those concepts. Students should also find this device helpful with their own cognitive efforts to organize, recall, and—most importantly—comprehend the material. The three parts are: (a) the practice; (b) the principles; and (c) the process, programs, and publics. An overview of the three parts and their chapters is given shortly. Before doing so, however, this introductory chapter first turns to some preliminary definitions that will help students formulate a perspective of fund raising that is congruent with the book's approach. In order to do so, it also introduces the concept of presuppositions, or assumptions, about fund raising and its purpose.

DEFINITIONS AND PRESUPPOSITIONS

As touched on earlier, unresolved definitional issues have created confusion and denied us common terminology. This section reviews some of those issues and provides students with meanings of terms that are essential to understanding fund-raising management as presented in this text. An extensive discussion of definitions is found in Kelly (1991a; see particularly chap. 3); furthermore, these issues continue to unfold throughout the chapters that follow this introduction and overview.

Fund Raising

In its *Glossary of Fund-Raising Terms*, the National Society of Fund Raising Executives (NSFRE) Institute (1986) defined "fund-raising [sic]" simply as "the seeking of gifts from various sources as conducted by 501(c)(3) organizations" (p. 40). Before examining such definitions, students first should be aware that there is inconsistency throughout the literature on the style of the terms *fund raiser* and *fund raising*. Representative of this confusion is NSFRE's usage, which does not hyphenate the latter term when used as an adjective in its name, but does hyphenate the term at other times (e.g., in the title of its *Glossary*). NSFRE traditionally hyphenated both terms when used as noun and verb. Other authors spell both terms as one word (fundraiser and fundraising), often in the interest of simplicity and—in the case of Steele and Elder (1992), who wrote their book specifically for library fund raising—to facilitate online retrieval of the literature.

Regardless of any such commendable intentions, the *Associated Press Stylebook* and other authorities advocate spelling *fund raising* and *fund raiser* as two words, without a hyphen, and fund raising with a hyphen when used as an adjective. This is the style adopted for this book.[2]

---

[2]It also is the style NSFRE is gradually adopting. The lexicographer who worked with a task force on revising the NSFRE *Glossary*, which was published in 1996, recommended the usage just described. In addition, the editorial policy of NSFRE's monthly journal changed in Fall 1993, when the hyphen for fund raising and fund raiser was dropped in the first issue of the redesigned journal, *Advancing Philanthropy*.

Students may think a debate about lexicon is trivial; actually it is significant in that staff fund raisers are such a new phenomenon we do not even agree on what to call them. Many organizations, particularly colleges, universities, and hospitals, use the term *development*—in part because of the negative connotations of *fund raising*. Indicative of this negative factor, a 1990 survey found that only 37% of Americans believe fund raisers are "trustworthy" ("Less than half," 1990). A practitioner at Tufts University phrased it another way: "Fund raising is like sex between your parents. You know it goes on, but you don't want the details" (Bailey, 1987, p. 34).

Development practitioners generally define their function more broadly than fund raising, equating the latter term to just one step of the fund-raising process—that of solicitation. According to Payton (1981), "To equate *development* with *fund raising* . . . will outrage many who have struggled for years to create a larger vision of the field. In their view, development is both broader in scope and deeper in purpose than simple fund raising would imply" (p. 282; italics in original).

Through their quest to broaden the fund-raising function beyond solicitation, many education practitioners have adopted the term *institutional advancement*. The Council for Advancement and Support of Education (CASE), which—along with NSFRE—is one of the three major fund-raising associations, advocates this umbrella term for the functions of fund raising, public relations, alumni relations, government relations, publications, and—to a lesser extent—student recruitment (Carbone, 1987). The third of the fund-raising associations is the Association for Healthcare Philanthropy (AHP). Formerly the National Association for Hospital Development (NAHD), it changed its name in 1991 in part because continual confusion over the term *development* prompted numerous telephone calls about hospital construction.

Other terms recently have emerged in the literature, such as *resource development* and *philanthropic fund raising*. The latter term apparently seeks to differentiate between fund raising for charitable organizations and fund raising for other types of nonprofit organizations to which gifts are not tax deductible, such as political parties.[3] Then too, its recent usage may be attributable to a growing sensitivity on the part of fund raisers to increased charges of commercialization through such ventures as cause-related marketing. The latest word from practitioner authorities, as espoused by Henry "Hank" Rosso (1991), cofounder of The Fund Raising School, is that fund raising currently is known as "resources development" (p. 51). Yet those who support the euphemism *philanthropic fund raiser* recently backed a drive to change the name of NSFRE to "the Council for the Advancement of Philanthropy" (Knott, 1992, p. 198).

Only the terms *fund raising* and *fund raiser* are used in this book to describe the process and activities related to helping charitable organizations obtain private gifts and to describe those specialists who are responsible for doing so. Clarity in describing practitioners and what they do outweighs any negative connotations associated with the terms. Furthermore, a basic assumption of this book is that fund raising is an honorable occupation, one that can contribute significantly to the well-being of organizations and our democratic society. I agree with practitioners such as Broce (1986), who stated, "Helping institutions generate resources

---

[3]The critical difference between charitable and other nonprofits is examined in chapter 2.

to reach new goals is a source of great satisfaction" (p. xi), and I applaud Payton et al. (1991), who explained, "When the fund-raising process is undergirded by an examination of the organization's mission and case, it is a task that can be carried out with dignity. The person seeking the gift should never demean the request by clothing it in apology" (p. 14).

Contrary to much of the literature, this book distinguishes between fund raisers who are paid specialists and volunteers who assist in the process of obtaining gifts. It is my contention that fund raisers are skilled communicators who are trained to manage relationships with strategic publics and who add compensated value to the organizations they serve. As demonstrated in subsequent chapters, fund raising is more specialized and continuous than can be handled on an ad hoc basis by volunteers or senior managers trained in other areas. Just as anyone can do "PR" when it is defined as getting publicity, anyone can do fund raising when it is defined as simply seeking gifts for charitable organizations (NSFRE Institute, 1986).[4]

For the purposes of this book, therefore, fund raisers are those people who are *paid* to manage donor relationships, thereby helping charitable organizations obtain private gifts. They generally work full time. They are either fund-raising consultants (i.e., external practitioners serving a number of clients) or staff fund raisers (internal practitioners who are employed by one organization). They are not paid solicitors, or those employees of for-profit companies hired to solicit gifts. Contrary to conventional wisdom, fund raising is more than solicitation. Those who only solicit and who do not manage relationships are not fund raisers. As discussed in the chapter on ethics, it is imperative that the behavior of paid solicitors be separated from legitimate practice. Defining who is and who is not a fund raiser is the most important issue facing the field.

Drawing from my earlier work, I define fund raising as a subfunction of nonprofit public relations, similar to investor relations in the business sector. Just as some companies are publicly owned corporations that require a function to manage relationships with shareholders, some nonprofits are charitable organizations that require a function to manage relationships with donors. Both types of organizations—publicly owned corporations and charitable nonprofits—are registered with agencies of the federal government, the Securities and Exchange Commission (SEC) and the Internal Revenue Service (IRS), respectively, and both functions—investor relations and donor relations—are regulated to different degrees by those agencies. Both functions involve social exchanges dealing with money, although one is commercial, or for-profit, in nature and the other is philanthropic in that some of the benefits from the exchange spill over into society (Douglas, 1983).

To clarify this important distinction, in a for-profit exchange the benefits are fully captured by the actors involved. For example, a person exchanges money for 10 shares of stock a company is selling through an initial public offering based on the rationale that the money and stock are of comparable value and that he or she—the inves-

---

[4]The term *PR* is not used in this book except in direct quotations. The abbreviation has been labeled by the Public Relations Society of America (PRSA) Special Committee on Terminology as denigrating and not in the best interest of public relations. It often is used in a derogatory sense and does not accurately reflect an emerging profession that defines itself as managerial and scientific. As I told a fund-raising consultant who insisted on using the term during a symposium at which I was speaking, its equivalent for what he does is *FR*, which the audience admitted has an unsavory and even obscene sound to it.

tor—and the corporation will profit from the exchange. In a philanthropic exchange, others benefit from actors giving and receiving a gift. For example, a person gives money to build a new classroom building at a university based on the rationale that the university will return benefits of value to him or her, including—but not limited to—carrying out the person's objective to help educate students. In addition to both the donor and the university benefiting, students benefit from the exchange, as does society in gaining a more educated citizenry.

The tax-exempt status of charitable organizations and the tax deductibility of gifts to them can only be preserved if gifts are philanthropic in purpose and, as economist Richard Steinberg (1993a) emphasized, generate goods that benefit more than just the purchaser. The closer gift giving and "getting" move toward commercial transactions, the more likely public opinion will turn against charitable organizations and government will move to rescind the special tax benefits conferred on these organizations. Van Til (1990) stated in his second of 11 guidelines for effective practice, "Philanthropy is no longer a matter of purely 'private' action and behavior; those active in the field should recognize that it is a field of lively public policy and concern, and quite likely to remain such" (p. 277). Payton (1987) further explained, "Philanthropy owes its credibility to its altruistic imperative—to remain philanthropic it must by definition give first place to the other rather than to the self. It is not that self-interest does not often yield altruistic benefits; what matters is that acts guided primarily by self-interest are called something else. They are not philanthropic in intent" (p. 39).

Based on this perspective and drawing from leading definitions of public relations, fund raising is a management function that identifies, builds, and maintains relationships between charitable organizations and donors for the purpose of exchanging resources to attain philanthropic goals that benefit others, as well as those involved in the exchange. More simply, this book defines fund raising as follows:

Fund raising is the management of relationships between a charitable organization and its donor publics.

There is much support in the literature for the idea that fund raising is a function that deals with relationships. For example, Payton et al. (1991) directly stated, "Philanthropy is about relationships" (p. 13). The third of Van Til's (1990) 11 guidelines was, "Philanthropy is most appropriately seen as a relationship between donors and recipients mediated by varying images of the public good" (p. 277). Lohmann (1992b) said, "In giving and receiving, individuals establish, symbolize, and demonstrate their ongoing relations and mutual obligations" (p. 201). Nudd (1991) stated, "Whether it is called development, advancement, attracting philanthropic resources, cultivating voluntary support, or friend raising, the key to fund raising [*sic*] success is *relationship building*" (p. 175; italics in original). Most recently, Patricia Lewis (1996), president and chief executive officer (CEO) of NSFRE, raised and answered the critical question: "So, what do fund raisers do? We specialize in building long-term relationships between philanthropic organizations and the individuals, corporations and foundations that support them with money, material resources, time and expertise" (p. 3).

Furthermore, communication is the basis of relationships; as such, the management of an organization's formal communication with donor publics is the defining characteristic of fund raising. Senior practitioner and author James Greenfield (1991) stated, "Fund raising is a unique form of communication" (p. 14). He called communication "the science of donor relations" (p. 228). Students should keep in mind that the archaic meaning of the word *communicate* is to share.

Presuppositions About Fund Raising

Public relations scholar James Grunig (1992) defined presuppositions as "a priori assumptions about the nature of truth, of society, of right or wrong, or simply of how things work in the world" (p. 8). Building on early versions of Grunig's work, I identified two categories of presuppositions about fund raising: asymmetrical and symmetrical (Kelly, 1991a; see chap. 15). Asymmetrical presuppositions assume that fund raising involves manipulating donors for their own good, as well as for the financial benefit of a good cause. When practitioners and others hold asymmetrical presuppositions they assume that the organization knows best and that if potential donors "just understood" they would willingly give. This know-best assumption leads them to assume further that, because of the worthiness of the mission, donors benefit from giving primarily because the organization benefits (i.e., the donor benefits from "doing good"). Fund raising is competitive, and the more dollars raised, the more important and valuable the organization is. Finally, fund raising is analogous to marketing; it is effective if it generates targeted amounts of revenue.

In contrast, symmetrical presuppositions assume fund raising is the means by which charitable organizations and donor publics interact in a pluralistic system to fulfill their interdependence for their benefit, as well as society's. Practitioners and others who hold such presuppositions support an "idealistic" approach to raising private gifts. Donors give not because they are persuaded, but because they have their own reasons for doing so. A decision to make a gift is based on mixed motives of interest in self and interest in a common good. Fund raising concentrates on the juncture where the interests of donors and the organization meet. Rather than generating revenue, its primary value to the organization is its management of environmental relationships with donors. In other words:

> *The purpose of fund raising is not to raise money, but to help charitable organizations manage their interdependencies with donor publics who share mutual goals and objectives.*

Analysis of the literature suggests that the practice of fund raising largely has been built on asymmetrical presuppositions. For example, many practitioners assume their "cause" is for the good of society; they rarely question the self-interest of their organization. Yet value judgments about which cause is greater, or more worthy, often "turn the waters murky." Illustrating, the people of Great Britain gave roughly three times more money in the late 1960s to prevent cruelty to animals than they gave to prevent cruelty to children (Whitaker, 1974). Americans give more money each year to education than they do to human services organizations, although poverty, homelessness, and other such problems continue to plague our society. As Payton (1987) stated, "It is very difficult to understand that one's own good cause isn't necessarily someone else's" (p. 44).

Drawing from the work of J. E. Grunig and White (1992), asymmetrical presuppositions steer fund-raising practitioners toward actions that are unethical, socially irresponsible, and ineffective. Such presuppositions are linked to ethics and effectiveness in later chapters. For now, an example is provided by consultant G. Douglass Alexander (1990), who attributed fund-raising abuses to the "unrealistic size of goals" for capital campaigns and related the following story: "I know of a development officer whose campaign was short of the goal. So he purchased a $1-million term life-insurance policy on himself, declared victory in the campaign, and shortly thereafter got another job. Needless to say, he also let the policy lapse" (p. 26).

Similar to conclusions reached by public relations scholars, it is argued here and throughout the book that asymmetrical presuppositions have led to unrealistic expectations of fund raising, have made it less effective than it could be, and have limited its value to the organizations it serves. This book advances a symmetrical approach to fund raising, based on the idealistic presuppositions just given.

Public Relations: An Academic Home for Fund Raising

Public relations is the organizational function that concerns itself with helping organizations in all sectors of our society manage their relationships with the various publics with whom they are interdependent. The authors of the most widely used public relations textbook, Cutlip, Center, and Broom (1994), offered this conceptual definition: "Public relations is the management function that establishes and maintains mutually beneficial relationships between an organization and the publics on whom its success or failure depends" (p. 6). J. E. Grunig and Hunt's (1984) definition is more parsimonious: "Public relations is the management of communication between an organization and its publics" (p. 6). Pavlik (1987) defined public relations as "the business of relationship management" (p. 118). These definitions emphasize public relations as a managerial rather than a technical function and are based on systems theory, which also is fundamental to fund raising.

From 1985 to 1996, J. E. Grunig led a team of scholars in the most comprehensive study of public relations to date. Sponsored by the International Association of Business Communicators (IABC) and known as the Excellence Project, this research resulted in the first general theory of public relations. Summarizing a few key concepts of that theory, organizations succeed and survive in environments made up of publics that affect or are affected by the organizations' behavior. Public relations helps manage these interdependencies by controlling strategic publics through persuasion or manipulation (asymmetrical public relations) or by adaptation through collaborative negotiation and strategies of conflict resolution (symmetrical public relations). Symmetrical public relations, which J. E. Grunig (1992) argued is synonymous with excellence, contributes to organizational effectiveness by using research to not only manage communications with strategic publics, but also to counsel senior management on adjusting the organization's behavior when it is in disharmony with the needs and interests of those publics. Its functional purpose is to establish two-way dialogue with publics from which mutual understanding will emerge.

Obviously, public relations is more than mere publicity or publications, which is a viewpoint commonly held by lay people. J. E. Grunig (1992) explained, "Public relations and communication management describes the overall planning, execution, and evaluation of an organization's communication with both external and internal publics—groups that affect the ability of an organization to meet its goals" (p. 4).

Traditionally, there have been six publics with whom public relations has been concerned: media, employees, community, government, consumers, and investors. The Body of Knowledge Task Force of the Public Relations Society of America Research Committee (PRSA, 1988) recently added the seventh public of donors to the function's domain. That task force, which—for the first time in 1988—defined the subject matter of public relations and codified its body of knowledge, incorporated the subheading, "Fund-Raising [sic]," as the seventh element and function of the practice, along with media, employee, community, government, consumer, and investor relations. In other words, the public relations function has developed seven specializations to manage organizational relationships with important stakeholders.[5]

A national survey of academic public relations programs I conducted in 1991 documented that 73% of the educators ($N = 79$) believe fund raising is a specialization of public relations (Kelly, 1992). Almost three fourths of those public relations programs housed in schools of journalism and mass communication incorporate fund-raising concepts in their public relations courses, and—at the time of the study—nine offered a separate course on fund raising. Observation since the study leads me to believe that today, at least 20 public relations programs have a separate course on fund raising. In other words, public relations offers an academic home that has been missing throughout fund raising's history.

According to Lohmann (1992a), whereas most of the major concepts in philanthropy began as subspecialties within existing disciplinary frameworks, "fundraising [sic] emerged entirely outside the organized knowledge industry of the universities, with its order of disciplines and sciences" (p. 309). The study of voluntary organizations grew out of sociology, charity and community organization came from researchers within social work, and nonprofit organization was the province of public administration. The study of fund raising, however, came from those practicing the function.

Ironically, historians have studied foundation giving, psychologists have studied individual giving, and sociologists have studied all three sources of gifts: individuals, corporations, and foundations (Lohmann, 1992a). No academic discipline until now has claimed fund raising as part of its domain.

Because of its birth outside of universities, fund-raising knowledge has not been oriented to science; rather its "parents" defined the function as more of an art. Dunn (1986) affirmed: "Fund raising is often viewed by its practitioners as an art, not a science. They may contend that development is not susceptible to analysis and management in the traditional sense" (p. 2). Illustrating this view, scholar Bruce Cook (1994a) quoted a chief fund raiser for a university, who stated, "There's not much science involved in it. It's basically an art. We have some technical things that we do. We've become better at doing them, but I don't think they would hold up under good scientific analysis" (p. 468). Rosso (1991) called fund raising a "complex art form" (p. 30).

A fundamental assumption of this book is that fund raising is a science. It can be observed, measured, and analyzed; theories can be conceptualized about it, and, in the form of hypotheses, they can be tested, confirmed, or disproved. This scientific approach has emerged only in the last few years, and it has come from the ivy-covered walls of academe. Whereas other disciplines, as evidenced by some citations in this

---

[5]An eighth specialization is member relations, unique to nonprofit organizations and of particular importance to associations.

book, have demonstrated an interest in various aspects of fund raising, only public relations appears to offer a "goodness-of-fit" for the entire function.

Practitioners, on the other hand, increasingly have turned to marketing as an explanatory framework for what they do. Although a few marketing educators have conducted research on fund raising (e.g., Harvey & McCrohan, 1990), the move to define the function as marketing comes primarily from the practice, not from academics. This groundswell was documented in my earlier book through a critical analysis of the fund-raising literature (Kelly, 1991a; see chap. 5). For example, consultant and author Jerold Panas (1984) directly stated, "Successful fundraising [sic] is simply effective marketing" (p. 176). He compared raising gifts to marketing cigarettes, toothpaste, and toys, advising fund raisers: "Don't sell what you want. Sell what they want" (p. 116). Broce (1986) claimed, "Marketing is the skill that most appropriately describes fund-raising work: the selling of a nonprofit organization. Marketing encompasses all the media, as well as personal outlets and related ability" (p. 214).

A national study I conducted in 1992 provided evidence that such beliefs are widely shared. Only 27% of the 296 practitioners participating in that quantitative study disagreed with the statement, "Fund raising is analogous to marketing in the for-profit sector." Yet, as I have argued in earlier works, including an article for the NSFRE *Journal*, marketing is an inappropriate and flawed approach to fund raising (Kelly, 1991b). My arguments are based on three primary reasons:

1. In market exchanges the *quid pro quo* is fully captured, but in philanthropic exchanges some of the benefits spill over into society.
2. Marketing is concerned with consumer publics, but donors and consumers are not synonymous for all charitable organizations, such as those with missions in human services.
3. The marketer's defined role is to generate sales by changing an organization's products and services, but the acknowledged role of the fund raiser is to support an organization's program services by generating gifts.

Elaborating on the last reason, T. Hunt and Grunig (1994) explained that marketing managers contribute to the strategic management of corporations by identifying market opportunities that help define the organization's business portfolio (i.e., what businesses or products should make up the company). The public relations authors continued, "Marketing managers then develop programs to respond to the market opportunities by developing and selling appropriate products" (p. 380). A marketing mindset by fund raisers, therefore, increases the vulnerability of charitable organizations because gifts may be "traded" for autonomy, or the organization's freedom to pursue self-determined goals and objectives. Furthermore, contrary to Broce's (1986) declaration, marketing relies heavily on paid advertisements, which rank low in the list of techniques used in fund raising.[6]

I was not the first to recognize the danger. The late consultant Maurice Gurin (1987) asked the question: Is marketing dangerous for fund raising? His answer was

---

[6]Fund-raising techniques and the relationship of organizational autonomy to gifts are presented in chapter 9.

yes. J. R. Wood and Hougland (1990) examined the issue in their essay on the role of religion in philanthropy:

> Some observers have expressed concern that a market-driven approach may be damaging even for those nonprofits that maintain formal standards of ethics and accountability. Gurin has expressed the fear that commercialization threatens an organization's integrity in the sense that it may lose its ability to keep its larger objectives in sight. (p. 119)

According to J. R. Wood and Hougland, the marketing approach pervaded fund raising during the 1980s. Some blamed it on tax reforms, increased competition, and a "baby boomer generation" that was less responsive to "traditional appeals" (p. 117). High participation in cause-related marketing, which was invented by the American Express Company in 1981 to promote use of its credit card, characterizes fund-raising practitioners' acceptance of a marketing perspective. Drawing from historian Peter Dobkin Hall (1989), if matching gifts were a new form of corporate philanthropy in the 1960s, cause-related marketing was indicative of the "greedy" 1980s, an era of hostile mergers and acquisitions built on self-advanced loans of debt.

Regardless of reasons, Payton et al. (1991) declared: "Marketing may be value-neutral; philanthropy and fund raising are not. Fund raising is always more than marketing" (p. 15). These authors argued, "The complex psychological relationship that arises from fund raising for a nonprofit organization is different from selling products and services in the marketplace" (p. 276). They added: "Philanthropy may soon go the way of patriotism—a valuable concept sacrificed to cheap emotional exploitation. Borrowing marketing and advertising techniques from business is one part of the problem" (pp. 279—280).

Finally, in an article directed at practitioners in education, Cindy Hall (1993), a marketer at Pennsylvania State University, provided the necessary distinction between marketing and public relations:

> You also need to understand how marketing differs from other disciplines—particularly public relations. Marketing, in its purest form, begins with the customer's needs; it tries to develop products and services to satisfy potential users. PR, on the other hand, begins with the organization's needs. It seeks to benefit both the campus and its audience by managing the relationship between the two. (p. 30)

Public relations, then, is a more appropriate discipline than marketing in which to house the fund-raising function.

Philanthropy and Charity

The second most important issue facing fund raising is reducing the high degree of misunderstanding about philanthropy, charity, and the overall purpose of private gifts, which—as discussed in chapter 2—are subsidized through our tax system. Critics argue that only *charity*, or serving the poor and needy, is appropriate for gifts that are tax deductible. Such arguments indicate a widespread naiveté that charity is the primary work of nonprofit organizations, which further reflects a lack of knowledge about the valuable role the third sector plays in our society.

For example, Teresa Odendahl's (1990) book, *Charity Begins at Home*, set off a debate over whether gifts for purposes other than charity, such as support for the arts, are also worthy of subsidization. Odendahl asserted that philanthropy, far from aiding the poor and the disenfranchised, ultimately promotes the interests of the wealthy. She concluded her book by calling for major changes in the tax laws.

Are gifts rightfully the province of charity? Is there a difference between charity and philanthropy, and if so, does fund raising deal primarily with one more than the other? A review of definitions establishes the terms of the debate and decreases the confusion.

The leading definition of *philanthropy* was conceptualized by Robert Payton (1988a), professor of philanthropic studies and founding director of the Center on Philanthropy at Indiana University–Purdue University at Indianapolis, who defined it as voluntary action for the public good, which includes voluntary giving, voluntary service, and voluntary association. Payton, as have others, identified two primary but distinctive thrusts in our efforts "to do good": (a) *compassion*, most closely associated with the giving of charity, and (b) *community*, our concern with civic improvement and social change (i.e., philanthropy). Lohmann (1992b) called philanthropy an "investment in civilization" (p. 163). He explained that positive social, or prosocial, behavior—a concept first advanced by psychology scholars in the 1970s—consists of mixtures of self-interested and altruistic behavior, "whether the prosocial behavior involved is philanthropic (for the common good of all who would benefit) [or] charitable (for the common good of others)" (p. 273).

Such authorities as Gurin and Van Til (1990) asserted that charity, which they defined as the direct intervention and assistance of human suffering, today falls primarily to government (e.g., welfare programs). Philanthropy, which translates from its Greek origins to "love of humankind," "takes a more impersonal and impassionate approach to bettering the human condition by institutionalizing giving" (p. 4).

More than 35 years ago, Robert Bremner (1960/1988), renowned scholar on the history of philanthropy and public policy toward children and youth, stated:

> Philanthropy has covered a wider field than charity; the problems of the poor have not been philanthropy's only or even primary concern. The aim of philanthropy in its broadest sense is improvement in the quality of human life. Whatever motives animate individual philanthropists, the purpose of philanthropy itself is to promote the welfare, happiness, and culture of mankind [*sic*]. (p. 3)

The problem, according to Payton (1987), lies in the flexible usage of the two terms, which often are used synonymously, although, as Payton said, "Philanthropy has succeeded charity as the embracing term" (p. 22). Public relations educator Scott Cutlip (1965/1990), who wrote the only comprehensive history of fund raising in the United States, said the term *charity* was replaced by *philanthropy* after World War I. As described in chapter 5, it was at the close of World War I that the occupation of fund raising came into being in the form of for-profit consulting firms.

Misunderstanding is exacerbated by legal definitions. When we refer to *charitable organizations*—or those nonprofits for which fund raisers work—we are not referring to charity, or programs dealing with the poor. Rather, as Simon (1987) pointed out, *charitable* is the term used by lawyers to refer to organizations described in 501(c)(3) of the tax code as serving religious, charitable, scientific, testing for public safety, literary, or educational purposes. Although confusing, the term has been reaffirmed by the Supreme Court, which has held that all 501(c)(3) organizations must conform to common-law charitable criteria.

Summarizing, charity and philanthropy are distinct concepts, although the term *philanthropy* is now used to encompass both. In a contemporary context, charity is a part of philanthropy, but only a minor part. Philanthropy is broader than serving the needs of the poor, which primarily are met through direct taxation, not tax subsidies. Fund raising, therefore, deals with philanthropy in the sense of investing in civilization, including assistance of human suffering. The greatest proportion of its practitioners, as discussed in chapter 3, work for organizations with purposes not defined as charity.

OVERVIEW OF THE BOOK

The text consists of 15 chapters, with the 14 following this introductory chapter organized into three parts: (a) the practice; (b) the principles; and (c) the process, programs, and publics.

Part I: The Practice: Parameters, Practitioners, and Professionalism

Continuing the alliterative device of titles starting with the letter *P*, Part I explores the parameters, practitioners, and professionalism of fund raising. Chapter 2, the Parameters, lays out the boundaries in which contemporary fund raising is practiced. It starts by looking at the tradition of philanthropy enjoyed by U.S. charitable organizations—a tradition that is the envy of other industrialized nations. Students are provided with a generational perspective of this tradition, as well as the American perspective of wealth, beginning with Andrew Carnegie's (1889/1983) admonition that to die rich is to die disgraced. The discussion concludes that—fundamentally—individual, corporate, and foundation donors make gifts because giving is a customary, admired, and expected behavior in our society and, therefore, fund raising does not affect whether donors give, but to which charitable organizations they give, the amount of their gifts, and the purposes for which their gifts are made.

This stage-setting chapter then turns to donor motivations, or the reasons beyond tradition for giving away money. The discussion resolves the two opposing viewpoints—donors give money as an act of altruism and donors make gifts to advance their self-interests—by adopting the mixed-motive model of giving. This model assumes that donors hold interest both in self and in a common good when making a gift. It further assumes that charitable organizations also have dual interests when obtaining gifts (i.e., their behavior is nether solely altruistic nor solely self-interested).

Those organizations and the larger nonprofit sector of which they are a part are the focus of the second half of chapter 2. Students are guided through a description of the sector, which one scholar called a "sprawling and unruly collection of animals" (Simon, 1987, p. 69) and another referred to as "a kind of Victorian attic of the unrelated and irrelevant castoffs of a profit-oriented civilization" (Lohmann, 1992b, p. 3). They are helped through this maze with a recent theory provided by philanthropy scholar Roger Lohmann (1992a, 1992b): the commons and its derivative concept of common goods. Based on shared values and interests, commons—or nonprofits—form to produce goods with external benefits, which are goods that benefit more than just the purchaser. Differentiating among the three sectors of business, government, and nonprofit, Lohmann (1992a) explained, "Markets produce private goods, states produce public goods, and commons produce common goods" (p. 320). Lohmann's distinction is important in that goods are desirable ends within the commons, but not necessarily beyond. Whereas widely used terms such as *public good* and *public interest* imply that any gift contributes to the good of an abstract "public," Lohmann's theory allows us to understand that a gift to one organization as opposed to another (e.g., pro-life vs. pro-choice) does not contribute to the *public* good, but rather to a good in which the donor and the recipient organization have common interests. As Lohmann (1992a) said, "Outside a reference group, any common good may be a matter of indifference or may even be considered a 'bad'" (p. 320). In short, philanthropy is not voluntary action for the public good (Payton, 1988a), but for particular common goods that, collectively, undergird our pluralistic democracy.

Finally, special care is taken to identify those nonprofits likely to have a fund-raising function because a list of such organizations does not exist and previous work has not found it necessary to deal with this distinction. Stereotypes and misconceptions about charitable organizations are discussed, and statistics are recalculated to describe the dimensions of the approximately 150,000 organizations on which this book concentrates.

Chapter 3 examines practitioners, or the people who are paid to raise money for these organizations. There are about 80,000 fund raisers in the United States, although only one third of them belong to the three major associations of AHP, CASE, and NSFRE. Under an array of job titles that hampers their identification, fund raisers work for organizations with diverse missions; however, an analysis of association membership reveals that the largest number of practitioners are employed by educational and health organizations.

Fund raising is an occupation for which there is high demand and which requires little experience. There is no prescribed program of education or specific personality traits that qualify one to be a fund raiser. Yet the occupation pays well, with a typical salary in 1995 of $54,650 for those belonging to CASE and top salaries of more than $140,000 (Mongon, 1996; R. L. Williams, 1996). Practitioners in fund raising earn more than those in public relations, with differences ranging from 20% to 50% more.

Fund raisers traditionally acquired their skills through an apprentice system that was supplemented by professional development offerings of the fund-raising associations. As the demand for fund raisers increased during the 1980s, a new venue for training emerged at colleges and universities. Fund raisers generally have high job satisfaction and a turnover rate comparable to members of other occupations, which is contradictory to common charges of "job hopping" by staff practitioners. Chapter 3 explores those charges and provides scientific evidence refuting them. It then turns to the feminization of fund raising, which it examines in depth.

During the 1980s, women moved from minority representation to the majority of practitioners. Fund raising offers career advantages for women, particularly those seeking to change careers or reenter the workforce. As is true in many occupations, however, women face widespread discrimination. Female practitioners are paid less than men and improvements have been slow and uneven. Women are victims of a backlash against their majority status, which has frozen gender proportions for the last 5 years. A two-tier hierarchy segregates female fund raisers into lower paying, lower status titles and positions.

Chapter 3 draws from findings of membership surveys by the three associations to document the gender gap in salaries and the differences in titles and positions between men and women in fund raising. Male members of NSFRE, for example, make $10,800, or 26%, more per year than female members (Mongon, 1992). Most women are clustered in fund-raising positions, such as annual giving, that have lower salaries and status than the positions most men occupy, such as major gifts. A hierarchy of positions is presented to help future practitioners understand workplace dynamics and plan successful careers. Other ways by which women can reduce the effects of gender discrimination are given.

Chapter 4 focuses on the issue of professionalism. Students are introduced to important elements and entities of the practice, including associations, research centers, and publications dealing with fund raising and the larger concepts of philanthropy and nonprofit management. The status of fund raising as a profession is analyzed using five common criteria: (a) body of knowledge, (b) program of formal education, (c) professional associations, (d) codes of ethics, and (e) professional autonomy and allegiance.

Given the state of research and theory described earlier, it is not surprising that fund raising lacks a body of knowledge. Chapter 4 identifies two primary reasons for the absence of this critical criterion of a profession: neglect by philanthropy scholars and substandard work by practitioner students. Analyses of master's theses and doctoral dissertations show the vast majority of that work emanates from departments of education, although few education faculty are scholars on fund raising. Regarding a program of formal education, fund raising is at the beginning of the second of three stages of progression to professionalism. Practitioners still largely control training; fund raising has no full-time faculty who exclusively teach and conduct research on it.

Based on the analysis of the five criteria, fund raising resides at the low end of the professional continuum. It is unlikely the occupation can improve its status in the near future without identifying an academic home that will provide it with a theoretical and educational foundation. Yet professionalization promises to improve the practice, making it more effective. Given current threats of increased regulation and loss of charitable privileges, discussed in chapter 7, the time necessary to advance fund raising without affiliating with an established discipline may not be available.

Public relations also is not a profession, but—unlike fund raising—it has the infrastructure in place to become one. It has a body of knowledge based on theory and research. Its 70-year-old program of education, which is grounded in the arts and sciences, provides a close match to fund-raising needs identified by studies and experts. Furthermore, the discipline claims fund raising as part of its domain, and public relations faculty teach courses, conduct research, and publish articles on the subject. The idea of affiliation is not as radical as it first may seem. Numerous past and current fund raisers started their careers as journalists and public relations practitioners (e.g.,

Maurice Gurin and Thomas Broce). Chapter 4 explores long-standing linkages between the two occupations and suggests future studies on the topic.

Part II: The Principles:
Historical, Organizational, Legal, Ethical,
and Theoretical

Part II consists of five chapters, all of which cover subjects rarely presented in the fund-raising literature but essential for academic study. Chapter 5 leads off by analyzing the historical context of fund-raising practice in the United States. Contemporary fund raising cannot be understood without first understanding the context in which the function evolved. Attorney Norman Fink (1993), who specializes in nonprofit and fund-raising law, added: "One must look to the past to forecast the future. The trends for the future do indeed have their seeds in the past" (p. 389).

A major thrust of chapter 5 is the newness of fund raising as a function systematically carried out by specialists, which dates back only to 1917. Furthermore, fund raising as an internal organizational function is less than 50 years old. Of particular significance is the recent evolution of the practice from an external consulting function to a predominantly staff function within charitable organizations. Whereas the end of World War I marked the beginnings of for-profit fund-raising firms, internal fund raisers employed continuously by organizations were a phenomenon that appeared only after the end of World War II. Consultant Robert Sharpe, Jr. (1989) explained, "Until the early 1950's, very few charities had professional staff members running fund-raising operations" (p. 40).

This evolution generally is ignored in the existing literature, and chapter 5 rectifies the knowledge gap by tracing fund raising through four distinct eras: (a) the era of nonspecialists from 1900 to 1917, (b) the era of fund-raising consultants from 1919 to 1941, (c) the era of transition from 1946 to the mid-1960s, and (d) the era of staff fund raisers from 1965 to the present. In so doing, it examines a critical difference in the function as practiced by external and internal practitioners, namely that consultants do not solicit gifts, whereas staff fund raisers do. This difference has gone largely unrecognized, which has resulted in much erroneous information about fund raising.

The second half of chapter 5 turns from chronological eras to stages through which fund-raising practice has passed. Four historical stages are documented, which represent four models, or different ways fund raising was practiced in the past. Unlike the eras, the models did not supersede each other, but rather the emergence of a new model added to the different ways of practicing fund raising. In other words, they describe *how* fund raising still is practiced today. They also describe the presuppositions held by organizations about fund raising. The four models are: (a) press agentry, (b) public information, (c) two-way asymmetrical, and (d) two-way symmetrical. Conceptualized and tested through an 8-year program of research, the theory of fund-raising models explains that the first three models are related to asymmetrical presuppositions and their practice is based on principles of persuasion, manipulation, and control. Only the newest model, two-way symmetrical, offers an ethical and socially responsible approach to fund raising. Its practice is based on principles of collaborative negotiation and conflict resolution. Whereas all four models constitute a descriptive theory, the two-way symmetrical model represents a normative theory of how fund raising *should* be practiced.

Chapter 6, on the organizational context of fund raising, documents continued use of the three older models. Results of two research studies are reported. The first, which empirically tested the models in a national survey, showed that the four models do describe the typical ways fund raising presently is practiced and provided supportive evidence as to their reliability, validity, and accuracy. It also found that press agentry—the oldest and least ethical model—is the one predominantly practiced by all types of charitable organizations.

The second study explored *why* charitable organizations practice the models they do. Theories from organizational behavior and public relations suggested that presuppositions about fund raising held by members of the dominant coalition—the powerful group of people who control the organization—determine the model practiced and whether the model is asymmetrical or symmetrical. The study showed that dominant coalitions support those fund-raising departments practicing press agentry and give less support to those practicing the two-way symmetrical model. Furthermore, dominant coalitions significantly influence the practice of the three asymmetrical models, but have little and nonsignificant influence on the two-way symmetrical model. In short, findings suggest that charitable organizations predominantly practice the press agentry model of fund raising because that is the model their dominant coalitions want them to practice. Yet the explanatory study also found that those organizations practicing the two-way symmetrical model in their major gifts program raise more total dollars in private support in a given year than those practicing the three other models.

Chapter 6 then turns to an examination of roles, or the daily behavior patterns of individual practitioners as they carry out their job responsibilities. Four fund-raising roles are conceptualized: (a) liaison, (b) expert prescriber, (c) technician, and (d) problem-solving process facilitator. Examples of the roles are identified through an analysis of the fund-raising literature. The theory helps explain variations in the behavior of practitioners, particularly the difference between the nonsolicitation role enacted and advocated by consultants (i.e., liaison) and other roles that include soliciting gifts. Following similar work in public relations, the four roles are collapsed into two major roles: manager and technician. Managers participate in strategic planning and decision making, utilize research, and direct programs, whereas technicians are limited to providing technical services to carry out plans and decisions made by others. The technician role is related to the practice of press agentry and public information, whereas the manager role is related to the more sophisticated two-way models.

Chapter 6 uses the line–staff management model to discuss structure and reporting lines. Unlike marketing, fund raising is a staff function, positioned high in the organization to advise and direct the behavior of top officials in building and maintaining relationships with donors. When the function is not integrated with other organizational components and key actors such as trustees and the CEO are not involved, the fund-raising process is ineffective. The chapter concludes by looking at variations from the management model presented, specifically, federations and affiliated foundations in which fund raising is a line function, and complex organizations, such as hospitals and research universities, in which the function is decentralized.

Chapter 7 moves to the legal context of fund raising. Although the practice largely is defined by laws and regulations, practitioners generally are uninformed, disinterested, and fragmented when it comes to legal issues. Regarding statues now in 47 states and the District of Columbia, Hopkins (1990) said fund raisers "are either unaware of such laws or blatantly ignore them" (p. 218). Similar indifference is found at the federal level where warnings are given, no improvement follows, and this is followed by more laws enacted. In 1987, for example, the IRS warned fund raisers to inform donors that only the amount of gifts in excess of the value of any goods or services returned to the donor is tax deductible, a rule that had existed since 1967. As defined by the IRS and the courts, a gift is "a voluntary transfer of money or property without receipt of or expectation of commensurate substantial financial benefit" (Ruge & Speizman, 1993, p. 609). Therefore, a payment of $100 for which the donor receives a dinner valued at $25 represents a tax-deductible gift of only $75. Congress threatened to enact legislation unless charitable organizations policed themselves more, and the IRS mailed about 400,000 pamphlets explaining the 20-year-old ruling. Writing in 1990, Hopkins said there was little leadership for improving compliance and predicted that a new law on disclosure of the nondeductibility of payments would be enacted. It was, in 1993.

This destructive cycle warrants special attention, and chapter 7 describes in detail the legal issues facing fund raisers and the organizations they serve. It examines the privileged status granted to 501(c)(3) organizations, including exemption from taxes and the right to receive gifts that can be deducted from taxable income and estates. It looks at questions raised about such economic privileges in relation to the behavior of the organizations that enjoy them, and concludes that all could be lost if changes are not made. Representative of threats, the Oversight Subcommittee of the House Ways and Means Committee held a series of hearings in 1993 and 1994, during which the IRS and state regulators urged Congress to introduce legislation to help them fight charity abuses. Chair of the subcommittee at the time, former Representative J. J. "Jake" Pickle (cited in Goss, 1993a) promised to introduce such a bill, saying, "Change is needed and is long overdue" (p. 39). The overriding issue, then, is whether changes will result from external regulation or self-regulation.

To facilitate self-determined change, students are introduced to key concepts and actors in the regulatory environment. Emphasis is given to the dual concepts of autonomy and accountability. To maintain freedom from government control, charitable organizations must increase their accountability, or continually reinforce public confidence in their performance. As N. S. Fink (1993) argued, at the root of privileges sanctioned by law is the question of whether 501(c)(3) organizations are providing and performing in society's highest interests. He concluded, "The answer is not all that clear" (p. 393).

Financial measures of accountability are particularly important. As decreed by law, "these entities must affirmatively engage in exempt functions" and their net earnings "may not inure to private individuals" (Hopkins, 1990, p. 209). It is expected, therefore, that organizations will spend most of their money on the program services for which they were granted charitable status. They demonstrate fulfillment of this basic criterion through such measures as low fund-raising cost ratios.

Chapter 7 provides a primer on accounting basics because accounting principles overlap with those of the law. They also are essential for understanding the three forces driving increased regulation: (a) abuses, (b) government's need for revenue, and (c) low accountability by those who control charitable organizations. Issues related to these three forces are presented. For example, excessive salaries, excessive endowments, and unfair competition with for-profit businesses are related to charges of low accountability.

Spurred by scandals involving private inurement (i.e., personal benefit), the charitable subsector has become the subject of scrutiny and criticism. Organizations that previously were ignored by the media and protected by a halo of their collective "good works" now find themselves defending the very reason for their existence. Elizabeth Dole (cited in G. Williams, 1992a), president of the American Red Cross, explained that for years organizations such as hers largely have been "free of public scrutiny, free to pursue our purposes, our own sense of what the public *should* want, and free to spend their money according to our own rules, standards, and priorities" (p. 8; italics added). She continued, "Those who survive in this new, more-public world are those who are willing to listen and live up to the expectations of the people who foot the bill" (p. 8).

A basic requirement for effective fund-raising management is compliance with IRS regulations. An overview of requirements is presented with an emphasis on tax laws introduced in 1994 (e.g., substantiation and *quid pro quo* rules). Regulations concerning noncash gifts, or gifts of property, and gifts that are not deductible, such as donated services and money spent to buy items at auctions, also are covered.

Chapter 8 examines the ethical context of fund raising, which has a causal relationship with the legal context. Stated another way, unethical behavior by charitable organizations results in increased regulation. The chapter describes the crisis of credibility currently faced by the subsector and places much of the blame on those organizations that seek financial support without investment—those looking to get something for nothing. The two means they employ are hiring paid solicitors and entering into joint ventures with for-profit businesses.

Paid solicitors, or solicitation firms, are defined and differentiated from fund-raising consultants and staff. Using the case of the United Cancer Council (UCC), the argument is made that charitable status does not carry an unequivocal right to survive and that hiring solicitation firms—which keep the majority of the money raised—in order to do so is reprehensible and socially irresponsible. The firm hired by UCC, Watson and Hughey, kept as much as 96% of the money given annually for 5 years, amounting to tens of millions of dollars. Research on recent reports by state regulators shows that, contrary to conventional wisdom, the clients of such firms are not new and small organizations with controversial missions, but organizations representing popular causes, many of which are well-known.

Chapter 8 follows efforts by state regulators to prosecute the Watson and Hughey firm (now renamed Direct Response Consulting Services) for alleged fraud and deception, including the use of sweepstakes mailings. Other solicitation firms, which have proliferated in the last decade, also are discussed, as well as "look-alike" charities that are closely associated with such firms and trade off the names and reputations of established organizations. The unethical and often illegal behavior of solicitation firms and their clients is the target of most efforts to regulate fund raising. Yet, until now, the practice has remained silent, refusing to condemn or disassociate these elements from legitimate fund raising. It can no longer afford to ignore this pressing issue.

The chapter then turns to joint ventures, or marketing agreements with for-profit companies, and discusses the four primary types: (a) cause-related marketing; (b) corporate sponsorships; (c) collection canisters, honor boxes, and vending machines; and (d) gambling. The dual purpose of joint ventures is to generate low- or no-cost income for 501(c)(3) organizations and to provide marketing advantages for companies. In exchange for income, charitable organizations authorize the use of their name, mission, logo, and sometimes programs and publics for selling a company's products or services. They also, it is argued, sell their integrity.

Joint marketing promotions are misleading. The amount of money received by the charitable organization, as compared to what the company gets, often is so little it amounts to deception. For example, such well-known organizations as the American Heart Association and the March of Dimes allow their names to be put on vending machines selling candy or gum. Consumers generally believe they are giving money to the organizations when making a purchase; however, the machines are owned by companies that give the organizations a few pennies of each dollar generated and keep the rest.

Organizations participating in joint ventures rarely inform consumers that a purchase made in the organization's name is not a gift. Money given through charitable gambling, for example, is not deductible from taxable income as a gift (although gambling losses can be deducted). In 1995, Americans wagered more than $7.6 *billion* on such games as pull-tabs and bingo, but only $780 *million* (10%) went to the sponsoring organizations (National Association of Fundraising Ticket Manufacturers, 1996). Government increasingly is interested in regulating these activities and in collecting taxes on the money gained through commercial ventures.

Paid solicitors and joint ventures have nothing to do with managing relationships with donor publics. Their use promotes unethical practice. N. S. Fink (1993), as have others, called for leadership "to develop a consensus on what is right and what is wrong in the sector" (p. 398). He warned:

> To avoid onerous regulation by government, bad apples need to be routed out of the barrel and exposed before they become national scandals. . . . The commercialism that has seduced many nonprofits into cause-related marketing, agressive direct-mail solicitations, commission fund raising, and inappropriate leveraging of tax-exempt funds has made it difficult to argue for legal incentives to giving or to defend against more regulation. (pp. 398–399)

In other words, only by adopting a critical voice and standards of ethical practice can fund raising hope to avoid its own undoing through punitive legislation.

Chapter 8 concludes by examining the predominant use of the press agentry model by the United Way of America (UWA) and its 2,000 local federations. Centralized under the UWA umbrella since 1970, the United Way system has dominated federated workplace fund raising until recently. The organizations constituting the system use emotion, competition, and coercion to propagandize the cause of "giving the United Way." Their press agentry practice has provoked three major charges: (a) manipulation, (b) mainstream beneficiaries, and (c) monopoly. The charges are supported and related to the 1992 UWA scandal when then President William Aramony was forced to resign and later was convicted of fraud. Based on systems theory, the conclusion is reached that unless the United Ways change, they will not long survive.

Systems theory is the foundation for the conceptual framework of fund raising presented in chapter 9. Charitable organizations do not exist in isolation, but are part of larger social, economic, and political systems—referred to as environments. Fund raisers serve in a boundary role between their organization and the environment in which the organization succeeds and survives. Included in the environment are those critical constituencies, or stakeholders, that can positively or negatively influence the organization's goals, including individual, corporate, and foundation donors. Fund raising contributes to organizational effectiveness by strategically managing environmental relationships with donors, helping the organization anticipate, adjust, and adapt to changes and opportunities.

Chapter 9 constructs the theoretical framework of fund raising by meticulously adding conceptual blocks to the foundation of systems theory. To do so, it borrows from such disciplines as management, sociology, psychology, and communication. It links the borrowed theories to time-tested principles of practitioners, thereby demonstrating validity in each step of the construction. By bonding scholarly knowledge with practitioner wisdom, concepts specific to fund raising emerge and are presented for the first time (e.g., the hierarchy of fund-raising effects). The end result of chapter 9 is a unified theory of donor relations that explains fund raising from the techniques it uses to the impact it has on society. The theory of donor relations incorporates fund-raising theories presented in earlier chapters, such as the models and roles, although they are not repeated in chapter 9.

Illustrating the chapter's method, a principle commonly espoused by practitioners is:

The larger the expected gift, the more personal the solicitation.

Theories drawn from communication differentiate techniques by levels of personalization and relate the levels to audience size. Theory predicts that as desired effects increase in difficulty, the probability of obtaining them increases by moving from mass to interpersonal communication. Chapter 9 presents a figure and description of the fund-raising techniques used to raise major and annual gifts, differentiated by three levels of communication: (a) interpersonal, which is direct communication between people; (b) controlled media, which is mediated communication through channels controlled by the organization; and (c) mass media, which is mediated communication through such uncontrolled channels as newspapers, television, and radio. The three levels descend in effectiveness.

Ideally, fund raisers would use only interpersonal techniques, such as face-to-face conversations and small group meetings; the ideal, however, would require almost unlimited financial and human resources. Practitioners, therefore, reserve interpersonal communication for the relatively small number of major donor prospects and rely on controlled communication techniques, such as direct mail and special events, to communicate with the larger number of prospects for annual gifts. Techniques based on mass communication, such as story placements and public service announcements (PSAs), are the least effective and are best utilized for such purposes as disaster relief. The conceptualization advances our understanding of fund raising by explaining why different techniques are used to raise gifts of different amounts, which previously was missing from the literature.

Chapter 9 pays special attention to factors related to donor behavior. It utilizes, for example, coorientation theory, which traces its beginnings to psychological studies about the mutual orientation of two individuals to some object. Public relations scholars have adapted the theory to corporations and publics, and chapter 9 further adapts it to charitable organizations and donor publics. The result is a model that defines giving behavior in the context of an environmental relationship and as a product of donors' views about a fund-raising opportunity and their estimates of the charitable organization's views about the same opportunity.

A principle handed down from veteran fund raisers is:

Belief in mission is the strongest reason for giving.

The societal problem the organization was formed to address, as described in its mission statement (e.g., promoting the arts in a community or helping homeless people), is paramount in fund-raising efforts. Paraphrasing Marshall McLuhan's (cited in Cutlip et al., 1994) famous declaration, the mission is the message. If real estate is dependent on the three factors of location, location, and location, then fund raising is dependent on mission, mission, and mission.

In addition to belief or interest in the organization's mission, practitioners rely on two other factors to identify donors: closeness or the degree to which prospects are connected to the organization and its work, and ability or capacity to give. The three factors correspond to the three predictor variables in J. E. Grunig's (e.g., Grunig & Repper, 1992) situational theory of publics: (a) problem recognition, (b) level of involvement, and (c) constraint recognition. Based on extensive research, the variables successfully segment stakeholders into four types of publics by the extent to which the members actively or passively communicate about an opportunity and the extent to which they behave in a way that supports or hampers an organization's pursuit of its goals.

Grunig's theory helps fund raisers identify those prospects with the highest probability of giving. Equally important, it reinforces practitioners' assertions that people who are not involved with the organization, do not care about its mission and program services, and do not have discretionary income or assets to give away, are of no concern to fund-raising efforts (i.e., they constitute a nonpublic).

The chapter concludes by discussing integrated relationship management, or consolidation of all functions that manage an organization's environmental relationships. Theories from business and management are applied to demonstrate the soundness of consolidation. Quite simply, a charitable organization succeeds and survives depending on how well it manages interdependencies with multiple stakeholders, not just donors. One department is needed, headed by a staff manager who is knowledgeable about and educated in both fund raising and public relations. Currently, the functions are either organized in separate departments or public relations is managed by fund raisers who are ill prepared. The second situation is termed fund-raising *encroachment*, which is examined in light of three studies on the subject.

Chapter 9 is the most important chapter in the text; it also is the longest. Without theory, fund raising is relegated to an occupation without scientific explanation, predictable outcomes, or any claim to professionalism. Students tempted to approach the chapter's subject with disdain are reminded of social psychologist Kurt Lewin's (1951/1975) adage: "There is nothing so practical as a good theory" (p. 169).

Part III: The Process, Programs, and Publics

Part III consists of six chapters, one each on the fund-raising process and donor publics, and four on the traditional programs of fund raising: annual giving, major gifts, planned giving, and capital campaigns. The final part of the book starts with chapter 10 on the process of raising gifts. Contrary to conventional wisdom, fund raising is not merely concerned with solicitation; it involves a multistep process that must continually be organized and managed, which requires the full-time attention of specialists. Chapter 10 presents a new conceptualization of the fund-raising process, a step-by-step description grounded in theory. Drawing from and expanding a public relations model, the process of fund raising is identified as ROPES.

ROPES is the acronym for the five consecutive steps of Research, Objectives, Programming, Evaluation, and Stewardship. Fund raisers first conduct research in three areas: (a) the organization for which they work, (b) the opportunity presented for raising gifts, and (c) the donor publics related to the organization and the opportunity. The last area commonly is referred to as *prospect research*. Practitioners employ both scientific and unscientific methods to gather essential information before they proceed to the next step of setting objectives that are specific and measurable. The objectives they set—many of which do not deal with dollars—flow from the charitable organization's self-determined goals and are shaped by research findings. Programming, the third step, consists of planning and implementing activities that will bring about the outcomes specified in the set objectives. Programming activities are broken down by cultivation and solicitation of donor prospects. The fourth step is evaluation, which includes both process and program evaluation. Stewardship, the fifth step, completes the process and also provides a loop back to its beginning (i.e., fund raising is cyclical due to the tendency of donors to make repeated gifts).

The fund-raising process is dependent on strategic planning by the organization, an ongoing process in which fund raisers must participate. Basically, fund-raising effectiveness is measured by how well the function helps an organization achieve its overall goals; therefore, organizational goals and strategies must first be in place before the fund-raising department can formulate its own goals and objectives. A principal component of strategic planning is *SWOT* analysis (Strengths, Weaknesses, Opportunities, and Threats), whereby the organization assesses its internal strengths and weaknesses in juxtaposition to opportunities and threats in the external environment. This management technique is used not only to establish the organization's strategic direction, but also serves at the departmental level for analyzing fund-raising opportunities.

Chapter 10 guides students through each of the steps in ROPES, pointing out differences in operationalization between the two primary programs of annual giving and major gifts. For example, because annual giving involves a large number of donor prospects, research on the publics requires group analysis, whereas the smaller number of prospects for major gifts allows individual attention. Similarly, fund-raising techniques selected in the programming step differ for the two programs. Care is taken to instruct students on research procedures, formulating output and impact objectives, such planning tools as a decimal system for outlining activities and tasks, evaluation by objectives, and elements of stewardship that must be fulfilled.

Focusing on the last two steps, chapter 10 presents the case for evaluating fundraising effectiveness by more than dollar goals. How the function should be evaluated is the third most important issue facing fund raising, following the need to define who is a fund raiser and to reduce misunderstanding about philanthropy. The purpose of fund raising is not to raise indiscriminate dollars, but to contribute to organizational effectiveness. It does so by meeting the objectives it formulated to support the organization's goals. A discussion of gift utility, delay factors in raising major gifts, and three levels of measuring effectiveness—drawn from the management literature—clarify the issue.

Stewardship, a step erroneously missing in public relations, is second in importance only to research. It consists of four elements: (a) reciprocity, which is broken down by acts of appreciation and recognition; (b) responsible gift use, which simply means that gifts be used for the purposes for which they were given; (c) reporting, which demands that donors be informed of their gift's use; and (d) relationship nurturing, which—in conjunction with the other elements—encourages donors to renew their gifts. A simple fact of fund raising is that most annual gifts and almost all major gifts come from individuals, corporations, and foundations who have given to the organization in the past; therefore, how donors are treated *after* they make their gifts largely determines future success. It also costs less to raise gifts from past donors than from new donors. Admitting he had no scientific evidence to back up his experiential claim, Squires (1992) argued, "It is 50 times harder to find a new donor than it is to renew a current donor" (p. 55).

Unfortunately, fund raisers and dominant coalition members currently do not take their stewardship responsibilities seriously, thereby undermining trust in America's charitable organizations. Illustrating, Independent Sector's (IS, 1994) biennial survey of giving and volunteering in the United States found that only 72% of the respondents agree that their gifts to charitable organizations are put to an appropriate use. In 1990, 80% agreed, representing an 8% decline in donor confidence during the early 1990s. Yet, as IS stressed, "Over the survey years, the belief that donations are used appropriately has [had] the highest association with increased rates of giving and volunteering" (p. 58). H. W. Smith (1993) warned, "'Stewardship' is not an empty concept; the recipients of charitable funds are in effect the stewards of those funds and are expected to use them in ways that accord with the goals of those who provide them" (p. 227). The ROPES process ensures that fund raising is carried out effectively; it also promotes ethical behavior.

Chapters 11 through 14 deal with the four programs traditionally used to raise gifts. The programs are categorized by the size of the gifts they generate: lower level or major. Dollar amounts defining the two gift types differ among organizations. Whereas such organizations as universities and hospitals typically use $100,000 as the criterion, this book—in order to be inclusive—defines major gifts as those of $10,000 or more and lower level gifts as all gifts below $10,000. Regardless of dollar amount, lower level gifts are raised through the annual giving program, and major gifts are raised through the major gifts program. Major gifts also are raised through planned giving, and both lower level and major gifts are raised through capital campaigns, with an emphasis on the second type. Planned giving and capital campaigns actually are *strategies* for raising major gifts.

Chapter 11 is on annual giving, often described as the bread-and-butter program of fund raising because it generates annual income that helps pay the organization's operational expenses. Annual gifts are synonymous with lower level gifts; they usually are unrestricted in purpose, meaning they can be used where most needed as determined by the organization's managers after receipt. In contrast, major gifts almost always are restricted and must be used for the specific purposes for which they were given, determined in advance of receipt. Annual gifts usually are made from donors' *income*, whereas outright major gifts are made from donors' income and *assets*, and planned major gifts typically come only from donors' assets. As operational expenses are reoccurring, the annual giving program is *repeated* each year, unlike the major gifts program and planned giving, which are ongoing, and capital campaigns, which are sporadic.

Chapter 11 begins by discussing three subjects of relevance to all programs: (a) the role of volunteers, (b) the principle of proportionate giving, and (c) different forms of gifts. Briefly, there has been confusion over the role of volunteers in fund raising because consultants—who do not solicit or handle gifts and, therefore, depend on others to do so—inappropriately refer to paid employees such as the CEO as volunteers. Furthermore, numerous volunteers who help the organization deliver its program services are essential to the charitable subsector, but fund raising relies on only a small number of volunteers, such as trustees. The principle of proportionate giving, based on our society's unequal distribution of wealth, holds that the majority of money will come from a minority of donors—both among programs and within. For any given organization, the major gifts program will account for the vast majority of dollars raised and only a relatively few gifts will account for most of that money. The principle has been affirmed through decades of practitioners' experience, and fund raisers abide by it when planning programming to meet solicitation objectives. Different forms of gifts are explained, including procedures for handling them. Gifts are grouped into cash, pledges, securities, real property, and personal property.

Chapter 11 continues by examining elements of the annual giving program, such as gift clubs, challenge grants, and corporate matching gifts. Also common are special projects, whereby donors are asked for restricted gifts. Practitioners acknowledge that people are more likely to give and to give higher amounts when the requested gift is for a specific purpose rather than for general operating needs. By breaking down operational expenses into fund-raising opportunities, both restricted and unrestricted options can be offered to donors—a move that will better meet their needs and still provide the necessary financial support for the organization.

The techniques used most heavily in annual giving are discussed, specifically, direct mail and special events. To communicate with the 10% of prospective donors who will provide 60% or more of the dollars raised through annual giving, the combination of a personal letter and a follow-up telephone call is recommended and described in detail. Chapter 11 ends by touching on the growing impact of new technologies, a subject raised in other chapters as well. The Internet promises to make communication with donors more two-way, and fund raisers must be prepared for the dialogue that will result.

The major gifts program is directed at the small portion of individuals, corporations, and foundations that own most of the wealth in the United States—prospects with the capacity to give $10,000 or more. As explained by theory, however, capacity, or the absence of financial constraints, is only part of the equation when identifying viable prospects. Virtually every major donor has a long-standing, carefully nurtured relationship with the recipient organization and the people who represent it. In almost all cases, major donors have made previous gifts to the organization. Students are advised against following the example of Beloit College in Wisconsin, which—in 1982—ran advertisements in *The Wall Street Journal* and *The New York Times* asking for a benefactor willing to invest $1 million in the college (Bergan, 1992). According to its president, inquiries were received from five possible donors; regardless, no gift ever was announced.

Chapter 12 presents a sample of the largest gifts made, emphasizing the relationship between donor and organizational recipient and the fact that mission largely determines gift size. Colleges, universities, and hospitals attract the largest gifts, followed by arts, culture, and humanities organizations, and independent schools. Whereas annual gifts directly increase the organization's spendable income, major gifts generally increase its assets: physical plant, equipment, reserves, and endowment. Endowments consist of multiple, separate funds established in perpetuity. Cash from gifts is invested to generate annual income, not all of which is spent; a portion is returned to the principal as a hedge against inflation. Because major gifts most often are made for endowed purposes, chapter 12 carefully explains the somewhat complicated financing such gifts entail (e.g., income is not available until 1 year after the gift is made).

Because major gifts usually are restricted, often with multiple conditions, negotiation is an inherent part of raising such gifts. Yet negotiation rarely is mentioned in the literature and only occasionally taught in professional development offerings. Chapter 12 rectifies the problem by introducing students to the principles of effective negotiation, drawn from the work of business educators and professional negotiators. Negotiation can be narrowed to two schools of thought: *positional bargaining*, in which each side takes a position, argues for it, and in a back-and-forth fashion works toward a compromise, and *principled negotiation*, in which the two parties look beyond position and concentrate on each other's interests, invent options for mutual gain, and strive to preserve the relationship (R. Fisher, Ury, & Patton, 1991). If the parties are involved in a one-time relationship that is not likely to be repeated (e.g., bargaining with a street vendor), positional bargaining is quick, efficient, and appropriate. If, however, the relationship is valued by the parties, the extra effort of principled negotiation is required. Principled negotiation allows fund raisers to think in symmetrical terms, adopting win–win strategies from the inception of the problem-solving process to its conclusion.

Personal attention in cultivating and soliciting prospects is critical in the major gifts program. A working model of moves management, a system refined by Cornell University, is described. Moves management focuses on planning and implementing regular interactions with prospects (i.e., it concentrates on cultivation). A scenario of an in-person solicitation is presented step by step to familiarize students with the techniques, actors, and dynamics involved.

Chapter 12 concludes by discussing yet another subject rarely mentioned in the literature: sexual harassment. To effectively manage the organization's relationships with prospects for major gifts, fund raisers must develop their own professional relationship with the gift source. This relationship sometimes is misinterpreted or exploited, particularly when the prospect is a man and the fund raiser is a younger woman. Sexual harassment can interfere with work performance and impair productivity. Above all, it is illegal. Fund raising is not a form of prostitution; no gift is worth anyone being harassed.

The discussion of major gifts continues in chapters 13 and 14, which examine planned giving and capital campaigns, respectively. Although both are strategies to raise major gifts, they represent diametrically different approaches. Planned giving is based on symmetrical presuppositions and two-way communication; it presents an unprecedented opportunity for growth. Capital campaigns, on the other hand, evolved from the press agentry model of practice with asymmetrical presuppositions; their continued use is questionable.

Planned giving is the managed effort by charitable organizations to generate gifts of assets from individuals through the use of estate and financial *planning* vehicles. Whereas other fund-raising programs are directed at all three donor publics, planned giving is concerned solely with individual donors. It previously was called *deferred giving* because financial benefits for the recipient organization usually are postponed until years after the donor makes the gift, typically after he or she dies.

Chapter 13 describes the largest transfer of wealth in the nation's history now underway. A staggering $10 trillion is expected to pass from one generation to the next during the coming 50 years (E. Greene, S. G. Greene, & Moore, 1993). Although people rightfully allocate most of their estates to family members, many—particularly those without surviving relatives—give some of their assets to charitable organizations. Planned gifts are sure to increase in the years ahead, and future fund raisers are advised to learn about this alternative to outright giving.

All practitioners are capable of raising planned gifts, contrary to much of the literature that extols the strategy as a highly complex area reserved for specialists trained in tax laws and finance. Three arguments are presented to refute the conventional wisdom. First, skills in relationship management, not in taxes and finance, are the necessary qualifications. Practitioner Michael Luck (1990) agreed: "If you are interested in leadership gifts, do not hire directors of deferred or planned gifts—hire directors of major gifts. You are asking potential givers to do great things, whether it be now, later or both. A major gift is a major gift regardless of its immediacy" (p. 31). Second, the estate and financial planning vehicle most commonly used also is the easiest one to understand, the charitable bequest. Consultant Fisher Howe (1991) affirmed, "Because a bequest is the simplest form of planned giving, an organization can begin without delay to encourage selected members of the support constituency to make provision for the organization in their wills" (p. 70). Third, lawyers, accountants, and financial planners—not fund raisers—handle and execute the technicalities of complex vehicles. Experts representing the organization's interests and those representing the donor's interests are active and *advocated* participants.

All planned giving vehicles are grouped into just three categories: (a) charitable bequests, (b) life income agreements, and (c) other vehicles. Life income agreements—as their name indicates—provide donors with income, usually until they die, from assets earlier transferred to a charitable organization that benefits from the remainder of the gift. Life income agreements consist of three primary vehicles: (a) the charitable remainder trust, (b) charitable gift annuity, and (c) pooled income fund. Other vehicles, which do not fit in the first two categories, include the charitable lead trust, remainder interest in a home or farm, and life insurance. Chapter 13 explains each vehicle in detail.

A critical issue in understanding planned gifts is the difference between face value and charitable remainder value. For example, because gifts made through life income agreements are encumbered for the term of the agreement in order to produce income for the donor and/or other individuals named income beneficiaries, funds are not available for use by the recipient organization until years after the gift is made. The charitable remainder, or the portion actually benefiting the organization, is substantially less than the value of the original gift, its face value. The difference, experts claim, usually is 50% (Moran, 1991). Fund raisers traditionally and wrongly have reported nonbequest gifts at their face value, knowing full well that their organizations actually will receive much less.

Reform recently was introduced by CASE (1994) as part of its new management and reporting standards for capital campaigns, which then became the basis for new reporting standards beyond campaigns (CASE, 1996). The standards dealing with planned giving require adoption of *present value discounting*, which promises to decrease reported fund-raising results dramatically. Counting the face value of planned gifts enables trustees, senior managers, and fund raisers to unethically inflate dollar totals, which also is a weakness of capital campaigns, the subject of chapter 14.

Capital campaigns are a strategy sporadically employed by charitable organizations to raise more money than usual in a fixed period of time. They were "invented" in 1902 by Charles Sumner Ward and Lyman Pierce, founders of the YMCA school of fund raisers and the leading historical figures of the press agentry model. Captital campaigns originally were used to raise gifts for physical capital needs such as buildings. By the 1950s, financial capital, or endowment, needs had been added to their purpose. Starting in the 1970s, campaigns expanded to include all purposes for which gifts are made, thereby encompassing annual giving, major gifts, and planned giving programs. Dollar goals increased as purposes and programs were added. Today, campaigns termed *comprehensive* rather than capital have the largest goals. Because they count every dollar raised during the campaign period, only about 25% of their goals represents *new money*; 75% would have been raised through the other programs without a campaign.

The evolution of capital campaigns is closely tied to the evolution of fund raising. The campaign strategy, with definitive beginning and end dates, was formed by the needs of consultants, the first fund raisers, whose primary service until the 1970s was providing full-time resident managers for a campaign's duration—after which they would move on to another organization's campaign. As increasing numbers of staff practitioners were employed, consultants changed their services from primarily full-time resident management to part-time campaign consulting. Their livelihood, however, remains dependent on campaigns, and they market them in favor of continuous programming. Based on evidence presented, chapter 14 concludes that capital campaigns are an artifact of fund raising's earlier eras and are no longer necessary or desirable.

Chapter 14 scrutinizes characteristics of campaigns, including feasibility studies, usage of volunteers, and committee reporting meetings. *Feasibility studies*, for example, are conducted by consultants to determine the likelihood that a proposed campaign can be successfully completed and a dollar goal reached. The fund-raising literature is adamant that the research be done by consultants because of their objectivity. Howe (1991) illustrated: "To be valid, a feasibility study must be made by an outsider. Survey respondents will speak candidly, if at all, only to a professional outsider who establishes confidence and guarantees confidentiality" (p. 61). Paradoxically, the literature is silent about the self-interests of consultants, who in most cases are retained as part-time counsel for the campaigns they recommend. Furthermore, supposedly confidential information sometimes is used to formulate plans for soliciting specific prospects.

Contrary to popular belief, campaigns are not very effective. Their fundamental purpose is to maximize income, not manage interdependent relationships with donors. Focusing solely on income, campaigns rely on smoke-and-mirror accounting for their success. Only a small portion of their goals represents new, or unique, money. Many campaigns fail, and even organizations that reach dollar goals often find themselves facing a deficit or unable to fund announced needs, termed *featured objectives*. As Luck (1990) asserted, "Few capital campaigns have achieved both the monetary and need targets. . . . Everyone brags about philanthropic achievement in terms of money raised but rarely do they mention that they missed the mark for funding several defined programmatic needs" (p. 32). Planned gifts, which will not benefit the organization for an average of 20 years, account for much of the money raised, often as great as half the goal. The problem is compounded by the traditional practice of reporting nonbequest gifts at their face value, or about 50% more than their worth to the organization. Campaigns commonly include government, or public, funds in their private support totals, distort the value of art and real estate, and count gifts twice by reporting pledges in one campaign and again as cash gifts in the next. Totals also are artificially inflated by extending the length of campaigns to 9 or even 20 years!

Chapter 14 assesses current practice in light of CASE's (1994) new management and reporting standards, which—among other reforms—instructs fund raisers to separate planned gifts from outright gifts and report the former at face and discounted present values in reports to CASE and to trustees. The impact of the standards will be to deflate campaign goals and announced results. Although the standards apply only to educational organizations and adherence is not a requirement of CASE membership, it is predicted that the dissemination of valid statistics—which CASE started at the end of 1996—will alert donors and other stakeholders to deceptive practices and document the ineffectiveness of campaigns. Chapter 14 recommends the continuing major gifts program as an alternative to the historical model. Luck (1990) concurred: "Established long-range development programs make better sense than a series or 'string' of three- to five-year campaigns which rarely achieve all the goals set at the beginning of the campaign" (p. 32).

Chapter 15, the final chapter of the book, examines the three sources of gifts, or donor publics: individuals, corporations, and foundations. There are approximately

37,600 active U.S. foundations, which collectively account for 8% of all gift dollars (Renz, Lawrence, & Treiber, 1995). They consist of four types: (a) independent, (b) corporate, (c) community, and (d) operating. Independent foundations are by far the largest group, accounting for 88% of the total number, 86% of the assets, and 78% of the annual dollars. Chapter 15 describes independent, corporate, and community foundations in detail, excluding operating foundations because they are not viable prospects for fund raising (i.e., they operate their own program services). The historical development of each type is traced, and operational differences are pointed out. For example, independent and corporate foundations are required by law to give away an amount equal to 5% of their assets each year, whereas community foundations are exempted from this requirement. Community foundations raise gifts as well as make grants. Unlike the other types, therefore, they employ fund raisers. A commonality among all three types is that a small number account for the majority of grant dollars. Illustrating, only about 1% of all independent foundations, or roughly the top 400, give 55% of the dollars.

Foundations, as is true of all major donors, are basically conservative in their giving. Education traditionally receives the largest share of grant dollars. Close to one third of both grants and dollars represent renewed gifts, and almost 90% of all dollars are restricted in purpose. Relationships with foundations, as with corporations and individuals, can best be understood as environmental interdependencies. Whereas the dependency of charitable organizations on donors is widely and often inaccurately portrayed in the literature, much less is said about the dependency of donors *on* charitable organizations. Foundations, for example, would cease to exist without charitable organizations (i.e., there would be no reason to grant them tax-exempt status or gift deductibility for their donors). As with all donor publics, foundations do not give for the sake of giving; rather mixed motives direct their grants to specific interests that may or may not coincide with those of an organization. Fund raisers manage foundation relations effectively when they identify overlapping interests and needs. Greenfield (1991) explained, "The best time to ask any foundations or corporations for money is when a special project is planned that is matched to their current priorities" (p. 123).

A widespread misunderstanding about corporations is that their giving—more so than giving by foundations or individuals—is motivated by self-interest. Chapter 15 eradicates this fallacy by conceptualizing a continuum of motivation to explain the mixed motives of corporate philanthropy. Points along the continuum are encompassed under the rubric of *enlightened self-interest*, although the term generally refers to a balanced, or center, position. The benefits corporate donors seek from their relationships with charitable organizations are grouped into five categories: (a) marketing, (b) tax savings, (c) social currency, (d) public relations, and (e) social responsibility. Emphasis on the benefits they expect shifts their position along the continuum, with apparent differences over time and among specific companies.

Although some companies currently emphasize short-term marketing benefits, recent research shows that major corporate donors still seek benefits from all five categories, but—in contrast to the past—they demand measurable results from their giving, quantified and documented by recipients. Chapter 15 traces the evolution of corporate philanthropy from a passive, scattergun activity to strategically managed programs with set objectives. Today, contributions must generate outcomes that support the corporation's objectives—requirements similar to those imposed by foundations. According to H. W. Smith (1993), the modern approach to corporate philanthropy "begins with the view that corporations exist primarily for the purpose of making money for their shareholders and that any money given to charity must bear some relationship to the interests of a company and its shareholders" (p. 220). A greater degree of accountability is called for; specifically, fund raisers must pay more attention to stewardship. Corporate donors complain that they do not receive enough appreciation and recognition for their gifts, and reporting on what gifts accomplished is less than acceptable. In short, unsatisfactory performance on the part of charitable organizations has contributed to charges that corporate giving is motivated by self-interest.

Chapter 15 points out further commonalities between corporations and the other two donor publics. Only a few, or less than 0.01% of all 6 million U.S. companies, contribute most of the dollars (Doty, 1994; U.S. Small Business Administration, 1995). Corporations are conservative in their giving, and education is the favored recipient. Corporations are dependent on charitable organizations. At the society level, companies depend on gifts to protect our capitalistic system and avoid big government. On the community level, nonprofits are critical partners in building local economies in terms of employment, services, and quality of life.

Regarding the last and most important of the three donor publics, individuals account for almost 90% of all gift dollars (American Association of Fund-Raising Counsel Trust for Philanthropy, 1997b), and there are about 170 million adults in the United States with diverse interests in charitable organizations. Just 400 of the wealthiest Americans have combined assets greater than all U.S. foundations. As with the other sources, a minority of individuals provide the majority of gift dollars. Only about one fourth of all U.S. households itemize deductions on their federal income tax returns and deduct charitable contributions, yet they give two thirds of all dollars from living individuals (IS, 1994).

Unlike foundations and corporations, the favored recipient of individuals is religion. However, religious organizations receive the biggest share of their gifts from individuals who make less than $40,000 per year, whereas wealthy individuals tend to give to other types of organizations, such as education. Individuals who are major donors are conservative in their giving, perpetuating the *status quo* from which they obtained their wealth.

Chapter 15 dissects patterns of individual giving to demonstrate that individuals give for altruistic reasons and also seek benefits in return. Members of religious congregations, for example, make gifts to their churches or temples partly for the direct benefits they receive as members (e.g., the employed services of a minister and a building in which to worship). Individuals, then, are dependent on charitable organizations. Due to the interdependency of all three donor publics, fund raisers have no need to apologize for requesting gifts from well-researched prospects. Philanthropy provides donors with a way to put their beliefs into action, beyond what they can express through the ballot box and the marketplace.

As do their counterparts, individuals have objectives they wish to accomplish with their giving. And increasingly they demand greater accountability. J. Michael Cook (cited in Dundjerski, 1995), CEO of the accounting firm of Deloitte & Touche and head of UWA's strategic planning committee, declared, "People these days don't just give you money and say, 'Here it is and go do some good.' There is an increasing expectation of impact, of accountability, measurement, and demonstrated results" (p. 28).

Chapter 15 ends with a discussion of the growing concentration of wealth in our country and concludes that fund raisers must make special efforts to ensure that their organization's donors are inclusive of people from across the economic spectrum. Widespread support is necessary to protect the well-being of the charitable subsector, which—in turn—promotes the pluralism undergirding our democratic society. Effective fund-raising management, students are urged to remember, goes beyond raising dollars.

MISSING: WOMEN, MINORITIES, AND AN INTERNATIONAL PERSPECTIVE

Two caveats are necessary before the book proceeds to Part I. First, women and minorities are conspicuously absent from the literature dealing with fund-raising history. Rather than documenting fund raising as an occupation developed solely by White men, the absence of references to women and minorities reflects our historical biases toward gender and race, as well as the sparse research in this field. It is recalled that most of the fund-raising literature has been written by practitioners; a review of the literature shows that the practitioner authors are predominantly White males. Similar to other functions in our society, the contributions of women and minorities have been ignored and require the attention of scholars with the skills to delve into primary sources to reconstruct a more accurate historical record.

This process currently is taking place in philanthropy as it relates to giving. Historian Kathleen McCarthy (1992), for example, documented women's significant contributions to American charitable organizations with missions in the arts. Although women's giving generally was more modest than men (partially because—until state laws were changed in the late 1800s—a married woman's property belonged to her husband), there were exceptions. Catharine Lorillard Wolfe, unmarried and an heiress to a tobacco fortune, was among the 105 charter subscribers to New York's Metropolitan Museum of Art. She donated more than 100 of her paintings to the museum when she died in 1887, "along with $200,000 for additional acquisitions" (p. 118). As McCarthy stated in the preface to her book, "Women's roles as donors have been virtually ignored" (p. xii).

Similarly, Emmett Carson (1989, 1991), president of the Minneapolis Foundation and former program officer at the Ford Foundation, documented the long and prestigious tradition of philanthropic activity that has existed in the African American community for more than 200 years. In 1852, William Lloyd Garrison (cited in Carson, 1989) commended African Americans in Boston for forming "societies, both among men and women, for mutual improvement and assistance" (p. 94). Reviewing the findings of a 3-year national study he directed in the mid-1980s on the charitable giving and volunteer behavior of Blacks and Whites, Carson (1989) concluded: "There is a widespread opinion among many that blacks do not contribute to charitable organizations. This view is unsupported by the data" (p. 98). Carson found, for example, that an equal percentage of Blacks and Whites with incomes of more than $25,000 make contributions of more than $1,000—20% of each group.

Parallel studies on women and minorities in fund raising have yet to be conducted. Our limited knowledge of contributions to the development of the fund-raising function by those who were not White and/or male begs for historical studies. The Joseph and Matthew Payton Philanthropic Studies Library, a component of Indiana University's Center on Philanthropy, houses the archives of several pioneering firms in fund raising.[7] During the 1993 dedication ceremony for the library's new facilities, I casually glanced through some of the documents and identified a number of female fund raisers—often the wives of the firms' founders—who actively participated in raising gifts in the 1930s, 1940s, and 1950s. It is hoped that students reading this text will become interested in unveiling these "shadowed" faces through historical studies that utilize both primary and secondary sources.

Focusing on the more recent past, I personally have met a number of women at conferences and seminars who have mentioned in passing their longevity in fund raising. Right now they are nameless faces, about whom we know little. This also would be a good topic for a thesis or dissertation. For example, a qualitative study of senior women in NSFRE, using depth interviews with a purposive sample of those who have worked in fund raising for 20 years or more, would add much to our knowledge. The sample would be relatively easy to identify in that NSFRE requests information about gender and year of entry into fund raising on its annual membership and dues form. Some areas of inquiry might be changes in fund-raising practice over the last two decades, role models and mentors for these women, and perceived differences between fund-raising management by males and females. Similar studies on minorities' contributions are badly needed, and targeted samples easily can be obtained as the NSFRE membership form breaks down ethnic background by such categories as Black, Hispanic/Latino, Asian/Pacific-Islander, and American Indian.

Turning to the book's focus on the United States, although it is hoped its concepts will be useful in other countries with a viable nonprofit sector, this textbook primarily is concerned with managing fund raising in the context of U.S. society. Arguments in support of this focus are numerous. For example, Dorsey (1991) and the Institute for Public Policy and Administration (1988), both cited at the beginning of the chapter, argued that the nonprofit sector is very much an American phenomenon. Although some European countries have voluntary sectors, they are considerably smaller and less important than America's. Former Yale University President Kingman Brewster (1989) explained:

> The United States relies more heavily than any other country on the voluntary nonprofit sector to conduct the nation's social, cultural, and economic business—to bring us into the world, to educate and entertain us, even to bury us. Indeed, the United States can be

---

[7]The Payton Library, endowed by Mr. and Mrs. Robert Payton and named for their deceased sons, has the most comprehensive collection of works on fund raising, philanthropy, and nonprofit management. It contains about 12,000 books, monographs, journal articles, working papers, and videotapes—including more than 2,500 dissertations. All materials other than reference items can be checked out through the Interlibrary Loan network. Information on its services and the *Philanthropic Studies Index*, a compilation of citations to relevant works, is available on the library's World Wide Web site: *http://www-lib.iupui.edu/philanthropy/payton.html*.

distinguished from all other societies by virtue of the work load it assigns to its "third sector," as compared to business firms or government agencies. (p. v)

According to Brian O'Connell (cited in Young, 1993), founding past president of Independent Sector, there are general similarities but also marked differences between philanthropy and fund raising in the United States and in other industrialized countries. He stated, "In most of those countries—for example, Japan, England, Germany—there is not a long-standing practice of voluntary contributions" (p. 313). In particular, non-U.S. corporations do not recognize any philanthropic obligation primarily because of traditional reliance on government funding for those activities supported by gifts in the United States.

Be that as it may, this textbook is limited due to its exclusive focus on American fund raising. The implications of ignoring fund raising in other industrialized nations of the world cannot be minimized. Studies on philanthropy and the nonprofit sector have expanded in scope beyond national boundaries. As Lohmann (1992a) stated: "This is no longer a parochial Anglo-American topic. We are witnessing an extraordinary international outburst of creativity and energy in the study of nonprofit organizations . . . fundraising [*sic*], and all related topics" (p. 311). Yet this surge of scholarly activity is new and unable to support a global perspective at this time. It is hoped that students interested in different cultures will pursue studies on international fund raising. As their work adds to the growing number of comparative studies, future fund-raising textbooks will find it possible—and necessary—to incorporate an international perspective.

SUGGESTED READINGS

Broce, T. E. (1986). *Fund raising: The guide to raising money from private sources* (2nd ed.). Norman: University of Oklahoma Press.

Burlingame, D. F., & Hulse, L. J. (Eds.). (1991). *Taking fund raising seriously: Advancing the profession and practice of raising money.* San Francisco, CA: Jossey-Bass.

Crowder, N. L., & Hodgkinson, V. A. (Eds.). (1991). *Compendium of resources for teaching about the nonprofit sector, voluntarism and philanthropy* (2nd ed.). Washington, DC: Independent Sector.

Cutlip, S. M., Center, A. H., & Broom, G. M. (1994). *Effective public relations* (7th Ed.). Englewood Cliffs, NJ: Prentice-Hall.

Grunig, J. E. (Ed.). (1992). *Excellence in public relations and communication management: Contributions to effective organizations.* Hillsdale, NJ: Lawrence Erlbaum Associates.

Kelly, K. S. (1991). *Fund raising and public relations: A critical analysis.* Hillsdale, NJ: Lawrence Erlbaum Associates.

Lohmann, R. A. (1992). *The commons: New perspectives on nonprofit organizations and voluntary action.* San Francisco, CA: Jossey-Bass.

Magat, R. (Ed.). (1989). *Philanthropic giving: Studies in varieties and goals.* New York: Oxford University Press.

Payton, R. L. (1988). *Philanthropy: Voluntary action for the public good.* New York: American Council on Education and Macmillan.

Rosso, H. A., & Associates. (1991). *Achieving excellence in fund raising: A comprehensive guide to principles, strategies, and methods.* San Francisco, CA: Jossey-Bass.

Van Til, J., & Associates. (1990). *Critical issues in American philanthropy: Strengthening theory and practice.* San Francisco, CA: Jossey-Bass.

PART I

THE PRACTICE: PARAMETERS, PRACTITIONERS, AND PROFESSIONALISM

2

The Parameters
of Fund Raising

The practice, principles, process, programs, and publics of fund raising cannot be understood without first understanding the larger concepts that delineate the boundaries in which fund raising takes place. This chapter, then, examines America's philanthropic tradition, donor motivations, the nonprofit sector, and the charitable subsector—or those nonprofits to which gifts are tax deductible. Special care is taken to estimate the number and describe the dimensions of those organizations most likely to have a fund-raising function.

AMERICA'S PHILANTHROPIC TRADITION

Americans give generously. Throughout our country's history, they customarily have given away their money, as well as their time, to serve a common good—their interpretation of what is in the best interest of society. As one observer stated, Americans will give "to build something, to fight something, or to save something" (J. Fink, 1990, p. 136).

This giving tradition is exemplified best by our response to national disasters. In a short 5 weeks after Hurricane Andrew swept through South Florida in August 1992, one organization, We Will Rebuild, received $6 million in cash contributions and an additional $11 million in pledges. "These contributions came pouring in from almost every state from Alaska to Maine. . . . School children, retirees, church groups and thousands of individuals and companies sent donations," reported Tracey Becken (1993, p. 16), a loaned executive to the organization. The gifts largely were unsolicited and separate from the millions of dollars spent on relief efforts by the federal government, such major foundations as the Florida-based Knight Foundation, and charitable organizations that deal with disasters, such as the American Red Cross. Speaking at a fund-raising conference in the aftermath of the hurricane, Red Cross President Elizabeth Dole (cited in "Fund-raisers," 1993) summarized American generosity: "The idea of giving to others is ingrained in our nature, taught by our parents who were taught by theirs" (p. 8).

Americans gave an estimated $150.7 billion to charitable organizations in 1996, which was 7.3% more than the amount given in 1995 (AAFRC Trust for Philanthropy,

1997b). Gifts have increased every year since the American Association of Fund-Raising Counsel (AAFRC) began tracking them in 1959. U.S. giving represents 2% of our country's gross domestic product (GDP). Total gift dollars equal half the combined profits of all Fortune 500 companies and exceed the budgets of most countries in the world (O'Neill, 1989; "Profits up," 1997).

Where do these gifts come from? Gifts by individuals, including bequests, traditionally account for almost 90% of the total—86.5% in 1996 (AAFRC Trust for Philanthropy, 1997b). Foundations and corporations essentially provide the rest—7.8% and 5.6%, respectively, in 1996. According to the Nonprofit Almanac 1996–1997 (Hodgkinson, Weitzman, Abrahams, Crutchfield, & Stevenson, 1996), nearly 75% of all U.S. households contribute to one or more charitable organizations each year. The proportion has remained stable since the mid-1980s. In 1993, for example, 73% of the households made gifts (IS, 1994). Independent Sector's (IS, 1996) most recent biennial survey on giving and volunteering found that 85% of all Americans would be likely to give if they were asked to do so. These high proportions are remarkable in light of U.S. Census Bureau statistics that show about 12% of adults 18 to 64 years old in the United States live in poverty ("America's poor," 1993). As Gurin and Van Til (1990) explained, although other countries also have a philanthropic tradition, the pervasiveness and very fundamentalism of American philanthropy make it unique in the world.

Students' Perspective

Students are very much a part of this tradition, or what some refer to as "America's voluntary spirit." In his essay on teaching philanthropy, Robert Payton (1990), who was a fund-raising practitioner before he became a professor, provided an overview of students' involvement:

> Students act as Big Brothers and Big Sisters; students sit with Alzheimer's victims; students organize and staff shelters for the homeless and serve food to the hungry; students raise money for art films and blood drives and cancer research and Afghan refugees; students fast, march, sit in, sing, and pray for human rights and civil rights and animal rights; students design posters and stuff envelopes and repair toys and collect canned goods and used clothing and signatures on petitions; students run long distances, crowd into small cars, dance until they drop, wear rhetorical T-shirts, and wear costumes to celebrate ethnic diversity. ... Some students hand out literature denouncing abortion, and others distribute condoms to prevent AIDS. Students staff the booths of art fairs and book fairs and help alumni in telethons to increase annual giving from alumni and even parents. (p. 171)

Every student, then, brings his or her personal experience of philanthropy to the study of fund raising. This has both constructive and potentially detrimental consequences. In many cases, students already have acted out roles as volunteers, and as donors and solicitors of lower level gifts. Their familiarity with helping, giving, and helping others to give is a plus. On the other hand, experiences dealing solely with lower level gifts tend to distort their perception of fund raising as an act of begging, with little understanding of the social exchange involved in raising both lower level and major gifts.

Indeed, the average college student may find it difficult to accept the fundamental concept of philanthropy, primarily because he or she generally has little discretionary income to give away. My experience has been that the eyes of students glaze over when I lecture about the process of raising a $10,000 gift. The thought of giving away even $100 is outside the realm of reality for most students (and, perhaps, for most educators!). This barrier can be surmounted through a historical perspective of fund raising, which is provided in chapter 5, and through an emphasis here that philanthropy is a characteristic of American society. In other words, fund raising is not begging, unsavory manipulation, or part of metaphysical phenomena, but identifying, building, and maintaining relationships with individuals, corporations, and foundations who, *characteristically*, give away money.

What does philanthropy cover? Everything from Girl Scouts selling cookies door to door to Walter Annenberg—who made a fortune from *TV Guide* and *Seventeen* magazines—giving $365 million in cash to three universities and one private school and pledging another $500 million to the nation's public schools, all in 1 year (E. Greene, 1994b). (In case students negate the Girl Scouts' efforts, they should know that this charitable organization generates about $400 million annually from its cookie sales.)

Using popular music as a spectrum for giving and receiving (E. Greene & Moore, 1993), philanthropy is country singer Willie Nelson founding Farm Aid, which—since it began in 1985—has raised $12 million through annual concerts to provide services for family farmers. It is pop singer Gloria Estefan coordinating a 1992 benefit concert that raised $3 million to aid victims of Hurricane Andrew. There is the rap group Run DMC working with Special Olympics International, the heavy metal group Poison helping People for the Ethical Treatment of Animals (PETA), and the punk rock group Fugazi donating all proceeds from its concerts in the District of Columbia to local charities. Philanthropy is Nashville-resident Garth Brooks giving $1 million in the wake of the Rodney King riots to the United Way of America for a children's community center in South-Central Los Angeles ("Annenberg gives," 1993). Just as philanthropy runs the gamut from country to rap, so does it pervade all aspects of American life.

American Perspective of Wealth

Turning from music to popular literature, the 1978 bestseller *Jackie Oh!* (Kelley, 1978) offered the following and enlightening quote, reportedly from sister Lee Radziwill about why the late Jackie Kennedy Onassis' second marriage was unpopular with Americans:

> But people aren't used to men like [Ari] Onassis who exhibit their wealth. The wealthy Europeans are ostentatious with their money. They want to show everyone how rich they are, to buy every good thing that money can buy, to enjoy themselves, and even, sometimes, to have the pleasure of wasting money. Rich Americans, on the other hand, are more strait-laced with their money. They establish libraries, they're philanthropic, they support political movements. It's as though they must buy forgiveness for having so much wealth. (pp. 321–322)

Whereas a tradition of helping and giving characterizes our entire society, those who have acquired wealth through our capitalistic economy are held—and often hold themselves—to a philanthropic standard that is unusual in the modern world.

In 1889, legendary philanthropist Andrew Carnegie (1889/1983) authored a five-part essay, "The Gospel of Wealth," which defined this philanthropic standard. Carnegie stated that the duty of America's wealthy was to set an example of unostentatious living, provide moderately for family members, "and, after doing so, to consider all surplus revenues . . . simply as trust funds, which he [sic] is called upon to administer" (p. 104). Adjusting his gifts to 1996 dollars, Carnegie gave away $3.5 billion during his lifetime (Hafner, 1996). John D. Rockefeller, Jr. also gave $3.5 billion, but the giant in philanthropy was his father and Carnegie's contemporary, John D. Rockefeller, Sr., whose gifts totaled an amazing $5.4 billion in today's currency!

Peter Dobkin Hall (1989), a philanthropy historian at Yale University, convincingly argued 100 years after the essay was published that Carnegie had arrived at his gospel by applying Darwinism to giving. According to Hall, Carnegie reasoned that if capitalism was to survive, it must be a self-renewing system. "And," said Hall, "only by putting back into the social organism what [wealthy capitalists such as Carnegie and Rockefeller] had taken out could its future be assured" (p. 183). Dramatically summarizing his gospel, Carnegie (1989/1983) proclaimed, "He who dies rich dies disgraced" (p. 108).

This philosophy remains evident today. Billionaire Walter Annenberg (cited in E. Greene, 1994b) recently stated, "If you have been fortunate economically in life, I think you have a very important obligation to share and support others less fortunate than you" (p. 11). Echoing Carnegie, he added, "And if you don't understand that, you're a rather shabby citizen" (p. 11). Annenberg has given and pledged almost $2.5 billion over the course of his life, including $50 million to the United Negro College Fund, two grants totaling $150 million to the Corporation for Public Broadcasting, and a pledge of 53 paintings with an estimated value of $1 billion to the Metropolitan Museum of Art in New York. When making his $865-million commitment in 1993, the then 85-year-old announced that he plans to give away as much as he can before he dies. Referring to fortunes accumulated and placed in foundations such as his, which—with assets of $1.4 billion in 1995 (Foundation Center, 1997)—is among the nation's 15 wealthiest, Annenberg (cited in Bailey, 1993) declared: "These are public funds. They don't belong to anybody in a foundation" (p. 10).

Touching on the giving away of business dollars, Joseph Galaskiewicz (1989), a professor of sociology and strategic management at the University of Minnesota and a leading scholar in corporate philanthropy, has advanced an explanation of corporate giving that he identifies as contributions used as *social currency* by those who head companies. Often referred to as "old boy network philanthropy," Galaskiewicz said this approach "is better understood as status competition among very powerful actors within an economic elite" (p. 252). Galaskiewicz concluded after numerous studies and a review of the literature that "giving is the norm in many business elite subcultures, and those who want to remain in the inner circles had best conform and make the appropriate contributions" (p. 252). In other words, a well-researched explanation of corporate philanthropy is that American corporations make gifts because their senior managers are expected to do so by business peers (i.e., a standard of philanthropic behavior exists in the business sector, as well as among individuals).

Foundations, the third primary source of gifts, currently are required by law to give away each year an amount equal to 5% of their assets. As Sheldon (1991) explained, their purpose is "to provide support to charitable organizations through grants" (p. 243). By legal definition, then, they are expected to behave philanthropically.

There are 94 billionnaires in the United States and about 60,000 households have annual incomes of $1 million or more (IRS, 1995; P. Newcomb, 1995). The number of $1-million-plus households increased 1,350% during the 1980s due to "an explosion of private wealth unmatched since the Industrial Revolution" (McNamee, 1993, p. 7). Every year, 700,000 companies report contributions on their tax returns (H. W. Smith, 1993). Grants from foundations have totaled over $10 billion annually since 1992 (Renz et al., 1995). Approximately 8,500 foundations have assets of at least $1 million.

According to Novak (1988), the economist Walter Williams cited figures showing that 80% of funds contributed throughout human history have been donated by Americans. Schuster (1985) found in his international study of the arts that "all European countries are quite envious, at the moment, of the American tradition of private support" (p. 41).

Summarizing this section, individuals, corporations, and foundations in the United States characteristically give away money. They do so for many reasons, but the one reason fundamental to understanding fund raising is that donors make gifts because giving is a customary, admired, expected, and even legally required behavior in our society. Fund raising, therefore, is not about convincing, persuading, or manipulating donors to give money because their inclination to do so is based on a tradition beyond the influence of practitioners. Contrary to conventional wisdom, fund raisers affect not whether donors give, but to which charitable organizations they give, the purposes of their gifts, and the amounts of the gifts—all of which are determined by the relationships identified, built, and maintained with them.

DONOR MOTIVATIONS

There traditionally have been two opposing viewpoints about donor motivations that have divided the philanthropy and fund-raising literature: (a) donors give money as an act of altruism, which is natural to the human condition (e.g., M. Hunt, 1990); and (b) donors make gifts to advance their self-interests, which some interpret as social control by the wealthy (e.g., Odendahl, 1990). Bremner (1990) explained that in reaction to the first viewpoint many studies on donor motivations were undertaken by scholars primarily so they could conclude "that the motive was self-serving or not entirely altruistic" (p. xiv). He added, "Motives for giving are much more complex than many observers or students of philanthropy have assumed" (p. xiv).

Consultant Jerold Panas (1984) based his book about the motivations of major donors on an assumption of complexity. Reviewing Annenberg's giving record, for example, Panas stated: "Who can be certain of the impetus which motivates this generosity. Likely, Walter Annenberg himself cannot be certain" (p. 4). Both the altruistic and self-interested viewpoints are found in Panas' book, which draws from the author's experience and an unscientific study of $1-million-or-more donors. Panas cited colleague Arthur Frantzreb, who said, "The act of philanthropy is a spiritual act—an act of love expressed for one's fellow man [sic]" (p. 106). In support of this altruistic viewpoint, Panas described fund raising as the "magnificent business of helping others undertake consequential acts of kindness and generosity" (p. 169). Yet he emphasized early in his book that self-interest was a factor in the giving of many well-known philanthropists of the past.

Illustrating, Panas (1984) described Sears, Roebuck and Co. founder Julius Rosenwald's many gifts during the 1920s to establish schools, shops, and housing units for southern African Americans, but also pointed out that critics charged such efforts were related directly to African Americans' ability to buy goods from the new Sears catalogs. Rosenwald, according to Panas, insisted that his name be attached to gifts, resulting in 5,000 "Rosenwald Schools" across the South by 1935. As the ability of African Americans to pay for merchandise grew, Rosenwald prospered. "What truly motivated his giving? A selfishness? An over-expanded ego? Or a strong commitment to help the needy," Panas asked, and then responded, "Likely all of these factors and more" (p. 6).

This textbook adopts a mixed-motive model of donor motivations that assumes donors hold interests both in self and in a common good when making a gift. The model is supported by recent scholarly work on philanthropy. Van Til (1988) first discussed the concept of mixed motives in his book on mapping the third sector. He later stated, "Modern philanthropy is in many ways an arena in which mixed motives prevail" (Van Til, 1990, p. 34). Jeavons (1991) confirmed this assessment in his historical analysis of religious fund raising: "Mixed motives are the rule, not the exception, of our experiences in philanthropy" (p. 55).

Van Til (1990), as do other contemporary scholars, approaches philanthropy as a social exchange. "Philanthropy *does involve* a complex exchange of money, power, values, and expectations between the donor and the donee" (p. 31; italics in original). Gifts, he said, may "be traded for some mix of power, influence, and the commitment of values" (p. 29).

The French sociologist Marcel Mauss (1925/1954) was the first to challenge the notion that giving to others is a pure altruistic act. His ground-breaking book approached gifts as a means of receiving something in return. In subsequent years, other sociologists conceptualized the theory of social exchange, which explains human interaction on the basis of reward expectations (e.g., Blau, 1964/1986). Alvin Gouldner (1960), whose work is discussed shortly, suggested that many acts labeled altruistic are, in fact, part of an exchange framework. Richard Titmus (1970) moved the concept of social exchange beyond individuals and advanced the idea of a society in which citizens feel responsibility toward one another, as well as themselves.

Both social exchange theory and mixed motives are placed in the theoretical context of fund raising in chapter 9. The following description of the mixed-motive model is provided here to help students comprehend information presented before that critical chapter. Similarly, the relationship between giving and tax savings is discussed later in this section, although tax laws primarily are covered in chapter 7. Finally, it must be emphasized before proceeding that the mixed-motive model adopted by this book also assumes that charitable organizations, like donors, hold dual interests in self and the common good (i.e., the motivations of organizations when obtaining gifts are not solely altruistic). This important assumption rarely is touched on in the philanthropy and fund-raising literature. As Payton (1988b) stated, "The self-interest of donors is often lamented; less often heard is concern about the self-interest of recipients" (p. 7).

Mixed-Motive Model of Giving

Addressing the debate between altruism and self-interest, Payton et al. (1991) admitted, "Altruism can be a powerful force in human affairs, but it is a less reliable force than egoism most of the time" (p. 10). They concluded, "We assume that human beings have a legitimate self-interest and a concern for others at the same time. Fund raising thus uses self-interest to help people go beyond self-interest" (p. 11).

Altruism and self-interest—or egoism—are not mutually exclusive. Students likely are familiar with the golden rule: Do unto others as you would have them do unto you. Much of our day-to-day understanding of altruism is based on such moral codes, generally derived from religion and taught to us as children. But Tuleja (1985) pointed out, "The Golden Rule works not in spite of selfishness, but because of it" (p. 24). J. E. Grunig and White (1992) explained, "The rule is selfish because it mandates that people should think of how they would like to be treated by others and then treat others in the same way" (p. 46). Their logic is sound, but they confuse self-interest with selfishness. Professor of philosophy Mike Martin (1994), whose book *Virtuous Giving* won the top research prize in 1995 from NSFRE, clarified: "Selfishness is a pejorative term which means immoral self-seeking. It implies disregard of others and inappropriately or excessively seeking personal advantages at their expense" (p. 126). In contrast, self-interest refers to one's overall good, the desire for that good, or desires for things that promote that good. Such motives are permissible and even desirable. Similarly, egoism is different from egotistical, which refers to objectionable forms of self-absorption, such as arrogance and narcissism.

Almost 40 years ago, Gouldner (1960) conceptualized the "norm of reciprocity," which holds that "those whom you have helped have an obligation to help you" (p. 173). He asserted, "The conclusion is clear: if you want to be helped by others you must help them; hence it is not only proper but also expedient to conform with the specific status rights of others and with the general norm" (p. 173). Gouldner argued in his seminal article that the norm of reciprocity is a universal component of all moral codes. He added that people tend toward egoism, as Payton et al. (1991) noted. Egoism, as defined by Gouldner (1960), is "a salient (but not exclusive) concern with the satisfaction of one's own needs" (p. 173). But, he explained, "There is an altruism in egoism, made possible through reciprocity" (p. 173).

What we define as altruism, then, incorporates self-interest, and egoism is not mutually exclusive of altruistic behavior. As Ralph Waldo Emerson (cited in Lord, 1983) said, "It is one of the beautiful compensations of this life that no one can sincerely try to help another without helping himself [*sic*]" (p. 113). Giving money, therefore, reflects neither pure altruism nor pure egoism; it involves mixed motives for giving: to fulfill the donor's interests in self and in a common good, as represented by the mission of the charitable organization receiving the gift. And as Lowenberg (1975) stated, "Reciprocity, a basic process in social interaction, is also the norm in fundraising [*sic*]" (p. 8).

Evidence of donors attributing their giving behavior to reasons of self-interest are difficult to find in the literature. For example, study after study of donor motivations show that whereas savings on taxes have an effect on giving, they rarely are found to be a significant reason for making a gift. Almost all such studies are based on surveys of donors after they have made a gift, and as Jenkins (1989) argued, such post hoc self-reports "are likely to be colored by a desire to present a favorable image" (p. 300).

Economist Jerald Schiff (1989) said he and others in his discipline are distrustful of such surveys, believing that respondents are unable or unwilling to provide truthful and accurate answers. He supported the distrust with findings of a 1974 study that showed when asked if tax deductibility made a difference in gift decisions, 82% of the respondents said it did not for themselves, but 56% said it did for people in general. Schiff concluded, "A typical response was that *I* do not allow my charitable giving to be influenced by taxation, but *others* do" (p. 131; italics in original).

Rather than rely on self-reported motivations, economists build models of charitable giving by observing donor behavior as documented on income tax forms. (Students will appreciate that economists believe people provide truthful and accurate information on their tax forms, but not on surveys.) They make predictions by noting variations among cases and inferring the causes of the variations. According to Schiff (1989), "Economists generally believe that much behavior can, in fact, be explained by concentrating on prices [the cost of the gift after subtracting the amount of taxes saved] and income. Other factors, such as attitudes, may play a role . . . but only a *small* role" (p. 134; italics in original). In other words, economists rely on the financial self-interest of donors to explain giving behavior, whereas donors and the scientists who use self-reported data emphasize altruistic reasons.

However, there is support from economists for the mixed-motive explanation. For example, Schiff (1989) found in an earlier study that altruistic tendencies were significant determinants of giving. Furthermore, as Auten and Rudney (1989) pointed out, econometric studies "typically find that price and income account for less than half of the variation in giving among taxpayers" (p. 85).

Another economist, Richard Steinberg (1989), who has conducted extensive research on fund raising and philanthropy, conceptualized two levels of motives for giving:

1. Raise the amount of a "local public good," or what this book refers to as a common good (e.g., increased medical research).
2. Receive some private good (benefit) in return for the gift:
    a. Tangible (e.g., front-row seat at the opera).
    b. Intangible but externally observable (e.g., greater prestige).
    c. Internal benefit (e.g., feel good about act of giving).

The two levels, Steinberg (1989) argued, are inextricably intertwined; therefore, "It seems reasonable to allow for both sorts of motivation in any theory of giving" (p. 146).

The appropriateness of exchanging tangible benefits for gifts, students should note, was legally supported by the Supreme Court in the early 1990s when it endorsed the *dual character theory*, which recognizes that gifts can be both a purchase and a contribution (Arthur Andersen & Company, 1992). As discussed in chapter 7, IRS regulations follow this theory with the stipulation that the fair market value of goods or services returned to the donor must be subtracted from the gift amount before a charitable deduction is claimed.

As opposed to surveys, anthropologist and feminist scholar Teresa Odendahl (1989) employed qualitative methodology to study the giving behaviors of wealthy donors, particularly those who create foundations. The findings of her in-depth interviews with 135 individuals support the mixed-motive model. For example, one interview subject commented, "I think my funding comes out of both helping others as well as how it affects me" (p. 172). Another stated, "There is some of just writing checks to friends. And there is some sort of feathering your nest in the hospital in your area or whatever. And there is just giving because you have the money to give away, giving to organizations that you think are doing the kind of things that you want to see done or you think are important" (p. 172).

Turning from individuals to corporations, management scholars Arthur White and John Bartolomeo (1982) concluded that corporate giving has an obvious double agenda—part altruism and part self-interest. Businesses, unlike the two other gift sources, generally are more candid about mixed motives because they represent an acceptable and legitimate way to rationalize corporate contributions. White and Bartolomeo supported their conclusion with summarized findings from their study of 219 CEOs on ideologies of corporate philanthropy:

> About 7 in 10 claim to be motivated by a desire to help the needy in the communities in which their company has plants/locations and by a desire to do what is ethically correct. But 2 out of 3 also emphasize the goals of improving local communities in order to benefit their own employees and of protecting/improving the environment in which to work and do business. . . . and about a quarter expect that their corporate giving will result in increased revenues/profitability and in an enhanced ability to recruit quality employees. (pp. 62–63)

Foundations, although philanthropic by definition, also have objectives for their giving, which have been defined by the founders and/or trustees and staff. They target their grants to generate outcomes that will fulfill the objectives; they do not give just for the sake of giving. The self-interests of specific foundations can be found in their guidelines for funding. No matter how worthy a proposed project, if it does not fall within the guidelines of a foundation (i.e., meet an interest, such as improving health care for children in the Midwest), the probability of obtaining a grant is unlikely. As Jenkins (1989) explained, a project must interest the prospective donor; therefore, self-interest is involved.

Van Til (1990) capsulized, "Altruism survives as a powerful philanthropic motive, but it is mixed with the more directly individual gains" (p. 29). He added, "At the least, most philanthropic contributions are traded, in part, for the return of a tax 'write-off'" (p. 29).[1]

---

[1]Van Til's conclusion is misleading. As discussed shortly, gifts from most donors do not result in tax savings, although most of the *dollars* given are claimed as charitable deductions.

The Charitable Deduction: How Important?

Contrary to fund-raising lore, the tax deductibility of gifts is vital to sustaining America's philanthropic tradition. The United States is distinctive in the degree to which it subsidizes charitable organizations through its tax system. Economist Charles Clotfelter (1989) elaborated, "Its provisions for the deductibility of charitable gifts in addition to the tax exemptions accorded to nonprofit institutions are unparalleled in scope" (p. 105). Tying this discussion to the one just concluded, Simon (1987) stated, "Neither charitable trust law nor charitable tax law requires subjective altruism, despite the teaching of St. Paul" (p. 86).

The nonprofit sector has enjoyed a "favorite child" status throughout most of its history (Hopkins, 1990). A federal income tax was implemented in 1913, from which nonprofits were exempted. Fearful that the high taxes imposed at the beginning of World War I would cause a decrease in gifts, Congress passed the Revenue Act of 1917, which established a charitable contributions deduction of up to 15% of taxable income. Between 1917 and 1969, the only substantive changes in the law were to increase incentives for giving. Hopkins (1990) summarized, "As the income tax system evolved, it generously accommodated the philanthropic impulse by means of exemptions and deductions. State income tax systems followed suit, as did other federal, state, and local laws that provided a variety of other exemptions and exceptions for charitable groups" (p. 205).

According to Jenkins (1989), tax privileges traditionally have been justified on the grounds that private initiative is "essential for social innovation and the promotion of social plurality" (p. 293). All major social action in the United States, such as abolition, women's rights, and the environmental movement, began in the nonprofit sector. Unlike business, which is driven by profit motives, and government, which has to build consensus before acting, the third sector is free to experiment with new strategies for social change and can quickly respond to emerging needs (Weisbrod, 1988). In a democracy built on pluralism, therefore, it is appropriate for government to subsidize the work of the nonprofit sector, including tax deductions for charitable gifts. Schiff (1989) explained, "Utilizing deductibility, in effect allows individuals to direct foregone tax revenue into their favored uses" (p. 131). The charitable deduction, then, is an "incentive by which the tax law encourages desirable behavior" (Clotfelter, 1989, p. 117).

It is important for students to realize that although taxpayers may make gifts, only those who itemize their deductions on federal income tax returns are allowed to *deduct* gifts.[2] Only about 36% of all individual households file itemized returns and of those, just 26% deduct charitable contributions (IRS, 1995; IS, 1994). The 64% of all U.S. households that file simplified tax returns take an overall standard deduction, waiving their right to deduct gifts.

According to Clotfelter (1989), the standard deduction was first adopted in 1941 and "effectively eliminated the charitable deduction for a majority of taxpayers" (p. 111). In the Economic Recovery Tax Act of 1981, Congress provided gradual extension of an "above the line" charitable deduction to nonitemizers over a 5-year period, thereby giving every taxpayer an opportunity to deduct gifts. The percentage

---

[2]Taxpayers also deduct gifts from estates on which taxes are owed, which is discussed in the chapter on planned giving.

of individual returns claiming charitable deductions increased from 28% in 1980 to 36% in 1985 (IRS, 1995). Congress reversed its direction with the Tax Reform Act of 1986, which ended the nonitemizer deduction. Since 1990, the percentage of individual returns claiming contributions has held steady at 26% (IRS, 1995).

The 1986 act, according to Hopkins (1990), eliminated, reduced, and threatened all deductions, exemptions, and other tax preferences. Today, there are only three primary deductions available to individual taxpayers: state income taxes, interest on home mortgages, and charitable contributions. Those who currently deduct gifts usually are people who own their own homes and deduct interest paid on their mortgages (IS, 1996). They also are the most affluent taxpayers. The average household income in 1995 for itemizers who claim charitable deductions—excluding people who made more than $200,000—was twice as much as the average income for individuals who file simplified tax returns ($61,000 vs. $30,500; IS, 1996).[3] These itemizers gave six times the amount given by nonitemizers ($1,730 vs. $270). Indeed, as demonstrated in chapter 15, households that itemize and deduct gifts, roughly one fourth of all taxpayers, account for two thirds of all gift dollars from living individuals.

As N. S. Fink (1993) warned, "It was and still is argued that tax incentives for charitable giving favor the rich—as indeed they do, for those who give" (p. 393). Because our marginal tax rates rise with income, the rate of subsidy for gifts is greater for the wealthy. The top tax rates and income brackets as of 1997 are 36% for married couples with taxable income (i.e., after all deductions) exceeding $140,000, and 39.6% for those with taxable incomes exceeding $250,000 (Quinn, 1993). Therefore, a gift of $10,000 would cost $6,400 for a couple in the 36% tax bracket (i.e., the couple would save $3,600 in taxes), but the same gift would cost $360 less, or only $6,040, for a couple in the 39.6% bracket. Clotfelter (1989) commented:

> The charitable deduction has come in for sustained and vigorous criticism for its alleged favoritism toward high-income taxpayers. Because the tax savings per dollar obtained from the deduction rises with one's marginal tax rate, high-income taxpayers enjoy a bigger proportional tax reduction in their giving than taxpayers at lower income levels. (p. 122)

Magat (1989) predicted that deductibility increasingly will be regarded as a benefit for the rich, which will garner political sympathy for challenges to the deduction. Introducing a different and important dimension, he continued, "Furthermore, especially in an atmosphere of deep concern for large government deficits, more credence may be given to the view of some economists (and legislators) that philanthropic giving that is deductible is a 'tax expenditure,' since the government loses tax revenue equal to the deduction" (p. 23).

The last part of Magat's statement is misleading, which provides an opportunity to distinguish between tax deductions and tax credits. The federal government does not lose an amount equal to the deduction, that would be a tax credit. Deductions are subtracted from the amount of *income* on which taxes are owed (i.e., taxable income), whereas credits are subtracted directly from the amount of *taxes* owed. Clarifying, a

---

[3]IS purposely excludes upper income households, or those that earn more than $200,000 per year, from its biennial surveys on giving and volunteering in the United States. Its findings, therefore, conceal the significant impact wealthy individuals have on fund raising.

charitable deduction reduces taxable income dollar for dollar, but it reduces the amount owed in taxes by only the percentage of the tax rate assessed on the remaining income. At the highest current rate of 39.6%, a $100 gift reduces a taxpayer's bill by $39.60 (keeping in mind that deductions can reduce taxable income to a lower bracket with a lower tax rate, thereby increasing savings). In other words, the government loses tax revenue equal to 39.6% or less of each deduction.

To date, there are no tax credits for charitable contributions. If they did exist, they would cost the government 100% because taxpayers would pay $1 less in taxes for every $1 given. The difference in savings for donors between deductions and credits obviously is significant, which is a critical point to remember in later discussions about a proposed tax credit for gifts to some organizations but not to others.

Regardless, the current charitable deduction represents lost revenue for government, roughly $16 billion annually at the federal level alone. And as Hopkins (1990) emphasized, "Mounting federal deficits are today causing Congress to look everywhere for revenue" (p. 205). Annual federal deficits have ranged from $107 billion to $290 billion during the first 6 years of the 1990s, resulting in a national debt that now stands at $5 trillion. As Congress struggles to curtail the flow of red ink, it increasingly gauges public support for the charitable deduction. Efforts to balance the budget have prompted calls for tax reform, including proposals for a flat tax system that would eliminate deductions—even the one for charitable contributions (Rosenman, 1995).

Given these ominous circumstances, it is disturbing that so many fund raisers continue to scoff at the importance of the charitable deduction. Consultant and author Irving Warner (1992a), for example, began one of his columns in a trade newspaper by stating: "Sooner or later, Congress will end the tax deductibility of contributions to charitable organizations. I won't mourn the loss" (p. 35). Warner claimed that during his almost 50 years as a fund raiser he has never been concerned about the effect of taxes, although he neglected to mention that the charitable deduction was well established when he began his career in 1950. Saying "dozens of studies in philanthropy have shown that taxes are way down the list of why people give money away," Warner declared, "Raising money is not dependent upon tax deductions" (p. 36). He further asserted, "Competent professionals know what will motivate potential donors to give to their causes. . . . The competent professional doesn't need tax deductions and would function just as well without them" (p. 36).

In contrast to such naive assessments, practitioner representatives of NSFRE testified before Congress in May 1996 on the importance of the charitable deduction and the detrimental effects of some tax-reform proposals (Marlowe & Company, 1996). Their urgent message, which refuted fund-raising lore, was basically the same as the one presented here: Our philanthropic tradition is reinforced by our tax code, through which government helps defray the cost of gifts with tax deductions. This is not to say tax reform is unnecessary or reductions of the federal debt and annual deficits are unimportant; like most citizens, reflective fund raisers desire solutions to these grave problems. Yet they know that decreasing or eliminating gift incentives in order to simplify the tax system and generate revenue would greatly harm the nonprofit sector on which our country depends.

Would Americans stop giving if there were no tax savings? Certainly not. After all, tens of millions of individuals who make gifts each year do not itemize their deductions and, therefore, receive no tax benefit. A significant follow-up question, however, is: Would Americans, collectively, continue to give at the same level as they do now if there were no tax savings? Most likely not. Economists have extensively studied the price elasticity of gifts (i.e., the percentage change in giving for each 1% increase in price), and their consensus is that the percentage change is slightly greater than 1. In other words, even a 10% increase in the price of giving leads to a decrease of more than 10% in the amount given. Econometric estimates suggest that the elimination of the charitable deduction would result in gifts from wealthy taxpayers falling the most (Clotfelter, 1989). A study by Price Waterhouse, the Big 6 accounting firm, found that 1994 contributions claimed by itemizers would have dropped by $20 billion if there had been no charitable deduction (Marlowe & Company, 1996). The study further revealed that if nonitemizers had been allowed to take a deduction, an additional $4 billion would have been contributed.

Moving from individuals to corporations, Galaskiewicz (1989) reported the findings of what he believed are the two definitive studies on the effect of price on corporate giving. Employing time-series data and econometric analyses, both studies used the price of giving as a predictor variable with the amount of contributions as the dependent variable. Their findings agreed: As the cost of making contributions went up, the amount of contributions significantly declined. "Given these empirical findings," Galaskiewicz stated, "it is surprising that surveys have not always found that executives always give high priority to tax matters in making company contributions" (pp. 250–251).

Illustrating the discrepancy between findings of studies that measure giving behavior and those that measure self-reported motivations, A. White and Bartolomeo (1982) found that of the 219 CEOs they interviewed, only 26% said tax laws provided great or substantial incentives for the company to give, 36% said they provided some incentives, and another 36% said they provided very slight or no incentives. Little has changed in the 15 years since the interviews. In a recent thesis study by one of my graduate students, 181 corporate donors, on average, disagreed that tax savings are a benefit they receive from giving to a local United Way (Duhé, 1996). Tax savings ranked at 12 out of 13 tangible, intangible, and internal benefits measured in the survey. The benefit most typically agreed on was "satisfaction of doing a good thing."

Foundations are exempt from income taxes; however, those who create and contribute to them, whether individuals or corporations, benefit from our tax system by deducting their gifts. Reflecting on the explosive foundation growth that occurred after World War II, the late Paul Ylvisaker (1987) stated, "The foundation movement was ready for takeoff by 1950; lift was provided by a federal and state tax structure that made foundations an attractive shelter for the great personal and corporate affluence of the postwar period" (p. 375). Statistics show that foundation growth is closely related to changes in tax rates (Renz & Lawrence, 1993).

Concluding this discussion, although the self-reported motivations of donors generally rank tax deductions as not among the most important reasons for giving, studies of giving behavior show that tax savings do affect the amount of gifts made (i.e., they are important). Clotfelter (1989) summarized, "Federal tax policy has a substantial impact on the level and distribution of charitable giving in the United States" (p. 124). More broadly, Jeavons (1991) stated, "While people will generally offer the most positive (socially acceptable) answer if queried about the reasons for their giving, their behaviors in giving may provide more trustworthy information about their real motives and intentions" (p. 55).

Before leaving this section, it is appropriate to address research needs and suggested problems and theories for thesis and dissertation studies. Donor motivations, as discussed in chapter 9, have captivated the attention of students conducting research on fund raising. Literally hundreds of studies have attempted to answer the fundamental questions: Who gives and why? The results, as also discussed in subsequent chapters, have been disappointing to say the least. Exhibiting redundancy and disregard for theoretical grounding, the studies have not produced what scholars refer to as "usable knowledge" (Kelly, 1997b). Later chapters identify several reasons for these deficiencies and offer solutions; the discussion here focuses on one overriding factor: the necessity to design studies that build on previous work.

The scientific method requires researchers to provide a review of the literature relevant to their study and to place their inquiry within the context of what has been discovered in the past. The larger perspective allows them to properly interpret their findings and add to a cumulative body of knowledge. Without comparisons, findings may be interesting, but are meaningless; they represent an isolated search for truth that has little value.

The scarcity of serious work on fund raising hampered earlier attempts to study donor motivations. Furthermore, student researchers were not exposed to or chose to ignore findings emanating from disciplines other than their own. These reasons for poor scholarship are no longer excusable. As demonstrated in this chapter, the literature on donor motivations is rich in research possibilities. Scholars from fields such as economics, history, management, and sociology have invested their time and resources to establish parameters for those who follow. Duhé's (1996) study, for example, drew from this book, particularly the section on corporate donors in chapter 15, and both her thesis and my explanations of corporate giving were guided by the work of Galaskiewicz (e.g., 1989) and others.

Students are urged to explore donor motivations as a possible topic for their contribution to fund-raising knowledge. They are warned, however, that their efforts will be deemed worthless if not built on previous work. A simplified rule I give my graduate students is that the purpose of a master's thesis is to test theory, whereas the purpose of a doctoral dissertation is to build theory. Both require a comprehensive literature review.

THE NONPROFIT SECTOR

Of the three societal sectors separate from family, students likely are least familiar with the nonprofit sector. This is not surprising given that about 80% of our country's labor force works for businesses, 13% for government entities, and only 7% for nonprofits (Van Til, 1992). Yet that percentage of employment translates to roughly 10 million jobs (Hodgkinson et al., 1996). According to Marlowe (1993), nonprofits provide almost as many jobs as the agriculture, mining, construction, and transportation industries combined. "It is," he claimed, "the third-largest industry in terms of the number of establishments" (p. 5). Indicative of the sector's unrecognized importance, the New York-based New School for Social Research (1996) advertises its Nonprofit Management Program by emphasizing that one in seven people in New York City works for nonprofits.

Students will recall from chapter 1 that the nonprofit sector often is defined by what it is not, rather than what it is. As Douglas (1983) pointed out, adoption of the synonymous term *third sector* has merit in that "it draws attention to what organizations constituting it are not" (p. 16). They are not businesses or government entities; they are all those U.S. organizations that do not fit into the first two sectors. They range from day-care centers and neighborhood churches to major research universities and metropolitan hospitals. Their one common characteristic is that they have qualified for exemption from federal income tax under the Internal Revenue Code.

Organizations apply to the IRS for tax-exempt status. If approved, they are registered as a nonprofit and classified according to the Internal Revenue Code, which contains 29 categories of different kinds of nonprofits (Bowen, Nygren, Turner, & Duffy, 1994). Four of the 29 categories are described in single sections of the code, 501(d), 501(e), 501(f), and 521(a). The remaining 25 are organized in just one section, 501(c), with each category assigned a separate number, 501(c)(1) through 501(c)(25). Because all but a few nonprofits are classified under this section, the IRS commonly uses 501(c) as a proxy for the nonprofit sector—a rule generally followed by this book. Based on the IRS' (1996) most recent statistics, then, there are 1.16 million nonprofits, of which the majority (54%) are classified as charitable organizations according to 501(c)(3). The five other largest categories in descending order are social welfare organizations, fraternal beneficiary societies, business leagues, labor and agriculture organizations, and social and recreation clubs.

Although it provides the most reliable statistics available, IRS registration is an imperfect measure of the nonprofit sector's dimensions. Very small nonprofits with annual incomes of less than $5,000 do not have to apply for tax exemption, although some choose to do so (Bowen et al., 1994). Due to our country's constitutional separation of church and state, religious organizations, including churches, synagogues, their auxiliaries, subordinate units, conventions, and associations, need not apply for recognition of exemption unless they desire a ruling. Organizations that serve charitable purposes but are incorporated as government agencies, such as public libraries, also are exempt from registering as a nonprofit. Illustrating the number of those missing, there are more than 350,000 churches in the United States (Hodgkinson, Weitzman, Toppe, & Noga, 1992). As O'Connell (1991) claimed, "When these and all the less formal neighborhood and community groups are added in, the figure [for all nonprofits] is something over two million" (p. 38). Unbeknownst to most, Americans utilize or interact with nonprofits every week of their life.

And the sector is a rapidly growing part of our society. In 1946, less than 100,000 nonprofits were registered with the IRS (Dorsey, 1991). By 1963, their number had increased 400% to about 500,000. During the next 33 years, the number of nonprofits more than doubled and—as just given—now totals 1.16 million. About 26,000 new nonprofits are added each year (IRS, 1996). As Dorsey (1991) stressed, "Approximately 72% of the groups currently on IRS rolls were granted exempt status after 1960" (p. xvii). The "independent sector," according to Hodgkinson et al. (1996), grew faster than business or government in the last two decades. Its collective operating expenses more than doubled between 1984 and 1994, from $225 billion to $500 billion annually. Dorsey (1991) attributed this growth, as well as the sector's centrality in our democracy, to what he described as the "persistence of Americans in forming voluntary organizations and developing nongovernmental institutions to solve community problems" (p. xiv).

The result has been an incredible variety of organizations known as nonprofits, which, until recently, the IRS identified by 140 different purpose codes (Hodgkinson & Toppe, 1991). In truth, differences among nonprofits are often easier to find than commonalities (e.g., local homeless shelters and national football leagues). As Simon (1987) said, "The sprawling and unruly collection of animals that populate the nonprofit world—from churches to civil rights groups to garden clubs to the National Council on Philanthropy—makes this field hard to grasp and study all at once" (p. 69).

The reason for much of the difficulty is that the very concept of a nonprofit sector is a recent phenomenon. Before the 1970s, there was no effort to treat nonprofits as part of a unified sector. P. D. Hall (1990) explained, "The Department of Commerce's national income accounts, which originated the concept of a sectored economy after the Second World War, had no 'nonprofits' category until a decade ago" (p. 244). The terms *nonprofit, voluntary, independent,* and *third* sector were coined just 20 years ago by the Filer Commission in response to a Congressional investigation of tax-exempt organizations (National Commission on Private Philanthropy and Public Needs, 1977). According to P. D. Hall (1990), "For the first time, all charitable tax-exempt agencies, from giant grant makers through grass-roots activist organizations, were treated as part of a unified 'nonprofit sector'" (p. 247). He continued, "Disregarding vast differences of scope and scale, kinds of goods and services produced, sources of support and clientage, it posits a single characteristic—tax-exempt status under the federal tax code—as the criterion for inclusion in the sector" (p. 244). In other words, diverse types of organizations, whether they are foundations that make gifts, charities that raise tax-deductible gifts, or associations to which gifts are not deductible, are lumped into one sector, which we refer to as nonprofit.

Estimates of the sector's size vary greatly because estimators differ in which organizations they choose to include. Whereas some scholars and practitioners focus only on those registered with the IRS, others include every possible group, such as parents of high school band members who have organized to purchase new uniforms for their children. IS, the coalition that speaks for the sector nationally, defines its constituency beyond corporate donors as 501(c)(3) organizations—including foundations—to which gifts are tax deductible *and* 501(c)(4) organizations (social welfare) to which gifts are not deductible (Hodgkinson et al., 1996).[4] It excludes all other nonprofits classified under the Internal Revenue Code; however, it includes estimates for unregistered religious groups in many of its reports. Illustrating how definitions affect estimated size, IS reported that the independent sector consisted of 1.03 million organizations in 1994, whereas IRS records for 1994 show 1.14 tax-exempt organizations (Hodgkinson et al., 1996; IRS, 1996). IS researchers Hodgkinson et al. (1992)

---

[4]IS often breaks down data on its constituency and reports figures applicable to only 501(c)(3)s that are not foundations, which allows this book to utilize many of its descriptive statistics.

admitted, "Counting the number of institutions in the independent sector is a challenge" (p. 16).

Roger Lohmann (1992a), a professor of social work at West Virginia University, argued, "At present, no one may be completely sure whether the 'nonprofit sector' is the same thing as or something quite different from the 'voluntary sector' or the 'independent sector' or the 'nongovernment sector'" (p. 313). A consistent pattern behind attempts to label the sector, he said, is "in each case, an adjective highlighting a single characteristic is used to modify the term *sector*, with the implication that this modifier (and the characteristic it signifies) represents the central or critical characteristic" (p. 316). He maintained that any meaningful sector must be construed simultaneously as an economic, social, political, and cultural unit.

The Commons

Lohmann (1992a, 1992b) conceptualized a theory of a meaningful nonprofit sector that meets the criteria he gave. It describes the essence of *why* a sector separate from business and government exists in our society: "to create a protected space for the collective expression of what people find most important in their lives" (Van Til, 1992, p. xi). Based on the metaphor of the commons, Lohmann's theory provides an elegant framework for "capturing" Simon's (1987) sprawling and unruly collection of animals.

Commons, or nonprofits, according to Lohmann, are characterized by four dimensions: (a) uncoerced participation, (b) shared purposes and resources, (c) mutuality (i.e., a community of shared values and interests), and (d) fairness, or justice. Linking the last dimension to earlier discussions, Jeavons (1991) described fairness as "a function of reciprocity, treating others as one would like (or has a right) to be treated oneself" (p. 60).

A way for students to perceive the nonprofit sector within the commons framework is to picture their own campus commons, quad, or green. Here we have a microcosm of nonprofit purposes that are embodied in more than 1 million organizations. The commons is:

- A place to rally and to celebrate.
- A place to demonstrate against authority.
- A forum of free speech and expression.
- A political arena for debate among those seeking votes.
- A social area to meet and gather with people who share "common" interests.
- A recreational area to throw around a frisbee or just enjoy a brief walk between classes.
- A setting for learning through reading and self-contemplation or through informal discussions in small groups.
- A place to appreciate beauty, whether the beauty is nature's as expressed in trees, arts' as expressed in architecture, or humans' as expressed in an attractive person.

The list easily expands with the use of the campus commons for concerts, crafts fairs, used-book sales, dance exhibitions, and blood drives. Older students use the commons as a playground for their children, and administrators and academics use it for their business, such as student-recruitment activities. The point is that if students think of all the uses of the commons on their own campus, they can then grasp and appreciate the diverse purposes for which we as a society use the nonprofit sector.

Lohmann's (1992a, 1992b) theory defines the goods and services of the nonprofit sector as common goods, and differentiates them from private goods, which are produced by the business sector, and public goods, which are produced by government. Common goods, he explained, are desirable ends that are pervasive and indivisible within a commons, but not necessarily beyond. Their benefits are shared regardless of payment; however, benefit is restricted to those with interests in the goods. In contrast, a private good is one whose benefit is restricted to those who have paid for it (e.g., a car), whereas a public good benefits all members of a society regardless of payment or interest (e.g., military defense). *Common goods*, therefore, is both an important concept for understanding and a more precise term for labeling the missions and outputs of nonprofits. Although most scholars use the term *public good*, Lohmann's theory makes it clear that nonprofits—including charitable organizations—produce common goods. Lohmann (1992a) explained, "In no meaningful sense, for example, can associations of bird watchers, antique car collectors, charismatic cultists, or volunteers counting whales be considered engaged in the private production of public goods" (p. 319).

Common goods, by definition, are not universally desired. Indeed, a common and the good it produces may be considered "bad" by people in other commons (Lohmann, 1992a). The National Association for the Advancement of White People (NAAWP) was formed to benefit people who believe in the supremacy of the White race. Its mission and outputs conflict with those of the National Association for the Advancement of Colored People (NAACP). The National Rifle Association and Handgun Control hold reverse positions. Churches teach doctrines that are antithetical to other churches' doctrines. Whereas some people concerned about abortion participate in pro-choice groups, others join groups that are pro-life. One common good as opposed to another is not "better" by consensus, and one's own good cause is not necessarily someone else's. Individually, commons are valued by a minority of people. Collectively, commons promote social plurality on which democracy depends. As John Gardner (cited in O'Connell, 1993), cofounder of IS, declared, "If you can't find a nonprofit institution that you can honestly disrespect, then something has gone wrong with our pluralism" (p. 15).

An amazingly symmetrical sector emerges from this arena of conflict. J. Fink (1990) described:

> For every civil liberties group that advocates an expansionist or activist interpretation of constitutional rights barring school prayer, capital punishment, or religious displays on public property, there has been a counterpart conservative citizens' movement that takes the opposing view. Pro-choice groups are more than matched by right-to-life groups. Thus, for those of conservative, liberal, or moderate political views, local initiative through voluntary action and philanthropic work remains one of the most accessible and direct means for redress of social problems. (pp. 136–137)

In other words, the nonprofit sector plays a critical role in our society—one that cannot be met by the first two sectors of business and government. A former president of the Lilly Endowment, John Mutz (1993), expounded on the sector's role during a fund-raising symposium at Indiana University's Center on Philanthropy. "Nonprofits," he maintained, "create public space where meaningful dialogue can occur." They promote public discourse and frame issues of public concern. They represent "a place for those who cannot be heard" and also act as an "escape valve." The third sector allows diametrically opposed organizations, such as NAAWP and NAACP, to coexist—a testament to the principles of freedom under which the United States was founded and continues to be sustained. Without the sector's public space, without the public discourse it nurtures, and without the public voice it bestows, one can convincingly argue that our democratic society would not long survive.

Focusing on the charitable subsector of nonprofits, Lohmann's (1992a, 1992b) theory provides a seminal explanation of philanthropy that this book adopts and builds on to explain fund raising. His theory emphasizes the individuality of each gift and the purpose for which it is made. It recognizes that in addition to altruism, donors have motives of self-interest for giving—which, on the most basic level, are interests supportive of the common good produced by the recipient organization. Therefore, if I make a gift to a pro-choice group, as opposed to an organization with a mission advocating pro-life, I am *not* contributing to the good of the so-called public, but rather to the good of people who share my interests in the organization's work.

Carnegie (1889/1983) argued in his Gospel of Wealth that a gift for one purpose, such as beautification of a park, is of no less value to society than a gift for another purpose, such as building a university—although Carnegie did rank founding a university as the first of seven "best uses" to which wealthy Americans could devote their surplus money. He stated, "There is room and need for all kinds of wise benefactions for the common weal" (p. 107). It is up to the donor, Carnegie believed, to determine what is best for society—a park, a university, or a collection of art. According to Carnegie, a donor should give "for that purpose which is seen by him [*sic*], as trustee, to be best for the good of the people" (p. 107).

Ylvisaker (1987), speaking on behalf of foundations, stated, "Philanthropy is far more than grant making; it is a constitutional statement by society that there should be a private counterpart to the legislative process, a freestanding alternative that allows for independent considerations of the public interest and private allocations of resources for public needs" (p. 376). Kirstein (cited in Lord, 1983) said, "Apart from the ballot box, philanthropy presents the one opportunity the individual has to express his [*sic*] meaningful choice over the direction in which our society will progress" (p. 111). Senior practitioner and author Marianne Briscoe (1994b) gave a fund raiser's viewpoint: "Philanthropy enables people to make possible what they, individually, belive is important" (p. 11).

Donors, then, advance their beliefs about what is best for society by collectively supporting a diverse—and often conflicting—array of charitable organizations. Or as Briscoe (1994b) said, "Donors give to organizations and causes like themselves" (p. 11). Lohmann's theory of the commons helps us understand why fund raisers must match an organization's mission and outputs with the interests of prospective donors. Its related and more powerful lesson is that most people are not interested in a given organization's work, or as Lohmann (1992a) said, the common good is "a matter of indifference" (p. 320). For example, whereas one student might make a gift to an animal rights group and another might make a gift to a drug treatment center, their classmates might give to neither because they are not concerned about animal or drug abuse—other social problems concern them more. Practitioners who manage fund raising effectively do not define their donor prospect pool as the general population; rather, as described in later chapters, they rely on research to identify individuals, corporations, and foundations who have interests "in common" with the organization.

THE CHARITABLE SUBSECTOR

Students likely have a preconceived view of the charitable subsector as one populated by small and poor organizations. The widely accepted stereotype holds true for the majority of the subsector's members; however, it does not apply to the minority of members on which this book focuses—those charitable organizations likely to employ fund raisers. As Jencks (1987) explained, most dollars from tax-deductible gifts go to organizations that "are seldom indigent and are often quite affluent" (p. 322). Media reports, books, and journals—including works by philanthropy and nonprofit scholars—commonly distort the subsector's composition by ignoring large and relatively wealthy organizations. The incomplete, and therefore inaccurate, descriptions skew our understanding of fund raising and the organizational context in which practitioners work.

Public relations textbooks, for example, generally assume that all charitable organizations possess few staff and dollars. Careers in such organizations, they warn students, are characterized by dependence on volunteers and deficient budgets. The authors rarely discuss such organizations as the Shriners Hospitals for Children, which had financial assets of $4.8 billion in 1995 (S. G. Greene & Williams, 1996).[5] Nor do they point out that Stanford University's institutional advancement staff totaled approximately 600 in 1990 (including 200 fund raisers)—a size equivalent to the largest public relations departments at the largest corporations (e.g., AT&T in 1990). If these textbook authors approached the business sector with the same stereotypical mindset, they would ignore large corporations like AT&T because the vast majority of U.S. businesses are small and poor. By doing so, they would disregard the businesses that employ the greatest number of practitioners.

Furthermore, as is the case in other disciplines, each public relations text creates its own typology of nonprofits. Whereas business and government usually are assigned their own chapter to familiarize students with these potential employers, nonprofits are scattered haphazardly among multiple chapters without any attempt to explain their collective distinctiveness or their critical role in our society. It is little wonder that the nonprofit sector is largely unacknowledged and unappreciated by even highly educated people. Of particular concern to public relations students, my 1991 study of public relations programs showed that almost one third of the programs' graduates take their first job with nonprofits (Kelly, 1992). Hopefully, the information presented in this chapter will aid authors of other texts in portraying the third sector and charitable organizations more accurately.

---

[5]Shriners was named Shriners Hospitals for *Crippled* Children until mid-1996.

Segmenting the Subsector

All nonprofits are exempt from federal income tax, but those nonprofits classified as charitable enjoy the dual privileges of tax exemption and tax deductibility of gifts—the right to receive gifts that donors can deduct from taxable income. Nonprofits must qualify for this special status by demonstrating to the IRS that their mission is charitable in purpose. Reviewing the description, charitable organizations originally were limited to those with religious, educational, charitable, and scientific missions (Bowen et al., 1994). The definition was expanded over the years as other missions were added, including preventing cruelty to children and animals, serving literary purposes, testing for public safety, and fostering international amateur sports competitions—which joined the description in 1976.

Students will recall that almost all nonprofits are classified under Section 501(c) of the Internal Revenue Code, although some are described in other sections. Similarly, most nonprofits to which gifts are tax deductible are contained in 501(c)(3), although small pockets of deductibility also are found among the other 501(c) categories. For example, gifts to some fraternal lodges, 501(c)(10), cemetery companies, 501(c)(13), and war veterans groups, 501(c)(19), may be deductible (R. Anderson, Ericson, Thee, & Williams, 1991). The IRS, similar to its practice with nonprofits, uses 501(c)(3) as a proxy for all charitable organizations—a rule again generally followed by this book. Based on IRS (1996) statistics, then, of the 1.16 million registered nonprofits, 626,226 (54%) are classified as charitable.

As with nonprofits overall, IRS registration is a reliable but flawed measure of the charitable subsector's dimensions. The imperfections are particularly disconcerting for the purposes of this book. As previously mentioned, government organizations legally defined as charitable are not included in the 501(c)(3) category. Public colleges and universities, for example, usually are covered under Section 115(a) of the Internal Revenue Code of 1954; yet, as demonstrated in the next chapter, public and private educational organizations are among the leading employers of fund raisers. Religious organizations also employ fund raisers, but most are not accounted for in 501(c)(3). Compounding the problem, religious organizations are exempt from requirements on filing, as well as from registration. Only 16% of those that are registered file the annual information return, Form 990, with the IRS (Hodgkinson & Toppe, 1991).

Another problem not mentioned earlier is that organizations with multiple branches performing similar functions are permitted to register as a "family" under an IRS provision known as "group exemption," although they may register all branches (Bowen et al., 1994). Therefore, the single group registration for the 2,400 chapters of the Red Cross, which employ hundreds of fund raisers, inappropriately decreases the number of potential employers, whereas the registration of nearly 6,500 affiliates of Future Homemakers of America, which employ few fund raisers, inappropriately inflates the number (Bowen et al., 1994; "Philanthropy 400," 1996). Bowen et al. (1994), who deconstructed the IRS' computerized database, Exempt Organizations/Business Master File (BMF), to calculate the number of viable 501(c)(3) organizations in 1991, often repeated a complaint that students probably share at this point, "We are reminded again of how difficult it can be to answer a seemingly simple question: How many active charitable nonprofits are there?" (p. 16).

Estimating the number of charitable organizations likely to employ fund raisers is even more difficult. No list exists, and no previous effort has been published. The dimension of fund-raising employers has not been a major concern of scholars conducting research on philanthropy and nonprofit management. Practitioners who have written about fund raising have adopted authorities' statistics without questioning their relevance. The following discussion maps the uncharted territory and fills an important void in fund-raising knowledge.

Starting with the official "head count" of the IRS (1996) and rounding figures to thousands, there are 626,000 charitable organizations. Past studies by scholars have shown that, excluding religion, 70% to 75% of all registered organizations do not file a Form 990 with the IRS (Hodgkinson & Toppe, 1991; Hodgkinson et al., 1992). These organizations do not file, scholars explain, because their total income is less than $25,000, which exempts them from filing requirements. For example, Hodgkinson and Toppe (1991) concluded that because of the $25,000 minimum, only "one-quarter of all 501(c)(3) organizations are required to file a tax return" (p. 406). Bowen et al. (1994) found a comparable percentage of *nonfilers*, which they also attributed to small incomes; however, their meticulous study further documented that an "overwhelming number of nonfilers simply do not exist" (p. 14). According to these scholars, the IRS does not remove inactive organizations from its database unless officially notified; therefore, "Comatose organizations may exist within the active file for a very long time" (p. 6). The first step they took in deconstructing the BMF was to remove 35,000 organizations that the IRS was unable to locate.

The first step in this book's effort to estimate the number of potential fund-raising employers is to reduce the number of registered charitable organizations by 70% because defunct entities are of no interest and groups with annual incomes of less than $25,000 cannot afford to pay salaries, except perhaps for a part-time CEO. The remaining organizations, or *filers*, total just 188,000.

The second step is to remove private foundations. It is ironic that even this step is overlooked by fund-raising authors. Although private foundations are classified as 501(c)(3) organizations, their purpose—as stated earlier—is to give money; they do not raise money. Bowen et al. (1994), who are employees of the Andrew W. Mellon Foundation, confirmed the step: "A sharp distinction needs to be drawn between . . . grantmaking foundations and public charities. They serve different functions, have been established for different reasons, [and] are treated quite differently under the tax code" (p. 40). The number of private foundations, according to the IRS (1996), is 44,000; however, Hodgkinson et al. (1992) reported that about 2% of all foundations are nonfilers, which have already been subtracted. Therefore, 43,000 private foundations (98%) are removed from the 188,000 filers to obtain a balance of 145,000 charitable organizations.

As with other components of the nonprofit sector, counts of foundations vary by the criteria used for selection. For example, IS researchers Hodgkinson et al. (1992) reported that there were 38,000 foundations registered with the IRS in 1989, of which 37,000 were filers. On the other hand, Renz et al. (1995), researchers at the Foundation Center, reported that only 32,000 foundations were *active* in 1989. Statistics should not be adopted without questioning their relevance. Providing some verification for the number of foundations used here, IRS economist Alicia Meckstroth

(1994) stated, "Private foundations, which primarily provide grants to other nonprofit organizations, represent approximately 23 percent of the total number of 501(c)(3) organizations that are *required* to file information returns with the IRS" (p. 363; italics added). Using her percentage, 23% of 188,000 filers is 43,000—the number just subtracted.

The third step is to augment the 145,000 remaining charitable organizations to compensate for those organizations that are not included in category 501(c)(3) but are potential employers of fund raisers. This final step, unlike the first two, lacks research guidance. For example, Bowen et al. (1994) admitted that despite extensive efforts, they were unable to find any estimate of the number of "governmentally sponsored public charities" (p. 4). Among those missing are government hospitals, state museums, public school districts, and municipal tourist attractions, such as annual festivals. Yet agencies at all levels of government hire fund raisers, particularly in the current era of deficit reduction and budget cutbacks.

According to a recent media report, more than 3,000 public schools and school districts have fund-raising units, as do the 60 largest public library systems in the country (Demko & Gray, 1996). A 1992 survey found that half of the 53 government hospitals studied had fund-raising departments, all of which were 6 years old or less. Several federal agencies, such as the National Fish and Wildlife Service, have fund raisers on staff.

More than half of all 3,600 U.S. colleges and universities are public institutions ("Almanac," 1993), and almost all of them employ fund raisers. Of the 20 colleges and universities that raised the most money in 1995, 8 were public institutions (Council for Aid to Education, 1996). Certainly some of the thousands of religious organizations not registered with the IRS employ fund raisers. A conservative figure to add, then, is 5,000, which brings the total number of potential fund-raising employers to 150,000 charitable organizations.

My decision to estimate conservatively is justified given that in spite of research guidance, the group selected through the first two steps is by no means "pure." For example, it includes the two largest 501(c)(3) organizations, but neither has a fund-raising function (Hodgkinson & Toppe, 1991). They are the Teachers Insurance and Annuity Association and College Retirement Equities Fund (TIAA-CREF), which—together—constitute a $120-billion retirement and insurance program for 2 million educators. These membership benefit organizations trace their beginnings to a gift of $10 million from Andrew Carnegie in the early 1900s to support pensions for college professors (Curti & Nash, 1965). Similar nonprofits are usually classified under 501(c)(11).

Regardless of such aberrations, the 150,000 estimate is more accurate than any figure previously available. Its composition is supported in part by the AAFRC Trust for Philanthropy (1997b), which includes gifts to government entities in its reports of U.S. giving and defines private foundations as one of three gift sources. Recapping, only 188,000 of the 626,000 organizations classified as 501(c)(3)s are active and have incomes of $25,000 or more—which are essential characteristics of potential fund-raising employers. Of those organizations, only 145,000 raise gifts; the other 43,000 are foundations. Approximately 5,000 government agencies and religious organizations not included in category 501(c)(3) have fund-raising programs. The total number of organizations likely to employ fund raisers, therefore, is 150,000.

Additional dimensions of this small but important segment of the charitable subsector are suggested by findings from previous studies. Excluding foundations and such membership benefit organizations as TIAA-CREF, Hodgkinson et al. (1992) found that 40% of all 501(c)(3) filers have annual expenses less than $100,000, 32% have expenses between $100,000 and $500,000, and 28% have expenses greater than $500,000. Based on these percentages, the 150,000 potential employers can be broken down into three financial groups: (a) small organizations, about 60,000, which rely on external fund-raising consultants; (b) mid-size organizations, about 48,000, which use consultants and/or have one-person fund-raising departments; and (c) large organizations, about 42,000, which employ one and often more staff fund raisers. In other words, the highest concentration of internal practitioners is in a minority of large organizations that spend more than $500,000 per year.

Hodgkinson and Toppe (1991) reported that only 15% of all filers—excluding foundations and membership benefit organizations—have assets and expenses of $1 million or more. This elite group, representing only 4% of all registered 501(c)(3)s, possesses 86% of the subsector's assets. As Hodgkinson et al. (1992) concluded from their analysis, the charitable subsector is "dominated by a small percentage of very large organizations in terms of their share of total financial resources" (p. 185). In 1995, just 400 organizations, or less than 1% of the estimated 150,000 fund-raising employers, received 16% of all gift dollars—$1 out of every $6 raised ("Philanthropy 400," 1996).

The pattern of a few commanding the bulk of the wealth mirrors comparative figures for the business sector in which less than 1% of all U.S. companies hold 80% of the total assets (Hodgkinson, 1990). As documented in chapter 15, a small percentage of individuals, corporations, and foundations own most of the wealth in the United States and provide most of the gift dollars. Joseph "Joe" Mixer (1993), who was named NSFRE's 1997 Outstanding Fund-Raising Executive, explained, "The allocation of resources among small and large nonprofit organizations parallels the concentration of wealth and power in the economy and society in general" (p. 250).

Turning to organizational types, statistics repeatedly have documented that educational and health organizations, primarily colleges, universities, and hospitals, are the wealthiest charitable organizations. Drawing from the most recent IS study and heeding the previously given exclusions, educational and health organizations hold 78% of the subsector's $686 billion in assets and account for 80% of its $458 billion in annual expenses (Hodgkinson et al., 1996). The proportions may be even higher given that IS figures do not include such large government agencies as public universities and hospitals. Bowen et al. (1994) provided a dramatic comparison: In 1991, the median income of research universities—meaning half have larger incomes and half have smaller incomes—was $200 million, whereas the median income of historical societies was $80,000. The documented wealth of educational and health organizations suggests that they are the leading employers of fund raisers. It is not surprising, then, that of the three major fund-raising associations, one is specialized for practitioners in education (CASE) and one is specialized for those in health care (AHP). Only NSFRE is a general membership association.

The segment of the charitable subsector just described is the one in which fund raisers are most likely to work. It bears little resemblance to the stereotype of small and poor organizations. Chapter 2 concludes by examining and refuting other common misconceptions.

Misconceptions

Charitable organizations, like all nonprofits, are not prohibited by law from making a profit, only from distributing their profits to those who control the organization, known as the *nondistribution constraint* (NDC). Indeed, almost all charitable organizations strive to end their fiscal year in the black, with income slightly exceeding expenses. If they did not, annual deficits would soon force them into bankruptcy. They often save profits, and a substantial number have accumulated millions and even billions of dollars in the form of endowments. As Steinberg (1993a) stated, "Under the NDC, nonprofits can earn 'profits' (what else are endowments but retained earnings?" (p. 15).

A corollary of NDC is that employee salaries must be reasonable, although lay people, as well as educators, usually assume nonprofit compensation is necessarily lower than for-profit compensation, "a requirement stronger than the law requires" (Steinberg, 1993a, p. 17). In other words, salaries in the charitable subsector can—and sometimes do—exceed those for similar positions in the business sector.

Gifts are by no means the primary source of income for charitable organizations. Client fees and dues, government grants and contracts, and investment earnings from endowments and reserves also are important sources. As Clotfelter (1989) asserted, "Nonprofit organizations receive a sizeable part of their funding from self-generated revenues and government support" (p. 111). The figures he presented showed that, overall, 30% of income comes from gifts, 30% from government, and 40% from fees and dues combined with investment earnings. The percentages, however, vary by organizational type.[6] For example, Bremner (1989) found that human services organizations receive the greatest proportion of their income from government (39%), followed by fees and dues (30%), gifts (21%), and investment earnings (10%). Table 2.1 lists these two sets of findings with those of four comparable studies to shatter the misconception that gifts constitute the majority of income for charitable organizations, and by implication, that donors are their most important public (i.e., government and clients are equally important to financial well-being).

Based on averages of the figures given in Table 2.1, gifts—in aggregate—account for only 25% of charitable organizations' income. Government provides about 30%. The latter average is supported by experts, who estimated that annual incomes of 501(c)(3) organizations in the early 1990s totaled almost $500 billion, of which $150 billion, or 30%, came from government (Wulff, 1995). Government funding, as documented by Bremner (1989), is higher than average for human services organizations. The primary reason is that many such organizations are contracted by local, state, and federal governments to carry out welfare and other assistance programs on their behalf. Contractual services paid for by government sometimes represent as

---

[6]The organizational types used here and systems for classifying charitable organizations by mission are discussed in chapter 3.

TABLE 2.1
Income of Charitable Organizations by Percentage From Sources

	Donor Gifts	Government Grants/ Contracts	Client Fees/Dues	Endowment/Investment Earnings
Hodgkinson and Weitzman (1986)	27%	27%	38%	8%
Rudney (1987)	22%	35%	36%	7%
Bremner (1989)[a]	21%	39%	30%	10%
Clotfelter (1989)	30%	30%	40%	(combined fees, dues, and investment earnings)
Harvey and McCrohan (1990)	25%	25%	50%	(combined fees, dues, and investment earnings)
Hodgkinson, Weitzman, Toppe, and Noga (1992)	27%	26%	38%	9%

[a]Human services organizations only.

much as 90% of a human services organization's income. As discussed shortly, those operating federal programs currently are facing a financial crisis because of severe cutbacks in welfare funding.

Reliance on client fees and dues also differs by types of organizations. Those with missions in health, education, and arts, culture, and humanities typically receive the largest portion of their annual income from charges to clients, or users of their services. Colleges and universities, for example, earn 70% of their income from client fees (Bowen et al., 1994). In contrast, religious organizations generally do not charge for their services; therefore, fees and dues are not their principal source of income, nor are government grants and contracts. Similarly, organizational type predicts the proportion of income supplied by investment earnings. Whereas colleges and universities typically have an endowment, relatively few public/society benefit organizations have invested gifts or profits to generate income for future years.

Further variations exist within types. Some educational and health organizations, unlike their counterparts, receive only a small portion of their income from client fees and dues (e.g., libraries and community health agencies). The line blurs, however, when fees subsidized by government are recognized (e.g., financial aid for college students and Medicare payments for patients of nonprofit hospitals). A few organizations are more atypical. Shriners Hospitals, for example, relies on investment earnings from its unrestricted endowment for 53% of its income ("Philanthropy 400," 1996). In comparison, investment earnings represent less than 15% of the incomes of similar organizations.

Returning to human services organizations, students may be unsurprised to learn that Goodwill Industries International is 1 of just 18 large organizations to which the United Way system historically allocated about 50% of its funds ("Charity chiefs," 1992). They also may find it reasonable that the organization raised $113 million in gifts in 1995 ("Philanthropy 400," 1996). However, students likely are unaware that gifts accounted for just 11% of Goodwill's income of $1 billion in 1995. About 90% of its annual income traditionally comes from sales of products and services (e.g., used clothes sold at thrift stores), which are defined as fees and dues.

Gifts, then, are only part of the income mix for charitable organizations overall. As with the other sources, gifts as a proportion of income varies by organizational type and within types. Religious organizations, for example, receive almost all their income from gifts.

Lohmann (1992b) categorized charitable organizations into three types by their degree of dependency on gifts. Type A organizations receive less than 20% of their income from gifts (low dependency). Type B organizations are the exact opposite in that 80% or more of their income comes from gifts (high dependency). Type C organizations fall between the two polar types with gift proportions ranging from 21% to 79% of income (moderately low to moderately high dependency). Lohmann estimated that 47% of all organizations are Type A, 27% are Type B, and 26% are Type C. Based on these percentages, roughly half the organizations likely to employ fund raisers have low gift dependency and only one fourth are highly dependent on gifts.

Charitable classification does not mean that organizational employers necessarily serve the poor. Students will recall the definitional differences between charity and philanthropy given in chapter 1. As stated there, the greatest proportion of fund raisers work for organizations with purposes other than charity—an assertion documented in chapter 3. An often ignored fact is that only a small portion of the charitable subsector mostly or exclusively serves the poor (Cnaan, 1993). For example, less than 30% of all human services organizations deal primarily with needy people. Nonprofit nursing homes and drug treatment centers have a lower concentration of Medicaid patients than their for-profit counterparts.

I discussed these and other misconceptions related to fund raising in my earlier book (Kelly, 1991a; see chap. 3). Their common acceptance attests to widespread ignorance about the nonprofit sector, particularly charitable organizations. As Shannon (1991) lamented, "Our citizenry at large, and even great segments of the print and electronic media, do not really understand the history, the elements, or the important function this sector plays in the day-to-day operation of our social, economic, and governmental systems" (pp. 355–356). The absence of understanding leaves the sector vulnerable to misguided actions that threaten to harm or even destroy its organizations.

In 1995, Republicans, who had gained control of Congress in the 1994 elections, initiated legislation in fulfillment of their Contract with America—a document that outlined promised action to reduce taxes and balance the federal budget by the year 2002. The contract proposed to cut an estimated $60 billion from welfare programs, which would severely reduce government funding for thousands of human services organizations and, simultaneously, increase demands for their services (Wulff, 1995). With little acknowledgment of the substantial portion of income such organizations receive from government, Republican leaders argued that the nation's charities would do a better job of helping the poor than the federal government had done. Philanthropy, they said, would provide the means for taking care of lower income people who would lose federal assistance—a position demonstrating misunderstanding about the degree to which the subsector deals with the poor and the difference between philanthropy and charity.

Citizens offered little rebuttal. Not only were they unaware of charitable organizations' reliance on government dollars, but they did not realize the extent to which the affected organizations serve people other than the needy. Rosenman (1995) explained, "While the family of a homebound senior citizen might think that it is simply charity that brings a hot meal to the loved one's door, the staff and volunteers of the not-for-profit organization that delivers the meal understand that without government funding programs, dinner would not be served" (p. 53). Rosenman listed some of the endangered services most citizens take for granted and warned:

> Millions of people helped by government programs, especially by taxpayer-supported services delivered through charitable organizations, will face tremendous dislocation under the new congressional directives. Many of these people, including a considerable number who think of themselves as well-informed, middle-class voters, are unaware that they benefit directly from expenditures of federal funds. (p. 53)

Whereas citizens generally were silent, leaders of the nonprofit sector loudly and vehemently opposed the proposed cuts. The projected burden was too large and unrealistic, they protested. Private support could not make up for such enormous cutbacks in government funding. Studies provided by scholars in 1996 showed that gifts would cover only 5% of the cuts (G. Williams, 1996d). Even if giving increased substantially, only a small portion of the new dollars would go to organizations primarily helping the poor. Traditional patterns of giving predicted that the bulk of any increase would go to organizations with other missions, such as higher education and the arts. Julian Wolpert (cited in G. Williams, 1996d), professor of urban affairs at Princeton University and author of one of the studies, asserted, "Most of the donations that charities raise go to support community churches and synagogues, Y's, museums, public radio and television, universities, and parochial schools—services that donors themselves use—and these funds are largely unavailable for helping the neediest" (p. 38). If the federal cuts were implemented, Wolpert warned, organizations that do serve the poor, particularly those located in inner cities, "may be overwhelmed as both they and their clients lose government support" (p. 38).

The arguments presented by the opposing sides had two significant consequences: The Council for Advancement and Support of Education (CASE, 1996) revised its reporting standards to make reports of fund-raising results more realistic, and Republicans countered the nonprofit defense by proposing that donors to organizations serving the poor be given a tax credit for their gifts.

CASE (1994) had adopted management and reporting standards for capital campaigns in 1994, primarily because the way gifts were counted and what was included in totals artificially inflated campaign results—which were then heralded in the media and widely disseminated. The standards, which are described in chapter 14, promise to substantially reduce the amount of dollars attributed to campaigns. It took CASE 4 years of controversy and compromise to get them approved; yet just 2 years after their adoption (and before the first figures were released), CASE (1996) issued new standards for all fund-raising efforts. Basically the same as those for capital campaigns, the inclusive standards also promise to significantly lower dollar totals. The rules had not been revised for almost 15 years, which strongly suggested that their revision and release in 1996 were related to Congress' flawed assumptions about the fund-raising capabilities of charitable organizations.

CASE's president and CEO at the time, Peter McE. Buchanan (cited in J. Moore, 1996b), admitted that the political climate prompted the changes: "There are tendencies to believe that private philanthropy can assume a much greater role than is possible" (p. 28).[7] By accurately reporting fund-raising results, he said, we "can begin to be more realistic about what philanthropy can do" (p. 28). As of 1997, CASE is developing a general version of the reporting standards for use by charitable organizations of all types.

Turning to the second consequence, in 1996, Republicans introduced multiple pieces of legislation proposing a tax credit for gifts to organizations that primarily aid the poor (Murawski & Williams, 1996). Representative Nancy Johnson, the Connecticut Republican who now chairs the House Ways and Means Subcommittee on Oversight, which monitors charitable organizations, told a group of nonprofit leaders in Summer 1996 that the idea of a tax credit was especially popular with Republicans who want charities to help relieve the federal government of its welfare burden. She said the tax credit also was gaining favor with Democrats in Congress. Republican presidential candidate Robert Dole had earlier announced that if elected, he would implement a tax credit of up to $500 per year for gifts to organizations fighting poverty (J. Moore & Williams, 1996a). Dole's plan would have cost the Treasury as much as $120 billion in its first 5 years.

Students will recall that a credit provides greater tax savings for donors than a deduction. Many nonprofit leaders, therefore, viewed the proposed credit as a bribe to entice donors into giving to organizations serving the poor rather than to organizations serving clients with higher incomes. Hospitals and colleges, among others, would not be eligible for the tax credit. As most versions restricted the credit to organizations devoting 75% or more of their services to the needy, such groups as the Salvation Army and the American Red Cross also would not be eligible because they serve people regardless of income level. Critics charged that by offering a more generous tax break to supporters of some charities, lawmakers would in effect be saying that one type of organization is more deserving of gifts than others.

The proposed tax credit is divisive and damaging. Restricting it to organizations helping the poor discriminates against organizations with equally important missions. The legislation foreshadows attempts to implement graduated categories of gift deductibility and tax exemption, which would greatly weaken the charitable subsector.

Dole failed to win the presidency, but the 1996 elections maintained a Republican-controlled Congress, which Representative Johnson predicted will give serious consideration to the proposed tax credit (Murawski & Williams, 1996). Before the election took place, legislation mandating more than $55 billion in federal welfare cuts was passed by Congress and signed into law by Democratic President Bill Clinton (Adler, 1996).

To protect against misguided action and avoid future harm, society's understanding about the nonprofit sector and charitable organizations must be increased. Knowledgeable and ethical fund raisers are fundamental to meeting the challenge.

---

[7]In November 1996, Buchanan announced his resignation from CASE ("People," 1996). He will be replaced by Eustace Theodore in October 1997.

SUGGESTED READINGS

Bowen, W. G., Nygren, T. I., Turner, S. E., & Duffy, E. A. (1994). *The charitable nonprofits: An analysis of institutional dynamics and characteristics.* San Francisco, CA: Jossey-Bass.

Clotfelter, C. T. (1992). *Who benefits from the nonprofit sector?* Chicago: University of Chicago.

The Foundation Center. (1989–1996). *The literature of the nonprofit sector: A bibliography with abstracts, Volumes 1–8.* New York: Author.

Hall, P. D. (1992). *Inventing the nonprofit sector and other essays on philanthropy, voluntarism, and nonprofit organizations.* San Francisco, CA: Jossey-Bass.

Hammack, D., & Young, D. R. (Eds.). (1993). *Nonprofit organizations in a market economy: Understanding new roles, issues, and trends.* San Francisco, CA: Jossey-Bass.

Hodgkinson, V. A., Weitzman, M. S., Abrahams, J. A., Crutchfield, E. A., & Stevenson, D. R. (1996). *Nonprofit almanac 1996–1997: Dimensions of the independent sector.* San Francisco, CA: Independent Sector and Jossey-Bass.

O'Neill, M. (1989). *The third America: The emergence of the nonprofit sector in the United States.* San Francisco, CA: Jossey-Bass.

Powell, W. W. (Ed.). (1987). *The nonprofit sector: A research handbook.* New Haven, CT: Yale University Press.

Salamon, L. M. (1992). *America's nonprofit sector: A primer.* New York: The Foundation Center.

Weisbrod, B. A. (1988). *The nonprofit economy.* Cambridge, MA: Harvard University Press.

Wuthnow, R. (1991). *Acts of compassion: Caring for others and helping ourselves.* Princeton, NJ: Princeton University Press.

3

Fund-Raising Practitioners

This chapter looks at the people who are paid to raise money. It discusses where these fund raisers work, where they come from, their salaries, and other characteristics. Particular attention is given to the feminization of fund raising and the differences in pay and positions between male and female practitioners. Gender discrimination is an important problem. If inequities are not corrected, fund raising will be perceived as less attractive by individuals considering it for a career. Charitable organizations will not achieve their potential if they continue to undervalue the talents and skills of women—the majority of fund raisers.

NUMBER AND SCOPE

About 80,000 people currently are employed as fund raisers full time, either within or as consultants to U.S. charitable organizations. This is an informed guess. The Department of Labor recognizes fund raising as an occupation but groups fund raisers with other types of workers, such as "membership solicitors," and does not provide a breakdown of their number (U.S. Department of Labor, 1991, p. 233; see also U.S. Bureau of the Census, 1993). Because no inclusive list of charitable organizations exists, determining a precise count of staff practitioners is nearly impossible. The array of titles held by such fund raisers contributes to the difficulty.

In 1990, John Kuhnle (cited in Millar, 1990), vice president of a recruiting firm, estimated that there were only 25,000 fund raisers in the country. Indeed, approximately 23,500 practitioners belonged to the three major fund-raising associations in 1993. Yet if fund raising follows the pattern of other occupations, association membership represents well under one half of all practitioners. Conry (1991) reported that some of the senior practitioners she interviewed placed the number of fund raisers at "nearly 40,000, many of whom are not members of professional organizations" (p. 151). Plans to create a database on every fund raiser in the United States led CASE to estimate the number at 50,000 (Bailey, 1992). Most recently, NSFRE maintained that there are 60,000 "professional fund raisers" (Fleishman, 1995, p. 34). I believe the rare figures cited in the literature are too conservative and have set the number one third higher than the most recent estimate.

As determined in chapter 2, only 150,000 charitable organizations are likely to employ fund raisers. These organizations are not equal in their ability to hire the estimated 80,000 staff practitioners and consultants. Students will recall that the potential employers were broken down into three groups based on the amount of money they spend each year and just 42,000 have budgets greater than $500,000. These large organizations are the ones most likely to have practitioners on staff.

A study I conducted showed that organizations represented in NSFRE employ a median of two staff fund raisers (Kelly, 1994a). The median department also has two support-staff employees. About one third (36%) of NSFRE's members work in one-person departments, whereas 25% work in departments of five or more fund raisers and six support staff. Slightly less than 2% of the organizations have 100 or more practitioners. Although not generalizable to all fund raisers, the findings add to previously presented evidence that staff practitioners work for large charitable organizations, not stereotypical small and poor charities. Employment of consultants is addressed later in this chapter.

JOB TITLES

Reluctance to use the term *fund raiser* has spawned numerous euphemisms. Among the more common job titles are director of development, vice president for institutional advancement, chief advancement officer, resource development officer, and institutional resources director. Some of the more unusual include public support associate for the Louisiana Capital Area Chapter of the American Red Cross, scientific resources manager for the Missouri Botanical Garden, and donor acquisition officer for the Lesbian & Gay Community Center in New York City.

Pertinent to this book's orientation, some charitable organizations title their chief fund raiser vice president of university relations or community relations director. Although this person has responsibility for public relations programs, advertisements for such positions generally stress experience and skills in fund raising as priority qualifications. Illustrating, Fig. 3.1 is a reproduction of an advertisement from Bucknell University seeking candidates for the position of vice president for university relations. Although, as stated in the ad, this senior position "is responsible for managing and developing an integrated external relations program" for all the university's "constituencies," the reproduction highlights the fact the university actually was searching for a fund raiser experienced in managing relations only with donors. In cases such as these, the pseudo job title reflects a situation of fund-raising encroachment, as well as the organization's reluctance to use the term *fund raiser*. Encroachment, which is the management of the public relations function by a manager not trained in public relations, is discussed in chapters 6 and 9.

On the other hand, a few organizations appear to want a practitioner trained in both fund raising and public relations. The Mid-America Chapter of the American Red Cross (Chicago), for example, advertised the availability of the position of chief advancement officer, who "is responsible for planning and directing comprehensive communications and fund-raising strategies and programs" ("Professional opportunities," 1993, p. 55). Qualifications included "breadth and depth of working with the media and the philanthropic community." Furthermore, applicants certified by either a public relations association (PRSA and IABC) or a fund-rais-

BUCKNELL

Bucknell University
Vice President for University Relations

Bucknell University seeks nominations and expressions of interest in the position of Vice President for University Relations.

Founded in 1846, Bucknell is a highly selective institution offering degree programs in liberal arts and sciences, engineering, management, music and education. Serving a student population of 3,350 undergraduates and 200 graduate students, Bucknell has 238 full-time and 30 part-time faculty, 95% of whom hold doctorates or appropriate terminal degrees. The University is located in Lewisburg, a historic community in central Pennsylvania.

Bucknell has just completed a strategic plan to direct its educational vision into the 21st Century. The University ding requirements to fulfill its strategic directions.

Reporting to th , the Vice President University Relations is responsible for managing an ng an integrated external r program, designed to advance the University s among its constituencies. With B ell's sesquicentennial in 1996, the Vice Pr the opportunity to plan, organize, dev and implement a major fund-raising

Ca tes must have proven nagement and le ship skills in conceptualizi and framing st gies for **fund raising**, a in cultivating an **soliciting major gift** oth indepen-den y and by using the President ustees, volun-teers nd professional staff.

Please subm information in confidence to:

Bucknell University S
Vice President fo Relations
ent Network
Box 792
Nantucket, MA 02554

Bucknell University is an EEO/AA employer as is
Educational Management Network.
Nominations of and applications from women and members of minority groups
are especially encouraged.

FIG. 3.1. Help wanted ad. From *The Chronicle of Higher Education* (1992, April 1, p. B41).

ing association (NSFRE and AHP) were preferred. Such positions are relatively rare, and few practitioners today are trained in both public relations and fund raising.

Even though most organizations continue to masquerade the function of fund raising, there is evidence that practitioners increasingly are referring to themselves as fund raisers. For example, editorial policy for CASE's journal, *Currents*, dictated until recently that the term *development* be used for references to education fund raisers. Around 1993, there was a noticeable change in the policy, and the terms *fund raiser* and *fund raising* now are predominantly used.

TYPES OF ORGANIZATIONAL EMPLOYERS

A refrain running through this textbook, with which students already are familiar, is the definitional inconsistencies hampering an understanding of fund raising. One of the most convoluted areas is the classification of nonprofits, including charitable organizations, by their mission. Multiple systems exist, and authors often make up their own typologies and terminology.

Currently, the largest classification effort is the National Taxonomy of Exempt Entities (NTEE). The NTEE project is under the auspices of the National Center for Charitable Statistics, which formerly was managed by IS and now is housed at the Urban Institute's Center on Nonprofits and Philanthropy. Designed to cover all nonprofits in Section 501(c) of the Internal Revenue Code, NTEE consists of 26 major fields, each assigned one letter of the alphabet—from A for arts, culture, and humanities to Z for unknown or unclassifiable (AAFRC Trust for Philanthropy, 1996). The system uses a 9-digit alphanumeric code to identify organizations not only by major field, but also by their major purpose, type of governance, and clients' characteristics, such as age and geographic location. As Hodgkinson and Toppe (1991) proclaimed, "When all nonprofit organizations are fully classified, the system will provide a powerful analytical tool for a variety of purposes" (p. 405). Plans call for the IRS to add the NTEE code to Form 990 and eventually take over the classification. The Foundation Center, the foremost source of information on foundation giving, already uses the system.

The NTEE project, however, is not without problems or critics. Started in the early 1980s, it is 3 years behind schedule and has cost millions of dollars. Researchers announced in 1993 that thousands of errors had been found and fixing the system could take another 10 years (Goss & Williams, 1993). Illustrating, NTEE computer software incorrectly classified the Southern California–Southern Nevada End-Stage Renal Disease Network as a theater on the basis of the word stage and College Park Towers as a college when in fact it is a housing complex for senior citizens. Some scholars have criticized the project because it creates a system separate from the federal government's widely used Standard Industrial Code (SIC), which has existed for more than 60 years. They have invested their efforts in revising SIC classification of nonprofits, the results of which are scheduled for publication in 1997.

Focusing on just charitable organizations, NSFRE uses two different systems to classify the organizations for which its members work. The association uses its own taxonomy of 11 organizational types, as well as three types of for-profit consulting firms, for its membership surveys. Since 1992, it uses a six-category system for its annual membership and dues form. The simpler system had been adopted earlier by the AAFRC Trust for Philanthropy (1987) and represents broad organizational categories of NTEE's major fields. The system's six types of charitable organizations are: (a) arts, culture, and humanities; (b) education; (c) health; (d) human services; (e) public/society benefit; and (f) religion.

The six-part classification is adopted by this text, although reported findings of NSFRE's membership surveys and other studies are based on varying typologies. To complicate matters further, the AAFRC Trust for Philanthropy (1997b) has expanded its organizational types to eight, adding (g) environment/wildlife and (h) international affairs to the six just listed. As Payton (1990) warned, "The study of philanthropy is no place for conceptual purists" (p. 171).

Despite these inconsistencies, the types of organizations most likely to hire fund raisers can be identified and important distinctions made.

Largest Employers: Education and Health

Educational and health organizations are the leading employers of fund raisers, and those with missions in higher education hire more practitioners than any other type. As discussed in chapter 2, these organizations—primarily colleges, universities, and hospitals—hold 78% of all assets and account for 80% of all expenses of the charitable subsector (Hodgkinson et al., 1996). By measurements of wealth, they are the biggest organizations, and their wealth attests to both their ability to hire fund raisers and the results of doing so.

As also pointed out in the last chapter, the fact that CASE and AHP constitute two of the three major fund-raising associations confirms the prominence of educational and health organizations as fund-raising employers. The third association, NSFRE, represents fund raisers who work for all types of charitable organizations.[1] The three associations periodically survey their members and report findings, which are used throughout this chapter to describe fund-raising practitioners. Because of its general membership, NSFRE's findings are used most extensively. Not only are CASE and AHP specialized, but CASE's membership includes practitioners who work in functions other than fund raising, such as alumni and government relations. However, 47% of all CASE members are fund raisers and another 11% are managers of advancement, who usually are fund raisers (R. L. Williams, 1996). Their majority status lends relevance to CASE's findings, which are presented with those from AHP to enrich descriptions of the people who are paid to raise money.

Discussions, then, rely on data gathered by NSFRE through five surveys of its members, conducted from 1981 to 1995 by George Mongon, Jr. Findings from the 1992 study (Mongon, 1992) are particularly useful because they provide the latest information that can be generalized to the entire NSFRE population. Unfortunately, the most recent survey, conducted in 1995 (Mongon, 1996), is not a valid representation of NSFRE's members because those who are minorities or live in Canada were oversampled and findings were based on the nonrandom group without weighting their responses.

---

[1]AAFRC is not defined as a major fund-raising association because it is a small group restricted to only a few consulting firms, as discussed in chapter 4.

Random sampling procedures, which ensure every member of a population has an equal chance of being selected, allow researchers to infer findings to the population. Analysis of a nonrandom group, on the other hand, can seriously misrepresent a population. Illustrating, Mongon (cited in S. G. Greene & Murawski, 1996) claimed in an initial report presented at NSFRE's 1996 International Conference that—based on the 1995 survey (which purposely oversampled minorities, as well as Canadians)—NSFRE had increased its proportion of minority members from less than 10% in 1992 to 17% in 1995. The flawed finding was highlighted in a major newspaper article about the survey, which heralded in its lead, "Blacks, Hispanics, Asians, and other minorities now form 17 per cent of the 16,000 members of the National Society of Fund Raising Executives" (S. G. Greene & Murawski, 1996, p. 37). As reported, the dramatic growth would mean that about 2,700 NSFRE members are minorities; yet data from the association's *Summary Report of 1996 Membership* (NSFRE, 1996) showed that only about 650 members, or 5% of the 13,200 who provided ethnic information, are minorities. The final report of the 1995 study (Mongon, 1996) qualified the findings, thereby improving accurate interpretation (i.e., the results are representative of survey respondents only, not the entire population).

Returning to the subject at hand, Mongon (1992) found from a random sample of NSFRE's members that those fund raisers who work for educational organizations account for the greatest proportion of the association's membership (25.3%)—as they have since the first survey was conducted in 1981. Hospitals and medical centers continued as employers of the second highest proportion (14.1%). Under the 11-part taxonomy used by NSFRE for its surveys, national health organizations are separated from hospitals and medical centers; when added together, they represent 19.4% of NSFRE's members. In other words, education and health are the two types of organizations employing 44.7%, or nearly half, of all members of NSFRE. Furthermore, breakdowns by organizational affiliation and number of coworkers showed that large fund-raising departments are most often found within educational and national health organizations, as well as in large consulting firms.

Based on a quota sample of randomly selected NSFRE, CASE, and AHP members, Carbone (1989) found that the majority (66%) of fund raisers who belonged to the associations in the late 1980s were employed by educational and medical or health care organizations. This finding was not unexpected as Carbone defined his sample as 10% of the membership of each association, which resulted in almost half of those selected for study being practitioners who worked for such organizations by virtue of their membership in CASE and AHP. Be that as it may, Carbone's findings showed that 41% of the members worked for colleges, universities, and schools and 25% were employed by medical or health care organizations. Only 13% of the fund raisers worked for social services organizations (i.e., human services), 5% for cultural arts organizations, and 3% for religious organizations.

Carbone (1989) speculated, "Perhaps the rapid expansion of fund raising [*sic*] units in academe means that these institutions now employ four of every ten fund raisers in the nation" (p. 24). Such a possibility is reasonable, as Carbone stated, "It is not uncommon for large, complex research universities, both public and private, to have 50 to 100 staff members involved in fund raising (or institutional advancement) activities. This is particularly true in institutions that have decentralized these functions or that are conducting substantial capital campaigns" (p. 24). In evidence of his assessment, the University of Pennsylvania had a staff of 250 fund raisers working on its $1-billion capital campaign (Bailey, 1990b), which was completed in 1994.

Former CASE President James Fisher (1989) estimated that there were about 9,000 full-time fund raisers employed at colleges and universities in the United States and Canada. The estimate is outdated and too low; I would place the current U.S. figure closer to 25,000, with about 30,000 working for all types of educational organizations, including private and public schools.

My estimates are supported by Worth (1993), who stated in his historical overview of education fund raising, "Today, nearly every college and university in the nation—four-year and two-year, private and public—has at least one and in many cases dozens of development professionals on the institutional staff" (p. 22). He added, "A trend began to emerge in the late 1980s that may signal a new area of potential growth: the establishment of fund-raising foundations for public school systems in major cities across the country" (p. 26).

Evidence exists that this trend has significantly increased the number of education fund raisers. As given in chapter 2, more than 3,000 public schools and school districts have a fund-raising unit (Demko & Gray, 1996), which are termed *affiliated foundations*. Researcher Margaret Duronio (1994a), in the second of three preliminary reports on her 3-year study, "Fund Raisers at Work," cited a male practitioner in higher education who said "he knew that competition had dramatically increased when he met a development officer who managed a sophisticated program and a staff of 12 and was employed *by a public high school!*" (p. 12; italics in original).[2]

In 1991, *The Chronicle of Philanthropy*, which bills itself as "The Newspaper of the Non-Profit World," compiled and published a first-ever ranking of those 400 charitable organizations that raise the most money in private support ("Philanthropy 400," 1991, p. 1). According to the report, 141, or 35%, of the organizations were colleges and universities, "far more than any other kind of institution or organization" (p. 21). Higher education has retained its top position by wide margins in subsequent rankings, published annually each November. Illustrating, 138 colleges and universities, representing just 1 of 17 types of organizations in the newspaper's own taxonomy, dominated the 1996 ranking ("Philanthropy 400," 1996). They accounted for nearly one third of the total dollars raised by the 400 leaders and were more than three times greater in number than the 45 local United Ways that constituted the second largest organizational type. Combining two categories, the third largest type consisted of 42 health charities, hospitals, and medical centers. Missions in higher education and health, therefore, described almost half (45%) of the 400 charitable organizations raising the most money from individuals, corporations, and foundations. A fund raiser for the Memphis, Tennessee affiliate of Catholic Charities USA summarized in an earlier report, "Hospitals and colleges have been so far ahead in terms of fund raising overall" ("Philanthropy 400," 1993, p. 39).

Annual reports of giving by the AAFRC Trust for Philanthropy (1997b) consistently show that education receives the highest proportion of gift dollars (12%) after

---

[2]Duronio's introspective study of fund raisers, which is cited throughout this text, was commissioned by NSFRE and Indiana University's Center on Philanthropy in 1993. A book reporting the study's findings was published in late 1996 and is listed in suggested readings at the end of this chapter.

religion (46%). Of the percentage, colleges and universities receive the lion's share, 72%, or $13 billion, in academic year 1994–1995 (Council for Aid to Education, 1996). Health ranks third (9%) in the latest AAFRC (1997b) report, followed closely by human services (8%).

Finally, the estimated portions of the fund-raising population used by Duronio (1993) to draw a stratified sample for her study on fund raisers supports the conclusion that the largest number are employed by educational and health organizations. Duronio's estimated percentages resulted from a 1990 systematic analysis of the organizational affiliations of NSFRE, CASE, and AHP members—as determined by available sources (i.e., membership surveys or dues forms)—with duplications among the three associations removed (Duronio, personal communication, February 14, 1994). According to Duronio (1993), the proportions of fund raisers employed by all types of charitable organizations are, in descending order: 44% education, 22% health, 16% other (includes environment, public/society benefit, and all others not captured by the categories), 12% human services, 4% arts/culture, and 2% religion. Given her sample was stratified by these percentages, it is not surprising that practitioners responding to her national survey did not differ greatly from the estimated population. The most notable difference for the purpose of this discussion is that whereas Duronio had estimated that education and health account for 66% of all fund raisers (a proportion identical to Carbone's 1989 finding), 74% of her respondents work for those two types of organizations.

In short, individuals interested in pursuing careers in fund raising should first look to educational and health organizations for jobs, particularly colleges, universities, and hospitals.

Other Fund-Raising Employers

Returning to the 1992 NSFRE membership survey (Mongon, 1992), human services organizations, or national social service and regional and local service agencies combined, employ 13.5% of those fund-raising practitioners. Arts and cultural organizations account for the fourth largest type of employer (7.7%), followed by youth organizations (6.6%), religion (4.2%), environment and conservation organizations combined (1.7%), and retirement communities (1.6%). Relevant to earlier estimates of the number of practitioners, only 4.6% of NSFRE's members work as consultants. The breakdown of NSFRE employers is given in Table 3.1.

Table 3.1 presents data from two NSFRE sources: (a) the 1992 membership survey (Mongon, 1992), which was based on responses of 1,557 randomly selected members; and (b) a summary report of 1996 membership (NSFRE, 1996), which was based on demographic information taken from membership and dues forms returned by all members—15,965 as of June 28, 1996. Because they use different systems to classify charitable organizations, overlapping categories in the survey typology are collapsed to improve consistency.

The two sets of data are quite similar, although some difference is expected due to the margin of error (unreported, but usually plus or minus 3% or more) that must be taken into account when comparing findings from a random sample to those from a census of the population. For example, the 1992 survey data show that educational organizations employ 25.3% of all NSFRE members, whereas 1996 membership data

TABLE 3.1
Types of Charitable Organizations by Percentage of Fund Raisers They Employ

Source I Organization Type	% Fund Raisers	Source II Organization Type	% Fund Raisers
Education	25.3	Education	21.5
Health, hospitals, and medical centers[a]	19.4	Health	19.4
Human services[a]	13.5	Human services	18.7
Arts, culture, and humanities	7.7	Arts, culture, and humanities	6.1
Youth	6.6		
Religion	4.2	Religion	4.4
Environment and conservation[a]	1.7		
Retirement communities	1.6	Public/society benefit	2.9
Consultants	4.6	Consultants	7.5
Not employed	.4	Not employed	1.2
Not classified	15.0	Not classified	18.2
Total	100.0%		99.9%

Note. Source I: NSFRE Profile: 1992 Membership Survey (Mongon, 1992).
[a]Combines 2 of 11 categories.
Source II: Summary Report of 1996 Membership: NSFRE Demographic Information (NSFRE, 1996).

show that 21.5% of the members work for such organizations—a 3.8% difference that is more likely attributable to sampling error than to a decrease of education fund raisers over the 4 years separating the two sources. Regardless, both the survey findings and the membership demographics show that education and health are the largest employers of fund raisers. In fact, when NSFRE members who are not employed or not classified are removed from the two data sets, education and health account for the majority of practitioners (52.8% and 50.8%, respectively), although the proportions are smaller than those found by Carbone (1989) and Duronio (1993).

These figures provide the best indication currently available as to where fund raisers work; however, students should not forget the figures are valid only for the population of dues-paying NSFRE members. For example, the very existence of—demonstrating a need for—the two specialized associations of CASE and AHP may mean a greater proportion of fund raisers are employed in education and health than these figures indicate. Consultants increasingly view religion as "a ripe market" for their services because religious organizations "typically have no development staff" (Gonzalez-Campoy, 1996, p. 38), an assertion somewhat supported by the figures presented here. Yet religious organizations' low representation in NSFRE cannot be taken as proof that they have few fund raisers. It may be staff members are encouraged to join one of the smaller fund-raising associations specializing in religion (e.g., the Association of Lutheran Development Executives), rather than the general society of NSFRE. Furthermore, the relatively high cost of annual membership—$170 for national dues in 1997—may deter fund raisers for certain types of organizations, such as public/society benefit, from joining NSFRE—particularly as employers pay the dues of 77%

of the society's members. Answers based on scientific research are inconclusive or do not exist.

Be that as it may, the comparative data presented in Table 3.1 provide strong evidence that—collectively and in descending order—charitable organizations with missions in education, health, and human services account for most fund-raising jobs.

Employers With Diverse Missions

Within these patterns of employment, fund-raising practitioners work, or have the opportunity to work, for a diverse assortment of organizations. Interested in the environment? Such students might enjoy working at 1 of the 250 offices of Nature Conservancy, which raised $209 million in 1995 and ranked 15th in the latest listing of the 400 U.S. charitable organizations that raise the most money ("Philanthropy 400," 1996). How about the media? The Public Broadcasting Service (PBS), ranked at 16, raised $205 million in cash and noncash gifts. PBS, National Public Radio, and their parent entity, the Corporation for Public Broadcasting, have fund raisers on staff, as do nearly 1,000 affiliated public television and radio stations. Perhaps conquering disease is of special importance. The American Cancer Society and the American Heart Association, ranking 4th and 10th, employ hundreds of fund raisers across the country to help them attract $382 million and $256 million, respectively.

Religion? The Salvation Army, which is classified as a religious group by the IRS, is the top organization on the top 400 list, a position it has held since 1993 ("Philanthropy 400," 1996). Similarly, two other high ranking organizations have roots in religion although their missions are not primarily religious: Catholic Charities USA (third) and the national United Jewish Appeal (sixth). Campus Crusade for Christ is ranked at 23 with $185 million raised in 1995.

Many people are drawn to fund raising to help improve the day-to-day lives of individuals. Of those organizations with missions defined as human services, the Salvation Army is the leader, as well as holding the highest overall rank, raising $644 million in 1995—about $179 million, or 38%, more than the second ranked American Red Cross ("Philanthropy 400," 1996). YWCA of the USA, representing 339 affiliates, is ninth among all organizations, raising $284 million. And if a student's interest is the quality of life for boys and young men (but apparently only for those who are heterosexual and believe in God), Boy Scouts of America ranks at 14 and raises $225 million.

Arts and cultural organizations? The Metropolitan Museum of Art in New York City is at 62 on the "Philanthropy 400" (1996) list. Even jobs related to sports are available. Fund raisers for the U.S. Olympic Committee, for example, helped that charitable organization generate $74 million in gifts during 1995. The National Urban League is the biggest fund-raising organization in the category of public affairs, and if students are interested in international causes, World Vision raised $240 million in 1995 to earn its 13th place slot. Phillips Academy in Andover, Massachusetts, a pacesetter among thousands of primary and secondary, private and public schools, raised $20 million, and Harvard University, the grandaddy of all U.S. charitable organizations, ranks seventh on the top 400 list and now raises $323 million or more a year.

These and the other 400 leaders accounted for total gifts of $23.5 billion in 1995 ("Philanthropy 400," 1996). Representing just 0.1% of all organizational recipients in number, they consistently raise about 16% of all gift dollars—making them the General Motors of the charitable subsector. Thousands of practitioners work for them, but they only touch on the opportunities available in fund-raising careers.

Virtually every community of reasonable size contains job possibilities with a local United Way, a public school district, or a chapter of Boys and Girls Clubs of America, to name but a few. There are zoos, aquariums, dance companies, and symphony orchestras in major metropolitan areas. Historical societies, chapters of the Red Cross, and organizations to fight illiteracy can be found in all states. Groups concerned about the environment operate in every region. Half of all hospitals—about 3,000—are nonprofit (Copeland & Rudney, 1993), most of which have fund-raising staffs. Libraries in cities, as well as those housed in universities, look to private support for maintenance and enhancement. In short, career opportunities exist at the local, state, and national levels.

Unlike occupations for which programs of formal education exist, working for a consulting firm generally is not an option for beginning fund raisers. As given earlier, Mongon (1992) found that only 4.6% of all NSFRE members work as consultants (although self-reported data from 1996 membership forms placed the proportion at 7.5%). The majority of these external practitioners are independent counselors who work alone. Consultants have a median of 10 years or more of experience; none has less than 3 years. Furthermore, there is evidence that career opportunities in consulting are decreasing. Mongon's findings, for example, showed that the proportion of NSFRE members who are consultants dropped by one half between 1988 and 1992, from 10.3% to 4.6%. All three types—small firms, large firms, and independent consultants—lost ground during the 4 years. Other evidence of this decline is presented in later chapters.

Before turning to practitioner characteristics, it should be noted that "nontraditional" types of organizations hire fund raisers. For example, professional and trade associations increasingly are creating affiliated foundations to which tax-deductible gifts can be made to support the associations' missions and goals. Illustrating this trend, an issue of *The Chronicle of Philanthropy* announced job openings for a director of development for the American Welding Society Foundation in Miami, Florida, and for a vice president for "the AOPA Air Safety Foundation, a 501(c)(3) organization with a $4 million budget and affiliated with the Aircraft Owners and Pilots Association" in Frederick, Maryland ("Professional opportunities," 1992, pp. 47, 50). Affiliated foundations are described in chapter 6.

Government entities also increasingly are employing fund raisers, as explained in chapter 2. At the federal level, for example, the Smithsonian Institution is conducting its first capital campaign to raise $60 million for the National Museum of the American Indian, scheduled to open in 2001 (Reiss, 1993). Legislation passed by Congress in 1989 dictates that the federal government will provide two thirds of the new museum's cost, but the remainder must come from private gifts. In 1995, the Smithsonian raised a total of $36 million for the new museum and other projects and was ranked at 196 on the "Philanthropy 400" (1996) list. Current efforts to balance budgets and reduce deficits promise to expand career opportunities at all levels of the government sector.

CHARACTERISTICS

Fund raising requires no formal training for entry. It pays well, and the demand for fund raisers—even in recessionary times—outweighs the supply. Reflecting this open career path, practitioners come from various backgrounds and traditionally have been trained by the apprentice system. Whites greatly outnumber minorities and women outnumber men.

Among NSFRE members, the typical fund raiser—as defined by the person at the 50th percentile—is 45 years old, entered the field at age 30, has a bachelor's degree in some discipline, has held 2.3 fund-raising jobs, and earns a salary of $44,000 (Mongon, 1992). A more recent study by CASE showed that—separated from other institutional advancement functions—the average fund raiser in education makes $55,000 a year (R. L. Williams, 1996).

High Demand and Little Experience

In the late 1980s, Robert Carbone (1989), professor emeritus of higher education administration and one of only a few researchers to conduct introspective studies of fund raising, stated, "The basic profile of American fund raisers suggests a field characterized by relatively young workers" with "relatively short tenure as full-time fund raisers" (p. 26). Of Carbone's respondents, who were sampled from the three associations, the majority had 5 or fewer years of experience in fund raising. Carbone (1987) found a similar pattern earlier when he focused solely on education fund raisers. He speculated that most of those practitioners were filling new positions created by organizations enlarging or starting a fund-raising unit. "Given the difficulty in funding positions for new fund raisers," he said, "many of the people attracted to these positions are young and sometimes inexperienced workers" (p. 4).

According to Herman and Block (1990), fund raising became an increasingly important function with the expansion of the number of charitable organizations during the 1960s and 1970s, and the reduction in government funding in the early 1980s. Reviewing the "profound changes" that had taken place in the subsector during Ronald Reagan's presidency, Bailey (1988a) cited the following: "Charities are scrambling to find fund raisers, many of whom can command salaries well into six figures, along with numerous perquisites," (p. 19). She added, "Demand for fund raisers has skyrocketed, and salaries and perquisites have soared along with the demand" (p. 22).

In 1991, *Working Woman* magazine listed "development officer" as one of the 25 hottest careers, along with veterinarian, international accountant, and human resources manager. According to an article about the list in *USA Today*, these careers are recession proof because practitioners have specialized skills and are in the high-demand/low-supply category ("Careers," 1991). Bloland and Bornstein (1991) simply stated, "Development at present is a wide open field, with many positions available and remuneration at an all time high" (p. 108).

The number of fund-raising jobs, then, increased dramatically during the last decades, and this growth is predicted to continue into the new century. Demonstrating past gains, membership in NSFRE increased 467% in 15 years, from 3,000 in 1981 to 17,000 at the end of 1996 (Mongon, 1992; NSFRE, personal communication, October 27, 1996). The other fund-raising associations experienced similar growth. AHP, for example, went from 1,200 members in 1980 to 2,500 in 1996 (AHP, personal communication, November 1, 1996; Stehle, 1989). Indicative of future opportunities, the number of charitable organizations is expected to double by 2005 (Bowen et al., 1994).

Education and Training

According to Carbone (1987), the supply and demand imbalance of fund raising is influenced by "the relative sparsity of formal programs for preparing fund raising [*sic*] personnel" (p. 7). His research on education practitioners showed that the major factors in deciding to embark on a fund-raising career are volunteer experiences, working at other campus jobs, knowing someone in fund raising, and "happenstance" (p. 9). Mongon (1992) similarly reported that individuals largely discover fund raising through venues other than schooling. Whereas more than 90% of NSFRE members have a college degree and more than one third hold at least one graduate degree, there is no prescribed educational training for fund raisers.

The academic backgrounds of practitioners belonging to CASE, according to Carbone (1987), primarily are liberal arts for bachelor's degrees, professional fields for master's degrees (37% in education), and education for doctoral degrees (53%). The preponderance of education degrees at the graduate level, he said, is explained by education fund raisers' interest in the type of organization for which they work and by the convenience of late afternoon and evening classes offered by colleges of education. The implications of working practitioners pursuing graduate degrees in education are discussed in chapter 4.

Carbone (1987) was the first to scientifically document that on-the-job training is the single most important source of fund-raising expertise. Subsequent introspective studies (Bloland & Bornstein, 1991; Carbone, 1989; Duronio, 1993, 1994a, 1994b) confirmed the apprentice system by which most current fund raisers were trained. Bloland and Bornstein (1991) summarized, "In development there is a strong tradition of learning skills on the job" (p. 115). Workshops and conferences sponsored by professional associations supplement hands-on-experience and mentoring. CASE, for example, conducts about 65 fund-raising workshops across the country each year. Bloland and Bornstein explained, "In both development offices and association meetings, the teachers are successful senior development practitioners and consultants" (p. 115).

Within the last decade, fund-raising courses have been taught in colleges and universities. The number of such courses is unknown. As reported in chapter 1, Crowder and Hodgkinson (1991a) said approximately 57 colleges and universities offer more than 150 courses about the nonprofit sector, voluntarism, and philanthropy. CASE listed only 14 institutions with specific courses on fund raising (Unkefer & Chewning, 1992). A 1995 study on nonprofit curricula by a researcher at the University of San Francisco's Institute for Nonprofit Organization Management included some 300 colleges and universities (H. Hall, 1995a).

Differences in estimates can be attributed to three factors: (a) the recent interest in and rapid growth of nonprofit and fund-raising education have hampered compilation of comprehensive listings; (b) the subject of fund raising is embedded within courses and programs titled by broader concepts (e.g., the master's degree in the

Nonprofit Administration Program at San Francisco's Institute requires coursework in resource development skills); and (c) many of the fund-raising courses are offered through continuing education "certificate programs" for nonacademic credit (e.g., the Fund Raising Management Program at Goucher College in Towson, Maryland) or through nontraditional degree programs (e.g., the three-summer Master of Arts in Philanthropy and Development program at Saint Mary's College in Winona, Minnesota). Addressing these factors, Carbone (1989) stated, "Creation of academic courses for aspiring fund raisers, to say nothing of complete degree programs (most of which are in nonprofit organization management with only some attention to fund raising) is a recent trend in this country" (p. 14).

Whereas current practitioners learned fund raising through apprenticeships, they recommend newcomers learn through professional development offerings taught by part-time practitioner faculty. Duronio (1994b) found that 74% of the 1,748 fund raisers participating in her study learned their occupation on the job, but only 39% recommend this as the best way for others to learn. A mere 7% selected formal education as a means to acquire fund-raising knowledge and skills. Further discussion of education is reserved for the next chapter on professionalism.

Salaries and Compensation

Based on 1992 figures, 90% of all NSFRE members make more than $25,000 a year, and top salaries exceed $115,000 (Mongon, 1992). Entry-level positions in fund raising pay relatively well considering no prior training is required. Almost half of the practitioners with less than 3 years of experience earn $33,000 or more and about one third earn between $33,000 and $50,000. Younger practitioners also are paid quite well. Almost 20% of NSFRE members under age 25 make more than $25,000; 54% of those between ages 25 and 34 earn more than $33,000.

Related to the earlier discussion about the largest fund-raising employers, hospitals and medical centers pay the highest salaries, followed by education (Mongon, 1992). According to Mongon, 1 out of 5 fund raisers working for hospitals and medical centers (21%) and 1 out of 10 working for educational organizations (11%) earn more than $75,000. AHP reported that the median salary of its members in 1992 was $59,500 (D. Joseph, 1992), an amount substantially greater than the mean and median salaries paid to members of CASE and NSFRE. Practitioners who work for hospitals and medical centers indisputably are the top wage earners in fund raising. The two types of organizations with the lowest salaries, according to Mongon (1992), are arts, culture, and humanities and religion, in which almost one third of the practitioners earn less than $33,000.

About 12% of the fund raisers belonging to NSFRE receive a cash bonus in addition to their regular salaries (Mongon, 1992). Bonuses are paid by all types of charitable organizations, from arts to religion, but the extent to which they are used varies across types. Whereas 30% of the practitioners who work for hospitals and medical centers receive bonuses, only 9% of those working for educational organizations do so. The majority of bonuses are equivalent to 5% or less of regular salary; however, 1 of every 10 exceeds 20%, and half the fund raisers reporting such large bonuses have salaries greater than $115,000. In other words, some NSFRE members earn, with a 20% bonus, more than $138,000 per year.

Although the rising cost of health care may change the situation, fund raisers generally enjoy excellent fringe benefits. Among the benefits included in their compensation—often fully funded by employers—are health insurance, major medical, dental and prescription plans, eye coverage, disability insurance, tuition reimbursement, professional dues, club memberships, and car and mileage allowances.

Differences in salaries between minorities and Whites, referred to as the *race gap*, and between women and men, termed the *gender gap*, are discussed shortly. Before proceeding, another salary gap pertinent to this book's orientation is examined: differences in salaries between fund-raising and public relations practitioners.

Salary Differences Between Fund Raising and Public Relations

Numerous studies consistently have reported higher salaries for fund raisers than for public relations practitioners who work in the charitable subsector. For example, the annual survey of salaries conducted by the College and University Personnel Association (CUPA) has shown in each of the last 10 years that heads of fund raising at higher educational institutions earn substantially more than heads of public relations. In academic year 1995–1996, the median salary for chief development officers at all colleges and universities—disregarding size and type—was $75,000, as compared to $50,000 for chief public relations officers—a difference of $25,000 per year in favor of the fund raisers (CUPA, 1996). The difference in 1990–1991, according to CUPA figures, was about $19,000 ("Median salaries," 1991).

The gap in salaries between the two functions is growing. It widened by 17% between 1986 and 1996. The median salary for chief development officers increased $27,900 during the 10-year period, from $47,100 to $75,000—a gain of 59%, whereas the median salary for chief public relations officers increased only $14,600, from $35,400 to $50,000—a gain of just 41% (CUPA, 1996; "Median salaries," 1987). In other words, fund-raising heads made about 33% more than their public relations counterparts in 1986–1987, but due to proportionately higher salary increases over the last 10 years, they now make 50% more.

An incentive for cross-training in public relations and fund raising is that practitioners holding the position of chief development *and* public relations officer for all colleges and universities earn a median salary of $83,700, or $8,700 more a year than chief fund raisers who do not manage the public relations function and $33,700 more than chief public relations practitioners who do not manage fund raising (CUPA, 1996). Focusing on the second situation, men and women trained in public relations can increase their potential earning power by as much as 67% if they specialize in fund-raising management. Cross-training and related issues are addressed in later chapters.

Similar differences are found in organizations with missions other than higher education. IS compiled results from nine separate studies that—together—showed that the top fund raiser in all types of charitable organizations earns almost $10,000 more a year than the top public relations person, $64,000 versus $54,300 ("Cash," 1989). Moving away from senior managers, the IS report demonstrated that students entering the job market can expect to earn much more as fund raisers than as general public relations practitioners: Whereas the median salary for a public relations position is $35,000, a fund-raising/grant position pays $55,600, or 59% more.

I found the same pattern in both qualitative and quantitative studies about the two functions (Kelly, 1993b, 1993c). Interestingly, people in public relations largely attribute higher fund-raising salaries to a greater value of that specialization as compared to their own. Of those public relations practitioners in the first study who worked for an organization employing at least one full-time fund raiser and who answered questions about salary comparison, 12 of the 13 interview subjects reported that salaries for their function are lower than salaries for fund raising (Kelly, 1993c). When prompted to give reasons for the salary differences, the majority offered none or said fund raisers deserve more money because they contribute more to the "bottom line."

Illustrating the absence of common explanations for salary differences, a female public relations director at a private 4-year college in Louisiana admitted her salary is lower than that of the director of development even though she has worked at the college 4 years longer and has more education. No organization represented in the study pays public relations personnel more than it pays fund raisers.

In a national survey of 175 public relations managers, the majority (59%) of those respondents who knew enough about salaries in their organization to compare them reported that public relations salaries generally are lower than those for fund raising (Kelly, 1993b). The reasons for salary discrepancies given by these managers included their beliefs that fund raisers contribute more to the bottom line, have a higher perceived value, and are fewer in number than public relations practitioners. The difference in demand was emphasized by a female respondent in an earlier study: "There are few good fund raisers and when you find one, you are willing to pay for it, whereas there are a lot of public relations people" (Kelly, 1993b, p. 9).

Concluding this discussion, public relations students and practitioners who seek high salaries should consider fund raising as an attractive career option.

Minorities

Only a small percentage of fund raisers are minorities. As pointed out earlier, about 5% of all NSFRE members are minorities, according to self-reported data from 1996 membership forms (NSFRE, 1996). The last generalizable survey by Mongon (1992), however, found that almost 10% of NSFRE's members are minorities. Furthermore, their representation had substantially increased from just 2% in 1985. Sampling error may be responsible for some of the difference in proportions, but people of color also may be more willing to provide information about their ethnicity on survey questionnaires than on annual membership forms. Regardless, the number of minorities in NSFRE is disproportionately lower than their representation in the general population.

The other fund-raising associations have similar ethnic profiles. For example, CASE's most recent survey, conducted in 1995, showed that less than 6% of its members are minorities, up from less than 5% in 1990 (R. L. Williams, 1996). The proportion of minority members in 1986 was 3%, which was the same as it was in 1982. In other words, minorities gained just three percentage points in CASE membership over the 13 years the association conducted its four surveys. Equally dismaying, the number of members who are African Americans—the largest minority group—and those who are Asians actually declined between 1990 and 1995, with increases in Native Americans and Hispanics making up for the loss.

Yet Borum (1991) concluded from her doctoral study that there are few readily identifiable factors contributing to the disproportionately small number of African Americans in fund raising. Her statistical analysis revealed no significant differences between African Americans and Whites as measured by their education, professional profile, personal activities, interactions, and other personal information. Her data also suggested that African Americans generally are pleased with and productive in their fund-raising careers. Based on her findings, Borum said organizations should system-atically recruit African Americans more aggressively and African Americans should give more consideration to entering fund raising.

According to Mongon (1992), minorities in NSFRE tend to earn salaries in a pattern similar to Whites. For example, 69% of minorities earn between $33,000 and $75,000 per year and about 8% earn more than $75,000. A disturbing finding of Mongon's 1992 survey was that African Americans receive a less valuable benefits package from their employers than do other groups; however, the finding was not supported in NSFRE's 1995 survey in which African Americans and other minorities were oversampled (Mongon, 1996).

Membership surveys by CASE have found that minorities are paid less than Whites, but the difference is not statistically significant when other factors, such as years of experience and primary responsibility (e.g., fund raising vs. alumni relations), are taken into account. In 1990, the average salary for minorities was $2,000 less than for Whites (R. L. Williams, 1996). The race gap grew worse by 1995, when the difference in average salaries nearly tripled to $5,800. As in the earlier study, however, statistical analysis showed that ethnicity is not significantly related to salary; other factors explain salary variations between minorities and Whites (Lafer, 1996).

Touching on a few other statistics, one in five minority practitioners belonging to NSFRE entered fund raising in the previous 3 years (Mongon, 1992). For example, 23% of African American practitioners have less than 3 years of fund-raising experi-ence, and 56% of Asian practitioners have less than 5 years. Twice as many African Americans are employed by educational organizations and retirement communities than by other organizational types. Asians work almost exclusively at hospitals and medical centers. More Hispanics are employees of national social agencies and youth organizations than of other types of organizations. Native Americans are best repre-sented in national health agencies, retirement communities, and hospitals and medical centers. Finally, African Americans and Hispanics are among the most educated in fund raising; 23% and 19%, respectively, hold a doctorate degree, as compared to 8% of all NSFRE members.

As Borum (1991) recommended, more needs to be done to increase the repre-sentation of minorities in fund raising. Special efforts are required to raise their awareness of the occupation and the characteristics that make it a desirable career choice. Organizations must aggressively recruit minority candidates when filling jobs. Discrepancies in salaries and benefits should be continually monitored. As minority fund raisers gain experience, they must be promoted into positions of power and visibility. Only by serving in senior positions will they be able to help organizations attract more people of color to fund raising and reflect the growing diversity of our society.

In support of such objectives, CASE sponsors an annual Forum for Minority Institutional Advancement Officers. African American practitioner Charles Stephens, chief development officer for Indiana University's Center on Philanthropy, served as national chair of NSFRE in 1992 and 1993. His leadership role helped stimulate greater concern about multiculturalism, and diversity committees now are incorporated in NSFRE's structure—from the national board of directors to local chapters.

Diversification is desirable not only because it is the right thing to do, but because doing so will increase the effectiveness of fund raising and charitable organizations. Sanford Cloud, Jr. (1993), president and CEO of the National Conference of Christians and Jews, pointed out that both minorities and women recently have joined the once very exclusive, White-male club of major donors (e.g., actor Bill Cosby and his wife Camille gave $20 million to Spelman College in 1988). Cloud rightfully argued, "If the fund-raising profession hopes to interact effectively with the evolving diversity of philanthropy, the profession itself is going to have to work harder to diversify its ranks" (p. 52).

J. E. Grunig (1992) and his public relations colleagues identified support for minorities and women as 1 of the 12 characteristics of excellent organizations. As Grunig asserted, "Excellent organizations recognize the value of diversity by employing female and minority workers and taking steps to foster their careers" (p. 17).

Job Satisfaction and Turnover

Fund raisers who are members of NSFRE generally have high job satisfaction, although about 40% say they want more management responsibility (Mongon, 1992). Only about 2% are interested in finding another job. Their satisfaction is reflected in job stability. Whereas the typical fund raiser has held 2.3 fund-raising jobs, 35% of all NSFRE members have worked for only one employer, and only 4% have worked for five or more employers.

A topic of hot discussion in fund-raising circles is the supposedly high turnover rate among staff fund raisers. One line of thought is that such practitioners change jobs frequently because of dissatisfaction. A more predominant viewpoint is that staff fund raisers jump from organization to organization to seek ever higher salaries. Both charges rely on anecdotal evidence and are contradicted by research findings such as those just cited from NSFRE's 1992 survey. Assumptions are being made that are detrimental and without factual basis.

Illustrating, Bloland and Bornstein (1991) assumed staff fund raisers change jobs often even though they did not examine the issue in their study on professionalization. The authors stated, "For an occupation in which time spent in one location is viewed as adding considerably to the worth of the practitioner, development currently operates with a high rate of turnover" (p. 108). Carbone (1989) made the same assumption in his study of professionalism, also without measuring the issue. One of the open-ended questions he asked the sample of association members was: "Other than a steady increase in the number of fund raising [sic] positions in recent years, what best explains why many fund raisers make relatively frequent job changes?" (p. 55).

Carbone (1987) gathered data about job tenure in his earlier study on education fund raisers. He found that the average number of years his respondents had served in their positions was 4 and 84% had been in the positions for less than 5 years. The latter finding should not have been surprising given Carbone—as students will recall—speculated that most of those practitioners were filling new positions. Yet, based only on univariate analysis, he concluded that fund raisers have a high number of job changes, although he blamed "job hopping" on "itinerant fund raisers whose frequent moves help keep the years-in-service figures low" (p. 7). Carbone further found that only about 20% of his respondents were actively seeking employment elsewhere. He admitted, "This is not a particularly high proportion of job seekers, given opportunities in the field" (p. 7).

Mongon (1992) concluded, "Job changes in this field traditionally have been considered to be more frequent than the national average in other fields. In fact, statistics do not support this" (p. 6). Adding to findings already presented, analysis of NSFRE data showed that higher salaries are related to a higher number of jobs—up to four. Having five or more employers has an inverse relationship with salary (i.e., fund raisers who change jobs frequently make less money, not more). It is unlikely, then, that staff practitioners engage in job hopping to increase their earnings.

Duronio's (1993) empirical findings also do not support the charges. When asked to indicate their plans in relation to staying with their present employer, 68% of the 1,748 members of AHP, CASE, and NSFRE said they intended to stay as far as they could see into the future or it was unlikely they would ever leave. Duronio additionally found that 86% of her respondents have a commitment to their organization equal to or greater than their commitment to their career in fund raising.

In her follow-up interviews with 82 practitioners, selected randomly from geographical strata of the quantitative study's respondents, Duronio (1994a) found that whereas almost 60% plan to change jobs sometime in the future (e.g., 30% said they would probably change jobs at some point to seek advancement), 40% have no plans to change jobs. Furthermore, 71% of those interviewed averaged 3 or more years with each of their employers.

In light of such findings, it is difficult to understand the widespread criticism of staff fund raisers. Michael Adams (1993), former practitioner and now president of Centre College, for example, claimed turnover is "clearly epidemic today and perhaps borders on the unethical" (p. 135). Consultants have been particularly vocal. One interviewed by Duronio (1994a) stated, "My most important criticism of the field is the low tenure of staff. . . . We have a profession that demands one kind of behavior and a group of professionals who for the most part behave differently. A good portion are motivated by the '80's, me-first' mentality" (p. 26).

Critics do not take into account the demand-side market of fund raising, and as Duronio (1994a) argued, it is "important to distinguish favorable market conditions for changing jobs from moral judgements of fund raisers" (p. 27). She rightfully added, "I'm concerned about a harsher standard applied to fund raisers and their integrity or the implication that they need to have a stronger commitment to the organization than staff in any other area" (p. 23). Duronio (1996) reported in an overview of her study, "Our research data suggest that turnover in the field is related not only to the rapid growth in the field, but to the resulting opportunities for advancement and competition among organizations for experienced fund raisers" (p. 16). Adding to her conclusions, overall U.S. employment has shifted from longer to shorter tenure, a trend generally ignored by critics.

Summarizing this discussion, contrary to common charges, scientific evidence indicates that staff fund raisers do not differ from members of other occupations in the degree to which they value and pursue long-term employment.

Personality Traits

Students may wonder about personal characteristics, or traits, of fund-raising practitioners. There is no evidence that individuals with certain attributes make better fund raisers. One problem in identifying personality traits that contribute to success is, of course, defining what constitutes success. Another problem is that past studies on this topic have been flawed by their measurement of a hodgepodge of characteristics without any theoretical basis.

The late John Miltner (1990)—a practitioner in higher education—designed his dissertation research to identify personal characteristics and skills that could be used in hiring and evaluating senior fund raisers. Miltner measured numerous variables, which he grouped into four categories: (a) communication/social skills, (b) managerial/administrative abilities, (c) educational/professional training, and (d) personal experiences. Statistically, only age and experience of the fund raisers and their staff had any relationship to what Miltner defined as success—increases in dollars raised that exceeded the median of the sample.

Willard (1984)—who like Miltner earned his PhD in education—obtained almost identical results 6 years earlier from his dissertation study. Out of 20 personal characteristics the literature repeatedly linked to effective fund raisers, only the 3 interrelated variables of age, years of fund-raising experience, and years of full-time work experience significantly correlated with effectiveness, defined as increases in dollars raised between two time periods. Willard concluded that beyond experience, there are no specific characteristics to serve as a guide for hiring and evaluating senior fund raisers.

The practitioner literature remains filled with references to "Mom-and-apple-pie" traits desired in fund raisers, such as an appreciation for hard work and the ability to inspire people. Respondents to Duronio's (1994b) study listed the personal characteristics of the "best fund raiser" they know (p. 20). The top five characteristics were: integrity, honesty, commitment, intelligence, and outgoing personality—none of which distinguishes fund raising from any other occupation. For now, students should not look for any "right" combination when assessing their potential for a fund-raising career. However, the theory of public relations excellence, summarized in chapter 1, does suggest that characteristics traditionally regarded as feminine are related to practicing fund raising the way this book recommends.

Providing a transition to the discussion on feminization, J. E. Grunig and White (1992) reviewed literature on differences in the orientations of men and women and stated, "The conventional wisdom has been that these differences make men more suitable as managers because of their preference for competition and 'toughness'" (pp. 49–50). They continued, "Recently, however, researchers have begun to realize that women's preferences for nurturance and relationships may be exactly what is needed by managers in the future" (p. 50). Relating masculine and feminine characteristics to presuppositions about the world, these scholars found that a feminine worldview closely describes the approach to public relations they theorized is the most effective and ethical, whereas the masculine worldview—based on competition and aggressiveness—describes an approach that is ineffective in the long run. They concluded, therefore, a majority of female practitioners "could move the field toward excellence" (p. 50).

FEMINIZATION OF FUND RAISING

During the late 1980s, women moved from minority representation to the majority of fund-raising practitioners. Today, more than half the members of the three major fund-raising associations are women, and their rise to majority status has been dramatic. From 1981 to 1992, the proportion of female members in NSFRE increased from 38% to 58% (Mongon, 1992). In CASE, 39% of the members were women in 1982, but by 1990 the percentage had jumped to 55% (Conry, 1991). Women represented only 15% of AHP's membership in 1977, 42% just 10 years later, and in 1992 they were the majority at 52% (Bumgarner, Georges, & Luna, 1987; D. Joseph, 1992).

As Boris, Daniels, and Odendahl (1985) explained in their gender study of foundation staffs, previous research has shown that women have greater opportunity in fields that require no formal training—those open to "gifted amateurs" (p. 72). Given its high demand and relatively high salaries, fund raising has been an attractive option for women who are seeking to change careers or reenter the workforce. Their technical skills, including word processing, and their experience as administrators or volunteers generally qualify them for entry-level positions.

This open career path has been and continues to be a boon for individual women. For example, those with a liberal arts degree who cannot seem to get beyond glorified secretarial positions in corporations find greater status and rewards as fund raisers. Women stuck in low-paying jobs as news bureau assistants look across the hall to the fund-raising department and decide the higher salaries paid to annual giving staff outweigh any journalistic aspirations. And former members of the Junior League point to their success at raising money as volunteers—as well as their social connections with prospective donors—to attain salaried positions when other doors are closed for lack of paid experience. In an era when women face difficult choices between career and family, fund raising is one of the few occupations currently offering reentry with little or no penalty for taking time off to have and/or raise children.

Collectively, however, the picture is not so rosy. Women historically have been paid less than men, and a gender gap persists. Concern that the new female majority will depress salaries and prestige has caused a backlash against women. As a result, a two-tier hierarchy segregates female practitioners into lower paying, lower status titles and positions.

Gender Gap

NSFRE first identified a gender gap in its 1985 survey, which showed that two thirds of its female members earned less than $33,000 per year (Mongon, 1992). The proportion dropped to one half in 1988 and one third in 1992. Mongon cited the improvement as evidence that the gap was closing. Yet, as he also noted, only one tenth of NSFRE's male members make less than $33,000. At the highest end of the salary range, 20% of the men are paid more than $75,000 and 4% earn over $115,000. In contrast, only 4% of the women have salaries greater than $75,000 and a mere 0.3% earn more than $115,000. Mongon stated, "Clearly our sample has found few women in key positions which men have typically occupied" (p. 17).

Whereas the median salary for all NSFRE members is $44,000, men earn $52,000 a year as compared to only $41,200 for women (Mongon, 1992). In other words, male members of NSFRE earn $10,800, or 26%, more than female members. Stated another way, women make 79 cents for every $1 men make. Although Mongon maintained the difference is narrowing, he admitted, "There continues to be a significant gap between salaries earned by male fund-raising executives and those earned by females" (p. 24).

Mongon (1992), as do most authors of reports about gender discrimination, blamed much of the salary difference on the difference in years of experience between men and women (medians of 11 vs. 7 years), thereby implying time will solve the problem as women gain experience—which further implies that women should be patient. For example, Mongon argued that few women are in the highest paid groups because less than 5% of them have been in fund raising for 20 or more years. As he stated, "Prior to 1970, females in the profession were rare" (p. 4). He did not explain why the salary gap remains when the amount of experience is controlled. In each of the six categories of experience included in his study, men make at least 20% more than women.

Mongon's 1992 findings provide a dismal synopsis of what NSFRE's female members can expect as they move through their fund-raising careers. They are at a disadvantage in their first jobs: With 3 or more years of experience, men earn $12,500, or 42%, more than women. After accruing 5 to 9 years of experience, women narrow the gender gap to 20%, although their salary is still $7,600 less than men's. Women earn their highest salary when they have 20 or more years of experience, $53,500—an amount men surpass when they have only 10 to 14 years of experience. At the senior stage in their career, women make $16,000 less than their male counterparts and the gender gap is 30%.

Obviously, discrepancies in salaries cannot be explained by experience alone. Sophisticated statistical techniques are needed to dissect the problem, which NSFRE does not employ but CASE does. Before examining findings of CASE's membership surveys, it is necessary to warn students about a common misuse of statistics that disguises the degree of salary discrimination.

A gender gap usually is calculated and reported in three ways, all of which were used earlier. The amount of cents women earn for every $1 men earn is determined by dividing the mean or median salary of women by the comparable salary for men; it is reported in one direction. Subtracting the women's salary from the men's salary yields a dollar difference that can be used interchangeably (i.e., men make $x more, or women make $x less). The third way involves dividing the dollar difference by one of the two salaries to provide a percentage. This is where problems arise. The percentage, which is supposed to enhance understanding of what the dollar amount means, differs by the salary used as the denominator.

Many researchers use the men's salary in order to report that women make x% less than men. This is meaningless and misleading information. The percentage represents the proportional *decrease* in salary men would have to endure in order for salaries to be equal. On the other hand, the percentage obtained by using the women's salary as the denominator provides the proportional *increase* in salary women need to gain parity with men. As the objective of salary comparison is not to reduce men's salaries but to help women attain financial equity, only the second percentage is valid when describing a gender gap. Furthermore, the first percentage is always smaller than the second (except when dollar differences are minimal). Its use, whether from ignorance or on purpose, makes differences between salaries appear less serious than they actually are.

Illustrating, the difference between the median salaries of NSFRE male and female members with 3 to 4 years of fund-raising experience is $11,000 (Mongon, 1992). Mongon reported the difference as a proportion of the men's salary; that is, women earn 26%, or about one fourth, less than men. As a proportion of the women's salary, however, the difference is 36%; that is, men make over one third more than women. The first percentage is easily misinterpreted as meaning an increase for women of only 26% would result in equal salaries when actually a 36% increase is needed. Students should critically question reports on gender gaps that only address how much less women make proportionately and never mention percentages on how much more men make.

Turning to CASE, whereas the average fund raiser in education earns $55,000 per year, male fund raisers are paid $61,600 and female fund raisers are paid only $48,200, representing a 28% gender gap. More insightful breakdowns of findings from the four studies conducted by CASE are limited to a composite of its members (i.e., fund raisers combined with practitioners in other functions).

Roger Williams (1996), the lead researcher for CASE's 1995 study, reported that the gender gap in institutional advancement is closing by one penny a year. From 1986 to 1995, women gained about eight cents in their average salary and—similar to NSFRE members—now earn 78 cents for every $1 men make. Williams called this "good news" in that "the situation is getting incrementally better" (p. 14). I disagreed with his "just be patient" interpretation in an opinion piece published by CASE *Currents* (Kelly, 1997a). At the penny-per-year rate, female advancement officers can expect to reach salary parity with their male counterparts in 2017—nearly a quarter century away!

I also presented calculations of the financial penalty for being a women. In 1986, female members of CASE were paid $11,600 a year less than male members (Turk, 1986). In 1990, they were paid $13,000 less (R. L. Williams, 1996). Although proportions improved, the dollar difference had not changed by 1995—women still brought home $13,000 less. Wages lost by women during those 10 years totaled $124,400. Multiplying the average annual loss over a 40-year career, women who entered advancement in the late 1980s can expect to earn $500,000 less than men—primarily because of their gender.

Such comparisons are useful for drawing attention to discrimination; however, they overstate the effect of gender because they do not account for other factors causing salary differences. Fortunately, more precise information is available. Researchers have employed the statistical technique of multiple regression in all four CASE studies to separate the effects of gender and 12 other independent variables on salary. The 13 variables measured over 13 years consist of personal and institutional characteristics logically related to salary, such as advancement experience, age, department budget, and institutional enrollment. Although it mentioned the regression analysis, R. L. Williams' (1996) published report on CASE's 1995 study largely ignored the results—a problem returned to shortly. To obtain the results, I contacted researchers at Pennsylvania State University who actually analyzed the data.

Regression analysis of 1995 data showed that a male member of CASE earns $4,800 more than a female member who matches him on each of the other variables (Lafer, 1996). Stated another way, all other factors being equal, men are paid $4,800 more a year just because they are men. Of the 12 other variables, 4, including ethnicity and tenure in current position, were not significantly related to salary; 8 variables in addition to gender accounted for some portion of salary differences. The four variables that explained most of the variation (80%) in 1995 salaries were, in descending order: (a) institutional type, or governance (working for a private—as opposed to a public—institution adds $5,200 to a practitioner's paycheck); (b) gender; (c) educational level (an additional degree is worth $3,400); and (d) title (a high-ranking title pays $2,200 more). Overall, regression analysis of data from CASE's four studies found that whereas other variables have some effect on salary, gender had the greatest effect in 1982, 1986, and 1990, and the second greatest effect in 1995.

Researchers analyzing the CASE studies also have divided the dollars women lost because they are not men by the women's average salaries to provide an index for comparing the gender gap over time (Lafer, 1996). The proportional difference between men's and women's salaries that cannot be explained by experience, age, or other variables was 12% in 1986, 14% in 1990, and 10% in 1995. The percentages, which represent salary increases needed to eliminate inequities, demonstrate slow and uneven progress; however, the percentage was 20% in 1982 when CASE conducted its first study. In other words, the financial penalty imposed on female advancement officers solely because of their gender was reduced by half between 1982 and 1995.

Progress, therefore, has been made, but the rate of reform is unacceptable. Women, including female students preparing to enter fund raising, should not be asked to wait 20 or more years before they are fairly compensated. As R. L. Williams (1996) rightfully concluded, the field "must now decide how to promote and pay them equitably or risk demoralizing the majority of its work force even more" (p. 21).

Backlash Against the Female Majority

Prompted by 1988 findings that for the first time NSFRE's female members outnumbered male members by 52% to 48%, *The Chronicle of Philanthropy* published a front-page article titled, "Influx of Women Into Fund Raising Poses Paradox: They're Effective, But Pay and Prestige Could Suffer" (Goss, 1989). Steven Ast (cited in Goss), head of a recruiting firm, summarized the predominant viewpoint: "The field is becoming feminized. And it's not good for the field and not good for women" (p. 1).

Female practitioners quoted in the article generally agreed with the assessment that women would bring down salaries and prestige, as did the male vice president at the university where I was working at the time, who said charitable organizations needed to hire more men. My reaction and that of other female fund raisers at the University of Maryland was disbelief and frustration. We applauded the comments of Rita Bornstein, then vice president for development at the University of Miami. Bornstein (cited in Goss, 1989), who had just completed a $400-million capital campaign 20 months ahead of schedule, countered, "If fund raising lacks status it is an occupational, not a gender, problem" (p. 10). She continued, "Discrimination against women is a bad response to a problem that's probably being defined wrong" (p. 10).

Bornstein was correct. The problem is not that the presence of women decreases pay and prestige, but that this happens because our society undervalues women. Instead of attacking the real problem, those in positions of power decided the proportional growth of female practitioners had to be curbed to protect fund raising. Illustrating the extent to which discrimination is accepted as an appropriate solution, the one finding from CASE's most recent survey that R. L. Williams (1996) chose to report first—two places before the gender gap—was: "After surging in the '80s, the feminization of advancement has leveled off" (p. 8). I doubt many women said to themselves, "That's certainly good news." The evidence he presented also was flawed. Based on the gender of those responding to the 1990 and 1995 surveys, Williams claimed the proportion of female CASE members had dropped 1.1%—a figure without statistical meaning as the survey's reported margin of error was plus or minus 3.1%, which means any change less than the error in either direction probably is due to sampling a population rather than taking a census.

Regardless, the finding of unchanged feminization is supported by membership figures of the three fund-raising associations: Female proportions have frozen at the levels achieved in the early 1990s. As of 1997, representation of women in NSFRE, CASE, and AHP remains essentially the same as the percentages cited earlier, which suggests a backlash is at work and is affecting the gender mix as intended. In the meantime, salaries overall have continued to rise and fund raising has not suffered a decline in prestige. For example, R. L. Williams (1996) reported, "Reflecting the increasing importance of advancement to campus aspirations, the average salary in the profession has climbed nearly 27 percent over the last five years" (p. 14). The increase, according to Williams, belies "the theory that more women in a given career field result in depressed wages for all" (p. 8). Only after giving this finding did Williams finally report that the gender gap of $13,000 found in 1990 "failed to shrink at all by 1995" (p. 8).

Before turning to the two-tier hierarchy resulting from discrimination, it is important to emphasize that the principal researchers for recent association studies have been male members who are full-time practitioners. For example, George Mongon, Jr. is a fund-raising consultant, and Roger Williams was head of public relations for Penn State and Georgetown University before joining a consulting agency in 1996. Their interpretation of findings often differs from mine and likely those of other women. Furthermore, these practitioner investigators lack methodological expertise; they rely on academic research centers to analyze the data. Findings are filtered through their insufficient understanding, which results in published reports based on elementary statistics and without required insight (e.g., significant and nonsignificant findings are not differentiated).

By utilizing male practitioners, CASE and NSFRE demonstrate disregard for the majority of their members and indifference to scientific objectivity and research skills.

I strongly urge the associations to rethink their criteria for selecting investigators for future studies.

Two-Tier Hierarchy

Julie Conry (1991), now director of development for the School of Nursing at Ohio State University, examined the gender issue in fund raising and drew parallels to the feminization of public relations and foundation grantmaking. Although gender has been studied extensively in the latter two fields, comparative work has not been conducted in fund raising. This area is rich in research possibilities for students searching for a topic for their thesis or dissertation study.

Occupations that have switched from male to female majorities are characterized by *pink-collar,* or *velvet, ghettos.* According to Conry (1991), gender transitions historically follow a similar pattern. Males in the occupation continue to dominate the highest status, highest paying positions, and as women gain access to previously male positions, the jobs become "deskilled" and redefined with consequent losses in pay and status. She elaborated, "Economists have observed in many studies of job segregation that within institutions women start at the bottom and move to the middle, while men start at the middle and move to the top" (p. 149). Feminist scholars argue that pressures, both personal and professional, keep the vast majority of women clustered in low to mid-management positions and that few actually break through the *glass ceiling,* or the invisible barrier to senior management.

As students will recall, multiple regression analysis showed that three variables in addition to gender explained most of the variation in 1995 salaries of CASE members: institutional type, educational level, and title. The published report did not break down institutional type by gender, and bivariate analysis indicated women and men are almost equal in holding an additional degree (R. L. Williams, 1996). However, women are at a disadvantage when it comes to having a high-ranking title. About 80% of all female CASE members are clustered at the bottom half of ranked titles, from the mid-level of director down to the lowest title of coordinator. In contrast, 85% of all male members are found at the top half of titles, from director up to vice president. Whereas four of every five coordinators are women, only one in four vice presidents is female. These figures attest to a two-tier hierarchy in institutional advancement and the presence of a glass ceiling at the mid-level of director. They also suggest that women lose more money than the amount regression analysis attributed solely to gender because women are less likely to have a high-ranking title, which was worth $2,200 in 1995. In short, title and gender are interrelated.

Providing further evidence of a two-tier hierarchy in fund raising, the membership survey conducted by AHP in 1992 found "substantial pay inequities between the sexes" (D. Joseph, 1992, p, 37). It also found that senior managers are rewarded to a greater degree than their junior colleagues. Between 1991 and 1992, the median salary for heads of fund-raising departments increased 3%, whereas assistant and associate directors experienced a 10% *decrease* in median salary, from $40,000 to $36,000. A breakdown of the two levels by gender was not provided; however, given Mongon (1992) concluded from the NSFRE study conducted the same year that men tend to dominate senior positions and women fill the majority of junior positions, the AHP findings suggest a "redefinition" of lower level positions is taking place.

TABLE 3.2
Hierarchy of Fund-Raising Positions

Highest status	*Major gifts*
	Planned giving
	Special gifts
	Corporate relations
	Foundation relations
	Annual giving
	Gift clubs
	Grant writing
	Prospect research
	Direct mail/Phonathons
	Special events
Lowest status	Gift records

Women occupy those positions, or specializations, that have lower status in the fund-raising department, which has the "Catch 22" effect of paying them lower salaries and—because of their heavy representation—lowering the value of those positions even more. Table 3.2 presents a hierarchy of fund-raising positions, which are labeled by what this book refers to as programs, publics, and techniques. Keeping in mind that status is a reflection of both salary and organizational power, the positions are listed in descending order from those with the highest status to those with the lowest.

All of the positions listed in Table 3.2 do not exist in every fund-raising department and in many instances, a given practitioner is responsible for more than one. Although arguments can be made about their exact order, these positions are the ones commonly found in the literature; however, their status usually is implied but not openly discussed.[3] Illustrating, a male vice president in higher education stated, "Those $25-a-year donors are wonderful . . . . But let's be honest with ourselves. A major gift program can bring in more money in a year than the annual fund can bring in a decade. And the bigger dollars are more important" (Edwards, 1989, p. 72).

Linking the hierarchy of positions to gender, Doris Critz (1981), who started her career in 1970 at Vassar College, compared fund raising to religion, saying, "In both fields, women have long been the backbone of the everyday activities, carrying out essential, mundane, unpaid or low-paid responsibilities, while men have filled the top leadership roles" (p. 285). She argued that stereotypes of what women are "good at" create problems for those seeking higher status positions:

> Too often they are channeled into more traditional areas such as the annual fund, phonathons, direct mail, special events and benefits . . . with male candidates given more serious consideration for positions in corporate and foundation solicitation, major and

---

[3]Planned giving is placed below major gifts although it currently has higher status. As explained in chapter 13, the position traditionally has been occupied by experts in financial planning and tax laws, who usually are not trained in fund raising and—of importance here—are men with high salaries. This book holds that the purpose of planned giving is to raise major gifts and that fund raisers, not people from other occupations, should manage the process; therefore, planned giving is subordinate to the major gifts position.

special gift responsibilities, direction of capital campaigns, and deferred giving programs. (p. 288)

Yet, she continued, "Not until women have paid their dues in these other areas are they considered eligible for the more demanding and exciting 'big money' positions of the development operation" (p. 288).

The value of the hierarchy presented in Table 3.2 is its ability to demonstrate—perhaps for the first time—the ordered distance in status between those positions related to raising major gifts and those related to lower level annual gifts (i.e., the two primary programs). This list will help both male and female students understand "the lay of the land" in fund-raising departments. It also provides women with a map for planning careers that extend beyond the bottom tier of positions.

Annual giving and the six positions listed below it can be viewed as "women's work," which Marxist-feminist scholars argue equates work in the labor market with work in the home: supporting, keeping things orderly, managing social activities, and reciprocating. Furthermore, Phillips and Taylor (1980) explained, "The work of women is often deemed inferior because it is women who do it. Women workers carry into the workplace their status as subordinate individuals, and this status comes to define the value of the work they do" (p. 6).

In 1988, a compensation study of higher education fund raisers by Brakeley Recruiting (1988) found that female practitioners were most strongly represented in the lower status positions. Focusing on title of director and following the descending order of Table 3.2, women represented only 36% of the directors of major gifts, 19% of planned giving, 42% of corporate and foundation relations, 60% of annual giving, and 78% of prospect research. The last position was the lowest paying of those included in the study. The second lowest salary was for annual giving. Conry (1991) explained, "Both research and annual fund positions are regarded as typical entry-level training jobs in fund raising because the work is routine, structured, and offers few opportunities for donor interaction" (p. 156). She added, "The negligible numbers of men in these departments suggest they are bypassing this entry route to more direct line and management roles" (p. 156).

Personal observation attests to this trend. When I first became a staff fund raiser in the mid-1970s, it was usual for both men and women to enter fund raising by taking positions in annual giving and working their way up to corporate relations and major gifts. In the late 1980s, I witnessed a number of men stepping into the higher status positions without starting at the beginning of the pipeline. Women, on the other hand, often stayed in lower status positions long after they had mastered the responsibilities and skills of the jobs.

Evidence of the trend at the highest job title was provided by Duronio and Loessin (1991), who found that 2 of the 10 chief fund raisers in their qualitative study of higher education practitioners were men who had no fund-raising experience at any other level than vice president.

The most recent information on the two-tier hierarchy comes from NSFRE's 1995 membership survey, which students are reminded was based on a nonrandom sample. The 1995 survey collected data on fund-raising positions for the first time and compared them with salaries. The positions and salaries were broken down by gender in the initial report, but were presented without gender breakdown in the final version.

No attempt was made to account for different titles. Of the respondents, 100% working in prospect research are women, as are 82% of those who work in special events, and 68% in annual giving (S. G. Greene & Murawski, 1996). On the other hand, women represent only 30% of the respondents working in planned giving. Planned giving officers earn a median salary of $51,000, whereas practitioners in annual giving earn only $39,400 (Mongon, 1996).

The NSFRE study also found a gender gap within positions. For example, male respondents who work in annual giving make $12,600, or 36%, more than the position's female majority (S. G. Greene & Murawski, 1996). Not all the findings, however, support assertions made in this discussion. For example, 70% of the respondents who work in major gifts are women, and respondents working in prospect research earn a higher median salary than those who work in annual giving, $41,000 versus $39,400 (S. G. Greene & Murawski, 1996; Mongon, 1996). Titles may explain some of the unexpected results. For example, many of the women in the major gifts position may be assistant or associate directors, rather than the head of major gifts.

Regardless, both supporting and conflicting findings underscore the need for studies using random samples to test the two-tier hierarchy in fund-raising departments of all types of charitable organizations. This would be an excellent topic for a master's thesis, which could draw on previous gender studies in public relations and foundation grantmaking. Organizational and feminist theory would provide guidance.

Undervaluing Women

A female fund raiser in higher education described the current situation: "Women start at lower salaries and are not given the same raises and promotions as men. There is a set of built in social attitudes that undervalues women's work and worth" (Conry, 1991, p. 149). Another stated: "As long as the old-boy network is still in a position of power, it is very difficult for women to rise above a certain level of management" (S. G. Greene & Murawski, 1996, p. 38).

The fund-raising literature, which—as pointed out in chapter 1—has been written primarily by male practitioners, insinuates and sometimes advises that women are handicapped when it comes to raising major gifts. Jerold Panas (1984), for example, said women may need assistance in securing appointments with major donor prospects, implying men do not. He further generalized that young women have difficulty soliciting older women and widows because such women—who, demographically, are the key prospects for planned giving—are more comfortable with men. Without any elaboration, he added, "Young, attractive women are not effective in soliciting large gifts from middle aged men" (p. 184)—who are key prospects for major gifts. Unlike other women, however, Panas said nuns are very effective for calling on male and female prospects, but they are even more effective when they wear their habits!

John Detmold (1981), who made a career as a fund raiser for such private women's colleges as Wells, Smith, and Mills, stated, "Women *can* be tops at this task of soliciting funds, but most of them approach it initially with fear and trepidation, if not actual loathing. For many women, *solicitation* is still a dirty word" (p. 157; italics in original).

Such stereotypical attitudes perpetuated in the male-dominated literature no doubt have hampered women in their attempts to move into fund-raising positions with higher status. Illustrated by an article published nearly 20 years ago (McIlquham,

1978), female fund raisers have long complained that male managers believe women are not capable of handling solicitations involving major gifts. Women cited in the article said gaining entry-level jobs was relatively easy, but advancing to higher status positions was difficult. Among the barriers they reported were not being taken seriously, being barred from corporate meetings, not being allowed to travel, and not being given the opportunity to speak for their organizations.

It also can be surmised by Panas' (1984) statement about young attractive women that concerns about sexual harassment by male donors have been used to deter female fund raisers from moving into major gifts positions. Rather than blame perpetrators, some male managers tend to view sexual harassment as a liability of being a woman; therefore, it is for their own good they be kept "at home" and out of situations in which offensive and unwelcomed conduct might occur. Sexual harassment is addressed in chapter 12.

Women must confront prejudice and barriers. From the time they enter the pipeline, female fund raisers are advised to keep their sights on the highest titles and progressively move toward the major gifts position. I believe experience in the lower level positions makes managers more effective; however, women should not linger in such positions as annual giving. Once responsibilities and skills are mastered, they should pursue promotion to positions with higher status and pay. Information contained in this book will help them in their career advancement.

The discussion continues by describing action women can take to reduce the effects of gender discrimination. Before proceeding, it is important to reassure students that in spite of discrimination, fund raising still offers career advantages to women. As Conry (1991) noted, "Many commentators and practitioners share the view that the current intensive market demand for competent fund raisers of any gender will continue into the immediate future, creating widespread entry-level opportunities for women" (p. 147). She concluded after her critical analysis, "Even the lower salaries women are paid in fund raising are often superior to what they could command in similar occupations" (p. 157). A "take charge" stance by women would improve the situation.

Applying Public Relations Theory

The public relations theory of roles, which is discussed more fully in chapter 6, identifies factors contributing to gender discrimination and suggests a way to overcome them.

All public relations practitioners starting at the entry level carry out the role of *technician*. They initially are hired on the basis of their written and oral communication skills. If they fail to move beyond the technician role to the role of *manager*, they often are relegated to positions at or slightly above entry level throughout their careers. Public relations researchers have found in numerous studies that women tend to enact the role of technician, which studies also have shown is related to significantly lower salaries than those paid to managers. Furthermore, Broom and Dozier (1986) found in their longitudinal studies from 1979 to the mid-1980s that the number of women classified as technicians increased over time, whereas those classified as managers barely changed. Women, then, remain in the lower paying technician role regardless of experience. Broom and Dozier concluded, "Professional growth in public relations [is] a function of the practitioner's gender and role" (p. 55).

Applying the theory to fund raising, managers employ environmental scanning and other research methods to contribute to decision making in their organizations and strategically plan fund-raising programs. Technicians, in contrast, concentrate on producing and implementing fund-raising techniques, such as designing direct mail, writing grant proposals, and staffing special events. They carry out their duties separate from the management team, often without full knowledge of how the techniques fit into the fund-raising plan or the intended results beyond set dollar goals.

Dozier, Chapo, and Sullivan (1983) argued that the technician role often defines a ghetto for women, providing a place to put them so they can be used but paid less than their male colleagues. In other words, one reason female fund raisers occupy lower status positions and earn less than men is because the expectations of women and the role they predominantly carry out are as technicians, not managers.

Men dominate higher status positions in which they have the opportunity to fulfill the manager role. In their positions low in the hierarchy, women rarely are exposed to management skills. As Wetherell (1989) concluded from her study of gender and public relations, "People cannot practice or even prefer what they do not know" (p. 201).

Female fund raisers, Conry (1991) predicted, will find career progress difficult because they are "fulfilling the expectations of some that their ultimate success will be limited to technical roles rather than management" (p. 159). Yet Cutlip et al. (1994) stressed that practitioners who understand roles are in a position to adopt different behavior patterns and develop strategies for dealing with others' expectations of them. "This understanding," they stated, "may be particularly important for women, as research shows that role differences are associated with both salaries and access to the organizational decision-making process" (p. 46).

Women in fund raising, therefore, can reduce gender discrimination by learning those skills that public relations research has shown are related to the manager role, such as strategic planning, which are covered in this book. Enacting the manager role does not mean women should rid themselves of feminine traits. As stated earlier, characteristics traditionally regarded as feminine are closely aligned with the approach to fund raising this book recommends. However, adopting the manager role while maintaining theoretically prescribed qualities will not be easy.

Feminine characteristics have been used in the past to justify women's relegation to lower status positions. Drawing from McIlquham's (1978) article, Conry (1991) stated, "The characteristics attributed to women as making them more effective fund raisers—being more verbal, more sensitive, less afraid of emotion, more detail-oriented, more nurturing, and more creative—also are cited as the very reason many barriers exist" (p. 164). New management theories advocate these traits for managers in the highest positions, which will help women break out of ghettos and ascend the departmental ladder.

Improving Salary Negotiation

Mongon (1992) partially credited decreases in the gender gap to more information about salaries and the result "that women were able to point to what was 'normal' for the field and help discourage salary discrimination relative to their male counterparts" (p. 16). Female fund raisers must use available figures to negotiate better salaries. First, however, they must learn negotiation skills, and more basically, they must realize that negotiation is required. Critz (1981) described the problem:

> Too often women are offered (and accept) the lower ranges of the pay scale for a given job, whereas a male with equal qualifications will be offered pay at a higher rate. Women must be prepared to negotiate for equal salaries . . . and not settle gratefully for bargain-basement compensation . . . . They must also be prepared to be labeled as "agressive" when they do this, compared to their male counterparts who are considered to have a healthy sense of self-worth. (p. 289)

Poor negotiation was a major reason given for women's lower salaries in AHP's 1990 membership survey. T. Richardson Miner, Jr. (cited in E. Greene, 1990), then chair of AHP's board of directors, said women "were unprepared to fight for compa-rable pay" (p. 19). NSFRE President Patricia Lewis (cited in S. G. Greene & Murawski, 1996), the only woman currently heading a fund-raising association, blamed some of the gender gap on women who enter fund raising with only volunteer experience "and are willing to take any money rather than no money" (p. 38). Generalizing, Conry (1991) said female job candidates "will accept less, work for less, and offer a standard of performance that is a bargain from the employer's point of view" (p. 155).

Findings of its 1990 survey prompted AHP to establish a special committee to study "the ways women negotiate for salaries, work responsibility, and job titles so it can help them to be compensated more fairly" (E. Greene, 1990, p. 19). NSFRE concluded from its 1995 survey that it also needs to help its female members under-stand negotiation (S. G. Greene & Murawski, 1996). But resolution must start with those beginning their careers. Mongon's findings given earlier provide evidence that women are poorer than men (pun intended) at negotiating their first salaries. Similar findings have been reported by the other associations. CASE's 1995 study, for example, showed that the widest salary gap (32%) is among newcomers who have less than 2 years of experience (R. L. Williams, 1996). When female fund raisers begin their careers at salaries lower than men, catching up is difficult if not impossible.

Because public relations has a female majority and a gender gap similar to fund raising, I usually spend at least 30 minutes on salary negotiation when teaching the first course of the public relations curriculum. My female students seem actually shocked that a counteroffer is not only advised, but expected by a prospective employer. The women tend to think of employer representatives as father figures, who will do the best they can for them; questioning the sincerity of such authorities is ungrateful and rude. We do some role playing in class that helps both the women and men better understand the dynamics of negotiation, and I often tell them some "war stories" about my own mistakes.

My first position with fund-raising responsibilities was a case in point. The job was offered to me with a salary $3,000 less than I was making at the time. The dean who offered it emphatically told me the lower salary was the best he could do. During a courtesy interview with me, the vice president of university relations—who was mentioned earlier—repeated twice that people should never take cuts in salary to get a new job. I chose not to listen, accepted the lower salary, and found out 3 months later from the vice president that he had arranged with the dean—prior to the offer—to cover the $3,000 shortfall or whatever was needed to hire me. As he said, "I tried to tell you." So I tell my students. Figure 3.2 summarizes commonsense advice to help future practitioners, particularly women, negotiate better salaries.

Accepting Mobility

According to Conry (1991), "In spite of the gains women have made in numbers in fund raising in the last ten years, one stubborn issue remains to foil many with ambitions to advance: the issue of mobility. Career advancement in fund raising, more than at any other time in its history, requires the willingness to relocate to achieve greater responsibilities" (p. 165).

Women must accept mobility as part of careerist values. As in most occupations, fund raising rewards individuals who take the greatest risks, including those who are willing to move to new opportunities. Relocation offers a solution to female practitioners stuck in low status, low paying positions. When doors to promotion are closed, the logical choice is to seek employment elsewhere. Unfortunately, most women view relocation as an option available only to men, which contributes to gender discrimination.

Avoid all discussion of salary until you have been offered a job. Once you have been selected as the top candidate, the employer's representative will go to great lengths not to have to revert to his or her second choice. That gives you substantial power and a lot of room for negotiation. After researching comparable salaries, such as those reported in this text, establish a desired figure before you sit down with the representative; also determine an "absolutely have-to-have" figure as your bottom line. If the offer made is at or just above your desired figure, add 10% and counter-offer. If the offer is less, counter-offer with your desired figure. Do not apologize or act embarrassed.

If you are uncomfortable, feel pressured, or cannot make up your mind, it is absolutely acceptable once an offer is made to state (not ask) that you need 24 hours to give it serious consideration. The more senior the position, the less likely an employer expects an on-the-spot decision. In fact, a quick acceptance might make you appear too eager (perhaps there is something that was missed in your background check), or it may make the employer representative question whether he or she offered you too much money, which would mean the person had burdened the organization with unnecessary cost.

By asking for a small amount of time you demonstrate your maturity in making such a serious life decision (how many of us buy a car on the spot?), your sincere interest in the job, and your desire to bring quick closure to the negotiations for your benefit, as well as that of the employer. At the same time, you remove yourself from a situation that could result in a regretful decision and give yourself time to consider factors and inevitably raise unasked questions that are essential to your decision.

Reply within 24 hours. Ask any new questions and then accept or reject the offer. Remember, once you have accepted an offer you cannot reenter negotiations. The subject is closed. Do not go back on your word. Knowing that you have negotiated your salary to the best of your ability and in good faith will help keep you satisfied with your decision even when the untold negative aspects of the job become familiar.

FIG. 3.2. Negotiating salaries.

Willingness to move does not equate to job hopping. The option of changing jobs in a high-demand market leads to career advancement by staying with or leaving employers. Female fund raisers who are unwilling to relocate consider their careers geographically bound, but expect employers not to notice. They notice, and salaries and status reflect it. An employee without choices receives little consideration.

Reporting findings from AHP's 1987 membership survey, Bumgarner et al. (1987) flatly stated, "Women's lack of mobility not only limits their opportunities but results in being taken for granted" (p. 17). They quoted a female vice president, who said, "Without mobility you will have a nice career, but not a great one" (p. 17).

Societal norms make it easier for women, particularly those who are married, to accept relocation for male partners than for themselves. Yet men no doubt have endured tremendous pressures when determining their willingness to uproot loved ones in order to pursue opportunities hundreds or thousands of miles from their current home. Just as men have found relocation decisions difficult and have not taken them lightly, women must weigh their desires to advance against their responsibilities and the needs of their families. They should not underestimate people who care about them. Those who truly are life partners often will not only accept but applaud a decision involving change.

In conclusion, gender discrimination must be acknowledged and addressed. Multiple studies have documented injustices for more than 10 years. Despite repeated findings, neither the fund-raising associations nor organizational employers have taken the necessary steps to solve the problem. Immediate action is required, including implementation of equity goals. Women's abilities to manage relationships with donors should be rewarded—not devalued.

SUGGESTED READINGS

Boris, E. T., Daniels, A. K., & Odendahl, T. J. (1985). *Working in foundations: Career patterns of men and women.* New York: The Foundation Center.

Broom, G. M., & Dozier, D. M. (1986). Advancement for public relations role models. *Public Relations Review, 12*(1), 37–56.

Carbone, R. F. (1986). *Agenda for research on fund raising* (Monograph No. 1). College Park: University of Maryland, Clearinghouse for Research on Fund Raising.

Carbone, R. F. (1987). *Fund raisers of academe* (Monograph No. 2). College Park: University of Maryland, Clearinghouse for Research on Fund Raising.

Creedon, P. J. (Ed.). (1993). *Women in mass communications* (2nd ed.). Thousand Oaks, CA: Sage.

Duronio, M. A., & Tempel, E. R. (1996). *Fund raisers: Their careers, stories, concerns, and accomplishments.* San Francisco, CA: Jossey-Bass and NSFRE.

Kelly, K. S. (1993). Public relations and fund-raising encroachment: Losing control in the nonprofit sector. *Public Relations Review, 19*(4), 3493–65.

Odendahl, T., & O'Neill, M. (Eds.). (1994). *Women and power in the nonprofit sector.* San Francisco, CA: Jossey-Bass.

Toth, E. L., & Cline, C. (Eds.). (1989). *Beyond the velvet ghetto.* San Francisco, CA: International Association of Business Communicators (IABC) Research Foundation.

4

Professionalism of Fund Raising

Fund raising is more than just an occupation. It enjoys some of the characteristics of a profession, such as active associations with certification programs and codes of ethics. This chapter examines the professionalism of fund raising, introducing students to entities and elements that affect its status. It draws from previous studies to evaluate the extent to which fund raising meets professional criteria. Although the analysis shows progress has been made, it also reveals that the infrastructure necessary to becoming a profession currently is incomplete. In particular, fund raising lacks a theoretical body of knowledge and a program of formal education.

Rather than delay professionalism until deficiencies are addressed, chapter 4 explores the alternative route of incorporating fund raising within public relations—an occupation for which the infrastructure of a profession already is in place.

CRITERIA OF A PROFESSION

The issue of professionalism, as Carbone (1989) argued, is best approached not by whether a particular occupation is or is not a profession, but rather by placing the occupation on a continuum of professionalism that gauges how closely it resembles the so-called "true professions," such as medicine and law. Carbone did just that with fund raising and concluded it is *"an emerging profession*—an occupation that has moved steadily along the professional continuum; an occupation with the potential to attain greater professional stature" (p. 46; italics in original).

Public relations is defined similarly by its scholars. Cutlip et al. (1994), for example, stated, "The relatively young practice of *public relations is an emerging profession*" (p. 26; italics in original). They supported their assertion by comparing the occupation to criteria basic to a profession, concluding, "Strict interpretation of the criteria would preclude calling public relations a 'profession'" (p. 49). J. E. Grunig and Hunt (1984) reached the same conclusion after an analysis based on a parallel set of professional characteristics; however, they added an important distinction: "Public relations has the necessary infrastructure to be a true profession" (p. 82).

Five common criteria similar to those used by the authors just cited are employed here to evaluate the status of fund raising as a profession: (a) a body of knowledge based on theory and research, (b) a program of formal education, (c) professional associations, (d) codes of ethics, and (e) shared values of professional autonomy and allegiance. These criteria are drawn from the extensive literature on professionalism first developed in sociology during the 1950s and 1960s.

Before examining the five criteria, it is necessary to emphasize that neither fund raising nor public relations has made much progress in achieving a sixth and vital criterion of a profession: recognition by society that the service it provides is unique and essential.

Unique and Essential Service

Addressing uniqueness, Carbone (1989)—like most scholars—did not differentiate between the fund-raising service of volunteers and the service of paid practitioners. He argued, in fact, that fund raising cannot qualify as a profession because volunteers raise money. At the first stage of the professionalization process, the work must become a full-time occupation. Yet many fund-raising departments rely on volunteers, who Carbone defined as "part time, amateur . . . fund raisers" (p. 14). Furthermore, he implied that because thousands of amateurs obviously have the same skills as practitioners, the service provided by fund raising is not unique.

Bloland and Bornstein (1991) also adopted this premise in their study on the professionalization of fund raising. They stated, "Sharing expertise with amateurs considerably weakens the occupation's power to define its work, and establish juris-dictional control and legitimacy" (p. 105). In addition, Bloland and Bornstein claimed many fund-raising activities are purely administrative and not unique to the function. "Except for the technical aspects of the work related to tax laws and planned giving, much of it could be conducted by another administrative unit" (p. 105).[1]

Similarly, the service of public relations commonly is not recognized as unique (i.e., anyone can do public relations). Representative of this viewpoint, a *Cosmopolitan* magazine article, "Thinking of a Career Switch? Try PR!," characterized public relations practitioners as "'people persons' who often enter the field after puttering around in a few other areas, such as publishing, secretarial work, or sales" (Newman, 1992, p. 96). According to the author, public relations work consists primarily of persuading journalists that publicity for an organization is newsworthy.

The question of uniqueness of service is dependent on the definitions used to describe both fund raising and public relations. As explained in chapter 1, when fund raising is defined as simply seeking gifts for charitable organizations, anyone can do it. Likewise, when public relations is defined as getting publicity, it is not unique to members of a particular occupation. As defined in this book, however, both public relations and fund raising provide unique services that cannot be duplicated by people outside the occupations. Be that as it may, this uniqueness is not widely recognized by society.

Turning to the question of how essential the service is, arguments can be made that both fund raising and public relations are fundamental to preserving our democratic

---

[1]This assertion is startling given coauthor Rita Bornstein, who was mentioned in the last chapter, was a fund raiser before becoming president of Rollins College in Florida in 1990—about the same time she wrote this essay with her husband, education professor Harland Bloland.

society as we know it. Gurin (1991) summarized the case for fund raising: "Fundraising [sic] is what makes philanthropy work, and philanthropy is what makes our pluralistic democracy work" (p. 149). Cutlip et al. (1994) argued that by helping organizations be responsive to others, public relations "contributes to making our democratic process—as well as the social, economic, and political systems—more effective in meeting social needs" (p. 22). They elaborated, "Public relations serves society by mediating conflict and by building relationships essential to the dynamic consensus needed to maintain social order . . . . In other words, public relations facilitates adjustment and maintenance in the social systems that provide us with our physical and social needs" (p. 22).

As with uniqueness, the essential services provided by fund raising and public relations are not widely recognized. In fact, both routinely are treated to disparaging remarks, with fund-raising practitioners often referred to as *hucksters* and those in public relations called *flacks*. J. E. Grunig and Hunt (1984) explained that society and particularly journalists have never forgotten the press agentry origins of public relations: "That is why they call public relations people 'flacks'—publicists who shoot all their weapons at the press in the hope that some of the flak will hit home" (p. 30). Philanthropy author and columnist Waldemar Nielsen (1992) reported that fund raisers frequently are viewed with disdain, particularly by staff members of foundations: "They are seen as hucksters or snoops" (p. 41).

Burlingame and Hulse (1991) underscored the latter occupation's "poor public image" in their preface to the book *Taking Fund Raising Seriously*, and stated, "Only by addressing fundamental issues about fund raising and its role in a democratic society will the disparity between its negative public image and its importance to the third sector be reconciled" (pp. xxii–xxiii). In the same book, Payton et al. (1991) proclaimed, "There is widespread academic bias against fund raising and fund raisers but very little solid argument to justify the prejudice" (p. 3). Payton (1990) simply said, "Fund raising, the least respected field of all, is endemic to applied philanthropy" (p. 177).

Providing an appropriate summary for this discussion, NSFRE President Lewis (1993b) declared, "I'll know that we are 'grown up' as a profession when nobody feels the need to apologize for being a fund raiser" (p. 10). The chapter now turns to an examination of the five basic criteria for measuring professionalism.

Body of Knowledge

Bloland and Bornstein (1991) asserted, "The most important strategy for gaining professional status is the development of a substantial, legitimate knowledge base" (p. 114). They added, "Creating a theory base that is changed by research, and a research base that is informed by theory is considered by many students of the professions to be the most important tactic in the professionalization process" (p. 117).

Abbott (1988) stressed the significance of scholarly knowledge: "Any occupation can obtain licensure (e.g., beautician) or develop a code of ethics (e.g., real estate). But only a knowledge system governed by abstractions can redefine its problems and tasks, defend them from interlopers, and seize new problems" (p. 9).

As emphasized in chapter 1, fund raising's body of knowledge consists primarily of intuitively based, untested principles generated by practitioners—the sum of which

Carbone (1986) described as a body of lore and experience but limited theoretical knowledge. "Up to now," he maintained, "research on fund raising has been sporadic, scatter-gun, and often pedestrian" (pp. 22–23).

The relatively dismal state of research and theory on fund raising was described and documented in my earlier book (Kelly, 1991a; see chap. 4). For example, the first comprehensive bibliography on philanthropy (Layton, 1987), published in 1987, referenced 1,614 publications, of which only 9 books and 11 articles—or slightly more than 1%—dealt with fund raising. The bibliography's author explained, "While there is an enormous practical literature on fund-raising [*sic*], there is almost nothing which examines the phenomenon of 'getting' with the same depth and comprehension that the phenomenon of giving has received" (p. xv).

Two factors are responsible for this deficiency: (a) philanthropy scholars have ignored fund raising, and (b) the void left by their absence has been filled with research produced by practitioner graduate students that is redundant, less than rigorous, and inadequate.

Neglect By Philanthropy Scholars.   As just given, Payton et al. (1991) charged that academics are biased; they added, "Scholars, even those interested in philanthropy, have neglected fund raising" (p. 3). Indeed, as supported by Layton's (1987) findings, scholars have been more interested in studying philanthropy from the perspective of donors than from the perspective of fund raisers. Their disinterest and neglect have contributed significantly to fund raising's lack of the criterion deemed most important by the literature on professionalism.

Although interrelated, philanthropy and fund raising are not synonymous. Giving money and raising money represent the two distinct sides of the philanthropic coin. Research concentrating on just one side produces findings that are limited in explanation. Yet as Ostrander and Schervish (1990) noted, most scholars conceptualize and study philanthropy as a world of donors. This exclusive focus, they continued, "runs the risk of obscuring issues that are of concern to recipients" (p. 67). Generally, philanthropy scholars assume that fund raising is something charitable organizations do, not a function carried out by trained practitioners (Kelly, 1997b). They approach giving as a generic act, isolated from relationships with specific organizations. The effects of fund-raising action, planned and implemented to evoke responses from prospective donors, such as cultivation activities, rarely are considered in accounts of giving behavior. The scholars usually equate fund raising to solicitation, only one part of the process through which gifts are raised. Studies, therefore, have produced knowledge that is insufficient and incomplete for understanding fund raising and philanthropy.

As discussed in the next chapter, philanthropy and nonprofit organizations did not become subjects of recognized scholarly inquiry until the 1970s, although a few individuals, such as Bremner (1960/1988), made valuable contributions earlier. The Program on Non-Profit Organizations (PONPO) was established in 1977 at Yale University. During the 1980s, similar academic research centers were founded, including centers at the City University of New York, the New School for Social Research, Seton Hall University, New York University, Case Western Reserve University, the University of San Francisco, the University of Missouri–Kansas City, Boston College, and Johns Hopkins University. Starting in the mid-1980s, most of the centers broadened their mission beyond research to include educating future managers and providing technical assistance to nonprofits (P. D. Hall, 1992b). By the early 1990s, 21 centers were in operation (Independent Sector, 1993). Today, 34 centers exist, as does the Nonprofit Academic Centers Council, which was formed to coordinate and facilitate center activities.[2] The university centers, according to pioneer scholar David Horton Smith (1993), had a median budget of $300,000 per year in 1992, and at least two received research grants of about $1 million around that time.

In addition to this growth of academic centers, scholars interested in philanthropy and nonprofits have been supported since 1983 by annual spring research forums sponsored by IS. The Association for Voluntary Action Scholars, which was founded in 1971, changed its name in 1989 to the Association for Research on Nonprofit Organizations and Voluntary Action (ARNOVA) to accommodate membership of scholars in the new domains. As of 1997, ARNOVA has more than 1,000 members from 40 countries. It holds an annual 3-day conference each fall. Graduate students are encouraged to join at a reduced rate. Table 4.1 lists addresses for the World Wide Web sites of ARNOVA, IS, and other organizations and entities discussed in this chapter.

There currently are three academic journals devoted to research on philanthropy and nonprofits: (a) *Nonprofit and Voluntary Sector Quarterly (NVSQ)*, sponsored by AR-

TABLE 4.1
World Wide Web Sites

Association for Healthcare Philanthropy (AHP)	http://www.go-ahp.org
Association of Professional Researchers for Advancement (APRA)	http://weber.uwashington.edu/dlamb/apra/resource.htm
Association for Research on Nonprofit Organizations and Voluntary Action (ARNOVA)	http://www.wvu.edu/~socialwk/A/arnova.html
Center on Philanthropy, Indiana University	http://www.tcop.org
Council for Advancement and Support of Education (CASE)	http://www.case.org
Independent Sector (IS)	http://www.indepsec.org
Institute for Nonprofit Organization Management, University of San Francisco	http://www.cps.usfca.edu/fundraising
International Society for Third-Sector Research (ISTR), Johns Hopkins University	http://www.jhu.edu/~istr
National Society of Fund Raising Executives (NSFRE)	http://www.nsfre.org
Nonprofit Sector Research Fund, Aspen Institute	http://www.aspenist.org:80/dir/polpro/nsrf/NSRF1.html
Nonprofit and Voluntary Sector Quarterly (NVSQ)	http://www.yale.edu/isps/ponpo/nvsq
Program on Non-Profit Organizations (PONPO), Yale University	http://www.yale.edu/isps/ponpo
Public Relations Society of America (PRSA)	http://www.prsa.org

[2]The newest center was created at Harvard University's John F. Kennedy School of Government in 1997 (S. Gray, 1997). Harvard's Business School already was conducting research and teaching classes on philanthropy and nonprofit management—attesting to increased attention on the third sector.

NOVA in affiliation with Yale's PONPO; (b) *Nonprofit Management & Leadership*, sponsored by the Mandel Center for Nonprofit Organizations at Case Western and the Centre for Voluntary Organisation at the London School of Economics and Political Science; and (c) *Voluntas*, sponsored by the International Society for Third-Sector Research (ISTR), which was founded in 1992 and is housed in Johns Hopkins' Institute for Policy Studies.

In September 1990, Indiana University announced it had received $15 million from the Lilly Endowment and a group of anonymous donors for development of the university's 3-year-old Center on Philanthropy, including a 10-year program to finance scholarly and applied research (Bailey, 1990a). In 1991, the Nonprofit Sector Research Fund was established at the Aspen Institute in Washington, DC with a mandate "to support independent, high-quality research that will benefit practitioners, policymakers, and others interested in the nonprofit sector" (Boris, 1992, p. 105). The initial funders were the AAFRC Trust for Philanthropy, the Ford Foundation, the Charles Stewart Mott Foundation, the Rockefeller Brothers Fund, and an anonymous donor. In its first 3 years of operation, the fund awarded about $2 million in research grants.[3] Finally, in the last 10 years, some of America's largest foundations have supported individual research projects on philanthropy and nonprofits, including Lilly, Ford, Mott, and the Kellogg Foundation.

Despite this rapid development of a research infrastructure, fund raising has not benefited from a corresponding gain in its body of knowledge. The effects of the millions of dollars spent by the entities just described have been indirect and minimal for fund raising. In illustration, only 3% of the 472 articles published by *NVSQ* during its first 20 years (1972–1992) dealt with fund/resource raising (Brudney & Durden, 1993). Even this low percentage overstates the attention paid to fund raising. The authors, who identified the 25 topics covered most often in the journal, included the broader area of philanthropy—such as studies on giving—in their operational definition of fund/resource raising.

The recent surge in research on philanthropy and nonprofits has disguised the fact that few of the studies have focused on fund raising. For example, Lewis (1993b) cited philanthropy research to support her assessment, "We are meeting many of the key benchmarks of full recognition as a profession" (p. 9). In evidence of a body of knowledge, she pointed to the 2,800 books, monographs, articles, papers, videotapes, and audiotapes in NSFRE's library. I can attest from firsthand observation that most of those works are either nontheoretical practitioner literature or scholarly publications that seldom—if ever—mention the fund-raising function.

Substandard Work By Practitioner Students.   Just as neglect by philanthropy scholars has contributed to fund raising's lack of a theoretical body of knowledge, so too has the substandard research that has been conducted on the function. As described in my previous book, fund-raising research consists primarily of work by practitioners pursing graduate degrees in education as part-time students.

---

[3]Doctoral students should investigate how their areas of interest for a dissertation study fit within the Aspen Institute's funding framework. Dissertation awards of up to $20,000 are considered. Applications are reviewed in two cycles per year, with deadlines of January 1 and June 1. To request information and application materials, call (202) 736-5800, or e-mail *nsrfund1@aol.com*. Information also is available at the fund's World Wide Web site, given in Table 4.1.

The studies overwhelmingly have been administrative in nature in that their purposes have been to help organizations raise more money—as opposed to building theory (basic research) or scientifically examining the occupation (introspective studies). In particular, a substantial portion of the research has been what I term *the search for magic buttons*, or practitioner students' preoccupation with cross-situational attitudes and beliefs that underlie donor behavior. CASE's former director of research, Judy Grace (1993), evaluated the work similarly: "Much of the past research has been institution-specific and oriented toward short-term goals. Fund-raising studies have consisted of, for example, descriptions of alumni donor behavior at one institution at a particular time" (p. 380).

Commenting on such studies and their preponderance, Brittingham and Pezzullo (1990) concluded that research on fund raising is limited, fragmented, and of marginal quality. They also attributed much of the literature's weakness to practitioner students who produce dissertations on fund raising but do not pursue subsequent research on the subject. They explained, "The topic of fund raising is more likely based on the student's employment in the field of development rather than on an organized research program" (p. 86). Few fund raisers who complete dissertations publish the results or seek careers as scholars; instead, the terminal degree is used for career advancement in fund raising. Significantly, Brittingham and Pezzullo reported, "Most dissertations appear to emanate in higher education administration programs" (p. 85).

Carbone (1986) argued that serious research on fund raising should not be conducted by part-time practitioner scholars. He outlined reasons comparable to those just given, adding, "Many fund raisers who complete graduate study do so in fields where methods are inappropriate or where methodological requirements are extremely modest" (p. 23). Soon afterward, Carbone (1987) documented that the majority of fund raisers with doctoral degrees who belong to CASE had majored in education.

Given Carbone's and Brittingham and Pezzullo's (1990) membership in the education discipline (i.e., all three held faculty appointments in education at the time of their studies), their early criticisms were markedly courageous. Their leadership and self-critical perspectives encouraged me to explore this issue further.

To do so, I reviewed the abstracts of doctoral dissertations and master's theses related to fund raising from 1985 to 1992, as compiled by Indiana University's Center on Philanthropy through University Microfilm Incorporated—the depository service for these manuscripts. Whereas the abstracts do not provide an explicit indicator of the student author's academic discipline, other information helps pinpoint it (e.g., type of degree and faculty adviser's name). Somewhat easier to interpret, codes based on academic disciplines must be used to select up to three headings that best describe the "subject" of the study. Selected subject headings almost always include the student author's major; however, they also represent the individual's choice in describing his or her work. Illustrating, Miltner (1990) selected his major discipline of education as a subject heading for his dissertation on fund raisers' personal characteristics, but he also listed political science and business.

Regardless, my review of fund-raising dissertations and theses indicated that about 80% were from colleges or departments of education. In other words, of the recent 200 or so graduate studies that represent much of the research on fund raising, 160 likely developed in education curricula, rather than in communication, economics, management, psychology, sociology, or other disciplines that logically and theoretically are more closely related to the practice.

In light of this assessment, I requested a more thorough analysis from bibliographer Janet Huettner and her staff at the Center on Philanthropy. A keywords search of all thesis and dissertation abstracts produced during the 90 years from 1903 through the first half of 1993—and a review of each abstract selected—resulted in 317 studies that pertained to and discussed fund raising in detail (Huettner, personal communication, November 1993). Attesting to the newness of the function and research on it, 93% of the studies (296) were produced after 1964. A total of 488 subject headings were used by the 317 student authors to describe their work. These subject headings, or academic disciplines, are broken down by percentages in Table 4.2.

As shown in Table 4.2, education accounts for 70% of the subject headings used to describe all fund-raising theses and dissertations. Even though the percentage is remarkably high, the number of studies generated by the education discipline likely is underrepresented because of multiple headings. A follow-up analysis concentrated on just the first subject heading of only doctoral dissertations produced since 1980. The

TABLE 4.2
Subject Headings of Fund-Raising Dissertations and Theses 1903–1993[a]

Subject Heading/ Academic Discipline	Number	% of Total
Architecture	1	0.2%
Art/Fine arts/Theater	11	2.2%
Black studies	2	0.4%
Business	38	7.8%
Communication (journalism, mass communication, public relations, speech)	16	3.3%
Economics	17	3.5%
Education	**340**	**69.7%**
Gerontology	1	0.2%
Health sciences	7	1.4%
History	5	1.0%
Library science	3	0.6%
Music	2	0.4%
Philosophy	1	0.2%
Political science	8	1.6%
Psychology	4	0.8%
Recreation	1	0.2%
Religion/Theology	15	3.1%
Social work	5	1.0%
Sociology	10	2.0%
Urban and regional planning	1	0.2%
Total	488	99.8%

[a]Of 317 studies analyzed, 296 (93%) were produced after 1964.
Note. From Janet Huettner (personal communication, November 1993)
Indiana University Center on Philanthropy

assumption was made that student authors who chose multiple headings to describe their study selected their academic discipline first, although they were not so instructed. The third analysis resulted in 205 doctoral dissertations, of which 80% were self-categorized as studies in education. As a point of clarification, whereas the vast majority of the studies dealt with fund raising for educational organizations, others dealt with different types of charitable organizations (e.g., hospitals) or with general fund-raising problems (e.g., cost effectiveness of direct-mail techniques).

Clearly, education professors who have advised these dissertations and theses have had a tremendous impact on our understanding of fund raising. Yet, aside from Carbone and a few others, faculty members in education rarely conduct research or write about fund raising, which raises questions about their qualifications to guide the numerous fund-raising studies by their graduate students.

A review of the literature on fund raising and the broader areas of philanthropy and nonprofits revealed works by only a handful of education professors. This is not to say those contributions are not valuable or that encouraging graduate research is not admirable. The point here is that *most* faculty in the education discipline do not contribute to our knowledge about fund raising through their own work (i.e., their research interests, as demonstrated by publications, are not related to fund raising), yet the vast majority of all theses and dissertations on fund raising come out of that discipline.

Of the 850 U.S. members of ARNOVA (1997), the foremost association for philanthropy and nonprofit scholars, only 17, or 2%, are professors who list education as their academic discipline, and only 2 of the 17 list fund raising as one of their research interests. M. R. Hall (1992) reported that at the 1990 national meeting of the Association for the Study of Higher Education, only 4 of the 54 sessions had any connection to fund raising, and, she added from personal observation, "Almost none of the scholars attended those four" (p. 576).

With no apparent expertise, many education professors approve and advise fund-raising studies designed by practitioner students, who, in turn, hardly ever publish their findings in scholarly journals—thereby circumventing the knowledge-building process of review, criticism, and dissemination. Among other ramifications, the flawed pattern has resulted in the same studies being conducted repeatedly (e.g., Miltner's 1990 duplication of Willard's 1984 efforts, discussed in chapter 3). As J. D. Grace (1993) remarked, "Applying accepted social-science methodologies to a field not well understood by most graduate faculty leads to findings not always useful to practice" (p. 382).

This discussion prompts two suggestions. The first, and most obvious, is that education faculty members—as well as those in other disciplines—should develop an acceptable level of expertise in fund raising or decline to chair committees on the subject. Second, academic centers and professional associations should explore programming to help faculty learn more about fund raising. For example, the Center on Philanthropy could sponsor faculty scholarships to seminars, and CASE could subsidize faculty subscriptions to its journal, *Currents*. Fund raising can no longer afford to ignore this issue, and students must be cognizant of its consequences.

Substandard research and philanthropy scholars' neglect have been permitted due to apathy on the part of practitioners. Carbone (1987), for example, found that education fund raisers "exhibit only a modest understanding and sense of concern for the elements which most scholars consider basic identifying characteristics of established professions" (p. 14). The majority of those studied (58%) believe "increasing the fund of knowledge and the theoretical base" is only somewhat or not important (p. 14). Although the percentage was smaller, Carbone (1989) found a similar viewpoint among fund raisers for all types of organizations: Nearly one third (32%) are not sure or do not think a body of knowledge is important.

Yet as Rosso (1991) stated in the preface to his experience-based book, fund raising cannot become a profession until a body of knowledge has been expanded and verified through academic research. Bloland and Bornstein (1991) elaborated, "Without a dynamic changing theory and research base, an occupation is considered a static enterprise, trapped in its own rigidities, and not a profession" (p. 118). Providing a conceptual bridge to the next criterion of education, they continued, "The development of theory and research find their most natural homes in the academy. Teaching and learning theory seem to be best accomplished by formal courses in universities and colleges taught by professors who make the field their scholarly interest" (p. 118).

Program of Formal Education

"One of the unequivocal hallmarks of every recognized, respected profession is a program of formal education" (Commission on Undergraduate Public Relations Education, 1987/1993, p. 3). Fund raising currently does not have such a program. There are no departments or faculty of fund raising within colleges and universities. Students reading this book are spread among disciplines, from business to social work. Study is dispersed because fund raising, unlike related concepts, emerged solely outside the academy. Training traditionally came from those who practiced the function. Without an academic home, practitioners still control fund-raising education—and they prefer to keep it that way.

After interviewing 40 senior fund raisers, Bloland and Bornstein (1991) concluded, "There is little interest among practitioners in the creation and support of university graduate programs and graduate degrees in fund raising, philanthropy or related areas, but strong support for on-the-job and association training programs" (pp. 120–121). Carbone (1989) reported a similar finding after gathering data from 754 fund raisers: "Advocates of more formal preparation in academic institutions are definitely in the minority" (p. 31). Duronio (1993) said that of the 1,748 practitioners she studied, "Only 7.3% of the respondents recommended Formal Education (college/graduate school formal courses, programs, or degrees)" (p. 4).

Second Stage of Progression. According to J. E. Grunig and Hunt (1984), education for professions progresses through three stages:

> In the first stage, students essentially work as apprentices for skilled practitioners, usually outside the formal educational system. In the second stage, this apprentice system moves inside the formal educational system, where the skilled practitioner can teach several students at once. In the third stage, the academic scholar and teacher replaces or supplements the skilled practitioner. The scholar–teacher begins to research, analyze, and criticize the profession rather than simply pass on existing practices. (p. 80)

Fund raising only recently moved into the second stage of this progression. As emphasized in chapter 3, on-the-job training was the traditional means for acquiring fund-raising knowledge and skills. Seminars and conferences taught by senior practitioners enhanced workplace training as the number of fund raisers increased. Such educational opportunities were and still are sponsored by professional associations, as well as by proprietary organizations run by practitioners (e.g., The Fund Raising School was started as a business in 1974 by three California practitioners, including Hank Rosso and Joe Mixer, and became a nonprofit a few years later). In the mid-1980s, fund raising began moving inside the formal educational system (e.g., The Fund Raising School was incorporated in Indiana University's Center on Philanthropy in 1988).

Today, an ever-growing number of colleges and universities are offering fund-raising courses. A review of recruitment literature and advertisements documented that—as described by J. E. Grunig and Hunt's second stage—most of the courses are taught by practitioners, although education faculty also were identified. For example, all courses for the certificate program at Goucher College, mentioned in chapter 3, are taught by full-time fund raisers. New York University's School of Continuing Education offers a Fundraising Management Certificate for students completing 6 of more than 14 courses, all taught by practitioners. In 1996, the University of Chicago, through its Center for Continuing Studies, launched one of the most expensive certificate programs: 3 weeks of practitioner-taught instruction in Managing Institutional Advancement for a cost of $5,350! Education entrepreneurs use the Internet to create national markets. The University of San Francisco, for example, awards a Development Director Certificate to nonprofit employees who take five online courses over 10 months. The 8-week courses are taught by adjuncts who are full-time fund raisers; tuition totals $5,600.

Nontraditional degree programs also rely on practitioners. For example, the summer program leading to a master's degree in philanthropy and development at Minnesota's St. Mary's College consists of less than 8 weeks of classes taught by fund raisers, as well as education faculty. The weekend Institutional Advancement Program at Vanderbilt University in Nashville, Tennessee—which draws practitioner students from as far away as Michigan and Texas—awards a master's degree in higher education administration. Whereas the program is housed in Vanderbilt's education unit, Peabody College, fund raisers are responsible for much of the instruction on key subjects (e.g., the two-semester professional seminar revolves around guest lecturers). All the classes are held on weekends and are open to education students pursuing doctoral degrees. The Union Institute in Cincinnati, Ohio, formerly the Union for Experimenting Colleges and Universities, began a PhD program in Philanthropic and Leadership Studies in 1988. Its core faculty in 1990 consisted of three institute administrators, a former CASE president who lives in Maryland, and two former fund raisers who are full-time college presidents in New York and Florida. Its doctoral students similarly are practitioners who work outside Ohio and rarely come to campus. For example, Miltner (1990) was vice chancellor for advancement at the University of California at Irvine while earning his degree at Union.

Moving from certificates and nontraditional formats, formal degree programs in philanthropy and nonprofit management include required and elective courses on fund raising, almost all of which are taught by practitioners. Representative of the stage-two status of fund-raising education is Indiana University, which offers two master's degrees: Master of Arts in Philanthropic Studies (MA) and Master of Public Affairs in Nonprofit Management (MPA). The MA program is multidisciplinary and based in the Center on Philanthropy, whereas the MPA program is housed in the School of Public and Environmental Affairs. Both programs use full-time faculty to teach the broad subjects (e.g., Robert Payton instructs students on the history, culture, and values of philanthropy), but rely on The Fund Raising School and its practitioner instructors to teach fund-raising principles and skills.

Fund raising has not been integrated into degree programs because it lacks a theoretical body of knowledge, which makes it suspect to academics. Case Western, for example, requires no fund-raising courses for its Master of Nonprofit Organizations Degree. An administrator at Case Western's Mandel Center explained, in developing the degree program, "our faculty felt that fund raising was not a scholarly discipline, although it's an important part of managing non-profits" (H. Hall, 1995a, p. 42). Students enrolled in the Case Western program are allowed to count elective fund-raising courses, taught by practitioners, toward their degree requirements.

Publication of this theory-based textbook will remove a major deterrent to fund raising's acceptance; however, changes in educational programs will depend on the availability of full-time faculty who are prepared—and willing—to teach and conduct research on the subject. As Peter McE. Buchanan (1993), the recently retired president of CASE, pointed out in his essay on professionalism, "There is no established professorate for the field" (p. 371).

Other information about Indiana University sheds more light on the situation and may be useful to students. The Center on Philanthropy's Philanthropic Studies Program offers three different fellowships to recent graduates with bachelor's degrees. The Jane Addams Fellowships encompass all disciplines, the Andrew Carnegie Fellowships are reserved for those who have earned an undergraduate degree in business, and the Hearst Minority Fellowships are for students of color. All three fellowships cover 10 months of study and an internship, provide a stipend of $15,000, and waive tuition and fees—including costs for attending The Fund Raising School and a national conference. Applications, which can be requested by calling (317) 274-4200, must be submitted by the beginning of February for the following academic year.

Started in 1997, Indiana's center also offers an Executive Master's Program for practitioners who only have summers to spare to earn an MA. The program consists of 2 or 3 weeks of courses each summer for 2 to 3 years. Information can be obtained by calling the number just given. Although publicity has diminished in recent years, Indiana awards a Doctorate of Education (EdD) in Higher Education with a Cognate in Institutional Advancement. The Fund Raising School currently offers nine different courses, such as Principles & Techniques of Fund Raising. As of 1997, 56 sessions of the courses, lasting 2 to 5 days, are taught in 19 U.S. cities. Tuition ranges from $295 to $695 per course. More than 15,000 practitioners have attended the school.

Summarizing, fund raising has moved into the formal educational system but practitioners still control the transfer of knowledge and skills. Whereas movement from the workplace to an academic setting signifies progress, it also represents fund raisers' desire for increased legitimacy—as well as colleges and universities' desire for increased income. Although only a small minority of the practitioners Carbone (1989) studied advocate academic education, the overwhelming majority endorse degree programs as one of the best means for elevating fund raising's professional status. One third of NSFRE's members believe educational opportunities or degree-granting programs are the way to enhance the "professional image" of fund raisers (Mongon, 1992, p. 23).

Practitioner Control.   Practitioners realize a program of formal education is necessary to advance professionalism, but they do not want to turn over the training of newcomers to educators, whom they distrust. Carbone (1989) quoted a hospital fund raiser: "What's needed now is a curriculum plan assembled by professionals (not academics) to guide these training methods" (p. 30). Given that the study of fund raising emanated from the practice and that philanthropy scholars have ignored the function, practitioners' wish to retain control is not unexpected. It is, however, unrealistic.

When addressing this issue at professional conferences, I have found that senior fund raisers generally do not welcome overtures to incorporate their function within established academic programs (junior practitioners are more receptive). Some practitioner faculty members with The Fund Raising School, for example, have told me they would prefer to "bring fund raising" into the university setting as a new and separate curriculum. They point to such disciplines as business that came from the practice and were successfully transferred to higher education. Yet business entered the academy more than 100 years ago when, in 1881, Joseph Wharton made a gift to the University of Pennsylvania to establish the business school that still bears his name (Curti & Nash, 1965).

Today's universities and colleges require credentials apart from practitioner expertise (e.g., a PhD degree). Bloland and Bornstein (1991) affirmed, "Housing knowledge generation in institutions of higher education requires that a different kind of fund-raising professional be added to the field: the professor, who specializes in research and theory building, whose home is an academic department and not the development division" (p. 119). Furthermore, tradition and limited resources have made academic structures very rigid, with little flexibility for adding new curricula. Most universities and colleges today are contracting rather than expanding; they are eliminating and merging established programs (e.g., moving library science to schools of communication). In view of the circumstances, it is highly doubtful that fund raising can achieve formal educational status as a stand-alone program in the foreseeable future.

Remaining in stage two of practitioner-taught classes is not the answer. Bloland and Bornstein (1991) emphasized, "The potentiality for needed change through restructuring or innovation is restricted if knowledge of skills and control over instruction is the exclusive property of current practitioners" (p. 115). They warned, "Unless an occupation has a continuous flow of new ideas and modified techniques from sources that go beyond practitioners, it may lose its connection to changes taking place in the larger institution or the society and become obsolete" (p. 115).

Communication scholar Melvin DeFleur (1993) explained that full-time faculty with PhDs perform two different but connected roles. The first role is *curator*, much like the person who directs a museum. "The PhD acts as a curator of ideas—the existing knowledge in his or her field that has accumulated thus far. This provides a body of information that is incorporated into various courses and passed on to students" (p. 24). The second role is *innovator*. DeFleur stated, "Few of us would be content with courses that offered only a static body of knowledge to which no new insights, concepts or theories were added over time" (p. 24).

The vital role of innovator is most dramatically illustrated by advances in technology. Imagine, for example, the difference in computer science education (and in most of our lives) if that discipline had been taught solely on the basis of how computing was done in the days of vacuum tubes, without the infusion of research findings on semiconductors. In other words, formal education's dual roles are to teach not only *how* something is practiced, but how it *should* be practiced. According to DeFleur (1993), non-PhDs—who lack advanced training in research and scholarship—can effectively carry out the curator role as college instructors; however, without a flow of new knowledge, the courses they teach will be stagnant repetitions of the same old ideas. "For the most part," he argued, "it is the faculty with the doctorate who produce the research and scholarship needed to keep knowledge in their fields moving ahead" (p. 3).

J. E. Grunig and Hunt (1984) asserted, "A profession cannot advance simply by passing on what practitioners have done in the past, as is the case when experienced practitioners pass on their 'anecdotal' experiences" (p. 80). Specifically addressing the current state of fund-raising education, Bloland and Bornstein (1991) admonished, "A preoccupation with skill development, important as it may be, combined with a neglect of theory construction and research, will be costly to the occupation" (pp. 116–117). Carbone (1989) said the thesis of his study on fund raising as a profession was, quite simply, "Competence is not enough!" (p. 7).

Professional Associations

According to J. E. Grunig and Hunt (1984), the ideal professional association is one like the American Bar Association, which licenses practitioners, publishes strong research journals, and serves nearly all those working in the profession. Fund raising benefits from a number of active associations, but it does not have one encompassing association with that kind of power or membership.

The three major associations for fund raisers are AHP, CASE, and NSFRE. Due to information already presented and the upcoming discussion about their histories, only an overview of the associations is provided here.

The Major Three.   AHP, CASE, and NSFRE are headquartered in Washington, DC or just outside the nation's capital in northern Virginia. Each has a different membership structure: NSFRE is based on individual members, CASE has organizational members with additional fees for each employee representative above the allotted number, and AHP offers membership to individuals with graduated dues for multiple members from the same organization. As of 1997, NSFRE's membership consists of 17,000 practitioners who work for all types of charitable organizations.[4]

---

[4]NSFRE offers reduced dues to full-time students enrolled in a degree program and persons employed in the field for 1 year or less. The special membership for newcomers, called "Interns," is limited to 2 years. Neither interns nor students are allowed to vote. NSFRE also is testing discounted dues for practitioners who work for small grassroots organizations. If approved, the lower fees will be available in 1998.

CASE has almost 3,000 organizational members, primarily colleges and universities, and 15,000 member representatives. More than half of its member representatives—as discussed in chapter 3—are fund raisers. AHP serves 2,500 fund raisers who are employed by more than 1,500 hospitals and health care organizations in the United States and Canada.[5] In total, only about 27,000 practitioners, or one third of the estimated number of U.S. fund raisers, belong to the three major associations.

Whereas AHP is the smallest of the three, CASE is the wealthiest, with an annual income approximately one third greater than NSFRE's income. Because its members are educational organizations, CASE is a 501(c)(3) to which gifts are tax deductible; AHP and NSFRE have affiliated foundations to carry out their fund raising. AHP is centralized, CASE is organized by eight geographic districts, and NSFRE has 149 chapters across the country.

All three associations offer professional development programming. For example, AHP annually sponsors an Institute for Healthcare Philanthropy, an international conference, and 13 regional programs with multiple workshop sessions. NSFRE sponsors both a 2-day First Course and a 2-day Survey Course about 24 times each year in various U.S. locations. About 1,500 chapter programs are held annually, as well as an international conference that attracts approximately 4,000 practitioners. CASE also holds an Annual Assembly (i.e., international conference) and sponsors about 140 conferences, workshops, and institutes per year, of which nearly half are on fund raising (e.g., the Summer Institute in Educational Fund Raising). CASE has an *Institutional Advancement Professional Area Guide* (Unkefer & Chewning, 1992) to provide recommended sequences for its conferences and publications by level of experience.

The three associations publish practitioner journals and newsletters, including CASE *Currents*, NSFRE *Advancing Philanthropy* (formerly the NSFRE *Journal*), and *AHP Journal* and *AHP Connect*. They also sell numerous books, pamphlets, videotapes, and audiotapes. None publishes a research journal.

AHP sponsors an annual award for excellence in writing about fund raising, named for legendary consultant and author Harold "Si" Seymour. CASE sponsors the annual John Grenzebach Awards for Outstanding Research in Philanthropy for Education, funded by the consulting firm of Grenzebach Giler & Associates and cosponsored by the AAFRC Trust for Philanthropy.[6] NSFRE sponsors the Staley/Robeson/Ryan/St. Lawrence Prize for Research, endowed by the firm of the same name.

NSFRE has a Research Council, which was established in 1991. The council sponsored the first think tank on fund-raising research in 1995; developed and revised a research agenda, which outlines gaps in fund-raising knowledge; and awards up to five grants per year, ranging from $1,000 to $2,000, to underwrite studies (see Kelly, 1996).[7] In 1993, CASE established a Commission on Philanthropy to encourage

---

[5]NSFRE and CASE also have Canadian members. Furthermore, during the early 1990s, NSFRE increased its presence in Mexico City, and CASE established an office in London as a base for European operations. Both groups believe there is an international market for their services and likely will continue to expand beyond the United States.

[6]One of the Grenzebach awards is for the outstanding dissertation, which includes a prize of $2,000. Doctoral students can obtain information by calling Paul Chewning, CASE's vice president for professional development, at (202) 328-5914.

[7]Students seeking funding for their master's or doctoral study can obtain grant guidelines by calling Cathlene Williams, NSFRE's director of education and research programs, at (703) 519-8469.

research and spearhead major initiatives. The commission was responsible for revising the reporting standards released in 1996 and currently is conducting a literature review of advancement.

AHP and NSFRE offer two levels of certification: They share one baseline credentialing program and independently operate programs to certify senior practitioners. Before 1997, AHP awarded the base credential Certified, Association for Healthcare Philanthropy (CAHP). NSFRE's credential was Certified Fund Raising Executive (CFRE). The programs were consolidated in 1996, and members of both associations—as well as nonmembers—now earn the CFRE credential. The CFRE Professional Certification Program is administered by NSFRE. A joint board currently is revising standards, including the single written examination that will be implemented in 1998. Future requirements are expected to emulate NSFRE's model.

To qualify, applicants must be employed as a fund raiser and have a minimum of 5 years of full-time practitioner experience within the previous 8 years. The process consists of three steps: (a) completing a 6-page application that documents experience, with heavy emphasis on the amount of dollars raised; (b) passing a written examination—geared to individuals with only 5 years of experience—that consists of 200 multiple-choice questions, of which only 70% need to be answered correctly; and (c) review of the application and exam by the CFRE Professional Certification Board. Roughly 70% of those who take the exam pass it, and there is no limit to the number of times it can be retaken if not passed. NSFRE's Survey Course, taught by local practitioners, usually is offered just prior to each exam to provide a review of baseline knowledge. The exam is scheduled about 30 times each year at various U.S. locations. As of 1997, fees for the course and certification total $520 for AHP and NSFRE members and $660 for nonmembers, not including travel expenses.

Certification must be renewed every 3 years by providing evidence of continuous employment in the field, successful fund-raising performance, professional service, and at least 12 contact hours per year of continuing education. Only about one fourth of NSFRE's members, approximately 4,000 practitioners, are now designated CFRE.

The two associations administer their second-tier programs separately. AHP, headed by President and CEO William McGinley, offers the credential Fellow, Association for Healthcare Philanthropy (FAHP) to certified practitioners who successfully complete an additional written and oral examination. NSFRE's senior credential is Advanced Certified Fund Raising Executive (ACFRE). Working fund raisers who are CFREs, have been recertified at least once, and have a minimum of 10 years of full-time experience are required to pass a written exam and successfully complete a portfolio review and oral evaluation by a peer committee. The cost is $1,100. ACFRE designation is conferred for life, and only 30 NSFRE members held this credential at the end of 1996.

Because they require practitioner employment and rely heavily on dollars raised, the certification programs exclude full-time educators—those who study and teach fund raising rather than practice it. The exclusion reflects poorly on the occupation's status in that associations affiliated with professions certify educators as well as practitioners. Fund raising, including college and university courses on the subject, is taught mostly by practitioners; hence, there has been no need to question experiential standards as the primary criteria by which fund-raising knowledge and proficiency are judged. I was able to earn the CFRE credential in 1993, even though I was an educator, because I could document fund-raising experience within the previous 8 years.[8] In 1996, I had no continuous performance to qualify for recertification. I appealed to the newly formed certification board, urging adoption of equivalent standards for educators. My credential was renewed, but requirements have not been changed to date. The action coupled with nonaction suggests that educators will be treated as aberrations until fund raising progresses to the third stage of education.

CASE does not offer certification; most notably, it currently does not participate in the credentialing program shared by AHP and NSFRE. According to Charles Stephens (1995), CASE was actively involved in 1993 when it and the two other associations "set out with missionary zeal to develop one baseline credential for all fundraisers [sic]" (p. 70). Stephens, who was NSFRE's chair in 1993, commented 2 years later, "Turf and competition concerns, some petty and some not so petty, and elitism have made this an odyssey of considerable frustration on all sides" (p. 70). Partially explaining CASE's absence in the resulting program, he reported, "CASE subscribes to the belief that the only credential worth considering is an academic degree" (p. 70). Then CASE President Buchanan (1993) retorted, "NSFRE has created a certification program, but some development officers—including some so certified—view it with disdain" (p. 371). Buchanan (cited in Bailey, 1992) earlier had said the publication of CASE's professional area guide was a step toward "meaningful professional certification" (p. 26). The new president may change CASE's position once again.

Regardless of association membership, fund raisers generally are not supportive of certification. Carbone (1989) found that only about one third (35%) of those he studied believe their peers would willingly seek a credential, even if required for entering or continuing in fund raising. Almost one half (46%) do not think credentialing is an important issue or are unsure. Duronio (1994a) quoted a female fund raiser for a health organization, who criticized, "The exams are just not that demanding and there is no standardization" (p. 22). A male fund raiser for an arts organization argued, "Certification is a total scam. I know people who are certified who don't know what they're doing. This is a half-baked attempt to professionalize the field but this isn't the way" (p. 22). Stephens (1995) said practitioners depreciate certification because they assume fund raising "is a skill-based profession, and the only real measure of capability is how much money one raises" (p. 70). His frustration with the associations' inability to develop common standards led him to conclude, "A federal government-administered licensing program . . . is the only logical course to bringing fundraising [sic] full professional and respected status" (p. 70).

As attested to by their World Wide Web sites, presented in Table 4.1, the major associations provide technologically advanced ways to communicate with them. CASE has been the leader among the three. It was the first to establish a home page in 1996. The site features a Freebies section that includes classified ads for jobs, listings of conferences, articles, and bibliographies. Its Advancement Links Center opens the door to more than 200 related sites. Netscape Navigator is the recommended Web browser. CASE also offers fax on demand, called FastFax Service. To receive a menu

---

[8]Based on a review of occupational titles, I was the first full-time faculty member, who was not an administrator, to be certified by NSFRE.

of what is available for free and for sale, phone (202) 274-4700 and touch 1 on the numerical pad when prompted. Reprints of popular *Currents* articles, for example, can be delivered to fax machines instantly at a cost of $5 to $10 by entering document numbers and credit-card information.

The old-fashioned way to reach CASE is by calling (202) 328-5900. The telephone number for AHP is (703) 532-6243. NSFRE has a toll-free number to facilitate inquiries and service, (800) 666-FUND (3863).

Other Associations.   There are several specialized fund-raising associations with purposes related to programs, affinity, and types of charitable organizations. The National Committee on Planned Giving (NCPG), based in Indianapolis, Indiana, provides professional development education and research on planned giving. It—as does the American Council on Gift Annuities (ACGA)—has a code of ethics for fund raisers and financial planners. The Association of Professional Researchers for Advancement (APRA), headquartered in Westmont, Illinois, has a national network of local chapters. It holds an annual conference and publishes the newsletter APRA *Connections*. African-American Fund Raising Officers, Inc. and Women in Development of Greater Boston are just two examples of affinity groups that offer peer support to their members. Representative of specialized groups for types of organizations are the National Catholic Development Conference (NCDC), which was founded in 1968 and now has about 1,200 members, and the Fund Raising and Financial Development Section of the Library Administration and Management Association—an affiliate of the American Library Association.

A description of professional associations would be incomplete without including AAFRC and IS. Founded in 1935, AAFRC is the oldest fund-raising association and the occupation's leading voice. Its membership is limited to a few consulting firms that traditionally have been the largest and most prestigious—a characteristic returned to shortly. Based in New York City, AAFRC has been the primary source of national data on charitable giving since 1959. In 1985, it established the AAFRC Trust for Philanthropy to foster research and education and "to increase public recognition of philanthropy for its pervasive and beneficial influence in shaping the life and character" of our society (Van Til & Associates, 1990, p. ii). The trust sponsors books (e.g., Van Til & Associates, 1990) and research awards (e.g., the Grenzebach Awards). More detailed information on AAFRC is given in chapter 5, which traces its prominent role in fund-raising history. Its current situation, however, warrants a brief discussion here.

Since the beginning of the 1990s, AAFRC has experienced serious membership losses in both quality and quantity. Some of the best-known firms have dropped out of the association (e.g., Brakeley, John Price Jones and Marts & Lundy), and the number of members has steadily declined, from 34 in 1989 to only 22 member firms in 1996 (AAFRC Trust for Philanthropy, 1989, 1996). These changes reflect the evolution of fund raising, which has resulted in a turbulent environment for consultants. Attesting to unstable conditions and the problems they have created for AAFRC, the association hired and let go two presidents between 1992 and the end of 1996, when it began a search for its third CEO in 5 years.

Also in 1996, a new association was incorporated to serve independent consultants and small consulting firms, the Association of Philanthropic Counsel (APC). Its founding members could not join AAFRC due to the small size of their businesses, and previously had no alternative except to join an association in which consultants represent a minority (all belonged to NSFRE). Those starting APC described it as "a strategic response to the changing and challenging conditions" faced by today's counselors (APC, 1996, p. 1). A goal shared by current and potential members is to "compete more effectively with larger firms" (p. 1).

Whether and how AAFRC will adapt to the new environment in which it operates is not known at this time. Similarly, APC's impact is hidden in the future. For now, AAFRC retains its leadership position in fund raising and is treated accordingly throughout this book; technically, however, it is no longer the only association devoted solely to consultants.

AAFRC and the three major fund-raising associations belong to IS, the Washington, DC-based coalition of approximately 800 organizations. Since it was founded in 1980, IS has played a key role in advancing research and formulating public policy on philanthropy and nonprofits. It is the sector's leading voice on national issues. Activities conducted by the umbrella association are directed at the sociopolitical and economic context in which fund raising is practiced. For example, in the late 1980s, IS launched its "Give Five" campaign to instill a standard for all Americans of contributing 5% of their household income and volunteering 5 hours per week.[9] In 1994, Sara Meléndez was selected to succeed Brian O'Connell as president of IS, which reflects a trend to increase diversity in the nonprofit sector's leadership. The presidents of AAFRC, AHP, CASE, IS, NCDC, NCPG, and NSFRE—known as the Consortium—hold semiannual meetings to discuss issues of mutual interest.

Concluding this description of associations, Carbone (1989) pointed to the lack of an "overarching and unified professional society" and a "single code of ethics that covers all members" as barriers to the professionalization of fund raising (p. 17).

Codes of Ethics

Codes of ethics provide guidance on what professions and their affiliated associations define as acceptable behavior. They also serve as "a basis for imposing appropriate punishment on members whose behavior conflicts with accepted norms" (Carbone, 1989, p. 40). In other words, an important consideration when examining codes of ethics is the presence or absence of penalties that can be levied on people who do not follow prescribed conduct. Codes have limited effect if there are no systematic means of enforcing them.

Stephens (1995) charged, "There must be a common code of ethics by which all fundraisers [sic] will be judged. Standards of professional practice and enforcement procedures must be part of that code" (p. 70). He elaborated, "The penalties for breaking the rules must be very clear to professionals and clients/employers alike; moreover, the administration of punishment in instances of wrongdoing must be quick and sure" (p. 70).

Each of the fund-raising associations has its own code of ethics. AHP's and CASE's codes have no enforcement component, whereas NSFRE implemented an enforcement process in 1993—one that appears unnecessarily burdensome and centralized.

---

[9]As discussed in the chapter on theory, the campaign had no measurable effect on giving or volunteering and was abandoned in 1995.

Drawing from an *NSFRE News* article ("Expanded," 1993), the Ethics Committee is responsible for enforcement, but the association's paid president controls procedures. To initiate a complaint, members must first request an official (and required) form from the president's office in Alexandria, Virginia. They must provide details of the violation and return the form to the president. She apparently reviews the complaint before turning it over to the Ethics Committee, which meets only periodically. Be that as it may, President Lewis (cited in "Expanded," 1993) stressed the need for enforcement when she announced NSFRE's revised Ethical Principles and Standards of Professional Practice: "Regaining and retaining the public's trust in philanthropy is what these guidelines and enforcement procedures are all about, because we will succeed in our missions only if Americans continue to give. And they will give only if they believe their money is being used wisely" (p. 6).

Criticizing fund raising's prolonged reluctance to enforce ethics, consultant David Thompson (cited in Goss, 1990) exhorted, "The mark of a profession is that you discipline your members" (p. 20). The problem extends beyond association membership. AAFRC, AHP, CASE, IS, and NSFRE rarely comment on the unethical or even illegal behavior of nonmembers. For example, not one of them publicly rebuked the solicitation firm of Watson and Hughey (now renamed Direct Response Consulting Services) when it was sued by 22 states for fraud in the late 1980s. The associations' silence implies that their members act no differently than accused criminals, thereby bolstering negative perceptions of all fund raisers. Avoiding lawsuits seems to be more important than building an ethical reputation for the field.

Carbone (1989) assessed the codes of AHP, CASE, and NSFRE and concluded, "Each of them addresses some core ethical issues, although the language of each differs, as does the total content" (p. 15). Illustrating differences, whereas CASE prohibits granting or accepting favors for personal gain, NSFRE only requires full disclosure of all relationships that might pose, or appear to pose, possible conflicts of interest.

The ethical issue receiving the most attention recently has been NSFRE's stand on commissions. Fearing lawsuits on restraint of trade from solicitors, the association dropped its ban on such fees in 1989, but reinstituted it in the 1993 code. As discussed in the next chapter, such standards historically have distinguished fund raisers who work for a salary or set fee (i.e., staff practitioners and consultants) from paid solicitors who often work on commission.

Carbone (1989) found that practitioners belonging to the three major fund-raising associations overwhelmingly rate codes of ethics as important, but only 34% agree that fund raisers are intimately aware of the codes and that their work, almost without exception, is guided by the norms. Just 5% agree peer enforcement of ethical standards exists. "Given the structure of the fund raising [*sic*] field at present," Carbone concluded, "it does not appear likely that broad scale efforts to implement enforcement mechanisms will be forthcoming in the near future" (p. 42).

Professional Autonomy and Allegiance

Autonomy and allegiance differentiate a profession from an occupation. Members of a profession value autonomy in their work; they insist on the freedom to perform in a way they consider right (J. E. Grunig & Hunt, 1984). Professionals also hold allegiance to both the organization that pays them and to the profession responsible for their expertise. Unlike members of an occupation, they gauge their performance by professional standards, as well as by organizational evaluation (i.e., approval of peers generally is valued as much or more than approval of supervisors). Grunig and Hunt referred to this dual allegiance as "serving two masters" (p. 64).

According to Carbone (1989), "Professionals enjoy a high degree of autonomy; they have the 'bottom line' on most, if not all, matters relating to their practice. This element amounts to a license to control their own activities" (p. 18). He added, "This characteristic signifies that professionals enjoy freedom from external interference with their own professional judgment regarding identification and achievement of goals and objectives" (p. 27). Fund raisers as a group have not reached this hallmark.

Carbone (1989) found that 80% of the practitioners he studied have little autonomy in performing their function; 25% do not even control their work time or the activities in which they engage. Carbone interpreted comments by respondents about "lack of respect," "little understanding," and "no appreciation" as "other ways of saying that fund raisers often lack decision-making power" (p. 28). Similarly, numerous complaints about "unrealistic expectations" suggested that "the selection of goals and methods used to attain them are imposed on many fund raisers" (p. 29). Carbone hypothesized that fund raisers' degree of autonomy "is directly related to their prominence in organizational policy making" (p. 18). As distance from the policymaking group increases, autonomy diminishes. In other words, autonomy is associated with the role practitioners enact—manager versus technician. Carbone concluded that fund raisers in aggregate are "implementors of decisions rather than bottom-line decision makers" (p. 29).

Turning to allegiance, Carbone (1989) stated, "Professionals believe in collegial establishment of standards of practice and in the creation of mechanisms for maintaining these standards" (p. 32). Basic to such standards is peer evaluation. Therefore, Carbone asked fund raisers in his study to what extent they agree their competence and the quality of their work are best judged primarily by other fund raisers rather than by managers who employ them. He described the responses as "quite startling" (p. 32). Only 17% agree that peers are better suited to judge performance; 59% flatly disagree.

Explaining the low level of professional allegiance among fund raisers, one of Carbone's (1989) respondents commented, "Success equals the dollars you raise; that's what we are evaluated on" (p. 36). Indeed, as discussed in my earlier book (Kelly, 1991a; see chap. 14), the fund-raising literature provides strong evidence that practitioners' performance generally is evaluated by dollar totals. There are few references to criteria other than meeting financial goals. Related to this assessment, none of the fund-raising associations sponsors program awards based on peer evaluation. CASE, for example, uses only data from its Survey of Voluntary Support of Education—dollar amounts and institutional characteristics—to select winners for its annual competition, the Circle of Excellence in Educational Fund Raising.

Carbone (1989) concluded, "Standards by members of the profession is not a deeply ingrained or well-understood concept among fund raisers" (p. 34). It is unlikely practitioners will value the judgements of their colleagues until theory and research help them define how fund raising should be practiced. Without such knowledge, their work will continue to be evaluated by the amount of money they raise.

PUBLIC RELATIONS: AN ALTERNATE ROUTE

Whereas Carbone (1989) began his report on professionalism by describing fund raising as an emerging profession, he stated at the end, "No one should be startled to learn that fund raising has not yet attained even the stature of some highly regarded, but imperfect, occupations" (p. 43). Similarly, Bloland and Bornstein (1991) referred to fund raising as an occupation throughout their essay and implied that professional status "is far in the distance" (p. 121).

Based on the discussion of common criteria just given, fund raising must be placed toward the lower end of the continuum of professionalism. In particular, its lack of a theoretical body of knowledge and its recent entry into only the second stage of education define it more as an occupation than a profession. The two criteria are interrelated. Without a theoretical foundation, fund raising is not a legitimate subject for teaching at the college and university level. It is closer to a trade, such as plumbing, which more appropriately is taught in vocational schools. Yet fund raising will not accumulate a body of knowledge based on theory and research until scholar teachers replace practitioner instructors in programs of higher education.

Resolution of the dilemma is not inconceivable, but would require many more years—time that may not be available given the current environment of fund raising. As documented in later chapters, issues of law and ethics demand greater professionalism as quickly as possible. A viable solution is to incorporate fund raising within the study and practice of public relations.

Public Relations' Professional Status

Public relations also resides below the "true profession" end of the continuum. However, the infrastructure necessary to become a profession has been in place for more than a decade. Public relations has a theoretical body of knowledge, a program of formal education, a premier association with established procedures for enforcing its code of ethics, and—at least conceptually—shared values of professional autonomy and allegiance.

Due to this book's purpose, the following discussion merely summarizes public relations' status as related to four of the five professional criteria. Only the education criterion is examined in detail. Students are referred to cited works for more information, as well as to the public relations books included in the various lists of suggested readings.

As described in chapter 1, public relations has an established body of knowledge, which was formally codified in 1988. Serious research began in the late 1960s when scholars replaced practitioners in the classroom. Scholars first "borrowed" theories from the mother disciplines of communication, sociology, psychology, and other social sciences to guide research and develop theoretical concepts that would explain the organizational function they and their students studied. Starting in the mid-1980s, research undertaken by a team led by James Grunig and sponsored by IABC produced the first general theory of public relations (e.g., J. E. Grunig, 1992). Today, more than 425 full-time educators belong to the public relations divisions of the major academic associations for communication (e.g., the Association for Education in Journalism and Mass Communication). Public relations has two scholarly journals: *Public Relations Review* and the *Journal of Public Relations Research*.

In contrast, a concerted effort to study fund raising only began in June 1990, when Indiana's Center on Philanthropy hosted the symposium "Taking Fund Raising Seriously" (Burlingame & Hulse, 1991), which resulted in the book of the same title. There are no full-time faculty or scholarly journals devoted to fund raising.

Of particular relevance to this discussion, public relations' body of knowledge encompasses fund raising as one of the practice's specializations, and faculty in the discipline have built on emerging theories to explain the function. There has been little resistance to accepting problems related to fund raising as important and worthy of study. From 1992 through 1994, academic papers dealing with fund raising were awarded "Top Three Honors" by the public relations divisions of all four major communication associations (e.g., Kelly, 1993b). Articles about research on fund raising have appeared in the public relations journals just named (e.g., Kelly, 1993c), as well as in other communication journals. Furthermore, papers and articles that approach fund raising from a public relations perspective have been presented at academic meetings and published in refereed journals concentrating on philanthropy and nonprofits (e.g., Kelly, 1993a).

Delaying discussion of education and moving to the third criteria, public relations has one premiere association, although—like fund raising—it benefits from a number of associations with narrower missions. PRSA is the leading public relations association in the country, with a membership of 18,000 individuals. Founded in 1947 when the American Council on Public Relations merged with the National Association of Public Relations Counsel, the New York City-based society has 16 professional interest sections (e.g., Educational and Cultural Organizations), 10 geographic districts, 108 local chapters, and 200 student chapters. PRSA offers professional development programming, a national conference, and practitioner publications (e.g., *Public Relations Strategist*).

PRSA's accreditation program for the base credential Accredited Public Relations (APR) has been in place for 30 years. Candidates must have 5 or more years of experience; however, the process relies on testing knowledge and proficiency, not documenting experience. Both educators and practitioners are eligible. Unlike the shorter, multiple-choice exam of NSFRE, PRSA's written examination covers 7 hours and consists of a mixture of question formats, including one essay question for which 2½ hours are allotted. Candidates also must pass an oral exam administered by accredited peers.

These differences are not surprising given that—until now—fund raising has not had even one textbook on which to base tests of knowledge, whereas public relations had Cutlip and Center's (1952) textbook from the inception of accreditation and currently uses the seventh edition of that book, as well as numerous other texts. Similar to NSFRE, only about one fourth of PRSA's members are accredited. Reaccreditation is required every 3 years for individuals who became APRs after 1992.

Accredited members with 20 or more years of experience in practice or teaching may apply for the senior credential APR, Fellow PRSA. Candidates must document exceptional contributions and performance through a peer-review process. Only 308 (2%) of the association's members held this credential at the end of 1996.[10]

---

[10]I earned PRSA's senior credential in 1996, the same year I petitioned the CFRE Professional Certification Board to change standards excluding educators.

PRSA has played a major role in building knowledge and formalizing education. Through its affiliated foundations, it has subsidized research projects, scholarships, compilation of bibliographies since 1957, and scholarly journals, such as *Public Relations Review*, which it published from 1975 to 1989. It was the professional and financial stimulus for the Body of Knowledge Project, and its Research Committee continues to update listings and abstracts of the literature important to public relations. As Cutlip et al. (1994) stated, "Much credit for the advance toward professionalism goes to the Foundation for Public Relations Research and Education, a [charitable] organization established by PRSA in 1956 to foster basic research and education" (p. 139). IABC, the second largest association, also has invested heavily in research and education (e.g., sponsoring the Excellence Project for 10 years).

PRSA's Code of Ethics was first adopted in 1954 and has been revised five times since, most recently in 1988. Whereas many of its standards are similar to those of NSFRE (e.g., disclosure of possible conflicts of interest), enforcement procedures are more sophisticated and less centralized. PRSA's code requires members to report unethical or illegal behavior by other members and to appear before a judicial panel if called as a witness. Judicial panels operate in each of the association's 10 districts, with a 35-year-old national Board of Ethics and Professional Standards overseeing the confidential proceedings. Complaints of code violations can be made to the closest judicial panel or to the national board. They can originate from a member or nonmember. No forms are required. The ethics board is responsible for investigating complaints—including soliciting a response from the accused—and deciding whether or not to file charges. Disciplinary cases are referred to judicial panels for hearings. Findings and recommendations are delivered to PRSA's National Board of Directors, which imposes punishment. Penalties range from warnings and reprimands to censure, suspension, and expulsion.

Adherence to its code and enforced compliance are limited to individuals who belong to PRSA. However, as public relations' premiere association, the society frequently comments through the media and other channels on the unethical and illegal actions of nonmembers, including organizations. It does so by pointing out where such behavior is incongruent with PRSA's code of ethics.

Professional autonomy and allegiance are strongly advocated in the practitioner and scholarly literature of public relations. Virtually all definitions conceptualize the function as one with a high degree of freedom that counsels senior managers and develops programming to meet organizational needs. Like fund raisers, however, practitioners in aggregate have not achieved this distinction. According to the theory of roles (e.g., Broom & Dozier, 1986), excellent departments are headed by a manager and are autonomous. Practitioners exposed to the theory are using it to change behavior patterns in the workplace.

Allegiance is demonstrated by the high value public relations practitioners place on collegial approval of their work. In evidence, the most prestigious program award is PRSA's Silver Anvil, which is based on peer evaluation. Other associations conduct similar competitions. For example, IABC sponsors the annual Gold Quill Awards to set standards for and honor excellence in communication. A common means of evaluating performance is the public relations audit, which brings in practitioners from outside the organization to judge the efficiency and effectiveness of a department and its members.

Finally, public relations instruction has been offered by colleges and universities for nearly 75 years. Edward Bernays, a full-time consultant, taught the first course in 1923 in the journalism department of New York University's School of Commerce, Accounts, and Finance. The academic discipline of public relations grew out of journalism education, just as its practice began with former journalists. In 1987, the Commission on Undergraduate Public Relations Education (1987/1993) identified sequences or degree programs at more than 160 institutions, not counting programs residing in departments other than journalism and mass communication (e.g., speech). As touched on earlier, PRSA currently charters student chapters (PRSSA) at 200 colleges and universities which—to be chartered—must teach at least five public relations courses. More than 5,000 students earn undergraduate or graduate degrees in public relations each year.

Public relations, then, has the infrastructure necessary to become a profession. It remains an occupation because "the majority of practitioners have not been exposed to that infrastructure and thus have not become professionals" (J. E. Grunig & Hunt, 1984, p. 82). Whereas practitioners in the past most often were trained in journalism, people now entering the field increasingly are graduates of public relations programs, where they acquired prerequisite knowledge and professional values. The stream from higher education moves public relations steadily toward professionalism.

Meeting Fund Raising's Educational Needs

Chapter 1 outlined the premise that public relations offers an academic home for fund raising. Among other points made, about three fourths of the programs already incorporate fund-raising concepts in their courses and a growing number teach separate courses on the function (Kelly, 1992). Universities with such fund-raising courses include Brigham Young, Ohio State, West Virginia, San Jose State, Florida, South Carolina, Georgia, and my own institution, the University of Southwestern Louisiana (USL). The courses are evenly split between undergraduate and graduate students, and increasingly, full-time faculty are teaching them. This chapter delves into the premise further by comparing the public relations curriculum to the educational needs of fund raising.

According to J. E. Grunig and Hunt (1984), educators and practitioners agree that five elements are essential to the public relations curriculum: (a) a broad liberal education, (b) communication skills, (c) knowledge needed to manage the function, (d) knowledge of organizations for which students will work, and (e) practical experience. Fund raisers also agree that a liberal education is best suited for their occupation. The skills they say are important to their work are mostly communication skills. Evidence suggests that fund raisers value principles of management and learning about organizational employers. Their endorsement of practical experience is unquestionable.

P. M. Buchanan (1993) stated, "I believe a substantial segment of advancement executives agree that an undergraduate liberal arts education is the best possible preparation for the field" (p. 375). Payton et al. (1991) recommended the same curriculum, which includes the study of literature, languages, philosophy, history, mathematics, and sciences (physical, biological, and social). In contrast to most professional curricula, liberal arts' purpose is to provide general knowledge and develop general intellectual capabilities. Predicting that fund raisers will be impatient with such a program, Payton (cited in "Philanthropy 2000," 1993) argued, "But I strongly believe this field requires . . . that they be liberally educated as well as technically competent" (p. 15).

Robert Fogal (1991), founding editor of *New Directions for Philanthropic Fundraising* proclaimed, "The development officer must be part psychologist, sociologist, anthropologist, economist, and historian" (p. 281). Pray (1981) urged practitioners to take "a hearty dose of social science courses," warning, "If the development officer has not acquired some working knowledge of behavioral psychology, has not studied at least a little of the culture of groups, has not been led to do some severe introspection about personal behavior and attitudes, he or she . . . has placed a serious limitation on potential for success in the profession" (p. 388).

Although public relations is defined as professional education because it is prescribed training for a specific "profession," its curriculum primarily is liberal arts. The Commission on Undergraduate Public Relations Education (1987/1993) recommended that no more than 25% of the credit hours required for a baccalaureate degree come from professional courses of communication and public relations. "The traditional arts and sciences remain the solid basis for undergraduate education of public relations students, essential to their functioning professionally in a complex society" (p. 4). The Accrediting Council on Education in Journalism and Mass Communication (ACEJMC), which authorizes professional accreditation for schools and departments housing the majority of public relations programs, requires at least 90 semester hours outside the major, with at least 65 of those in liberal arts.

According to the fund raisers interviewed by Bloland and Bornstein (1991), career preparation should include "a liberal arts education, some business administration skills, experience in some other administrative position, talent in writing and speaking, and a pleasant personality" (p. 108). When asked to list the top skills of the "best" fund raiser they know, Duronio's (1993) respondents gave 12, of which more than half deal with communication. Whereas "organizational skills" was the most frequently reported skill, the second was simply "communication skills," followed by "listening" and "writing" (p. 4). Others were interpersonal skills, grantsmanship (i.e., writing proposals), motivating others, and verbal skills. Cleo Phillips (cited in "Forum," 1996), a senior manager of a recruiting firm specializing in fund raising, said organizations are "looking for people who can write" (p. 25). He explained, "This is a business of communication, and in case statements, proposals and letters to donors, development professionals are articulating the mission of the organization. They must be able to do it in a compelling way" (p. 25). As Conry (1991) asserted, fund raising always has been "highly dependent on skillful communicators" (p. 157).

Theory, writing, and public speaking/presentations are among the professional communication courses recommended by the Commission on Undergraduate Public Relations Education (1987/1993). It defined the subjects for five professional courses in public relations: principles, techniques, research/evaluation, strategy/implementation, and supervised work experience (i.e., internships). In alignment with its body of knowledge, public relations courses should be grounded in the social sciences. The commission further recommended that students minor in business with coursework in management, marketing, and other areas.

These guidelines are followed by most public relations programs. For example, undergraduate students majoring in public relations in my ACEJMC-accredited department, which is housed in USL's College of Liberal Arts, must take the recommended professional courses, and others, such as communication law. The major discipline represents only 27% of the 134 credits required for graduation; 98 credits come from noncommunication courses, primarily the liberal arts. Among the required courses are economics, statistics, and 13 credits in a foreign language. Students must take an internship for which they earn three credits—and usually minimum wage. About 80% of the public relations students minor in business by taking 18 semester hours in that discipline.

Graduate programs in public relations generally have a dual focus on management and social science theory and research. Both were recommended by the National Commission on Graduate Study in Public Relations (1985). A cognate area, or minor, usually is required. For example, if one of my master's students plans to conduct a thesis study on fund raising for secondary schools, he or she must take 6 graduate credit hours in education to better understand the mission and operations of those organizations.

Whereas minors are desirable because they enrich research and furnish knowledge about future organizational employers, majoring in disciplines related to specific types of organizations is not advised for students planning careers in public relations. J. E. Grunig and Hunt (1984) explained, "Students will become organization people, identifying so closely with the organization for which they work that they lose the professional's ability to see that organization as an outsider" (p. 80). An outsider's perspective is equally critical to fund raisers; therefore, the current situation of practitioners who work for educational institutions studying fund raising in academic units of education is detrimental. Such fund raisers will be unable to objectively question and counsel senior managers about the organization's behavior, thereby diminishing their effectiveness and the organization's potential for success.

The public relations curriculum offers a good fit for meeting the educational needs of fund raising. Furthermore, fund raising, public relations, and the latter's parent discipline of journalism traditionally have been linked in practice, although such linkages have been unexplored and often denied. Illustrating, Jonathan Spinner (1994), a fund raiser and nonprofit manager for more than 20 years, criticized my 1991 book for conceptualizing fund raising as a specialization of public relations, refuting, "I know of very few (actually, *not one*) public relations professionals who wish to have any real involvement with fund raising (p. 59; italics in original). Spinner, as do others, ignores the public relations backgrounds of numerous fund raisers. The chapter concludes by pointing out linkages in practice.

LONG-STANDING LINKAGES

A national survey on hiring trends, conducted by a recruiting firm in 1990, found that more than 75% of the responding 400 CEOs and fund raisers believe "marketing and/or public relations" are the careers with the "most transferable skills" to fund raising (Development Resource Group, 1990, p. 2). Without providing percentages, Bloland and Bornstein (1991) reported, "A number of vice presidents for development began their careers in advancement—alumni relations, public relations, or admissions" (p. 108). They listed journalism first among the graduate degrees held by the fund raisers they studied.

According Duronio (1993), 88% of her respondents had worked in some other field before entering fund raising. The broad area of education was the most frequently mentioned (27%), followed by "Advertising/Marketing/Public Relations" (18%). Harrah-Conforth and Borsos (1991) compared fund raising to "similar professions and businesses, such as public relations or advertising" (p. 29), and concluded from their historical research, "Fund raising in its new-found professional glory is becoming indistinguishable from business, advertising, or public relations" (p. 31).

The occupational linkages are not a recent phenomenon. Many present and past fund raisers came out of journalism and public relations. For example, Broce (1986) and Gurin (1985) began their careers as newspaper reporters and then worked in public relations. Broce majored in journalism and English in college (as did Rosso) and said his first job with fund-raising responsibilities was as "director of public relations and development" at a small university. Demonstrating a conventional bias that partially explains why linkages have not been more apparent, he recalled his reaction to learning that his job included fund-raising duties: "I became alarmed. I wanted to cut and run. As a former newspaperman, I barely trusted public relations 'hacks,' and I knew that fund raisers—I had never met one—certainly were a class all to themselves" (p. x).

Gurin (1985) entered fund raising at age 50, after 5 years as a journalist for the now defunct *Philadelphia Record* and 14 years as a public relations practitioner. Like Broce, he admitted, "I also never lost the newspaperman's view of public relations as somewhat degrading" (p. xii). Gurin's partner in his first fund-raising firm, Lewis Bowen, also had worked for newspapers and in public relations (e.g., financial reporter for the New York *Herald Tribune* and national publicity director for the Red Cross).

In his prologue to the recent book about him (Knott, 1992), Milton Murray—who was named NSFRE's 1991 Outstanding Fund-Raising Executive—paid tribute to "the professional who skillfully shoehorned me from public relations into philanthropy at an important juncture in my career" (p. xxi). Murray founded the public relations function at the College of Medical Evangelists, now Loma Linda University in California. He began a fund-raising program while serving in that position from 1949 to 1961. Until his retirement in 1995, Murray was director of philanthropic services for the Seventh-Day Adventist Church. He is certified by NSFRE, is a Fellow of AHP—and is accredited by PRSA.

Combined backgrounds in journalism, public relations, and fund raising strike a personal note. My undergraduate degree is in journalism, but—similar to many such graduates—my first job after college was in public relations, in my case working for a state college. In less than 4 years, I moved to a state research university and a position that combined public relations and fund-raising responsibilities, primarily because I recognized the growing power of fund raisers at public institutions. In quick succession, I accepted another position as associate director of development for the same university, thereby becoming a full-time fund raiser exactly 5 years after starting what I thought was going to be a career in journalism.

Stepping back to the function's beginning, pioneer Robert Duncan (cited in Cutlip, 1965/1990) described early fund-raising consultants as a "modest little band" composed of former YMCA secretaries and newspaper journalists (p. x). As substantiated in chapter 5, many of fund raising's historical figures were former reporters. I pointed out this journalism lineage in my earlier book, as well as the fact that a number of the first consulting firms started out as both fund-raising and public relations companies (Kelly, 1991a; see chaps. 11 and 13).

Fund raising's linkages to journalism and public relations are of interest for two reasons. First, they lend historical and applied support to the appropriateness of public relations as an academic home for fund raising. Second, they are unexplored relationships representing fertile ground for research. Whereas public relations' emergence from journalism is well documented, there are no studies on the parallel movement to fund raising. Practitioners and scholars in journalism and mass communication are ignorant about their field's ties to fund raising. Students interested in the journalistic beginnings of prominent fund raisers should consider historical studies to record this ancestry.

Similarly, little is known about fund raisers who have a public relations background. Yet PRSA's membership directory lists numerous individuals with fund-raising titles. For example, Frances Driscoll, APR, is vice president of public relations and development at Roger Williams Medical Center, and Wesley "Pat" Pattillo, APR, Fellow PRSA, was vice president of development at Southern Baptist Theological Seminary before becoming the executive director of the National Foundation for Youth. A casual comparison with NSFRE's directory identified several practitioners who are members of both associations, and some are accredited in public relations and certified as fund-raising executives. Pattillo, for example, is a CFRE. Ralph Frede, former vice president in charge of public affairs and development at Baylor College of Medicine and currently an independent consultant, and Michael Radock, former vice president of public relations and fund raising for the University of Michigan and now an adviser with the Mott Foundation, belong to NSFRE and hold PRSA's senior credential.

These and other practitioners were interviewed by a group of my graduate students in 1996 as part of a class research project. Findings revealed a strong conviction in the indivisibility of fund raising and public relations. Illustrating, the director of development for libraries at a large state university, who has a master's degree in public relations and is certified by NSFRE, stated, "I don't think you can do fund raising without good public relations [skills]. Fund raising as a whole is a communication process, so whether I'm working with volunteers or asking for gifts, it's all grounded in communication and the practice of public relations" (Brasseaux, Grayson, Parker, Shields, & Sutley, 1996, p. 17). A population exists for introspective studies on overlaps between the two functions, which would add to our knowledge of fund raising and provide insight on professionalism.

SUGGESTED READINGS

Carbone, R. F. (1989). *Fund raising as a profession* (Monograph No. 3). College Park: University of Maryland, Clearinghouse for Research on Fund Raising.

Grunig, J. E., & Hunt, T. (1984). *Managing public relations*. New York: Holt, Rinehart & Winston.

Kelly, K. S. (1992). Fund raising: Functional element in public relations education. *Journalism Educator, 47*(2), 19–25.

Public Relations Society of America (PRSA), Research Committee, Body of Knowledge Task Force. (1988). Public relations body of knowledge task force report. *Public Relations Review, 14*(3), 3–40.

PART II

THE PRINCIPLES: HISTORICAL, ORGANIZATIONAL, LEGAL, ETHICAL, AND THEORETICAL

5

Historical Context
of Fund Raising

Although antecedents of the fund-raising function can be traced to the founding days of our country, systematic efforts to raise money in the United States did not begin until the early 1900s. Fund raising has gone through a dramatic evolution that has not been readily apparent or well documented in the literature. This chapter first examines the evolution in detail. It then describes the four historical stages through which the practice of fund raising has passed. These stages also represent four models, or the different ways fund raising has been and is practiced.

A premise of this chapter is that current fund raising and its future practice cannot be understood without first having a solid grasp of the historical context in which the function evolved. Payton (1990) agreed, "Practice should indeed be informed by theory and history" (p. 177). Nonetheless, there is evidence that today's practitioners have little understanding of their function's history. For example, the examination currently used by NSFRE to test knowledge required for certification includes no questions on history. Rosso's (Rosso & Associates, 1991) book, *Achieving Excellence in Fund Raising,* and Mixer's (1993) book, *Principles of Professional Fundraising,* which won NSFRE's top research prizes in 1992 and 1994, respectively, include no chapter on history and contain only one or two brief mentions of fund raising's past.

Fostering such ignorance hampers efforts to advance the practice for the benefit of practitioners, charitable organizations, and society. As the proverbial question asks, "If we don't know where we've been, how can we possibly know where we're going"? Or as NSFRE President Lewis (1993a) stated, "Our future will be surer if we understand our past" (p. 9).

ONE GOOD BOOK

In contrast to most of our anecdotal knowledge about fund raising, we are fortunate to have a solid, well-researched book on its history from 1641 to the early 1960s. Scott Cutlip (1965/1990), the father of public relations education, provided us with this valuable work in 1965. The book was reissued in 1990, with 18 additional pages consisting of a preface by Cutlip and an introduction by John Schwartz (1990), former president of AAFRC and a founding member of IS.

When he originally wrote the book, Cutlip was part of the Wisconsin Philanthropy Project, which was headed by historian Merle Curti, who had obtained the first grant to underwrite research on philanthropy. According to Cutlip, he had started out to write a history of public relations, but conversations with Curti—who was highly critical of public relations—turned him instead to researching the history of fund raising.[1]

Cutlip's book *Fund Raising in the United States* is—and has remained for over 30 years—the only comprehensive history on fund raising (Layton, 1987). As such, it has been the primary reference for all subsequent works that touch on fund raising's past. Unfortunately, the combination of the book's publication date and fund raising's rapid and dramatic evolution have left a tremendous gap in our knowledge. As Cutlip himself pointed out in the preface to the reissue, there has been an "exponential growth of professional fund raising in the past quarter century" (p. ix).

At the time his history was published, the most recent gift figures available were from 1964, when the total amount given to U.S. charitable organizations was $13.6 billion, which was worth $72.5 billion in 1994 dollars (AAFRC Trust for Philanthropy, 1995). In comparison, giving in 1996 was estimated at $150.7 billion, or more than 11 times the highest amount with which Cutlip and the fund raisers he studied were familiar and about twice as much in inflation-adjusted dollars (AAFRC Trust for Philanthropy, 1997b). Given this difference in financial scope, the 32 years that have passed since the book's publication, and other important changes discussed shortly, there is a desperate need to add to our historical knowledge of fund-raising practice since the 1960s.

Students searching for an appropriate research topic for a thesis or dissertation should consider studies on the history of fund raising from 1960 to the present. A comprehensive study complementing Cutlip's would be of greatest value; however, such a study likely is beyond the reach of even a dissertation (perhaps a faculty member would be interested). As an alternative, students might consider recent histories of fund raising for one type of charitable organization (e.g., nonprofit hospitals), or they might select just one decade to study fund raising for all types (e.g., the Reagan years of the 1980s). Studies limited to state and regional organizations also would be of value as we know little about the effect of geographic location on fund-raising practice. Finally, historical studies of just one major charitable organization, similar to the work by Eleanor Brilliant (1990) on the United Way system, would contribute to our knowledge about fund raising. There are primary and secondary documents available at the Payton Philanthropic Studies Library at Indiana University to support such work. In addition, NSFRE and CASE have fairly good libraries with very helpful staff.[2]

---

[1]Thirty years later, Cutlip finally found the opportunity to finish his history of public relations. He had retired as dean emeritus of the Henry W. Grady College of Journalism and Mass Communication at the University of Georgia, where he went from the University of Wisconsin. In his "leisure time," he wrote two major books, *The Unseen Power: Public Relations. A History* (1994) and *Public Relations History: From the 17th to the 20th Century. The Antecedents* (1995), published by Lawrence Erlbaum Associates. In 1995, PRSA awarded Cutlip its highest individual honor, the Gold Anvil, in recognition of his outstanding achievements in advancing the practice of public relations.

[2]These libraries also contain valuable papers and publications to support research on the history of fund raising before 1960. For example, the Payton Library has microfilmed the Charles Sumner Ward Papers, which include personal correspondence, campaign materials, newspaper clippings, and scrapbooks dating from the early 1900s to 1920.

Some Caveats

Returning to Cutlip (1965/1990), this chapter—as do other parts of the book—draws heavily from that seminal work. However, much of Cutlip's rich research is absent due to space limitations and purposeful efforts to avoid duplication. Students should refer to the 500-plus-page book.

Furthermore, this chapter is not intended to provide either a history of philanthropy or of the nonprofit sector, but rather to focus on fund raising, which has been neglected in most studies. The broader topics are covered elsewhere. In particular, students are referred to Gurin and Van Til's (1990) historical essay on philanthropy, and to the work of P. D. Hall (e.g., 1987, 1992a) on the history of the nonprofit sector. Valuable information not covered here also can be found in the literature about philanthropy as it relates to specific types of charitable organizations (e.g., Curti & Nash's 1965 book on philanthropy's role in shaping higher education). These works and others are listed in suggested readings at the end of the chapter.

Students also are alerted that they may recognize discrepancies in the history related here and references to fund raising in other works. Most of these discrepancies can be explained by the age of Cutlip's (1965/1990) book and the necessary reliance of later authors on the book. Two areas in particular stand out. First, Cutlip's research focused almost exclusively on fund-raising consultants, as opposed to staff fund raisers. This is understandable given that external consultants were the dominant fund raisers up to the time Cutlip's book was published. As explained shortly, fund raising as an internal function is a recent phenomenon, yet—students will recall from chapter 3—staff practitioners now greatly outnumber consultants, representing nearly 95% of all fund raisers. There is a significant difference in the function as practiced by internal and external practitioners: The first solicit gifts, but the second do not.

The time gap in our knowledge has resulted in much erroneous information about fund raising. For example, in their essay on trustees, Herman and Block (1990) stated, "The evidence available in highly regarded histories of U.S. philanthropy and fund raising suggests that 'paid staff' have long been a part of fund raising" (p. 223). They concluded that whereas employees were under the direction of volunteers when it came to raising money in the 19th century, fund raising became professionalized during the early 20th century, "thus shifting the general relationship between volunteers and paid fund raisers" (p. 225). Similarly, P. D. Hall (1987) cited Cutlip when he reported, "In the 1920s . . . the Community Chests, the YMCA, and the universities all professionalized their revenue-generating operations" (p. 15). In the introduction to his book on philanthropic giving, Magat (1989) said, "Fund raising itself has come to be a major subindustry of the nonprofit world. Curiously, it consists to a great extent of for-profit firms and individual entrepreneur-consultants" (p. 8).

The second area responsible for discrepancies was Cutlip's focus on small gifts that resulted in big totals for such organizations as the March of Dimes and the American Cancer Society during the 1930s and 1940s. According to Schwartz (1990), the late Si Seymour criticized Cutlip for ignoring major gifts in his history. In a 1965 letter to philanthropy scholar F. Emerson Andrews, Seymour (cited in Schwartz, 1990) charged, "Cutlip missed altogether the important point that the dimes and the dollars were mostly sound effects for the appeal to larger gifts" (p. xx). Yet Cutlip (1965/1990) repeatedly pointed out his intended emphasis on what he termed *people's philanthropy*, or the number of donors, not the size of gifts. Unfortunately, much of the subsequent literature has neglected the historical role of major gifts, treating them as if they were a relatively new element. To set the record straight, Cutlip clearly stated, "Year in, year out the fund-raising campaign depends quite heavily on the large, wealthy donor for the bulk of its funds" (p. 317).

With these caveats in mind, the chapter now turns to the evolution of the fund-raising function.

EVOLUTION OF THE FUND-RAISING FUNCTION

Fund raising as an organizational function is new. According to *The Oxford English Dictionary* (1989), the leading authority on historic use of words in English, the term *fund raiser* first appeared in print just 40 years ago, in the late Vance Packard's (1957) book, *The Hidden Persuaders*. English professor Richard Turner (1991) claimed the term *fund raising* goes back only to the late 1930s.

This newness is shrouded in much of the literature on nonprofits, philanthropy, and fund raising. Discussion of the function's history often begins with the first solicitation for Harvard College in 1641 (e.g., Worth, 1993). Education fund raisers, in particular, relegate their beginnings to the three clergymen who met with mixed success on an early mission to England: One was hanged, one became an English rector, and the third returned home with the money.

Almost all related histories point to America's colonial colleges as the birthplace of fund raising. Many exaggerate the extent of solicitation efforts and mistakenly portray the first educational institutions as charities highly dependent on private gifts. Broce (1986), for example, claimed the first settlers enacted the philanthropic spirit they brought with them by "building churches, schools, and colleges with their own money" (p. 10). Starting with Harvard and Virginia's College of William and Mary, Broce said, "Americans contributed generously to provide their children with educational opportunities" (p. 10).

Yet P. D. Hall (1992a, 1993b) convincingly argued that the conventional notion of charitable organizations dating back to this period is erroneous. Hall (1993b) explained, "The colonial colleges were state enterprises, and they were supported primarily by government funds until the early nineteenth century" (p. 181). Even churches—except those in the handful of colonies that tolerated religious diversity—were supported by taxation, not contributions. Hall could identify only a few nonprofits, such as the Masons and Benjamin Franklin's library and fire company, that date back to the mid-1700s. He stated, "Legislatures in the colonial and early national periods were intensely hostile to voluntary associations of any kind" (p. 181).

Even after the late 1770s, according to Hall, establishment of charitable and other nonprofits was concentrated very selectively, primarily in areas of New England and the upper Midwest. The West and the South remained generally hostile to such activity. Hall (1993b) added, "Major urban centers like New York and Pennsylvania sharply limited both the powers of nonprofit corporations and the rights of individuals to donate or endow them" (p. 182).

Cutlip (1965/1990) concluded from his research:

Organized philanthropy supported by systematic fund raising is a twentieth-century development in the United States. Philanthropy, in America's first three centuries, was carried along on a small scale, largely financed by the wealthy few in response to personal begging appeals . . . . There were few organized drives, in the modern sense, before 1900. World War I and the decade that followed provided the seedbed for the growth of today's fund raising. (p. 3)

In other words, early activities related to gifts did not signify the beginning of fund raising as an organizational function. They were sporadic efforts carried out by amateurs in response to specific financial needs. However, as pointed out in Kelly (1991a; see chap. 13), early fund-raising-like activities did provide antecedents of the models—discussed later in this chapter—that would emerge in the 1900s when systematic fund raising began.

Following Cutlip's definitive work, most contemporary authors make some distinction between pre-1900, fund-raising-like activities and the function we know today. Broce (1986), for example, stated, "Systematic solicitation of the general public began in the early 1900s," (p. 10). Worth (1993) said, "Fund raising before the twentieth century was generally amateur and personal, a transaction between two individuals, with no role for organization, strategy, or professional managers" (p. 19). The distinctions made by such authors, however, generally are not as clear as they should be and others blatantly ignore fund raising's recent genesis (e.g., Panas, 1984).

This chapter, then, marks the beginning of the fund-raising function at 1900, and traces its evolution to the present. In doing so, it identifies four distinct eras: (a) the era of nonspecialists from 1900 to 1917, (b) the era of fund-raising consultants from 1919 to 1941, (c) the era of transition from 1946 to the mid-1960s, and (d) the era of staff fund raisers from 1965 to the present. Table 5.1 outlines this evolution with appropriate benchmarks; publication of Cutlip's book is included to emphasize changes that have occurred since its writing.

As presented in Table 5.1, the fund-raising function primarily consisted of part-time efforts by nonspecialists until World War I. The end of the war delineated the start of the era of fund-raising consultants, who would dominate the practice for 30 years. Following World War II, private universities began to hire fund raisers for their staffs. During the 1950s, other types of charitable organizations followed suit. In 1960, there were enough staff fund raisers and consultants who did not belong to AAFRC to begin their own professional association, NSFRE. About the same time Cutlip's book was published, consulting firms began to change their services in response to the growing number of staff practitioners. By 1967, there were enough staff fund raisers employed by hospitals to create the specialized association now known as AHP. There was a surge of practitioner employment by public colleges and universities during the 1970s, which paved the way for the formation of CASE. In 1980, IS was founded to promote research on the nonprofit sector and to protect its organizations from government regulation. By that time, the practice was dominated by staff fund raisers.

TABLE 5.1
Evolution of the Fund-Raising Function

Era of Nonspecialists

1913 • American Alumni Council (AAC) founded

• Federal income tax law enacted

1917 • American College Public Relations Association (ACPRA) founded

• Revenue Act of 1917 establishes charitable contributions deduction

World War I

Era of Fund-Raising Consultants

1919 • First fund-raising consulting firms started

1935 • American Association of Fund-Raising Counsel (AAFRC) founded

1940 • U.S. giving totals $1.2 billion

World War II

Era of Transition

1949 • First university staff fund raisers join ACPRA

1950s • Charitable organizations hire staff fund raisers

1955 • First fund-raising registration law enacted

1960 • National Society of Fund Raising Executives (NSFRE) founded

1964 • U.S. giving totals $13.6 billion

Era of Staff Fund Raisers

1965 • Book on history of fund raising published (Cutlip, 1965/1990)

• First AAFRC firm starts part-time counseling to replace resident campaign directors

1967 • Association for Healthcare Philanthropy (AHP) founded

1970s • Public colleges and universities hire staff fund raisers

1974 • Council for Advancement and Support of Education (CASE) formed by merger of AAC and ACPRA

• The Fund Raising School founded

1980 • Independent Sector (IS) founded

1989 • U.S. giving exceeds $100 billion for the first time

Era of Nonspecialists

According to a CASE article on the history of institutional advancement ("Years in review," 1988), Williams College established the first alumni association in 1821, and Brown University organized the first alumni fund in 1823. The first mention of public institutions in this chronology was more than 70 years later, when the University of Michigan hired its first full-time, paid alumni secretary in 1897. This early difference in organizational behavior between private and public educational institutions is repeated throughout fund-raising history. Private institutions advanced the function much earlier than their public counterparts, although today there are only minor differences in their fund-raising behavior.

On February 21, 1913, 23 men who were responsible for organizing former students at U.S. colleges and universities gathered for the first time at Ohio State University and founded the Association of Alumni Secretaries, which later became the American Alumni Council (AAC). Fund-raising duties were apparent in the reports of some, but not all, participants of that meeting. For example, William Field (cited in Association of Alumni Secretaries, 1913), secretary of Carnegie Institute of

Technology (now Carnegie Mellon University), said the only distinctive thing accomplished by his alumni organization in its brief history was the establishment of small scholarships by three of the graduating classes. "Our men are not wealthy as a whole and therefore they are limited to helping in a small way," he explained (p. 7).

In other words, almost a century passed from the time the first alumni association was established until staff employees of colleges and universities who managed relations with alumni formally organized. Furthermore, fund raising was only a portion of the responsibilities of only some of those staff members.

To verify the part-time nature of these nonspecialists in fund raising, we must leap ahead to the 1920s and 1930s. The results of a survey presented at the 1938 AAC conference—the 25th anniversary of the alumni organization's founding—showed that only one fifth of the respondents were involved in raising general funds for their institution (Carter, 1988). Describing his job as alumni secretary at the University of North Carolina–Chapel Hill in the late 1920s and 1930s, Maryon "Spike" Saunders (cited in Carter, 1988) explained that although fund raising was a part of his job, organized drives were irregular and only a minor portion of his responsibilities. He stated, "The bottom line was getting the alumni to understand the goals of the university and promoting good will toward it" (p. 19).

The American Association of College News Bureaus, later renamed the American College Publicity Association and then the American College Public Relations Association (ACPRA), was founded in 1917. Similar to alumni secretaries, some of these early public relations practitioners were involved in sporadic fund-raising efforts during the time. The historical evidence supporting their involvement is sparse. Cutlip (1965/1990) mentioned in passing that Whiting Williams, first executive director of the Cleveland Federation for Charity and Philanthropy, which was established in 1913, had been a fund raiser and public relations practitioner for Oberlin College.

Interestingly, the founding dates of the two associations coincided with the introduction of the federal income tax in 1913 and creation of the charitable contributions deduction in the Revenue Act of 1917—both of which would accelerate the specialization of fund raising.

Focusing on organizations other than colleges and universities, the Progressive movement was in force during this period of U.S. history. Scholars, social workers, and "muckrakers" actively sought reform to problems raised by the rapid industrialization and urbanization that followed the Civil War. The first 17 years of the century marked the founding of many of our largest charitable organizations, including the Boy Scouts, Girl Scouts, National Tuberculosis Association, American Cancer Society, NAACP, National Urban League, and others.

As discussed in Kelly (1991a; see chaps. 2 and 13), CEOs and trustees primarily carried out fund raising for such organizations—as well as for colleges and universities—as part of their overall duties. In addition, fund-raising federations representing multiple organizations in various communities frequently hired percentage-paid solicitors to collect gifts. William Allen (cited in Cutlip, 1965/1990), director of the Bureau of Municipal Research and National Training School for Public Service in New York City in 1912, described a common approach to fund raising during this era:

At present our philanthropic activities rely chiefly upon "personal equation" methods of raising funds. Mrs. Earnest lunches with Mrs. Gushing and describes a visit to the day nursery that is suffering dreadfully for want of money. . . . After appeals in person begin to affect one's invitations to dinner and to other social functions . . . the paid collector is tried. (p. 64)

Students should not assume philanthropy was minimal during this era. On the contrary, historians generally identify the first decade of the 1900s as the early years of large-scale philanthropy. For example, John D. Rockefeller, Sr. established the General Education Board in 1902 with a gift of $130 million. Andrew Carnegie, who earlier had published his Gospel of Wealth, established the Carnegie Corporation in 1911 with his largest gift. The United States had more than 14,000 millionaires, and as Hiebert (1966) pointed out, just 1% of all Americans owned 54% of the wealth in 1900. With Carnegie and Rockefeller leading the way, "The march of large-scale philanthropy and benevolent foundations across the national landscape began" (Cutlip, 1965/1990, p. 33).

Representative of the era of nonspecialists, William Lawrence, an Episcopal bishop, raised more than $2 million for Harvard College during 1904–1905 while serving as volunteer president of the alumni association. As a trustee of Wellesley College in 1914, Lawrence conducted a drive to raise almost $2 million for that institution. Secretaries of the Young Men's Christian Association (YMCA) carried out fund raising as part of their paid duties. The YMCA "campaign method" was introduced at the beginning of the era of nonspecialists. According to Arnaud Marts (cited in Cutlip, 1965/1990), founder of one of the early consulting firms, "The campaign was definitely developed by secretaries of the Young Men's Christian Associations about 1901–1902" (p. 158). Its innovators were Charles Sumner Ward and Lyman L. Pierce, who—with other secretaries—raised about $60 million in capital funds for the YMCA from 1905 to 1915.

Employees Ward and Pierce raised money for organizations other than the YMCA during this period. In 1911, for example, Ward conducted a campaign for a hospital in Salem, Ohio. According to Carlton Ketchum (cited in Cutlip, 1965/1990), cofounder of another pioneer firm, "Prior to World War I, professional campaign service was usually provided on the basis of a fee of 5% of the amount subscribed" (p. 91). Although Cutlip claimed Ward did not work on a percentage arrangement in such campaigns, he speculated that Pierce probably did. Yet Harrah-Conforth and Borsos (1991) found evidence in the Pierce scrapbooks at the State Historical Society of Wisconsin that, on occasion, "Ward at least was not above taking a commission as his form of payment" (p. 23).

Foreshadowing the era of fund-raising consultants, the first commercial firm actually was started in 1913, by Frederick Courtenay Barber. A former newspaperman, Barber had worked for Ward as a publicist in the 1911 Salem hospital campaign. Barber's criticized behavior and his relationship to the YMCA campaign method are discussed later in the section on fund-raising models. An important point to emphasize here is that consultants disavowed Barber's firm as their progenitor. Cutlip (1965/1990) explained, "Almost from the start, Barber . . . operated on a percentage fee basis" (p. 83). The commissions he charged, Harrah-Conforth and Borsos (1991) reported, ranged from 5% to 15% of the amount raised. They said Marts—representative of the early consultants—believed the commissions and other behavior gave fund raising a bad name, so he strived "to draw clearcut distinctions between Barber and the YMCA men" (p. 23). Due to such efforts, 1919 generally became accepted as the date when the first "authentic" firms were started.

Summarizing this first era from 1900 to 1917, fund raising was carried out part time by nonspecialists, primarily CEOs, other employed staff, trustees, and volunteers. In colleges and universities, some alumni relations and public relations practitioners assumed fund-raising tasks. As the YMCA secretaries moved from nonspecialists to specialists, they sometimes adopted the payment mode of paid solicitors, as did the first fund-raising firm. Such percentage-based commissions would be ruled unethical by the association founded in the following era—AAFRC.

Congress declared war on April 6, 1917 and armistice was declared on November 11, 1918. Although World War I lasted only 19 months, it had a major impact on systematic fund raising.

Era of Fund-Raising Consultants

As Cutlip (1965/1990) stated, "Many were the consequences that would flow from the pervasive, powerful dynamism of our participation in World War I. Among them was the big nationwide fund drive" (p. 110).

The American Red Cross War Council was created by President Woodrow Wilson at the beginning of the war to combine all relief efforts and concentrate them in the hands of a single organization. "The champion money-raiser" Ward was hired and—along with Pierce—served for the duration of the war on loan from the YMCA. Fund raising's newfound power was dramatically demonstrated in the war's early months when the Red Cross raised $114 million in just 8 days! According to Cutlip, the Ward-directed campaigns raised a total of $690 million. The figures are even more impressive when it is taken into account that Americans also gave almost $14 billion through five drives for Liberty Loans during the same short period. Working on those loan drives was another important historical figure, John Price Jones.

Jones, who graduated from Harvard in 1902, was a newspaper reporter for 13 years. Upon joining an advertising agency in 1917, he was loaned by his firm to work on the Liberty Loan drives in New York City. In this position, he learned fund raising from Guy Emerson, another former journalist, who had been trained by Bishop Lawrence. After the armistice, Jones directed the Harvard Endowment Fund campaign, which raised $14.2 million in less than 1 year. In November 1919, the same month the campaign was completed, Jones incorporated his commercial fund-raising firm.

One month earlier, in September 1919, Ward started the firm of Ward, Hill, Pierce & Wells in New York. He had resigned from the YMCA early in 1919, after 35 years as a secretary, and had first established Ward & Hill Associated before starting the new company. Other consulting firms quickly formed. For example, brothers Carlton and George started Ketchum Inc. also in September of that year. Cornelius Smith (cited in Cutlip 1965/1990), a former reporter for the Baltimore *Sun* and a founder in 1919 of the fund-raising firm Will, Folsom & Smith, said that in the post-WWI days of fund raising "almost anyone of good appearance with a flair for selling, organizing, and publicizing could conduct successful campaigns to raise moderate sums for popular

causes" (p. 169). Cutlip explained, "In the hindsight of history it appears obvious that
the nation's newly discovered philanthropic potential—so dramatically uncovered in
World War I—would be exploited to meet the dammed up needs of colleges, hospitals,
preparatory schools, libraries, and the mushrooming social agencies" (p. 157).

Over the next 10 years, the number of consulting firms multiplied as the demand
for fund raising continued and those trained in the older firms broke away to start
their own companies. Bremner (1960/1988) reported that there were 20 fund-raising
firms in New York City by the end of the 1920s. Cutlip (1965/1990) identified five
firms whose founders were influenced by Ward, including Marts & Lundy, Ketchum,
and Tamblyn & Brown, which he termed *the Y school* of commercial fund raisers.[3] He
described these fund raisers' deep sense of religious motivation, adding, "Yet this
motivation did not make them immune to the quest for power and profit" (p. 164).
Harrah-Conforth and Borsos (1991) stated, "Fund raising under the tutelage of Ward
and Pierce became not only a source for gathering enormous sums of money but also
became a breeding ground in which one sector of the first generation of professional
fund raisers received their training" (p. 22).

Cutlip (1965/1990) contrasted the Y school with John Price Jones, who admired
efficient business methods and derogatorily referred to the Y fund raisers as "the
Christers" (p. 43). Like the Y school, the Jones firm begot its own school of
consultants, such as Si Seymour and George Brakeley, Jr. Indicative of Jones' impact
on current fund-raising practice, Brakeley, John Price Jones is a well-known contemporary firm, and Seymour first articulated many of the basic principles still followed
by practitioners. Cutlip concluded that to Ward and his disciples, fund raising was an
art; to Jones and those who adopted his approach, it was a business.

Harrah-Conforth and Borsos (1991) divided fund raisers into two similar categories: (a) the Christian philanthropic tradition of the Y school, and (b) the business
tradition of John Price Jones. They argued that a tension between fund raising as a
calling and fund raising as a job has persisted through three generations of practitioners. Although they admitted "in-house development offices have generally taken the
place of external fund-raising firms at universities and hospitals" (p. 30), they based
their historical analysis almost exclusively on consultants.

Ignoring differences in what later are identified as models of practice, fund-raising firms
during this era shared much in common. According to Harrah-Conforth and Borsos, the
fixed fee, as opposed to commissions, became professional dogma by the end of the 1920s.
This change was fundamental to consultants' goal of making fund raising more dignified
and worthy of respect. Related to the goal, consultants adhered to a nonsolicitation role
to further distance themselves from paid solicitors. Solicitors—who ask for and collect
gifts, usually for a percentage fee—appeared in American philanthropy early on. Cutlip
said they disappeared from the fund-raising scene after World War I, but their perpetual
abuses haunted owners of the first commercial firms. Cutlip's assertion was premature
given the activities of paid solicitors today, which are discussed in chapters 7 and 8.

Nonsolicitor Role of Consultants.   A distinctive characteristic of fund-
raising consultants is that they do not solicit or receive gifts; they only advise and

---

[3]Ward's firm still exists today as Ward, Dreshman & Reinhardt, Inc., which moved to Columbus, Ohio
in 1969.

manage others who actually carry out the activities. Bintzer (1981) affirmed, "Counsel will not solicit gifts but will use all his [*sic*] knowledge and powers of persuasion to equip the client's staff and volunteers with the skills they need to seek gifts successfully" (p. 220).

Most of the scholarly and practitioner literature ignores the nonsolicitor role of consultants. For example, in her entire chapter on hiring and working with consultants, Geever (1991) never once mentioned that they do not solicit gifts. In fact, she warned readers not to hire consultants and turn all fund raising over to them. As a historic aside, in 1979, Geever's company became the first consulting firm headed by a woman to be admitted into membership in AAFRC, which during its first 45 years commonly was referred to as a "male club."

The nonsolicitation distinction is critical because staff fund raisers *do* solicit and receive gifts on behalf of their employers. Until the late 1940s, charitable organizations were dependent on consultants, who—in turn—were dependent on others, particularly trustees and CEOs, to undertake solicitations. In evidence, Cutlip (1965/1990) said Jones once confessed that although "he had been instrumental in raising nearly a billion dollars he had never personally asked anyone to contribute to any cause" (p. 182). Worth (1993) emphasized the nonsolicitor role of the YMCA fund raisers: "The task of solicitation was carried out by volunteers and institutional leaders, with Ward providing the strategy, the method, and overall direction of the campaign. Ward did not personally solicit gifts, yet he raised millions" (p. 21).

Contemporary consultants adhere to nonsolicitation primarily to differentiate themselves from companies that only solicit gifts (i.e., solicitation firms). Two related reasons underlie the distinction: the voluntary spirit of philanthropy and the requirements of state regulations, particularly registration costs.

According to the AAFRC Fair Practice Code, now called the Standards of Membership and Professional Conduct, "Member firms also believe it is the best interest of clients that solicitation of gifts should generally be undertaken by volunteers" (AAFRC Trust for Philanthropy, 1987, p. 120). The code emphasizes that the voluntary nature of philanthropy dictates solicitors not be self-interested parties who are paid to raise money. Contemporary consultants bemoan the widespread decrease in use of volunteer solicitors and the corresponding increase in gift solicitations by fund-raising staff.

I admit some sympathy for their calls for involvement of nonpractitioners in the fund-raising process. Certainly, as discussed in chapter 8, organizations that turn their fund raising over to paid solicitors are acting in a socially irresponsible manner. Furthermore, consultants—who own or are employees of for-profit firms—are warning internal practitioners that undue emphasis on fund raising as paid solicitation may lead society and its representative government to misunderstand the function and reduce or eliminate such benefits as the charitable deduction.

However, the first reason for nonsolicitation is flawed. Consultants hold that fund-raising employees generally should not solicit gifts because they have a self-interest in whether the gift is obtained. Yet many so-called volunteers traditionally used by consultants are paid (e.g., CEOs and other managers), usually more than fund raisers, and their self-interest in whether the gift is made is as great if not greater. Although trustees are unpaid volunteers, they have ultimate responsibility for ensuring that the organization obtains necessary resources, as discussed in the next chapter.

Therefore, trustees have (or should have) a high level of self-interest in the success of solicitations.

The second and less discussed reason underlying the nonsolicitor role is that state regulations are more rigorous for external paid solicitors than for consultants who do not solicit gifts. The most noteworthy difference is in registration costs, which usually are higher for solicitors than for consultants. For example, two of the most populated states, California and Ohio, require annual registration with a $200 fee and a $25,000 bond for solicitors who receive and have custody of funds, but they have no registration requirements for consultants (AAFRC Trust for Philanthropy, 1997a). Similarly, New York, Florida, Maryland, Massachusetts, Minnesota, Pennsylvania, and Virginia require a registration fee and a bond of $10,000 to $50,000 for solicitors, but require no bond from consultants, only a registration fee that is lower or equal to the fee required from solicitors. In all, 41 of the 50 states have some registration requirements with financial ramifications for solicitors and/or consultants. In most of those states (71%), it pays not to handle gift funds.

Other Commonalities of Early Firms.   Harrah-Conforth and Borsos (1991) pointed out that during the era of fund-raising consultants, Ward and Pierce "set a standard for fund-raising counsel to remain out of the limelight of campaigns" (p. 23). Jones also had learned the painful lesson that commercial firms must stay in the background to remain profitable. When his firm took credit for the successful completion of the Johns Hopkins University campaign in the mid-1920s, it was attacked by a director of a Rockefeller foundation that had given millions of dollars to Hopkins. According to Cutlip (1965/1990), "Thereafter Jones, in public utterances, was careful to claim only that he had 'assisted' in raising the money" (p. 286).

Transcending one generation, J. Patrick Ryan (cited in Harrah-Conforth & Borsos, 1991), founder of Staley/Robeson/Ryan/St. Lawrence, described the tenet:

> I don't need anyone to know who my firm is or who I am, nor does any member of our firm need to be known as to who they are, except by the president of the institution, the chairman of the board, some of the key volunteers we're working directly with, and staff members who know we are helping them. . . . So there is nothing we do, or should do, that brings attention to us or, therefore, our career. So, it's a behind-the-scenes function. (p. 29)

The consulting firms offered similar services. Of particular significance during this era and the next was resident campaign direction. As Gurin (1985) explained, a firm's employees were assigned by the owners to work with the client organization on its premises, but under the firm's supervision. These resident directors often stayed on site for 2 years to direct a campaign, usually far away from home and family. Harrah-Conforth and Borsos (1991) said the primary evidence they used to conclude that the second generation of fund raisers (i.e., those over age 60) adhered to "true philanthropic values" was the descriptions given by members of that generation about the suffering and professional hardships they had endured as resident directors. In short, until the mid-1960s, consulting firms relied heavily on field campaign direction for much of their income.

Viewed from this perspective, the external nature of consulting firms and the absence of staff practitioners encouraged early fund raisers to package their services as directors of campaigns with definitive beginning and end dates. J. P. Smith (1981) emphasized this point in a later era, arguing that when charitable organizations "rely on consultants and hired hands, as opposed to professional staff, there is no alternative to a respite from the campaign" (p. 66). Partially explaining why the campaign structure—which was shaped by the needs of external consultants—is still popular today, Broce (1986) said, "The campaign introduced the sense-of-urgency factor that many of us still believe is essential to success" (p. 11). Lord (1983) simply called the campaign "the greatest invention in fund raising since the bake sale" (p. 67).

Discussing the period identified here as the era of fund-raising consultants, Bintzer (1981) stated, "Their success resulted from two conditions: 1) their own well-developed expertise and proven procedures and 2) the lack of any similar (or even remotely akin) expertise within the staff of the client" (p. 217). Bintzer, who worked as both an external and internal fund raiser (e.g., president of the John Price Jones Company and chief advancement officer of Drexel University), is one of the rare sources that explicitly addresses the transition of fund raising from consultants to staff practitioners, which he labeled "the evolution in the management of philanthropy" (p. 217). According to Bintzer, increased competition for the philanthropic dollar and other environmental factors "forced the creation of the skilled, professional, full-time, in-house staff to cope with these challenges" (p. 217).

Sixteen years after the first consulting firms were started, AAFRC was founded on May 13, 1935. The trade association was established by nine large fund-raising firms, most of which were owned by former journalists, and remained a closed group until it opened membership to other firms in 1949—after the first staff fund raisers joined the college public relations association, ACPRA.

Era of Transition

Federated fund-raising drives during the height of World War II (1943–1945) raised a total of $900 million, as compared to the $690 million raised in World War I (Cutlip, 1965/1990). The National War Fund was created to represent 17 member agencies in a series of appeals. Seymour (1947) managed the work of the federated fund, which traced its ancestry to the National United War Fund started in the closing days of World War I.

Declaring that fund raising had greatly matured during the 20 years between the two World Wars, Cutlip noted changes brought about by the Great Depression. In the 1930s, dimes-and-dollars drives, pioneered by such organizations as the March of Dimes, became prevalent and large-scale capital fund drives—dependent on wealthy donors—were halted. The depression also taught Americans that the resources of government must be brought to bear on needs that could not be met by private philanthropy. As a result, during World War II, the federal government joined the USO in providing recreational facilities for soldiers and sailors. The U.S. military assumed the former duties of the Red Cross, taking over the maintenance of base hospitals, recruitment of ambulance sections, and provision of medical supplies.

To fill the void resulting from loss of responsibilities, the Red Cross started its Blood Donor Program on January 9, 1941, which—Cutlip (1965/1990) stressed—"proved a great asset, both during and after the war" (p. 416). In evidence, the Red Cross raised $666 million during the 4 years of World War II, even though "it still had to compete with the appeals for the USO, for War Bond drives, and the expanded demands of community chests and other fund drives across the nation" (p. 417). Cutlip called the Red Cross "the greatest fund raiser of modern times" (p. 529), elaborating, "The power of a good cause, careful organization, sound planning, intensive publicity, and systematic solicitation of money has never been more effectively demonstrated" (p. 422). Unlike in World War I, the fund-raising efforts were managed by the Red Cross' own public relations director—G. Stewart Brown, a former journalist—and his headquarters staff (i.e., consultants were not put in charge).

Senior managers and trustees of charitable organizations who witnessed the success of the Red Cross embraced fund raising in the post-WWII years to meet what Cutlip (1965/1990) described as "the pent-up demands for buildings for colleges, churches, and other institutions plus the continuing needs of relief and welfare" (p. 493). They began hiring internal staff in the first years after the war to address fund-raising needs on a full-time, continuous basis.

According to Pray (1981), a 1936 ACPRA survey showed that less than 50% of the colleges and universities represented had alumni funds. The proportion did not change much by 1942 when another survey was conducted. However, Pray reported that the first fund raiser joined ACPRA in 1949, and by 1952, there were 13 fund raisers in the association. As he explained, fund raising for education on an institutionalized basis came "with agonizing slowness over the years" (p. 1).

The fact that Francis Pray, who became a renowned fund-raising consultant, was editor of ACPRA's journal, *Publicity Problems*, during World War II adds validity to his evidence about the transition to staff fund raisers. Pray (1981) himself first assumed fund-raising responsibilities in 1946, when as director of public relations he took on his college's alumni fund. He said most alumni funds in those days relied heavily on class agents and stressed participation—getting as many gifts as possible, even $1 gifts, "to raise the percentage" (p. 2) of alumni participating in what then constituted the annual giving program.

In his editor's note to an article by Frank Pearsall (1943)—publicity director for the two private secondary schools, The Northfield Schools—Pray provided historical insight on the beginning of internal fund raisers. Pearsall came to the Northfield Schools in the late 1920s as an employee of Marts & Lundy to direct a $3-million campaign. At the conclusion of the campaign in 1929, he accepted a position on the schools' staff, eventually moving from publications to "the institution's public relations and fund-raising program" (p. 8). Pearsall described the program in 1942: "A staff of four workers man the public relations office, of whom two are engaged exclusively in fund raising and mailing activities" (p. 8). With direct mail as their principal technique, the Northfield practitioners raised an average of $57,000 in annual giving. Pearsall explained, "Few large gifts are included in these totals; the aim from the beginning having been a great number of gifts rather than large individual donations" (p. 8).

Turning to the other education association, John Price Jones (1946) contended in *The Yearbook of Philanthropy 1945–46* that annual giving belonged to alumni funds and the AAC. Jones quoted the *AAC News*: "The number of colleges in which an annual giving plan is in effect has increased with each year, which is further evidence that the type of appeal which is generally called the Alumni Fund, or the Loyalty Fund, is receiving wide acceptance by the graduates of our colleges" (p. 46).

Both alumni relations and public relations claimed fund raising as part of their function, which was reflected in an intense competition between AAC and ACPRA to recruit fund raisers as members in the postwar days. AAC had an Educational Fund Raising Committee and ACPRA had a Development Section (Linehan, 1961). The introduction of staff practitioners fueled long-standing turf battles between the two groups. Illustrating the adversarial relationship, Carter (1988) found from her interviews with pioneers in alumni relations that "ACPRA members were too aggressive for the easy going alumni directors' tastes" (p. 19).

In 1958, the two associations held a joint conference at the Greenbrier Hotel in West Virginia in an attempt to work out their differences. In his introduction to the monograph on the Greenbrier conference, Porter (1958) wrote:

> In the years since the end of the second World War, a new administrative area in higher education clearly has emerged. It is an area which does not even have a commonly-understood name, as yet; it is sometimes called Development, sometimes called University (or College) Relations . . . . The precise dimensions of this new area also lack definition . . . . It obviously includes public relations, alumni relations, and fund raising. The recognition of this new area of administration grew out of the realization on many campuses that these three activities . . . obviously have much in common and, just as obviously, often work at cross-purposes. (p. 1)

Whether self-categorized as public relations or alumni relations personnel, the new fund raisers and their organizations followed a tradition carried over from earlier eras. Annual giving, or raising lower level gifts for operational needs, was managed by staff, whereas campaigns, or raising gifts to meet capital needs, were managed by consultants. This division of labor between internal and external fund raisers helps explain why conventional wisdom during past eras held that the annual fund should be suspended during a capital campaign, which was disproved as fund raising evolved (Pray, 1981).

Research I conducted in the libraries of NSFRE and CASE provided evidence that—apart from a few exceptions related to annual giving—the first full-time staff fund raisers did not appear on the scene until the late 1940s. Furthermore, the first fund-raising employees of colleges and universities (i.e., those who joined ACPRA and AAC before 1970) overwhelmingly worked for private, as opposed to public, institutions.

Chronologically examining books and early volumes of ACPRA's journal, only a handful of references to staff fund raisers were found before 1946. For example, John Price Jones (1949) made no mention of internal practitioners in his 1949 book, yet in Pollard's 1958 book, *Fund-Raising for Higher Education*, there are references to staff who raise gifts full time. The first chronological reference Gurin (1985) made to staff fund raisers in his autobiography was in the late 1960s, when he terminated counseling service for Manhattan College, but the campaign momentum was maintained by the "college's vice president for development" (p. 46). Addressing all types of organizations, Sharpe (1989) summarized, "Until the early 1950's, very few charities had professional staff members running fund-raising operations" (p. 40).

A review of the members-news section in ACPRA's journal through 1955 revealed that private universities primarily hired the early internal fund raisers for education. For example, a 1949 issue reported that Howard Thompson became assistant to the vice president for university development at Cornell University in February of that year and the private institution's third member of ACPRA ("For your information," 1949). "His duties at Cornell are to assist in the intensive fund-raising campaign, which is advancing vigorously, as readers of the New York City newspapers have lately been much aware" (p. 22). In the same section, the University of Bridgeport—another private institution—announced that its public relations office had appointed two "special development fund assistants" (p. 22).

As a point of clarification, the term *development* has a long history in education fund raising. According to Cutlip (1965/1990), it was first suggested by President Ernest DeWitt Burton of the University of Chicago for the institution's 1924–1925 campaign. Worth (1993), drawing from consultant Robert Stuhr, also placed the term's origin in Illinois during the 1920s, but for a capital campaign for a different private university, Northwestern.[4] The early use of *development* by educational institutions and its adoption by hospitals and other organizations help explain why the term *fund raiser* did not appear in print until 1957.

In 1955, the year John Price Jones sold his consulting firm, the State of New York passed what Cutlip (1965/1990) described as a "trail-blazing legislative act requiring registration and reporting by fund-raising organizations and professional fund raisers" (p. 343). During the next 10 years, 25 other states followed New York's lead. Also in 1955, AAFRC established its new central office in New York City. It was first headed by David Church, a former Jones executive and newspaperman. In effect, 1955 marked the passage of AAFRC from a largely unknown trade association to the leading national voice for the fund-raising occupation.

In 1959, it began tracking gifts and disseminating the data in its annual report, *Giving USA*, which was first published in 1955 and now is the foremost source of statistics on philanthropy (AAFRC Trust for Philanthropy, 1997b). AAFRC later began publishing *Giving USA Update*, a quarterly newsletter about legal, economic, and social developments affecting the charitable subsector. Joined by NSFRE, AHP, CASE, and IS in later years, it undertook an active lobbying role on behalf of 501(c)(3) organizations and fund raising.

In 1960, the National Society of Fund Raisers—renamed NSFRE in 1978—was founded in New York City with 137 members. NSFRE's beginning demonstrated a need for an association other than AAFRC, AAC, and ACPRA to serve a growing number of practitioners. Consultant Bruce Flessner (cited in H. Hall, 1993b), a partner of Bentz Whaley Flessner, identified the time line separating the eras of transition and staff fund raisers in a provocative charge made at the 1993 NSFRE International Conference: Although organizations now employ thousands of practitioners, giving as a percentage of GDP has not changed since the early 1960s "when most nonprofits either had no fund raisers or only a very few" (p. 24). The unchanged statistic, Flessner argued, prompts legitimate questions about whether fund raisers have made any real difference, which this book addresses in later chapters.

---

[4]Some observers, such as Hawthorne (1950), claimed Stuhr was a development officer on the staff of Northwestern University during its 1920s campaign, which would qualify him as one of the first staff fund raisers. Unfortunately, writers do not differentiate staff from resident campaign directors, who—although they occupied offices on site for long periods of time—were employees of consulting firms. Research based on primary sources is needed to verify the claim.

Era of Staff Fund Raisers

In 1965, the consulting firm of Bowen & Gurin, Inc.—a member of AAFRC—added part-time campaign counseling to its repertoire, having decided that providing resident campaign direction would dwindle in importance for the firm (Gurin, 1985). According to Gurin, the turning point was a campaign for the Hackley School in Tarrytown, New York, which could not afford a resident director. A music instructor at the school was appointed half-time director of development, and Gurin's firm supervised and worked closely with him for the duration of the campaign. Gurin himself visited the school twice a month for a charge of 2 days' service. Reflecting on this fund-raising milestone, he stated:

> This experience showed us that a campaign could succeed if we provided only part-time counseling and relied for day-to-day campaign direction on a member of the client's staff who could serve effectively under our supervision. It started us re-examining the basis for resident campaign direction, and it was the beginning of a turning point in our concept of the role of a fund-raising counseling firm in providing campaign services. (p. 19)

When Gurin's firm decided in the late 1960s to completely discontinue resident campaign direction and to provide only campaign counseling, it was alone among AAFRC firms to take this approach. Less than 20 years later, Gurin reported that some firms still offered resident campaign direction, but all offered campaign counseling. Harrah-Conforth and Borsos (1991) concluded from their historical study, "The days of resident (or field) managers . . . are quickly fading" (p. 30). Gurin (1985) identified the main reason: "Contributing importantly to this trend has been the greatly strengthened development staffs at major institutions who are capable of day-to-day campaign management" (p. 127).

Functional Changes.   Among those institutions with increased in-house fund-raising capability were hospitals. The National Association for Hospital Development was founded in 1967, and renamed AHP in 1991. Attesting to the recent emergence of staff practitioners, a survey by the association showed that 50% of its members' departments were less than 7 years old in 1988 (Stehle, 1989).

Whereas private universities began hiring staff fund raisers immediately after World War II, few public institutions established fund-raising departments before the 1970s. Brittingham and Pezzullo (1990) stated, "Almost all coordinated and centralized development activity in higher education is less than 40 years old, with only 25 percent of all institutions reporting a centralized development function as recently as 1970" (p. 82). The 25% primarily were private universities. According to Wheat (cited in Worth, 1993) fund-raising programs at public colleges and universities were, on average, 12 years old in 1987. Therefore, public institutions—in particular universities—typically began managing fund raising as a staff function in 1975. Economic and sociopolitical factors related to the 1970s benchmark, such as decreased state appropriations, are described in Kelly (1991a).

Supporting my assessment but giving the wrong decade, Royster Hedgepeth (1993), now vice chancellor for advancement at the University of Massachusetts–Amherst, said fund raising for public institutions "is essentially a phenomenon of the 1980s" (p. 323). He continued, "To be sure, there have been some notable post-World

War II exceptions, such as the University of Michigan and the Kansas Endowment Association. But in general, the widespread, concerted pursuit of private funds by public universities is a relatively new element in American philanthropy" (p. 323).

Exceptions in addition to those mentioned by Hedgepeth occurred in parts of the country other than the Midwest. For example, Mixer (1993) said he became the first full-time fund raiser for the largest public system of higher education, the University of California, in 1959, when he was hired as "statewide gifts and endowments officer" (p. xix). Regardless, public institutions did not hire staff fund raisers in mass until the 1970s.

CASE was formed in December 1974 through the merger of AAC and ACPRA.[5] Until then, animosity between members of the two associations had thwarted efforts to consolidate. Pray (1981) reminisced, "Only someone who remembers how fiercely and, occasionally, with what anger specialists in the early days of fund raising, public relations, and alumni affairs fought to keep their individual turf can appreciate how far we have come in submerging individual differences in a common emphasis on institutional well-being" (p. 3).

At the Greenbrier conference 16 years earlier, representatives of ACPRA and AAC had "hammered out the concept of the contemporary organization of college and university relations" (Pray, 1991, p. 2). The term *advancement* was conceived to encompass the three functions, and, according to Dittman (1981), "Today the organization of the 'advancement' division is essentially what was proposed in 1958: a coordinating officer (usually vice-president), an alumni program officer, a public relations officer (incorporating public information, publications, special events, and the like), and a fund-raising officer (usually director of development)" (p. 227).

Fund raisers eventually assumed most of the coordinating officer positions, much to the surprise of practitioners in the older functions. As discussed in chapters 6 and 9, relations among the specializations are not as harmonious as leaders envisioned.

Turning to other types of organizations, The Fund Raising School also was founded in 1974, when practitioners Hank Rosso, Joe Mixer, and Lyle Cook formed a for-profit business that later was changed to a nonprofit (Mixer, personal communication, March 1996). The school's creation signified the existence of a market of fund raisers in need of training, presumably practitioners who were—or hoped to be—employed by different types of charitable organizations. A synopsis of the evolution of fund raising at New York's Metropolitan Museum of Art illustrates the emergence of this market. Before 1975, the museum had only one person in its fund-raising office (Stehle, 1992a). It conducted its first capital campaign between 1975 and 1981, raising $98 million. By 1992, the museum employed a fund-raising staff of 17. In 1994, the Metropolitan Museum of Art raised $62 million in 1 year and publicly launched a $300-million capital campaign, the largest to date for an American museum (AAFRC Trust for Philanthropy, 1995; "Philanthropy 400," 1995).

By the beginning of the 1980s, according to Bintzer (1981), the dominant role for consultants was "campaign-advisory" (p. 219). NSFRE's 1988 survey (Klein, 1988) showed that the greatest use of consultants during the previous 2 years was to conduct feasibility studies for capital campaigns (45%), followed by campaign advisement

---

[5]CASE's first president was Alice Beeman, the first woman to head a national fund-raising or public relations association.

(43%). Consultant usage then dropped substantially to assistance with planned giving (23%) and annual giving (21%). By the end of the decade, organizations with large fund-raising staffs were launching campaigns without hiring consultants to serve as advisers. A university president interviewed by Cook (1994a) explained, "We had no consultants during [our last] campaign, and I think that's fairly typical of a larger institution because a larger institution is able to bring its own resources [to the effort]" (p. 306). In other words, contemporary employment of consultants is positively related to capital campaigns and negatively related to the number of staff fund raisers.

Contextual Changes.   As the function was internalized, important changes took place in the overall context in which fund raising is practiced. Specifically, the newest era coincided with the beginning of government intervention, which in turn spurred research on philanthropy and nonprofits.

As described in chapter 2, from the time the federal income tax was introduced in 1913 until 1969, the only substantive changes in the law were to increase incentives for giving. The Tax Reform Act of 1969 marked the first punitive action by government. Targeted primarily at private foundations, the act imposed strict and costly rules on their creation and operation (e.g., the mandated payout rate). Charitable organizations also were subjected to new regulations. For example, all 501(c)(3) organizations were required—for the first time—to file annual financial statements with the IRS (i.e., Form 990). Whereas such organizations had enjoyed a high degree of freedom in the past, the 1970s introduced government oversight and a different legal context for raising gifts, which is detailed in chapter 7. The 1969 tax act, according to P. D. Hall (1992b), "underlined the vulnerability of the charitable tax-exempt universe" (p. 406).

Fears of further Congressional action prompted leaders to establish the National Commission on Private Philanthropy and Public Needs—more commonly known as the Filer Commission for its chair, the late John Filer, who was chairman of the Aetna Life & Casualty Company. Magat (1991) described the commission's significance: "The first major attempt to gather data systematically and produce analyses of the field did not occur until the Filer Commission was established in 1973. That entity commissioned 77 papers, which were published in five volumes in 1977" (p. 1).[6] Powell (1987) added, "These research papers provided scholars and policy-makers with a baseline knowledge, circa the mid-1970s, of the scope and operations of the nonprofit sector" (p. xi).

Until the 1970s, then, little was known about philanthropy and the organizations for which fund raisers work. As stated in the opening lines of the commission's recommendations, "On the map of American society, one of the least charted regions is . . . the Third Sector . . . . [which] remains something of a terra incognita, barely explored in terms of its inner dynamics and motivations, and its social, economic and political relations to the rest of the world" (Filer, 1993, p. 51). Illustrative of the lack of knowledge uncovered by the commission, gifts were expected to be the principal source of income for charitable organizations, but researchers found that government provided a substantial portion of the subsector's funding.

---

[6]The Filer Commission actually issued seven volumes, one of recommendations and six of research papers.

The Filer Commission originally hoped its work would be institutionalized by the federal government in the form of a bureau of philanthropy within the Department of the Treasury. President Jimmy Carter's administration declined to cooperate. "So," P. D. Hall (1993a) explained, "the research effort initiated by the commission had to be carried forward in other ways. One of these was the creation of an academic base for nonprofits research" (p. 278).

The Program On Non-Profit Organizations (PONPO) was established in 1977 at Yale University's Institution for Social and Policy Studies, largely through the efforts of then Yale President Kingman Brewster and John D. Rockefeller, III, who personally pledged $250,000 to start the center. Brewster (1989) stressed that at the time PONPO was founded, nonprofit organizations lacked any connective theory of their governance or their function in society.[7] By the end of 1980, PONPO had received more than $1 million in gift commitments—primarily from private foundations—to sponsor research on "the philosophical basis and the long-term societal aspects of the third sector" (P. D. Hall, 1990, p. 250).

A second "way" the Filer Commission's research was carried forward was through IS, which was founded in 1980. P. D. Hall (1993a) stated, "At the same time [PONPO began], efforts were under way to create an umbrella organization, Independent Sector, for all national philanthropic and voluntary organizations that would count among its goals the promotion and dissemination of research" (p. 278). In addition to research, IS assumed a major role in mediating relations between its constituency and the federal government, thereby becoming the sector's leading voice on national issues.

In 1989, U.S. giving exceeded $100 billion for the first time, and staff practitioners dominated fund-raising practice.[8] Mongon (1992) identified "a decrease in the proportion of workers in . . . consulting positions" (p. 24) as a trend supported by NSFRE's survey findings. Consultants now constitute only 7.5% of the fund raisers belonging to NSFRE (1996). They represented just 6% of the 1,748 members of AHP, CASE, and NSFRE included in Duronio's (1993, 1994b) study. Students should keep in mind that AAFRC had only 22 member firms in 1996.

Edith Falk (cited in Gonzalez-Campoy, 1996), cofounder of the AAFRC firm, Campbell & Company, described the changed conditions for consultants: "Twenty years ago, we would come in and run campaigns from the inside. Today, since more organizations are hiring full-time development officers, we are doing more assessments of development programs and many more feasibility studies (p. 36). Gonzalez-Campoy (1996) elaborated, "Whereas consultants once worked directly with a volunteer leader, they are now more likely to work with a *staff* leader—that is, with another fund-raising professional" (p. 38; italics in original).

Evidence suggests that even in their new advisory role, consultants are losing ground. Mongon (1992) reported, "Despite the cost of counsel, respondents admit to following their advice 'exactly' or 'almost all of it' only 21.2 percent of the time

---

[7]Brewster also admitted that the hyphenated spelling of *nonprofit* in PONPO's name was a stylistic mistake in 1977, as it is today.

[8]The AAFRC Trust for Philanthropy (1989) originally reported that the $100-billion benchmark was broken in 1988, when it estimated total giving at $104 billion; however, the 1988 estimate was later revised to only $98 billion, making 1989's total of $107 billion the official milestone (AAFRC Trust for Philanthropy, 1996).

compared to 45 percent just four years ago!" (p. 14). Gonzalez-Campoy (1996) pointed out that "as traditional markets close or require less from consultants" (p. 38), they are scouting different types of clients, such as religious organizations, which are believed to have few staff fund raisers.

Rosso (1991) arbitrarily dated the fund-raising function from World War II, stating, "In the contemporary period, the planning, directing, and implementing of fund raising [*sic*] plans are more the responsibility of an in-house practitioner than they have ever been in the past" (p. xvii). He briefly added, "The phenomenon of program management by in-house staff is increasingly apparent and will continue to be so into the future" (p. xvii).

FOUR MODELS OF FUND RAISING

The chapter now turns to models of fund raising, or the different ways fund raising was practiced in the past and still is practiced today. These models complement the historical eras just discussed in that they constitute a theory describing *how* fund raising has been practiced. Unlike the chronological eras, however, the models did not supersede each other, but rather the emergence of a new model added to the different ways of practicing fund raising.

The models have been conceptualized and tested through a program of research spanning the last 8 years. In 1989, I used public relations models as an analytical tool to exam the history of U.S. fund raising. Based on the qualitative analysis, I concluded that fund raising has evolved through four historical stages, which also represent four models of practice. I also found evidence in the literature that these models continue to be used by contemporary charitable organizations (Kelly, 1991a).

In the second phase of theory building, I empirically tested the models in a national survey of 296 fund-raising practitioners. Findings of the 1992 study showed that the models do describe the typical ways fund raising presently is practiced and provided supportive evidence as to their reliability, validity, and accuracy (Kelly, 1994a, 1995b). A third phase of the program, undertaken in 1993, investigated *why* charitable organizations practice the models they do (Kelly, 1995a).

Results from the second and third phases of research, as well as illustrations of the models' continued use, are given in chapter 6. A reanalysis of the historical study is presented here. This section first introduces the fund-raising models and their characteristics. It then documents the four historical stages and the models they represent, drawing from many of the sources cited earlier.

Characteristics of the Models

In 1984, James Grunig (J. E. Grunig & Hunt, 1984) introduced four models of public relations, which he derived from the combinations of communication direction (one-way vs. two-way) and balance of intended effects (asymmetrical vs. symmetrical). Applying those models to the specialization of fund raising, I identified and identically named four typical ways fund raising has been and is practiced: (a) the press agentry model, (b) the public information model, (c) the two-way asymmetrical model, and (d) the two-way symmetrical model.

These models are representations of the values, goals, and behaviors held and enacted by charitable organizations when they practice fund raising—simplified in the same way a perfect vacuum is simplified in the physical sciences. As explained by J. E. Grunig and Hunt (1984): "In scientific usage, a model is a representation of reality. The human mind can never grasp all of reality in total, but it can isolate and grasp parts of that reality. It then uses those parts of reality to construct ideas. Those ideas model reality, although they also simplify it by not including all of reality" (p. 21). Due to simplification, then, not everything any single organization or fund raiser does will fit any of the four models perfectly. Furthermore, the models are not practiced exclusively. Organizations and their fund raisers use all four models to some extent; however, they practice one model predominantly.

Table 5.2 presents the four models of fund raising with their major characteristics. Students will recognize from the earlier discussion names of historical figures associated with the three oldest models. Starting with the first, the leading historical figures of the press agentry model are Charles Sumner Ward and Lyman Pierce, the YMCA fund raisers who developed the "whirlwind campaign method" beginning in 1902. The purpose of press agentry is to propagandize a cause. The nature of communication of the model is one-way from organization to donor, with little research conducted. Its effects are unbalanced; that is to say, the model is asymmetrical because communications are intended to affect the receiver (e.g., change prospective donors' behavior), but not the organizational source. The press agentry model is dependent on emotions to raise money, and truth is not an essential factor. Its practice is based on principles of manipulation and control. As such, this oldest model also is the most unethical and socially irresponsible of the four.

TABLE 5.2
Characteristics of Four Models of Fund Raising

	Models			
Characteristics	*Press Agentry*	*Public Information*	*Two-Way Asymmetrical*	*Two-Way Symmetrical*
Beginning date	1902–	1916–	1919–	1980–
Purpose	Propagandize a cause	Disseminate needs information	Scientifically persuade giving	Reach mutual understanding
Nature of communication	One-way Unbalanced effects Truth not important	One-way Unbalanced effects Truth important	Two-way Unbalanced effects	Two-way Balanced effects
Model of communication	Source→Receiver	Source→Receiver	Source↔Receiver (Feedback)	Group↔Group
Nature of dependency	Emotions	Enlightenment	Accessibility	Agreement
Nature of research	Little	Little	Formative Evaluative of money	Formative Evaluative of autonomy and accountability
Leading historical figures	Charles Sumner Ward Lyman L. Pierce	Bishop William Lawrence Ivy L. Lee	John Price Jones	Few educators and "reflective practitioners"

The historical figures identified with the public information model are Bishop William Lawrence and Ivy Lee, who—together in 1916—developed an approach different from press agentry to raise $9 million for the Episcopal Church Pension Fund. The purpose of the public information model is to disseminate needs information. Whereas the press agentry model is dependent on emotions, the public information model relies on "enlightenment" (i.e., fund raising is dependent on rational, intelligent, and compassionate donor publics). The nature of communication is one-way and asymmetrical. Similar to press agentry, little research is conducted by its practitioners. In contrast, truth is important.

The leading historical figure of the two-way asymmetrical model is John Price Jones, whose devotion to research and planning was a distinguishing characteristic of the consulting firm he founded in 1919. The purpose of this model is to scientifically persuade giving, and the nature of communication is two-way, with unbalanced effects. The two-way asymmetrical model is dependent on the accessibility of donors (i.e., the degree to which they are open to influence). It uses formative research to shape persuasive communications that will be readily accepted. Results are evaluated by indiscriminate dollar totals.

As given in Table 5.2, the purpose of the two-way symmetrical model is to reach mutual understanding with donor publics. The nature of its communication is two-way between groups, with balanced, or symmetrical, effects. Rather than source to receiver, the group-to-group distinction emphasizes this model's orientation to systems theory and the environmental interdependencies of donors and charitable organizations. In contrast to the reliance of press agentry on donor emotions, of public information on enlightenment, and of two-way asymmetrical on accessibility, the two-way symmetrical model is dependent on donor agreement with the organization's mission and the means by which it carries out that mission (i.e., its purpose and program services).

The two-way symmetrical model uses formative research not only to match donor interest and shape communications, but also to sometimes change the organization's behavior when it is in disharmony with strategic donor publics (i.e., it balances the needs of the organization and its donors). Practice of the model is based on principles of collaborative negotiation and conflict resolution. In accord with systems theory, fund raising is evaluated by how well it protects and enhances organizational autonomy and accountability, more so than by the amount of money it generates. No historical figure is associated with this newest model; a few current educators and "reflective practitioners" defined its characteristics.

Whereas the four models constitute a positive theory in that they describe how fund raising is practiced, the two-way symmetrical model provides a normative theory of how fund raising *should* be practiced to be ethical and effective. Paraphrasing public relations scholars J. E. Grunig and L. A. Grunig (1992), only the most recent model represents a break from the predominant worldview that fund raising is a way of manipulating donor publics for the benefit of the organization. Although some may argue with use of the term *manipulation*, preferring instead the term *persuasion*, I agree with J. E. Grunig (1989b), who said "changing the word does not change the mindset" (p. 18).

Press Agentry Stage and Model

As given earlier, Marts credited the development of the campaign method of fund raising to the YMCA and dated its beginning at 1901–1902 (Cutlip, 1965/1990). In 1902, Lyman Pierce began a campaign to raise $300,000 toward construction of a new YMCA building in Washington, DC. Pierce called in Charles Sumner Ward, a Y secretary from Chicago, to help raise the last $80,000 when the campaign stalled in 1905. Together, they met the goal through an intensive 1-week drive, after which they adopted the collaboratively developed programming as their standard practice of fund raising.

Cutlip (1965/1990) proclaimed, "The whirlwind, intensive campaign to raise large sums of money in a short period of time by bombarding the public with surefire appeals and by recruiting scores of volunteers to solicit many times their number had its origins in the Young Men's Christian Association" (p. 38). Distinctive programming elements, including the two highlighted by Cutlip, were a short public time period, an army of volunteers, a competitive atmosphere, gimmicks—such as a clock—to apply pressure on volunteers and prospective donors, and a great deal of publicity and emotion.

In agreement, Harrah-Conforth and Borsos (1991) said the approach of the YMCA secretaries was "characterized by heavily publicized competition among teams of volunteers" (p. 31). Bintzer (1981) stated, "They brought their skills to bear on training volunteers, whipping up enthusiasm, *promoting the cause*, scheduling report meetings, holding a victory dinner, and then departing the scene" (p. 216; italics added).

Ward (cited in Cutlip, 1965/1990) himself called his way of practicing fund raising the "intensive method" (p. 82). He told his campaign assistants, "The press, pulpit, and the active *propaganda* form an educational force by which practically every individual in a community may be reached" (p. 92; italics added). He candidly disclosed the origins of his strategy: "To get the agony over with quickly was the main idea which prompted this movement" (p. 41).

According to Cutlip (1965/1990), Ward "put his emphasis on systematic organization and on pressure created through saturation publicity" (p. 92). Both Ward and Pierce "were impelled by a missionary zeal, regarded their work as 'Christian stewardship,' and said so on many occasions" (p. 43). From their fervor and intensive method, the press agentry model developed and spread in use.

Three campaigns directed by Ward before World War I serve to describe the first historical stage of fund raising and its press agentry model. In 1911, Ward took on his first hospital campaign while still a YMCA secretary.[9] Cutlip (1965/1990) reported, "Ward was a strong believer in a saturation publicity drive to build a favorable opinion climate for the competing teams of solicitors. He usually hired a local newspaperman for the publicity task" (p. 82). Ward hired Frederick Courtenay Barber for the Salem City Hospital campaign.

Reminiscent of P. T. Barnum of circus fame—who is the historical figure identified with the press agentry model of public relations, as opposed to fund raising—Barber was described by Cutlip (1965/1990) as a "flamboyant showman," who also was "a

---

[9]Cutlip and others do not explain why or how Ward and Pierce, who were employed by one organization, spent considerable time on and received substantial payment for work done on behalf of other organizations.

hard drinker" (p. 80). He combined "his flair for showmanship with the lessons Ward had taught him" (p. 83) to start the first fund-raising firm 2 years after the Salem campaign.

Carlton Ketchum (cited in Cutlip, 1965/1990), who once worked for Barber's firm, pronounced him "a man of great inherent ability, but with absolutely no self-control and very few principles" (p. 87). Marts (cited in Cutlip, 1965/1990) said Barber was "a spectacular personality who organized community campaigns with all the fanfare and spectacle of a circus" (p. 83). He elaborated:

> [Barber] put on a great show and charged substantial fees, and I suspect in many cases operated on a percentage basis. A friend . . . has told me of the parade which Barber organized as a part of his campaign publicity. At the head of the parade, in a beautiful phaeton, with high stepping horses, rode Barber himself, in a frock coat and a high silk hat. The contrast between the Barber type of circus and the Lyman Pierce and Charles Ward type of behind the scenes campaign is very striking. (p. 83)

Students will recall that Marts believed Barber gave fund raising a bad name and that pioneer consultants later disavowed his firm. Yet Barber's behavior cannot be distanced from the fund-raising practice of Ward and Pierce, the forefathers of the Y school to which Ketchum and Marts—among others—belonged. Harrah-Conforth and Borsos (1991) affirmed, "Despite later attempts to draw clearcut distinctions between Barber and the YMCA men, clippings in the Pierce scrapbooks . . . reveal evidence of carnival-like, fund-raiser-center campaigns with cartoons and pictures of Pierce featured prominently in local campaign coverage" (p. 23). As mentioned earlier, these authors and Cutlip found evidence that both Ward and Pierce took commissions at least on occasion. The Y school, then, represented the press agentry model with its characteristics of propagandizing a cause, dependency on emotions, and a cavalier regard for truth.

"Having perfected his campaign methods in terms of thousands, Ward now decided the time was right to go after millions" (Cutlip, 1965/1990, p. 85). In November 1913, Ward launched a campaign to raise the unprecedented sum of $4 million in just 2 weeks for new buildings for the YMCA and YWCA of Greater New York. Cutlip called the campaign a "whirlwind assault on New York's pocketbook" (p. 85). Collectively addressing the early campaigns, he said Ward was not only raising money, but also "teaching persons of means the often painful lesson of their obligation to support charitable causes and conditioning the public to the *high-pressure fund drive* which today is commonplace in our society" (p. 87; italics added).

Although not stressed by Cutlip, the New York campaign illustrated the principle of proportionate giving, which is explained in chapter 11, and the artificialness of high-dollar goals for broad-based drives. Piecing together information provided by Cutlip and by Marts (1953), just 7 donors gave $1.7 million (41%) of the total $4.1 million raised, another 393 donors gave $1.9 million (47%), and the remaining 17,000 donors contributed less than $500,000 (12%). In other words, the publicity, armies of volunteers, and manufactured emotion and pressure can be viewed as elaborate theatrics—involving a cast of thousands—primarily undertaken to provide a conducive setting for soliciting just 400 wealthy donors, who gave almost 90% of the money. Seymour (cited in Schwartz, 1990), it is recalled, described the dimes and dollars raised in later campaigns as "sound effects for the appeal to larger gifts" (p. xx). About 50 years after the New York campaign, historian Daniel Boorstin (1962) coined the term *pseudoevents*, which appropriately fits such press agentry efforts.

In May 1914, Ward launched his first campaign for an educational institution when he attempted to raise $3 million for the University of Pittsburgh in just 10 days. Two Pitt students, Carlton and George Ketchum, were chosen to assist Ward during the 5 months of planning that preceded the 10-day campaign.

The discrepancy between the longer "quiet time" of planning and the announced time limits of the campaign's public phase is important because it reveals again the theatrics of press agentry fund raising. The drama of short constraints for the public phase imposes an artificial sense of urgency so that emotions can be sustained and pressure brought to bear. As Cutlip (1965/1990) stated, Ward and Pierce "exulted in their dramatic, last-minute push to meet a goal deadline by a fixed date and hour" (p. 52).

Ward's campaign for Pitt failed to reach its $3-million goal. Cutlip (1965/1990) presented his research findings:

> The president's report concerning this campaign states that in the allotted ten days "nearly $2,000,000 was raised" and that "the (Alumni Fund) Committee will double its efforts until the remaining amount is raised." The records in the University of Pittsburgh Library give nothing to indicate that the remaining million was ever raised. Carlton Ketchum thinks $2.1 million was raised. Ward was retained and paid a fee by the Alumni Fund Committee, presumably out of the funds raised. (p. 86)

The failure of the campaign also is important because it and similar failures of press agentry fund raising rarely are mentioned in the literature (i.e., the literature—most of which is written by senior practitioners—generally ignores or whitewashes failures). For example, in his 1961 book, Marts reported that Pittsburgh was the first college to use the new campaign method *effectively* as a means of raising capital funds. He further reported that Pierce, who was general secretary of the Pittsburgh YMCA at the time, participated as a volunteer worker in the "successful campaign" (p. 110). The issue of overlooked failures is returned to shortly.

The press agentry model quickly spread beyond the application of Ward and Pierce. Significantly, it was adopted by the new fund-raising federations that had been formed to combat social problems in the Progressive movement of the early 1900s. The federations first relied on letter appeals, personal calls on prospective donors by the organizations' trustees or paid secretary, and—in many instances—paid solicitors. Cutlip (1965/1990) quoted William Norton, a federation pioneer: "Although this combination of methods . . . produced more money than had been raised by the separate agencies previously, the increase did not satisfy the pressure of the agencies for funds. Consequently the campaign method of raising money became . . . universal. It produced larger sums than any known means of fund raising" (pp. 25–26). Cutlip concluded, "Fund raising for the new federations accelerated the spread of the 'whirlwind' money-raising campaign, as the Ward–Pierce technique was coming to be called" (p. 75).

Headed by publicists, who Cutlip frequently referred to as good propagandists, the federations concentrated on getting their names before the general public through the mass media. Cutlip (1965/1990) explained, "The federation idea had brought the need for the intensive fund-raising campaign which in turn had necessitated intensive publicity" (p. 81). Saying there was "understandable concern about the publicist's exploitation of the fear motive," Cutlip declared, "Yet something as new, as flamboyant, and as tainted with overtones of *'press agentry'* . . . would naturally draw the fire of many conservative businessmen and publicity-shy social workers" (p. 81; italics added). The long-standing relationship between the press agentry model and federations, such as today's United Way system, is discussed further in chapter 6.

Keeping in mind that the models did not supersede each other, Ward and Pierce used press agentry to raise funds for the Red Cross War Council during World War I. Whereas the dollar results reported earlier were impressive, fund raising was characterized by pressure, competition, emotion, and even coercion. Cutlip (1965/1990) illustrated with the following description of the first Red Cross campaign: "A quota was set for each city, town, and hamlet to give it a goal to reach. . . . City was matched against city in the fund-raising competition—an old technique of Ward's. . . . All media vied to promote the cause of the Red Cross and thus prove their patriotism. As the Kansas City Star thundered, 'Kansas City must have no slackers'" (p. 117).

Students should understand that wars—as do other manmade and natural disasters—create their own sense of urgency (i.e., the urgency of need is not artificially induced). Given America's tradition of philanthropy, it is not surprising that an intensive, systematic model of fund raising during a national emergency would generate a great deal of money.

The press agentry model was perpetuated after the war when those trained by Ward and Pierce founded their own firms based on ideas about mass persuasion that came out of the work of the Red Cross. For example, the $15-million campaign for the Presbyterian Church Pension Fund, directed by Marts' firm in the late 1920s, was conducted "in the new post-World War I pattern of high-pressure methods and widespread solicitation" (Cutlip, 1965/1990, p. 286). Cutlip commented, "Marts himself knew the art of using emotion-laden publicity methods" (p. 288). When a starving, retired Presbyterian minister was found slumped against a wall in a midwestern city, Marts' firm dramatized the incident to promote the campaign. Marts evaluated the technique employed as "one of the most striking newspaper releases for stirring a lot of action and emotion" (p. 288).

Press agentry continued to be heavily used decades after the second and third models of fund raising were introduced. For example, the oldest model was evident in the Red Cross drives of World War II. As Cutlip (1965/1990) claimed, "It is doubtful if any appeal for funds has achieved the support of publicity equal to that achieved by the Red Cross and its allies in loading the nation's news channels with fervent heat-moving Red Cross appeals during the Second World War" (p. 419). The 1945 drive, which raised $231 million in 31 days, was the most intensive and lucrative. Some of the applied fund-raising techniques were booklets, leaflets, billboards, posters, magazine features, movie promotions and collections, speeches, window displays, calendars, and media ads. The "avalanche of publicity" (p. 420) also included a plea by President Franklin D. Roosevelt in his last address on radio. Cutlip summarized, "Every known tool of the public relations practice was used to enroll and guide 4 million volunteer workers . . . . [who were] asking many, many others to give—and to give now" (p. 422).

According to Marts (1961), the intensive campaign method had raised more than $75 billion by the early 1960s. However, he also reported that the giving public had repeatedly rebelled against this way of practicing fund raising:

> The first time was in the mid-1920's when hundreds of colleges took up the new "campaign" methods with a rush and all over the land began to pressure their alumni to "pay their debt to alma mater." . . . Too much was said about the fact that alma mater had given them an education below costs and that they should now pay up. This worked well enough once, but when alma mater made a big point of the same debt a few years later in a second appeal to the same alumni, some cynicism and resentment resulted. (p. 55)

The Christian philanthropic tradition credited to Ward, Pierce, and their followers stands in juxtaposition to their press agentry practice. Furthermore, unlike the impression given in most of the literature, the model was not as pragmatically successful as commonly assumed. Although it generated billions of dollars, there is evidence of frequent failures and ethical abuses.

Scattered throughout the middle of his book, Cutlip (1965/1990) provided illustrations of Y-school campaigns that failed to reach their goals. The 1919 Red Cross drive, for example, "failed dismally and set off a wave of bitter criticism" (p. 209). A 1925 campaign managed by Tamblyn & Brown for the Cathedral of St. John the Divine in New York City finally ended after a time period three times longer than announced, a $5-million shortfall in its $15-million goal, and media charges of misrepresentation and hypocrisy.

Cutlip (1965/1990) said the Y fund raisers were familiar with criticism about their way of practice. Pierce, for example, was to hear complaints "many times before his career as a professional fund raiser ended with his death on the eve of World War II, and so would others" (pp. 334–335).[10] Cutlip concluded, "Ward's systematic organization of solicitation that brought the strongest possible pressure on those catalogued as able to give was bound to outrage many. But the system brought in the cash to meet campaign goals!" (p. 87).

Public Information Stage and Model

Cutlip (1965/1990) stated early in his book, "The American genius for system and efficiency was first applied to fund raising by two YMCA workers and an Episcopal bishop" (p. 38). Using "an entirely different approach" from Ward and Pierce, Bishop William Lawrence and Ivy Ledbetter Lee introduced the public information model of fund raising in 1916. Lawrence had raised substantial funds for two colleges as a volunteer during the era of nonspecialists. In 1915, he took leave from his diocesan position to become the full-time director of a campaign to raise $5 million for the Church Pension Fund, which would support retired Episcopal clergy and the families of those who were deceased.

Lee, a former journalist, was the best known of the early 20th-century publicists. Unlike press agents of the period, he based his practice on principles of openness and

---

[10]Ward died in 1929.

truth to help his clients, such as the Rockefeller family, deal with the mass media and public opinion. According to J. E. Grunig and Hunt (1984), "Lee viewed the public as made up of rational human beings who, if they are given complete and accurate information, would make the right decisions" (p. 34). Lee is the historical figure associated with the public information model of public relations.

Convinced that publicity "was the great problem" for the upcoming campaign's success, Lawrence consulted his friend Edward Bok, the famous editor of *The Ladies Home Journal*. Bok's advice was to "depict, describe your pathetic cases," because, he said, "People give when their sympathies are touched" (Cutlip, 1965/1990, p. 96). "Elated by this guidance from a distinguished editor, Lawrence returned to New York and invited Ivy Lee to his office for a conference" (p. 96). Lee rejected the advice, saying that repeated cries for help had made it impossible to depict an old parson or his widow and orphan in such a way as to move people to contribute. He told Lawrence, "The sympathies of the American people are bruised and raw.... Moreover, in the long run emotional appeals lose their force. The American people, intelligent, just, and generous to a cause that appeals to them, want facts and figures" (pp. 96–97).

Lee's views on enlightened donor publics and their desire for information formed the foundation of the public information model developed by Lawrence and Lee and applied to the Church Pension Fund. Cutlip (1965/1990) reported, "A campaign of publicity based on facts more than on emotion is what these two shrewd students of public behavior agreed upon in conferences over the next week" (p. 97).

The public information model of fund raising reflected Lawrence's New England distaste of public display. He was repelled by the high-pressure and theatrical campaigns of press agentry. Lawrence (cited in Cutlip, 1965/1990) wrote in a magazine article, "I dislike the word 'campaign' in this connection almost as much as I abhor 'appeal.' 'Campaign' suggests force or pressure, methods whereby people are dragooned to give. 'Appeal' suggests a call upon the sympathies and emotions of people, melting them to give. Both methods are weak and liable to bring reaction" (p. 51).

In contrast to Ward's campaigns that were measured in days, the Church Pension Fund drive was scheduled to run for 14 months, beginning January 1, 1916. By the deadline on March 1, 1917, the $5-million goal had been surpassed but "the flood of contributions continued" (Cutlip, 1965/1990, p. 99). By September 1917, the dollars raised totaled $9 million, making philanthropic history. Cutlip declared, "Bishop Lawrence had established himself, on the eve of World War I, as America's champion fund raiser" (p. 99).

Lawrence's biographer attributed the bishop's success to his belief in enlightened people. "To be sure, he spent untold hours in securing the right publicity, in the arranging of lists, in the writing of letters in his own hand. But fundamental was his faith in the sense of responsibility of the average man and woman" (Cutlip, 1965/1990, p. 268). Lawrence also had become an expert in communication, utilizing both the mass media and such techniques as direct mail. His biographer pointed out the high degree of attention the bishop paid to preparing a printed solicitation: "He always did this with the utmost care, writing and re-writing, and being most particular as to the printing and even the type and color of paper used" (p. 268).

Cutlip (1965/1990) attested, "Lawrence possessed a shrewd sense of publicity and paid much attention to the press" (p. 97). Describing the activities of what students of public relations will recognize as a journalist-in-residence—a characteristic of the public information model of public relations—Cutlip said Lawrence took advantage of slow news days during which to place stories; he added a local angle by having each bishop make an announcement in his own diocese; he deluged the newspapers with facts on the general problem of retirement for all elderly citizens; and by simply adding the name of his organization to the release, he linked his cause to a broader issue of concern on the media's agenda, which helped ensure headline coverage.

Ivy Lee left his consulting firm to work for the American Red Cross War Council during World War I. As head of publicity, he worked closely with Ward and Pierce. At the conclusion of the war, he recommended that the publicity department be demobilized, and he returned to his practice. According to Cutlip (1965/1990), Lee "took his newly enlarged public relations firm into the fund-raising field in its early years" (p. 263). For example, his firm managed the 1919–1920 endowment campaign that raised $14 million for Princeton University—Lee's alma mater. He "publicized the little gift as well as the large" (p. 263).

Similarly, Bishop Lawrence returned to his diocesan duties, but in 1923 undertook the campaign for Harvard, "An Opportunity for National Service." The campaign was geared to large gifts and was not directed at alumni because "Alma Mater's sons had been put through the John Price Jones fund-raising wringer only three years before" (Cutlip, 1965/1990, p. 266).

Little more was heard from these men as fund raisers. Lawrence published his memoirs in 1926, and Lee died in 1934. Yet their model of raising gifts continued. For example, Guy Emerson, who was trained by Lawrence during the Church Pension Fund drive, became a leading fund raiser. More importantly, many of the national health and human services agencies founded during the first decades of the 20th century adopted the public information model.

Until the Church Pension Fund, campaigns largely had been conducted on a local or regional level (e.g., the Greater New York YMCA–YWCA campaign of 1913). The techniques refined by Lawrence were capable of reaching donor publics spread across the country. Many charitable organizations turned to publicity and direct mail as the mainstay of their fund-raising program. Cutlip (1965/1990) illustrated with the National Tuberculosis Association:

> A painless way of raising money would not long go unnoticed by the increasing number of nonprofit organizations springing up in that period . . . . Thus began the annual Christmas seal sale of stamps to "fight T.B." that today annually brings in some $26 million from the mailing of 40 million letters carrying some 12 billion seals to prospective givers. About one out of three letters brings results. The device of the seal to get money, and of high-powered publicity to sell it, had been harnessed together in a new pattern of public fund raising. (p. 57)

Before turning to the third stage of fund-raising practice, it is necessary to emphasize the asymmetrical dimension of the public information model. Although truth is a characteristic and its practitioners do not exploit emotions, the model still is intended to bring about unbalanced effects (e.g., change the behavior of prospective donors but not the organization's). Evidence is found in presuppositions held by its leading historical figures.

Biographer Ray Hiebert (1966) said Lee believed that—similar to lawyers—the publicist does not question the client's motivation, but promotes the client's interest as far as public opinion will permit. Transposed to the public information model of fund raising, no effort is made to balance the organization's needs with the needs of donor prospects; the model is asymmetrical because the organization is right and its interests take precedence. Little research is conducted before communicating. Messages consist of incomplete information, selected to place the organizational sender in a favorable light. Cutlip (1965/1990) recognized a common dimension between Lawrence's approach and the Y-school method: "Like Ward and Pierce, Bishop Lawrence realized that a fund drive must be built upon a platform of public opinion conditioned by *persuasive* publicity" (p. 96; italics added).

Two-Way Asymmetrical Stage and Model

The third fund-raising model emerged from the work of John Price Jones and the firm he founded in 1919. As Pierce was starting the Washington, DC campaign in 1902, Jones was graduating from Harvard. He took a job for 2 years as a secretary to a congressman and then became a reporter for *The Washington Post*, where he stayed for 7 years before moving to New York to work for other newspapers. When he joined an advertising agency in 1917, he was drafted to handle publicity for the Liberty Loan drives, which started him on a career in fund raising.

Cutlip (1965/1990) stated, "Jones came from the world of journalism to bring *a new approach* and new intensity to the art of getting people to give money. He developed a lucrative fund-raising business quite independent of the influence and ideas of the Ward-Pierce-Y school" (p. 170; italics added). Reminiscent of Edward Bernays, who is the leading historical figure associated with the asymmetrical model of public relations, Jones used research to market the needs of his clients. J. E. Grunig and Hunt (1984) described Bernays: "Like other practitioners of the two-way asymmetric model, he most often practiced this role by finding out what the public liked about the organization and then highlighting that aspect . . . or by determining what values and attitudes publics had and then describing the organization in a way that conformed to these values and attitudes" (p. 40).

Identically, Jones used research to find out what donors liked about his clients and to determine the values and attitudes of their prospective donors—the findings of which were then used to shape fund-raising messages. "He undergirded fund appeals, from the early twenties on, with thorough research on the institution to be served, its degree of support, and the case to be presented in the fund appeal" (Cutlip, 1965/1990, p. 183). Curti and Nash (1965) said Jones' fund-raising campaigns for Smith and five other women's colleges "began with careful planning, including a survey of the needs of the colleges and of the social and economic status of alumnae and other potential donors" (p. 204). According to these scholars, "Special attention was given to the kind of publicity likely to be most effective in view of the traditions of the college and the psychology and values of the alumnae" (p. 204). Finally, Cutlip cited one of the recommendations made by a Jones executive at the end of the 1930s Depression: "Greater care must be taken insofar as the larger givers are concerned to determine interests and attitudes so as to make the most effective appeal along the *avenue of least resistance*" (p. 318; italics added).

Emphasizing this distinguishing characteristic of the two-way asymmetrical model, Cutlip (1965/1990) stated, "Jones brought to fund raising a deep appreciation for the value of research and planning" (p. 170). He added, "Jones's fetish for research, for careful record keeping, and for thorough planning made the methodical Charles S. Ward appear slovenly and haphazard by comparison" (p. 170). In other words, the newer model of fund raising—unlike those that had preceded it—employed two-way communication through formative research on donor publics. Its intended effects, however, were still unbalanced in that research was conducted not to help the organization adapt to donors' needs and interests (i.e., affect the organization), but to make prospective donors believe and behave as the organization wished (i.e., persuade them to give).

The impact Jones had on how fund raising was practiced after his firm's founding was documented earlier. To provide evidence of the continuation of the two-way asymmetrical model after Jones sold his firm, the discussion turns briefly to the 1956–1960 campaign, "A Program for Harvard College," which was directed by Kersting, Brown & Company. Many of the firm's employees, such as Robert Duncan, had been trained by Jones. Not surprisingly, then, Cutlip (1965/1990) reported, "Although Kersting & Brown was the firm operating behind the scenes in this Harvard drive, the methodical, relentless ways of John Price Jones were fully utilized by his former aides" (p. 482). The campaign used new tools of mass persuasion, including public opinion polls. For example, "An opinion survey of Harvard's alumni was conducted, well after the drive was under way, and results of this poll guided efforts that culminated in pushing alumni participation in the campaign to some 26,000 givers" (p. 484).

Verifying the asymmetrical dimension of this model, the survey had found that alumni volunteers did not want to resolicit alumni who had already given (i.e., research showed that the organization should change its planned behavior by not resoliciting donors). However, many of the volunteers indicated they were ready to give again, so Harvard implemented a series of direct-mail packages targeted solely at the alumni workers, which brought in $1 million.

Similar to the one-way models, the two-way asymmetrical model historically has been criticized. According to Cutlip (1965/1990), "Evidence of a deepening resentment of what John Price Jones called the 'scientific method of raising funds' began to appear in the mid-twenties and has grown into the crescendo of criticism of the never-ending list of money appeals we hear so frequently today" (p. 330). The criticism serves as a transition to the fourth stage of fund raising. It also represents a symbolic farewell to Cutlip's history, which ended at the mid-1960s.

In the original work and its reissue, Cutlip repeatedly raised questions about ethics and what this book refers to as accountability to donors and other publics. His extensive research on fund raising led him to conclude that both the media and government regulators must intervene to preserve the pluralistic system nourished by the function. Before continuing, students need to understand the worldview Cutlip derived from his research, which he synthesized in the epilogue of his book: "America's philanthropy is typically American—born of the cooperative and generous spirit bred on the frontier, required by the problems of large-scale industrialization and urbanization, made possible by the enormous accumulation of capital wealth, and energized by the *high-pressure, publicity techniques*" (pp. 530–531; italics added).

In the absence of the two-way symmetrical model, therefore, Cutlip disregarded the differences he had observed among the different ways fund raising historically had been practiced and collapsed the three models of press agentry, public information, and two-way asymmetrical into one asymmetrical approach that used manipulation to raise gifts. It was on this dimension that he based his conclusions about media and government intervention. He stated, for example, "It seems clear that federal legislation, requiring annual registration and uniform, public accounting for all nationwide fund-raising agencies, is the only effective solution to this problem" (p. 533). "The mass media," he said, "bear a large share of the responsibility for waste, misdirection of gifts, and frauds in today's philanthropy. These media do too much promoting and too little reporting in the field of philanthropy" (pp. 534–535).

During the intervening years between his book's publication in 1965 and its reissue in 1990, little apparently had changed to alter Cutlip's conclusions (i.e., fund raising still was predominantly asymmetrical). In his preface to the book's reissue, Cutlip asserted, "Our people's philanthropy [is] financed by organized high pressure fund raising" (p. xi). Cruel exploitation, he said, had accelerated since he wrote the book, and efforts to curb it had failed. He called on the media to do more to combat charlatans. After a review of regulatory action in the 1970s and 1980s, he ended his preface with "the dictum of *caveat emptor*—to paraphrase, givers beware" (p. xvii).

Two-Way Symmetrical Stage and Model

Whereas the three older models developed within a 20-year span at the beginning of this century, 60 years elapsed before the two-way symmetrical model emerged. Its beginning date is 1980, although no historical figure or specific event is associated with the model or date.[11] Instead, 1980 marks the presence of a new legal context and conceptual framework that demanded fund raising be approached in a new way.

Government nurtured philanthropy through favorable legislation for more than 50 years, which helps explain the time gap between the third and fourth stages. The federal tax system encouraged gifts by means of deductions, and federal, state, and local laws provided a variety of tax exemptions for charitable organizations. Simplistically stated, because of the subsector's "favorite child" status with government, there was little reason before the 1970s to develop a way of practicing fund raising that was different from the ways it historically had been practiced.

As discussed earlier, the Tax Reform Act of 1969 heralded changed conditions. From then to the present, the federal government has engaged in continuous oversight, with threats of further intervention always on the horizon. In the 1970s, states stepped up their efforts to regulate fund raising, particularly the high costs associated with paid solicitors. Starting in 1980, the Supreme Court declared laws limiting fund-raising costs unconstitutional in a series of three landmark cases. Regulators turned to stricter registration, reporting, and disclosure requirements—in addition to prosecution and education—to control fund-raising behavior.

---

[11]This is not to say events significant to fund raising did not take place in 1980. As reported earlier and in the following discussion, in 1980, IS was founded, the Supreme Court ruled that fund raising is protected under the First Amendment of the Constitution, scholar Henry Hansmann published his seminal article on the theory of contract failure, and practitioner Joel Smith was using symmetrical concepts to write an essay criticizing capital campaigns.

Government did not act in isolation. Cutlip's conclusions just given epitomize calls for regulation that have multiplied over the last three decades. In his introduction to the reissue of Cutlip's book, Schwartz (1990) described the current regulatory climate as "cloudy, even stormy" (p. xxiii), due to public perceptions and public policies. Schwartz stated, "In recent years, the public perception of the worth of charities has become more cynical and questioning" (p. xx). He illustrated the threat of public policy by pointing to Congressional hearings in the mid-1980s that dealt with such proposals as capping gift deductions, which would have cost charitable organizations billions of dollars each year.

Government intervention after 1969—spurred by public distrust—can be interpreted as a revolt against the asymmetrical models of fund raising. Although abuses by paid solicitors provoked much of the action, it became increasingly clear that a more ethical and socially responsible approach was the best defense against further regulation.

Just as the legal context demanded a different approach, so too did the conceptual framework that began forming with the Filer Commission's research, published in 1977. Studies since then have advanced knowledge about philanthropy and nonprofit organizations. Two representative theories are presented here to demonstrate how the recent scholarly work called for a symmetrical model of fund raising.

In a groundbreaking article, economist Henry Hansmann (1980) defined nonprofits as organizations that obey NDC, which—as explained in chapter 2—means profits can be made but not distributed to those who control the organizations. For-profit companies, which exist to make profits for their owners, have an incentive to take advantage of consumers and other publics through asymmetrical information, termed *contract failure*. NDC reduces this incentive in nonprofits. Therefore, Hansmann concluded, nonprofits exist to foster a degree of trustworthiness. In other words, charitable organizations behaving in an untrustworthy fashion are at odds with the tax-exempt status granted to them by government. Payton (1990) applied the theory to fund-raising practice when he said, "Philanthropic values imply (and sometimes assert) a higher morality than marketplace values. In addition to truthfulness, a value prided (by lip service) in both sectors, there is an explicit assertion of concern for the well-being of others in philanthropy that is supposed to be different from the self-interest of the marketplace" (pp. 182–183).

Revisiting Hansmann's theory, Steinberg and Gray (1994) emphasized that although NDC reduces the financial incentive for taking advantage of people, it does not provide a direct, positive motivation for acting trustworthy, as Hansmann also noted. Steinberg and Gray gave examples of contract failure by nonprofits, one of which parallels the press agentry model: "An organization may employ a high-pressure or borderline deceptive fundraising [*sic*] campaign in order to maximize funds available for 'the cause'" (p. 303).

The older models, then, based on manipulation, untruthful or incomplete information, and preoccupation with dollar totals, are incompatible with Hansmann's theory, which required an approach to fund raising based on trustworthiness. Payton et al. (1991) stated, "In the vocabulary of the ethical fund raiser, 'trustworthiness' is a powerful, omnipresent word" (p. 7).

Also representative of the conceptual framework, scholars adopted social exchange theory to explain philanthropy. Sociologists Susan Ostrander and Paul Schervish (1990) summarized the theory's application: "Donors and recipients both give and get in the social relation that is philanthropy" (p. 93). The exchange, they said, is distinguished by "an interaction between donors and recipients that revolves around an effort to match what donors have to give to recipients with what recipients have to give to donors" (p. 95). Advocating symmetrical practice, they argued, "Contributions are mobilized most strongly when donors see their interests and concerns to be the same as those of recipients or closely identified with them" (p. 93). In other words, social exchange theory holds that fund raising is dependent on agreement between prospective donors and charitable organizations. "The values of reciprocity, cooperation, mutual respect, accountability, and commitment," Ostrander and Schervish asserted, are the basis of donor–recipient relationships (p. 95).

The two theories just presented serve as a reminder that serious research on fund raising lagged more than a decade behind research on philanthropy and nonprofits. For example, *The Nonprofit Sector: A Research Handbook* (Powell, 1987), which was described in a testimonial on its cover as "the bible of researchers on the non-profit sector," reported findings from studies conducted during PONPO's first 10 years. Yet in the entire 24 chapters, covering 463 pages, there are no studies dealing specifically with the fund-raising function, and the term fund raiser is not even listed in the book's index. One of the contributing authors responded when I asked him why so little attention had been paid to fund raising, "Not much of anything good has been written about it." The "Catch 22" circumstances of a deficient literature and neglect by philanthropy and nonprofit scholars delayed recognition of the two-way symmetrical model.

In the mid-1980s, Carbone (1986) evaluated fund-raising knowledge as a product of lore and experience. Jacobson (1986) commanded, "We need to develop a conceptual framework of theory and research that is powerful enough to *critically examine* the process of fund raising" (p. 38; italics added). The two obstacles singled out by these fund-raising scholars, a body of lore and a missing critical voice, help explain why the practice changed little between 1919 and 1980.

Without theoretical knowledge, experience in the particular models—propagated through the apprentice system of training—dictated that fund raising generally was practiced the *way* it was because that was how it had been practiced in the past. When scholars began studying fund raising, they criticized it for poor ethics, negative social consequences, and ineffectiveness. They also began suggesting changes to resolve dilemmas. In their traditional role as critic, they did not accept fund raising as it was practiced as "the way fund raising is" or the way it must be practiced; they looked at the function as an essential component of our democratic society that could be improved. In short, they began to define how fund raising *should* be practiced.

Reflective practitioners contributed to the normative model. Symmetrical concepts advanced by some of these fund raisers are presented here to document contributions and endorsement from the field (i.e., whereas my research, informed by practitioner experience, led to conceptualization of the newest model, others advocate two-way symmetrical practice). Before citing examples from the literature, it is necessary to point out that, historically, many defined fund raising in symmetrical terms but practiced one of the asymmetrical models.

Illustrating, Seymour (cited in Cutlip, 1965/1990) established symmetrical policies for the National War Fund during World War II, including the principle that the fund "would do its best to represent both the organizations seeking money and the Americans giving money" (p. 406). Regardless, his asymmetrical approach to fund raising is evident throughout his writings, including his condemnation of people who criticize high-pressure campaigns as "innocents who still think that there is substantial nourishment to be found in 'quiet special gifts efforts'" (p. 485). According to Harrah-Conforth and Borsos (1991), the second generation of fund-raising consultants "believe that fund raising is, or should be, backed by a philosophy deeper than merely meeting financial goals" (p. 31). Yet no evidence can be found that this group of fund raisers ever measured their impact or fund raising's by anything other than dollar totals.

Turning to current reflective practitioners, Joel Smith (1981) promoted numerous symmetrical concepts in a seminal essay denouncing capital campaigns, which he wrote in 1980 while working at Stanford University.[12] For example, Smith, who now is vice president of development for Health Sciences at West Virginia University, charged that fund raisers involved in capital campaigns solicit and accept gifts for big-dollar goals rather than for what they contribute to organizational priorities—a concept he termed *gift utility*. In an article published shortly afterward, J. P. Smith (1982) stated, "Much of the art of fund raising lies in bringing about a match—sufficient but rarely perfect—between the legitimate preferences of donors and our own needs" (p. 36). Smith urged charitable organizations to reach an internal understanding of fund-raising needs, to translate those needs into fund-raising objectives, and then to match those objectives with the interests and preferences of donor prospects. He added, "In doing that, we must understand that there is nothing wrong in donors having ideas of their own" (p. 36).

In another seminal work, David Dunlop (1987), director of capital projects at Cornell University, recommended a symmetrical approach to raising *ultimate gifts*, or extremely large major gifts that represent a substantial portion of individual donors' assets. "Ultimate gift fund raising," Dunlop said, "depends on our ability to build and develop long-term relationships with a few special givers" (p. 10). He advised:

> If we want to go beyond the annual and special gifts to the gifts that are of the greatest importance to the giver, we need to look beyond our own particular needs and campaigns and causes. We must look instead at the needs and interests of the giver and respond to those needs—even as we go about the business of serving our institution. (p. 13).

As given in chapter 1, this book defines fund raising as the management of relationships between a charitable organization and its donor publics. Dunlop (1987) provided a similar definition for the major gifts program: "the business of enhancing the prospect's relationship with the institution" (p. 11).

In a more recent essay on major gifts, Dunlop (1993) categorized fund raising into three "methods": (a) speculative, (b) campaign/project, and (c) nurturing. He endorsed the third method, which he described: "Almost all the time, talent, and other resources invested in this type of fund raising focus on nurturing the prospective

---

[12]J. P. Smith's (1981) essay was reprinted in *Educational Fund Raising: Principles and Practice*, edited by Worth (1993).

givers' sense of commitment to the institution and to the purpose for which their gifts are sought" (p. 101).

Following the multistep fund-raising process, Dunlop (1993) said that when identifying prospective donors, "The information that will be most helpful is the common currency of any friendship" (p. 105). He elaborated, "Look for shared values and shared interests that can provide the basis for involving the prospect in the life of the institution" (p. 105). Moving from research to cultivation, he maintained, "We must provide opportunities for our friends to give their personal, moral, political, and spiritual support, along with their financial support. The chance to express feelings of caring plays an integral part in developing the sense of commitment so essential to giving very large gifts" (p. 107).

Focusing on solicitation, Dunlop (1993) urged fund raisers to develop a two-way dialogue with donor prospects, discussing their beliefs, values, and giving capabilities. "Given appropriate attention, the givers themselves will decide when they wish to give" (p. 101). Finally, in his earlier article, Dunlop (1987) argued against traditional methods of evaluating fund-raising programs: "If you count the numbers of givers based on when they happened to become givers, as opposed to looking at those who are developing relationships, you're not measuring the thing that really matters" (p. 11). Likewise, "If you measure the dollars that happen to flow in during, say, 1987, you're not looking at the process. You're just totaling the cash register tape at the end of the process" (p. 11).

It is important to note that neither persuasion nor other forms of manipulation are mentioned—or presumably practiced—by Dunlop, whose ideas have made him a very popular speaker at practitioner conferences and seminars. Furthermore, Cornell University, where Dunlop has been employed for more than three decades, recently completed a capital campaign that raised $1.5 billion, which demonstrates that his symmetrical approach successfully raises money.

The discussion now turns to the purpose of the two-way symmetrical model, its dependency on donor agreement, and its practitioners' use of principles of collaborative negotiation. These three characteristics form the core of Jake Schrum's (1993) essay on fund-raising ethics. Schrum, who was a vice president of development and planning before becoming president of Texas Wesleyan University in the early 1990s, advocated reaching mutual understanding with donors:[13]

> We should welcome the opportunity to interact with our donors in ways that allow them to teach us about their goals and perspectives while we enhance their understanding of the intricacies of the [organization]. As we learn about them, so too can they learn about us. Our willingness to understand their needs will, in many cases, encourage them to understand ours. If we handle these situations sensitively and openly, we can contribute to greater understanding on both sides of the table. (p. 365)

Addressing donor agreement and utilization of negotiation, Schrum (1993) said if a donor wants to make a gift that "might muddle the institution's mission" or compromise its integrity, fund raisers are obligated "to explain to that donor why such a gift would be harmful," always being "sensitive to the history, philosophy, and

---

[13]Schrum, Adams, and Bornstein, cited in earlier chapters, are just 3 of more than 65 college presidents who are former fund raisers (Dorich, 1991).

emotions that lead [the donor] to want to share [his or her] resources in certain ways" (p. 365). He advised fund raisers to try to enlighten such donors and then negotiate terms that would allow acceptance of their gifts. Sometimes, he admitted, agreement cannot be reached because of deeply held values, reasons, or attitudes. "In the end, the fact remains that we must refuse some gifts" (p. 366). Some donors also will conclude that the charitable organization cannot fulfill their philanthropic needs.

Schrum's discussion of these symmetrical concepts within the context of ethics lends support to this book's premise that the newest model is the most ethical and socially responsible of the four. Other reflective practitioners provide further evidence. For example, Payton et al. (1991) gave an evolutionary perspective, stating, "Fund-raising practice as it becomes more professional becomes more open, more candid, more accountable to those who have given their money and other resources to advance the organization" (p. 9).

Using the metaphor of a double agent, consultant David Boaz (1991) proposed five principles of practice that emphasize symmetrical fund raising based on ethics and balanced effects. "One, if we are fully and equally agents of both the charity and the donor, then we must avoid the manipulative stunts" (p. 46). Cultivation timetables, he said, often are nothing but plans "for sucking in a person or institution so that in the end, they really would have no choice but to produce the gift" (p. 46). He argued, "We are going to have to start taking a stand here. We are not in the business of forcing or tricking people into giving" (p. 46). He continued, "Two, we must *fully* inform and involve donors whenever possible. We are often tempted to try to keep donors at arm's length. 'Just give us the money and come to the dinner in your honor, but don't bother us about the way we do our work'" (p. 46; italics in original).

Boaz (1991) parsimoniously stated the third principle: "Use gifts for what they're given for. Period. Always" (p. 46). "Four, tell the pure simple truth. . . . Be a channel of open, candid, two-way communication between donor and charity" (p. 46). He concluded, "Five, don't raise money for something that's not worth doing. . . . We are the front-line of society's evaluation process of not-for-profit entities. Let's not sell our integrity for a high salary or fee" (p. 47).

These examples document that the two-way symmetrical model does exist in the "real world." As demonstrated in the next chapter, however, the three asymmetrical models are prevalent in contemporary practice. Although the newest model offers practitioners and the charitable organizations they serve a more effective way to practice fund raising ethically and in a more socially responsible manner, it remains underutilized. Its adoption is hampered by the small number of scholars currently studying fund raising and by the absence of a program of formal education through which research findings can be disseminated and future practitioners trained.

J. E. Grunig and Hunt (1984) said it was only after full-time faculty replaced skilled practitioners in the classroom that the two-way symmetrical model of public relations was developed. This chapter closes with a similar conclusion: Until fund raising finds an academic home with scholar teachers, the symmetrical model will remain underutilized.

SUGGESTED READINGS

Andrews, F. E. (1950). *Philanthropic giving.* New York: Russell Sage Foundation.
Curti, M., & Nash, R. (1965). *Philanthropy in the shaping of American higher education.* New Brunswick, NJ: Rutgers University Press.
Cutlip, S. M. (1990). *Fund raising in the United States: Its role in America's philanthropy.* New Bruns-wick, NJ: Transaction. (Original work published 1965)
Cutlip, S. M. (1994). *The unseen power. Public relations: A history.* Hillsdale, NJ: Lawrence Erlbaum Associates.
Gurin, M. G., & Van Til, J. (1990). Philanthropy in its historical context. In J. Van Til & Associates, *Critical issues in American philanthropy: Strengthening theory and practice* (pp. 3–18). San Francisco, CA: Jossey-Bass.
Hall, P. D. (1987). A historical overview of the private nonprofit sector. In W. W. Powell (Ed.), *The nonprofit sector: A research handbook* (pp. 3–26). New Haven, CT: Yale University Press.
Kelly, K. S. (1994). Building fund-raising theory: An empirical test of four models of practice. *Essays on Philanthropy, 12.* Indianapolis: Indiana University, Center on Philanthropy.
Street, W. D. (1985). *A beacon for philanthropy: The American Association of Fund-Raising Counsel through fifty years: 1935–1985.* New York: American Association of Fund-Raising Counsel.

Fund Raisers' Autobiographies and Biographies

Gurin, M. G. (1985). *Confessions of a fund raiser: Lessons of an instructive career.* Washington, DC: Taft Group.
Knott, R. A. (1992). *The makings of a philanthropic fund raiser: The instructive example of Milton Murray.* San Francisco, CA: Jossey-Bass.
Schwartz, J. J. (1993). *Modern American philanthropy: A personal account.* New York: Wiley.

6

Organizational Context
of Fund Raising

Most fund raisers today are employees of charitable organizations. As such, they carry out their duties as part of a system that includes trustees, CEOs, other managers, and staff. Their efforts to raise gifts are inseparable from the behavior of other organizational members and from the collective behavior of the system.

Chapter 6 continues the discussion of the four ways organizations typically practice fund raising, reporting the results of two quantitative studies designed to test the models and explain their use. Role theory is adopted to conceptualize four individual behavior patterns enacted by practitioners. Utilizing the line–staff management model, working relationships between the head of fund raising and key actors in the organization are examined. Variations in the function's structure and operation are described.

PRACTICE OF THE OLDER MODELS

Despite changed conditions described in chapter 5, charitable organizations continue to practice the three older models. The following discussion draws from the fund-raising and philanthropy literature to demonstrate current use of the press agentry, public information, and two-way asymmetrical models.

Press Agentry

It is recalled that the oldest model, press agentry, is dependent on emotions to raise money, and truth is not an essential factor. Its practice is based on principles of manipulation and control. Attesting to widespread use of the model, Payton (1987) said, "Manipulation of emotion for various purposes is practiced on a national and even world-wide scale in our time. . . . Philanthropy, after all, is the product of persuasion, not of logical demonstration. The abuses of rhetorical technique in a good cause are so familiar as to be commonplace" (p. 41).

According to Cutlip (1965/1990), the fund-raising model developed by Ward and Pierce "today is a fixed feature of Americans' civic lives" (p. 528). Given the historical linkage between press agentry and fund-raising federations, it is not unexpected that contemporary practice of the model is evident in the behavior of the 2,000 local United Ways. As Cutlip, Center, and Broom (1985) stated, "The Ward-Pierce campaign format has endured the test of time and can be easily recognized in today's annual United Way drive" (pp. 39–40). The authors described the campaigns with which most students are familiar:

> Each autumn, in cities across the nation, a charity fund drive is staged to raise large sums of money for the community's volunteer social and welfare services, under the banner of "United Way". . . . These whirlwind campaigns to raise money in a few weeks' time bombard the public with heart-tugging appeals. Scores of volunteers are recruited to solicit funds from many times their number. The pattern has changed relatively little since it was developed by the YMCA in the early 1900s. (p. 152)

Because press agentry is the least ethical and socially responsible of the four models, its practice by the United Way system is examined in detail in the chapter on ethics.

Continuing the discussion here, Cutlip (1965/1990) asserted, "Use of the emotional rather than the education approach to getting money for popular philanthropy continues, though perhaps not to the same extent as was practiced in the early 1920's" (p. 236). "Nevertheless," he said, "tearful appeals, such as stories and photographs of pathetically crippled children, continue to be used in much of twentieth-century fund raising" (p. 21).

Such comments bring to mind Jerry Lewis' annual Labor Day telethon for the Muscular Dystrophy Association (MDA), which has been criticized by activists—including many muscular dystrophy patients—who charge that it "demeans the disabled by presenting them as 'objects to be pitied'" ("Jerry Lewis," 1992, p. 6). Disability activists held demonstrations during the 1992 telethon to protest this way of fund raising. As reported in the media, "The protesters have contended that the association exploits people with the disease to evoke pity and wring money from viewers" ("Over," 1992, p. 30). *The Encyclopedia of Bad Taste* (Stern & Stern, 1991) described MDA's telethon as "television's crowning supplication," that "wheedles, begs, scolds, shames, entertains, and counts money all night and all day; it is guaranteed to leave any viewer wrung out, agog, and aghast" (p. 290). Bremner (1989) generalized, "Television and movie celebrities hold well-publicized 'pitythons' to raise money for sufferers of children's diseases" (pp. 315–316).

Connecting religious fund raising to the oldest model, Van Til (1990) stated, "Some of what passes for religion is more nearly the manipulation of lonely and anxious individuals (and their donations)" (p. 278). J. R. Wood and Hougland (1990) provided a 1980 example of what they defined as manipulative fund raising by the Rex Humbard Ministry. A letter signed by Humbard urged receivers to join the "Prayer Key Family" by sending monthly contributions to his ministry. The purpose of joining was so Humbard could pray for them as members. He began his letter by saying he wanted to pray for the person, "but your name was not there" (p. 114). Extraordinary benefits promised by Humbard, which—as the authors pointed out—were beyond his to deliver, included healed bodies, mended homes, and meeting "every one of your financial needs" (p. 114).

James Smurl (1991), professor of religious studies at Indiana University, claimed the pledges solicited by contemporary religious fund raisers and televangelists often are more like tithes than voluntary donations. "More ominously still, these 'pledges' are accepted from the elderly poor and from the emotionally vulnerable. Whether through oversight of, or insensitivity to, the possibility of doing harm to donors, the result is that the tithes gathered tend to serve the needs and wants of the collectors more than anyone else" (p. 14).

In 1992, the United Jewish Appeal (UJA), the foremost Jewish charitable organization in the world, commissioned a study on trends in philanthropy, which found that the primary reason Jews do not give to UJA is, "They are put off by the group's 'hard sell' solicitation techniques" (E. Greene, 1992, p. 12). Whitaker (1974) described card-calling dinners used by the UJA to raise money for Israel. People attending such functions must say how much they are going to give when their name is called. He quoted a New York trustee: "It was really a type of blackmail. It is still used today in a great deal of fund-raising [*sic*], but it is most open in the Jewish world" (p. 43).

Warner (1994) argued, if "Jewish fund raising is pushy, unrelenting, and involves pressure tactics" (p. 53), then other types of organizations use the same model. He described a meeting to raise money for a Catholic maternity hospital at the home of then Cardinal McIntyre of Los Angeles: "The chairman of the hospital campaign called each man present, by name, and asked what he was going to give to the hospital. The pressure was palpable. Each rose, stated an amount, and was greeted by applause, some loud, some not so loud, depending on the amount. That sure sounds like the stereotype of Jewish fund raising to me" (p. 53).

Press agentry is not limited to organizations with missions in religion, health, or human services. Korten (1989) condemned practices among those involved in international aid, saying, "The exploitation of the starving child for fund-raising purposes is perhaps development's equivalent to child pornography" (p. 43). Critics charge that some environmental organizations use blatant scaremongering as a fund-raising strategy; they rely on half-truths about dwindling natural resources and on emotions fearing their loss. Addressing all organizational types, Payton (cited in "Philanthropy 2000," 1993) maintained, "There's a great deal of dishonesty, exaggeration, distortion, misrepresentation and errors of omission in the language we use in justifying giving in the name of the good cause" (p. 14).

At least one group concerned with domestic violence admitted that the estimate of battered wives it used for publicity and fund raising during the O. J. Simpson trial was considerably overblown (Berger, 1996). In 1996, a Sacramento, California-based organization was criticized for inflating the city's number of homeless children by more than 5,000% in fund-raising advertisements. Managers responded that the figure depended on what counts as being homeless, and even if their figure was too high, using a large number helped raise public consciousness about the homelessness problem. Berger (1996) admonished, "The mentality that seems to be at work in these cases is one that justifies deceit in the name of a just cause" (p. 2).

Public Information

The purpose of the public information model is to disseminate needs information. It relies on rational, intelligent, and compassionate donor publics. Current practice of the model is most easily identified in national organizations that primarily raise lower level gifts through direct mail.

Illustrating, the Carter Center in Atlanta, Georgia, founded by former President Carter and his wife Rosalynn, attributes much of its fund-raising success to its "thinking man's" direct-mail campaign ("Philanthropy 400," 1995). In 1994, the campaign consisted of five different letters, each providing information on one of the center's programs, such as its work to relieve health problems in Sudan. Explaining that the letters are designed to appeal to reason rather than emotions, a senior manager declared, "It doesn't have to be [about] a starving child. . . . People will respond to a solid, well-thought-out case presented in a direct-mail piece" (p. 52). The Carter Center raised $43 million in 1994, mainly through gifts averaging less than $40.

There is some evidence that literature, or needs information, is related to raising lower level gifts. Panas (1984), for example, advised, "Campaign literature is certainly important. . . . It is probably effective for smaller gifts. But for the major donor, it will likely take something different to make the sale" (p. 121). In a quantitative study I conducted on alumni giving, I found that reading annual giving literature and two organizational magazines discriminated donors of lower level gifts from nondonors (Kelly, 1979).

Because there has been little scholarly work on fund raising, philanthropy and nonprofit scholars have gained their knowledge of the function from books and articles written by practitioners. Their reliance on practitioner sources, as well as their personal observations, have resulted in conceptualizations of fund raising that correspond to the asymmetrical models. In other words, contemporary use of the older models, including public information, is demonstrated by some scholars' theories. Steinberg (1987), for example, conceptualized a model of philanthropy in which donors exchange gifts for factual literature. According to the model, donors are motivated to give, but are uncertain as to which organizations have the most desirable characteristics in terms of type, quality of service, and efficiency in converting donations to program services. Literature allows them to make their gift decisions.

Whereas Ostrander and Schervish (1990) recommended two-way symmetrical practice, as discussed in chapter 5, they conceptualized two other strategies used by charitable organizations to gain attention and favorable response from donors, based on practitioner authorities (e.g., Panas, 1984). One of these, the "need-based strategy," parallels the public information model. "Recipients take it as a given that donors wish to contribute and be involved in projects that seek to address community needs, and that if given the chance to do so, they will come forward and give what they can" (p. 87). The scholars continued, "Possible specific fund-raising tactics might include mailings to lists of donors who have given to similar programs. Mailings would likely include substantial amounts of concrete, explicit information about the need or interest being addressed" (p. 87).

The second strategy parallels the two-way asymmetrical model. Before proceeding to the third model, it is important to note that Ostrander and Schervish's work provides overall support for the theory of the models. Students are reminded that the models are representations of the values, goals, and behaviors held and enacted by organizations when they practice fund raising. Similarly, the organizational strategies of Ostrander and Schervish (1990) are composites of rationales, complex goals, and practices. The strategies, or modes of interaction between recipients and their donors, are the *"different ways* that people on the . . . recipient sides of the relation come to think about and carry out philanthropy" (p. 76; italics added). Also congruent with the models, Ostrander and Schervish said their strategies are not mutually exclusive: "A particular . . . recipient probably participates in more than one at a time" (p. 76).

Two-Way Asymmetrical

The purpose of the two-way asymmetrical model is to scientifically persuade giving. To do so, it uses formative research to shape persuasive communications that will be readily accepted by prospective donors.

Ostrander and Schervish (1990) explained that unlike the needs-based strategy, which is more recipient centered, the "opportunity-based strategy" shifts toward the donor, with needs expressed as opportunities. "The goal of the transaction is to *persuade* the donor of the value of this opportunity. It is a strategy that requires that the recipient have more specific knowledge about the donor and what the donor might want and value than is the case with a needs-based strategy" (p. 88; italics in original). They added, "This strategy requires that the recipient group obtain information about potential donors that anticipates what they might want as the basis for an appeal" (p. 89).

Panas (1984) advocated this approach for raising major gifts: "Individuals require their own needs to be met. Listen carefully. See how you can mold the needs of the potential donor to the opportunities of the proposed program. . . . The *trick* is in making certain that what they want most is what you want most" (p. 172; italics added). Reminiscent of John Price Jones, Panas instructed, "Research your prospect with finite care and painstaking attention" (p. 194). He pointed out that not everyone who has the financial resources to give does so, and asked: "How do you find the 'right button'? And when you do, how do you most effectively push it?" (p. 9). Linking the two-way asymmetrical model to marketing, Panas said, "Good marketing means helping the major donor want to share in your dream. This means proper interpretation and effective persuasion" (p.115).

R. L. Williams (1993), the lead researcher for CASE's 1995 membership study, recommended asymmetrical practice. Public relations staff, he said, should conduct opinion polls to assess the strengths and weaknesses of the organization's reputation. "With that information they can then devise communications strategies to *market* the institution as they wish the public to see it and to influence the public's behavior toward it. This shaping of institutional identity and reputation is of extreme importance to fund raising" (p. 292; italics added).

Rosso (1991) also emphasized this model's dual dimensions of two-way communication and unbalanced effects in his explanation of the fund-raising cycle—again illustrating the relationship between the third model and marketing:

> Creative communication is a two-way instrument. It transmits what the market is both willing to receive and [what it] requires to help it understand the organization's mission goals and objectives. Such communication stands ready to receive feedback or questions to verify that the market is receiving and understanding the transmitted message. (p. 13)

The guru of fund raising as a marketing function is consultant James Gregory Lord, whose axiomatic books are filled with two-way asymmetrical advice. For example,

Lord (1983) commanded: "It's essential to listen to the donor community. If we can find out what's on *their* minds and where *they're* going, we'll be in a strong position to shape our offering accordingly" (p. 11; italics in original). He stressed the superiority of the two-way asymmetrical model over the one-way models: "The marketing approach is far more appropriate to the people business of fund raising. It's also more effective" (p. 77). Rather than trying to tell people how they should think and what they should do, Lord said, "It's much easier to relate our program to what people already want" (p. 11). He gave the example of a zoo that wanted to get a specific businessman interested in its building campaign. Because the businessman was interested in education and projects promoting free-enterprise values, the zoo proposed that he "invest" in an education department for young people, which would teach them about animal societies and how the "basic principles of competition, cooperation, adaptation and survival were related to the children's own future in a free society" (p. 14).

The zoo got the gift, but it is doubtful that the dollars raised supported the organization's mission and goals in any meaningful way. Instead, Lord's example illustrates a marketing mindset whereby charitable organizations are overly willing to change their program services to attract gifts. As Rosso (1991) argued, "Fund raising should never be undertaken simply to raise funds; it must serve the larger cause" (p. 4). His assertion prompts a concluding comment: Although they espouse two-way asymmetrical practice, Rosso, Lord, and other proponents often define fund raising in symmetrical terms.

EMPIRICAL TEST OF THE MODELS

The four models were tested in a national survey of 296 fund raisers (Kelly, 1994a, 1995b). Whereas researchers have attempted to define "ideal" models of fund raising (e.g., C. H. Webb, 1982) and characteristics of "effective" models (e.g., Loessin & Duronio, 1989), this study represented the first time theoretical models were used to explain how fund raising is practiced differently in different charitable organizations. The following discussion includes details on the methodology and statistical analysis of the study to enhance students' understanding of research.

Methodology

The population defined for study was members of NSFRE who work for the six major types of charitable organizations, as classified by the AAFRC Trust for Philanthropy (1987). A stratified sample of 597 was generated from self-reported information on employer type and yielded a response rate of 50%.

To measure the models of fund raising, four items were developed for each of the four models based on their characteristics. For example, as the purpose of the two-way asymmetrical model is to scientifically persuade donors to give, and as that model uses formative research in its programs, one of the items designed to measure it was: "Before starting, we look at attitude surveys to make sure we describe the organization in ways our prospects will be most likely to support." All 16 items were measured for how well they describe the way fund raising is practiced both for annual giving and for major gifts programs.

A fractionation scale was used to measure the models and a set of fund-raising activities (e.g., organizing volunteers and developing grant proposals). Respondents were asked to give a number on a scale from 0 to as high as they wanted to go. They were told that 100 was the average response on all of the items. To reduce a positive skew resulting from the open-end scale, scores were transformed by computing their square roots; therefore, a score of 10 (the square root of 100) represented an "average" response.

The type of organization for which respondents work was measured by color coding the 4-page questionnaires, which were keyed to the stratified sample (e.g., questionnaires printed on blue paper were mailed to those who work for health organizations, whereas those who work for public/society benefit organizations were sent ivory questionnaires). Single indicators were used to measure demographics.

Findings

The 296 usable questionnaires provided a relatively well-balanced proportion of respondents from each of the six organizational types. Demographics of the respondents were very similar to those of the general NSFRE membership (Mongon, 1992). Representativeness and sampling procedures allowed the findings to be generalized to the population.

Using SPSS® software, additive scales were formed from the items used to measure the fund-raising models as practiced in both programs. To estimate their reliability, Cronbach's alpha was computed for the resulting eight indices to show the extent to which each of the items in an index measured the same concept. Mean scores were computed for the indices and were correlated with the 16 fund-raising activities as a test of the models' validity. Factor analyses were conducted to determine the accuracy of the models. Finally, mean scores on the models were broken down by the six types of organizations. The findings supported the models as conceptualized, but also suggested some revisions in their measurement.

Mean Scores and Reliability.   Table 6.1 presents the mean scores of the respondents on the models and the items used to measure them for the two primary programs. The scores provide strong evidence that the press agentry model of fund raising is the model predominantly practiced today.

Means on the press agentry model are the highest of the four models, 9.67 for the annual giving program and 9.25 for the major gifts program, with a standard deviation of 3.11 and 3.56, respectively. Mean scores on the two-way symmetrical model are higher than those on the two-way asymmetrical model, 7.15 versus 6.16 ($t = 5.59$, p .00) for annual giving and 7.67 versus 6.11 ($t = 8.47$, p .00) for major gifts. The unexpectedly high scores on the newest model largely are attributable to respondents' strong identification with the first item measuring the symmetrical model: "The purpose of this program is to develop mutually beneficial relationships between the organization and its donors." As explained in chapter 1, fund raisers practicing one of the three asymmetrical models believe that donors benefit from making a gift primarily

TABLE 6.1
Mean Scores on Items and Scales Measuring Fund-Raising Models Practiced
for Annual Giving and Major Gifts Programs

Variable	Annual Giving (AG) Program Mean	AG Standard Deviation	Major Gifts (MG) Program Mean	MG Standard Deviation
Press Agentry Model				
The more people who know about our cause, the more dollars we will raise.	11.33	3.57	10.81	4.36
Favorable publicity in the media, scores of volunteers, and appeals that touch people's hearts are fundamental to this program.	10.91	4.89	10.02	5.30
In this program, fund raisers fulfill many roles, including cheerleader, evangelist, and arm twister.	10.04	4.59	10.10	4.93
Fund raising and campaigning mean essentially the same thing.	6.22	4.75	5.86	5.13
Mean for Press Agentry Model	*9.67*	3.11	*9.25*	3.56
Cronbach's alpha for reliability of scale	.62		.68	
Public Information Model				
Nearly everyone is so busy writing solicitation materials or producing publications that there is not time to do research.	7.88	4.60	7.23	4.89
In this program, we disseminate factual information, which prospective donors then use to make a rational decision to give.	10.05	3.80	10.34	4.36
Basically, people want to help; they just need to know about our particular needs and be asked for their gift.	10.74	3.40	10.67	4.14
Fund raising is more of a neutral disseminator of gift needs than an advocate for the organization or a mediator between management and donors.	4.94	4.65	4.68	4.71
Mean for Public Information Model	*8.47*	2.54	*8.33*	3.07
Cronbach's alpha for reliability of scale	.35		.56	
Two-Way Asymmetrical Model				
After completing the program, we do research to determine how effective it has been in changing people's attitudes and behaviors toward giving.	5.70	4.47	5.61	4.62
Our broad goal is to persuade donors to give—primarily because that is what the organization wants them to do.	7.60	4.42	6.98	4.66
Before starting, we look at attitude surveys to make sure we describe the organization in ways our prospects will be most likely to support.	6.15	4.96	6.30	5.29
Before beginning, we do research to determine public attitudes toward the organization and how they might be changed.	5.36	5.20	5.64	5.39

(continued)

TABLE 6.1. (continued)

Variable	Annual Giving (AG) Program Mean	AG Standard Deviation	Major Gifts (MG) Program Mean	MG Standard Deviation
Mean for Two-Way Asymmetrical Model	6.16	3.28	6.11	3.54
Cronbach's alpha for reliability of scale	.60		.67	
Two-Way Symmetrical Model				
The purpose of this program is to develop mutually beneficial relationships between the organization and its donors.	11.69	4.33	12.20	4.71
Before starting, we do surveys or informal research to find out how much management and our donor prospects understand each other.	4.81	4.79	5.67	5.24
Our purpose is to change the attitudes and behavior of management as much as it is to change the attitudes and behavior of prospects.	7.37	5.72	7.54	6.20
The organization believes fund raising should provide mediation to help management and donors negotiate their collaboration and possible conflicts.	4.59	4.87	5.08	5.21
Mean for Two-Way Symmetrical Model	7.15	3.23	7.67	3.64
Cronbach's alpha for reliability of scale	.56		.63	

Note. Scores are the square roots of responses on a fractionation scale for which respondents were told that 100 is a typical response on all of the items. Thus, a mean of 10 in this table represents this typical response.

because the charitable organization benefits. It is on such a basis that asymmetrical fund raisers would describe "mutually beneficial relationships."

As shown in Table 6.1, the mean scores for the three asymmetrical models decrease slightly when moving from annual giving programs to major gifts programs. Conversely, the mean score for the two-way symmetrical model increases by .52 when moving from annual giving to major gifts. In other words, fund raisers tend to move toward symmetrical concepts when raising major gifts. Table 6.1 also shows that Cronbach's alphas for reliability of the eight model indices generally are acceptable, although lower than that recommended for highly reliable scales. Further analysis pinpointed specific items that could be modified to increase reliability in future studies.

Validity.   To test validity, Pearson product–moment correlations were computed between the model indices and the 16 fund-raising activities. Importantly, none of the activities had a negative correlation with any of the four fund-raising models (i.e., all the models use the activities to some extent). This point was best illustrated by the relatively equal correlations between the four models as practiced in major gifts programs and the activity of editing newsletters and periodicals. All four correlations were significant at p .01, indicating that fund raisers engage in this activity no matter what model they practice for raising major gifts.

A definite pattern between the models and the activities emerged. Technical elements of fund raising, such as staging special events, preparing publicity material, and producing public service announcements, were significantly related to the practice of the one-way models. The more managerial activities, such as scripting group meetings with major prospects, researching donor attitudes and behaviors, planning cultivation moves, meeting informally with opinion leaders, and participating in strategic planning for the organization, were significantly related to the more sophisticated two-way models.

Whereas correlations between a majority of technical activities showed as strong of a relationship with the two-way models as they did for the one-way models, none of the eight managerial activities showed comparable relationships with the one-way models. In other words, fund raisers who practice the two-way asymmetrical or symmetrical models use managerial and technical activities to conduct their annual giving and major gifts programs, but fund raisers who practice the press agentry or public information models rely primarily on technical activities.

In general, the 16 fund-raising activities correlated moderately, logically, and consistently across the two primary programs with the models as conceptualized, thereby supporting their validity.

Accuracy.   Accuracy was tested by factor analyzing the items comprising the four models. Factor analysis helps identify underlying, not directly observable, constructs. It was employed to determine whether the models describe fund raising empirically or whether some other configuration of items would describe actual fund-raising practice more accurately.

The 16 items were factor analyzed using principal components analysis with a varimax rotation. Both the analysis for annual giving and the one for major gifts produced a three-factor solution with eigenvalues greater than 1.00. After grouping the items that had high loadings for the same factors, the underlying constructs were identified as Press Agentry, Public Information, and Two-Way Communication.

Four of the five items loading on the Two-Way Communication factor dealt with conducting research on or gathering information from donor publics before and after the organization communicates with them. The underlying construct, therefore, corresponded to the two-way communication dimension shared by the two-way asymmetrical and symmetrical models and emphasized the important role research plays in their practice. None of the items representing the one-way models loaded on this factor.

The fifth item loading highest on the two-way factor, "The organization believes fund raising should provide mediation to help management and donors negotiate their collaboration and possible conflicts," measured the symmetrical model. The combination of variables suggested that fund raisers may hold "mixed motives," meaning they believe in some symmetrical concepts but still engage in asymmetrical practice. Mixed motives offers an explanation of why such asymmetrical proponents as Rosso (1991) often define fund raising in symmetrical terms. The evidence also supports the mixed-motive model of public relations, conceptualized by J. E. Grunig and L. A. Grunig (1989) and found by researchers in the Excellence Project (J. E. Grunig, L. A. Grunig, Dozier, Ehling, Repper, & White, 1991).

As touched on earlier, the "mutually beneficial relationship" item from the two-way symmetrical indices appeared to have a halo effect. Its loading on the Press Agentry factor confirmed the problem. The item was deleted in subsequent analyses to better discriminate between asymmetrical and symmetrical concepts.

Together, the three factors explained 41% of the variance of all 16 items as practiced in annual giving programs and 55% of their variance when practiced in major gifts programs. Findings attested to the models' accuracy. Drawing from results of their reliability and concurrent validity, the conclusion was reached that the four models capture variations in the fund-raising behavior of U.S. charitable organizations. In short, the models do exist in the real world.

Different Organizational Types.   Findings showed only a weak relationship between the four models and the six types of organizations: (a) arts, culture, and humanities; (b) education; (c) health; (d) human services; (e) public/society benefit; and (f) religion. Mean scores on the models broken down by organizational type differed little from the mean scores for all respondents: Press agentry was the model predominantly practiced by all types, and the two-way asymmetrical model was the least practiced.

One-way analysis of variance (ANOVA) was conducted to confirm the absence of differences. Scheffe tests showed that no group among the six was significantly different at the .05 probability level. In other words, the mission of a charitable organization, whether it is arts or religion, makes no difference in the predominant practice of the press agentry model.

It is important to emphasize that this study focused on staff fund raisers; NSFRE members self-categorized as consultants were excluded from the sample. Theory predicts, however, that consultants do not differ from the findings of this study. J. E. Grunig and Hunt (1984) said the pressure to keep clients often means consultants must give clients the services they demand. As documented shortly, this ordinarily means fund-raising consultants have little choice but to practice press agentry.

Several graduate students across the country currently are testing the four models on different samples of fund raisers. Their findings will add to the ongoing process of refining theory to help us better understand the fund-raising function and manage it more effectively. Other students interested in conducting such studies are encouraged to do so.

EXPLANATORY STUDY OF THE MODELS

Whereas the study testing the models explained *how* charitable organizations practice fund raising, the third stage of theory building investigated *why* these organizations practice fund raising the way they do. Stated another way, research on the models moved from descriptive studies to an explanatory study in 1993 (Kelly, 1995a).

Before reporting findings, it is necessary to briefly discuss the concept and theory that guided the study's design—the dominant coalition and power control.

Dominant Coalition and Power Control

The dominant coalition was first conceptualized by Thompson (1967), who referred to it simply as the "inner circle" (p. 140). He and other organizational scholars concluded that no one person can control an organization today. Hage (1980) explained, "The team approach, the variety of specialists, the complexity of the environment, the need for joint decision-making make the stamp of one man or woman less and less likely. This is the era of the dominant coalition" (p. 158).

Following such scholars, J. E. Grunig (1992) advanced a power-control theory, which holds that organizations behave the way they do because the people who have power in an organization, the dominant coalition, choose that behavior. Those with power, Grunig stressed, cannot be assumed by formal positions or titles. An extensive literature review on what constitutes excellent public relations revealed that dominant coalition members determine the philosophy of the function and the model practiced. According to Grunig, adoption of the two-way symmetrical model "is the key choice made by effective organizations," but "the public relations department does not make that choice" (p. 24); the group controlling the organization decides on the model. Managers of the function contribute to the decision only if they are part of the dominant coalition and have power within it. Furthermore, the dominant coalition's choice is influenced by presuppositions held by its members.

I used early drafts of Grunig's work to identify two categories of presuppositions about fund raising, asymmetrical and symmetrical, described in chapter 1. Based on the power-control theory, the way in which members of the dominant coalition think about fund raising dictates how a charitable organization practices it (i.e., the fund-raising model predominantly used). Research on dominant coalitions, then, would help explain why organizations practice fund raising the way they do.

Explanatory Findings

Data were gathered from the same sample of NSFRE fund raisers used in the previous study. Practitioners were asked to identify *who* was represented in the dominant coalition of their organization. They were instructed to check all of the 12 individuals and groups listed that applied and were given an "other specified" option. The fractionation scale, used to measure the models, also was used to measure the degree of the dominant coalition's support of and influence on the fund-raising function. Single indicators measured 11 characteristics of the respondents and their organizations.

Members of the Dominant Coalition.   Dominant coalition members and the proportion of organizations in which they are members are presented in Table 6.2. Responses to the "other" option did not uncover any important groups or individuals overlooked in the list provided.

Of the 295 respondents answering the question, almost all (94%) identified their CEO as a member of the dominant coalition; 19 said the CEO is not a member. The second situation is not inconceivable. For example, the CEO may be near retirement age and serving more as a figurehead than as a leader. Trustees are members in only 80% of the organizations.

As 67% of the respondents reported that they are the head of the fund-raising department, it was somewhat suspicious that 63% said the fund-raising head is a member of the dominant coalition. A cross-tabulation of those who reported they are fund-raising heads with responses to the dominant coalition item showed that the high percentage of fund raisers in the dominant coalition is an indication of the function's status in charitable organizations and not a flaw of self-reported data.

TABLE 6.2
Kendall Correlation Coefficients for Representation in the Dominant Coalition With the
Dominant Coalition's Support of and Influence on Fund Raising

| | | Degree Dominant Coalition | |
Members of Dominant Coalition	In % of Organizations (N = 295)	Supports Fund Raising	Influences Fund Raising
Chief executive officer (CEO)	94%	.01	.01
Trustees/Directors of board	80%	−.01	−.00
Head of fund raising	63%	.13*	.11*
Chief financial officer (CFO)	52%	.00	−.05
Chief operating officer (COO)	35%	.03	−.05
Head of public relations	30%	.01	.01
Individual major donors	16%	.02	.10*
Corporate major donors	10%	−.01	.07
Employees	8%	.03	−.03
Clients/Customers	8%	−.04	.01
Government	8%	−.07	−.03
Foundation major donors	5%	.00	.04

*p .05

Membership, as predicted by theory, is not analogous to other indicators of organizational status. Whereas 63% of the fund-raising heads are dominant coalition members, 77% of the respondents said their fund-raising department reports to the CEO.

The chief financial officer (CFO) and the chief operating officer (COO) were identified as members of the dominant coalition in 52% and 35% of the organizations, respectively. The latter finding may be attributable to a high percentage of CEOs who also are the COOs of their organizations. Or it may indicate that COOs, who presumably are in charge of program services, have little control in 65% of the organizations represented in NSFRE. Such situations would contribute to low accountability to clients and support charges of undue attention on donors, keeping in mind that almost twice as many fund-raising heads than COOs are dominant coalition members. Milofsky and Blades (1991), for example, claimed health charities concentrate on donors at the expense of clients, although both constituencies have a legitimate interest in the organizations. Arguing that health charities will be accountable only when forced, they urged clients to form activist groups to demand greater representation in the decision processes of the organizations. The nonprofit scholars warned, "As services become less important than fund-raising [*sic*], organizational competence can suffer" (p. 389).

Clients, as well as employees and government, are not well represented in the dominant coalitions of NSFRE organizations (8% each). Individual and corporate major donors, however, were identified as dominant coalition members in 16% and 10% of the organizations, respectively; foundation donors are members in only 5%. Whereas Milofsky and Blades (1991) verified donors' interest in charitable organizations, they also stated, "There is much anecdotal evidence that program decisions have been determined by fund-raising concerns or by the ideological or religious convictions of major donors" (p. 389). The dual issues of accountability and autonomy are discussed in chapters 7 and 9.

The head of public relations was identified as a dominant coalition member in 30% of the organizations. As more than twice as many fund-raising heads are members, the findings provide evidence of encroachment, which is returned to later in this chapter.

Dominant Coalition's Support and Influence.

Moving from who is represented to the impact the dominant coalition has on fund raising, respondents were asked to indicate the extent to which they believe the dominant coalition they had identified supports the fund-raising function and influences the way fund raising is practiced. Table 6.2 presents Kendall correlation coefficients for these relationships.

Only membership of the fund-raising head has a significant relationship with increased support for the function. Although relatively small, the relationship is logical in that admittance to the dominant coalition would place increased importance—and, therefore, support—on the function represented. The head of fund raising also is related to the degree of influence. More interesting, there is a positive and significant relationship between membership of individual major donors and the extent to which the dominant coalition influences the way fund raising is practiced.

Connecting these findings to the four fund-raising models, Table 6.3 reports Pearson correlation coefficients for the dominant coalition's collective support and influence with the models as practiced in annual giving and major gifts programs. There is a significant *inverse*, or negative, relationship between support of the dominant coalition and the two-way symmetrical model as practiced in annual giving programs. In contrast, there are significant and positive relationships between support and the model predominantly practiced by the population in both annual giving and major gifts programs, press agentry. The statistics provide empirical evidence that the dominant coalitions of charitable organizations support those fund-raising departments practicing the press agentry model (i.e., they encourage its utilization) and give less support to those practicing the two-way symmetrical model, thereby discouraging more ethical and socially responsible fund raising.

TABLE 6.3
Pearson Correlation Coefficients for the Dominant Coalition's Support of and
Influence on Fund Raising With Four Fund-Raising Models as Practiced
in Annual Giving and Major Gifts Programs

Dominant Coalition's Support and Influence	Models							
	Two-Way Symmetrical		Two-Way Asymmetrical		Public Information		Press Agentry	
	AG	MG	AG	MG	AG	MG	AG	MG
Extent to which the dominant coalition *supports* the fund-raising function	-.12*	.03	.11	.08	.04	.10	.16**	.15*
How much the dominant coalition *influences* the way fund raising is practiced	.06	.09	.14*	.11	.16**	.13*	.28**	.15*

Note. AG = Annual Giving Program. MG = Major Gifts Program.
*p .05. **p .01.

Justifying this interpretation, the correlation coefficients for the relationship between how much the dominant coalition influences the way fund raising is practiced and the four models show that the dominant coalition significantly influences the practice of the three asymmetrical models, but has little and nonsignificant influence on the symmetrical model. Clearly, the powerful elites who control NSFRE organizations prefer fund raising that is based on principles of persuasion, manipulation, and control of donors, rather than an approach that strives for mutual understanding. This preference, although expressed in relatively small correlations, lends credence to the earlier discussion about the explanatory power of presuppositions held by the dominant coalition on why organizations practice fund raising the way they do. Findings suggest that charitable organizations predominantly practice the press agentry model because it is the model the dominant coalition wants them to practice.

Organizational Characteristics.   Correlations were computed for the models and 11 organizational and practitioner characteristics. Table 6.4 presents the results of those computations.

Only two organizational characteristics have a significant relationship with any of the four models. The larger the organization, as measured by its number of employees, the more likely it will practice the two-way symmetrical model in its major gifts program. Furthermore, organizations that practice the two-way symmetrical model in their major gifts program raise more total dollars in a given year than those practicing the three other models.

The second finding provides empirical evidence that the normative model is the most pragmatically effective. In total, respondents helped their organizations raise $4.3 billion the year before the study, with a median of $1.3 million in gifts. Pearson correlations between the amount of private dollars raised and mean scores on the models yielded only one significant and positive relationship: Dollars increased as scores increased on the two-way symmetrical model as practiced in major gifts programs. In contrast, the model predominantly practiced, press agentry, had nonsignificant and low correlations with the reported gift amounts.

On the surface, this finding appears at odds with the billions of dollars raised each year and the success stories that fill trade and practitioner publications. If press agentry is predominantly practiced, but the model has no relationship to raising more money, why do dollar totals continue to increase? The answer consists of three parts.

First, gift totals increase simply because of inflation (i.e., money is worth less each year). Almost all charitable organizations report their fund-raising results in *current dollars* that do not account for the impact of inflation. When converted to *inflation-adjusted dollars* and compared to previous years, results rarely show a continuous upward slope: Gift totals often stay at the same level or even decrease. Illustrating from the macro perspective, yearly totals of U.S. giving since 1959, as documented by the AAFRC Trust for Philanthropy (1996), increased every year in current dollars, but when adjusted for inflation, decreased in 25% of the years and did not move in many others. During the first 6 years of the 1990s, for example, giving barely kept pace with inflation in 2 years and lost ground in 3; "real" growth occurred only in 1995, when giving increased 5.5% in inflation-adjusted terms.

TABLE 6.4
Correlation Coefficients for 11 Organizational and Practitioner Characteristics With
Four Fund-Raising Models

Demographic Variables	Models							
	Two-Way Symmetrical		Two-Way Asymmetrical		Public Information		Press Agentry	
	AG	MG	AG	MG	AG	MG	AG	MG
Organization								
Number of people employed by organization[a]	.10	.15*	−.00	.01	.03	.06	.00	.04
Number of professional fund raisers employed[a]	.00	.04	−.02	−.02	.02	.06	.02	.04
Number of all people working in fund raising[a]	.04	−.07	−.00	−.08	−.01	−.08	−.01	−.09
Total dollars raised in private support[a]	.11	.13*	.09	.07	.11	.10	−.02	.05
Type of charitable organization[b] *(Arts, Culture = 1/ Religion = 6)*	.00	−.00	.03	.06	.04	.05	−.02	.03
To whom the fund-raising department reports[b] *(Junior Management Level = 1/CEO = 3)*	−.03	−.06	.05	.04	−.01	−.05	.09	.02
Practitioner								
Years of fund-raising experience[a]	.11	.13*	.06	.13*	.02	.09	.07	.15*
Age[a]	.01	.03	.01	.02	−.13*	−.11	.03	.05
Head of fund-raising department[b]	−.03	−.05	−.10*	−.09	−.06	−.09	.12*	.14**
Gender[b] *(Female = 1/Male = 2)*	.08	.02	.09	.11*	−.07	−.04	−.10*	−.03
CFRE certification[b]	.05	.08	.02	.05	−.01	.04	.02	.04

Note. AG = Annual Giving Program. MG = Major Gifts Program.
[a] Pearson correlation coefficients. [b] Kendall correlation coefficients
*p .05. **p .01.

Second, as described in chapter 2, America enjoys a tradition of philanthropy. Giving is a customary, admired, expected, and even legally required behavior in our society. Fund raising, therefore, does not affect whether donors give, but to which charitable organizations they give, the extent of their giving, and the purposes of their gifts. Flessner (cited in H. Hall, 1993b), it is recalled from chapter 5, charged that private support as a percentage of GDP has not changed from the early 1960s even though the number of fund raisers has increased dramatically. Indeed, U.S. giving has represented about 2% of GDP for more than three decades (AAFRC Trust for Philanthropy, 1997b). The unchanged percentage supports the concepts presented in chapter 2—which are developed more fully in chapter 9—that fund raisers do make a difference, but not by affecting whether or not donors give. Although the percentage has not changed, gift totals have grown proportionately as our country's GDP has increased. In other words, fund raisers' aggregate difference has been their contribution to keeping private support steady at 2% of GDP (i.e., they reinforce a giving behavior).

Third, fund raisers use all four models to some extent although they practice one predominantly. It is likely that symmetrical fund raising is responsible for a significant portion of private support raised each year. As suggested by earlier findings, fund raisers tend to utilize the two-way symmetrical model more when raising major gifts, which typically account for most of the dollars raised by organizations that conduct both annual giving and major gifts programs—a description fitting 96% of those represented in NSFRE. For example, the leading employers of fund raisers—colleges, universities, and hospitals—rely on major gifts for about 80% of their gift income. The symmetrical concepts recommended by Dunlop (1993) for raising major gifts, which were presented in chapter 5, illustrate the relationship.

Beyond the question of continual increases, other evidence indicates that the model predominantly practiced is not as pragmatically effective as might be assumed. A remarkable 80% of the NSFRE members surveyed in 1992 reported that they had *not* met their dollar goals in each of the 5 years before the survey (Mongon, 1992). More than one fourth (27%) had not reached their goal in even 2 of the previous 5 years. Generalizing the findings, the vast majority of organizations represented in NSFRE fail to achieve their fund-raising goals in at least 1 year in every 5, and failure is becoming more common. In the 1988 survey, only 67% had not met their goals, meaning the failure rate increased by 13% between 1988 and 1992. As Mongon (1992) commented, "There has been a noticeable change in results within the last four years" (p. 12). Editorial comments were conspicuously absent in the report on NSFRE's 1995 survey, which found that 100% of the respondents had not met their dollar goals in each of the 5 prior years (Mongon, 1996). Almost three fourths (72%) were unsuccessful in 2 of the 5 years, keeping in mind that the 1995 findings are not generalizable.

In short, this study's finding that the two-way symmetrical model is related to higher fund-raising totals supports the thesis that charitable organizations can do well while doing good.

Practitioner Characteristics.   Four of the five practitioner characteristics have a significant relationship with one or more of the models. Only certification by NSFRE has no relationship, which indicates that the process does not distinguish between ineffective and effective fund-raising management.

Table 6.4 shows that younger practitioners tend to follow the public information model when raising annual gifts. Female fund raisers prefer the press agentry model for annual giving programs, and males favor the two-way asymmetrical model when raising major gifts. Experience has an equally significant relationship with the two-way models and press agentry in the major gifts program. Because fund raisers traditionally have been trained in the workplace, we can hypothesize that some learned their craft under mentors who were knowledgeable about research and other means of two-way communication, whereas some were exposed only to older strategies.

Related to training, professionalism was not measured in the explanatory study. Yet J. E. Grunig and Hunt (1984) argued that professionalism discriminates between the use of asymmetrical and symmetrical models in public relations. They claimed most professionals would be uncomfortable practicing the asymmetrical models as their efforts would be confined to promoting the organization's interest without question. On the other hand, only a professional could practice the two-way symmetrical model as it requires practitioners to get outside the organization's mindset in order to help it reach mutual understanding with important publics. Therefore, fund raisers with high levels of professionalism (e.g., training in a program of formal education and strong values of professional autonomy) hypothetically practice the two-way symmetrical model. Students contemplating future explanatory studies should incorporate measurements of professionalism as predictor variables, perhaps drawing from the criteria of a profession examined in chapter 4.

Returning to this study's findings, heads of fund-raising departments predominantly practice the press agentry model. Their position, as reported in Table 6.4, is negatively related to their scores on the other three models, but positively and significantly related to press agentry practice in both annual giving and major gifts programs. Their association with the oldest model must be discarded if charitable organizations are to think and behave more symmetrically.

According to power-control theory, department heads can move their organizations toward symmetrical fund raising only if they are members of the dominant coalition and have the knowledge, training, and experience necessary for practicing a two-way model. If they are not members of the dominant coalition, organizational change is unlikely. If they are a dominant coalition member but lack knowledge of and expertise in the two-way models, they also will lack power within the coalition. J. E. Grunig and L. A. Grunig (1989) predicted that in the latter case, functional managers would serve the dominant coalition in an advisory role, rather than in a counseling and managerial role.

The first situation accounts for 37% of NSFRE's members. The head of the fund-raising department is not a member of the dominant coalition and the organization predominantly practices the press agentry model. These fund-raising heads are basically technicians, as opposed to managers. They are unable to change asymmetrical presuppositions about fund raising because they are excluded from the group that controls the organization. Cook (1994a) documented this situation in his qualitative study on the role of university CEOs in fund raising. One of the chief fund raisers he interviewed stated:

> I've often felt that presidents, many presidents, really don't look at the chief development officer as a central officer of the university. That person may be titled vice president, that person may report directly to the president, but he or she is not really in on the major decision making of the institution. The provost or the senior vice president [COO] and the vice president for finance [CFO] are the two people who work more closely with the president on decision making on a day-to-day basis, whereas the development officer is really peripheral to that. (pp. 296–297)

In the second situation, the head of fund raising is a member of the dominant coalition, but the organization still predominantly practices the oldest model. Fund-raising heads are unable to change asymmetrical presuppositions because they have little or no expertise in the two-way models. They were admitted to the power elite primarily because of a need for fund-raising skills. As J. E. Grunig (1992) explained, top managers of a function are included in the dominant coalition when they can help the organization manage relationships with a strategic public deemed important by decision makers. This situation accounts for the majority (63%) of NSFRE's members.

Former CASE President Fisher (1985) attested to its commonness: "We are accepted at the academic conference table largely out of a pressing need for us rather than out of appreciation for what we are and what we do as professionals" (p. 12). Bloland and Bornstein (1991) reported that the 40 senior fund raisers they interviewed "see their relatively high status as dependent upon current demands for income in a time when many other sources of income have leveled off or been reduced" (p. 120). Describing the situation as "precarious" with constant fears "that unrealistic demands will be made upon them," the researchers concluded, "Development vice presidents see their position as enhanced or protected primarily in terms of whether they are able to secure continually increasing resources" (p. 120).

To enlighten understanding of the function's status, the chapter turns now to an examination of the roles fund raisers enact, which also provides insight on how future practitioners can gain power in organizations and thereby change the way fund raising is practiced.

ORGANIZATIONAL ROLES OF FUND RAISERS

Roles are the daily behavior patterns of individuals. They are important concepts in organizational theory because they explain how people behave in carrying out their job responsibilities and predict the outcomes of the action (Katz & Kahn, 1978). The public relations theory of roles, conceptualized and refined by Glen Broom and David Dozier of San Diego State University, paves the way for conceptualizing roles of fund raisers.

Major Roles of Technician and Manager

As introduced in chapter 3, the two major roles are technician and manager. The two-part typology provides a simplified way to examine the relationships among roles, practitioner behavior, and the models. Based on their research findings, Broom and Dozier (1986) said practitioners enacting the manager role use formative and evaluative research in their work. Environmental scanning, for example, is employed to help organizations manage interdependencies with strategic publics. Such practitioners are more likely to participate in decision making. Technicians, on the other hand, consider themselves creative personnel. They view their work more as an art than as management science.

J. E. Grunig (1992) distinguished between the two roles: "Managers conceptualize and direct" programs, whereas technicians "provide technical services" (p. 19). Technicians are found in every department, but "managers are a necessary component of excellent departments" (p. 19). Quantitative findings presented in the initial report of the Excellence Project (J. E. Grunig et al., 1991) showed that participation in critical management activities, especially strategic planning, is associated with the manager role and both the role and participation in such activities are characteristics of excellent public relations departments. The project's 1995 report (Dozier, L. A. Grunig, & J. E. Grunig, 1995) ranked knowledge to enact the manager role as the most important of 20 key characteristics of excellence.

Numerous studies conducted by University of Maryland researchers and others (e.g., Kelly, 1994b; Wetherell, 1989) have found that the technician role is empirically—as well as conceptually—related to the one-way models of public relations, whereas the manager role is related to the more sophisticated two-way models. Dozier (1992) explained the relationship between technicians and the one-way models: "Organizations that practice the press agentry and public information models need technicians. Staff are not involved in strategic planning and problem solving under these models. Once strategic decisions are made and action plans drawn, the technician is brought in to implement" (p. 345).

His explanation sheds light on the situation in which heads of fund-raising departments are not members of the dominant coalition and the organization predominantly practices press agentry. The chief fund raiser enacts the technician role because that is what the model practiced by the organization requires. Duronio and Loessin (1991) provided an evolutionary description in their qualitative study of fund-raising effectiveness in higher education:

> Many veteran fund raisers told us that in the not too distant past, when the development officer typically was not part of the executive administrative team, executive staff members and trustees defined the institution's mission and set priorities and then handed the development officer the "shopping list" of projects in need of private funding. (p. 207)

The head of fund raising for most—but not all—of the 10 institutions studied by Duronio and Loessin now is a member of the organization's executive staff (i.e., a dominant coalition member). The move to executive status, the researchers speculated, is fairly new, citing Gilley, Fulmer, and Reithlingshoefer (1986), who identified fund raisers as one of "the new power brokers" (p. 84) in higher education. Indicative of the second situation, Duronio and Loessin (1991) found that formal planning, goal setting, and evaluation, which they had assumed would be integral to effective practice, "were not particularly characteristic of the fund-raising programs in our ten institutions" (p. 217). They reported, "In most institutions, management was generally perceived more as a routine housekeeping chore than as a critical factor affecting overall fund-raising performance" (p. 214).

In other words, department heads have been admitted to the dominant coalition, but do not enact the manager role. It is not surprising, then, that their organizations continue to practice the press agentry model. To affect change, senior practitioners must adopt managerial characteristics, including use of research and strategic planning, which will build their expertise in the two-way models.

The typology of manager and technician roles did not emerge until the research program in public relations was well underway. To identify the roles of fund raisers, it is necessary to return to the beginning of the theory.

Four Fund-Raising Roles

Using a classical deductive approach in the late 1970s, Broom (Broom & Smith, 1979) drew from the literature to first conceptualize four theoretical roles: (a) communication facilitator, (b) expert prescriber, (c) communication technician, and (d) problem-solving process facilitator. Broom (1982) then operationalized the roles by developing 24 self-reported measures of activities—six Likert-like statements for each of the four roles. The measures were used to test his theoretical roles in a national survey of PRSA members. Results showed that his indicators of role activities were highly reliable, and subsequent studies by him and others added evidence as to their reliability and validity (Dozier, 1992).

The following discussion extrapolates the four roles to fund raisers. Anticipating that Broom's use of the term *communication* may hamper understanding by some future practitioners, I have modified the labels of two of the four roles, which are renamed: (a) liaison, (b) expert prescriber, (c) technician, and (d) problem-solving process facilitator. The changes are minor, they do not muddy the conceptual waters, and they are based on precedent. Broom (Cutlip et al., 1985, 1994) has argued that fund raising is a part of public relations. The term *liaison* was used previously by Dozier (1984) to label a role related to communication facilitator. And Dozier and Broom (1995) recognized limitations of the term *communication* and explicitly excluded it from their definition of the public relations function.

According to Broom (Cutlip et al., 1994), "Practitioners adopt roles in organizations by taking on patterns of behaviors to deal with recurring types of situations and to accommodate others' expectations" (p. 42). As with the models, every practitioner plays all of the roles to some extent, but one of the four will emerge as the dominant role.

Liaison.   The liaison role is the traditional role of fund raisers. It was the one predominantly enacted by the first full-time practitioners, consultants, who—it is recalled—do not solicit gifts but advise senior managers and volunteers on doing so. As depicted by its label, the role casts practitioners as liaisons in the fund-raising process: They act as facilitators, interpreters, and mediators in bringing together organizational representatives with prospective donors.

A major concern of fund raisers in this role is removing barriers in donor–recipient relations. The characteristic underscores a danger of the liaison role: Practitioners tend to concentrate on concerns about donors rather than larger issues related to the program services, policies, and actions of the organization. In addition, the role's reliance on other actors to carry out activities and meet goals leaves fund raising vulnerable to ineffective amateurs and criticisms of inefficiency.

Evidence of this role commonly is found in the literature written by consultants. For example, consultant Fisher Howe (1991) stated, "Only occasionally do development officers visit foundations, corporations, or other prospects, and then it is with the chief executive or a board member, who, in most organizations, does the asking" (p. 95). Although Howe conceded that fund raisers for universities and hospitals personally solicit contributions (i.e., enact a different role), he asserted, "But by and large, development officers initiate, prepare, point the way, assist, and accompany, but do not themselves do the asking" (p. 95). Lord (1983) said, "The development officer, in most cases, should not be expected to personally solicit contributions or recruit volunteers" (p. 101). The fund raiser, according to Lord, is not to do, but to see that things get done by others. He acknowledged, "This job description has been modeled for us, to a great extent, by the development officers who are in business—the outside fund-raising consultants" (p. 104).

Gurin (1985) argued that acting as a liaison is the only proper fund-raising role:

> Professional fund raisers are properly functioning when they advise and assist volunteers in becoming effective solicitors. This distinction has been drawn so clearly so often over so many years that it is difficult to understand how some so-called professionals in the business have not heard of it or, knowing it, evidence no inclination to observe it. (p. 106)

Yet Duronio and Loessin (1991) found that only 4 of the 10 universities they studied have strong volunteer participation, suggesting enactment of roles other than liaison. They concluded, "Involving volunteers in fund raising is not a prerequisite for fund-raising success in all institutions" (p. 214).

Relating this role to consultants is theoretically logical in that its conceptualization by Broom (Broom & Smith, 1979) was drawn from the consulting literature. Furthermore, based on his research, Dozier (1984) maintained that external consultants play different roles than do practitioners inside organizations. This is not to say staff fund raisers do not practice the liaison role to some extent, or even predominantly in a few organizations. NSFRE's 1992 study (Mongon, 1992) showed that 10% of its members did not solicit any gifts during the year before the survey. As consultants represented 4.6% of the respondents, we can hypothesize that only about 5% of all staff fund raisers belonging to NSFRE predominantly enact the liaison role. Furthermore, 40% and 50% of the respondents said practitioners more so than volunteers solicit top- and midlevel gifts, respectively. Findings reflect the historical evolution of the function, as Mongon noted, "This suggests a dramatic departure from practice several decades ago" (p. 14).

Expert Prescriber. The expert prescriber role can be considered the exact opposite of the liaison role (Dozier, 1992). Fund raisers in this role act and are viewed as the only ones in their organization with the skill and the responsibility for raising gifts. Senior managers and trustees are content to leave fund raising in the hands of the "expert" and assume relatively passive participation. The fund raiser decides which organizational needs and donor prospects are addressed, develops the programming, and carries out most activities. Little effort is made to bring top officials or managers into the process other than requesting their token representation in selected cultivation activities and solicitation calls.

The expert prescriber role is seductive to practitioners because it is gratifying to be seen as the authority. The role is equally seductive to trustees and managers because they do not have to "bother" with fund raising once they have turned it over to the expert. Handing over responsibility is particularly attractive to those who have not been educated about the newer models and perceive fund raising as "distasteful." However, there are dangers inherent in the role of expert prescriber. Its predominant enactment can compartmentalize fund raising and remove it from the mainstream of the organization's operations. Commitment to raising money and responsibility for success are left with the practitioner, often leading to unrealistic expectations and dissatisfaction with results. The role obstructs the diffusion of fund-raising thinking throughout the organization, lessening its ability to effectively manage environmental interdependencies with donor publics.

Evidence of this role also is found in the literature. For example, consultant Kay Sprinkel Grace (1991b), who advocated a core fund-raising team composed of the CEO, two trustees, and the chief fund raiser, criticized the expert prescriber role:

> There has been a movement among some organizations—principally colleges, universities, and hospitals—toward "staff-driven" fund raising, thereby minimizing the need for a full development team that involves board members and other volunteers. In this approach, development staff members initiate and execute the vast majority of the fund raising [sic] responsibilities, including major donor solicitations. (p. 162)

Providing empirical evidence, Winfree (1992) found that only 57% of total major gift dollars to colleges and universities in his sample were solicited with "nondevelopment personnel" having played a significant role in the process (p. 6). In other words, 43% of the dollars were raised without the involvement of the CEO, program service managers, trustees, or other volunteers. Generalizing the findings to Winfree's population, almost half of all major gift dollars raised by the 4-year U.S. colleges and universities that received one or more $1-million-plus gifts from 1985 to 1987 were raised solely by staff fund raisers.

This conclusion—which Winfree ignored—suggests that the predominant enactment of the expert prescriber role is increasing, at least in institutions of higher education. Winship (1984) concluded from an earlier study of 68 representative colleges and universities that only 23% of major gifts—which he defined as gifts of $100,000 or more—were raised by staff fund raisers. Commenting on what then seemed a high percentage of gifts raised by practitioners, Winship said, "That should not be surprising, yet it carries a message to those who feel that senior development officers should be manager and orchestrators, but not solicitors" (p. 1).

Documenting dangers of the expert prescriber role, Carbone (1989) quoted a female fund raiser with 10 years of experience: "In general, organizations tend to have unrealistic expectations of their development professionals; tend to see them as (isolates) who should do their work without commitment from and integration with the rest of the organization" (p. 29). Conry (1991) attested to others' expectations of expert prescribers: "In a climate of increasing competition for the private dollar, [organizations] are trying to buy expertise and acquire fund raisers who can turn on money machines" (p. 156).

In my earlier work, I cited numerous examples from the fund-raising literature advocating a behind-the-scenes role for practitioners (Kelly, 1991a). I used secondary research and critical analysis to refute what I termed *the myth of the invisible fund raiser*, showing that consultants perpetuated this viewpoint and that staff fund raisers were quite productive in personally cultivating and soliciting gifts. The emphasis given to using volunteer solicitors, I argued, created misconceptions and misunderstandings about the fund-raising function. The theory of roles provides a fuller explanation. Both patterns are accurate descriptions of how individuals behave in carrying out their fund-raising responsibilities, and they are more appropriately recognized as the liaison and expert prescriber roles. Some practitioners predominantly enact one, some adopt the other.

Juxtaposition of the two roles is common. Harrah-Conforth and Borsos (1991) concluded from their historical study dealing primarily with consultants, "Professional standards demand that fund raisers hide themselves in order to shift the focus of acknowledgement and interest toward the cause and the donors; therefore, fund raising remains a behind-the-scenes career" (p. 29). The personal attributes Carbone's (1989) respondents assigned to themselves are incongruent with such a role: "'self-starters,' 'gregarious,' and 'entrepreneurial,' with strong 'ego needs' and considerable 'pride in personal achievement'" (p. 36). The theory of roles reduces confusion about the contradictory information.

Technician.   Practitioners in the technician role are not involved in setting fund-raising objectives or in other decisions related to how the process is managed. They are not part of the management team; they are concerned with producing and implementing the various techniques used in raising gifts. Effectiveness of the function—in terms of supporting the organization's mission and goals—is dependent on the planning and strategic decisions of others, as well as their ability to communicate decisions to the fund-raising staff.

Whereas all practitioners begin their careers in this role, fund-raising departments composed solely of technicians will contribute little to organizational success. Responding to criticism of the role's label, Dozier and Broom (1995) stated, "A technician by any other name would still be a technician: a creator and disseminator of messages, intimately involved in production, operating independent of management decision making, strategic planning, issues management, environmental scanning, and program evaluation" (p. 22).

Evidence of the technician role is readily available. According to Payton (1986), most of the fund-raising literature is aimed at technicians. He defined a technician as a person indifferent to purpose, who focuses instead on process and technique. "They tend to know everything about a subject except what it is for" (p. 8). Out of courtesy, Payton presumed most senior fund raisers are not technicians, but he hypothesized that they know quite a bit about technical things, such as how to use direct mail and organize a fund-raising committee, but they know little about why they do these things.

Although he advocated the liaison role, Howe (1991) also described fund raisers as technicians. "Development officers, on the whole . . . are the drones who do the work, prepare the materials and recommendations, and then send the chiefs in to see the prospects while they stay in the background" (p. 95). Delineating their "duties," Howe emphasized prospect research and then listed the following in order: "They write proposals. They draft correspondence. They arrange cultivation events. They maintain files and record systems. They generate ideas" (p. 95). Generally, it is rare for external fund raisers to execute any but the last of the duties listed; thus, it may be that Howe and other consultants perceive a technician role for internal staff but reserve a role more in keeping with counseling senior managers, such as liaison, for themselves.

Three college presidents who once were fund raisers similarly outlined technician responsibilities as the "important things" staff practitioners do to help presidents be effective: prospect research, bringing opportunities to the president, generating reports, proposal writing, record keeping, drafting letters, and "hounding the president" to meet obligations (Pray, 1981, p. 355). Whether such role expectations are sent by

CEOs, consultants, or others, limiting staff fund raisers to a technician role reduces their contribution to the charitable organizations they are hired to serve.

Problem-Solving Process Facilitator.

Practitioners enacting the problem-solving process facilitator role consult *and* collaborate with others in the organization. They are part of the management team, guiding organizational members through the 5-step process of fund raising. The interaction begins with research and continues as a joint effort through setting objectives, programming (including cultivation and solicitation), evaluation, and stewardship.[1]

Managers responsible for program services and operations supply much of the information for decisions at each of the steps because they are the ones most knowledgeable about and intimately involved in the organization's offerings, policies, and actions. As Broom (Cutlip et al., 1994) stressed, they "are also the ones with the *power* to make any needed changes" (p. 43; italics in original), which may be necessary to balance relations with donors. These managers assist in enhancing accountability and protecting autonomy. When not involved, they are likely to be uninformed about fund-raising objectives, unenthusiastic about efforts to achieve them, and uncommitted to the function's position in the organization.

Evidence of the problem-solving process facilitator role is embedded in the fund-raising literature. Consultant and staff practitioner Kent Dove (1988) described today's ideal fund-raising head as "a helper in problem solving and goal accomplishment" (p. 41). The first of Broce's (1986) "Nine Cardinal Principles of Fund Raising" was, "Institutional or organizational objectives must be established first" (p. 17). Fund raising grows out of the aspirations and directions of an organization, he said; therefore, an early priority in planning any program to raise gifts is a review of organizational goals. He instructed, "The fund-raising officer should participate, as should the institution's key leaders, including volunteers" (p. 18).

Pray (1981) endorsed the problem-solving process facilitator role:

> More and more chief development and advancement officers have proved themselves capable of assuming prominent posts in development strategy . . . working directly with trustees, making themselves highly visible in public meetings, and *partnering* appropriate staff, volunteers, or other colleagues in . . . negotiations with important foundations, corporations and individual donors. (p. 179; italics in original)

Comparing this behavior pattern to the roles of liaison and technician, Pray (1981) argued, "We begin to suspect that the folklore of what is appropriate behavior grew out of a lack of ability of the earlier development people to play this *more important role*, more than it did out of the reality of the situation" (p. 180; italics added). Competent fund raisers, he said, are becoming colleagues rather than merely assistants. Pray also discredited the expert prescriber role: "Fund raising is not, cannot be, and will not successfully work as a separate entity. . . . At best, the officer with prime responsibilities is a coordinator and facilitator, playing the role of helping the other elements within the organism function effectively in winning support" (p. 5).

Mixer (1993) drew from a range of social science literature to identify four "leadership styles," which parallel the fund-raising roles. As "coach director" (liaison),

---

[1]The 5-step process of fund raising, ROPES, is the subject of chapter 10.

the fund raiser takes "an advisory stance" while "board members, other leaders, and staff appear as players and stars on the field" (p. 155). In contrast, the "authoritative executive" (expert prescriber) avoids "consultation and participation with others" and is evident when "the chief executive dislikes or shuns fundraising [*sic*]" (p. 154). The "laissez-faire official" (technician) "gives little or no overall direction" and "find[s] it difficult to marshall effective fundraising [*sic*] programs" (pp. 156–157). The "collegial facilitator" (problem-solving process facilitator) consults extensively, "asking for input from board members, volunteers, and staff, while synthesizing and suggesting direction and trends" (p. 155). Mixer concluded that the fourth style's "active engagement" of others "produces greater results than passive or limited participation" (p. 156).

In the only article linking public relations role theory to fund raising, educator John Ledingham (1993) stated without elaborating, "Today's development director has progressed from a communication facilitator to a problem-solving process facilitator who recognizes the importance of reaching significant publics and gaining their support" (p. 368).

Research on Fund-Raising Roles

Broom (1982) found that public relations practitioners who rate high on the technician role show no tendency to score high on the other three roles. Conversely, those scoring highest on any one of the other three roles—liaison, expert prescriber, or problem-solving process facilitator—also score relatively high on the other two, but not on the technician role. Intercorrelation among the three nontechnician roles convinced him that they are part of a common underlying role, the manager.

Dozier (1983) reached the same conclusion after conducting exploratory factor analyses of three separate studies measuring Broom's roles. Findings confirmed that the three intercorrelated roles should be collapsed into one, and he urged reduction of the roles typology from four to two.

The two major roles of manager and technician provide a parsimonious description of practitioner behavior; as such, their use is adopted for most of this text. However, as Broom (Cutlip et al., 1985) emphasized, important conceptual distinctions are lost when the three roles are combined into the manager role. These distinctions are critical to understanding the behavior patterns of fund raisers.

The public relations scholars have chosen to treat all three of the nontechnician roles as conceptually distinct but equal components of the manager role. Yet the discussion of fund-raising roles indicates that the problem-solving process facilitator role is superior to the other two. Predominant enactment of the liaison role with its nonsolicitation posture is not a viable option for staff practitioners. The expert prescriber role isolates the function and excludes organizational actors important to success. The problem-solving process facilitator role, on the other hand, integrates fund raising in the overall management of charitable organizations.

The public relations scholars themselves allude to the last role's superiority. For example, Dozier and Broom (1995) said the expert prescriber role "leads to passive management involvement," whereas the problem-solving process facilitator role "leads to strong management 'ownership' of solutions reached" (p. 8). Dozier (1992) related the liaison role to both the public information and two-way symmetrical models, but he stressed, "The problem-solving process facilitator role is essential in organizations practicing the two-way symmetric model" (p. 330).

Students looking for a thesis or dissertation topic should consider studies on the four roles of fund raisers conceptualized here. Derived from theory and an analysis of the literature, the roles now need to be tested in the field and refined in order to advance our understanding of fund raising. The program of research undertaken in public relations facilitates such studies.

Broom's (1982) 24 indicators are available for modification. For example, only one word would have to be changed in the statement, "I make communication policy decisions" (Dozier, 1992, p. 331). Responses could be measured with the 7-point, never-to-always scale used by Broom (1982) or the fractionation scale I used in the studies on the fund-raising models (testing the roles and models in the same study would have added value). A stratified sample from NSFRE could include consultants and staff fund raisers, providing insightful comparisons of the predominant roles among types of fund raisers and charitable organizations. Samples from the other associations also are recommended. Given the discussion of feminization and role theory in chapter 3, studies should measure gender and break down results by male and female practitioners. Students now have a better grasp of why women enacting the technician role make less money and hold lower status positions than men. Research findings would add to our knowledge and suggest ways to combat gender discrimination.

Until now, there have been few studies on fund-raising roles because practitioners—who have conducted much of the research as part-time students—have not considered organizational roles an important problem. Less than half (46%) the education fund raisers Carbone (1987) studied believe it is "very important" to clarify the "central roles" of practitioners (p. 15). Yet as Carbone pointed out, such efforts are "deemed vital to the process" (p. 15) of moving an occupation toward greater professionalism.

Public relations has laid a conceptual and methodological path that fund-raising students and scholars should follow, although curves, turns, and even new routes always are encouraged.

FUND RAISERS AS STAFF MANAGERS

Effective fund-raising management requires practitioners enacting the manager role, predominantly the role of problem-solving process facilitator. Adoption of the three other roles prevents charitable organizations from practicing the two-way symmetrical model.

K. S. Grace (1991b) identified four organizational problems fund raisers encounter, which are associated with the roles of liaison, expert prescriber, and technician. The most prevalent problem is the fund-raising function is not understood by trustees, senior managers, and others in the organization. Second, fund raising is considered peripheral. Third, limited authority is coupled with great responsibility. To illustrate the third problem, Grace pointed to situations in which decisions about program services are made without consultation with fund raisers or consideration of the effects on fund raising. Fourth, horizontal and vertical relationships between the function and other organizational units are weak or nonexistent. Advocating an integrative role, she proclaimed, "Successful fund raising requires and deserves support from the entire organization" (p. 142).

Staff Versus Line Functions

Effective management also requires that fund raising be approached as a staff function, as opposed to a line function. It serves the organization by counseling and supporting those with the responsibility and authority to run it. Figure 6.1 presents an organization chart distinguishing between line and staff functions.

Solid connecting lines in Fig. 6.1 represent the reporting relationships from the board of trustees, which has legal and fiduciary responsibility, through the CEO and COO to the line managers, who are responsible for carrying out the organization's mission (i.e., program services and operations). Broken lines represent the reporting relationships of staff functions to the CEO, which reside outside the hierarchy of trustees, senior managers, and line managers. Similar to legal and human resources departments, fund raising is positioned high in the organization to contribute to its overall well-being, but does not have authority or responsibility to produce its services. Pace (1983) explained, "The job of staff officers is to advise top officials and to support and assist line officers" (pp. 16–17). In other words, fund raising is not a line function that independently generates income (i.e., a money machine), but rather a staff function that spans departmental boundaries to manage the organization's efforts to obtain gifts.

Students will note that Fig. 6.1 combines fund raising and public relations in one vice-presidential position. The reason for doing so is discussed shortly. They should also note that marketing is a line function, with responsibility for service production and use. As described in chapter 1, marketing's defined role is to generate consumer demand by changing an organization's products and services. Fund raising supports marketing and other line functions, but it does not change what the organization does.

The line–staff management model originated in the military and now is used in most large organizations (Cutlip et al., 1994). Staff functions become increasingly necessary as organizations grow in size and complexity. For example, the larger and more complex an organization, the more likely it will have an internal legal department. Similarly, charitable organizations that are small and have low complexity, such as a local shelter for the homeless, usually do not have a staff function for fund raising, whereas large charitable organizations with high complexity, such as a research hospital, do. Outside consultants provide services to organizations not large or complex enough to need a particular staff function in-house. In the case of fund raising, consultants advise and direct managers, trustees, and other volunteers in raising gifts.

The distinction between staff and line functions promotes the integration of fund raising with other organizational units. The fund-raising process is seriously impaired without the participation of trustees, senior officers, and line managers. Needs they prioritize as greatest may not be addressed. Prospective donors with whom they have relationships likely will be ignored. Essential knowledge about plans and operation of program services will be absent from negotiations determining the use of major gifts. Evaluation will be based on criteria other than supporting the organization's goals,

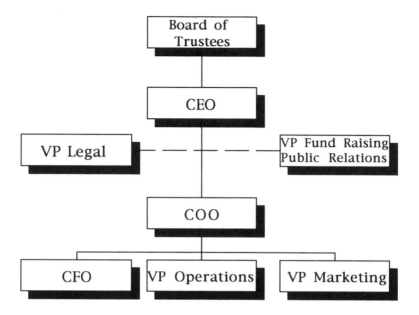

FIG. 6.1. Line and staff organization chart.

and appropriate recognition, reporting, and continued cultivation will be decided in isolation of those responsible for running the organization. Overall, when other units are not meaningfully involved, fund raising is less relevant to the organization's mission and more distant from its management.

Working With the Board

Board members, whether called trustees, directors, governors, or something else, are, as O'Connell (1993) argued, "trustees in the literal and legal sense of the term" (p. 19). By legal definition, trustees hold the charitable organization in trust for the common good. O'Connell explained, "No matter how the organization is structured or the degree of authority delegated to staff, committees, or affiliates, the board and therefore the trustees are ultimately accountable" (p. 19).

Drawing from earlier work, Herman and Block (1990) termed the prescriptive ideal of what a board should be—on which most of the trustee literature is based—the "heroic model" (p. 226). This model places boards at the hierarchical peak in charitable organizations. A tripartite system, presented by Houle (1989), divides activities into a staff–executive–board pattern that differentiates the work to be done (staff), the administration of the work (executive), and the establishment of policies to guide it (trustees). According to Herman and Block (1990), trustees have three chief areas of responsibilities under the heroic model: (a) hire and fire the CEO; (b) define and reevaluate the organization's mission and major goals, develop a strategic plan, and approve budgets and policies consistent with the plan; and (c) ensure the organization obtains the resources necessary to meet the plan. Ideally, then, boards embrace fund raising as one of their main duties.

Illustrating this expectation, Howe (1991) began his book, *The Board Member's Guide to Fund Raising*, with what he referred to as the first principle for trustees: "The board must establish the organization and procedures to get the fund-raising job done. In turn, board members must be involved, individually and personally" (p. 1). Broce (1986) emphatically stated, "The board must be involved in fund-raising programs from the planning stage through the solicitation stage" (p. 204).

Scholars recently have challenged the heroic model. Middleton (1987), for example, asserted, "Most of the data indicate that boards do not formulate policy but rather ratify policy presented to them by staff" (p. 152). Herman and Heimovics (1990) concluded from the results of a 1989 management study that CEOs, not trustees, commonly carry the burden of responsibility for organizational outcomes.

It is recalled from the explanatory study of the fund-raising models that trustees are members of the dominant coalition in only 80% of the organizations represented in NSFRE, whereas CEOs are members in 94%. The findings support challenges to trustees' superordinate position. Only those who are members of the powerful inner circle control the charitable organizations for which they are accountable.

Herman and Block (1990) reached two major conclusions after reviewing the literature on trustees and fund raising: (a) Little research has been conducted on the extent of board involvement; and (b) Evidence strongly suggests that many or even most boards do not meet prescriptive expectations. Yet as the scholars insisted, "The board cannot divorce itself from its fiduciary responsibility; thereby it always remains responsible for funding both policy and program decisions" (p. 227). O'Connell (1993) argued, "One of the most inappropriate things a board can do is to call for increased income and leave it to the staff to produce.... The board is accountable—and the board leads" (p. 126).

The gap between prescriptive behavior and findings of descriptive studies is partially explained by the line–staff management model. The board has ultimate responsibility for ensuring the organization obtains necessary resources. In small organizations with low complexity, trustees must also take responsibility for the strategy and tactics necessary to achieve fund-raising results. In larger, more complex organizations, they delegate management responsibility to the CEO or the CEO's designee (i.e., the staff manager). This does not mean trustees remove themselves from fund raising; they work as volunteers under staff direction (Carver, 1990). Although the authority and responsibility for managing donor relations lie with the function, trustee participation is vital. O'Connell (1993) affirmed, "Good development directors . . . are good in large part because they know—and will tell you—that they can succeed only to the extent that the board and staff leadership are committed to and involved in the fundraising [*sic*]" (p. 127).

This explanation is congruent with other attempts to account for variation in trustee involvement. For example, Block, Leduc, and Carroccio (cited in Herman & Block, 1990) said the board's role in fund raising is partly determined by the age of the organization. In early stages of the life cycle, board members' involvement is indistinguishable from the work of staff. In later stages, the board's hands-on role is taken over by staff but trustees still participate, most noticeably by networking and serving as the organization's representatives. Aging would necessitate "staff who could devote the appropriate concentration of time that is required" (p. 228).

O'Connell (1993) differentiated board involvement by fund-raising complexity and amount of gifts. If an organization conducts several programs using several techniques and has a yearly goal of more than $75,000, a staff function usually is needed. He stated, "The basic rule is for the board to do everything possible on its own and to hire a staff only when that will help the volunteers reach even higher results" (p. 129). Consultants, he maintained, can substitute for staff for all but the annual giving program; however, he advised trustees, "If you're going to grow and sustain the momentum, you will need an individual who is good and is employed full-time" (p. 128).

This book assumes that a staff function, headed by a manager, is responsible for the process of raising gifts. The board retains ultimate responsibility for financial resources, but has delegated management of the organization's fund-raising efforts to staff designated by the CEO. Trustees serve in a volunteer capacity and are directed by staff. Similarly, the staff manager provides direction, counsel, and support for the CEO's involvement. As Lord (1983) stated, "The senior development officer who does not form close working relationships with the CEO and the trustees won't be able to accomplish very much. This officer has to be able to direct their activities with respect to development" (p. 102).

Working With the CEO

Effective fund raising is dependent on all organizational members, but particularly those who control the organization. CEOs, as found in the explanatory study of the models, are almost always dominant coalition members. The power and credibility of their office makes their involvement in fund raising imperative. The CEO generally is the only person capable of speaking for the whole organization; he or she is, literally, the person in charge. "And," as one university president stated, "most donors . . . want the privilege and the opportunity to talk to the person in charge" (Cook, 1994a, p. 366).

Every gift would be easier to raise if the CEO was involved, but then there would be little reason for top officials to designate a department for fund raising. Furthermore, the size and complexity that necessitated a staff function in the first place also demand time and attention from the CEO. Evidence suggests that about one third of the CEO's time is spent on fund raising (P. M. Buchanan, 1993). Staff managers, therefore, are selective in directing the attention of the CEO to those situations and opportunities when the person in charge must speak for the organization. Their involvement primarily is with prospects for major gifts.

On the other hand, CEOs are dependent on their staff managers (i.e., the relationship is interdependent). If the fund-raising manager does not successfully meet set objectives, the CEO is accountable to the board. When unmet objectives negatively impact program services and operations, the CEO bears responsibility. Professional reputations of CEOs increasingly are tied to fund-raising results. And on a personal level, most CEOs are not trained in fund raising and rely on staff managers for counsel, as well as direction.

A chief fund raiser and a CEO interviewed by Cook (1993) illustrated the working relationship. The fund raiser said, "My role is to be a manager of the process and a manager of the CEO's time and effort in development" (p. 3). The CEO stated, "I learn from my own staff. I don't hesitate to follow their advice and determination as to what amount of money should be requested, or when, or how, or who" (p. 8).

To build and maintain such a relationship, the staff manager must develop an affinity with the CEO and earn his or her trust and confidence. If need be, the practitioner must educate the CEO about what it takes to raise money. The head of the function helps instill fund raising as an inherent element in everything the CEO does.

Stephen Trachtenberg (1993), president of George Washington University, presented his expectations of a chief fund raiser. The first 6 of his 11 basic rules simply were: Be loyal and honest, share my enthusiasm, push me, don't waste my time, and support me. He compared the CEO to a political candidate, with the head of fund raising serving as the campaign manager. "Put me in the right place at the right time and brief me with accurate and thoughtful research" (p. 20). Addressing another rule, "raise money," he stated:

> We need to make some calls together, but you should also make calls alone. I expect you to manage your own portfolio of major prospects in addition to the ones I handle or those we handle together . . . . I expect you to be turning up new ground, discovering new prospective donors, and then bringing me in when you are ready to close the big gift. (p. 20)

Expanding on the CEO's dependency, fund-raising experience and success have become required qualifications for those who head charitable organizations. Professional reputations frequently are won or lost based on dollars raised. One university president interviewed by Cook (1994a) explained, "If you succeed in helping to raise a lot of money, not only will you get things done, but people will forgive you for a lot of things that otherwise they might have a harder time with. . . . The incentive . . . is enormous and the penalty for not doing that is also enormous" (p. 278). A chief fund raiser declared, "A solid development effort can make or break their presidency. They probably didn't realize that when they became president" (Cook, 1993, p. 5). Bornstein (cited in M. A. Fisher, 1993), the former fund raiser and now college president, wistfully said, "I wish I'd known how much success in fund raising means to success as a president" (p. 40).

Unfortunately, such an emphasis can be detrimental to effective management of the function. CEOs often feel pressured to take credit and shortcuts when it comes to attracting private support. In turn, they may apply pressure on staff to generate indiscriminate dollars. Attesting to the rewards of fund-raising "success," in 1989, George Langdon, Jr. was hired by New York's American Museum of Natural History for a salary of $225,000, free use of a $2.2-million penthouse, and much more because, according to media reports, "he had just led a successful drive to raise $85-million as the president of Colgate University" ("New York," 1992, p. 37).

Outcomes of such pressures can take many forms, including unrealistic expectations and increased use of and goals for capital campaigns. Solutions to these and other problems are incorporated in subsequent chapters. Suffice it to say here that sometimes fund raisers must weigh what they know is appropriate against sportslike games undertaken to help CEOs make a name for themselves—and then act accordingly.

Staff managers have a right to expect essential support from CEOs, without which fund raising cannot be effectively managed. Cutlip et al. (1994) listed four legitimate expectations: (a) positive leadership; (b) strategic planning embracing all policies and programs; (c) adequate budget to do the job, including funds for research and evaluation; and (d) reasonable availability for consultation and "public appearances" (p. 61). To this list, we must add a fifth and overarching expectation: (e) an understanding of philanthropy.

Touching on these briefly, a chief fund raiser interviewed by Cook (1993) complained, "I find that an awful lot of presidents really don't understand philanthropy. They want the money but they are not willing to work at relationship fund raising to get the money. . . . [they] either don't devote the time to that or it's not their style" (p. 2).

In an unscientific survey of selected NSFRE members (Hedgepeth, 1994), 67 senior fund raisers ranked the appropriate roles for the CEO as follows: (a) leader, (b) visionary, and (c) definer of organizational mission. The ordered fund-raising roles for trustees were: (a) example for board and donors, (b) motivator of board, (c) and recruiter of key volunteers. According to the respondents, misunderstanding about role definitions is the greatest source of conflict among the actors of chief fund raiser, CEO, and trustee volunteer.

Verifying the CEO's roles as leader and visionary, Winfree (1992) found that the top reason fund raisers gave for using the CEO in the solicitation of major gifts was the simple fact that he or she "is the school's president" (p. 12). A chief fund raiser in Cook's (1994a) study asserted, "The president's role is to explain what the vision is that you hope the donor will consider funding" (p. 292).

Strategic planning, as discussed in chapter 10, is mandatory for effective fund-raising management. Block, Leduc, and Carroccio (cited in Herman & Block, 1990) explained:

> Fund raising is an outgrowth of strategic directional planning, a process that examines and seeks an understanding of the management and program strengths and weaknesses . . . an understanding of the service needs of the organization's constituents; an understanding of the organization's attraction to existing and potential stakeholders; and familiarity with the organization's competition. (p. 228)

CEOs must ensure strategic planning takes place before fund-raising efforts are started. Ignoring this essential step severely handicaps the function and diminishes the CEO's contribution. A chief fund raiser described one of the likely results: "The presidents that have the hardest time are the ones that don't know what the hell they want to raise money for, and are confused, or have so many things they want to raise money for that the donors say, 'What is your real priority?'" (Cook, 1994a, pp. 459–460).

Broce (1986) elaborated, "Donors give gifts to meet objectives, not simply to give money away" (p. 19). Broce's first cardinal principle of fund raising, students will recall, was organizational goals must be in place. Only then, he argued, can the second principle of establishing fund-raising objectives be carried out. He stated, "How I pity people hired to 'raise money' without any idea how the money is going to be used in the life of the institution. They might just as well stand on busy corners with tin cups" (p. 18).

Finally, staff managers have a right to expect adequate budgets. According to K. S. Grace (1991b), goal displacement is a primary threat to managing the function for optimum results. "Development officers are frequently hired with the admonition that they will have to 'raise their own salary' in the first year—or every year—to justify their jobs" (p. 144). The condition constitutes goal displacement because it diverts focus from raising gifts for program services to fund raising for the practitioner's own salary.

Salaries, benefits, and projected expenses must be included in the organization's operating budget before a fund raiser is hired. Failure to do so is a dereliction of duty by trustees and senior managers, one largely responsible for unethical fund raising. If funding cannot be earmarked, the board and the CEO retain responsibility for raising gifts until necessary funds are found (O'Connell, 1993). Hiring internal practitioners to raise their own salary or paid solicitors whose fees come from the money collected is irresponsible and violates fundamental principles. Quite simply, if those who control a charitable organization do not care enough about attracting private support to engage in fund raising themselves (with or without the assistance of a consultant) or to provide funding for a staff function, they have no right to seek gifts from others. Our tradition of philanthropy and the theory of the commons demand their commitment first.

Broce (1986) stated, "Governing boards often hear the old saw that 'it costs money to make money,' and I subscribe to that theory" (p. 231). Indeed, the American Cancer Society spent $83 million on fund raising in 1995 to raise $382 million, representing a 22% fund-raising cost ratio ("Philanthropy 400," 1996). Habitat For Humanity spent $16 million, KCET Community Television of Southern California in Los Angeles spent $10 million, the New York Public Library spent $5 million, and the Lyric Opera of Chicago spent $2 million. Their cost ratios ranged from 9% to 25%. Chapter 7 addresses the issue of cost ratios; the point here is that socially responsible organizations invest resources in fund raising before looking outside for financial support.

The investment is worthwhile. In 1994, Catholic Charities USA spent $17 million on fund raising, and only 80 of its 160 affiliates had fund raisers on staff ("Philanthropy 400," 1996). In 1995, it increased its fund-raising budget to $27 million and the number of affiliates with practitioners to 136. As a result, the human services organization raised 25% more in 1995 than it had in 1994, $419 million, and jumped from seventh to third place in the "Philanthropy 400." Its president, the Reverend Fred Kammer, said the rise in ranking proved the investment paid off. Conventional wisdom, Boardman (1993) reported, holds that fund raisers generate three times their salary the first year. A 1986 expenditure study of higher education showed that the median for the average amount raised per fund-raising staff member was $738,500 annually—22 times the average salary of $33,000 paid to CASE members in 1986 (Boardman, 1993; Turk, 1986)! Clearly, fund raising is deserving of the financial support of trustees and CEOs.

) commented in the overview of her 3-year study, "Interestingly, no
that fund raisers may require and expect more of their organizations
~..cr staff members" (p. 18). She then presented a conclusion students are
urged to remember: "An organization is not automatically a good place to work just
because its cause is worthy" (p. 18).

Working With Other Departments

If one characteristic predicts effectiveness, it is that concern for fund raising is not
housed in the executive suite but permeates the organization. Bintzer (1981) explained:

> Every part of the institutional family bears some degree of responsibility for the fund-
> raising process. Stated another way, although not every action within a [charitable
> organization] must be bent to fund-raising purposes, no action should be undertaken
> without careful consideration of its possible effect on the fund-raising program. (pp.
> 220–221)

Such a mindset signifies an externally focused organization that is entrepreneurial,
integrates private support with other income sources, and values accountability to
donors—although donors are not singled out from other strategic publics.

Line Managers.   In a survey by NSFRE's Advanced Executives Task Force
("Experienced," 1993), senior practitioners identified the following as their most
challenging professional obstacles: (a) managing expectations, organizational relationships, politics, and change; (b) building understanding of fund raising and getting
cooperation within the organization; and (c) understaffing. Boardman (1993) illumi-
nated, "Traditionally, development officers have been stronger in strengthening relationships externally than in building alliances internally" (p. 268).

As described earlier, the process of raising gifts is ineffective without the involvement of those responsible for the organization's program services and operations. The
staff manager, therefore, spends a considerable amount of time interacting with line
managers. A chief fund raiser in Cook's (1994a) study portrayed the role in universities:

> I think the chief development officer, especially in a large institution like mine, really is
> a manager. . . . Less than 20% of my time is spent on fund raising . . . . What I have to do
> is make sure that I have the budget for my people, make sure that I do the political work
> with the deans and all . . . . So you manage the process within your own organization. (p.
> 444)

Public Relations Managers.   There is general consensus that cooperation
of the public relations department is essential to fund-raising success. The function
depends on communication techniques produced by public relations, such as brochures, videotapes, and newsletters, as well as publicity in the mass media. Public
relations also provides support for special events, writing proposals, and donor
recognition. A widespread belief among practitioners of both departments is that
public relations creates the climate in which successful fund raising takes place.

In some organizations, the departments are separate, with the heads of both reporting to the CEO. In others, they are consolidated in one department. It is recalled that the consolidated structure was endorsed for colleges and universities at the 1958 Greenbrier conference and named advancement. Other types of organizations, sensing a symbiotic relationship, followed suit. Gearhart and Bezilla (1991) presented the argument for consolidation: "The successful fund-raising effort requires extremely close cooperation among all advancement personnel. Experience has shown that the best way to achieve this cooperation is to integrate all advancement offices under one senior officer" (p. 46).

This book also endorses the one-department structure, but it places an emphasis on managing relationships with all strategic publics on whom an organization depends, not just donors. The manager of such a department, as given in Fig. 6.1, is responsible for fund raising and public relations. He or she has been trained in both (i.e., cross-trained) and recognizes that an organization has many stakeholders, including clients, employees, government officials, community residents, and donors—all of whom contribute to its success. Accordingly, the manager ensures programming is planned and implemented to meet the needs of those groups.

In contrast, consolidated departments today generally are headed by an individual trained only in fund raising, who concentrates almost exclusively on donor publics. The resources of the department, including public relations staff, are utilized primarily to achieve fund-raising objectives. Other important stakeholders are ignored or underserved, leaving the organization vulnerable to loss of support and even attack by those who have been neglected. Illustrating the danger of such situations, Haberman and Dolphin (1988) stated, "The clinic that concentrates on cultivating major donors but lets relations languish with another external public, its patients, will find occupancy in its impressive new facilities well below capacity, perhaps suggesting second thoughts to some donors" (p. 139).

The term for managing public relations primarily for donor relations is *fund-raising encroachment*. The full implications of encroachment cannot be understood without first understanding systems theory. As already introduced, organizations are systems that operate within an environment. Their success and survival depend on how well they manage interdependencies with publics and other organizations in their environment. More information about systems theory is presented in chapter 9; therefore, further discussion of the relationship between fund raising and public relations is delayed until that chapter. Similarly, discussions about working with trustees, CEOs, and line managers are continued in subsequent chapters.

FUND RAISERS AS DEPARTMENT MANAGERS

The median fund-raising department of NSFRE members, as pointed out in chapter 3, consists of two practitioners and two support staff. Almost all departments conduct both annual giving and major gifts programs (Kelly, 1995b). Therefore, the division of labor in the typical department is relatively simple, with the two primary programs split between the fund-raising head, who serves as the major gifts officer, and the second practitioner, who organizes annual giving. Support staff handle donor records and gift processing, and the five fund-raising steps—from research to stewardship—are managed by the one department. The organization has only 90 total employees, which facilitates internal communication about donor relations (Kelly, 1994a). The head of the fund-raising department reports to the CEO and interacts with line managers on a regular basis. The function is centralized, which provides a high degree of control.

This typical department does not describe the work situation of many fund raisers. Students will recall that one fourth of NSFRE's members work in departments with five or more practitioners and some work with 100 or more. Chapter 3 listed 12 fund-raising positions commonly found in larger departments (e.g., prospect research and planned giving). Just as organizational size and complexity determine the need for the staff function, they also affect the structure of the organization and, therefore, the structure of the fund-raising function and the responsibilities of the department manager.

Robbins (1990) defined an organization's structure as "how tasks are to be allocated, who reports to whom, and the formal coordinating mechanisms and interaction patterns that will be followed" (p. 5). He and other organizational sociologists have identified several structural characteristics, among the most cited of which are complexity and centralization. Mixer (1993) argued that the most pressing issue for fund-raising managers of large organizations is "solving questions about structure, centralization, decentralization, coordination, and control" (p. 247). Before examining those questions, the chapter looks at two types of charitable organizations different from others in that their missions primarily are to raise gifts. Federations and affiliated foundations do not operate to provide program services, but to provide funding for organizations that do. In other words, fund raising in such organizations is a line, not a staff, function.

Federations and Affiliated Foundations

Federations are established for the purpose of raising gifts for multiple, loosely coupled charitable organizations. Affiliated foundations exist to raise and manage private funds for a single organization.

Federations.   As touched on in chapter 5, federations have a long history in U.S. philanthropy, predating the internal fund-raising function. The concept was imported from Great Britain and first tried in Colorado in 1877, when the Denver Society was founded (Cutlip, 1965/1990). It failed after 21 years, mainly because it relied on commission-paid solicitors, who kept most of the money, and its member organizations stopped limiting their appeals.

The impetus for federations historically has been efficiency and economy: One appeal, once a year, on behalf of numerous charitable organizations would save time and money. It also would save donors, particularly corporations, from decisions about which organizations were most deserving of their support. Federations are structured to reflect their purpose, with a board usually composed of representatives of both member organizations and corporate donors. Paid CEOs, managers, and staff carry out the mission, which sometimes includes public relations and lobbying as well as fund raising.

The function generally is limited to conducting annual giving programs targeted at businesses and their employees—and, to a lesser extent, at workers in government and nonprofits. Whereas the early federations spent considerable effort on soliciting community residents, contemporary programming concentrates on the workplace. One of the exceptions is the United Negro College Fund, founded in 1943, which also raises major gifts from individuals, corporations, and foundations. More typical are state and regional organizations of the Independent College Funds of America, founded in 1948, which solicit unrestricted annual gifts from companies in their geographic area. A percentage of the gifts is used to pay federation expenses; the remainder is distributed proportionately to member colleges and universities, which retain their right to solicit corporate donors for major gifts.

Until recently, the United Way system monopolized workplace solicitations. About 172 other national federations now raise money through employee campaigns (J. Moore, 1993). Almost all participate in the Combined Federal Campaign—the annual solicitation of more than 4 million federal employees and military personnel. Providing some idea of total number, Earth Share represents some 40 environmental groups at the national level, but there also are about 18 state and regional federations raising money solely for environmental groups. Hundreds of others raise gifts for organizations with different missions.

Regardless of scope or beneficiaries' purpose, the fund-raising function in federations differs significantly from the one described earlier. The department manager has limited interaction with the people who utilize the gifts (i.e., line managers of member organizations). In turn, those who run the member organizations have little or no interaction with the people who contribute the gifts—in the case of workplace solicitations, they usually do not even know the employee donors' names. More information on federations is given in chapter 8.

Affiliated Foundations.   Affiliated foundations, also called *institutionally related foundations*, are outgrowths of charitable organizations that receive substantial government funding. They are found most often at nonprofit hospitals and public colleges and universities, although other types of organizations, such as CARE, also have foundations. Unlike federations, affiliated foundations are a relatively new type of organization.

Nonprofit hospitals began receiving federal Medicare and Medicaid payments in 1965 (Hansmann, 1987). Public colleges and universities, it is recalled, did not hire staff fund raisers until the 1970s. Started in the time frame identified by those dates, the impetus for affiliated foundations historically has been to keep private gifts separate from government, or public, funding. The new fund-raising organizations solved auditing problems and provided additional advantages, particularly to public colleges and universities.

Affiliated foundations preserve an arm's-length relationship between state treasuries and gifts and also furnish financial flexibility not available through procedures tied to state appropriations (Hedgepeth, 1993). For example, foundations allow public institutions to buy property quickly by avoiding the lengthy process required when using state money. The many financial benefits range from purchasing alcohol, for which state funds cannot be used, to earning income from investments and for-profit ventures, which—unlike tuition—does not have to be "given" to the state for appropriation back to the institution.

A foundation also enables an institution to build volunteer leadership with a board of directors when politically appointed trustees are uninvolved in fund raising and constituency relations. Underlying all benefits is protection of private funds from legislatures that may substitute gift income for tax-generated funding.

At some public colleges and universities, affiliated foundations serve more as a bank than as a fund-raising organization. At others, they are a replacement for the institution's fund-raising department, with large staffs and multimillion-dollar budgets. In between are state systems that have a central foundation with fund-raising staff, as well as fund-raising departments within each institution. The first situation presents no conflict with the function's operation as advocated earlier. The fund-raising department reports to the institution's president and is funded with institutional funds. Hedgepeth (1993) expressed the desirability of this situation: "The development office is more likely to be integrated into the senior management structure of the institution and involved in institutional decision-making" (p. 326).

In the second situation, the fund-raising function is similar to that in federations because it is isolated from program services for which gifts are raised. As is often the case with federations, the beneficiary institution has no function of its own and is dependent on the separate organization. Fund raisers report to the CEO of the foundation, usually another practitioner, who reports to the board of directors. Practitioners' salaries are paid with foundation funds, which institutional trustees and CEOs foolishly consider a savings. In such situations, Hedgepeth (1993) explained, fund raising is estranged from the managers who are responsible for carrying out the institution's mission. Institutional officials assume the role of supplicants seeking grants from the foundation and have little say in "merging foundation actions with institutional goals and opportunities" (p. 327). Mixer (1993) added, "These related foundations also present problems of divided authority, external control, and inappropriate allocations with respect to … their host organizations" (p. 231).

Illustrating problems associated with the second situation, a colleague at the multiuniversity system of the State University of New York (SUNY) related the following incident. The affiliated foundation of one of the SUNY universities was interviewing candidates for a fund-raising position. During a meeting with the search committee, one candidate asked who he would be working for. The chairman of the foundation's board of directors replied, "Me, I guess; the board pays your salary." The answer shocked at least one person in the room—the university's president, who thought he was in charge.

The third situation of essentially two fund-raising departments also differs from earlier descriptions of how the function should operate. Competition and conflict largely displace fund raising's purpose of managing relationships between the organization and its donors. Hedgepeth (1993) addressed this situation, which sometimes includes multiple foundations (e.g., a separate foundation for athletics): "Efforts to attract major gifts and enlist top volunteers may be competitive at best and work at cross-purposes at worst" (p. 328).

Similar problems are common in large charitable organizations, depending on their degree of centralization and complexity. The discussion now turns to those structural variables.

The Issue of Decentralization

Centralization is the extent to which decision making is concentrated at the top of the organizational hierarchy (Hage, 1980; Robbins, 1990). Complexity is the extent of specialization, or differentiation of skills, within the organization. The two are inversely related. To illustrate the effects of these variables on the fund-raising function, the following discussion touches on three national charitable organizations and on hospitals and research universities, concentrating on the last.

The March of Dimes Birth Defects Foundation is an example of a centralized structure (Mixer, 1993). It is a top-down, national organization, headquartered in White Plains, New York. It creates chapters as local fund-raising units and holds the power to hire, promote, and fire local staff. Headquarters dictates how fund raising is managed through rigid policies and procedures. It also, Mixer said, relies on "a highly centralized direct-mail process that it pioneered" (p. 227). The March of Dimes' high degree of centralization is related to its program services. It was established to fight polio, and the programs it chose through which to accomplish its mission dealt with medical research (i.e., development of a vaccine). When its mission was attained, it adopted a new one, fighting birth defects, also largely through research. Its missions, therefore, have been national in scope and its services primarily centralized (i.e., most funding goes to research centers selected by headquarters).

The Girl Scouts of the USA, in contrast, has decentralized program services and a low degree of centralization. Its programs are available in virtually every community. Mixer (1993) described the Girl Scouts as "almost completely decentralized, securing private support through local units" (p. 225). The national office, based in New York City, retains some control with the power to renew or deny charters through a review process every 5 or 6 years. Annual cookie sales also are coordinated through the national office. In 1993, the organization was criticized for using too much of the profits for administration (Skolnik, 1993).

The American Red Cross has a hybrid structure to match its programs of local service and national disaster relief (responsibility for blood drives is shared). The 2,400 chapters, according to Mixer (1993), are somewhat autonomous in that they hire their own CEOs and exercise considerable authority in fund raising. The local functions solicit gifts for such services as swimming classes in life saving, whereas the central function in Washington, DC conducts appeals for disaster relief. However, as Mixer pointed out, competition occurs when national appeals conflict with chapter solicitations. Goal displacement results from quotas assigned by the national office and requirements of membership in the United Way (e.g., members are not allowed to raise gifts during annual United Way campaigns).

Moving away from geographically dispersed organizations and adding the second structural variable, hospitals have high complexity because they require highly specialized personnel (e.g., heart surgeons), as well as unskilled labor (e.g., janitors). Research universities share a similar degree of complexity. Specialized professionals demand authority and autonomy; therefore, hospitals and research universities almost always have a decentralized structure (i.e., program services are carried out by relatively autonomous line functions). Mixer (1993) called them arenas of freedom and linked the effect of their structure to fund raising: "Large organizations whose principal delivery services require highly trained professionals, such as doctors or specialized teaching faculty, face unique forces that propel decentralization" (p. 229).

In a completely centralized function, all fund raisers and programming are managed by one department reporting to the CEO. In a fully decentralized function, fund raising is assigned to the organization's program service units, and practitioners termed *component fund raisers* report to line managers. The degree of decentralization that can be accommodated without eroding the function's effectiveness currently is an issue of great concern to practitioners at complex organizations.

Focusing on research universities, the fund-raising function was centralized until the mid-1980s, although some units, such as medical and law schools, ventured into fund raising earlier. M. R. Hall (1992) found that 61% of the 213 research universities represented in her 1989 study had component fund raisers for their business school and/or engineering school. Another 13% planned to establish such positions by 1991. The majority of the component fund raisers (65%) had been hired after 1984. Hall concluded, "Increasingly, research universities are decentralizing their development structure and function" (p. 569).

Recognizing this trend, CASE began offering special conferences for deans, other unit managers, and component fund raisers in the late 1980s. Evans (1993) described the phenomenon as "a centrifugal force that is always pushing even the most centralized of programs toward some level of decentralization" (p. 283). Yet most senior fund raisers in education, he said, prefer a centralized structure. M. R. Hall (1993) similarly reported that among her respondents, of which 65% were heads of central departments, "most development professionals favored centralization" (p. 53).

Their preference is understandable but misguided. According to organizational sociologists, centralization is more efficient (Hage, 1980); however, functional structure must be congruent with organizational structure. A centralized fund-raising department in a decentralized organization will cause friction and disorder. It eventually will give way to the larger structure.

Newness of the staff function and shortage of research have disguised this basic principle. Nevertheless, practitioners are grappling their way to understanding. Estey and Wilkerson (1994) concluded from their informal survey of fund-raising heads at 10 universities, "The larger an institution, the more likely it is to benefit from a decentralized arrangement. The key factor, however, is the intricacy of the organization, not its enrollment, staffing, or endowment. The more complex the campus, the more splintered its missions, messages, and prospect pools" (p. 25). They quoted William McGoldrick, then vice president for institute relations at Rensselaer Polytechnic Institute, who recounted his department's move toward decentralization: "Development staffers used to formulate goals on the basis of institutional priorities and then go out to raise the money. Now we have to think in a new way—*with* the deans about *their* fund-raising priorities" (p. 26; italics in original).

E. Ryan (1994b) gathered written comments about the issue from five practitioner experts. Michael Worth, author and vice president for development and alumni affairs at George Washington University (President Trachtenberg's chief fund raiser), rightfully said decentralization is more practical at complex organizations even though centralization is more efficient. Ted Gibbens, vice president for development at Pomona College, maintained that decentralization is not appropriate for liberal arts colleges, which—unlike research universities—do not have semiautonomous units. Burr Gibson, executive chair of Marts & Lundy, predicted, "Over time, deans of the most powerful schools will insist on having their own development offices. It will be difficult for any major university to remain fully centralized" (p. 39).

Unfortunately, too many fund-raising heads have taken a reactive rather than a proactive stance on the issue, formulating hybrid structures when forced to do so. The mixed structures try to placate line managers while keeping the function as centralized as possible. Evans (1993) defended hybrids, arguing that the chief fund raiser in a decentralized structure has no direct authority for setting fund-raising goals and planning. Furthermore, decentralization creates problems of coordination and "ownership" of donor prospects. E. Ryan (1994b) elaborated, "When there's not enough control—always a risk in decentralized development systems—all divisions might inadvertently gang up on one major prospect" (p. 34).

E. Ryan's (1994b) five experts agreed that coordinating interaction with prospects is the primary problem necessitating a "mixed model" (p. 39). Curt Simic, president of the Indiana University Foundation (an affiliated foundation that acts as the university's central department), asserted, "Prospect control (I prefer 'management') must be centrally coordinated" (p. 37). Whereas most of the experts said only solicitations require coordination, Simic claimed cultivation contacts also need to be cleared by the central office.

Hybrid structures, as E. Ryan (1994b) reported, also differ by their restrictions on the fund-raising programs units are allowed to conduct. Simic said units at his university can solicit annual gifts, "but when it comes to a major ask, we decide which program has the best chance of success at the highest gift level" (p. 34). Margarete Hall, vice president for institutional advancement at Gallaudet University (whose research is the basis for much of this discussion), argued that units should be able to solicit both annual and major gifts. Of those she studied, only 32% raised gifts of less than $1,000, whereas 64% raised gifts of more than $1 million; 100% reported gifts of $1,000 to $10,000 (M. R. Hall, 1992). Her findings suggest that units in hybrid structures are permitted to raise large annual gifts and—to a lesser extent—major gifts, but annual giving below $1,000 most often is reserved for the central department.

Lower level annual gifts generally are unrestricted, meaning they can be used as managers see fit. Their flexibility is highly valued. Furthermore, unrestricted gifts account for only 27% of all gift dollars to private colleges and universities and only 10% to public institutions (Kelly, 1991a). When a university decentralizes its annual giving program, M. R. Hall (1992) explained, "It shifts the decision about the use of these limited, flexible resources from the president to the deans" (p. 571). It is not surprising then that hybrids prefer to keep annual giving centralized. In addition to protecting CEO prerogatives, many central departments retain control because they use a portion of the money to subsidize salaries and program expenses.

Regarding salaries, 41% of the component fund raisers in M. R. Hall's (1993) study were paid by the academic unit for which they worked, whereas 30% were paid by the central department, and another 30% were paid jointly. Yet the majority of the component fund raisers (54%) reported jointly to the dean of the unit and to the central department. According to Sabo (1994a), the "dynamic" of dual reporting in hybrid structures "may lead development officers to feel torn" (p. 30). Mixer (1993) emphasized "[A] classical management principle asserts that a person, whether staff member or volunteer, should report to only one superior. Frustration, anxiety, mistrust, and confusion result from individuals' having two masters" (p. 126).

There is considerable agreement in the literature that fund-raising effectiveness increases as the function moves closer to program services. For example, Evans (1993) said fund raisers housed in units "are often closer to and more knowledgeable about the units they serve" (p. 281) than central fund raisers who act as account executives. Connecting this proximity to donors, he added, "A prospect will find it easier to become interested in and attached to a unit with a mission close to the prospect's beliefs and values" (p. 282). Hedgepeth (1993) concurred, saying fund-raising managers "must recognize that most donors relate to the college or department from which they graduated, or to some special interest they have developed in their life" (p. 331). In other words, unit goals are more important to donors than broader organizational goals, and integration in units best prepares fund raisers to interact with prospects.

M. R. Hall (1992) found that cooperation between faculty and fund raisers increased by 34% when the function was housed in units rather than the central department. Faculty "became involved in the identification and cultivation of potential donors" (p. 577). Ideas growing out of lunchroom discussions and hallway meetings resulted in donors participating in meaningful work of the organization. When the function moves into units, Hall stated, "Fund raising becomes integrated ... in faculty activities" (p. 577).

In contrast, Worth (cited in E. Ryan, 1994b) described the outcome of many hybrids: "an atmosphere of excessive competition, withholding of information, fragmentation, and missed opportunities" (p. 37). The issue of decentralization must be resolved. The fund-raising function should be structured to complement the organizational structure.

The University of Pennsylvania has a near match of the structure I recommend for complex organizations. The central department pays the salaries of all fund raisers, regardless of where they work (Sabo, 1994a). Multiple practitioners are housed in the university's 15 schools and centers. The senior fund raiser in each unit reports to the central department's "director of school and center development" (p. 30), with a dotted-line relationship to the respective dean. Unit fund raisers conduct both annual giving and major gifts programs. Task forces composed of practitioners from the schools and the central department raise gifts for general university needs. A Prospect Action Advisory Committee (PAAC) meets every 2 weeks to negotiate and agree on prospect assignments for solicitation. No approval is necessary for cultivation. Under the formal policies guiding PAAC's work, once a prospect is assigned, no other unit can solicit the individual or organization. Units can, however, always request reassignment.

Explaining the reasoning behind Pennsylvania's structure, Vice President Virginia Clark (cited in Sabo, 1994a), the department manager who oversees fund raising, stated, "The philosophy is to make the system as effective and efficient as possible while being mindful of our donors" (p. 30). She added that the university is "raising more money than in the past" (p. 30). Although Clark did not discuss basic requirements for successful decentralization, two appear obvious when comparing the fund-raising structure at her institution to current hybrids.

First, the organization must make a commitment to finance the function. When commitment is missing, component fund raisers are paid by units or through "shared" arrangements, which often leads to hiring less expensive and experienced practitioners, who—in turn—become frustrated with their salaries and dual reporting. Based on simple economics, loyalty in the workplace is related to who supplies the paycheck. Or as Estey and Wilkerson (1994) concluded from their survey, "Where the central office pays, it generally controls" (p. 26). My endorsement of central-paid salaries is not intended to control fund raisers housed in units, but to instill an allegiance to the larger organization and ensure equitable and competitive pay. Illustrating the value of doing so, Clark (cited in Sabo, 1994a) said Pennsylvania's PAAC works because "everyone comes as a representative of the university rather than of individual schools" (p. 32).

Second, those positioned high in the organization, particularly the CEO and the head of the central department, must accept that fund raising cannot be top heavy. Gifts are made to help the organization carry out its mission, which—by definition—is accomplished at the line-function level. In complex organizations, relatively autonomous line managers and staff must be brought to the forefront to interact with donor publics. This is not to say broad needs are not addressed or senior managers have little to do with fund raising, but rather a focus on program services, combined with leadership and direction set through strategic planning, best serves the organization.

Estey and Wilkerson (1994) found three common characteristics at universities with high degrees of decentralization: (a) strong support for fund raising from the top, (b) clear rules, and (c) solid administrative support. Expanding on the third, the central department should provide services to units, including research, records management, and technical assistance. The department's personnel, including its manager, must predominantly assist other practitioners; they must refrain from acting as major gifts officers. As Estey and Wilkerson advised, "To make such a system work, it's important to establish your central development office as an ally of the unit offices, not a competitor" (p. 25).

The recommended structure is backed by the management literature. For example, two of the eight characteristics of excellent companies identified by Peters and Waterman (1982) are relevant to this discussion: Excellent organizations are decentralized and have "simultaneous loose-tight properties," which the authors described as "the coexistence of firm central direction and maximum individual autonomy" (p. 318). Kanter (1983) said such organizations substitute leadership for structure to set direction, constrain decisions, and "keep everyone's mind on the shared vision" (p. 275). Like the University of Pennsylvania, they employ "task forces, quality circles, problem-solving groups, or shared responsibility teams" (p. 241). J. E. Grunig (1992) concluded from his review of the literature that an excellent organization plans strategically, "empowers people, imposes few structural controls, and relies on communication for collaboration and cooperation" (p. 233).

Regardless of complexity, staff managers recognize the value of these principles and incorporate them in fund raising to the degree appropriate for their organization.

SUGGESTED READINGS

Birnbaum, R. (1992). *How academic leadership works: Understanding success and failure in the college presidency*. San Francisco, CA: Jossey-Bass.

Carver, J. (1990). *Boards that make a difference: A new design for leadership in nonprofit and public organizations*. San Francisco, CA: Jossey-Bass.

Dozier, D. M., Grunig, L. A., & Grunig, J. E. (1995). *Manager's guide to excellence in public relations and communication management*. Mahwah, NJ: Lawrence Erlbaum Associates.

Hall, M. R. (1993). *The dean's role in fund raising*. Baltimore, MD: Johns Hopkins University Press.

Herman, R. D., & Associates. (1994). *The Jossey-Bass handbook on nonprofit leadership and management*. San Francisco, CA: Jossey-Bass.

Herman, R. D., & Heimovics, R. D. (1991). *Executive leadership in nonprofit organizations: New strategies for shaping executive-board dynamics*. San Francisco, CA: Jossey-Bass.

Mixer, J. R. (1993). *Principles of professional fundraising: Useful foundations for successful practice*. San Francisco, CA: Jossey-Bass.

O'Connell, B. (1993). *The board member's book: Making a difference in voluntary organizations* (2nd ed.). New York: The Foundation Center.

Robbins, S. P. (1990). *Organization theory: Structure, design, and applications* (3rd ed.). Englewood Cliffs, NJ: Prentice-Hall.

7

Legal Context
of Fund Raising

Fund raisers are not lawyers, tax specialists, or accountants. They depend on others in the organization who have expertise in these areas. Yet fund raisers cannot carry out their duties effectively without knowledge of the laws, tax rules, and accounting standards that—to a great extent—define and direct the practice. Equally important, staff managers must understand the regulatory issues facing their organizations if they are to counsel dominant coalition members and constructively affect decision making.

This chapter describes serious problems requiring leadership and change. Regulation has rapidly increased in the last few years and more is expected. The privileged status granted to charitable organizations is under attack on the local, state, and federal levels. Analysis of the current legal environment, aided by such concepts as autonomy and accountability, reveals a strong correlation between government intervention and irresponsible behavior. Fund raisers must guide their organizations in taking corrective action. Information provided in the chapter, including IRS requirements, prepares future practitioners for both basic and larger responsibilities.

The discussion does not claim to be a comprehensive presentation of all legal principles affecting fund raising. Some are covered elsewhere in the text, and technical components are left to experts. A point-in-time discussion about the volatile regulatory environment is guaranteed to be outdated by the time it is read. Resources listed in this and other chapters should be utilized to keep up with recent developments—a prerequisite of effective practice.

CALL FOR ACTION

Attorney Betsy Bush (1991) maintained, "Principles of regulation of fund raising and charitable organizations should be part of every fund-raising executive's education from the beginning" (p. 214). Yet, as she pointed out, current fund raisers largely are ignorant of the legal context in which they and their organizations operate. NSFRE's certification exam, for example, includes no questions on fund-raising law.

Practitioners also demonstrate an indifference toward regulatory issues affecting the charitable subsector as a whole. Acting more as technicians than managers, they generally prefer information about how to raise gifts, rather than how to protect the tax deductibility of gifts. Many, if not most, assume that the legal environment in which gifts are raised is and will remain the same as it was last year or 10 years ago. Attorney Bruce Hopkins (1990) elaborated, "Probably most people in the philanthropic community take the charitable deduction for granted, assuming that it will always exist. This is dangerous and ignorant thinking" (p. 213). He added, "Today's custodians of American philanthropy cannot responsibly operate on the assumption that present law in regard to this field will be tomorrow's law" (p. 205).

Absent and Fragmented

Current regulatory debate about the subsector's future is widespread and intense, with proposals ranging from payment of local property taxes to elimination the federal gift deduction. Attorney Norman Fink (1993) summarized, "The ground rules have changed. The nonprofit sector—for all its good work and high purpose—has lost its status as the sanctified 'vestal virgin' and has been thrust out of the temples and into the marketplace. Nonprofits had been creeping in that direction already" (p. 394).

The debate, unfortunately, is carried out mainly by regulators, lawyers, and accountants; conspicuously missing are fund raisers. According to Bush (1991), not only are they absent from discussions about state regulation, but "most are unaware of the changing climate affecting fund-raising laws in their state and in the states in which their organizations solicit" (p. 201).

Fragmentation, in addition to lack of knowledge and indifference, is responsible for practitioners' absence. Although the Filer Commission defined the nonprofit sector 20 years ago, and efforts were taken in this book to define the charitable subsector and its members, a strong identification across organizational types does not exist. Essentially, fund raisers and their employers claim to be part of a cohesive subsector when it suits their purposes, but do not act as one when it comes to addressing legal issues.

Regulatory debate at the federal and local levels focuses on large organizations, particularly hospitals, colleges, and universities. Yet at the state level, these same types of organizations—as well as religious organizations—are exempt from most fund-raising laws (Bush, 1991). Federal and local deliberations attempt to separate "purely public charities," or organizations that provide most of their services to the poor at no charge, from organizations that do not. Those such as hospitals and universities that serve people of various financial means and rely on client fees for the majority of their income are being segregated for different legal treatment. The trend is evident and alarming.

For example, *The NonProfit Times*' list of the 100 biggest charities ("NPT 100 Directory," 1992) excluded colleges and universities because of questions about whether they perform charitable acts and therefore should be tax exempt. Two former tax researchers for the Department of the Treasury, John Copeland and Gabriel Rudney (1993), estimated that only about 5% of the expenses of America's some 3,000 nonprofit hospitals go to providing free or low-cost care to the needy. Therefore, they argued, a good place to start financing health-care reform is by ending tax breaks for nonprofit hospitals, which would save almost $4 billion a year. In 1994, health care legislation considered by Congress, but not passed, included harsh new standards on the amount of charity care that nonprofit hospitals would have to provide (S. G. Greene, 1994b). Hospitals, colleges, and universities—as well as other large organizations—are primary targets in legal battles against exemption from local property taxes, which began in the early 1990s and continue to spread across the country (Berton, 1994; Burns, 1993).

Supporting the divisive trend, critics such as Odendahl (1990) called for changes in the Internal Revenue Code to establish different categories of exempt status. Columnist Irving Warner, who—students will recall from chapter 2—claimed that fund raising is not affected by tax benefits accorded to donors (Warner, 1992a), argued shortly afterward that NSFRE and other fund-raising associations should be leading a campaign to enact "a sliding scale for tax deductions—giving bigger tax breaks to people who contribute to groups that have more 'virtue'" (Warner, 1992b, p. 42). Warner's definition of virtue was based on helping the poor, or charity, rather than on philanthropy. In 1996—students also will recall—Republican leaders proposed to offset cuts in federal funding for social welfare by awarding tax credits (in contrast to deductions) for gifts to organizations fighting poverty (Murawski & Williams, 1996). The idea of different tax benefits continues to gain popularity with members of the 105th Congress, including Democrats, because lawmakers commonly view organizations serving the poor as "core charities," which deserve more help in attracting gifts. Such distinctions translated into law would result in universities and hospitals, among others, losing their full charitable status.

On one hand, then, the largest employers of fund raisers need a strong and unified subsector to avoid onerous regulation. On the other hand, they and their fund raisers ignore issues about state regulation because they are not among the organizations affected. A university, for example, can conduct solicitations nationwide, utilizing direct mail, phonathons, and other techniques such as grant proposals to corporations and foundations, without registering in any state except Massachusetts (Bush, 1996).[1] Contradictorily, a human services organization must comply with the statues of each and every state in which it solicits. The exemptions have served as a barrier to building an inclusive approach to fund-raising law. Many would agree with Bush (1991), who questioned the exemption of universities and hospitals: "Why should smaller organizations, such as social service agencies and arts groups, bear the brunt of registration and filing requirements alone?" (p. 215). To instill public confidence and ward off further regulation, NSFRE President Lewis (1993a) recommended that every organization register in all states whether they are required to or not.

Adding to the fragmentation, state laws have been directed primarily at paid solicitors, who—as demonstrated in this chapter and the next—are responsible for much of government's intervention. Their unethical and illegal practices, Bush (1991) explained, "are the experiences that inform state regulators and legislators and shape fund-raising regulation" (p. 208). Staff fund raisers appropriately disassociate themselves from paid solicitors; inappropriately, however, they do not criticize them, nor do they participate in discussions about how regulations can curb solicitors' behavior without imposing undue requirements on legitimate practice.

---

[1]Universities and other educational organizations do not have universal exemption, which is illustrated later in this chapter. According to the AAFRC Trust for Philanthropy (1996), 24 states have statutes that may require registration by the affiliated foundations of public institutions. Eight states changed their educational exemptions between 1992 and 1996. Fund raisers must continually monitor the regulatory environment.

Bush (1991) warned that if fund raisers remain ignorant of the law and indifferent to legislative developments, government officials will be less likely to believe that self-regulation is a realistic alternative to increased regulation and more likely to believe that fund raisers do not have a place in the regulatory debate. She concluded, "It is a field that can no longer be left to staff accountants and attorneys" (p. 203).

Custodians of Philanthropy

In agreement with Bush, staff managers take a larger view of their responsibilities than just obtaining private support for one charitable organization. They accept their role as what Hopkins (1990) called custodians of philanthropy. As such, their interest in the law extends to all levels of government and to functional, organizational, and societal concerns.

Staff managers know their efforts to raise gifts are part of a system and—as explained in the last chapter—cannot be separated from the behavior of other organizational actors or from the system's collective behavior. More precisely, they believe the degree to which they, their organization, and its dominant coalition behave ethically and in a socially responsible manner is directly related to effectiveness in fund raising and freedom from regulatory constraints (i.e., ethical and legal issues are intertwined and both affect fund-raising results). Staff managers uphold self-regulation as superior to imposed regulation and recognize their critical position in advancing the alternative course. They realize an organization's lawyers and accountants pursue functional objectives different from those of fund raising. Lawyers, for example, primarily concern themselves with their client's standing in courts of law, whereas fund raisers concentrate on the more powerful court of public opinion.

Staff managers understand that the legal context in which gifts are raised is constantly changing, regulations affecting one part of the charitable subsector affect all, and success and survival of their organizations are dependent not on raising increasing amounts of dollars, but on protecting the privileged status that allows them to do so. Acquiring the necessary knowledge about enacted and proposed laws, they counsel members of the dominant coalition, implement proactive policies, and help their organizations avoid crises. In short, fund raisers serve as guardians of gifts, the organization's conscience, and agents of accountability.

Joel Fleishman (1995), who holds various positions, including professor of law and public policy at Duke University, advocated these larger responsibilities in a speech reprinted by NSFRE. He argued that fund raisers must take the lead in championing self-regulation, which, he asserted, is the best way to maintain society's trust and thereby keep government interference at bay—a description of accountability, which is discussed shortly. Addressing recent betrayals of trust, Fleishman declared, "Nothing poses a greater threat to the continued vibrancy of the not-for-profit sector than such failures, and no one can influence not-for-profits' behavior and attitude toward accountability more than fund raisers can" (pp. 33–34). He continued: "Fund raisers have every reason to *demand* accountability and propriety of their organizations. A fund raiser's capacity to produce funds depends on his or her organization's public reputation, a reputation that is likely to suffer as a consequence of any publicly noted failure of accountability" (p. 34; italics added).

To fulfill their responsibilities, fund raisers must engage in ongoing scanning of the regulatory environment. Continual surveillance is required to keep up with changes and identify emerging problems. Subscriptions to trade publications and journals assist practitioners. *The Chronicle of Philanthropy*, for example, has full-time reporters covering the regulatory beat. Started in 1988, the biweekly newspaper is invaluable for keeping up with all aspects of the practice. Similarly, e-mail discussion groups on the Internet, known as listservs, offer practitioner-to-practitioner advice on legal issues as well as most other topics of interest to fund raisers. Scholars also lend their informed voices. Table 7.1 presents a basic list of resources with subscription costs.

Environmental scanning has become easier with the phenomenal growth of World Wide Web sites. Many of those listed in Table 4.1 provide timely information on state and federal legislation. CASE's home page, for example, tracks bills affecting education as they move through Congress. A guide to Internet resources is available on *The Chronicle of Philanthropy*'s site: http://philanthropy.com. Access to data from diverse sources, including formal research and opinion leaders, is recommended.

TABLE 7.1
Resources for Continual Surveillance

Publications[a]	
The Chronicle of Philanthropy; (800) 347-6969.	$67.50 (24 issues)
The NonProfit Times; (201) 734-1700.	Free to full-time U.S. executive managers at organizations with $500,000+ annual gross incomes, $59 for others (12 issues)
The Philanthropy Monthly; (203) 354-7132.	$65 for 501(c)(3) organizations, $84 for individuals (10 issues)
Fund Raising Management; (516) 746-6700.	$54 (12 issues)
Fund Raising Regulation Report; (800) 753-0655, ext. 4456/7.	$108 (6 issues)
Internet Listservs[b]	E-mail to listserv address, leave subject line blank, type subscribe line in message space, and send.
Discussion of Fund-Raising Issues: listproc@listproc.hcf.jhu.edu sub FUNDLIST <your name>	Discussion of Nonprofit Issues: listserv@rain.org subscribe USNONPROFIT-L <your name>
Forum for Corporate & Foundation Relations: cfrnet-request@medicine.wustl.edu subscribe CFRNET <your name>	Forum for ARNOVA Scholars/Managers: listserv@wvnvm.wvnet.edu subscribe ARNOVA-L <your name>
Forum for Prospect Research: listserv@bucknell.edu subscribe PRSPCT-L <your name>	Discussion of Technical Services: majordomo@acpub.duke.edu subscribe FUNDSVCS [no name]
Forum for Planned Giving: listserv@indycms.iupui.edu subscribe GIFT-PL <your name>	Forum for Consultants: listserv@jtsa.edu subscribe CONSULT-L <your name>

[a]Rates are for 1 year at 1997 U.S. prices.
[b]All subscriptions are free. Acceptance takes less than 5 minutes and includes instructions.
A regularly updated directory of listservs about fund raising can be found at the Web site: http://www.fundraiser-software.com/listserv.html.

PRIVILEGED STATUS

A historic and deeply rooted cultural belief in the United States is that our country's social needs, to the greatest possible extent, should be addressed by private voluntary action, rather than by government (Clotfelter, 1992). Cutlip (1965/1990) explained, "Voluntary action, supported by voluntary giving, is the pragmatic American answer to the host of problems that have arisen in the past and will arise in the future" (p. 538).

To sustain this belief, society, through its representative government, has granted economic privileges to charitable organizations to assist them in carrying out their work. Charitable status provides two primary types of benefits: exemption from taxes and access to tax-deductible gifts. Organizations classified 501(c)(3) under the Internal Revenue Code are exempt from federal income taxes, excise taxes, and estate and gift taxes.[2] Although not guaranteed by federal designation, they generally also are exempt from state and local income taxes, property taxes, and sales taxes. They additionally are exempt from paying taxes on money derived from bingo games, and they pay lower postal rates than for-profit companies. Similarly, government forfeits part of its revenue by allowing donors to deduct gifts from income and estates on which taxes are owed. Illustrating some of these benefits, a nonprofit hospital may own property worth $5 million, have an annual income of $30 million, including $1.5 million in gifts, and purchase $2 million worth of products each year, but—unlike a for-profit hospital—it pays no property, income, gift, or sales taxes. At the federal level alone, nonprofits—not just charitable organizations—cost the Treasury about $36.5 billion each year (Gaul & Borowski, 1993).

In return, these organizations must carry out program services in support of their tax-exempt purpose. The only fundamental restraints placed on them are they cannot distribute profits to those in control (i.e., NDC), are prohibited from participating in electoral campaigns, and cannot engage in a substantial amount of lobbying. Historically, they have been subject to minimal audit and regulation, with even financial disclosure required only since the Tax Reform Act of 1969. In other words, charitable organizations traditionally have enjoyed a high degree of independence, as well as economic privileges. Cutlip (1965/1990) presented the basic philosophy: "There must never be a bar to a group of American citizens organizing to meet a problem they deem urgent and in having the freedom to go to the public with their appeal for money" (pp. 537–538). The First Amendment, Lohmann (1992b) emphasized, establishes strong normative barriers against excessive government interference in the pursuit of common goods.

In three landmark cases during the 1980s, the U.S. Supreme Court established the free-speech rights of charitable organizations and their fund-raising function. Fund raising, it proclaimed, is protected under the First Amendment of the Constitution because it involves the "communication of information, the dissemination and propagation of views and ideas, and the advocacy of causes" (*Village of Schaumburg*, 1980, p. 632). The Court also ruled that imposed limits on the amount of money organizations can spend on fund raising violate those organizations' constitutional right of

---

[2]Private foundations, which also are designated 501(c)(3), must pay a federal excise tax on their investment income—one of several differences in their legal status, discussed in chapter 15.

free speech (*Maryland*, 1984). In the third case, it ruled that point-of-solicitation disclosures of fund-raising costs and qualifications for licensing also are unconstitutional (*Riley*, 1988).

The decisions sanctioned a degree of free speech for charitable organizations far greater than that allowed for businesses, thereby reaffirming their special status. Unfortunately, the Court also extended full First Amendment protection to those who commit abuses and fraud. As discussed in chapter 8, all three cases resulted from lawsuits filed by paid solicitors and organizations employing them. The decisions invalidated local and state laws intended to curb their behavior.

Status Questioned

In April 1993, the *Philadelphia Inquirer* ran a seven-part, investigative series condemning nonprofits, which later was published as the book, *Free Ride: The Tax-Exempt Economy* (Gaul & Borowski, 1993). Reporters Gilbert Gaul and Neill Borowski argued that the nonprofit sector is too big and has been growing too fast. It costs $100 million a day in lost tax revenues; in 1992, that equaled 12% of the federal deficit. The money forfeited, they claimed, is not used to generate goods for society but to benefit those who populate the sector. Without distinguishing between charitable and other nonprofits, the reporters centered their investigation on accumulation of tax-exempt wealth, compensation and self-dealing, commercial activities, fraud, and abuse of the public trust. For example, they criticized the large endowments found in the sector and questioned why taxpayers should subsidize unreasonable salaries and such perks as country club memberships. Exempt organizations such as nonprofit hospitals, they charged, unfairly compete with businesses that do pay taxes. Based on their findings, Gaul and Borowski challenged nonprofits to justify the favorable tax treatment they receive, particularly at a time when new revenue sources are needed to balance the federal budget.

In his review for *The Chronicle of Philanthropy*, journalist David Johnston (1993a) concluded that *Free Ride*'s authors made a compelling case that reform is long overdue, taxpayers are chumps whose pockets are being picked, and the problems are not limited to a few rotten apples, as often claimed. He said, "Only political ostriches in non-profit America will ignore the prospect that Congress will covet the money lost through the tax exemptions described in this book" (p. 35). He then raised a critical question: "But if they end some kinds of exemptions, will it be the profiteers who suffer or the legitimate charities?" (p. 35).

Peter Dobkin Hall gave his reaction to *Free Ride* in a message on Internet's ARNOVA forum (June 21, 1994): "While I don't agree with everything in the book, I think it performed an enormously important service. Nonprofiteers tend all too often to think that their high purposes exempt them from the normal obligations of corporate citizenship . . . . This is why one prominent ethicist once described the nonprofit sector as 'an ethical black hole.'" He added: "Our failure to recognize what is happening to the sector and our continuing resistance to criticism presents—as it did in 1969—our greatest danger. (Or as Pogo would say, 'We have met the enemy—and he [*sic*] is us.')."

It is recalled from chapter 5 that Schwartz (1990) described the regulatory climate as stormy. Reviewing events during the summer of 1993 and winter of 1994, NSFRE's government relations consultant, Howard Marlowe (1994a), continued the climate metaphor, stating, "Not since 1969 has the summer Washington air seemed so chilly for the private, philanthropic sector" (p. 4). His report emanated from the first of a series of hearings held by the Oversight Subcommittee of the House Ways and Means Committee, then chaired by Representative Jake Pickle. Spurred by the IRS and state regulators, the subcommittee investigated abuses in the charitable subsector and promised change. Marlowe described the outcome: "Now it's a different season, and the winter winds are a lot colder than they have been in decades. . . . As I write, the Oversight Subcommittee . . . is preparing to make recommendations for sweeping new federal regulation of not-for-profits. . . . Even if legislation is not passed this year, Congress will act in the next year or two" (p. 4).

Status Endangered

The movement to increase regulation is driven by three forces: (a) abuses, (b) government's need for revenue, and (c) low accountability. Identifying the first force, Mixer (1993) stated, "Concerns by the general public and legislators over fraud, excessive costs, commercial ventures, tax avoidance, improper accounting practices, and further abuses of charitable purposes have stimulated this trend" (p. 249).

A national debt of $5 trillion and annual deficits as high as $290 billion have Congress searching everywhere for revenue. Drastic cuts in federal appropriations during the 1980s and mid-1990s transferred many financial responsibilities to state and local governments, which now view exemptions from property, sales, and other taxes as withholding badly needed revenue.[3] Greenfield (1991) summarized, "Government at all levels is desperate for added sources of revenue, so desperate that traditional 'sacred cows' are being sacrificed" (p. 212).

Accountability is the degree to which organizations continually reinforce public confidence in the integrity and effectiveness of their performance (Dressel, 1980). Widespread criticism of the charitable subsector is based on charges of insufficient accountability. When accountability is low, demands for government intervention increase. As Kanter and Summers (1987) explained, the ultimate test of charitable organizations' performance is whether representatives of society, starting with the IRS, believe they deserve their special status.

The three forces cannot be easily separated. Abuses are related to low accountability, and the presence of both allows government to reap new revenue through corrective measures. Before examining the driving forces in more detail, it is necessary to introduce concepts and actors essential to understanding the current legal context of fund raising.

KEY CONCEPTS AND ACTORS

Self-regulation has not worked up to this point. A general mindset among charitable organizations appears to be, "We'll behave any way we want until we are forced to behave differently." Without change, society may move to revoke the economic

---

[3]The term *devolution* is used to describe this downward shift in government responsibility.

privileges and freedom it has granted. Without tax exemptions and tax-deductible gifts, it is doubtful the subsector can survive.

Autonomy and Accountability

When we discuss the high degree of freedom traditionally enjoyed by charitable organizations, we are talking about the concept of autonomy, or the ability of an organization "to govern itself without outside controls" (Dressel, 1980, p. 1). Jon Pratt (1991), executive director of the Minnesota Council of Nonprofit Organizations, asserted, "Nonprofits consider their autonomous nature one of their distinct qualities" (p. 219). Their vital role in sustaining our democratic society, he argued, is based on the assumption that they are not subject to external control by government. According to Pablo Eisenberg (1994), president of the Center for Community Change and cochair of the National Committee for Responsive Philanthropy, the customary defense against government intrusion is that "the autonomy of the non-profit world . . . must be preserved at all costs" (p. 46). However, he pointed out, nonprofit leaders have failed to define where the balance lies between independence and accountability to government and society.

Autonomy is a necessary and valued trait of charitable organizations, but any discussion of their independence must also deal with accountability, or the degree to which they reinforce public confidence. Stated another way, a high degree of autonomy cannot be protected when accountability is low. Dressel (1980) explained, "Account-ability, the requirement to provide evidence that autonomy is responsibly used, is the price of autonomy" (p. 96).

Accountability is both general—to society as a whole—and specific—to such stakeholders as donors, clients, and government (McConnell, 1981). Charitable organizations, therefore, must explain themselves, demonstrate their service is worth the cost, and defend their essential character on two different levels.

On the general level, accountability is closely related to the concept of social responsibility, which simply defined means organizations behave as good citizens. They have an obligation to serve societal needs because society grants them the opportunities to operate (J. E. Grunig, 1992). As pointed out by J. E. Grunig and Hunt (1984), almost all discussion about social responsibility is concerned with for-profit companies; yet these scholars rightfully argued, "It is as important for governmental and nonprofit organizations to be socially responsible as for business firms" (p. 48). A former president of the General Electric Company explained the basic philosophy: "We know perfectly well that business does not function by divine right, but, like any other part of society, exists with the sanction of the community as a whole. . . . Today's public opinion, though it may appear as light as air, may become tomorrow's legisla-tion—for better or worse" (Cutlip et al., 1994, p. 21).

On the specific level, charitable organizations are answerable to constituencies who are affected by or may affect the organization's behavior. Government, for example, constitutes a stakeholder group to which such organizations must continually dem-onstrate integrity and effectiveness. Johnston (1993a) simply stated, "To ask anyone to justify a favorable tax treatment is more than appropriate" (p. 35).

Yet Milofsky and Blades (1991) concluded that ideas about what accountability means are not well worked out or readily apparent in the subsector. They said, "In the absence of clear theories of accountability, excess is likely to be commonplace" (p. 391). In a later study, Blades and Milofsky (1992) reported, "It is not hard to find important organizations whose fiscal and administrative practices beg serious questioning" (p. 28). "Fraud, distortion, and incomplete information seem widespread" (p. 10). In other words, insufficient understanding about the concept of accountability has contributed to its low presence among charitable organizations. Their failure to demonstrate that they are responsible—and therefore require only minimal control—invites government intervention. Supporting this assertion, N. S. Fink (1993) charged that current behavior "has made it difficult to argue for legal incentives to giving or to defend against more regulation" (p. 399). As Dressel (1980) stated, "The only justification for autonomy is performance in service of society that surpasses what would be achieved under regulation" (p. 96).

Concluding this discussion, the term *trust* denotes both faith and stewardship. Charitable organizations are dependent on society's faith in them, which often is referred to as "the public trust." The organizations also are held in trust for the common good. When those in control disregard their obligation to continually prove that trust is justified, other mechanisms for accountability—exposure in the media, condemnation by watchdog groups, and proposed laws by regulators—take over. The end result is a transfer of control to government, which entails a greater loss of autonomy than if self-corrective action had been taken. McConnell (1981) explained, "Accountability often emanates from external intervention, but intervention often goes well beyond reasonable requirements for accountability" (p. 38). To safeguard autonomy, organizations must be accountable for the use of resources and the attainment of results (Dressel, 1990)—commonly measured by accounting principles.

Accounting Basics

"Accounting is an important part of fund raising," affirmed Richard Larkin (1995, p. 21), a certified public accountant (CPA) who has worked with charitable organizations for more than 26 years. According to Larkin, an organization's accounting practices affect both its success in attracting private support and the satisfaction its donors derive from the philanthropic relationship. He maintained, "Fund raisers are uniquely positioned to help both parties meet their goals. To do so, however, a fund raiser must understand some basic accounting and financial-reporting concepts" (p. 21).

All organizations have income, expenses, and assets. Income for charitable organizations overall, as explained in chapter 2, comes from four sources: (a) fees, dues, and charges; (b) government grants and contracts; (c) gifts; and (d) endowment and investment income. As required by tax law, expenses are allocated to three functional categories: (a) program services, (b) management and general, and (c) fund raising. Program services are the purpose for which the organization was granted tax-exempt status. Expenses for this functional area must be commensurate in scope with the organization's financial resources. Assets are divided into two categories: (a) physical capital, or physical plant (i.e., real estate and buildings) and equipment; and (b) financial capital, or endowment and reserves.

Endowment and reserves represent previous income invested by the organization to provide future income. Reserves, more appropriately termed *operating reserves*, are funds set aside by the organization's dominant coalition to compensate for future fluctuations in annual cash flow, such as income shortfalls or unanticipated expenses. Whereas only earnings from the invested funds may be needed to cover fluctuations some years, the principal also can be spent whenever necessary. Therefore, as prescribed by accounting standards, reserves should be reported on financial statements as "unrestricted net assets," meaning all the money is available for immediate spending.

An *endowment* consists of multiple, separate funds—each of which is also referred to as an endowment (i.e., the term applies to the collective whole and its individual parts). Unlike operating reserves, endowments are established to generate income in perpetuity. The principal is not meant to be spent, nor are all of the earnings; a portion usually is returned to the principal as a hedge against inflation (e.g., $6,000 of earned income may be needed in 2007 to pay for the same thing that cost $5,000 in 1997). The portion of earnings that can be spent is set by organizational policy and is dependent on the performance of the total investments. A common rate in 1997 is 5% of the principal's value. An endowment of $100,000, then, provides only about $5,000 each year, but it does so year in and year out.

Two types of endowments traditionally and erroneously have been grouped together (S. G. Greene & Williams, 1995). *Pure endowments* are established when donors stipulate that their major gifts be endowed. Donors may further restrict the use of income from the invested principal (e.g., spendable income can only be used to buy books), or they may leave the endowed gift's purpose unrestricted (i.e., income can be used as the recipient organization sees fit). Regardless, only the income can be spent; by law, the principal must remain intact in perpetuity. Therefore, accounting rules hold that endowments of this type, also called donor-designated endowments, be recorded as "permanently restricted assets."

Board-designated endowments, on the other hand, are established when dominant coalitions choose to endow organizational profits, including excess unrestricted gifts. Because the funding is free of restrictions, income from this type of endowment always can be used as the organization sees fit. The principal also can be spent. Unlike pure endowments, preservation of the principal is not a donor stipulation protected by law, but simply the intention of those who created the endowment—which can be modified or dissolved by taking similar action. Like operating reserves, all the money technically is available for immediate spending whenever the dominant coalition decides it is needed. Therefore, new accounting standards mandate that these quasi endowments be recorded as unrestricted net assets, the implications of which are addressed shortly.

Financial Measures of Accountability

Regulators, watchdog groups, the media, and donors use various financial ratios to measure the accountability of charitable organizations. The most common two are the ratio of program expenses to total expenses and the fund-raising cost ratio (amount of money spent on fund raising divided by amount of money raised).

The first ratio measures the extent to which resources are used to advance the organization's purpose. It is expected that annual expenses for program services will be higher than those for management and fund raising combined, sometimes referred to as overhead. A high program expense ratio indicates that the organization is fulfilling its mission. A low ratio signifies that overhead is excessive. The standard for the National Charities Information Bureau, one of the two major watchdog groups discussed later in this section, is that at least 60% of annual expenses be for program services.

The fund-raising cost ratio should not exceed 25% on an annual basis. The national average for organizations represented in NSFRE is 20% (Greenfield, 1991). Studies by CASE and AHP in the early 1990s found lower ratios: 16% for colleges and universities and 12% for hospitals and medical centers.[4] In support of my recommended ceiling, 74% of the NSFRE members responding to Mongon's (1995) study said fund-raising costs should not exceed 24% of the amount raised. Only 5% said a ratio of 35% or higher was acceptable. Becky Gonzalez-Campoy (cited in "Forum," 1995), formerly a staff practitioner at Minnesota Public Radio, declared, "You have to spend money to earn it—but you don't need to spend as much as 30 percent to 40 percent of your donations on administration and fund raising" (p. 20).

If the fund-raising cost ratio is high, the function is not being managed efficiently. High cost ratios also result from hiring paid solicitors. Low cost ratios are achieved when fund raising includes a major gifts program and has a prospect pool with a high proportion of previous donors. Quite simply, costs increase as the average gift size decreases and the process targets new, rather than renewed, donors.

Wilson "Bill" Levis (1991), then manager of the Nonprofit Quality Reporting Project at Baruch College of City University of New York, estimated that the cost ratio for raising an average gift of $10 from new donors was 100%, whereas it was only 25% for an average gift of $1,000. Gifts of the same two sizes from renewed donors cost just 35% and 10%, respectively. Greenfield (1991) provided cost guidelines that also support variations by gift size and donor status. Drawing from several studies, he reported that direct-mail *acquisition*, or recruiting new donors through mail solicitations, costs $1 to $1.25 per $1 raised, whereas direct-mail *renewal* costs 20 cents per $1 raised. He said planned giving programs and capital campaigns, which concentrate on major gifts, respectively cost 25 cents and 5 to 10 cents per $1 raised.

Clearly, maintaining donor relationships is cost efficient. The net dollars raised from previous donors are significantly greater than those from first-time donors. Nevertheless, charitable organizations must continually invest in acquiring new donors; not doing so results in a shrinking donor base that eventually will disappear. Similarly, relationships with major donors usually start with lower level gifts. Not investing in annual giving in order to lower fund-raising costs is shortsighted and foolhardy.

Staff managers strive for a balance in their function, keeping costs reasonable through stewardship and major gifts, and simultaneously investing in the acquisition of new donors and annual giving. Budgets are broken down by programs, activities, and techniques so that costs and return on investment (ROI) can be measured for each. These individual cost ratios vary greatly. A special event, for example, likely costs 50% of the gross proceeds, whereas a series of cultivation and solicitation visits to a

---

[4]A 1995 survey of AHP members found an extremely high median ratio of 36% (AAFRC Trust for Philanthropy, 1996). The finding is suspect due to the survey's 20% response rate; however, AHP ratios have been steadily increasing, which prompts numerous questions in need of scientific answers. For example, what is the relationship between the immoderate ratios and the high salaries reported by fund raisers who work for hospitals and medical centers? Overall, research on the topic is scant, and basic questions about measurement are only now being asked. In 1996, NSFRE's Research Council launched the first large study on measuring fund-raising costs, guided by James Greenfield's expertise. Students are encouraged to explore this topic as it relates to their own research interests.

corporation costs about 20% of the resulting gift (Greenfield, 1991). These are internal measurements of efficiency that help managers plan, budget, and evaluate their programming. They do not have to be shared with prospective donors or other publics. However, the two-way symmetrical model dictates that the overall fund-raising cost ratio for the year, as well as the ratio of program service expenses to total expenses, be widely reported to the organization's strategic publics.

Disclosure of annual ratios is backed by such experts as Larkin (1993), the CPA cited earlier, who also is the technical director of the Not-for-Profit Industry Services Group of Price Waterhouse. He advised fund raisers to use financial statements that include the two common ratios to demonstrate management performance, thereby strengthening the organization's case for support.

In opposition, Levis (1991) argued that fund-raising cost ratios are misleading and create negative attitudes. He and others assume uncontrollable circumstances cause an "unbalanced" function in many charitable organizations: Some only have access to lower level gifts, some are dependent on more expensive techniques, and some—particularly newer organizations—have to spend more on fund raising to acquire donors. Underlying these assumptions is the presupposition that organizational need overrides fund-raising potential when setting dollar goals. With little scientific evidence to support them, the assumptions have been granted the status of law and are constantly perpetuated in the literature, as demonstrated by Hopkins (1995):

> Many variables can account for the expense of a charity's fund-raising efforts in a given year—some of them having little or nothing to do with the merits of the organization or its cause. Some fund-raising methods are inherently more expensive than others. Controversial programs may impede an organization's fund-raising efforts, driving up costs. Fund raising in the early years of an organization's existence also tends to be more costly, so that fledgling charities often must spend more on fund-raising efforts than organizations with a well-developed constituency and fund-raising program. (p. 27)

I believe the assumptions are seriously flawed and that their widespread acceptance has more to do with avoiding accountability than with explaining reality. Providing supportive evidence, the study testing the fund-raising models, reported in chapter 6, showed that only 4% of the organizations represented in NSFRE do not have a major gifts program (Kelly, 1995b). Therefore, organizations with fund-raising staff rarely lack the means to achieve a balance between large and small gifts. Furthermore, no organization is confined to one or two techniques; the numerous choices available, categorized by effectiveness, are presented in chapter 9. Logically, and as confirmed by experience, after even 1 year of fund raising, every organization has a nucleus of former donors. Decisions to utilize ineffective and, therefore, expensive techniques or to place a higher priority on donor acquisition than on donor renewal result in high cost ratios, which indicate low accountability.

The credibility of the assumptions and the defense of high ratios are grounded in the presupposition that organizational need is the overriding factor when setting dollar goals—a characteristic of asymmetrical fund raising. Representing a different perspective, the fund-raising process described in chapter 10 requires managers to qualify the needs of the organization by its potential to raise gifts. Both factors are examined in the first step of research, including such critical measures of potential as prospective donors' interests and needs. Based on findings from both sides of the philanthropic exchange, attainable dollar goals are set in the next step. Following the multistep process increases efficiency—as well as effectiveness—and lowers cost ratios for any organization, regardless of variables such as age. Due to the flawed assumptions they hold, defenders of high ratios ignore such a possibility. Levis (1991), for example, urged regulators, watchdog groups, and the media to find other ways of measuring accountability because "high cost percentages are not abuses, so other criteria must be applied" (p. 270).

Among those who disagree with Levis' popular claim is U.S. Supreme Court Justice William Rehnquist. In the dissenting opinion he authored for the *Maryland* (1984) case, Rehnquist argued that a high fund-raising cost—in this case, the amount paid to a solicitation firm—"betrays the expectations of the donor who thinks that his [*sic*] money will be used to benefit the charitable purpose in the name of which the money was solicited" (p. 811). The dissenting opinion, signed by four of the nine justices, supported a Maryland statute that prohibited charitable organizations from paying fund-raising expenses of more than 25% of the amount raised.

No one indicator provides ample evidence of an organization's accountability. Milofsky and Blades (1991), for example, said fund-raising cost ratios are not as important as evidence that the organization concentrates primarily on its tax-exempt purpose. Yet they admitted, "Donors have a legitimate interest in knowing whether the money they give is used as promised and whether it is actually used to help people rather than spent in administration and fund-raising [*sic*]" (p. 388). Blades and Milofsky (1992) said that although ratios do not measure effectiveness, they should be publicized "since the public has been educated to care about this issue" (p. 15).

Society increasingly expects 501(c)(3) organizations to be forthright about the percentage of money spent annually on program services, management and general, and fund raising. Staff managers understand the importance of financial measurements of accountability and freely disseminate them. As Boris and Odendahl (1990) stated, "Disclosure is the keystone of trust and stewardship upon which the sector is built" (p. 200).

New Accounting Standards

A network of independent agencies govern the accounting standards for charitable organizations. Colleges and universities, for example, follow the standards set by the National Association of College and University Business Officers (NACUBO). NACUBO, as do other agencies, follows standards set by the Financial Accounting Standards Board (FASB) and the American Institute of Certified Public Accountants (AICPA). Recently implemented and proposed changes in FASB and AICPA standards address legal and ethical problems presented in this book. In other words, new accounting rules represent external corrective action to make charitable organizations behave more responsibly.

FASB Standards on Endowments. FASB's stated intention for changing its standards was to promote "more relevant, comparable, and understandable financial reporting" (S. G. Greene, 1993, p. 29). One of the four major changes made was introduced earlier: differences in classifying and reporting endowments and reserves.[5] Effective in 1995, the revised rules, known as Statements 116 and 117, depart dramatically from traditional accounting practices; regardless, they apply to all organizations covered by existing CPA audit guides.

Under the 1995 standards, endowments are classified by the presence or absence of donor restriction. Pure endowments, which are established to fulfill the intention of donors, are permanently restricted assets and are so reported on financial statements. Board-designated endowments, on the other hand, are unrestricted net assets—like operating reserves—and must now be reported as such. In the past, both types of endowments were treated the same: classified and reported as restricted assets.

The change, critics charge, is harmful because users of financial statements might assume all unrestricted net assets are available for immediate spending on operation, even though the organization has designated some as permanent endowment. They say such views could have a chilling effect on income, particularly gifts from donors. NACUBO representative Ingrid Stafford (cited in S. G. Greene, 1993), for example, protested at a hearing, "We feel uncomfortable saying it is all unrestricted, because that implies it is available to be spent" (p. 31). Yet, as already explained, preserving the principal of board-designated endowments is merely the intention of those responsible for their creation. Unlike pure endowments that are legally protected, all the money can be spent, although dominant coalitions generally choose not to do so. Responding to Stafford's objection, FASB member James Leisenring (cited in S. G. Greene, 1993) stated, "It seems universities want to change the law to call things what they're not" (p. 31).

As described later in this chapter, excessive endowments consisting of unrestricted net assets indicate low accountability. Students should understand that setting aside profits results in less money available for current program services. In moderation, investing in the organization's future is admirable; however, constantly choosing future security over the immediate needs of known and unknown clients is irresponsible. Larkin (1993) explained, "In the not-for-profit world, increasing net assets is not the criterion for success. (In fact, increasing net assets can sometimes imply that a not-for-profit is not doing its job.)" (p. 47).

AICPA Guidelines on Joint Costs.

As part of its efforts to prepare new audit standards for nonprofits, AICPA (1993) proposed revised guidelines for calculating *joint costs*, or apportioning part of a solicitation's cost to program service expenses. Joint costs constitute a long-standing issue of concern. Basically, charitable organizations have argued that solicitations do more than raise money; they also educate donors and nondonors about societal problems and organizational efforts to address those problems. Cutlip (1965/1990) traced arguments about the educational value of fund raising back to the early 1900s.

---

[5]The other three changes are: (a) certain volunteer services and property use now are classified as income, which is explained in the later overview of IRS regulations; (b) gift pledges that are written and legally binding now must be reported as income for the total amount in the year the pledge is made, which is discussed in chapters 10 and 14; and (c) gifts designated by donors for other organizations can no longer be counted as income by the distributing organization that first receives the gift (e.g., a federation), which is covered in the next chapter (Larkin, 1995).

Before 1987, organizations mostly used a "primary purpose" rule in accounting for costs (G. Williams, 1992b). All expenses of an activity that contained a fund-raising appeal, such as a mailing, phonathon, or special event, had to be counted as a fund-raising expense. Standards issued by AICPA in 1987 allowed organizations to shift some of their expenses for solicitations to the program-services category. What followed was widespread abuse, whereby high percentages of fund-raising expenses were allocated to program services.

Organizations closely associated with paid solicitors often defined their services as little more than public education in conjunction with solicitations. Superficial phrases of advice, such as "Keep your workplace free of cancer hazards," included in a 1993 mailing from the Walker Cancer Research Institute (WCRI), a client of the solicitation firm of Watson and Hughey, were used to justify as much as 99% of program service expenses.[6] David Ormstedt (cited in G. Williams, 1992b), Assistant Attorney General in charge of Connecticut's Public Charities Unit, said, "A significant number of charities exist only because of the existence of the accounting rule" (p. 31).

Equally serious, well-known organizations not using paid solicitors assigned too much of their fund-raising costs to program expenses in order to keep fund-raising cost ratios low and program–expense ratios high. Increased reliance on such ratios to evaluate organizations convinced many to maximize—on paper—the amount they spent on program services and minimize the amount spent on fund raising. Acceptable ratios often meant the difference in attracting more gifts, gaining entry to federated campaigns, obtaining a satisfactory rating from a watchdog group, or winning praise in the media. Steven Arter (cited in S. G. Greene & Williams, 1992a), a Pennsylvania investigator at the time, reported, "I have had officials of charities say to me, 'If we have to abuse the accounting rules to compete, then we'll do it. Otherwise, we feel we're doing a disservice to our organization'" (p. 1).

Some organizations and their lawyers insisted that regulators had "grossly exaggerated the problem, unnecessarily alarmed the public, and hurt the reputations of all non-profits" (G. Williams, 1992b, p. 30). Attorney MacKenzie Canter, III, now a partner in the Washington, DC law firm of Copilevitz & Canter, said the accounting policy made perfect sense. As documented in the next chapter, Canter represents such Watson and Hughey clients as WCRI, and his partner Errol Copilevitz also works with organizations closely tied to solicitation firms. Copilevitz was the lead attorney for the National Federation of the Blind of North Carolina, a group of organizations using solicitors, in the 1988 Supreme Court case (*Riley*).[7] The two frequently are identified in media reports as defense lawyers for solicitors and organizations charged with fraud (e.g., "Pa. sues," 1996).

On the other side, state regulators urged AICPA to return to the original primary purpose rule or to set a ceiling on the proportion that organizations could shift to program expenses. The accounting group did neither, but it did propose revised guidelines that would strengthen, clarify, and illustrate its standards for joint costs (AICPA, 1993).

---

[6]The WCRI mailing is discussed further in chapter 8.

[7]Copilevitz maintains a separate practice in Kansas City, Missouri, which he prefers to use for public identification.

Under the new guidelines, no portion of the costs of fund-raising appeals produced by paid solicitors receiving commissions can be counted as program expenses. The standard, unfortunately, does not cover solicitation firms that base their fees on hourly or per-piece rates. However, charitable organizations cannot charge to program services any of the costs of mailings that use vague slogans without other information about nongiving ways people can help the organization accomplish its goals and ways receivers of such messages can utilize the organization's programs.

To count part of the costs of a solicitation as program services, an organization must meet *all* criteria in the three areas of purpose, audience, and content. Regarding purpose, the organization must prove it intended to educate receivers of the solicitation. One way is to demonstrate that the same technique had been utilized with similar or greater numbers for purely educational purposes, without any attempt to solicit gifts. For example, if fund raisers intend to assign direct-mail costs to program services, they should schedule a series of nonsolicitation mailings to the same donor public (e.g., a newsletter). Another way given by AICPA for proving purpose is to regularly evaluate the results of the educational part of solicitations. Instead of just counting dollars received from a phonathon, for example, practitioners could send questionnaires to a sample of participants, measuring awareness or understanding gained from the telephone calls.

Guidelines for meeting criteria in the two other areas are equally stringent. To meet the audience requirement, the organization must prove the solicitation was targeted at people clearly interested in its program services, not at people who were selected because of their presumed ability to give. To meet the content requirement, the solicitation must include a message with the potential to affect the behavior of receivers in ways other than contributing. For example, instead of simply telling people to stop smoking, AICPA recommended that specific instructions, references, and available resources that would help people do so be included in the solicitation.

The new guidelines spell out, for the first time, a variety of methods organizations can use to calculate the percentages of solicitation expenses. For example, those relying on direct mail can use the physical units method, which requires making a line-by-line count of the text of each mailing. A 100-line letter devoting 35 lines to educating the reader about the mission of the organization and nongiving behavior that can help fulfill both its mission and the reader's needs (e.g., an organization fighting AIDS that addresses the practice of safe sex) is considered a communication that is 35% program services and 65% fund raising. Under the guidelines, organizations must explain in audited financial reports what type of solicitations were involved in joint costs and the method used to determine how expenses were allocated to each category.

As of 1997, AICPA's new guidelines are still in preparation. The delay of 4 years largely is attributable to opposition by the National Federation of Nonprofits, a trade association representing about 400 charitable organizations and solicitation firms, which generally solicit only lower level gifts through direct mail. The federation, based in Washington, DC, vehemently opposed the changes on joint costs and issued a harshly critical report to the media. Following set procedures, AICPA had invited reaction to its revised guidelines before making them final. Just 306 written comments were received. Based on its own analysis of the comments, which totaled less than its membership, the National Federation of Nonprofits (1994) reported that 90% of those commenting cited deficiencies in the proposed accounting rules and more than half asked AICPA to withdraw or significantly modify them.

Ormstedt (1995) provided an explanation for the federation's action when he emphasized the current absence of controls over joint costs: "The opportunity for direct mailers and telemarketers to make money from fund raising for incorporeal charities is now remarkable" (p. 13). He predicted that if accounting groups do not act soon, "litigation is inevitable" (p. 15). State regulators, he said, would not attack the concept that solicitations can involve public education, but instead would go after those organizations allocating 80% or more of their fund-raising costs to program services. "Once a precedent is set, states will be able to erode this threat to accountability" (p. 15). Underscoring the seriousness of the situation, he declared, "If there is to be another major U.S. Supreme Court case in this field, it will be over this issue" (p. 15).

I agree with Ormstedt's assessment, and following the lead of Larkin (1995), who chaired AICPA's Not-for-Profit Audit Guide Task Force, I believe the revised guidelines will be adopted in the near future—regardless of resistance by the National Federation of Nonprofits. Legitimate organizations and their fund raisers should anticipate adoption and begin complying with the new rules now. Working closely with financial officers and others, staff managers must first decide whether or not part of the costs of future solicitations should be allocated to program services. A reasonable decision for most is to keep solicitation expenses separate and utilize joint costs only for activities with nonsolicitation objectives, such as cultivation and stewardship (e.g., inviting donors to a special event for clients). Abuses of joint costs have made it very difficult to convince officials and legislators that public education through solicitations is an authentic program service (Bush, 1991).

Whatever the decision, policies must be developed to ensure consistency. Another accounting group, Accountants for the Public Interest (API, 1990), explained, "The key to useful functional expense analysis is consistency. Each organization must establish specific criteria for classifying expenses—and then remain steadfast in applying them for financial reporting" (p. 15). Copies of AICPA's (1993) new guidelines can be ordered by calling (800) 862-4272. FASB's publications are available on the group's Web site: *http://www.fasb.org*.

The IRS

The IRS, a unit of the Treasury Department, enforces the Internal Revenue Code, which defines such fundamental issues as what constitutes a charitable organization and a tax-deductible gift. As such, the IRS plays a dominant role in defining and directing fund-raising practice. This is not to say practitioners and their employers do not interact with other federal agencies. The Federal Communications Commission (FCC), for example, prescribes acceptable on-air recognition of corporate donors for public radio and television stations. The SEC influences the transfer, receipt, and sale of securities given to organizations. The Federal Trade Commission (FTC), which enforces consumer-protection laws, has the authority to step in when fund-raising abuse crosses state boundaries. Because it oversees telemarketing, its interaction primarily has been with paid solicitors; however, the behavior of these firms has prompted concerted efforts during the last decade to place all interstate fund raising under FTC jurisdiction.

Be that as it may, the IRS currently commands center stage when discussing the legal context of fund raising. It has the power to revoke organizations' charitable status and to levy fines and penalties on donors and organizations who do not comply with its rules. An overview of IRS regulations is given in the final section of this chapter. The discussion here details two elements of the service's oversight that must be understood before examining the forces driving regulation: (a) IRS Form 990, and (b) unrelated business income tax (UBIT).

IRS Form 990.   Touched on in earlier chapters, Form 990, Return of Organization Exempt from Income Tax, is the annual information return to the IRS that must be filed by nonprofits, except those exempted (e.g., religious organizations). Similar to her recommendation about state registration, NSFRE President Lewis (1993a) recommended that every organization file an IRS Form 990 every year whether required to or not, and then comply with laws about making it available to interested parties. Demonstrating such a proactive stance, Volunteers of America is not required to file a 990 because it is classified as a religious organization, but Arthur Smith (cited in Skolnik, 1993), then director of communications, reported, "We do it anyway" (p. 30).

There are four versions of the 990, including a short form for small nonprofits, 990EZ, and a business income tax return, 990-T, which is discussed shortly (API, 1990). Form 990-PF is filed by private foundations and is used by fund raisers for prospect research on foundation donors. Charitable 501(c)(3) organizations file Form 990 and Schedule A. The return reports financial information, including a Statement of Revenue and a Statement of Functional Expenses (i.e., program services, management and general, and fund raising). It also describes program accomplishments for the year. Schedule A requires the organization to list, by name, the salaries and benefits paid to its officers, trustees, "key employees," and the five other highest paid employees. Information must be provided on activities related to insider dealing (e.g., loans to trustees) and to maintaining tax-exempt status (e.g., lobbying).

The importance of the 990 cannot be minimized. Levis (cited in "Form 990," 1992) explained, "Taking Form 990 seriously means taking several responsibilities seriously—the law, ethics and public accountability, industry statistics, not-for-profit policy making, media and public credibility, and donors' use of Form 990" (p. 8). Although they are not responsible for filing the form, staff managers participate in its preparation, most notably by providing complete and accurate figures on fund raising. They also serve as the organization's conscience, ensuring that all information meets the highest standards. The IRS Form 990 is the cornerstone of an organization's reputation, and fund raisers give it the attention it deserves.

Staff managers recognize the importance of sharing vital information on the Form 990 with donors and other publics, including the media. If trustees, senior managers, or other dominant coalition members are hesitant to do so because some of the information might be questioned, fund raisers counsel them to change the questionable behavior to bring it in line with expectations of strategic publics.

This prescribed role, unfortunately, has been underrepresented in the past. Levis (cited in "Form 990," 1992) reported in 1992 that more than 50% of the 990s filed annually "are incomplete, inaccurate or both" (p. 8). Many organizations refused or were reluctant to make the form available to those who asked to see it. In 1996, a federal law was enacted to correct the problems. The new law increased the fines for failing to file an accurate Form 990 and significantly extended publics' right of access to the forms.

Under previous law, only those persons who presented themselves at an organization's principal office during regular business hours were legally entitled to inspect the forms (Murawski, 1996). Copies did not have to be provided. Members of the media, in particular, criticized this low standard of disclosure and publicized the number and names of well-known organizations unwilling to comply even at that level. Illustrating, when the University of Oklahoma refused to provide its 990 for *The Chronicle of Philanthropy*'s 1995 survey of top fund-raising organizations, the executive director of the university's affiliated foundation, Ron Burton (cited in "Philanthropy 400," 1995), defiantly told the reporter, "We don't work for you" (p. 53).

The 1996 law requires organizations to make their Form 990s for the previous 3 years available by mail to *anyone* who requests copies and pays reasonable duplicating and postage costs (Murawski, 1996). The fine for not complying within 30 days is $5,000 per offense. Failure to file complete and accurate 990s on time with the IRS evokes fines of $20 and $100 a day for small and large organizations, respectively, up to a maximum of $10,000 and $50,000. In short, the normative role for fund raisers just given is now sanctioned by government and enforced through penalties.

UBIT.   Charitable organizations must pay taxes when they engage in income-producing activities that bear little relation to their purpose. Defined by Meckstroth (1994), "Unrelated business income is the income earned by an organization that is not related to its tax-exempt mission" (p. 361). Only an insubstantial portion of an organization's activities can be devoted to unrelated business, otherwise its tax-exempt status may be jeopardized (API, 1990).[8] Income from such activities that exceeds $1,000 is taxed at regular corporate rates. Information must be submitted on Form 990-T, "Exempt Organization Business Income Tax Return." Exceptions include revenue from businesses staffed at least 85% by volunteers and the sale of donated goods. Fund-raising events such as dinners also are excluded. Royalties are not taxable, which has led to legal battles about the definitional difference between that form of earned income and business income.

The IRS was aggressive in enforcing UBIT during the late 1980s and early 1990s. Some universities, for example, discovered they owed taxes on income from commercial entertainment and professional sports events held in their campus auditoriums or arenas. Although they argued that all such activities were related to their broad charitable purpose, the IRS disagreed, saying the only criterion used in booking the events was profitability.

Joint ventures, or marketing agreements with for-profit companies, also were targeted. In 1991, the IRS proposed charging UBIT on money received from corporate sponsorships, one of five types of joint ventures discussed in chapter 8. Congress opposed the move, which would have taxed such popular events as football bowl

---

[8]API's 75-page guidebook explains the basic principles of nonprofit accounting in a relatively simple manner, which makes it a useful resource for students. The 1995 edition is listed in suggested readings at the end this chapter.

games, and passed legislation in 1992 exempting most sponsorships (Hopkins, 1996). The bill, however, was never signed by then President George Bush. As of 1997, there is no law defining whether or not UBIT is owed on a sponsorship payment. Because the Congressional action received much more media coverage than the president's nonaction, most fund raisers today mistakenly assume that the legislation was enacted and, therefore, sponsorship income is tax free. Their deficient knowledge could be costly.

Taxation of unrelated business activities was subsumed in the first half of the 1990s by the IRS' efforts to curb unfair competition, an issue covered later in this chapter. Although challenges are less visible today, problems related to UBIT are embedded in current and broader attacks against charitable organizations' privileged status.

State Regulations and Regulators

The federal government shares oversight responsibilities with the states, and, according to N. S. Fink (1993), "each year, as new abuses appear, the states add to the regulations" (p. 398). Bush (1991) identified the three areas of state regulation: (a) registration, (b) disclosure, and (c) reporting. She stressed the importance of differentiating between what the fund-raising practice views as reasonable requirements for states to demand and those that can be considered unreasonable and burdensome. States, she argued, have a right to know what activities are taking place within their jurisdiction. It is reasonable for them to require disclosure of facts not protected under the First Amendment, which can help citizens make informed decisions. Furthermore, it is appropriate for states to collect information they need to answer questions from citizens.

On the other hand, Bush (1991) argued that the situation is "chaotic" (p. 210) because each state has tried to come up with its own formula to stop abuses. Nonstandardized state regulations, she said, are a costly burden for charitable organizations. Writing at the beginning of the decade, she urged fund raisers to push for adoption of a uniform registration form, one that could be filled out once, photocopied, and sent to multiple jurisdictions. States and associations began working toward a common form in 1992 (G. Williams, 1994e). As of 1997, 20 states and the District of Columbia allow organizations to use the 3-page Uniform Registration Statement (Craig, 1997b). Progress also has been made in reporting requirements, with 40 states now accepting copies of IRS Form 990 for annual reports (Fleishman, 1995). Variations in disclosure rules, however, have not been significantly reduced. In other words, recent changes have improved the situation, but efforts to achieve greater standardization still are needed.

It is recalled from chapter 5 that 41 of the 50 states have registration laws for consultants and/or paid solicitors; 47 of the states and the District of Columbia have registration, disclosure, and reporting laws affecting those groups and/or charitable organizations (AAFRC Trust for Philanthropy, 1997a).[9] The laws differ among the jurisdictions. For example, in Washington, DC, all types of organizations, including colleges and universities, must apply for a license and pay an annual fee of $80. There are no registration requirements for paid solicitors or consultants. Much more typical is its close neighbor Maryland, which

---

[9]Counties and municipalities also have laws regulating charities, consultants, and paid solicitors; estimates range as high as 17,000 jurisdictions for just registration requirements (Craig, 1997a).

requires annual registration for organizations, with fees ranging from $0 to $200 depending on the amount of private support raised. Educational institutions and hospitals are exempt. Maryland requires only a $200 registration fee from consultants, but a $300 fee and a $25,000 bond from paid solicitors.

I received an abrupt introduction to legal variations in 1982, when I left a position at the University of Maryland to become the vice president for development and public relations at Mount Vernon College in Washington, DC. After a few months on the job, I thought I was doing well until I got a notice from the district government informing me that my institution was not allowed to raise private gifts because its license had lapsed! A useful warning for all fund raisers is that, generally, solicitation activity without complete registration in pertinent states is punishable by fines of about $5,000 per state.

Practitioners should check AAFRC's summary of state regulations, published annually in *Giving USA Update*, to monitor laws in states where their organization is located and where it solicits gifts. Direct inquiries to appropriate offices of those states (e.g., Office of the Attorney General) are strongly recommended to avoid harmful surprises. For example, in 1993, Hawaii became one of the first states to make it illegal for charitable organizations to exchange or rent names unless they have obtained permission from the people on their mailing lists (Goldstein, 1994). Ignorance of the law is no defense; diligence and research are required.

To understand regulation, practitioners must understand the historical context from which it emerged; specifically, experiences with paid solicitors have shaped fund-raising laws. Starting in the late 1970s, the consumer-protection theory of regulation led states to enact laws directed at solicitors (e.g., requiring disclosure of fund-raising costs to prospective donors). Connecticut regulator Ormstedt (1995) explained:

> The primary targets of states in those days were professional telephone solicitors. There were (and still are) some telemarketers who would pass themselves off as volunteers, lie about the nature of the organization for which they were soliciting, lie about how contributions would be used and, in short, say anything necessary to separate people from their money. From the perspective of the states, their greatest offense was that year after year the charity for whom they solicited was lucky to see 10 cents of any contributed dollar—and the public was kept completely unaware. (p. 12)

After the 1980s series of Supreme Court decisions, 23 states found they had unconstitutional fund-raising laws (Bush, 1994). For example, states could not limit the percentage of gift dollars paid to solicitors (*Maryland*, 1984), nor could they require disclosure of costs (*Riley*, 1988). A footnote to the 1988 ruling, however, said it would not be a violation of free-speech rights if solicitors were required to disclose that they are paid for their work. The decisions also gave regulators the go ahead to continue enforcing laws against fraud and to educate citizens about those who exploit philanthropy.

About the same time the Court issued its third decision, 22 states sued the solicitation firm of Watson and Hughey, now based in McLean, Virginia and renamed Direct Response Consulting Services (G. Williams, 1993a). Regulators charged that the firm's sweepstakes mailings constituted fraud by leading donors to believe they would receive substantial cash prizes instead of the few pennies they got. Bush (1994) identified the sweepstakes as "a seminal moment in fund-raising regulation" (p. 30) because of their dramatic and negative impact. The scheme, she said, resulted in a "stiffening of regulations on fund raising in at least 20 states, including a handful of states that went from no fund-raising regulation to extensive regulation, virtually overnight" (p. 30). "The regulatory landscape suddenly got more difficult" (p. 30).[10]

The Supreme Court's cumulative decisions, coupled with the concurrent charges against Watson and Hughey, set off a flurry of legal activity during the late 1980s as states modified and/or enacted laws to conform with the rulings and still combat abuses. The outcome was current registration, disclosure, and reporting requirements, as well as laws prohibiting deception.

Focusing on disclosure and reporting, states such as Ohio, Michigan, and Tennessee mandate that paid solicitors disclose their status. Tennessee, for example, requires them to inform donor prospects, prior to solicitation, that they are "professional solicitors"—using those exact words—who will receive a portion of the solicited funds as costs, expenses, and fees (G. Williams, 1991). Federal district courts have upheld such disclosure laws since 1988 (G. Williams, 1993b). A larger number of states require paid solicitors to file copies of their contracts and year-end financial reports, including fund-raising costs, for each campaign conducted in the state. Regulators are now using the laws and the information gained to prosecute and to publicize.

As can be expected with government intervention, efforts to curb the abusive behavior of paid solicitors also have resulted in costly regulations for legitimate fund raising. For example, nine states, as of 1997, require a disclosure statement that must appear on every written solicitation received in those states. In 1987, New York became the first to require a statement informing donor prospects that they could write to a state office for financial information filed by the soliciting organization (Bush, 1994). West Virginia, Pennsylvania, Florida, and New Jersey have statements that must be reproduced *verbatim*, giving each state's regulatory address and toll-free telephone number. Maryland, North Carolina, Virginia, and Washington have similar requirements. The nine statements easily fill one fourth of a standard page. As more states adopt such rules, printing, paper, and postage costs for interstate direct-mail packages will go up. Bush (1994) commented, "This is getting to be an expensive requirement for groups soliciting nationwide" (p. 32).

Ending this discussion on a positive note, the progress in standardization described earlier will save time and money. The uniform registration form now in use was developed by the two professional associations of state regulators: the National Association of Attorneys General (NAAG) and the National Association of State Charity Officials (NASCO). NAAG and NASCO meet jointly each year to discuss issues and—to some extent—coordinate action, thereby reducing barriers to interstate enforcement. They are key actors in the regulatory environment, and a dialogue with them is strongly recommended. Bush (1994) summarized, "It is in the best interest of fund-raising executives and not-for-profit managers to recognize the validity of regulation and actively promote smart, consistent, non-punitive laws" (p. 28).

---

[10] Amazingly and contradictory to basic editorial requirements, Bush (1994) neglected to name Watson and Hughey/Direct Response Consulting Services as the firm responsible for the sweepstakes.

Watchdog Groups

The two major watchdog groups reporting on charitable organizations are the National Charities Information Bureau (NCIB), based in New York City, and the Philanthropic Advisory Service (PAS) of the Council of Better Business Bureaus, located in Arlington, Virginia. Using similar sets of standards of acceptable practice, they conduct organizational audits and publicly report whether an organization meets standards in the four areas of fund raising, governance, financial management, and public information. One of PAS' standards, for example, calls for an organization to provide on request an annual report containing information related to the four areas. Their work embodies self-regulation, encouraging organizations to be accountable and to adhere to ethical and socially responsible norms outlined in the standards. Both are widely quoted in the media as authorities on issues facing the subsector. As Bush (1994) stated, their "statements on charitable accountability carry a lot of weight with the press and with the public" (p. 33).

NCIB and PAS are nonprofits that provide reports on individual organizations as a free service. They promote informed giving and implicitly advocate giving to organizations that comply with their standards. Both concentrate solely on organizations that solicit nationally, excluding hospitals, churches, and educational institutions. Using detailed questionnaires, as well as other auditing tools, NCIB and PAS review about 100 and 200 organizations each year, respectively. Blades and Milofsky (1992) pointed out that although the primary purpose of their questionnaires is to provide service to "the public," "a parallel product is that in completing the forms charities must engage in a process of self-examination and public disclosure" (p. 19). They added, however, that only a fraction of the organizations selected for review by NCIB bother to answer its questionnaire. "A substantial number of charities refuse to register with it, will not participate in its self-regulation system, and often launch virulent attacks on the NCIB if that organization asks questions that are too searching" (p. 7). According to J. R. Wood and Hougland (1990), some religious organizations respond to PAS' inquires by declaring, "We are accountable only to God" (p. 11).

NCIB was started in 1918. Its nine standards have been revised over the years with the help of charitable organization managers, accountants, and others. It only reviews national organizations with annual incomes of at least $250,000. It has detailed reports on 400 organizations on file, but in 1994, President James Bausch announced plans to increase the group's activity so that it will have reports on the 500 largest charities, excluding the types traditionally not covered.

PAS was established in 1977. It has 22 standards and utilizes 160 Better Business Bureaus and branches across the country to report on local charitable organizations and disseminate educational materials. Although it collects and distributes information on thousands of organizations, PAS only conducts full audits on the most asked about national charities (i.e., those that have been the subject of citizen inquiries). In 1994, the watchdog group announced it would implement a new standard on disclosure of joint costs (G. Williams, 1994f). The standard, which goes beyond AICPA's proposed guidelines, would require organizations apportioning direct-mail costs to tell potential donors that the mail itself is part of their program services. PAS Vice President Bennett Weiner (cited in G. Williams, 1994f) justified the new standard: "If people who receive the letters want to support educational methods conducted through direct-mail appeals, then they will. If they don't, they won't. But at least people will be given the information to make that decision" (p. 33).

Shortly before the standard was to be implemented, PAS postponed the date until sometime in 1995 (G. Williams, 1994g). The postponement primarily was due to opposition by the National Federation of Nonprofits, the trade association of organizations and solicitation firms that also has delayed adoption of AICPA guidelines. The association, students should note, was called the Nonprofit Mailers Federation before renaming itself in mid-1994. Lee Cassidy (cited in G. Williams, 1994g), its executive director, said he was pleased by the postponement and welcomed the chance to express his members' concerns more fully, but he revealingly added, "I'm still not at all convinced the disclosure PAS wants is really useful to the contributing public" (p. 32).

As of 1997, the standard still has not been implemented, although PAS said it would not back away from its plan and would use the delay to explore a disclosure requirement on joint costs for telemarketing. The National Federation of Nonprofits, cloaked in its impressive new name, also has opposed NCIB in recent years. For example, it sponsored a report attacking the watchdog group's consistency in evaluating organizations—which revealed that more than several of the federation's members have failed to meet NCIB's standards.

Both PAS and NCIB produce publications (e.g., PAS publishes the brochure, "Tips on Solicitations by Police and Firefighter Organizations"). They also provide free 1- to 4-page summaries of their audit reports on individual organizations. Requests are limited to three summaries at one time and must be accompanied by a stamped, self-addressed large envelope. This information offers rich research possibilities for students. For example, organizations could be identified for a study on annual reports in the charitable subsector, perhaps using the concept of social responsibility as a theoretical base. Compliance with acceptable financial ratios could be studied (e.g., fund-raising costs). Using watchdog standards as measures of accountability, a thesis might explore patterns among types of organizations and over time. Furthermore, valuable comparisons could be made between efforts at self-regulation and government intervention. Issues are discussed throughout this chapter that represent unstudied problems on which NCIB and PAS reports would shed light.

Additional watchdog groups monitor charitable organizations and fund raising. For example, the Evangelical Council for Financial Accountability (ECFA) concerns itself with conservative Christian charities. It requires its 850 member organizations to meet reasonable standards of ethics, governance, and disclosure. It sets no ceiling on fund-raising costs, although it may question expenses exceeding 25%. ECFA scrutinizes solicitations, demands independent accounting audits, and makes periodic on-site reviews. The group damaged its reputation in the 1980s when it allowed Jim Bakker's PTL ministry to continue as a member in good standing and to display the ECFA seal to prospective donors while conducting fraudulent activities (Tidwell, 1993). It was criticized again in 1996 for not keeping its members out of the New Era scam, although it received praise for its damage-control role in the aftermath of the scandal (Blum, 1996). Both PTL and New Era are returned to in the next chapter on ethics.

No description of watchdog groups is complete without mention of the media. A donor participating in a round-table discussion about regulation, sponsored by

NSFRE, accurately described their role: "With watchdog agencies, there's always the question of who will watch the watchdogs. But this is where the press comes in—making information available to the people. The press can be invaluable in uncovering abuses and keeping people honest" ("Forum," 1995, p. 18). Whereas in the past the media tended to ignore or revere the charitable subsector, controversies and scandals have convinced journalists to be more critical. Bush (1991) offered a lawyer's perspective: "The charity appeal gone sour is a story the media cannot resist" (p. 212).

The increased scrutiny has created tension and revealed an absence of understanding about the media's watchdog role. Eisenberg (1994) explained, "Because they were accustomed to kid-glove treatment by the press and were not used to criticism, many non-profit leaders cried 'unfair' and 'foul' when attacked" (p. 46). Studies on the relationship between journalists and managers of charitable organizations are badly needed and would be timely. Other research suggestions related to fund-raising law are given in chapter 8, which also continues the discussion of the National Federation of Nonprofits.

With these key concepts and actors in place, the chapter now turns to the forces driving regulation. Bush (1994) endorsed such an examination, saying, "A sign of professional maturity is the willingness to tackle the difficult, and sometimes tedious, arena of government relations and meet head on the outside forces shaping today's fund-raising climate" (p. 32).

FORCES DRIVING FUND-RAISING REGULATION

As given earlier, three forces are driving the movement to regulate charitable organizations and their fund-raising function: (a) abuses, (b) government's need for revenue, and (c) low accountability. One issue is used to examine the first force, two to examine the second, and three to examine the third.

Abuses: Overvaluing Gifts of Property

Some charitable organizations, particularly those with missions related to relief and hunger, depend heavily on donated products, or gifts of inventory from businesses. There is a great deal of variation in how recipient organizations value and record such gifts for accounting purposes. Whereas some assign liquidation or wholesale value to donated products, others assign retail value, and some assign outrageously high values. Choosing a greater value makes an organization look more efficient on paper: Gift income is increased, as are expenses for program services because the products ostensibly are used for the organization's tax-exempt purpose.

In 1992, state regulators in Connecticut and Pennsylvania filed lawsuits against six organizations—including the Watson and Hughey client, Cancer Fund of America—alleging that they had participated in schemes to inflate their incomes and program expenses by millions of dollars by passing virtually worthless, highly over-valued products from one to another (S. G. Greene, 1992). Their goal was to increase their ratio of program expenses to income to 75% or more (S. G. Greene & Williams, 1992b). By doing so, they would be eligible to join Independent Charities of America—a federation challenging the United Way system—and participate in the Combined Federal Campaign.

Sketching just one chain of transactions, in 1990, Viking-Penguin Publishers donated five truckloads of damaged paperback books to Feed the Children, an organization of Larry Jones International Ministries in Oklahoma City, Oklahoma. Feed the Children was not charged by state regulators because—many believe—it is protected by its religious classification (i.e., it is exempt from most fund-raising regulation, including the reporting laws of Connecticut and Pennsylvania). Among criticisms leveled against the organization, it counts the distribution of tens of millions of dollars' worth of paperback books to other charities as part of its program services. It also allocates most expenses for its direct-mail and television solicitations to program services. It was sued for trademark infringement by the much older and established Save the Children and was rejected for membership by the leading coalition of international relief and development organizations, Interfaith (S. G. Greene & Williams, 1992b).

After recording the Viking-Penguin books at near-retail value, Feed the Children shipped all five truckloads to other organizations, including two truckloads to the Children's Wish Foundation International in Atlanta, Georgia. That organization, in turn, donated one truckload to United Citizens Against Drugs in Santa Ana, California—although the books remained in Atlanta. The California organization donated 1,440 cases to Famine Relief Fund in Warrenton, Virginia. The Virginia organization had the books shipped from Atlanta to an out-of-state project of the American Indian Relief Council, also based in Warrenton.

According to regulators, Children's Wish, United Citizens, and Famine Relief all counted the paperbacks as part of their expenses for program services, although the books had little to do with their tax-exempt purposes (S. G. Greene & Williams, 1992b). A spokesperson for United Citizens Against Drugs, which was created by paid solicitor Mitchell Gold, said books help teach people to read and reading helps people stay away from drugs! Each of the organizations valued the damaged paperbacks at $230 or more a case, although their estimated worth was $30 to $40 a case. The organizations denied wrongdoing, saying "they relied on the advice of their accountants" (p. 23). All six named in the lawsuits used the same accounting firm, Brown & Company of Washington, DC. That firm closed in 1991, and its head, Brian Brown, became CEO of the American Indian Relief Council.

Commenting on such cases, Gary Paisley (cited in S. G. Greene, 1992), vice president for finance and administration at Food for the Hungry, admitted that overvaluing product donations had become a common game to keep overhead low. The variation in accounting practices, he claimed, rewarded those who played the game most aggressively by manipulating their figures. Paul Thompson (cited in S. G. Greene, 1992), executive director of World Vision Relief and Development, said, "There has been such a lack of standards in the industry for some time that it has been a real problem" (p. 29). Larry Jones (cited in S. G. Greene & Williams, 1992b), in contrast, responded, "I just find it difficult to have a wrong way to feed a hungry child" (p. 25).

The litigation lasted 3 years. By 1995, Pennsylvania and Connecticut had reached out-of-court settlements with all six organizations ("Commodities," 1995). The organizations agreed to pay back the money they had raised in each state during the questioned years and to change how they handled donated products. None acknowledged wrongdoing.

In the meantime, the IRS had begun to audit the books of 12 organizations that rely on donated products, including Feed the Children (S. G. Greene & Williams, 1992b). In 1993, the IRS changed its Form 990 to require organizations to break down their income and expenses into cash and noncash for the first time (G. Williams, 1994c). Although the change was aimed at those who abuse product donations, it affected all organizations that accept noncash gifts. Museums, for example, now must separate the value of artwork they receive if they count such gifts as part of their fund-raising income. Organizations spend a total of more than $2 billion each year to compile data for the 990 ("Form 990," 1992). Every corrective change imposed by government increases the cost.

Summarizing this first driving force, a CPA who has worked on versions of Form 990 observed, "The trend by the IRS is toward more and more regulation of the non-profit industry because of what groups with legislative or watchdog powers see as abuses by non-profits" (G. Williams, 1994c, p. 32).

Government's Need for Revenue

Hopkins (1995) included the following among reasons for increased regulation:

> [One] factor is the federal government's deficit. Tax laws are being written with the revenue impact [as] the primary consideration. A similar phenomenon is playing out at the state level. Many lawmakers are interested in narrowing the range of the exemptions from sales, use and property taxes. It is not that these lawmakers are suddenly seeing the performance of less charity in their jurisdictions, but that they are desperate for additional tax revenue. (p. 30)

Federal: Postal Subsidies End.   An economic benefit enjoyed by charitable and other nonprofits is that, except for first-class mail, they pay substantially lower postage rates than businesses. Congress traditionally approved annual subsidies for the U.S. Postal Service (USPS) to make up differences between the reduced rates and the actual cost of delivering the mail. Arguing that the Treasury could no longer afford to subsidize nonprofit postage, Congress passed legislation in 1993 to overhaul the system.

The enacted law provides the USPS with only $29 million each year until 2035, as compared to the last annual subsidy of $612 million (H. Hall, 1994c). To compensate, increases in nonprofit rates were approved in 1993 and are being phased in over a 6-year period. The increases range from 1% to 3% annually for standard and periodical mail.[11] First-class mail is not affected because a nonprofit rate does not exist. Early estimates predicted that elimination of mail subsidies would erase $1.5 billion from annual federal deficits ("Top Clinton," 1992).

The mandated increases are in addition to general rate hikes, which the USPS regularly seeks. In 1995, for example, rates went up 3 cents for first-class mail, an average of 19.3% for periodical nonprofit mail, and 3.9% for what was then known as third-class nonprofit mail (H. Hall, 1994b). Besides raising its prices, the USPS continues to cut its expenses by offering graduated discounts to organizations that

---

[11]An exception was made for organizations serving the blind. Also worthy of note, the USPS changed its categories of bulk mail in 1996. Third-class and fourth-class mail became *standard* mail. Second-class mail now is called *periodical* mail.

make their bulk mailings easier to deliver. Rate changes implemented in October 1996 provided the largest discounts to date and were proclaimed a break for nonprofits (H. Hall, 1996b). Those that sort their standard and periodical mail more precisely (e.g., by carrier route), deliver it to more appropriate postal facilities (e.g., bulk mailing centers), and apply barcodes, or ZIP code designations that can be read by automated equipment, pay less postage under the new rates.

Whereas charitable organizations take advantage of the discounts to save money, very few produce enough mail to qualify for the lowest rates. The discounts primarily benefit those that solicit mass audiences through direct mail; savings are much smaller for organizations that selectively target donor publics. Therefore, when the 1993 rate increases are completed in 1999, postage will cost significantly more for most fund-raising efforts—although rates for nonprofits still will be lower than commercial rates.

The 1993 law also tightened eligibility for nonprofit rates. Applying the same guidelines used by the IRS to determine UBIT, products or services promoted in standard and periodical mail must be substantially related to the tax-exempt purpose for which the organization was granted a nonprofit postage permit (H. Hall, 1994c). Mailings or parts of mailings that do not qualify are subject to commercial rates. For example, if paid advertisements exceed 10% of the content of any publication sent at periodical rates, such as alumni magazines, commercial postage is due on the advertising portion. Periodicals mailed at standard rates, such as church bulletins, are exempt from the new rules—but not from previously banned ads. All standard mail other than periodicals must fully conform. For example, if an organization pays UBIT on income derived from selling a product or service, it cannot promote that product or service in any nonperiodical material sent at standard rates.

Rules issued before 1993 banned all offers—including advertisements—for affinity credit cards, insurance policies, and travel tours from standard nonprofit mail. In other words, abuses of postal privileges in the past led to corrective regulation before Congress decided to end federal subsidies. Fund-raising managers comply with USPS rules, recognizing the necessity to protect the less-than-commercial rates still available to their organizations.

State and Local: Tax Exemptions Challenged. In 1994, 35 states filed suits contesting charitable organizations' exemptions from local property taxes (Berton, 1994). Berton summarized in *The Wall Street Journal*, "Institutions that once basked in community goodwill now find themselves challenged by budget-conscious towns, cities and even whole states fighting to make them either pay property taxes or give specific payments or services to help offset the loss of the taxes to the community" (p. 1).

The issue, referred to by the acronym *PILOT*, payments in lieu of taxes, is the subject of intense debate over the charitable subsector's privileged status and government's need for more revenue. Indicative of its importance, PILOT commanded segments on the *CBS Evening News* and *60 Minutes* in 1996. Its pervasiveness is demonstrated in the following discussion, which outlines recent action in geographically diverse areas. As Berton (1994) stated, "Protests against tax-exempt organizations are arising all around the country. . . . Taken together they add up to a kind of citizens' revolt" (p. 1).

In the summer of 1994, most types of charitable organizations in Philadelphia, Pennsylvania were asked to pay fees up to 40% of the amount they would have to pay if they were not exempt from property taxes ("Philadelphia," 1994). Excluded were churches, synagogues, and human services organizations, which were defined as purely public charities. Organizations asked for fees could reduce the amount by paying the money quickly or by increasing services they provide free to city residents. The mayor said he hoped to generate $33 million in cash and services.

About the same time, a Pennsylvania judge ruled that Washington and Jefferson College, a private institution with 1,100 students, must pay property taxes because it failed to qualify as a charity under state law ("Pa. judge," 1994). Illustrating the trend to segregate organizations relying on client fees, the judge decreed, "Providing education is not of itself a charitable function" (p. 47). The college had been sued by the City of Washington, which, according to the media report, "has been searching for more tax revenues" (p. 47). If it lost its appeal, the college would owe about $465,000.[12] A lawyer who monitors tax trends claimed the 1994 decision gave other local governments strapped for cash new ammunition. She declared, "Governments increasingly are saying to non-profits, You have land; we need money" (p. 47).

In 1993, 20 of Pennsylvania's 224 nonprofit hospitals were forced to make payments or provide services in lieu of property taxes after city commissioners decided the majority of nonprofit hospitals were acting more like for-profit businesses than charitable organizations (Burns, 1993). Also in 1993, Texas enacted a law requiring nonprofit hospitals to provide a minimum amount of charity care and perform other services in exchange for exemptions from property, sales, and franchise taxes (Texas does not have an income tax; "Texas," 1993). Nonprofit hospitals must spend a sum equal to at least 4% of their annual net income on caring for the poor, education, or research; failure to do so means loss of exemptions. The state senator who sponsored the legislation warned, "Hospitals cannot enjoy a tax exemption if they fail to return benefits to the community that are reasonably related to the hospital's financial capacity and the value of the tax exemption" (p. 43).

Elaborating on the relationship between PILOT and financial capacity, Briscoe (1994b) stated, "Just as the privilege of great personal wealth comes with a serious obligation to practice philanthropy, so the most heavily endowed nonprofits must practice a higher standard of citizenship" (p. 11). She advised charitable organizations with sizable assets to voluntarily make payments in lieu of property taxes—advice that I endorse and extend to those with high incomes. Wealthy organizations must be sensitive to growing perceptions of their "cost" to communities. For example, many large universities and nonprofit hospitals make considerable demands on police and fire departments, for which they pay no property or other taxes. Individuals and corporations taxed for such services are likely to resent multimillion-dollar entities paying nothing, particularly when tax bills go up. To maintain good relationships and avoid full taxation, socially responsible organizations with the financial means voluntarily make payments.

Contradicting this advice, N. S. Fink (1993) argued against PILOT. He said no matter how well-intentioned, voluntary payments "are what lawyers call an 'admission

---

[12]The Pennsylvania Supreme Court ruled in 1995 that Washington and Jefferson College is a charitable organization and, therefore, qualified for exemption from property taxes.

against interest'—in other words, an acknowledgment that a tax might be valid" (p. 391). He added, "And, of course, these payments establish precedents" (p. 391). Although Fink recognized government's need for revenue as a force driving regulation, he recommended that organizations resist overtures to pay fees. Functional objectives for lawyers, as stated earlier, differ from those of fund raisers.

NSFRE and its Government Relations Committee took a lawyerlike stand in 1993 against the City of Des Moines, Iowa, which planned to ask nonprofits to make payments for fire and police protection (Lyddon, 1994). The proposed payments were based on a percentage of the property tax that would be assessed if the organization's real property were not exempt; therefore, those with less valuable property would pay only a few dollars, whereas those with large and valuable holdings would pay much more. NSFRE pronounced the initiative dangerous because it would create conflict between organizations, set precedent for repeal of tax-exempt statutes, and erode the belief that the charitable subsector's work is worthy of special treatment. Its arguments stressed the value society receives from "the third sector as a whole" (p. 9), which supposedly outweighs the value of individual organizations and reasons for taxing them. NSFRE's views on the issue have not changed. A position paper opposing PILOT was approved by the association's board of directors in 1997 (NSFRE, 1997).

Reflective practitioners, in contrast, hold views similar to mine (e.g., Briscoe, 1994b; Greenfield, 1991). They recognize that—given the current regulatory environment—paying a fair share for the costs of police, firefighters, water, sewage, garbage, roads, or other services is inevitable for large, financially sound organizations. Indeed, a number of such organizations, as well as others of moderate size and capacity, already make payments for the free services they receive from their communities (e.g., Syracuse University in New York and St. Olaf College in Minnesota). Whereas voluntary payments demonstrate social responsibility, refusal and resistance incite taxpayers' resentment and invite more serious and costly intervention.

In the November 1996 elections, Colorado residents voted on a referendum that would have eliminated property tax exemption for the state's charitable organizations, including churches (G. Williams, 1996c).[13] Backers rallied support for the measure by promising that the new revenue would allow local governments to cut tax bills. More than $70 million would be collected each year from the formerly exempt organizations; for example, the YMCA of Metro Denver would owe $750,000—an amount far greater than any voluntary payment it might have considered. G. Williams (1996c) summarized: "More and more state and local governments have been asking charities to volunteer to pay at least a share of the property taxes they would owe if they were businesses. Many institutions have agreed to do so. But no state has considered anything as draconian as Colorado has" (p. 42). The referendum was soundly defeated; however, experts agree that the idea of imposing property taxes on nonprofits almost certainly will spread to other states.

PILOT, then, should not be viewed as a threat, but as a strategic opportunity to prevent further erosion of privileged status. In addition to voluntary payments, in-kind contributions and community service are strongly recommended (e.g., sharing facilities with other nonprofits). Such proactive behavior provides alternative ways to

---

[13]Inconsistent with the Philadelphia case and Washington and Jefferson College, Colorado's proposed law included churches, synagogues, and mosques, but excluded schools, colleges, and universities.

meet obligations for small organizations unable to afford payments and reduces perceived tax liabilities for those with greater affluence. The Nature Conservancy's Western Pacific Region, for example, holds "pioneer days," during which managers open up nature preserves to communities—complete with wagon rides (Skolnik, 1993). The Southern Baptist Convention, headquartered in Fort Worth, Texas, produces videos for the local United Way, Chamber of Commerce, and Convention and Visitors Bureau on a cost-recovery basis.

Scholar Jon Van Til concluded from his analysis of PILOT, distributed on Internet's ARNOVA forum (June 6, 1996), "It is clear that nonprofits can no longer expect local governments to provide them with tax exemption as a matter of entitlement." I would expand his assessment: Government's need for revenue demands that each charitable organization continually demonstrates its value from the local to the federal level (i.e., be accountable).

Low Accountability

In 1993, PAS released the findings of a national opinion poll on Americans' attitudes about regulation (Gallup Organization, 1993). The study found that 81% of the 1,000 respondents were very or somewhat concerned about the amount of money charitable organizations spend on fund raising and other expenses not directly related to their stated mission. A dismaying 74% said more government regulation is needed to ensure that organizations fulfill the promises they make to donors. As stated in a popular news magazine, failing to spend most of what is raised on program services is the "ugliest offense in the charity world" ("Other," 1992, p. 46).

Excessive Salaries

The UWA scandal in 1992 shattered common misconceptions that all charitable organizations are poor and pay their employees substandard wages. Disclosure of former UWA President William Aramony's salary and benefits totaling $463,455 per year ignited widespread public anger—which was fueled by later charges of fraud. Compensation in the subsector became the subject of intense media scrutiny, and CEOs found themselves defending their salaries in public for what was likely the first time. Elaine Chao (cited in Sebastian, 1992), who UWA first hired to replace Aramony at less than one half the salary, proclaimed, "We've gotten a wake-up call from Americans. They want greater accountability" (p. A7C).

The call fell on deaf ears. Instead of defining what was excessive and taking a stand against such payments, leaders generally upheld a free market approach. High salaries and benefits, they argued, are necessary to compete with business and government in attracting top talent. Their defense concentrated on individual worth of managers rather than on protection of the employers' privileged status.

It is recalled that obedience to NDC is a fundamental restraint placed on charitable organizations in return for the economic privileges they receive. Students also will recall the corollary of NDC given in chapter 2: Salaries paid to employees must be reasonable. Steinberg (1993a) explained, "Some forms of executive compensation could represent disguised profit distribution" (p. 17). The IRS determines if salaries are reasonable by looking at what people in comparable positions make, among other measures. It uses the findings, in turn, to decide whether or not an organization meets criteria for exemption from taxes and for access to tax-deductible gifts. In other words, the issue of excessive salaries strikes at the very definition of charitable status. Whereas leaders of the subsector largely missed this point, the government did not.

Studies and investigations by the media showed that senior managers of large charitable organizations are—overall—well compensated, some are paid questionably high salaries, and some are given ludicrous rewards that mock the law. *The Chronicle of Philanthropy* found that at the time of the UWA scandal the median salary for CEOs of 189 large organizations was $190,022 (Goss & Moore, 1994). About one third were paid $200,000 or more, which equaled or surpassed what the President of the United States made. The highest paid CEO was the president of Memorial Sloan-Kettering Cancer Center in New York, who made more than $1 million in salary and benefits in 1992.

The Chronicle also found that high salaries are not limited to CEOs or to one organizational type. Based on figures from the 189 organizations' Form 990s, it reported total 1992 earnings for the two highest paid employees of each organization (Goss & Moore, 1994). The general manager of the Metropolitan Opera made $390,000, the president of the National Wildlife Federation made $275,000, and a professor of medicine at Cornell University, Wayne Isom, was the highest paid employee for all types of organizations, making $1.8 million annually! The chief fund raiser of the National Multiple Sclerosis Society, Thor Hanson, made $250,000, whereas Elizabeth Dole, president of the Red Cross, made just $200,000. The presidents of CARE and Los Angeles-based KCET public television each made $250,000, the president of the American Bible Society made $212,000, and the CFO of the Boy Scouts of America made $424,000—almost as much as UWA's Aramony.

Investigations by nontrade media documented cases of flagrant exploitation. For example, *New York* magazine revealed in 1992 that the president of New York's American Museum of Natural History, George Langdon, Jr., earned a base annual salary of $225,000, which was $100,000 more than his predecessor made ("'New York,'" 1992). He also received the free use of a $2.2-million penthouse, maid service, a car and driver, and 44 vacation days a year. As pointed out in chapter 6, Langdon was hired by the museum in 1989 and given such high compensation because of his fund-raising credentials. During his first 3 years as president, the museum reduced the hours it was open to clients and froze salaries for most employees.

At the University of Pittsburgh, outgoing president Wesley Posvar was paid a $3.3-million retirement package in 1991 (Rotstein, 1992). A storm of criticism forced a partial payback, but the situation did not improve with the arrival of J. Dennis O'Conner, who spent $500,000 during his first year on renovations for his office and residence and on the ceremony installing him as Pitt's new chancellor. Reporting the expenditures in early 1992, local journalists drew a connection between O'Conner's spending and the UWA scandal. Columnist Sally Kalson (1992), for example, stated, "People who give money to non-profit institutions don't like it when their donations are spent on obscene executive salaries and perks. It makes them mad, which makes them stop giving. And if you thought it was hard to win their support to begin with, wait until you try to win back their lost faith" (p. 21). She concluded, "When this kind of abuse becomes accepted operating procedure, it's time to strip down the operation and start all over again" (p. 21).

Less than 2 weeks after media reports appeared, Pennsylvania's governor backed a disclosure bill that would force the University of Pittsburgh—as well as other private universities receiving state aid—to open its financial records to public inquiry (Reeves, 1992). The governor justified his action, saying, "These places are empires. Everyone saw what happened at Pitt" (p. 1). Chancellor O'Conner resigned about 3 years later.

The media's exposure of excessive salaries, benefits, and perks had two contradictory effects: Some senior managers were given raises because boards of trustees felt freer to push salaries closer to those at the upper limits, and the federal government stepped in to curb what it viewed as abuses (Goss & Moore, 1994). Briefly demonstrating the first effect, the general manager of the Metropolitan Opera made $471,000 in 1995 (Blum, Demko, Gray, & Hall, 1996), or 21% more than he made in 1992. The president of CARE made $325,000 in 1995, or 30% more than the position paid 3 years earlier. George Langdon, Jr. is no longer at the American Museum of Natural History; however, his successor, Ellen Futter, earned a base salary of $321,000 in 1995, or 43% more than Langdon's 1992 salary. At UWA, the board hired Betty Beene in 1996 to replace Elaine Chao as president and authorized a 41% increase in salary to pay Beene $275,000 (H. Hall, 1996c).

As already described, the House Oversight Subcommittee held a series of hearings during 1993 and 1994 to investigate abuses. In 1994, Representative Pickle's subcommittee and President Clinton's administration joined forces to recommend new laws that would help the IRS crack down on behavior resulting from low accountability. The legislation incorporated two important provisions: (a) allow the IRS to levy penalties on employees and trustees who receive or approve unreasonably high salaries or other inappropriate benefits, and (b) require organizations to make their Form 990 more accessible (G. Williams, 1994a).

Many nonprofit leaders criticized the legislation as unjustified government meddling. They argued that public opinion, not imposed penalties, was the best way to keep salaries in line. Incongruently however, leaders also attacked the provision to make the Form 990 and the salary figures it contains more accessible. They argued that the form does not provide enough information to help people make an informed judgment about whether salaries are reasonable. Some said access to salary figures could negatively affect gift income. One anonymous CEO explained, "We don't want to go out of our way to do anything that might discourage people from giving" (Goss & Moore, 1994, p. 34). Both NSFRE and IS endorsed and lobbied for passage of the legislation—although reports said support among some of IS' members was less than enthusiastic. In Summer 1996, Congress passed the legislation and President Clinton signed it into law (Murawski & Williams, 1996).

Before 1996, the only penalty the IRS could impose for illegally using funds to benefit managers, trustees, or others was revocation of the organization's tax exemption, an extreme punishment rarely imposed. The subsector's inadequate response to charges of excessive salaries accelerated efforts to make it easier for the IRS to intervene. The new law provides a set of less severe penalties—termed *intermediate sanctions*—for excessive compensation, insider dealing, and other irregularities. Pickles (cited in "House panel," 1993) had summarized the law's intention early on: "The IRS needs an interim sanction, something short of revocation, as a tool to punish those individuals who misuse a charity's name and assets" (p. 30).

As of 1996, individuals who receive improper financial benefits must return to the organization the portion of the benefits the IRS deems excessive and pay the government a fine equal to 25% of the returned amount (Murawski, 1996). Refusal to pay the fine or refund the money evokes additional fines of 200% of the excessive amount. Board members and managers who approved the illegal benefits are subject to a 10% penalty, up to $10,000. The law applies to trustees and all employees who have a substantial influence over organizational decisions. Legal experts say that in addition to senior managers, high-paid employees, such as doctors at nonprofit hospitals and professors at universities, could be considered influential and subject to the new law.[14] Organizations must disclose on their Form 990 the amount of any penalties their employees or trustees pay, who was fined, and the nature of the excessive benefits for which they were penalized.

The 1996 law on making Form 990s more accessible was described earlier. Sensing initial resistance to the new requirements, Barber (1996) argued that compliance offered an "opportunity to restore public confidence" (p. 56). He urged organizations to go further then required by adding the following statement to their customary declaration of tax-exempt, tax-deductible status: "A copy of our completed federal information return, Form 990, is available on request from any office" (p. 56). He appropriately reasoned:

> Congress passed the new law at least in part because of a perception that the non-profit community had not been forthcoming, as required by law, with information about programs and finances. Instead of waiting for further escalation of the tug-of-war over this information—a tug-of-war non-profit participants will surely lose—it is time for a new posture of openness and candor. (pp. 56, 58)

Excessive Endowments

Briscoe (1994b) stated, "Every nonprofit runs the risk of acting greedily or irresponsibly. Those with great wealth are particularly vulnerable to criticism" (p. 11). The issue of excessive endowments deals with funds endowed by boards rather than at the request of donors.[15] As previously explained, board-designated endowments represent excess profits that have been invested by an organization's dominant coalition to provide future income. Sound fiscal management dictates that a reasonable amount of unrestricted assets be accumulated to protect against shortfalls and to ensure continuity of services. Endowments of excessively large amounts, however, are not necessary safeguards but indicators of great wealth and low accountability. Briscoe (1994b) asked, "Can an organization be too rich?" (p. 11). "Is it unethical to capitalize programs rather than to fund them outright?" (p. 10). In many cases, the answers are yes.

In November 1993, a new watchdog group, the American Institute of Philanthropy (AIP), published a researched rating guide that assigned grades from A to F to 300 large organizations, based on the percentage of income they devoted to program services. Daniel Borochoff (cited in Goss, 1993e), AIP's founder and sole

---

[14]Relevant to the discussion on autonomy in chapter 9, some lawyers believe the IRS could hold major donors to the standards of the new law, "since they often influence a charity's policies and programs" (Murawski, 1996, p. 39).

[15]In contrast, the term *endowment* generally is used in subsequent chapters to refer only to pure endowments, or those designated by major donors.

employee, explained, "The bottom line is, people want to know how much is going to the charitable purpose" (p. 31). In assigning the grades, Borochoff also took into account how much money the organization had available in board-designated endowments. The principal of such endowments, it is recalled, can be spent—although dominant coalitions generally choose not do so. Borochoff divided the organization's unrestricted net assets by its annual expenses to determine how long the organization could survive without additional fund raising. He adopted the rule that endowment should equal less than total operating costs for 3 years. If it equaled 3 or more years, he started lowering the organization's letter grade; if it equaled 5 years, the organization flunked. Both Boys Town of Omaha, Nebraska, and the Shriners Hospitals for Children of Tampa, Florida received an F for that reason.

Boys Town.   Father Flanagan's Boys' Home, better known as Boys Town, had a board-designated endowment of $568 million in 1992 (Goss, 1994a). Based on Borochoff's figures, it could survive for 6 years without raising any additional money. Boys Town has been criticized for its excessive endowment—formally named the "Father Flanagan Foundation Fund"—since the Tax Reform Act of 1969 first required charitable organizations to disclose their finances.

Founded in 1917 by Father Edward J. Flanagan, Boys Town began sending out letters in the 1940s at Christmas and Easter to solicit small gifts that would "bring happiness to homeless and unwanted boys" (Bremner, 1989, p. 327). Donors gave so willingly that in 1970, the first year for which figures were publicly available, 34 million solicitations raised about $18 million. Boys Town's financial statement showed that the Flanagan Fund, which also was started in the 1940s, totaled over $200 million in 1970—more than the combined unrestricted *and* restricted endowments of all but the richest universities. Its investment income was $6 million that year, and operating costs totaled only $9 million; therefore, just $3 million, or 16%, of the amount raised was needed for operation (i.e. all expenses for program services, management and general, and fund raising).

In 1972, the now defunct Omaha *Sun* newspaper published a Pulitzer Prize-winning series on the organization's finances (Goss, 1994a). Its investigation revealed that whereas Boys Town sent out "desperate pleas for donations, it had more than enough income without fund raising to operate its facilities" (p. 34). The series convinced the organization to stop raising money for a year and to establish two research centers at a cost of $70 million. Bremner (1989) said the criticism forced the board to "put Boys Town's wealth to more productive use" (p. 327).

In 1994, a few months after AIP published its rating guide, Boys Town—which now operates "towns" in 16 cities—sued the watchdog group and Borochoff for libel because of the F rating (Goss, 1994a). The lawsuit charged that Boys Town had been defamed and its ability to attract gifts had been undermined. It sought $2 million in damages and a ban on the guide's distribution. Its CEO, the Reverend Val Peter (cited in Goss, 1994a), asserted, "The watchdog has become an attack dog. Somebody has to muzzle it" (p. 34). Peter claimed his organization would have to serve 6,000 fewer children if it spent down its endowment. Borochoff countered that he never said any charity should run through its unrestricted net assets, but a total equal to less than 3 years of operating expenses was sufficient.

Because the 8-page guide included "several sentences about the general topic of fraud and abuse among charities," the suit alleged that the F grade "led donors to believe that the charity was guilty of such 'corrupt or criminal action'" (Goss, 1994a, p. 34). The judge presiding over the case said Boys Town was foolish to bring the suit: It had a "strong likelihood of losing" and would get bad publicity from such a verdict (S. G. Greene & Williams, 1996, p. 26). In mid-1996, the two parties settled out of court (Dundjerski, 1996). AIP did not pay any money to Boys Town or change its rating; however, Borochoff did announce that future AIP guides would present two sets of grades: one accounting for endowments and one ignoring them.

Adding the second grade seriously weakens AIP's original intention of warning donors to think twice before giving more money to an organization that already has millions of dollars in unrestricted assets. Other watchdog groups agree that a big concern "is the number of organizations that try to stimulate a rush of donations by citing urgent social needs—even though they have large surpluses that could be spent fighting problems" (S. G. Greene & Williams, 1996, p. 25). A spokesperson for NCIB, which flunks organizations for having endowments greater than 2 years of expenses, charged, "Charities are saying, 'Children are hurting,' 'Wrongs need righting,' but they are not using all the money sent in response to their pleas to tackle the problems they cite" (p. 25).

These characteristics were apparent in a direct-mail solicitation Boys Town sent to my husband in November 1996. The cover letter, signed by Reverend Peter, used simulated handwritten underlining to emphasize three times that my husband's gift could make "*a lifesaving difference.*" The letter sensationalized the hardships suffered by one of the organization's clients and began with the headline: "This story is shocking . . . a boy kept in a cage!" It ended with the plea: "We need much, much more help to take care of more and more children." Yet a 20-line disclosure on the back of the gift-response card revealed that Boys Town's endowment totaled $533 million at the end of 1995. Also in 1995, Boys Town earned a profit of $10 million when its income of $107 million, including $63 million in gifts, exceeded its expenses of only $97 million ("Philanthropy 400," 1996). Rather than using the surplus to expand current services, the organization added the money to the resources it has set aside. Boys Town reported in 1994 that it *turns down* eight to nine applicants for every child it admits ("Orphanage," 1994).

The disclosure defended Boys Town's excessive endowment, which it described as a "savings account to care for children today, tomorrow and the day after tomorrow." The funds are preserved so that future and unborn clients may be served, or to achieve what Boys Town calls "intergenerational equity"! "We spend as much as we feel we can on kids today. . . . If the Lord blesses us with more donors we will be able to do more of the Lord's work." Prospects were assured that every dollar received from mail solicitations would be spent on program services because the Flanagan Fund pays all fund-raising costs, which represented 32% of the dollars raised in 1995. In response to criticism, the statement also assured prospects that gifts would be spent "right away." There was no mention, however, of surpluses from other income that the organization regularly invests rather than spends.

Speaker of the House Newt Gingrich has praised Boys Town as an example of nonprofit initiatives that should replace government welfare programs because they are more effective and efficient ("Orphanage," 1994). His and others' esteem largely is based on images retained from the 1938 movie, *Boys Town*, starring Spencer Tracy and Mickey Rooney. Inspired 60 years ago, before the Flanagan Fund was started, the Hollywood version bears little resemblance to the organization today. Boys Town acts as if it is more interested in perpetuating its existence than in helping young people. Its recent and past behavior demonstrates an "above reproach" mindset and low accountability. Its fund raising is asymmetrical, characterized by a disregard for truth and candor. If unrestricted assets are available to meet program service expenses, solicitations imploring help are dishonest. If gifts will be added to endowment or used in place of other income that will not be spent, solicitations should so inform donor prospects.

Shriners Hospitals for Children.

Boys Town's endowment pales in comparison to the vast unrestricted assets accumulated by the Shriners Hospitals for Children. In 1995, Shriners' board-designated endowment totaled $4.8 billion—more than all endowments for any college or university except Harvard (Council for Aid to Education, 1996; S. G. Greene & Williams, 1996). The 1993 AIP rating guide estimated that Shriners could survive 13.5 years on the funds it had set aside (Goss, 1993e). The estimate was confirmed by a spokesperson who admitted that, based on 1994 figures, "the group has enough money to run for 14 years without raising a penny" (Beddingfield, 1995, p. 90). Yet Shriners consistently ranks among the 20 organizations raising the most private support each year; in 1995, for example, it ranked at 18 in the "Philanthropy 400" (1996). Blades and Milofsky (1992) called Shriners an awesome fund-raising and resource-accumulating machine.

Shriners operates 22 hospitals that provide free treatment to children with orthopedic problems or severe burns (S. G. Greene & Williams, 1996). It is rooted in a system of fraternal organizations with chapters in nearly every American community. A portion of members' dues is paid to the national organization, providing a stream of annual gift income. Shriners takes pride in the fact that it does not charge patient fees or collect government funds; it relies exclusively on gifts and earnings from its invested assets. Its unbalanced dependency is the reason given by the organization for preserving and adding to its mammoth endowment. S. G. Greene and Williams (1996) reported, "To keep expanding its programs, says Molnar [Executive Vice President Lewis Molnar], the Shriners needs as large an endowment as it can build" (p. 27). Shriners never explains why it needs to continually expand (after all, there are many U.S hospitals specializing in children's care) or why other means of increasing income are not viable options. For example, it could charge minimal patient fees, such as cost-recovery payments based on the financial capacity of the child's parents, or collect government funding for which it is eligible, such as reimbursements for patients covered by Medicaid.

Regardless, Shriners has relentlessly pursed its goal of building an endowment as large as possible. Its strategy has been relatively simple: It creates huge annual surpluses through aggressive fund raising and capped expenses and adds the surpluses to its endowment each year. As its endowment has grown and investment income has increased, Shriners has spent progressively more on program services, although its intense fund raising continues. The following discussion traces the organization's behavior over the most recent 9 years for which statistics are available.

In 1987, Shriners spent less than 33% of its income on operation (Milofsky & Blades, 1991). It designated $343 million, or more than two thirds of its income, for endowment! In 1990, the organization used 56% of its $414 million in income to pay all expenses. It added the remaining $183 million to its endowment, which then totaled $3.3 billion (Blades & Milofsky, 1992). According to Blades and Milofsky, successful health organizations, in general, spend about 90% of their income and maintain unrestricted assets equal to about 1 year's operating expenses. The National Easter Seal Society, for example, spent 96% of its 1990 income of $288 million on operation. It increased its endowment by $13 million, to $212 million. Whereas Easter Seal's endowment at the beginning of the decade could pay expenses for less than 1 year, Shriners' endowment could pay expenses for 14 years.

In 1994, Shriners spent 60% of its income and added $195 million to its endowment, which then totaled $4.2 billion—nearly $1 billion more than just 4 years earlier (Beddingfield, 1995; "Philanthropy 400," 1995). Gifts accounted for $198 million, or 40%, of the organization's income, an amount nearly equal to that added to endowment. In other words, fund-raising results were devoted almost entirely to increasing the organization's assets, not to treating sick children. In 1995, Shriners spent 73% of its income of $429 million on operating expenses ("Philanthropy 400," 1996). The majority of the income was generated by its endowment, which—as already given—totaled $4.8 billion, or $.6 billion more than 1 year before. Although it could then survive for more than 15 years without any additional money, Shriners designated its 1995 surplus of $114 million for endowment.

According to Robert Anthony (1996), the Harvard Business School professor whose work prompted FASB's first nonprofit accounting standards, "At a well-managed non-profit group, revenue should approximately equal expenses. A bottom line that reports a large surplus signals that the group did not provide the quantity of services that its supporters had the right to expect" (p. 46). Boris and Odendahl (1990) added, "Actions that contribute to the perception that philanthropic agencies are profit-maximizing entities undermine the legitimacy of the sector" (p. 197). Shriners' endowment earnings of more than $225 million annually explain why Congress, in its search for new revenue, continues to consider proposals to charge a 5% excise tax on the investment income of all exempt organizations (Hopkins, 1990).

Due to its endowment-building strategy, Shriners failed its review by PAS in 1992; specifically, it did not meet the standard that a reasonable percentage of income—at least half—must be spent on programs and activities directly related to the purposes for which the organization exists ("Watchdog," 1992). Shriners responded that "it believed its expenditures on program services were reasonable in view of its long-term commitment . . . to provide a continuing source of investment income in future fiscal years" (p. 33). At the rate it is growing, Shriners' endowment could be large enough by the year 2000 to generate 100% of the money needed for annual operation.

It should also be noted that in 1986, *The Orlando Sentinel* reported that the temples of the Shrine of North America, the Shriners' related fraternal organizations, were raising money through charity circuses ostensibly for the hospitals, but were keeping much of the proceeds for temple uses ("Other," 1992). Cutlip (1965/1990) called the

Shrine circuses a "multimillion-dollar myth" (p. xiii). He cited a 1980s study showing that only 1% of the circus revenue was donated to Shriners' hospitals; $1 million "was used to provide long-term, low-interest loans for Shrine employees" (p. xiii). According to a temple spokesperson, current solicitations clarify gift purposes ("Other," 1992).

FASB's accounting standards now require organizations to report on their financial statements that board-designated endowments are unrestricted net assets available for immediate spending. The 1995 change will help prospective donors, such as those solicited by Boys Town and Shriners, weigh the need for their gift against the amount of resources the organization has set aside for the future. Briscoe (1994b) warned managers: "Be sensitive to the strengthening public view that those making little use of their assets . . . are indeed challenging the public trust that makes it possible for them to build such reserves" (p. 11).

Unfair Competition

Small businesses charge that government subsidies in the form of exemptions from taxes provide an unfair advantage to charitable organizations selling products and services similar to theirs. University bookstores and hospital gift shops, for example, offer products commonly available from for-profit companies. Although students may argue—as many universities have—that bookstores are closely related to the purpose of an educational organization, they need only look around the next time they go in one. Many of the items for sale, such as clothing, food, greeting cards, and cosmetics, have little to do with education and are available at commercial outlets, usually within a block.

Between 1989 and 1994, the tax-exempt status of 15 YMCAs across the country were challenged in local and state courts (Berton, 1994). The lawsuits were filed by owners of private health clubs who claimed the YMCAs were competing with them for customers. A number were ordered to pay property taxes because they "did not provide enough free services to needy clients" to warrant their special status (Stehle, 1990, p. 25). Small-business leaders applauded such decisions, saying they established a level playing field between for-profits and nonprofits. Property tax exemption was upheld or restored to most of the YMCAs.

In June 1994, small-business representatives testified at a subcommittee hearing of the House Committee on Small Business that nonprofit hospitals, universities, and YMCAs "are abusing the privileges of tax-exempt status to muscle in on their for-profit counterparts" ("Small-business," 1994, p. 32). They asked legislators to take steps to reduce what they see as unfair competition undermining everything from laundry businesses to computer stores. The chairman of the Business Coalition for Fair Competition, which represents 40 companies and trade associations, called on Congress to "engage in a thorough examination of non-profit organizations' benefits for, and burdens on, our national economic activity" (p. 32). The then Democrat-controlled Congress took no action.

Charitable organizations generally have ignored charges of unfair competition leveled against them, at the same time increasing activities that are inherently commercial (e.g., catalog sales by museums, testing services by hospitals, and dormitory rentals to nonstudents by colleges). They also have not paid UBIT on the profits they make. According to Hopkins (1990), "This entire subject is currently woefully unappreciated by nonprofit organizations across the country" (p. 208). When managers do think about the issue, they regard it solely as one of competition. Yet, as Hopkins argued, it is a definitional issue about qualification for tax exemption: "It pertains to the role of nonprofit organizations in contemporary United States society" (p. 206).

In 1996, the Pennsylvania state legislature gave serious consideration to a proposed law that would prohibit nonprofits from opening new offices or adding programs that compete with local businesses (AAFRC Trust for Philanthropy, 1996). Although the law did not pass, N. S. Fink (1993)—among others—predicted that the issue of unfair competition would continue to reappear as federal, state, and local governments look to tax exemptions as a new source of revenue. Any organization wandering from its defined mission in search of income, he cautioned, can find itself in commercial competition with taxpaying businesses.

Providing a fitting conclusion to this section, Milofsky and Blades (1991) stated, "The excesses of a few organizations can have enormously damaging effects on the fund-raising capacity and political support that other nonprofit organizations receive" (p. 391). N. S. Fink (1993) explained, "Public perception often becomes reality in politics" (p. 394). Unfortunately, Eisenberg (1994) reported, "business as usual" (p. 45) has been the overall response to the issues used here to examine the three forces driving regulation. He warned, "Unless some action is taken now, the crisis among non-profits is likely to get worse, not better. The press most certainly will maintain, if not intensify, its scrutiny. And the public will not so easily tolerate further disclosures of excessive compensation packages, unethical practices, and refusal to be accountable" (p. 46).

OVERVIEW OF IRS COMPLIANCE

Knowledge of IRS regulations enables fund raisers to meet legal obligations of their organization and function. It also allows them to help donors meet their philanthropic goals. Fund raisers, however, *never* act as tax advisers to donors; to do so would be inappropriate and unwise.

Electoral Campaigns and Lobbying

Organizations categorized as 501(c)(3) are prohibited from directly influencing the selection of candidates for elective office. They "must not participate or intervene (including publishing or distributing statements) in a political campaign on behalf of, or in opposition to, a candidate" ("IRS revokes," 1993, p. 40). The ban also includes political fund raising and contributions. The IRS revoked the tax-exempt status of the Reverend Jerry Falwell's Old Time Gospel Hour for 1986 and 1987 for improperly engaging in political activities ("IRS revokes," 1993). The organization was ordered to pay $50,000 in back taxes because it devoted personnel and church income to political fund-raising efforts. Violations by conservative religious groups have increased in recent years, particularly in relation to candidates' positions on abortion.

As with all organizational funds, gifts may not be used for electoral campaigns. The president of a Maryland state university was forced to resign in the late 1980s for using money from his discretionary account in the university's affiliated foundation to buy tickets to fund-raising dinners for candidates. Staff managers guard the use of gifts and counsel others about the strict ban against participation in political campaigns.[16]

In contrast, 501(c)(3) organizations—except churches and private foundations—are allowed to influence legislation, although the amount of lobbying activities cannot be substantial and federal funds cannot be used. Lobbying includes attempting to influence public opinion about any legislation and communicating with government officials or employees who may participate in formulating legislation. Providing technical advice or assistance to government or "appearing before a legislative body on matters which might affect the organization's tax-exempt status" are not considered lobbying (API, 1990, p. 53).

Decisions now being made at all levels of government demand greater involvement by charitable organizations. Only through dialogue and collaborative negotiation can leaders of the subsector hope to influence legal outcomes. Yet experts claim that organizations have not been as active in lobbying as they should be and as present law allows. Bob Smucker (1991), IS' senior vice president for government relations, argued that when organizations forgo lobbying they may find themselves challenging laws in the courts after enactment. Lobbying is a less costly and complex way to affect the legal environment.

In addition to the two restrictions already mentioned, the Lobby Disclosure Act of 1995 requires all organizations that lobby at the federal level to disclose the issues on which they seek to influence government and the amount of money they spend doing so (AAFRC Trust for Philanthropy, 1996). Charitable organizations do not have to register if all costs related to lobbying do not exceed $20,000 in a 6-month period; however, experts generally recommend registration for even those that spend little. Lobbying expenses must be reported on the IRS Form 990.

Not included in the 1995 law were provisions, known as the Istook Amendment, which would have severely limited lobbying by organizations receiving federal grants—although new versions of the provisions continue to appear in proposed legislation (AAFRC Trust for Philanthropy, 1996). The restrictions would prohibit any organization that receives government money from using more than 5% of its budget for advocacy work, including lobbying and public-interest litigation. Current law only prohibits an organization from using federal money—but not its own money—for lobbying. Given the subsector receives about 30% of its aggregate income from government, numerous organizations would be affected by the lobbying cap if enacted.

The Istook Amendment emanated from charges by Republican lawmakers that recipients of federal grants lobby for increased spending on social service programs and "liberal causes" (Murawski, 1995c, p. 47). Demonstrating a disregard for such organizations' free-speech rights, a high-ranking Republican proclaimed, "Government should assist the needy, not those whose business it is to lobby the government

---

[16]The ban attracted national notice in 1997, when House Speaker Gingrich was reprimanded and fined for giving inaccurate information to a House subcommittee investigating the connection between several 501(c)(3)s and the political action committee (PAC) that Gingrich had helped found and run. The IRS currently is reviewing whether any illegal activity occurred.

in the name of the needy" (p. 47). Congressional leaders have vowed to keep pushing for the restrictions.

Such proposals present a dangerous threat, which—paradoxically—underscores the need for more effective communication with government. Trustees and senior managers can no longer afford to sit back, expecting the subsector's privileged status to remain unchanged. When necessary, they must aggressively oppose legislation that will harm their organizations and America's philanthropic tradition. With equal vigor, they must condemn those who abuse the tradition under the cloak of being charitable.

Fund-raising managers share responsibility for alerting dominant coalition members to problems and opportunities requiring lobbying. They identify such situations through their constant surveillance of the regulatory environment. In addition to pending legislation, several laws already in the Internal Revenue Code deserve attention, starting with the 3% floor on deductions.

3% Floor

In 1993, Congress made permanent a 3% floor on deductions, which was first implemented in 1991. It is recalled from chapter 2 that there are only three primary deductions currently available to individuals: state income taxes, interest on home mortgages, and charitable contributions. Taxpayers with high adjusted gross incomes (AGI) must subtract from their total deductions 3% of the amount by which their AGI exceeds a standard income figure. The income figure is adjusted for cost of living each year; it was $117,950 in 1996. Illustrating, an individual with an AGI of $250,000 in 1996 had to subtract $3,961 from his or her deductions (3% of $132,050). The floor saves the federal government billions of dollars in deductions each year, for example, $12.5 billion in 1992 (G. Williams, 1994b).

A major concern for charitable organizations is that Congress has a history of raising such floors. Medical expenses, for example, used to be mostly deductible for individuals filing itemized tax returns; today, the floor is so high, few have enough expenses to qualify. Similar increases in the floor for the three remaining deductions would discourage high AGI donors from making gifts. Fund-raising managers must monitor this issue closely and urge dominant coalition members to take action if Congress threatens to raise the floor.

1993 Omnibus Budget Reconciliation Act

The Omnibus Budget Reconciliation Act of 1993 added two major provisions to the Internal Revenue Code that significantly impact fund-raising practice. The changes were designed to prevent overvaluation of tax-deductible gifts, termed *substantiation requirements*, and to separate gifts from purchases of goods and services, termed *quid pro quo regulations*. The substantiation requirements legally were assigned to donors who claim gifts of $250 or more on their tax returns; however, for all practical purposes, the responsibility for fulfilling the requirements rests with fund raisers. First, they must provide acknowledgments needed by such donors, and second, they must educate donors to keep the acknowledgment for their tax records.

The *quid pro quo* regulations codified the IRS' position that organizations should provide donors with information regarding the amount of their contribution that is deductible. The IRS had warned fund raisers in 1987 to inform donors that only the amount of gifts in excess of the value of any goods or services returned to the donor is tax deductible. According to the rule, which had existed since 1967, the *fair market value* of goods or services received by the donor, generally their retail price, must be subtracted from a gift payment before tax deductibility is claimed. Compliance did not improve, which resulted in the 1993 *quid pro quo* regulations.

Reluctance to educate donors was attributable to ignorance, disregard for the law, and a marketing approach to fund raising whereby excessive benefits are exchanged for gifts. Booster clubs for university athletic programs, for example, typically have relied on donor benefits to attract and retain members. Benefits often included clothing, meals with coaches, stadium parking, travel with the team to away games, complimentary game tickets, the right to buy tournament tickets, and first-choice seating for season tickets. Jeffrey Gray (1993), then associate athletic director for advancement at the University of Maryland, explained, "Traditionally, athletic fund raising has been characterized by a *quid pro quo* attitude on the part of the donor and the recipient institution" (p. 222).

In the early 1990s (before Gray was hired), an annual gift of $250 to the University of Maryland Terrapin Club "entitled the member to a silver terrapin pin, free home game tickets, and, most importantly, priority for the purchase of ACC [Atlantic Coast Conference] Tournament tickets" (C. F. Smith, 1992, p. 154). Furthermore, the executive director of the affiliated Maryland Educational Foundation, the chief athletic fund raiser, "received, above his salary, a percentage of all the money he raised" (p. 154).

Congress partially addressed this widespread problem in 1988, by adding a special rule to the Internal Revenue Code in 1988. Under the rule, a taxpayer who receives preferred-seating privilege at athletic events in recognition of a payment to an educational institution can deduct only 80% of the payment as a charitable contribution; the cost of tickets is nondeductible (Arthur Andersen & Company, 1992). Despite the 1988 law, few athletic fund raisers informed donors that goods or services provided to them were not deductible. Instead, they continued to use such benefits to "market" gifts.

As a scholarly aside, research has documented that there is no relationship between success of athletic teams and giving to colleges and universities. The question has been studied longer than any other in higher education fund raising, with studies spanning more than 70 years (Brittingham & Pezzullo, 1990). Brittingham and Pezzullo summarized the findings:

> The body of research is completely at odds with the conviction of both fund raisers and donors. No evidence of any substance suggests that success in intercollegiate athletics is associated with increased total giving to an institution or to athletic giving other than in the most limited time periods or in anecdotal cases. This conviction, that successful athletic teams breed successful fund raising, will no doubt withstand the myriad research evidence to the contrary, as athletic boosters want so desperately to believe it and most advancement officers and presidents use athletic events to cultivate donors. (p. 82)

Under the laws implemented in 1994, organizations that fail to comply with the *quid pro quo* regulations are subject to fines up to $5,000 for each illegal activity.

Regarding substantiation, penalties are imposed on any organization that knowingly provides a false written acknowledgment. The federal government expects the two provisions to add about $500 million to the Treasury by 1999 (Ruge & Speizman, 1993).

Substantiation Requirements.

Donors must substantiate any contribution of $250 or more when filing federal income tax returns. A canceled check is no longer acceptable verification; instead, donors need a written statement that the money given was a charitable gift and that no goods or services were received in exchange. Although I strongly recommend that gifts of all sizes be acknowledged in writing, fund raisers must take special care to send donors who give $250 or more prompt and appropriate acknowledgments, as required by law. Acknowledgments can take the form of letters, postcards, or computer-generated forms. I recommend a combination of a computer-generated receipt with a personal thank-you letter for donors of $250 or more.[17] Acknowledgments must tell the donor to retain the receipt and must include the name of the charitable organization, the date the gift was received, and the exact amount of a cash gift (noncash gifts are discussed shortly). If no goods or services were provided to the donor, the acknowledgment must explicitly say so. Sample wording is:

> Please retain this receipt as proof of your gift for federal income tax purpose. No goods or services were provided to you; therefore, the full amount of your gift is a deductible contribution.

If the donor did receive goods or services in exchange for the gift, *quid pro quo* regulations must be followed.

Quid Pro Quo Regulations.

When gifts involve goods or services for donors, the fair market value of those goods or services must be subtracted from the amount given to determine the amount eligible for deduction. Organizations are required to provide the breakdown in writing if a gift exceeds $75; however, donor relations are managed more effectively when the same service is provided for gifts of all sizes. By informing donors of the amount of their gift that is deductible, fund raisers reinforce philanthropic behavior and reduce confusion with *quid pro quo* exchanges.

Special events with solicitation objectives illustrate the regulation. If a donor pays $100 to attend a dinner and the meal is valued at $40, the fund raiser must tell the donor in writing that only the portion of the payment exceeding the value of the meal, $60, qualifies as a charitable contribution. The respective amounts should be stated when making the solicitation and clearly indicated on any ticket, receipt, or thank-you letter (Ruge & Speizman, 1993). Turning to goods, if a donor makes an $80 gift and receives a photograph worth $10, fund raisers must inform the donor that he or she made a deductible gift of $70. Acknowledgments must contain the same four elements required for the substantiation rule: (a) instructions to retain the receipt, (b) the name of the charitable organization, (c) the date the gift was received, and (d) the exact amount of a cash gift. Sample wording for the breakdown of benefits received is:

---

[17]Personal acknowledgments increase fund-raising effectiveness; therefore, acknowledgments for gifts of less than $250 should be as personalized as cost efficiency allows.

Your gift is deductible as a charitable contribution only to the extent that it exceeds the value of goods and/or services you received in exchange. Goods and/or services [Describe] with an estimated fair market value of $_____ were provided to you. The deductible portion of your gift is $_____.

The IRS reaffirmed two exceptions to cover moderate use of incentive and recognition items in fund-raising programs (i.e., goods provided to donors before and after making a gift). The dollar amounts for both are adjusted for inflation at the beginning of each calendar year and issued by the IRS. Practitioners need to stay current with these figures.

The first exception is low-cost items bearing the organization's name or logo. Such premiums are not considered substantial if, in 1997, the gift amount was $34.50 or more and the total cost of premiums received by the donor did not exceed $6.90. In illustration, fund raisers can include a $2 ink pen imprinted with the organization's name in direct-mail solicitations to donors who give $50 or more and still preserve the full deductibility of the gifts.

The second exception recognizes proportional giving. If the fair market value of all goods or services received is not more than 2% of the gift amount or $69 in 1997, whichever is less, then the goods or services are not considered substantial and the entire gift is deductible. Modifying the example given earlier, if the donor received the same photograph worth $10 but had made a $500 gift, the full $500 is eligible for deduction because $10 is 2% of the amount contributed and less than $69.

Both exceptions underscore a reasonable approach to incentives for giving and recognition for doing so. Few donors appreciate receiving benefits that represent a substantial portion of their gift. If either of the two exceptions is met, acknowledgments to donors (e.g., printed gift receipts) should contain the four required elements with such a statement as:

Under IRS guidelines, the estimated value of the benefits you received is not substantial; therefore the full amount of your gift is a deductible contribution.

Response to the Laws. Shortly after implementation, gifts to federations through payroll deductions were exempted from the substantiation requirements unless $250 or more is deducted from a single paycheck. Workplace solicitations, such as United Way campaigns, encourage employees to pledge annual gifts that are paid in installments through payroll deductions. Employers usually transfer the gift installments to federations in bundles, without individual names. A federation receiving the money, therefore, does not know the identities of the employee donors or how much money each contributed. Issuing acknowledgments is nearly impossible. Until the new law, few realized the degree to which federation donors are anonymous. The IRS ruled that gifts totaling $250 or more through payroll deductions do not need a receipt; however, federations must issue a general statement that no goods or services were provided (e.g., printed on a pledge card).

As previously explained, the *quid pro quo* regulations did not change the criteria of gift deductibility. Yet their implementation caused an outburst of complaints from organizations relying on donor benefits. The Arts & Business Council in New York, for example, reported that its performing- and visual-arts members were "having a terrible time trying to figure out how to value many of the benefits they provide in return for gifts" (Stehle & Williams, 1994, p. 27). Among the benefits mentioned was a discount on ticket prices for employees of corporate donors. Museums also complained about valuing benefits they offer, such as discounts on gift shop purchases, use of facilities for receptions, and free admission to galleries and lectures. John Taylor (cited in Stehle & Williams, 1994), director of gift records at Duke University, commented, "Without intending to, the government may be eliminating the fundraising tools a lot of organizations have used" (p. 28).

The intention is not as misdirected as Taylor believes. The Supreme Court has ruled on what constitutes a gift for charitable deduction and, according to R. Anderson et al. (1991), its definition clearly spells out "there is no expectation of ANY *quid pro quo*, including special admissions, seating, or other privileges or benefits" (p. 41). The IRS regulations likely will curb excessive benefits and a marketing approach to fund raising. Furthermore, the requirements encourage accountability. As Patricia Rudebusch (cited in Stehle & Williams, 1994), director of major gifts at the Public Broadcasting System, stated, "A lot of what is in the law is just good donor relations" (p. 22).

The overview of IRS compliance now turns to regulations in effect before 1994 about which fund raisers must be knowledgeable.

Noncash Gifts

Acknowledgments for noncash gifts, except securities, must describe the property that was donated, with the amount of specific detail increasing with the value of the gift. The recipient organization *does not* place a value in the acknowledgment. Valuation of the gift is the donor's responsibility. The substantiation requirements obligate organizations to identify those noncash gifts worth $250 or more in order to provide receipts to donors. "Good faith estimates" of fair market value are acceptable for gifts worth less than $500. The acknowledgment, however, does not include the estimation; it only describes what was donated and—in compliance with *quid pro quo* regulations—states the value of any goods or services received by the donor. Acknowledging all contributions, as recommended earlier, eliminates the problem of determining which noncash gifts should be valued at $250 or more.

If an individual's total of noncash gifts, including securities, exceeds $500 in 1 year, he or she must file IRS Form 8283. The amount is $5,000 for corporations. Fund raisers should provide these forms to donors and remind them of their obligations to complete them. In the case of certain noncash gifts of more than $5,000, a qualified appraisal of the property must be obtained by the donor, and the Form 8283 must be signed by the appraiser. Also when the value is in excess of $5,000, a representative of the organization—usually the fund-raising manager—must fill out and sign the donee acknowledgment section of the form, verifying the property described was received. A written acknowledgment additionally is required, but it still does not place a value on the gift; that is the purpose of Form 8283. If the organization sells the property within 2 years, it must file IRS Form 8282, which includes the sale price, and provide the donor with a copy of the form.

Other rules governing noncash gifts are presented in chapters 11 and 15. Staff managers take special care to see that policies controlling such gifts' acceptance and handling are developed, adopted, and reviewed regularly.

Nondeductible "Gifts"

Fund raising is defined by the presence of philanthropic exchanges, as measured by the deductibility of gifts. This does not mean the function deals only with those donors who actually deduct their gifts from taxable income; indeed, about 56% of all contributing households do not file itemized tax returns so they cannot claim charitable deductions (IS, 1994). Likewise, fund raisers sometimes engage in activities that generate funds that are not eligible for tax deduction. These activities technically then are not fund raising. Practitioners must have a clear understanding of the differences to ensure they *predominantly* concern themselves with philanthropic exchanges.

"Fund Raisers." The long-standing rule on fair market value (i.e., retail price) helps differentiate between fund raising and so-called "fund raisers," or activities that primarily involve *quid pro quo* exchanges. The first results in gifts, the other generates earned income. "Fund raisers" consist of selling a product or service. The difference between the sales price and fair market value determines if the activity technically is marketing or fund raising. For example, companies offer such products as watches and athletic footwear that can be personalized with an organization's identification and sold by volunteers—typically its members. The organization receives a portion of the sales price; however, if the price represents fair market value, none of it is tax deductible for the buyer even though a portion goes to charitable purposes. Using a more common example, if the price paid for Girl Scout cookies is comparable to what the cookies cost at the local grocery store, no gift is involved in the exchange. The income is not subject to UBIT if at least 80% of the sales are made by volunteers.

Students likely are familiar with "fund raisers" involving a service, such as car washes conducted by university-sponsored organizations. Because volunteer labor is used, the difference between expenses and sales provides a profit for the organization. However, the price paid for such services almost always is equal to or less than their retail price (e.g., $5 for a Student Government Association car wash vs. $10 for a commercial car wash). There is a zero or negative difference when the fair market value is subtracted from the sales price; therefore, no gift is involved.

R. Anderson et al. (1991) provided several examples to clarify further the rule distinguishing fund raising from "fund raisers." An organization decides to sell Christmas cards to "raise" money for its programs. The cards are purchased at wholesale prices and are resold at prices comparable to retail prices for similar cards offered at regular stores. This is a market exchange. The difference between the amount received from the customer and the wholesale cost of the cards is part of the purchase price of their fair market value. The difference is *not* a tax-deductible contribution, according to IRS regulations. For the organization, it is a sales profit.

An organization sponsors a symphony concert to raise money for its programs. It pays a fee to the symphony, a separate organization, to cover all expenses related to the benefit (e.g., hall rental and musicians' salaries) and receives all revenue from ticket sales. It sells tickets at prices approximating what the symphony usually charges for its concerts. As the prices are about the same as the established admission charge for similar events, there is no gift involved in the exchange. No part of the ticket price is deductible, and the funds are earned income.

The ticket price also is not deductible for those buyers who do not use the ticket (i.e., do not attend the concert). Not using the ticket, or any other product or service, does not entitle taxpayers to any greater right to a deduction than if they did use it. Those who wanted to support the organization but did not intend to use the ticket could have made a qualifying charitable contribution by giving the money and refusing to accept the ticket. Potential customers should always be given the opportunity to be donors instead.

Once, I was responsible for putting on a benefit basketball game to raise money for a scholarship fund at the University of Maryland. Rather than just selling tickets, I offered local businesses the option of contributing to the scholarship fund at a level equivalent to the purchase of a block of tickets. The gifts allowed me to distribute free tickets to human services organizations working with young and disadvantaged people in the area. A good-sized crowd was guaranteed for the game, about half the money raised represented tax-deductible gifts, and new relationships with local businesses were started.

Auctions. Many fund raisers have long told people who buy items at "charity auctions" that they can take a tax deduction for the difference between the amount they paid for an item and its fair market value. Their advice is wrong. The IRS currently does not regard any portion of an auction purchase as a gift; the person making the winning bid has, in so doing, set the fair market value of the item (G. Williams, 1994d). Therefore, there is no charitable portion, and no deduction is allowed.

It is likely the policy will be changed. Due to the *quid pro quo* regulations, the IRS began a review of its policy on auctions in 1994. Marc Owens (cited in G. Williams, 1994d), director of the IRS Exempt Organizations Technical Division, agreed that people often bid large amounts of money for items of little value and bid more than the market value for items with a commonly known price (e.g., meals at a popular restaurant). In those cases, he said, an argument was possible that a gift had been made. Fund raisers claimed people would stop going to auctions if the policy was not changed.

Anticipating that changes will be made, practitioners using auctions should take the following action. Have appraisers set the fair market value of every item before the event. Display the appraised value on the items. Provide the buyer of each item with a receipt stating the market value, the amount paid, and the amount of the purchase, if any, that is eligible for deduction. Monitor the IRS policy closely and make necessary adjustments. Auctions—as is true of all special events—are time consuming and labor intensive. They are among the least efficient techniques for raising gifts.

Gambling. Money given to participate in games of chance, including raffles, lotteries, drawings, puzzles, or other contests, is not tax deductible as a gift (R. Anderson et al., 1991). Stated another way, transferring funds for these and other forms of gambling, such as Las Vegas nights, does not qualify as a charitable contribution, although individuals can deduct gambling losses from their taxable income. Practitioners are strongly urged to inform consumers of this fact at the point of sales (e.g., printed notification on tickets and promotional literature). Congruently, organizations must pay UBIT on income from most forms of gambling; however, federal law exempts bingo if such games are legal in the state and community in which they are played. Gambling is another type of joint venture discussed in the next chapter.

Free Services. No gift deduction is allowed for a contribution of services, no matter how valuable such services actually may be to the charitable organization (Arthur Andersen & Company, 1992). Practitioners demonstrate a high degree of confusion about this rule. Many refer to donated services, such as printing an invitation, as gifts-in-kind. Although fund raisers can ask individuals and businesses to contribute their services free of charge (e.g., to reduce costs of producing a special event), they must not claim the contribution is deductible as a gift. Companies, however, can deduct services as business expenses, and they and individuals can deduct certain costs incurred while volunteering, such as transportation, meals, and lodging, if they keep records of their expenditures. The term *gifts-in-kind*, which is a misnomer, should be reserved for noncash gifts of property, if used at all. Illustrating this rule, the donation of advertising space by a newspaper is not deductible as a gift, nor are legal services donated by an attorney.

One of the major changes made in FASB accounting standards has added to the confusion by defining donated services as noncash gifts and requiring organizations to count the value of certain ones as income (Larkin, 1995). Under the 1995 standards, volunteer services must be reported on financial statements as income if either of two criteria is met: (a) the services create or enhance nonfinancial assets; or (b) the services require specialized skills, are performed by persons possessing those skills, and would have to be purchased if volunteers were not available. If services do not meet either criteria, recording their value is banned. The accounting standards also define the use of property as a noncash gift and require organizations to report donated use as income—based on the property's fair market value. As with volunteer services, tax laws governing the deductibility of gifts prescribe different treatment.

Other Nongifts. Giving the use of property does not constitute a charitable contribution (Arthur Andersen & Company, 1992). For example, allowing an organization to use office space free of charge does not entitle the donor to deduct the lost rent as a gift. Contributions to individuals, no matter how charitably motivated, ordinarily do not qualify as tax-deductible gifts. For example, giving money to a homeless person does not qualify, nor does a personal contribution to a member of the clergy for his or her unrestricted use. Fund-raising practitioners must be alert to situations when a gift is intended to primarily benefit an individual, such as a particular employee, rather than his or her organization. I know of one case in which a company owned by a full-time professor made a gift to the professor's university for the purpose of reducing his teaching load so he could spend more time working at the company.

The importance of knowing about and complying with these rules was emphasized by Hopkins (1995) in his discussion of reasons for increased regulation:

> The IRS sees scandal in fund raising, especially in what officials perceive to be misleading solicitations—those that advise prospective donors that gifts are deductible as charitable contributions when they in fact are not (because they are not gifts at all) or when only a partial deduction applies (because the payments are partly a purchase of a service or product). . . . Such fund-raising practices are tainting the IRS' attitude toward charitable fund raising in general, with unfavorable consequences for the future. (p. 30)

The overview and chapter conclude by returning to the 1993 Omnibus Budget Reconciliation Act. Two resulting changes in the Internal Revenue Code represent incentives for giving. Recent federal action, however, threatens to reduce incentives.

Incentives for Giving

N. S. Fink (1993) contended, "Across the board, it is the Internal Revenue Code that purports to reflect the societal values of the time. Where the majority of elected representatives have found 'good,' they have provided incentives, and where they have found 'bad,' they have instituted penalties" (p. 393).

Appreciated Property.   Good news emerging from the 1993 legislation was a change in deductibility for gifts of *appreciated property*—securities, real estate, and personal property that have increased in value from the time of purchase. Prior to the Tax Reform Act of 1986, such gifts were fully deductible at their fair market value. The 1986 act significantly lowered the deduction for taxpayers who, because they had many gift and nongift deductions, were subject to the new Alternative Minimum Tax (AMT). In such cases, deductibility of appreciated property was limited to the original cost to the donor, not full market value. For example, a gift of stock valued at $10,000 that 20 years before had cost the donor $1,000 provided a deduction of only $1,000. Many donors decided to keep such assets.

Due to 1993 legislation, gifts of appreciated property by any taxpayer, even one subject to AMT, can be deducted at fair market value. Students should understand that when appreciated assets are sold, the seller faces capital-gains taxes on the asset's appreciated value. Giving such assets to charitable organizations is advantageous to taxpayers because capital-gains taxes are avoided and a deduction at full market value is used to reduce taxable income, thereby lowering taxes owed to the government. Major and planned gifts typically involve gifts of appreciated property.

Unfortunately, as of 1997, Congress—with support from the Clinton administration—is promising to lower the tax rate on capital gains, which would decrease the financial benefits donors derive from giving appreciated property. The tax rate is either the rate paid on ordinary income or a set capital-gains rate, whichever is smaller. As most capital gains are realized by individuals in high income brackets, the set rate—rather than the income tax rate—usually determines the amount of taxes paid or saved. Therefore, when we talk about capital-gains taxes, it is appropriate to concentrate on the set rate, which is 28% as of 1997. Proposed legislation would reduce the rate to about 20%, although the Republican platform for the 1996 election called for a more drastic cut to 14%. A fundamental principle of fund raising is as rates go down, gifts go down, and *vice versa*.

Higher Tax Rates.   The higher the tax rates, the lower the costs of making gifts; therefore, giving increases when rates increase. The 1993 legislation created a fourth income tax bracket and a 10% surtax on net income above $250,000. An IS study estimated that these rate changes would increase giving by $1.6 billion annually because wealthier taxpayers would save more in taxes by making gifts (Marlowe, 1994b). Similarly, gift and estate tax rates were raised. Estates greater than $600,000, the amount exempted under current law, are subject to heavy progressive taxes up to 55%. Experts predicted that the higher rates would increase planned gifts.

In mid-1997, however, Congressional leaders and the President agreed to a balanced-budget plan that would reduce gift and estate taxes, likely by raising the lifetime exemption to $1 million or more (Tax Watch, 1997). The plan also included cutting the capital-gains tax (Tax Watch, 1997). Finally, the Republican-controlled Congress has vowed to revamp the Internal Revenue Code, with some proposals calling for a flat income tax that would eliminate all deductions. Given the problems presented in this chapter, the charitable subsector is poorly positioned to defend tax incentives for giving. Some loss is expected.

Information and publications about IRS regulations can be obtained by calling (800) TAX-1040 (829-1040), or the IRS Exempt Organizations Technical Division at (202) 622-8100. Supplementary information is available on the service's Web site at *http://www.irs.ustreas.gov.*

SUGGESTED READINGS

Accountants for the Public Interest (API). (1995). *What a difference nonprofits make: A guide to accounting procedures* (2nd ed.). (Available from Author, 1012 14th Street, N.W., Suite 1103, Washington, DC 20005.)

Blazek, J. (1993). *Tax planning and compliance for tax-exempt organizations: Forms, checklists, procedures* (2nd ed.). New York: Wiley.

Council for Advancement and Support of Education (CASE) and National Association of College University Business Officers (NACUBO). (1995). *The impact of FASB standards 116 & 117 on development operations.* Washington, DC: CASE.

Covington, S. (1994). *New age of nonprofit accountability.* (Available from National Committee for Responsive Philanthropy, 2001 S Street, N.W., Suite 620, Washington, DC 20009.)

Fuerst, R. A. (Ed.). (1996). *What fundraisers need to know about state and federal regulation, New directions for philanthropic fundraising* (No. 13). San Francisco, CA: Jossey-Bass.

Gaul, G. M., & Borowski, N. A. (1993). *Free ride: The tax-exempt economy.* Kansas City, MO: Andrews & McMeel.

Greenfield, J. M. (Ed.). (1994). *Financial practices for effective fundraising, New directions for philanthropic fundraising* (No. 3). San Francisco, CA: Jossey-Bass.

Greenfield, J. M. (1996). *Fund-raising cost effectiveness: A self-assessment workbook.* New York: Wiley.

Hill, F. R., & Kirschten, B. L. (1994). *Federal and state taxation of exempt organizations.* Boston, MA: Warren, Gorham, & Lamont.

Hopkins, B. R. (1996). *The law of fund-raising* (2nd ed.). New York: Wiley.

Kearns, K. P. (1996). *Managing for accountability: Preserving public trust in public and nonprofit organizations.* San Francisco, CA: Jossey-Bass.

8

Ethical Context
of Fund Raising

Whereas compliance with the law is the floor for conduct, ethical fund raising requires adherence to higher standards of practice. Independent sector (IS, 1991) explained, "The essential test of ethical behavior is 'obedience to the unenforceable'" or "self-imposed law" (p. 3).

Chapter 8 examines the ethical context of fund raising, with an emphasis on organizations that misuse the function and abuse philanthropy. Solicitation firms receive special attention because they are responsible for much of the criticism and regulation directed at fund raisers. Joint ventures with for-profit companies, such as cause-related marketing and corporate sponsorship, also are scrutinized and found lacking in ethics. Charitable organizations employing paid solicitors and joint ventures sell their names and missions for a quick buck, which eventually will damage their well-being, as well as the entire subsector's. As Eisenberg (1992) warned, "Non-profits have nothing to sell but their integrity. Undermining that, they will be in real danger of losing their soul and public trust that sustains them" (p. 42).

The discussion ties presuppositions about fund raising to unethical and ethical practice. Symmetrical rules on individual behavior are presented, and a fundamental principle is advanced: The ends of fund raising do not justify the means. The chapter concludes with a case study on use of the press agentry model by those organizations collectively known as the United Way.

Norms to guide practitioners in their daily work are found throughout the book. The discussion here concentrates on prominent issues of widespread concern and consequences. They—and others already covered in the chapter on law—are the ethical issues that practitioners mentioned frequently in interviews with Duronio (1994a), for example, accountability, paid solicitors, *quid pro quo* exchanges replacing philanthropy, and the United Way scandal.

Briscoe (1994a) argued that the public trust should be "the first and primary stakeholder in an ethical dilemma in fundraising [*sic*]" (p. 110). She ranked donors second in priority, organizations third, and fund raisers last. As given in the next chapter, the theory of donor relations holds that social, economic, and political sanction is the highest of seven effects of fund raising programming. In other words, protecting the privileged status granted to charitable organizations by society is the foremost objective in fund raising and the primary concern when discussing ethics.

ORGANIZATIONS AND ETHICS

As previously asserted, effective fund raising is dependent on the behavior of other organizational actors and the collective behavior of the system. Ethics cannot be separated from this dependency.

Organizational Influence

In her comments for future discussion, Duronio (1994a) asked, "How is individual responsibility for ethical conduct supported and/or undermined by organizational practices and values?" (p. 16). Quantitative evidence was presented in chapter 6 that the values of the dominant coalition affect how fund raising is practiced and that press agentry, the least ethical model, is preferred. Fogal (1991) observed, "*How* a not-for-profit organization or institution conducts fund raising says a great deal about . . . the organization's character" (p. 264; italics in original).

According to Briscoe (1994a), a poll conducted at the 1993 CASE National Assembly revealed that practitioners believe pressures from and decisions made by management largely are responsible for unethical behavior in fund raising. These findings are similar to those from studies on ethics in business.

Public relations scholar Mark McElreath (1997) cited a study from the 1960s that showed the majority of managers feel pressure to compromise personal ethics to achieve corporate goals. The Ethics Resource Center (1990), based in Washington, DC, claimed employee misconduct often is driven by a company's management style, agressive goal-setting, and incentive and reward systems. Most of the headline-making business scandals, it said, are caused by employees who choose to disregard the law because the reward is so great or because they believe the company expects them to do whatever is necessary to meet budgets, schedules, or sales quotas.

To promote ethical practice in fund raising, Briscoe (1994a) said department heads "must foster cultures where open discussion about ethics is accepted and encouraged" (p. 119). "They must create a climate in the workplace where values and stakeholder analysis are as much a part of decision making as fulfilling plans and meeting campaign goals" (p. 111). She maintained, "It is the responsibility of the fundraising [*sic*] manager to bring the relevant standards out of the organization's subconscious and to have them articulated for the guidance and assurance of board, officers and staff" (p. 115).

Organizational Codes of Ethics

A 1987 survey of 2,000 U.S. corporations, conducted by the Ethics Resource Center (1990), found that 85% had codes of ethics. To the best of my knowledge, no similar study has been conducted on charitable organizations. This would be an excellent subject for a master's thesis, whereby a survey would determine the extent to which the subsector incorporates codes of ethics. There is some evidence that the nonprofit sector lags behind its for-profit counterpart. Walters (1983), for example, found that although less than half the corporations in his study rigorously monitor and enforce their codes of ethics, a significantly smaller percentage of nonprofit associations do likewise.

Indicative of this lag, Boris and Odendahl (1990) reported, "Compared to business ethics or government ethics, the literature on philanthropic ethics is sparse and not well developed" (p. 189). Yet, as IS (1991) stated: "Concerns about lapses in ethical conduct touch every part of society. But, the public expects the highest values and ethics to be practiced *habitually* in the institutions of the charitable, nonprofit sector" (p. 5; italics in original).

I found from the explanatory study of the fund-raising models that less than half the organizations (44%) represented in NSFRE have some form of policy to control the acquisition of gifts; one half (50%) do not have a policy but rely on fund raisers to abide by a code of professional ethics or judge gifts on a case-by-case basis (Kelly, 1995a). Similarly, Lombardo (1991) found that of the 12 charitable organizations in her study about corporate donors, "only four had formal guidelines or policies addressing potential conflicts of interest with benefactors" (p. 96).

Absence of policies demonstrates a disregard for ethics and an organizational culture that invites unethical behavior. Without formal guidelines, as McElreath (1997) pointed out, "Practitioners are legally and professionally vulnerable if their clients or the organizations they work for engage in unethical or illegal activities" (p. 96). Adoption of a code of ethics deters bad actions and fosters good reputations.

McElreath (1997) presented the four parts of a comprehensive code of ethics: (a) a credo, "which is an overarching statement of organizational philosophy and values" (p. 70); (b) general guidelines for decision making; (c) specific rules that prohibit certain actions and require others; and (d) definitions, rationales, and illustrations. Adapting his work to fund raising, a sample credo is:

> A reputation of integrity is our organization's most valuable asset. We protect that asset by operating honestly and ethically. We will keep our word. We will not compromise our principles for short-term advantage. No illegal or unethical conduct is in the organization's interest. No employee will ever be asked by a supervisor to compromise his or her own ethical standards.

General guidelines provide direction. For example, they tell fund raisers that benefits returned to donors must not be excessive and gifts must be used for the purpose for which they were given. McElreath (1997) quoted a guideline from the Eli Lilly Company, which I recommend every organization copy: "Employees should not do anything—or be expected to take any action—that they would be ashamed to explain to their family or close friends" (p. 72). Specific rules prescribe behavior. A sample is: "Copies of our Form 990 will be provided to interested parties no later than 2 working days after the request." Definitions, rationales, and illustrations offer greater detail for situations commonly related to ethical problems. A sample rationale is: "Decisions to assign a portion of solicitation expenses to programs services must be approved by the Board of Trustees because joint costs have been abused in recent years." A sample illustration is:

An attorney calls to inform you that his or her client has selected our organization for a major gift. Ask for the client's name and other relevant information. If the individual, corporation, or foundation is unknown to you, do not make any commitment to accept the gift. Tell the lawyer you would like to arrange a meeting with the prospective donor and appropriate managers. If you have to make an immediate decision and have any doubts about the donor's reputation, do not accept the gift. Remember, our organization is known by the company it keeps.

The ancient advice of Socrates holds true: The way to gain a good reputation is to endeavor to be what you desire to appear. A code of ethics champions the vital principle that "good" behavior pays off. Unethical behavior, in contrast, damages organizations and threatens the survival of the charitable subsector.

CRISIS OF CREDIBILITY

It is recalled from chapter 7 that 74% of the respondents to a national opinion poll said more mandatory regulation of charitable organizations is needed (Gallup Organization, 1993). One third of the respondents also said they believe these organizations had become less trustworthy in the year before the study, and 52% thought they had become less trustworthy in the last decade. Joel Fleishman (1995), who in addition to being a law professor is the director of Duke University's Center for Ethics, Public Policy, and the Professions, warned, "The greatest threat to the not-for-profit sector is the betrayal of public trust, the disappointment of public confidence" (p. 32). He continued, "When government has intervened, it has done so in response to public disenchantment triggered by scandal within the sector" (p. 32).

Era of Scrutiny

In the late 1980s, 22 states sued the solicitation firm of Watson and Hughey for its deceptive sweepstakes mailings (G. Williams, 1993a). The mailings also were the subject of CBS' *60 Minutes* and two congressional hearings, which led to an unsuccessful bill that would have put interstate fund raising under the jurisdiction of the FTC.

In 1989, Jim Bakker, the founding minister of Praise the Lord (PTL), was convicted and sentenced to serve 45 years in prison on 24 counts of fraud and conspiracy.[1] An affidavit from the case stated, "The fraud perpetrated by Bakker is one of the largest, if not the largest, consumer frauds prosecuted as a federal mail fraud violation to date in this country" (Tidwell, 1993, p. 58). Media reports described the excessive compensation Bakker and his former wife Tammy Faye drew from gifts and other PTL income, including antique cars, a jet aircraft, and a number of luxurious homes. Scandals involving other television evangelists, such as Oral Roberts and Robert Tilton, soon followed.

In February 1990, the Reverend Bruce Ritter was forced to resign as CEO of Covenant House—which helps homeless and runaway youths—because of misuse of funds, including no-interest loans to friends and family members, and allegations that he had had sexual relations with several of the organization's male clients. The *New*

---

[1]Bakker was released in July 1994 after serving less than 5 years in a minimum-security prison.

York Post reporter who broke the story and then wrote a book about it, Charles Sennott (1992), said the scandal was the result of an organization that had allowed its ambitions for power and size to overwhelm its responsibilities. Using emotional letters written by Ritter, Covenant House increased direct-mail gifts from $22 million in 1983, to $71 million in 1989. The manipulative fund raising, according to Sennott, exaggerated the extent of teenage prostitution to get donations and portrayed Ritter as a tireless priest burning the midnight oil to send out the next letter.

Two years later, in February 1992, UWA President William Aramony was forced to resign following media reports about his annual compensation of $463,455, his pension worth $4.4 million, and his hiring of family and friends—to which charges of fraudulent use of UWA funds soon were added. UWA's internal investigation concluded shortly afterward that Aramony's management style had "led to numerous unethical and illegal activities" (Millar, 1992c, p. 1). Citing at least $360,000 worth of expenses during the previous 4 years, the investigation's report stated, "Expense claims which Mr. Aramony submitted to UWA for such items as first-class travel, limousine services, and gifts to friends are dwarfed by the expenditures Mr. Aramony approved for questionable consulting fees, ill-founded transfers of funds to spin-offs, high salaries, and benefits for senior executives" ("Text," 1992, p. 23). The report, as given in the opening lines of the its executive summary, "reveals a story of excess and of values lost" (p. 22). Interim President Kenneth Dam (cited in Millar, 1992c) declared, "This will certainly outrage people who have given their hard-earned money week by week to help the United Way help those in need. They will and should feel betrayed" (p. 1).

In June 1993, *The Chronicle of Philanthropy* ran a cover story on the crisis of credibility faced by the subsector. According to reporter Kristin Goss (1993b), the United Way scandal set off an attack by the local and national media. Organizations that once enjoyed a halo effect were now "portrayed as greedy and out of touch, begging the American people to dig deep into their pockets to give, then using those donations to pay fat salaries and build empires" (p. 1). Many senior managers bemoaned the 1990s as the decade of "non-profit bashing" (p. 1). Media representatives said the era of giving charitable organizations the benefit of the doubt was over; scandals had permanently changed the way they viewed these entities.

Pablo Eisenberg (1994), cochair of the National Committee for Responsive Philanthropy, reported, "The general reaction by non-profit leaders to press coverage of abuses was that the problem was 'a few bad apples in the barrel,' not large-scale wrongdoing by many of their colleagues" (p. 45). A handful of leaders welcomed the increased scrutiny, saying it would make organizations more responsible. They recommended more self-criticism and self-correction and called for a commitment to disclosure, accountability, and censure of those who abuse tax-exempt status. Mark Rosenman (cited in Goss, 1993b), vice president of social responsibility at the Union Institute in Washington, DC, argued that the subsector needs "clearly defined normative standards, and we haven't done that" (p. 41). Peter Goldmark (cited in Goss, 1993b), then president of the Rockefeller Foundation, stated, "One of the things our field suffers from is an unwillingness, when the facts are all out and all put together, to take a stand and say whether you find something broadly acceptable or not" (p. 41). We should be the first, not the last, he said, to be willing to look at our own problems. More recently, Fleishman (1995) summarized the ethical framework for fund raising: "The public expects, and has a right to expect, not-for-profits to behave properly, to abide by the rules, to do the right thing" (p. 32).

Proclaiming this the "era of scrutiny," NSFRE President Lewis (1993a) asked, "How did we get here . . . to the climate where proposals to regulate fund-raising practices and practitioners are on the increase?" (p. 9). Much of the answer to her question lies with those organizations that seek gifts and other income with little or no investment—those looking to get something for nothing.

Something for Nothing

Greenfield (1991) defined fund raising as "a combination of friend-raising (relationship building) and money-raising designed to meet needs for public benefit this year, next year and for years into the future" (p. 143). Using symmetrical concepts, he said, "Gifts satisfy donor aspirations; a 'quick buck' is never going to be a reliable source of gift income or of donor satisfaction" (pp. 143–144). He argued that anyone who offers to produce cash for the organization with "no effort" on its part, is signaling danger: "A red flag should go up every time those words are heard!" (p. 144).

Illustrating that such advice often goes unheeded, the subsector was rocked by yet another scandal in May 1995 when the Foundation for New Era Philanthropy, based in Radnor, Pennsylvania, filed for bankruptcy (Hanchette & Williams, 1995). The 6-year-old nonprofit, founded by John G. Bennett, Jr., had *invited* charitable organizations and donors to turn over their money for 6 months with the promise that the *investments* would be matched dollar for dollar by anonymous philanthropists and returned at twice the value. Religious organizations stepped forward, and in the end, more than 1,300 charities and individuals—including such prominent institutions and millionaires as Drexel University and Laurance Rockefeller—took advantage of the offer that seemed too good to be true.

It was. The anonymous philanthropists, according to government investigators, never existed, and the SEC charged Bennett with running an illegal pyramid, or Ponzi, scheme, whereby he used income from new investors to pay off promises to earlier investors (Hanchette & Williams, 1995). Claims filed against New Era totaled $536 million, of which $225 million represented lost investments (G. Williams, 1996a).

Moving from headline-making scandals to practices permeating the subsector, there are two primary means by which organizations seek something for nothing: hiring for-profit solicitation firms and entering into joint ventures with for-profit companies. In both cases, little or no investment of time or money is required of the organization. The outcome of the first is high fund-raising cost ratios and loss of society's trust. The outcome of the second is donor expectation of *quid pro quo* exchanges and loss of society's trust. When its trust diminishes, society—through its representative government—moves to revoke the privileged status it has granted to charitable organizations.

SOLICITATION FIRMS

The most important issue facing fund raising is defining who is and who is not a fund raiser. A high degree of confusion exists. State regulators, for example, generally refer to both consultants and solicitors as "professional fundraisers [*sic*]" (e.g., Office of the Attorney General, 1992, p. 9). They also equate fund raising with solicitation, only one step in the process of raising gifts. Trade media, on the other hand, use the term *professional fund raisers* solely to describe paid solicitors; the adjective "professional" rarely is used when describing consultants or staff practitioners. In its glossary of terms, the NSFRE Institute (1986) defined *solicitor(s)* as "volunteers and institutional staff who ask for contributions" and "professional solicitors [who] are paid to solicit for programs or causes" (p. 93). The fund-raising associations prohibit or discourage commission-based fees through their codes of ethics; yet, except for AAFRC, they do not exclude solicitors from membership.

Of overriding concern, in its landmark decisions during the 1980s, the Supreme Court failed to differentiate legitimate practitioners from what it called "professional fund raisers" (*Maryland*, 1984, p. 810). All three cases involved paid solicitors and organizations employing them. Cumulatively, the Court held that attempts to dissuade fraud by paid solicitors should not come at the expense of the First Amendment rights of charitable organizations.

Citizens for a Better Environment sued the Village of Schaumburg, a suburb of Chicago, because the organization was denied a permit for solicitation under an ordinance requiring that 75% of the amount of gifts raised would be used for charitable purposes (*Village of Schaumburg*, 1980). Although the village argued that the ordinance was justified because it served as a protection from fraud, the Supreme Court agreed with lower courts that the ordinance was unconstitutional because it unduly intruded on organizations' rights of free speech. Preventing fraud, the Court ruled, could be achieved in less intrusive ways.

The solicitation firm of Joseph H. Munson Company sued Maryland's Secretary of State over a statute that prohibited "a charitable organization, in connection with any fund-raising activity, from paying or agreeing to pay as expenses more than 25% of the amount raised" (*Maryland*, 1984, p. 787). Regulators' justification for the law was that "any organization using more than 25% of its receipts on fundraising [*sic*], salaries, and overhead was not charitable, but was a commercial, for-profit enterprise" (p. 799). The Court claimed no correlation existed between high solicitation costs and fraud; therefore, although the percentage limitation would restrict costs, it would not prevent fraud. The statute was unconstitutionally too broad.

The National Federation of the Blind of North Carolina, a group of organizations that uses and is closely associated with paid solicitors, sued North Carolina District Attorney Randolph Riley over a law consisting of three provisions: (a) paid solicitors could only collect a "reasonable fee" from gifts they solicited, (b) solicitors had to disclose the percentages of gifts they received as earnings in the past, and (c) solicitors had to qualify for a required license before soliciting (*Riley*, 1988, p. 669). The Court concurred with lower rulings that the law was not sufficiently narrow to represent the state's interest in fraud. The majority opinion proclaimed, "We reaffirm simply and emphatically that the First Amendment does not permit the State to sacrifice speech for efficiency" (p. 688).

Whereas the majority opinions on the three cases were written by Justices White, Blackmun, and Brennan, respectively, Chief Justice Rehnquist wrote all three dissenting opinions. Rehnquist generally held that the Court underestimated the reasons why a community or state might conclude that regulation of paid solicitors was necessary. He argued that attempts to regulate solicitors were not attempts to infringe on the

First Amendment rights of charitable organizations and their fund raisers, but rather attempts to prevent fraudulent behavior. Limitations on solicitors' fees, he contended, would serve governmental interests and help ensure that gifts would be spent on charitable purposes. Justice Rehnquist's arguments influenced my thinking on regulation, paid solicitors, and fund-raising cost ratios.

Defining Paid Solicitors

This book uses the terms *paid solicitors* and *solicitation firms* to differentiate members of that occupation from fund raisers. The solicitation terms are interchangeable as contemporary paid solicitors almost always work for solicitation firms. The techniques they employ are telemarketing and direct-response marketing (i.e., direct mail). They deal exclusively with lower level gifts from mass donor publics. They do not raise major gifts; however, promotions of planned gifts, such as suggested wording for adding bequests to wills, sometimes are included in gift-response forms. Some solicitation firms join with a charitable organization to sponsor entertainment events, such as circuses or Las Vegas nights, or to sell products and advertising. They primarily use telemarketing to make the sales and give a portion of the profit to the organization. Although the solicitors imply differently, gifts are not involved because of the product or service exchanged. These activities, therefore, are joint ventures and the solicitation firms also are termed *commercial coventurers* (Office of the Attorney General, 1992).

State registration regulations and the literature suggest four characteristics that further distinguish paid solicitors from fund-raising consultants and staff. First, as previously pointed out, they base their fees on commissions, or percentage of money raised. Second, they defer payment for their services until solicitation results are received. Third, they have custody of or access to gift funds (e.g., joint bank accounts). Fourth, they incur expenses on behalf of a charitable organization (e.g., paying for the production of direct mail or the deposit on a circus). All four characteristics do not have to be present to define a company as a solicitation firm. For example, some charge hourly or per-piece fees rather than commissions; however, they still defer payment and may handle gifts or incur expenses.

Fund raisers must help legislators, regulators, the media, donors, and other publics understand critical differences between their behavior and that of solicitation firms. Unfortunately, practitioners demonstrate their own degree of misunderstanding. Ignoring those that use direct mail, Mixer (1993) described what he called commercial fund-raising firms:

> These companies hire salespersons to make high-pressure telephone solicitations from temporary banks of phones in boiler-room operations located in prospects' hometowns. Donations go into accounts controlled by the firms, expenses are deducted, and net proceeds paid to the charity. The extraordinarily high expenses and the soliciting tactics continue to give fundraising [sic] an exceedingly poor image. (p. 249)

He argued that such companies should be distinguished from "ethical firms" that also employ solicitors but do not control funds received and are paid on a set fee basis. Yet he admitted, expenses for even those firms are high.

Mixer's and others' attempts to distinguish between unethical and ethical solicitation firms miss the point. These firms have nothing to do with relationships between charitable organizations and donors. No process is involved when they raise gifts—typically, there is no research, no cultivation, and no stewardship. For example, even simple acknowledgments rarely are sent to donors after receipt of their gifts. Fund raising is more than solicitation; therefore, paid solicitors are not fund raisers. They are commercial salespeople whose behavior should be regulated as such.

Given the Supreme Court's decisions, efforts to define who are fund raisers must start within the practice. To begin, paid solicitors should be barred from membership in fund-raising associations, which must also speak out against their abuses of philanthropy. They should not be allowed to make presentations at meetings, as they were at NSFRE's 1996 International Conference. Nor should the lawyers they hire to fight regulation be keynote speakers, as was the case at the 1996 Symposium on Fund Raising, sponsored by Indiana University's Center on Philanthropy.

A female fund raiser in higher education interviewed by Duronio (1994a) declared, "If we were any good at policing our own, we wouldn't have the bad apples we have, but we don't have a strong enough sense of standards of practice or values or ethics to say 'this behavior will not be tolerated'" (p. 15). NSFRE President Lewis (1993a) admitted that practitioners are timid about speaking out against solicitation techniques that "stretch the bounds of trust" (p. 9). Without singling out paid solicitors, she argued that some techniques are within the letter but not the spirit of the law—they mislead the easily led and easily confused. Illustrating Lewis' point, a male participant in NSFRE's round-table discussion on regulation related the following story about a 78-year-old woman for whom he holds power of attorney:

> Recently I noticed that she had written four $200 checks to one particular organization. Instead of sending her a thank-you for her donation, the organization continued to send her more solicitations as if she had never given. Because of her age, she did not remember that she already had sent a contribution. When I asked her about it, she said she never meant to give them $800. . . . This kind of thing happens to a lot of older people. ("Forum," 1995, p. 18)

Right to Survival

The paid-solicitation industry has thrived because of asymmetrical presuppositions about fund raising and the widely held misconception that charitable organizations—due to their noble purposes—have a right to survive no matter what the costs. Clarine Riddle (1990), then Attorney General of Connecticut, warned:

> An attitude on the part of some charities that they have an absolute right to survive leads those charities to justify their manipulation of the donor on the ground that they may do whatever it takes to induce someone to contribute. The drive for short-term results at any cost will slowly but inevitably destroy one of our civilization's most precious assets. (p. 29)

The consulting firm of Staley/Robeson/Ryan/St. Lawrence (1988) argued that all organizations conducting fund raising must examine their goals more closely, asking themselves, "Does our mission reflect a genuine need of contemporary society?" (p. 1). The firm said some organizations begin to believe "existence *is* the fulfillment of a mission" (p. 1; italics in original). It concluded that those without relevant missions "cannot survive for long and, indeed, perhaps they should not" (p. 1).

No charitable organization has an inviolable right to exist. As Lohmann's (1992b) theory differentiates, government provides public goods "that are indivisible and uniformly available to all" (p. 185). Common goods produced by charitable organizations are not available to all and they reflect the mutuality and meaning of quite distinct commons. Lohmann commented, "Of course, nonprofits attempt to argue that their common goods are public goods, but they are being disingenuous" (p. 269).

Stated differently, one's good cause is not another's. Assuming that the "general public" benefits and therefore *should* care about a particular common good is sanctimonious and arrogant and leads to unethical behavior. Failure to identify a commons (i.e., others who share an interest in the good) should result in failure of the organization. A question fund raisers must continually ask themselves is: Who cares whether this organization lives or dies? As Bush (1991) concluded, "When fund raisers or nonprofits feel their constitutional rights (or simply their right to exist) outweigh those of the public, then tax-exempt status and privileges are called into question by public officials" (p. 217).

The Case of United Cancer Council.   In 1990, the IRS revoked the tax exemption of the United Cancer Council (UCC), based in Carmel, Indiana ("Big charity," 1993). The IRS pulled the exemption retroactive to 1984 because the organization spent too much on fund raising and failed to carry on a mission-based program "commensurate in scope" with its financial resources (p. 34). The IRS also charged that UCC operated to improperly serve the private interests and commercial purposes of Watson and Hughey, the solicitation firm. UCC's relationship with the company, the IRS said, amounted to a joint venture to produce mailing lists.

According to the IRS, UCC spent as much as 96% of its annual gross income on fund-raising costs associated with the Watson and Hughey contract! Regardless, UCC sued the IRS, asking the U.S. Tax Court to restore its exemption. IS filed a friend-of-the-court brief supporting the IRS in the hope of influencing the decision. Whereas the coalition had not spoken out against the firm earlier, the former chair of its government relations committee said the brief would help the court "see the necessity of deciding the case against Watson and Hughey and their friends," yet avoid "an opinion that would be a slashing, broadsword attack on the (non-profit) sector" ("Big charity," 1993, p. 34). Also signing the IS brief were the American Heart Association, American Lung Association, and American Cancer Society ("Charity coalitions," 1994).

In contrast, the National Federation of Nonprofits filed a friend-of-the-court brief in support of UCC ("Charity coalitions," 1994). The federation argued that the IRS was wrong to find fault in the relationship between UCC and Watson and Hughey. Students will recall from chapter 7 that the federation's name at the time was the Nonprofit Mailers Federation and that the Watson and Hughey firm now is Direct Response Consulting Services. Those who have poor reputations often change their names rather than changing the way they behave. As also described in the previous chapter, the trade association protects the interests of its members—some 400 organizations and solicitation firms—by opposing all efforts to regulate fund raising and establish standards of ethical practice. Adding to examples already given, the association successfully convinced a federal court in 1995 to strike down a California law that required solicitors to limit their fees to no more than 50% of the *net* proceeds from each campaign ("Cal. limit," 1995).

Members of the National Federation of Nonprofits have a high stake in the UCC court case. Experts predict that if the IRS wins a broad victory, it could have grounds to pull the tax exemption of many charities that the service thinks have improper relationships with solicitation firms ("Charity coalitions," 1994). Ormstedt (1995), the Connecticut regulator cited in chapter 7, said the case "is landmark in its potential to strip the privilege of tax-exemption from those that do not deserve it" (p. 13; italics added). The trial started in 1992, and a decision still is pending as of 1997.

Steinberg (1993b) provided background information on UCC that demonstrates the fallacy of assuming a charitable organization's right to exist. UCC was formed in 1962 as an umbrella organization for more than 88 American Cancer Society chapters that had quit the society or been expelled for participating in United Way campaigns. The local affiliates paid dues to UCC and prohibited it from fund raising in their geographic regions. For 20 years, the organization relied mostly on affiliate dues; it did little fund raising. Steinberg claimed that in 1982, UCC was near bankruptcy. In fact, former board members testified at the trial that UCC had an annual income of about $40,000 from dues and, in 1983, faced a projected deficit of only $13,000 (G. Williams, 1992c). Pointing to problems of "competing" with the larger, better-known American Cancer Society, they argued that "Watson and Hughey provided the solution" (p. 22). Few questioned why the board members did not give or raise the $13,000 themselves, or why the affiliates served by the organization did not offer the financial means to its survival.

According to Steinberg (1993b), UCC asked the Watson and Hughey firm to conduct a national direct-mail campaign. He explained, "The charity could not solicit funds in regions covered by member affiliates, so it was handicapped in that it could only ask for money in places where it *provided no services*" (p. 13; italics added). Because UCC had insufficient funds to pay for such a campaign, it also asked the firm to advance the funds and absorb any losses. The firm agreed, with the provision that it would retain the exclusive right to market all mailing lists developed. As explained by the Association of Direct Response Fundraising Counsel (1992), the acquired donor list is the primary product of a mail campaign directed to nondonors. Its value lies in future fund raising from those identified; therefore, it is of considerable worth to the organization and to others in the direct-response marketplace. UCC signed the original contract in 1984 and renewed it until 1989.

During the 5 years, Watson and Hughey created 165 fund-raising packages, or almost 3 every month, which were sent to nearly 80 million people (G. Williams, 1992c). Of those packages, more than 70% were sweepstakes mailings that offered cash prizes to recipients, which, as Steinberg (1993b) admitted, "were probably not very effective at securing long-term donor commitment" (p. 2). Steinberg also emphasized that the Watson and Hughey firm was not paid by commission, but rather it received a fee based on the number of mailings—which helps explain the high volume of mail generated. Based on federal tax court papers, an estimated $27 million was raised over the 5-year period; UCC netted just $2.5 million, or 9% (Podolsky, 1995). The rest went to fund-raising expenses, including the solicitation firm's fees. "This,"

Steinberg (1993b) said, "is presumably why the IRS believes UCC's expenditures were 'incommensurate' with resources" (p. 2).

He argued, however, "The organization was prospecting for new donors, willing to spend lots of money now on people who rarely give in the effort to find the few reliable donors that will give time and again in the future" (p. 13). Yet documents submitted to the U.S. Tax Court by Watson and Hughey showed that the firm earned $7 million from renting mailing lists, including UCC's donors, to its other clients and its own for-profit operations between 1986 and 1989 (G. Williams, 1992c).[2] The IRS said the firm's "free-wheeling use" of the list sharply reduced its value to UCC because "excessive solicitation by others uses up or dilutes the benefits to be reaped from one's own mailing list" (p. 21).

Due to adverse publicity and lawsuits directed at the sweepstakes and the solicitation firm, UCC did not renew its contract with Watson and Hughey in 1989. According to Steinberg (1993b), the organization signed instead "a traditional contract with a more 'respectable' fundraiser [sic]" (p. 2). Shortly thereafter, UCC filed for bankruptcy.

Hiring Paid Solicitors.

A UCC lawyer in the tax-exemption case, Leonard Henzke, accused the IRS of imposing vague and harmful restrictions on the organization's fund-raising efforts, which, he claimed, violated its First Amendment rights (G. Williams, 1992c). He, as well as the board of directors, maintained that the fund-raising contract with Watson and Hughey was beneficial—without it, UCC would have failed. If the revocation were upheld, Henzke warned, the verdict would discourage volunteers from serving on charity boards and establishing exempt organizations to advance unpopular and controversial causes.

Boards, as discussed in chapter 6, are accountable by law for the organization. It is their responsibility to ensure necessary resources are available and inappropriate for them, as O'Connell (1993) argued, to call for increased income and leave it to others to produce. Discussing the use of paid solicitors, Greenfield (1991) said, "One of the primary responsibilities of every board member in any nonprofit organization is to initiate professional fiscal methods and controls. Hiring out this responsibility is a mistake and a lapse in stewardship" (p. 79). Organizations that cannot attract board members who are willing to accept full fiduciary responsibility have lost a basic requirement for existence.

The defense that paid solicitors enable new, small, and unpopular organizations—with few resources and undeveloped donor constituencies—to get established is seriously flawed. Certainly, UCC was not new, nor was its mission to fight cancer controversial. Indeed, organizations charged in lawsuits with solicitation firms almost always have conventional, not unpopular, missions. Reports now issued by state regulators document that "popular causes," large organizations, and those that are well-established are the dominant users of solicitation firms.

Reviewing a State of Massachusetts report (Office of the Attorney General, 1992), for example, no controversial causes could be identified by organizational name for the 128 campaigns conducted by paid solicitors during 1991. On the other hand,

---

[2]Many Watson and Hughey/Direct Response Consulting Services' clients have missions supposedly dealing with cancer, which—by interchanging mailing lists—results in an array of solicitations confusing to prospective donors. A personal example is given shortly.

Heritage Publishing raised more than $1 million in the name of the Child Protection Program, but only 23% of the money went to that organization. The same firm raised more than $250,000 for the Multiple Sclerosis Association, but forwarded only 10%. The U.S. Organization for Disabled Athletes got only 20% of the $1.5 million raised in its name by Heritage. Although Reese Brothers forwarded almost 75% of the $1.4 million it raised for Mothers Against Drunk Drivers (MADD), with which the firm has a close relationship, only 19% of the $262,000 it raised for "Just Say No" International went to the organization's fight against drugs.

Review of other regulators' reports yielded similar findings. In California during 1993, for example, Stephen Dunn & Associates turned over 89% of the $836,000 it solicited for the California Institute of Technology, but returned only 21% of the $64,000 it solicited for the San Francisco Museum of Modern Art, and left the Sierra Club with a bill for $11,000 on top of taking the entire $7,500 raised (Attorney General, 1994). Non-Profit Telemedia solicited funds for such organizations as Veteran's Wish Fund, Heart Support of America, Operation Doctor, Help Hospitalized Children's Fund, Disabled Children's Relief Fund, and America's Missing Children—none of which received more than 15% of the money raised.

Solicitation firms do not serve new, small, and unpopular causes, which is economically logical given the for-profit motives of the firms. Those for whom it would be difficult to solicit money are not viable clients. Rather, clients of paid solicitors are charitable organizations seeking gifts for which no investment is required (i.e., getting something for nothing). The dominant coalitions of the organizations have decided that any return, even 10% of the dollars generated, is profitable and, therefore, acceptable. As the Massachusetts report (Office of the Attorney General, 1992) stated: "Why would a charitable organization use a professional solicitor? Some do so because this arrangement involves little or no work for the charity. Many times, the charity does nothing except take in the money" (p. 10). Such reasoning is unethical, shortsighted, and a betrayal of "the public trust."

Regarding the UCC case, Steinberg (1993b) argued that the IRS commensurate test should be based on whether expenses for program services are commensurate with an organization's *net* income (i.e, after subtracting costs such as fund raising), not its *gross* income. UCC's expenditures would have been commensurate using this different measure. The current test, Steinberg said, implies that financial means are "available" before fund-raising costs are paid. He protested, "It is logically impossible for a charity to spend money it does not have" (p. 13).

His latter statements are correct; UCC should have failed before 1984. It had no identifiable commons. Those who controlled the organization were unwilling to invest in its tax-exempt purpose. Those it primarily served, its member affiliates, did not demonstrate support for its continuance. The only reason it survived was because the paid-solicitation industry earns millions of dollars exploiting such situations. As argued in the beginning chapters of this book, the nonprofit sector is essential to preserving our society as we know it. As also argued in chapter 6, however, socially responsible organizations invest resources in fund raising before looking outside for financial support. Organizations that hire paid solicitors because they lack the means to raise funds have no right to survive.

Publicity on Paid Solicitors

State regulators are concentrating on publicity and prosecution to curb fund-raising abuses. Nine states are leading the efforts to educate citizens about paid solicitors: California, Florida, Maine, Massachusetts, Minnesota, New York, North Carolina, Ohio, and South Dakota. Each publishes regular reports on solicitation activities and publicizes its findings through the media.

For example, Massachusetts' report for 1991 (Office of the Attorney General, 1992) showed that an average of only 28% of the money raised by solicitation firms in that state went to the organizations for which the gifts were intended. Of the 128 campaigns conducted, almost one in five forwarded 10% or less of the dollars raised. The report explained that the organization is very aware of the percentage being charged by the solicitation firm, but "donors may not be so well informed and may believe that a high percentage of their donations are going to the charitable purpose which led them to donate" (p. 10). Demonstrating both an increase in fund raising and the number of organizations hiring solicitors, only 39 consulting and solicitation firms registered to conduct business in Massachusetts in 1981, but 176 registered in 1992, including 63 solicitation firms.

On the other side of the country, 161 paid solicitors registered in California in 1993 (Attorney General, 1994). They raised slightly more than $192 million in gifts that year, but only $63 million, or 33%, of the total went to the organizations on whose behalf the solicitations were made. California's report, which deals only with solicitation firms, emphasized, "Simply put, two out of every three dollars donated to charities which used these commercial fundraisers [*sic*] did not go to charity at all, but instead went to solicitation expenses and to fundraiser [*sic*] profits" (pp. 8–9). Solicitors took 75% or more of the money raised in over half of the 516 campaigns conducted! The report reminded residents, "The vast majority of California's 68,000 registered charities *do not use* commercial fundraisers [*sic*] to solicit the public, but instead rely on trained charity staff and volunteers who are directly accountable to the charity's officers" (p. 2; italics in original).

In the Midwest, the State of Minnesota Office of the Attorney General (1994) reported that during 1993–1994, 40 solicitation firms conducted 137 campaigns for 121 different organizations. Only 36% of the $11.4 million raised went to the sponsoring organizations, a percentage that has been relatively consistent since the Office of the Attorney General began publishing reports in 1989. Minnesota's report concentrates on solicitors that use telemarketing; noticeably missing are firms specializing in direct mail, such as Direct Response Consulting Services.

An analysis of regulators' 1996 reports by one of my graduate students showed that cost ratios remain excessively high and the same solicitation firms are profiting from the plunder (Devillier, 1996). For example, 48 campaigns conducted by Non-Profit Telemedia in 1995 returned 25% or less of the dollars raised. Based on figures from just seven states, Non-Profit Telemedia kept $13 million in gifts. Reese Brothers, which recently relocated from Pennsylvania to Vienna, Virginia, retained 75% or more of the dollars it raised in 36 separate campaigns conducted in five states. Non-Profit Telemedia, Heritage Publishing, and Reese Brothers were the three solicitation firms keeping the most gift dollars in 1995. Similar to previous reports, police and firefighters dominated the listings of organizations hiring paid solicitors.

Police and Firefighters. Regulators' reports provide evidence that the heaviest users of paid solicitors are police and firefighter organizations. Of the 128 campaigns conducted in Massachusetts during 1991, more than one third (36%) were for organizations that included the terms *police* or *firefighters* in their names (Office of the Attorney General, 1992). The report warned, "Donors should realize that it is generally *not* the police or fire *department* who will benefit from the donation, but rather the police or firefighter *organization*, such as a union or other fraternal membership group" (p. 8; italics in original).

Gifts to such organizations generally are used to build retirement funds or for union purposes, such as legal expenses incurred in bargaining. Paid solicitors often offer premiums, including police stickers for the donor's vehicle. People find it difficult to refuse when asked to support authority figures who are responsible for the safety of their community. Police stickers imply that those who display them will be treated differently than those who do not.[3] The State of Minnesota Office of the Attorney General (1994) stated in its top-ranked tip for smart giving, "Law enforcement or fire fighter appeals seem to confuse consumers. Your local police or fire departments *do not* generally solicit money. Police or fire fighter associations *do* request money for their purposes, which may or may not be charitable in nature. Do not allow yourself to feel intimidated" (p. 7; italics in original).

A review of other state regulators' reports confirmed the large number of these organizations employing paid solicitors. The 1993 report from the Florida Department of Agriculture and Consumer Services (1993), for example, listed 58 organizations under "Fraternal Order of Police" alone. In 1992, Fraternal Order of Police, District #5, spent 78% of its total expenses of $1.1 million on fund raising. The Florida Police Benevolent Association spent $4.5 million, or 58% of its expenses, on fund raising. The Pinellas County Council of Firefighters had expenses totaling $643,000, of which 78% represented fund-raising costs. Florida's report, unfortunately, only lists charitable organizations; it does not name or give information on solicitation firms.

When asked to identify the biggest problem or challenge faced by state regulators, an Assistant Attorney General for the State of Washington replied: "Professional fundraising [*sic*] on behalf of police and firefighter organizations. . . . The complaints we get indicate high pressure tactics; for example, if you don't donate to the firefighters you'd better hope your house doesn't catch on fire. Also, solicitors claim to represent the consumers' own local police and fire departments" (Mehegan, Bush, & Nacson, 1994, p. 19). An Assistant Attorney General in Louisiana responded: "The most complaints fall in the area of false law enforcement charities. They range from solicitors calling on behalf of funds that don't exist to people who have been told they will be arrested or have their license plates pegged if they don't donate" (p. 14).

In 1997, the FTC and the Attorneys General of all 50 states formed an unprecedented alliance to publicize fraudulent fund raising for "badge-related" organizations ("FTC," 1997). Called "Operation Alert," the program is targeted at two kinds of fraud: solicitations for sham organizations that are presented as causes benefiting police, firefighters, and sheriffs, but are owned by paid solicitors who keep all the

---

[3] I personally can attest that such stickers issued in Maryland can, indeed, mean the difference between a speeding ticket and a warning.

money; and solicitations for "real" badge-related organizations that mislead donors about the identity of solicitors and the purposes for which gifts are raised.

News reports announcing the program quoted numerous representatives of badge occupations who expressed outrage at fraud committed in their names. They blamed unscrupulous solicitors pretending to be officers, particularly those running bogus operations, and emphasized that many states prohibit law enforcement personnel from personally soliciting gifts. Little was said about the actual fraternal organizations that hire solicitation firms to raise money on behalf of their members. Fraud involving sham organizations is repugnant, but regulators' reports indicate that real police and firefighters are responsible for most of the crimes.

Prosecuting Paid Solicitors

Although publicity efforts by regulators may one day prove more effective, the Attorney General of Maine, Michael Carpenter (cited in G. Williams, 1991), stated, "What justifies our existence is the aggressive criminal prosecution of fraudulent conduct that directly protects the legitimate fund-raising community and the charitable giving public" (p. 30). Criminal action against paid solicitors has increased dramatically since the beginning of the decade. Describing the situation in 1991, Ormstedt (cited in G. Williams, 1991) said, "The level of enforcement activity nationwide is higher than I've ever seen it in the 18 years I've been doing this. More states are becoming committed to doing something about [fraud]—at least to try to make a dent" (p. 30).

Unfortunately, prosecution has not stopped those with a sufficiency of lawyers to protect their deficiency of ethics. In 1991, the Watson and Hughey Company reached out-of-court settlements with the 22 states, including California, which had sued it and some of its clients for the infamous sweepstakes mailings (G. Williams, 1993a). The solicitation firm and the organizations admitted no wrongdoing, but agreed to make changes in their operations. In the biggest settlement, involving 10 states, the firm and its clients—including UCC and the Walker Cancer Research Institute (WCRI)—agreed to pay $2.1 million and to disclose an unusual degree of financial detail in their future solicitations.

In 1992, California again sued Watson and Hughey for unfair business practices, along with WCRI—based in Aberdeen, Maryland (G. Williams, 1993b). The state charged the firm and organization for using a direct-mail campaign designed to create the impression among donors that gifts would go for cancer research, even though less than 1% of the money raised from 1988 through 1990 went for that purpose. Of more than $9 million raised, WCRI spent only $68,000 on research grants!

WCRI lawyer MacKenzie Canter, III, argued that the state failed to take into account the cost of public education messages incorporated in the direct-mail pieces. As discussed in the last chapter, platitudinous advice and other abuses of joint costs led to pending revisions of accounting standards. Canter further argued that no deception took place because fund-raising costs also were included in the solicitations. Watson and Hughey changed its name to Direct Response Consulting Services in 1992.

The California lawsuit was a key case watched closely by regulators across the country. Legal experts predicted that if California won, other states would try the same approach (G. Williams, 1993b). In January 1994, 3 months before the case was scheduled to go to trial, Direct Response Consulting Services and WCRI settled the lawsuit, again out of court ("Cal. suit," 1994). Both agreed to try to raise $185,000 for a special cancer-research fund, and WCRI agreed to stop doing business in California. WCRI, it should be pointed out, continually fails to meet the standards of such watchdog groups as NCIB (e.g., too many board members are paid by or have financial interests in the organization). WCRI is headed by Dr. Evan Harris Walker, also of Aberdeen, Maryland—a small town located about 30 miles north of Baltimore.

Watson and Hughey. An entire book could be devoted to the unsavory legacy Jerry C. Watson and Byron "Chat" Hughey have given to fund raising. Their lawyers and the practice's unwillingness to confront their behavior have allowed them to "legally" exploit America's philanthropic tradition. Bush (1994), it is recalled, did not even name the Watson and Hughey Company in her article describing the negative impact of the firm's sweepstakes mailings on fund-raising law, published in NSFRE's magazine, *Advancing Philanthropy*. Readers simply were informed that the firm responsible "is still in business under another name" (p. 30). When I protested this serious omission, NSFRE refused to publish my letter to the editor because I was unable to provide legal documents naming the company, only articles from the trade and mass media! The association presumably was more interested in avoiding a lawsuit than in unmasking unethical behavior.

Syndicated columnist Ann Landers raised her voice against the firm, only to find its lawyers banging at her door (Landers, 1993b). As she stated in a semiretraction, "There is nothing illegal in asking people to contribute to charities which give very little money to charitable work, so long as that fact is disclosed, even though it appears in fine print" (Landers, 1993a, p. 9A).

In December 1993, my mother-in-law—an 87-year-old widow living in Duluth, Minnesota—showed me a sweepstakes mailing she had just received. She was convinced that the suggested $7, $10, or $15 "tax deductible gift" was worth the chance to win the $2,500 prize heralded on a governmentlike certificate, titled "IOU Form," that was made out to her ("Pay to the order of") and sent from Washington, DC. What made the offer even more enticing was that the donation would be used to fight cancer. "This extraordinary cash giveaway" was sponsored by the National Cancer Research Center, a "project" of WCRI, which—as just stated—is located in Aberdeen, Maryland, not Washington, DC. A 1,400-word disclosure sheet, crowded with dense and difficult-to-read text, identified Direct Response Consulting Services as "the paid professional fundraiser [sic]" used to assist WCRI in the solicitation of funds.

The personalized letter attached to the certificate was signed by vice president in charge of fund raising, Steven Blementhal, and stated more than once that the IOU Form was a facsimile. The letter also referred to the disclosure sheet for details. The disclosure statements—which I was most interested in reading but my mother-in-law was not—reported that in the last fiscal year, WCRI raised more than $6 million, of which less than 3% went to program services. Fund-raising costs, if one took the time to add them up, amounted to 95% for fund raising and public education "in conjunction" with solicitations. The public education consisted primarily of such slogans as "Check up—get one each year" and an 800 telephone number from which the caller could obtain the name of the closest federal cancer center!

Embedded within the disclosure sheet's crowded text was the statement: "A portion of the money included in the program service category was expended pursuant to voluntary agreements settling causes of action regarding certain previous mailings." My mother-in-law is bright, but even if she had read it, I doubt she would have understood its meaning: The organization had been sued for alleged deception and had agreed to spend more on program services during the last fiscal year to comply with the terms of the out-of-court settlement—which obviously also dictated disclosure of the fact.

The letter told my mother-in-law that Steve was giving her a "special opportunity" because she was "part of a group with a record of past generosity to charitable causes." (Obviously, her name was on a donor list acquired from similar solicitations.) Saying that WCRI's purpose is "to fight cancer," Steve urged her to send a gift because her help was "desperately" needed. Reflecting a very different tone, the disclosure sheet was filled with caveats, disclaimers, and legally required information from regulators. For example, the names of 23 states that prohibit sweepstakes were listed. The mailing neglected to mention that the IRS does not allow charitable deductions for money given to participate in games of chance; instead, it stated that gifts to the project "are tax deductible to the full extent of the law." The disclosure sheet ended by suggesting that WCRI be included as a beneficiary in the receiver's will and provided the language for adding a bequest.

Given Watson and Hughey's lawyers, the solicitation likely was perfectly legal, but it also was perfectly unethical. Jerry Huntsinger (1994), owner of direct-mail companies in Virginia and California, provided insight on the ethics of such solicitations in a candid newspaper column:

> I don't think the "general public" has lost confidence in fundraising [sic] appeals. I don't think they ever had any confidence in the first place! . . . . The people being interviewed and polled today are not your traditional elderly, female donors who have been the primary force in direct mail fundraising [sic] for the past 30 years. . . . Fundraising [sic] copy has always involved the dredging up of deep emotions. Emotions about someone who desperately needs to be helped. . . . We thought our elderly, female, positive thinking donor would live forever. (p. 56)

He advised readers of *The NonProfit Times* to "try something other than your normal bait and switch story" in order to "deregulate" fund raising from the older donor (p. 57).

Perhaps in an effort to reach new donor types (or perhaps because he is getting older), my husband received a solicitation in May 1994 from the American Institute for Cancer Research (AICR), an organization created by Watson and Hughey in 1981, the same year WCRI was founded (Landers, 1993b). The mailing was a localized appeal to prospective donors living in Breaux Bridge, Louisiana—a town of about 7,000 citizens. The response card suggested a gift of only $5, which indicated that it was an acquisition mailing to build salable donor lists (i.e., the cost ratio for new donor gifts of $10 or less from direct mail is 1:1 or higher).

The fact that both my husband and his mother were solicited by Watson and Hughey within 6 months in two different parts of the country attests to the magnitude of damage inflicted by these paid solicitors. It refutes those who imply that the problem of fraud is small, such as Hopkins (1995), who questioned the need for regulation. "Are there many fraudulent and otherwise misrepresented charitable solicitations? Are there many unscrupulous charities or ill-meaning fund-raising efforts? . . . . The truth is that no one knows" (p. 28). He criticized the increasing number of state laws when there are "absolutely no data defining the reason for their existence or the magnitude of the problem they are supposed to rectify" (p. 28).[4] Whereas Hopkins ignored secondary and anecdotal evidence like the information presented in this section, his criticism rightfully emphasizes the absence of scientific research on paid solicitors, which students are urged to address (some suggestions are offered later). Without studies to support legal action, solicitors will continue to prey on the elderly.

My husband can protect himself, but he and I are powerless to stop the solicitations my mother-in-law receives or her responses. Her small gifts, which gradually diminish her savings, have kept her on Watson and Hughey's lists. Between 1993 and 1995, she was the target of multiple direct-mail solicitations from the following organizations that identified themselves as clients of Direct Response Consulting Services in McLean, Virginia:

> American Institute for Cancer Research (Washington, DC)
> Cancer Fund of America (Knoxville, Tennessee)
> National Children's Cancer Society (St. Louis, Missouri)
> Pacific West Cancer Fund (Seattle, Washington)
>   Cancer Center for Detection and Prevention (a Pacific West project)
> Project Cure (Dallas, Texas)
>   The Alzheimer's Disease Fund (a Project Cure program)
>   Center for Advanced Heart Research (a Project Cure program)
>   Center for Alternative Cancer Research (a Project Cure program)
> United Children's Fund (Knoxville, Tennessee)
>   A Child's Wish (a United Children's project)
> Walker Cancer Research Institute (Aberdeen, Maryland)
>   National Cancer Research Center (a Walker project).

All the solicitations my mother-in-law showed me involved sweepstakes. Little had changed except the "prizes" had gone up in value. For example, WCRI's National Cancer Research Center touted a chance to win $25,000 in 1994, up from $2,500 in 1993. Chances of winning were "no worse than" 1 in 200 million! The 1,600-word disclosure sheet stated that just 4% of the $4 million raised the year before had been used for program services. Minnesota regulators previously had sued Watson and Hughey and its clients over sweepstakes mailings. Yet, because its reports of solicitation activities concentrate on telemarketing rather than direct mail, neither the renamed firm nor any of the organizations just listed that solicited my mother-in-law were included in the 1993–1994 report published by the State of Minnesota Office of the Attorney General (1994).[5]

---

[4] A FTC officially recently estimated that fraudulent fund raising costs Americans more than $1.4 billion each year ("FTC," 1997). I believe the financial loss is much greater, perhaps as high as $5 billion annually.

[5] In January 1997, Minnesota charged Direct Response Consulting Services and its client United Children's Fund with mailing deceptive and misleading appeals ("Minnesota," 1997). Attorney General Hubert H. Humphrey, III, said that gifts sent in response to letters promising to fight cancer had been used primarily to pay fund-raising expenses. The charity, he reported, had raised more than $2.5 million nationally in recent years but had not spent any of the money on cancer programs. The charity's president, Rick Bowen, said he was "shocked" by the lawsuit and hoped to settle out of court. Richard Wolf, current general counsel for the solicitation firm, claimed the appeals were legal because they had been "verified" by lawyers and accountants before being mailed.

The clients of Direct Response Consulting Services generally take a low profile to avoid drawing attention to their disreputable operations. They rarely are mentioned in the trade media except when lawsuits are brought against them or their failures to pass review are included in watchdog summaries—both of which are published in back pages under small headlines. AICR is an enigma. It has participated in the "Philanthropy 400" surveys since *The Chronicle of Philanthropy* began ranking organizations in 1991 (i.e., AICR released its Form 990 for publication in each of the last 6 years). For example, it reported gift income of $23 million in 1994, which placed it at 273 on the list of organizations raising the most money ("Philanthropy 400," 1995). AICR's cost ratios, as given on its Form 990s, also have appeared reasonable—keeping in mind abuses of joint costs. For example, the listing just cited showed that AICR spent only 22% of its gift dollars on fund raising and 64% of its total income on program services. Contradicting these figures, the same newspaper issue that displayed them also disclosed that AICR had failed its latest evaluation by NCIB; specifically, it did not meet the four standards that call for spending at least 60% of annual expenses on program services, ensuring fund-raising cost ratios are reasonable over time, an independent board, and no payment to board members ("Watchdog," 1995).

Whereas AICR, like other clients, regularly failed watchdog reviews in the past, it met all of PAS' standards in 1996 ("Watchdog," 1996). The converted behavior—if it exists—could be related to AICR's leadership role in a new initiative of the National Federation of Nonprofits, discussed shortly. Its recently acquired legitimacy allows AICR to advance the self-interests of Jerry Watson and Chat Hughey in the public forum by serving as a supposedly credible spokesperson for their firm and its clients.

Direct Response Consulting Services' exploitation of my mother-in-law—representing millions like her—was featured in a 1995 *U.S. News & World Report* article about cancer charities closely affiliated with the infamous firm (Podolsky, 1995). Such organizations are termed *look-alikes*.

Look-Alikes.   Students should not assume, as many practitioners claim, that the one solicitation firm selected for analysis here is an aberration. Numerous such firms exist. Almost every issue of *The Chronicle of Philanthropy* names at least one solicitor that has been accused of wrongdoing, along with its clients. For example, although more than $9 million was given to the U.S Marine Corps Reserve Toys for Tots Foundation between July 1992 and December 1993 to buy Christmas toys for needy children, not $1 was spent on toys (Goss, 1994c). Most of the money went to pay the fees of Steve Cram & Associates of Falls Church, Virginia.[6] In 1994, the Pennsylvania Attorney General's Office launched an investigation of the Toys for Tots Foundation and three other organizations that had used Steve Cram & Associates to handle their direct-mail solicitations (Goss & Williams, 1994).

The foundation and the Watson and Hughey clients are examples of look-alikes, or 501(c)(3) organizations that adopt names similar to those of well-known organi-

---

[6]Steve Cram & Associates is a familiar name in state regulators' reports—one often related to extremely high cost ratios (e.g., Attorney General, 1994). Its location, as well as others' mentioned in this chapter, prompts the question: Why are cities in northern Virginia a common site for solicitation firms and charities accused of wrongdoing? A study exploring this pattern and possible relationships with Virginia's fund-raising regulations and proximity to the federal government would be informative.

zations in order to facilitate solicitations by misleading donor prospects. Most were created by or have close relationships with solicitation firms. All spend millions on national fund-raising campaigns and administration, but conduct few program services. Former Pennsylvania investigator Steven Arter (cited in Goss, 1993c) commented, "The sad fact of the matter is, anybody can start a charitable organization and go out and raise money, and as long as I'm giving something to a charitable purpose, I'm pretty much untouchable unless someone can prove fraud" (p. 31). Due to the Supreme Court decisions, "A charity can't be barred from fund raising, even if it pays its solicitor 95 percent of the funds raised" (Bush, 1994, p. 31).

Hundreds of look-alikes have emerged in recent years, and the gift dollars they drain from legitimate organizations are substantial. The American Cancer Society estimates that millions are annually lost to cancer look-alikes because donors are misled into believing their gifts are going to the society or another reputable organization (Montague, 1990). The same problem exists for heart disease and other health and human services missions.

In illustration, the U.S Marine Corps Reserve Toys for Tots *Foundation* was created in 1991, and despite its name, it has no official affiliation with the local "Toys for Tots" drives conducted for 50 years by the United States Marine Corps Reserve (Goss, 1994c). Yet the foundation uses the established program to generate gifts. A December 1993 solicitation letter from the foundation, for example, described the older program and told prospective donors that *"our* toy drives" are "not enough" because the then New York-based foundation had thousands of "Dear Santa" letters from children who would not have toys for Christmas, many from the reader's geographic area ("A sampling," 1993, p. 33; italics added). The foundation's letter, which also included a photograph of a Marine with his arms around two children, continued in characteristic press agentry style: "Although it's impossible to wipe away the pain that a child experiences when a parent dies . . . or when a child suffers from a crippling disease . . . or when a child's parents are too poor to provide any 'extras' . . . it is possible to give a child a moment of joy" (p. 33; ellipses in original). As just mentioned, not $1 was spent on toys during the 18 months preceding the solicitation. The foundation had relocated from New York to Quantico, Virginia before the Pennsylvania investigation began.

Established organizations are doubly hurt by look-alikes: Not only do they siphon gifts, but the well-known organizations often are blamed for the unethical solicitation techniques used. They have gone to court to enforce their rights under federal trademark laws, which grant exclusive use of name, insignia, and other unique symbols to those who first create them. Yet trademark litigation is expensive and not always useful. Some terms, such as *veterans*, have been ruled too commonplace to be protected. Even after suits are won, compliance often is less than satisfactory.

Confusion among donors is high; they find it increasingly difficult to distinguish between "good" and "bad" organizations. Efforts to educate people about the proliferation of charities that have similar names and claim to sponsor similar programs have been localized, minimal, and seemingly ineffective. Many legitimate organizations complain about such publicity, saying it only damages their fund-raising programs. Some actually accuse state regulators of grandstanding and feeding the media's "nonprofit bashing." An underlying consensus appears to be that the less said about the problem, the better. I disagree and align myself with former Attorney General Riddle (1990):

> Legitimate charities cannot afford to pretend that there is no problem or, when finally confronted with it, blame the government for bringing the fraudulent charities to the public's attention. It is well past the time when defensiveness and closemindedness will work. For the sake of philanthropy, we have to work harder to maintain the high standard of conduct charities should expect from themselves. (p. 29)

New Initiatives and Research

Ormstedt (1995) predicted that initiatives by state regulators in the foreseeable future will remain focused on publicity and prosecution. "First and foremost, the states will use their common law and statutory authority to prosecute charities that deceive the public as to the nature and extent of their programs. . . . Second, states will continue to develop more sophisticated programs to inform the public about the activities of charities" (p. 14). He singled out abuse of joint costs as a problem that will command increased efforts by regulators. Correspondingly, he urged organizations to take action in support of self-regulation. "Charities must ask themselves whether it is in their best interest to defend, or to be apathetic to, the use some make of accounting gimmicks that breed public distrust of all charities" (p. 15). Promoting ethical behavior as the alternative to more laws, Ormstedt accused the fund-raising associations of having codes of ethics that are "mere window-dressing," and advised them and others to "adopt and *enforce* effective codes of professional conduct" (p. 15; italics added).

The FTC is cooperating "more closely than ever" with state regulators to crack down on deceptive solicitations (Goss, 1993c, p. 26). In 1994, for example, Heritage Publishing Company of Sherwood, Arkansas agreed to pay $200,000 after the FTC charged that it had made fraudulent telephone and direct-mail appeals to donors across the country ("Ark. company," 1994). Proposed legislation would allow the IRS to tighten its criteria for granting tax-exempt status in order to prevent "the spread of sham charities created to benefit a professional fund-raising company" (Goss, 1993c, p. 31). Pending laws would lift privacy restrictions barring the IRS from sharing findings of its investigations with state regulators.

Both levels of government oversight, however, are seriously understaffed. The IRS assigns only about 500 agents nationwide to the task of monitoring 1.16 million nonprofits, of which more than 626,000 are classified 501(c)(3)s; in other words, there is only one agent for every 1,250 registered charitable organizations (H. T. Davis & Thomas, 1996; IRS, 1996). The service currently audits only about 2% of the Form 990s filed every year (Fleishman, 1995). NAAG reports that there are fewer than 90 state-employed attorneys with ongoing responsibility in charitable regulation, and one third of them are located in either New York or California. As of 1997, the IRS is in its second consecutive year of budget cuts, and Congress has pledged to further reduce its size and clout (J. Moore & Williams, 1996b). The headquarter's charity division, which decreased from 85 to 73 professionals in the previous 3 years, has been ordered to layoff 18 more employees. A former IRS commissioner warned, "If the revenue service is less efficient—and it will be—then the bad guys [sic] will have less chance of getting caught" (p. 1).

Turning to the other side, a group of approximately 40 organizations and solicitation firms formed a "public-interest law firm" in late 1995 to challenge the states' "egregious laws" (Murawski, 1995d, p. 32). The new initiative is being led by the National Federation of Nonprofits, guided by Executive Director Lee Cassidy and three lawyers: Geoffrey Peters, Seth Perlman, and Erroll Copilevitz. The lawyers said the group's first action would be against registration regulations. According to Jon Pratt in a message on Internet's ARNOVA forum (October 17, 1995), members of the group had disclosed earlier that targeted states "will be carefully selected for their inability to mount an adequate defense," either because of weak laws or a lack of "seasoned legal counsel." Public announcement of the initiative revealingly featured AICR as representative of the organizations willing to pay $5,000 each to initially fund the court challenge. AICR's Executive Vice President Kelly Browning (cited in E. Greene, 1995) ironically proclaimed:

> These regulatory issues have been on the minds of a number of non-profits across the country for a number of years and finally people are at the point where they feel like something needs to be done to take a more proactive stance. A lot of the regulatory initiatives throw the baby out with the bath water. They really harm a lot of legitimate non-profits in an attempt to get what the regulators see as the bad guys [sic]. (p. 27)

Other contributors to the initiative, as reported by Pratt in his Internet message (October 17, 1995), include the American Military Society, Christian Appalachian Project, Priests of the Sacred Heart, Council for Government Reform, American Kidney Fund, and National Federation of the Blind—the group responsible for the Supreme Court's 1988 decision (*Riley*). Pratt described, "The organizations involved tend to be lesser known groups with a single office and little presence (other than mail and telephone solicitations) in the states in which they seek funds."

Responding to news of the litigation project and its backing by the National Federation of Nonprofits, Richard Allen (cited in Murawski, 1995d), chief of the Public Charities Division in the Massachusetts Attorney General's Office, protested, "I'm frustrated that this segment of the charitable sector would seek to spend time and resources to handcuff charity regulators rather than work with us to prevent fraud and deception that is occurring in every state on a daily basis" (p. 32). Some regulators appropriately saw greed behind the initiative—the self-interests of solicitation firms and their team of lawyers. Francine Giani (cited in Murawski, 1995d), director of Utah's Consumer Protection Division, reacted: "These are the guys [sic] who are making money off the charities. They stand to gain so much. It's just a joke" (p. 32).

In late 1996, the public-interest law firm, deceptively named Charities USA, announced that it would soon sue the City of Los Angeles, California "over its requirement that charities register there before soliciting" (G. Williams, 1996b, p. 31).[7] Geoffrey Peters, who described himself as a volunteer lawyer for the organization, even though it is housed in his McLean, Virginia offices, stated, "It would be nice to be able to negotiate with regulators about problems that we have in common and how

---

[7]The group changed its name a few months later to American Charities for Reasonable Fundraising Regulation, and redirected its efforts to other locations after a federal judge struck down key parts of Los Angeles' registration laws (Craig, 1997a).

to solve those problems, but first you have to get their attention" (p. 31). At the same time Peters presented plans for the lawsuit at the 1996 annual meeting of the National Federation of Nonprofits, the National Council of Nonprofit Associations—a group representing 25 state coalitions of charitable organizations, including the Minnesota council headed by Pratt—announced at the 1996 joint meeting of NASCO and NAAG that it planned "to work more closely with state regulators on efforts to help tax-exempt groups better understand and follow state laws" (p. 31). Regulators praised the latter initiative.

The fund-raising associations have been silent about the National Federation of Nonprofits and its litigation. CASE, in fact, is a member. Their silence reflects poorly on the occupation's leadership and commitment to self-regulation. In the absence of practitioner criticism, paid solicitors will continue to damage the reputations of all fund raisers and their organizations. As Fleishman (1995) asserted, "We cannot rely on the government alone to guard the integrity of the not-for-profit sector" (p. 32).

Students interested in fund-raising law and ethics should consider the rich possibilities for research in these areas. To the best of my knowledge, no studies except the one by Devillier (1996) have been conducted on state regulators' publicity efforts to educate citizens. Not only would descriptive and comparative studies be welcomed, but quantitative studies could be designed to measure the impact of such efforts on citizens' awareness and understanding. Some states likely are only now considering public-education programs; pre- and posttest measurement would be valuable. We have no case studies chronicling the legal actions against solicitation firms or the organizations that hire them. All documents filed with state regulatory offices are public information, and regulators' reports are free on request. A thesis or dissertation on IRS action in recent years would contribute to our knowledge. Surveys on practitioners' attitudes toward paid solicitors and their use would help bring this vital issue to the forefront of debates about ethics.

JOINT VENTURES

When charitable organizations enter into marketing agreements with for-profit companies, they are engaging in *joint ventures*. The dual purpose of joint ventures is to generate low- or no-cost income for 501 (c) (3) organizations and to provide marketing advantages for companies, also called *commercial coventurers*. In exchange for income, the charitable organization authorizes the use of its name, mission, logo, and sometimes programs and publics for selling a company's products or services. There are five common types of joint ventures: (a) cause-related marketing; (b) corporate sponsorships; (c) collection canisters, honor boxes, and vending machines; (d) gambling; and (e) joint ventures with solicitation firms. The fifth type was addressed in the description of paid solicitors at the beginning of the previous section; the other four are discussed here.

By definition, joint ventures involve market, or *quid pro quo*, exchanges. The company is not making a gift as a corporate donor; it is buying the rights to use the charitable organization's name and other intangible and tangible assets. Consumers are not making gifts as individual donors; they are buying the product or service offered by the company. Whereas both the company and consumers may be motivated to engage in the market exchange because some benefits will flow to the charitable organization, their philanthropic intent is expressed in a commercial transaction. Furthermore, the benefits received from the transactions are significantly greater for the company and consumers than for the organization. The difference often is so great that it amounts to deception. PAS has criticized some joint marketing promotions as vague and misleading. One of its standards of ethical practice is that consumers be told exactly how much or what percentage of the sales price will be received by the organization (J. Moore, 1994).

Because it is derived from market exchanges, the money generated by joint ventures must be treated as earned income, not gifts. Although the income may take the form of royalties on which taxes are not owed, it also may be declared unrelated business income subject to UBIT. Fund-raising managers establish policies, in consultation with the finance and marketing departments and approved by the board of trustees, that guide the organization in its decisions about such agreements. Special care should be taken to counsel members of the dominant coalition about the dangers of joint ventures. They must understand that the organization's reputation will be damaged if there is less than full disclosure about the amount received from a purchase. They must realize that UBIT may have to be paid on the income. They must be made aware that joint ventures encourage and educate donors to expect a "return" from supporting the organization's mission. The more joint ventures are used, the more confusion there will be about what is and what is not a gift. Organizations may one day approach prospective donors for gifts and find themselves soliciting consumers who ask, "What do I get in return?"

The same outcome can be predicted for activities known as "fund raisers," which—as discussed in chapter 7—rely on the sale of products or services to generate income. "Fund raisers" are not included here because they do not always involve for-profit companies, the charitable organization's volunteers generally sell the product or service, and those activities require considerable investment in money and/or time. In other words, they are not joint ventures.

Cause-Related Marketing

Cause-related marketing, as denoted in its name, is a marketing strategy used by for-profit companies to sell products and services. The company pays a percentage of the profits or a set amount to a charitable organization in exchange for use of the organization's name and mission. It was invented by American Express in 1981, when the company increased the use of its credit card in California by advertising that it would give state arts groups a sum equal to 1% of the sales charged to the card (Bailey, 1988a). In 1983, American Express took the new strategy national, running a mass advertising campaign that tied use of its card to the Statue of Liberty restoration project. Results were impressive: Card usage increased 28%, the number of new cards issued rose more than 45%, and the Statue of Liberty project got $1.7 million (Dannelley, 1986).

Hundreds of other companies quickly adopted cause-related marketing. The Walt Disney Co., for example, used Children's Miracle Network—a Utah-based federation that raises money for children's hospitals—to help cable companies sell subscriptions to the Disney Channel (C. Smith, 1990). Mr. K's Pizza used the Leukemia Society of

America and the American Diabetes Association to sell frozen pizza ("2 charities," 1991). In the second case, both charitable organizations sued the New York company for delinquent payments in violation of their joint-venture agreements.

The U.S. Olympic Committee introduced an additional feature for its 1984 games in Los Angeles—the license to use the name of the organization on the products sold, as well as in the advertising. Greenfield (1991) commented: "Was there a public benefit? Yes. Was there a licensing agreement with proprietary rights enjoyed by both parties? Yes. Does such marketing mislead the public in promoting philanthropy? Yes, because the exchange was not a gift" (p. 145).

Cause-related marketing dominated the 1980s. As advertising prices climbed and other marketing strategies proved less effective, companies increasingly turned to charitable organizations to get what Shell (1989) described as "the best of all promotional worlds: higher visibility, a unique image niche resulting from association with worthy projects and stronger ties to the community" (p. 8). Schwartz (1990) claimed it became a substitute for corporate gifts, citing static contributions after 1985 as evidence. He said some stockholders asked, "If we can make money and improve our image through cause-related marketing, why do we even have a corporate contributions budget?" (p. xxvi).

Cause-related marketing spewed *affinity* credit cards in the mid-1980s and ventures with long-distance telephone services in the early 1990s. "Built-in" constituencies became viable markets for companies looking for customers. Colleges and universities, in particular, began generating low-cost income by allowing companies to use their identification and alumni mailing lists. At my own university, LDDS Communications (1993) became the "official long distance carrier" for the *Ragin' Cajuns* (p. 37). An advertisement in the alumni magazine told readers:

> As a participant in the program, you can take advantage of group buying power to substantially reduce your phone bill. And LDDS will donate a portion of your monthly payment to the University of Southwestern Louisiana Alumni and Athletic Associations, no strings attached, to help them continue to meet their ambitious goals. (p. 37)

Few have questioned whether alumni might one day view their monthly payments on phone services or credit cards as their "annual gift" to alma mater. Estimates in 1994 placed the number of charitable and other nonprofits participating just in affinity credit-card programs at 7,000 or more (Zapler, 1994). The IRS, it should be noted, has ruled in a few cases that individuals can claim a charitable deduction for the portion of their affinity credit-card bill that is forwarded to a 501(c)(3) organization.

In contrast, the IRS regards the income an organization receives from phone services and affinity credit cards as taxable at the corporate rate of 34%. It has ruled on several occasions that a charity must pay UBIT on money it earns from referring customers to a long-distance telephone company in exchange for a percentage of the profits. In one *Private Letter Ruling*, which the IRS periodically issues without naming the involved parties, an affiliated foundation of a professional association wanted to recruit association members to sign up with a phone service that would give the foundation a portion of the collected revenues ("Charity told," 1995). The foundation planned to promote the agreement in its publications with ads stating that people who became customers would be helping to support the foundation's work. The IRS ruled that the agreement was not related to the group's charitable or educational purpose, and, therefore, taxes would have to be paid on any money earned from the deal. The foundation had asked that the earnings be considered royalties.

Royalties are payments made for the rental of something of value that belongs to another organization. They are exempt from taxation. Whereas earned income from royalties cannot be taxed, payments received for providing a commercial service or product are subject to UBIT. The difference between the two forms of earned income has been the source of continuing legal battles over cause-related marketing.

Since the late 1980s, the IRS has decreed that UBIT is owed on money generated by affinity credit cards, that is, payments received from companies for allowing them to print the nonprofit's name and logo on their credit cards (J. Moore, 1992). Among the first to sue was the Sierra Club, which argued that earnings from its affinity credit-card program are not business income but tax-exempt royalties it receives in exchange for licensing the use of intangible assets—its name and logo (S. G. Greene, 1994a). The club won its case in late 1994, but the IRS appealed the decision. Commenting on the legal battle, the club's finance director warned, "This is just Round 1," and experts agreed that the struggle will continue until new laws clarify the legal definitions of royalties and unrelated business income (S. G. Greene, 1994a, p. 33). As of 1997, a decision on the case still is pending.

In the meantime, the University of Oregon and Oregon State University, which had been paying UBIT on the approximately $300,000 in income they receive from affinity credit cards annually, filed lawsuits against the IRS (Zapler, 1994). As reporter Stephen Greene (1994a) stated, "At stake are millions of dollars in non-profit revenues that would flow to the federal Treasury each year if the government's position were to prevail" (p. 33).

Greenfield (1991) hypothesized that cause-related marketing was "a fad" of the 1980s, an idea whose time may have passed as consumers become tired of "the gimmick" and sales fall off (p. 143). He added, "Never philanthropic, this early promise for 'found money' for nonprofit organizations began to evaporate at about the same time that corporations became disillusioned with its promises of added profits" (p. 212). His assessment, unfortunately, was premature.

Building on the Olympic Committee model, the Arthritis Foundation announced in 1994 that it had entered into an agreement with McNeil Consumer Products, a subsidiary of Johnson & Johnson, to allow its name to be used on a new line of over-the-counter pain relievers (J. Moore, 1994). The company expected the four "Arthritis Foundation" products to attract many of the estimated 40 million consumers who suffer from arthritis, thereby giving it a marketing advantage over competing brands that consist of the same ingredients. In exchange, the foundation was to get at least $1 million a year (in violation of PAS' standard, the amount of the sales price going to the foundation was not disclosed). Advertisements for the product line featured spokesperson Julie Andrews, the actress who first became famous for her role as Mary Poppins.

Managers at other organizations said the venture "could become a new kind of cause-related marketing that everyone will have to get into down the road" (J. Moore, 1994, p. 28). A research director at the Center for the Study of Commercialism in Washington, DC, however, harshly criticized the agreement: "We are very concerned that this kind of deal between non-profits and businesses really compromises the non-profits' integrity" (p. 28).

The concern was well-founded. In late 1996, McNeil dropped the Arthritis Foundation line after 19 state Attorneys General charged that the products had been advertised deceptively (J. Moore, 1996a). Ads, regulators alleged, implied that the pain relievers contained new medication rather then the same ingredients of other brands. In one television commercial cited, Julie Andrews stated: "The Arthritis Foundation is working, too, to find a cure. But until they do, they've helped to create *new* Arthritis Foundation pain reliever, for pain relief we can count on" (p. 64; italics added). McNeil agreed to pay $2 million to cover costs of the investigations and to support research on arthritis at the National Institutes of Health. It also offered refunds to consumers. Contrastingly, the Arthritis Foundation, which approved the ads, paid no penalties and demonstrated no remorse. Its response was that it hoped to find another company that would pay to use its name on products.

Other national organizations have followed in the foundation's footsteps. In August 1996, the American Cancer Society announced an agreement giving Smith-Kline Beecham, the British drug manufacturer, exclusive rights to use the society's name and logo in advertisements and on packaging for NicoDerm antismoking patches (J. Moore, 1996a). The company expects the society's affiliation will be viewed by the 46 million U.S. smokers as an endorsement, thereby generating hundreds of millions of dollars in sales ("Endorsement," 1996). It will pay the society $1 million a year for 3 years. The society will get an additional $1 million in 1997 from the Florida Department of Citrus, a state marketers' association. The American Cancer Society, March of Dimes, and American Heart Association agreed to put their widely recognized names on Florida orange juice in exchange for money (J. Moore, 1996a). The organizations claim the payments represent royalties; the IRS may challenge their claim as the number of charitable identities displayed on store shelves increases.

Announcements of the agreements set off a wave of criticism and negative newspaper editorials. Robert Lawry (cited in J. Moore, 1996a), director of the Center for Professional Ethics at Case Western Reserve University, commented, "As sympathetic as I am to the need for non-profits to have an extra dollar in their pocket and to do good work, this seems to be an inappropriate way to go about the process" (p. 64). He added, "For the sake of making that extra money, there is a real blurring of some lines that ought to be kept as clear as possible" (p. 64). Another ethicist predicted that the trend could result in health organizations someday endorsing everything from tires and chewing gum to sneakers. "We're going to end up with the health equivalent of the Olympics," he said ("Endorsement," 1996, p. 5B). The 1996 Olympic Games, as students probably know, were severely criticized for their commercialism. The reputation of the U.S. Olympic Committee was irrefutably damaged, and international officials promised cutbacks in the amount of cause-related marketing for future games.

Corporate Sponsorships

Whereas the first type of joint venture is a marketing strategy, a corporate sponsorship is an advertising medium by which products or services can be marketed. Corporations purchase advertising exposure much as they would when buying space or time in more traditional media, such as magazines. Providing an example, in 1991, General Mills sponsored a re-created shark exhibit at New Orleans' Aquarium of the Americas to sell its Shark Bites Fruit Snacks ("Big G," 1991). The sponsorship cost $60,000 and included signage and identification on the exhibit, as well as half-price admission to the aquarium for children with proof-of-purchase of the snack food. The cultural organization's former director of special events related the origin of the joint venture: "General Mills asked us to create a local marketing vehicle to generate display activity for Shark Bites in New Orleans" (p. 7).

Patricia Martin (1996) confirmed, "Corporate sponsorship is not philanthropy" (p. 30). The American Library Association's decision to use sponsorships, she said, "fundamentally changed the way our development office worked" (p. 30). She elaborated, "We had to learn a new language: *deals, trade overlays* and *return-on-investment* replaced *pledges, recognition* and *stewardship* in our speech" (p. 30). Based on her experience, Martin advised, "To succeed in sponsorship, an organization must see itself as a marketing opportunity for companies" (p. 30).

Corporate sponsorships, also called *event sponsorships*, are big business. International Events Group (IEG), which publishes a directory and an industry newsletter now named *IEG Sponsorship Report*, projected that sponsorship spending in North America would reach $5.4 billion in 1996, up from only $850 million in 1985 (International Events Group, 1996). For more than 10 years, the Chicago-based group has held an annual event-marketing seminar that attracts hundreds of sponsors, agents, and *properties*, which is the term used for charitable organizations. According to IEG, "Sponsorship relies on borrowed imagery. Sponsors *buy the right* to associate their product or service with the goodwill and audience a property fosters" ("Assertions," 1991, p. 2; italics added). Lexus, for example, promoted its new luxury car in 1991 by signing "a low-six-figure-per-year deal to be official car" of Jazz at Lincoln Center in New York City and "a $50,000 deal for the Ambassador Foundation's jazz programs in Pasadena, Calif." ("Lexus," 1991, p. 1). IEG explained why corporations find sponsorships attractive:

> Companies have never needed sponsorship more because making an impact with traditional media has never been tougher. . . . Sponsorship is the only marketing platform that links companies with leisure pursuits such as sports, culture, entertainment and causes—precisely the type of communication to which today's consumers will respond. ("IEG's ninth," 1991, p. 1)

Seemingly unaware of this perspective from the "other side," many charitable organizations traditionally viewed sponsorship payments as corporate gifts. They were shocked when, in 1991, the IRS ruled that payments from companies to organizers of two college football games in Texas, the Mobil [Oil] Cotton Bowl and the John Hancock [Insurance] Bowl, were not charitable gifts but taxable business income that the 501(c)(3) organizations received in exchange for advertising (J. Moore, 1992). Panic ensued as all types of organizations contemplated paying 34% in taxes on "gifts" made in relation to events.

Congress stepped in, passing legislation in 1992 that excluded sponsorship payments for most public events from UBIT. The bill also defined *qualified* sponsorship payments, or those exempt from taxation. Payments would not be subject to UBIT if made without expectation of receiving a substantial return benefit (Hopkins, 1996).

In other words, to qualify for exemption, sponsorship payments would have to meet a fundamental rule governing the tax deductibility of gifts—charitable intent. Whether or not the sponsored event was related or unrelated to the recipient organization's exempt purpose was irrelevant. The type and degree of benefits returned to the funder would determine whether the payment constituted business income or gift income. As explained in chapter 7, the 1992 bill was never signed.

Mistakenly assuming that the legislation was enacted, many organizations returned to "business as usual." They continued to engage in this type of joint venture and to treat all money received from companies as gifts. Fund raisers who understood the warnings from the federal government developed policies differentiating sponsorship payments from corporate contributions. When money is provided by a corporation for the expressed purpose of marketing its products or services (e.g., advertisements are required, there is a contract describing exposure, and complimentary admissions are issued), it is an unqualified sponsorship payment, and the income likely is subject to UBIT. When a corporation transfers funds in its own name with no expected return other than recognition (e.g., displaying a company's name or logo), it is a qualified sponsorship payment, or a corporate contribution. However, if the contribution is made in the name of a specific product or service of the corporation (e.g., Miller Lite beer, instead of the Miller Brewing Company), a portion of the gift—depending on the amount of recognition provided—should be considered payment for advertising and be designated taxable income.

The last point is clarified by the difference between product advertising and corporate, or institutional, advertising. The purpose of the first is to sell a product or service; it is a marketing technique. The purpose of the second is to enhance reputation; it is a public relations technique.

In 1993, the IRS issued proposed regulations dealing with corporate sponsorships, but those rules also were not enacted (G. Williams, 1995). As Hopkins (1996) pointed out, there is much proposed law, but as of today there is no law to determine whether or not a sponsorship payment is taxable. The 1992 bill, he predicted, eventually will be adopted.

Honor Boxes With No Honor

Collection canisters, honor boxes, and vending machines primarily generate profits for businesses. Students likely have seen these devices in restaurants, convenience stores, or gas stations. Typically, canisters are placed by cash registers to encourage customers to deposit their change in support of a "cause." Vending machines and honor boxes offer a small food item, such as gum balls or mints, in exchange for a specified amount. The devices range from commercial equipment with sophisticated labeling to cardboard boxes with handwritten signs.

Most people assume the devices are placed in their locations by the charitable organization identified on them and that the money given belongs to that organization. Wrong! Companies manufacture the devices and sell them to salespeople who place and maintain them. Most of the money is kept by the person who owns the device, with the charitable organization receiving only a small amount, usually about $1.50 per device each month. Exploiting philanthropy, this industry has become widespread and lucrative. It also is attracting increased attention from state regulators. The Office of the Attorney General of the Commonwealth of Massachusetts (1992) warned, "While the amount of money a person may place in a canister or honor box may be small, the total amount of money raised is significant" (p. 6).

While recently waiting for my car to be repaired, I counted six honor boxes and vending machines in the lobby of the service center. Among them was a cardboard box with lollipops for 25 cents, "sponsored" by the National Exchange Club Foundation for the Prevention of Child Abuse. A sign featured pictures of pathetic-looking children and a notice that a "portion goes to child abuse prevention." Much more sophisticated was a vending machine selling gum, "sponsored" by the American Heart Association. Aside from its well-known name and logo, the only information offered was "Fund Raising [sic] Program." Another vending machine, sponsored by the March of Dimes, displayed more information. A label listed Curtis Products and informed the consumer that "15% of purchase goes to March of Dimes." It also stated that $10 million had been "generated" since 1985.[8]

Shortly after moving to Louisiana, my husband responded to a newspaper advertisement about a small business opportunity. The business turned out to be a franchise to place honor boxes with candy bars at local sites. The franchises, which were then being sold for $7,500, included joint-venture agreements with charitable organizations that would get about 1% of the wholesale price of the candy. Therefore, if a franchise holder paid $100 wholesale for candy bars and sold them in an organization's name for $200, he or she would get $100 and the company selling the candy would get $100, of which $1, or 0.5% of the amount "given" would be transferred to the charity. My husband turned down the opportunity.

Whereas businesses' involvement can be explained—although not condoned—by for-profit motives, it is difficult to understand why organizations would lend their name to such deception. Yet *The Washington Post* concluded from its investigation that the reason is simple: "Even if charities get only a tiny amount of the money raised from the devices, they still are getting thousands of dollars with little or no effort" ("'The Washington Post,'" 1993, p. 37). Through licensing arrangements with third parties, charitable organizations sell their integrity and ridicule the trust of their publics.

In the wake of consumer complaints and media reports, several states have begun regulating these devices. For example, a 1995 Alabama law requires a disclosure label in a conspicuous place on all candy containers sponsored by charitable organizations ("Ala. charities," 1995). The label must state exactly what portion of the sales proceeds will be used for program services and what portion is paid to collect the money and maintain the equipment. There is little doubt more states soon will enact similar laws. There also is little doubt the IRS will be interested in UBIT on the income received by organizations.

---

[8]Until late 1996, the March of Dimes had a contract with Curtis Products, guaranteeing the charity 10% (not 15%) of revenues from the company's vending machines across the country (Blum, 1997). The charity received $15 million between 1980 and 1995. It canceled the contract after Michael Curtis, owner of the company and one of the charity's trustees, failed to forward revenue or make payments on $2 million he owed from previous years. New York State regulators currently are investigating whether the March of Dimes violated disclosure laws by not reporting the credit it extended to Curtis.

Gambling

Charitable gambling is a big industry. It is legal in every state except Arkansas, Hawaii, Tennessee, and Utah (National Association of Fundraising Ticket Manufacturers [NAFTM], 1996). Money spent on charitable gambling has increased 144% since 1985. Based on figures from only 31 states and the District of Columbia, NAFTM reported that, in 1995, Americans bet $7.6 billion, but just 10% went to the sponsoring organizations. Averages for states that supplied the most complete figures showed that organizations received a slightly smaller portion, 9%; 74% of the gross receipts were used to pay prizes to winners, 3% to pay taxes to government, and 14% to pay expenses to commercial coventurers. As it has in previous years, Minnesota held the dubious honor of leading the nation in total receipts: Its residents gambled away about $1.4 billion, of which only $77 million, or 6%, went to organizations that provided their names, missions, and—sometimes—volunteers. In South Carolina, just 1% of $90 million was returned. Stated another way, South Carolina charities get about one penny of every dollar wagered.

Slightly more than half the money from charitable gambling is generated from game tickets, also known as pull-tabs, jar tickets, break-opens, instant bingo, and Lucky 7s (NAFTM, 1996). Bingo accounts for over one third of the annual gross receipts. Other popular forms of what coventurers prefer to call *gaming* are raffles and Las Vegas, or casino, nights. As pointed out in chapter 7, charitable organizations must pay UBIT on income from gambling except for bingo, which is exempted by federal law. Money given to participate in games of chance is not tax deductible as gifts. Failure to inform consumers of this fact, as well as the small percentage of proceeds received by the organization, is unethical. It also, unfortunately, is standard practice.

Whereas organizations of all kinds rely on gambling revenues, bingo traditionally has been identified with the Roman Catholic Church, whose schools and parishes conduct games as "fund raisers" and joint ventures. A study of the fund-raising function in New England Catholic elementary and secondary schools found that one third of the $12 million raised by the 195 responding schools the year before the study came from bingo (New England Association of Catholic Development Officers [NEACDO], 1993). Another third came from special events. According to the NEACDO report, bingo is an artifact of previous eras when money was raised by nonspecialists. The fund-raising function moved into Catholic high schools in the 1970s and into elementary schools and parishes by the mid-1980s. Although only 22% of the Catholic elementary schools in the New England study employed fund raisers in 1993, 77% of the high schools had practitioners on staff. The report concluded that net profits from bingo are diminishing.

It is likely that bingo and other forms of gambling will soon disappear as a source of income for charitable organizations. Legalization of noncharitable gambling is quickly reducing the profitability of this type of joint venture. Illustrating, Louisiana's Charitable Gaming Division reported that $49 million was distributed to charities from bingo in 1992, but only about $40 million was expected for 1993 (Redman, 1993). Competition from the state-sponsored lottery, video poker machines, riverboat gambling, and Native American casinos has changed Louisiana gambling since 1991 from a $900-million industry consisting primarily of bingo and horse racing to an expanded $4-billion industry (which will grow even more when a $1-billion casino opens in New Orleans). Legislators are sympathetic to the fate of organizations finding it harder to raise money from joint ventures with bingo halls, but the state gets little revenue from such gambling, whereas it gets a substantial amount from the lottery and commercial games. In 1995, charitable gambling represented just 6% of the Louisiana gambling industry's total gross income (NAFTM, 1996). States, like other levels of government, need money.

Charitable organizations are partly responsible for the recent flourish of legalized gambling. In 1987, the U.S. Supreme Court ruled that Native American tribes are entitled to run on their reservations, free of state regulation, any form of gambling allowed elsewhere in the state ("Charity gambling on the way out," 1993). Congress passed the necessary legislation 1 year later, and federal and state lawmakers concluded, "The same laws which permit church-run gambling also pave the way for full-scale casinos on Native American reservation land" (p. 8). Furthermore, by promoting games of chance, charitable organizations helped make gambling socially acceptable, which allowed states to implement lotteries. One result is what critics are calling an epidemic of gambling addiction.

According to the IRS, organizations are drawn into gambling joint ventures "by the promise of getting steady income for very little effort" (S. G. Greene & Williams, 1993, p. 31). An IRS official explained: "A for-profit operator becomes attractive to charities that just don't have much money. The operators walk in and say, 'We can get it going for you, we can give you the initial money to get it going. It's easy to do'" (S. Greene & Williams, 1993, p. 31). The IRS announced in late 1995 that it was stepping up its scrutiny of gambling. Marc Owens (cited in "Charity gambling and pay," 1995), the division director introduced in chapter 7, stated, "The propensity of tax-exempt organizations to use gambling of almost every form to generate revenue has not gone unnoticed" (p. 41). Owens said the service was particularly interested in making sure the large sums of money such activities bring in have been raised legally.

Charitable gambling is corrupt and reform is urgently needed. Journalist David Johnston (1993b) asserted, "From cheating players with dishonest pull-tabs to skimming the winnings to using non-profit groups to launder money from whorehouses and drugs, charity gambling is a growing scandal" (p. 39). This type of joint venture, according to Johnston, has drawn scam artists and organized crime. For example, investigative reporters in Minnesota found that 78% of the Form 990s filed by 2,000 organizations revealed problems ranging from bad accounting to thievery. One third had excessive expenses, indicating that the coventurers were diverting proceeds by inflating their fees and costs.

The Pennsylvania Crime Commission found that racketeers operated bingo games for charities—including churches and synagogues—and skimmed millions of dollars from the take, leaving the charities with as little as 1.7% of the receipts (S. G. Greene & Williams, 1993). The South Carolina Tax Commission proclaimed in a 1992 report that the state's $90-million bingo industry "is permeated with fraud, misrepresentation and the diversion of monies" (S. G. Greene & Williams, 1993, p. 29). Illustrating, games operated by coventurers on behalf of an unnamed national organization grossed more than $35 million in South Carolina over 3 years, but the organization received only $250,000, or less than 1%, and all but $20,000 of the amount went to administrative expenses. A commission spokesperson stated, "For the most part, these charities didn't give a rip about what [the coventurers] were doing. As long as they got their monthly check, they didn't care about it" (S. G. Greene & Williams, 1993, p. 29).

Johnston (1993b) concluded, "Corruption has become so common that the whole barrel stinks" (p. 38). He urged leaders to take a stand, at least so they can say they tried to put a stop to it. "Now," Johnston admonished, "the best that can be said is that they knew and looked the other way" (p. 39).

Similar conclusions can be drawn about all types of joint ventures. They do not involve philanthropic exchanges, and their dangers and abuses must be acknowledged. Rosenman (1992) argued that charitable organizations often operate more like for-profit companies than like entities whose purpose is to serve society. As a result, he said, "It's no longer as clear why non-profits are different from other organizations—and therefore deserving of special tax status and other perquisites" (p. 40). Providing a summary to the related discussions of solicitation firms and joint ventures, Rosenman charged, "In the face of such wrongs, too many charities have remained silent. We have ignored the unethical—and possibly illegal—activities we have witnessed, failed to condemn the worst among us, and implicitly colluded in the loss of the special qualities that distinguish the non-profit world" (p. 41).

PRESUPPOSITIONS AND ETHICS

The ends of fund raising do not justify the means. According to Boris and Odendahl (1990), "Since the goals of philanthropy are usually considered worthy and above question, the ethical implications of the means are not often seriously examined" (p. 189). Decisions about how gifts will be raised, Smurl (1991) argued, must be based on "morally warranted premises and presuppositions" (p. 14).

The four fund-raising models, or the means by which charitable organizations raise gifts, reflect two different sets of presuppositions: asymmetrical and symmetrical. Whereas symmetrical presuppositions lead to ethical practice, asymmetrical presuppositions promote the idea that the purpose for which gifts are raised excuses unethical behavior. The latter viewpoint, unfortunately, is common. Payton et al. (1991) confirmed, "The philosophy of fund raising is often a crude form of pragmatism ('vulgar pragmatism,' one might say)—opportunistic and manipulative. If it works, it's good (or good enough)" (p. 276).

Blades and Milofsky (1992) illustrated the viewpoint in their discussion of protests against Jerry Lewis and the annual Labor Day telethon for MDA. They described Lewis' response to criticism that the show he hosts demeans the disabled:

> Without him, millions of dollars would not be raised. That money does good for many, and therefore, he argued, his efforts are justified. The fact that he portrays disabled kids as cute victims is unimportant if this ploy is the very device that causes people to donate. The donated money more than offsets whatever (hypothetical) symbolic damage is caused by the appeal. (p. 27)

Calling them "Jerry's Orphans," Blades and Milofsky said muscular dystrophy patients who have turned protesters "are one manifestation of a broad movement among the disabled to challenge images of helplessness conveyed by fundraising [sic] appeals and practices embedded in organizational policies that critics claim conflict with the interests of clients or potential clients" (p. 7).

In his book about the disability rights movement, Shapiro (1993) reported that among all fund-raising telethons, the harshest criticism has been directed at MDA's Labor Day event. Other organizations, he said, have gotten rid of the pity approach. For example, the National Easter Seal Society now uses its telethon to highlight the accomplishments of disabled people. MDA, on the other hand, has denied charges and held firm in its support of Lewis. Significantly, in 1992, MDA announced a $9-million shortfall caused by the weak economy and protests by activists during its telethon ("Muscular-Dystrophy," 1992). The 1993 Easter Seal Telethon, in contrast, broke its previous record by raising $48 million ("Easter Seal," 1993).

Shapiro (1993) presented another example of an organization that responded to client demands even when fund-raising concerns were at issue. In 1991, the Association for Retarded Citizens (ARC) changed its name to The Arc because it was urged to do so by many of its clients who do not like to be called "retarded." ARC's officials, according to Shapiro, were concerned that money would be harder to raise with a name that did not clearly state the organization's purpose, but made the change anyway because they wanted to show their respect for the people served by the organization.

Metaphors and Asymmetrical Presuppositions

Over the past 20 years, increased attention has been given to the role of metaphors in management theory and practice. One of the main ways of approaching metaphors is as indicators of the presuppositions held by managers about their situations and actions. Kay (1994) recommended such an "interpretist perspective" in his essay on the leadership process in nonprofits. The perspective, Kay said, "reflects a belief in the interrelationship of thought, language, sense making, and reality, including action" (p. 287).

Turner (1991) took this approach in his study of metaphors used by fund raisers. He explained, "The presence of the metaphor suggests an orientation of values and perceptions of reality that are significant and worthy of comment" (p. 38). "Metaphors are not detachable figures that we choose to use or not to use. Rather, they are part of the way we articulate ourselves and our understandings about the people and the things around us" (p. 43).

To identify fund-raising metaphors, Turner examined practitioner literature such as the NSFRE *Journal* (predecessor to *Advancing Philanthropy*) and *Fund Raising Management*, the commercial monthly magazine. He found that the most prominent metaphors are military images: *prospects bombarded with solicitations, enlist volunteers, target prospects,* and *capturing a gift.* He questioned the appropriateness of such images, saying that a military campaign may be a useful metaphor for creating a sense of urgency, "but the metaphor is perhaps not so useful for the sense of mission and for the position taken toward the people the campaign will address (the enemy?)" (p. 44).

Professor of philosophy Allen Buchanan (1993) reported the results of a similar study during a presentation titled "Talking Philanthropically." He said that whereas fund raisers insist there is no conflict of party interest in the philanthropic exchange, their language reveals otherwise. He, like Turner, pointed to the pervasive use of war metaphors: *targeting donors, launching campaigns, hit on prospects, volunteers in trenches*, and *divide-and-conquer strategy*. There would be no need for these metaphors, Buchanan argued, if a conflict did not exist.

Using game theory, prevailing metaphors of military and war suggest widely held presuppositions about relationships with donors as win–lose situations—either the donor or charitable organization can win, but not both. Fund raisers holding such presuppositions approach donors with the intention of winning (i.e., their intended effect is unbalanced, or asymmetrical). In contrast, Steele and Elder (1992) advocated symmetrical presuppositions, saying the ultimate goal of fund raising is "reaching a win–win outcome for both donor and recipient" (p. 65). They elaborated: "Following a successful solicitation, both giver and receiver should believe that their best interests have been served. The prospect is not an adversary, not a quarry or prey who must be trapped, cornered, or captured" (p. 65).

Turner (1991) said fund-raising traditions are apparent in the language practitioners use. Furthermore, he stated, "The pervasiveness of the metaphor and the casual way in which we use and regard such usages suggest the degree to which they are part of the fabric of our conceptions" (p. 42). In other words, warlike terms to describe fund raising may be shrugged off as harmless jargon, but their extensive and common use actually demonstrates ingrained acceptance of asymmetrical concepts, such as manipulating donors for the good of the organization.

A. E. Buchanan (1993) linked the discourse of fund raising directly to ethics. He said ethics has to do with character, and language illuminates character, providing keys that tell us something about attitudes and motivation. He concluded from his analysis that fund raisers' discourse reflects badly on their characters.

Turner (1991) claimed gender and race affect linguistic choices. Therefore, he predicted, "The increasing feminization of fund raising as a profession will influence the metaphors fund raisers use, pushing back the prominence of military metaphors and substituting metaphors that emphasize cooperation and mutual dependence" (p. 45). If his prediction proves accurate, women will have advanced adoption of symmetrical presuppositions.

Symmetrical Presuppositions

Barbara Marion (1994), NSFRE's 1995 Outstanding Fund-Raising Executive, former national chair of the association, and a longtime member of its ethics committee, discussed 12 values for ethical decision making in fund raising, which—collectively—describe symmetrical presuppositions about the practice. The 12 values are honesty, integrity, promise-keeping, fidelity/loyalty, fairness, caring for others, respect for others, responsible citizenship, pursuit of excellence, accountability, safeguarding the public trust, and duty. Marion used each of the values to define rules. For example, communications with donors should be open, honest, and clear, avoiding exaggerated claims and misleading descriptions. Integrity prohibits bending the organization's mission to get funding, allowing activities to drag the organization away from its mission, or looking the other way at bad policies or questionable tactics.

Based on promise keeping, fund raisers abide by the spirit and terms of a gift and do not allow the misuse of funds. They do not put personal interest above organizational interest, or organizational interest above mission interest. They do not manipulate or exploit prospects; they honor donor motivations and avoid doing harm. As Marion emphasized, respect requires candor about needs and the manner in which the organization's program services will or will not solve society's problems. It means being cautious about how prospect research is conducted and diligent about how information is protected. Responsible citizenship requires adherence to all laws and to the concept of social responsibility. Fund raisers are committed to excellence in their own work and that of their organization.

Defining rules on accountability, Marion (1994) included full disclosure of how funding is used (e.g., disseminating information on fund-raising cost ratios), being "a scrupulous steward" of contributed dollars, confronting issues—even difficult ones—directly and quickly, and planning for the future of the organization "by projecting future demands and cultivating for future support" (p. 54). She said fund raisers serve as guardians of philanthropy, safeguarding and advancing "the integrity and reputation of those organizations which depend on voluntary support" (p. 54), avoiding even the appearance of impropriety. Regarding the last value, she argued that practitioners have a special duty "to act in the best interests of the donor" (p. 55). Contradicting asymmetrical presuppositions, she explained, "It means we have a duty to give information that allows an informed decision, a duty to assure that the legitimate interests of the donor are protected, a duty to avoid manipulation or intimidation, and a duty to seek funds only for worthy organizations" (p. 55).

Lending support for ethical practice, the "Donor Bill of Rights," developed in 1993 by AHP, CASE, NSFRE, and AAFRC, also is based on symmetrical presuppositions. The bill emphasizes disclosure, social responsibility, two-way communication, truth, and interdependency. It represents an imperfect but first stand against paid solicitors. For example, the bill declares that prospective donors have the right "to be informed whether those seeking gifts are volunteers, employees of the organization, or hired solicitors." Its 10 tenets, in many ways, are stronger than the codes of ethics of the individual associations.

Furthermore, the bill's preamble is highly congruent with the framework for fund raising presented in this book. It adopts the concept of *common good*, rather than the nebulous *public good*. It identifies philanthropy as an American tradition of giving and sharing. It acknowledges the dual levels of accountability to the "general public," as well as to the specific publics of donors and prospective donors. Finally, it advances self-regulation by assuming that charitable organizations must continually demonstrate their worthiness of confidence and trust. Ethical fund raising begins with adoption of Marion's (1994) symmetrical rules and the Donor Bill of Rights, which is reproduced in Fig. 8.1.

Jeavons (1991) advised practitioners to avoid approaches, or what this book considers models, that are inconsistent with the core values of the organization. Describing press agentry, he said fund-raising practices that "manipulate potential donors by playing on their fears or guilt, or that are in any sense finally false will ultimately destroy the cause they seek to support" (p. 71). He declared, "Noble ends cannot be long sustained by ignoble means; giving and getting need to be marked by grace, not greed" (p. 71).

With this warning in mind, the chapter concludes with an examination of the United Way system and its predominant practice of the press agentry model.

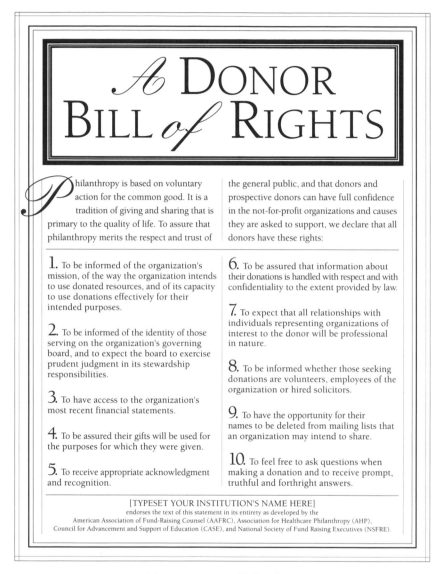

A DONOR BILL of RIGHTS

Philanthropy is based on voluntary action for the common good. It is a tradition of giving and sharing that is primary to the quality of life. To assure that philanthropy merits the respect and trust of the general public, and that donors and prospective donors can have full confidence in the not-for-profit organizations and causes they are asked to support, we declare that all donors have these rights:

1. To be informed of the organization's mission, of the way the organization intends to use donated resources, and of its capacity to use donations effectively for their intended purposes.

2. To be informed of the identity of those serving on the organization's governing board, and to expect the board to exercise prudent judgment in its stewardship responsibilities.

3. To have access to the organization's most recent financial statements.

4. To be assured their gifts will be used for the purposes for which they were given.

5. To receive appropriate acknowledgment and recognition.

6. To be assured that information about their donations is handled with respect and with confidentiality to the extent provided by law.

7. To expect that all relationships with individuals representing organizations of interest to the donor will be professional in nature.

8. To be informed whether those seeking donations are volunteers, employees of the organization or hired solicitors.

9. To have the opportunity for their names to be deleted from mailing lists that an organization may intend to share.

10. To feel free to ask questions when making a donation and to receive prompt, truthful and forthright answers.

[TYPESET YOUR INSTITUTION'S NAME HERE]
endorses the text of this statement in its entirety as developed by the
American Association of Fund-Raising Counsel (AAFRC), Association for Healthcare Philanthropy (AHP),
Council for Advancement and Support of Education (CASE), and National Society of Fund Raising Executives (NSFRE).

FIG. 8.1. A Donor Bill of Rights.

UNITED WAY AND PRESS AGENTRY FUND RAISING

For most Americans, those organizations commonly known as the United Way symbolize the charitable subsector. They are highly visible in almost every community—raising and distributing billions of dollars each year. Their pervasiveness was demonstrated in 1992, when the scandal that erupted at UWA sent shock waves across the country. Disclosure of facts surrounding the forced resignation of CEO William Aramony was, according to Bush (1994), a "seismic jolt to the field" (p. 31). She asserted, "In many ways, this episode may have done more to erode the regulators' confidence in the integrity of the not-for-profit sector than the [Watson and Hughey] sweepstakes did" (p. 31).

The scandal's impact on fund raising warrants an examination of the United Way. Details reported by the media because of the scandal, in addition to findings of scholars, provide the material for a case study of organizations predominantly practicing the press agentry model—and the negative consequences of doing so. The discussion is broken down into three time periods: (a) prescandal, (b) scandal, and (c) postscandal. By taking a long-term perspective, current behavior can be tied to historical precedents and predictions about the future can be made. It also allows us to identify changes, most notably a shift in United Way fund raising toward the two-way models in the late 1970s and a proposed strategic plan in 1995 that promotes symmetrical concepts.

Students are cautioned to remember that organizations practice all four models to some extent, but they practice one predominantly. Although changes can be observed in United Way's tactics and strategies, its fund raising remains press agentry in character.

Prescandal

The "United Way of America" (UWA) was created in 1970 to bring a centralizing force and national image to the many community organizations conducting federated fund raising under diverse names, such as Community Chest, United Fund, and United Way (Brilliant, 1990). It successfully advocated nationwide use of a single name and a single logo—the highly recognized helping hand holding a rainbow. Before the 1992 scandal, the organizations were known individually and collectively as *the* United Way, singular. After the scandal, the organizations emphasized their independence by insisting that the correct name was the United Ways, plural.

The 2,000 United Ways (UWs) are autonomous in that each is a separate federation, governed by its own board. Each raises gifts in its own area—directly from businesses and individuals employed by businesses, government, and nonprofits. Each distributes the money to multiple organizations in its own community—its *members*. Regardless, the UWs behave as a system rather than distinct entities. Their commonness is evident in their operations, structure, the organizations they fund, and the way they practice fund raising.

UWA, based in Alexandria, Virginia, represents the system at the national level, interacting with the federal government, Fortune 500 companies, international labor unions, and large foundations. Proponents claim UWA is structured much like a trade association for the community-based UWs. Before the 1992 scandal, however, major corporate donors—not UWs—were predominantly represented on UWA's governing board. Only 1,300 of the 2,000 UWs pay dues to the national organization, generally 1% of the amount raised locally.

In total, the system raises about $3 billion each year on behalf of its members. UW membership traditionally has been restricted to organizations with health and human services missions. Other types of organizations, such as those with missions in education or arts, culture, and humanities, are not eligible. In 1995, 45,000 of the 626,000 charitable organizations registered with the IRS received funding from the UW system (S. Gray, 1995; IRS, 1996).

Members traditionally have been prohibited from soliciting gifts during about 3 months of each year, referred to as a *blackout*. This allows UWs to conduct their local campaigns, most of which are run in the fall. The campaigns, which were given as examples of the press agentry model in chapter 6, are characterized by emotional messages disseminated through the mass media. As Cutlip et al. (1985) described, "The drive is kicked off in September with fanfare and publicity; in press conferences, news stories, and public-service announcements (PSAs) over the air" (p. 152).

The messages play on emotions of neighbor helping neighbor and are designed to build social pressure on community residents to give. The lead of a newspaper article published in my area is typical:

> A car filled with a family and its borrowed belongings arrived at the small United Way office not too long ago. The sunny winter's day was in stark contrast to the trial by tornado they had endured only a few days before. Their home destroyed, their possessions scattered to the four winds, they were running out of places to go. (Delhomme, 1992, p. 1C)

Other press agentry characteristics include kickoff and reporting luncheons with supporting publicity, a large thermometer or clock to visibly record progress, scores of business people and community leaders heading dozens of committees—each composed of dozens of more volunteers—and a continual stream of communication to remind citizens of their obligation to give a "fair share."

Solicitation is carried out almost exclusively in the workplace with employees solicited by other employees, their supervisor, a senior manager, or the CEO. This adds to the social pressure already built by the community publicity. Employees often are reminded that 100% participation is the expected goal in order to successfully compete with other companies and organizations. They receive internal memoranda urging them to make their gifts through automatic payroll deductions. Written communication is reinforced by group meetings in the workplace, complete with videotapes and speeches by UW volunteers and staff. Cutlip et al. (1985) explained, "Organizational rivalries and internal pressures are used to make members of an organization—be it a college, a corporation, or an insurance agency—feel compelled to cooperate to demonstrate that their organization is a 'good community citizen'" (p. 154).

In addition, leadership positions in campaigns are evaluated highly when managers are considered for promotion in their corporations, thereby placing pressure on those eager for career advancement to not only volunteer but to ensure high participation of their coworkers. Reporter Bruce Millar (1992a), who covered the UW beat for *The Chronicle of Philanthropy* during the first half of the 1990s, summarized: "Critics say pressure to give is inherent in the United Way's system of raising money through on-the-job drives. The backbone of the system is competition between business leaders who don't want to be outdone in their commitment to the community" (p. 20).

In short, United Way uses emotion, coercion, and competition to propagandize its cause. Brilliant (1990) argued that the unique position the UWs have established in their communities has suppressed issues surrounding them. Large corporations and their high-profile executives, member organizations, and volunteer groups all have too much at stake to question the federations and their practices. Nevertheless, the UWs' press agentry fund raising provoked criticism long before the 1992 scandal. The historical criticism is broken down here into three major charges: (a) manipulation, (b) mainstream beneficiaries, and (c) monopoly.

Manipulation.   As just described, the manner in which the United Way system raises funds encourages coercion. For years, employees have complained that they often feel their good standing, promotions, raises, and even their jobs might be in jeopardy unless they make a gift. According to Millar (1992a), "United Way of America became so concerned about the number of complaints that in 1977 its board issued a statement declaring that the organization was 'unalterably opposed' to coercive fund-raising tactics" (p. 19). Still, a 1980 study commissioned by UWA found that 25% of the system's donors reported unfair pressure tactics (Cutlip et al., 1985). In 1989, an employee sued the Cleveland Electric Illuminating Company because he claimed he had been fired from his engineering job for "failure to cooperate with the company's policy of giving to United Way" (Melillo, 1989, p. 5). He described the solicitations as "extortion," saying, "the company was arrogantly dictating to people to give was for the wrong reasons" (p. 5).

Lawsuits and increasing complaints have prompted some companies to make all employee contributions to UW campaigns strictly confidential and/or to turn the in-house drives over to more junior employees. Yet Millar (1992a) reported that at many businesses, mandatory attendance at the annual company rally is a frequent precursor to complaints of managerial arm twisting. "Some employees regard the meetings as thinly veiled pressure from management" (p. 19).

Mainstream Beneficiaries.   United Ways historically have been criticized for not being responsive to emerging and important needs in their communities, supporting instead the same established organizations year after year. Until recently, such charges generally were accurate because the UWs—as is true of most federations—were committed to providing a stable funding base for the organizations they had agreed to support at some point in their history (Brilliant, 1990). Therefore, most UW gifts went to longtime members, who—because of their longevity and other factors—are "mainstream" and large, such as the Red Cross and the Boy Scouts.

In fact, the local chapters and affiliates of just 18 national organizations traditionally received about 50% of the total funds allocated by the United Way system ("Charity chiefs," 1992). In addition to the two just mentioned, others receiving most of the money included Catholic Charities USA, Goodwill, Salvation Army, and YMCA. Denoting a status higher than other members, such organizations were referred to as *partners* and usually had contracts guaranteeing them a fixed percentage of UW proceeds. Many of the partners were listed in chapter 3 as examples of large organizations that raise the most money.

Overall, funding followed a base-allocation process; zero-base budgeting, which allocates funds by priority need each year, did not exist. The result was that newer organizations with missions to serve needs not previously widespread, recognized, or considered important (e.g., AIDS, urban crime, and domestic violence) received only a minority portion of all United Way funding.

According to Grønbjerg (1993), pressure from civil rights and other advocacy groups forced most UWs to open their membership to newer groups before 1992. Yet the new members obtained very small levels of support "because only small increments of funds are available once older members have obtained their base allocations" (p. 76). Illustrating, from 1987 to 1991, new members of the Mid-America United Way in Chicago received—on average—10% of the allocations to older members ($50,000 vs. $500,000). This limitation was in addition to the one mentioned earlier that organizations with missions outside of health and human services were not eligible for UW membership. Furthermore, strict membership requirements and boards dominated by conservative business people kept out new and controversial organizations (Brilliant, 1990).

Completely abandoning funding procedures, proponents and critics agreed, would place members in financial chaos. Few engaged in comprehensive fund raising because of their long-nurtured reliance. Without some guarantee of future funding, members likely would step up their efforts and actively solicit gifts year round to stabilize finances—putting them in competition with the United Ways. Brilliant (1990) explained the situation in the late 1980s: On one hand, UWs were under pressure to broaden the base of agencies they funded and to be more inclusive; on the other hand, increased client demands and decreased government support required more funding for current members. The situation intensified during the first half of the 1990s.

Although no easy solution existed, the criticism of funding mainstream organizations at the exclusion of other causes was justified because of press agentry practice. Aware of their inability to fund a community's full range of charitable needs, UWs characteristically assumed that companies and employees in the community should give to the campaigns regardless of interest in the organizations receiving the money. And they used guilt, coercion, and competition to ensure that many did.

It is important to emphasize that the system has traditionally solicited unrestricted gifts. Until options for designating gifts were widely offered, which is discussed shortly, donors were asked to trust the UWs and their citizen review process to make the best decisions about which health and human services needs in their community should be funded and for how much. Given the system's history of successfully raising billions of unrestricted dollars, it could be assumed that donors were satisfied with this approach. The assumption is seriously flawed.

Research has documented that UW donors generally are not knowledgeable about the recipients of their gifts. In his study of giving to a midwestern United Way, Ledingham (1993) found little difference between donors' and nondonors' knowledge about which organizations are funded. For example, 45% of the donors inaccurately identified the American Cancer Society as a UW member. An earlier study for the United Way in Dade County, Florida found that knowledge of agency services among participants in four focus groups was "virtually non-existent" (Ledingham, 1993, p. 369). In a survey conducted by National/United Service Agencies, a competing fund-raising federation, the typical respondent estimated that 36% of the nation's charities receive support from the UW system, whereas National/United Service claimed only 7% of all nonreligious organizations are funded by UW ("Poll finds," 1992).

As these studies suggest, ignorance—not satisfaction—may explain much of United Way's historical success. Some donors give because they falsely believe their local UW serves more charitable organizations than it actually does and supports different organizations than the ones actually funded. Brilliant (1990) reported, "Both my own research and the extensive marketing surveys of the United Way itself suggest that widespread publicity about the United Way has not been matched by the transmission of accurate factual knowledge" (p. 4).

Monopoly.   The third and related criticism is that United Way monopolizes fund raising in the workplace. The system raises about 90% of its gift dollars from on-the-job campaigns ("Rise in gifts," 1992). The vast majority take place in the corporate setting.

Businesses not only employ 80% of all U.S. workers, but they are historically interdependent with federated campaigns. As explained by P. D. Hall (1989), the modern concept of federated campaigns—as well as community foundations—resulted from a search during the 1920s by progressive business leaders who were looking for a middle course between socialism and *laissez-faire* capitalism. According to Hall, "They were convinced that capitalism could be a humane and just system if the principles of efficient organization toward which they strove in their enterprises were applied to efforts to solve social problems" (p. 184). The Cleveland Federation for Charity and Philanthropy was created by the Cleveland, Ohio, Chamber of Commerce in 1913. It became the model for the national movement known as the Community Chest. Due to an aggressive education campaign by the U.S. Chamber of Commerce, more than 129 cities were carrying out these coordinated appeals by 1929.

Federated campaigns relied on businesses and other organizations for efficient access to centralized groups of prospective donors—employees. Companies traditionally granted permission for workplace fund raising with the explicit understanding that only one campaign, conducted by one federation, would be allowed each year. This "united approach" reduced costs, disruptions, and difficult decisions incurred by businesses when facing multiple solicitations. It appealed to business managers' principles of efficiency and economy.

Since the early 1980s, the Washington, DC-based National Committee for Responsive Philanthropy (NCRP), which—students will recall—is cochaired by Eisenberg, has been the leading critic of UW's monopoly of workplace fund raising. NCRP charges that the sole-access arrangement limits the ability of employees to contribute to organizations other than the traditional ones funded by UW. NCRP Executive Director Robert Bothwell (1993) complained, "Every study ever conducted on United Way shows that United Ways generally give most of their allocations to the same fat mainstream non-profits which have the most power and influence in any given community" (p. 40).

Such criticism undergirded the recent increase of competing federations. The National Black United Fund was founded in the early 1960s by African-American leaders who believed the federations now known as United Ways were not directing enough of their resources to inner-city needs and concerns, especially those of Blacks.

According to J. Fink (1990), the fund challenged the hegemony of the UWs over workplace solicitation. "As a result of litigation," he reported, "the fund opened the way for participation in the Combined Federal Campaign and some 500 other federated campaigns across the United States that had previously been limited solely to United Way" (p. 151).

About 172 national federations collectively raised $158 million in 1994, which represented approximately 5% of the amount raised by UW (S. Gray, 1995). Among the largest is Independent Charities of America (ICA), which is both a federation and an umbrella group for 11 other federations that represent such diverse organizations as the American Civil Liberties Union Foundation and the YWCA (Stehle, 1996a). ICA's slogan is "Share the American Way." Founded in 1988, it participated in only five campaigns in 1990. Two years later, ICA solicited gifts on behalf of 245 members in 2,500 on-the-job drives ("Charity federation," 1992). In 1995, it represented nearly 470 organizations and raised $38 million (Stehle, 1996a).[9] Charging 3% overhead on all gifts, ICA actively recruits new members. A press agentry tone is apparent in a 1992 advertisement for applications:

> There is a revolution in workplace giving going on, and your organization should be a part of it. Hundreds of at-work, payroll deduction fund drives are opening up to non-United Way organizations. Not just for "write-in-gifts," but for full and equal participation. [ICA] can get you in the door. (Independent Charities of America, 1992, p. 17)

In addition to those national in scope, multiple state and local federations have also recently emerged to challenge the UWs. For example, Community Shares of Colorado, which includes environmental and women's groups, was established in 1990 as an alternative to the Mile High United Way in Denver (Millar, 1993b). In 1992, the Denver UW raised 13% less than it had the year before, whereas Community Shares almost doubled its contributions.

Efforts to break the monopoly are directed at government and large businesses, where economies of scale make on-the-job solicitations more efficient. By 1995, 50 of the Fortune 500 corporations allowed other federations besides United Way to conduct campaigns (S. Gray, 1995).

UW Response.   United Ways selectively responded to some of the criticisms before the 1992 scandal. As already discussed, most opened their membership to new organizations, although new members obtained only a small portion of the funding. In the late 1970s, UWs began incorporating *donor-choice options* in their campaigns, whereby donors can restrict their gifts to specific members or even designate a nonmember organization as the recipient. Usage of donor options slowly increased over the next decade, and by 1991–1992, about 70% of all UWs allowed donors to

---

[9]In contrast to this rapid growth, Stehle (1996a) reported recent membership losses and internal conflicts at ICA, which some observers say could cause the group's collapse. It lost one federation in 1996, and at least two others are threatening to severe their ties. At issue are ICA's concentration on government campaigns and charges that its founder, Patrick Maguire, receives excessive financial benefits. For example, ICA will pay Maguire's consulting company almost $1 million in 1997.

restrict their gifts to members (Millar, 1994b). The year following the scandal, the percentage increased to 80%; however, only 35% of the UWs allowed donors to earmark their gifts for nonmembers. Adoption of donor-choice options marked a shift in United Way fund raising away from press agentry toward the two-way models.

As Brilliant (1990) emphasized, donor options were not a new idea to the UW system. The federations had practiced some form of designation throughout most of their histories. She explained, however, "Under the previously existing practice of donor option, the designated dollar generally did not go to the agency, and it had essentially no impact on the amount of money that the agency received" (p. 104). Describing it as "a fictional notion of a gift relationship," Brilliant said, "In short, the old form of donor option was on the whole more a matter of appearance than substance, and it was generally minimized in use, and even discouraged by local United Ways" (p. 104). Moreover, old forms were restricted to member organizations; the new form "was developed in order to allow for designations outside the United Way group of funded agencies and, therefore, was intended to serve as a *release valve*, at a time when there was pressure over the limited number of choices in giving at the workplace" (p. 105; italics added).

Many UWs resisted adopting the new options; those that did offer them found that donors increasingly took advantage of the choices. In 1992–1993, restricted gifts accounted for an estimated $377 million, or 13% of the total dollars raised (Millar, 1994b). Regardless, only 12% of all UW donors restricted their gifts, and 85% of those restricted gifts went to UW members. Critics such as NCRP's Bothwell (1993) charged that UWs allowing donor options conveyed the idea that restricted gifts somehow disappear from the common good of the community. As he pointed out, they do not disappear, they just are not controlled by the UWs.

More widespread and flexible usage of donor options evolved in the postscandal period after giving fell and then stayed below the 1992 level. Predictably, the change in fund raising also meant less money for member organizations. S. Gray (1995) summarized, "The popularity of earmarking is squeezing the amount of discretionary money available to local United Ways" (p. 22). The problem was compounded by efforts to extend access to UW membership during the same time. As the pie of unrestricted funds got smaller, it had to be divided into more slices. More members also reduced restricted funding for individual organizations because the options available to donors were expanded.

Illustrating, the United Way of the National Capital Area (Washington, DC) increased its number of members from 260 in 1993–1994 to 700 the next year and allowed donors to direct their gifts to specific members, including such nontraditional types as arts and environmental groups (Dundjerski, 1995). Of the $73 million raised in 1994–1995, an unprecedented 70% was restricted. As a result, annual UW allocations from unrestricted gifts fell dramatically, and many longtime members received fewer restricted dollars. Yet the amount raised was 4% more than the year before, which federation managers attributed to expanded membership; therefore, they announced that 843 organizations would be included in the 1995–1996 campaign (S. Gray, 1995). The Washington president defended greater donor options: "We live in a society where people want to make their own choices on a lot of things" (S. Gray, 1995, p. 29).

Scandal

In 1992, UWA President William Aramony was forced to resign amid allegations that for years he had used the organization's money to subsidize "a high-flying life style that included luxury apartments, personal trips, and kickbacks to his teen-age girlfriend" (Murawski, 1995b, p. 37). For more than 2 years, mass media across the country heralded charges of deception and fraud. In 1994, a federal grand jury indicted Aramony and two associates on charges that they "swindled more than $1-million from the charity to pay for personal expenses" (S. G. Greene & Millar, 1994, p. 31). The 71-count indictment filed against Aramony and two former UWA CFOs, Thomas Merlo and Stephen Paulachak, charged them with conspiracy, tax fraud, and mail fraud, among other illegal activities. All three were found guilty in April 1995, and Aramony was convicted on 25 criminal counts (E. Greene & Murawski, 1995).

The crimes embodied flagrant abuse of money and power. Over a period of at least 6 years, Aramony had used UWA funds to purchase a Florida condominium, help pay for an apartment in New York City, underwrite gambling trips to Las Vegas, and compensate his New York chauffeur to the tune of $78,000. Aramony transferred more than $325,000 of UWA's money to Volunteer Initiative America, a separate organization he created and appointed his son and Merlo to run. Embedded in many of the felonies were Aramony's sexual escapades, including his affair with Lori Villasor, who was 17 years old when then married 58-year-old Aramony began dating her in 1986. UWA funds paid for Aramony's visits to Villasor at her Florida home, supplements to Villasor's income, and lavish European vacations together.

Aramony's lawyers claimed he was a scapegoat for a negligent board of directors (E. Greene & Murawski, 1995). The UWA board, they contended, was aware of Aramony's conduct, but chose to indulge a CEO who had brought praise and fund-raising success to the organization.

In June 1995, the three defendants were sentenced to prison terms (Murawski, 1995b). Aramony was given 7 years in minimum-security prison with an earliest possible release in 2001. He and Merlo were ordered to return a total of $552,000 to United Way.

Following the break of the scandal, the United Ways scrambled to distance themselves from the national UWA. Full-page ads signed by members of local governing boards appeared in newspapers in nearly every community. The ads referred to UWA—perhaps for the first time—as the trade association for the UWs and vehemently asserted that money raised in the community stayed in the community. In my own area, the executive director of the United Way of Acadiana proclaimed in a news article: "We vacuum our own carpets and clean our own sinks around here. United Way of America is far removed from us" (Delhomme, 1992, p. 1C). Yet, as Grønbjerg (1993) argued, the Aramony scandal threw the legitimacy of the entire system into question.

At least 100 UWs, including many of the largest, announced they were withholding national dues (Millar & Moore, 1993). UWA's 1992 budget was cut by 19%; nevertheless, the boycott forced the organization to deplete its operating reserves and in April 1992, to borrow money to meet its payroll. In 1993, 1 year after Aramony's resignation, the number of dues-paying UWs decreased by 300. UWA's budget was reduced 25% (Skolnik, 1993). Resignations had resulted in a staff one third smaller than the year before.

   Aftermath.   In 1991–1992, the UW system had raised $3.2 billion (Millar, 1992b). The year following the scandal, total giving dropped 4%. UWA managers announced that although the federated drives had raised slightly more than $3 billion, 1992–1993 was "the worst fund-raising year United Way has seen since World War II" (Millar, 1993a, p. 33). Furthermore, based on findings from a national poll, managers predicted that local federations would still have to deal with the scandal in their next drives. Robert O'Conner (cited in Millar, 1993a), UWA vice president for research services, concluded, "The one legacy of the crisis is that people still are questioning whether their contributions are handled wisely" (p. 33).

   United Way raised only $3 billion again in 1993–1994 (Millar, 1994d). Totals in 1994–1995 and 1995–1996 were $3.08 billion and $3.15 billion, respectively (Dundjerski, 1995; Stehle, 1996b). In other words, 4 years after the scandal, private support was still $50 million less than in 1991–1992. Annual losses, without accounting for inflation or normally expected increases, totaled roughly $500 million—just one measure of the scandal's cost. Adding to the expense, the number of dues-paying UWs was still 300 fewer in 1996 than in 1992; the lost income from their annual dues represents a significant past and future cost.

   Fewer gift dollars resulted in lower allocations to member organizations. When coupled with increases in membership and donor choice options, cutbacks were severe for longtime members, particularly the 18 partners. For example, in 1992–1993, United Ways provided only 45% of the Red Cross gift income, whereas in the past they had supplied as much as 75% (Millar, 1994c). Red Cross chapters in Chicago, Denver, and San Francisco were among those hardest hit, with cuts of about $1 million each. Many of the smaller chapters that had received up to 95% of their gift dollars from United Way in 1988 were getting only about 40% in 1993.

   Due primarily to declining UW allocations, the Red Cross announced in 1994 that it was making big changes in the way it raises money (Millar, 1994c). The organization and its 2,400 chapters, which had relied on United Way funding for close to 40 years, set a goal to raise $1 billion annually by the year 2000. Plans included special training for chapter fund raisers, new initiatives to raise major and planned gifts, recruitment of more business executives for chapter boards, and a greater emphasis on soliciting foundations and corporations. Millar (1994c) reported, "Until recently, many chapters had limited their fund raising to special events and direct-mail appeals that generate, on average, gifts of $30 and $40. Some chapters had become so dependent on United Way support that they did no fund raising for nearly a half-century" (p. 24). The explicit implication of the changes was that fund raising had become a top priority for the Red Cross; implicitly, the large and powerful organization—ranked second in private support for 1994 and 1995 ("Philanthropy 400," 1995, 1996)—was going head to head against the UWs that funded it. The conclusion can be reached by reading between the lines that the American Red Cross is preparing itself for a permanent separation from the United Way.[10]

A precedent at the local level already exists. In 1996, the Salvation Army chapter in Washington, DC severed its 40-plus-year affiliation with the United Way of the National Capital Area, whose activities were described earlier. UW support for the chapter had eroded 40% in the previous 5 years, from $1 million in 1991 to roughly $600,000 in 1996, and the most recent amount consisted entirely of gifts earmarked by donors for the chapter (Stehle, 1996b). In 1995–1996, 81% of the money raised by the Washington UW was restricted for specific organizations, up from 70% the year before. Because unrestricted allocations had become so small, the Salvation Army chapter had stopped applying for them. Moreover, its restricted funding via the local UW had decreased $100,000 from 1994 to 1996. The chapter's division commander proclaimed, "Since the United Way can't—or won't—provide us with the funds, we have to go directly to the community we serve" (Stehle, 1996b, p. 33). A UW spokesperson responded: "It's ironic that the Salvation Army would complain, because some would have said that they monopolized the campaign in a previous time. Now we operate in a much more inclusive world, and much smaller organizations have every right to be in the campaign" (p. 33).

Unlike the Red Cross, which is concentrating on major gifts, the Salvation Army chapter is expanding its fund raising by soliciting business and government employees in its area. In other words, the former UW member is now a UW competitor in the workplace. National officials on both sides were quick to point out that their split was localized to the two Washington groups; however, as Stehle (1996b) reported, "The break could send shock waves through the United Way system if it is seen as a harbinger of eroding relations between United Ways and their biggest participants" (p. 33).

Finding themselves in a "Catch 22" situation, many of the UWs loosened their restrictions on members' fund raising, including lifting the ban on soliciting gifts during the federations' blackouts (Millar, 1994e). More members stepped up their fund-raising efforts. Fewer donors contributed to United Way campaigns. Only 35% of the employees at corporations that ran UW campaigns in 1995–1996 made a contribution, down from 37% the year before and 47% in 1989–1990 (Dundjerski, 1995; Stehle, 1996b). The number of companies that made direct grants similarly dropped, from 61% of those solicited in 1989–1990, to 51% in 1994–1995.

Press Agentry Values. Obviously, the unethical and illegal activities of Aramony damaged the United Way. Yet the scandal cannot be singled out as an isolated

---

[10]Ensuing conditions have delayed separation. Although it retained its second-place ranking, Red Cross' annual private support dropped $70 million between 1993 and 1995, from $536 million to $466 million (Marchetti, 1995). Managers claimed a 63% decrease in gifts for disaster relief was responsible, which—they speculated—was due to the absence of any major, dramatic natural disaster during the 2 years. Furthermore, the Red Cross posted a $60-million operating deficit in 1995, the first in its 111-year history. The shortfall largely resulted from a costly restructuring of the division that collects and distributes blood, which escalated in priority status after the organization was sued by the Food and Drug Administration in 1993 for alleged regulatory violations. The Red Cross also replaced its head of fund raising 1 year after announcing the $1-billion goal, and two different people filled the position in 1995 and 1996. President Elizabeth Dole, a driving force behind the fund-raising changes, took a 1-year leave of absence in 1996 to work on her husband's unsuccessful bid for the White House. Despite these setbacks, the Red Cross likely will continue to pursue separation from the United Way, which may occur as early as 2000.

and unrelated cause of the multiple problems the system now faces. Rather it must be viewed within the context of the UW's way of operating for most of its 27 years, specifically, its predominant practice of press agentry fund raising.

Most of the system's current problems can be traced to its traditional behavior, which prompted the three charges described earlier. When corrective action was taken, changes often were adopted reluctantly and for the purpose of raising more money, as opposed to improving ethics or donor relations. Yet, as a proportion of all U.S. giving, gifts to United Way have steadily declined for more than a decade. In 1984, its private support represented 3.1% of the gift dollars Americans gave to charitable organizations; by 1994, UW's share had fallen to 2.4% (Dundjerski, 1995). The difference represents about $1 billion a year in fewer gifts. One interpretation of these statistics is that reaction against United Way's fund-raising practice was evident in giving patterns before the 1992 scandal. Supporting this interpretation, Grønbjerg (1993) concluded from data gathered before 1992 that the system's resource base was declining at the same time the local UWs became "locations for turf battles among competing demands" (p. 76). Skolnik (1993) speculated that the scandal "may simply have been the rallying point for an insurrection that had been brewing for some time" (p. 29).

Students will recall that the fund-raising models reflect presuppositions held by practitioners and dominant coalition members. Asymmetrical presuppositions associated with the press agentry model include the beliefs that the organization knows best and that the number of dollars raised is a measure of importance and worth. With this concepts in mind, it is revealing to examine an opening passage in UWA's early report on the scandal, which attempts to explain why it happened:

> Because [Aramony] led a not-for-profit institution to record contributions and world-wide renown, Board members placed a significant degree of trust in him. The looseness and independence of Mr. Aramony's management style over the course of more than two decades resulted in a breach of that trust. Under his stewardship, UWA did not have a strong institutional culture open to examination by its local members and contributors. ("Text," 1992, p. 22)

In other words, fund-raising results were the primary justification given by the governing board for turning control of the system over to Aramony (which is congruent with claims made by his lawyers). He, in turn, instilled a culture that discouraged any questions about UWA's behavior—that he and the organization knew best. Critic Robert Bothwell (cited in E. Greene & Murawski, 1995) maintained, "What created Aramony was a system that had a virtual monopoly of workplace fund raising, and came to believe itself as the greatest charity on earth. The monopoly led to an arrogance of power that in fact led to a total disregard for the standards that other charities followed" (pp. 31, 34).

UWA's subsequent behavior provides the most damaging evidence that Aramony's actions were not an isolated mishap. Despite its pleas to donors to forgive, forget, and give, the national organization continued to operate under a philosophy that can best be described as "the public be damned."

In 1996, Elaine Chao, who had replaced Aramony as UWA's president, supposedly resigned after serving less than 4 years (H. Hall, 1996a). The organization announced that anonymous board members would pay Chao an "appreciation bonus" of $292,500—the exact amount the board had contracted to pay her if she were asked to leave before 5 years were up. Although private funds were to be used, the planned bonus violated UWA's Code of Ethics, which prohibits an employee from accepting any gratuity or favor for doing his or her job. The code, significantly, was instituted in 1993 under Chao's charge to clean up the organization after the Aramony scandal. The chair of UWA's board argued that the bonus would not conflict with the code because payments would be delayed until Chao was no longer an employee!

Due to media attention and public complaints, Chao finally declined the bonus; however, she claimed the criticism was unjustified and that she deserved the money because her salary at UWA had been less than half the amount paid to Aramony (H. Hall, 1996d). Eisenberg (1996) expressed the outrage of many observers when he insisted that the criticism was entirely justified given the 1992 scandal, the suspicious purpose of the bonus, and the lack of answers to questions about the payments (e.g., Would the anonymous board members funnel their portion of the bonus through UWA first in order to get a tax deduction?). Eisenberg concluded, "Ms. Chao's decision under pressure to decline the gift—after having planned to accept it—did little to remove the blemish United Way had caused itself in the first place" (p. 53).

In reaction to the scandal, letters from managers of other charitable organizations—including UW members whose allocations had been cut—filled the opinion page of *The Chronicle of Philanthropy* ("United Way after Chao," 1996). The majority of the letters rightfully blamed the organization and its dominant coalition for continuing problems. One manager declared, "Aramony's behavior was a product of the UWA culture—a culture that the board and President Aramony conspired to create. . . . The goodbye gift to Ms. Chao, and the way it was handled (poorly, leaving obvious questions unanswered), reflect the same culture" (p. 55). Another manager, responding to the defense that Chao would not have been an employee when she got the bonus, asked, "Perhaps this exempts Ms. Chao from the code of ethics, but does it exempt the organization?" (p. 55). "I wonder about a corporate culture that produced a William Aramony and then thought it appropriate to offer a $292,500 severance payment to a short-term employee" (p. 55). Overall, the letters cautioned UWA about excessive salaries and urged the board to hire a CEO who would identify with typical workers—those whose gifts constitute much of United Way's funding.

Disregarding such advice, a few months after Chao's departure, UWA hired its current president, Betty Beene, who—students will recall from chapter 7—is paid $275,000 a year, or 41% more than Chao (H. Hall, 1996c). Beene, who had just 12 years of UW experience, the latest as head of the United Way of Tri-State, defended her salary by pointing out that she took a $15,000 *cut* to assume her new duties!

Duhé (1996) found that corporate donors in southwestern Louisiana are very loyal to their local United Way. However, when asked what might cause a disruption in their support, corporate donors, on average, said they would be more likely to reduce their giving due to questionable practices at UWA or the local UW than for any other reason, including decreased company profits and campaigns by other federations.

Postscandal

In a speech titled "Dose of Reality," presented at the UW 1994 annual meeting, Cathleen Black (cited in Millar, 1994e), then secretary of the UWA board and president of the Newspaper Association of America, warned that changes in business and society were having a profound effect on fund raising for the system. She ticked off numerous trends including the dramatic increase in the number of charitable organizations, demands for accountability, and changes in the workplace such as downsizing and restructuring. Most alarming, she argued, was the erosion in direct corporate contributions. From 1982 to 1992, corporate giving grew twice as fast as gifts to United Ways. "The people who know us best . . . are increasingly steering dollars away to more specific causes—the environment, the arts, AIDS" (p. 27).

The speech was a milestone. Millar (1994a) reported, "Although the points that Ms. Black raised have been discussed among United Way leaders privately—and cited by numerous critics of United Ways—her speech marked one of the few times that a United Way representative made public remarks acknowledging the seriousness of the potential challenges facing the charity network" (p. 28).

In 1995, the United Way announced plans to remake itself, revisioning the system as "the community problem-solver," rather than "fund raisers who channel money to charities" (S. Gray, 1995, p. 1). The UWA strategic planning committee concluded after a year of deliberations that more had to be done to heed donor demands. J. Michael Cook (cited in S. Gray, 1995), chair of the committee and CEO of the accounting firm of Deloitte & Touche, explained that 10 years ago employees at his firm would not think twice about giving to the United Way. But since the Aramony scandal and other news about corruption, employees have been hesitant. "Now workers need to be shown a reason to give—and understandably so" (p. 30).

The strategic plan calls for the local UWs to abandon base allocations and adopt zero-base budgeting. Under the new approach, they would determine the most pressing health or human service needs in their communities and direct UW dollars to organizations addressing those needs (S. Gray, 1995). The plan also calls for greater emphasis on evaluation and stewardship. UWs are urged to create procedures for measuring the "value added" by UW gifts to the cities and towns they serve. For example, instead of simply reporting that it gave $1 million to a Red Cross chapter, a UW would tell donors and others how many people learned life-saving techniques or how much blood was collected for hospitals. The plan endorses more flexibility with employers and employees who want to restrict their gifts to organizations traditionally not eligible to receive UW funds. It also counsels UWs to expand fund raising beyond corporate settings in order to reduce their dependency on workplace solicitations.

Many of the recommendations incorporated in the 1995 strategic plan are based on symmetrical concepts (i.e., balanced effects and two-way communication between the UWs and their donors). However, adoption of the plan would intensify historical problems that potentially could destroy the United Way system.

Member organizations traditionally dependent on UW funding viewed the proposed changes as a threat—and some returned threats of their own. The YMCA of Greater New York, for example, announced it was expanding its own fund raising to offset previous and anticipated cuts (Dundjerski, 1995). The vice president for development and communications stated, "We're really going to have to escalate our fund-raising efforts and turn to government sources, corporations, foundations, and individuals. That's the only way you're going to make up for the loss" (Dundjerski, 1995, pp. 27–28).

Speaking for competing federations, Bothwell (cited in S. Gray, 1995) charged United Way with being arrogant once again. The UWs, he said, have been "deluded into thinking that they can bring together all of the community, when all of the community doesn't want to be under the United Way umbrella" (p. 22).

Forecasting possible outcomes, increased fund raising by member organizations will place greater demands on communities' resources. Donors subjected to numerous solicitations will question why they should contribute to their local United Way when they already give to the organizations that UW gifts support. The reason for a "United Way," meeting community needs through one campaign, will no longer exist. Without base allocations, more UW partners will consider separating themselves from the system. Loss of well-known beneficiaries, such as Goodwill and the Boy Scouts, would seriously decrease United Way's ability to attract gift dollars. Its monopoly on workplace fund raising will continue to erode as multiple federations demand access and employees demand more and different choices for their payroll contributions. In the absence of collaboration—an alternative UWA has yet to suggest—business leaders may one day decide that the efficiency and economy they sought in federations are no longer possible.

Adding to historical problems, many UWs believe a recent change in FASB standards jeopardizes their success. The revised accounting standards, implemented in 1995, prohibit organizations from counting as income any gifts they receive that are designated by donors for other organizations (Larkin, 1995). In other words, a United Way cannot include dollars from restricted gifts in its financial statements. Stated another way, donor-designated options lower fund-raising totals under the new rule. Illustrating, it is recalled that 81% of the money raised by the United Way of the National Capital Chapter in 1995–1996 was restricted for specific organizations. The percentage translated into $57 million, meaning that although $70 million was received by the UW, only $13 million could be reported on its financial statement as gift income ("Philanthropy 400," 1996).

UWs that measure the importance of gifts by the number of dollars raised complained that the new rule makes them appear unsuccessful. Donors, they protested, would think the federations were not doing their job, which could further reduce support. Notably, the 1995 strategic plan addressed this problem in its recommendation that UWs concentrate on measuring and reporting "value added" to communities by UW gifts rather than just citing the amount of dollars raised and handed out to community organizations.[11]

Because expenses do not change even though gift income is lowered, the accounting rule increases fund-raising cost ratios. Illustrating, the United Way of the National Capital Chapter's cost ratio was 33% in 1995–1996, whereas it would have been only 7% if the $57 million in restricted gifts had been counted ("Philanthropy 400," 1996). UWs argued that financial statements could not adequately explain the accounting

---

[11]As the FASB standards were adopted in 1993, the UWA strategic planning committee likely was aware of their scheduled implementation, which may have influenced the committee's decision to deemphasize dollar totals.

rule's effect on cost ratios. Therefore, they speculated, perceptions of high fund-raising costs will turn donors away. Ongoing communication to educate donors about the accounting rule would alleviate much of the problem (e.g., articles in a quarterly newsletter); yet UWs traditionally communicate with the bulk of their donors, corporate employees, only when they solicit them—once a year.

As of 1997, the strategic plan developed by UWA has had no observable impact. Rate of adoption by local UWs has not been publicly announced. The 2,000 federations appear to be more concerned with regaining campaign totals they had before 1992 than with remaking themselves for the future.

American society bears little resemblance to what it was in 1913 when the first Community Chest began. Since UWA was created in 1970, diversity and complexity have grown. Fund-raising practices from past eras are incompatible with contemporary societal needs. Although the strategic plan is not without potential danger, it is doubtful the United Way system will survive if if continues to operate as it has in the past. As committee chair Cook (cited in S. Gray, 1995) warned UW managers, "If we don't make these changes now, someone else will take our place" (p. 30).

The environments in which charitable organizations exist continually change, and organizations must adapt to changes or eventually fail. The relationship between an organization's survival and its environment is explained by systems theory, which begins the next chapter on the theoretical context of fund raising.

SUGGESTED READINGS

Anderson, A. (1996). *Ethics for fundraisers*. Bloomington: Indiana University Press.

Briscoe, M. G. (Ed.). (1994). *Ethics in fundraising: Putting values into practice, New directions for philanthropic fundraising* (No. 6). San Francisco, CA: Jossey-Bass.

Glaser, J. S. (1994). *The United Way scandal: An insider's account of what went wrong and why*. New York: Wiley.

Gray, S. (Ed.). (1993). *Leadership is: Everyday ethics*. Washington, DC: Independent Sector.

Independent Sector. (1991). *Ethics and the nation's voluntary and philanthropic community: Obedience to the unenforceable*. Washington, DC: Author.

Josephson, M. (1992). *Ethics of grant-making and grant-seeking: Making philanthropy better*. (Available from Josephson Institute of Ethics, 4640 Admiralty Way, Suite 1001, Marina del Rey, CA 90292-6610.)

O'Neill, M. (Ed.). (1990). *Ethics in nonprofit management: A collection of cases*. San Francisco, CA: University of San Francisco.

Sennott, C. M. (1992). *Broken covenant*. New York: Simon & Schuster.

Smith, D. H. (1995). *Entrusted: The moral responsibilities of trusteeship*. Bloomington: Indiana University Press.

Tidwell, G. L. (1993). *Anatomy of a fraud: Inside the finances of the PTL ministries*. New York: Wiley.

9

Theoretical Context
of Fund Raising

Fund raising is guided by theory, although time-tested principles of practitioners rarely are associated with their theoretical underpinnings. Chapter 9 identifies and discusses the theories on which fund raising is based and links them to principles commonly found in the literature. The theories, derived from such disciplines as management, sociology, psychology, and communication, have been adopted and refined for public relations. Their application to fund raising helps us understand the function from the macro level of society to the micro level of techniques, and in the middle at the meso, or departmental, level. Jacobson (1990) called for such an approach, stating, "The creative synthesis of relevant theories carefully culled from a wide spectrum of disciplines could contribute substantially toward establishing a theoretical knowledge base for the profession" (p. 467). By relating principles to theories and building each component on the others, chapter 9 results in a unified theory of donor relations.

SYSTEMS THEORY

A fundamental principle of fund raising is:

Make the case bigger than the organization.

The *case* is the charitable organization's "basic argument for philanthropic support" (R. L. Williams, 1993, p. 295). It is communicated through a formal or informal publication, the *case statement*, and emphasizes the relationship among gifts, program services, and benefits to donors. The case for support, Howe (1991) argued, should be based on a societal problem: "What is out there in the community that needs doing? Then the case can address what the organization does or will do to meet that focus problem" (p. 14). The case, according to Rosso (1991), must answer such questions as, "Why should any individual, corporation, or foundation contribute to a specific organization? and What benefits will accrue to the contributor who makes such gifts?" (p. 9). Rosso added, "A clear and complete statement of case gives evidence of the organization's readiness to seek gift support from its constituencies" (p. 9). The fifth of Broce's (1986) nine cardinal principles of fund raising was, "The case for the program must reflect the importance of the institution" (p. 22).

324

This principle is explained by systems theory; that is, organizations do not exist in isolation but are part of larger social, economic, and political systems that affect and are affected by the organizations' behavior. How an organization operates in relation to its environment (i.e., the larger system of which it is a part) determines its success and survival.

Systems theory is the foundation of our conceptual framework for fund raising. It explains how fund raising impacts society, why charitable organizations have the function, and what contribution the function makes to the effectiveness of such organizations. In other words, systems theory provides the "reason for being" of fund raisers and legitimizes the practice. The centrality of systems theory to fund raising was extensively discussed and documented in my earlier book (Kelly, 1991a; see particularly chaps. 6 and 10). To avoid duplication, it is presented here with related theories in the form of a primer, followed by discussions of selected parts. Grønbjerg (1993) authenticated a systems perspective for this text's subject: "It is not possible to understand the behavior of nonprofits, including their internal structures and processes of decision making, without paying careful attention to the complex organizational environments in which they operate and with which they interact on multiple levels" (p. 309).

Contemporary literature on organizations is grounded in open-systems theory as conceptualized by Katz and Kahn (1978). The theory holds that organizations are dependent on their environments for success and survival and that environmental factors help shape the behavior of organizations. Environments are both general and specific (Robbins, 1990). The general environment encompasses conditions that may potentially impact the organization (e.g., changes in the economy). The specific environment is the part with which management will be concerned because it is made up of those critical constituencies, or stakeholders, that can positively or negatively influence the organization's goals. It is unique to each organization, and it changes with conditions.

The nature and amount of interchange between an organization and its environment represents the degree to which it is an open or closed system (Cutlip et al., 1994). Closed systems are insensitive to their environments. They do not take in new information, they do not adapt to external change, and eventually they deteriorate. Open systems are responsive to environmental changes and depend on interchange with their environments.

A consequence of open systems is interdependence. An organization manages interdependencies between itself and strategic groups and organizations in its environment through an exchange process. Based on the resource dependence theory of Pfeffer and Salancik (1978), organizations are controlled by their relationships to external providers of necessary resources. The amount of control, or autonomy, given up by the recipient organization in order to obtain a resource is negotiable. However, the more the organization depends on a resource provided by an outside group, the more control that group has on the priorities and goals of the organization. Effectiveness rests on the organization's accountability, or how well it satisfies the needs and interests of those in its environment from whom it requires resources and other forms of support for continued operation.

Systems theory explains the relationships between charitable organizations and donors as environmental interdependencies. Donors are enabling stakeholders whose resources are needed to varying degrees by organizations, and donors look to recipients of their gifts for various returns (i.e., they engage in a social exchange; Blau, 1964/1986). Fund raisers serve in a boundary role between the organization and its environment. They are responsible for reducing the uncertainty of private support by managing relationships with donors. In their boundary-spanning role, with one foot in the organization and one outside, practitioners support other organizational components by helping them communicate across boundaries to external donors. Staff managers also conduct research, such as environmental scanning, in order to inform members of their organization's dominant coalition about issues and publics within the environment that may affect the organization's ability to succeed and survive (J. E. Grunig & Hunt, 1984).

Connecting the theory to the four models of fund raising, press agentry and public information reflect a closed-system orientation. Communication is one-way, outward from the organization to donors and potential donors. In contrast, the two-way asymmetrical and symmetrical models reflect an open-system perspective, with practitioners collecting as well as disseminating information. Information brought into the organization is used by the dominant coalition to make strategic and tactical decisions about donor relationships. Only the two-way symmetrical model, however, uses the information to make changes in the organization's internal operations and processes when adjustments are necessary to balance relations with donors.

Tempel (1991) applied systems theory to fund raising and advocated two-way practice: "For an organization to be successful in fund raising, it must be connected to its external environment. It must understand the changing needs of that environment and its facility to respond to the organization's need for human and financial resources to remain functional" (pp. 19–20). He argued that charitable organizations "must continually monitor the environment and either adapt to changes or attempt to change inhospitable elements" (p. 21).

Returning to the practitioner principle that began this discussion, Lord (1983) said the case for support must touch donor prospects "where they live and breathe" (p. 18). He elaborated: "They need to feel that investing in the program will make life better for them, for their children and grandchildren. They need to feel that the community and the nation will be strengthened—even that *civilization itself* will be advanced by what they do" (p. 18; italics in original).

Case statements in the past, particularly those formulated for capital campaigns, often used press agentry to frame gifts to a specific organization as the solution to problems of widespread concern. Illustrating, Gurin (1985) included in his autobiography the opening section of the case statement he wrote in 1958 for Princeton University's $53-million capital campaign. The document, "Not for Princeton Alone," began with the following statement, which—students should keep in mind—was written at the height of the Cold War with the former Soviet Union: "It is now conceivable, technologically, to annihilate a continent or to rid mankind [*sic*] of disease. How we respond to this challenge (and to others of equal urgency) will determine how we live—and whether we live" (p. 109).

Resolution of the challenge, with its obvious fear appeal, was to give money to Princeton for endowment and physical capital needs. Gurin claimed that legendary consultant Si Seymour considered the case statement a classic. Representative of what I believe is a growing distaste for press agentry, practitioners with whom I took the NSFRE Survey Course in June 1993 evaluated the same document—distributed without authorship—as pompous, melodramatic, elitist, and offensive. To this day, I believe few people who participate in the NSFRE course realize that the case statement's author is one of fund raising's revered pioneers or that it is used in the course because it is considered a classic!

Practitioner and author Kay Grace (1991a) provided examples of more recent case statements that instill a sense of purpose beyond the organization by realistically relating the organization's work to a bigger problem. The statement for the Yale University School of Medicine's capital campaign in the mid-1980s asserted: "We are in the midst of one of the most profound intellectual revolutions of all time, the revolution in the biological sciences. Its implications for understanding life processes and combating disease are boundless. . . . Yale is in the forefront of this revolution" (K. S. Grace, 1991a, p. 190). Stanford University's $1.1-billion Centennial Campaign, which ended in 1991, built its case for giving on the global needs Stanford meets through its education of talented men and women. Prospective donors were invited to invest in the university's role in shaping the next century.

As demonstrated by these two examples, the case for support flows from the organization's mission. It must be congruent with and not exaggerate the organization's ability to address societal problems. At the same time, however, the case must be based on a problem that concerns a sufficient number of potential donors. In other words, fund raising is dependent on the degree to which the organization and its donor publics share a common problem, as expressed by the organization's mission statement. K. S. Grace (1991a) explained, "Mission statements which answer the question 'why' position the organization so that it relates to the community need it is meeting" (p. 189). She continued:

> A mission statement that tells "why," followed by a purpose statement that tells "what" the organization is doing, establishes a feeling of strength and responsibility in the mind of the prospective donor. This strength does not negate the need for funds: It says, instead, that the organization is a good place for those who share *common* values and concerns to invest their charitable funds. It is a strength based on a relationship over time with the donor, one in which these values and concerns are shared, discussed, and accomplished. (p. 189; italics added)

With an overview of systems theory in place, a revisit to the parameters of fund raising, the subject of chapter 2, adds to our conceptual framework. Theories of philanthropy—explanations of giving—are grounded in systems theory and provide necessary building blocks for a theoretical understanding of fund raising—an explanation of "getting." The following section reviews and expands on America's philanthropic tradition, the theory of the commons, and social exchange theory. To assure accurate comprehension in these and subsequent discussions, key definitions are first summarized.

DEFINITIONS AND PHILANTHROPY THEORIES

Gifts come from three primary sources: individuals, corporations, and foundations. These groups constitute the three donor publics with which fund raising is concerned.

Gifts from individuals, including bequests, traditionally account for almost 90% of the total amount given each year; corporations and foundations essentially provide the rest (AAFRC Trust for Philanthropy, 1996). More than two thirds of the amount given by individuals comes from high-income households (Schervish & Havens, 1995).

Usage of the terms *people, prospects*, and *donors* represent all three sources of gifts. Lord (1983) explained: "The donor, too, is *always* a person. A foundation, corporation or committee never makes a decision. Only people make decisions" (p. 75; italics in original). Furthermore, as Steele and Elder (1992) stated, "The same principles that apply to raising money from individuals apply to raising money from foundations and corporations" (p. 104). In other words, the theories discussed in this chapter explain fund raising as it relates to all three donor publics.

There are two types of gifts: lower level and major. Adopting the parsimonious typology I presented in my earlier book, lower level gifts are raised through the annual giving program and major gifts are raised through the major gifts program (Kelly, 1991a). Definitional dollar amounts vary among organizations. For some, major gifts are defined as those of $10,000 or more, and lower level gifts are all gifts below $10,000. Other organizations, such as universities and hospitals, typically use $100,000 as the defining criterion. Major gifts also are raised through planned giving efforts, and both annual and major gifts are raised through capital campaigns, with an emphasis on the second type. Planned giving and capital campaigns actually are *strategies* for raising large gifts and should be incorporated in the two primary programs.

Although significantly fewer in number, major gifts typically account for most of the dollars raised by organizations conducting both programs. The *principle of proportionate giving*, based on our society's unequal distribution of wealth, holds that the majority of money will come from a minority of donors, even within programs. In annual giving, for example, 10% of the gifts typically account for 60% of the dollars (Rosso, 1991). In the mid-1980s, gifts larger than $5,000 accounted for more than 75% of the total dollars given to private colleges and universities and for about 66% of gift dollars to public institutions (Brittingham & Pezzullo, 1990).

Annual gifts usually are unrestricted in purpose, whereas major gifts almost always are restricted (except for those made through bequests). Clarifying this important characteristic, unrestricted gifts can be used where most needed as determined by the organization's managers after receipt. Restricted gifts, on the other hand, must be used for the specific purposes for which they were given, determined in advance of receipt.

Tradition of Philanthropy

America's philanthropic tradition is unique and deeply ingrained in our society. Whereas rich and poor alike make gifts, individuals who have acquired wealth through our capitalistic system are held to a special philanthropic standard. Representing a minority of the population, they provide the majority of gift dollars from individuals.

Almost three fourths of all U.S. households contribute to one or more charitable organizations each year, and they give about 2% of their income, on average (Hodgkinson et al., 1996; IS, 1994). The percentage holds across all income groups. Debunking a popular myth that the wealthy give away a smaller proportion of their larger incomes than less affluent Americans, Schervish and Havens (1995) found from reanalyzing national data that the average household gives about 2% of its income, regardless of size. The scholars stated: "This result contradicts the imagery of the caring poor contributing more than the uncaring rich. Both groups appear equally caring" (p. 84).

Giving also is a behavioral norm in the business sector. Corporations collectively give about 2% of their pretax income each year. Foundations, by legal definition, are required to behave philanthropically. Every year, they must give away an amount equal to 5% of their assets.

Gifts from individuals, corporations, and foundations have represented about 2% of the U.S. GDP for more than 30 years, ranging from a low of 1.7% to a high of 2.2% (AAFRC Trust for Philanthropy, 1996). Giving as a percentage of national income—a statistic different from GDP—hovers around 2.5% (Hodgkinson et al., 1992). Similarly, the 2% of household income represented by gifts varies little from year to year. The 2% of pretax income given by corporations essentially has stayed the same for 50 years, even though the allowable deduction was increased from 5% to 10% in 1981 (Bailey, 1994). In other words, about 2% of GDP, national income, household income, and corporate income, as well as 5% of foundation assets, define the parameters of fund raising.

This is a critical point for understanding the fund-raising function. Although percentages may fluctuate in the short term because of such factors as tax laws, the parameters appear invulnerable to efforts to substantially change them. In 1995, for example, IS announced that it was phasing out its "Give Five" campaign to get people to volunteer 5 hours per week and donate 5% of their income ("New drive," 1995). After conducting the public information campaign for more than 8 years, "surveys of donors and volunteers [led] officials to concede that Americans do not—and may never—give five per cent of their income away" (p. 16). Instead of trying to change donor behavior, IS launched a new campaign to reinforce giving, using the slogan: "Thanks for all you've given. Imagine what more could do" (p. 16).

As presented in previous chapters, the unchanged proportion of GDP represented by gifts prompted consultant Bruce Flessner's (cited in H. Hall, 1993a) charge that the statistic's flatness over three decades, during which charitable organizations progressed from employing few to thousands of practitioners, raised legitimate questions about whether fund raisers make any real difference. Such charges have gained widespread popularity but have not inspired scientific studies to seek answers. Instead, the GDP percentage has been accepted by practitioner leaders as unrefutable evidence damaging to fund raising. Warner (1995), for example, dedicated a column to solving what he termed *the 2% barrier*. Echoing Flessner, he proclaimed, "What is most alarming about the real lack of growth in donations is that even though we have more and more people involved in the business of seeking private contributions, they do not appear to be making a significant difference" (p. 67). Questions he raised included, "Are we stuck at 2 per cent because the fund-raising world is loaded with incompetent professionals?. . . . Have donors been saturated with so many appeals that they have grown tired of responding?" (p. 68). Contradictorily, he also asked, "Or is it likely that we would be raising far less than 2 per cent of the gross domestic product were it not for . . . the work of the thousands of new fund raisers who have inundated the non-profit world?" (p. 67).

The answer to the last question is yes. The overall answer is that fund raisers do make a difference. Flessner, Warner, and others have distorted the statistic's meaning by not accounting for growth in GDP. They mistakenly assume a higher percentage of GDP results from a higher amount of gift dollars, without regard to increases in GDP (i.e., they assume the denominator of the fraction remains constant). Because they erroneously believe that fund raising has an unmediated effect on the statistic, they misinterpret its stability as an absence of effect. They are wrong.

Although the percentage has not changed, gift dollars have grown proportionately as our country's GDP has increased by *billions* of dollars each and every year.[1] Those who foolishly lament this remarkable accomplishment misunderstand the statistic and fund raising's impact on giving behavior. The 2% represented by gifts most likely would drop without the efforts of fund raisers; however, Americans would continue to give because of our pervasive philanthropic tradition. In other words, the aggregate difference fund raisers make is keeping private support steady as a proportion of GDP (i.e., they reinforce giving behavior).

The stable statistics defining the parameters of fund raising support this book's approach: Fund raisers affect not whether donors give, but to which specific organizations they give, the purposes of their gifts, and the gift amounts. Fund raising is not about educating, persuading, or manipulating donors to give money because they already are predisposed to do so.

Schervish and Havens (1994) reached similar conclusions from their empirical study of wealthy individuals:

> First, fundraisers [*sic*] do not need to induce the financially well-off to become givers . . . . Nearly all upper income and all wealthy households are already participating in charitable giving and many from each group are substantial givers. Second, this means that much of the groundwork for fundraisers has already been done. . . . Third, this means that fundraisers should attend to getting wealthy donors to do more of what the wealthy and their peers are already doing. (p. 30)

The scholars argued that a primary task for practitioners "is to provide a *reason* for people who are already givers to focus on a particular cause" (pp. 30–31; italics added). They advised, "To attract the financial wherewithal of donors, fundraisers [*sic*] need to induce dedication and expanded commitment—but not initial engagement" (p. 31).

The first of six principles of philanthropic giving offered by Howe (1991) was: "People give money because they want to" (p. 6). He elaborated, "Asking for money, therefore, is not an act of arm-twisting; you are not trying to force someone to do something they don't want to do" (p. 7). Payton (1987) reaffirmed, "People give because they want to give" (p. 18).

---

[1]Richard Steinberg (personal communication, March 15, 1994) helped clarify my thinking on this subject, which has *not* been studied by him or other economists. He reminded me that giving is income inelastic in that a 10% rise in income causes a rise of less than 10% in giving—all else being equal. Therefore, he explained, even though gifts increase in dollar amount, we would expect them to decrease as a percentage of national income unless other factors intervene. Although national income is a different statistic, I extrapolated his research-based reasoning to GDP; that is, constancy of percentage provides evidence that fund raising helps counter the effect of inelasticity and generate the increased dollars necessary to keep pace with ever-rising economic indicators.

Theory of the Commons

Lohmann's (e.g., 1992a) theory also supports this book's approach. Commons—or nonprofits—form to produce common goods, which Lohmann defined as "desirable or preferred outcomes that are uncoerced, that are associated with shared purposes and pooled resources, and that engender a sense of . . . community and fairness" (p. 320). By definition, common goods are not universally desired or available. They are valued by a minority of people; for most, the common good produced by a specific organization is a matter of indifference or may even be considered a "bad." Whereas other theories of philanthropy deal with the so-called public good, meaning any gift to any charitable organization contributes to the good of an abstract *general public*, Lohmann's theory allows us to understand that gifts are made to support goods in which the donor and the recipient organization share common interests.

Public relations scholars help clarify this important distinction with their concept of publics (plural) as opposed to *the* public (singular). J. E. Grunig and Hunt (1984) explained: "A 'general public' is a logical impossibility. Publics are always specific; they always have some *common problem*. Thus, they cannot be general" (p. 138; italics added). Publics form around particular problems, which also are defined as issues, or opportunities. As J. E. Grunig and Repper (1992) asserted, they "seldom affect everyone in the population" (p. 127). The social problems addressed by charitable organizations, whether cultural, educational, religious, or other, are embedded in their missions (i.e., the reasons they exist). From mission statements to cases for support, K. S. Grace (1991a) stated, "Institutional needs are presented as opportunities for donors to invest in programs that are solving community *problems* effectively" (p. 189; italics added).

Redefined by Lohmann's (1992a) theory, philanthropy is voluntary action for particular common goods that, collectively, undergird our pluralistic democracy. O'Connell (1991) argued that the central value of philanthropy and voluntary effort "is the extra dimension they provide for people to do and see things differently" (p. 41). He continued, "They cannot take the place of business or government, but they do provide additional ways to address our needs [and] pursue our hopes" (p. 41).

In other words, when we examine giving behavior, we are concerned with the donor's *interpretation* of what is in the best interest of society—an interpretation with which we may or may not agree. For example, given increased militia action and the 1995 terrorist bombing in Oklahoma City, I may not believe that a $100 gift to the National Rifle Association Foundation is in the best interest of society, but other people obviously do. Pluralism is essential to our democracy, and the diverse common goods supported by philanthropy are essential to pluralism.

In a recent public relations thesis, fund-raising practitioner Diana Vandeventer (1993) applied theories of the Chicago School of Social Thought to the area of donor motivation. Through qualitative methodology, including in-depth interviews with major donors to the University of Northern Iowa, she found evidence that philanthropy provides a sense of community in a disengaged and fragmented society. Giving allows people to go beyond majority rule (government) and consumer demand (business) to join with others who think and believe as they do. As one of her interview subjects explained, "When I give it is on a personal belief. I eliminate anything that does not coincide with my personal belief of what will do the most good for the most people" (p. 88). Linking Vandeventer's findings to Lohmann's (1992a) theory, John Dewey (cited in Vandeventer, 1993), the eminent philosopher, psychologist and educator of the Chicago School, defined *community* as "a number of people held together because they are working along common lines, in a common spirit and with reference to common aims" (p. 10).

Schervish and Havens (1997) reached comparable conclusions through extensive empirical research on donor motivation, which involved multivariate analyses of 107 variables grouped in clusters. The variables, representing nearly all the factors suggested in the literature, were operationalized by matching them with national data collected through IS' biennial survey on giving and volunteering. The match resulted in five clusters: Youthful Experiences, Framework of Consciousness, Invitation to Participate, Discretionary Resources, and Community of Participation. Schervish and Havens defined the last cluster as "groups and organizations in which one participates." They explained, "Many communities of participation directly request and sometimes require time and money from their participants. But the important point is that being *connected* . . . is the basis for people becoming aware of needs and choosing to respond" (italics added).

Schervish and Havens' (1997) analyses showed that each of the five clusters is significantly related to giving but Community of Participation "is the cluster with by far the strongest and most consistent relationship to giving behavior." They concluded, "Charitable giving is largely a consequence of forging a connection between the existing inclinations and involvements of individuals and the needs of recipients." Linking Schervish and Havens' findings to public relations theory, Dozier and Ehling (1992) stated, "Conceptually, publics are defined by their *connection* to an organization in a particular situation" (p. 169; italics added).

Fund raisers raise gifts in support of common goods, not goods that are valued by all. Their efforts are bounded by voluntary participation, shared purposes, mutuality, and fairness. There is no such thing as the public for the purposes of fund raising, rather there are numerous publics of which some share an interest in particular common goods, and some of those are donor publics. Fund raising, then, concentrates on the juncture where the interests of donors and the organization meet.

Social Exchange Theory

Contemporary scholars approach philanthropy as a social exchange in that making a gift is not a one-way act. Culbertson, Jeffers, Stone, and Terrell (1993) explained that exchange theory, which is drawn from social psychology, "builds on the basic economic proposition that people normally work or pay only when they receive something in return that they see as justifying their inputs" (p. 7). Unlike a market exchange, the benefits given and received in a philanthropic exchange are not fully captured by the actors; some benefits spill into society (Douglas, 1983).

Ostrander and Schervish (1990) described the theory's application to philanthropy: "Donors have needs to be fulfilled as well as resources to grant, and recipients have resources to give as well as needs to be met. In other words, donors and recipients both give and get in the social relation that is philanthropy" (p. 93). Cook (1994a) provided a university president's endorsement of the theory's explanatory power:

Fund raising is obviously trying to get some money to advance the purposes of the university, but it goes beyond that. There are people who give to universities and in a very real way benefit from the giving. So really what you're trying to do is to connect the needs of the university to the interests and the needs of potential donors, and when you do that, everybody wins. (p. 105)

Lord (1983) advised practitioners: "The fact is that people give in order to *get*. They don't want to feel that they are 'giving away' their money. They want to feel that they are investing it, and getting something in return" (p. 5; italics in original). "It's a process of exchange; we owe them" (p. 31).

Based on exchange theory, fund raising deals with mixed motives for giving—interests in self and in a common good. Philosopher Mike Martin (1994) defined the mixed-motive model: "Philanthropic giving usually springs from a combination of altruism (caring for others for their sake) and self-interest (caring for one's own well-being)" (p. 123). He added, "Within limits, the resulting mixture of purposes is morally acceptable, even desirable, insofar as it strengthens the overall pursuit of good ends" (p. 17). Citing scientific studies during the past two decades, Martin concluded, "Mixed motives are typical in giving, and nothing is wrong with self-interested motives so long as they do not distort caring or entirely replace altruism" (p. 150). Martin argued that self-interest is not sufficient to create and sustain what he termed *caring relationships*; however, the presence of self-interest engages donors in relationships that are stronger and more enduring than ones based only on altruism. "In fact, altruism and self-interest become increasingly interwoven as caring relationships deepen" (p. 131).

Social exchange theory derives from the two important concepts of exchange and relationships. In his book about fund raising, Mixer (1993) stated, "Social exchange takes place between two parties that have some underlying relationship, be it participation in common activities, coexistence in a certain geographical area, or shared concerns about human conditions" (p. 243). Drawing from systems theory, he said, "No organization is self-sufficient, all must enter into exchanges with the environment" (p. 67). Jacobson (1990) summarized in his review of research on institutional advancement, "'Exchange,' a reciprocal process, is fundamentally rooted in the relationship between source and receiver" (p. 468).

Exchange. Whereas money is the primary benefit donors bring to the philanthropic exchange, organizations offer donors benefits that are internal (e.g., feel good about act of giving), intangible but externally observable (e.g., increased prestige), and even tangible (e.g., tickets to a concert), in addition to the overarching benefit of a common good (Steinberg, 1989). Both parties also perceive the relationship itself as a potential benefit. The outcome of exchanges, according to Gouldner's (1960) norm of reciprocity, is determined by the power of the parties relative to each other. "Given significant power differences, egoistic motivations may seek to get benefits without returning them" (p. 174).

Much of the literature on philanthropy assumes that, because of the money they give, donors are more powerful than the organizations that receive their gifts. M. W. Martin (1994), for example, argued that money is power, and power is easily misused to harm organizational recipients. When that happens, he said, it becomes "less blessed to receive than to give" (p. 98). Although Ostrander and Schervish (1990) defined philanthropy as "a social relation in which there is some kind of reciprocal exchange," they quickly added, "Recipients are dependent on donors for their organizational existence and for the well-being of their clients, consumers, and employees" (p. 74). The scholars had little to say about the dependency of donors on recipient organizations. Pratt (1991) even claimed that because of unbalanced power between grant-maker and grantseeker, "Honest communication between the two is difficult" (p. 221).

Stereotypes of small poor organizations and rich powerful donors underlie these flawed assumptions and contribute to a perspective of fund raising as begging. In assuming a dependency on donors, scholars ignore numerous studies such as those given in chapter 2 that show gifts account for only about 25% of the subsector's income, in aggregate, and as little as 2% for many employers of fund raisers (e.g., hospitals). They ignore the fact that many organizations are wealthy. For example, 50 of the top 400 charitable organizations in 1995 had incomes large enough to make them Fortune 500 companies if they were private businesses ("Philanthropy 400," 1996). It is unlikely that such organizations suffer from a power imbalance in exchanges with specific donors. Most seriously, scholars ignore the theories from which their work is drawn.

Blau (1964/1986) explained that the source of power in social exchange is one-sided dependence; "interdependence and mutual influence of equal strength indicate lack of power" (p. 118). He reminded us that wealth is not a perfect predictor of power because many benefits people desire, such as appreciation and respect, cannot be purchased in market exchanges. In other words, a charitable organization's power stems from the degree to which it is dependent on donors for money and its ability to provide donors with benefits they desire. And, contrary to the literature, the organization is not necessarily less powerful than its donors.

Ironically, the symmetrical approach to public relations has been criticized as impractical because of the opposite assumption that organizations inherently have more power than publics (J. E. Grunig & White, 1992). Critics argue that, due to their power, organizations are more likely to turn to egoistic motivations in relationships with publics than to a model that strives for balanced effects. J. E. Grunig and White defended the two-way symmetrical model by applying the norm of reciprocity, which they described as "the essence of what generally is called social responsibility" (p. 47). Organizations that are socially responsible, they countered, will act in fairness with publics, allowing practice of the normative model. In contrast to those in philanthropy, then, public relations scholars erroneously concede that all publics, including donors, are weaker than organizations—which they stereotype as large, publicly owned corporations. Assumptions about both powerful publics and powerful organizations are misleading.

Relationships.   A commonly accepted principle is:

Friend raising is as important as fund raising.

According to Gonzalez-Campoy (1996), "Successful fund raising boils down to one thing: building relationships. . . . This rule goes back to the roots of fund raising" (p. 36). Howe (1991) stated, "The essence of raising money lies in the relationship of an organization to its support constituency" (p. 75). K. S. Grace (1991a) simply said, "Fund raising is about relationships more than it is about money" (p. 185). Seymour

(1966/1988) elaborated: "Every cause . . . needs people more than money. For when people are with you and are giving your cause their attention, interest, confidence, advocacy, and service, financial support should just about take care of itself" (p. ix). More recently, philosopher Marilyn Fischer (1994), who has studied fund-raising ethics, stated, "The fund raiser's job, obviously, is to raise money. The fund raiser accomplishes this task by cultivating friends for the organization and enabling them to make informed financial, emotional and time commitments. The money is freely given by persons who share a sense of commitment to the organization" (p. 30).

K. S. Grace (1991a) differentiated fund raising based on relationships from what she called *tin cup* fund raising: "Tin cup donors give impulsively. They respond, and walk on; it is unlikely they will circle back and put more money in the same cup. In the long term, this approach to fund raising fails but in spite of this, organizations continue it" (p. 187). Impulsive gifts, Grace argued, provide little financial stability for the recipient organization. "For that, a relationship based on shared values must be developed" (p. 191). She urged fund raisers to "focus on relationship building, donor and community needs, and true investment and exchange" (p. 198).

As defined in the first chapter of this book, fund raising is the management of relationships between a charitable organization and its donor publics. The basis of donor relationships is communication. Howe (1991) supported this assertion:

> Although the concept of communication as the wellspring of all organizational activities is timeworn, it has validity. Every step in the progression of relationships with contribu-tors—initial awareness, increased knowledge and involvement, solicitation, and proposal writing—depends on how effectively an organization communicates with its support constituencies—prospective, current, and regular. (p. 76)

Paraphrasing Cutlip et al. (1994), communication helps parties in relationships make predictions about each other. It reduces uncertainty about the probable out-comes of future exchanges and provides a foundation for the continuing relationship between donor and organizational recipient. The public relations educators explained, "Communication, then, not only moves information from one party in a relationship to another, but also defines the relationships and social environment within which we all function" (p. 254). They also reminded us that the term *communication* is derived from the Latin word *communis*, meaning common, "So, 'communication' means to establish a commonness" (p. 401). Indeed, Lohmann (1992b) argued that the defining characteristics of commons are dependent on communication: "Free and uncoerced participation and fairness can only be realized, shared purposes and resources identi-fied, and a sense of mutuality and affiliation built up through talk, dialogue, commu-nication, and exchange" (p. 210).

Two-way communication is necessary for identifying, maintaining, and building relationships with donors. Quite simply, relationships do not work if one party always talks and never listens. As Culbertson et al. (1993) asserted, "Fruitful human relation-ships generally require accurate two-way communication, with respectful listening [and] openness by both source and receiver to a wide variety of ideas" (p. 280). The two-way asymmetrical and symmetrical models of fund raising are based on two-way communication; press agentry and public information are based on one-way commu-nication from organization to donor. In other words, relationship fund raising requires practice of the two-way models, although the two-way symmetrical model is most effective. Lord (1983) confirmed, "In the final analysis, if you've given your prospects some kind of opportunity to tell you what they want—and especially if you've responded to their interests—you'll be in a strong position to develop a sense of commitment to your program" (p. 40).

According to J. E. Grunig and L. A. Grunig (1991), "Public relations—managed communication—makes organizations more effective by building relationships with publics that can constrain or enhance the mission of the organization" (p. 260). The second word in the phrase, *relations*, "centers on ways in which people share meaning, take each other into account, influence others, and gain understanding as well as support and participation" (Culbertson et al., 1993, p. 6). *Public* simply means that the relations are organizational (i.e., they are not private relations between individuals). Systems theory explains that organizational relations involve and affect multiple publics. Responsibility for managing relationships with donor publics belongs to fund raisers. In systems theory terms, practitioners serve in a boundary role, reducing environmental uncertainty and buffering the organization by managing relationships with stakeholders who are donor publics—those who can constrain or enhance the organization's mission through their gifts.

STAKEHOLDERS AND BOUNDARY SPANNERS

A principle espoused in the literature is:

Fund raising begins with the organization's constituencies.

When identifying people likely to make gifts, practitioners are advised by experts such as Rosso (1991) to always start with those already served by and related to the organization. The fourth of Broce's (1986) nine cardinal principles of fund raising was: "The institution must start with *natural* prospects" (p. 21; italics added). He explained, "Significant private gifts rarely come from strangers" (p. 177).

Another principle, found particularly in articles and books about planned giving, is:

Fund raisers represent both the organization and the donor.

M. R. Hall (1993) described this boundary-spanning role: "A good development officer will be entrepreneurial, will have a sense that he or she is representing the donor to the institution as much as representing the institution to the donor, and will often act as a broker between the institution and the donor" (p. 95).

Stakeholders

The management literature refers to constituencies as *stakeholders*, or those groups and organizations that have an interest or a *stake* in the focal organization. Freeman (1984), for example, broadly defined a stakeholder as "any individual or group who can affect or is affected by the actions, decisions, policies, practices, or goals of the organization" (p. 25). Of particular relevance to donors, Brody (1988) defined stakeholders as "groups of individuals whose interests coincide in one or more ways with the organization" (p. 81). J. E. Grunig and Repper (1992) stated, "Stakeholders are people who are *linked* to an organization because they and the organization have consequences on each other" (p. 125; italics added).

Esman (1972) conceptualized four types of linkages organizations have with their environments that are critical for survival. J. E. Grunig and Hunt (1984) used the linkages to identify categories of stakeholders:

1. *Enabling linkages* with organizations and groups that "provide the authority and control the resources that enable an organization to exist" (p. 140). Examples of enabling stakeholders are members of the focal organization's governing board, government entities, such as Congress and state legislators, shareholders for publicly owned corporations, and donors for charitable organizations.

2. *Functional linkages* with internal and external groups and organizations that "provide inputs and take outputs," which divides this type in two (p. 141). The most common example of functional stakeholders linked by inputs are employees; volunteers also fit in this group. Consumers, or clients, are the most common example of those linked by outputs (i.e., they use the organization's products or services).

3. *Normative linkages* with organizations that "face similar problems or share similar views" (p. 142). These linkages provide cooperative arrangements whereby the focal organization is part of a larger whole. Examples of normative stakeholders for charitable organizations are associations, such as IS, and federations, such as the UWs.

4. *Diffused linkages* to people who "cannot clearly be identified by membership" in formal groups (p. 142). These linkages provide potential support for or opposition to the organization, depending on its behavior. Examples of diffused stakeholders are community residents and the media.

J. E. Grunig and Hunt argued that the four types of linkages and their resulting stakeholders explain why so many organizations have public relations programs targeted at such groups as government, investors, employees, consumers, community residents, and the media. In other words, the linkages define the publics with which the function of public relations traditionally has been concerned. Expertise in managing communication with specific stakeholders, in turn, has resulted in the public relations specializations presented in chapter 1: government relations, investor relations, employee relations, consumer relations, community relations, and media relations. As also discussed in chapter 1, donor relations recently has been defined as one of the seven specializations of public relations, which we now can understand in terms of systems theory and environmental linkages.

Donors are *enabling stakeholders* because they control resources that enable charitable organizations to exist. Although dependency on gifts varies for each organization, the charitable subsector would cease to exist without donors (i.e., there would be no reason for continuing the privileged status granted by society). Furthermore, donors are not functional stakeholders, which would describe a marketing perspective of fund raising. Donors are not necessarily consumers of the organization's outputs, nor should their importance be diminished by viewing them simply as providers of needed inputs.

Prospective donors are identified among stakeholders connected through all four types of linkages. A first step in fund raising, then, is to make a list of the people who have a stake in the organization, which Freeman (1984) called a *stakeholder map*. J. E.

Grunig and Repper (1992) explained that the list is compiled by "thinking through the consequences an organization has on people and that they have on the organization" (p. 126). Although some connections will be apparent, consequences regarding diffused stakeholders should be determined through environmental scanning, whereby practitioners conduct public opinion polls, study specialized and mass media, and confer with opinion leaders, among other research. A stakeholder map for a private university likely would include the following groups whose members may be prospects for gifts: trustees and previous donors (enabling linkages), vendors and faculty (functional input linkages), parents of current students, alumni, and employers of alumni (functional output linkages), community residents and friends (diffused linkages), and a regional federation that solicits businesses on behalf of institutional members (normative linkages).

The second step, according to Grunig and Repper, is to rank or assign weights to stakeholders to indicate their importance to the organization. Programming is then planned and implemented to communicate with the most strategic ones, working down the ranked list until available resources are used up. Communication at this stage is especially important "because it helps to develop the stable, long-term relationships that an organization needs to build support from stakeholders and to manage conflict when it occurs" (J. E. Grunig & Repper, 1992, p. 127). It must be emphasized that the analysis, by definition, encompasses all stakeholders of an organization, even those unable to make gifts (e.g., government agencies that provide public but not private funding). This critical point is returned to at the end of the chapter when integrated relationship management is discussed.

Although stakeholder analysis provides a beginning for fund raising, not all members of any one of its broad categories will be equally likely to communicate with the organization or enact a giving behavior. To increase probabilities, stakeholders must be segmented into *publics*, which form around a problem, issue, or opportunity. J. E. Grunig and Repper (1992) explained the subtle but significant difference between the two levels of relationships: "Many people in a category of stakeholders—such as employees or residents of a community—are passive. The stakeholders who are or become more aware and active can be described as publics" (p. 125). The two terms often are used interchangeably; however, indiscriminant efforts to raise gifts from stakeholders are inefficient. Illustrating as it relates to the private university just used as an example, only 25% of all individuals who have attended college ever make a gift to their undergraduate institutions, and only about 40% of those who earn a bachelor's degree make a gift (Brittingham & Pezzullo, 1990). In other words, affiliation as a stakeholder, by itself, is not a sufficient condition for giving.

Boundary Spanners

White and Dozier (1992) defined *boundary spanners* as "individuals within the organization who frequently interact with the organization's environment and who gather, select, and relay information from the environment to decision makers in the dominant coalition" (p. 93). Drawing from management scholars, fund raisers span organizational boundaries to perform two functions: external representation and information seeking. Practitioners most frequently act to represent the organization to the external environment. Staff managers, however, also employ environmental scanning, issues management, and strategic planning to research donor publics and represent their views to the dominant coalition.

Illustrating, Vincent Pellegrino (cited in M. Davis, 1994), vice chancellor for development at the University of Tennessee, Chattanooga (UTC), responded to a question about his work philosophy as follows:

> The fundamental challenge I face every day is to constantly refine the vision of the university. I know how the philanthropic community responds to the institution. Based on that, I need to effectively communicate that to the provost and the chancellor and the academic deans: This is what is going on in the minds of the community. And I'm the liaison from them back to the community. (p. A12)

Asked how he kept up with public opinion, Pellegrino answered:

> I'm always out gathering information, and not only in those sectors bounded by corporations and foundations. It's getting out into all the areas of the town to find out what the needs are. You've got to go out to the churches, to the non-profit organizations. You've got to ask what's going on and what they need from UTC. (p. A12)

It is important to note that Pellegrino referred to refining the "vision" of his university, not its mission. A fund-raising philosophy that focused on altering the mission to evoke a positive response from prospective donors is indicative of a marketing, or two-way asymmetrical approach. Pellegrino's philosophy, on the other hand, focuses on helping his CEO, senior managers, and line managers develop a symmetrical perspective—one that enables them to consider donors' potential reaction to their decisions. Furthermore, Pellegrino concerns himself with stakeholders other than donors, thereby expanding the vision of dominant coalition members. With this comprehensive perspective, the organization is able to adapt to its environment and increase its probability of success.

Although numerous members of a charitable organization are involved in fund-raising activities (e.g., trustees and the CEO), it is the specialist responsible for donor relations who is expected to ensure a continuing income of gifts (i.e., fund raisers reduce the environmental uncertainty of private support). White and Dozier (1992) summarized conclusions of management scholars: "Lack of information, ambiguity in information, or uncertainty regarding the likelihood of outcomes in given situations make decision makers uncertain. Under such conditions, boundary spanners play important roles in providing information about environmental contingencies" (p. 103). Grønbjerg (1993) connected fund raisers' organizational power to their boundary-spanning role:

> Individuals responsible for maintaining those external relationships that provide the most critical resources for the organization will be able to exercise the highest level of power in the organization, especially if they are able to reduce the amount of uncertainty associated with the resource. They have internal leverage because they can deprive the organization of access to the resources by how they manage the exchange relationship. (p. 292)

In addition to reducing uncertainty, practitioners protect and buffer the organization from its environmental dependencies. Describing the philanthropic arena, Van

Til (1990) argued that perspectives of donors, recipient organizations, fund raisers, and the broader community "often clash with each other dramatically" (p. xx). Burlingame and Hulse (1991) stated, "A fund raiser often must balance competing, sometimes conflicting, demands and expectations of staff, colleagues, volunteers, trustees, and donors" (p. xxii). Payton (1987) simply said, "To practice philanthropy is to engage in a constant struggle with the claims of self-interest" (p. 45).

Self-interest is the single most important word in fund raising. Fund raisers are effective when they accept—but do not take for granted or abuse—America's philanthropic tradition and focus on the interests and needs of donors. With this other-directed mindset, they conduct research to identify those prospects with whom their organization shares common interests. They rely on two-way communication and negotiation to manage the process by which gifts are acquired. The necessity of negotiation is most apparent in raising major gifts because such gifts usually are restricted. Brittingham and Pezzullo (1990) explained, "Negotiations over the size and conditions of large gifts . . . are often so detailed that the conversation and correspondence . . . come to resemble more closely negotiation for a contract" (p. 62). As Gottlieb and Healy (1990) asserted, negotiation is a necessary activity in situations involving two or more parties that have to make a decision about their interdependent goals and objectives. Grønbjerg (1993) described the contingencies organizations face in relations with donors, "They must decide how to link the priorities of funding sources to organizational missions and client or community needs, how to develop resource flexibility and cushion themselves against funding jolts, and how to engage in networking and other boundary-spanning activities in order to develop and maintain resources" (p. 275).

Fund raisers' boundary role helps us understand their pivotal position in determining the amount of organizational autonomy lost through the process of raising gifts. As Dressel (1980) argued, "Inevitably, there will be times at which those involved in the continuing interaction and negotiation . . . will differ as to the measure of institutional autonomy that should be awarded . . . and as to the nature, character, and source of appropriate constraints which may be placed upon the institution" (p. ix). Ostrander and Schervish (1990) elaborated, "Attention to recipient needs may not always remain prominent or determinant in the minds of those providing donor resources or in the minds of those who seek funding on behalf of ultimate beneficiaries" (p. 73).

AUTONOMY AND ACCOUNTABILITY

Two principles that on the surface appear in conflict are:

Fund raising should be need driven, not donor driven;

and

Enable the donor to develop a sense of ownership.

Brittingham and Pezzullo (1990) explained the first: "The literature on fund raising makes much of the point that fund raisers should not set their institution's priorities for fund raising; they should raise money for institutional priorities" (p. 57). In other words, the interests and needs of donors should not take precedence over those of the organization. Equating giving with investing, Lord (1983) advocated the second principle: "When we recruit investors, we must give them a share of ownership. . . . As many a businessman [*sic*] is fond of saying, 'There's no free lunch'—not from government, and not from philanthropy, either" (p. 31).

The two principles are based on theories about autonomy and accountability. As previously argued in relation to government, the two concepts must be discussed in tandem. Accountability, it is recalled, is both general to society and specific to such stakeholders as donors and clients. Social exchange theory prescribes that charitable organizations be accountable to prospective and current donors. Their needs, interests, wishes, and ideas must be addressed during the process of raising gifts. Accountability, Dressel (1980) reminded us, is the price of autonomy.

Like government, donors affect autonomy—the ability of an organization to govern itself without outside controls. Berdahl and Altbach (1981) divided the concept into two parts: autonomy of a *substantive* nature, defined as the power of an organization to determine its own goals and programs, and autonomy of a *procedural* nature, which is the organization's power to determine the means by which its goals and programs will be pursued. According to Dressel (1980), "No institution can receive support from public or private sources and maintain complete autonomy" (p. 1). He asserted, "Any discussion of autonomy must focus on the nature and extent of autonomy required for effective operation of the institution [and] on the institution's fulfillment of its responsibilities to society" (p. x).

L. A. Grunig, J. E. Grunig, and Ehling (1992) concluded from their extensive review of the management and sociology literature that all types of organizations "struggle constantly to achieve their mission—the goals selected by internal decision makers—in the face of constraints imposed by outside groups or interests" (p. 67). The reality of interdependence, as explained by systems theory, means that organizations have relationships with outside stakeholders, which constrain autonomy, whether such relationships are wanted or not. Absolute autonomy, then, is neither possible nor desirable for charitable organizations because all funding involves some loss, and such organizations are accountable to the stakeholders with whom they are interdependent and to the larger society.

At the same time, fund-raising managers hold autonomy as high in importance in the philanthropic exchange and protect their organizations from excessive loss. The seriousness of their responsibility cannot be minimized. In one of the rare essays about the concept as it relates to fund raising, Pratt (1991) stated, "Balancing the financial needs of an organization with the interests of government and private donors presents constant challenges to a nonprofit's concept of autonomy" (p. 220).

Autonomy Forfeited

In my earlier book, I examined the tension created by the desire of donors to shape an organization according to their ideas of what the organization should be and do, and the desire of organizational leaders to shape the organization according to their own ideas and interpretation of the mission (Kelly, 1991a; see particularly chaps. 7–9). I concluded from my critical analysis:

- All donors—individuals, corporations, and foundations—have potential for infringing on the autonomy of charitable organizations through their gifts.
- All types of charitable organizations are vulnerable to losing autonomy during the process of raising gifts.
- All gifts—major gifts, individually and collectively, and lower level gifts, collectively—have potential to negatively affect organizational autonomy.

I also provided a number of examples of organizations forfeiting high degrees of their autonomy in order to meet the demands of donors. Not surprisingly, public reports about such situations are rare. The following examples add to those reported earlier.

In 1991, critics charged that the Christian Science Church published an irresponsible biography of its founder, Mary Baker Eddy, in order to get a $90-million bequest left by the author's wife and her sister ("$90-million," 1991). According to the archivist for the church's headquarters, who was dismissed after 29 years, the biography "pretends to deify the founder" (p. 16), which is opposite to what the church teaches about Baker Eddy. The bequest required that the book, which the church had refused to publish for more than 40 years, be released by 1993 and be prominently displayed in the organization's 2,500 reading rooms around the world. As stipulated by the bequest, if the terms were not met, the money would be evenly divided between Stanford University and the Los Angeles County Museum of Art. In 1993, the church announced it had reached a compromise settlement with the two other organizations, which had sued it after the book's publication because—they claimed—all conditions of the gift had not been met ("Accord," 1993). Under the settlement, the church received half of the disputed bequest, which then totaled $100 million.

Texaco Corporation announced in 1992 that it was discontinuing its sponsorship of *Great Performances*, a PBS television series ("Aid," 1992). Although the oil company said it was withdrawing its approximately $900,000 annual gift because it was moving away from supporting classical types of works, a filmmaker who helped produce the series charged that Texaco's decision was due to the homosexual content of one of the shows. The company and the host station denied the charges. Yet a study published in *Columbia Journalism Review* found that public broadcasters have shied away from controversial shows because they worry that such programming might lead corporate donors to stop giving money ("Public TV," 1991).

When Texas billionaire Ross Perot was running for president in 1992, news reports described him as a donor who walks away from or attacks charitable organizations "that he cannot control or that do not meet his exacting standards" (Goss, 1992, p. 6). For example, the former chairperson of the Vietnam Veterans Memorial Fund claimed that Perot, who had given more than $170,000 to finance the design competition for the Washington, DC memorial, tried to dictate the design after it already had been decided. According to the chairperson, Perot was so displeased with the winning entry that he threatened to "wipe out" the group. "The bottom line is we went to Ross for help and we were very grateful to him. And then when we wouldn't change the design to suit his demands, he turned on us" (p. 7).

In 1994, Michigan State University was embroiled in a controversy over its search for a new dean to head its business school (Howes, 1994). Eli Broad, who gave $20 million to the school that bears his name, was displeased with the list of finalists for the position. He stated in a news report, "I am a bit disappointed . . . . The dean search—like it or not and we'll see—has been dominated by the faculty. The committee could have had some stronger non-faculty people on it" (Howes, 1994, p. 1D). Broad admitted that if the final candidate did not have the right qualifications, he would intervene with the university's president. On the other hand, the chairperson of the school's marketing and logistics department said outside intervention would be viewed very badly by the business school faculty. He added, "There are things that Broad can do for us and help us a lot, and there are things that are not in his purview from outside the university (p. 4D). According to the news report, this was not the first time Broad attempted to influence decision making at Michigan State. He was involved in that institution's decision to replace its president in 1992.

The University of California system was attacked by state legislators in 1996 when its Los Angeles campus, UCLA, acknowledged that it had admitted some students in large part because they had connections to major donors (Demko & Dundjerski, 1996). Fund raisers rated requests for preferential treatment according to the donor's importance to the university, and the rating was included in the student's application file. UCLA officials justified the action, saying that it was necessary "in order to maintain their fund-raising success" (Demko & Dundjerski, 1996, p. 27). Admission officers at other universities said it was not uncommon for donors to influence admission decisions.

Duronio (1994a) found that autonomy was an issue of concern among the 82 fund raisers she interviewed. A female practitioner in higher education related the following situation:

> We had a chair endowed by a donor who didn't like the person who held the chair. The dean was told to fire him or lose his own job. The person in the chair retired and solved the problem. Now we are going through a search to fill the chair. The academic community . . . knows the story so it has been hard to get good candidates. Now the donor wants to be on the search committee. Where is it going to end? (p. 15)

Nine of the university presidents Cook (1994a) interviewed for his fund-raising study commented on autonomy without prompting. One described the following encounter: "There was a prominent executive in Dallas that a number of years ago we were talking to about our graduate school of business, and he said, 'Fine, if you'll move it to Dallas.'. . . I mean, he was serious. He wanted it moved to Dallas. We can't do that. That is not part of our mission" (p. 450). Another president warned:

> That's a hard lesson that many people don't learn. . . . Look gift horses in the mouth, contrary to popular thinking. . . . It's very easy to prostitute yourself in this business—deliberately or inadvertently, it doesn't matter. And having once done it, it is easier to do it the second time. And then before you know it the program is not in your hands anymore. (p. 452)

Boris and Odendahl (1990) described the relationship between raising gifts of all sizes—not just major gifts—and autonomy, identifying it as a management issue with significant consequences:

Because revenue is both difficult to obtain and essential to ongoing operations, fund raising may begin to shape an organization's mission and dominate its activities. . . . mission may be shifted into areas that have greater appeal to donors. These are choices, often with ethical components, that the board and staff should confront and decide with clear understanding of the impact on the organization, its mission, and those it serves. (p. 196)

Pratt (1991) agreed, "Funding pressures act as incentives for an organization to adjust its original mission to more closely match current funder preferences" (p. 221). Addressing specific gifts, he added, "At a certain point, the funding process can shift the locus of control for key organizational decisions from the nonprofit board to the funding source" (p. 222). He focused on corporate donors, claiming, "Corporate giving officers actually have greater power over decisions in the organizations they fund than they do over many decisions made in their own companies. Based on the resource-driven willingness to adapt on the part of nonprofits, corporate grants undoubtedly influence nonprofit planning and service strategies" (p. 221).

Barbara Levy (1994), who has more than 20 years of fund-raising experience with arts organizations, discussed loss of both substantive and procedural autonomy to foundation donors. She said if a foundation grant "sidetracks the organization from its mission," or if it "adds unmanageable strain" (p. 43), the fund raiser should refuse it. She related her personal experiences: "I have, on occasion, convinced an artistic director to add an educational or touring component to a project in order to meet funding guidelines. It seemed logical. But adding such an element to an already tight budget meant something else had to give. It was several years before I began to consider the consequences" (p. 41). She continued, "Securing grants can make us, as development officers, appear effective. . . . But if the funded program ends up costing our organizations too much money or time, or detracts from its mission, the grant was too expensive" (p. 41). Levy linked lost autonomy to the very survival of organizations by describing how dance companies in the 1970s brought about their demise because of grants they pursued from a popular fund for dance-touring programs: "The funding appeared to be the answer to the financial crunch many of the companies were feeling. But the grants ended up supporting only the adjunct touring arm of the companies. The parent companies meanwhile fell deeper into debt, forcing many of them to close their doors" (p. 42).

M. R. Hall (1993) concluded from her study on fund-raising decentralization at 213 research universities, "Private gifts can and do alter institutional priorities" (p. 78). Almost one half of her study's respondents (47%) reported that a major gift had, in the past, caused a significant shift in priorities of an academic unit. The shift, however, was readily accepted by the unit (94%) and by the central administration (95%).

M. W. Martin (1994) argued that donors who seek power through giving are not necessarily selfish. He explained, "Rather than manipulating people and violating rights, they may be seeking power in order to improve the world by exerting responsible influence based on others' *voluntary* consent" (p. 143; italics added). Illustrating, a wealthy individual quoted by Panas (1984) remarked, "If I make a large gift to an organization I would expect to have some influence if change really was necessary" (p. 30). Such relations between donor and organizational recipient are very different from those described in most of the fund-raising literature. They also differ dramatically from the historical perspective presented by Curti and Nash (1965): "The optimum relationship seems over the years to have been one in which the donor gave little but his [*sic*] money" (p. 263).

Resource Dependence

A widely accepted fund-raising principle is:

Build a broad base of donors.

Rosso (1991) explained, "Broad-spectrum fund raising that seeks gifts from diverse sources promotes good health within the organization by making it more resilient, more aware of market requirements, more sensitive to changes within the environment, and more responsive to the service and support requirements of its constituencies" (p. 12). Although he neglected to include individual donors and unexplainably excluded small organizations, Rosso warned, "A dependency on single sources of funding—foundations, corporations, or government—is too risky for any but the smallest of agencies, and even these must understand that the playing field provided by the dominant funding source is 'tilted' to the funding source's advantage" (p. 292).

Resource dependence theory explains this principle. Pfeffer and Salancik (1978) conceptualized four strategies for avoiding external control, the most effective of which is to develop substitutable exchanges in order to diversify sources and loosen dependencies. Applied to fund raising, a broad base of donors—including individuals, corporations and foundations—and conducting both annual giving and major gifts programs reduce the possibility that a charitable organization will forfeit a high degree of autonomy to one or more donors. As M. R. Hall (1993) stated, "Smaller gifts from a larger number of donors counterbalance the potential for a single very large gift to have too great an influence on the priorities of the institution" (p. 106).

Providing scientific evidence, Grønbjerg (1993) employed resource dependence theory to conduct 13 case studies on the funding of social services and community development organizations. Among her sample, she identified an extreme case of lost autonomy, whereby an organization obtained the bulk of its funding from a major institution in the community. She described the relationship as approaching "a condition of cooptation" (p. 158) and hypothesized that similar relationships may characterize other organizations that also depend heavily on a single funding source. Her findings, she concluded, supported "the general argument that an organization that depends heavily on an exchange relationship with one particular funding source will be subject to considerable influence from that source" (p. 292).

Pfeffer and Salancik's (1978) other three strategies for avoiding external control—with examples relevant to fund raising provided—are as follows: (a) build an inventory (e.g., raise gifts to increase endowments, which produce income in perpetuity), (b) define terms of the exchange relationship (e.g., establish policies that standardize fund-raising decisions and describe unacceptable gift conditions), and (c) diversify and build alternative sources (e.g., seek a balance among donor gifts, government grants and contracts, client fees and dues, and endowment and investment earnings). Students should understand that developing substitutable exchanges and diversifying alternative sources do not reduce demands from external stakeholders; in fact, they create the potential for more—but diversification does reduce the focal organization's need to respond to any given demand.

Paradoxically, an organization, because of its external dependencies, often seeks to stabilize the exchange relationships that threaten its autonomy. One method used is *cooptation*, which Pfeffer and Salancik (1978) defined as "managing the environment by appointing significant external representatives to positions in the organization" (p. 161). The method's application to fund raising is evident in the principle:

Place your top donors on the governing board

Paul Franz (1981), former vice president of development at Lehigh University, explained, "A well-constituted board must have a good potential to raise funds, and this means that at least half of the members should have the capability to give and to solicit major gifts" (p. 163). In other words, single funding sources—as described by Grønbjerg (1993)—and organizational recipients try to coopt the other party in exchange relationships. Although cooptation stabilizes the relationship, it also can formalize external control.

It is recalled from findings of the explanatory study on the fund-raising models, reported in chapter 6, that the larger the organization, as measured by its number of employees, the more likely it will practice the two-way symmetrical model in its major gifts program. This finding suggests that larger organizations accommodate the interests and needs of major donors without forfeiting high degrees of autonomy (i.e., symmetrical fund raising balances accountability and autonomy). The interpretation is supported by management theories, which hold that larger organizations are less vulnerable in interdependent relationships with funding sources. Pfeffer and Salancik (1978), for example, stated: "Organizations that are large have more power and leverage over their environments. They are more able to resist immediate pressures for change" (p. 139). In other words, size may be a predictor of propensity for loss of autonomy from donors, and large organizations might best manage relationships with major donors who help finance them. Therefore, major donors who are members of the dominant coalition of large organizations likely do not represent a threat; in smaller organizations they do.

Based on her findings and resource dependence theory, Grønbjerg (1993) concluded, "To secure stable donation streams, nonprofits seek to institutionalize their relationships with donors. To do so, demands additional management efforts and almost always requires the organization to relinquish some control over its own operations. In extreme cases, the organization may cease to operate as a fully independent entity" (p. 164).

Confronting the Challenge

A tension between donor and organizational recipient logically is inherent in a social exchange in which both parties advance their self-interests, as well as a common good. M. W. Martin (1994) presented the recipient's case: "Philanthropic organizations are legitimately interested in their own survival, growth, resources, and reputation, in order to meet their philanthropic aims" (p. 17). Donors, he said, also have interests related to self. He suggested that people have a fundamental right to seek satisfaction of their needs, which he termed *individual autonomy* and defined as "the right and the ability to competently pursue one's interests and values" (p. x). Ideally, he argued, gifts augment autonomy by providing recipients with resources to pursue their interests and by offering donors opportunities to pursue theirs. M. R. Hall (1993) described this ideal in higher education: "Institutions seek donors whose interests overlap with the goals of the college or university. Institutional leaders try to avoid accepting gifts that skew priorities, drain resources from core programs, or give the donor an opportunity to dictate internal policy such as personnel decisions or admission decisions" (p. 76). J. P. Smith (1982) warned: "Sometimes a donor's preferences and purposes simply do not match ours. And then the honorable thing to do is to say no" (p. 36).

The tension also represents the recipient organization's struggle between accountability, which assures that it will provide the services society and strategic stakeholders want and need, and autonomy, which assures that it will remain independent. Illustrating, one of the CEOs interviewed by Cook (1994a) explained:

> You have to decide whether you're willing to admit potential supporters into the university's heart, or do you want to keep them out? Lots of presidents . . . want to keep [donors] the hell out. They're not going to raise money very well if they do that. . . . You've got to consult with them and so forth because that's the only way you're going to get people really involved in the place, if they have some kind of say in what's going on. And that's very delicate because you can't turn over your responsibility to them. (p. 452)

Describing the relationship between recipient and donor, M. R. Hall (1993) said a "creative tension develops that keeps each responsive to the other" (p. 76).

Physicists explain that tension is a necessary condition of movement and action; it is not necessarily cause for alarm or distress (Wolfenden, 1968). However, if a donor insists on calling the tune because he or she pays the piper, or if an organization claims the right to ignore those who support it because of absolute autonomy, there inevitably will be not just tension, but friction. And friction, according to physicists, "is apt to generate heat, and in certain conditions, explosion" (p. 206).

To avoid friction, fund raisers and dominant coalition members must acknowledge that it is in the charitable organization's self-interest to identify, build, and maintain *good* relationships with strategic stakeholders. L. A. Grunig et al. (1992) clarified, "Relationships limit autonomy, but good relationships limit it less than bad relationships" (p. 69). They elaborated: "Good relationships . . . make organizations more effective because they allow organizations more freedom—more autonomy—to achieve their missions than they would [have] with bad relationships. By giving up autonomy by building relationships, ironically, organizations maximize that autonomy" (p. 69). As Pfeffer and Salancik (1978) stated, "Organizations comply with the demands of others, or they act to manage the dependencies that create constraints on organizational actions" (p. 257).

Steele and Elder (1992) drew from my earlier work to present two principles for guiding fund-raising practice: (a) fund raising seeks consonance between a donor's wishes and an organization's needs, and (b) fund raising is judged to be successful when it results in gifts that contribute to the strategic vision for the organization. Explaining the principles, they argued that fund raising "should proceed in an open, ethical, balanced, win–win way" (p. 1) and that gifts should free an organization to achieve its goals rather than hamper or distract it from its mission. Fund-raising effectiveness, they said, should not be judged by the dollars raised, but by the extent to which gifts contribute to organizational autonomy. Subsequent research has both confirmed and advanced my thinking on the subject, which now focuses on the balance between autonomy and accountability.

I measured propensity to forfeit autonomy as part of the explanatory study on the fund-raising models (Kelly, 1995a). Generalizing the findings from the 296 respondents, one third of the fund raisers belonging to NSFRE believe that although donors' priorities do not control, they often do not blend with those of the organization. One fourth agree that it is not rare for donors to try to influence organizational policy, and almost one third agree that some gifts cause a significant shift in organizational priorities. One fourth of the organizations represented in NSFRE have changed their goals or shifted their priorities in order to acquire a particular gift. The 11 items measuring autonomy and the percentages of respondents who agreed or disagreed with each item are listed in Table 9.1.

Among other conclusions drawn from the findings, the majority of NSFRE members (61%) believe senior managers often have unrealistic expectations of fund raisers, which suggests that pressure is placed on practitioners to generate gift dollars regardless of the purpose of the gifts. The interpretation is supported by the finding that 38% of the respondents agreed that dollar amount determines the importance of gifts. Brittingham and Pezzullo (1990) reported that a major dilemma facing practitioners is "balancing institutional pressures toward improving the bottom line in fund

TABLE 9.1
Agreement and Disagreement by NSFRE Members With 11 Autonomy Items

Autonomy Variables	Agree	Disagree
Organizations must be flexible when prioritizing gift needs.	77%	9%
Senior managers often have unrealistic expectations of fund raisers.	61%	21%
Possible negative reaction by donors is often taken into consideration when planning new programs or policy changes.	54%	23%
No organizational policy to control acquisition of gifts.	50%	44%
Donors give for excellence and enhancement purposes, not for basics.	44%	34%
Importance of a gift largely is determined by its dollar amount.	38%	46%
Donor priorities do not control, but often they do not blend with those of the organization.	33%	34%
Some gifts cause a significant shift in organizational priorities.	31%	49%
Incidences of donors trying to influence organizational policy are not rare.	25%	60%
My organization has changed its goals or shifted its priorities in order to acquire a particular gift.	25%	75%
Announced fund-raising needs generally do not have a strong relationship to the purposes of gifts actually raised.	14%	73%

Note. $N = 296$. Percentages do not add up to 100% due to neutral, or "Neither Agree Nor Disagree," responses.

raising with issues of matching fund raising with institutional priorities" (p. 73). In other words, fund raisers often are compelled to ignore the real needs of their organizations and accept gifts that appear to have little relation to priorities and goals. They spend time and resources on such gifts because their performance is measured solely by the amount of indiscriminate dollars raised, not by the degree to which gifts support priorities and goals. This flawed evaluation leads fund raisers to concentrate on dollar amounts, which—in turn—leads them to accept gifts without negotiating terms that may substantially reduce their organization's autonomy. Illustrating the quandary in which many practitioners find themselves, a male respondent wrote "unfortunately" after he strongly agreed with the statement, "The importance of a gift largely is determined by its dollar amount."

Three fourths of all NSFRE members (76%) believe charitable organizations must be flexible when prioritizing gift needs, and one half of the organizations represented in the association (50%) have no policy to control the acquisition of gifts, which would protect autonomy. Only 15% of the organizations have a comprehensive written policy to guide practitioners in such important decisions as what can and cannot be accepted, or what potential costs of administrating the gift's purpose must be covered by the donor.

Theory predicted that there would be a positive relationship between loss of autonomy and practice of the three asymmetrical models. Analyses of the relationships between the autonomy measurements and the models did not support the prediction (Kelly, 1995a). For example, there was significant consensus across all but the press agentry model that senior managers in the respondents' organizations take possible negative reaction by donors into consideration when planning new programs or policy changes. These and other findings suggested that some of the items actually measured accountability to donors rather than propensity to forfeit autonomy.

Attempts to construct a scale from the 11 autonomy items were unsuccessful. All the items were first added into one scale, but correlations between the scale and the four fund-raising models were uninterpretable. The items were then factor analyzed in an attempt to group them by relatedness. Four factors were produced, but their underlying concepts could not be identified. Also, the reliabilities of the factor scales were unacceptably low, with Cronbach's alphas ranging from .23 to .39. These unsuccessful attempts to combine the autonomy items provided empirical evidence that autonomy was closely related to accountability and that the two must be approached in tandem.

Based on organizational theory and the findings of the explanatory study, I concluded that the dual concepts are best understood as a continuum with high autonomy at one end and high accountability at the other end. This continuum represents the balanced and unbalanced effects of the fund-raising models (i.e., their symmetrical vs. asymmetrical dimension). The symmetrical model strives to maintain a balance between autonomy and accountability, placing the organization in the middle of the continuum. Asymmetrical models invite situations in which either excessive amounts of autonomy are forfeited in exchange for a gift—placing the organization at the high accountability end of the continuum—or accountability to donors is ignored—placing the organization at the high autonomy end. Either extreme results in friction, which, as just pointed out, can cause an explosion.

Fund raising presents a double-edged sword: Without adequate funding, there is little autonomy because there is little freedom to pursue mission-related goals, but the needs and interests of donors also can limit autonomy. Pratt (1991) presented his version of the dilemma: "The difficult, ongoing challenge is for nonprofit boards and managers to successfully assert and maintain a strong focused mission and, simultaneously, get the resources necessary to carry it out" (p. 222). The critical question, then, is the extent and nature of the limitations that can be imposed on the autonomy of the organization without eroding its effectiveness and accountability.

Some degree of autonomy is naturally and rightfully forfeited in relationships with donors, but research to match interests and the explicit acknowledgment of and provision for donor needs in the philanthropic exchange prevent profound losses. Interdependencies with donors must be managed symmetrically—through negotiation, collaboration, and conflict resolution—to avoid the risk of great losses of autonomy. J. E. Grunig and White (1992) affirmed: "Excellent organizations realize that they can get more of what they want by giving publics some of what they want. Reciprocity means that publics, too, will be willing to give up some of what they want to the organization" (p. 46).

Charitable organizations that practice fund raising symmetrically will relinquish some of their autonomy to meet the needs of donors, but will gain more in the long run than if they ignored donors' self-interest. In short, they will carefully and constantly balance accountability in relation to autonomy. Pratt (1991) reached a similar conclusion: "Nonprofits and their funders need to seriously discuss the trade-offs between achieving donor expectations and supporting nonprofit initiatives. It is inevitable that the grantmaking interaction brings out conflicts and different viewpoints—even opposite conclusions on the same aspect of the relationship" (p. 222). Dressel (1980) endorsed a two-way symmetrical approach:

> Only simultaneous and sympathetic interaction of an institution with society directed at maximizing the performance of the institution and its services to society can attain a conception of autonomy that benefits both the institution and its supporters. Since there is no unanimity either within the institution or the society it serves, this is a continuing process of interaction and negotiation. (p. ix)

Providing a summary statement for the first third of this chapter, J. E. Grunig and Repper (1992) stated, "Managers who manage strategically do so by balancing the mission of the organization—what it is, what it wants to be, and what it wants to do—with what the environment will allow or encourage it to do" (p. 119). Brittingham and Pezzullo (1990) transposed the meaning to fund raising: "Each request for support for a particular purpose is a statement about what the institution would like to become (or remain) . . . . And each accepted gift, with all of its stipulations and restrictions, is a statement about what the institution is willing to become, how it is willing to see itself and the world" (p. 57).

THEORY OF MAGIC BUTTONS

A time-tested principle handed down from veteran fund raisers is:

Separate prospects from suspects.

Rosso (1991) presented the Linkage–Ability–Interest (L–A–I) formula to guide practitioners. According to the formula, prospects are separated from suspects by three factors: (a) linkage to the organization, (b) ability to give, and (c) interest in the organization's mission, goals, and priorities. All three factors, Rosso warned, must apply; elimination of just one invalidates the process and reduces the "gift candidate" (p. 29) from prospect to suspect. Illustrating, a suspect is someone like comedian Bob Hope who has lots of money (i.e., ability), but no linkage to or known interest in the organization.

Steele and Elder (1992) called soliciting gifts from wealthy strangers the "'Why don't you call Donald Trump?' syndrome" (p. 28). The name changes, but the phenomenon does not. Ridiculing such practice, E. W. Wood (1989) stated, "Asking someone who has a lot of money—but no relationship with your organization—to make a major gift is like asking an attractive stranger to marry you just because you think they're eligible" (p. 1). Broce (1986) elaborated: "Because people have accumulated wealth does not automatically mean that they will wish to grace your institution with gifts. Because a foundation has made a gift to one college in your state does not mean that it will automatically support yours. The reason for giving may well be no more than geographic, but there must be a *reason*" (p. 24; italics added).

Addressing reasons for giving, Schervish and Herman (1988) asserted, "Motivational research remains fundamentally flawed due to the inability of researchers to more than nominally differentiate 'motives' from other aspects of *subjective orientation* such as goals, attitudes, interest, and values" (p. 56; italics added). Based on empirical findings, the philanthropy scholars concluded, "Motivations at most constitute only part of a broader framework of meaning that is dynamic and practical" (p. 57). They added, "From our perspective, philanthropy is a form of purposive social action in which an individual's mode of consciousness and mode of practice are linked together in a coherently ordered strategy or logic" (p. 57).

Donor motivation has captivated the attention of those conducting research on fund raising almost to the exclusion of other equally or even more important problems. The search to identify cross-situational demographics, cognitions (i.e., thoughts and ideas), and attitudes that underlie donor behavior has dominated research for decades and is partly responsible for the slow accumulation of a scholarly body of knowledge on fund raising.

As documented in chapter 4, fund-raising researchers primarily are full-time practitioners who also are part-time graduate students in education curricula. Explaining their preoccupation with administrative studies about variables that may predict giving, Brittingham and Pezzullo (1990) said practitioner researchers "have naturally been drawn to studies of donors' behavior, just as practitioners have longed for a *simple list* of characteristics that could help them identify likely donors from longer lists" (p. 90; italics added). They concluded their review of the research with a poignant understatement: "The cumulative results of these studies have been somewhat disappointing, given their relatively high numbers" (p. 90).

The hundreds of fund-raising studies on the relationship between donor characteristics and behavior have been based on what I call the *theory of magic buttons*. This theory is not articulated by the researchers employing it, it is not grounded in any scholarly domain, and it is not espoused in the fund-raising literature. In fact, the literature, consisting almost entirely of practitioner wisdom, provides little support for the theory (i.e., face validity). Regardless, searching for magic buttons arguably is the most popular theory guiding past and current fund-raising research.

The theory of magic buttons holds that there is a causal linkage between giving behavior and donor demographics, cognitions, and attitudes, if just the right combination can be found. Based on this premise, it assumes that prospective donors are passive participants in the philanthropic exchange—that donor characteristics determine behavior. It assumes that some people have a natural inclination to give and others do not. Those that do, the theory presumes, can be manipulated to behave as the organization desires. Donor characteristics are assumed to be cross-situational and even cross-organizational (i.e., donors will enact a giving behavior regardless of the purpose for which the gift is made or its recipient). The theory is based on a powerful model of communication in that messages sent to the receiver, whether in person or through other channels, will result in the desired behavior. Paraphrasing the mystical voice in *Field of Dreams*, the 1989 movie about baseball, if you find the right buttons, they will give.

Magic Bullet Theory

The theory corresponds to the *magic bullet theory* of mass communication. This first theory of media effects, as described by Lowery and DeFleur (1995) in their popular textbook, held that "a media message would reach every eye and ear in the same way, like a symbolic 'bullet,' immediately bringing about the same changes of thought and behavior in the entire audience" (pp. 13–14). Also known as the "hypodermic-needle theory," it assumed communication would have powerful effects on attitudes and behavior: The "injection of information into a population" would bring rapid and desired results (Simmons, 1990, p. 18). Studies based on this theory viewed audiences as vulnerable to messages; they could be manipulated by those who controlled message design and delivery. Attesting to the theory's general acceptance, most people in the early 20th century thought that the media were powerful, manipulative, and therefore dangerous. According to Lowery and DeFleur (1995), "It was within this guiding framework that empirical research on the influences of mass communications was to begin" (p. 14).

Accumulated findings from studies starting in the 1940s discredited the magic bullet theory (e.g., Hyman & Sheatsley, 1947). By the early 1960s, researchers concluded that communication, especially mass communication, does not exert strong, direct, and powerful effects on audiences (Dozier & Ehling, 1992). People are not passive receivers of messages, but active participants in the communication process. For example, the theory of selectivity explains that generally only people who already hold attitudes and beliefs similar to those expressed in the message will attend to that message (i.e., pay attention). A corollary provided by the theory of cognitive dissonance is that people avoid information that is contrary to their views and seek information that is consonant (e.g., many more nonsmokers than smokers attend to antismoking messages). A more contemporary and elegant explanation is simply that people engage in communication when it is of relevance to them (J. E. Grunig & Hunt, 1984). Therefore, people cannot be easily manipulated by communication, and they resist unwanted persuasion.

Scholars further rejected the concept of a *general public*. In addition to theoretical differences already pointed out, Cutlip et al. (1994) explained: "The mosaic of the many different ethnic, racial, religious, geographic, political, occupational, social, and special-interest groupings that would be included make the general public concept of little, if any, value. Rather, effective programs that communicate and build relationships call for specifically defined 'target publics'" (p. 245). Dozier and Ehling (1992) specified: "The general public is of no relevance to organizations. Nor do organizations have resources to establish and maintain relationships with all peoples and all other organizations" (p. 169). Cutlip et al. (1994) summarized findings of the communication research: "In short, the notion of a monolithic and passive mass audience does not describe reality. Rather, the more accurate description suggests selected active receivers processing messages designed for the few, not the masses" (p. 235).

Although the powerful effects theory was first replaced with one assuming minimal effects, communication scholars now subscribe to theories in the middle range. Illustrating, three decades of research suggested that much of our media consumption results in information gain, but that the acquired *knowledge* has little effect on attitude or behavior. Rather than accepting the premise of minimal impact, scholars pursued new lines of inquiry in their belief that the media have some important effects. In the early 1970s, McCombs and Shaw (1972) conceptualized agenda-setting theory, which holds that the media do not tell us what to think, but they do tell us what to think about (i.e., media set the agenda for public discussion). Agenda-setting is now widely accepted as the major effect of the mass media (J. E. Grunig & Hunt, 1984).

Of interest to future fund raisers, agenda-setting theory appears to explain why missions of some charitable organizations attract more gifts at given times than others. Research has shown that the relative number of people concerned about a problem or issue parallels the relative media emphasis of that problem, as measured by the amount of space or time devoted to it. In other words, media attention is causally related to the number of people who believe a societal problem is important, or salient, to them. There is anecdotal evidence that, in turn, a problem's widespread salience translates into increased giving to those organizations whose missions deal with the problem. For example, Mary Leonard (1992), director of the precollegiate education program at the Council on Foundations, attributed increased foundation giving for primary and secondary education during the 1980s to media coverage of reports criticizing U.S. education. She stated, "Foundation staff and board members read the news about the reports, and their sense of concern over educational problems gave rise to a significant increase in the number of funders interested in educational issues" (p. 376). Leonard claimed that only a small number of major foundations were active in the field before the media attention.

The amount of attention media devote to a social problem is often unrelated to any objective measure of its importance. Research has shown wide discrepancies between real-world circumstances and mass media coverage (Rogers, Dearning, & Chang, 1991). Therefore, concern over the killing of animals for fur is treated as a social problem whereas the hunger of homeless children is not. In their agenda-setting study of AIDS, Rogers et al. explained why certain issues climb onto the news agenda and others do not: "Journalists and editors are trained to recognize and value issues which are 'newsworthy' by virtue of how much the issue reflects, or can be made to reflect, such newsworthiness criteria as sensation, conflict, mystery, celebrity, deviance, tragedy, and proximity" (p. 2). Their subjective decisions about the degree to which an issue is newsworthy "determine the extent of mass media coverage that an issue receives" (p. 2).

Agenda-setting theory has attracted a great deal of attention from communication researchers, who have produced more than 200 published studies, as well as hundreds of unpublished theses, dissertations, and scholarly papers. Ironically, it has escaped the interest of researchers studying fund raising, philanthropy, and nonprofit management, even though issues studied in agenda setting frequently are those many charitable organizations were established to address (e.g., diseases and drugs). The theory offers rich possibilities for fund-raising research. Although there have been broad probes into the behavioral consequences of agenda setting, there have been no studies comparing media attention to giving behavior. Students could track selected social issues through content analysis of such elite newspapers as *The New York Times*, which is a traditional agenda-setting source, and compare the prominence given those issues with gifts to related organizations. Other studies could analyze the content of television news and survey a sample of donors about the types of organizations to which they give.

Research has shown that, because the mass media constantly need new information, an issue stays in the news for a limited amount of time, often less than a month. Studies examining the extent to which fund raisers take advantage of issue prominence would add to our knowledge of effective practice. For example, gifts to public television and radio stations increased 15% during the first quarter of 1995 when practitioners incorporated messages about threats of federal cutbacks in their solicitations (Rocque, 1995). According to Rocque, "Many fund raisers said they were helped by the substantial press attention that had been paid to Congressional efforts to trim spending on public broadcasting" (p. 27).

McCombs and Shaw (1993), whose work began agenda-setting theory, encouraged such research: "If the content of media and public agendas also can be parsimoniously linked to subsequent behavioral responses, agenda-setting theory will have solved in three decades a problem that eluded the much larger field of attitude and opinion research for a considerably longer period of time" (p. 64).

Domino Model

Despite the body of communication research accumulated over 50 years, variations of the magic bullet theory still are accepted by many public relations practitioners. The theory obviously is also accepted by fund-raising researchers conducting studies on donor motivation. J. E. Grunig and Hunt (1984) presented their *domino model* to graphically illustrate the assumptions such people hold about powerful communication effects.

The model consists of four dominos—message, knowledge, attitude, and behavior—toppling each other in line. As Dozier and Ehling (1992) described, "The domino model . . . implies strong causal linkage between communication (or messages) from an organization and direct, immediate impact on the knowledge, attitudes, and behavior of publics" (p. 163). In other words, some practitioners believe that communication increases knowledge, after which knowledge leads to a positive attitude, which results in a desired behavior—all in an inevitable progression.

J. E. Grunig and Hunt (1984) explained the fallacy of the model in that it assumes each domino affects subsequent dominos in the progression and that effects only occur in the sequence given. Furthermore, they stated, "There is little evidence that the knowledgeable person's attitude or behavior will consistently be that advocated by the organization communicating a particular message" (p. 125). Whereas some studies have shown that knowledge does at times lead to favorable attitudes, other studies have shown that the most knowledgeable people often have the most negative attitudes—"when negative means those people oppose the organization's point of view" (p. 125). They further pointed out that not everyone to whom a message is directed will choose to expose him- or herself to the message, and not everyone who is exposed will remember it. The scholars summarized, "The dominos may fall, but only rarely do they fall in a line and topple each other" (p. 125).

Based on J. E. Grunig and Hunt's work, Dozier and Ehling (1992) calculated the probabilities associated with the domino model (i.e., the chances of messages being successfully communicated to members of a target public, resulting in changes in knowledge, attitude, and then behavior). The calculations are presented in Fig. 9.1.

Drawing from their collective observations, the authors assigned a 40% chance that members of a targeted public actually are exposed to (i.e., reached by) a communicated message (e.g., they may choose to throw away a piece of mail). They argued that there is only a 50% chance that the members reached by the message actually will learn (i.e., retain, understand, or know) the key message points communicated. There is only a 20% chance that those who learn the key message points actually will adopt an attitude consistent with the intention of the message. Finally, only 10% of those holding a desired attitude will behave in a manner consistent with the attitude. As given in Fig. 9.1, multiplying these probabilities shows that there is only a 0.4%, or 4 in 1,000, chance of achieving a desired behavior with any particular member of the targeted public. Dozier and Ehling (1992) concluded, "A practitioner might find better odds for success in Las Vegas or Atlantic City" (p. 166).

Patrick Jackson (cited in "Opinion," 1993), a well-known public relations consultant, said anyone who still believes information alone affects behavior should examine the AIDS epidemic, arguably the most publicized phenomenon in history. As he explained, everybody knows what AIDS is, everybody knows how to prevent it, yet few people take heed. Public information campaigns, research has shown, result in *awareness*, but do not have significant impact on behavior. Jackson said the most noticeable outcome of publicity on AIDS is that people wear red ribbons; the objective was to get them to wear condoms.

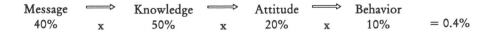

Message $\Longrightarrow$ Knowledge $\Longrightarrow$ Attitude $\Longrightarrow$ Behavior
40%   x   50%   x   20%   x   10%   = 0.4%

FIG. 9.1. Probabilities of powerful effects assumptions
(adapted from Dozlier & Ehling, 1992).

Representing a substantial body of research, a study conducted by the Ohio Department of Highway Safety in the early 1970s found that although 69% of the 25,000 drivers interviewed favored requiring seat belts in cars, only 28% used them when they drove (Gross & Niman, 1975). In other words, the majority of Ohio drivers held a positive attitude toward the behavior of wearing seat belts, but only a minority enacted a behavior consistent with that attitude. During the 1980s and 1990s, resolution of the seat belt issue moved from education to engineering and finally to enforcement, which J. E. Grunig and Hunt (1984) explained are progressively more effective means for changing behavior.

The fund-raising literature generally advocates principles supported by the research findings just presented. Unfortunately, it also contains evidence that many practitioners accept the domino model. K. S. Grace (1991a), for example, argued that "education" is required to bring donors to a giving behavior. Confusing the concept of publics with stakeholders, she called the educational process "maturation of the prospect": "Constituents must be moved from awareness, to understanding, to involvement and, finally, to commitment if they are to become stakeholders" (p. 185). Similarly, Rosso (1991) stated, "From awareness to understanding to acceptance is the direct path to people involvement and the process that is so necessary for constituency development" (p. 35). Howe (1991) said, "The interrelation of an organization with its supporters is a progression: first an awareness, then a familiarity and emerging interest, in turn an involvement, all leading to a contribution" (p. 75). The Cultivation Cycle, developed by G. T. "Buck" Smith (1977), is widely recognized as the standard formula for raising major gifts. Also known as the Five I's of Fund Raising, the popular formula is simply the domino model expressed in five steps: (a) identification, (b) information, (c) interest, (d) involvement, and (e) investment. Dunlop (1993) provided his version, the "Nurturing Fund-Raising Cycle" (p. 102): identification, information, awareness, understanding, caring, involvement, and commitment.

Donors are not passive participants who can be programmed to give; nor are they a predictable homogeneous group. As Steele and Elder (1992) warned, fund raisers must resist "the tendency to view people (and to treat them) as so many objects gliding along on a conveyor belt toward solicitation" (p. 22). Practitioners' acceptance of the domino model can be attributed to two factors: They have not been exposed to communication research, and they have confused fund-raising effects with a flawed progression of individual states. As presented later in this chapter, effects do form a hierarchy, with awareness as the lowest effect and behavior as one of the highest. The effects represent impacts of fund-raising efforts; they do not, however, represent a progression whereby an individual moves from a cognitive, to an attitudinal, to a behavioral state. The conceptualization will help future practitioners base their work on substantiated theory, not disproved models.

More serious is evidence that practitioners utilize the domino model to justify press agentry fund raising. In opposition to the L–A–I formula that demands that efforts be focused on prospects qualified by rigorous criteria, fund raisers practicing press agentry view all people as prospective donors. Illustrating, Howe (1991) asserted, "The potential for support is as wide as the number of people who can be reached by mail and as high as the largest gift of the most generous donor" (p. xvii). In the study measuring the four fund-raising models, reported in chapter 6, I found high agreement among NSFRE members with the statement: "The more people who know about our cause, the more dollars we will raise" (see Table 6.1). Mean scores on this item, which measured press agentry practice, were the second highest of the 16 items measuring the models: 11.33 ($SD = 3.57$) for the annual giving program and 10.81 ($SD = 4.36$) for the major gifts program, when 10 represented the typical response. Such views bode poorly for effective and ethical practice.

Answers to questions about who enacts a giving behavior and why are important to fund raising. Theories dealing with magic buttons, bullets, and dominos, however, seek simplistic solutions and fail to acknowledge the subject's complexity. All the social and behavioral sciences are concerned with the same fundamental question: Why do people behave as they do? (J. E. Grunig & Repper, 1992). Pat answers should not be expected. If philanthropy is a social exchange, then as prescribed by that theory, giving behavior must be analyzed by its dependence, not on the donor's attributes or prior conditioning, but on the exchange partner's behavior, which—in turn—is contingent on the donor's behavior (Blau, 1987). Theories that explain behavior in the context of organizational relationships provide the usable knowledge fund raisers need.

COORIENTATION THEORY

A widely endorsed principle is:

Match the organization's needs to donors' needs.

Rosso (1991) explained, "Fund raising is at its best when it strives to match the needs of the not-for-profit organization with the contributor's need and desire to give" (p. 7). Tempel (1991) argued:

> The organization must develop a program to understand what the gift source needs, what its preferences and perceptions are, and what it requires in the manner of value exchange. What are the philanthropic interests and needs of the prospective contributor? This knowledge serves as the basis for a meaningful exchange of values between the asking organization and the potential gift source. (p. 25)

Lord (1983) advised: "Understanding what people want is critical to the practice of fund raising. Not to ask them—to assume that we already know—is an oversight we can ill afford" (p. 17). He elaborated: "If we're not tuned in to what the donor community is saying, we can easily get in trouble—for we may end up trying to coerce people. We may find ourselves trying to convince people how they *should* think and what they *should* do" (p. 11; italics in original).

Coorientation theory supports the principle of matching needs; it explains the relationship between charitable organizations and donor publics and the critical role of agreement in efforts to raise both annual and major gifts. Annual gifts, it is recalled, usually are unrestricted, whereas major gifts almost always are restricted. Unrestricted annual gifts are made for general support of the organization's mission (i.e., the societal problem it addresses). Decisions about their use are left to senior managers and other members of the dominant coalition. The use of restricted major gifts, on the other hand, requires agreement by the donor and the dominant coalition before the gift is made. Although it is assumed general support of the organization's mission is a factor in most decisions to make major gifts, the specificity of the gift's use adds a second level of shared interest.

Coorientation models of relationships trace their beginnings to psychological studies about the mutual orientation of two individuals to some object. T. M. Newcomb's (1953) symmetry model was expanded by McLeod and Chaffee (1973), who based their model on the assumptions that behavior results from more than a person's internal thinking; it also is affected by the person's orientation to other people and perceptions of the views others hold. In colloquial terms, the theory describes the process of thinking about an issue as, "I think that you think that I think." Behavior, then, is defined in the context of relationships and is a product of both personal perceptions about an issue and perceptions of what others think about the same issue. Public relations scholars Glen Broom and David Dozier (1990) adapted the theory to corporations and publics, resulting in a model that represents the two sides of an organizational relationship. The model directs practitioners to examine perceptions that dominant coalitions and publics hold about each other and about issues that may or may not be of mutual concern or interest.

The coorientation model is further adapted here to explain a charitable organization's relationship to donors of annual gifts and major gifts. The appropriateness of applying coorientation theory is supported by findings from the study testing the fund-raising models, which showed a strong belief among practitioners belonging to NSFRE that the purpose of both their annual giving and major gifts programs is to develop *mutually beneficial* relationships between their organization and its donors (see Table 6.1). Mean scores on this item, designed to measure the two-way symmetrical model, were the highest of the 16 items measured: 11.69 (SD = 4.33) for annual giving and 12.20 (SD = 4.71) for major gifts, when 10 represented an average response. Figure 9.2 presents the coorientation model that identifies gift prospects for both programs.

The term *opportunity* can be used interchangeably with *problem* or *issue*. The fund-raising literature advocates use of the term in that gifts represent an opportunity for donors to help resolve a societal problem, as represented by the organization's mission. In addition, specific needs for which the organization seeks restricted gifts are referred to as *opportunities*. Indeed, those related to increasing physical and financial assets (i.e., facilities, equipment, and endowments) are regularly offered to major donor prospects as *named gift opportunities*, whereby the donor's name can be attached to the gift's use. Broce (1986) claimed the terminology emerged during the 1960s: "Money tends to flow to promising programs rather than to needy institutions. Most organizations dropped the word 'need' from the fund-raising vocabulary and replaced it with 'opportunity'" (p. 13). The term, then, conceptually describes any fund-raising effort. As given in Fig. 9.2, "fund-raising opportunity" represents the two primary programs of annual giving and major gifts, as well as single-unit efforts to raise a specific major gift.

The model consists of four elements: (a) the charitable organization's views of the fund-raising opportunity, (b) the donor public's views of that opportunity, (c) the organization's estimate of the donor public's views (i.e., perception), and (d) the donor public's estimate of the organization's views. *Agreement* represents the extent

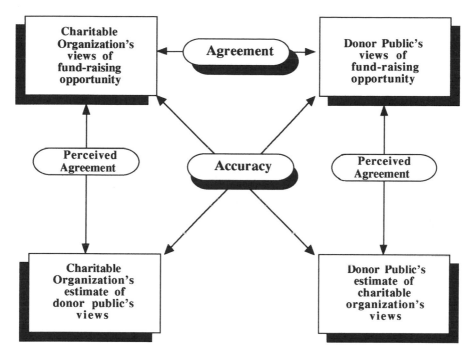

FIG. 9.2. Coorientation model: Identifying gift prospects
(adapted from Broom & Dozier, 1990).

to which the organization and the public hold similar views. *Accuracy* indicates the extent to which one side's estimate of the other's views is similar to the other's actual views. *Perceived agreement* describes how one side assesses the relationship in light of the opportunity, which affects if and how it interacts with the other side (e.g., planning programming or a response).

Coorientation States

The model suggests four coorientation states, defined by Broom and Dozier (1990). The first is *consensus*, when there is agreement between the organization's views and the donor public's views. Both sides essentially share the same views of the opportunity and each knows that such agreement exists. This state represents the ideal of a close match between the organization's needs and donors' needs. It also represents the mutually beneficial relationship sought by fund raisers in that a social exchange occurs that meets the self-interests of both sides. Whitaker (1974) described the state of consensus:

> The best and most durable relationships develop when the giver and the receiver fully agree in their sense of values as to what needs to be done and the exceeding importance of that need. For a purpose thus shared, and in complementary contribution to a common cause, both donor and recipient can be and usually are grateful to each other. (p. 202)

The second state is the exact opposite, *dissensus*. The organization and the donor public hold conflicting views and both are aware that disagreement exists. The only resolution is for one or both of the sides to change its own or the other's views. For example, the dominant coalition may decide to shift its priorities in order to accommodate the interests of a major donor prospect who disagrees with the opportunity offered. Although such accommodations are acceptable, the state of dissensus is dangerous in that fund raisers may be tempted to trade organizational autonomy in exchange for gifts or to manipulate donors to change their views (i.e., infringe on what M. W. Martin, 1994, called individual autonomy). John Ford (cited in McNamee, 1993), vice president for development at Stanford University, described this state, "When a donor comes with a very strong idea of what he or she wants and it doesn't necessarily align with the university's priorities—that's the trickiest gift of all" (p. 24).

Culbertson et al. (1993) directly linked the dissensus state to autonomy and accountability, referring to the second as "followership." Of the two available choices, following one's own set of preferences results in high autonomy, and following the other side's preferences results in high followership. They stated, "Extremely high followership to the exclusion of autonomy, or visa versa, is questionable in most situations" (p. 73). Supporting my thinking, they concluded, "Clearly some blend is called for. The nature of that blend is a challenging question with important ethical implications" (p. 73). The scholars also emphasized a critical point explained by coorientation theory: If perceived agreement and accuracy are high, autonomy and accountability do not yield different outcomes. "Following self and audience give nearly the same result. And no tug of war between the two perspectives seems likely" (p. 73). In other words, identifying donor prospects who share similar views with the organization is the most effective protection against loss of autonomy and the means by which fund raisers can successfully balance autonomy with accountability to donors.

The last two states of the coorientation model are false states based on inaccurate perceptions of the other side's views. If the dominant coalition thinks the public agrees with the organization about the fund-raising opportunity but is mistaken, then a state of *false consensus* exists. Fund-raising efforts will be inefficient, with few dollars raised and high cost ratios. For example, the dominant coalition of a nonprofit hospital may decide that upgrading the cardiac unit is critical to the organization's mission of quality health care for the community. Prospective corporate donors, on the other hand, may view cost containment as vastly more important than improved services. Furthermore, members of this public may view raising gifts for a state-of-the-art cardiac unit as wasteful if a similar facility is already available at another hospital nearby. Launching a major gifts initiative without recognizing the misperception on the part of dominant coalition members would be disastrous. For this reason, *feasibility studies* traditionally have been conducted before proceeding with capital campaigns.

False consensus also exists when the public is mistaken in its belief that there is agreement. Illustrating, individual donors may make annual gifts to an organization with a mission to alleviate homelessness only to find out later that the organization's program services consist of job training. If donors believe low-cost housing or reduced alcohol consumption provide better solutions to the problem, the relationship will end. Similarly, if donors discover that much of the money raised by an organization is not spent on program services but on fund-raising and administrative expenses, the relationship likely will terminate. Relationships resulting from false consensus are short-term or are maintained through an absence of full disclosure by the recipient organization.

The state of *false conflict* exists when either the organization or the donor public misperceives disagreement with the other side. This state calls for immediate two-way communication with the objective of increasing accuracy and understanding, not agreement or behavior. Only after accuracy is achieved can fund-raising efforts take place. This is the only state that justifies fund raisers thinking, as many are inclined to do, "If prospective donors just understood, they would be willing to give."

Required Research

Each of the four coorientation states requires different action and programming; therefore, research on both sides of the relationship must be conducted before fund raising starts. Broom and Dozier (1990) advised practitioners to gather data from members of the organization's dominant coalition and the specified public. Rating scores on items measuring views are used to calculate *D-scores*, the differences between the two sides' ratings for each item. The relative magnitude of the difference scores indicates the degree of agreement, perceived agreement, and accuracy.

Such research is similar to feasibility studies for capital campaigns and prospect research conducted for major gifts programs, both discussed in the next chapter. I recommend that all efforts to raise gifts be preceded by research on coorientational measures. Illustrating, the prospect pool for any annual giving program consists of only two basic segments: (a) previous donors who have demonstrated through past giving behavior that they agree with the importance of the common good and the organization's approach to producing the good; and (b) prospective donors who have not yet given, but who agree the common good is important and also agree with the organization's approach. Theory predicts that everybody else is *not* a prospect.

The "rest of the world" constitutes a nonpublic, also made up of two segments. First, there are those individuals, corporations, and foundations who agree with the importance of the good produced, but disagree with the organization's approach. An example might be donors who have high agreement on the importance of helping disadvantaged youngsters become productive citizens. Whereas some of these donors might give to the Boys and Girls Club, others might give to Big Brothers/Big Sisters, and still others might give to the YMCA or YWCA—all of which have different ways of accomplishing essentially the same good. The second nonpublic segment consists of individuals, corporations, and foundations who have little interest in the common good produced by the organization. Regardless of whether they agree with the approach or not, their disinterest obstructs them from paying attention to the fund-raising opportunity. More information is not the answer; members of this nonpublic simply do not care.

The last point is difficult for some dominant coalition members to grasp, given the purposes of charitable organizations as opposed to for-profit companies. How could anyone not care about feeding starving children in Third World countries? How could anyone not care about preserving our culture through a museum? How could anyone not care about finding a cure for cancer? And so on. Answers to such questions are rational, although emotion is not absent from their formulation. Most important, the answers are personal; they are embedded in what Schervish and Herman (1988) referred to earlier as *subjective orientation*. Steele and Elder (1992) affirmed, "People's reasons for giving are highly personal, unique to each individual, and closely linked to their values and attitudes" (p. 33). They warned fund raisers, "It is not our business to worry about how others assess their own giving priorities" (p. 13).

At the risk of offending worthy organizations, I care a great deal about higher education (i.e., I have high agreement on the importance of the goods produced by colleges and universities) because I work for that type of organization, which means I also am involved. On the other hand, I care little about private elementary education because it is not important to me, personally. I do not know anyone who currently attends a private elementary school, and I did not attend one. For these and other reasons, the missions of such organizations have little salience to my priorities. Similarly, I highly agree that providing shelter for homeless children is important, but I have little interest in providing shelter for homeless animals; nor am I interested in protecting animals from laboratory experiments.

Such personal preferences do not make me a bad person (I hope). Lohmann's (1992a, 1992b) theory helps us understand that the importance of common goods is specific to members of specific commons. M. W. Martin (1994) defended individual autonomy in giving decisions: "We should renounce the heavy-handed moralizing that insists every caring person must give to this or that cause. We should also oppose all forms of coercion that undermine autonomy in meeting philanthropic responsibilities" (p. 93). Echoing practitioner statements at the beginning of this discussion, fund raisers engage in ineffective and unethical practice when they find themselves trying to convince people how they should think and what they should do. Based on coorientation theory, staff managers focus fund-raising efforts on those donor publics with whom their organization shares common views. The discussion turns now to a theory that expands our understanding of how those publics are identified.

SITUATIONAL THEORY OF PUBLICS

A principle endorsed in the literature and related to others already given is:

Those closest to the organization are the best prospects.

A second is:

Belief in mission is the strongest reason for giving.

Often quoted is Benjamin Franklin's 200-year-old formula for raising gifts, a version of which was provided by Lord (1983):

> My practice is to go first to those who may be counted upon to be favorable, who know the cause and believe in it, and ask them to give as generously as possible. When they have done so, I go next to those who may be presumed to have a favorable opinion and to be disposed to listening, and secure their adherence. Lastly, I go to those who know little of the matter or have no known predilection for it and influence them by presentation of the names of those who have already given. (pp. 50–51)

The principles have been historically validated by practitioners. They also are explained by the situational theory of publics, conceptualized by public relations scholar James Grunig.

Practitioner Predictors

Steele and Elder (1992) graphically portrayed the first principle with three concentric circles, or rings, which defined stakeholders most likely, less likely, and least likely to give to annual giving and major gifts programs. They placed previous donors and people with "strong ties" to the organization in the center ring. Such groups as employees and clients were in the second, and national foundations and corporations in the third. Moving from the center outward, they advised, "You are not looking to make a convert out of a nonbeliever—someone in the outer ring. . . . You are mainly looking for people who already believe in your cause on some level" (p. 28). They applied the principle to annual giving donors: You probably throw a good deal of direct mail away without even opening it, "but every so often a piece will arrive that coincides with some feelings you have about a given issue, whether it is handgun control, civil rights, or an environmental concern. Whatever it is, you decide you must support that cause, and you write a check" (p. 30).

Unscientific and scientific evidence suggests that people's identification with the mission of the organization is paramount to giving. Panas (1984), for example, concluded from his interviews with donors of $1 million or more that their chief motivation was "belief in the mission of the institution" (p. 227). There was not a close second reason. File, Prince, and Cermak (1994) reported a similar finding from their study of 476 individuals who have established a charitable remainder trust of $1 million or more: "In our sample, the motivation to donate to a *specific* nonprofit was driven by a *perceived similarity* between the donor's goals and those of the nonprofit (86 percent said that this rationale was very important)" (p. 275; italics added).

Steele and Elder (1992) advised fund raisers, "The vast majority of major gifts will come from a relatively small number of prospects, most of whom will already be known to you" (p. 3). They added, "The simplicity of this idea belies its importance" (pp. 27–28). Broce (1986) elaborated, "Most major donors are close friends of the institution or have logical reasons to give to it. That is why prospect research and evaluation are so important. They are the processes by which we identify the legitimate prospects: which ones will give; how much they might give; [and] what programs they will likely support" (p. 177). Furthermore, Broce pointed out, "An institution cannot expect others to invest in it until those who are closest to the center do so" (p. 21).

Incorporating the L–A–I formula, K. S. Grace (1991a) argued that fund raising "depends on the organization's ability to recognize and encourage the linkages, ability and interest of its donors and to present funding opportunities that are based on an exchange of values" (p. 185). Linkage to the organization, ability to make a gift, and interest in the organization's mission, goals, and priorities—the criteria by which prospects are separated from suspects—also are the basis for the *principle of sequential giving*. As presented by Rosso (1991), the principle prescribes that gifts should be raised sequentially from the top down and from the inside out. Efforts begin with prospects for the largest gifts and with those prospects closest to the organization. Fund raisers then move down in gift amounts and focus their attention outward. The last solicitations are requests for lower level gifts from suspects, which yield few dollars and high costs.

Summarizing this collective wisdom, practitioners rely on three important factors to identify donors of both annual and major gifts: (a) closeness or the degree to which prospects are connected to the organization and its work, which can be defined as *involvement*; (b) belief or interest in the organization's mission, goals, and priorities, which can be defined as identification with a *problem*; and (c) ability or capacity to give, which can be defined as financial *constraints*. Consultant René Blanchette (1993), who has investigated the relationship between giving and various donor variables for about 10 years, provided some empirical support for this interpretation. In his APRA prize-winning essay, he concluded that giving behavior results from the interaction of financial capacity and "willingness." Discriminant analysis, a statistical procedure for identifying characteristics that separate groups, showed that strong support for an organization's goals discriminates donors from nondonors, whereas estimated income (i.e., a measure of capacity) is the foremost factor for gifts ranging from low to high amounts. He also found that desire for volunteer involvement and desire for additional information were highly correlated with giving.

Theoretical Predictors

The three factors on which practitioners rely correspond to the three predictor variables incorporated in J. E. Grunig's (e.g., Grunig & Hunt, 1984) situational theory of publics: (a) level of involvement, (b) problem recognition, and (c) constraint recognition. *Level of involvement* is the degree to which members of a population feel *connected* to a problem, issue, or opportunity involving an organization. *Problem recognition* is the degree to which population members think the problem is important. *Constraint recognition* is the degree to which the members believe they can personally do something to affect the problem. In the late 1970s, Grunig theorized that the three variables explain why people engage in a behavior and communicate in the process of planning the behavior. Extensive empirical research since has shown that the variables successfully segment stakeholders into publics by "the extent to which the members passively or actively communicate about an issue and the extent to which they behave in a way that supports or constrains the organization's pursuit of its mission" (J. E. Grunig & Repper, 1992, p. 125).

All combinations of the three variables generate eight possible publics, but Grunig (J. E. Grunig & Repper, 1992) collapsed these to four: (a) *active public*, who has high level of involvement and high problem recognition and does not feel constrained in doing something about the problem; (b) *aware public*, who has high problem recognition, but varies on involvement and beliefs about constraints; (c) *latent public*, who is low in problem recognition and involvement and has not thought about constraints; and (d) *nonpublic*, or everyone else, who has no involvement and does not recognize the problem. The situational theory, as its name indicates, holds that *how* people perceive a situation determines whether they will enact a behavior relevant to the situation (i.e., people respond differently to different situations); general attitudes and personal characteristics explain little variance in people's views of a given situation. Practitioners are advised to concentrate their attention and resources on the first two publics, active and aware. Members of the latent public should be monitored and selected for communication only when resources allow. Those constituting the non-public should be dismissed—"they are of no concern to an organization" (J. E. Grunig & Repper, 1992, p. 125).

The theory predicts that members of the nonpublic will not communicate (i.e., they will not attend to messages). Members of the latent public will passively process information. Active and aware publics, on the other hand, will actively seek information (i.e., they desire information). As J. E. Grunig and Hunt (1984) emphasized, information actively sought has greater impact on cognitions, attitudes, and behavior than information processed or ignored altogether. Information seekers purposefully select and thoughtfully integrate and interpret information (Culbertson et al., 1993). They are more eager to learn and more reachable than information processors. Because they have high problem recognition and often high involvement, they examine the contents of messages carefully and respond strongly to them. Information processors make little effort to seek new information, rationally select what they read or hear, or integrate diverse information for meaningful interpretation. They attend to pieces of information that come their way and grab their attention. Whereas information seekers can be counted on to invest time and energy in communicating with the organization (e.g., they will read long, detailed letters), information processors require attention-getting devices (e.g., short animated letters, large headlines, unusual layouts, and envelope "teasers"). In particular, information processors focus heavily on a message's source and on the setting in which they receive the message.

Information seeking and processing, as conceptualized by Grunig, are supported by Petty and Cacioppo's (1986) elaboration-likelihood model of persuasion. This psychology theory predicts that high involvement leads people to follow the *central route* to constructing attitudes, objectively evaluating incoming communication to elaborate on information already received. Highly involved people analyze issues more often, scrutinize the merits of new information, and prefer messages that contain multiple, reasoned arguments. Because they link new information to old, communication effects accrue and attitudes are more enduring. People with lower involvement follow a *peripheral route*, depending on superficial cues to develop attitudes. They pay less attention to message content and focus instead on situational or source cues, such as likability or credibility.

Application to Donors

The situational theory of publics explains how fund raisers effectively identify those donor publics with the highest probability of giving. Equally important, it reinforces practitioners' assertions that people who are not involved with the organization, do not care about its mission and program services, and do not have discretionary income or assets to give away, are of no concern to fund-raising efforts (i.e., they constitute a nonpublic). Looping back to practitioner principles, Grunig's (J. E. Grunig & Repper, 1992) three publics of active, aware, and latent emulate Benjamin Franklin's (cited in Lord, 1983) three descending levels of prospects: (a) those who know the cause and believe in it, (b) those who may be presumed to have a favorable opinion, and (c) those who know little of the matter and are influenced by the names of people who have already given.

The theory instructs fund raisers to spend their time and resources on active and aware publics, who seek information. Latent publics may be targeted for programming that emphasizes peripheral cues, but only when resources are not needed for the first two publics and can be expended at a higher cost ratio. Culbertson et al. (1993) explained the applicable economic principle: "The process of reaching all relevant publics becomes subject to decreasing marginal productivity. This suggests the practitioner should assign a priority to publics and be willing to halt expenditures before they cease to be cost effective" (p. 117). The three independent variables that predict publics must be understood as they apply to donors and measured through research on the organization's stakeholders.

Involvement.   Level of involvement is the most critical variable affecting decisions to give. Studies have found that it is positively and significantly related to information seeking and action taking (e.g., Heath, Liao, & Douglas, 1995). The variable is key, according to J. E. Grunig (1989a), because it has been shown to result from people's perceptions that a problem affects their self-interest. Compatible with the mixed-motive model of giving, public relations scholar Robert Heath (Heath et al., 1995) reported that people with high involvement "are likely to take actions selected to secure their self-interest," but that level of involvement also reflects people's altruism toward the well-being of others (p. 96). Indeed, involvement theory holds that perceptions of self- and altruistic interests are the motives for all collective action. Heath, who has successfully used the situational theory to predict people's behavior as it relates to specific corporations and environmental problems, no longer measures problem and constraint recognition because, he claimed, level of involvement is a condition of the second two variables. Like Rosso (1991), however, Grunig (J. E. Grunig & Repper, 1992) argued that all three variables must apply.

The concept of involvement was first used in mass communication research to explain how low-information advertisements on television successfully lead to purchase behavior of low-involvement products (J. E. Grunig & Hunt, 1984). Based on the findings, Grunig and Hunt concluded that when "a product costs little or the consumer does not perceive one brand of a product to be much different from another, the consumer will often purchase the product after simply hearing about it" (p. 369). "Publicity alone may be sufficient to get people to buy low-involvement products" (p. 369). Heath (Heath et al., 1995) concluded from his studies measuring involvement that "action taking," or behavior other than purchasing a product, "is engaged in with some sense of its cost as well as expected outcomes" (p. 96).

Extrapolating the research to fund raising, sending $25 to the Red Cross for emergency relief, dropping money in the Salvation Army bell-ringer's pot during the holidays, or making a small pledge over the telephone to a local theater group represent low-cost gifts that do not require a meaningful level of involvement. Expanding that idea, the majority of annual gifts, with an estimated average of $50, are similar to low-involvement products in that peripheral cues in solicitations, such as credibility of the message source, affect giving behavior. Higher level gifts, on the other hand, generally require a higher degree of involvement because the gift amount demands more thoughtful consideration of the request, its merits of reasoning, and its relevance to the donor's evaluation of the situation. As Payton (1987) argued, "Philanthropy becomes more planned and rational as it increases in scale" (p. 15).

Involvement also is differentiated by its two dimensions of internal and external, or cognitive and physical (J. E. Grunig & Repper, 1992). The first can only be determined by directly measuring the connection a person perceives between him- or herself and the charitable organization and its work. Physical involvement can be identified by affiliation, similar to mapping stakeholders (e.g., status as a client or volunteer). Attesting to the variable's explanatory power as it relates to volunteering in general, IS (1994) reported that its biennial surveys have consistently documented that "volunteers give more than nonvolunteers, and contributing households with a volunteer give a much higher percentage of their household income than contributing households which do not have a volunteer" (p. 91). In 1993, 90% of all volunteers made gifts, as compared to only 59% of nonvolunteers, and the average amount volunteers gave was 4.5 times higher.

Mixer (1993), touching on the close relationship between involvement and problem recognition, argued that by participating in any form of organizational activity, people soon find themselves identifying with organizational goals and plans (i.e., their problem recognition increases). "They feel they are a part of the agency and their *bonding* extends beyond their concern for the human needs served. . . . As a consequence, gifts flow readily from this involvement" (p. 25; italics added). Fund raisers, then, should always look first to those closest to the organization when identifying prospective donors. However, they must understand that affiliation represents only one dimension of involvement and only one of the three predictor variables. Many people affiliated with an organization are passive stakeholders. On the other hand, people not formally affiliated (i.e., members of a diffused category) may feel a connection to the organization's work and the purposes for which it raises gifts.

Problem Recognition.   Problem recognition discriminates those individuals, corporations, and foundations who believe a charitable organization's program services are important and needed from those who do not. The concept derives from the work of the Chicago School's John Dewey (cited in J. E. Grunig & Repper, 1992), who defined it as "the perception that something is lacking in a situation" (p. 135). Dewey also observed that publics arise around problems that have consequences on them. When the social problem addressed by an organization has salience for prospects, they are more likely to become donors, whereby they express their interpretation of what is best for society. As Schervish and Havens (1994) concluded from their research, "Giving reflects the connection between an organization's mission and a funder's moral purpose" (p. 31). Mixer (1993) added, gifts "offer an opportunity for people to 'do something' about offending problems" (p. 21).

Perceptions of importance, not attitudes, are the determining factor. Culbertson et al. (1993) explained, "People may feel the American Cancer Society is very commendable as gauged by rating scales or agree-disagree items. Yet they may consider it less important than supporting research on AIDS" (p. 45). Mixer (1993) listed 61 reasons why people do not give, compiled from "several thousand participants in over one hundred fund-raising workshops" (p. 29). Of the 11 mentioned most frequently, 5 relate to this discussion: (a) higher priorities, (b) not interested, (c) don't agree on policies, (d) don't believe in cause, and (e) can't afford to give.

Constraints. Constraint recognition encompasses physical, social, economic, or political obstacles to taking actions. Regardless, those dealing with economics logically have great impact on behavior that entails giving away money. As J. E. Grunig and Repper (1992) emphasized, people do not communicate about or enact behaviors related to problems they believe they can do little to resolve.

Prospects are unlikely to make a gift if they perceive financial constraints to doing so. Providing empirical evidence, IS (1994) reported that its surveys "have consistently shown that respondents who worried about having enough money in the future gave less as a percentage of household income than those who did not worry" (p. 93). In 1993, the average percentage of household income contributed by people who worried about money was 50% less than the average contributed by people who were not worried. The level of income contributed declined as the level of worry increased (e.g., people who worried a little gave 2% on average, whereas those who worried a lot gave only 1.2%). In contrast to *how much* people gave, their *behavior of giving* was unrelated to money worries (i.e., 73% of both worried and unworried people made gifts). These findings are similar to Blanchette's (1993) and are supported by our philanthropic tradition. Their meaning, however, must be clarified.

IS' surveys, like most national studies of philanthropy, operationalize giving behavior as having made one or more gifts of any amount to any and all charitable organizations. This "generic giving" is not the same thing as making a gift to a specific organization (i.e., the dependent variables are different). Furthermore, most national studies examine giving behavior primarily as it relates to lower level gifts; major donors, due to their small number and other factors, are not well represented. Illustrating, 56% of the contributing households sampled by IS (1994) gave a total of $300 or less. In other words, financial constraints are not a determinant of giving in general, but they do influence who will make annual and major gifts to specific organizations.

Constraint recognition was a significant predictor of nondonors in a study I conducted on journalism alumni's annual giving to the University of Maryland (Kelly, 1979). Although many of the nondonors had high levels of involvement and problem recognition, scores on constraints discriminated them from donors. Alumni who made annual gifts had more income, paid dues to the alumni association more often, and gave money to a greater number of other organizations. In sum, donors perceived fewer constraints to giving to the university than nondonors. I concluded that financial constraints can be an important factor in decisions to make even lower level gifts. As J. E. Grunig and Hunt (1984) explained, "Recognition of constraints stops many people from behaving in ways they would like to behave" (p. 367).

Touching briefly on two other aspects of financial constraints, annual giving programs based on broad, abstract needs, such as ensuring the continued excellence of the organization, do little to help prospects of lower level gifts see how their money can *make a difference*. Fund raisers must take special care to effectively communicate, with specific examples, how even low-involvement gifts of $50 will allow the organization to meet its broader goals. J. E. Grunig and Hunt (1984) warned, "Donors won't contribute to a fund-raising campaign if they don't think their donation will make much difference" (p. 358). Major gifts programs already demand such specificity; however, practitioners should utilize planned gifts for those prospects who perceive high constraints to making outright gifts.

Research.   The three situational variables must be measured to segment stake-holders into publics before planning fund-raising efforts. Given that each fund-raising opportunity represents a different situation, regular research is needed.

One strategy that will help fund raisers hold down research costs is Grunig's (J. E. Grunig & Repper, 1992) *nested model of segmentation*. The model assumes that *inferred* variables, or those that must be measured by questioning members of a population directly, are located within general, more easily observed *objective* variables, or those that can be measured from secondary sources. In other words, prospects' level of involvement, problem recognition, and constraint recognition can be associated with more readily available information such as gift history, participation in cultivation activities, and demographics.

Practitioners are advised to first conduct primary research measuring the predictor variables, as well as a range of objective variables. Statistical analysis groups respondents into publics that are active, aware, latent, and nonpublics and identifies significant characteristics unique to each group. Those characteristics are then matched to organizational records, and prospects are assigned codes based on their probability of giving. The coding system is used to guide programming; for example, prospects designated active might be targeted for a bimonthly letter about operations from the CEO. Based on the nested model, the objective variables can serve as surrogate predictors for multiple efforts; however, their generality—by definition—means they are less powerful than inferred variables, yield less precise results, and must periodically be reexamined. I recommend primary research for annual giving programs every 3 years and every year for major gifts programs.

J. E. Grunig and Hunt (1984) summarized this discussion with their simple but theoretically sound advice: "To raise funds, identify, cultivate, and solicit publics that have money to give and take interest in your organization" (p. 366).

FUND-RAISING EFFECTS

A principle given almost the status of law is:

The best prospects are previous donors.

As Lord (1983) stated, "Experience shows that the best prospects for the immediate future are those who have given in the past" (p. 49). This principle, as well as a number of others given in this chapter, was first formally presented in Seymour's (1966/1988) classic book, *Designs for Fund-Raising*. Previous donors have a higher probability of making a gift than nondonors, regardless of all other factors. Furthermore, Seymour claimed, the more a person gives, the more likely he or she will give more.

Another valued principle is:

Cultivation is the key to successful solicitation.

This was the eighth of Broce's (1986) nine cardinal principles of fund raising. Howe (1991) elaborated: "You cannot expect to receive donations from people until they know about your organization; you should not ask people for contributions until they are ready. Getting them ready is called cultivation" (p. 83). These two practitioner principles prescribe important outcomes for fund raising: renewal of previous donors and cultivation of both new and previous donors. They are explained by theories of communication effects.

The fund-raising process of ROPES, the subject of the next chapter, consists of the five consecutive steps of research, objectives, programming, evaluation, and stewardship. The process requires that objectives precede and govern programming decisions and that—in turn—evaluation is based on how well the programming met the set objectives. In other words, the intended effects of fund raising are specified in the objectives chosen early in the process. And contrary to conventional wisdom, fund-raising objectives and effects are not just dollar totals, nor do they deal exclusively with donors' giving behavior—other outcomes also are sought. As Steele and Elder (1992) asserted, "Fundraising [*sic*] is not simply about the checkbook; it is about communication" (p. 127).

Communication scholars break down *impact* objectives, or those specifying intended effects, by formation, change, or reinforcement of: (a) cognitions, (b) attitudes, and (c) behavior. Cognitions are further broken down to concepts dealing with awareness, knowledge, and understanding, each a progressively higher order of thinking. J. E. Grunig and Hunt (1984) drew from theory and research to conceptualize a taxonomy of public relations objectives, which they based on McLeod and Chaffee's (1973) coorientation model. More recently, T. Hunt and J. E. Grunig (1994) refined and presented the five impact objectives for programming: awareness, accuracy, understanding, agreement, and behavior. The objectives represent all intended effects of communication and are increasingly difficult to achieve as they ascend from awareness to behavior.

Although it is relatively easy to get people to form new cognitions or to change them (e.g., a story in the mass media can create awareness), it is much more difficult to affect attitudes and behavior. Situations calling for the formation of new attitudes or behavior are unusual (e.g., people's first exposure to new innovations, such as e-mail). Changing them rarely is achievable through short-term programming. As T. Hunt and Grunig (1994) explained, communication can change attitudes and behaviors of publics, but the objectives often take years to accomplish. "Only simple behavior generally can be changed in the short run" (p. 17). Dozier and Ehling (1992) elaborated, "Cognitive changes stimulated through communication can cause short-term behavioral changes when such behaviors are specific and easy to implement" (p. 175). J. E. Grunig (1992) defined four conditions that must be present for changing behavior in the short term: (a) the behavior must be a simple one, (b) the communication must be aimed at a well segmented public, (c) the communication must be supplemented by interpersonal support among members of the segmented public, and (d) execution must be flawless.

According to T. Hunt and Grunig (1994), "Accuracy and understanding generally are the most important objectives for public relations programs" (p. 381). Furthermore, they explained, "The 'understanding' that results from cognitive change also contributes over the long run to 'agreement' in attitudes and behaviors" (p. 18). Theories of effects, such as Hunt and Grunig's, have not been widely accepted: "Practitioners frequently assume blindly that their communication programs will change attitudes or behaviors—that they will *persuade* publics" (p. 17; italics added). Fund raisers should not make the same mistake.

Hierarchy of Effects

T. Hunt and Grunig's impact objectives are the basis of a hierarchy of fund-raising effects. They are supplemented and enriched by Broom and Dozier's (1990) levels of program impact criteria. Specifically, Broom and Dozier expanded effects about cognitions, attitudes, and behaviors by adding "repeat behavior" and "social and cultural change" at the highest levels (p. 87). The resulting hierarchy of effects of fund raising is presented in Table 9.2.

The hierarchy consists of seven effects, ordered from the lowest of affecting people's awareness of the organization, to the highest of maintaining the sanction granted to charitable organizations by our society (i.e., their privileged status). Paraphrasing Broom and Dozier, the highest effect, *social, economic, and political sanction*, underscores that the ultimate judgment of fund-raising programs will be based on their positive or negative impact on society and culture. Both individual practitioners and the subsector as a whole must pass this test. As concluded in chapter 7, the legal context of fund raising demands attention be paid to this long-term, but most important of all outcomes. Abraham Lincoln (cited in Lord, 1983) stated: "Public sentiment is everything. With public sentiment, nothing can fail. Without it, nothing can succeed" (p. 68).

Moving down to the second effect, it is appropriate that *repeat behavior* of previous donors is of a higher order impact than *behavior* of new donors. Similar to other practitioners, Lord (1983) presented criteria for separating prospects from suspects that correspond to the situational theory's predictor variables. But he also added that the prospect "should have some *history of giving*—to other organizations, if not to your own" (p. 85; italics in original). He warned, "It's very difficult to turn a non-giver into a giver" (p. 85). J. E. Grunig and Hunt (1984) confirmed the importance of this criterion: "If your organization must fill seats, sell products, or raise funds—i.e., if bringing about a behavior is a must—then you should do research to identify the people who are already active publics for the behavior you want and communicate to them what you have to offer" (p. 366). Despite such advice, public relations scholars, paradoxically, pay little more than lip service to reinforcing either attitudes or behavior, which is essential to effective public relations. Even Broom and Dozier (1990) provided weak justification for designating repeat behavior a high-level effect, saying only that maintaining desired behaviors over an extended time "are outcomes sought by many public relations programs" (p. 86). Fund-raising theories can contribute to public relations theory and practice, as well as the other way around.

TABLE 9.2
Hierarchy of Effects of Fund Raising

Social, economic, and political sanction
Repeat behavior
Behavior
Agreement
Understanding
Accuracy
Awareness

The high and separate placement of repeat behavior in the hierarchy of fund-raising effects is theoretically and pragmatically sound. Effects theory holds that changing behavior is more difficult than reinforcing behavior. Nichols (1992), drawing from theory and experience, argued that it takes five times as much work to acquire a new donor as it does to renew an existing one. Based on observation, practitioners estimate that about 75% of an organization's annual giving donors renew their gifts the next year (e.g., Mixer, 1993); therefore, reinforcing repeat behavior is a primary objective for annual giving programs. Practitioners also strongly assert that most major gifts come from previous donors. When fund raisers turn from donor renewal to donor acquisition, they traditionally use previous giving behavior to similar organizations as a criterion for qualifying prospects.

Repeat gifts cost significantly less to raise than new gifts. As given in chapter 7, for example, Levis (1991) estimated that the cost ratio for raising an average gift of $10 from new donors is 100%, whereas it is only 35% from renewed donors. An average gift of $1,000 from new donors cost 25%, but only 10% from renewed donors. Reflecting back to systems theory, continued funding by repeat donors reduces financial uncertainty by providing a relatively dependable stream of dollars.

The critical difference in probability of giving between an organization's previous donors and nondonors was documented by IS (1994), which found that 85% of its respondents would be very or somewhat likely to make a gift in response to a mail solicitation from an organization they had regularly supported in the past, but only 45% or less would be very or somewhat likely to contribute to organizations to which they had not previously given. Concerning solicitations by telephone, 56% said they would be likely to make a gift in response to an appeal from an employee or volunteer of an organization to which they had regularly contributed, but only 13% said they would respond similarly to an organization that was new to them. In short, individuals who are previous donors are about two to four times more likely to make a gift than nondonors.

Lindahl and Winship (1992b) used multivariate analysis to determine what combination of variables best predicts which alumni make annual and major gifts to Northwestern University. Although they incorporated 14 independent variables in their analysis, including internal data typically found in alumni records and external geodemographic data, they reported, "Past giving has by far and away the largest effect on current giving" (p. 52). Their findings, they said, confirmed fund raisers' traditional practice of using past giving as the main criterion for selecting prospects. Regarding major donors, their analysis showed that chances are only about 20% that a major gift will result from soliciting a prospect who has great financial wealth, but who has not given much in the past.

In a follow-up study dealing exclusively with major gifts, Lindahl and Winship (1992a) employed additional statistical procedures to develop predictor models. They found that different variables are important for individuals with different levels of past giving; however, they reported, "Although the full models tend to be superior overall, past giving by itself accounts for a *great majority* of the predictive power" (p. 1; italics added). Lindahl (1994) applied the findings to fund-raising practice, "Our study showed in a more definitive way the enormous weight that past giving has in the major gift prospecting equation" (p. 45). He advised practitioners, "Spending money to cultivate major gifts results in good relationships with prospects that, in turn, reap dividends of repeated donations" (p. 45).

Solicitation activities constitute a minority portion of the fund-raising process and only part of the programming step. Practitioners spend much of their time and efforts on cultivation of donor prospects. For such programming, practitioners seek effects other than behavior: *agreement, understanding, accuracy,* and *awareness.* Agreement also can be called attitudes but the selected term frames the effect within the coorientation model of relationships, emphasizing the state of consensus when both organization and donor publics agree with each other. Similarly, accuracy is drawn from coorientation theory but also can be called retention of a message, whereby members of a public know the organization's views and can articulate them.

Cultivation, especially if a symmetrical approach is taken, leads to repeat behavior and even changed behavior when time is allotted. Although donors of low-cost, low-involvement gifts may be influenced in the short term, higher level gifts require an investment of time. Lord (1983) explained, "If time is *not* provided, the development process will degenerate into a series of 'shakedowns'—in which the easy money is taken, and the building of relationships neglected" (p. 104; italics in original). Furthermore, J. E. Grunig (1992) argued, achieving short-term cognitive effects through symmetrical programs "maximizes the chances for long-term behavioral changes" (p. 15). He asserted, "Publics who are treated as equals of an organization and whose ideas are communicated to the organization—as well as the ideas of the organization being communicated to the publics—more often support . . . an organization than do publics whose behavior the organization tries to change directly in the short term" (p. 15).

Staff managers assign the highest effect of maintaining social, economic, and political sanction to every fund-raising effort. It is the overriding objective for all programming. They choose from among the remaining six effects to develop specific impact objectives. The techniques they employ to meet their objectives are differentiated by three levels of communication.

Fund-Raising Techniques

A well-known principle is:

The larger the expected gift, the more personal the solicitation.

A corollary is:

Cultivate and solicit important prospects in person.

Practitioners developed the "ladder of communication effectiveness" (Howe, 1991, p. 77) for selecting what this book terms *fund-raising techniques.* The ladder illustrates that personal communication has the most powerful effects and that effects become less powerful as communication becomes less personal. Rosso (1991) explained his version of the concept:

> In descending order, the ladder portrays the relative effectiveness of the various methods used to solicit gifts. Each step down the ladder indicates diminishing effectiveness in the soliciting procedure. Face-to-face solicitation by a peer of the prospect is the most

effective method; solicitation through media or by direct mail is the least effective. (p. 59)

Rosso divided the ladder into two levels: personal approach for prospects for major gifts at the top and impersonal approach for prospects for smaller gifts from midpoint to the bottom. Among the techniques in the upper level were personal visit by a team or one person (first and second) and personal letter with a follow-up telephone call (third). Included in the lower level—in addition to those techniques Rosso mentioned—were phonathons and special events. In other words, fund raisers utilize techniques based on interpersonal communication for major gifts programs and techniques based on other forms of communication for annual giving.

Howe (1991) explained, "The [direct-mail] letter is the principal medium for seeking regular, annual, 'small' contributions; a personal visit or formal proposal is always involved in soliciting major individual gifts or corporate and foundation grants" (p. 79). In an earlier essay, Howe (1985) presented a graph of techniques descending in their effectiveness from one-to-one conversation and small group discussion at the top, to brochure and news item at the bottom. He advised, "Use the highest rung on the ladder possible within your budget and manpower [sic] capabilities" (p. 19).

Principles about techniques are grounded in communication theory, which differentiates communication by levels of personalization and relates the levels to audience size. They are supported by effects theory in that practitioners are advised to move up from mass to interpersonal techniques as desired effects increase in difficulty to attain (i.e., from awareness to changing behavior). Fund raisers typically rely on less personal techniques to achieve objectives related to cultivation, particularly for annual giving prospects. Because of audience size and theoretical reasons already given, they also use these techniques for soliciting the majority of lower level gifts. As the amount of the gift increases and the number of prospects decline, they turn to more personal means for communicating. J. E. Grunig and Repper (1992) summarized the applied theories, "Specialized or local media, controlled publications, or interpersonal communication are [progressively] more effective ways of reaching publics than are the massive media" (p. 127). Figure 9.3 presents the techniques used by fund raisers in the two primary programs of major gifts and annual giving.

As given in Fig. 9.3, fund-raising techniques are differentiated by three levels of communication: (a) interpersonal, which is direct communication between people; (b) controlled media, which is mediated communication through channels controlled by the organization; and (c) mass media, which is mediated communication through such uncontrolled channels as newspapers, television, and radio stations. The three levels are presented in descending order of effectiveness. Starting at the top, they move from communicating with small, well-known audiences to communicating with larger, targeted audiences to communicating with mass, relatively anonymous audiences.

Interpersonal communication usually refers to oral, or verbal, communication and is limited to face-to-face situations. It is expanded here to include telephone conversations, personal letters, and personalized proposals because those techniques also provide effective means for communicating directly with selected prospects. *Controlled media communication* encompasses techniques, such as direct mail, videos, and paid advertisements, over which practitioners have control about what is said, how it is said, when it is said, and to whom it is said (Cutlip et al., 1994). *Mass media*

I.   INTERPERSONAL COMMUNICATION

• Major Gifts Program

- Face-to-Face Conversations
- Small Group Meetings
- Speeches
- Telephone Conversations
- Personal Letters
- Personalized Proposals

II.   CONTROLLED MEDIA COMMUNICATION

• Annual Giving Program

- Direct Mail
- Special Events
- Publications (Newsletters, Brochures & Flyers)
- Phonathons
- Videos and Films
- [Computers]
- Telethons (Television & Radio)
- Paid Advertisements, Billboards, Collection Signage

III. MASS MEDIA COMMUNICATION

• Annual Giving Program

- Editorials and Op-Ed Pieces
- News Releases and Story Placements
- Public Service Announcements (PSAs)

NOTE:

Interpersonal:	*Direct communication between people*
Controlled Media:	*Mediated communication through channels controlled by the organization*
Mass Media:	*Mediated communication through uncontrolled channels (e.g., newspapers, television & radio)*

FIG. 9.3. Fund-raising techniques by three levels of communication
and two primary programs.

communication covers techniques, such as news releases and PSAs, over which practitioners have little control. Instead, media *gatekeepers* (e.g., editors and program
directors) decide what is reported, how it is reported, when, and to whom. A
distinguishing characteristic between the third level and the other two is economic—who pays the bill for message dissemination.

Major Gifts.   The six techniques defined as interpersonal communication are
associated with the major gifts program. Logically, fund raisers use techniques from
the highest level of effectiveness to communicate with those donor prospects who
provide the majority of dollars raised. Their small number in relation to annual giving
prospects allows this personal attention. Techniques involving face-to-face situations
are the most effective. Lord (1983) stated, "If we really believe that people are more
important than dollars, then we owe it to our top prospects to visit them in person.
Besides, seeing people face to face works better than any other method" (p. 80). Cutlip
et al. (1994) affirmed this claim, "Communication scholars and practitioners historically have considered face-to-face interpersonal communication the most direct,
powerful, and preferred method for exchanging information" (p. 233). They stressed
the advantages of communicating in person, including close proximity and nonverbal
behavior—important to "relational communication" (p. 236). Proximity communicates intimacy, trust, and caring, among other attributes. Shaking hands enhances
intimacy, as does smiling, which also communicates liking. Eye contact intensifies the
other nonverbal behaviors.

Because they are based on oral, as opposed to written, communication, the in-person techniques of face-to-face conversations, small group meetings, and speeches have
additional advantages. Focusing on speeches, T. Hunt and Grunig (1994) stated:
"While a written message such as a newsletter, brochure, or advertisement is somewhat
impersonal, the *spoken word* carries the credibility of the speaker. Enthusiasm, concern, tolerance, understanding, and empathy are all best demonstrated through the
verbal and nonverbal act of meeting an audience in person" (p. 206; italics added).

A significant advantage of all techniques employing oral communication is that,
unlike those using written communication, they provide instantaneous feedback,
allowing alterations of the message and the delivery. Again focusing on speeches, T.
Hunt and Grunig (1994) explained, "The speaking situation is flexible and can be
altered to fit the response of the audience. With the print or audiovisual message, you
fire your shot and hope it hits the target. In a speaking situation, you can make
mid-course corrections" (p. 206).

Both verbal and nonverbal responses of donor prospects help fund raisers communicate more effectively. For example, if a prospect for a major gift shuffles his or her
feet during a small group meeting, practitioners can accelerate the discussion or shift
it to another aspect of the topic. Most important, they can listen to and learn the
prospect's view. The two-way models of fund raising rely on interpersonal techniques
more so than the one-way models.

Telephone conversations share the advantages of oral communication, although
the technique is less powerful because nonverbal cues are missing. Personal letters and
personalized proposals supplement the other techniques in managing relationships
with major donors. They also are the communication techniques *required* by most
corporate and foundation donors, who usually are treated as sources of major gifts.

Ideally, fund raisers would use only interpersonal communication, whereby every single prospect would receive personal attention. As Hendrix (1995) maintained, "In truly effective communication there can be no substitute for direct interaction" (p. 6). Such an ideal would require almost unlimited financial and human resources, specifically, hundreds or even thousands of staff members. Because donor prospects far outnumber fund-raising practitioners, it is nearly impossible for a charitable organization to use interpersonal techniques exclusively. The first of six barriers to interpersonal communication, as emphasized by Culbertson et al. (1993), is "the number of people available to interact" (p. 69). Two others are size of targeted public and space–time relationships (i.e., distance).

In terms of diffusion of innovations theory, the absence of techniques based on controlled and mass media communication would require large numbers of change agents in the field. It is not surprising, then, that those organizations conducting capital campaigns with billion-dollar goals employ hundreds of fund raisers to engage in interpersonal communication with major donor prospects. For example, Harvard University had a fund-raising staff of 271 employees in 1993–1994 to support its $2.1-billion campaign (Wise, 1994).

An alternative to numerous staff members is numerous volunteers who are trained and managed by practitioners. K. S. Grace (1991a) claimed that 2,500 volunteers were involved in fund raising for Stanford University's $1.1-billion capital campaign. Although the number is impressive, Grace neglected to mention that Stanford employed more than 200 fund raisers during its campaign or that only a few volunteers directly interact with donor prospects, particularly those for major gifts.[2]

In earlier eras, organizations such as the March of Dimes routinely utilized massive numbers of volunteers, primarily housewives, to solicit lower level gifts through door-to-door canvasing. Today, few organizations have access to such large numbers of volunteers because of changes in our society (e.g., the proportion of women who work outside the home). The March of Dimes now solicits most of its gifts by mail, maintaining a list of the names and addresses of 4 million people (Mixer, 1993). In short, human resources available for direct communication are limited in the everyday world. Cutlip et al. (1994) elaborated:

> In much of contemporary society, face-to-face contacts give way to mediated transmissions. Spoken words give way to written communication. Individually addressed letters give way to printed messages. Printed publications give way to broadcast words and pictures. Broadcast messages give way to networks of computers carrying digital signals. (pp. 233–234)

Logically, then, fund raisers rely on techniques that are less personal but have a wider audience reach for communicating with those prospects who provide the majority of gifts but only the minority of dollars raised.

Annual Giving.   The techniques defined in Fig. 9.3 as controlled media communication and mass media communication are associated with the annual giving program. They also are used to meet objectives dealing with cultivation of donors to both primary programs. For example, special events and publications are commonly used to cultivate major donor prospects, to reinforce and change their understanding

---

[2]The role of volunteers is discussed in chapter 11.

and attitudes about the organization and its work. Story placements in the mass media are mainstays for building awareness and accuracy among prospects for gifts of all sizes. It is not the intent of this discussion to describe each technique listed in Fig. 9.3; many are covered in subsequent chapters. Instead, selected techniques from the second and third levels of communication are briefly introduced because their usage in soliciting lower level gifts is not well understood. The section concludes by pointing out strengths and weaknesses of the conceptualization.

Direct mail is the technique used by fund raisers more than any other. Craver (1991) estimated in the early 1990s that it accounted for $25 billion each year, which represented almost one fourth of all gift dollars at the time. Unlike personal letters, which are mailed individually at first-class rates, direct mail disseminates thousands and even millions of identical messages at about one third the cost, using nonprofit bulk rates. Sole reliance on the technique, however, is expensive. Disabled American Veterans, for example, pays more than $6 million annually for postage alone and spends 33% of the money it raises on fund-raising expenses—a cost ratio higher than the 25% I recommend (H. Hall, 1996b; "Philanthropy 400," 1996).

Direct mail is broken down into two general categories based on intended receiver: (a) *in-house lists*, or people known to the organization (i.e., previous donors and prospective donors from such stakeholder groups as clients); and (b) *cold lists*, or unknown people whose names have been acquired by renting, exchanging, or buying other organizations' lists. Response rates between the two categories differ dramatically. Whereas in-house lists yield about a 75% response from previous donors and 25% from nondonors, cold lists generate a return of about 1% (Mixer, 1993). Furthermore, mailings to cold lists are considered successful if gifts average $20 (Craver, 1991), but in-house lists are used to solicit gifts as large as $500 (I recommend a lower limit for most situations). The second category of direct mail, then, shares many of the characteristics of techniques from the less effective mass media level. The first category is used by all types of charitable organizations; cold lists generally are not used by the largest employers of fund raisers—universities, colleges, and hospitals.

On the other hand, educational organizations are the heaviest users of phonathons, according to NSFRE's 1988 membership survey (Klein, 1988). Although only 41% of the association's members use phonathons, 73% of those identified with education employ this technique. NSFRE discontinued measuring usage of techniques after 1988. Earlier findings, which were limited to only four of what this book defines as techniques, showed the following usage rates: direct mail (83%), special events (77%), phonathons (41%), and videos (29%). Unlike individual telephone conversations, Mixer (1993) explained, phonathons "enable organizations to reach large numbers of prospects with personally tailored messages" (p. 114). They rely on phone banks staffed by volunteers or paid callers, usually employees or clients (e.g., students enrolled at a college). In spite of their use of paid callers, phonathons are *not* the same as telemarketing. The fund-raising technique deals exclusively with in-house lists. Telemarketing, which is carried out by paid solicitors, also uses cold lists, from which a response rate of 15% or less is promised. IS (1994) found that whereas 56% of its respondents said they would be likely to make a gift if called by an employee or volunteer of an organization to which they had previously contributed, only 6% said they would respond similarly to a call from a paid solicitor for an organization that was new to them.

Videos and films primarily are used for cultivation, although practitioners increasingly find videos effective for soliciting gifts in the $1,000 range from faraway prospects who cannot be visited in person (Dessoff, 1994). They simulate proximity and nonverbal behavior, with additional advantages of audiovisual media (e.g., client testimonials can be incorporated in a request for operating gifts). Unlike telethons, which are broadcast to mass anonymous audiences, videos are disseminated by mail to carefully segmented donor publics. Computers share the same advantages and more. By transmitting information through growing networks, they have the power to communicate directly to large, segmented groups. World Wide Web sites, which combine images with text and sound, are especially useful. Practitioners are able to inexpensively "show and tell" why annual gifts are needed (e.g., a video tour of the organization's facilities narrated by the CEO). Most important, computers—unlike videos—provide two-way communication, allowing quick feedback and prospect-initiated conversations. They are bracketed in Fig. 9.3 because their application to fund raising is only now being explored. Their potential is suggested by statistics: In 1996, 40% of all households contained personal computers, 30 million users were connected to the Internet, and about 1 million new users were coming online each month.

Paid advertisements, billboards, and collection signage—like telethons—solicit gifts from mass audiences. Still using controlled channels, they move fund raising away from targeted efforts, thereby constituting hybrids of the second and third communication levels. Their low order in the second level represents both their mixed status and their low usage by practitioners. They are, however, used. Focusing on just one type of paid advertisement, large national organizations, such as World Vision, Childreach, and Save the Children, produce *infomercials*, or program-length television advertisements (Mixer, 1993). Airtime and production costs average about $100 per gift. Rosso (1991) claimed that paid advertisements, which he also placed at the bottom of his ladder of effectiveness, attract "what are essentially impulse givers" (p. 61). When fund raisers cast a wide net to capture unknown prospects through controlled channels, they violate principles of effective practice and denigrate the purpose of their function.

Finally, the techniques defined as mass media communication are most effective when soliciting low-cost gifts related to crises, such as disaster relief. They are used more often, however, as components of *public information campaigns*, which rely on mass media appeals through editorials and news coverage in combination with controlled media and interpersonal techniques.

Ledingham's (1993) study on giving to a midwestern United Way is one of the few studies measuring fund-raising techniques, and his findings support practitioners' ladder of communication effectiveness and the conceptualization presented here. He found minimal differences between donors and nondonors in relation to exposure to mass media techniques and those at the bottom of controlled media:

> Givers are only somewhat more likely to recall UW televised PSAs, a UW billboard, a UW newspaper ad or radio message, and to have viewed a UW film at work than non-givers. . . . [On the other hand], UW givers are almost three times as likely to have attended a UW group meeting at work. And, they are more than twice as likely to have received a solicitation letter or memo at their place of employment. (p. 372)

The conceptualization of techniques advances an understanding of fund raising. Practitioner authors commonly have mislabeled techniques, confused them with programs and staff positions, and rarely explained beyond advocating face-to-face conversations why different techniques are used to raise gifts of different amounts. Rosso (1991), for example, argued that controlled media techniques are used by practitioners who are uncomfortable or inexperienced with the more "dynamic, more effective" (p. 63) form of personal solicitation. Presenting an even less helpful explanation, Tempel (1991) advised, "Different activities are used for different purposes and for different prospects to accomplish a variety of different results" (p. 26).

At the same time, the dichotomy between techniques used in major gifts programs and those used in annual giving programs is overly simplified; fund raisers utilize a combination of interpersonal, controlled, and mass media communication in both programs. Providing some empirical evidence, students will recall that the study testing the fund-raising models measured 16 activities to help determine the models' validity. Eight of those activities related to production of techniques at the three descending levels of communication (e.g., scripting group meetings, staging special events, and producing PSAs), and findings suggested that techniques at all three levels are used to some degree in both primary programs (Kelly, 1994a). Illustrating, correlations between scripting group meetings and the two-way symmetrical model were .30 for annual giving and .38 for major gifts, both significant at the .01 level.

Regardless of this weakness, the conceptualization explains important distinctions between the techniques predominantly used to raise major gifts and those used to raise lower level gifts. Research would add to the theory presented here. Students should consider introspective studies addressing such questions as: How much interpersonal communication do fund raisers use in annual giving programs? To what extent do they employ controlled media techniques to raise major gifts? Are there relationships between the techniques used and the mission of the organization, its size, the size and age of the fund-raising department, or the use of volunteers? Whereas an attempt was made to order the techniques according to their effectiveness and usage, the resulting list is only an estimate informed by observation and the literature. Studies building on this work, guided by effects theory, are needed.

INTEGRATED RELATIONSHIP MANAGEMENT

Based on systems theory, a charitable organization succeeds and survives depending on how well it manages interdependencies with multiple stakeholders, not just donors. Relationships with other groups, such as community residents and government officials, must also be effectively managed. One department is needed, headed by a staff manager who is knowledgeable about and educated in both fund raising and public relations. Integrated relationship management increases the organization's ability to respond to environmental demands and changes and to thrive as an open system.

Pfeffer and Salancik (1978) explained, "Organizations survive to the extent that they are effective. Their effectiveness derives from the management of demands, particularly the demands of interest groups upon which the organizations depend for resources and support" (p. 2). The scholars warned that an organization puts itself at risk when it does not recognize or it ignores groups on which it is dependent. Failure to consider other interests, according to J. E. Grunig and White (1992), can result in the organization losing the trust and support of the ignored stakeholders. Furthermore, when undue attention is paid to one stakeholder group at the expense of others, the organization is vulnerable to attack by those it has neglected (Kelly, 1994b).

Forty years ago, participants of the Greenbrier Conference recommended that educational organizations incorporate the functions of alumni relations, public relations, and fund raising in one department—institutional advancement (Porter, 1958). The conference, under the joint auspices of ACPRA and AAC, concerned itself "primarily with the *internal* mechanism of the college or university, not its relationship with the rest of society" (Porter, 1958, p. 3; italics in original). Its recommendations called for a Chief Administrative Coordinator who would be responsible for the merged department and report directly to the president. The new officer would be a person from any of the three previously separate functions, providing he or she had such competencies as a thorough knowledge of the institution.

Alumni and public relations practitioners, feuding with each other, were not threatened by the possibility of a fund-raising coordinator. Their perceived positions of strength were evident in the proceedings reported by Porter. Fund raising was the newest function; a preconference survey showed that 41% of the responding colleges and universities did not yet even have fund raisers on staff. Fund raising was dependent on the work of the other two areas: "Its effectiveness derives clearly from them" (p. 52). Fund raising had only one objective, "the raising of money" (p. 47). ACPRA–AAC conferees agreed that "the fund raiser should, in most cases, have status equal with that of the public relations officer and the alumni executive," but "fund raising does not have to be a policy job" (p. 53). Finally, Porter (1958) reported, "The fact that the fund raiser has but one principal objective does not make him [*sic*] a mechanic who should be subordinate to the big-picture planners of the public relations and alumni offices; nor does the fact that he sometimes produces spectacular and tangible results make him superior" (p. 53).

Not surprisingly then, 86% of the ACPRA respondents to another preconference survey selected the coordinated department as the ideal management structure. Pray (1981) presented his optimistic remembrance of advancement's beginnings: "We saw an alumni officer become the chief advancement officer at one institution, a public relations officer expand his [*sic*] duties to the total job at another, and the development officer at a third institution assume responsibility for alumni and public relations as well as for fund raising" (p. 400). Jacobson (1990) provided a conceptual definition of the unified department that closely resembles what this book advocates: "Institutional advancement is the management function responsible for maintaining and improving relationships between an educational organization and its publics for their mutual benefit. Communication is the major process by which this function is accomplished" (p. 435).

Flash forward to the late 1990s! At most educational organizations today, the fund raiser is in charge or public relations is a separate and usually weaker department. The alumni officer almost always reports to one of the other two; chief coordinating positions rarely are held by someone from alumni relations.

In a well-designed thesis, Thinesen (1992) documented the current role of public relations in higher education. Of the 254 public relations heads responding to her survey, 37% report to a fund-raising vice president, with another 26% reporting to managers outside of institutional advancement. Only slightly more than one third report to the president. Thinesen's study built on previous research by R. L. Williams (1991), who surveyed 165 presidents, and her comparisons to his results showed variations between the views of CEOs and public relations heads. For example, 68% of the public relations officers strongly agreed that public relations considerations should be a component of organizational policymaking, but only 15% of the presidents similarly agreed. Whereas only 50% of the CEOs think public relations should report directly to them, 85% of the public relations officers believe such a reporting relationship is important. Statistically significant differences were found between public relations heads who report to the CEO and those who do not. Of those with a direct reporting relationship, 87% said the CEO considers public relations implications in organizational policymaking, but 82% of those who do not report directly said the opposite. Thinesen concluded that information restrictions resulting from the weak relationship between presidents and their chief public relations officers contribute to the serious problems colleges and universities are facing today.

Fund raisers, by definition, concentrate on one stakeholder group: donors. When public relations and other functions such as alumni relations are subsumed under fund raising, there is danger that relationship efforts will concentrate on the concerns and demands of only donors. Such situations describe *fund-raising encroachment*, when public relations is managed by a fund raiser and is viewed as a support function for fund-raising objectives. Its practitioners are cast in technician roles and isolated from decision making. Strategic publics that can affect the organization's success and survival seldom are brought to the attention of the dominant coalition because public relations practitioners are denied access, and the manager who does have access—the fund raiser—is trained and rewarded to concentrate on donor publics. The organization is then handicapped by *environmental blinders* that prevent it from "seeing" problems and opportunities related to nondonor publics. Systems theory predicts that resulting imbalances produce crises and, eventually, dysfunction.

George Washington University President Stephen Trachtenberg (1993), it is recalled from chapter 6, presented 11 basic rules for chief fund raisers from a CEO's perspective. One not mentioned earlier, "Keep your eye on the ball," illustrates commonly held views that are related to encroachment and environmental blinders:

> Your focus must remain on fund-raising results. I realize you may have other responsibilities, possibly including public relations, alumni affairs, and other operations. Those *support* everything we are trying to do in fund raising as well as student recruitment . . . . But this is reality: If you're the chief development officer, people will judge your performance primarily by the bottom line. (p. 21; italics added)

The chapter turns now to studies documenting fund-raising encroachment in all types of charitable organizations. Before leaving the discussion on institutional advancement, however, it is necessary to point out that I define alumni relations as part of the larger function of public relations. Alumni are important stakeholders for educational organizations; they also are a natural constituency on which such organizations depend for gifts. Specialized practitioners' management of relationships with these groups is recommended and explained by public relations theory.

Encroachment

I conducted three studies to examine the current relationship between the fund-raising and public relations functions, reported in four publications (Kelly, 1993a, 1993b, 1993c, 1994b). Qualitative methodology first was employed to provide insight on the problem. Findings opened new lines of inquiry and created questions and hypotheses that were then tested in a large-sample quantitative study.

An exploratory study collected data through telephone interviews with 184 of the 284 members of the Educational and Cultural Organizations Section of PRSA, representing a 65% response rate (Kelly, 1993a). Cases were sorted by the factor of dominant/subordinate, which revealed that public relations is subordinate to fund raising in 40% of the organizations represented and is of equal status in 42%. An executive assistant to the president of a northwestern university stated, "There is great concern among PR people that they'll be gobbled up by fund raising. The bottom line is money . . . so fund raising directs the activities" (p. 53). Defending her separate department, the public relations director for a California college of design argued, "There are publics the fund raisers neglect, and I need to make that my priority" (p. 53).

In the second study, depth interviews with 19 public relations heads in Maryland and Louisiana examined factors leading to fund-raising encroachment, as well as its consequences (Kelly, 1993c). Of the 19 subjects interviewed, 7 are part of the fund-raising department, 3 are in departments other than fund raising, such as marketing, and 9 have a separate department. Public relations does not manage fund raising in any of the organizations. Analysis of data revealed that seven of the nine reporting separate departments are not autonomous from fund raising, do not have equal status, and do not have a stable structure. Illustrating, a chief public relations officer for a public university said his newly appointed president already had expressed interest in hiring a vice president with proven fund-raising abilities to oversee both the fund-raising and public relations departments. The practitioner did not appear threatened by impending encroachment and, indeed, already defined public relations as a support function for fund raising: "The role of the public relations department is to provide support services to fund raising—keeping the university's name out in front of the public so that when [the fund raiser] goes asking for donations, the public will know who we are and what we do. This is true for any nonprofit organization" (p. 355).

A number of those reporting separate departments, as well as others, distinguished between fund raisers' *bottom-line* contribution to organizational effectiveness and their contribution of *story telling*. For example, the chief public relations officer for a local United Way defined his department's function as "telling and selling of United Way stories through a number of outlets," whereas the fund-raising department "contributes to the bottom line by bringing in the money" (p. 356). This same practitioner complained that although he and the head of fund raising both report directly to the CEO, his department—unlike fund raising—has no power in decision making. The director of public relations for an aquarium/zoo complex said that comparing public relations to fund raising is like comparing a graduate student to a professor because fund raising is "a much larger and more complex function than public relations" (p. 357).

Such findings suggested that self-perception of public relations as a technical support function is an important factor in fund-raising encroachment. In other words, many practitioners do not fulfill the manager role prescribed by textbooks, nor do they practice two-way models of public relations. They act as technicians, concerned with producing and disseminating information. Their contribution to organizational effectiveness is minimal, and they know it. Fund-raising encroachment, therefore, is more likely to occur when public relations potential is low.

The third study, a national mail survey of 175 PRSA members, documented fund-raising encroachment in 23% of the cases, with variation among the types of organizations represented (Kelly, 1994b). Whereas 50% of the public relations practitioners working for private colleges and universities are supervised by a fund raiser, only 14% of those working for human services organizations are in the same situation. Indicators measuring organizational power showed that public relations, even as a separate department, does not have equal status with fund raising. For example, only 31% of the respondents disagreed with the statement, "Top management values fund raising more than public relations."

I also found that in the majority of cases the size of the public relations staff is smaller than the fund-raising staff, and salaries of public relations practitioners generally are lower than salaries of fund raisers (Kelly, 1993c). The top reason given for salary discrepancies was that fund raisers contribute to the bottom line. Only 26% of the most senior persons in public relations have the title of vice president or executive director, whereas 52% of the most senior persons in fund raising have a title at those levels. Finally, 51% of the respondents agreed that public relations best serves an organization when it supports primary functions such as fund raising.

Because of earlier evidence about self-perceptions, I measured the potential of the public relations department to practice the function as theory prescribes (Kelly, 1994b). Using 24 items designed to measure the four models of public relations and the two primary roles of manager and technician, respondents were asked to assign a numerical value that best described the extent to which their department or someone in their department has the expertise or knowledge to perform the tasks given in each item. Analysis of the responses showed that the departments have low potential to enact the manager role or to practice the two-way models. The highest mean scores were on the public information model and the technician role. Further analysis found small but significant correlations between the departments' potential and fund-raising encroachment. Expertise in the one-way models and the technician role was related to encroachment, whereas expertise in the two-way models and the manager role was related to its *absence*. Empirical evidence, therefore, confirmed that low potential on the part of public relations practitioners is related to encroachment by fund raisers.

These findings were supported by Thinesen's (1992) study. Both presidents and public relations heads agreed that public relations is most effective in carrying out task-oriented, or technician, responsibilities, such as writing news releases, producing informational publications, and managing special events, but is less effective in more strategic, or managerial, responsibilities, such as responding to crises and keeping the president informed about relevant trends and events in the external environment.

The situation is unlikely to change until most public relations practitioners are formally educated in the discipline and the purpose of fund raising is better understood. Until then, the overriding question is not, "Who should manage public relations?," but rather, "Who will manage the organization's relationships with stakeholders?"

This book endorses one department of integrated relationship management. It also holds that fund raising is more than merely raising money and can best be understood as a specialization of public relations. Managers of the integrated department, regardless of their background or title, must be trained in both fund raising and public relations.

Cross-Training

According to Freeman (1984), the biggest change in the management paradigm during the 1970s and 1980s was a move away from market fundamentalism—whereby the bottom line is assumed optimal—and toward proactive management that meets the concerns of all corporate stakeholders, not just the concerns of *stockholders*. The chairman of Cummins Engine Company, Henry Schacht (cited in J. A. Joseph, 1991), presented the argument in four points:

> (1) The existence of a corporation is dependent upon the consent of the various individuals and groups whose lives the corporation affects, (2) a corporation is a social organization formed to produce goods and services in a competitive environment and gets the right to produce these from the consent of those individuals and groups it affects, (3) those who have a stake in a business corporation will make claims on it, and (4) the long-term, self-interest of even the shareholder depends on a corporation's ability to satisfy the claims of other stakeholders. (p. 9)

The new management approach emerged from self-interest. As stakeholders can significantly affect a business' current and future operations, it makes sense to have them as allies rather than as adversaries who can organize boycotts, increase regulation, unionize, oppose facility expansion, or generate negative publicity. Similarly, a business does better if it is proactive, anticipating and meeting stakeholder concerns rather than reactively cleaning up after crises and repairing damaged relationships.[3]

The paradigm shift informs the practice of fund raising to the extent that donors are analogous to investors of publicly owned corporations (e.g., they both are enabling stakeholders). It reinforces theoretical arguments given earlier that donors are only one of multiple stakeholders with whom relationships must be managed. When one group is given undue attention or practitioners dealing with relationships are separated from each other, imbalances result that can lead to costly crises. The demands of all strategic publics can best be addressed through a single department that integrates the functions responsible for relationship management. With this structure, programming can be altered and resources shifted as problems or opportunities arise. Key to increased effectiveness, however, is a staff manager who understands fund raising and public relations.

Qualified candidates currently are difficult to find. A participant in the first encroachment study, a vice president for university relations at a midwestern university, underscored this point in a response not reported in the study's essay: "Very

---

[3]Unfortunately, as reported in chapter 15, changed conditions in the business environment of the 1990s, such as global competition, have driven many corporations back to market fundamentalism.

seldom do you have a public relations person with a firm grasp of fund raising or a fund-raising person with a firm grasp of public relations." The issue is not one of just skills, but as this practitioner expressed, *a firm grasp* of the two functions. This chapter and others provide the required understanding. The theories used to explain fund raising are the same theories that explain public relations. Focusing on the micro level of techniques, those listed in Fig. 9.3—with the exception of phonathons and telethons—are the same techniques public relations practitioners use to communicate with nondonor publics. The commonness of the two functions has been obscured by practitioners' flawed perceptions of each other's work.

At the beginning of a 1995 presentation on team building, sponsored by CASE, I asked fund raisers what words came to mind when they were asked to describe public relations. The first descriptors they gave were "newspapers, story tellers, and publications." Public relations practitioners, the other half of the 150-member audience, described fund raising as "money, schmoozing, and personal contact." When asked to react to the descriptors assigned to them, both sides essentially rejected the narrow perspectives. I know of few senior fund raisers who would describe their work as simply getting money, nor do senior public relations practitioners limit their role to media relations. The conventional wisdom of fund raising as solicitation and of public relations as publicity and publications represents definitions restricted to only parts of each function, which likely characterize the work of some practitioners, but not all. The perceptions, unfortunately, are perpetuated in each other's literature.

Unfairly selecting just one example, Steele and Elder (1992) compared the two functions to emphasize their differences—a comparison that was incongruent with much of their fund-raising book. The purpose of public relations, they said, is to promote a good image, but the purpose of fund raising is to raise money. Public relations "seeks a wide and diverse audience," whereas fund raising "focuses on donors" (p. 115). They assigned the lowest and easiest communication objective of awareness as the cross-situational goal of public relations, and giving (behavior) as fund raising's goal. As for techniques employed, they said public relations uses mass media and fund raising uses personal contact.

In contrast, the literature of each function describes the work very differently. Again using techniques, T. Hunt and Grunig (1994) instructed, "Speaking and speechmaking are as fundamental to public relations as writing" (p. 205). Steele and Elder (1992) said, "For obvious reasons, [fund raisers] need to have highly developed interpersonal skills. What is perhaps less obvious, they must also posses excellent writing skills" (p. 40).

Associations such as CASE, PRSA, and NSFRE need to emphasize the bigger picture—a firm grasp of the two functions. In addition, seminars designed to enhance knowledge about the work of colleagues specializing in relationships with other stakeholders would help produce the leadership needed (e.g., workshops on media relations for fund raisers and on planned giving for public relations people). Instead of looking for differences, practitioners should concentrate on commonalities—the most fundamental of which is relationship management. The theory of donor relations explains fund raising in this context. Applying theory to practice, Willmer (1993) advised senior officers heading the merged function at colleges and universities:

Learn to help others understand that institutional advancement means more than raising money. Stress that you are advancing the college when you help avert a lawsuit over campus expansion, when you work with state legislators to increase financial aid, [and] when you improve student retention through better campus communication. (p. 39)

The theory of donor relations presented in this chapter moves the emerging profession from unexplained art to a management function grounded in the behavioral and social sciences. Guided by this theoretical framework, practitioners can increase their effectiveness and take pride in their work. Lord (1983) summarized my intent: "In the business of raising money, we cannot allow ourselves to become mere technicians or manipulators....We should never feel ashamed or apologize for what we do" (p. 98).

SUGGESTED READINGS

Broom, G. M., & Dozier, D. M. (1990). *Using research in public relations: Applications to program management.* Englewood Cliffs, NJ: Prentice Hall.

Culbertson, H. M., Jeffers, D. W., Stone, D. B., & Terrell, M. (1993). *Social, political, and economic contexts in public relations: Theory and cases.* Hill-sdale, NJ: Law-rence Erlbaum Associ-ates.

Dressel, P. L. (1980). *The autonomy of public colleges.* San Francisco, CA: Jossey-Bass.

Frey, L. R., Botan, C. H., Friedman, P. G., & Kreps, G. L. (1992). *Interpreting communication research: A case study approach.* Englewood Cliffs, NJ: Prentice-Hall.

Grunig, J. E., & Hunt, T. (in preparation). *Managing public relations* (2nd ed.). Fort Worth, TX: Harcourt Brace.

Hunt, T., & Grunig, J. E. (1994). *Public relations techniques.* Fort Worth, TX: Harcourt Brace.

Newsom, D., & Carrell, B. (1995). *Public relations writing* (4th ed.). Belmont, CA: Wadsworth.

Nichols, J. E. (1992). *Targeted fund raising: Defining and refining your development strategy.* Chicago: Precept Press.

Pfeffer, J., & Salancik, G. R. (1978). *The external control of organizations: A resource dependence perspective.* New York: Harper & Row.

Steele, V., & Elder, S. D. (1992). *Becoming a fundraiser: The principles and practice of library development.* Chicago: American Library Association.

Wilcox, D. L., & Nolte, L. W. (1997). *Public relations writing and media techniques* (3rd ed.). White Plains, NY: Longman.

PART III

THE PROCESS, PROGRAMS, AND PUBLICS

10

The Fund-Raising Process

Fund raising is more than merely seeking gifts; it involves a process that must continually be organized and managed. Responsibility for process management belongs to the specialized practitioner, who attends to fund raising full time and focuses the CEO's and others' attention on it at critical points in the process. Defending the need for full-time management, M. R. Hall (1993) stated, "Attention may be the primary ingredient in success" (p. 8).

Chapter 10 presents the process for fund raising, conceptualized here as a descriptive and normative theory. The fund-raising process consists of five steps: Research, Objectives, Programming, Evaluation, and Stewardship. The steps form a convenient mnemonic device, the acronym *ROPES*. Learning the ROPES of fund raising provides future practitioners with a strategic approach to raising gifts and managing donor relations.

The process begins with *research* in three areas: (a) the organization, (b) the opportunity, and (c) the publics related to the organization and opportunity. Failure to conduct research in all of the areas (*oops!*) dooms fund raising to sporadic results that contribute little to organizational effectiveness. The second step in the process is setting *objectives* that are specific and measurable. Fund-raising objectives flow from the charitable organization's goals (i.e., their attainment directly supports organizational plans).

The third step, *programming*, consists of planning and implementing activities designed to bring about the outcomes stated in the objectives. These activities are grouped in two categories based on their desired results, cultivation and solicitation. Contrary to conventional wisdom, solicitation activities constitute a minority portion of the fund-raising process and only part of the programming step. Practitioners spend much of their time and efforts on cultivation of donor prospects. The fourth step is *evaluation*, whereby programming is monitored and adjusted (process evaluation) and results are measured and compared with the set objectives (program evaluation). Finally, *stewardship* completes the process and provides an essential loop back to the beginning of fund raising. Four elements are basic to stewardship: reciprocity, responsible gift use, reporting, and relationship nurturing. Also embedded in the last step are ethical elements that hold moral obligations and responsibilities to donors above other considerations.

The ROPES process draws from a public relations model by educator Jerry Hendrix (1995), ROPE, which does not include the stewardship step or account for the specialization of fund raising. In contrast, ROPES represents a comprehensive theory for integrated relationship management (i.e., it explains how relations with all publics, including donors, are and should be managed). Figure 10.1 displays the ROPES process.

ROPES AND PRACTITIONER DESCRIPTIONS

Raising gifts is not difficult, given America's tradition of philanthropy. To yield effective results year in and year out, however, relationships with donors must be managed scientifically, which requires hard work. The New England Association of Catholic Development Officers (1993) described fund raising as "brilliant in its simplicity" (p. 5). It offered a formula for conducting the two primary programs of annual giving and major gifts—paraphrased as follows:

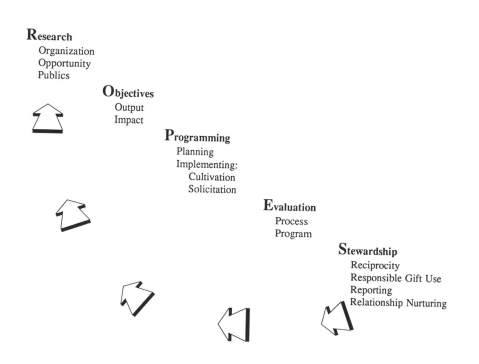

FIG. 10.1. Fund-raising process of ROPES.

Convene a committee of donor representatives. Have them make a list of potential major donors in the community, then go out and solicit them, accompanied by the CEO, who does the "ask." At the same time, mail letters to thousands of donor prospects who have some relationship to the organization (e.g., past clients, friends, and community business owners). Ask for an annual contribution, $25 or $100.

Such formulas contain some accurate advice (e.g., research is the starting point for both programs), but are incomplete, misleading, and based on asymmetrical presuppositions (e.g., the process stops at solicitation, there is no cultivation, and the needs of donors are ignored).

Other descriptions of fund raising found in the practitioner literature are of greater value and are congruent with the ROPES process. For example, consultant Ernest Wood (1989) offered the 4-step process of research, cultivation, solicitation, and recognition (i.e., the reciprocity element of stewardship). Wood argued that when raising major gifts, fund raisers spend 60% of their time and effort on cultivation, 25% on research, 10% on stewardship, and only 5% on solicitation. He stated, "There is no magic or mystery to the process, but it takes a lot of work coupled with honest caring" (p. 6).

Former staff practitioner Eugene Tempel (1991), who now is the executive director of Indiana University's Center on Philanthropy, outlined a management process for fund raising. Tempel's process, which he adopted from The Fund Raising School, consists of six steps: analysis, planning, cultivation, execution, control, and evaluation. Victoria Steele and Stephen Elder (1992), specialists in raising gifts for libraries, presented a 5-step "development cycle" (p. 3): identification, cultivation, solicitation, stewardship, and resolicitation. They defined and described the science—as opposed to the art—of fund raising as "a carefully orchestrated, purposive effort to raise substantial sums of money by identifying and cultivating potential donors and by soliciting gifts from them when their goals and wishes are congruent with the [organization's] goals and priorities" (p. 3). Table 10.1 provides a comparison of the three practitioner descriptions with the ROPES process.

TABLE 10.1
Comparison of ROPES Process With Three Practitioner Descriptions
of Fund Raising

ROPES	E. W. Wood (1989)	Tempel (1991)	Steele & Elder (1992)
Research	Research	Analysis	Identification
Objectives			
Programming			
Planning		Planning	
Implementing:			
Cultivation	Cultivation	Cultivation	Cultivation
Solicitation	Solicitation	Execution	Solicitation
		Control	
Evaluation		Evaluation	
Stewardship	Recognition		Stewardship
			Resolicitation

As shown in Table 10.1, there is a high degree of similarity among the four processes. Of particular significance, there is unanimous agreement about the importance of research and cultivation in fund raising. The most obvious discrepancy is the absence of setting objectives in the three practitioner models, although Tempel's planning step likely is intended to include objectives. Also, Tempel included a control step, which he did not directly explain; however, as his essay emphasized systems theory, we can assume the fifth step is included to remind practitioners to balance autonomy and accountability during the process of raising gifts, which supports the approach of this text. Steele and Elder added resolicitation after stewardship, which is implied in the continuous nature of ROPES. In short, the comparison provides evidence that ROPES is a valid description of the fund-raising process.

It also demonstrates agreement among leading practitioners and myself that effective fund raising is based on logical and orderly steps. Success is not attributable to happenstance, miracles, or unexplained phenomena; it is the result of planned action—well researched and systematically implemented. Fund raising also requires organizational commitment, practitioner expertise, and continual attention. As Rosso (1991) explained, there is no magic formula by which an abundance of gifts is available for a minimum investment of time, talent, energy, and money. Reality, he said, is that fund raising "moves in orderly fashion from preparation to planning to program execution . . . to evaluation and back to the renewal of the plan" (p. 9). The process, according to Rosso, "emphasizes the basic truth that fund raising cannot and should not be a haphazard and impulsively devised undertaking" (p. 9).

ROPES describes the process by which both annual and major gifts are raised. Although dollar amounts vary among organizations, for the purpose of this text, major gifts are defined as those of $10,000 or more and annual gifts are all gifts less than $10,000. Major gifts also are raised through planned giving and capital campaigns; however, I recommend that the two strategies be incorporated in the primary programs of annual giving and major gifts. In other words, ROPES applies to the four traditional programs of fund raising, but its application concentrates on the two primary programs.

The number of prospects and donors associated with each program affects the operationalization of the five steps. Specifically, the annual giving program involves a large number of people, which requires group analysis and the use of controlled and mass media techniques. The major gifts program, on the other hand, deals with a small number of people, which allows individual attention and interpersonal techniques. This chapter describes each of the steps, emphasizing variations between the two programs. Before doing so, it turns to a discussion of strategic planning, which—on the organizational level—precedes the fund-raising process and—on the departmental level—provides the foundation for ROPES.

STRATEGIC PLANNING

Strategic planning is an ongoing process involving renewal of the mission, formulation of basic purposes and goals, and the development and implementation of the policies and programs necessary to achieve those goals (Buchholz, Evans, & Wagley, 1989). Attesting to its widespread use, J. E. Grunig (1992) pointed out, "Strategic planning occupies a chapter or section in almost every basic book on management" (p. 237). He concluded from his review of the literature that excellent organizations plan strategically and excellent departments are integrated in the strategic-planning process.

Strategic planning begins with examination of the organization's mission. Using SWOT analysis (Strengths, Weaknesses, Opportunities, and Threats), the organization assesses conditions of the external environment, including social, economic, and political forces, and internal strengths and weaknesses, including available resources. Choices of short- and long-term goals derived from the first steps are outlined. Courses of action, or strategic alternatives, are assessed by such criteria as suitability, feasibility, acceptability (including legal and ethical considerations), and risk. The highest ranked strategic alternatives are selected and implemented. Finally, the effectiveness of the chosen strategies are reviewed and evaluated.

Moving down to the departmental level, goals are formulated in support of the organization's goals and strategies. Measurable objectives are specified to meet departmental goals. Based on these objectives, programs are planned and further broken down by activities and tasks. When implementation is complete, programs are evaluated by the degree to which they accomplished the set objectives. If objectives are met, goals will have been attained. In this systematic manner, the department advances the organization's strategies, thereby helping it achieve its overall goals and fulfill its mission.

Strategic planning requires participation of key representatives from throughout the organization. Not only is comprehensive input critical, but as Mixer (1993) explained, "Those parties most affected by the plan will give it greater support if they are consulted and involved during its creation" (pp. 96–97). According to the late communication scholar Robert Simmons (1990), widespread participation and the resulting plan enable an organization to integrate all its components. Every decision made and action taken is congruent with the mission of the organization. Simmons stated, "Strategic planning represents a powerful fusion of theory, methodologies, principles, and techniques drawn from management, the social sciences (including communication) . . . and scientific research" (p. 2).

There is increasing consensus in the literature that effective fund raising is inseparable from strategic planning. McNamee (1993), for example, linked it to multimillion-dollar gifts, and said a good strategic plan—with input by practitioners—will operate as a fund-raising blueprint for several years. Steele and Elder (1992) stated, "Since strategic planning articulates where you are currently and where you aspire to be in the future, it provides the rationale for your development program" (p. 57). Lord (1983) made the critical connection with systems theory: "The organization attempts to design its own future—based on the external environment, its opportunities and constraints. Strategic planning looks at forces outside the organization's control, forces like rising expectations for health care or a declining industrial base" (p. 34). With a fund-raising plan drawn from the process, Lord said, "an organization is seen as a quality operation—an intelligently managed enterprise, aware of its purpose and its environment, and ready to take advantage of opportunities as they arise" (p. 35).

Mixer (1993) devoted an entire chapter of his book to strategic planning. He also grounded it in systems theory and incorporated SWOT analysis to demonstrate how findings affect fund raising at the organizational level. Emphasizing the instability of environments, Mixer stated, "As economic and social conditions in the organization's market area vary, the needs and interests of clients, members, and donors will change, affecting the purpose and fundraising [sic] capability of the agency" (p. 94). Gagen-McCarthy (1993) connected strategic planning to autonomy and accountability. She argued that the ultimate measure of success for an organization—in her case a community foundation—was a balance between donor needs and community needs as determined by the organization. She said, "These dual and at times conflicting roles can be kept in appropriate balance with effective strategic planning. Planning gives control and direction to an organization" (pp. 27–28).

In the study testing the fund-raising models, 77% of the respondents reported that their department participates in strategic planning to an extent that is average or above ($N = 291$; Kelly, 1994a). The strongest correlations, as predicted by theory, were with practice of the two-way symmetrical model in annual giving and major gifts programs, significant at the .01 level. It is recalled from chapter 6 that participation in strategic planning is strongly related to enacting the manager role and that both are charac-teristics of excellent fund-raising departments. Staff managers base the ROPES process on the formulated plan they helped develop. As a result, everything done by their department is aligned with the organization's mission and contributes to achiev-ing organizational goals.

"Without the link to institutional goals," Broce (1986) declared, "fund-raising goals are meaningless" (p. 156). He adamantly defended the involvement of practitioners in planning, not only to ensure agreement between goals at the two levels, but also to protect the function's integrity. He urged practitioners to ask critical questions, such as: Will we be duplicating the services of other organizations? How will the project be funded after gift support runs out? If fund raisers are told to not worry about such details, Broce proclaimed, "That is irresponsible behavior" (p. 31). He continued:

> Sometimes the development officer will be told, "We won't set up the program unless we get the funding." The development officer's antenna must spring up at this response. He [sic] must challenge the organizational motive. Is the institution preparing the program just to get a grant? . . . The program must be one that can be presented and defended as part of the institution's basic mission. (p. 31)

According to Broom and Dozier (1990), "Strategic planning is deciding where you want to be in the future (the goal) and how to get there (the strategies). It sets the organization's direction proactively, avoiding 'drift' and routine repetition of activi-ties" (p. 23). When a sportswriter once asked hockey star Wayne Gretzky for the secret to his success, Gretzky supposedly replied: "The other players try to get to where the puck is. I try to get to where the puck is going to be." Although Gretzky undoubtedly uses a rare and gifted intuition to reach his goals, fund raisers must rely on managerial processes and tools.

SWOT Analysis

Kevin Kearns (1992), director of the nonprofit management program at the University of Pittsburgh's Graduate School of Public and International Affairs, applied strategic planning to nonprofit organizations and argued that SWOT analysis is its "principal ingredient" (p. 3). Based on his essay, the purpose of SWOT analysis is to assess the charitable organization's strategic position vis-à-vis changes in its external environment. Kearns recommended that—contrary to its alphabetical order—the analysis be conducted first with respect to the external environment before analyzing the internal environment. The logic of starting with opportunities and threats, he explained, is "that the organization must respond to the external environment, not vice versa" (p. 4). This suggests a symmetrical approach to managing relationships with such stakeholders as donors in that symmetrical practice seeks to adapt the organization to the environment, whereas asymmetrical practice seeks to control the environment. In other words, asymmetrical fund raising is incompatible with principles of strategic planning.

Unlike traditional methods of long-range planning that assume the future is a linear extension of the past, SWOT analysis, Kearns (1992) said, "assumes that goals and strategies emerge from the juxtaposition of opportunities and threats in the external environment and strengths and weaknesses in the internal environment" (p. 6). He warned that the most frequent and costly error in using SWOT is failure to link the assessments of the two environments. For example, organizational managers may develop strategies involving fund raising solely on the basis of perceived internal strengths or weaknesses without regard for what is happening outside the organization. On the other hand, they may perceive an external opportunity for fund raising without realistically weighing the internal conditions necessary to take advantage of the opportunity. Illustrating the second, managers at the University of Maryland held a series of meetings almost 1 year after launching a capital campaign in the late 1980s to decide how the cost of the campaign could be paid on a unit-share basis. Kearns said such problems result from "simple naive optimism or a more sinister form of institutional arrogance" (p. 8).

Kearns (1992) recommended that SWOT analysis be used not only to establish the strategic direction of the organization, but also at the departmental level as a way for practitioners to organize their thinking about specific situations and issues. The procedure he outlined provides a valuable analytical tool that has been adapted here for fund raising and is embedded in the research step of the ROPES process. It emulates *issues management*, the function primarily related to corporations that identifies issues in the environment and monitors, analyzes, and incorporates them in operational plans (Heath & Nelson, 1986).

SWOT, also presented in progressive steps, starts by identifying opportunities and threats in the external environment that could affect fund raising. Kearns (1992) explained, "Decision makers search for factors (manifest) or trends (emerging) that present the organization with either opportunities for growth or service enhancement or, conversely, threats to its core mission or supporting activities" (p. 5). As each opportunity and threat is identified, related internal factors are weighed. Fund raisers ask: What strengths of the organization will help us capitalize on this opportunity or avert this threat, or what weaknesses will prevent us from doing so? The second step of identifying strengths and weaknesses stimulates additional reflection on the preliminary list. These two steps, according to Kearns, "constitute a 'matching' exercise in which the objective is to identify salient links" (p. 11).

In the third step, practitioners map the interactions in a 2 × 2 matrix of opportunities and threats by strengths and weaknesses. Using a public school district as an example, fund raisers identify the external factor of increased corporate giving to primary and secondary education. The factor is perceived as a fund-raising opportunity that matches the school district's mission. The detected factor in funding (opportunity) with the school district's core purpose (strength) places that situation in the upper left quadrant of the matrix. Fund raisers also identify a trend in corporate giving for vocational education. Their school district concentrates on college preparation, although it does have a small vocational component. The funding trend (opportunity) with the school's curriculum (weakness) places that situation in the lower left quadrant. Environmental scanning further reveals a trend of growing criticism by individual donors about the poor academic performance of public school students. As this school district has a documented record of high academic achievement, the situation is placed in the upper right quadrant (threats/strengths). Finally, fund raisers identify a factor of taxpayers who do not understand why private gifts should be contributed to charitable organizations that are funded primarily by tax dollars. This situation, given the school district's public funding base, is placed in the lower right quadrant (threats/weaknesses). Figure 10.2 depicts a SWOT matrix mapping these four interactions, or fund-raising situations.

In Step 4, the situations, many more than those depicted in Fig. 10.2, are formulated as strategic issues and classified by four types: (a) comparative advantage (opportunity/strengths), (b) mobilization (threats/strengths), (c) investment/divestment (opportunities/weaknesses), and (d) damage control (threats/weaknesses). Comparative advantage, according to Kearns (1992), "represents the set of desirable circumstances toward which all organizations—public, private, or nonprofit—continually strive" (p. 14). The question that arises from this category of issues is: How can the organization leverage its strengths to achieve or enhance its comparative advantage, thereby capitalizing on a perceived opportunity? The question prompted by issues in the mobilization category is: How can the organization mobilize its strengths to avert a perceived threat or even transform that threat into an opportunity?

In the example of the school district, the fund-raising department may decide to target the majority of its efforts to acquire new donors from local corporations, as opposed to individuals or foundations (comparative advantage), and to stress the district's record of academic excellence in all communications with individual donors and prospects (mobilization). The situation about taxpayers who do not understand why private gifts should be contributed to public schools is categorized as a damage

	Opportunities	Threats
Strengths	Increased corporate giving to public schools	Increased criticism about poor academic performance by individual donors
Weaknesses	Increased corporate gifts designated for vocational education	Taxpayers who do not understand why private gifts should be made to public schools

FIG. 10.2. Fund-raising SWOT matrix for public school system.

control issue, which may result in a decision to set objectives and develop programming to increase understanding, thereby reducing threats to future fund-raising efforts. The situation about corporate gifts designated for vocational education is categorized as an investment/divestment issue. Fund raisers would bring the trend to the attention of district managers as part of the strategic-planning process. A departmental decision to ignore the trend or to incorporate it in fund-raising plans is inappropriate until a decision is made at the organizational level.

For example, managers may decide to invest in vocational training because of growing student demand, as well as the employment needs of corporations as expressed in their giving pattern. Vocational education would become a strategic priority, and the fund-raising department would establish objectives to support it. On the other hand, managers may decide to keep the district's vocational education program small in order to address higher priority needs. The availability of corporate gifts for such purposes would then be set aside when formulating fund-raising objectives. Dollars raised for vocational education would not support organizational strategy, would divert fund-raising resources from meeting priority needs, and would result in loss of autonomy in that the organization's direction would be determined by donors and resources may have to be shifted to fulfill their expectations. In such cases, fund raising would be donor driven rather than strategically managed.

Step 5 is issues clarification, which helps the department reach agreement on a set of questions that will reflect the critical choices facing it. For example, the comparative advantage issue for the public school fund raisers originally may have been framed as: How can the district leverage its mission as a charitable organization for primary and secondary education to capitalize on the perceived factor of corporate giving to such organizations? The clarification step reveals flaws in this framing. The interests of other important stakeholders, such as state and local governments, would suffer. Taxpayers would feel threatened that control of their public schools was being sold to corporations. Whereas corporate gifts might result, so too might lower public support. Step 5 stimulates discussion about critical assumptions, the organization's mission, and competing goals. From such discussions, the issue likely would be reframed, such as: How can our school district develop more corporate support for elementary and secondary education while (a) continuing to meet the needs of local communities, and (b) protecting our essential, publicly funded support?

Because multiple issues will be generated through SWOT analysis, each of the four quadrants of the matrix can be subdivided into its own 2 x 2 matrix to add more precision. Staying with the comparative advantage category, the upper left quadrant is broken down by most and least certain opportunities and current and potential strengths. School fund raisers identify a trend of increased giving by foundations to education other than colleges and universities, although the trend is newer than the environmental factor of corporate giving. As both deal with current strengths (i.e., the district's mission), the corporate factor is placed in the most certain opportunities/current strengths subquadrant (upper left) and the foundation trend in the one for least certain opportunities/current strengths (upper right). Two additional situations are added: a planned sex-education program matches well with established foundation funding to combat teen pregnancies, and a priority need for foreign-language laboratories is related to community relations efforts by foreign-owned companies with operations in the district's service area. The first is placed in the most certain opportunities/potential strengths subquadrant (lower left), and the second in the one for least certain opportunities/potential strengths (lower right). Based on the analysis, the corporate giving issue provides the highest comparative advantage and the foreign-owned companies' issue the least. Increased foundation giving and foundation funding to combat teen pregnancies require more research.

The sixth and last step is issue ranking. No organization has unlimited resources; therefore, it cannot address all issues simultaneously and with equal vigor—no matter how strong the opportunities or strengths. Fund raisers must establish priorities and reach consensus on them with members of the dominant coalition. Kearns (1992) offered the following criteria that should be used in establishing a rank ordering of fund-raising issues:

1. The *centrality* of the issue to the agency's mandate and mission.
2. The *urgency* of the issue in terms of both time and impact.
3. The extent to which the agency can *control* the issue.
4. The *cost* of addressing the issue.
5. The *public visibility* of the issue to clients, donors, and other important stakeholders.
6. The *pervasiveness* of the issue in terms of its impact on a wide range of agency goals and functions.
7. The extent to which the issue affects fundamental *values* of the agency.
8. The extent to which the issue requires additional *research* in order to clarify the choices.
9. The extent to which *competing agencies* are addressing the same issue. (p. 18; italics in original)

Kearns advised practitioners to assign percentages of effort to issues based on the priority ranking, which forces all organizational actors to recognize criteria and trade-offs. Providing insight on the importance of this last step, MacKeith (1994) found from her case studies that relationships between the fund-raising department and those responsible for program services often are problematic. She reported complaints by fund raisers that service providers (i.e., line managers and staff) are "out of touch with reality," "isolated," and "elitist" (p. 435). Service providers, on the other hand, complained that fund raisers are "only interested in money," "without compassion," and "callous" (p. 435). MacKeith concluded, "The discrepancy between client needs, as perceived by some service providers, and donor preferences, as perceived by the fundraisers [*sic*], appeared to be the main source of problems" (p. 437).

Strategic management, especially SWOT analysis, enables fund raisers to reduce internal tensions and to avoid laundry or wish lists generated by such antiquated forms of planning as *needs assessment*. As Kearns (1992) summarized, "SWOT *requires* decision makers to envision their organization interacting with factors in the dynamic external environment that can either facilitate or impede progress toward the mission of the enterprise" (p. 6; italics added).

Strategic Thinking

Strategic planning is not sporadic but ongoing. Similarly, fund raisers do not engage in SWOT analysis, formulate their plans, and then lock themselves behind closed doors. They continue to scan the environment, which rapidly changes, and are alert to opportunities not anticipated in the formulated plans. They understand that fruitful relationships require not only two-way communication and openness to ideas, but also "a measure of spontaneity" (Culbertson et al., 1993, p. 280). Prospective donors, they know, often start the fund-raising dialogue. In short, fund raisers think strategically and embrace *informed opportunism.*

Management scholar Robert Waterman (1987) identified informed opportunism as one of eight characteristics of "renewing organizations" (p. 6). He based the concept on a combination of information and flexibility, which successful organizations view as their main strategic advantage. Gilley et al. (1986) cited "opportunity consciousness" as a condition for excellence in higher education (p. 61). Drawing from other studies, they defined the concept as "a continuing attention to changes in the environment . . . to any change that can be turned to the advantage of the institution" (p. 61).

Opportunities are expected to occur that, if recognized and seized, will advance the organization and help realize its potential. Holt (1993) argued that institutional advancement practitioners must "allow for spontaneity, flexibility, creativity, and the occasional brilliant hunch when the situation warrants it" (p. 72). She stated, "Even the most meticulous, formula-driven planning process can't take the place of strategic thinking" (p. 72).

When I was the director of development at the University of Maryland at College Park, I made an appointment to visit an alumnus during a 1984 vacation in California. The alumnus, a wealthy businessman I will just call Michael, had not been on campus for almost 25 years and had made only one gift of $5,000. We knew a lot about him through research, but no one had ever met him. It was obvious when I sat down in his office that he was pleased I had called on him and that my visit had in some way spurred his own ideas about making a gift. He asked many questions about the university, and at the end of the hour he handed me a certificate of stock worth $500,000! He said he would decide later how the gift would be used because he had not had time to give it much thought. Needless to say, I was elated and made sure on my return to Maryland that thank-you letters were quickly sent from the chancellor of the campus and the president of the university system.

The work that had piled up on my desk during vacation demanded attention; yet I felt the university's new relationship with Michael was worth setting aside some of the tasks planned months before. I invited him and his family to the next month's meeting of the board of directors of the university's affiliated foundation so that directors and senior managers could express their appreciation for his gift in person. He came to Maryland and at the board's luncheon asked if he could say a few words. He stood up and told the group that he had regretted his decision as soon as I left his office! The room was deathly silent; the chancellor and president looked at me with dismay. Then Michael announced that I was too nice to have left with only $500,000, so he had brought with him stock worth an additional $1 million! As he handed me the certificate, he simply said, "Thanks for coming to California." The stock later sold, minus commission, for $2.6 million. In the summer of 1995, long after I had left Maryland, Michael gave another $2 million to the university.

The two-way symmetrical model of fund raising is grounded in informed opportunism, as well as in strategic planning. As the nature of its communication is two-way between groups, not source to receiver, practitioners are responsive to opportunities presented by members of donor publics. When I was an assistant dean at Maryland's College of Business and Management, a large grocery store chain headquartered on the West Coast contacted the university about funding merit scholarships for juniors and seniors majoring in business. The corporation had started hiring college graduates as managers, and part of its recruitment plan was to establish scholarships in selected areas of the country. Funding scholarships unrelated to financial aid or student recruitment was not one of our fund-raising objectives, nor was the grocery store chain a corporate prospect. It was not a previous donor, it had until then limited its employee recruitment to high school graduates, and it had no apparent relationship with the school. Yet the corporation had come to us because we could help it meet one of its important objectives. Rather than accept the $20,000 gift, which would be of little value to the school, or reject it, which would hamper the corporation's plans, I negotiated with managers to use the $20,000 to supplement faculty salaries and the budget of the student marketing association. The corporation gained the visibility among students it desired and the business school received funding for one of its top objectives, faculty salaries. About 7 months after the initial gift, we asked for and received a pledge from the same company for $150,000 toward the cost of a classroom in the school's new building.

Strategic planning is the basis of the fund-raising process, but practitioners also continually scan the environment and seize opportunities as they arise. They are not like the comic-strip character Ernest, who told his friend Frank, "Opportunity knocked once, but by the time I switched off the alarm system, removed the safety bar, loosened the guard chain and unlocked the dead bolt, it had gone" (Thaves, 1995). Harvey and McCrohan (1990) urged charitable organizations to adopt "an ongoing commitment to environmental scanning and strategic planning" (p. 61). They predicted, "Failure to monitor the increasingly changing context of fund raising will test the survival skills of even the largest and most sophisticated of today's philanthropic organizations" (p. 61).

Chapter 10 turns now to the 5-step process of ROPES. Formative research is conducted, objectives are established, and programming is planned and implemented to carry out the objectives. Ongoing and follow-up evaluation is performed to monitor and measure how well the programming accomplishes its objectives. Stewardship is the final step in fund raising, whereby obligations and responsibilities to donors are met and the success of future efforts is determined.

RESEARCH

The most important step in the ROPES process is the first, research. Without solid research, fund raising is reduced to hucksterism and panhandling—hit-and-miss activities without direction and with little respect. Research provides knowledge, formulates strategy, inspires confidence, and ensures that practitioners achieve desired results. Paraphrasing Cutlip et al. (1994), research is the essential ingredient that makes fund raising a management function, as well as a managed function.

Methods

Defined by Broom and Dozier (1990), "Research is the controlled, objective, and systematic gathering of information for the purposes of describing and understanding. In other words, it is the *scientific* approach to answering questions, providing more reliable answers in most situations than authority, personal experience, and historical precedent" (p. 4; italics in original). These scholars placed research methods along a continuum from very informal at one end, to very formal at the other end. Informal methods include casual scanning of the media, unstructured interviews, and anecdotal reports. Formal methods include large-sample surveys of publics. Methods at both ends and those in between yield valuable information.

The intent of the following discussion is not to instruct students in methodology, but to briefly introduce the various levels of research as applied to fund-raising practice. I strongly recommend that future practitioners take a separate academic course on research methods in the behavioral and social sciences.

Background reading is fundamental and is differentiated by browsing and structured searching (Culbertson et al., 1993). The first provides the breadth of perspective so important to strategic management. Fund raisers, for example, regularly read such news publications as *The Wall Street Journal*, *Time* magazine, and their local daily newspaper. They also subscribe to such business magazines as *Forbes* and *Fortune*. For structured searching, they rely on specialized and trade publications, secondary research, and online electronic services. Secondary research, such as reading about studies on similar and related topics in academic journals, provides an advanced starting point for primary research, or the organization's own efforts to gather information. Increasingly, the Internet is used for both browsing and searching.

Fund raisers talk with people. They meet with opinion leaders in their communities, attend government and civic functions, and pay attention to unsolicited feedback from stakeholders (e.g., complaint letters from clients). They record their observations, particularly *call reports* filed after in-person meetings with prospective and current donors. For annual giving, they utilize gift *response forms* to gather information on donors. They incorporate the three predictor variables of the situational theory of publics—level of involvement, problem recognition, and constraint recognition—in their informal research. For example, when scanning the environment, they ask themselves such questions as: Does this information indicate increased salience for the problem addressed by my organization? Do people have lower financial constraints to giving?

Qualitative methods are placed about midpoint on the continuum. They should not be confused with informal methods because qualitative research involves systematic formal design and analysis. The difference is noted by referring to data, as opposed to information. Of particular value to fund raisers are in-depth interviews and focus groups. Both methods primarily utilize open-ended questions, and study participants are selected for their representativeness of the population of interest. Because scientific sampling procedures are not used, results are not generalizable; however, findings do provide rich insight on the problem being studied. For example, whereas focus groups previously were viewed as a preliminary research method, requiring confirmation by quantitative methods, studies employing them can stand on their own as appropriate and self-contained *if* their purpose is to increase understanding rather than to project results (L. A. Grunig, 1990).

Depth interviews are based on carefully designed, standardized interview guides, which ensure data are collected from every case on specified variables while allowing the interviewer to pursue additional lines of inquiry. Interviews generally are conducted in person so that both verbal responses and nonverbal cues can be recorded. The guide then directs analysis of the data, supplemented by the interviewer's observations and perceptions. The use of this research method in fund raising, although flawed, is illustrated by *feasibility studies*, which traditionally are undertaken before capital campaigns. Because they supposedly are unbiased, consultants usually conduct the studies using proprietary interview guides developed through experience. A purposive sample of between 25 and 75 major donor prospects is selected by the client organization, and open-ended questions elicit the interview subjects' reactions to the proposed campaign and their intended giving behavior. The major flaw in the application is that findings are used not to increase understanding, but to predict the likelihood of the campaign being completed successfully and a specific dollar goal reached.

Focus groups typically consist of 7 to 10 people gathered in one location for a discussion focused on a specific issue. The discussion is led by a moderator with some training in interviewing and group-process management, who encourages the expression of a variety of ideas and asks probing questions to help participants clarify meanings. Answers are recorded on videotape or audiotape and transcribed into written format. Data are analyzed by looking for consensus, patterns, and insightful comments. Fund raisers use focus groups not only in the formative research step, but throughout the process. For example, focus groups are helpful for testing the case for support, rating prospects for major gifts, and getting reaction to a planned direct-mail series. Practitioners often tap volunteer leadership committees, which Culbertson et al. (1993) described as "blue-ribbon groups" (p. 40) because they are selected for their expertise and experience rather than for their representativeness.

Although I endorse methods along the full continuum, only quantitative research employing statistical procedures yields findings that are scientifically reliable. The three common methods are surveys, experiments, and content analysis. The large-sample survey is the most frequently used quantitative method in fund raising. Findings are generalizable to the population from which the sample is selected, enabling practitioners to make predictions. Among its multiple uses, it allows fund raisers to measure variables that theory predicts are critical to the practice (e.g., coorientation factors). Surveys can be conducted by mail, by telephone, or in person, with cost increasing in the same order. Content analysis was touched on in chapter 9 in relation to agenda-setting theory; research using field experiments is suggested later in this chapter.

Following Hendrix (1995), the initial step in ROPES is broken down into research in the three areas of organization, opportunity, and publics. Although the first step is readily accepted in fund raising, practioners generally concentrate on only the last of the three areas and usually that research is limited to prospects for major gifts. The importance of what is termed *prospect research* is supported in the literature and demonstrated by the existence of a specialized association dedicated to this area, the American Prospect Research Association, which changed its name in 1995 to the Association of Professional Researchers for Advancement (APRA). Even with their limited perspective, fund raisers emphasize the first process step and conduct more research than public relations practitioners. Broom and Dozier (1990) explained, "Not only does research play a minor part in public relations practice, it often is greeted with skepticism or hostility" (p. 10). J. E. Grunig (1993) added, "Far more practitioners talk about theory and research than use it" (p. vii).

Research on the Organization

The fund-raising process starts with gathering and interpreting information on the organization. Practitioners must be thoroughly familiar with the organization's history, finances, personnel, program services, and past fund-raising efforts. They develop a solid working knowledge about operations and clients. They gain a complete understanding of how annual gifts will serve organizational goals and learn all they can about projects requiring major gifts. In accordance with SWOT analysis, they assess internal strengths and weaknesses.

Practitioners interview key managers and trustees. They analyze such documents as reports, budgets, and IRS Form 990 before conducting research in other areas. Focus groups are helpful for studying a broad spectrum of stakeholders. Fund raisers also are advised to do a monthly stint as a volunteer, greet new clients for a day, sit in on program service sessions, and join employees outside their department for lunch. Attesting to the importance of research on the organization, Loessin and Duronio (1993) concluded from their study on characteristics of successful fund raising: "The most important factor in making decisions about fund-raising programs may be insight into one's own institution" (p. 48).

This area of research is not new. According to Cutlip (1965/1990), the John Price Jones firm digested 20 volumes of records in preparation for the capital campaign it directed during the 1920s on behalf of the Washington National Cathedral. Cutlip further described the detailed research: "Jones and his staff, upon acquiring the Washington Cathedral account, made an extensive survey as to the Cathedral's comprehensive needs, its general policy, future plans, past fund-raising activities, and relations with the lay public" (p. 285). It is recalled that Jones, the historical figure identified with the two-way asymmetrical model, placed great emphasis on research and planning. In a 1925 memorandum to his staff, Jones (cited in Cutlip, 1965/1990) made clear his belief that fund-raising success results from concentration on the first steps of the process:

Facts first.
Then analysis.
With complete information, intelligently classified, a reasonable plan will reveal itself.
If there is time, make a preliminary test.
Beware of irrelevant stunts. Every shot should be carefully aimed at the target.
Think it out first, then write. After that it probably won't need much talking over. (p. 184)

Research on the Opportunity

A logical progression from knowledge about the organization is research on the opportunity. The outcomes of strategic planning, including SWOT analysis, set the direction of the fund-raising department and suggest the opportunities it will pursue. Practitioners study the opportunities before incorporating them in objectives.

Research on the opportunity is grounded in coorientation theory. As described in chapter 9, coorientation emphasizes the importance of determining the degree of agreement and accuracy between a charitable organization's view of a fund-raising opportunity and the views of its donor publics before programming begins. If differences are found, the organization must change its intended behavior or correct misperceptions.

Providing an applied example, the University of Miami undertook a 10-month, $15,000 research effort in 1993 to measure the views of regional opinion leaders—including corporate CEOs—in preparation for its planned capital campaign (Schreiber, 1993). According to the associate vice president for university relations, administrators were trying to "assess perceptions of the University of Miami, its role in South Florida, and where there may be some gaps between what *we see as reality* and what opinion leaders perceive about the institution" (Schreiber, 1993, p. 27; italics added). An outside research firm conducted initial interviews to reveal issues and establish baseline information. Drawing from those findings, an on-campus research center designed a mail survey of some 2,000 opinion leaders. Results of the quantitative study were used to develop programming to address opportunities and problems.

This type of study differs from traditional feasibility studies in that the latter almost always are limited to qualitative research on a small number of major donor prospects. In the past, according to Lord (1983), feasibility studies had a one-way purpose, "to test the feasibility of reaching the dollar goal, period" (p. 40). He described current studies in two-way asymmetrical terms, saying they are an effective way to listen to people, to gain information for shaping campaign strategy and identifying tactics to use to obtain gifts from specific prospects. He summarized, "A feasibility study enables us to get the answers 'from the horse's mouth,' so to speak" (p. 40). This approach disregards the possibility of behavior change by the organization and ignores the fact that consultants promise confidentiality to interview subjects.

Research on the opportunity should be two-way and symmetrical; it should not be confined to capital campaigns. All fund-raising programs, specifically annual giving and major gifts, benefit from research in this area. Formal to informal methods help practitioners determine how "in sync" their preliminary plans are with the views of donor publics.

Research on the Publics

Effective, efficient, and ethical fund raising demands that prospective donors be matched to the organization and the opportunity—which only can be accomplished through research. Defined by Allen (1991), "Prospect research is the systematic acquisition and recording of data about donors and prospects that provide the basis to establish, maintain, and expand the 'exchange relationship'" (p. 217).

With unlimited resources, all members of donor publics would be researched individually. Because such an approach is unrealistic, fund raisers segment prospects and conduct single-unit analysis on major donor prospects and group analysis on annual giving prospects.

Corporations and foundations generally are researched at the single-unit level. They require personal attention because their gifts usually involve multiple decision makers. Their relatively small number facilitates this attention. Although many contribute lower level gifts, corporations and foundations are identified mainly with major gifts, which makes single-unit analysis cost efficient. Individuals are researched as members of segmented groups or as single entities, depending on their capacity to give (i.e., annual vs. major gift). The three publics are further divided into previous donors and prospective donors. Nudd (1991) justified the basic segmentation, "Although it is important to attract gifts of all sizes (and new donors whatever the gift level), organizations can no longer afford to treat everyone the same" (p. 178).

At this point, research recommended in chapter 9 takes place. Capsulizing the earlier discussion, fund raisers conduct studies to determine which prospects have interests and needs that match those of the organization. J. E. Grunig's (e.g., J. E. Grunig & Repper, 1992) situational theory of publics helps practitioners target their efforts on those with the highest probability of giving. The seventh of Broce's (1986) nine cardinal rules of fund raising was: "Prospect research must be thorough and realistic" (p. 23). He elaborated: "Before significant fund raising can take place, the staff must identify and evaluate those persons, foundations, corporations . . . from which it reasonably can expect to receive support. 'Blue-sky' prospect identification is dangerous" (pp. 23–24).

Group Analysis. Although annual gifts are defined as all gifts of less than $10,000, when we discuss the annual giving program we typically are speaking of an average amount of about $50. Charitable organizations have access to numerous individuals capable of making such gifts. Because of the large number and the small gift average, prospect research for annual giving generally is confined to group analysis.

Practitioners systematically collect, store, and analyze information about previous donors. A computer is essential. Many software packages on the market are specifically designed for fund raising. To name just a few for Macintosh and DOS/Windows systems, there are MACTRAC and GiftMaker Pro, DONOR II, the Raiser's Edge by Blackbaud, Fund-Master and FM Light by Master Software Corporation, and Results PLUS by Metafile. No particular package is recommended; practitioners should assess their needs and try demonstrations of different ones. User satisfaction can be checked through queries to some of the Internet resources listed in Tables 4.1 and 7.1. Opinions of subscribers to the Forum for Prospect Research would be particularly valuable.

In addition to such basic demographics as name, address, and telephone number, practitioners also collect information on occupation, employer, age, and spouse's name from response forms and checks. Records usually include the amount of each gift, the date it was received, the technique to which the donor responded (e.g., direct-mail package 3), the purpose of the gift, and the date of the gift receipt and acknowledgment. Affiliation and stakeholder membership are noted (e.g., volunteer, employee, or client). Each donor's record should contain fields in which cultivation activities can be logged, such as events attended and newsletters sent. As recommended in chapter 9, periodic surveys measuring the situational theory's predictor variables allow fund raisers to assign codes based on the donor's probability of giving. In the absence of such research, other procedures improve effectiveness and efficiency.

Donor information is analyzed for three purposes: (a) to segment previous donors for more effective communication, (b) to identify prospects who share characteristics in common with donors, and (c) to identify annual giving donors who are capable of making a major gift. For the first purpose, variables are selected to segment previous donors into smaller, more homogeneous groups. Programming and messages can then be designed to communicate more effectively with each group's members. At the most basic level, previous donors are segmented by gift amount and date of last gift. Disabled American Veterans, for example, segments its 6.5 million direct-mail donors into more than 100 categories, primarily using amount and date of gift (H. Hall, 1994a). Fund raisers for colleges and universities use the terms *LYBUNT* and *SYBUNT* when separating previous donors into those who gave "Last Year But Unfortunately Not This (year)" and those who gave "Some Year But Unfortunately Not This."

Statistical analysis should be employed to select variables for meaningful segmentation. For example, donors of gifts greater than $50 may be older and more likely to be married than donors of lower gifts. Messages can be personalized based on differences between the two groups. Analysis also reduces costs. By analyzing gift records of 50,000 individuals who contributed less than $10 in response to any one mailing, Covenant House discovered it was losing $2,000 each time it mailed to these donors (H. Hall, 1994a). It now sends solicitations only to individuals who contribute $10 or more.

Statistical analysis also enables fund raisers to identify prospects by characteristics they have in common with donors—the second purpose for analyzing donor information. As Blanchette (1993) stated, "In-house databases are becoming increasingly rich sources of significant information. Statistical techniques can sift that information for variables highly correlated with giving to produce more sophisticated segmentation and target populations" (p. 1).

In the study I conducted on annual giving by journalism alumni to the University of Maryland, I used discriminant analysis to identify characteristics that separate donors from nondonors (Kelly, 1979). Of 45 independent variables tested, 15 accounted for 87% of the difference between the two groups. Because many of the 15 were inferred variables, or variables that must be measured by questioning members of the population directly, I ran an additional analysis with only those variables of the original 45 that were available from alumni records (i.e., objective variables) or measured readership of various university publications. The second analysis showed that only five variables could successfully predict 72% of the time who was a nondonor, a donor of less than $50, or a donor of $50 or more (as compared to a random probability of 33%). The five predictor variables were readership of three publications (including annual giving literature), year of graduation, and number of years the individual had paid dues to the alumni association (3 consecutive years was significant). I postulated that the publication variables easily could be measured through a short, annual readership survey, which included respondent identification. By adding results to alumni records, qualified prospects for the two levels of gifts could routinely be separated from suspects with a low probability of giving.

The third and last purpose for analyzing donor information, identifying prospects for major gifts, requires the services of commercial firms who compare the organization's records to complex databases. There are different variations of the procedure, referred to as *electronic screening*. Some databases consist of the names and addresses of wealthy individuals (e.g., those who own a great deal of stock). Others contain U.S. Census Bureau and marketing data that target demographics related to gift capacity, such as age of the individual and wealth of the neighborhood where he or she resides. Consulting firms develop donor profiles of people who can contribute specific amounts, using giving behavior, proprietary research, and their own predictions about characteristics. Illustrating, Nature Conservancy hired Marts & Lundy in 1993 to screen all of its donors before beginning a capital campaign to raise $300 million (H. Hall, 1994a). The firm's analysis found that 1.5% of the Conservancy's 438,000 direct-mail donors were relatively affluent and resembled others who give large amounts to charity. Screening charges run roughly $10,000 for detailed analyses of 8,000 to 10,000 donors. A minimum of 5,000 cases usually is required.

Single-Unit Analysis.   Fund raisers never begin communication with a major donor prospect without first gathering information on the individual, corporation, or foundation. Practitioners obtain the necessary information from three sources: (a) public sources, (b) peers of the prospect, and (c) the prospect. The first source consists of reference materials such as directories, and public records such as courthouse documents. Large departments have at least one full-time staff person for researching just public sources. These prospect researchers usually are trained in library science, not social science research. They rarely analyze annual giving donors or interact with prospects for major gifts. In addition to retrieving information, they develop biographical profiles, maintain prospect files, record contacts, and disseminate internal reports. Eric Siegel (1993), director of development operations at the University of California, San Diego, recommended one full-time researcher for every $10 million raised annually or for every four fund raisers with responsibilities for major gifts.

Reference materials are found in departments of all sizes. They are available in print and electronic forms. A basic collection of directories and journal subscriptions, according to Siegel, annually costs about $5,000, whereas a state-of-the-art library costs about $20,000. He estimated that fee-based online search services run about $12,000 per year. "Database searching," Siegel (1993) declared, "is now considered the most efficient, cost-effective way of conducting donor research" (p. 260). Electronic reference materials are available from both fee-based services and the Internet. Until recently, fund raisers relied on fee-based services, primarily Dialog; as of 1997, World Wide Web sites increasingly are used.

Bobbie Strand (1996), a longtime expert in prospect research and currently a principal consultant with Bentz Whaley Flessner, described fee-based online search services as an investment: Although often costly, the information typically found can pay handsome dividends. Strand provided an example of researching one individual for which online fees totaled $34; however, items uncovered included existence of a family foundation, membership on four corporate boards, dozens of stock transactions with dates and company names, and the prospective donor's year of birth. She proclaimed Dialog "a gold mine of data" (p. 53) and recommended the following from its collection of databases: ABI/Inform, which gives the sale price of privately owned companies; BioMaster Index, which indexes more than 675 biographical directories; and Foundation Directory and Standard & Poor's, which present classic reference works on foundations and corporations. For-fee search services other than Dialog include Nexis, which contains databases on property holdings and similar public records throughout the United States; NewsNet, the largest online collection of newsletters, including *Foundation Giving Watch* and *Corporate Giving Watch*; and CDA/Investnet, which supplies detailed information on officers', directors', and others' stock holdings in companies whose stock is publicly traded.

Whereas fee-based services can be faster and more reliable, the Internet offers information that is harder to find elsewhere and usually is free. A good place to start is APRA's Web site, listed in Table 4.1. Another valuable site is Internet Prospector, a monthly online newsletter to which fund raisers from across the country contribute. To get there, type *http://plains.uwyo.edu/prospect/*. E. Ryan (1996) recommended several other popular sites: SEC's Edgar (electronic data gathering and retrieval), which contains financial statements on publicly owned companies and mutual funds, *http://www.sec.gov/edgarhp.html*; NewsLink, which features free links to 3,000 newspapers, magazines, and broadcasting companies, *http://newslink.org/menu.html*; and WhoWhere, which lists people's and organizations' e-mail addresses, URLs, phone numbers, and street addresses, *http://whowhere.com/*.

Within the next few years, practitioners will routinely access thousands of databases from their computers. To address transitional needs, the discussion touches on a few basic reference tools offered in print form (most of which are also available in electronic form). Students are advised to read Siegel's (1993) overview of the vast array of reference materials on the market. Also useful is former librarian Helen Bergan's (1992) handbook, *Where the Money Is*, which describes more than 200 resources. Demonstrating the move to electronic form, Bergan's (1996) newer book, *Where the Information Is*, concentrates on fee-based online services and the Internet.

The Bibliography and Genealogy Master Index, which covers most major biographical publications, is the recommended starting point for research on individuals. Other tools are the Marquis Who's Who series, particularly *Who's Who in America, Who's Who in Finance and Industry*, and the regional volumes. Haines Criss-Cross Directories, available for 50 major U.S. cities, list the value of residential property and tell who lives there. The classic works for corporate prospects are *Standard & Poor's Register of Corporations, Directors and Executives* and Dun & Bradstreet's *Million Dollar Directory*. The Foundation Center's *National Directory of Corporate Giving* is a guide to 600 direct-giving programs and 1,700 corporate foundations. Illustrating the use of journals, the June issue of *Black Entrepreneur* annually lists the top businesses owned and/or controlled by African Americans. The Foundation Center's flagship publication and the classic reference work for foundations is *The Foundation Directory*, published annually. The center's database, which contains information on more than 40,000 active grantmaking foundations and corporations, is available through Dialog or on CD-ROM. The CD-ROM version, *FC Search*, costs $995 as of 1997.

Plans call for adding the database, including descriptions of recent grants to the center's Web site at *http://fdncenter.org/index.html*.

Reference materials are drawn from public sources (e.g., databases built from corporate reports filed with the SEC). Their use for prospect research generally creates few ethical problems. In contrast, public records about individuals that are not incorporated in reference materials constitute a sensitive area, one practitioners are advised to avoid. Documents such as probate files, divorce settlements, and civil actions are open to "the public" and contain information rarely found elsewhere. However, their use should be reserved as a last resort when research based on other sources fails to find information deemed *essential* for communicating with the prospect. Ethics is returned to shortly.

Peers of the prospect, the second source of information, are used informally and in focus groups. Referred to as *prospect rating*, or screening, sessions, small groups of individuals are convened to assess "prospects' abilities to make gifts at specific levels" and to comment on suggested "cultivation and solicitation strategies" (Allen, 1991, p. 221). The moderator asks participants to consider each prospect's financial capacity, interests in common with the organization and its work, linkage to the organization, readiness to give, and philanthropic nature. Questions about financial capacity are often framed as time windows, such as, "Has the prospect recently sold a business, inherited money, or made extraordinary profits in the stock market?" Participants almost always are previous donors, and moderators strive to keep the meetings professional and confidential. They discourage gossip, record only relevant information, and collect all written materials at the end of the meeting.

Focus groups dealing with donor diversity also are recommended. For example, Von Schlegell and Hickey (1993) urged fund raisers to use this research method to learn more about women prospects because recent studies suggest there is "a profound difference in the philanthropic behavior of women and men" (p. 26). Colgate University conducted focus groups of alumnae to discuss their motives for giving and attitudes about cultivation and recognition. The data, according to Von Schlegell and Hickey, helped Colgate's fund raisers match the interests of women to specific major gift opportunities. Similar research on members of different ethnic groups would be valuable.

The third source of information is the prospect, and as Jon Thorsen (1993), then president of APRA, admitted, "The most valuable information is still what prospects relay in person" (p. 64). Steele and Elder (1992) explained, "Through careful questioning, you can check on the validity of your assumptions about a person; elicit new information, uncover values, attitudes, and needs that are relevant to the potential gift; and locate the prospect's position in relation to the giving process" (p. 67). Nudd (1991) agreed: "One of the most likely and most dependable places to learn about the prospect is *from the prospect*" (p. 180; italics in original). Fund raisers complete and file call reports after meeting with prospective donors.

Based on the research findings from all three sources, practitioners analyze each prospect's likelihood of making a major gift. They often synthesize the information into categories, such as propensity to give and common interest, and assign a subjective number (e.g., 1 to 5, with 5 as highest likelihood). The ratings are added to paper or computerized files and are regularly reviewed as the fund-raising process continues and new information is received. Nudd (1991) asserted, "Whether it is scanning the business and social columns in the newspaper, reading trade magazines aimed at the industries from which funding is being sought, asking for information while networking with colleagues, or picking up on a signal from the donor" (p. 177), prospect research is an ongoing activity.

It also faces ethical challenges about privacy rights. Allen (1991) described one aspect: "It is not uncommon to learn about a family member's drug or alcohol problem, an unknown bankruptcy, extramarital affairs, and other family secrets" (p. 225). Nudd (1991) related an incident in which a student worker in a fund-raising department mistakenly sent a Dun & Bradstreet report on alumni-owned businesses to one of the alumni owners. In an angry telephone call the alumnus announced, "If you want to know something about my business, all you have to do is ask me," and hung up (pp. 187–188).

The best way to prevent problems is to develop and adhere to strict policies on information selection and the maintenance of files. Information that could damage a prospect's reputation or cause embarrassment should not be recorded, nor should it be passed on indiscreetly by word of mouth. Files should be secured, including coded access to those on computers. The formulated policies should be disseminated to strategic stakeholders. Dunlop (1993) provided three helpful guidelines: Follow the Golden Rule (i.e., treat prospects the way you would want to be treated), be open and honest about what you intend to do with the information you receive, and make sure the information you seek is appropriate to your need to know at the time. APRA has an Ethics Code for Research on Potential Donors, which, Thorsen (1993) pointed out, serves as a base for ethical practice.

OBJECTIVES

An old adage states, "If you don't know where you want to end up, then you need not fret about which direction you go!" (Broom & Dozier, 1990, p. 12). Or as baseball legend Yogi Berra (cited in Lord, 1983) reportedly said, "You've got to be very careful if you don't know where you are going, because you might not get there" (p. 32).

Departmental goals evolve from the organization's goals and strategies. Based on the research step, goals are broken down into objectives. The objectives are formulated to state the results desired from programming. Without objectives derived from organizational goals, which J. P. Smith (1981) called an institutional agenda, "fund raising is destined to be more random than rational—an amateurish activity around which serendipitous events will occasionally occur, but by which they are rarely caused" (p. 63).

This text defines *goals* as general statements that express broad, desired results, whereas *objectives* are specific statements that express results as measurable outcomes. Rosso (1991) adopted similar terminology, saying fund-raising objectives move from global needs (goals) to specific quantitative expressions. "This specificity," he said, "establishes a natural link to program budgeting, program cost, and identification of program needs that provide the rationale for all fund raising" (p. 11). Broom and Dozier (1990) agreed with this approach:

Writers sometimes use the terms "goals" and "objectives" interchangeably, but the usual meanings make goals the more global statement of program results. Goals indicate the more general and ultimate outcome the total program is designed to achieve. Objectives describe the specific results to be achieved by a specified date for each of the well-defined target publics. (p. 40)

As Broom and Dozier explained, objectives serve three critical purposes. They give focus and direction to designing programming, provide guidance and motivation to those working in the programs, and spell out the criteria for assessing program results. In other words, fund-raising objectives state where the department is going, how it is going to get there, and how it will know if the desired ends have been reached. Neither goals nor objectives are expressed solely in terms of dollar totals; other ends are sought.

Hendrix (1995) presented two criteria for formulating objectives: (a) each objective must be stated in the form of an infinitive phrase that expresses a specific, desired result; and (b) each objective must be verifiable. Meeting both criteria facilitates evaluation. Describing the first, an infinitive phrase consists of the word *to* plus a verb plus the complement, or receiver of the verb's action. For example, the fund-raising department may want the annual giving program to result in previous donors renewing their gifts. The phrasing of the objective in the infinitive form could be: To renew gifts from previous donors. The second criterion requires that the desired result be stated in quantified, measurable terms, and that a time frame or target date be set for its accomplishment. The objective just given, therefore, could be reworded: To renew gifts from at least 80% of last year's donors to this year's annual giving program, ending on December 31, 199–.

Other desired results would be formulated. The fund-raising department, for example, may want the annual giving program to attract restricted gifts for a special purpose, such as purchasing a new computer system, increase accuracy about the organization's work among nondonors, and solicit more prospects. The department may want the major gifts program to attract endowed funding for one service staff position, increase the number of major donors, and cultivate more prospects. These objectives could be worded:

Annual Giving Program:
Objective 1—To attract restricted gifts totaling at least $100,000 for the computer project by December 31, 199–.
Objective 2—To increase accuracy about the organization's work by 50% among nondonors on the in-house list, ending December 31, 199–.
Objective 3—To solicit 20% more prospects during 199– than in 199– through direct mail.
Major Gifts Program:
Objective 1—To attract endowed gift(s) totaling $1.5 million to fund one staff position by December 31, 199–.
Objective 2—To increase the number of major donors from 199– to 199– by 10%, as of December 31.
Objective 3—To conduct 25 in-person meetings with qualified, nondonor prospects during 199–.

The time to think about evaluation is at the time objectives are set. In this way, practitioners build in the means by which their programming results will be measured. Illustrating, Objective 3 for annual giving can be measured by comparing the number of direct-mail solicitations sent 1 year with the number sent the previous year, and for major gifts by counting the number of in-person meetings held with qualified, nondonor prospects during the calendar year. Objectives 1 and 2 for the major gifts program can be measured by checking gift records at the conclusion of the program, keeping in mind that Objective 1 may have a 2-year time frame because of the large amount of money required. Whereas Objective 1 for annual giving also can be measured by in-house counting, Objective 2 requires pre- and postprogramming research, such as mail surveys, to determine if and how much accuracy increased among nondonors. These examples illustrate the two types of objectives: (a) output, and (b) impact.

Output Objectives

Output objectives represent the work to be produced. They are, according to Hendrix (1995), "stated intentions regarding program production and effort (or output)" (p. 22). Objectives 3 for annual giving and major gifts, just presented, are output objectives, one dealing with solicitation and the other with cultivation. Another example applicable to both fund-raising programs is: To form a leadership committee of at least 15 volunteers by February 1, 199–. K. S. Grace (1991b) provided two other examples in her essay on managing for results. Using a United Way, she presented the following, repeated for individual, corporate, and foundation donors:

> Objective 1—By September 1, 199–, information about United Way Donor Option giving to be promoted among existing donor base through newsletter or direct mail.

> Objective 2—By September 5, 199–, staff to complete analysis and assessment of existing donor base and convert record keeping to new software. (p. 147)

Output objectives, then, deal with administration, as well as cultivation and solicitation. They are intentions to implement activities and tasks that likely will contribute to a program's eventual success, but do not deal directly with the consequences.

As Hendrix (1995) explained, output objectives often are referred to as support or process objectives. They are of a lower order than those dealing with impact, such as affecting giving behavior. A fund-raising department that based its programming entirely on output objectives would be ineffective and have low accountability. It would essentially concentrate on production without taking responsibility for what it accomplished (i.e., its contribution to organizational effectiveness). Practitioners are warned not to confuse the two types of objectives, although both are important.

The importance of output objectives is dependent on the degree to which the output contributes to desired impact. When the relationship is weak, the objectives are of little value. For example, theory predicts that output objectives focused on publicity in the mass media contribute almost nothing to impacts related to agreement or behavior. Such situations are common in public relations, whereby output objectives are unrelated to the actual impact the programming is supposed to achieve. The abuse is so widespread, Hendrix argued that in an ideal world practitioners would not use output objectives. His condemnation is understandable given the public relations function's poor record in documenting how it contributes to organizations' goals and strategies. Furthermore, practitioners often claim that success in attaining output objectives, such as the number of news releases sent or the number of brochures published, has some vague spillover effect on impact. Senior managers frequently respond, "Prove it."

Fund raising, on the other hand, relies on outputs that logically have a causal relationship to the impacts sought. Maintaining in-house mailing lists, forming volunteer committees, soliciting more prospects through direct mail, and making in-person cultivation calls likely improve conditions necessary for effective fund-raising management. The evidence, however, is largely anecdotal. This is a fertile area for master's theses and doctoral dissertations. Graduate students could utilize field experiments to test causal relationships between output and impact. For example, a study on annual giving could include a comparison of gift results—including proportion that gave and average gift size—between a sample of prospects who received a financial report from the organization the year before (treatment group) and a sample who did not receive the report (control group), with other variables such as previous giving record held constant. Cross-organizational surveys of practitioners about the number and type of contacts required to obtain major gifts could be conducted. If fund-raising production is a factor in giving, then studies are needed to provide statistical evidence that relationships exist. As T. Hunt and Grunig (1994) argued, output objectives have little value unless previous research has shown that the outputs contribute to desired impact.

The call for such research is not new. Lindahl (1992) concluded that cost-efficiency studies like the one he conducted at Northwestern University are flawed without systematically recorded data on all cultivation and solicitation contacts with prospective donors and related costs. In the later study on predicting alumni donors to Northwestern, Lindahl and Winship (1992b) also concluded that future research needs to explore "the critical importance" of staff interactions with prospects as related to giving behavior (p. 62). The researchers, it is recalled, found that the strongest predictor of both annual and major gifts was past giving. Challenging practitioner wisdom, they asked, "If development staff had approached those with the highest capacity (regardless of past giving) over the past few years, would the results have been better than if the staff had approached alumni based primarily on past giving levels?" (p. 62). Lindahl and Winship (1992a) subsequently announced they planned to incorporate the variable "development effort" in future predictive models (p. 18).

Impact Objectives

Impact objectives "represent specific intended *effects*" of programming on targeted publics (Hendrix, 1995, p. 22; italics added). As explained in the last chapter, the effects of fund raising—listed in Table 9.2—are used by practitioners to formulate impact objectives. The effects from which they choose are: awareness, accuracy, understanding, agreement, behavior, and repeat behavior. Combined with the two basic intentions of reinforcing or changing, they represent all possible impacts of the function.

Hendrix rightfully pointed out that there is no linear progression among the effects: People do not move from cognitive, to attitudinal, to behavioral states in an uninterrupted and predictable course (i.e., the domino model). The selection of each effect is situational, depending on the needs of the organization. However, the importance of previous donors demands that fund raisers pay special attention to the sixth effect, repeat behavior. They rely on research to prudently set impact objectives dealing with nondonors because changing unfavorable attitudes or behavior are the most difficult effects to attain. Their reversal takes time and cannot be accomplished with one organized effort. Hendrix (1995) said a useful guideline for practitioners is the military adage, "Don't fight a losing battle" (p. 24). At the lower end of the hierarchy, accuracy is selected to improve communication, as dictated by the coorientation model of relationships, and awareness is regularly selected as an investment for future efforts.

Once output and impact objectives have been formulated, they must be reviewed and approved by members of the dominant coalition. This part of the second step cannot be overlooked. Not only does approval ensure that objectives support the organization's goals and strategies, but evaluation of fund-raising programs and practitioners' performance will be based on the extent to which the objectives are met. Revisions or changes should be carefully negotiated to avoid setting unrealistic expectations.

Peters and Waterman (1982) found that America's best run companies build objectives and measurements into every aspect of the organization. Feedback and evaluation are used to monitor and reevaluate programs on a continuous basis. The ROPES process requires the same standards of managerial excellence for fund raising. As described in this section, the second step makes the process highly compatible with *management by objectives* (MBO), a well-established procedure for agreeing on desired and achievable results in advance of the work and then evaluating the work by the cooperatively set objectives. In fund raising, therefore, objectives precede and govern programming decisions.

PROGRAMMING

The programming step consists of two parts, planning and implementing. Implementation is broken down by programming designed to achieve objectives dealing with cultivation and programming designed for solicitation.

Planning

The first part of programming results in a written fund-raising plan. A convenient format is to divide the plan by the two primary programs of annual giving and major gifts, both subdivided by approved objectives. Under each objective, a synopsis of the research supporting and shaping the objective is given, followed by an outline of the activities and tasks required to accomplish the objective, including selected techniques. Planning tools are used to present time lines and personnel assignments. The means by which the objective will be evaluated and plans for stewardship are described. Budgets are a fundamental component, including line items for research. Overlapping objectives, such as those dealing with administration or planned giving, can be addressed in a third section.

Drafts of the plan are submitted to those who approved the objectives earlier (i.e., dominant coalition members) and to members of the fund-raising department who helped draft the plan. Key volunteers and donors should also be asked to react. Addressing the last groups, Lord (1983) advised, "Authentic involvement in the planning process can promote a sense of ownership among prospective donors and volunteers. People are simply more motivated to work for, and invest in, the realization of plans they themselves have helped to develop" (p. 33). Oral presentations with audiovisual materials and procedures for recording feedback are recommended.

Once the plan is approved, it becomes a blueprint for the department's day-to-day work. As K. S. Grace (1991b) asserted, a fund-raising plan provides the basis for managing staff and volunteers, "balancing priorities, working with major donors on funding priorities, and responding objectively to the demands placed on the fund raising [sic] professional staff" (p. 145). In other words, a plan approved before programming starts is the strongest deterrent to those inside and outside the organization who would make fund raising a catch-all solution to financial problems or attempt to bend the function to their wishes. It proclaims, in effect, "If it's not in the approved plan, we can't do it." The plan educates important participants about the systematic nature of fund raising and increases its credibility.

Activities and Tasks.   Planning tools help make the written plan clear and concise. I recommend a *decimal system* for outlining activities and tasks. Each objective is assigned a number to the left of the decimal point, with two levels of numbering to the right. The *activities* necessary to accomplish the objective are numbered one place to the right of the decimal point, as illustrated with the annual giving program's first objective, presented earlier:

1.   To attract restricted gifts totaling at least $100,000 for the computer project by December 31, 199–.
1.1   Recruit members who are interested in the computer project to the program's volunteer leadership committee.
1.2   Identify and research individuals, corporations, and foundations with demonstrated interest in computers.
1.3   Conduct a series of breakfast meetings with the CEO and prospects for gifts of $5,000 or more.
1.4   Use e-mail to inform and solicit individual prospects who regularly use computer communication.
1.5   Incorporate computer project in all direct mail solicitations, including check-off option on response card.

Each activity is then broken down by the *tasks* required to complete the activity, numbered two places to the right of the decimal point. Selecting just Activity 1.1, for example:

1.1   Recruit members who are interested in the computer project to the program's volunteer leadership committee.

1.11 Draft and obtain approval for a description of responsibilities, including hosting one breakfast meeting.

1.12 Compile a list of prospective members.

1.13 Send personal letters from the volunteer chair requesting a meeting.

1.14 Schedule meetings.

1.15 Hold orientation session for computer subcommittee.

Once the tasks are completed, the activity is completed; when all activities are done, the objective should be met.

Gantt charts are helpful for presenting estimated time needed for completion. The chart shows the tasks to be completed on the vertical axis and the time required to complete them on the horizontal axis, usually in units of weeks. The tasks are sequenced from top to bottom, so that the ones at the top must come first and those at the bottom last. The name of the staff member responsible for the task is listed below it. In one glance, then, the Gantt chart provides information on what will be going on, when, and by whom. Also useful are the program evaluation and review technique (*PERT*) and the critical path method (*CPM*), which allow managers to allocate time more precisely. These and other planning tools are fully described in such textbooks as J. E. Grunig and Hunt (1984; see chap. 8).

Techniques.   During program planning, fund raisers select the techniques they will employ to communicate with donor publics. The techniques were listed in the last chapter in Fig. 9.3, broken down by the three levels of communication and the two primary programs of fund raising. It is recalled that techniques based on interpersonal communication, such as face-to-face conversations and personalized proposals, are used predominantly in the major gifts program, whereas annual giving relies on techniques based on controlled and mass media communication, such as special events and story placements. As emphasized in chapter 9, however, both programs use techniques from all three levels to some extent, which was demonstrated in the illustration of the decimal system just given.

The techniques commonly are mislabeled in the literature as *vehicles* or *methods* and often are confused with programs, publics, and other elements of fund raising. Described by Rosso (1991), for example: "Fund raising [*sic*] methods include the annual fund, direct mail, phone-a-thons, telethons, special events or benefits known as fund raisers, special gifts, gift clubs, capital campaigns, grantsmanship, and planned giving" (pp. 11–12). Similarly, Mixer (1993) listed "14 basic methods" of fund raising that included techniques such as phonathons, programs such as major gifts, and donor publics such as foundation solicitations. Students are advised to disregard such confused definitions and adopt the terminology introduced in this text.

On the other hand, there are numerous books available on the technical aspects of techniques: how to organize a direct-mail effort, how to run a phonathon, and how to write effective fund-raising letters, to name just a few. This how-to literature is a resource for future practitioners, and examples are given as suggested readings and references in this text. Because the fund-raising books have no theoretical basis, more helpful information is found in textbooks on communication techniques, such as T.

Hunt and Grunig (1994), also cited in this book. The necessary linkage between the two bodies of literature—one lacking theory and the other not specific to fund raising—is the conceptualization of techniques presented in chapter 9.

The theory guides the selection of techniques and helps fund raisers justify their decisions in the written plan. Basic to the theory is an understanding that mass and controlled media techniques are less effective than interpersonal techniques as set objectives ascend from awareness to behavior. However, because human and financial resources available for communication always are limited, donor publics are segmented by their number and the size of their probable gift, and corresponding limitations are placed on the techniques used. Scarcity of human resources was discussed earlier; relevant to this discussion is an emphasis on cost factors.

The cost of techniques per exposure decreases as communication moves down from interpersonal to mass media. Illustrating, in-person visits to one donor over the course of 2 or 3 years can easily total $2,500 (Lindahl, 1994). Lindahl and Winship (1992b) explained, "The cost of personally soliciting major gift prospects is very high, involving many hours of professional, clerical, and volunteer time in the process" (p. 55). They estimated that every 100 to 200 prospects for major gifts translates into the cost equivalent of one full-time fund raiser. In contrast, editorials and PSAs reach thousands of people at no distribution cost. Even paid advertisements and telethons, which can be very expensive, have a low per-exposure rate.

Cost efficiency, then, demands that interpersonal techniques be reserved for prospects for larger gifts. Practitioners compensate by segmenting donor publics and personalizing communication as much as possible. As Lord (1983) stated, "The plan for a broad-based campaign may call for soliciting smaller gifts by telephone, mail or even television. Even here, the more personal we can get, the better the results will be" (pp. 80–81). Practitioners are aided by principles of effective communication, readily available in communication texts.

Cutlip et al. (1994), for example, provided the "seven Cs" of effectiveness: credibility, context, content, clarity, continuity and consistency, channels, and capability of the audience (pp. 402–403). Briefly demonstrating their application to fund raising, credibility is an attribute of both the organization and the source of the message. Perceived status, reliability, and expertise of the person who signs a direct-mail letter amplifies the value of the information. The content of the letter must have relevance for the receiver, and rules of continuity and consistency require repetition; therefore, direct mail consists of three or more separate mailings.

Sharpe (1993b) recommended that practitioners focus their messages on the needs of the donor publics they wish to reach. Using prospects for planned gifts as an example, he explained, "It is a fact of life for fund raisers that the programs and approaches that work with a high-powered, mid-career corporate executive may not be as effective with that executive's aging parent" (p. 31). Simmons (1990) provided theoretical support, describing the act of communication as a social exchange: "Your success in transmitting information to other persons depends on knowledge of an audience and its wants; if you do not learn what a targeted audience expects in exchange for its attention to a message and then do not provide it, successful communication is unlikely" (p. 19).

The fund-raising plan includes samples of messages that will be used in programming with a description of their intended receivers. The messages are drawn from a *message platform*, or theme of about five words, that summarizes the case for support, which—in turn—is derived from the organization's mission. The platform allows practitioners to develop consistent messages segmented to appropriate groups. Levner (1993) provided an example from Morehouse College, a prestigious institution for African American men and the alma mater of Martin Luther King, Jr. The powerful fund-raising theme was "Morehouse Men Speak for Themselves," and messages were built around testimonials from graduates in positions of prominence and influence.

Budgets.   Financial implications of programming are presented in budgets. Neither planning nor budgeting is a one-person job. All practitioners in the department should participate, including estimating and itemizing *variable costs* that will be incurred in implementing the plan. Variable costs are those associated with activities and tasks, such as printing, entertainment, photographers, travel, rental fees for special events, and postage (Cutlip et al., 1994). The staff manager adds the estimated variable costs to the department's *fixed costs*, such as salaries and benefits, phone, supplies, and service contracts. In addition to these two categories, fund-raising budgets should include three critical line items: (a) research, 10% of the total budget; (b) stewardship, about 2% of the amount of dollars expected to be raised; and (c) contingency, 15% of the budget to cover changes and unplanned opportunities.

I recommend that the plan contain a budget for each objective, as well as comprehensive budgets for the programs. The budgets should include *line-item justification*, which is a supplementary section of text to explain unusual or complex items. For example, a line item of only $1,000 for the series of breakfast meetings described in Activity 1.3 earlier would prompt an explanation that the expense is for fixed costs; the meetings will be hosted, and paid for, by members of the computer project subcommittee. Formulating a budget for each objective meets one of Cutlip et al.'s (1994) three guidelines for budgeting: "Communicate the budget in terms of what it costs to achieve specific results" (p. 372).

The two other guidelines are: (a) know the cost of what you propose to buy, and (b) use the power of your computer to manage the program. Addressing the first, fund raisers responsible for annual giving must be knowledgeable about printing and postage costs; those responsible for major gifts should have a solid grasp of expenses related to travel and entertainment. Elaborating on the last guideline, Cutlip et al. (1994) advised practitioners to develop a master spreadsheet, as well as spreadsheets for specific projects. "By tracking each project and linking each to the master spreadsheet, you can estimate cash-flow requirements in advance and monitor expenditures against cost estimates" (p. 372). The guidelines help fund raisers calculate cost ratios, or financial measures of accountability, that should be reported to donors and other organizational stakeholders.

Budgets are management tools. Used in conjunction with other aspects of program planning, they provide guidance for scheduling staff resources, purchasing goods and services, tracking costs, and linking costs to performance and results. The fund-raising plan also includes evaluation and stewardship, which are covered later in this chapter. The discussion turns now to implementing programming.

Implementing

Programming generally concentrates on two areas, cultivation and solicitation—neither of which is well understood by those outside of fund raising. Steele and Elder (1992) pointed out that the very vocabulary used to describe programming, cultivating prospects and soliciting gifts, suggests to some lay people that fund raising is a "kind of institutional prostitution" (p. 10). Illustrating, Arthur Schafer (cited in E. Ryan, 1993), director of the Centre for Professional and Applied Ethics at the University of Manitoba, stated in an article published by CASE, "To compete effectively, campus fund raisers must often sail close to the wind; to put it crudely, sucking up to major donors is more the rule than the exception" (p. 62). Broce (1986) discredited such misconceptions:

> Many people think that tricks or gimmicks must be employed to butter up prospective donors. This assumption fails to take into account the intelligence and perception of most donors, and makes fund raising appear mysterious and "unnatural.". . . People are sensitive. They do not want to be "handled" or catered to. They do want to be respected and appreciated. Respect is conveyed through dignified treatment and thoughtfulness in making use of their time. (pp. 217–218)

Solicitation is often thought of as begging or conning people out of money. Milton Murray (cited in Knott, 1992) told a story from 25 years ago when he was consulting for a 2-year college. He asked the academic dean for a list of alumni in order to start an annual giving program. Dropping the list on Murray's desk, the dean said, "I'm eager to see how you con them out of money." Murray replied, "My friend, if that's your point of view, I'm not going to be able to do anything for you. Your alumni should be giving out of loyalty and appreciation for what this institution has done for them. If you think you have to 'con them out of money,' that means you don't deserve it, and if you don't deserve it, then I can't help you" (p. 198).

Cultivation. Much of programming is designed to meet objectives dealing with cultivation; for the major gifts program, it constitutes the majority. If fund raising is a function concerned with relationships, as attested to in earlier chapters, it should not be surprising that cultivation is critical to the process of raising gifts. Dunlop (1993) explained, "When we recognize that an institution's interests in fund raising go beyond the processes of asking and include processes to develop a sense of commitment, the focus of our planning shifts from raising dollars and cents to building attitudes" (p. 101). Other impact objectives dealing with awareness, accuracy, and understanding are as necessary as those specifying giving behavior.

Cultivation is not sucking up or "schmoozing." Prospective donors, especially those for major gifts, resent unwanted and inappropriate attention. Social interactions unrelated to the organization's mission, such as playing golf, contribute little to the relationship. Cultivation is managed communication by which fund raisers continually seek to *inform* prospective donors about and *involve* them in a charitable organization's work. The simple rules of friendship apply. Drawing from decades of experience, Dunlop (1993) advised: "Let your friendships grow naturally. Don't assume familiarity that is not based on the experience of your relationship with the prospect. The best way I have found to judge the appropriateness of initiatives is to apply the same standards you use in your personal friendships" (p. 109).

Congruent with theory and research presented in chapter 9, practitioner definitions emphasize information and involvement as the two essential factors in cultivation. Worth (1993), for example, defined cultivation as "the process by which an institution develops a relationship with a prospective donor by providing information and involving the individual in the institution's planning and life, with the goal of engendering that person's commitment and support" (p. 415). Focusing first on involvement, the sixth of Broce's (1986) nine cardinal principles of effective fund raising was: "Involvement is the key to leadership and support" (p. 23). He elaborated, "The meaningful involvement of individuals is a full-time, never-ending task. It must be sincere, it must be constant, and it must be real" (p. 23). Lord (1983) agreed: "Involvement, it is said, is more important than information. If we want people to invest their time and resources in a program, we have to give them *authentic* involvement in the cause" (p. 29; italics in original).

Culbertson et al. (1993) drew from communication research to provide the theoretical basis: "There is reason to believe that involvement enhances genuine, long-term behavioral support" (p. 98). They gave examples dealing with fund raising:

> Membership in a collegiate sports hall of fame. Naming a building after someone who contributes to its construction. Putting up a plaque that identifies a hospital room as "Constructed with a generous gift from Jody Smathers, 1900–1986." Naming someone to an advisory board that defines goals and philosophies for a . . . charitable organization . . . . These and countless other strategies help build behavioral involvement. One can scarcely help feeling involved in the face of widespread recognition and/or "immortalization" in bronze. (pp. 98–99)

Culbertson (1992), warned, however, that genuine involvement exists only when the person feels he or she has done or at least can do useful things for the organization. Simply enhancing prestige, without a feeling of active personal involvement, has little impact on a person's supportive behavior.

As demonstrated by the examples Culbertson et al. (1993) gave, stewardship, or the organization's responsive behavior to donors *after* they have made a gift, provides opportunities for increasing involvement. J. Patrick Ryan (1994), president and CEO of Staley/Robeson/Ryan/St. Lawrence, explained, "Giving grows as our involvement grows—and involvement is never more timely than after a person donates" (p. 64). He added, "Virtually no one makes one major lifetime gift and walks away" (p. 64).

File et al. (1994) found that physical involvement of donors who have created charitable remainder trusts of $1 million or more dramatically increased after they made their planned gifts. Only 13% said they were highly involved with the recipient organization before the trusts were created, whereas 49% reported high involvement after the gift ($N = 476$). Volunteering, for example, more than doubled from 18% to 48%.

Turning to information, the glossary of the NSFRE Institute (1986) distinguished between two types of techniques used for cultivation, special events and "published materials." It explained that events, such as dinners and meetings, are used to involve important prospects in an organization's affairs and that material is "literature specifically designed to enhance interest in and enthusiasm for the work of an organization, preferably personalized to some degree" (p. 25). Broce (1986) divided cultivation into individual and mass cultivation and touched on techniques appropriate to each. Regarding individual cultivation, he stated, "Activities may range from a visit by the chief executive officer . . . to a personal letter conveying important information" (p. 218). Lord (1983) listed techniques used for mass cultivation: direct mail, including letters and publications, and "all the activities that come under the heading of public relations" (p. 38), including news coverage in the print and broadcast media, editorials, PSAs, and special events.

The dichotomy in cultivation parallels that found in other steps of the fund-raising process, namely, programming differs by gift capacity and number of prospects. Whereas prospects for major gifts are cultivated through both involvement and information, annual giving prospects are cultivated primarily through information. The literature reflects this dichotomy, but concentrates almost exclusively on cultivation of major donors. A further emphasis on those capable of making the largest gifts promotes unbalanced programming, which, according to resource dependence theory, is not in the best interests of the organization. For example, Nudd (1991) said, "Continued success (and in some cases continued existence) will depend on the ability to develop and maintain a close relationship with 'the few' who have the ability and the willingness to make a difference for the organization" (p. 176). She argued that if 90% of the total dollars raised comes from 10% of an organization's donors, then cultivation should be focused on the 10% capable of making such gifts. "And not a week should go by without significant attention being given to the care and cultivation of those at the top of the major donor list!" (p. 176).

Illustrating the danger of such a narrow focus, File et al. (1994) reported from their study of $1-million-plus donors: "There was some indication that the donors believed that their large gifts entitled or obligated them to intervene in the management of the organizations. One-third of the donors said that they were highly likely to complain to the management" (p. 278). The researchers argued that this finding did not reflect dissatisfaction, "but rather was the expression of feelings of *ownership* and high involvement" (p. 278; italics added). They advised nonprofit managers to treat "negative messages or complaints" as opportunities "to increase the day-to-day involvement of [major] donors in improving operations, services delivery, fundraising [*sic*], and donor relations" (p. 280). The researchers, whose study was based on marketing theories, did not address the issue of autonomy or the desirability of maintaining a broad base of donors to avoid external control.

A model program in cultivation of major donors is the one directed by David Dunlop (1987, 1993) at Cornell University. The program is grounded in *moves management*, a systematic strategy originally developed by G. T. "Buck" Smith (1977). It qualifies contacts with prospects by the quality, quantity, frequency, and continuity of the contacts. The contacts, also termed *initiatives*, are classified by quality into two categories: foreground and background initiatives. Foreground initiatives are activities planned with a specific prospect in mind (e.g., a private tour of facilities conducted by line managers). Background initiatives are activities planned for groups of people that include two or thousands of prospects (e.g., advisory councils and annual reports). The initiatives, using all three levels of techniques, are planned and implemented by members of the fund-raising staff, who Dunlop (1987, 1993) refers to as *moves managers*. Information about each contact is recorded in a computer system, and tracking software generates monthly reports on the cultivation of all prospects for major gifts.

Similar systematic efforts are needed for annual giving donors. Not only should such contacts as informational mailings be recorded, but a cultivation plan designed to instill cognitive involvement should be developed (i.e., reinforcing perceived linkages between prospects and the organization and its work). To the degree that it is cost efficient, prospects for lower level gifts should be encouraged to forge physical connections, such as volunteering. Eugene Dorsey (cited in Mixer, 1993), former chair of IS, recommended that people be invited to make firsthand visits to see where the need is being met and not just see, but feel the need and develop a sense of interrelatedness and connectedness. Illustrating this approach, UJA believes sponsoring trips to Israel is one of its most effective ways for strengthening the bonds American Jews feel to Jewish charities (E. Greene, 1992). A study it commissioned placed this cultivation activity at the top of the organization's priority list and recommended that the program be expanded to include more types and different lengths of trips so that people of different ages and gift capability could participate.

The most effective cultivation flows naturally from the organization's routine operations—it is closely tied to program services. M. R. Hall (1992) related how when she was a component fund raiser for a business school, a professor mentioned in an informal conversation that it would be interesting to have business executives discuss their own leadership practices with graduate students enrolled in a seminar on organizational leadership. The result was a series of executive guest lectures that enhanced the academic program and provided quality cultivation of potential donors. She also used business executives as judges for the school's annual case competition, when teams of graduating MBA students presented written and oral analyses of a selected corporate problem. The experience of interacting with faculty and the professionally postured students during the 2-day, round-robin event received high praise from the visiting judges. Many of them later joined the school's board of visitors and became donors.

Fund raisers view everything that happens in their organization as a potential opportunity for cultivation. They also think strategically when natural, external opportunities present themselves.

During a cultivation call in 1979 when I was the associate director of development at the University of Maryland, the alumnus I was visiting told me that another alumnus, who I will call George, was soon to be promoted to president of the state's major utility company. The next day, I found a photograph in a university yearbook of George racing across the finish line during a 1950 track meet. With the support and cooperation of my supervisors—Patrick Hunt, then director of university relations, and Michael Worth, then director of development—I had the photograph enlarged, framed, and sent to George the week he was named president, along with a note handwritten by our chancellor, which simply read, "Once a winner, always a winner." In the years that followed, George became a valued volunteer, donor, and professional friend. He also became chairman of his company, one of the largest corporate donors in the state, and chairman of the University of Maryland's Board of Regents.

Cultivation requires multiyear programming, particularly for major donors. Panas (1984) said the average cultivation period for a very large gift is about 7 years. Nudd

(1991) reported that a national survey of senior practitioners suggested an average of nine separate cultivation contacts should take place before a major gift is solicited. Steele and Elder (1992), who defined cultivation as orchestrated involvement, provided the rule of thumb: "The typical major gift requires thirteen contacts over the space of two to three years" (p. 25). Underscoring both cultivation's importance and the investment required, they told of one practitioner who when asked how she obtained a $20-million gift for her university, replied: "Simple. We cultivated the donor for twenty years" (p. 25). As Lindahl (1992) concluded from his empirical study on cost efficiency, "Results support the idea that development is a very long-term process and that, in some instances, the longer the delay, the greater the payout" (p. 111).

Senior managers and other members of the dominant coalition must be active in cultivation and understand the necessary commitment of time and resources. Steele and Elder (1992) argued that the fund raiser is the CEO's moves manager. Addressing directors of libraries, they said, "Very often, you will be in the position of taking direction from your fundraiser [sic], who will say, 'I need you to host this dinner, take this trip, and call these people and say these things to them'" (p. 41). To avoid unrealistic expectations, O'Shea (1993) advised practitioners to counsel managers, using data from a historical analysis of past gifts to the organization. Samuel Hook (cited in O'Shea, 1993), then vice president for development at Centenary College in Shreveport, Louisiana, capsulized this discussion, "Point out that development depends on relationships, and that 15 minutes does not constitute a relationship" (p. 34).

Solicitation.   A revered practitioner principle is:

People do not give unless asked.

It appears in almost all the literature on both annual giving and major gifts programs, warning fund raisers that those who do not ask rarely receive the gift. Calling it "the greatest commandment of all," Panas (1984), for example, concluded his 65 Tenets of Success with, "You must ask for the gift" (p. 198). He illustrated the principle with a story about a dying widow and her minister, who hoped the woman—because of her high involvement—would make a planned gift to his church. Instead, Panas said, the widow's entire estate went to her deceased husband's alma mater because the president of that institution visited the hospital and asked for a gift; the minister did not. Regardless of Panas' press agentry overtones, gifts to specific organizations rarely occur without solicitation, or implementing programming designed to request gifts.

Steele and Elder (1992) stated, "Donors give if asked to give but do not give if they are not asked. When all is said and done, the number one reason people give is because they are asked" (p. 35). Providing supporting evidence, IS (1994) found that respondents to its national survey "were more than twice as likely to give if they were asked to contribute than if they were not asked" (p. 79). Of the respondents, 77% reported they had been asked to give in 1993, and 84% of them made contributions; in contrast, only 38% of those who had not been asked made gifts. J. P. Smith (1981) summarized practitioner wisdom on implementation, "The two most frequent errors are to ask too hastily and to fail to ask at all" (p. 63).

Solicitation is the easiest part of fund raising. Howe (1991) stated, "It is proverbial that the success of fund raising is 90% in prospect identification, research, cultivation, and preparation, and 10% in the asking" (p. 81). Fund raisers do not solicit gifts, particularly major gifts, unless they have good reason to expect that the prospect will say yes. As explained by theories presented in the last chapter, practitioners spend much of their effort on seeking a *goodness of fit* between their organization and its donor publics. Steele and Elder (1992) commented: "If the fit is right, the decision to give will follow naturally. If the fit is not right, a decision not to give may follow, and that is fine, too" (p. 67).

The last of Broce's (1986) nine cardinal principles of fund raising was: "Solicitation is successful only if Cardinal Principles I through VIII have been followed" (p. 25). Reviewing the first eight principles in the order Broce assigned them: (a) organizational goals must be established first, (b) fund-raising objectives must be established to meet organizational goals, (c) fund-raising programs are determined by the kind of support needed (which was not used in this text because I recommend that all organizations have annual giving and major gifts programs, as well as planned giving), (d) the organization must start with natural prospects, (e) the case for fund raising must reflect the importance of the organization, (f), involvement is the key to volunteering and giving, (g) prospect research must be thorough and realistic, and (h) cultivation is the key to successful solicitation. "It is at this point," Broce stated, "that well-motivated donors, thoroughly informed and involved, seize the opportunity to make investments in an organization or institution in whose present operation or future growth they have significant interest and concern" (p. 25).

Solicitation's placement in the fund-raising process, Broce (1986) said, "comes as a surprise to those who believe that solicitation alone *is* fund raising" (p. 40; italics in original). He elaborated: "Many organizations want to skip the other steps—planning, prospect identification, cultivation—and just go ask people for money. This is defeating, just as defeating as the approach of the organization that is always talking about the need to raise money but never gets started" (p. 215). Broce rightfully argued:

> The successful fund raiser knows that only when all the earlier steps have been accomplished successfully does solicitation come easily. It is then that the person (or foundation or corporation) is meaningfully involved with the organization, understands and appreciates the goals, recognizes their importance to him [*sic*], and welcomes the opportunity, when offered, to make [a gift]. (pp. 40–41)

When most lay people think about asking for money, they immediately conjure up images of face-to-face conversations with strangers. No wonder, then, solicitation is viewed as uncomfortable and unpleasant. Fund raisers, however, do not solicit strangers. Furthermore, face-to-face conversations constitute only one technique employed to solicit gifts. Most lower level gifts are solicited by direct mail. Major gifts from corporations and foundations usually are solicited by personal letters or personalized proposals. Howe (1991) claimed corporations invite organizations to submit a request for a gift, sometimes preceded by a visit. He said, "There is no personal asking after the initial discussion that led to the invitation to submit a proposal" (p. 85). According to Greenfield (1991), "Asking is simple; there are only three ways: by mail, by telephone, or in person" (p. 14). In spite of its oversight of techniques used by many organizations, his reductionist typology is useful.

As the degree of intimacy increases, so do fears of rejection. New practitioners do not find it difficult to ask for gifts in writing, although they sometimes "beat around the bush" without getting to the purpose of the communication. Telephones present greater challenges, but the combination of a letter and follow-up telephone call, advocated by Rosso (1991) and described in the next chapter, helps practitioners overcome their hesitation. Finally, in-person techniques, including face-to-face conversations, do not take place in isolation. If communication has been clear, the prospect signals his or her willingness to be solicited when granting an appointment for the meeting. As Mixer (1993) stated, "The prospect knows either directly or indirectly that a request for funds will be made" (p. 45). Steele and Elder (1992) agreed, explaining that fund raisers build "incremental commitment" with the prospect along the way so unexpected requests are unnecessary; "everyone will know what is going on and where things stand" (p. 70). My experience confirms the claim of fund raiser turned college president Michael Adams (1993): "It is often more difficult to get an appointment with a prospect than to get the money" (p. 136).

The fear of being turned down is grounded in misunderstanding about the fund raiser's role. Practitioners, as Adams (1993) explained, solicit gifts on behalf of an organization; "they are not asking for themselves" (p. 133). Rejection should never be taken personally. The requested gift is not a symbol of personal acceptance or approval. Steele and Elder (1992) advised, "Remember that the 'you' that is involved in soliciting funds is the 'institutional you'—not the 'personal you'" (p. 11). They continued, "You are acting in a professional capacity as an official representative of your institution" (p. 11). Dennis Murray (1995), also a former fund raiser and now president of Marist College, added a critical point, "Success in fund raising comes only after an organization demonstrates that it is accomplishing something worthwhile" (p. 19).

When fund raisers represent an organization that is worthy of support, as demonstrated *to* them by the actions of those who control and carry out the work of the organization, solicitation is a prideful and exhilarating experience. Among my fond memories of practice is an incident that occurred when, as the associate dean, I was in charge of fund raising for the College of Journalism at the University of Maryland. During a break in a meeting about a new continuing education program for advertising practitioners, Joe—a member of the school's board of visitors who was responsible for getting the program started—took me aside to tell me he had just sold his advertising and public relations company for "millions of dollars." With a smile on his face, he asked me to keep the news quiet for a while. "I'm only telling you so you can get ready to ask me for a gift!"

I fully agree with Tempel (1991), who stated, "Fund raising based on the strengths of the organization assumes a dignity that flows from those strengths, obviating any need on the part of staff or volunteers to apologize for the solicitation process" (p. 23).

EVALUATION

The third most important issue facing fund raising—following the need to define who is a fund raiser and to reduce misunderstanding about philanthropy—is how the function should be evaluated. Far too frequently, success or failure is determined by the amount of dollars received in a given year. Fund raising is thought to be effective when it generates the most money possible at a reasonable cost. The approach is flawed in three fundamental ways: (a) it ignores *gift utility*, or what the money was raised for; (b) it does not account for *delay factors* in raising major gifts; and (c) it measures only impact objectives dealing with donor behavior. In short, common evaluation procedures confuse efficiency with effectiveness and misapply the two managerial concepts.

Effectiveness and Efficiency

Charitable organizations are effective when the goals they formulated through strategic planning are met. In its guide to accounting procedures, API (1990) instructed, "To determine a nonprofit's success you must refer to its goals: these are the group's self-determined replacement for the bottom line of profit-making" (p. 14). Effectiveness, then, is measured by comparing the results achieved with the results sought. Efficiency, on the other hand, is a measure of the proportion of resources used to produce outputs or to attain inputs—cost ratios. Although efficiency may help an organization be more effective, the two concepts are not interchangeable. Moving down one level, the fund-raising department contributes to organizational effectiveness when it meets the goals and objectives it formulated to support the organization's goals. It increases efficiency when it keeps fund-raising cost ratios low.

Gift Utility.   Fund raising is not an end in itself, but rather a means to an end. As Rosso (1991) asserted, "It draws both its meaning and essence from the ends that are served" (p. 4). Its purpose is not to simply raise indiscriminate dollars. When fund raising "focuses almost exclusively on gathering financial resources," Payton et al. (1991) argued, it "neglects or even betrays its own larger purposes" (p. 4). Yet Payton (cited in "Philanthropy 2000," 1993) reported, "The trend is toward measuring success in very narrow financial terms: who can raise the most money, who can conduct the biggest campaign" (p. 15). Presenting a fundamental problem with such evaluation practices, Brittingham and Pezzullo (1990) explained, "Too much concern for the bottom line in fund raising discourages both fund raisers and other institutional officers from discussing the relationship between raising funds for institutional priorities versus increasing the overall amount of support raised" (p. 60).

The concept of gift utility, or the degree to which a gift contributes to organizational goals and priorities, was introduced by practitioner Joel Smith (1981). Smith challenged the idea that a gift's dollar amount was more important than its purpose. By pointing out "rather dramatic differential utility among gifts" (p. 64), he attacked the larger issue of evaluating fund raising by dollar totals or efficiency ratios. For example, a $1-million gift restricted for a purpose not related to the organization's goals (e.g., an unneeded chapel for a college) contributes less to effectiveness than a $10,000 gift made in support of the goals. Smith stated, "How regrettable it is, then, that so many fund raisers and the institutional leaders who employ them are preoccupied by big numbers instead of promoting an understanding of which gifts are the most useful, which the least, and what is the approximate order of the many that fall between those extremes" (p. 64). He urged practitioners to discourage the notion that the success of their programs ought to be judged by the bottom line. The fascination with large numbers, he said, "is shortsighted and superficial; it ignores the entire subject of utility" (p. 64).

Delay Factors.   Lindahl's (1992) cost-efficiency study at Northwestern University showed that dollars received in a given year are a poor basis for measuring fund-raising efficiency, let alone effectiveness. He identified delay factors in raising major gifts, showing that the majority of activity and, therefore, costs precede receipt of dollars by a number of years. Most of the costs for raising major gifts, which often are pledged and then paid in multiyear installments, are associated with the year the pledge is made.[1] He found that responses to solicitation techniques predominantly used in annual giving programs, such as direct mail and phonathons, have less than 1 year's delay between the asking and the receipt of the gift—which is one reason such gifts are referred to as annual. But outright major gifts have delays of 4 to 5 years from solicitation activity to the final payment on the pledge. Those from planned giving could not be analyzed properly within the 6-year period Lindahl set for his study. He hypothesized that a minimum of 15 years of data is required to determine the typical delay factors of planned gifts, although he later said uncited studies have found 25 years to be the norm for charitable bequests, the most widely used planned giving vehicle.

In other words, costs incurred in a given year have a weak relationship to the dollars received from major gifts, which Lindahl estimated constitute 80% of the total for colleges and universities. He recommended that organizations change their reporting procedures to reflect the fund-raising process rather than "cash-in numbers" and change their evaluation of practitioners from a short-term to a long-term strategy (p. 115). He warned: "Using short-term or cash-in results as the main evaluation criteria can cause an excellent staff member to look ineffective or an average staff member to look outstanding. Personnel should be evaluated both on long-term (two- or three-year) results and on how well and how often they relate to the prospects" (p. 119).

In a later essay, Lindahl (1994) advised practitioners, "First, begin to track the quantity and quality of development contacts and not just the total numbers of dollars given to the institution" (p. 46). Second, he said, "make personnel decisions based on the success of building and keeping key relationships with the donor population" (p. 46). Translated in the terminology of this chapter, Lindahl recommended evaluating fund raising on multiyear assessment of impact objectives dealing with giving behaviors and on output objectives dealing with cultivation.

Three Levels of Effectiveness.   In my earlier book, I also recommended evaluating the process of fund raising, including cultivation of prospective donors, and a 3-year time frame for evaluating dollar results (Kelly, 1991a; see chap. 14). Drawing on the work of J. P. Smith (1981, 1982), I argued that dollar totals should be broken down by their gift utility so the function's contribution to the organization's goals could be more accurately determined. I further proposed three progressive levels for evaluating fund-raising effectiveness, based on systems theory.

At the highest level, effectiveness is measured by fund raising's impact on all stakeholders of the organization. Pfeffer and Salancik (1978) explained, "Effectiveness is an external standard of how well an organization is meeting the demands of the various groups and organizations that are concerned with its activities" (p. 11). Fund raising, then, contributes to organizational effectiveness when it helps the organiza-

---

[1]Recognizing this phenomenon, FASB changed its accounting standards in 1995 so that written pledges must be recorded in full as gifts received at the time the pledge is made.

tion adapt to its environment (i.e., fund raising is perceived as useful by stakeholders and helps fulfill their expectations of the organization). Staff managers who head a department of integrated relationship management would rely on this level of evaluation.

The second level measures effectiveness by the impact of fund raising on donors. Managers ask: To what degree did our fund-raising efforts satisfy the interests and needs of donors? Illustrating, Carnegie Mellon University's fund-raising department conducted a multiyear evaluation that focused primarily on alumni donors to the annual giving program (Dundjerski, 1994). As part of the evaluation, a survey of 595 donors showed that 79% are satisfied with the process of raising gifts, but that numerous improvements could be made. For example, 40% of the donors said they do not receive enough information about the university, as opposed to solicitations. An alumnus who gives several thousand dollars each year commented, "Even fairly consistent givers make a joke of the fact that every envelope they get from Carnegie Mellon is just another piece of mail asking for money" (p. 24). Donors claimed they would give more if they were treated with more consideration. In other words, the university's fund-raising department discovered it was not spending enough time on programming dealing with cultivation. Carnegie Mellon, it should be noted, consistently ranks high in lists of the most dollars raised; its private support in 1995, for example, totaled $42 million ("Philanthropy 400," 1996).

The most basic level for evaluating fund-raising effectiveness is to measure the impact of the function on the charitable organization itself (i.e., to what degree did gifts support the organization's mission, goals, and strategies?). The ROPES process ensures that fund-raising managers routinely evaluate their department's work at this level. Kanter and Summers (1987) supported the three levels of measuring effectiveness:

> The ideal performance assessment system in a nonprofit organization would acknowledge the existence of multiple constituencies and build measures around all of them. . . . an explicit but complex array of tests of performance that balances clients and donors, board and professionals, groups of managers, and any of the other constituencies with a stake in the organization. (p. 164)

Evaluation by Objectives

The fund-raising department's goals are derived from the organization's goals and strategies. Departmental goals are broken down into measurable objectives. Following the ROPES process, practitioners set objectives before programming starts and build into the objectives the means by which results will be evaluated. If the objectives are met, the departmental goals are fulfilled, and fund raising helps the organization attain its goals (i.e., it contributes to organizational effectiveness).

The set objectives deal with both cultivation and solicitation and consist of both output and impact objectives. Impact objectives focus on the six effects of awareness, accuracy, understanding, agreement, behavior, and repeat behavior. When conducting evaluation, fund raisers are careful not to substitute measurement of one effect for another or measurement of output as an indicator of impact. For example, desired results dealing with agreement cannot be determined by measuring the level of awareness (i.e., prospects know of the organization's work; therefore, they hold positive attitudes about making gifts). Similarly, desired results dealing with giving behavior cannot be determined by measuring the number of mailings sent to prospects, or the number of calls made. Process evaluation is conducted during programming to monitor progress and to make adjustments when necessary. Program evaluation measures results after programming is completed.

Process Evaluation.   Waiting until programming is over to evaluate results is risky. Fund raisers may find that part of their planning was flawed and that changes in programming could have increased results. As the environment is constantly changing, conditions affecting fund raising also change. Staff managers establish procedures for assessing progress toward attainment of set objectives. For example, if an impact objective for the annual giving program is to renew gifts from at least 80% of the previous year's donors by the end of the fiscal year, some acceptable percentage of renewed gifts should be achieved by midyear. A 3-year average percentage of the number of renewed gifts received by midyear could be compared to the current year. If the percentage is lower than average, new activities can be planned and implemented, such as an additional mailing. Murray (1995), whose manual on fund-raising planning is grounded in systems theory, endorsed process evaluation: "Key indicators of fund-raising gains—monetary and nonmonetary—should be tracked" (p. 23).

Process evaluation, as indicated by its name, is particularly useful for monitoring output objectives, or those dealing with the process of raising gifts. Counts of production and distribution are readily available during programming. For example, say it was determined in the planning phase that, in order to achieve fund-raising goals, 20% more prospects for annual giving should be solicited through direct mail than the year before. A periodic check of mailings that showed only 5% more prospects had been solicited would signal that the objective may not be reached by the end of programming, thereby endangering achievement of the goals. Adjustments easily can be made.

The moves management system at Cornell University relies on process evaluation to achieve output objectives related to cultivating major donors. Moves, or cultivation activities, are recorded on computer and tracked during programming. According to Dunlop (1987), "Our means of measurement is the number and type of contacts each of our top prospects has with the institution" (p. 11). He explained, "If we can monitor their experiences—and initiate additional experiences of the right sort at the right time—we can deepen that person's relationship with the institution. And the deeper that relationship, the more likely that person will eventually consider our institution for an ultimate gift" (p. 11). Monthly reports are used to evaluate programming and the work of moves managers responsible for producing the activities.

Program Evaluation.   As Murray (1995) explained, evaluation "is how an organization links plans to performance" (p. 23). When programming is completed, members of the fund-raising department evaluate their efforts by comparing the results attained with the results sought, as expressed by the set objectives. They employ evaluative research, both informal and formal, to determine the achieved results. Whereas in-house counting tells them if output objectives and impact objec-

tives dealing with giving behavior were reached, survey research and other methodologies are needed to assess programming designed for impact objectives other than
giving. For example, to measure whether understanding has increased among prospects for major gifts, fund raisers might conduct interviews with a selected sample and
compare the findings with previous assessments. By *listening* to donor publics through
evaluation research, practitioners engage in two-way communication, and the research
itself provides quality interaction (i.e., research serves as a cultivation activity).

Fund raisers also measure efficiency. Given Lindahl's (1992) findings on delay
factors for major gifts, fund-raising cost ratios should be averaged over a 5-year period,
as well as calculated annually for the department and for each program and activity, as
recommended in chapter 7. The standard of 25% or less should be upheld for the
average and the annual department ratios. Murray (1995) endorsed program evaluation
and the important distinction between effectiveness and efficiency: "A formal evaluation determines whether the development department accomplished its goals
(whether it was effective) and whether goals were reached at an acceptable cost
(whether the department was efficient)" (p. 23). He argued that "the fairest and most
appropriate method for evaluating the fund-raising operation" is one based on objectives that flow from strategic planning, "a thorough assessment of the organization
and its environment" (p. 23).

Reports on evaluation findings should be widely circulated among dominant
coalition members, line managers, and volunteer leaders. Evaluation reports, based on
agreed objectives and quantified evidence, increase understanding of and appreciation
for fund raising's contribution. Findings also are used to improve future efforts. By
keeping complete records, practitioners identify what worked and what did not work
(Cutlip et al., 1994). The knowledge gained informs subsequent decision making.

Concluding this discussion, neither the fund-raising function nor its practitioners
should be evaluated by dollar totals. Payton (cited in "Philanthropy 2000," 1993)
presented ethical reasons at the practitioner level: "If professionals come to measure
their effectiveness by the dollars they directly raise, there will be a strong tendency
for them to manipulate and exploit both the cause they serve and the people from
whom they raise money" (p. 13).

Organizations promote unethical behavior when they impose evaluation by dollars
rather than by objectives. They also demonstrate a high degree of irresponsibility and
ignorance about fund raising. When applying for a new position, one of the first
questions fund raisers should ask is: How will I be evaluated? If the answer is by dollars
raised, my advice is to turn the job down. Expectations will be unrealistic and success
unlikely.

STEWARDSHIP

Fittingly, the term *donor relations* often is used as synonymous with the stewardship
step, although its meaning is much more limited than this book's unified theory.
Greenfield (1991) said the purpose of donor relations is to thank those who have made
gifts and to "establish the means for continued communication that will help to
preserve their interest and attention to the organization" (p. 148). He reminded fund

raisers, "Donors are and will always remain the best prospects for more giving" (p. 40).

Unfortunately, donor relations also is the name given to service units assigned stewardship responsibilities within fund-raising departments. These units usually consist of clerical and other low-paid staff who produce letters, publications, and special events. Staff members, almost all of whom are women, do not know the donors, they were not part of earlier steps in the process, and their work is standardized as much as possible (i.e., stewardship is operationalized as technician tasks). Incongruent with principles of effective practice, department heads responsible for creating these service units argue that fund raisers can spend their time more productively on prospective donors rather than on those who have already given. Worth (1993) claimed such units are new, but predicted, "Continued growth in this area may be a trend of the 1990s" (p. 13). He applauded the "better departments" that have added "professional positions" (p. 13) to assume responsibility for donor relations.

I strongly disagree. Stewardship must be managed by those fund raisers who were responsible for each step in the process of raising the gifts. Standardizing and assigning the final step to others violates donor expectations embedded in the philanthropic exchange. It also violates principles and theories about the importance of previous donors, who are more likely to give than nondonors, whose gifts cost less to raise, and whose continued relationships are essential for future fund raising and the organization's success. As Worth (1993) himself emphasized, "Because the best prospects for new gifts are past donors, programs that provide careful stewardship and provide donors with timely information on the impact of their gifts can pay significant dividends in continued support" (p. 13).

The fund-raising process is not complete without stewardship. Obligations and responsibilities to the donor must be met. Furthermore, the last step provides an essential loop back to the beginning of the process for new efforts. Research takes place during stewardship when fund raisers employ two-way communication to learn more about donors' interests and needs. Continued interaction represents cultivation of prospects who have already made gifts. In other words, good stewardship ensures that the process is continuous; it does not stop and then later start with entirely different and unknown publics. This last step makes the ROPES process superior to those previously applied to public relations, which end at evaluation and have no stewardship component (e.g., ROPE). Such descriptions ignore crossovers in situational publics and the critical objective of reinforcing desired behavior. Stewardship is necessary for all relationship management.

Horton (1981) expressed a view commonly found among fund raisers: "The idea of stewardship is often in our minds, of course—reporting back to donors on the benefits derived from their gifts. There could be almost no end to this. Perhaps it will suffice to say we do what we can in this area, knowing that if time allowed we could always do much, much more" (p. 267). In contrast, Greenfield (1991) ended every chapter in his book with a discussion about stewardship. He explained: "Fund raising concentrates too much on asking for money. More time and attention should be given to the relationships needed to sustain donor interests" (p. 17). Minimizing donor relations for major gifts, he proclaimed, is "the greatest sin of omission among development staff" (p. 167).

The stewardship step in ROPES consists of four progressive elements requiring fund raisers' attention and action: (a) reciprocity, (b) responsible gift use, (c) reporting, and (d) relationship nurturing. Although he did not present them together or order them the same, Rosso (1991) incorporated all four in his sage advice to practitioners:

> In accepting the gift, it is incumbent upon the organization to return a value to the donor . . . . The receipt of the gift should mark the beginning of a continuing and important relationship with the contributor. A gift is received with the tacit promise that it will be used wisely. Proper stewardship requires periodic reports to the donor that the money indeed is so used. (pp. 6, 14)

Before discussing the elements, a broader perspective adds to our understanding and anchors the fifth step in ethical practice.

The concept of stewardship is multifaceted, with both religious and secular meanings. Christianity, for example, holds that resources are not owned by people but are temporarily granted to them by God. Good stewardship means using both monetary and nonmonetary resources for God's greater good. A secular translation is that charitable organizations serve as stewards of the gift resources granted to them by donors. It is incumbent on them to use the resources for the purposes they were given, most basically to advance the common good. Applying the sacred viewpoint to the work of nonprofit managers, Jeavons (1994) concluded that stewardship is thought of too narrowly as only dealing with the management of funds. The original meaning, he argued, is larger and fuller—responsibility for overall administration. "Steward speaks of a person who is concerned with the right ordering and management of all the affairs and concerns—including what we now call economic concerns—of a household or community" (p. 111).

Stewardship for fund raisers, then, means much more than sending acknowledgment letters or periodic reports. As stewards, staff managers are attentive to every aspect of the organization's behavior that may affect relations with donors. They are, as asserted in chapter 7, agents of accountability, guardians of gifts, and the organization's conscience. Jeavons (1994) declared, "Real stewardship has inescapably moral obligations and responsibilities" (p. 115).

Reciprocity

The norm of reciprocity is a universal component of all moral codes (Gouldner, 1960). Studies by anthropologists have shown that it is cross-cultural and fundamental to all people: Human interaction requires stable practices of give and take (Becker, 1986). For individuals, reciprocity is a mandatory virtue (M. W. Martin, 1994); for organizations, it is the essence of social responsibility (J. E. Grunig & White, 1992). In short, when donors make gifts, the organization receiving the gift must reciprocate.

Lombardo (1995) drew from studies on the cultural meaning of gift giving to explain reciprocity in donor relations: "Gifts create an obligation for the recipient to repay the giver, and an expectation of reciprocity on the part of the giver" (p. 297). Repaying helps maintain social balance, and, as M. W. Martin (1994) explained, "Mere taking upsets the balance" (p. 70). He added, "So can mere giving when it is wholly one-sided and when benefactors refuse to accept expressions of appreciation or in other ways place themselves above recipients" (p. 70). As Becker (1986) emphasized, reciprocity affects respect of self and the other party. When socially ingrained expectations of reciprocity are not met, respect is put at risk. Conversely, when they are met, they strengthen a sense of *equal worth*. Lombardo (1995) elaborated, "An unbalanced relationship has been temporarily created, which can be put into balance through reciprocity. The expectation of reciprocity also contributes to the bonding power of gift exchange, since an initial gift is the start of a continued exchange between people" (p. 297).

In other words, charitable organizations are not only obligated to reciprocate, but they must reciprocate if the philanthropic exchange is to remain in balance. Reciprocity protects against loss of autonomy. It also engenders mutual respect, thereby strengthening the relationship between organization and donor. Regarding gift renewal, scholars have found that patterns of reciprocity encourage further helping. How foolish those fund raisers are who regard stewardship as technician tasks without any understanding of reciprocity's critical role in donor relations!

At the applied level, reciprocity simply means that organizational recipients show gratitude for gifts. Gratitude is broken down by acts of appreciation and recognition.

Appreciation.   The most common and expected way of demonstrating appreciation is to say, "Thank you." The thank-you message must be timely and sincere. Acknowledgment and thanks generally should be sent within 24 hours after a gift is received. Mixer (1993) agreed: "An immediate acknowledgement serves to assure the donor that the gift is welcomed" (p. 12). Negative reaction results when a donor's cancelled check is returned before his or her gift has been acknowledged. "The relationship begins to wither as the donor wonders if the gift is appreciated or needed" (p. 12).

Expressing appreciation is not difficult; however, it does require an investment of time and strategic thinking. Fund raisers responsible for the annual giving program should compose thank-you messages *before* gifts are solicited, drawing from the message platform used in programming. An acknowledgment plan, segmented by graduated dollar amounts, should be formulated and approved. The larger the gift, the more personal the acknowledgment. For example, gifts of less than $100 might be acknowledged with a printed thank-you card, whereas donors who give $1,000 or more would receive two personal letters, one from the CEO and one from the volunteer chairperson.

Creativity enhances communication. When I was in charge of annual giving for the University of Maryland, we stamped each check in red with the message, "Thanks Again," so donors would be reminded of the university's appreciation when they received the canceled check from their banks, and later when they went through their checks to itemize tax deductions. A small private school for underprivileged children in Chicago sent handwritten thank-you notes from all its students when a family foundation made its first grant to the school, which was the largest ever received (Lies, 1994). The foundation president rated the acknowledgments highly, which reinforced repeat giving. The president of another family foundation that gives to the same school stated, "I can assure you that as we reevaluate some of the organizations to which we give small grants and decide which to cut back on, this school will never be among them" (Lies, 1994, p. 22).

When Michael, the major donor mentioned earlier in this chapter, decided to designate $1 million of his gift of stock to support *American Journalism Review*, owned by Maryland's College of Journalism, I immediately called each member of the school's board of visitors. I asked the board members, including some of America's best known journalists, editors, and publishers, to call Michael, whom they had never met. The day after the gift was designated, he talked to or had telephone messages from 14 media leaders, such as Donald Graham, publisher of *The Washington Post*, and William Raspberry, syndicated columnist, who all said the same thing, "Thanks a million!"

Research and two-way communication increase effectiveness of appreciation activities. Fund raisers at Carnegie Mellon University, for example, found from their 1993 survey that new donors are more likely to remain loyal if they are thanked for their initial gift and more likely to give again if other signs of appreciation follow (Dundjerski, 1994). As a result, a "thank-a-thon" is held after every annual giving solicitation, whereby students call donors to thank them, update them about the university, and receive feedback. Donors are not asked for another gift. Tying this discussion to future efforts, Howe (1991) advised, "The more prompt and personal the expression of appreciation, the more favorable the carryover toward further giving" (p. 32).

Recognition. According to J. P. Ryan (1994), "Recognition displays your institution's style and gratitude. It shows good stewardship. It says you're thoughtful, attentive, and caring" (p. 64). Most forms of recognition also are used as incentives for giving (i.e., they are incorporated in programming to suggest gift levels). The organization in effect tells prospects, "If you give this amount, you will receive these benefits." Recognition, then, usually represents fulfilling a promise. The benefits returned to the donor must be appropriate, particularly in relation to the size of the gift. They must reflect well on the organization, comply with the law, be in good taste, and protect the organization's autonomy. Fund raisers rely on sensitivity and good judgment, as well as research and formal policies.

For annual giving, the most common forms of recognition are publishing donors' names in gift reports, returning low-cost premiums, and awarding membership in gift clubs to those who give $100 and up. A more effective form of recognition, which I recommend, is simply to personalize all future communication, thereby recognizing the donor's special status to the organization.

The Carnegie Mellon survey found that 64% of the donors who give less than $1,000 do not consider it important to see their names published in the university's special fund-raising report (Dundjerski, 1994). Many said they found it embarrassing to be listed with major donors. Based on the findings, the fund-raising department now publishes an insert for the alumni magazine that only lists the names of donors who give at least $1,000. The change saved the department $40,000 per year. Donors to Carnegie Mellon are adamant about not wanting to receive premiums. Of those who give less than $1,000, only 2% expect a gift in return. A fund raiser elaborated, "A lot of the donors said, 'If you're going to be sending me a premium, then you're showing me you don't need my money'" (Dundjerski, 1994, p. 23).

Forms of recognition that return goods or services to the donor are subject to IRS *quid pro quo* regulations. Greenfield (1991) suggested that public broadcasting stations, which are "notorious for 'premium' benefits for gifts of $100" (p. 115) helped bring about the new regulations because of their heavy use of such "give backs" as coffee mugs, t-shirts, tote bags, and umbrellas.

Gift clubs also are affected by the regulations. Costs of club benefits, such as meals or free tickets, must be subtracted from the value of the gift for tax purposes, and organizations are responsible for informing donors of their legal deduction. Fund raisers at Carnegie Mellon found that the university's donors do not want their gifts used for membership benefits (Dundjerski, 1994). Because a majority specified special events, Carnegie Mellon now charges fees to attend donor-recognition events. Furthermore, the survey found that clubs do not have much influence on the size of an individual's gift. Of those who give less than $1,000 a year, 84% said they would not increase their contribution to become a member of a gift club.

Forms of recognition for donors of major gifts run the gamut from commemorative plaques to VIP parking privileges to naming exhibits, rooms, buildings, and even entire organizations after them. Named gift opportunities, in particular, are widely used because, as Lord (1983) pointed out, they provide "tangible and public recognition for major investments" (p. 57). Due to their public nature, they must be handled with concern for reaction from other donors and stakeholders. In 1996, for example, the San Diego Museum of Art ended gift negotiations with cigarette manufacturer Philip Morris Companies that would have resulted in a named exhibit ("San Diego museum," 1996). The decision followed a public outcry by antitobacco activists, who said the museum was accepting tainted money.

Formal written policies, approved by the board of trustees, are strongly recommended. Greenfield (1991) similarly urged consistent policy, with guidelines for each primary form of recognition the organization decides to offer. He provided a sample in an appendix to his book (see Appendix A). Policies also help fund raisers avoid returning benefits to donors that result in high loss of autonomy.

Despite the cautionary tone of this discussion, recognition of major donors is an extremely satisfying part of fund raising. The pleasure of giving back to someone who has helped your organization is an add-on value to the practice. Whether bringing together corporate sponsors of endowed scholarships with their student recipients, dedicating a new building to a donor's family, or sending a scrapbook of newspaper clippings about new program services to the foundation that underwrote the grant, recognition activities are joyful, memorable, and fun. Only those who lack imagination and a sense of caring find reciprocity an administrative burden. Fred Novy (cited in Lies, 1994) presented his perspective as head of a small family foundation: "Something as corny as a public ceremony can have an impact. We gave money to a hospital many years ago for some cause. At one of their functions, they hung a medal around my neck. That was my own personal Olympics" (p. 22).

Yet, according to J. P. Ryan (1994), few organizations receive top marks for recognizing major donors. "Some lack an *attitude of gratitude*" (p. 64; italics added). Not only do I like Ryan's descriptive term, but it points out that exploitation of even major donors by charitable organizations is not unusual. Some give almost nothing in return for the benefits they receive, violating the norm of reciprocity. Ryan reminded practitioners, "You promised the recognition, and in some way it helped motivate that major gift" (p. 64). In other words, fund raisers who consider reciprocity an option ignore issues of ethics, as well as social responsibility, and endanger future gifts. As Ryan concluded, "Giving appropriate major donor recognition is one of the most important things development officers can do for their institution's well-being" (p. 64).

Responsible Gift Use

Accountability demands that gifts be used for the purposes for which they were given. The element is so reasonable it almost defies questioning. Unfortunately, adherence is not the norm.

Uses of major gifts, which are almost always restricted in purpose, are determined before receipt. When those gifts are made for endowment or facilities, their use spans time, usually to perpetuity. Problems arise years after the gifts were made when organizational managers face new needs and goals. Names on buildings in need of renovation are removed so that prospective donors can be offered a named gift opportunity. At colleges and universities, names of schools are separated from the buildings in which they are housed for the same reason. Yet most fund raisers, disregarding limits of named gift opportunities, continue to promise perpetual use.

Restrictions on endowed gifts for a specific unit of an organization are "bent" to include funding for other units. Similarly, endowed gifts with purposes that have become outdated are redefined without consulting the donor or his or her descendants. The perennial story of millions of dollars in unused scholarships attests to acceptance of endowed gifts with restrictions that cannot be met (e.g., the recipient must be a resident of a specific county who has a specific grade point average and plans to attend a specific college with the intention of studying a specific discipline). Illustrating problems with major gifts of property, Ostrower (1989) claimed that 90% of the art in U.S. museums was accepted with such restrictions as the works are not to be sold, cannot be loaned, always must be shown together, or shown only a certain number of days a year. Compliance often is viewed by later managers as a strain on scarce resources.

To ensure adherence to responsible gift use, fund-raising managers negotiate major gifts with an eye to the future and a perspective of the organization's well-being beyond dollar totals. They help their organization renegotiate the terms of gifts that have become outdated. When necessary, they remind others in the organization that purposes of gifts must be followed otherwise they, the fund raisers, cannot assure future donors that their gift's use will be honored. Without such assurance, few donors would be willing to entrust their resources.

Unrestricted annual gifts present other problems. These gifts are solicited with some implication of their use stated in broad terms, such as helping the organization find a cure for cancer. Once received, many—if not most—organizations comingle the gift dollars with income from other sources, such as client fees. When the time comes for fund raisers to report to donors what their gifts have accomplished, accountants offer little help beyond unsubstantiated generalities. Paying the light bill, administrative salaries, and interest on loans are not uses for which annual gifts are made—at least few donors likely would think so. Although finance officers and others might balk, I strongly recommend that unrestricted gift dollars be dedicated to budget line items that meet donors' interests and needs (e.g., grants for cancer research).

Doing so would still support the organization's annual operating costs, but would also provide fund raisers with greater specificity for solicitations and reporting and provide donors with greater assurance that their gifts are used as intended.[2]

Organizations primarily funded by government present special problems due to the nature of public funding. Fiscal controls imposed on government dollars often mean that unrestricted annual gifts are used to fund purposes that are difficult to fund with government dollars and, as a consequence, rarely are used to fund the organization's core program services, which already are funded by government dollars. Illustrating, government dollars for travel and entertainment expenses, including meals and alcohol purchases, are limited and tightly controlled. In many cases, a large portion of unrestricted gift dollars is used for such purposes as the CEO's discretionary fund, from which travel and entertainment easily can be paid. Equally troublesome are those organizations that use most of the unrestricted dollars raised to pay for fund raising because salaries and expenses are not covered by government funding.

Public colleges and universities are among the worst offenders, particularly those with new fund-raising departments. Annual giving solicitations stress unrestricted gifts that will advance the institution's work. Options to restrict gifts to specific purposes are limited, although donors sometimes can designate their gifts to specific units. Designated gifts usually are used at the unit level in ways similar to those just described (e.g., discretionary funds for deans). Many institutions tax units for the designated dollars raised, which helps pay for fund-raising costs. Reporting to donors is difficult; asking for gifts each year is an exercise in tedious fabrication.

I recommend that fund-raising managers at such organizations sit down with CEOs and others to negotiate more responsible gift use. Portions of discretionary funds should be dedicated to purposes of interest to both donors and those controlling the funds, who should also be prepared to explain mutual benefits of other expenses (e.g., travel funds spent to interview a prospective faculty member). Projects related to program services that supplement government funding should be identified each year before the annual giving program starts, which would allow fund raisers to tell prospective donors about ways their gifts will make a difference. Internal agreement must be reached on moving expenses of the fund-raising department from gift receipts to mainstream funding, which would involve reallocation of staff lines and budgets and, perhaps, lobbying for new resources. Good stewardship cannot be achieved when donors are misled about how their gifts are used. M. W. Martin (1994) explained:

> Trust makes philanthropy possible. We give voluntarily only when we trust that our money and efforts will not be misused. Fundraisers [sic], in particular, have a fiduciary relationship with donors: they have a shared understanding and trust to carry out the intentions of their constituencies. . . . We are justifiably outraged when our money is used fraudulently or in other ways that subvert our intentions to help others, and we are easily disillusioned when that occurs. (p. 48)

---

[2]Trust in responsible gift use is decreasing. Whereas 71% of Americans in 1989 believed that most charitable organizations are honest and ethical in their use of donated funds, only 60% held the same belief in 1995 (IS, 1996).

Reporting

Accountability also demands that donors be informed of their gift's use. The study conducted by Carnegie Mellon showed that 33% of the donors who give less than $1,000 would increase the amount they give if fund raisers took the time to let them know more about specific projects for which their gifts would be used *and* about the impact of their last gift (Dundjerski, 1994).

More than 50 years ago, David Church (cited in Jones, 1946), then vice president of the John Price Jones firm, told managers of charitable organizations, "It requires no great courage on my part to make the prediction that you are going to be faced with constantly increasing demands from your contributors for an accounting of your stewardship and if you do not give a satisfactory accounting you will face growing difficulties in raising the funds required to carry on your work" (p. 82). Church strongly recommended that annual reports be compiled and sent to donors; yet today, few organizations do so.

Lists of donors' names, such as those published by Carnegie Mellon, meet obligations of recognition, but not reporting. As accountant Richard Larkin (1993) urged, fund raisers must send financial statements to donors. An annual report, complete with financial data and evidence of how gifts helped the organization meet its goals, is required.

Both recognition lists and annual reports should comply with the management and reporting standards recently issued by CASE (1994, 1996). Touching on critical standards that often are abused, fund-raising totals should not include government money (even when the public funds were allocated to match a private contribution), donated services, funds from contracts that carry an explicit *quid pro quo* relationship between the source and the organization (including sponsored research grants), client fees and dues (including alumni membership dues), investment earnings on gifts, sales of merchandise, and pledges. Addressing the last exemption, CASE (1996) specified that only gifts in hand should be counted in annual fund-raising reports, which differs from its standards for capital campaigns and FASB's 1995 accounting rule on pledges—discussed in chapter 14.[3] The 1996 standards fail to distinguish between written pledges that are explicitly binding and oral pledges that are simply promises. Whereas CASE excludes all pledges from annual fund-raising reports, it instructs organizations to follow FASB's rules when preparing their financial statements, thereby perpetuating the use of two sets of figures. I disagree and recommend that CASE's (1994) standards on capital campaign pledges be followed.

Of all the reporting standards issued by CASE in 1994 and 1996, the most controversial are those dealing with planned gifts, which are explained in chapters 13 and 14. For the purposes of this discussion, students need only understand that gifts derived from certain planned giving vehicles traditionally have been reported at their face value, which is significantly greater than their actual value to the organization. The practice is deceptive; it artificially inflates fund-raising totals and causes high confusion among donors and other strategic publics. CASE's standards prescribe corrective action, and all organizations—regardless of type—should follow them as a threshold for reporting requirements.

---

[3]The CASE standards also disagree with FASB's rule on donated services, which—in turn—is incongruent with tax regulations governing the deductibility of gifts. Resolution of differences in accounting rules is needed, and some action is expected in the near future.

Relationship Nurturing

The head of fund raising for Carnegie Mellon, Eric Johnson (cited in Dundjerski, 1994), justified time and resources spent on stewardship: "It's easier to get a second gift from a donor who is treated well the first time than it is to get a new gift" (p. 22). Treating donors well goes beyond reciprocity, responsible gift use, and reporting; the relationship so important to the philanthropic exchange must be nurtured. K. S. Grace (1991b) said whereas "traditional notions of stewardship refer to the gift and ensuring that it is spent wisely and in accordance with the donor's wishes," contemporary fund raisers have adopted "an expanded sense of stewardship, one that includes continued relationship building with the donor" (p. 158). "This new view of stewardship," she argued, "lets people know on a regular basis that you care about them, respect their support, appreciate their gifts, and want their interest and involvement" (p. 158).

The most effective means of nurturing relationships is quite simple: Accept the importance of previous donors and keep them at the forefront of the organization's consciousness. Information and involvement are critical, and both should flow naturally from the organization's work. For example, when special events are planned, donors—as well as other strategic publics—should always be considered as possible invitees. Events honoring clients, needs for speakers, and legislative hearings offer ongoing opportunities for increasing donors' involvement. Similarly, donors should be at the top of the list for all external communications. News releases of major announcements, for example, should be sent to donors at the same time they are sent to media. The possibilities present themselves on a weekly basis. Cost considerations, of course, must be balanced with gift amounts. The point is that the organization should be in contact with donors of both annual and major gifts at times other than solicitations.

Lord (1983) concurred: "If donors only hear from us when we're asking for money, they'll be less likely to respond. Build ongoing relationships with your contributors. Invite them. Recognize them. Involve them. Ask them. Send them information before others receive it" (p. 92). Stressing the interdependent nature of donor relations, Seltzer (1987) advised practitioners: "Your constituents expect a certain regularity and consistency from you. Just as you hope that their donations will become a tradition, they expect that your communication with them will be both predictable and continuous" (p. 184). He added, however, do not make assumptions about what your donors want, ask them. Only through research can fund raisers determine the amount of contact their donors desire. Lord (1983) asserted, "Good stewardship is well worth the extra effort it requires. It is the bedrock on which the future of an organization is built" (p. 93).

Despite such expert endorsement, too many organizations are unwilling to invest in this final fund-raising step. According to K. S. Grace (1991b), "Although boards and administrators acknowledge the importance of stewardship, they frequently balk at the cost of providing events and opportunities that have no direct fund-raising impact" (pp. 158–159). J. P. Ryan (1994) argued that stewardship must be budgeted as a line item, roughly 2% of the dollar goal. Staff managers educate members of the dominant coalition and insist on adequate financial support.

Finally, the staff manager, as in all steps of the fund-raising process, focuses the attention of others in the organization on stewardship. It cannot be carried out by practitioners alone. Advising directors of libraries about fund raisers' responsibilities, Steele and Elder (1992) warned, "You should not expect them to take over the care and feeding of everyone who has ever made a gift; it is up to the people who have established relationships with past donors to maintain those relationships" (p. 42).

Practitioners ensure that expressions of appreciation are provided, plan recognition activities, monitor gift use, establish a system of reporting, and develop strategies for nurturing relationships. A key issue, however, is that others in the organization must be as concerned with stewardship as the fund-raising department. A CEO who never takes the time to call a donor to say thank you without prompting, never writes his or her own letter of gratitude for a major gift, or never initiates involvement of previous donors in the organization's work, is a CEO who is taking money under false pretenses. Commitment and enthusiasm cannot be sustained if fund raisers witness a low degree of stewardship on the part of those who said the gift was necessary beforehand, but who have no time or inclination to be a good steward once the gift is received.

TESTING ROPES

The ROPES process for fund raising has been conceptualized in this book; it now needs to be tested in the field. Students interested in a topic for a master's thesis should consider a study utilizing the new theory. Some investigation already has occurred. In 1994, graduate students enrolled in the fund-raising seminar I teach at USL conducted 14 depth interviews with members of the Baton Rouge Chapter of NSFRE. Incorporated in the standardized guide developed by the students were items measuring the percentage of time fund-raising departments spend on the five steps of ROPES. The findings of their exploratory study provide evidence that the ROPES process has face validity and that the proportion of time spent on each step deviates little from the theory presented here.

Based on the collected data, the students calculated that, on average, respondents' departments spend 12% of their time on research, 15% on setting objectives, 48% on programming (23% cultivation activities, 22% solicitation activities, and 3% other), 9% on evaluation, and 16% on stewardship (Duhé, Tyler, Constantine, Devillier, Hollems, Deranger, & Mouton-Allen, 1994). Of particular interest, each case was categorized by the fund-raising model predominantly practiced, and a comparison was made of time allocation between those practicing one-way and two-way models.

As predicted by theory, there is a difference in the average time spent on the research step between departments practicing a one-way model and those practicing two-way asymmetrical or symmetrical fund raising, although the difference is not as great as theory predicts—9% versus 16%. Average amounts of time spent on the 4 other steps are almost identical between the two groups, with one dramatic difference: Time proportions spent on cultivation and solicitation in the programming step are reversed between the one-way and two-way models. Departments identified as predominantly practicing a one-way model devote an average of only 28% of their programming to cultivation, 61% to solicitation, and 11% to other activities. In contrast, respondents practicing a two-way model reported that their programming consists of 71% cultivation activities, only 25% solicitation, and 4% other, on average. These findings suggest that fund-raising departments practicing press agentry and public information concentrate the majority of their programming on solicitation, whereas those practicing a two-way model emphasize cultivation.

A large-sample quantitative study testing the differences would add to the theories of the models and the fund-raising process. Students considering this topic should also gather data on budget allocations for each of the five steps of ROPES, which would provide a comparative guide for resource allocation.

The 1994 exploratory study also examined the extent to which Louisiana charitable organizations use the traditional programs of fund raising. Student researchers found that all but 1 of the 14 organizations have an annual giving program. Two of the organizations have no major gifts program, and half do not raise planned gifts. Four of the 14 organizations have conducted a capital campaign in the past, 4 others were planning one at the time of the study, and 6 have never conducted nor were they planning a capital campaign. The book turns now from the process of fund raising to the programs used to raise private gifts.

SUGGESTED READINGS

Bergan, H. (1992). *Where the money is: A fund raiser's guide to the rich* (2nd ed.). Alexandria, VA: BioGuide Press.

Bergan, H. (1996). *Where the information is: A guide to electronic research for nonprofit organizations.* Alexandria, VA: BioGuide Press.

Bryson, J. M. (1995). *Strategic planning for public and nonprofit organizations: A guide to strengthening and sustaining organizational achievement* (Rev. ed.). San Francisco, CA: Jossey-Bass.

Burkhart, P. J., & Reuss, S. (1993). *Successful strategic planning: A guide for nonprofit agencies and organizations.* Thousand Oaks, CA: Sage.

Council for Advancement and Support of Education (CASE). (1996). *CASE management reporting standards: Standards for annual giving and campaigns in educational fund raising.* Washington, DC: Author.

Murray, D. J. (1994). *The guaranteed fund-raising system: A systems approach to developing fund-raising plans* (2nd ed.). Poughkeepsie, NY: American Institute of Management.

Philanthropic Services for Institutions, Seventh-Day Adventist Church. (1991). *Accent on recognition: Saying thank you to donors and volunteers.* Silver Spring, MD: Author.

Rossi, P. H., & Freeman, H. E. (1993). *Evaluation: A systematic approach* (5th ed.). Thousand Oaks, CA: Sage.

Worth, M. J. (Ed.). (1993). *Educational fund raising: Principles and practice.* Phoenix, AZ: American Council on Education and Oryx Press.

11

Fund-Raising Programs:
Annual Giving

Chapter 11 covers annual giving, the first of the two primary programs. The next chapter deals with major gifts. Three subjects essential to understanding both programs lead off this chapter's discussion: the role of volunteers, the principle of proportionate giving, and different forms of gifts (i.e., cash, pledges, securities, real property, and personal property).

Annual giving raises lower level gifts, whereas the major gifts program raises major gifts. This book adopts $10,000 as the amount differentiating the two types, although many large organizations define major gifts as those of $100,000 or more. Fund raisers for such organizations use the term *special gifts* to distinguish gifts of $10,000 to $99,999 from those of higher amounts. This intermediate category also is used in capital campaigns (Worth, 1993). Indicative of the practice's failure to adopt common terminology, Rosso (1991) placed special gifts within the annual giving program, saying they generate income for special purpose needs. The gifts, in other words, are lower level and restricted to a specific project. Because I define major gifts at $10,000 and recommend that annual giving feature more opportunities for restricted gifts, the term's usage is avoided in this book.

Definitional confusion also exists about programs. Planned giving and capital campaigns, discussed in chapters 13 and 14, respectively, traditionally have been defined as separate from the two primary programs. They actually are strategies to raise major gifts and should be approached as such. Although the four traditional programs are reinforced in the literature, some support for the new two-program typology is available. Worth (1993), for example, argued that planned giving, rather than being a program, "is more properly a tool that is used with increasing frequency in major gift fund raising" (p. 11). Similarly, he said a capital campaign "is more accurately described as a fund-raising strategy than a distinct element of the development program" (p. 12).

ROLE OF VOLUNTEERS

The role of volunteers in fund raising requires clarification, as well as description. The very term *volunteer* commonly is misused. The problem stems primarily from the nonsolicitation characteristic of consultants, who have written much of the literature. The absence of theory explaining the multistep process of raising gifts has, until now, contributed to the confusion. Consultants define volunteers—on whom they are dependent to solicit gifts—as any person who is not a fund raiser, regardless of that person's paid or unpaid affiliation with the organization. When discussing volunteers, the literature actually is referring to four distinct groups: (a) volunteers for program services; (b) senior managers of the organization, particularly the CEO; (c) trustees; and (d) volunteers for fund raising.

Volunteers for program services are important stakeholders who also may be donors, but they usually are not involved in fund raising. According to IS (1994), an estimated 89 million Americans volunteered in 1993, but less than 5% reported fund-raising work in a given month. The kinds of jobs reported most frequently were serving as an aide to clergy, teaching Sunday school, other volunteer work for religious organizations, and assisting elderly or handicapped individuals.

In an ideal world, all charitable organizations would have hundreds of volunteers involved in their program services. They would have a high-level office of volunteer management to ensure that people willing to contribute time and talent were identified and provided with rewarding experiences. Quality interactions of numerous volunteers help protect organizations' privileged status and cultivate prospective donors. In the real world, the use of volunteers in program services varies dramatically among organizations. The Boy Scouts of America has about 15,000 volunteers; CARE, which has some 9,000 employees, has few. Hospitals traditionally rely on volunteers to serve their patients; colleges and universities rarely bring students in contact with any volunteers.

The CEO and line managers should not be referred to as volunteers. As argued throughout this book, fund raising—when managed effectively—is an integrated function that by definition requires the participation of those who control and carry out the work of the organization. Their refusal to participate represents a breach of trust with donors and an unworthiness of support. By virtue of his or her office, the CEO is the interpreter of organizational plans. Line managers, and, in some cases, line staff, are the program service experts. If fund raising is to advance the organization's goals, then the involvement of these key employees is necessary to the process of raising gifts—it is not voluntary. Their participation in the major gifts program is especially critical. The CEO must interact with the most affluent and influential prospects, who expect face-to-face contact. A university president explained, "Someone will give $25 or $100 to the annual fund without much concern for who the president is or a relationship with him [sic], but they're not going to plunk down a million dollars without a relationship with the president. It's as simple as that" (Cook, 1994a, p. 391).

Mixer (1993) pointed out that line managers and staff develop reputations and personal relationships with clients and other persons interested in their work. "These linkages," he said, "produce fundraising [sic] opportunities with foundations and corporations as well as wealthy individuals" (p. 229).

As a related aside, just as CEOs are not volunteers, neither are they the chief fund raiser in organizations with staff practitioners. The literature paradoxically refers to them in both roles, often simultaneously. The issue largely is one of semantics. To emphasize the importance of the CEO's participation, authors have overstated the case. The CEO is no more the chief fund raiser than he or she is the chief financial officer or the chief legal officer. Unfortunately, even senior practitioners espouse the flawed role, yet when questioned, admit that they—not the CEO—manage the fund-raising process. Perpetuating the myth denigrates the practice and hampers fund raising's acceptance as a management function.

On a conceptual level, trustees should not be thought of as volunteers for many of the same reasons given for senior managers. Their participation is not voluntary; it is part of their responsibilities and is necessary for effective fund raising. On an applied level, however, trustees represent the critical core of fund-raising volunteers, particularly for the major gifts program. Franz (1981) advocated the philosophy widely shared by practitioners: Volunteer leadership positions are filled by trustees. He stated, "Generally, fund-raising leadership must come from within the family" (p. 163). Murray (1995) elaborated, "Leaders, in a fund-raising sense, are those who have affluence or influence or both and are willing to use them to accomplish the organization's fund-raising goals" (p. 21). He continued, "In most organizations, leadership will come from the board or be generated by the board" (p. 21).

The fourth group consists of fund-raising volunteers who are not trustees. Their number and participation vary among organizations, but generally they are used for nonsolicitation activities in the major gifts program and for implementing such solicitation techniques as direct mail and special events in the annual giving program. Whereas a local United Way uses many volunteers in a complex committee structure, a university likely will have only one or two committees with a few members. The idea of armies of volunteers soliciting prospects is a characteristic of the press agentry model of fund raising and an artifact of earlier eras before staff practitioners dominated the field.

Luck (1990) challenged the principal advice in the literature: "Fund raisers should do most of the fund raising and not depend solely on volunteers" (p. 30). Supporting my conclusion, he argued, "The idea of assigning prospects to volunteers and training them to be fund raisers is part of philanthropic legend—it is just not worth the time and energy" (p. 30). Focusing on the major gifts program, he stated, "Volunteers may be of help in writing letters of introduction, making telephone calls or making verbal requests for attention from their colleagues, friends and acquaintances on behalf of the fund-raisers [sic]" (p. 30). Wilkerson and Schuette (1981) addressed annual giving: "Although conventional wisdom assumes the volunteer to be central to the solicitation process, as the size of constituencies increases and annual giving programs become more complex it can become costly and inefficient to maintain large cadres of volunteers" (p. 30).

Major Gifts Program

As a general rule, the board of trustees serves as the volunteer committee for the major gifts program. Members participate in all steps of the fund-raising process at the direction of the staff manager, who must have full access to members. For larger boards, a fund-raising committee, headed by the board's chair, spearheads the work. Howe (1991) emphasized that unlike other board responsibilities that adhere to a policy-only role, "Development committee members get directly involved in fund-raising activities" (p. 128). The role of trustees has three parts: to lead by example, to endorse objectives, and to provide a network for reaching prospective donors.

Explaining the first, Murray (1995) stated, "There is only one standard for board participation as donors: 100 percent" (p. 22). People cannot be asked to give without those who hold the organization in trust first expressing their commitment. Trustees also must make gifts at a level proportionate to their involvement so as to set appropriate gift levels for other donors. They are the most involved; therefore, they must give the most. Indeed, many of the largest gifts raised through the major gifts program are expected to come from the board. Panas (1984) reported that of the 30 persons he interviewed who gave $1 million or more, 20 were on the board of directors of the recipient organization. Addressing the second part of their role, Murray (1995) argued that an obligation of trustees is to be actively involved in fund raising because their involvement lends legitimacy to the programs. "Their participation is their stamp of approval, which can be powerful in motivating others to support the organization" (p. 21). Finally, trustees must use their knowledge and contacts to identify, cultivate, and solicit prospects for major gifts. Murray admitted that whereas trustees might not participate in all steps of the process, they must be willing to help in some.

Similarly, Rosso (1991) presented four ways trustees are of value to fund raising—none of which involve solicitation. Trustees testify to the worth of the organization's services, attract other volunteers to work, identify and help cultivate potential donors, and serve as *door openers*. He explained the last, "The personal contacts that many trustees have with major prospects are valuable assets for the fund raising [*sic*] program" (p. 135).

In other words, contrary to much of the literature, the role of volunteers in the major gifts program is not one of solicitor. Studies, such as Altizer's (1992), have provided evidence that trustees and volunteers are used more for identification and cultivation than for solicitation of major gifts. This does not minimize their contribution. As demonstrated in the last chapter, solicitation is only a minority portion of the fund-raising process, and programming for major gifts concentrates on cultivation. Volunteers are particularly valuable in the research step. Those who are not trustees often are tapped for prospect rating sessions. Stanford University used more than 1,200 volunteers during its capital campaign to identify prospects for gifts of $10,000 or more.

Annual Giving Program

Volunteer leadership for the annual giving program commonly consists of one committee with a volunteer chair to serve as spokesperson and a small group of 10 to 15 individuals to personally solicit prospects for the program's largest gifts. A mixture of board members and nonboard members is recommended. It is strategically unsound to occupy all or even most trustees with raising lower level gifts because of their pivotal role in the major gifts program. Furthermore, recruiting nonboard members for the annual giving program provides an opportunity to build a closer relationship with volunteers who may later become trustees.

It must be pointed out here that not all trustees have the affluence and influence to be effective leaders in raising major gifts. Board members are not, or should not be, recruited only on the basis of their fund-raising potential. Systems theory demands diversified boards that also represent such stakeholders as clients, community residents, or government agencies. Weick's (1979) principle of requisite variety, derived from systems theory, holds that there must be at least as much diversity inside the organization as outside for the organization to build effective relationships with all strategic groups in the environment. People of diverse backgrounds offer other points of view that are essential to success and survival. Such trustees may be excellent candidates for volunteer positions in the annual giving program. Regardless of their wealth, however, they must make an annual gift. As Herman and Block (1990) stated, "Board members with modest economic means are no less responsible as organizational leaders, and therefore their financial contribution, at whatever level, represents an important message about their commitment" (p. 229). Generally speaking, discretionary income should allow an annual unrestricted gift of at least $100 for all but a few of America's hundreds of thousands of board members. The amount represents little more than the cost of two tickets to a sports event or dinner at a restaurant.

Whether trustees or fund-raising volunteers, all members of the committee must be donors. Lord (1983) explained, "This is the cardinal rule of fund raising: A volunteer must make a personal commitment before asking others. That is a given" (p. 79). He added, "The volunteer who solicits others without the benefit of a strong personal example is like the shoemaker who goes without shoes" (p. 53). Those who sign direct-mail letters, host a cultivation luncheon, or solicit top prospects by telephone can be effective examples and endorsers only if they make their own gift first.

Any specific activity requiring volunteers, such as a labor-intensive special event, should be structured as a subcommittee with a chair who is a member of the annual giving committee. In addition, I recommend that a vice chair be recruited with the understanding that he or she will assume the chair's position the next year. A vice chair ensures continuity of the program, reduces chances that the chair will become overburdened, provides a ready replacement in the event the chair is forced to resign due to illness or other circumstances, and gives the vice chair a trial period during which he or she can learn more about the organization, its annual giving program, and the responsibilities of leadership.

Management and Research

Contrary to what the literature insinuates, volunteers are not free labor. Their recruitment, training, staffing, and stewardship are expensive. As L. Fischer and Schaffer (1993) stated, "Inefficient management can raise costs to the point that volunteers cost more than they give" (p. 137). When the required investment is not acknowledged and accounted for, fund raisers, as Luck (1990) advised, often eliminate volunteer participation, which eventually reduces the effectiveness of their programs.

There has been little—if any—research on volunteer costs in fund raising. Fischer and Schaffer's (1993) book on program service volunteers suggests that paid staff spend 1 hour to support 6 hours of volunteer work and that the cost of a volunteer is

$2 per hour less than the cost of paid staff. The authors warned, "If there is no allocation for these costs—if staff are expected somehow to fit these activities into their workload—they are more likely to resent than appreciate the contributions of volunteers" (p. 134). Dissertations or theses studying volunteer costs and benefits would advance fund-raising knowledge.

In the absence of such studies, I recommend Fischer and Schaffer's book—co-winner of NSFRE's top research prize in 1994—as a guide to volunteer management. The scholars presented 12 principles of recruitment and retention that evolved from their review of the literature and an analysis of 57 case studies of exemplary programs.

It is recalled from chapter 6 that little research has been conducted on trustee participation in fund raising and that evidence suggests many boards do not live up to the behavior prescribed in the literature (Herman & Block, 1990). Lending credence to the gap between principles and practice, Rosso (1991) reported that the most common problem mentioned by the thousands of practitioners who have taken courses from The Fund Raising School is "trustee apathy and lack of willingness to become involved in fund raising" (p. 133). This would be an excellent topic for a doctoral dissertation. An overriding research question could be: To what extent do trustees participate in fund raising? Secondary questions could examine their participation within the theoretical framework of ROPES (i.e., the degree to which trustees participate in each of the five steps). Of particular interest would be their involvement in solicitation activities in comparison to the other parts of the process (e.g., research and cultivation). Theories of organizational roles might be useful. Unlike other topics, there is a body of scholarly literature on which to base studies, although the literature primarily has been written by nonprofit management scholars who demonstrate an inadequate understanding of fund raising. Previous studies have not differentiated between organizations that have staff fund raisers and those that do not. The perspective of the CEO has been the one most studied; rarely has the fund raiser's perspective been examined.

Concluding this discussion, the two primary programs of annual giving and major gifts are dependent on the involvement of trustees. Their key role is recognized by staff managers, who invest heavily in the board's participation. They work closely with the nominating committee to ensure that members are recruited who can fill leadership positions for both programs and that expectations about involvement in fund raising are clearly understood and accepted as a *condition* of membership. Staff managers help design orientation programming for new trustees that includes sessions on the organization's philosophy of fund raising (i.e., the model predominantly practiced) and the skills trustees must have to carry out their assignments. Attendance should be mandatory. Herman and Block (1990) advised, "The board's capacity for fund raising depends on communicated and accepted expectations, relationship-building skills, confidence, recognitions and celebrations of fund-raising achievements, and a commitment to the organization characterized by a strong feeling of psychological ownership toward it" (p. 239). Hank Bauer (1993), an attorney and member of the Oregon State University Foundation Board, presented five simple rules for practitioners: Recruit us honestly, keep us informed, make the most of our time, "sweat the small stuff" (p. 43), and ensure enjoyment.

PRINCIPLE OF PROPORTIONATE GIVING

The principle of proportionate giving was first presented by Seymour (1966/1988), who formulated the *Rule of Thirds* to describe giving patterns to capital campaigns—the traditional program with which consultants are closely identified. Seymour explained, "In any substantial capital campaign you have to get about a third of the money from the top ten gifts, another third from the next 100 largest gifts, and the last third from everybody else" (p. 32). He illustrated his rule by analyzing Harvard's late-1950s campaign. Of the 31,696 gifts made, the top 15 accounted for 36% of the total dollars raised, the largest 130 gifts totaled 69%, and the remaining 31,566 gifts accounted for just slightly more than 30%. Furthermore, the 23,124 gifts of less than $1,000, or 88% of all gifts made to the campaign, amounted to less than 5% of the money raised. Writing in the mid-1960s, Seymour added, "As goals have risen higher and higher, more and more has to be expected from fewer and fewer, to the point today that about 1 percent of the list can make or break any really big campaign" (p. 32).

The proportion has changed even more dramatically during the last 30 years, as documented in my earlier book (Kelly, 1991a). In the late 1980s, for example, 0.1% of all donors to the University of Miami's capital campaign provided 50% of the total gift dollars. Lindahl (1994) reported that of the $32.4 million raised for Northwestern University's Campaign for Great Teachers during the early 1990s, 90% came from 1% of the donors. The importance of those few donors who can make or break a fund-raising effort extends beyond capital campaigns to major gifts programs and planned giving. It also applies to the annual giving program.

Rosso (1991) described proportionate giving as the time-honored principle of the "arithmetic of fund raising" (p. 54). He explained, "The arithmetic concept as it pertains to the annual fund means that a large amount of the money to be raised will come from a small number of contributors who are encouraged to provide what will necessarily be larger gifts" (p. 54). He estimated that 10% of all annual gifts typically will produce 60% of the money required to meet the dollar goal. Another 20% will account for 15% to 25% of the goal, and 70% of the gifts will account for the remainder, 15% to 25%. In other words, only 30% of those donors who contribute lower level gifts will provide 75% to 85% of total dollars raised through an organization's annual giving program.

The principle largely is explained by our capitalistic economy; that is, the unequal distribution of wealth determines gifts of unequal amounts. Vermeulen (1995) claimed that "the United States is the most economically stratified nation in the industrial world" (p. 4). The richest 10% of the population owns 66% of the country's wealth; just 1% owns one third. Fund raisers abide by the principle when planning programming to meet solicitation objectives, unlike lay people who often suggest equal gifts from hundreds or thousands of donors—"If everyone just gives $10 we can raise the amount we need." As Dove (1988) warned, "One of the most common fallacies regarding gift ranges and distribution patterns is the notion that a campaign can succeed if everyone in the constituency gives the same amount. It never works. Why? This type of approach is not fair or equitable to donors. Wealth is not distributed democratically in this society" (p. 75).

The principle of proportionate giving is supported by Pareto's economic principle (cited in Gottlieb & Healy, 1990), which holds that in most aspects of life, a critical few efforts, around 20%, produce the great bulk of results, around 80%. This has become known as the 80/20 rule. Illustrating, 80% of a company's business is attributable to 20% of its customers, and 80% of a manuscript produced by a research organization can be traced to about 20% of the staff (Simmons, 1990). Virtually every person who has studied business knows the 80/20 rule and swears to its reliability. Of theoretical interest, Pareto conducted work in the early 1900s that provided the foundation for systems theory (L. A. Grunig et al., 1992).

Based on the inviolable principle, fund raisers devise *gift-range charts*, which provide a blueprint for solicitation—regardless of program, amount of dollar goal, or monetary definition of major versus annual gifts. Table 11.1 presents a gift-range chart for an annual giving program with a dollar goal of $200,000. As shown, the chart estimates the number of gifts needed in each range to meet the goal and the number of prospects needed to obtain those gifts. Such estimates also are referred to as the gift-scaling technique (Rosso, 1991).

According to the chart presented in Table 11.1, of the estimated 1,322 donors necessary to raise $200,000, only 102, or 8%, are expected to contribute $120,000, or 60% of the goal. The 750 donors making gifts of less than $100 will account for 57% of the gifts but only about 7% of the dollars raised. The number of prospects needed to obtain a sufficient number of gifts in each range varies from a multiple of four at the highest ranges to a multiple of two at the lowest. Fund raisers planning this annual giving program predict that they will have to identify slightly more than twice as many prospects (2,768) as gifts needed.

Reflecting the principle of proportionate giving, gift patterns to all fund-raising programs are configured in a *pyramid of donors*, whereby the number of donors decreases as the amount given increases. The pattern holds for annual giving, major gifts, planned giving, and capital campaigns. Collapsing all programs into one donor pyramid shows that the largest number of donors are at the base, which represents the lowest level of gifts; a small number of donors are at the pyramid's peak. Indeed, the terminology of building a *broad base* of donors through the annual giving program derives from the pyramid configuration.

TABLE 11.1
Gift-Range Chart for Annual Giving Program With Dollar Goal of $200,000

Range of Gifts	Number of Gifts	Number of Prospects	Subtotals	Total
$7,500	2	8	$15,000	
5,000	5	20	25,000	
2,500	10	40	25,000	
1,000	25	80	25,000	
500	60	180	30,000	*$120,000*
250	120	240	30,000	
100	350	700	35,000	
100	750	1,500	15,000	$200,000

As Graham (1992) pointed out, the shape of an organization's overall donor pyramid may vary from that of other organizations. Some may be elongated, representing few donors at the lowest and midlevels, whereas others are flatter, representing multiple donors at the lowest level and few at the highest and midlevels. Converting the pyramid to types of triangles, I believe the ideal is an equilateral triangle that has three sides of equal length. This symmetrical shape demonstrates the presence of a broad base of donors, a strong representation of midlevel donors, and enough major donors to reach dollar goals efficiently in relation to fund-raising costs. An isosceles triangle, which is asymmetrical with sides of unequal length, indicates that the organization is dependent on a few donors of large gifts (an elongated shape)—raising questions about autonomy—or indicates that fund raisers are inefficiently focusing on donors of the lowest gift level (a flat shape).

Rosso (1991) addressed the latter case, saying gifts of \$5, \$10, or \$15 are costly to raise. Steele and Elder (1992) said annual gifts of less than \$25 cost the recipient organization money. Such gifts should be appreciated and acknowledged but not actively solicited (i.e., when suggesting gift amounts, fund raisers should not ask for less than \$25). On the other hand, fund raisers who neglect annual giving in favor of raising major gifts mistakenly assume they serve their organization best by maximizing gift income. Major gifts do account for the majority of dollars raised, and the larger the gift, the lower the fund-raising cost. However, annual giving, by providing a broad base of support from many donors, protects autonomy and legitimizes the organization's purpose and work. As Mixer (1993) pointed out, major gifts make dollar goals possible, but "small donations in large volumes attest to broad public acceptance of the needs being met" (p. 240). If fund raisers concentrated only on major donors, it is likely society would revoke the privileged status granted to charitable organizations because there would be little support for subsidizing philanthropy limited to the wealthy. Under current law, public charities that fail to demonstrate gifts from numerous donors are subject to reclassification as private foundations, which—as discussed in chapter 15—have a less beneficial status.

To achieve an equilateral shape for the pyramid of donors, I recommend a robust mixture of fund-raising programs, gift amounts, techniques (e.g., face-to-face conversations, personal letters, and direct mail), and sources of gifts (i.e., individuals, corporations, and foundations). Rosso (1991) endorsed such a mixture because it makes the organization "more resilient" and "more responsive" (p. 12). Even Lindahl (1992), whose study supported greater resource allocation for the major gifts program, admitted that annual giving should not be completely ignored: "A balanced approach is essential" (p. 122). Fund raisers are advised to plot the number and amounts of previous gifts to determine their organization's donor pyramid and to identify weaknesses that require attention.

Closely related to proportionate giving is the principle of sequential giving, introduced in chapter 9. This principle also was developed by consulting firms, such as Brakeley, John Price Jones, to guide capital campaigns (Greenfield, 1991). Recommended here for all fund-raising programs, gifts are raised sequentially from the top down and from the inside out. A helpful device is visualizing concentric circles with the organization at the center, trustees in the inner circle, previous donors in the second circle, qualified prospects in the third, and suspects in the outer circle.

Superimposing the concentric circles on the gift-range chart, solicitation starts with prospects for the largest gifts in the chart and with those prospects closest to the organization, trustees. Practitioners then move down the chart in gift amounts and focus their attention outward. The last gifts solicited are those in the lowest range. Budgets and time are allocated accordingly.

DIFFERENT FORMS OF GIFTS

Gifts come in different forms, which are grouped for the purpose of this discussion into five categories: (a) cash, (b) pledges, (c) securities, (d) real property, and (e) personal property. The annual giving program usually deals with only the first three categories, whereas the major gifts program deals with all five. Cash includes checks, money orders, charges to credit cards, and *electronic fund transfers* (EFT). Checks are the most common gift form, regardless of category. Payments by credit cards and EFT are offered to donors of annual gifts as convenient options that also save the organization money.

Using EFT, donors authorize their banks to automatically make gifts directly from their checking or savings accounts to the recipient organization every month or at other regular periods. A record of each deduction appears on the donor's bank statements. Only a small percentage of donors elect to use EFT, although Mixer (1993) reported that almost 20% of Amnesty International's 20,000 monthly "Partners of Conscience" make their gifts through electronic transfers. EFT presents problems of accountability. Fund raisers often view bank statements as a substitute for acknowledgment, thereby failing to express appreciation for the gifts. Almost all EFTs are set up to continue indefinitely, until the donor takes the initiative to stop the transfers. By not reminding donors of their automatic gifts and by not asking for a renewal, fund raisers manipulate people who are vulnerable, such as the elderly. EFT should be used only as a service for those donors who want to give small monthly amounts, and fund raisers should send annual acknowledgments and requests for renewal.

EFT and credit cards reduce unfulfilled pledges to the annual giving program, which run between 10% and 30%. Pledges are written commitments or oral promises to make a gift. They are commonly used in the major gifts program to schedule multiyear payments. Pledges are sometimes used in the annual giving program to schedule monthly or quarterly gift payments, which is expensive to administer given the size of the gifts and the cost of mailing reminders. Greenfield (1991) declared, "Pledges are an administrative burden; they cost the organization money for record keeping, billing and collections" (p. 60). Also in annual giving, oral pledges are the basis for such techniques as phonathons and telethons, whereby donors promise gifts of a specific amount over the telephone.

Organizations increasingly are soliciting pledges on the Internet. A few, such as the Red Cross, have an online giving option on their Web site, which allows donors to charge gifts to credit cards (see *www.redcross.org*). Dangers of transmitting credit-card numbers in cyberspace have inhibited adoption of online gifts; however, experts predict that advances in security software will soon make such financial transactions common.

Securities include publicly traded stock, closely held stock, bonds, and other financial instruments. The SEC requires brokers to set up accounts for the transfer, receipt, and sale of securities given to charitable organizations (Greenfield, 1991). Publicly traded stock is this category's most common form. Indeed, publicly traded stock that has appreciated in value is the primary form of major gifts across all five categories (AAFRC Trust for Philanthropy, 1996). When accepting gifts of publicly traded stock, fund raisers follow three steps suggested by the IRS: (a) value the stock by calculating the mean average price on the date ownership was transferred, (b) verify the calculation with a broker and the next business day's edition of the stock exchange listing in such newspapers as *The Wall Street Journal*, and (c) confirm the gift's value in writing to the donor (Greenfield, 1991). The stock in most cases is sold immediately to ensure that the gift's full value is available for the purpose intended by the donor. Retaining the stock in the hope its value will increase can backfire—stock prices go down as well as up. In particular, major donors who have been asked for and have given a specific amount for a restricted purpose are not pleased when they find out there is not enough money to fund the purpose for which they made their gift.

Closely held stock, or nonpublic stock, is handled differently. Contributed by one of the few owners of a closely held corporation, such as a family business or a new entrepreneurial firm, the stock has no ready market for selling and converting it to cash. In most cases, the recipient organization holds the stock until it is bought back by the corporation. The donor or the donor's spouse cannot purchase it (Brown & Feagin, 1994). Rarer and more complex are shares in so-called *S corporations*, businesses for which the shareholders—not the incorporated entity—pay income taxes. Under a new provision enacted in 1996, donors can deduct gifts of such stock as charitable contributions; however, unlike other types of stock, recipient organizations must pay UBIT on earnings from S corporation stock and capital-gains tax if the stock is sold (Murawski & Stehle, 1996).

Gifts of real property most often consist of real estate. They include primary residence, vacation home, farm, ranch, commercial building, subdivision lots, and undeveloped land (Sapp, 1993). The gift can be made three ways: (a) outright, (b) as a bargain sale, or (c) as an undivided partial interest.

When making the gift outright, the donor deeds the property to the organization, which sells it unless it is of use or there is an investment reason for keeping it. The purpose for which the donor gave the property must be fulfilled. A *bargain sale* means that the donor sells the property to the organization for a price below its fair market value. The difference between the sale price and the market value constitutes the charitable gift. The organization then sells or keeps the property. An undivided portion of real property can be conveyed in any percentage. For example, a donor can give one half of the interest in his or her farm, thereby making the organization a coowner. When the property is sold, both share the proceeds proportionately. Fund raisers keep in mind that, generally, real estate is not readily converted to cash; therefore, it should not be used to fund urgent needs. Also, property subject to debt creates problems that must be thoroughly analyzed before acceptance.

The last category, personal property, runs the gamut from highly valuable works of art to old clothes. It includes antiques, collections, manuscripts, books, vehicles, and boats. Although the category is identified with the major gifts program, some organizations solicit low-value property as annual gifts (e.g., Goodwill). Tax deductions for gifts of personal property depend on their related use to the tax-exempt purpose of the organization. Property directly usable for the mission can provide greater deduction value than property that is not. For example, an individual donor may receive a smaller deduction for a gift of art to a hospital than he or she would get for giving the artwork to a museum. Special rules apply for corporate donors when contributing property, particularly products (e.g., drug manufacturers donating drugs). The tax deductibility of products is covered in chapter 15.

As already alluded to, the last three categories often include gifts of appreciated property. When appreciated securities, real property, and personal property are given to a charitable organization, taxes on capital gains are eliminated. Students will recall from chapter 7 that donors also can deduct the fair market value of such gifts, as opposed to their original value. The securities or property must be owned for 1 year. In other words, gifts of appreciated property provide significant tax savings, making them an attractive option for major donors. Such gifts are frequently used in planned giving.

Pledges are not deductible from taxable income. Deductions for gifts of cash are limited to 50% of the taxpayer's adjusted gross income (AGI). Gifts of appreciated property are limited to 30% of AGI. Donors can carry forward any unused portion of their gift deduction for up to 5 additional years.

Knowledge of tax laws helps fund raisers recognize advantageous situations. For example, funding a named gift opportunity with publicly traded stock that is worth a great deal more than its original price and that pays very low dividends may appeal to a prospective donor. On the other hand, stock that has depreciated in value should not be given directly to the organization. As Sapp (1993) advised, "It is to the donor's advantage to sell the securities to establish a tax-deductible loss and then donate the cash proceeds" (p. 120).

Finally, IRS Form 8283 must be filed by individuals who make gifts of securities, real property, and personal property that are worth more than $500. The amount is $5,000 for corporations. If gifts of real or personal property exceed $5,000 in value, the donor must obtain a qualified appraisal. Securities are treated differently. Publicly traded stock does not require an appraisal at any amount; closely held stock must be appraised if the value exceeds $10,000. If the organization sells the property or securities within 2 years, it must file IRS Form 8282. If the sale amount is substantially less than the value claimed by the donor for tax purposes, the IRS may ask for an explanation. More serious questions arise if the buyer is also the original donor.

ANNUAL GIVING

Annual giving is the basic fund-raising program. Practitioner-experts are in high accord that annual giving—sometimes called the annual fund—should be started first, followed by major gifts, and—after strong relationships have been built with donors—planned giving should be introduced (e.g., Worth, 1993). Rosso (1991) stated, "The annual fund is the cornerstone and the key to success for all aspects of the resources development program" (p. 51).

Cook (1994b) used a baseball analogy to describe its relation to other programs: "A base hit might be an annual gift, a home run might be a capital or major gift, and a grand slam might be an ultimate gift" (p. 14). He elaborated by quoting a CEO, who said, "It's the home run that wins the game, unfortunately. But you've got to have the singles, too, and you've got to move the runner over, and sometimes it's the single you hit today that's the home run 5 or 10 years from now" (p. 15).

The purpose of the annual giving program is to provide funds for the operation of the organization. Gifts represent annual income used to pay annual operating expenses (i.e., they are spent the same year they are received). As the expenses are reoccurring, the program is *repeated* each year, unlike the major gifts program and planned giving, which are ongoing, and capital campaigns, which are sporadic. An overriding objective of the annual giving program, therefore, is to engender repetitive giving behavior. The program usually is run according to the calendar year, which also is the tax year. Fund raisers at educational institutions adhere to the academic year, fall to summer, although some have switched on the assumption that most donors think of their gifts within a tax year framework. Greenfield (1991) emphasized that timing of requests has to make sense: "Donors are not likely to respond to arbitrary schedules invented by nonprofit organizations" (p. 58).

Adding further definitional clarification, gifts to annual giving programs usually are made from donors' *income*. They average about $50, although some types of organizations solicit and receive annual gifts averaging $250 or more (e.g., museums and symphony orchestras). Gifts traditionally have been unrestricted in purpose. The time between solicitation and receipt is less than 1 year. Finally, annual gifts—one would think from their name—are made once a year. This is a point of contention among fund raisers and a source of complaint from donors.

Multiple Solicitations

Practitioners strongly agree that one solicitation does not make an annual giving program. Organizations relying on one request are wasting their time and money. Prospects are busy people, dealing with their own situations, who must be asked at least three times during a 12-month period. The question is, however, once they have made their gifts, should donors be asked to give again? Greenfield (1991) presented the dominant viewpoint, arguing that annual giving does not mean only one gift each year: "Its true purpose is to ask for multiple gifts throughout the year" (p. 54). He illustrated the appropriateness of multiple solicitations by pointing out that churches ask for gifts 52 times each year at weekly services. Saturation, he said, has not happened.

Not only does Greenfield ignore differences between making gifts while participating in free religious services and making gifts in response to at-home solicitations, but he assumes that maximizing gift income outweighs other considerations. Because gifts are of a low amount and previous donors are the best prospects, repeat solicitations are viewed as an efficient strategy. Some people will give; it may be because they want to contribute more or because they simply cannot remember if they have already given that year. Others will not give, but the solicitation still is cost efficient because of the higher response rate from previous donors. If a few get angry or upset, the loss of their future gifts is not financially significant. Major donors, on the other hand, are carefully protected from multiple solicitations.

A minority of fund raisers, with whom I stand, disagree with the dominant viewpoint. (It should be added that Greenfield's thoughts on this topic are inconsistent with most of his work.) Income maximization—held in check only by saturation—is not optimum. A long-term and larger perspective is needed. Maintaining relationships is essential for the continued well-being of the focal organization and the charitable subsector as a whole. Graham (1992) described the behavior of annual giving donors as "habitual involvement" (p. 10). She explained, "As discerning as donors may be, they tend to give to some of the same organizations year after year. It may be difficult to attract their gifts the first two or three years, but once you get past year three, the habit is set. If you are reliably consistent, they will be too" (p. 10).

Multiple solicitations breed frustration and discontent. Some donors think repeat requests are a mistake, not a deliberate strategy. In a round-table discussion about donors' perceptions of fund raising, a trustee for several charitable organizations said, "One thing that I don't want is to get calls or another application for a donation when I just sent one... It seems many organizations are just not bothering to track whether a household has already made a gift" (Lies, 1994, p. 21). More serious are complaints such as those expressed by John E. Moore (1993), a fund-raising volunteer and retired market research manager for Procter & Gamble. In an opinion piece titled "I Already Gave, So Why Do Charities Keep Asking?," he stated:

> Each spring I write checks to the charities to which I contributed last year, plus perhaps one or two new ones. This makes me feel happy. Unfortunately, this sense of contentment is short-lived. . . . Many fund raisers seem to regard my contribution as a signal that I want to be bombarded with requests for additional funds throughout the year. . . . I'm still searching for an effective way to get my message to all multiple solicitors. It is a simple one: "I already have given, and once a year is all I can afford. . . . Send me one solicitation and one thank-you card. Then leave me alone." (pp. 40–41)

Contrast his opinion with that of direct-mail expert Roger Craver (1991): "Every organization that is worthy of public support has a valid reason to communicate with its supporters and to seek their support at least once a month" (p. 71). Craver added, "The key to successful direct mail is the *continual and assertive resolicitation* of an organization's contributors" (p. 67; italics added). Yet IS (1994) reported that whereas people are most likely to respond to mail solicitations from organizations they regularly support, "the likelihood of response fell off if the organization asked for more contributions after the person had contributed or if the organizations suggested an increased donation amount" (p. 74). Looking only at those who answered "very likely," just 11% said they would respond to a repeat solicitation and only 4% said they would give to an appeal that suggested an increased amount.

One gift for one year should be the general rule. The last thing fund raisers want is to make their organizations appear greedy. Research on donor publics can help determine their prospects' opinion on multiple solicitations. Avoiding donors' animosity may save the organization more money than any gifts that might be raised. NSFRE stresses during its 2-day Survey Course that it is much more costly to acquire a new donor than to get a current donor to renew—10 times more expensive using direct mail. Unfortunately, NSFRE also advocates multiple solicitations of annual giving donors.

Upgrading

As just touched on, respondents to IS' survey reported a dislike for being asked for an increased gift amount, which fund raisers refer to as *upgrading*. Some clarification is necessary before discussing this program element.

The fund-raising process requires practitioners to not only ask for the gift, but also to suggest a specific amount, or at least provide a gift range. The situational theory of publics explains that giving behavior is dependent on the degree to which prospects believe their gifts can make a difference (i.e., constraint recognition). Suggesting an amount, usually employing the verb "consider," addresses constraints by relating the gift's size to its impact. As Lord (1983) stated: "'Whatever you can do' is a recipe for failure. It suggests that the organization is ambiguous about the whole enterprise" (p. 81).

Specificity is demanded for major restricted gifts as the costs of the restricted purpose are known. For annual giving, a floor amount, such as $25, must be suggested to avoid raising gifts that cost the organization money. Previous donors should be asked to renew their gifts at the same level they gave the year before, specifying the amount. This not only provides another opportunity for stewardship, but as Dove (1988) pointed out, "Seldom do donors give more than they are asked to give" (p. 75). In short, suggesting a dollar amount is theoretically and pragmatically sound.

Gifts of the same amount this year are worth less to the organization than they were 3 years ago. To offset inflation and increased costs, fund raisers periodically ask previous donors to upgrade their unrestricted gifts. The purpose is not to get people to give more, but to preserve the impact of their gifts. I hypothesize that much of the dislike reported by IS (1994) is the result of frequent and indiscriminate requests for increased dollars, without the benefit of research or reason—just that the organization could use more money. Squires (1992) advised: "Make your requested upgrades reasonable—and don't ask for them too often. . . . Make them modest and specific, with well-argued 'reasons why' the donor can help by increasing his or her gift modestly at this time" (p. 55).

In addition to simply asking for an increase, practitioners traditionally have employed four devices for upgrading gifts: (a) gift clubs, (b) challenge grants, (c) corporate matching gifts, and (d) specific projects.

Gift Clubs.   Gift clubs are established by mutually exclusive dollar ranges starting at the $100 level—such as $100 to $249, $250 to $499, $500 to $999, $1,000 to $2,499, and so on—to promote gift increases. The clubs are assigned names denoting ascending prestige, which often are related to the organization or its mission. For example, a business school might use the Managers' Club, the Executives' Society, the Presidents' Club, and the Chairpersons' Circle (Mixer, 1993).

Despite their longevity and popularity with fund raisers, gift clubs have little effect on upgrading. Practitioner observation suggests that clubs tend to generate gifts at the minimum amount (e.g., $100 for the $100 to $249 club) and that donors tend to stay in the same dollar categories year after year, despite rising costs and inflation (Mixer, 1993). It is recalled from chapter 9 that Carnegie Mellon University found that 84% of its donors who give less than $1,000 a year would not increase their contribution to become a member of a gift club (Dundjerski, 1994). Donors said they already are giving as much as they can afford. They also do not want the benefits of club membership. Carnegie Mellon fund raisers, who believe the clubs enhance camaraderie and the spirit of giving, are studying ways to revamp them to better meet donor needs.

Gift clubs are more effective as a device for segmenting annual giving donors than for upgrading them. Clubs help ensure that appropriate attention is paid to the minority of prospects whose gifts will account for the majority of funds raised. They allow practitioners to target programming and provide stewardship by gift ranges—which, students are reminded, may not be the most meaningful criterion for segmentation. Large departments have a staff person assigned to support the club structure, which serves the major gifts program as well as annual giving. The lowest level club should not start below gifts of $100 because anything less likely would not be cost efficient. Ranges are necessary to capture those gifts made for restricted purposes at amounts higher than a gift club's minimum. Regardless of the designation of club membership, references to payments or dues are inappropriate; donors make gifts, not payments.

In response to the *quid pro quo* regulations, some organizations are letting donors refuse club membership, changing benefits, or dropping gift clubs completely (McNamee, 1994). Not using benefits, as explained in chapter 7, does not affect the deductibility of gifts; donors must specifically refuse them in advance. Recognition events are being changed to cultivation events with guest lists that are not pegged to giving levels. Most tax experts think cultivation activities do not create a *quid pro quo* situation, although the IRS has not explicitly exempted them. According to experts, the IRS *is* interested in benefits reserved for club membership, such as free magazine subscriptions, use of such facilities as a YMCA's racquetball courts, and the drinks and hors d'oeuvres served at receptions. Gift clubs, if they are to be preserved, must be critically examined and adapted to the new regulatory environment. Eradicating the pretense that they are related to upgrading is a first step.

Challenge Grants.   Challenge grants are a device valued for their ability to create a sense of urgency, compelling annual giving donors to increase their gifts. A major donor, whether an individual, corporation, or foundation, pledges an amount of money with the stipulation that the pledge will only be paid if an equal or greater amount is raised from other donors within a specified time period. The challenge acts as a matching grant for prospects' gifts.

As used in the annual giving program, the challenge grant can be unrestricted or restricted. Unrestricted grants often focus directly on upgrading, as well as acquiring new donors. They limit matches to increases over amounts previously given and to new gifts. Trustees often are the source for such grants. Restricted grants are used to generate lower level gifts for special purposes, usually in addition to gifts already made for unrestricted support. Private universities, colleges, and schools traditionally have relied on the challenge concept with their reunion classes.

Problems associated with challenge grants include overuse and abuse. Challenges quickly lose any effect they might have on upgrading when they are routinely employed. A standard practice at some organizations is to ask one corporation every year to put up a set amount, such as $200,000, so that annual giving prospects can be asked to *stretch* their gift capacity year after year. The challenge grant often is for a restricted purpose, unbeknown to prospects who are told their unrestricted gifts will be matched. The absence of sincerity when issuing a challenge represents manipulation of donors. Too often, the source of the grant and fund raisers agree beforehand that the pledge will be paid whether the challenge is met or not.

In the major gifts program, challenge grants are confined to purposes that allow naming opportunities for *other* donors. One of the fallacies held by lay people, including some major donors, is that other people are willing to make major gifts in support of someone else's project—selected and named by the original donor. Challenge grants so conceived are doomed to failure. An example of their appropriate use is provided by the Kresge Foundation, the nation's leading grantmaker for buildings and facilities. All of Kresge's grants are challenge grants, which are made only after 20% to 50% of the dollars needed for a capital project have been raised. Most important, the foundation's dollars can be used to match gifts for named opportunities related to the project, such as $50,000 to name a room in honor of a donor or $5 million to name the building itself.

Several states have programs that emulate challenge grants for increasing endowments at state colleges and universities, whereby government funds match major gifts in some proportion. For example, Florida's Eminent Scholars Program, established in 1980, matches 70% of $600,000 gifts to fund $1-million endowed chairs, which are named by the donor (C. Anderson, 1992). Other states include Minnesota, Maryland, Virginia, and Louisiana. Federal agencies such as the U.S. Department of Education use challenge grants to leverage their impact on the program services offered by charitable organizations. Heavy reliance on *public* challenge grants can result in fund-raising programs that are driven by government interests rather than by the needs of the organization. Although such grants require private gifts, government funds—by definition—are not philanthropic. They should not be counted in fund-raising reports (CASE, 1996).

Corporate Matching Gifts.   Corporate matching gifts double, triple, quadruple, and sometimes quintuple the amount given by individual donors. According to CASE ("Matching gifts," 1996), about 1,000 parent companies and 5,300 subsidiaries have formal programs to match gifts made by their employees to charitable organizations. Because 88% of the participating companies limit their matches to gifts of less than $10,000, corporate matching gifts are primarily associated with the annual giving program. This is not to say the device is never used for major gifts. A one-to-one match, offered by 84% of the companies, means that an annual gift of $5,000 generates $10,000. Slightly more than one half of the companies also match gifts made by members of their board of directors, who often are officers and directors of other matching gift companies. When allowed by company policies, these executives sometimes use multiple matches to increase their gifts to $25,000 or more.

Corporations began matching employees' gifts more than 40 years ago, when General Electric started its program in 1954 as an experiment to see whether corporate matches would stimulate alumni support for colleges and universities (E. Ryan, 1994a). Representative of mixed motives, an underlying factor was—and continues to be—recognition of U.S. business' need for highly skilled workers and college campuses as the key source of those workers. Corporate needs beyond employee recruitment have since expanded the scope of the programs, with experts predicting even greater expansion during the last years of the 1990s. Independent schools, or those dealing with private secondary and elementary education, were included early on.

Today, 41% of the participating companies match gifts to at least one type of charitable organization other than education, and 13% match gifts to all 501(c)(3) organizations, although education continues to dominate (e.g., 100% of the companies match gifts to colleges and universities; CASE, 1995). Dollar amounts broken down by organizational types are not available; however, in 1991–1992, matching gifts represented 47% of all corporate support to independent schools and 10% to colleges and universities (E. Ryan, 1994a). Since their beginning, corporate matching gifts have totaled about $2 billion.

The donor must take the initiative to have his or her gift matched. The procedure is relatively simple, although many donors are not aware of it or choose not to take advantage of the programs. Each corporation requires its own form, which usually is available from the human resources department. For 83% of the corporations, donors fill out the form and send it with their gift to the recipient organization (CASE, 1995). Fund raisers complete the form and return it to the corporation. Checks are received in most cases within 3 months.

Increasingly, companies are eliminating forms and electronically processing the transactions, which makes the procedure more convenient for donors. Elimination of forms and improved communication are credited by General Electric for doubling its program during the first 3 years of the 1990s (E. Ryan, 1994a). Fund raisers also must focus on communication and donor convenience to encourage matching gifts.

CASE operates the National Clearinghouse for Corporate Matching Gift Information, which tracks trends and promotes this upgrading device. Among other resources, it annually publishes the *Matching Gift Leaflet Series*, designed for insertion in mailings to prospective donors. Attesting to program expansion beyond education, there currently are four versions of the leaflets, listing the companies that match gifts to: (a) higher education; (b) secondary and elementary schools, both public and private; (c) arts and cultural organizations, including museums, performing arts groups, and public television and radio; and (d) nonprofit hospitals, health, human services, environmental organizations, and United Ways. The leaflets can be purchased at bulk rates; information can be obtained by calling (800) 554-8536.

Rather than placing the burden on prospective donors to search listings for their employer's name, fund raisers take a more proactive approach when they identify those prospects who are affiliated with matching gift corporations. CASE offers printed and electronic versions of *Matching Gift Details*, which describes each of the 6,300 programs. The computer software version for Windows provides easy access to data and allows practitioners to compare company names with employment information recorded in their database ("Matching gifts," 1996). Prices start at just under $1,000. Targeted programming may include a series of receptions hosted by employees who already use a specific company's match, or personal letters signed by such individuals. Retired employees should not be forgotten; 42% of all participating companies match retirees' gifts (CASE, 1995). Special attention should also be paid to the corporations that make matches greater than one-to-one (14%). A few match every $1 given with $5.

Corporate matching gifts represent a win–win–*win* situation. Not only are they a means by which annual gifts can be increased at no cost to the individual donor, but they provide the basis for relationships with corporate donors. They represent a three-way interdependency among corporations, charitable organizations, and individuals linked to both entities. Problems, however, can arise from poor stewardship and abuse.

Stewardship must be provided to both corporate and individual donors; matching gifts would not exist without either one. Not providing reciprocity, responsible gift use, reporting, and relationship nurturing to the corporation leaves the programs vulnerable in this era of cost containment and downsizing. A receipt and thank-you letter—whether required or not—should be sent to the officer who forwarded the matching gift check. General Electric's program manager advised fund raisers to refrain from such recognition items as plaques and just make acknowledgments more meaningful: "A well-researched letter on how you're using matching gift dollars presents a much more compelling case for continued support" (E. Ryan, 1994a, p. 30).

Roughly one half of the participating companies specify that their matching contribution be used for the same purpose as the individual donor's gift, whereas the other half specify unrestricted use (CASE, 1995). Furthermore, although it is appropriate to credit the individual donor with his or her gift plus the matching amount, corporate funds are the source of the matching gift and should be so documented for accounting purposes. In other words, credit must be given to both donors, but the gift must be counted only once. Clear policies and two-way communication help alleviate stewardship problems.

As long as there have been corporate matching gifts, there have been those who abuse them. A contributions specialist with Phillip Morris stated, "Fraud and related problems are inherent in such a program" (E. Ryan, 1994a, p. 30). Early abuses by colleges and universities were responsible for the development of reporting standards at educational institutions (Fogal, 1991). In 1982, CASE and NACUBO (1982) issued management reporting standards for fund raising that defined how gifts should be counted. The standards were revised in 1996 (CASE, 1996).

Schemes that have been exposed in the past and are suspected today include *bundling*, whereby employees collect contributions from people who do not work at a company and bundle the money together to submit as a single gift to be matched by the employer. Others are employees using corporate matching gifts to pay for their children's tuition and fees at independent schools, and fund-raising practitioners giving money to employees to submit as their personal gifts for matching. As with all aspects of fund raising, corporate matching gifts require adherence to ethical practice. A starting point is to follow CASE's (1996) *Management Reporting Standards*; a copy should be in every fund-raising office, regardless of organizational type.

Special Projects. Special projects are simply another way of saying that fund raisers ask for *restricted* gifts when they want to upgrade annual giving donors. The device usually is employed as part of a multiple solicitation strategy, after the donor already has made an unrestricted gift. Practitioners acknowledge that people are more likely to give and to give higher amounts when the requested gift is for a specific purpose rather than for general operating needs.

The common knowledge, although untested, prompts the question: Why don't more annual giving programs feature restricted gift opportunities? The answer is twofold: Organizations prefer misconception to reality and place the convenience of managers above the interests and needs of donors.

As described in chapter 2, about 70% of all charitable organizations registered with the IRS have annual incomes of less than $25,000. No doubt these organizations, who do not employ fund raisers, rely on unrestricted gifts to operate. In aggregate, however, all gifts—unrestricted and restricted—account for only 25% of the subsector's income; client fees and dues, government grants and contracts, and investment earnings provide the majority of income. Of particular relevance to this discussion are client fees, or charges for program services, which represent income that can be used where needed (i.e., fees can pay basic expenses). Although the proportion of income received from client fees differs among organizations, it is significantly greater than gifts for the largest employers of fund raisers. Gifts to universities and nonprofit hospitals pale in comparison to student tuition and patient charges. The cost of operating such organizations is not dependent on annual gifts, which represent 5% or less of income. In other words, dedicating the annual giving program to raising unrestricted funds has little basis in reality.

The misconception of reliance on gifts is perpetuated in the literature. Graham (1992), as do almost all authors, characterized annual giving as critical to survival: It "pays for operations on a yearly basis," and "it must be unrestricted money that can be spent on the essentials of day-to-day operation" (p. 91). The accuracy of such descriptions as applied to different sizes and types of organizations rarely is questioned. The time has come for a new approach.

Fund raisers must carefully examine the need for unrestricted gifts in light of other sources of income and adjust their annual giving program accordingly. I hypothesize that few work for organizations with no funding alternatives. As advocated in the last chapter, identifying budget line items, known as *budget replacement*, still supports operational costs but also provides restricted opportunities for annual giving. Illustrating, U.S.A. Harvest, an organization in Louisville, Kentucky that collects and distributes donated food, asks corporate donors to take over monthly utility bills (H. Hall, 1995b). A local tire company pays the monthly telephone bill, about $5,000 per year, and another company pays the electric bill. According to the organization's founder: "Companies come to us and want to help, and I say, 'Well you can pay the phone bill.' The company likes it because they know the money is not going into a dark pit" (H. Hall, 1995b, p. 33).

Repeatedly asking for gifts for general purposes is less productive and less effective. Pray (1981) explained, "It is particularly difficult to keep annual giving programs fresh and lively. Their goals all too often seem merely to be more money" (p. 24). Bruce Loessin (cited in H. Hall, 1995b), vice president for alumni relations and development at Case Western Reserve University, stated, "A slush fund is what many donors expect when you ask them for an unrestricted gift" (p. 35).

Senior managers highly value unrestricted gifts because of their flexibility. The funds can be used where needed, which does not have to be determined until after receipt. Often framed as the means by which managers can grasp unexpected opportunities, the gifts also provide a way to cover unexpected expenses and shortfalls in income from other sources.

No one would argue that unrestricted gifts are not a valuable resource for management; they can—and often do—contribute to organizational effectiveness. Unfortunately, most organizations do a poor job of reporting to donors what actually is accomplished with their unrestricted gifts. The problem also is one of balance, ensuring that managers' preferences for unrestricted funds do not outweigh the interests and needs of annual giving donors. Restricted and unrestricted options should be offered and gift use conscientiously reported. Undue attention on unrestricted gifts indicates that managers simply have not made an effort to break down their organization's operating costs by gift opportunities.

Increasingly, fund raisers are recognizing that preferences of donors must be taken into account when planning the annual giving program. Whereas foundation donors have always been reluctant to make unrestricted gifts, they have become even more so in recent years (H. Hall, 1995b). The percentage of foundation dollars for general operating support dropped from 17% in 1987 to about 12% in 1993. Individuals, who traditionally have been more willing to make unrestricted gifts than either foundations or corporations, are demonstrating a marked change. For example, the percentage of unrestricted gifts to McMaster University's annual fund fell from 84% in 1991 to only 45% in 1994 (H. Hall, 1995b).

In short, the view that managers know best how gifts should be used is quickly losing its predominant position. Some organizations have reacted with press agentry tactics, trying to manipulate donors to go back to making unrestricted gifts. McMaster University, for example, may adopt a new gift response form that requires people to do more paperwork if they want to restrict gifts for particular programs (H. Hall, 1995b). On the other hand, reflective practitioners in charge of annual giving are moving toward two-way symmetrical fund raising.

Warwick (1995) stated, "You can hardly turn around these days at gatherings of fundraisers [sic] without hearing talk about 'donor choice.' The growing emphasis on offering options to donors in United Way campaigns has a lot to do with that conversation" (p. 20). Others attribute the movement to differences between older and younger donors. A survey conducted by the University of California at Santa Cruz, for example, found that its alumni, most of whom are in their late 30s to mid-40s, would gladly make gifts—but not for unrestricted purposes (Aldrich, 1994). According to the assistant chancellor for university advancement, the young alumni "expressed interest in specific restricted projects, not general support, thus following what seems to be an age-based trend" (p. 28). Due to the research findings, annual giving donors are allowed to select projects they feel most inclined to support.

Regardless of whether younger people actually have different preferences or whether changes in United Ways have had a ripple effect, the annual giving program is in transition—moving from an unwarranted concentration on unrestricted gifts to donor friendly options. New initiatives emerging from strategic planning are being listed on gift response forms, along with the option, "Use my gift where needed most." Fund-raising managers are analyzing projected budgets to identify budget-replacement items that can be added to the forms, such as purchasing computers and funding staff training. Research, including focus groups, helps them select those options that are of interest to prospective donors. Theory predicts that the transition to the two-way symmetrical model will increase fund-raising effectiveness. In terms of dollars, giving and gift amounts increase as specificity about gift purpose and personalization of communication increase.

Techniques

As a general guideline, the 10% of prospective donors who will provide 60% or more of the dollars raised through annual giving should be segmented for interpersonal communication. Who constitute that important 10%? A good place to start is by identifying previous donors in the group. Practitioners might produce a computer listing of all annual gifts from the previous year by decreasing dollar amounts, with running cumulative totals. They then could identify the gift amount at the point in the listing where the cumulative total equals 60% of the total dollars (e.g., $250). Using an amount $1 less, they would instruct the computer to select donor records by a "greater than" dollar amount (e.g., 199– GIFT = > $249 BUT < $10,000). If the organization has gift clubs, identification could be made by club membership. For example, previous totals may show that donors assigned to the clubs from $500 to $9,999 accounted for 60% or more of the dollars raised. Selection then would be made on membership in the appropriate clubs. Research and suggestions from members of the volunteer committee identify other individuals, corporations, and foundations who are likely to make a large annual gift.

These important prospects should be cultivated and solicited through such techniques as personal letters, telephone calls, and face-to-face conversations, as well as through such controlled media as special events and publications. Fund-raising managers plan the activities and personally solicit many of the gifts. The very top prospects often are assigned to the annual giving committee for solicitation. Practitioner wisdom holds that each volunteer should be assigned about five prospects (Rosso, 1991); therefore, a committee of 10 to 15 can handle up to 75 prospective donors. Although some volunteers may be comfortable designing their own strategy, such as holding informal conversations with prospects they know, I recommend a more structured approach. Specifically, the combination of a letter and a follow-up telephone call should be employed to request a gift or an in-person meeting at which the gift will be solicited. The combination, which utilizes two-way communication, works well for both volunteers and fund raisers.

Letter and Follow-Up Phone Call. A personal letter followed by a telephone call is recommended not only for soliciting top gifts but for all communication that seeks desired behavior from key individuals. In other words, whether asking a person to serve as a volunteer, host an event, give a speech, attend a meeting, or make a gift, a letter and a follow-up phone call increase the probability of an affirmative answer. This assertion is made without benefit of research; studies on interpersonal techniques are absent from the literature. Furthermore, although Rosso (1991) also recommended the combination, he and other authors have not described it. The following discussion, then, is drawn from my experience in fund raising and presents a how-to description of the combination as executed by staff practitioners.

The personal letter presents the request for a gift or for a meeting to discuss a gift in a professional manner, well thought out and written, and carefully edited and formatted. The risk of inadvertently saying the wrong thing, which sometimes happens in oral communication, is minimized. In addition, organizational affiliation and title, as given on the letterhead and in the closing, provide symbols of credibility sometimes missing in conversations. The letter starts by stating its purpose (e.g., consideration of a gift), summarizes the case, and ends by telling the prospective donor that he or she will receive a telephone call from the fund raiser: "I will call you within the next two weeks to discuss this request. In the meantime, thank you for your consideration."

New practitioners often make the mistake of giving *their* telephone number and asking the prospect to call them. They worry about appearing too assertive, so they leave the initiative to the prospect. Underlying their action is a fear of rejection: if they call, they might be turned down. It is easier to believe that prospects agreeable to the request will send a check or call. The approach does not work; it places an unreasonable burden on the prospect. Most important, it sends a message that can only be described as arrogant: "I want something from you, but I want you to stop what you are doing and contact me. I am waiting."

A second mistake is to include the "I will call you" statement and then not make the follow-up call. Practitioners who put off calling are still hoping the prospect will take the responsibility for action. I was one of them.

A donor, who I will call Norman, helped me understand the ramifications of what I was doing at a point in my career when I should have known better. Soon after becoming the vice president for development and public relations at Mount Vernon College in Washington, DC, I identified Norman as a prospect for a computer project because his daughter was an alumna, he owned a computer business, and he was a director of a private foundation, among other reasons. As neither the president nor I had met him, I wrote a letter for the president's signature asking Norman to meet with us to discuss the project, which concluded by saying that I, the vice president, would call to get his response. I put off calling for 1 week, and then most of the next. Convinced that the silence boded poorly for our requested meeting, I finally dialed the telephone. After telling a secretary my name and then holding for what seemed much longer than the actual 1 minute, this cheerful voice came booming over the line: "I was wondering if you were going to call; I've been waiting. The letter's right here on my desk. Now, tell me what I can do." He sounded as if I had passed a test. I realized later that Norman was teaching me the importance of fund raisers taking that extra step toward those from whom they request support. We had the meeting, which led to a major gift to purchase the college's first personal computers, and Norman became chairman of Mount Vernon's board of trustees a few years later.

The 2-week time frame I recommend between letter and telephone call, although arbitrary, is designed to give the prospect enough time to consider the request and to bring fairly quick closure, accounting for mail and work days. Making a follow-up call within 1 week after the letter is mailed often results in preempting the letter, which is frustrating and unsatisfactory for both the fund raiser and the prospect. Waiting more than 2 weeks risks the possibility that the request will have been replaced or forgotten. A rule to remember is that prospects generally are busy people: Get on and off their personal agenda as quickly as possible. Using weeks rather than days provides slack for those times when other fund-raising responsibilities interfere with making the follow-up calls.

Because a deadline has been self-imposed, the letters must be carefully tracked. Computer software featuring a calendar can be used to provide daily reminders of pending calls. A less technologically advanced but reliable method is to tuck a copy of each letter—with the prospect's daytime telephone number written under the inside address—into the corner of a desk pad where it is constantly visible. Attempted contacts and other information can then be recorded on the letter copy (e.g., "left message Wednesday, 2/6, 10:30 a.m.," or secretary's name). Given other activities and tasks, fund raisers generally can handle only about 10 such letters at any one time.

I recommend three follow-up telephone calls. In other words, when the prospect is unavailable, practitioners should leave three phone messages—no less and no more. New practitioners mistakenly believe that by leaving one message the burden of responsibility has been shifted to the prospect and that no return call means the request is declined. Busy people do not immediately respond to one message; they have other priorities and concerns. Second and third calls, usually spaced 2 days apart, are often not only necessary, but perceived by the prospect as an indication of the request's importance and the fund raiser's sincerity. On the other hand, more than three calls may be perceived as unwanted attention. To protect future relationships and bring closure to the communication, after three uncompleted calls, a second letter should be sent, briefly expressing regret that a conversation was not possible and promising to keep the prospect informed of the organization's activities and progress.

More commonly, the telephone conversation does take place, during which practitioners should refrain from talking too much. When a letter has been sent beforehand, the fund raiser need only introduce himself or herself—including organizational affiliation—reference the letter, and then be quiet. Let the prospect do the talking. Listen carefully and have a pencil on hand to record responses. This is not to say practitioners are not prepared. They always review letters before placing calls so that details are fresh in their mind. If the request is for a meeting, they have precleared dates on hand for all who might participate (e.g., the CEO). They review the three possible outcomes—agreement, no decision, or decline—and mentally prepare their response to each.

When the prospect has finished relaying his or her decision, or absence of one, fund raisers summarize what they think they heard and suggest a follow-up action. For example, if the prospect agrees to make a gift, the fund raiser proposes to confirm the agreement in a second letter, which basically will state, "I am delighted that you have decided to make a gift of $x to our 199– annual giving program." If no decision has been reached, further interaction is proposed, such as having someone else contact the prospect or calling back in 2 weeks. If the request is declined, permission is sought to keep the communication door open (e.g., "If it's all right with you, I'm going to keep your name on our list of friends so that you continue to get information about our program").

In short, fund raisers strive to keep the ball in their court. Above all, they are professional and polite. They always close the conversation with an expression of appreciation on behalf of the organization (e.g., "Thank you for taking the time to discuss this request with me").

Whereas techniques based on interpersonal communication are utilized to raise annual gifts from the small number of prospects who provide 60% or more of the dollars, fund raisers turn to techniques of controlled and mass media to communicate with the majority of prospective donors. In contrast to the combination just described, there are numerous resources available for acquiring basic knowledge about the techniques.

Direct Mail and Special Events.

A comprehensive treatment of the various techniques used in annual giving is beyond the scope of this book. Indeed, the techniques represent areas of specialized communication and a cross-section of several disciplines, including advertising, broadcasting, journalism, marketing, and public relations. Attesting to the techniques' requirement for technical expertise, entire industries exist to support their use. For example, graphic artists and printers set the standards for publications, and vendors trained in broadcasting and film produce telethons and videos.

I strongly recommend that future practitioners take a separate academic course on public relations techniques, which covers planning, production, and dissemination of almost all the techniques employed in fund raising, as given in Fig. 9.3. Students also are advised to make use of fund raising's how-to literature, examples of which are cited in this book.

The discussion here focuses on direct mail and special events because they are the two most commonly used techniques in annual giving. The information on direct mail emphasizes the need for specialized knowledge, providing a sketch of elements likely unknown to most students. The presentation of special events concentrates on issues of efficiency and effectiveness.

Direct mail is based on principles of direct-response marketing, and a substantial body of research is available for study. The typical direct-mail package consists of five pieces: (a) #10 carrier envelope, (b) letter, (c) brochure or other insert, (d) response form, and (e) #9 return envelope (Craver, 1991). Current technologies provide the means to individually address the package, insert short personal references (e.g., "Your gift last year of $35 was used to buy supplies"), and add postscripts that appear to be handwritten. Studies suggest that people read the letter's postscript first, then the name of the sender, and only then the opening lines of the letter's text. Experts rely on field experiments to test the copy and design of each package before mass quantities are produced. November is by far the most popular month for direct-mail solicitations, followed by September and August (Kleid Company, 1996). The end of the tax year and delays caused by holiday mailings in December are responsible for November's popularity.

Postal regulations on direct mail are complex. The technique is subject to USPS rules on eligibility, preparation, and rates for standard nonprofit mail, introduced earlier in chapter 7. Adding a few basics, a permit must be obtained from a postal facility and a bulk mail account established. The assigned permit number allows an organization to print a facsimile of a stamp, called an *indicia*, on carrier envelopes. Most organizations also have a business-reply permit and print that indicia on return envelopes to encourage donor response. An amount of money sufficient to cover all postage is deposited in the bulk mail account before each mailing, which requires careful planning and budgeting.

A point sometimes overlooked by new fund raisers is that the per-unit cost of return mail is much more expensive than the per-unit cost of outgoing mail. Because multiple units—usually in the thousands—are sent out, direct mail benefits from bulk rates (e.g., the cost of each package sent at the 1997 basic letter rate for standard nonprofit mail is 13.2 cents). Returns, on the other hand, are sent back individually, not in bulk; therefore, first-class postage must be paid, which is 32 cents in 1997. If return envelopes include a business-reply indicia, the USPS charges about twice the amount of first-class postage for handling each return. Fund raisers, then, must anticipate response rates and make cost-efficient decisions.

Paying for business-reply postage is recommended for direct mail designed to acquire new donors because the anticipated response rate is low, 25% or less, and expenses are incurred only for those return envelopes sent back (i.e., there are no charges for unused envelopes bearing the indicia). Stamping first-class postage on return envelopes with a postal meter is much cheaper when higher responses are expected, such as 50% or more from a mailing targeted at previous donors. Even applying first-class stamps usually is cost efficient, keeping in mind that—as with metered mail return postage is paid whether envelopes are used or not. To hold fund-raising costs down, practitioners sometimes decide donors should pay for returning their gifts to the recipient organization. The decision violates principles of direct-response marketing and generally is not recommended.

Standard nonprofit mail is divided into two categories: letters and nonletters. Requirements and rates for letters pertain to direct mail consisting of small packages. Defined by the USPS, letters are packages 6⅛ inches by 11½ inches or smaller, not thicker than ¼ inch, and weighing no more than 3.3 ounces (H. Hall, 1996b). Postage is determined by piece, and the basic rate in 1997, as given earlier, is 13.2 cents. Nonletters include direct mail of large packages, or those exceeding the height, width, and thickness of letters. Postage for nonletters is calculated by piece if individual packages weigh 3.3 ounces or less; if they are heavier, a pound rate plus a per-piece charge is used. The basic rates in 1997 are, respectively, 19.5 cents and 44.5 cents plus 10 cents.

Regarding preparation, direct-mail packages must be designed with automation in mind. Mail processed manually is subject to delays and to basic rates—the rates without discounts just given, which are the highest. Paper with dark fibers or a return address not printed within a specified area will send mail to the manual sorter or back to the organization (Hotaling & Sabo, 1993). To qualify for discounts that reduce basic rates, packages must have preprinted barcodes on the carrier envelope, be sorted in 3-digit or 5-digit ZIP code order, and—bundled and bagged—be delivered to a mail facility. Direct mail letters with barcodes, sorted by ZIP codes, and delivered to a bulk mailing center cost only 8.6 cents per unit in 1997, or one third less than the basic rate of 13.2 cents (H. Hall, 1996b).

Rate changes implemented in 1996 offer greater discounts for more precise preparation. Illustrating, the USPS has moved to delivery-point barcodes with 11-digit ZIP codes and now offers discounts for direct mail sorted by carrier route, which requires sorting packages according to the "walk sequence" of addresses on a specific postal route. Applied to the example just given, the new discount lowers the per-unit cost of letters to 6.6 cents, or half the basic rate (H. Hall, 1996b). Few charitable organizations, however, produce enough mail to take advantage of such discounts. As argued in chapter 7, the greatest savings are realized by organizations that solicit unknown mass audiences—characteristic of press agentry practice. Fund raisers who selectively target their efforts must be satisfied with more moderate savings, although they strive to attain the lowest appropriate rates by learning about and keeping up with postal regulations.

The USPS employs mail-design analysts and automation readability specialists who will review package design before printing. It offers booklets, periodicals, and newsletters, such as the *Postal Bulletin* and the monthly *Memo to Mailers* and *Mailroom Companion*. The 1996 *Max It* guide explains the latest rates and requirements. Free copies can be obtained by calling (800) THE USPS (843-8777). Another source of information is the service's Web site, from which the publications just given can be downloaded. To get there, type *http://www.usps.gov*.

I recommend that, generally, direct mail be limited to in-house lists. Its purpose, as Armstrong (1995) asserted, "is to target people who already agree with you and convince them that your organization is the best means of achieving your shared goals" (p. 42). Armstrong added, "No direct mail letter has successfully changed anyone's mind about anything" (p. 42). Regardless, students should be aware of the multimillion-dollar industry involved in renting and exchanging cold lists. The reference book *Standard Rate and Data* describes more than 20,000 "markets" and listings available from for-profit and nonprofit organizations (Craver, 1991). Exchanges and rentals are handled directly or through *list brokers*. Many large charitable organizations, such as the American Lung Association, the Arthritis Foundation, the National Wildlife Federation, and the Mayo Clinic, generate substantial income from renting their in-house lists. Donors are heralded in paid advertisements as "ideal targets" for other organizations. The income is treated either as exempt royalties or is subject to UBIT, as determined by IRS guidelines. The issue currently is the basis of numerous court cases. Cold lists rented by charitable organizations include subscription lists to such commercial magazines as *Mirabella*, *Mademoiselle*, *The New Yorker*, and *GQ*.

Students likely now understand why they and other people receive unwanted solicitations from organizations with which they have no connection. An ethical question faced by fund raisers is whether a donor has the right to keep his or her name from being rented or traded. Warwick (1995) provided an unconditional answer:

> Let me put it to you straight: If more fundraisers [*sic*] don't start offering this option without further fuss, bother, and procrastination, we may all soon find that the law requires us to do so. . . . Every nonprofit organization that makes its list available for rental or exchange owes it to its donors to disclose that fact—and to give them a chance to opt out. Privacy rights demand it as a matter of plain decency. (p. 20)

The purpose of solicitations using cold lists, for both direct mail and telemarketing, is to acquire donors, not gifts (i.e., donor acquisition). Even with careful matches between organizations with similar missions, the response rate is extremely low, gifts are small, and costs are high (Craver, 1991). Howe (1991) described donor acquisition from cold lists as "a deep-sea trawler operation to catch anything it can" (p. 34).

Successful users of such mailings, he said, almost always are high-profile national organizations, usually with an advocacy mission, such as Planned Parenthood and Right to Life. In contrast, Mixer (1993) claimed, "New and small agencies find this method helpful in quickly generating a donor base" (p. 116).

I hypothesize, in the absence of any research, that only a minority of fund raisers utilize cold lists. The mailing-list industry is subsidized by paid solicitors, who have expertise in both list selection and direct mail, and by those organizations that hire them. In support of my hypothesis, when I took NSFRE's Survey Course, the practitioner instructor on annual giving stressed donor acquisition using cold lists. He carefully explained how each list must be tested by mailing the intended package to a sample of about 4,000 and that—even with testing—the typical response for the entire mailing is 1.5% or less. Yet when I asked, only 2 of the 19 participants in the class said they dealt with rented or exchanged lists. A female fund raiser employed by a symphony orchestra described a more strategically sound approach. Her organization sponsors a free concert each year during which a raffle for season tickets is held, producing thousands of names with addresses. In other words, she has no reason to *buy* prospects because they identify themselves through a demonstrated interest in the organization's work.

Moving to the second most commonly used technique, special events can play a critical role in fund-raising management; however, they are among the least efficient of all techniques when used to solicit annual gifts. Solicitation events generally cost a great deal—often one half or more of the money raised. They are extremely labor intensive—often requiring thousands of hours of staff and volunteer time. Much of their expense encumbers funds far in advance of such revenue predictors as ticket sales, and their success or failure often is determined by such unpredictable factors as the weather. H. Hall (1993a) summarized, "Special events can be the black hole of fund raising. Unless managed correctly, they can easily eat up more time and money than they're worth" (p. 35). Grønbjerg (1993) concluded from her case studies, "Organizing special events is an exercise in the management of uncertainty" (p. 138).

Types of solicitation events, often called "fund raisers," range from kiss-a-pig contests that generate gifts of $1, to charity balls that charge $1,000 or more. There are rubber duck races, fashion shows, auctions, preperformance dinners, street dances, Keystone Cop jail-and-bail competitions, running marathons, swimming marathons, walk-a-thons, golf tournaments, craft shows, buy-a-celebrity contests, festivals, circuses, benefit concerts, and scores of others. They run the spectrum from the ridiculously absurd to the traditionally revered. A common denominator is that they return goods or services, including entertainment, to the donor.

Events often are identified with women. Probably because it is the fund-raising technique with which they are most familiar, female volunteers and donors—at least until recently—have demonstrated a preference for special events over more cost-efficient techniques. Events constituted the socially acceptable way for their mothers to raise and give money, and their mothers before them. Men, who benefited from a different tradition, including owning money to give outright, use special events but also are comfortable with solicitation techniques that do not provide products or services.

When I was vice president at Mount Vernon, a women's college, one of my constant frustrations was that alumnae leaders—most of whom were quite wealthy—responded to virtually every fund-raising plan by suggesting a special event: an art auction, a fashion show, or a dinner party. Whereas they had few reservations about asking friends and acquaintances to buy tickets priced high enough to include a $100 contribution, they were reluctant to solicit outright gifts of $100 for the college. This concentration on events hampered the annual giving program and, on one occasion, would have resulted in a financial loss if the event had not been canceled.

J. W. Gray (1993) provided a gender balance by describing the male-dominated arena of college athletics:

> One would be hard-pressed to find an athletic fund-raising program that does not sponsor at least a golf tournament annually. Auctions, raffles, bingo games, dinners, and receptions have become a very time-consuming portion of many athletic fund-raising programs. These types of events are extremely labor-intensive. Often, the dollars raised are relatively small when compared to the amount of time and energy required of staff and volunteers for a successful event. (p. 226)

J. W. Gray (1993) argued that the technique should be reserved for objectives dealing with cultivation, rather than solicitation. He explained, "By making the *involvement* of prospective donors the primary purpose of the event, you will not be disappointed when your six months of planning and preparation result in minimal dollar returns" (p. 226; italics added). Greenfield (1991) agreed with this assessment, stating that special events for solicitation purposes "consume an inordinate amount of time for their net results" (p. 49). In short, many practitioners advise that raising money should be the last reason for holding an event.

In addition to their low cost efficiency, solicitation events may interfere with the philanthropic relationship between the sponsoring organization and its donors (i.e., effectiveness is questionable). Donors may view the gift as a market exchange rather than one based on philanthropy. Grønbjerg (1993) explained, "Special events resemble fees or service charges in that both require marketing products or services to customers who are willing to pay for them" (p. 122). She concluded that they "blur the line between commercial and donative transactions" (p. 125). Consultant Mark Randall (cited in H. Hall, 1993a) argued: "Special events say, 'If you buy a ticket, you will have a good time or maybe win something.' If your cause is worthwhile, you shouldn't have to hawk tickets or sell chances" (p. 35). Effective fund raisers, he said, "don't waste their time running Jell-O jumps and Mickey Mouse events" (p. 35).

Donor relationships also may fail to develop when an event overshadows the organization. A few years ago, the executive director of the Boys and Girls Club in my area complained to me about the club's annual Duck Race: "People remember the event but not our name as the sponsor."

Providing an illustration of special events, numerous Boys and Girls Clubs throughout the country—as well as other organizations—raise gifts by racing rubber ducks. The races are based on a commercial package sold by Great American Duck Races, located in Arizona. The package includes thousands of rubber ducks, which are numbered and offered to donors for a $5 adoption fee. On an announced date, the ducks are dumped into a designated waterway and those that float to the finish line first win prizes for their adoptive "parents." The event is dependent on big numbers: hundreds of volunteers and program service staff spending thousands of hours to solicit thousands of donors, only some of whom attend the race. The duck races generally net between $10,000 and $100,000. They would almost always lose money if time was calculated at minimum wage and treated as an expense.

In contrast, many Boys and Girls Clubs raise larger annual gifts through a second event called "Steak & Burgers," which is efficient and effective. Using the club in my area as an example, each year, board members and past donors sell tickets to a dinner that brings together donors and young club members. Individual tickets are $100, and a table seating five adults and three youngsters sells for $500. As most donors are corporations, table sales dominate, thereby requiring a minimum amount of volunteer time. The youngsters are served steak; the adults get hamburgers. Although the dinner is used to solicit new donors, its primary objective is to renew previous donors. The interaction between the organization's clients and those who financially support its purpose strengthens ongoing relationships. As the club's executive director told me, "Nobody sells what we do better than the child."

Generally, I agree with Greenfield (1991) and others that special events are better used for purposes such as research, cultivation, and stewardship than for solicitation. If selected and implemented strategically, however, they do have their place in the solicitation mix. The in-person contact emulates more powerful techniques based on interpersonal communication. Events provide a fund-raising role for volunteers and board members who are not comfortable with asking for a gift without returning a product or service. For those organizations that have a large volunteer corps in place, events offer a means to increase volunteers' involvement while advancing the organization's goals. On the other hand, recruiting large numbers of volunteers in order to carry out solicitation events is wasteful. Justifying the use of events because they generate publicity is a sham; there are easier and cheaper ways to get exposure through the mass media.

As Greenfield recommended, policies and procedures should be established to guide the management of special events, particularly when implemented by volunteers. Policies should include requirements that all contracts be reviewed by the organization's legal department before signing. Volunteers should be required to work closely with the finance department. No special event should ever be produced without insurance. If someone is hurt or if property is damaged, the organization and/or its employees may be sued. Small events often can be insured at no cost by adding a temporary rider to a regular policy. Specialized insurance calls for careful shopping and brokers who are known and trusted.

I learned about the importance of insurance while organizing the benefit basketball game at the University of Maryland mentioned in chapter 7. The game featured the varsity team against a team of alumni who were professional basketball players. Less than 1 week before the event, one of the university's attorneys asked me what arrangements I had made for insurance on the professional players, some of whom were making seven-figure salaries. If one was injured during the game, he explained, we could expect expensive claims against the university. Last-minute investigation revealed that a comprehensive policy would cost thousands of dollars, almost equal to the amount I planned to raise from the event. Fortunately, the state's insurance commissioner took pity on me and facilitated the purchase of a special 24-hour rider that provided adequate protection at an inexpensive cost.

Quid pro quo regulations now require fund raisers to print a disclosure statement about returned benefits on special events material, such as invitations and tickets. A sample statement is:

> Under the Internal Revenue Code, the amount of the contribution that is deductible for federal income tax purposes by purchasing this ticket is limited to the excess of the amount you paid for your ticket, [$200], over the value of the benefits you will receive at the special event. We estimate that the value of those benefits is [$75] . Therefore, your income tax charitable deduction resulting from the ticket purchase will be [$125].

It is appropriate to end this chapter on annual giving with a note about new technologies. Techniques will change as technology rapidly advances. By the time students are established in their careers, direct-mail packages and phonathons may be replaced by videos and interactive television. Fax on demand may be routinely used for cultivation. Online gifts may dominate broad-based solicitation. Stewardship might include annual reports on CD-ROMs and computer disks with screen savers featuring the organization's name as inexpensive tokens of appreciation. The Internet surely will affect how fund raisers communicate with donor publics. Of particular significance, communication will be more two-way, with the former *receivers* of messages becoming active *senders*. In other words, the new technologies promise to empower donor publics, and fund raisers must be prepared for the dialogue that will result.

SUGGESTED READINGS

Fischer, L. R., & Schaffer, K. B. (1993). *Older volunteers: A guide to research and practice*. Thousand Oaks, CA: Sage.

Gayley, H. T. (1991). *How to write for development: Better communication brings bigger dollar results* (Rev. ed.). Washington, DC: Council for Advancement and Support of Education.

Gee, A. D. (Ed.). (1990). *Annual giving strategies: A comprehensive guide to better results*. Washington, DC: Council for Advancement and Support of Education.

Graham, C. (1992). *Keep the money coming: A step-by-step strategic guide to annual fundraising*. Sarasota, FL: Pineapple Press.

Greenfield, J. (1994). *Fund-raising fundamentals: A guide to annual giving for professionals and volunteers*. New York: Wiley.

Harris, A. L. (1991). *Raising money and cultivating donors through special events*. Washington, DC: Council for Advancement and Support of Education.

Kachorek, J. (1991). *Direct mail testing for fund raisers*. Chicago: Precept Press.

Levine, J., & Baroudi, C. (1994). *The Internet for dummies* (2nd ed.). San Mateo, CA: IDG Books.

Peirce, S. P. (1992). *Gift club programs: A survey of how 44 institutions raise money*. Washington, DC: Council for Advancement and Support of Education.

Zeff, R. (1996). *The nonprofit guide to the Internet*. New York: Wiley.

12

Fund-Raising Programs: Major Gifts

Fund raising is incomplete without a major gifts program. Pray (1981) stated, "No matter how broad the base of support, no matter how many contribute to the annual fund, if the development staff and the president and trustees are not able to stimulate the truly significant big gifts, all else is window dressing" (p. 58).

Due to our capitalistic economy, wealth is not distributed equally. Some people simply have the capacity to make gifts of large amounts. Similarly, a small proportion of U.S. companies and foundations control most of the wealth belonging to such organizations. Their gifts are larger than those of others. Because of their larger gifts, wealthier donors account for most of the dollars raised.

Major gifts are made from people's *income and assets*. They traditionally have been defined as those made *outright*. Unlike planned gifts that are *deferred*, outright gifts mean the donors transfer their income and/or assets to the organization immediately or pay in installments over an agreed period of time. The pledge period should not exceed 5 years (CASE, 1994). Whereas annual gifts directly increase the recipient organization's spendable income, major gifts generally increase the organization's assets. Assets, as explained in chapter 7, are of two types: (a) physical capital, or the organization's physical plant and equipment; and (b) financial capital, or endowment and reserves. Because assets and capital are synonymous, the major gifts program sometimes is referred to as the *capital program*. The alternate name is inaccurate. Although most major gifts are made for capital purposes (e.g., to construct a new building or to create an endowed fund), sometimes major gifts are solicited and used for operating expenses (e.g., to underwrite the salary of a new staff position for 1 year).

Major gifts usually are restricted to specific purposes. Worth (1993) elaborated, "Few major gifts are unrestricted or directed to current operating needs. They usually are designated for a specific endowment or facility, reflecting the interests and experiences of the donors" (p. 14).

Donors who make major gifts are well-known to the organization and its fund raisers. They often are trustees. Adams (1993) explained, "Virtually every major gift donor has a long standing, carefully nurtured relationship with the institution or cause—and, by extension, the people who represent it" (p. 135). In almost all cases, major donors have made previous gifts to the organization. Heetland (1993) estimated that 90% are past donors. He endorsed advice given to him by a seasoned fund raiser: "Don't look for wealthy people and hope that some will become your friends. Rather, look at your friends and hope that some of them are wealthy" (p. 10).

The dollar amount that constitutes a major gift varies by organization. Major gifts are defined here as those of $10,000 or more. Heetland (1993), citing another expert, defined major gifts as "those gifts which play a major role in reaching the fund-raising goal" (p. 11). Based on the principle of proportionate giving, he claimed that the top 100 gifts will account for 90% of what an organization raises, concluding, "A simple definition of major gifts then becomes the top 100 prospects" (p. 11).

For some organizations, those 100 prospects will have the capacity to make gifts of $1 million or more, what the literature refers to as *ultimate*, *mega*, or *principal* gifts. For other organizations, $10,000 may be the largest amount they can realistically expect to receive. Practitioners claim that most gifts of $1 million or more are made by people worth $20 million and up ("NSFRE chapters," 1993). Not all organizations have access to prospective donors with this degree of wealth. On the other hand, almost all organizations have access to individual, corporate, and foundation prospects with the capacity to give at least $10,000, which generally requires an income of $200,000 and/or assets of $500,000. In other words, all organizations are capable of raising major gifts as defined by the amount used in this book; however, their mission determines if they will receive the very largest ones.

LARGEST GIFTS

The organizations receiving the largest gifts are colleges and universities (with private institutions leading the way) and hospitals (Jencks, 1987). Following close behind are arts, culture, and humanities organizations (Odendahl, 1990) and independent schools. The largest gifts are made by individuals, and wealthy individuals are more likely to make gifts to these types of organizations than to others. Cnaan (1993) explained, "The fact that the rich donate more to education and culture, the middle classes more to social and medical services, and the poor more to religion suggests that all classes tend to support services from which they benefit and that perpetuate their interests" (p. 187). Broken down further, out of the 3,600 U.S. colleges and universities, just 60 elite institutions traditionally receive one half of all private dollars given to higher education (Council for Aid to Education, 1991). Within universities, engineering and business schools receive larger gifts than schools of social work or education (Myers, 1993).

Illustrating rules and exceptions, Michael Bloomberg, who heads the news and financial information company Bloomberg L.C., gave $55 million to Johns Hopkins University in 1995—the largest gift ever received by that institution (AAFRC Trust for Philanthropy, 1996). Bloomberg is an alumnus of Hopkins, chairman of its board of trustees, and chairman of its current $900-million capital campaign. He previously had made an $8-million gift to the university. Also in 1995, Gordon Wu, a Hong Kong entrepreneur and self-made billionaire, pledged $100 million to Princeton University's school of engineering and paid the first $20-million installment (AAFRC Trust for Philanthropy, 1996). Wu and two of his children graduated from Princeton. His gift—as of 1997—is the largest by a foreign individual to a U.S. institution and is among the largest gifts to higher education historically.

The largest gift by any donor to a college or university is contested and difficult to determine because of varying gift forms and conditions. Louisiana State University (LSU) claims the $125-million pledge it received from oilman Claude B. "Doc" Pennington in 1981 is the largest gift (Bailey, 1993). Its claim is flawed. The gift is a trust, consisting of stock, and gas and oil royalties, set up to make payments to LSU over 20 years. After 12 years, less than half of the pledged amount had been paid, and given depressed gas and oil prices since the mid-1980s, it is unlikely the trust will yield the full amount by 2001. The Pennington Biomedical Research Center, which was established by LSU as the purpose of the gift, has been heavily subsidized by state appropriations.[1]

New York University (NYU) claims a bequest it received in 1994 from the late British historian Sir Harold Acton surpasses Pennington's gift, although the total value of the bequeathed property has not yet been determined (AAFRC Trust for Philanthropy, 1996). Regardless, NYU reported that the 57-acre estate—located in Florence, Italy—and the collection of art it contains are worth "hundreds of millions" (AAFRC Trust for Philanthropy, 1995, p. 147). As stipulated in Acton's will, the estate and artworks cannot be sold by the university, which significantly diminishes the gift's value.

Walter Annenberg gave $120 million *each* to the University of Pennsylvania (Penn) and the University of Southern California (USC) in 1993 (Bailey, 1993). Annenberg also gave $100 million to the Peddie School the same year. He previously had given about $40 million to Penn in the 4 years before, $50 million to USC, and $44 million to the Peddie School, from which he graduated in 1927. The 1993 gifts actually were made from the Annenberg Foundation and represent the largest foundation grants made to any type of organization since the Foundation Center began tabulating such information in 1973 (Bailey, 1993).

Before Annenberg's gifts, the distinction of having made the largest gift was held for 15 years by Robert Woodruff, former chairman of Coca-Cola, who gave company stock worth $105 million to Emory University in 1978 (McNamee, 1993). In inflation-adjusted dollars, Woodruff's gift likely remains the largest. His gift represented the corpus of the Emily and Ernest Woodruff Fund, which already had been giving 40% of its income to Emory. According to McNamee, Woodruff was cultivated for 40 years, including weekly breakfasts with the dean of Emory's medical school.

In contrast, except for a previous gift of $1,500, Henry and Betty Rowan had no formal ties to Glassboro State College, when—in 1992—they made a $100-million gift to the New Jersey public institution (McNamee, 1993). The gift was added to the college's endowment, which increased from $0.5 million to $100.5 million! Mr. Rowan, who attended colleges in Massachusetts, said his gift to Glassboro reflected his interest in "creating something new" in southern New Jersey, where—significantly—his multinational company, Inductotherm Industries, has its headquarters, and which lacked a public engineering school (Blumenstyk, 1992, p. A27). At Rowan's request, the college currently is using the endowment income "to create an engineering

---

[1]LSU likely has been counting on a bequest from Pennington, who was worth $550 million when he died in mid-1997.

school and to provide scholarships to the children of the employees of his company" (Blumenstyk, 1992, p. A27). Glassboro's president hopes the state will eventually assume the operating costs of the engineering school so that the endowment income can be used for other purposes, such as expanding the college's teacher education programs for which it primarily has been known. Glassboro was renamed Rowan College of New Jersey in 1992, despite a lawsuit filed by an alumnus who objected to the new name because the college would still be supported primarily by state taxpayers ("Effort," 1992).

Staying with public institutions but moving down in dollar amounts, Peter Haas, Sr. of the Levi's jeans family and his wife Mimi made an *unrestricted* gift of $15 million in 1994 to the University of California at Berkeley to be used at the discretion of the university's chancellor ("U. of Cal.," 1995). Mr. Haas graduated from Berkeley in 1940. Businessman Curt Carlson gave $10 million in 1994 to the University of Minnesota for a new building to house the Carlson School of Management—named for him in 1986 when he gave $25 million (AAFRC Trust for Philanthropy, 1987, 1995).

Organizations with missions other than education also receive multimillion-dollar gifts. In 1994, Ronald Perelman, chairman of the Revlon cosmetics company, gave $10 million to the Solomon R. Guggenheim Museum in New York City to commission a sculpture for the museum's new building and for unrestricted support ("Diabetes," 1994). Perelman, who serves as president of the Guggenheim, made another $10-million gift to the museum's capital campaign the following year ("Ronald," 1995). Fashion designer Bill Blass gave $10 million in 1994 to the New York Public Library to renovate its catalog room (AAFRC Trust for Philanthropy, 1996). The room was then named for Blass, who has been a trustee of the library since 1986. In 1994, the family of Robert Wood Johnson, IV, great-grandson of the founder of Johnson & Johnson, gave $10 million to the New York-based Juvenile Diabetes Foundation ("Diabetes," 1994). Mr. Johnson was at the time cochair of the organization's capital campaign; his daughter was diagnosed with diabetes 6 years earlier.

Billionaire philanthropist George Soros gave $6 million in 1994 to the Drug Policy Foundation to encourage treatment of drug abuse as a medical problem rather than a criminal offense (AAFRC Trust for Philanthropy, 1995). Two years later, Soros announced a $50-million gift to assist legal immigrants in the United States after the 1996 welfare reform law substantially reduced their access to food stamps and Social Security benefits (Demko, 1996a). Soros, a Hungarian-born financier who is a naturalized U.S. citizen, previously had concentrated his giving in Eastern and Central Europe. For example, the foundations he has established in 25 countries gave away more than $350 million in 1995, but his U.S. foundation, Open Society Institute–New York, accounted for less than $5 million, or 1.4% of the total (Demko, 1996b). Soros now says he will spend as much as he feels is necessary to alleviate domestic social problems.

On Valentine's Day in 1993, Joan Kroc, widow of the founder of McDonald's Corporation, gave more than $60 million in company stock to 121 Ronald McDonald Houses around the country (Stehle, 1993). The independent homes, which provide temporary housing to families with seriously ill children in nearby hospitals and medical centers, each received about $500,000, which Kroc stipulated be used solely for endowments. In many cases, the gift was bigger than the home's entire annual budget. Kroc gave $50 million in 1995 to Ronald McDonald Children's Charities to be distributed to organizations helping young people ("Ronald," 1995). Although she had considered making the gift in multiyear installments, Kroc gave the money in one lump sum.

Kroc's decision raises the issue of time and prompts a comparison of two recent gifts to illustrate critical differences between major outright gifts and major planned gifts. Jon Huntsman, a petrochemical industrialist, pledged $90 million to the University of Utah in 1995 (AAFRC Trust for Philanthropy, 1996). He is paying his gift in annual installments over 5 years. Also in 1995, financier John Loeb and his wife, Frances Lehman Loeb, pledged $70.5 million to Harvard University (AAFRC Trust for Philanthropy, 1996). Their gift, consisting of most of their assets, will be transferred to Harvard when they die. The university will then pay the Loeb's children lifetime annuities from the assets. Only after all the children die—which may be as long as 50 years—will Harvard have complete access to the gift, whereas Utah will benefit from Huntsman's total gift by 2000. Regardless, Harvard publicly announced in 1995 that it had "received" one of the largest gifts in its history. As touched on in earlier chapters and explained more fully in chapter 13, reporting planned gifts at their face value without adjusting for time and payouts distorts fund-raising results.

In early 1997, media reports revealed that Charles Feeney, a self-made businessman from New Jersey, had given away more than $610 million in the previous 15 years—anonymously (S. G. Greene, Moore, & Williams, 1997). Whereas major donors usually are well-known to recipients, Feeney kept his identity hidden from almost all the organizations receiving his gifts, which ranged from universities and hospitals to human services groups to IS, NSFRE, and academic centers on philanthropy. The gifts, which actually came from Feeney's two Bermuda-based foundations, were channeled through the Atlantic Philanthropic Service Company, a for-profit consulting firm in New York that billed itself as an adviser to wealthy anonymous donors. In fact, the company had no other clients besides Feeney. Because the foundations are located outside the United States, they are not subject to U.S. laws, including public disclosure regulations. Secrecy was further assured by making recipients agree in writing that if they disclosed any information about the gift they received, they would have to return the money.

Critics charged that the measures went beyond protecting privacy and raised questions about accountability. Ironically, Joel Fleishman, who was quoted extensively as a proponent of high accountability in earlier chapters, is president of Atlantic Philanthropic Service Company and responsible for much of the subterfuge. Good intentions do not necessarily translate into a "good" major gift.

LARGEST RETURNED GIFT

The largest gift ever *returned* to a donor—at least the largest ever publicized—occurred in 1995. In March of that year, Texas billionaire Lee Bass, a member of one of the world's richest families, asked for, and got, $20 million back from Yale University (Adler, 1995). Bass had given the money in Spring 1991 to endow a new undergraduate course in Western civilization. After nearly 4 years, the course was still not underway and Bass added a new demand to approve faculty appointments, to which Yale refused to agree.

Returning the gift was a notable embarrassment for the university, which was in the middle of its $1.5-billion capital campaign. The story broke the same day the media announced the Loebs' planned gift to Harvard, which was beginning its $2.1-billion campaign. Lee Bass, his father Perry, and his three older brothers, Sid, Edward, and Robert, have a combined fortune of about $7 billion (P. Newcomb, 1995); all are Yale alumni. Bass family members had given the university a total of $85 million between 1990 and 1995 (S. G. Greene, 1995).

The ensuing controversy centered around campus politics, specifically, conservative versus liberal ideologies. It was grounded in the recipient organization's obligation to honor understandings reached with donors. According to reports, Lee Bass' $20-million gift was attributable in some degree to a speech by a highly regarded conservative scholar at Yale, who condemned how Western civilization was being taught on U.S. campuses in this era of multiculturalism (Lenkowsky, 1995). In 1991, Bass agreed to establish an endowed fund to underwrite an intensive, year-long course designed to address the problem. Yale's president at the time, Benno Schmidt, claimed that 2 years of discussion had preceded the gift (Mundy, 1993). It was structured so that $14 million was to endow seven chairs in Western civilization, $4 million was to hire four junior faculty, and $2 million was to cover program costs (S. G. Greene, 1995). Before he left office in 1992, Schmidt appointed five of the seven chairs, including the scholar who had made the pivotal speech. When Richard Levin assumed the presidency more than 1 year later, he decided to restructure the project in a way that would not involve hiring *additional* professors. According to Adler (1995), the new president apparently had reservations about the project: "After rejecting one outline of the proposed course, he authorized a committee to look at other ways to use the money—reportedly without mentioning it to Bass" (p. 59). In short, Yale altered the original terms of the gift.

Critics charged that Yale reneged on what it promised to do. The gift, they said, had sparked a heated political debate on campus. Western civilization was the rallying cry for opponents of multiculturalism, faced off by those advancing multicultural perspectives. In Fall 1994, a right-wing student periodical suggested that radical faculty members and administrators, embarrassed at the thought of giving such prominence to Western civilization, hoped to use Bass' money for more fashionable subjects such as lesbian studies. Responding, Yale officials pointed out that all the topics that would be covered in the proposed course were already being taught at the university. The course, officials later claimed, *duplicated* existing undergraduate courses. Yale's defense was that it had not been devious, just bumbling in its administration of the gift (Adler, 1995).

When the student periodical broke the news, Bass reiterated that he wanted the money used precisely as specified, and he added a new demand—approving faculty members who would design and teach the course. Bass (cited in S. G. Greene, 1995) explained, "In order to assure that the original spirit and intent of the program should be implemented, I requested the opportunity to approve the designation of professors named as Bass professors" (p. 13). Yale's reluctance to agree, he said, led to "our mutual decision that the gift should be returned" (p. 13).

Leslie Lenkowsky (1995), president of the Hudson Institute, a conservative think tank, argued that after nearly 4 years, Bass had tired of waiting for Yale to use his gift for the purpose he intended, and was mistrustful that it would do so at all. Asking for faculty approval was more a symptom of the rift than a cause of it, indicating how much the relationship between donor and recipient had already broken down. Yale's response, Lenkowsky said, was predictable—it would refuse to give veto power over its faculty to a donor. In other words, Bass knew his new terms could not be met. Lenkowsky presented what he called the most important lesson of the controversy:

> Fund raising today is often thought of as a matter of persuasion, organization, and skill, an activity that could, to a significant extent, be carried on with minimal regard for the character of the institution it purports to serve. In truth, however, it is ultimately a matter of building trust, of persuading potential donors that their gifts would serve worthy purposes and be administered faithfully. What an organization is—and does—is critical for success. (p. 46)

Lenkowsky raised valid points. Fund raising is not free of values—social, political, or economic. By definition, it reflects the value system of the organization, whose behavior speaks louder than any crafted communications. Trust is the basis for relationships with donors.

On the other hand, Lenkowsky and other commentators missed what I believe were significant factors contributing to Yale's unenviable situation, which are presented here as three questions. Did the pressure of a capital campaign, publicly announced in 1992, force fund raisers to place more importance on the *amount* of Bass' $20-million gift than on its *purpose*? Was the gift amount insufficient for funding the endowed positions promised by the university? Given the first two questions, were poor negotiations between Bass and Yale fundamentally responsible for the problem? The three factors of capital campaigns, endowments, and negotiation are framed as questions because without access to proprietary information their relevance to Yale is conjecture.

Capital campaigns are the subject of chapter 14; however, preview information on two characteristics are necessary for this discussion. First, campaigns are notorious for concentrating on dollar amounts. A competition of who can raise the most dollars has emerged in recent years, particularly among private universities that have completed or launched campaigns with goals of $1 billion or more. Second, in order to successfully reach the goal, experts recommend that about 40% of the dollars must be raised during what is called the *advance gifts/nucleus fund phase*, generally a 1-year period before the campaign is publicly announced (Worth, 1993).

In Summer 1991, Stanford University finished the first ever $1-billion campaign, raising $1.3 billion. That same summer, Yale started its advance gifts/nucleus fund phase for—not coincidentally—a $1.5-billion campaign. According to media reports at the time, Harvard, which had just selected a new president, was getting ready to start its delayed campaign—rumored to be the largest yet. It was in this context of campaign competition and high dollar goals that Lee Bass made his gift in 1991. The $20 million was counted in the critical advance gifts phase, although it actually was made several months before the official start. Obviously, $20 million would have been considered a big step toward reaching the recommended 40% of the campaign's goal within 1 year. It is not difficult to imagine, then, that Yale's fund raisers and President Schmidt were more interested in the amount of Bass' gift than the purpose for which it was made.

The influence of the capital campaign factor is supported by Yale officials' later arguments that the proposed course on Western civilization actually duplicated existing courses. Campaigns, as documented in chapter 14, place inordinate pressure on fund raisers to produce dollars, often at the expense of the gift's usefulness, or utility, for the organization. The discussion turns now to endowments and negotiation. The Bass gift continues to serve as a framework, but the perspective is expanded to cover elements of the major gifts program about which future practitioners must be knowledgeable.

ENDOWMENTS

Endowments consist of multiple, separate funds that originate with gifts and are established in perpetuity.[2] A generally accepted standard is that $10,000—this book's defining criterion of a major gift—is the minimum amount required to set up and maintain an endowment fund (C. Anderson, 1992). Cash from the gift is invested to generate annual income, not all of which is spent. A portion is returned to the principal to protect the fund's future spending power. *Spendable income*, or the percentage of the principal's value available each year to support the purpose for which the endowed gift was made, is determined by internal policy and varies among organizations and over time. About 5% appears to be a common spendable rate in the late 1990s. A NACUBO survey cited by Synodinos (1992) found that the 396 U.S. colleges and universities with the largest endowments spend an average of 4.5% of their endowment each year.

Endowments can grow in three ways: additional gifts, higher than expected earnings on investment, and earnings returned to principal—which is dependent on the spending rate. Only the third option can be controlled by the organization. As Synodinos (1992) advised, "Don't spend all your earnings; retain enough to stay ahead of inflation" (p. 23). In short, the perpetual nature of endowed gifts demands that fund raisers match expected spendable income with estimated expenses *before* gift acceptance.

Recalling the structure of the Bass gift, $14 million was to be used to endow seven chairs. At $2 million each and a spendable rate of 5%, only $100,000 would be available during the first years to pay expenses for each holder of the chairs. Although the amount may seem sufficient to students, chairs usually are filled by full professors (i.e., educators with the highest academic rank), and professors at such institutions as Yale—particularly those deemed worthy of appointment to an endowed chair—often command salaries greater than $100,000. Furthermore, salaries are only part of the expense for a chair position. Office space, furniture, equipment, clerical support, travel funds, and research assistance also must be included. Fringe benefits, such as retirement and medical insurance, currently run about 30% of salary for any personnel position. As a rule of thumb, fully loaded expenses for a full-time employee at all types of organizations are roughly twice the salary paid.

---

[2]This discussion deals only with pure endowments, which were differentiated from board-designated endowments in chapter 7.

Few endowed positions cover 100% of expenses, a fact rarely discussed in the fund-raising literature. When accepting gifts for such purposes, organizations assume financial responsibility for some related costs. Problems occur if the financial implications are not thoroughly analyzed and explicitly defined before acceptance. This may have been a factor in the Bass controversy. Before explaining, students must understand the significant difference between appointing a person already on the payroll to an endowed position and hiring a new person. The first represents budget replacement in that the gift frees up operating income. Expenses not covered by the gift are easily absorbed because they already are budgeted. A new person, on the other hand, means added expenses for the organization.

Yale's President Levin reportedly restructured the Bass project in order to avoid hiring additional professors. The decision suggests that the spendable income generated by the $14 million was being fully used to support the five Bass chairs appointed by Levin's predecessor 2 years earlier and that the institution was unwilling—whether for political or financial reasons—to subsidize the two vacant chairs to the extent necessary. Similarly, the $4-million endowment to hire four junior faculty members represented spendable income of only about $50,000 for each position, which required a financial commitment from Yale. It is impossible to say if the impact of new hires versus appointment of existing faculty was taken into account by those negotiating the terms of the gift; however, it can be surmised that an absence of commitment to the purpose of the gift made Yale's financial commitments more burdensome to its administration.

Yet fund raisers for Yale, which had a $4-billion endowment in 1995 (Council for Aid to Education, 1996), likely have more experience in raising endowed gifts than most practitioners. The vast majority of America's colleges and universities have endowments smaller than their annual operating budgets (Synodinos, 1992). This presumably is also true for other types of charitable organizations. C. Anderson (1992) explained, "Until recently, most institutions haven't made concerted efforts to raise endowments" (p. 27).

The scene is rapidly changing as fund raisers and dominant coalition managers increasingly adopt a long-range view. An endowed gift raised this year is a gift that does not have to be raised the next year, or the year after. In systems theory terms, endowed gifts reduce environmental uncertainty by stabilizing funding streams. Their importance to the well-being of organizations cannot be minimized. Furthermore, endowed funds named by the donor are attractive to prospects for major gifts because they provide long-lasting recognition—some would say a piece of immortality. Unfortunately, endowment financing is not well understood by lay people or by inexperienced practitioners.

Illustrating, in his essay on the predicted shortage of faculty members with PhDs, communication professor Melvin DeFleur (1993) commended Brown University for its fund-raising efforts to address the shortage. He described:

> Brown University announced in September 1992 a funding drive that will include 65 endowed assistant professorships. Each will be financed with an endowment of $1 million to cover the person's salary, graduate assistants, travel needs and research costs. This should enable that institution to compete strongly for the very best talent available. (p. 23)

I applaud DeFleur's selection as an excellent example of how fund raising can identify and help resolve organizational problems with far-reaching and significant consequences. I regret, however, that he passes on misinformation about endowment financing. He, like others, assumes that 100% of the earnings are available each year for spending. As with the Yale junior faculty positions, spendable income from a $1-million endowed fund would only be about $50,000. Such an amount would hardly cover salaries, benefits, and support expenses, let alone graduate assistants' salaries, funds for travel, and research costs. For most disciplines, the $50,000 would be used entirely for the assistant professor's salary and benefits. Even more misleading are $1-million chairs, such as those mentioned in the last chapter, that are offered by public universities and partially funded by state challenge grants. In almost all cases, they represent supplemental, not primary, funding for the position.

Misinformation creates confusion and frustration among donors, employees, and other stakeholders. Taken to an extreme, ignoring organizational costs related to endowed gifts may result in the purpose of a gift not being carried out as promised or in the organization excessively subsidizing expenses with income from other sources. "Pricing" of all endowed purposes—not just personnel positions—must be formulated, agreed on by the dominant coalition, and stated in official policy. In the absence of policies, gifts are negotiated under different terms on a case-by-case basis, leaving the organization vulnerable to one of the two situations just given.

Through a comparison of two benchmark studies sponsored by CASE, Winship (1984) and Altizer (1992), Shoemaker (1992) provided evidence that progress has been made in this aspect of fund-raising practice, but more improvement is needed. In the 1980s, only 25% of the colleges and universities studied required a gift of $1 million to endow a full professorship (i.e., a chair), whereas 50% required at least that amount in the 1990s.[3] Donors' cost to endow a professorship still varied dramatically among organizations, ranging from $100,000 to $2 million. In the 1980s, 57% were willing to negotiate the minimum gift amount, but only 43% were willing to do so in the next decade. In the 1980s, only one third required full funding before filling the endowed professorship; the percentage increased to 53% in the 1990s.

Clarifying this point, institutions have in the past and continue to appoint professors to positions that are only partially funded, thereby assuming the majority of expenses until pledge payments are complete. A more prudent practice is to wait until the entire gift is received, or to ask the donor to increase his or her payments to cover the annual expenses during the pledge period. Furthermore, endowed gifts for all purposes require a *1-year delay* before implementation because a full year is needed for the fund to generate spendable income. This simple investment principle is often overlooked.

Moving beyond professorships, the two CASE studies found a variety of purposes for endowed gifts, including visiting faculty, junior faculty, librarian, dean of a chapel, artist in residence, book funds, department enhancement, athletic department support, alumni center maintenance, student scholarships, loans, prizes, and even projects to endow a student. E. Ryan (1992) reported one of the more unusual purposes: endowing the football team at USC, the Trojans. In 1992, 32 of 85 team positions, including the quarterback,

---

[3]Although full professorships and chairs were used interchangeably in the two studies, professorships usually are defined as a separate category one level below chairs and priced accordingly.

were endowed through gifts of $250,000. Each fund reportedly generated $23,000 for player scholarships, representing a spendable income rate of 9.2%—almost double that recommended. Started in 1985, the USC Athletic Endowment Program reflected innovation but also a disregard for IRS rulings on *quid pro quo*. Ryan described: "For $250,000, a die-hard alumnus could call that position his own—along with a tax break, a free lifetime membership in the Scholarship Club of Donors, and fancy seats on the 50-yard line at every game. It was a crazy idea—and it worked" (p. 41). The fund raiser responsible for the program described it as "a great gimmick" (p. 41).

The operating budgets of all types of charitable organizations contain line items that may be appropriate for endowment, although those dealing with people generally have a higher value for both managers and donors. Most organizations are labor intensive; therefore, endowed funds for personnel can have a significant impact on reoccurring expenses. Donors find supporting people an attractive gift opportunity because designated recipients carry the given name in perpetuity, thereby providing a *living tribute* to the name and the gift's intention. This is particularly true for personnel positions that are central to the organization's mission, such as the conductor of a symphony orchestra, the chief of staff at a hospital, or the head curator at a museum.

Linking gifts for financial capital to those for physical capital, some organizations have instituted policies requiring a matching endowment for gifts that name buildings. Illustrating, a new administration building that costs $2 million might require a total gift of $3 million to provide income for the building's long-term maintenance. The strategy relieves the operating budget of additional expense and helps ensure that the name given by the donor does not disappear in a few years. According to Shoemaker (1992), 30% of the institutions studied in the 1990s included endowment for long-term maintenance in the amount a donor must give to name a building. Fund raisers representing the majority indicated that negotiations for maintenance endowment goes on behind the scenes *after* the building gift has been made. As with endowments, donors' costs for naming buildings, other physical facilities, and equipment vary dramatically among organizations, with some requiring 100% financing for construction, renovation, or purchase, and others asking for 25% or less.

Shoemaker (1992) reported that only 60% of the institutions in the 1990s study had a specific policy on named gift opportunities. She observed, "In the comments to a question about how negotiable that policy was, the words 'flexible,' 'at the discretion of,' and 'we're usually willing to work with the donor or family' crop up more often than, for example, 'not usually negotiable'" (p. 37). Negotiation obviously is an important aspect of the major gifts program. Before discussing that topic, two remaining elements concerning endowments must be presented.

Fund raisers commonly rely on a *Memorandum of Understanding* (MOU) to state the terms of an endowed gift and to guide its administration in perpetuity. The document is drafted by practitioners, revised during negotiations, and signed by the donor(s) and the highest officials of the organization, usually the CEO and the chair of the board of trustees. Richard Struck (1993), director of resource development for Methodist Hospital Foundation in Minnesota, advised, "It's absolutely necessary to discuss and document gift arrangements, including pledges, as a significant and key step to encourage ultimate donor satisfaction and follow through" (p. 37). The MOU,

Struck said, is based on the journalism maxim, "If it isn't written out, it isn't thought out" (p. 39).

Key provisions of the MOU in suggested order are:

1. Name of the fund.
2. Purpose.
3. Designation: If applicable, a specific unit of the organization.
4. Funding: Description of the gift, including whether it is outright or planned, its form, amount, and pledge payments.
5. Operation: Financial terms, including a statement on investment policy, preservation of principal, spendable income, 1-year delay of implementation, and any special considerations.
6. Reporting: Promised communication about fund disbursements and impact on program services.
7. Recognition: Consent to use names publicly and any special forms of reciprocity (e.g., naming a building in recognition of a fund for program service support).
8. Additional gifts: Statement that additional gifts can be made to the fund at any time.
9. Future use: Also known as an exit clause, allows organization to access the fund if restricted purposes are no longer viable.
10. Signatures/Dates.

Clarifying the provision about future use, it is possible that the purposes for which an endowed gift is made will not be relevant to the organization's mission in future years. Stories abound about antiquated endowments, such as providing potatoes to young women attending college. To avoid legal complications, MOUs must be futuristic and acknowledge possible changes in conditions. Struck (1993) presented the following wording for the provision:

> If, in the future, the ABC Hospital no longer offers the *specified* services supported by our gift, then this fund may be used as an endowment to support a patient care program as closely identified with the foregoing or wherever the need is greatest, as determined by the Foundation's Board of Directors. In either case, such a decision will be considered carefully by both the ABC Hospital and the ABC Hospital Foundation staffs with notice to available Doe family members prior to any final action. (p. 38; italics in original)

Signing the MOU marks the beginning of the stewardship step. Although signatures can be handled by mail, Struck recommended a small, dignified special event to commemorate the occasion—bringing together top officials and the donor(s) who have made a commitment to the organization's future. A signed copy of the MOU is given to the donor and copies are filed in appropriate departments of the organization, including fund raising and the department responsible for endowment management. Struck (1993) concluded, "The time, patience and effort committed to ensure understanding also ensures that we don't rush our donors, that we demonstrate the value of their emotional needs and gift objectives, and will help them reach their goals" (p. 39).

According to Rick Nahm (cited in Shoemaker, 1992), then senior vice president for institutional planning and development at the University of Pennsylvania, good stewardship is essential to raising endowed gifts, but current practice falls short of the mark. He argued that stewardship should include not only reporting to donors on how the intent of their gift is being followed, "but also telling them how you're investing their funds" (p. 38). Because investments can do poorly and spendable income by definition is conservative, it is important to explain investment policy up front and keep donors informed about returns, both good and bad, at least once a year.

NEGOTIATION

A major mistake in Yale's handling of the Bass gift was its failure to renegotiate terms with the donor in private. Once problems about the gift became public knowledge in Fall 1994, the probability of resolving them through renegotiation greatly decreased. Experts agree that to reach successful outcomes, negotiation must take place in private and stay private (e.g., Gottlieb & Healy, 1990). A key concept is saving face, which is difficult to uphold when the two parties take or are thrust into public stances. Alignments and adjustments that might have been possible in private become unacceptable in the glare of public scrutiny (i.e., any positional changes might be perceived as "backing down").

Bass' demand for approval of faculty appointments, an infringement on autonomy and academic freedom, constituted an insurmountable barrier to resolution—which he likely knew when presenting the new terms. The best possible settlement, then, was to agree to disagree and return the $20 million, with the hope that the relationship would be preserved. It would have been far more damaging for Yale to have won the renegotiations, but lost the relationship with Bass. Time will tell if the action was successful.[4]

What happened in the original negotiations is impossible to determine, although earlier discussions suggest that Yale representatives did not heed principles of effective negotiation or of fund raising. It may be that actors without authority, such as interested faculty members, had a hand in formulating the terms, which were rubber-stamped by an administration eager to acquire money. Regardless, anyone who was knowledgeable about the organization, either through experience or research, should have evaluated the gift's usefulness and been alert to its political ramifications. As Brittingham and Pezzullo (1990) emphasized, "Restrictions are viewed as acceptable to the extent that they match the institution's existing priorities and values or at least do not conflict with them" (p. 71). In short, the problems with the Bass gift did not occur in 1994, but in 1991 when the gift was negotiated and accepted.

M. R. Hall (1992) illustrated how such problems can transpire and can be resolved through negotiation. Drawing from her interviews on decentralization at universities, she related a situation in which a donor wanted to establish a degree program in free enterprise at a business school. The school's dean and component fund raiser decided such a program would be academically unacceptable, but that the donor's intent might

---

[4]In May 1996, Robert Bass and his wife Anne gave $20 million to Yale for renovation of its residential colleges ("Scripps," 1996). The gift, university officials noted, was not intended to make up for the $20 million returned to Lee the year before.

be accomplished with other gift options. As a result of negotiation, the donor endowed a nondegree program in entrepreneurship, which focused on the study of small business management. The dean reported that his impression from conversations with central fund raisers was that they saw little difference between the two gift purposes and probably would have encouraged the donor's interest in free enterprise. The school then would have faced a choice of initiating a degree program against its judgment, using the gift for purposes other than intended, or returning the gift.

M. R. Hall (1993) also identified situations when gifts accepted by central fund raisers were financially inadequate to fully implement the gifts' purposes, which resulted in shifting resources from higher priority projects. She quoted a dean describing such a gift: "It is driving other expenditures, which is causing severe dislocations in our operating in the meantime. The expenditures are far in excess of the gift" (p. 78).

Negotiation is an inherent part of soliciting major gifts. Brittingham and Pezzullo (1990) explained, "The relationship between donor and institution may be seen as a gift relationship for public and ceremonial purposes, but it also has elements of a contractual or business-type relationship, particularly in private negotiations before the actual donation" (p. 62). They added, "While support from foundations and corporations often overtly acknowledges the contractual or purchase aspects of the funds, support from individuals may also take on overtones of contracts and purchases" (p. 62). Furthermore, as Mixer (1993) pointed out, "The willingness of the organization to negotiate and adjust its needs to the interests of prospects makes positive giving decisions more likely" (p. 121).

Despite its importance, negotiation receives little attention in the fund-raising literature. It is briefly endorsed, most notably in relation to planned giving, but principles and skills seldom are discussed. With occasional exceptions, negotiation is not taught in seminars or professional development workshops offered by such organizations as NSFRE, CASE, or The Fund Raising School. This void in practitioner knowledge is detrimental to the function and the organizations it serves.

Based on the work of business educators Marvin Gottlieb and William Healy (1990), fund raisers are effective as negotiators when guided by three principles: (a) See the negotiation process as a *conference* rather than a contest or confrontation, (b) operate with the objective of *reaching agreement* rather than triumph, and (c) approach negotiation from the perspective of *common concern* rather than selfish demand. The following describes the five stages of negotiation:

1. *Identify and plan.* Appropriate situations are targeted, and research is conducted to gather all information that could bear on the negotiation.
2. *Establish contact.* Parties meet; positions and issues are questioned, probed, and examined. Ranges are estimated on the most critical issues.
3. *Present proposal.* Based on the needs, limits, personalities, and other variables uncovered during the contact stage, a proposal is presented for consideration.
4. *Resolve conflict.* Differences are examined, and alternative solutions are considered and weighed against the substantive needs and the desire to build and maintain a working relationship.

5. *Confirm and act.* On reaching a satisfactory resolution of differences, both parties confirm their understanding of all the terms of the agreement—first orally, then in writing (e.g., an MOU). This should be facilitated quickly before memories fade or other issues enter the situation.

The five stages closely resemble practitioner advice on soliciting major gifts, although—until now—the advice has not been linked to the process of negotiation. The omission may be an artifact of earlier eras before the mixed-motive model of philanthropy was advanced. In other words, giving defined as pure altruism would not require negotiation, but current theories that account for the self-interest of donors legitimize negotiation as an essential aspect of soliciting major gifts. The omission is exacerbated by a misunderstanding of negotiation.

In a rare essay directed at fund raisers, attorney Gerard Mantese (1994) touched on the misunderstanding, saying negotiators are visualized as either tough and abrasive (which would be inappropriate to fund raising), or as a nice person and a pushover (which would be detrimental to organizational interests). There is a third view—largely unacknowledged by fund raisers—that dominates the literature on negotiation and negotiators: "They can be decent and polite, but firm" (p. 49).

Actually, scholars have identified four *communication styles* negotiators can assume: collaboration, accommodation, avoidance, and competition (e.g., Gottlieb & Healy, 1990; Hocker & Wilmot, 1995). Mantese (1994) referred to the theoretical grounding: "Negotiation is a basic mode of communication. It can cement a relationship or sever it" (p. 49). In reverse order, *competitors* desire to meet their party's needs and concerns at the expense of the other party. Resolution is win–lose (Gottlieb & Healy, 1990). *Avoiders* make no attempt to address any conflicts; they are both uncooperative and unassertive. Resolution is lose–lose. *Accommodators* are cooperative, but unassertive; they place the needs and concerns of the other party above their own. Resolution is win–lose. *Collaborators* make maximum use of both cooperation and assertiveness; their aim is to satisfy the needs of both parties. Resolution is win–win. According to Gottlieb and Healy, reaching a mutually satisfactory agreement is the best long-term outcome of any negotiation, and collaboration is the most effective of the four styles in achieving the objective. Collaboration, they explained, is a problem-solving approach "that allows the parties involved in a negotiation to satisfy their substantive interests in a mutually satisfactory way, while building or maintaining a good working relationship" (p. 13).

The collaboration style corresponds to the two-way symmetrical model of fund raising and the problem-solving process facilitator role of staff managers. Among characteristics listed by Gottlieb and Healy (1990), collaborators are receptive/effective listeners, mission/team focused, and plans/discussion balanced. They rely on creative problem solving and two-way communication. The scholars stated, "The collaborator is driven by finding a solution that is pragmatic and addresses both the substantive or factual issues at hand as well as building relationships for long-term pay back" (p. 75). Linking negotiation styles to public relations, J. E. Grunig and L. A. Grunig (1992) concluded, "The collaborative model could be another name for the two-way symmetrical model" (p. 315).

Students may recognize that *compromise*, the style of negotiation with which they probably are most familiar, has so far been missing from the discussion. Gottlieb and Healy (1990) explained the style's familiarity: "In the United States we are taught throughout school that the democratic process is built on compromise, and we come to accept it as the preferred mode of settling disputes" (p. 40). Yet, they argued, "The concept of compromise actually gets in the way of good problem-solving negotiation" (p. 14). Recent research has revealed that compromise often plants seeds for future discontent. Each party has given up something it wanted (i.e., settled for less), and often needs have not been met. "In fact," Gottlieb and Healy said, "compromise might be looked at as a settlement in which both parties sooner or later realize that they had neither their substantive or relationship needs satisfied—what we call a 'lose–lose'" (p. 16). Fund raisers are advised to set aside predispositions toward seeking compromise and employ collaboration, which produces better and more acceptable outcomes for both parties.

Another fallacy about negotiation concerns power. Many people wrongly assume that the party holding the purse strings, such as the prospective donor, has greater power than the other party. Although power is related to money, a more important determinant in negotiation is the degree of dependency on the outcome. Gottlieb and Healy (1990) simply stated, "The power rests with the side that can most easily walk away from the deal" (p. 28). Fund raisers who are evaluated by dollar amounts are at a disadvantage when negotiating with major donor prospects. They are overly dependent on the outcome of the negotiations, sometimes to the extent that getting the gift overrides any concessions they have to make. Yet organizations prefer that fund raisers be tough rather than soft when making concessions. Addressing college and university advancement officers, Benjamin (1989) presented a professor's viewpoint: "It will sometimes be compelling or advantageous to trade a little of our educational capital to business, the community, or the legislature. But when you must make such a trade, be tough about it. Be as tough as the other side is" (p. 11).

Organizations provide fund raisers with the power they need to negotiate good outcomes when evaluation is based on contribution to organizational effectiveness, not dollar goals. Fund raisers enhance their power by understanding systems theory and the interdependency between the organization and its donors (i.e., prospects also are dependent on negotiation outcomes to fulfill their own needs). Practitioners realize that they have gotten to the point of negotiation because the prospect has interests in the potential gift. As Gottlieb and Healy (1990) asked, "Why would they be talking to you if they didn't see some potential benefit to them?" (p. 37). Fund raisers who are effective negotiators focus on their professionalism and the strengths of their organization, thereby increasing their power base. Gavin Kennedy (1983), a commercial negotiator, stated, "There is nothing so awe-inspiring as a richly deserved reputation for being good at your business" (p. 166). Fund raisers are not intimidated by what Kennedy called "props," or symbols of wealth and authority. Finally, fund raisers gain power when they are well prepared. Gottlieb and Healy (1990) explained, "There is great power in having done thorough preparation; knowing where you are going and truly knowing the needs of the other party" (p. 37).

As part of preparation, fund raisers are advised to identify negotiable variables and nonnegotiable constants in collaboration with line managers and members of the dominant coalition. This allows them to determine in advance what concessions are agreeable to the organization. For example, the timing of the gift may be a negotiable variable, whereas the site of the gift's purpose may be a nonnegotiable constant. The variables are then used during negotiation to change the shape of the gift proposal, or what Kennedy (1983) called "the package." He claimed that the first challenge was always about pricing, and advised, "Don't change the price, change the package" (p. 224). For example, if a prospect objects to the amount of $2 million to endow a chair, fund raisers could present options about combining an outright gift with a planned gift, or endowing a lower level personnel position. Exploring options helps establish an atmosphere of trust and a creative problem-solving climate, while minimizing defensiveness (Gottlieb & Healy, 1990). Options are generated by asking *what if* and *if–then* questions. The most useful word in negotiation is *if*.

Fund raisers look for opportunities to build on areas of agreement, and are willing to spend time investigating the prospect's rationale and needs. They use reflective statements, paraphrasing, and empathizing to demonstrate and confirm their understanding of the prospect's position. According to Gottlieb and Healy (1990), "The more options there are on the table with perceived value for both parties, the easier the process of trading off becomes" (p. 39). Trading off consists of weighing, evaluating, and deciding which of all possible options will work most effectively for the organization and the donor. Gottlieb and Healy advised, "Be open-minded and accept reasonable, creative alternatives to the positions you came into the negotiation holding" (p. 102). The scholars cautioned, however, "Remember that being collaborative doesn't necessarily mean being 'Mr. Nice Guy' [*sic*] all the time" (p. 185). Meaningful negotiation involves conflicts, and fund raisers who do not assertively protect and advance their organization's interests end up failing their organization. Kennedy (1983) presented the rule, "In conceding, be more like Scrooge than St. Francis" (p. 222). He added, "Never concede anything without getting something back in exchange" (p. 223).

Negotiation should include *bridging*, or building an ongoing relationship with the donor. Assurances of stewardship are a first step. Gottlieb and Healy (1990) explained, "Bridges are built with promises of follow-up, and the fulfillment of those promises" (p. 40). Reminiscent of Yale's controversy, they warned that bridges fall into disrepair when negotiators promise what cannot be delivered or the organization fails to deliver what was promised.

The greatest failure in negotiation, however, is failing to negotiate. Gottlieb and Healy (1990) offered the following advice, which I recommend to future fund-raising practitioners: "Look for opportunities to apply collaborative negotiation rather than passively accepting someone's offer, withdrawing, or immediately looking for a compromise position" (p. 181). By definition, negotiation involves two parties in a *voluntary* consent to a *joint* decision; both have a veto (Kennedy, 1983).

PROCESS

The process of raising major gifts is the same regardless of the definitional amount. Practitioners continually ask themselves: From whom are our top gifts going to come, and how are we working with those prospects today? Allocating time and effort for qualified prospects ensures that strong, genuine relationships develop.

Students will recall from the study testing the fund-raising models that practitioners tend to move away from press agentry toward the two-way symmetrical model when raising major gifts (Kelly, 1995b). Accelerating this move is a growing acceptance by practitioners that the major gifts program is more about relationships than it is about generating money—an approach extended in this book to all of fund raising. Luck and Evans (1993) stated:

> Everyone is searching for a "magic" formula to successfully entice prospective contributors. In reality, the "magic" is quite simple—major gift solicitation is based on the basic foundation of building solid relationships. To truly succeed, you must fully embrace a *philosophy* that focuses on cultivating and nurturing relationships. (p. 12; italics added)

Nudd (1991) agreed, "Only if development professionals feel deep inside that the relationship with the donor is more important than the gifts requested can they truly be effective" (p. 186).

Personal Attention

Describing an identification process closely emulating stakeholder analysis, Heetland (1993) argued that the place to begin when looking for major donor prospects is a review of "categories of friends" (p. 10), such as past donors, employees, volunteers, and clients. Once potential prospects are qualified through research, he recommended that fund raisers compile a list of the top 100 prospects, prioritized by capacity to give. The top-100 list, which is regularly reviewed and maintained, helps keep practitioners focused on the cultivation of those donors who will give the majority of money. Heetland asserted, "The single most important function in a successful development program is the cultivation of major donors" (p. 11).

Heetland's advice is helpful, particularly for fund raisers in small departments who have responsibilities for both primary programs. All too often, major donor cultivation is pushed aside by the more immediate demands of annual giving programming. Representing the other end of the spectrum, the University of Pennsylvania has 57 fund raisers working solely on the major gifts program (Myers, 1993). Each officer is assigned 150 qualified prospects for gifts of $25,000 or more, representing a total prospect pool of around 8,500. Not only does Penn conduct traditional prospect research on such variables as capacity to give, but it also relies on findings from an alumni census and a survey of rated prospects that measure the extent to which the university is a high priority among potential donors. The 150 prospects assigned to each officer include 50 who are estimated to be ready for solicitation within 12 months; the other 100 are expected to give in future years.

Based on a moves management system, Penn's fund-raising department developed three overall objectives to guide interactions with prospects and evaluation of practitioners' work. First, each officer must make 200 meaningful moves per year. He or she plans 5 to 6 moves per week for approximately 40 weeks, which allows for vacations, holidays, training sessions, and other downtime. Second, the moves should consist of 50% cultivation, 30% solicitation, and 20% stewardship. Both the number and composition of the moves are tracked through call reports and a computer system.

Third, each officer must close 25 major gifts per year for a total of at least $625,000 (25 x $25,000). Myers (1993) summarized: "Throughout the year, major gift officers continually make moves, update a portfolio of active prospects, identify new ones, and close major gifts. Staff members understand that each task is equally important in the cycle of contacts and gift income" (p. 18). The Penn program offers a standard that can be adapted to departments of all sizes.

Cultivation activities also vary from the simple to the highly complex. Illustrating the latter, the University of Notre Dame implemented a "fly-in" program in the 1970s to cultivate major donor prospects in preparation for a capital campaign. Described by R. L. Williams (1993), the program consisted of 20 weekends over 15 months, during which the public relations staff brought about six couples at a time to the campus. The university sent private planes to pick them up, and they were personal guests of then President Theodore Hesburgh from Friday evening to Sunday morning. Weekends included a get-acquainted dinner with the president, presentations about the university and the upcoming campaign, an overview of academic programs, site visits to special points of interest, a private mass celebrated by Father Hesburgh, and an intimate dinner atop the university library. According to Williams, "Before leaving, the guests were told a university representative would soon call on them to discuss their campaign commitment" (p. 290). The 125 couples who participated subsequently pledged an average gift of $600,000 each, which accounted for $75 million of the campaign's goal.

Few organizations have the resources to duplicate such an effort; however, spending money to cultivate prospects for major gifts is a necessary and worthwhile investment. Too many organizations fail to budget sufficient funding for cultivation, which results in fund raisers spending too much time in their offices. Hosting prospective donors on site generally is the most effective form of cultivation, but usually the organization must first go to the prospect, whether the distance is 10 or 3,000 miles. Travel is critical to raising major gifts, and the more practitioners and other organizational representatives are "on the road" talking with prospects, the more likely they are building relationships that, in turn, reap dividends of gifts and repeated gifts.

Luck and Evans (1993) advised: "Befriend your prospective donors. Build a solid relationship between them and your organization, and they won't let you down" (p. 12). Emphasizing stewardship, Heetland (1993) quoted one fund raiser on what she called her key to success, "I get prospects to make the first gift and then I keep thanking them until they give again" (p. 12). Lindahl (1994), drawing from his empirical research, simply stated, "Stewardship is the name of the game" (p. 47).

In-Person Solicitation

The technique associated most closely with soliciting major gifts is face-to-face conversation. The technique actually is used in combination with others such as the personal letter and follow-up phone call, which are first employed to obtain an appointment for a meeting. The meeting usually involves the fund raiser and one to three other organizational representatives, referred to here as the team. Broce (1986) outlined a scenario of an in-person solicitation that closely aligns with my experience as a fund raiser, although I have added to his description and used a female practitioner to present the technique.

An appointment with the prospect is requested and confirmed in advance. The request for the appointment, most often in the form of a personal letter, clearly states the purpose of the meeting. The fund raiser is responsible for writing the letter, which is signed by the person she deems most appropriate to ask for the meeting. For example, if the chair of the board of trustees knows the prospect and plans to attend the meeting, the letter is written for his or her signature. Such letters often come from CEOs because they, more than any other person, speak for the organization. Regardless of who signs the letter, the fund raiser makes the follow-up telephone call to obtain the prospect's response to the request and drafts the confirmation letter, which is signed by the person originally requesting the meeting. If the appointment is denied, the fund raiser drafts a responding letter that leaves the door open for future communication.

The fund raiser prepares the team for the meeting by writing and distributing pertinent research findings and a personalized draft proposal, which provides details of the requested gift (e.g., the shared interest prompting the solicitation and a proposed budget). The fund raiser follows up to answer any questions or to make changes in the proposal, which will be presented at the meeting. She arranges to meet with the team shortly before the meeting to review the role of each—often a rough *script* of the meeting is drafted and sent to participants in advance. Meetings generally are held in offices because they are formal and professional; however, they are held in the prospect's home when he or she does not have an office or when the gift is requested from more than one family member. The meetings should not take place in a social setting, such as in a restaurant over a meal.

After 1 or 2 minutes of casual preliminaries, the person who signed the letter requesting the meeting opens the conversation by saying that he or she appreciates this time to talk about a significant gift to the organization. Broce (1986) explained, "This statement makes everyone more comfortable, gets everything in the open, relaxes the prospect, and permits the topic to come to the surface, no matter how much unrelated talk may follow" (p. 228). It must be repeated that the meeting's purpose is not surprising to the prospect because it was clearly stated when the appointment was requested. In other words, by agreeing to the meeting, the prospect already has communicated his or her willingness to talk about a gift.

The CEO or another team member with expertise presents the case and explains how the proposed gift will help meet an identified goal. He or she asks for the gift, naming a specific amount. As Steele and Elder (1992) recommended, the verb *consider* is commonly used (e. g., "Would you consider a gift of $50,000 to help us carry out this plan?"). The verb places appropriate emphasis on the prospect's right to make or not make the gift (i.e., his or her individual autonomy) and acknowledges the seriousness of the decision—it is not one that can or should be made spontaneously. The prepared proposal, clearly marked as a draft, is given to the prospect. At that point, it is the donor's turn to react and for the team to listen carefully. Details of the gift are discussed and negotiated using the proposal as a guide. For example, the suggested time period for pledge payments may be adjusted to accommodate the donor's needs. Other changes are noted by the fund raiser on her copy of the proposal (others attending the meeting also have copies to which to refer).

The fund raiser summarizes the agreed upon changes, making it clear to the donor that she, the practitioner, is responsible for incorporating them in the final proposal. In this way, she ensures that open lines of communication are available for further discussion if needed during revision. As Broce (1986) stated, "It is important to be sure that the prospect has the staff member's name and telephone number" (pp. 228–229).

The donor usually gives some indication of how the request has been received; however, the size of the gift requested and the presentation of the draft proposal, usually consisting of about 10 pages, demands that the donor be given time for thoughtful consideration of the request. In short, final closure is not sought. Instead, the fund raiser agrees to incorporate any changes that came out of the meeting and to send a revised proposal within the next 5 working days. The CEO, or another team member, asks the prospect when it would be convenient to talk again about the revised proposal and the prospect's decision. By agreeing to a follow-up contact, the prospect indicates his or her willingness to continue the negotiations.

The fund raiser is responsible for seeing that the meeting is brought to a timely close, usually at the end of 1 hour. Each member of the solicitation team thanks the prospect for his or her time and consideration of the important request. Immediately following the meeting, the team members spend about 30 minutes debriefing, during which they compare what each other heard and thought. A cup of coffee at a corner cafeteria with a tape recorder on the table produces valuable information and perceptions that otherwise might be lost.

Back at the office, the fund raiser writes the letter thanking the prospect for the meeting, which is signed and sent within 2 days by the person who signed the original letter. The proposal is revised and sent to the prospect within the promised time, with copies sent to those who attended the meeting. The fund raiser reminds the CEO or other team member to make the follow-up telephone call at the time the prospect indicated would be convenient. The call may lead to a second meeting or bring closure to the solicitation. The fund raiser confirms the outcome in a letter either thanking the donor for the gift or suggesting dates and times for another meeting.

Once the gift is promised, stewardship begins. An essential first activity is that each person who participated in the solicitation expresses his or her own appreciation to the donor. A letter from the fund raiser is particularly important because she must intensify her professional relationship with the donor to effectively manage the stewardship step.

SEXUAL HARASSMENT

Fund-raising managers are not behind-the-scenes technicians. To help their organizations manage relationships with donor publics, they forge their own professional relationships, some of which develop into friendships. The friendships, however, are *professional*, not personal. The distinction is critical for two reasons: (a) It acknowledges the practitioner's organizational role as the basis for the friendship and (b) guards against inappropriate behavior on both sides. Explaining the first reason, Broce (1986) stated, "The development officer must remember that the relationship should exist between the prospect and the institution. Personal friendships can and should develop during the course of a program. But the development officer must not place himself [sic] in the forefront at the expense of the institutional relationship" (p. 219). Schafer (cited in E. Ryan, 1993) addressed the second reason: "Many people are apt to misconstrue business relationships as personal ones. Professionals typically guard against these misunderstandings by confining their gestures of friendliness within careful limits" (p. 62).

A problem only starting to receive attention is sexual harassment of fund raisers by major donors and prospects for major gifts, collectively referred to in this discussion as donors. After first qualifying that the problem is "hardly rampant," Sabo (1994b) reported: "Still, it happens. Male donors come on to female development officers and, less frequently, female donors make moves on male officers. One fund raiser reports several incidents of young men on the staff being harassed by older male donors" (p. 15).

The pervasiveness of the problem actually is unknown. Evidence collected to date is strictly anecdotal. There have been no scientific studies on sexual harassment by donors, which highlights this area as an excellent one for master's theses. In a preliminary study on the problem, one of my graduate students conducted in-depth interviews by telephone with three female practitioners, each of whom had 15 or more years of experience and worked in a different part of the country (Constantine, 1994). She found that all three subjects had been victims of sexual harassment during their career. One related how she had been inappropriately approached by donors and board members; another told of donors who were overly friendly and who wanted dates rather than meetings; and the third talked about a former CEO who would grab her in the presence of donors. Quantitative studies are needed to determine the extent of the problem.

In the absence of research, fund raising appears to be an occupation conducive to sexual harassment. The majority of fund raisers are women, and men still constitute the largest portion of major donors, including representatives of corporations and foundations. The major gifts program is dependent on building long-term relationships through interpersonal communication, which involves face-to-face situations. The process, particularly cultivation, usually includes meals, entertainment, and even meeting donors in private homes—situations that can be misconstrued as social activities or even dates. In addition, events often feature alcohol, which can undermine professional behavior. McNamee (1993) summarized, "The relationships that result in major gifts are the result of long, painstaking cultivation of prospects who by the end of the process feel a deep and abiding tie to the recipient institution, its people, and its purposes" (p. 21).

It must be emphasized that both sexes are victims of harassment. For example, a number of male fund raisers have told me how older female donors sometimes treat them as on-call escorts, expecting excessive personal attention in the face of promises and threats related to their gifts (e.g., changing a will). Regardless, men are far more often the harassers, and women, particularly those who are young and single, are far more often the targets of sexual harassment (Tata, 1993). The discussion, then, concentrates on male donors and female fund raisers.

This is not to say sexual harassment is a "women's problem." It cuts to the core of effective fund raising, influencing the very nature of donor relationships. It potentially can interfere with work performance and impair productivity. Above all, it is illegal.

Employers are held responsible when they knew, or *should* have known, that harassment occurred but did nothing to stop it (Sabo, 1994b). Liability extends to the acts of nonemployees as well as employees. In short, sexual harassment is an organizational problem, and donors' conduct must be addressed. A brief background on the general problem provides the necessary perspective.

Sexual harassment is not a new phenomenon, but the term has only recently been used to label behavior that is *unwelcomed and offensive* and primarily directed at women (J. T. Wood, 1992). Many people had never heard the term until it was added to the national lexicon by law professor Anita Hill's charges against U.S. Supreme Court nominee Clarence Thomas in 1991. According to Wood, the earlier absence of a name negated the behavior, made it invisible, and denied that it existed or mattered. Because naming defines reality, those who were sexually harassed had no legitimate way to label what occurred, much less to enlist others' help with the "problem that had no name" (p. 352). Targets were defined as complainers and prudes without a sense of humor. Harassers were defined as men who were merely forward or pushy. Their acts were described in inappropriate terms of dating and romance, such as *overtures*, *advances*, or *passes*. Harassment was just something that happened, which implicitly condoned the behavior and advised victims to tolerate it. Sexual harassment now has a name. It has terms to help describe it, including *target* and *harasser*. It is recognizable, and it is illegal.

The U.S. Equal Employment Opportunity Commission (EEOC) defines sexual harassment as:

> Unwelcome sexual advances, requests for sexual favors, and other verbal or physical conduct of a sexual nature . . . when submission to or rejection of this conduct explicitly or implicitly affects an individual's employment, unreasonably interferes with an individual's work performance, or creates an intimidating, hostile, or offensive working environment. (Sabo, 1994b, p. 11)

The definition covers the two types of harassment: (a) *quid pro quo*, when an individual is asked by a person in power to perform sex or do sexual favors in exchange for professional advancement; and (b) *harassing environment*, when verbal or physical conduct creates a working environment that is intimidating, hostile, or offensive (Bovet, 1993). Men and women generally agree on what behaviors are classified as *quid pro quo*, but they have conflicting ideas about what constitutes a harassing environment (Tata, 1993). Women perceive more situations as harassing, including unwelcomed requests for dates or other social engagements, unnecessary or inappropriate touching, and offensive use of obscene language, gestures, or humor. Single and divorced women report more harassment than married women, and younger women are harassed more than older women.

Although sexual harassment then had no name, its legal ramifications began with Title VII of the original Civil Rights Act of 1964, which made it unlawful to discriminate against a woman with respect to the conditions of her employment. In 1986, the Supreme Court ruled unanimously that harassment was indeed a form of gender discrimination prohibited by the 1964 law (Bovet, 1993). The Court further recognized harassing environment for the first time and declared that employees have a right to work free from discriminatory intimidation, ridicule, and insult.

Stringent penalties for sexual harassment were imposed for the first time when Congress passed the Civil Rights Act of 1991, the same year it also confirmed Justice

Thomas. Employers are subject to up to $300,000 in compensatory and punitive damages for each occurrence (Bovet, 1993). In 1993, the Supreme Court ruled on the problem for the second time, unanimously defining sexual harassment as "conduct making the workplace environment 'hostile or abusive' to a 'reasonable person'" (Kaplan, 1993, p. 34). Viewed as a landmark victory for working women, the decision knocked down a standard emerging from lower courts that the harassing behavior must be so severe that it seriously affects a female employee's psychological well-being. Furthermore, the Court's test was not whether harassment actually impaired a plaintiff's productivity, but whether the acts simply made it harder for one to perform a job.

In a rare article on sexual harassment by donors, a female fund raiser related an incident that happened early in her career when she was a vice president at a small college (Sabo, 1994b). A group of wealthy foreign businessmen had expressed interest in donating a building, and the woman spent several days hosting the group during a visit to the campus. One evening, the woman received a call at home from the college's male president, who said, "Before I tell you the question, I want you to know that the answer is no" (p. 11). The question relayed the businessmen's request for the woman to spend the night with them. The woman declined and—presumably with the president's approval—turned further interactions with the prospective donors over to the college's male academic dean. No gift was ever made.

The woman's point in telling the story was that sexual harassment by donors does exist; unfortunately, she and the article's author overlooked more serious points. The president, even though he supposedly preempted the decision, passed on a blatant request for sexual favors. He obviously did not inform the businessmen that their behavior was inappropriate. By relaying the request to an employee, he added the power of his office to their harassment. Finally, replacing a woman with a man is not an acceptable solution to harassment because it makes it more difficult for the woman to perform her job.

Male practitioner J. Terry Jones (cited in Sabo, 1994b), vice president at Pitzer College, was a copresenter of the first session on sexual harassment by donors at the 1991 CASE Annual Assembly. He told a story about a major donor at another university who asked Jones to seat a young and attractive female staff member next to him during a campaign kickoff dinner. Jones said he learned from such experiences to simply say, "That would be inappropriate" (p. 11). He continued, "I tell my staff members I would never knowingly put them in a situation of being harassed. We'd either find a different approach to the prospect or consider terminating the relationship. No gift is worth anybody's being harassed" (p. 15). Yet Jones, as do others, centered the discussion on "the *dilemma* of keeping a donor *happy* while not jeopardizing someone's safety" (p. 11; italics added).

A female practitioner at Harvard Law School presented the dilemma in terms implying that fund raising is a form of prostitution (Sabo, 1994b). "You're paid to develop relationships, paid to do *whatever it takes* to make donors and alumni *feel good* about the institution. That might place you in a position where you normally would say no and just walk away—but you must remember the institution as well" (p. 12; italics added). She did add, however, "People are not paid to accept uncomfortable situations" (p. 14).

The so-called dilemma between carrying out fund-raising responsibilities and sexual harassment represents a dangerous mindset, one that is particularly alarming for young female practitioners. Sabo (1994b) described how easily the mindset can be rationalized: "In a purely social environment, you might smack someone who brushes up against you or makes a suggestive comment about your sex appeal. When a gift is on the line, though, you might be tempted to ignore such behavior and assume it simply goes with the territory" (p. 12). Authors such as Sabo—a female free-lance writer for CASE—do not help matters when they describe fund raising using such sexual phrases as "wooing donors" (p. 11).

Experts agree that sexual harassment is not an act of sex; it is an act of power (Bovet, 1993). In most cases, there are power differences between the two actors involved, with the harasser having more power than the target. It is assumed, then, that a woman asking for money from a wealthy man, who is in the position to give it, creates a power dynamic that makes the situation ripe for sexual harassment. Although there is a correlation between the two, however, money and power are not the same. As with negotiation, power comes from being able to walk away from the gift. Again, those fund raisers who are evaluated by dollar totals are at a disadvantage and may be more willing to put up with harassment because their professional success depends on obtaining the money. In short, redefining how fund raising and its practitioners are evaluated would go a long way toward eradicating sexual harassment by donors.

The responsibility and burden for addressing the problem belong to the employer, specifically, the fund-raising department. To protect staff against sexual harassment and organizations against lawsuits, managers should take the following measures: Have a clear, written policy defining sexual harassment and prohibiting it by donors as well as others; establish a complaint procedure; inform staff what steps to take if they are harassed; assign a high-level officer to field and follow-up on complaints; conduct workplace training; and reinforce organizational commitment on a regular basis. As attorney Rita Risser (cited in Sabo, 1994b) stated, "The absence of a policy and of a complaint procedure allows employees to believe the institution will ignore, tolerate, or even condone harassment" (p. 15).

The policy should be articulated to the organization's constituencies, including donors. In-house workshops reduce employer liability and help practitioners defend themselves. Women are advised to be forthright, reacting to unwelcomed and offensive behavior with such statements as: You probably don't realize it, but that makes me uncomfortable. Some people advise the use of humor, but as Sabo (1994b) rightfully pointed out, "Witty comebacks do not spring naturally to everyone's lips, especially young fund raisers just beginning their careers" (p. 13). Role playing different scenarios in workshops provides young practitioners with the opportunity to think through responses to difficult situations before they happen.

Most basically, the problem should be openly discussed, or as the Harvard Law School fund raiser said, "Get the topic off the taboo list" (Sabo, 1994b, p. 14). The discussion must extend beyond the fund-raising department to include trustees, senior managers, line managers, and volunteer leaders.

Sabo's article contained a story by another female practitioner who told how she once had remained silent after a drunken trustee literally jumped her in a car one night. Afraid of alienating the harasser and *disappointing* her female president, she vowed to never be caught alone with the man again. "It didn't matter. A year later, in a room full of people, the same trustee got behind her in a buffet line and placed his hand on her rear" (p. 12). Before she could react, the chair of the board of trustees, who had witnessed the incident, yanked the harasser out of the room and read him the riot act. The woman stated, "That was an important experience because it made me realize I could talk to other people, that harassment wasn't just something women are supposed to handle and be strong about" (p. 12). Years later, she still described her ordeal as "extremely upsetting" (p. 12).

According to J. T. Wood (1992), sexual harassment evokes intense emotions, "from shame and feeling wrong or stupid, to feeling violated, to guilt about *allowing* it to occur, to entrapment with no viable alternatives, to resentment of others who implicitly or explicitly enabled harassment, to rage at being impotent to stop [it]" (p. 360; italics in original). Perhaps the most common and serious result is loss of self-esteem. Harassment emphasizes a woman's gender role over her abilities and professional duties. Whether in the form of dramatic incidents or seemingly inconsequential remarks, it says: "You are a woman and, therefore, both different and inferior."

I remember a board meeting I had spent weeks organizing, during which a member, who had to leave early, indicated that he wanted me to step out of the room with him. Thinking that he had some unfinished business, I was taken aback when he said he just wanted me to know how "sharp" I looked that day and that he had not been able to keep his eyes off me during the meeting. His comments reduced me from a competent manager to an object whose primary value was physical. When I rejoined the meeting, I felt isolated from the other board members and unworthy of participating in the discussions.

Most of the male donors I dealt with during my years as a fund raiser were gentlemen of the highest caliber. They treated me as a professional with courtesy and respect. Given their exemplary behavior, the donors would have been appalled at the number of times their gifts were attributed to my sexuality by male employees of my own organization. In other words, I was the target of more harassing remarks inside than outside, particularly from line managers and staff who viewed fund raising as something unsavory.

I remember walking across campus one day with a dean and his all-male department chairs on our way to a lunch in celebration of a $1-million gift I had helped raise for their school. I was feeling quite pleased with myself, when the dean winked at his colleagues and said that I must have been *really good* to have gotten the male donor to part with $1 million. The insinuation that I had traded sex for money prompted laughter from everyone else, but I felt like the wind had been knocked out of me. This type of "good-natured kidding" was rarely directed at male fund raisers, but women were different. The gifts we raised were suspect because of our gender.

Stories and anecdotes about sexual harassment in fund raising open the door to further conversations; however, without scientific studies our understanding will remain deficient. Until recently, the literature was silent on the problem, which is not surprising as most authors are men who probably never experienced harassment. Its significance can no longer be ignored, particularly as the majority of fund raisers today are women.

SUGGESTED READINGS

Altizer, A. W. (1992). *Seeking major gifts: How 57 institutions do it.* Washington, DC: Council for Advancement and Support of Education.

Brehmer, D. A. (Ed.). (1996). *Communicating effectively with major donors (New directions for philanthropic fundraising*, No. 10). San Francisco, CA: Jossey-Bass.

Matheny, R. (1994). *Major gifts: Solicitation strategies.* Washington, DC: Council for Advancement and Support of Education.

Miner, L. E., & Griffith, J. (1993). *Proposal planning and writing.* Phoenix, AZ: Oryx Press.

Muir, R., & May, J. (Eds.). (1993). *Developing an effective major gift program: From managing staff to soliciting gifts.* Washington, DC: Council for Advancement and Support of Education.

Nichols, J. E. (1994). *Pinpointing affluence: Increasing your share of major donor dollars.* Chicago: Precept Press.

13

Fund-Raising Programs: Planned Giving

Planned giving is the managed effort by charitable organizations to generate gifts of assets from individuals through the use of estate and financial *planning* vehicles. It is a fund-raising strategy, not a separate program. Its purpose is to raise major gifts by providing donors with an option in addition to outright giving. It expands the prospect pool by focusing on assets—rather than income—as a measurement of gift capacity. Planned giving concerns itself solely with individual donors, whereas other fund-raising efforts are directed at all three donor publics. It previously was called *deferred giving* because financial benefits for the recipient organization usually are postponed until years after the donor enacts a giving behavior (i.e., makes the gift), typically after he or she dies.

The only certain things in life are death and taxes, according to the oft-quoted adage. Another warns, "You can't take it with you." As trite as it sounds, and perhaps as callous as discussions about death may first seem to those who are young, such homespun principles help explain planned giving. People acquire assets during their lifetime. Although they may spend or give away some while alive, most of their assets are disposed of after death in the form of their estate. Death cannot be avoided nor assets kept. Stated another way, assets become discretionary within the context of dying.

Cash, securities, and property transferred during a lifetime or after death are subject to federal taxes under gift and estate tax laws. Our democratic society, which supports a capitalistic economy, imposes these taxes to curtail the unencumbered passing of wealth from one generation to another. In other words, society—through its representative government—demands a share of excess assets accumulated through the economy it supports. An exception is granted to assets contributed to charitable organizations: They are deductible from taxable estates, just as gifts are deductible from taxable income. On this basis of accumulated assets, death, and taxes, planned giving emerges as a logical and laudable means by which organizations designated as charitable acquire funds to advance their common goods.

Age and assets are positively related. Generally, young people do not have enough income or assets to give away—a statement unlikely to surprise students. Income increases as people grow older, freeing up some portion that can be perceived as discretionary (i.e., not needed to meet current basic needs). Individuals at this stage in their life convert some of their discretionary income into assets (e.g., buying a house). They also may elect to give some to 501(c)(3) organizations with which they share common interests. Or they may elect to buy a second car. Regardless, most do not perceive any portion of their assets—as opposed to income—as discretionary, preferring instead to keep all for potential and unknown future needs. When people are older still they face decreased income, but the assets they have accumulated throughout their lifetime have increased and often appreciated in value. Individuals at this stage may convert some of their discretionary assets into future income (e.g., retirement plans). They also may elect to give some to 501(c)(3) organizations. Or they may—once again—elect to buy another car. Staff managers understand this standard progression of personal economics and initiate the fund-raising process to accommodate those donors who wish to contribute gifts of assets through estate and financial planning vehicles.

Of particular importance, planned giving is a strategy by which charitable organizations can build their endowments, helping to secure their future. Planned gifts, unlike outright major gifts, often are unrestricted or restricted only to areas of operation, such as support for a particular program. Decisions about whether to spend or invest the gift income, therefore, rest with the organization's dominant coalition—although, as stressed in chapter 7, this privilege should not be abused. Because their financial benefit for the organization usually is deferred, planned gifts are not raised to meet immediate needs but for ongoing and future needs; therefore, restricted gifts for endowment also can be requested. The concept of making a gift that principally will benefit the organization in the future blends well with the concept of extending that future to perpetuity. The size of planned gifts usually meets or exceeds the minimum amount required for establishing an endowed fund. Rosso (1991) summarized, "Planned giving is an ideal fund raising [*sic*] method to attract gifts for endowment purposes" (p. 288).

The vehicles used in planned giving were last defined by the Deferred Giving Program created by Congress in the 1969 Tax Reform Act (Brain, 1991). They include the charitable bequest, charitable remainder trusts, the charitable gift annuity, pooled income fund, and charitable lead trust. Their degree of complexity varies from simple to highly complex. To facilitate understanding, they are grouped here in three categories: (a) charitable bequests, (b) life income agreements, and (c) other vehicles. Charitable bequests are gifts made through a will, which legally decrees how an individual's assets are to be dispersed after death. Life income agreements—as their name indicates—provide donors with income, usually until they die, from assets earlier transferred to a charitable organization that benefits from the remainder of the gift. Other vehicles, which do not fit in the first two categories, include the charitable lead trust, remainder interest in a home or farm, and life insurance.

Bequests are *revocable*, meaning donors can change their mind and "unmake" the gift because they retain ownership of the assets. Life income agreements are *irrevocable* because ownership is transferred. Vehicles in the third category are mixed: Most require irrevocable gifts, although some, such as life insurance, can be used to make a revocable gift.

Before describing the vehicles in more detail, issues surrounding this fund-raising strategy must be examined and clarified. Specifically, planned giving presents an unprecedented opportunity to generate income for charitable organizations, all practitioners and their organizations are capable of employing planned giving, and financial benefits returned to donors—often of high value—are sanctioned by our tax laws, which must be protected by rigorous adherence to the spirit as well as the letter of the law.

UNPRECEDENTED OPPORTUNITY

The largest transfer of wealth in the nation's history has begun: A staggering $10 trillion is expected to pass from one generation to the next during the coming 50 years (E. Greene et al., 1993). Cornell University economists Robert Avery and Michael Rendall (cited in E. Greene et al., 1993) predicted that total assets transferred from Americans aged 50 or older in 1993 will peak at $355 billion around the year 2017. The 20 years during which students likely will be active practitioners, 2000 to 2020, will witness the transfer of $5 trillion. These mind-boggling figures illustrate the opportunity for fund raising and the necessity of learning about planned giving (i.e., it is not optional). In press agentry terms, consultant André Donikian (cited in H. Hall, 1993b) warned, "If you're going to share in this feeding frenzy, you better prepare yourself and your institution to do so," adding that most practitioners focus on income tax savings "when the real action" is transfer-tax savings (p. 25).

The Depression generation, which economists describe as the most financially fortunate of this century, now is poised to pass its aggregate wealth to the postwar baby-boom generation. Members of the older era were in the workplace during the economic prosperity following World War II and enjoyed an amazing 524% growth in their real net worth between the ages of 20 and 30 (Connell, 1993). In comparison, their children—the baby boomers—experienced only a 34% increase in wealth between the same ages. Many older Americans also receive generous retirement benefits, including employer pensions, which help preserve the accumulated and appreciated assets about to be transferred. Schervish (1993) stated, "Although some of these inheritances will be relatively modest sums passing from middle-class parents to their children, a significant number of such intergenerational transfers will be from the wealthy" (p. 26). Linking this opportunity for planned giving to raising outright major gifts, he pointed out that the number of millionaires will triple during the next 20 years, from approximately 1.5 million to 4.5 million.

The average estate of the Depression generation, predicted by previous IRS breakdowns, consists of 31% stock, 23% real estate, 17% bonds, 17% other, including life insurance, and only 12% cash (E. Greene et al., 1993). Consultant Robert Sharpe, Jr. (1993b) defined the demographic pool to which efforts should be targeted as individuals aged 65 to 84, a growing segment of the population. He elaborated, "By the year 2000, some 30 million people will be in this group that is likely to make deferred gifts; by 2010, the number will increase by another 10 percent" (p. 31). Sharpe, it should be noted, defined individuals aged 55 to 65 as the critical constituency for outright major gifts, which is logical given the progression of personal finance just described.

A fundamental issue in planned giving is allocation of assets between future generations of an individual's family and society at large. Interests in spouse, children, and other relatives almost always take precedence. For example, among wealthy taxpayers, only 8% of married men and women make charitable bequests and those bequests total less than 10% of their estates (E. Greene et al., 1993). The numbers change dramatically for wealthy individuals who are not married. More than 50% of all single women and 33% of all single men make charitable bequests—which, among single men, total nearly 50% of their estates. Setting aside the factor of wealth, Hartsook (1993) reported that the number of single and childless households is increasing each year. He said census studies predict nonfamily households will soon account for 23% of the total population.

The opportunity now presenting itself is not entirely optimistic. As documented shortly, the most heavily used planned giving vehicle is the charitable bequest. Yet only 2 out of 10 Americans make a bequest gift, and the number has been decreasing. According to Donikian (cited in H. Hall, 1993b), IRS figures showed that 22% of the more than 2 million people who died in 1976 made bequests; the percentage had dropped to 20% by 1988. Furthermore, wealthy Americans, who own most assets, are giving less through bequests. The percentage of their aggregate assets bequeathed to charitable organizations decreased from 13% in 1976 to 6% in 1990 (E. Greene et al., 1993).

The transfer of wealth clearly represents a challenge as well as an opportunity for fund raising. NSFRE found that only 52% of the organizations represented in its 1988 membership survey employ planned giving, with religious organizations being the most active at 78% and cultural organizations the least at 20% (Klein, 1988). Efforts to raise planned gifts were not measured in subsequent studies.

THRESHOLD OF KNOWLEDGE

All practitioners are capable of raising planned gifts. Skills in relationship management, not in taxes and finance, are the necessary qualifications. Most gifts and dollars raised through planned giving are generated by the simplest vehicle, the charitable bequest—easy to understand and explain. Responsibility for technical details belongs to the organization's legal and financial experts and to donors' expert advisers.

Planned giving is treated almost as an anomaly in the literature. Whereas other aspects of fund raising are heralded as an art that can be carried out even by amateur volunteers, planned giving is extolled as a highly complex area reserved for specialists. For example, Jordan and Quynn (1994) advised senior managers to hire an "outside professional," such as an attorney or certified public accountant, for their staff because "fund raisers who lack background in finance, law, and taxes can find planned giving intimidating" (p. 20). Other fund-raising efforts are described in terms of asymmetrical presuppositions, such as persuading donors, but symmetrical practice is strongly endorsed when planned giving is addressed. Brain (1991) explained what he and others view as a primary difference between this strategy and the rest of fund raising: "The contributors' objectives come first. In both annual giving and capital fund raising, the needs of the organization come first" (p. 99). I advocate all aspects of fund raising be practiced symmetrically and managed by fund raisers.

Necessary Qualifications

The complexities of estate and financial planning have been misused to make planned giving and, therefore, fund raising appear to be a highly technical occupation that is difficult to master. Many organizations structure the effort as a program separate from the rest of the function and staffed by experts on tax laws and finance. Such an approach is unnecessary and detrimental to effective fund-raising management. It results in duplication of responsibilities, intra- and interorganizational competition, lower responsiveness to prospective donors' needs, and an undue emphasis on life income agreements and other nonbequest vehicles. When I assert that public relations practitioners are capable of specializing in fund raising, those educators who disagree with me unfailingly base their opposition on the complexity of planned giving.

The ability to manage relationships with individual prospects and donors supersedes technical knowledge when raising planned gifts. William Moran (cited in Colton, 1992), then director of planned giving at St. Luke's Hospital Foundation in Kansas City, Missouri, argued that to be successful, fund raisers must focus on building relationships, not on the mechanics of vehicles. Donovan (1993) advised practitioners that planned giving basically requires "the development of your communication skills to better serve your charitable organization and your donors" (p. 28). Although a separate specialist may once have been necessary to ensure attention was paid to potential donors of assets, a number of those specialists, such as Ronald Sapp (1993), former director of planned giving at Johns Hopkins University, now agree that planned giving has moved from a technical orientation to a "'donor friendly' orientation" (p. 117). What fund raisers need is an understanding of the overall strategy and a threshold of knowledge about the various vehicles employed.

Broce (1986) agreed: "I believe that all members of a fund-raising staff should have a working knowledge of deferred-gift methods, no matter how limited. Deferred giving is a *method* of making a contribution" (p. 166; italics added). Insisting that organizations must be willing to invest staff time and money in research and training, he stated: "This does not mean that the professional fund raiser must be a walking-talking expert on the tax laws. But he [sic] must know where to go for information and counsel" (p. 162). Access to legal, financial, and tax experts, as Broce affirmed, is a prerequisite for conducting planned giving.

Students who are daunted by acquiring even a threshold of knowledge should take heart from Gurin (1985), who admitted in his autobiography: "I must confess that if there is one thing my mind apparently does not care to retain, it's the various ways of making planned (deferred) gifts. I can rehearse them for use on a particular occasion, but then I promptly forget them" (p. 91). He continued, "Heaven help me if I'm asked without warning to list the various ways of making planned gifts and recite their individual advantages" (p. 92). Although it is hoped the ability to list and recite the distinctive characteristics of planned giving vehicles will be gained from this text, the most important thing for future practitioners to know is that such vehicles exist and should be explored for the prospective donor's benefit, as well as the organization's.

Besides which, the easiest vehicle to understand is the one most commonly used, the charitable bequest. A description of the characteristics that make it user friendly for both donors and practitioners is reserved for later in this chapter. The point here is that contrary to the impression given in much of the fund-raising literature, the simple bequest dominates the planned giving arena.

Dominance of Simple Bequests

Evidence supporting this critical point was provided by a survey conducted by the National Committee on Planned Giving (NCPG; Bigelow & Lumpkin, 1993). Based on a demographic sample of 150,000 households, the survey found that 6% of all individuals in the United States have included a bequest to a charitable organization in their will. In contrast, only 0.6% have executed any of the various life income agreements that command most of the literature's attention. Generalizing these findings, the ratio of bequests to life income agreements is 10:1.

William Moran (1991) further claimed that 80% of all *dollars* generated by planned gifts comes from bequests and only 20% from other vehicles, such as life income agreements. Yet fund-raising practitioners, he said, spend most of their time pursuing the 20%. Their attention, he argued, is misplaced. "Like other fund raisers who spend all their time on special events and neglect major gift prospects, they simply ain't where the money is" (p. 38).

Moran, who holds a law degree and advanced certification from both NSFRE and AHP, has been a leading advocate for demystifying planned giving through recognition of the simple bequest's importance.[1] Using data on gifts to colleges and universities from 1978 to 1989, collected by the Council for Aid to Education (CFAE), he demonstrated that twice as many dollars were given through bequests than through all other planned giving vehicles combined.[2] For example, in academic year 1988–1989, bequests accounted for 22% of the gift dollars from individuals, whereas only 11% was generated by other vehicles. Even so, Moran argued, the data disguised the importance of bequests because the comparison was similar to comparing apples to oranges.

Bequest figures represented actual receipts available for immediate use by the organizations, whereas gifts from other vehicles were reported by CFAE at their *face value*, as opposed to their actual value. Funds from life income agreements, for example, are not available for the organization's use until years after the agreements are executed because gift principals are dedicated to producing income for donors, usually for their lifetime. Although dependent on returns from the invested principal and the number of years the donor draws income, the amount the organization actually receives almost always is less than the original gift. In other words, the *charitable remainder* of such gifts becomes available for use only after financial obligations to donors have been met. The passage of time during which funds are encumbered, as well as payments to donors, Moran pointed out, means the worth of the remainder, calculated to its present value, is substantially less than the amount originally transferred, its face value. Income tax laws reflect these gift conditions, allowing donors only a partial charitable deduction, or the difference between the value of the assets transferred and the amount the government expects the donor to get back in income payments.

---

[1]Moran currently is executive director of St. Vincent's Foundation in Birmingham, Alabama.

[2]The Council for Aid to Education was named the Council for *Financial* Aid to Education until the late 1980s. Its original abbreviation is used in this chapter to simplify presentation of the organization's data.

Moran illustrated his point by breaking down the value of a $10,000 gift made through one type of life income agreement, a pooled income fund, by a couple aged 70 and 65 years old. Based on a life expectancy of 23 years and an interest rate of 8%, Moran calculated that the $10,000 gift had a charitable remainder value of only $2,084. Moreover, the recipient organization, as is often the case, paid the expenses of an outside financial firm to administer the fund, a 1% annual fee for the length of the donors' lives, which further reduced the charitable remainder value by $1,120. "So this apparently major gift of $10,000," he concluded from his analysis, "is hardly 'major,' with a present value of only $964!" (p. 40). He then presented a principle students are urged to remember: "As a rule of thumb, for the vast majority of life income agreements, the charitable portion is 50 percent or less of the sum transferred" (p. 40).

Returning to the CFAE data on gifts to colleges and universities, Moran adjusted the nonbequest gifts to 50% of their face value for the 10-year period. His calculations showed that, on average, 86% of all planned giving dollars were made through bequests and only 14% through other vehicles. For 1988–1989, 80% of the dollars came from bequests and 20% from all other vehicles—which provided the basis for his 80/20 proportion, or a ratio of 4:1.

The importance of the charitable bequest is supported by the few practitioners and scholars who have studied planned giving. For example, Sharpe (1993b) found an unadjusted ratio of almost 2:1 between bequests and other vehicles in his analysis of CFAE figures for 1991–1992. Of the $1.6 billion received from planned gifts, 64% came from bequests and 36% came from nonbequests. An additional consideration is that bequests frequently are the means by which donors fund life income agreements for others, such as a spouse or child. Based on their interviews with a purposive sample of 476 individuals who have established a $1-million or more charitable remainder trust (another type of life income agreement), File et al. (1994) found that 75% funded the trust through their will; only 25% created the trust during their lifetime—a ratio of 3:1.

No comprehensive statistics currently exist on planned giving results or the dollars attributable to different vehicles. Annual reports by the AAFRC Trust for Philanthropy, for example, present separate estimates of bequests, but include planned gifts other than bequests in the large, general category of gifts from living individuals, $10 billion and $120 billion, respectively, in 1996 (AAFRC Trust for Philanthropy, 1997b). Furthermore, Sharpe (1993b)—who founded the National Planned Giving Institute in 1967, now located at the College of William and Mary in Williamsburg, Virginia—claimed AAFRC estimates of bequests do not correlate closely with other available data. He hypothesized that planned gifts to all types of charitable organizations totaled $20 billion or more in 1991, based on a historical norm of 20% to 30% of the dollars given by individuals, derived from his studies. The best indicators of planned giving's importance, he said, are CFAE reports, which analyze gifts to higher education (and also provide separate statistics on private schools). Findings from 1993–1994, then, suggest that planned giving accounts for 16% of all gift dollars and 40% of the dollars given by individuals (CFAE, 1995). As just discussed, CFAE reports also suggest that almost two thirds of all planned giving dollars come from bequests and probably represent as much as 80% of the income generated when nonbequest gifts are adjusted to reflect their charitable remainder value.

NSFRE agrees with this assessment, as demonstrated in its survey course on fund raising. Consultant James Holcomb, who taught the session on planned giving when I took the course in 1993, estimated that as much as 85% of all planned giving dollars come from bequests. Reasons why bequests have been downplayed are provided later in this chapter. The discussion turns now to the expertise contributed by others to the process of raising planned gifts.

Reliance on Experts

Planned giving is not synonymous with estate and financial planning, which is the province of lawyers, accountants, and financial planners with the necessary knowledge of tax laws and finance. Fund raisers rely on such experts within their organizations to handle and execute the technicalities of planned giving vehicles. Indeed, the decision about what vehicles the charitable organization utilizes greatly depends on the expertise available in its legal and finance departments. Organizations without the necessary skills retain outside counsel or establish a network of experts willing to volunteer their services. Regardless, professionals other than fund raisers are responsible for the intricate details involved in accepting gifts of assets. As summarized by planned giving consultant John Brown (Brown & Feagin, 1994), current and future fund raisers must have enough knowledge to bring a donor to the midpoint on the road of giving, then call in the expert.

Furthermore, experts representing the donor's interests are active and advocated participants in the process of raising planned gifts. Breaking down that statement, lawyers, accountants, and financial planners retained by donors are key actors in planned giving and provide much of the necessary technical expertise. For example, File et al. (1994) found that every donor in their study of 476 individuals who have established a large charitable remainder trust hired a professional expert to attend to the actual creation of the trust. Almost three fourths of the expert advisers (73%) were lawyers, 18% were bank officers, 5% accountants, and 4% were professionals at financial advisory and investment firms. A second adviser was retained by 28% of the donors to check on the work of the first. Jordan and Quynn (1994) referred to such advisers as "allied professionals who work with our prospects and donors" (p. 20). They included, in addition to those just listed, life insurance agents and real estate brokers.

The involvement of donor advisers is increasing. Based on findings of the NCPG survey, Bigelow and Lumpkin (1993), authors of the survey's report, concluded, "It is clear that donors are relying more and more on their own technical advisors, both legal and financial, to consider the details and advise them on the wisdom of making a certain type of gift" (p. 16). This trend should reassure future practitioners, although, as discussed shortly, it also is cause for concern at a broader level.

As to their advocated participation, there is unanimity in the fund-raising literature that the donor's own expert adviser is an essential participant during the negotiation of a planned gift. Broce (1986), for example, stated:

> It is important to ensure that the potential donor is always represented by his or her legal counsel. Most donors ask their attorneys to participate as a matter of course, and the institution's representative should insist on it. A potential donor who does not normally

retain an attorney should be assisted in finding one with expertise in estate planning. (p. 167)

Clarifying Broce's last point, assistance should be limited to providing the prospect with a list of reputable attorneys or other experts; fund raisers should never recommend a specific adviser.

Reasons for advocating expert representation are both pragmatic and philosophical. Because it usually deals with older individuals, who often are single, and because the donor usually is dead when the organization receives its principal financial benefits, planned giving is susceptible to charges of manipulation by family heirs or others with interest in the estate's distribution. Fund raisers must avoid real or perceived impropriety, and an effective safeguard is to insist on the participation of the donor's own expert adviser. Brain (1991) warned, "The organization should exercise extreme caution against the use of high-pressure sales techniques when negotiating with prospective donors.... Never, under any circumstances, should the donor be pressured or unduly persuaded" (p. 110). More directly, Hartsook (1993) advised that fund raisers "not become so intertwined with the structuring of deferred gifts that it causes future questions concerning conflicts of interest" (p. 47).

Philosophically, as pointed out earlier, planned giving is based on symmetrical presuppositions in that the organization's self-interest does not take precedence over the donor's self-interest. The literature recommends that in all cases the donor's needs must come first. For example, Sharpe (1993b) stated, "In planning deferred gifts with older donors, consider the donors' financial and other needs first, their families second and the charity third—an approach our experience has shown will work, while remaining well within accepted ethical norms" (p. 31). Participation of advisers ensures an appropriate focus on the donor.

Donor advisers are evident in the fund-raising process beyond negotiation. For example, practitioners traditionally have developed cultivation activities for advisers (e.g., mailings to local attorneys about program service needs and vehicles available to their clients). Many organizations have a planned giving advisory committee through which volunteer professionals become familiar with the organization's program services, as well as function as a technical resource. Such activities often result in advisers recommending planned gifts to their clients, thereby participating as part of solicitation. In conclusion, it is not necessary nor is it appropriate for fund raisers to duplicate the expertise of those trained in estate and financial planning.

Before leaving the topic of donor advisers, two serious trends must be addressed. The first involves ethics. Some advisers have engaged in *selling* planned gifts to charitable organizations (Greenfield, 1991). They recommend to a client that he or she make such a gift as a means for financial gain and then offer that gift to organizations contingent on payment of a finder's fee to the adviser. This practice is incongruent with the defining characteristic of a gift, charitable intent. The primary motivation for making the gift is financial benefit for the donor as he or she does not care to which organization the gift is made and for the adviser who will profit from the sale of the gift. Because charitable intent is diminished, paying finder's fees is unethical for fund raisers and their organizations, regardless of how such practice is viewed by members of other occupations. It is against the code of standards adopted by the two leading associations that deal with planned giving, NCPG and the American Council on Gift Annuities (ACGA).

The second trend involves the marketplace and no clear-cut solution is offered. Outside experts have expanded their role from providing technical advice and attention to controlling the arrangement and management of planned gifts, often without any involvement of the charitable organizations to which the gifts are made. Some clarification is needed.

The majority of planned giving vehicles can be executed without the participation or even the knowledge of the recipient organization. Bequests, for example, are made through the execution of a will, which usually involves only the donor and his or her attorney. Vehicles with the term *trust* in their name, such as charitable remainder trusts, create fiscal entities that legally operate as self-contained trusts. Assets given through these vehicles actually are made to the trust created, not to the organization named as its charitable, or ultimate, *beneficiary*. The donor appoints a trustee to manage the trust until its termination. The trustee and the ultimate beneficiary do not have to be the same; in fact, donors can name themselves as the trustee. In other words, although this chapter talks about assets transferred to charitable organizations and the organizations' management of the funds, trusts are not controlled by the organizational beneficiary unless it also is named trustee by the donor. In the early 1990s, the control of trusts shifted drastically from 501(c)(3) organizations to the financial services industry.

Spurred by the transfer of wealth now underway, trust companies, commercial banks with trust departments, life insurance companies, investment banks, and mutual fund companies are marketing planned gifts, particularly charitable remainder trusts, to current and new clients. Their involvement increased by at least 50% between 1991 and 1993, according to a survey conducted by consultant Russ Alan Prince (cited in Goss, 1993d).

Planned giving represents a largely untapped source of income for commercial firms. Financial companies acquire more assets to manage when they arrange charitable remainder trusts because they almost always are named trustees. They charge the trusts management fees, which usually equal 1% of a trust's value annually for the years of its existence. Insurance companies make money because many donors, having transferred assets to create charitable remainder trusts, buy life insurance policies for their family heirs to replace the dollars given away. Such gifts also are used as a marketing tool in that they identify insurance agents with "the moral high ground" (Goss, 1993d, p. 31). Prince (cited in E. Greene, 1994a) summarized: "The whole financial industry is going after this en masse. They are recognizing the opportunities for them in the planned giving field" (p. 24).

Reflective fund raisers, who described this trend as "an invitation to disaster" and "dangerous," identified two major potential problems (Goss, 1993d, pp. 32–33). In light of their for-profit missions, commercial firms might promote the tax and financial advantages of planned gifts with little or no mention of their charitable intent. Paid advertisements, on which they rely to market their products and services, could trumpet tax breaks, thereby inviting scrutiny from federal lawmakers seeking new revenues to reduce budget deficits. As discussed shortly, if planned giving comes to be seen as simply a tax dodge, Congress could move to restrict or even eliminate its deductions. Also worrisome, commercial managers who represent the donor might invest trust funds in such a way as to provide a generous income for their clients, while eroding the value of the corpus of the agreement that eventually goes to the charitable organization. The organization serving as both trustee and beneficiary tries to balance the interest of the donor with its own self-interest. An intermediary might not do so.

Other problems can be envisioned. For example, members of a volunteer advisory committee may now be competitors with each other and with the charitable organization. Although often unrestricted in use, planned gifts executed without the involvement of the organizational beneficiary could be restricted to purposes it does not regard as priority needs. If its representatives, including fund raisers, are not part of the dialogue, there is no opportunity for articulating needs or for negotiation, which might result in restricted dollars of little value to the organization.

Leadership action is required. IS, NCPG, NSFRE, and other associations must develop a proactive plan to work with the financial services industry to ensure that charitable intent is the basis of every planned gift. Just as 501(c)(3) organizations have strived to include the donor's expert adviser in the process, for-profit companies must provide some degree of representation for the recipient organization. Compelling reasons for voluntary cooperation would be demonstrated if only one or two organizations refused to accept planned gifts arranged and managed without their involvement, thereby causing significant negative tax consequences for the donors' estates. Consideration may have to be given to tax-law changes that would require the approval of the charitable beneficiary before vehicles establishing trusts are executed. Due to the lucrative market, Prince (cited in Goss, 1993d) argued that nothing is going to stop companies from stepping up their planned giving activities; therefore, he advised, "What you're left with is either working with them, or watching them run over you" (p. 33).

COMMENSURATE SCOPE

All charitable organizations are capable of generating income through planned giving. They can limit their efforts to the simple bequest or they can selectively add other vehicles that match their expertise and constituencies' needs.

The only fundamental requirement for raising planned gifts is organizational commitment to a long-term perspective. According to knowledgeable practitioners, few financial benefits will be received for a minimum of 3 years. Schmeling (1990), for example, warned, "In the initial years of a planned giving program—anywhere from three to eight years, depending upon prior donor relationships—planned giving is all expense with little, if any, income" (p. 2). The time delay becomes about five times longer when talking about a specific gift. Lindahl (1992), it is recalled from chapter 10, hypothesized that a minimum of 15 years of data are required to determine the typical delay factors of planned gifts, although 25 years may be the norm.

Once begun, however, studies show that planned giving generates at least $4 for every $1 invested, representing an acceptable 25% fund-raising cost ratio (Greenfield, 1991). Organizations must adopt a long-term perspective and invest resources wisely. As Sharpe (1993b) put it, an investment now will generate financial returns "in as *little* as three to five years" (p. 31; italics added). Illustrating an even shorter time frame, the United Way of San Diego County (California) generated more than $2 million, primarily in bequests and charitable remainder trusts, only 2 years after starting planned giving efforts in 1992 (E. Greene, 1994a). It previously had received only $8,000 in planned gifts during its entire 72-year history.

Are all organizations capable of offering a comprehensive planned giving effort? The answer is no, but all organizations can utilize the charitable bequest to obtain gifts of assets. This basic vehicle requires minimum investment of staff and financial resources. No special training is needed because bequests are easy to understand and explain. Much of the programming relies on controlled media techniques, which are relatively inexpensive. Whereas some organizations do not have donor prospects with the financial capacity to make a gift through such vehicles as life income agreements, all have prospects with the capacity to make a gift through a charitable bequest. Members of a church, for example, include individuals who—although they cannot do so during their lifetime—can give $10,000 or more from their estate after they have no further need for the assets. Unlike other vehicles, bequests entail little administrative and financial management costs because there is no transfer of funds until after the donor's death.

The scope of the planned giving effort must be commensurate with the organization's capabilities and its constituencies' needs. The first step of the fund-raising process, research on the organization, opportunity, and publics, determines whether the effort should be limited to bequests or include other vehicles.

Research on the Organization

Charitable organizations with in-house legal staff and a sophisticated finance department may be capable of offering a full array of planned giving vehicles. For example, hospitals and universities already have much of the infrastructure in place to handle complex life income agreements and other nonbequest vehicles. They usually have experience in managing or farming out the management of endowment funds, have refined systems for accounts payable and receivable, have dealt with large noncash gifts in the past, and have the necessary oversight committees as part of their boards of trustees (e.g., an investment committee). Illustrating, fund raisers at the California Institute of Technology, which offers numerous vehicles, work closely with such campus offices as trust accounting, the treasurer, and the property manager (Netherton, 1994). Of particular importance, these organizations have resources available to underwrite a comprehensive effort.

Long-term expenses related to managing funds and reporting to donors are incurred when offering nonbequest vehicles. Life income agreements, for example, allow donors to name multiple income beneficiaries. The NCPG survey (Bigelow & Lumpkin, 1993) found that although 52% of all such gifts have a payout for a single life, 22% have a payout for two or more lives, and the remaining specify a term of years up to 20 or a combination of life plus a set number of years. According to Abrams and Foster (1995), payments to donors and other income beneficiaries generally are made quarterly; however, monthly payments are not unusual. Recipient organizations are required to file annual federal and state tax returns on each agreement and to provide income beneficiaries with appropriate tax information and forms (Sapp, 1993; Seltzer, 1987). Expenses, therefore, can be substantial and—depending on the number and ages of the income beneficiaries—can extend for a very long time.

Organizations also assume some degree of financial risk when they enter into life income agreements. Poor money management, market conditions, and other factors can result in low returns and even financial debt. As Michael Seltzer (1987)—a program officer at the Ford Foundation—pointed out, the remainder of life income gifts may be much smaller than originally expected, depending on investment expertise. That is the organization's risk, as are the effects of waiting to use the gift monies.

Staff managers carefully research the organization and counsel trustees, the CEO, and other members of the dominant coalition about the required expertise and costs for different vehicles. Examples of questions guiding the research are: Is the organization capable of buying gift annuities, paying quarterly or even monthly income payments, creating a pooled income fund, and administering it? Although a for-profit financial firm can be hired to handle administrative details and provide investment services, the organization retains fiduciary and oversight responsibilities that it must be capable of performing. Seltzer (1987), who advises the Ford Foundation's board about grants to strengthen philanthropy, explained, "An organization interested in receiving substantial contributions of any sort must be sure that it can demonstrate that it is adequately prepared to handle such contributions" (p. 179).

Outsourcing administration also reduces net income; few organizations can afford to have all vehicles handled externally. Furthermore, without some internal involvement, donor confidence in the organization's ability to manage funds may be diminished. Brown and Feagin (1994), for example, argued that charitable gift annuities, which are less complex than other life income vehicles, should be handled internally because they represent a test of financial management that will affect later and larger gifts. Only those vehicles the organization is prepared to fully support should be offered.

Research on the Opportunity

As already described, the overall opportunity for raising planned gifts is positive. However, practitioners must conduct primary research to determine the feasibility of an effort for their organization. In addition to determining donor interest, they should investigate the estate and financial planning needs of their constituencies. Questions guiding the research include: Can those closest to the organization afford to give away assets during their lifetime? Are they concerned about estate taxes? Do they understand the benefits of making out a will? Organizational needs 10 to 25 years in the future should be specified as areas for restricted support and compared to the preferences of potential donors.

Clarifying this point, time delays inherent in planned giving prohibit offering specific gift opportunities with suggested funding levels. Many things can change from the time a gift is solicited to the time funds are available for use by the organization, not the least of which is inflation. For example, an international relief agency that asks for planned gifts of $25,000 to annually feed a child in Haiti may find—we would like to hope—that there no longer are hungry children in Haiti when funds from the gifts finally can be used. Even if the situation has not changed, the agency likely will find the amount available is not enough to pay inflated costs (e.g., $35,000 may be needed to produce sufficient annual income). Because of delays that can extend as long as 25 or even 50 years, organizations must define general areas of support and basic program services congruent with their mission to which donors can restrict planned gifts (e.g., feeding children in poverty-stricken countries). Suggested funding levels must be placed within the context of inflated dollars, and named opportunities for purposes requiring exact amounts should be avoided unless funded in combination with an outright gift. In short, fund raisers cannot ignore donors' preferences for designating the use of their gift; however, in planned giving, funding needs must be generalized to accommodate the deferred nature of the gifts.

Research on the Publics

Demographics, personal finance, and relationship with the organization are key variables for determining those individuals likely to constitute donor publics for planned giving. It is recalled that prospects are aged 65 to 84, although some practitioners, such as Hartsook (1993), recommend not soliciting individuals beyond 75 years old—presumably because of feebleness. Given that people are living longer and many senior citizens are in better physical and mental condition than their younger counterparts, age ceilings are arbitrary. There is evidence the same may be true for age floors. The NCPG survey (Bigelow & Lumpkin, 1993) found that planned giving donors are evenly divided among age groups ranging from under 45 years old to 70 and older. A surprising 58% of those who have made a charitable bequest and 53% who have executed a life income agreement are younger than 60 years old. Acknowledging that younger donors were over-represented in the sample, Bigelow and Lumpkin still concluded, "These results have startling implications for charitable organizations . . . . [They] may need to move toward a more segmented approach that targets planned giving prospects of various ages rather than focusing primarily on older prospects as is common with many organizations" (p. 1).

Practitioners must conduct research to determine age variations among their organization's potential donors. A survey, for example, could detect interest in different planned giving vehicles by age groups. Results would then be used in conjunction with the organization's capability and willingness to extend the time delay between fund-raising effort and resulting income in order to make decisions about vehicles that will be offered and minimum age and gift amount required for each. In other words, even if 45-year-olds express interest in charitable remainder trusts, the organization may be unable to expend resources from which it will not receive financial gain for 35 or more years, as opposed to the more typical delay of 15 years for 65-year-olds. Other generalizations discussed here should be similarly researched.

Hartsook (1993) advised, "Your task is to identify prospects—friends of your institution—who fit those age-qualified categories. To narrow your prospect pool even more, you can look for those prospects who fit the age category and do not have children" (p. 48). Individuals who are single, divorced, or widowed are more likely to make a planned gift than those who are married. The absence of children increases the probability for such vehicles as the charitable bequest. Because they live longer than men, women constitute the majority of prospects. Two thirds of the 8 million households headed by those aged 75 or older are unmarried people, and two thirds of the population from age 70 on are females (Connell, 1993). Demographically, then, the generalized prospect pool consists of elderly individuals who are not married, have few or no family heirs, and primarily are women. Fund raisers must ask if these demographics are well-represented among their organization's constituencies.

Financial capacity focuses on assets, not standard measures of wealth and affluence. Elderly individuals generally have assets valued 10 to 20 times greater than their income. For example, an older donor with an annual income of $35,000, who gives $35 to the annual giving program, may have assets valued at more than $600,000. Such situations are not uncommon. Paid ownership of a house in today's real estate market represents an asset of about $125,000, based on the national median. A farm owned by a middle-class widower may be worth more than $1 million. When the values of real estate, stock, pension, and life insurance are added together, the total often is surprisingly high. Sapp (1993) stated, "With the wide variety and flexibility that planned giving offers, donors never before thought of as major gift prospects are able to make major gifts" (p. 117). Moran (cited in Colton, 1992) advised fund raisers, "Look for assets, not wealth" (p. 51).

Personal finance divides prospects into two groups: individuals with sufficient capacity to make an irrevocable planned gift and those without the capacity. Some irrevocable vehicles—because of the cost involved in administrating them—require a minimum gift of $50,000. More importantly, all irrevocable gifts require donors to forfeit control over the assets given. Not knowing what the future holds, individuals value flexibility and strive to keep enough assets for their largely unknown needs—the amount required determined by each person. To protect donor interests, I recommend that, as a general rule, individuals whose assets total less than $600,000 not be solicited for irrevocable gifts. The $600,000 cutoff emulates the credit granted for federal gift and estate taxes, discussed shortly. It provides an arbitrary but ethical criterion. Only organizations with numerous prospects owning assets worth more than $600,000 are advised to offer life income agreements and other vehicles requiring irrevocable gifts.

As touched on by Schmeling (1990) and Hartsook (1993), prospects for planned giving are defined by their relationship with the organization. They may be former or current trustees, donors, volunteers, clients, members, alumni, employees, and community residents. In other words, prospects are identified among natural constituencies, moving progressively outward from those closest to the organization to those most removed. Broce (1986) explained: "As in all other kinds of fund raising, the best prospects for a deferred-giving program are those closest to the institution. Therefore, the best initial prospects should be members of the governing board and previous contributors" (pp. 169–170). Although their study's purposive sample prohibits generalization, File et al. (1994) found that all 476 donors who established a charitable remainder trust of $1 million or more had a relationship with the organizational beneficiary before establishing the trust. The highest ranked forms of involvement were being a previous donor (76%) and serving on the board of directors (52%).

Fund raisers must pay special attention to the interests and needs of trustees and donors of annual and major gifts when determining the scope of their organization's planned giving effort. If these stakeholders, for example, express little interest in a pooled income fund, the vehicle should not be offered. Past giving remains the strongest indicator of those who will make a planned gift to a particular organization; however, there are some unique qualifications.

Anecdotal evidence suggests older donors stop making annual gifts after retirement because they do not have as much discretionary income as before. Status as current donor and recency of last gift, therefore, may not be reliable indicators for predicting prospects likely to give assets. I recommend that fund raisers identify lapsed annual giving donors who are elderly and develop programming to continue communication with them.

Similarly, there is some empirical evidence that previously making an outright major gift may not be a strong predictor of those who make a planned gift. Lindahl (1992, 1994) reported that an analysis of Northwestern University's donors showed outright past giving was statistically significant only for prospects of outright major gifts and not for prospects of planned gifts made through irrevocable trust agreements. The key variables for the latter were age and past irrevocable trust gifts. Drawing from these findings, individuals who do not believe they have sufficient income and/or assets to give a large amount outright, may, as they grow older, be interested in making a gift of assets that returns financial benefits to them, and once having done so, likely will repeat the behavior.

Finally, individuals who are not viable prospects for annual or major gifts—and, therefore, rarely have been solicited—may be prospects for planned giving because of differences between income and assets. Employees, clients, and community residents often fall in this group. For example, tenured faculty at some universities earn relatively low salaries but have pension plans valued at more than $1 million. Former clients of organizations that charge little for their services should not be overlooked. The March of Dimes, in light of the Depression generation's transfer of assets, began research in the early 1990s to identify the parents of children who were helped by the organization when it was fighting polio in the 1940s and 1950s (E. Greene et al., 1993). Bequests from a public school art teacher and a librarian in Cleveland, Ohio recently endowed a $1-million chair in English at nearby Hiram College ("$12-million," 1993). Lindahl (1994) found that "overnight stars," or "never givers" (p. 45) who make major gifts almost always are donors of planned gifts. The overriding rule on status as previous donor, then, prevails for planned giving, but with qualifiers that require expanded research and programming, particularly long-term cultivation.

PROTECTION, NOT EXPLOITATION

Planned gifts are encouraged and subsidized by our tax system, and financial benefits returned to donors can be great. Individuals save money on gift and estate taxes, as well as on income and capital-gains taxes. Charitable intent, however, must be the overriding reason for making the gift. If benefits are primary, the payment loses its qualification. Brain (1991) explained, "If there is no charitable intent, there is no valid gift; and if there is no gift, there are no tax benefits under the law" (p. 99).

The system is so advantageous for both donors and charitable organizations, finance columnist Jane Bryant Quinn (1994) stated, "If the tax code didn't exist, America's charities would have to invent it" (p. 61). Focusing on life income agreements, she presented a 6-step procedure highlighting the financial benefits:

(1) You donate cash savings, or stocks or land that have run up in value. (2) You win substantial tax breaks. (3) The charity invests your money for growth. (4) Now, or in the future, the charity starts paying you (and your spouse or another person) a lifetime income. (5) When the last beneficiary dies, the charity gets the remaining money. (6) You

can, if you want, replace some of the money you gave away by using tax savings to buy life insurance to leave to your kids. (p. 61)

Quinn described the three tax breaks. If the gift is in the form of appreciated property, the donor avoids capital-gains tax on the appreciated amount, up to 28% in 1997. The asset is sold by the recipient organization tax free, and the donor receives income based on the entire amount. A portion of the gift is deductible from taxable income, with the amount varying by size of the income payments returned to the donor and his or her age, among other factors. The gift reduces the donor's estate, saving gift and estate taxes if net worth exceeds the federal credit.

Each individual currently is entitled to a lifetime *unified credit* of $600,000 on gifts and estate. Assets totaling $600,000 or less are exempted from federal taxation at death if the amount does not exceed the unused portion of the unified credit.[3] Assets beyond the credit, however, are subject to a heavy, progressive federal tax, up to 55% for the transfer of $3 million or more (Marlowe, 1994b). For married couples, everything can be passed from one spouse to the other without any serious tax impact. However, after the second spouse dies, if the estate exceeds $600,000, tax rates can climb to more than 60% when state and local taxes are added to the federal tax.

The implications for fund raising are clear: Individuals with assets greater than $600,000 have a choice of leaving a significant portion of the excess to Uncle Sam or reducing their estate by contributing some of the assets to charitable organizations with whom they share common interests. For example, if a donor whose estate beyond the unified credit will be taxed in the 50% bracket makes a planned gift of $100,000, the actual cost of the gift is only $50,000 because the other $50,000 would have gone for taxes. In addition, the allowance for married couples helps explain why individuals who are unmarried are more likely to make a planned gift.

Unlike the limitations placed on charitable deductions from taxable income (e.g., maximum of 30% of AGI for gifts of appreciated property), estate-tax deductions are unlimited. Experts maintain that most Americans can avoid or significantly reduce estate taxes with the right planning. They advise clients to utilize available vehicles such as life insurance to provide survivors with money, or charitable remainder trusts to help shelter assets.

Illustrating the first, which is related to Quinn's (1994) sixth step, Clymer (1993) presented a scenario of a married couple with $2 million in assets who want each of their two children to inherit one half of their estate after both the husband and wife have died. Without any estate planning, Clymer said, the IRS would get $512,800, or almost 37% of the estate not covered by the unified credit. With planning, they can pay the IRS, pass the full $2 million to their children, and give $320,000 to a charitable organization.

For 4 years, the husband and wife make outright gifts of $80,000 to a charitable organization of their choice. Because they are in the 31% income tax bracket, the deduction of their gift saves them $24,800 each year in taxes, providing them with a total savings of $99,200 and the recipient organization with a total gift of $320,000 at the end of the 4 years. The couple use their annual tax savings to buy a "second-to-die,"

---

[3]Students will note that the "credit" actually is a deduction because it reduces the amount of assets on which tax is owed, not the amount of tax. Also, students will recall from chapter 7, action is underway in 1997 to raise the amount of the credit, probably to $1 million.

or *survivorship*, life insurance policy with a face value of $813,000, which is fully funded after 4 years at a total cost of $99,200. As its name indicates, a survivorship policy on a married couple pays its benefit on the death of the second spouse when heavy estate taxes are levied. It is one example of using life insurance to replace assets given away. To accomplish their financial planning objectives, the couple in the scenario name their children as owners and beneficiaries of the policy. After both the husband and wife die, the children get the $2 million, and the $813,000 value of the insurance covers the $512,800 estate tax due and all but $20,000 of the amount given to the charitable organization. As Clymer (1993) stated, "Planned giving offers some fairly simple solutions to your prospects' estate planning problems" (p. 42).

Brain (1991) provided an example of how charitable remainder trusts can benefit donors, which has been modified slightly for the purpose of this discussion. A widow, who has total assets of $800,000, owns a farm that has increased in value from $25,000 when she and her late husband bought it to a current value of $400,000. Income from the property is only 1%, which is not enough to help support her. By giving the property to a 501(c)(3) organization through a charitable remainder trust, she avoids the capital-gains tax on its fair-market value, gets an income at a minimum of 5%, gets an immediate income tax deduction based on the gift's charitable remainder, saves estate taxes by reducing her assets below the unified credit, thereby sheltering the remaining assets of $400,000, and contributes to an organization of her choice. Pragmatic financial benefits enjoyed by such donors, Brain emphasized, are "all legal and all sanctioned under the nation's tax laws" (p. 99).

It is argued throughout this book that the deductibility of gifts from taxable income is essential to sustaining America's tradition of philanthropy, although it generally is not the primary reason for making a gift. Similarly, savings on gift and estate taxes influence planned gifts, although they are not—or should not be—the primary motivation.

There are reasons other than those provided by the tax system for making a planned gift. First and foremost is the desire to provide financial support for an organization's mission and program services. The NCPG survey (Bigelow & Lumpkin, 1993) found that the strongest motivating factor for making all types of planned gifts is a desire to support the specific charitable organization. Bigelow and Lumpkin concluded, "Donors are clearly motivated by a charitable intent that goes beyond any benefit to themselves, thus reinforcing the overall significance of the philanthropic spirit in America" (p. 3). The second strongest factor is the ultimate use of the gift by the organization, which supports my recommendation that, even with time delays, general areas to which donors may restrict their gift should be offered as much as possible. Other motivating factors in descending order of importance are to enhance income, avoid tax on capital gains, long-range estate and financial planning issues (all three representing financial benefits returned to donors), create a lasting memorial to oneself or a loved one (verifying the common use of planned gifts to establish endowments), and relationship with a representative of the organization (confirming the importance of cultivation in the process of raising planned gifts). The degree of importance of the last factors varies among donors utilizing different types of vehicles.

Just as most donors of annual gifts do not qualify for gift deductions because they do not file itemized income tax returns, many donors of planned gifts have assets valued at less than the unified credit. In fact, Hartsook (1993) claimed the majority of planned gifts come from estates of $250,000 to $500,000. Some individuals who make such gifts do so because they have no children, other family, or friends to whom they wish to leave their assets. In short, the reasons for making planned gifts are diverse, representing—as with all gifts—mixed motives. Be that as it may, their tax consequences must be acknowledged and protected.

Current exploitation of nonbequest gifts for financial gains threatens the very tax laws that subsidize planned giving. The culprits are not all external to the charitable subsector. Many organizations market planned gifts, particularly life income agreements, as tax-savings devices with little mention of their charitable purpose. For example, New York City's United Jewish Appeal–Federation of Jewish Philanthropies (UJA–FJP) drew an outcry of criticism in 1994 for its paid advertisements promoting the tax and financial advantages of life income agreements (Stehle, 1994b). Copy for one of its print ads referred to the federation as "experienced in the field of financial and retirement planning" and stated: "Investing with a charity could give you a greater return on your money than investing yourself. But choosing the right charity to invest with is an important financial decision" (pp. 23–24).

Critics charged that ads placing so much emphasis on returned benefits could leave donors and—more directly—public policymakers with the impression that charitable organizations are just like commercial financial firms and deserve to be treated in the same way. As Sharpe (1989) warned 5 years earlier, "If you act like a tax shelter, Congress will eventually treat you like one, and the prevailing mood in a revenue-starved Congress is not a kind one toward tax shelters" (p. 40). The ads also positioned the New York federation in direct competition with for-profit firms, which could prompt charges of unfair competition to federal, state, and local governments because the 501(c)(3) organization enjoys such special privileges as property tax exemption. Furthermore, the earnings it promoted for one type of life income agreement, the charitable gift annuity, were higher than those offered by most other charitable organizations, which voluntarily adhere to rate ceilings set by ACGA in order to avoid peer competition. One critic summarized, "The ad pits charities not only against the financial community, but it also pits charity against charity" (Stehle, 1994b, p. 25).

The dangerous outcomes of its behavior largely were ignored by New York UJA–FJP officials, who said the criticism did not bother them and that they believed the ads were appropriate and effective. The head of planned giving, Neal Myerberg (cited in Stehle, 1994b), defended the ads by using arguments based on asymmetrical presuppositions, with which students should now be familiar. Assuming the ends of fund raising justify the means, Myerberg argued, "This organization does a lot of good for thousands of people" (p. 24). He insinuated that donors must be manipulated for their own good and for the good of the organization, saying, "There are a lot of people out there who can make substantial gifts to help this community, and we're just trying to teach them how. Sometimes you've got to bring in people who don't have a philanthropic bone in their body and teach them how to be philanthropic" (p. 25).

Rather than relying on research to identify prospects who share common interests, Myerberg (cited in Stehle, 1994b) defined the federation's "donor population" as "many hundreds of thousands of prospects who don't [give] and who aren't by any means affiliated with us" (p. 26). This unknown mass audience requires paid advertising for communication because other techniques, such as direct mail, are very difficult to use, he explained. Advocating competition, he chided fund raisers who "usually stick within the narrow set of their own donor lists" (p. 26) and advised them to reach out beyond their natural constituencies to the general population. Finally, he and other officials assumed success is measured by the dollars raised, pointing out that 106 individuals had made or were in the process of making a planned gift. The federation, which already was raising $157 million annually ("Philanthropy 400," 1995), did change some of the ads for the second phase of its campaign to give more emphasis to charitable purpose.

Staff managers understand the dangers of inappropriately emphasizing benefits returned to donors and reserve planned giving as an option for those whose primary concern is supporting the organization's work. The discussion now turns to the three categories of vehicles used to make planned gifts, which are presented in Table 13.1.

CHARITABLE BEQUESTS

Charitable bequests also are referred to as testamentary gifts because they are transmitted through "the last will and testament" of the donor. As outlined by Sapp (1993), there are three types: (a) specific, (b) residuary, and (c) contingent. A specific bequest simply names a specific dollar amount or a noncash asset, such as stock, that the donor gives to the organization. Donors also can specify a percentage of their estate, as opposed to a dollar amount or asset. A residuary bequest transfers all or a percentage of the estate to the organization *after* expenses have been paid and specific bequests to other beneficiaries have been dispersed—the residual. A contingent bequest is conditional in that the organization receives the gift only in the event that named individual beneficiaries predecease the donor.

Specific bequests are by far the most prevalent. According to the NCPG survey (Bigelow & Lumpkin, 1993), 78% of all charitable bequests are specific, with 47% of the donors naming a specific amount and 31% naming a specific percentage (noncash assets were not measured). Only 10% and 12%, respectively, made residuary and contingent bequests.

The available evidence, presented earlier, clearly indicates that the simple bequest is the planned giving vehicle most used. As such, it is an important strategy for raising major gifts and represents great opportunity for growth. Many people do not have wills, and of those who do, many just do not stop to think about naming charitable organizations as beneficiaries. Furthermore, bequests are easy for prospective donors to understand and for even new practitioners to master.

Charitable bequests can be incorporated in new wills or added to an existing will through a short separate document known as a *codicil*. Although wording should always

TABLE 13.1
Planned Giving Vehicles

Charitable Bequests	Life Income Agreements	Other Vehicles
	Charitable remainder trusts	Charitable lead trust
	Annuity trust	Remainder interest in home or
	Unitrust	farm
	Charitable gift annuity	Life insurance
	Pooled income fund	

be checked by the organization's and the donor's attorneys, Seltzer (1987) presented this sentence for making an unrestricted bequest in a new will: "I hereby give, devise and bequeath the xyz charity _____(identify the property given, such as 'the sum of $_____') to further the objects and purposes of the xyz charity" (p. 179). The following is a sample codicil for a specific bequest that could be included in mailings to planned giving prospects:

In addition to the will I executed on (Date of Will), I now desire to add this provision

for _____ [formal name of charitable organization printed here] _____

located at _____ [street address, city, state, & zip code printed here] _____

namely to provide _____
Specify percentage of estate or dollar amount, or describe asset.

to be used for _____
Specify your choice or "Where most needed."

Dated: _____ Signed: _____
Witnessed: _____

Please check wording with your attorney to assure that your wishes will be honored in your state.

The example assumes donors may wish to restrict their gift and that a listing of general areas of support and basic program services is provided. Hartsook (1993) endorsed this approach, urging fund raisers to specify projects that planned gifts eventually can support. Some practitioners recommend the organization's federal IRS identification, or tax-exempt, number be included in the suggested wording. Also, revocable *living trusts* recently have increased in use as a substitute for the standard will. Communication with donors should refer to such documents.

If the least technical vehicle is the most used, why then is so much emphasis placed on planned gifts other than bequests? According to Moran (1991), CEOs bear much of the responsibility, as do accounting practices that record nonbequest gifts at their face value. He explained that a CEO will denigrate a $250,000 bequest that will be received sometime in the future and revere a $50,000 life income gift, with an actual charitable value of about $25,000, because it "impacts *his* [sic] fund raising for the year" (p. 42; italics added). Because of flawed accounting methods and CEO preference, Moran (1991) argued, "Planned-giving officers are hired with the idea that a technician is needed for those sophisticated life income agreements. The charity would be better off with someone who can encourage very simple bequests" (p. 42). He said the bias for immediate outcomes is reflected in professional development seminars, which spend a disproportionate amount of time on the complexities of life income agreements and little time on how to generate bequests.

Moran (1991) admitted that bequests are given short shrift because they are revocable. They generally are considered incomplete gifts, or as he described them, "mere expectancies" (p. 42). They are difficult to track because there is no immediate transfer of funds and donors often do not inform the recipient organization. Indeed, three fourths of the 710 NCPG survey respondents who have included a charitable bequest in their will have not notified the organization about the gift (Bigelow & Lumpkin, 1993). The majority (65%) indicated their reason for remaining silent has to do with privacy; only 4% said their decision is due to the possibility they might change their mind.

Getting to the crux of the problem, evaluation, Moran (1991) stated, "Current bequest receipts are often the result of fund raising done many years before, and by a fund raiser who has long since moved on from the charity" (p. 42). He added, "It is difficult to even determine the fund raiser who helped obtain the bequest. After a solicitation, donors will not run out and immediately change their estate plans. Often they wait until circumstances combine to compel them to revise their estate. This may be years after their decision to include the charity" (p. 42).

Moran neglected to stress that those who evaluate the fund-raising function, CEOs and other senior managers, favor short-term gifts over planned gifts in general. Commenting on the problem as it relates to colleges and universities, Worth (1993) explained, "Presidents and deans sometimes overvalue the annual gifts that can help them increase their spending now, while discounting the importance of planned gifts that will benefit their successors" (p. 17).

Returning to the issue of revocability, Moran (cited in Colton, 1992) said people have three fears related to giving away their assets: (a) dying too young and not leaving sufficient funds for their family, (b) living too long and not having enough money to live on, and (c) catastrophic illness. In other words, irrevocable planned gifts are frightening for many people because they do not know what the future will hold. Giving away their assets under such circumstances would be illogical. This perspective is not limited to those with less financial worth, according to empirical evidence.

Steuerle (1987) found that wealthy individuals tend to retain their assets during their lifetime, making their largest contributions as bequests. He investigated the timing of their giving by comparing estate tax returns filed in 1977 with the decedents' income tax returns in the years prior to death. Although the evidence indicated an increasing propensity to give with age, it also showed that older people tend to postpone their giving until death even though their tax savings would be greater by giving during their lifetime. He hypothesized that the wealthy prefer to accumulate and control their wealth until death rather than consume or give it away. A revocable bequest through a will, therefore, represents the safest and most desirable planned giving vehicle for most individuals. Moran (1991) summarized the implications for fund raising, "As long as life's uncertainties and perils exist for donors, revocable gifts will continue to form most of planned giving" (p. 42).

Practitioner wisdom, as transmitted through NSFRE's Survey Course, holds that irrevocable vehicles are beyond the realm of possibility for many, if not most, people. Bequests allow donors to leave their assets flexible during their life and still provide a major gift. Of particular significance, NSFRE practitioner instructors claimed that only about 5% of such donors change their minds (i.e., once a charitable bequest is included in a will, it rarely is removed). The NCPG survey (Bigelow & Lumpkin, 1993) provided support for this claim. It found that of the respondents who have included a charitable bequest in their will, only 8.8% have ever taken such a bequest out. As the bequest portion of the survey had a sampling error of plus or minus 3.7 at the 95% confidence level, we can be 95% sure that only between 5.1% and 12.5% of all charitable bequests actually are revoked; at least 87.5% remain in donors' wills once they are made. Commenting on the finding, Bigelow and Lumpkin (1993) stated, "This should reassure charities that are concerned about the reliability of bequest expectancies, and should also encourage them to provide appropriate forms of stewardship and cultivation to bequest donors" (p. 3).

Revocability, then, is not as serious an issue as some believe; it is unlikely to have detrimental effects on fund-raising results. Rather than viewing it as a negative characteristic of bequests, revocability is positive in that donors highly value it but rarely employ it. In terms of game theory, it provides a win–win situation. The charitable bequest is the planned giving vehicle of choice precisely because it is simple and revocable.

Moran (cited in Colton, 1992) advised practitioners, especially those just starting efforts, to "concentrate on revocable assets—bequests—not irrevocable assets" (p. 51). He offered several recommendations to resolve current incongruencies: redirect planned giving to concentrate on bequests, change accounting practices so that only the charitable remainder value of nonbequests is counted in dollar totals, and hire relationship-building fund raisers, not technicians (Moran, 1991). He concluded, "If most planned gifts come through estate settlements, then that is where we should do our fund raising. . . . We should spend 80 percent of our time where 80 percent of the contributions come from" (p. 42).

In transition to the next category, there is evidence that the use of nonbequest vehicles is growing as planned giving increases. For example, total giving to colleges and universities in 1991–1992 increased only 5% over the year before, but the dollars generated by planned giving increased 12% and those from nonbequest gifts increased 25% (CFAE, 1993). In 1992–1993, giving again increased only 5%, but planned giving increased 10% and nonbequest gifts increased 13% (CFAE, 1994). The same pattern emerged in 1993–1994 (CFAE, 1995). Over the last 20 years, the dollar amount from bequests has risen 113% and the amount accounted for by nonbequest gifts has leaped 433%—keeping in mind that bequests usually represent dollars received, whereas nonbequest gifts traditionally have been reported at face value at the time they are executed.

A nonrandom survey by Prince (cited in E. Greene, 1994a) of 879 affluent individuals—defined as those with liquid assets from $400,000 to more than $10 million—found that 261 (30%) made a planned gift during the 12 months from June 1993 to June 1994. This finding represented a 37% increase over the previous 12 months, attesting to overall growth in planned giving. The survey showed that, even among its wealthy purposive sample, bequests still are the vehicle most used (51%), followed by life income agreements (35%), and then other vehicles (15%).

LIFE INCOME AGREEMENTS

Life income agreements provide irrevocable gifts for charitable organizations and income for donors, generally for the remainder of their life. Gifts are encumbered for the term of the agreement in order to produce income for the donor and/or for any other individuals named income beneficiaries, usually a spouse. Therefore, funds are not available for use by the organization until years after the gift is made. The charitable portion is less than the value of the assets originally given, typically 50%.

Vehicles in this category are attractive to people who want to make a major gift but do not want to give up the income their assets might earn. Sapp (1993) explained:

> Loss of income is a frequent barrier to giving. Some individuals would like to make gifts but cannot afford to give up the annual income they draw from the assets that would form the gift. Potential donors often assume that the only alternative is to provide for a future gift in their will. This need not be the case. Special provisions in the tax code allow donors to make a charitable gift while retaining the right to income during their lives. (p. 123)

The vehicles also provide three forms of tax savings for donors: a partial income tax deduction, elimination or reduction of capital-gains taxes, and savings on gift and estate taxes. Clarifying the first, irrevocability defines whether a gift may be deductible on income taxes (i.e., revocable gifts, such as bequests, are not deductible from taxable income because ownership of the assets is not transferred). Deductions for life income gifts are based on the fair market value of the assets given, minus the projected return to the donor as determined by IRS rules, including actuarial tables, or probabilities of life expectancy (Abrams & Foster, 1995). In other words, the amount eligible for deduction on federal income taxes is equal to the value of the gift's charitable remainder, or the amount the organizational beneficiary likely will get.

Donors fund life income agreements with cash, publicly traded stock, closely held stock, real estate, and tangible personal property (Bigelow & Lumpkin, 1993). Related to the second tax savings, vehicles in this category are particularly attractive to potential donors who desire more income and who own appreciated assets that produce little. For example, publicly traded stock that has grown in value but is not producing any or much income can be given through a life income agreement. The recipient organization sells the appreciated stock and then invests the cash from the sale in something that will provide more income for the donor, who has avoided capital-gains tax on the sale of the stock. Subsequent income payments, however, are not tax free.

Financial benefits returned to donors can be problematic when prospects offer *hard-to-value assets*, or assets other than cash and publicly traded stock, to fund life income agreements (Bigelow & Lumpkin, 1993). Stated differently, financial risk increases when closely held stock, real estate, and tangible personal property are accepted.

For example, an organization might accept a piece of real estate to fund a charitable remainder trust, only to find out later that the property is contaminated and cannot be sold until thousands of dollars are spent to comply with Environmental Protection Agency guidelines. In such a case, the donor theoretically is not liable and still is entitled to his or her life income payments, even though there is no principal to earn interest from which the payments can be made. Staying with just real estate, potentially contaminated property, encumbered property, fractional interest in property, and property producing unrelated business income represent high risks to the recipient organization and can even threaten its tax-exempt status. Furthermore, findings from the NCPG survey (Bigelow & Lumpkin, 1993) provided evidence in support of practitioners' belief that donors using hard-to-value assets are motivated more by financial planning concerns than by charitable intent. I recommend that, in general, organizations limit life income agreements to those funded with gifts of cash and publicly traded stock. Real estate that can be easily sold may be appropriate in some cases. Exceptions should be carefully scrutinized by the organization's experts before acceptance.

Policies in addition to those dealing with types of assets must be established to protect the charitable portion of gifts made in this category. Prior decisions are needed on payout, number of income beneficiaries, minimum age, and minimum gift amount for each vehicle. Although parameters are set by laws and voluntary standards, there is flexibility in limiting the size of the payments returned to donors and the number of income beneficiaries. The minimum age of donors and others who will receive payments and the minimum gift amount for each vehicle are a function of organizational policy, not law.

Life income agreements are not easily understood by donors or fund raisers. Bigelow and Lumpkin (1993) concluded from the NCPG survey, "The use of life income giving vehicles to make a long-term gift to charity is not only the most complex area of the planned giving profession, it is also the most confusing to donors" (p. 15). Contributing to their conclusion, the survey's 175 respondents who have made a life income gift had trouble distinguishing among different vehicles. An amazing 80% of the 500 individuals who originally reported they had executed a life income agreement later said they had made a mistake in responding positively to NCPG's screener questionnaire! The following discussion attempts to reduce such confusion, but still provide students with the threshold of knowledge they need to integrate planned giving in their future work. Specific questions, particularly about the tax consequences for individual cases, should be directed to legal and financial experts.

As given in Table 13.1, life income agreements consist of three primary vehicles: (a) charitable remainder trusts, (b) the charitable gift annuity, and (c) the pooled income fund. Charitable remainder trusts are by far the most popular. The NCPG survey showed that, after removing vehicles inappropriate to this category (e.g., installment bargain sales, discussed shortly), 64% of the life income agreements executed by its respondents were charitable remainder trusts, 25% were charitable gift annuities, and only 11% were pooled income funds. Among the affluent, Prince (cited in E. Greene, 1994a) found that of those who utilized life income agreements, 85% made their gift through a charitable remainder trust, 7% through a charitable gift annuity, and 8% through a pooled income fund.

Charitable Remainder Trusts

A charitable remainder trust enables a donor to give a 501(c)(3) organization cash, stocks, or other assets to establish a self-contained trust, from which the donor receives income. The gift is invested by the organization and produces income for the donor and/or one or more other individuals until those designated die or a fixed term of up to 20 years expires. At that point, the organization keeps the amount remaining in the trust—hence the name, *remainder* trusts.

There are two types of charitable remainder trusts that differ primarily in the way payments to donors are calculated: the charitable remainder *annuity trust* and the charitable remainder *unitrust*. Outlining commonalities first, both types generally require a minimum gift of $50,000. Both must provide donors with payments at a legal minimum of 5%. For both, if the invested assets constituting the trust earn more in interest income than needed to pay the donor, the excess is added to the principal, thereby increasing the amount ultimately payable to the organization (Sapp, 1993). However, if the income earned is less than required to meet payments, the difference is taken from the principal, thereby reducing the amount that will go to the organization. Stated another way, payment is drawn from the trust's income when possible, and from the principal when income is not sufficient.

A charitable remainder annuity trust provides the donor with a *fixed payment* (i.e., a set dollar amount) that must be equal to at least 5% of the value of the contributed assets at the time the life income agreement is signed. For example, if a donor puts $50,000 cash in an annuity trust and is promised a 6% rate of return, he or she will receive $3,000 each and every year, regardless of the value of the trust. Using a charitable remainder unitrust, the donor receives payments equal to a *fixed percentage* of at least 5% of the value of the trust created by the given assets, as calculated at the beginning of each year. For example, if a donor puts $50,000 cash in a unitrust and is promised a 6% rate of return, he or she will receive $3,000 the first year, and subsequent payments will increase or decrease in accordance with the trust's value, adjusted annually.

There are two variations of the unitrust that are useful for accommodating situational needs of organizations and donors. The *net income* unitrust limits payments to the lesser of the agreed-on percentage rate or the actual income earned. According to Sapp (1993), "This variation, which leaves principal and appreciation intact for the life of the unitrust, is especially useful when funding a unitrust with non-liquid assets that are earning little or no income" (p. 125). For example, if a prospective donor wishes to fund a charitable remainder trust with a gift of real estate, the net income unitrust gives the organization time to sell the property and reinvest the proceeds, free of any obligation to make payments before income is available. A further variation is the net income *with make up* unitrust. It uses income earned in excess of the agreed percentage to make up for earlier shortfalls, which is useful when the donor wishes to minimize payments in early years and shift to increased payments during retirement (Sapp, 1993).

Younger donors generally prefer the unitrust, hoping their income will increase as the trust grows over time. Older donors find the annuity trust more attractive because they can count on receiving a set amount of money. Furthermore, donors can make additional gifts to a unitrust, but not to an annuity trust, which enhances the unitrust's attractiveness as a long-term, financial planning vehicle for younger donors. Suggested minimum age reflects these differences: about 60 years old for those who wish to receive income from a charitable remainder unitrust and 65 years old for those choosing the charitable remainder annuity trust.

A concern for fund raisers as of 1997 is that the popularity of charitable remainder trusts—as well as other life income vehicles—will diminish if Congress reduces the set tax rate on capital gains, which leaders have promised to do. At the current rate of

28%, a gift of stock that has appreciated $50,000 represents a $14,000 savings in capital-gains tax. A proposed rate of 20% would decrease the savings by $4,000. Prince (cited in Murawski & Moore, 1995), who claimed most charitable remainder trusts are funded with appreciated assets, found in a nonrandom survey of 388 donors who have established such trusts that a majority (55%) would not have done so if the capital-gains rate had been 21% at the time of their gift. He reported, "They all say giving a gift is real important, but they drop out in five seconds if you lower the capital-gains tax" (p. 32).

Charitable Gift Annuity

Although they share similar names, the charitable gift annuity is different from the charitable remainder annuity trust. They both pay fixed-dollar amounts, or annuities, to donors, but the charitable gift annuity is a *contract* by which a 501(c)(3) organization legally guarantees income for a maximum of two individuals for life (Sapp, 1993). Its distinctive characteristic is that it always pays, regardless of investment returns or market conditions. If a charitable remainder annuity trust—or any other life income vehicle—runs out of money, the income stops, whereas payments from a charitable gift annuity cannot be discontinued.

Among other differences, the minimum amount typically required to fund the charitable gift annuity is $5,000 to $10,000, considerably less than charitable remainder trusts. Some religious organizations offer gift annuities for as little as $500, which explains why this option often is called middle America's life income vehicle (Johnston, 1994). It also is the simplest and easiest to understand; a single sheet of paper is sufficient for its terms.

Gift annuities appeal to older people because the income payments are tied to the age of the donor (and one additional beneficiary, if named) at the time the gift is made. The older the donor, the higher the payments. For example, voluntary standards set in 1997 recommend that donors aged 70 be paid 7.7% of the amount they put in an annuity, every year until they die, and that donors aged 55 get only 6.7% annually. Younger donors, who are not old enough to reap a significant rate of return, sometimes choose a variation, the *deferred* charitable gift annuity, which allows the principal to grow in value and bases delayed payments on the donor's age at the time income will begin, as stipulated in the agreement. Suggested minimum age generally is 65 for the standard gift annuity and 35 for the deferred variation.

When the economy is down or uncertain, a fixed rate of return is more appealing to donors than fluctuating rates tied to market performance. Therefore, in the early 1990s, low returns on many commercial investments, such as certificates of deposit and bonds, produced a boom in gift annuities (Stehle, 1994c). When tax-law changes made contributions to individual retirement accounts (IRAs) nondeductible for those with annual salaries of $50,000 or more, younger people began using deferred annuities to create a "charitable IRA" (Aldrich, 1994, p. 26). For the organization, the charitable gift annuity offers a distinct advantage over other vehicles in this category. Because it is a contract and not a trust, funds do not have to be kept intact (unless required by state law) so the organization can spend the estimated portion of the gift not needed to cover promised payments to the donor (i.e., financial benefits can be immediate).

Some organizations, however, have made a deliberate decision not to offer gift annuities due to the unique risk of promising future payments regardless of unforeseen financial circumstances. As Johnston (1994) explained, "That promise commits the charity's resources, right down to the last sharpened pencil in the fund-raising office" (p. 45). Those wanting to offer them without the obligation of future payments can *reinsure* gift annuities through a commercial insurance company (Seltzer, 1987). In such cases, the organization sells the annuity for an amount less than it should ultimately receive (i.e., at a discount), thereby transferring its legal obligation. Many of those who reinsured annuities in the late 1980s and early 1990s, it must be emphasized, committed a disservice to their donors because numerous insurance companies failed and income payments were discontinued (Brown & Feagin, 1994).

The charitable gift annuity is the most standardized of the life income vehicles. Laws and voluntary standards structure the vehicle so the charitable portion will approximate 50% of the amount originally transferred to the organization. Commercial annuities sold by insurance companies—and increasingly by national banks—students should note, pay back as much as 95% of the amount invested, attesting to the charitable intent necessary for making such gifts (Johnston, 1994).

As already touched on, rate ceilings are set by ACGA, which was called the Committee on Gift Annuities from its founding in 1927 until it changed its name in 1994. The council, located in Dallas, Texas, meets every 3 years to recommend the standards charitable organizations should follow in offering annuities, based on prevailing interest rates. Its primary purpose is to help organizations avoid competing with each other on the financial performance of this vehicle, which has been in use since before the Civil War (Johnston, 1994). According to ACGA, which has 1,900 members, about 86% of all organizations offering gift annuities follow its recommendations (Murawski, 1995a; Stehle, 1994b).

This is not to say all pay the maximum rates; some, such as the University of Pennsylvania, purposely set rates lower than the ceilings so a larger portion of the gifts will benefit the organization. Addressing the New York UJA–FJP advertising campaign that offered higher than recommended rates, ACGA's chair stated, "To deviate from the rates puts us back to a situation that existed before there was a gift-annuities council, to a position when we competed on the basis of rates of return rather than on the basis of your cause and mission" (Stehle, 1994b, p. 25). In the 1920s and 1930s, rates offered by some organizations were so favorable experts say the organizations were, in effect, making contributions to their donors.

ACGA temporarily stopped setting rate ceilings when a class-action lawsuit was brought against the council and its members in 1995 for allegedly engaging in price fixing and violating SEC regulations (Murawski, 1995a). In response, Congress passed the Charitable Gift Annuity Antitrust Relief Act to exempt the vehicle from antitrust laws (i.e., using uniform payout rates does not constitute price fixing) and the Philanthropy Protection Act to exempt charitable organizations offering gift annuities and other planned giving vehicles from registering with the SEC. President Clinton signed the legislation in December 1995, which effectively rendered the lawsuit moot. The judge, however, refused to dismiss the case, which prompted further legislation in mid-1997. ACGA resumed setting rates at the beginning of 1997.

The new federal laws supersede all applicable state antitrust and securities laws; if state legislatures disagree with either or both of the measures, however, they have until 1999 to override them. Illustrating unresolved issues at stake, the Philanthropy Protection Act holds that charitable gift annuities are not commercial investment products, yet most states did not make this distinction at the time the bill was enacted. The vehicle generally was regulated under state laws governing the sale of commercial annuities by the insurance industry. Sapp (1993), for example, reported that some states' insurance regulations prohibited the use of real estate and tangible personal property to fund gift annuities. Organizations located in states such as California and New York needed a license to offer them (Johnston, 1994). New York's law required 5 or more years of operation before applying for a license, keeping funds intact and separate from other resources, and investing most of the money in government bonds. California required licensing fees that sometimes totaled as much as $30,000. As states respond to the new federal laws, fund raisers must check regulations and carefully monitor the situation. They also should refrain from inappropriate marketing activities.

According to Johnston (1994), there was a surge of regulatory interest in charitable gift annuities in the early 1990s, much of which resulted from the growing use of advertising to generate gifts. Johnston explained:

> Traditionally it was long-time supporters who were offered charitable gift annuities. Now national charities run ads in major newspapers seeking annuities from strangers. That makes charities look like commercial enterprises soliciting business. And, of course, society expects businesses to pay taxes and, when appropriate, to be regulated to protect the public. (p. 46)

Finally, fund raisers often approach the low-cost charitable gift annuity as a means by which donors can be cultivated and upgraded to larger planned gifts. Effective stewardship often leads to the execution of additional gift annuities or other vehicles.

Pooled Income Fund

The pooled income fund is best understood as a *charitable mutual fund* in that it comingles gifts from multiple donors and pays them income based on their proportionate share in the fund. Brain (1991) explained, "The contributor receives income from the fund each year based on his or her share of the net earnings of the fund, or in the same manner that an investor in a mutual fund would receive income" (p. 98). When the donor dies, his or her share of the fund's principal goes to the organization, to be used as directed by the donor at the time the original agreement was executed (Sapp, 1993).

Because of the pooled income fund's distinctive characteristic of combining many gifts, the amount required for each is relatively low. Like the charitable gift annuity, its minimum gift is only $5,000 to $10,000. Unlike the charitable gift annuity, income fluctuates. Size of the payments depends on the fund's performance and is not tied to the donor's age. The fund's previous 3 years of performance determines the expected rate of return for gifts ("New ruling," 1994). Gifts to new funds, without sufficient history, must use the assumed rate of return set by the IRS each year for newly created funds. In 1997, the rate is 7.2%. Additional gifts of smaller amounts, usually $2,000, can be made.

Pooled income funds, therefore, are attractive to donors who lack the financial capacity to fund a charitable remainder unitrust, want a higher rate of return than they would get from a charitable gift annuity (often because they are not old enough to qualify for the top rates), and seek growth opportunity. The suggested minimum age usually is 60.

Like charitable remainder trusts, the pooled income fund allows donors to name more than two income beneficiaries, but like the charitable gift annuity, the term of its agreement is for life only (i.e., a fixed number of years is not an option). Different from the other life income vehicles, payments to donors are taxed as ordinary income; other vehicles produce payments that are tax free and taxed as ordinary income and capital gains, depending on the specifics of the gift.

Donors were attracted to new pooled income funds in 1995, when the IRS decreased its assumed rate of return at the same time interest rates were expected to rise (Murawski, 1994a). The assumed rate for new funds was lowered from 8.4% to 6.8% to reflect a 3-year drop in interest rates. The lower IRS rate meant that donors making a gift to a newly created fund in 1995 could take a higher income tax deduction at the time of their gift and still expect higher than assumed payments (i.e., the lower the government's estimate of how much the donor will receive, the higher the tax deduction). Because of the favorable conditions for donors, a number of organizations established pooled income funds in 1995.

On the other hand, many organizations reported that charitable gift annuities remained more attractive to prospective donors. For example, David Lawrence (cited in Murawski, 1994a), director of development at the Mayo Foundation for Medical Education and Research in Rochester, Minnesota, explained why his organization had decided against offering a pooled income fund. "We find that gift annuities are simpler for people to understand, and they achieve generally similar objectives" (p. 27). Pooled income funds returned about 6% to 7% to donors in 1994, as compared to the 1994 gift annuity rate of 6.9% recommended for donors aged 70 (Murawski, 1994a).

Concluding this category, in addition to the three vehicles described here, donors sometimes are provided with income through an installment bargain sale or a remainder interest in a home or farm. A bargain sale, it is recalled from chapter 11, is an outright major gift whereby the donor sells an asset to an organization for a price below its fair market value, the difference being the charitable portion. When the sale price is paid in installments to the donor over a number of years, some authors increase the confusion about planned giving by incorporating such outright gifts in the category of life income agreements (e.g., Bigelow & Lumpkin, 1993). A remainder interest in a home or farm, as discussed shortly, gives donors the right to use the property for life. Some organizations under certain conditions will provide lifetime income to the donor in addition to lifetime residency. This is the exception rather than the rule, which justifies my placement of such gifts in the category of other vehicles.

OTHER VEHICLES

As given in Table 13.1, the last category consists of three vehicles, which—because of their characteristics—do not fit in the first two categories: (a) the charitable lead trust, (b) remainder interest in home or farm, and (c) life insurance. Whereas bequests are revocable and life income agreements are irrevocable, the first two vehicles in this category require irrevocable gifts, and the third can be used to make either an irrevocable or revocable gift. Pension plans share characteristics with life insurance and are discussed in relation to that vehicle.

Charitable Lead Trust

The charitable lead trust is planned giving's oxymoron. It is responsible for much of the confusion, absence of concise definitions, and overuse of qualifiers in discussions about planned gifts. Unlike all other vehicles, the purpose of the charitable lead trust is to provide *immediate* financial benefit to the recipient organization and to *defer* principal financial benefits to the donor. It is the exact opposite of charitable remainder trusts in that the organization receives income from the transferred assets for the lifetime of the donor or a fixed period, after which the assets revert back to the donor or named beneficiaries; in other words, lead versus remainder.

Abrams and Foster (1995) listed four variations of the lead trust formed from two factors: (a) how the income payments are calculated, annuity trust or unitrust; and (b) to whom the assets revert, "grantor" or "nongrantor" (p. 31). Payments from an annuity trust, students now understand, are a fixed amount, whereas those from a unitrust are a fluctuating amount adjusted annually—keeping in mind that, with a lead trust, the payments are made to the organization. A grantor lead trust, whether an annuity trust or a unitrust, returns the assets to the donor. A nongrantor lead trust returns them to other beneficiaries, either individuals or entities. Tax savings differ between grantor and nongrantor trusts: The first only provides a deduction on income tax; the second only provides a reduction for gift and estate taxes. These variations are useful for meeting objectives of different donors.

The charitable lead trust is the most flexible vehicle in its requirements, but the most limited in use. Any type of asset that produces revenue, particularly a closely held business, can be used to fund the trust. There are no minimum age requirements because the organization does not have to wait to receive its financial benefits. The minimum gift amount and the size of income payments to the organization are completely negotiable. There is no limit on years for fixed terms, although the minimum usually is 10.

On the other hand, the lead trust appeals primarily to people with the capacity to give away $1 million or more, who have large estates, who have used up their lifetime unified credit that reduces taxable estates, and who want to pass assets intact to heirs. Its distinctive use is helping donors who own a closely held business pass the business to their children. According to Sapp (1993), "The use of lead trusts has diminished steadily through the 1980s due to changes in tax rules. Given the current limitations, charitable lead trusts are used far less than the life income plans" (p. 129).

Remainder Interest in Home or Farm

The IRS breakdown of an average estate given at the beginning of the chapter, which was based on the statistical mean of individuals with a great many assets and those with few, showed that stock was the leading asset. In contrast, Donikian (cited in H. Hall, 1993b) logically argued that most people have their assets in real estate, life insurance, and pensions. All three can be transferred without being part of a will (i.e., they can be given irrevocably during the donor's lifetime). Insurance and retirement policies also can be used to make revocable gifts.

If unmortgaged real estate is being used as a residence or farm, an individual (or a married couple) can transfer ownership to a charitable organization while retaining the right to use the property for life. The donor claims an income tax deduction for the *remainder interest* in the property at the time the agreement is executed. The amount is an actuarially calculated partial value, based on age and worth of the property (Sapp, 1993). The gift also reduces the donor's estate, which may result in savings on gift and estate taxes if assets owned exceed the unused portion of the unified credit. At death, the life residency ends and the organization takes full possession of the property. Seltzer (1987) described this vehicle as "give it but live in it" (p. 174).

Its execution is relatively simple; all that is needed is a properly drawn deed. There are minimal administrative responsibilities for the recipient organization. According to Seltzer (1987), the donor, while living at the residence or farm, still is responsible for paying real estate and other taxes on the property. Capital improvements, such as a new roof, are tax deductible as gifts to the charitable organization because the organization owns the property. A word of caution: If the property is not maintained by the donor resident, its value can decrease (e.g., he or she may not have sufficient funds to make needed capital improvements).

Gifts of remainder interest in home or farm are attractive to individuals of moderate means who have no children. Illustrating, a retired professor and his wife once approached me about their wish to use the remainder interest in their home to endow and name the honors program at the university where I worked. Although they were in their 70s and the home was worth more than $250,000 at the time of the negotiations, a decision was reached after consulting with the chief operating officer that the gift's value was less than the amount required to fund the program in perpetuity. Unfortunately, therefore, I had to turn the gift down, but the gracious couple convinced me that this vehicle provides a donor-friendly option for individuals who want to make a major gift but lack the capacity to make the gift outright.

Life Insurance

Life insurance policies are used three different ways in planned giving: (a) given as irrevocable gifts, (b) used to make revocable gifts, and (c) purchased to replace assets given away either outright or through other vehicles. Donors make an irrevocable gift by naming a charitable organization the *owner and beneficiary* of a life insurance policy that is new, existing, or paid up. The gift entitles them to deduct premiums and/or the "present value" of the policy (approximately the cash surrender value or the cost basis, whichever is less) from income on which they owe taxes (Sapp, 1993, p. 122). The organization is able to use the policy's cash reserve (i.e., financial benefits can be immediate). A critical point is that the age of the policy is progressively beneficial for the recipient organization. As Sharpe (1993a) stated, "In general, the older the life insurance policy, the better it is for the donee institution" (p. 17).

A new policy has high administrative obligations, particularly if premiums are paid quarterly or monthly. In most cases, the organization bills the donor for the premium, the donor pays the organization, and the organization pays the insurance company the premium. Because they usually come from income rather than assets, premiums on new policies potentially can deter outright giving. As they generally are tax deductible, payments may be viewed by donors as their annual gifts for the years it takes to pay for the policy. Experts, such as Brown (Brown & Feagin, 1994), advise fund raisers to consider new life insurance a last option in planned giving. Disregarding such advice, many charitable organizations engage in joint ventures with insurance companies, referred to as "life insurance endowment programs," whereby commercial agents market new policies to the organization's constituencies (Sharpe, 1993a, p. 16). Addressing such ventures, Sharpe argued that donors should deal with their own agent and company: "If I were the trustee, CEO, or chief development executive, I would not want my institution involved in any life insurance scheme that gives the institution's implied endorsement to any company, agent, or policy" (p. 16). As pointed out earlier, many insurance companies went out of business in recent years.

The same obligations mitigate the benefits of existing policies. In addition, the organization must decide if it will assume the expense or let the policy lapse if a donor stops making premium payments. A paid-up policy, on the other hand, involves little if any administrative work. This variation is attractive to individuals who own life insurance policies they no longer need (e.g., a policy on the donor's life purchased for the benefit of a spouse who died first). Unlike life income agreements, the value of the gift is not eroded by payments to the donor.

Gifts of new policies have raised regulatory questions about whether a charitable organization has an insurable interest in the donor and, therefore, whether the premiums should be deductible from taxable income. Some states say the organization has no legitimate interest (i.e., there is no potential loss to the organizational beneficiary when the donor dies). Sharpe (1993a) advised fund raisers to avoid the question of insurable interest and the deductibility of premiums by urging donors to give policies they already own.

Donors make a revocable gift by naming a charitable organization the first, second, or contingent *beneficiary* for part or all of the proceeds from their new, existing, or paid-up life insurance policies. This variation acts much like a charitable bequest made through a will and is equally promising for generating gifts of assets. Sharpe (1993a) agreed: "I am convinced that the best source of life insurance gifts is from existing policies by being named as first, second, or last beneficiary" (p. 17). It is the contractual right of policyholders to submit policy change forms naming 501(c)(3) organizations as a beneficiary on existing life insurance policies—as well as on pension plans and annuity policies. According to Sharpe (1993a), more than $9 trillion of life insurance currently exists. A U.S. family, on average, has about $122,000, and 86% of all Americans are insured. Therefore, he concluded, "More than 86 percent of your donors could make a life insurance gift without purchasing a policy by simply using a change of beneficiary form which any policyholder can request from the life insurance carrier" (p. 17).

Pension plans act like revocable gifts of life insurance in that charitable organizations can be named a beneficiary of the asset. Illustrating, Planned Parenthood of America offered the following as 1 of 15 ways donors can leave their legacy to the organization: "When you retire, designate Planned Parenthood contingent beneficiary of your pension benefits—a legacy that would come to Planned Parenthood only if everyone you want to provide for predeceases you" (Seltzer, 1987, p. 182). Students are reminded that revocable gifts are not deductible on income taxes; therefore, if the organization only is named beneficiary, not owner of the vehicle, insurance premiums, pension contributions, and annuity payments are not deductible.

The third and final way of using life insurance is as *asset replacement*, whereby a policy is purchased to replace assets given away either outright or through other planned giving vehicles. A donor gives assets to a charitable organization and replaces the dollar value of the assets with life insurance payable to family members or other heirs. The income tax savings from the gift may be sufficient to pay for the replacement insurance. Premiums, however, are not deductible. Asset replacement is a strategically sound practice for donors because life insurance, unlike other inherited property, is not subject to gift and estate taxes.

Similar to life income agreements, many organizations traditionally have reported irrevocable gifts of life insurance at their face value rather then at their actual value. Gifts made through a charitable lead trust and remainder interest in a home or farm also have been incorrectly recorded. Counting the face value of irrevocable gifts enables trustees, senior managers, and fund raisers to unethically inflate dollar totals—a subject addressed in the discussion that follows.

ROPES PROCESS

The research step was already outlined; however, two overlapping points about research on the opportunity and publics warrant emphasis: needs of the organization must be matched with the needs and interests of prospective donors, and planned giving concentrates on those with whom the organization shares common interests. Regarding the first, Connell (1993) urged fund raisers—who generally are younger—to acquire a better understanding of senior citizens and to monitor the issues and problems with which they are concerned. He recommended regular reading of such publications as *Modern Maturity*, the monthly magazine of the American Association of Retired Persons, which has a paid membership of more than 35 million Americans over age 50. Supporting the second point, Abrams and Foster (1995) advised, "Identify people motivated to support your institution and its mission so you can focus your limited time on situations most likely to result in meaningful gifts" (p. 27).

The second step of setting objectives varies little from the procedures outlined in chapter 10. Output objectives help track the process of raising planned gifts. Impact objectives deal with the degree to which planned giving and its vehicles are understood and positively regarded by donor publics, as well as measures of enacted behaviors (e.g., to increase the number of donors to the pooled income fund by 10 during the fiscal year). The discussion here concentrates on the remaining three steps of ROPES.

Programming

Regardless of the scope of the effort, planned giving is effective when it is integrated with fund raising's two primary programs. Its purpose is to raise major gifts, but because income and other standard measures of affluence are not reliable indicators of accumulated assets, the strategy must extend beyond prospects assigned to the major gifts program.

The prospect pool is drawn from both annual giving and major gifts, with additional research to identify individuals who do not fit typical criteria. Information is disseminated through cultivation activities. For example, articles in periodicals and newsletters provide testimonials from donors who have utilized the vehicles offered. Seminars and small group meetings are held on financial and estate planning. A series of direct-mail pieces, which might include a brochure on why women need wills, is sent to qualified prospects. Generic publications about different vehicles and topics are available from numerous vendors and can be purchased in bulk quantities with customized information, such as the charitable organization's name and address, printed on them. Response forms for all annual gifts include check-off options requesting planned giving material.

The importance of cultivation cannot be minimized. Somewhere around one half of all planned gifts are not known to the organizational beneficiary until after the donor's death. Focusing on ultimate gifts, which are large major gifts usually arranged through planned giving vehicles, Dunlop (1987) argued that individuals make these gifts "when they want to—because it's the right time in their own lives, not necessarily because it's the right time for the institution" (p. 10). Hartsook (1993) and Moran (1991) agreed, explaining that donors usually change their financial and estate plans only when circumstances compel them to do so, such as at marriage, births, divorce, retirement, or other life-changing events. Even when solicited, donors often do not enact a giving behavior until years later, and—depending on the selected vehicle and parties involved in its execution—the organizational beneficiary may or may not be notified.

The literature touches on this phenomenon, but usually only in regard to bequests. Practitioner authors advise fund raisers to gather information from annual giving prospects about whether a bequest for the organization already has been included in their will. Rarely acknowledged is that donors utilizing other planned giving vehicles must be similarly canvased. The NCPG survey (Bigelow & Lumpkin, 1993) found that 49% of all donors who have executed a life income agreement have done so without the knowledge of the organizational beneficiary. Of those who have made bequests, 74% have not notified the organization. The NCPG survey also found that of the 181 donors who had made their bequests known to the charitable beneficiary, only 10% reported they did so because the organization asked them; 90% undertook notification on their own initiative. Bigelow and Lumpkin (1993) commented, "This indicates that there is significant room for charitable organizations to expand their efforts to identify bequest donors" (p. 11). Greenfield (1991)—one of the few to do so—recommended that information about all types of planned gifts be gathered and disseminated through direct-mail response forms. For example, forms should include such options to check as, "Yes, I have made a gift to the xyz organization through a charitable remainder trust," and "Yes, I would like more information about how to make a gift to the xyz organization through a charitable remainder trust."

Interpersonal communication is employed once prospects identify themselves. Those requesting information promptly are sent personal letters, which include notification that a follow-up telephone call will be made to answer any questions. If the prospect desires, meetings are scheduled. Because requests are for major gifts, solicitation activities emulate that program (e.g., face-to-face meetings are used whenever possible). The simplicity of bequests allows an exception. Such gifts can be solicited through written communication by providing simple wording that can be used to include a bequest when executing a will or to add a bequest through a codicil, examples of which were given earlier. Solicitations for other revocable gifts can similarly be made (e.g., asking prospects to use policy change forms to name the organization contingent beneficiary of existing life insurance policies).

As part of the major gifts program, planned giving is utilized in conjunction with outright gifts to fund specific needs of the organization and purposes of interest to its donors. Illustrating, an individual may be a prospect for a named gift opportunity, such as endowing a staff position, but lacks the discretionary income and assets necessary to fully fund it. The combination of outright and planned gifts may provide the solution, keeping in mind that funds from the planned gift likely will not be available for use for some time. Greenfield (1991) affirmed, "Every major gift situation has opportunities for estate gifts and planned giving" (p. 184).

In all programming, empathy with prospective donors is critical. Hartsook (1993) reminded practitioners that prospects for planned gifts generally are older than those for annual and major outright gifts. He and others advised: Do not be patronizing, allow time for reflection, and use type larger than normal in written communication.

Evaluation

Because of its long-term time frame, planned giving cannot be evaluated by annual dollar totals, nor can the overall fund-raising function in which it is integrated. Evaluation beyond dollars is strongly recommended in the literature, demonstrating again the symmetrical characteristic of this strategy. Brain (1991), for example, explained that although the effectiveness of other programs is measured by dollars raised, planned giving should be measured by process evaluation—number of prospects identified, number of prospects cultivated, and number of calls made.

This is not to say program evaluation using dollar measurements is impossible or undesirable. Estimates of dollars generated help evaluate fund raising in relation to current expenditures (e.g., we can expect $x during the next 5 years from this year's programming). Illustrating, practitioners at Brown University estimate the future restricted and unrestricted income that will be produced by the life income agreements executed in a given year (Netherton, 1994). They calculate their estimates using planned giving software—discussed shortly—that incorporates information about payment rates, donors' ages, and life expectancies, among other factors. Such measurements are valid and ethical, in contrast to the traditional practice of reporting irrevocable gifts at their face value.

Reform of misleading accounting practices was introduced by CASE (1994) as part of its new management and reporting standards for capital campaigns, which provided the foundation for CASE's (1996) revised standards for all fund-raising efforts. The reporting standards are based on the mechanism of *present value discounting*, which the financial world uses to recognize current value of an asset that will not be realized until some time in the future. The present value of a future interest simply is what the future amount would be worth in terms of today's dollar value. The standards use the Applicable Federal Rate (AFR) as the discount factor for calculating the present value of planned gifts, in addition to the donor's actuarial life expectancy, income to be paid to the donor, and the number of beneficiaries. In other words, the standards advocate reporting planned gifts at the amount they will actually be worth to the organization.

As explained by CASE (1994, 1996), when an outright gift is made for the recipient organization's immediate use—including endowment purposes—and no benefits are returned to the donor, its current, full fair-market value is the amount available to the donor for income tax deduction. When a return benefit is given and/or the organization cannot have immediate and complete access to the transferred amount, the deduction will be less than the gift's full fair-market value. In such cases, the Internal Revenue Code requires that the AFR be used to determine the gift's present value for deduction. The CASE standards hold that planned gifts should be credited at the same amount as that allowable as a deduction by the IRS, before any limits specific to the donor's situation are imposed.

I strongly endorse crediting planned gifts at their present value and urge fund raisers to adopt it for all reporting. The AFR, or monthly discount rates issued by the IRS, can be found in such publications as *The Wall Street Journal*, *The Chronicle of Philanthropy*, and *Planned Giving Today*. Software programs designed to calculate tax and financial consequences of the different vehicles regularly are updated to account for the monthly rates.

Vance Peterson (1994), then vice president for institutional advancement at Occidental College in Los Angeles, California, and chair of the advisory group that devised the campaign standards, stated, "While discounting to present value represents a substantial change from past practice, many people strongly support its use as a more realistic indicator of the future value those dollars will have when the institution actually is able to spend them" (p. iv). Accountants associated with AICPA and FASB, students should note, refer to planned gifts other than bequests as "split-interest gifts" (Larkin, 1995, p. 25).

The CASE advisory group spent 4 years developing the campaign standards, and, according to Goss (1994b), their release was delayed an entire year largely because of objections to the reporting requirements for planned gifts. The first version called for counting only their present value. After meeting fierce resistance from some fund raisers, who claimed the lower valuations would deter donors and unfairly shrink campaign totals, the association decided on a compromise—allowing planned gifts to be reported at both their present and face values. Under the final standards, organizations can choose to report only the face value to their constituencies, including donors, but they must report both face and present values to their governing board and to CASE.

Peterson (1994), who now is the president of Sierra Nevada College, presented the argument used by those opposing present value discounting: "Even though the institution may pay back a substantial amount to the donor and will not be able to spend the asset for some time into the future, many donors consider the current face value of the asset as the amount that he or she gave to the institution" (p. iv). Such arguments denigrate donors, portraying them as ignorant and egotistical. Individuals capable of making irrevocable gifts are intelligent enough to understand that the organization does not benefit from the full market value of their gift. After all, they were allowed only a partial deduction for income taxes and most of them regularly receive income payments. The argument more accurately reflects the desires of those trustees, CEOs, other managers, and fund raisers who wish to perpetuate the practice of inflating dollar totals.[4]

Goss (1994b) illustrated the misrepresentation: "In practical terms, that means that if a donor endows a professorship with a $1-million deferred gift, it might only be worth $750,000 when the donor dies, leaving the university to come up with the rest of the money" (p. 27). To be ethical and socially responsible, evaluation using dollars raised must be based on the present value of gifts. CASE standards are a significant step forward in promoting such practice. The compromise, however, weakens them, as do their current application only to CASE members and the fact that compliance is not a condition of membership. The standards are discussed further in the chapter on capital campaigns.

Stewardship

Unlike other fund-raising efforts, stewardship for planned gifts begins years before the organization usually receives financial benefit. Reciprocity, responsible gift use, reporting, and relationship nurturing still must be provided to donors.

Bigelow and Lumpkin (1993) found that one half of the bequest donors whose gifts are known to the recipient organization said they had not received any form of recognition. The authors chastised such inattention, stating, "There is clearly room for improvement in the degree to which charitable organizations properly recognize bequest donors, whether that stewardship is as elaborate as a recognition event or as simple as a thank-you letter or a listing of bequest donors" (p. 2). Keeping in mind that 49% of the life income gifts in the NCPG survey are not known to the organizations, 84% of all donors of such gifts reported they had not been recognized in any significant way. Only 3% received even a letter of thanks.

A convenient mechanism for expressing appreciation and providing recognition is a special gift club, called the "Heritage Society," or a similar name. It emphasizes, without differentiating by gift size, that members have helped ensure the organization's future, which also encourages others to make planned gifts. There is widespread agreement that a special club should be created to honor donors of revocable gifts, such as bequests, but donors of irrevocable gifts often are awarded membership in clubs originally established for outright gifts, graduated by gift size. This poses no problem if the planned gifts are discounted to present value; however, membership based on face value is deceptive and diminishes the integrity of the clubs (i.e., a gift of $50,000 through a charitable remainder trust is worth substantially less than an outright $50,000 gift). Due to the compromise on reporting face and present values, the CASE standards are "silent on the question of how an institution should publicly recognize its donors" (Peterson, 1994, p. iv).

---

[4]My assumptions and those held by opponents of present value discounting should be tested through scientific research. An excellent topic for a master's study would be donors' self-reported beliefs about the monetary value of their planned gifts to the organizational recipient. Another study, based on coorientation theory, could measure perceived value on both sides of the relationship, thereby determining the degree of accuracy and agreement between the views of dominant coalition members and donors. Turning to a different area of research suggested by this discussion, Peterson's career move from college fund raiser to college president in 1996 reflects a growing trend that is in need of study. Master's theses on the number and experiences of practitioners who have become CEOs of educational and other types of charitable organizations would add to our knowledge. The last such study (Dorich, 1991) was conducted 7 years ago; its findings provide a basis for design and comparison.

Responsible use of planned gifts requires vigilance and perseverance on the part of fund raisers. Extensive efforts must be made to gather information about each gift and its conditions—if any—before the donor dies. Only in this way can practitioners ensure that the donor's wishes will be carried out and that restricted gifts will match the organization's priority needs. In particular, restricted gifts made for endowment cannot be easily changed because the donor is not alive to approve the changes. Although the doctrine of *cy pres* allows the courts to direct a modified application of donated funds, the modification must be as close to the original intentions of the donor as possible (Ostrower, 1989). Requirements that must be met include "evidence that the original purpose has become impossible, impractical, or illegal" (p. 284), which is difficult to provide except in extreme cases. Illustrating, a donor left a bequest to Amherst College in the 1960s to provide scholarships for "deserving American born, Protestant, Gentile boys of good moral repute, not given to gambling, smoking, drinking or similar acts" (p. 284). Amherst's charter did not allow such religious restrictions, so it refused to accept the bequest until court action altered the gift's conditions.

According to Ostrower (1989), some organizations accept planned gifts with restrictions that are perceived as onerous, hoping they will find some way to get around them in the future. Others have started to turn them down. She concluded that little is known about the day-to-day ways charitable organizations are managing their restricted gifts made through bequests and other vehicles. Clear communication in programming, gift-acceptance policies, and adherence to ethical standards during stewardship alleviate problems with responsible gift use.

Most irrevocable gifts require long-term financial management and reporting. A surprising finding of the NCPG survey was that an amazing 66% of the life income donors did not know how well their vehicle was performing. Bigelow and Lumpkin (1993) attributed this finding to either a lack of attention to detail or a high degree of confusion; however, it may be that many organizations do a poor job of reporting to donors. Even for revocable gifts, regular reports about the organization should be sent to donors during their life, and reports about the use of gift funds later should be sent to surviving family members.

Brain (1991) addressed the last element of stewardship, simply stating, "Any failure to nurture this relationship is unfair to both the individual and the organization" (p. 101). An axiom transmitted through the NSFRE Survey Course is that planned giving promotes rather than detracts from annual giving. Demonstrating, the University of California at Santa Cruz found that more than 75% of its alumni who attended small group meetings about planned giving make annual gifts, compared to only about 10% for alumni in general (Aldrich, 1994). According to a study by the Direct Marketing Association (1995), the most generous donors are people who already have included bequests for charitable organizations in their will. These individuals contribute an average of $558 per year, or $385 more than the national median.

As presented here, an integrated approach to planned giving is not complicated and fits well with the primary fund-raising programs. It is easily adopted by departments of all sizes, even those with only one practitioner. Providing some support for this approach, Schmeling (1990) began the first chapter of his manual by stating, "Planned giving is the cultivation of donors for the purpose of receiving major gifts . . . . [it]

should be an integral part of your organization's comprehensive and balanced development program" (p. 2).

The approach is quite new. Writing in the mid-1980s, Gurin (1985) observed that most organizations hire a specialist who searches for "new donors" rather than focusing on individuals who are closest to the organization (p. 92). At NSFRE's 1994 conference about 10 years later, Harvard University fund raiser Susan Feagin (Brown & Feagin, 1994) predicted during her presentation with husband John Brown that the staff position of major gifts soon will blend with the planned giving position. Her prediction, interestingly, was based not on definitional, structural, or operational issues, but on the asymmetrical–symmetrical dimension of fund-raising practice. She explained, the planned giving officer was the first to be perceived as an advocate for the donor. "Major gifts people are moving that way," enabling the two positions to merge.

A forerunner to this prediction was Rensselaer Polytechnic Institute's (RPI) fund-raising department, which incorporated planned giving in its major gifts program in 1988 (Killoran & Estey, 1993). As a result of the merger, RPI practitioners emphasized planned gifts as a supplement and option to outright giving, resulting in more and larger gifts. Dollars generated from planned gifts were nearly double 3 years later.

Attorney Lynda Moerschbacker (cited in "NSFRE chapters," 1993), a specialist in planned giving, listed advantages of an integrated approach in addition to increasing gift income: more coordination, including shared research findings on specific prospects; a structure designed for donor convenience rather than for functional convenience; eliminating duplication between two programs with the same purpose, and an office atmosphere of greater cooperation and less competition. Moerschbacker argued that major gifts are either immediate or deferred; therefore, she maintained, "There is no such thing as planned giving" (p. 54).

LEARNING AND RESEARCH OPPORTUNITIES

Opportunities to learn more about planned giving abound. The fund-raising associations, such as CASE, offer professional development seminars. The National Committee on Planned Giving (1994) publishes *A Guide To Starting A Planned Giving Program*, which is packaged with such resource materials as the association's syllabus, bibliography, and calendar of training sessions. Other publications are available for self-study. For example, Jordan and Quynn's (1995) book, *Planned Giving: Management, Marketing, and Law*, is accompanied by an IBM-compatible disk with more than 140 sample items, including policies, procedures, agreements for various vehicles, newsletters, brochures, checklists, and IRS forms. Publisher information is listed in the suggested readings section at the end of this chapter.

Computer software provides learning experiences as well as a tool for implementing programming. Practitioners in planned giving were among the first fund raisers to insist on having computers on their desks. "And," as Netherton (1994) explained, "specialized programs for planned giving carved out a solid niche in the software market years ago" (p. 38). A number of software companies, such as PhilanthroTec, PG Calc, and Comdel, offer programs. PG Calc's Planned Giving Manager, for example, comes in DOS/Windows and Macintosh versions. The software, featuring color graphics, produces customized diagrams of different vehicles by inputting prospect information. Cost in 1997 is about $1,800, plus an annual update and service fee of $500. As previously suggested for other fund-raising software, practitioners should seek opinions of those who already use various programs before purchasing.

Similar to learning, research possibilities on planned giving are unlimited. Students will have no difficulty identifying problems in need of study. A keyword search of dissertation and thesis abstracts from 1980 to 1994, as compiled by Indiana University's Center on Philanthropy through University Microfilm Incorporated, revealed only two studies on planned giving: a theory-building work on negotiation (Parsons, 1993), and an analysis of demographics and attitudes of one university's alumni (Eldridge-Karr, 1991). Two other studies simply found that planned giving efforts, along with other organizational variables, were significant predictors of greater gift-dollar productivity. Aside from Bigelow and Lumpkin (1993), Steuerle (1987), and the Direct Marketing Association (1995), the few studies cited in this chapter were limited to single organizations (e.g., Lindahl, 1992) or nonrandom samples (e.g., File et al., 1994).

A survey of NSFRE members, based on a random sample, could measure the degree to which charitable organizations currently employ planned giving and what vehicles they offer. Respondents could be asked to estimate the proportion of dollars generated by each vehicle, with appropriate distinctions between present and face values. They could provide counts of those planned giving donors who previously made planned gifts, outright major gifts, annual gifts, or no gifts at all. Questions about the placement of the effort in the departmental structure and about demographics of donors would increase our understanding.

Another study could test the fund-raising models for differences that may exist in planned giving. The literature promotes a symmetrical approach, suggesting that fund raisers predominantly practice the two-way symmetrical model, as opposed to the predominant use of press agentry in annual giving and major gifts programs that I found among NSFRE members (Kelly, 1995b).

Both quantitative and qualitative methods would be valuable for examining the issue of notification. For example, what proportion of planned gifts are unexpected? Has the proportion changed since the financial services industry started actively marketing charitable remainder trusts in the early 1990s? Why do donors not notify organizations of their gift? Do fund raisers encourage notification? How? Little is known about this issue. A related issue concerns the doctrine of *cy pres* and how organizations routinely handle planned gifts that are restricted to purposes other than priority needs.

In short, students are strongly encouraged to pursue research on planned giving. Much work needs to be done if organizations are to benefit from the unprecedented transfer of wealth now underway.

SUGGESTED READINGS

Jordan, R. R., & Quynn, K. L. (1995). *Planned giving: Management, marketing, and law.* New York: Wiley.
Lochray, P. J. (1993). *Charitable giving today: Taxes, techniques, and trusts.* Englewood Cliffs, NJ: Prentice-Hall.

National Committee on Planned Giving. (1994). *A guide to starting a planned giving program.* (Available from Author, 310 North Alabama, Suite 210, Indianapolis, IN 46204-2103.)

Tueller, A. B. (1995). *Practical guide to planned giving, 1995.* Washington, DC: Taft Group.

White, D. E. (1995). *The art of planned giving: Understanding donors and the culture of giving.* New York: Wiley.

14

Fund-Raising Programs: Capital Campaigns

At the 1992 National Assembly of CASE, then President Peter McE. Buchanan (cited in H. Hall, 1992) exclaimed, "I wish to hell we could get rid of campaigns, I really do" (p. 20). Capital campaigns are an artifact of fund raising's earlier eras when external consultants dominated the field. Increasingly, practitioners and strategic publics are questioning their purpose, the motivations behind them, and their effectiveness. An alternative is a continuous effort to raise major gifts, which is more appropriate for the current era of staff fund raisers.

Capital campaigns are a strategy sporadically employed by charitable organizations to raise more money than normal in a fixed period of time, with an emphasis on increasing the organization's assets through major gifts. J. P. Smith (1981) defined them as "concentrated, full-throttled efforts to achieve predetermined dollar goals for a variety of purposes during a specified period of time" (p. 60). Dove (1988) stated, "A capital campaign is an organized, intensive fundraising [*sic*] effort on the part of the third-sector institution or organization to secure extraordinary gifts and pledges for a specific purpose or purposes during a specified period of time" (p. 1). Except for the press agentry modifiers of "full-throttled," "intensive," and "extraordinary," these and other definitions differ little from this book's earlier description of the fund-raising process for the two primary programs of annual giving and major gifts.

Capital campaigns, as denoted by their name, traditionally were used to raise gifts for the organization's capital needs—to increase its assets. As previously explained, assets are of two types: (a) physical capital, or the organization's physical plant and equipment, including buildings; and (b) financial capital, or its endowment and reserves. Campaigns today commonly are comprehensive in purpose, raising money for both operations and assets.

EVOLVING PURPOSE

Capital campaigns were invented by Charles Sumner Ward and Lyman Pierce, founders of the YMCA school of fund raisers and the leading historical figures of the press agentry model. First introduced in 1902, the campaigns concentrated solely on physical assets during the first decades of their use, specifically gifts for new buildings. They properly could have been called physical capital campaigns. They were used by all types of organizations, although the heaviest users were large organizations, such as universities and hospitals. Examples of these campaigns were given in chapter 5. Broce (1986) highlighted the purpose of many universities' early campaigns by pointing to their remnants: "The traveler on a trip across the nation sees a large number of 'memorial stadiums' and 'memorial student union buildings.' They are the evidence of bygone campaigns to honor Americans who lost their lives in World War I" (p. 11).

By the 1950s, financial capital, or endowment, needs had been added to the purpose of campaigns. Some types of organizations, particularly those with religious missions, however, reserved their use for physical capital (e.g., building a new church). During both periods, consulting firms were hired to manage the campaigns through full-time resident directors. Annual giving, or efforts to raise operating income rather than assets, was the province of staff employees. Pray (1981) described the situation for colleges and universities:

> The campaign as part of a staff program was relatively late in coming. Institutions in need turned to professional firms for campaign direction and in many cases for staffing [excluding solicitation]. Between campaigns many institutions did little aggressive fund raising except for the increasing number of alumni funds.... many barely self-supporting. (p. 57)

The 1960s introduced the $100-million campaign. The high dollar totals were only possible because the purpose of campaigns, particularly those for universities and hospitals, then encompassed endowment and building needs—an evolutionary factor rarely acknowledged in the literature. Practitioner authors, such as Broce (1986), instead pointed to reasons of peer incentive:

> Inspired by the success of Harvard University's $82 million program, other major private universities launched capital campaigns, many in excess of $100 million. At first most people doubted that such goals could be reached, but when Duke, Stanford, Chicago, and other universities met or exceeded them, many other organizations and institutions began to have confidence in their own abilities. Large campaigns, conducted by teams of workers operating with short deadlines, spread throughout the nation. (p. 13)

It was during this decade, according to Seymour (1966/1988), that a new philosophy of fund raising emerged: Money tends to flow to promising programs rather than to needy institutions. The purpose of campaigns moved from capital needs of the organization to opportunity for raising more money, and a competitive mindset about the strategy was instilled.

Starting in the 1970s, campaigns added annual giving to their purpose and also encompassed planned giving. All gift monies received or generated by the organization during the campaign period, including planned gifts that would not be usable for many years, were counted toward campaign totals. Worth (1993) explained, "Today's campaigns represent an intensive cranking-up of all elements of the development program" (p. 12). The definitional issue was addressed by adopting the term *comprehensive campaign* to signify that the effort was for operating as well as capital needs. Again, the change in purpose enabled organizations to set increasingly higher dollar goals.

The U.S. economy supported the escalation. During the 1980s, private giving increased 12% each year, on average (AAFRC Trust for Philanthropy, 1996). Universities and hospitals were quick to adopt a rolling campaign strategy—concluding a campaign 1 year and announcing another 4 years later. According to R. L. Williams (1993), comprehensive campaigns became a staple of educational fund raising in the 1980s: "As an expanding economy offered the opportunity for philanthropic growth, colleges and universities rushed to orient themselves to the world beyond their gates—to great financial benefit" (p. 289). Hedgepeth (1993) said a primary force driving public institutions to fund raising during the 1980s was early success of a small number of campaigns by public universities. "As one success quickly followed another, skepticism quickly changed to a rush to get on the campaign bandwagon. Public universities realized they had found a potential source of economic growth and rushed to take advantage of it" (p. 323).

In 1987, Stanford University publicly launched the first capital campaign with a goal of $1 billion or more. By 1990, six other organizations were conducting $1-billion campaigns, and a few years later, four more joined what Alexander (1990) called the "Billion Dollar Campaign Club" (p. 26). The 11 organizations consisted of 8 private universities (Boston, Columbia, Cornell, Harvard, New York, Stanford, University of Pennsylvania, and Yale), 2 public universities (University of California at Berkeley and University of Michigan), and a major federation, the United Jewish Appeal–Federation of Jewish Philanthropies (UJA–FJP) of New York City, discussed in the chapter on planned giving.[1]

By 1996, two of the private universities had formed a $2-billion club. Harvard University was in the middle of a 7.4-year campaign to raise $2.1 billion. Columbia University, having exceeded its $1.15-billion goal for a 7-year campaign started in December 1988, announced in December 1995 that it was extending the campaign to the year 2000 and increasing its goal to $2.2 billion—or $100 million more than the goal previously set by Harvard ("Columbia," 1995). The 12-year duration of Columbia's campaign, which actually consists of two campaigns conducted back to back, seriously weakens that institution's claim to the highest goal. Harvard's shorter effort, therefore, is more appropriately the largest campaign—as of 1997—and is treated as such in this book.

In 1985, 1988, and again in 1992, roughly one third of the respondents to NSFRE's membership survey said their organizations were in a capital campaign (Mongon, 1992). Although this proportion held across different organizational types, almost one half the educational (47%) and religious (48%) organizations were in a campaign in 1992.[2] Attesting to their heavy use by colleges and universities, Thieblot (1992) stated, "Today, any campus that is not openly pursuing an announced campaign objective is probably in the quiet phase of its next such effort" (p. 9). Illustrating, Columbia University—during the time Buchanan was its vice president for university development and alumni relations before going to CASE—completed a campaign in 1987 that raised $605 million and began a new $1.15-billion campaign about 1 year

---

[1]Another public university will soon join this group. UCLA is planning a forthcoming campaign to raise more than $1 billion (Osterholt, 1996).

[2]NSFRE's 1995 survey (Mongon, 1996), based on a nonrandom sample, found that 39% of the respondents' organizations were in a capital campaign. The proportion of educational organizations was greater than in previous surveys, 59%.

later, at the end of 1988 (H. Hall, 1992). In 1995, when it had raised almost $1.3 billion and the campaign was scheduled to end, Columbia extended the campaign until 2000 and added slightly less than $1 billion to the goal ("Columbia," 1995).

During the period when campaigns evolved from capital to comprehensive purpose, the number of organizations employing staff practitioners increased dramatically. Consultants, recognizing the shift in the field, moved away from full-time resident direction to part-time campaign counseling, starting with Gurin's (1985) firm in 1965. Although external fund raisers diversified their repertoire of services, they remained—and currently remain—dependent on campaigns for their livelihoods. Consultant George Brakeley, III (1993) described the dependence: "An institution might turn to counsel at almost anytime. Most typically, however, this occurs at one of three junctures: before a comprehensive campaign, during a campaign, or between campaigns" (p. 161).

Not surprisingly, as the number of staff practitioners increased, the use of consultants correspondingly dropped. For example, Harvard, with a fund-raising staff numbering 271, is not using a consultant for its $2.1-billion campaign (Wise, 1994)—a decision likely to have shocked those who managed its earlier campaigns, such as John Price Jones and Si Seymour. In 1995, Ketchum Inc., one of the country's largest fund-raising consulting companies and an original member of AAFRC, announced it would close its doors (Stehle, 1995).[3] Its demise, observers said, was the result of its failure to adjust to a rapidly shifting marketplace.

One of the company's key problems stemmed from its continued emphasis on providing full-time resident directors to work on capital campaigns. Compounding the problem, it pursued the big education and health accounts—organizations that employ the largest number of staff practitioners. Ketchum's CFO blamed the trend first identified 30 years earlier: "A lot of clients are moving away from using resident directors supplied by outside counsel to staffing and running their own campaigns" (Stehle, 1995, p. 35). The company ignored another threat in its environment: Plans for health care reform virtually halted capital campaigns for nonprofit hospitals, which constituted about 40% of its business. In the early 1990s, Ketchum directed between 15 and 20 hospital campaigns annually; after President Clinton was elected on a platform that included health care reform, the number dropped to 4 or 5 a year. In an editorial, John McIlquham (1995), founder of *The NonProfit Times*, called the firm's closing "the end of a tradition" and "yet another sign that the art and science of development is continuing its metamorphosis" (p. 15).

What is surprising, given the evolution of the fund-raising function, is that charitable organizations with established internal staffs continue to use a strategy developed for the convenience of consultants, who now play a diminishing role in its use. As explained in chapter 5, the campaign structure, with definitive beginning and end dates, was shaped by the needs of external practitioners in the absence of staff fund raisers. Sporadic programming is no longer necessary or desirable.

This was one of three major arguments underlying former CASE President Buchanan's (cited in H. Hall, 1992) condemnation of campaigns. He maintained: "We do in this business the dumbest thing I think I have ever seen: We gear up for a campaign

---

[3]A reconstituted Ketchum is in business today as part of a Texas consulting firm that bought its name and other assets.

and we hire new people; we put together a communications program; we put all of that wonderful apparatus together and then we have the campaign; and then what do we do? We shut it down" (p. 20). Drawing from the taped version of his remarks (P. M. Buchanan, Peterson, & Welter, 1992), he continued: "What do we do 4 years later? We crank it up again. We continue to do this over and over and over again." He said it would be "a whole lot cheaper" and "a whole lot better" if organizations engaged in continuous fund raising. A panelist with Buchanan, Linda Welter (P. M. Buchanan et al., 1992), who had just completed a $172-million campaign for Wellesley College, responded: "Sooner or later I think people are going to come around to the idea that these things are too time-consuming and wasteful of resources to get into. And I agree with you. In my favorite world, there would be no such thing [as campaigns]. We would just continue."

UNDERLYING MOTIVATIONS

The second of Buchanan's (cited in H. Hall, 1992) three arguments was that campaigns' multimillion-dollar goals represent "fascination" with "money" rather than mission (p. 20). Goals are determined for competitive reasons, not need. Organizations, particularly colleges and universities, are challenging each other to wage the largest capital campaign. Dominant coalition members are telling fund raisers, "The important factor is not what we need to raise or what we can raise, but what we have to raise to beat our competitor." Alexander (1990) reprimanded, "Too often, campaign goals are based on what rival institutions report they have raised, rather than on analysis of an organization's greatest needs and careful evaluation of the giving climate among its donors" (p. 26).

The collective result looks much like a game of poker—with million-dollar stakes. While Stanford was in its $1.1-billion campaign, Columbia set its campaign goal at $1.15 billion. When Stanford closed its campaign with $1.27 billion, Yale University launched its campaign for $1.5 billion. As already noted, Harvard's $2.1-billion goal spurred Columbia to extend its campaign and increase its goal to $2.2 billion.[4]

More serious because it is more common is the "I'll-see-you-and-raise-you" mindset for the hundreds of campaigns with goals of less than $1 billion. A college will announce a $150-million campaign and a fund raiser at another college in the same geographic area will decide the amount for its next campaign must be $175 million, regardless.

The same mindset is apparent in other types of organizations. A study by the Walter and Elise Haas Fund (Blake, 1994), an independent foundation created by the inventor of Levi's jeans, found that the combined capital-campaign goals of only 49 organizations in San Francisco, California far outstrip the giving capabilities of the city's foundation, corporate, and individual donors. Excluding the billion-dollar campaigns

---

[4]Reported results at the conclusions of campaigns also reflect this competitive mindset. Four of the eight private universities conducting billion-dollar campaigns had completed their efforts by 1996 ("Status," 1996). Stanford finished in 1992 with $1.27 billion. The University of Pennsylvania's campaign ended in 1994 with a slightly higher total, $1.33 billion. Cornell closed its books in December 1995 at $1.5 billion. In an unexpected and questionable move, New York University halted its campaign before Cornell, in February 1995, and reported that it had raised exactly $1 billion—not $1 more. A fifth private university, Boston, which publicly announced a $1-billion campaign in May 1988, had disappeared from progress reports by 1996.

of Stanford and the University of California at Berkeley, large campaigns were trying to raise $614 million from 1993 to 1997, or triple the $186 million sought by 41 campaigns during the preceding 5 years, 1988 to 1992. Just 11 arts and humanities organizations accounted for almost one half the combined goal ($269 million), followed by education, public society/benefit, human services, health, and religion. As the study concluded, even if receipts for campaigns grew at the same rate of 9.5% per year as they did between 1988 and 1992, there would be more than a $200 million shortfall in performance against targets. For goals to be met, 1997 giving would have to increase to more than 500% of the 1992 level! Blake (1994), the author of the study's report, simply stated, "The total appears quite unrealistic" (p. 28).

Two outcomes were predicted: (a) many campaigns likely will fail or significantly reduce their goals, and (b) there will be a redistribution of total charitable resources to some recipients and away from others. Expanding on the second, because the heaviest users of campaigns are large organizations with the biggest budgets, campaign success could significantly reduce gifts to many small organizations. Blake (1994) further hypothesized, "Other organizations with capital needs may conclude that they must join the fray with campaigns of their own, and they would be correct, as capital gifts to non-campaigning organizations would shrink, too" (p. 3). The campaign overload found in San Francisco, according to the study, is not unique; other U.S. areas likely are experiencing similar incongruencies between unrealistic goals and gift capacity.

Fueling the competition is the assumption that organizational prestige is a function of greater resources. Respected higher education author and former university president Clark Kerr (1991) noted, "Private fund-raising [*sic*] by both public and private institutions has, in recent times, increasingly become a mechanism for competitive advantage" (pp. 10, 15). Highly visible campaigns for colleges and universities, proponents argue, help attract top faculty, students, public funds, and subsequent private funds. Worth (1993) elaborated:

> In this concept of excellence, I suspect, lies at least one explanation for the much-criticized mega-campaign goals. The college's fund-raising goal is set to be greater than that of some rival college or university, probably one perceived as being just a bit higher in the institutional pecking order. Decisions about the campaign's length and types of gifts it will include then follow to produce the desired dollar result. (p. 408)

The escalating competition is played out in the public spotlight, and Worth, among others, admitted that society's perception of campaigns increasingly is one of organizational greed rather than need. Campaigns have a strong publicity component. Indeed, the CASE campaign standards offered the following definition: "The capital or comprehensive fund-raising campaign is a vehicle for focusing *attention* upon the needs and aspirations of an institution" (Peterson, 1994, p. iii; italics added).

Many experts defend the use of campaigns because of their publicity, or what they call public relations, value. Campaigns, they argue, produce more than gifts; they have spillover effects not specified in programming objectives. Mixer (1993), for example, stated, "The acceptance of the case and goodwill generated by the promotional efforts of the campaign contribute long-term benefits" (p. 141). Greenfield (1991) asserted that a campaign can improve an organization's overall public image. Addressing colleges and universities, Thieblot (1992) said, "Setting an ambitious goal—and meeting it—has great public relations value on campus and off. . . . And because some people consider an institution's level of philanthropic support one measure of its quality, success in fund raising can sometimes mean success on other important fronts—including enrollment" (p. 9). She added, however, "Some campaign planners are wondering if donors will start to reject large campaign goals and see them as reflections of greed more than need" (p. 9).

Setting ever-larger goals, J. P. Smith (1981) argued, does not elevate donor sights to larger gifts: "The much more probable result is that their constituents will be put off, that they will perceive those programs as reaching way beyond what even the most faithful among them thought of as a legitimate realm of need—in short, as grasping for all that they can get" (p. 67). Dove (1988), who wrote the most widely recognized book on capital campaigns, said today's goals are "likely to startle most people who care about an institution" (p. 170). Although some will be sympathetic, he said, "with many, many people, the institution has the burden of making a persuasive case that is awfully difficult to make convincingly" (p. 170). He asked:

> How much credibility can there be in a claim that an unusually large goal is a realistic reflection of what an institution needs, that it has done the kind of institutional soul-searching that warrants the assertion that these really are worthy objectives that are critical to the quality of the institution? Is the institution coming across as grasping, as reaching for some dramatically large amount hoping that somehow it might get it but willing to settle for less? (pp. 170-171)

Such questions are well-suited to Harvard's $2.1-billion campaign, which began in 1992 when the market value of that charitable organization's endowment was $5.1 billion—the highest of any U.S. college or university by $1.5 billion ("Endowments," 1993).[5]

Greenfield (1991) said the first question that always must be asked is whether a capital campaign is truly needed. He argued that all other means of gaining funds must be exhausted first, that the money needed by a certain date can only be raised through a campaign. Major gifts, he stressed, can be raised outright and through planned giving without a campaign. Organizations and staff tend to conclude too quickly that a campaign is in order. "They have all the wrong reasons: a quick fix, an easy solution to major funding needs, a path to glory and their own reputation for success." (p. 172). Broce (1986) agreed, presenting his version of the fundamental question: "Is there a real need to conduct this campaign, and, if so, is there some urgency about it?" (p. 53). Other than wanting more money, few organizations could answer the question both affirmatively and truthfully.

Because of their reliance on widespread publicity, capital campaigns build awareness among and beyond the organizations' natural constituencies. The attention they attract has long been considered a positive aspect; however, in light of multimillion-dollar goals and questions about greed, that aspect may now be one of their strongest negatives. Vance Peterson (1994), chair of the advisory group that devised the CASE campaign standards, explained:

---

[5]The gap between Harvard and the university with the second highest endowment, Yale, doubled during the next 3 years. In 1995, Harvard's endowment totaled $7 billion, whereas Yale's endowment was $4 billion (Council for Aid to Education, 1996).

The recent trend toward campaigns that raise hundreds of millions or even billions of dollars has boosted the visibility of fund raising in general and the role of campaigns in particular. This visibility has also heightened the pressure on fund raisers and financial managers to ensure their campaigns' success. At the same time, and in part because of their sheer size, campaigns are being scrutinized with growing intensity. (p. iii)

CASE's Buchanan (cited in H. Hall, 1992) stated, "The most acute concern that we all have had about our campaigns is the fact that they have had an impact on the public arena that has been questionable at best, and a lot worse if you want to press that question" (p. 20).

Press Agentry to Two-Way Asymmetrical

Dove (1988) reported that the strategy of Charles Sumner Ward, the "master campaigner," became "the foundation on which today's capital campaigns are still built" (p. 3). Contemporary campaigns, he said, "have many of the traditional characteristics of the campaigns that Ward organized seventy years ago" (p. 14). Among those, which were identified in earlier chapters of this book, are a great deal of publicity, competitive atmosphere, devices to stimulate a sense of urgency, emphasis on proportionately few major gifts, and extraordinary efforts to reach the dollar goal. Emotions, particularly excitement, remain the bedrock of campaigns. Broce (1986) supported these characteristics, as demonstrated by the following axioms:

Few people give money because of publicity, but fewer give without it. (p. 50)

To create and maintain a sense of urgency, a demanding pace must be set for the program. (p. 48)

The challenge gift has become an important tool with which to create momentum. (p. 48)

Without one or two staggeringly large gifts—perhaps 20 percent of the total goal—the campaign may fail. (p. 51)

Involvement is the key to *sacrificial* giving. (p. 49; italics added)

Summarizing their press agentry value, Dove (1988) stated, "Besides the sheer volume of dollars that can be raised when a heightened sense of urgency and importance is *created*, and the psychological and motivational strategies that can maximize giving in a campaign's excitement, institutions will occasionally simply want to bring to themselves the special attention that a campaign provides" (p. 13; italics added).

According to Rosso (1991), campaign jargon, such as *tactics* and *logistical support*, is "distinctly militaristic in expression" (p. 93). Indeed, Broce (1986) stated, "A capital campaign has often been called the 'moral equivalent of war'" (p. 52). In short, contemporary campaigns are based on asymmetrical presuppositions and much about them emulates the oldest and least ethical model of fund raising, press agentry.

On the other hand, campaigns today feature characteristics notably different from their earliest predecessors. In addition to changes already discussed, research is considered an essential step, fewer volunteers are involved, and the time frame is longer. These characteristics, particularly the two-way communication undertaken for research purposes, have moved capital campaigns closer to the two-way asymmetrical model of fund raising.

Campaigns rely on prospect research and feasibility studies to identify potential major donors and gain information about how campaign messages should be shaped to scientifically persuade giving. Touching briefly on prospect research, Levner (1993) recommended a marketing perspective as "especially useful for people involved in capital campaigns" (p. 39). Marketing research that provides information about where prospective donors are going or want to go is essential, she said. "Only then can you develop strategies to 'lead them there'" (p. 39). She used an organization needing a new building or a multimillion-dollar endowment to illustrate how findings are used to shape "powerful campaign communications": "Unfortunately, you can't assume your supporters share your vision. Your job is to convince your audience that the new building will place *their* town on the map artistically, or that a larger endowment will catapult *their* alma mater to national prominence" (p. 39; italics in original).

Feasibility studies also are based on asymmetrical presuppositions. Their application for researching the opportunity is suspect. They ostensibly are conducted to determine the likelihood of a proposed campaign being successfully completed and a dollar goal reached, but two major flaws reduce the validity and reliability of their findings. First, as pointed out in chapter 10, the studies are qualitative and include only a small number of donor prospects, providing a skewed and partial picture. The Haas Fund study (Blake, 1994) stated: "Most feasibility studies are quite parochial in scope. Consultants talk to an agency's close friends and wealthy supporters and then extrapolate from their sample a prediction of total revenues. Macroeconomic analysis, or an audit of the competitive environment for capital gifts in the community, is notably absent from such studies" (p. 30).

The second flaw rarely is acknowledged: Consultants conducting feasibility studies may distort findings in order to acquire lucrative campaign contracts. The fund-raising literature is adamant that feasibility studies be conducted by external consultants and not by staff because objectivity is required. Broce (1986) explained:

> In conducting the precampaign survey, the consultant has the advantage of being able to ask hard questions and receive hard answers. Prospects will often confide to an outsider any doubts they may have . . . comments they would not wish to make to someone closely identified with the institution. They can also be more open about their own financial situation and commitments. (pp. 55-56)

The literature says nothing about the self-interest of consultants, who in most cases are retained for the duration of the campaigns they recommend. If objectivity is necessary to measure campaign feasibility, then logically any consultant conducting a study should be barred in advance from bidding on work recommended by its findings.

The Haas Fund study (Blake, 1994) agreed. Among its suggestions for coping with the current overload of capital campaigns was that organizations "commission feasibility studies from fundraising [*sic*] consultants different from those who are to run the subsequent campaigns" (p. 5). It presented its reasons based on San Francisco organizations: "Of the 30 agencies which did feasibility studies for their campaigns, 18 [60%] retained the consultants to help run their campaigns. Although this may be an efficient approach, it also raises the possibility of a conflict of interest, as there may be a built-in incentive to recommend a launch" (p. 30). The study also found a wide variation in the predictive value of consultants' findings. Whereas more than one half the organizations said the information they received was right on target or useful, 43% said it was flawed or totally off the mark.

When I took NSFRE's Survey Course in 1993, I asked about consultants' self-interest in relation to conducting feasibility studies. The consultant practitioner teaching the session on capital campaigns said she was not aware of the issue ever being raised and that, anyway, valuable information would be lost by changing consultants. Her response supported my limited observation that confidentiality promised to donor prospects participating in feasibility studies is not always honored (i.e., supposedly confidential information is used to formulate tactics for soliciting specific prospects). Attesting to their flawed validity and reliability, she added that many firms such as hers would be reluctant to base plans for campaign management on findings from a different consultant.

The self-interest of organizations and dominant coalition members also can distort findings. When I was a staff fund raiser at the University of Maryland in the late 1980s, a well-known consulting firm issued a preliminary report recommending the university postpone a capital campaign for at least 5 years while essential staffing and cultivation took place. Although the recommendation was based on 18 months of internal and external study, a revised report was issued a few months later—at the request of the then chancellor—that recommended the campaign be started immediately. The same firm was hired to serve as campaign consultant for the next 6 years.

It must be emphasized in defense of consultants that their long-term interests are not served by arbitrarily recommending campaigns because a record of failure would eventually damage their reputations and thereby diminish their ability to attract future clients. Illustrating what likely is a common outcome, the firm of Community Consulting Service Co. (CCS), a former member of AAFRC, completed a feasibility study for PRSA's affiliated foundation in 1994. Based on its findings, the firm recommended that a proposed campaign be delayed at least 1 year and the dollar goal cut in half. As a member of the foundation's Board of Trustees, I was pleased to accept the report; however, I lamented the loss of $25,000 paid to CCS for interviewing approximately 50 individuals in order to tell trustees what should have been obvious without a study: The foundation was not prepared to conduct a capital campaign. For example, it had no fund raiser on staff or experience raising gifts; in fact, it did not have an annual giving or major gifts program! Paradoxically, CCS' recommendations to prepare the foundation for an eventual campaign did not address any of these shortcomings. In other words, the self-interest issue extends to consultants marketing campaigns in favor of continuous programming.

Contemporary campaigns do not use armies of volunteers to solicit gifts; however, a complex volunteer-committee structure has been maintained to involve donor prospects in the strategy. Stated another way, volunteers and prospects for major gifts are often the same people (Thieblot, 1992). Numerous committee positions (e.g., a committee for major gifts, one for special gifts, one for general gifts, one for corporate gifts, one for foundation gifts, etc.) are used as an asymmetrical device for cultivating and soliciting donors. Broce (1986) advised fund raisers to get the best prospects involved early as volunteers in important roles: "See that they attend meetings and strategy sessions that thoroughly inform and deeply commit them to the success of the program" (p. 49). Volunteers are urged to make their gifts first, before soliciting other prospects.

Committee reporting meetings create artificial deadlines and provide much of the urgency on which campaigns depend. Welter (P. M. Buchanan et al., 1992), who was a staff practitioner at Harvard before becoming assistant vice president for resources at Wellesley College, described reporting meetings as bringing peers together to show, by using statistical reports, which volunteers have accomplished their solicitation assignments. As used by Harvard, she said, the meetings were "an act of actually shaming those who had not done their work." Welter was hired by Wellesley to bring the Harvard model to the campaign planned for the women's college, but, believing pressure tactics would not work well with female prospects, she turned reporting meetings into focus groups. Rather than pressing volunteers to complete their assignments, she structured the meetings around such questions as: Did this mailing make sense? Did this proposal work? What has worked for you? These two variations represent the press agentry and two-way asymmetrical approaches to managing campaign volunteers.

As campaigns evolved in purpose, their lengths were extended to accommodate ever-larger goals. Whereas Ward spent 5 months to plan a campaign and 10 days to execute it, contemporary campaigns devote about 2 years to planning, 1 to 2 years to the "quiet phase" of raising pace-setting gifts, and 5 or more years to the public phase. The typical time frame for the entire effort is 8 to 10 years, although some organizations have stretched the duration even longer, as attested to by Columbia University's 12-year campaign. New York and Boston Universities officially started $1-billion campaigns in the mid-1980s that originally were not scheduled to conclude until 2000, representing about a 15-year period.[6] UJA–FJP's campaign, started in 1989, has no set date for completion. Endeavors sustained over 10 or more years, most experts argue, do not qualify as actual campaigns because a sense of urgency is greatly diminished or absent, among other differences. The longer time frame—which facilitates more sophisticated planning and ongoing research, as well as larger dollar goals—demonstrates movement from press agentry to two-way asymmetrical fund raising. It also provides a framework for presenting basic principles about capital campaigns.

Campaign Phases

According to CASE (1994), campaigns consist of four phases: (a) precampaign planning, (b) advance gifts/nucleus fund phase, (c) general public phase, and (d) postcampaign accounting. The first phase forces the organization to focus on planning for fund-raising purposes. This may be the greatest advantage of campaigns in that organizations that do not regularly engage in strategic planning and/or isolate fund raising from overall management are obligated to change their behavior before conducting a campaign. Mixer (1993) identified "necessary strategic planning and strengthening the case of the agency" as one of the positive aspects of campaigns (p. 141). Yet, as Welter (cited in H. Hall, 1992) pointed out, sporadic planning is less

---

[6]As already noted, New York unexpectedly ended its campaign in 1995, 10.4 years after its start, and Boston has disappeared from recent progress reports on billion dollar campaigns ("Status," 1996).

effective than ongoing planning. "Due to the time it takes to plan capital campaigns, such plans are already inadequate to meet the changing needs before the drive reaches completion" (p. 20). She concluded, "Campaigns and their ever-increasing monetary objectives will not equip us to move through an environment that unfortunately is going to be in perpetual change" (p. 20).

The advance gifts/nucleus fund phase, also termed the *quiet phase*, marks the official beginning of a campaign. Experts recommend that about 40% of the dollar goal be raised during this period—before the campaign is publicly announced (Worth, 1993). Rosso (1991) argued that at least one gift of 10% and two gifts of 5% of the goal must be sought at the campaign's beginning. Therefore, a $1-billion campaign requires one gift of $100 million and two gifts of $50 million. There is strong consensus that 95% of the dollar total will come from 3% to 5% of the donors (Thieblot, 1992) and that the nucleus fund phase, which concentrates on such prospects, tests the campaign's viability (Worth, 1993). If advance gifts fall short of expected amounts, the campaign is aborted before the public phase.

Much of the responsibility for successfully completing the second phase rightfully belongs to the organization's trustees. Broce (1986) offered a 20/20 rule: "I say that to be successful the board must commit itself to contribute 20 percent of whatever dollar goal is selected and commit to solicit from others the next 20 percent of the goal" (p. 46). For a $1-billion campaign, therefore, the board is expected to collectively give $200 million and raise an additional $200 million before any public announcement is made. Broce called these requirements "point-of-no-return checkpoints" (p. 46). Reminding board members of their necessary and extraordinary participation may be the one remaining role best enacted by consultants. Broce explained, "Better than any staff officer, the consultant can face the board squarely and say, 'Unless you will be committed to the success of this program through your own sacrificial giving and enthusiastic leadership, there will be little or no chance for success'" (p. 53). He commented:

> This pronouncement makes many board members uncomfortable, especially those who up to this point have favored the idea of more money flowing into the coffers from a capital campaign but have expected the bulk of the gifts to come primarily from new sources. It may be their first collective realization that, on all prospect lists, their names come first. (p. 54)

During the general public phase, both major and lower level gifts are solicited, although efforts still focus on the "critical few" prospects who are able to make major gifts (McGoldrick, 1993, p. 151). Programming is guided by the principles of sequential and proportionate giving, with nondonors who have the capability of making only a small gift reserved for the closing months of the campaign. The crucial role of major gifts requires interpersonal communication by a large fund-raising staff. Using an example mentioned earlier, Harvard University had 271 staff practitioners in the academic year it publicly launched its campaign, 1993–1994 (Wise, 1994). The expense of a campaign is a function of the goal, as well as other factors. Harvard's $2.1-billion goal mandates that its practitioners raise $1 million a day during the public phase (although advance gifts likely reduced that quota to about $600,000). To support campaign programming, the university increased its fund-raising budget by $1.8

million a year, to $24.2 million in 1993–1994. At the conclusion of the 7.4-year campaign, from the beginning of its advance gifts phase in July 1992 to its scheduled date for completion in December 1999, Harvard will have spent around $187 million on fund raising, or 9% of its goal.

Serious problems arise when organizations depend on raising unrestricted outright gifts through the campaign to cover fund-raising expenses. Too often, annual giving dollars are spent for campaign costs, not for announced needs. In such cases, lower level gifts from the majority of donors are used to subsidize the cultivation and solicitation of major donors, who restrict their gifts. Not only are such practices unethical, but they can be financially damaging. The University of Connecticut was left with a $2.6-million deficit when it concluded a $50-million campaign in 1987 because although the campaign surpassed its goal, it did not attract enough unrestricted money to cover the cost of raising the funds ("Give & take," 1992).

Many public universities financed their capital campaigns during the 1980s by levying a "tax" of about 5% on gifts received. As gift taxes were an awkward subject to raise with major donors, who generally are solicited in person and restrict their gifts, the problem usually was avoided by using unrestricted dollars to pay taxes on all gifts. Such a tax system was approved at the University of Maryland to underwrite its $200-million capital campaign in the late 1980s. It never was implemented because powerful deans in Maryland's decentralized structure simply refused to have large portions of unrestricted gifts to their programs used as campaign taxes. Although ethics had a hand in their decision, the primary reason was that unrestricted money was too valuable to lose. I disapprove of such funding methods for all programs. Symmetrical fund raising demands responsible gift use worthy of trust.

In addition to interpersonal communication, campaigns require a heavy emphasis on controlled and mass media communication, specifically publications and publicity. "Campaign publications are essential," Broce (1986, p. 50) proclaimed. They generally include a special logo, case statement, brochures, packets for volunteers, letterhead, various sizes and types of envelopes, pledge forms, pocket folders, mailing labels, event invitations, commemorative certificates, note cards, and a multi-issue newsletter. The case statement, which functions as "the rhetorical primer and the 'copy platform' for all campaign communications" (R. L. Williams, 1993, p. 295), can cost as much as $50,000. Total publication expenses excluding salaries often are $300,000 or more, even for a small campaign with a goal of $10 million.

Videos, special events, media placements, news releases, and PSAs are the publicity techniques commonly used to promote visibility and excitement. In an informal poll, R. L. Williams (1993) found that two thirds of the universities conducting campaigns had established a new communication unit dedicated to assisting with fund raising. The University of Pennsylvania, for example, created an eight-person unit before publicly launching its $1-billion campaign in 1989. Stanford employed a separate 18-person staff to generate publicity for its campaign.

The mass media, it should be noted, usually confuse the date a campaign is publicly announced with the date it actually began (e.g., *Newsweek* [Hancock, 1994] reported that Harvard's campaign is for 5 rather than 7.4 years). Organizations encourage this less than truthful information. According to Nicklin (1992), whereas most do not count the nucleus fund phase in their time frame, they do count the advance gifts raised. For example, the University of Michigan, which began raising advance gifts for its $1-billion campaign in July 1990 and scheduled the public phase to end in September 1997, consistently refers to its effort as a 5-year campaign even though the duration is 7.2 years ("Status," 1996; Stehle, 1992b; "Univ. of Michigan," 1996). G. David Gearhart (cited in Nicklin, 1992), then senior vice president for development and university relations at Pennsylvania State University and author of a book on capital campaigns, condemned such practice: "It's misleading. It says that an institution may have raised X dollars in five years, when that's not true" (p. A34).

Controlled and mass media communications account for a small portion of the dollars raised, but experts consider them necessary for legitimizing the campaign and providing an atmosphere of festivity and achievement in which the dollar goal can be reached. J. P. Smith (1981) explained: "It is widely assumed that the enthusiasm and momentum of a campaign make it possible to set and to meet goals that could not otherwise be accomplished. This argument . . . claims that the esprit of a campaign—its enthusiasm and sense of urgency—create a dynamic that takes the program further than would otherwise be possible" (pp. 64-65). Yet their "promotional nature," CASE (1994) admitted, "can create misunderstanding about the purposes of campaigns and what they will achieve" (p. 1).

The fourth phase defined by CASE, postcampaign accounting, is covered shortly in relation to effectiveness. Practitioners have identified two other campaign phases: (a) the plateau of fatigue, which McGoldrick (1993) said hits about 1 to 3 years into the general public phase; and (b) the transitional phase, the 2 years before a campaign formally ends. Broce (1986) addressed the first when he warned that it is very difficult to maintain a campaign's intensity for more than a short period of time. Keeping in mind the advance gifts/nucleus fund phase lasts for 1 to 2 years, Broce advised, "Three to five years is about as long as the fund-raising organization can remain geared up" (p. 48). During the transition phase, fund-raising heads must figure out how to move from campaign to postcampaign programming. When external consultants directed an occasional campaign in the past, the organization could look forward to a rest. Now internal practitioners face such questions as: Which staff members must be let go? Are there enough volunteers not burned out who still can be used? How will the organization deal with donors who feel they do not need to contribute again because organizational needs were supposedly satisfied by the campaign? Welter (cited in H. Hall, 1992) said, "Transition environments feel different, they feel weird, they feel uneasy" (p. 20). Buchanan (P. M. Buchanan et al., 1992) agreed, "Transition is a very, very hard time."

According to Mixer (1993), at the conclusion of capital campaigns, fund-raising personnel is reduced, which leads to serious disorganization of the department, morale problems, and declining gift production. Leadership is exhausted and desirous of returning to neglected, ongoing duties. Nahm and Zemsky (1993) described the outcome for college and university presidents: "When they reach their announced goal, there is little of the euphoria with which they began their campaigns. Glad their ordeal is over, these leaders publicly welcome the chance to spend more time on campus, while privately wondering if this may be the moment to bring their administrations to a successful close" (pp. 58-59).

In November 1994, Harvard University President Neil Rudenstine took a 3-month sabbatical to recover from severe fatigue and exhaustion. Citing the president's immersion in the "$1 million-a-day fund-raising campaign," *Newsweek* journalist LynNell Hancock (1995) reported: "After three years of intensive nonstop toil in a hypermetabolic climate, Rudenstine hit the wall. His life was devoured, his sleep habits scrambled, his waking minutes assaulted by a hail of never-finished tasks" (p. 56).

It is difficult to understand why any members of an organization's dominant coalition would propose conducting a capital campaign. The fund-raising department is placed under severe production quotas and left in disarray at the campaign's conclusion. Attesting to the heavy burden, James Osterholt (1996), who was in charge of fund raising for UCLA, left that institution after 21 years because of its forthcoming campaign. He explained, "As this effort moved from planning to implementation . . . . It became clear that internal support for my leadership was not unanimous" (p. 44). Volunteers, who also are prospective donors, are subjected to rigid schedules and reporting meetings often designed to shame them into action. Trustees are expected to give and get much of the dollar goal. Presidents and other senior managers are diverted from their primary duties and often experience exhaustion. Mixer (1993) summarized, "Capital campaigns require substantial commitments of time, energy, and funds" (p. 141). Are they worth it?

J. P. Smith (1981) concluded they are not. He argued that campaigns force organizations "to hurry, to claim present commitments at the expense of the longer view, so that, again and again, the emphasis is on large numbers—large numbers now" (p. 65). Their result, he said, "is haste and waste, a lot of relatively indiscriminate activity that may produce apparently impressive results. But when such results are more carefully analyzed, they can be soberly disappointing" (p. 65). The discussion turns now to the effectiveness of capital campaigns.

EFFECTIVENESS

Presenting his third and final argument against capital campaigns, CASE President Buchanan (cited in H. Hall, 1992) stated, "We have the juxtaposition of raising enormous amounts of money at the same time our institutions go into deficit. And then people say, 'What the hell is going on here?'" (p. 20). Too many campaigns, he asserted, cannot answer the question, "Where did the money go?" (p. 20).

A paradox of campaigns is that many organizations successfully reaching dollar goals find themselves facing a deficit or unable to fund announced objectives. Almost all do not meet stakeholders' expectations. Before examining the inconsistency, however, it must be stressed that not every campaign succeeds. For example, the United Negro College Fund failed to meet its campaign goal of $250 million by its publicly announced deadline of December 31, 1993 ("United Negro," 1993). The organization fell more than $60 million short even though, as mentioned in chapter 2, Walter Annenberg gave $50 million, or 20% of the goal, to launch the campaign. The shortfall was blamed on the poor economy and simultaneous campaigns at one half the fund's 41 member colleges, which are private, historically Black institutions. The deadline was extended, but no completion date was set.[7]

---

[7]The fund completed its campaign in 1995, with a reported total of $280 million ("Press clippings," 1996).

In contrast to publicity surrounding the announcement of campaigns, failures rarely are reported in the mass media. The Haas Fund study (Blake, 1994) explained: "Organizations that do not reach targets do not typically admit failure. They revise targets downward, slow down or cancel projected construction projects, and delay the finish dates for their campaigns" (p. 3). The study found that of the 41 San Francisco organizations conducting a campaign during the period 1988 to 1992, most extended their deadlines, 8 reduced their goals, and only 18 had completed their campaigns at the time of the study's report. Of those that had finished, four (22%) failed to reach at least 95% of their revised goals. Consultant Marion Simon (cited in Demko, 1996c) provided insight on why campaigns usually are assumed to be successful when she offered the following press agentry advice to organizations facing failure: "Revise the goal downward, declare victory, and tell your story from the most positive perspective. People who are in development think everybody in the world knows exactly what's going on. You can just say, 'Hey, we've raised more money than ever before'" (p. 24).

Whereas deception may account for much of the misunderstanding about the effectiveness of campaigns, another point often overlooked is that organizations have succeeded in raising large amounts of private dollars *without* using them. For example, the University of Texas Southwestern Medical Center raised about $100 million in gifts and pledges during 1988, including $60 million in 1 month (Bailey, 1988b). The organization, with only two fund raisers on staff, had no capital campaign underway or even contemplated. Buchanan (P. M. Buchanan et al., 1992) illustrated the same point by referring to his alma mater, Cornell University, which had one of the best fund-raising records in recent history. Its staff practitioners, he said, "drove those numbers right off the roof, and they hadn't had a campaign for many years." He continued: "They finally collapsed [in 1988] because the trustees wanted a campaign. I understand that dynamic."

Returning to the inconsistency between financial well-being and campaigns, Nahm and Zemsky (1993) identified two "disturbing maxims" (p. 57) about current fund raising: (a) it costs more than it raises, and (b) it is donor driven rather than need driven. Elaborating on the first as related to colleges and universities, they argued that to attract lead gifts in campaigns, an institution "builds buildings and names them for donors who provide less than half of the construction funds and none of the operating funds. It establishes and fills endowed chairs, though the income from the donor's gift may supply less than half of the cost of maintaining a faculty member and none of the 'extras' associated with a chair" (p. 57).

Some discount named gift opportunities, for example, allowing donors to put a down payment on a chair with a pledge to pay later, or to finance the gift through planned giving vehicles. Payments stretch over years, yet the chair is filled and costing the organization real money. Nahm and Zemsky (1993) added, "The harshest criticism, however, is reserved for those institutions that announce the successful completion of a campaign on Monday and a major budget crisis on Tuesday. Both the donor and campus communities feel betrayed and are quick to place blame on an administration that clearly did not know what it was doing" (p. 58).

According to J. P. Smith (1981), campaigns provide only occasional symptomatic relief rather than contributing to the continuing financial health of the organization. Stanford University, representing numerous cases in higher education, announced budget deficits during and at the conclusion of its campaign—which raised $1.27 billion, or $1.7 million more than its goal—and continued to deal with reductions for at least 3 years after the "successful" campaign officially ended in February 1992 (Leatherman, 1994). Representing other types of organizations and campaigns at lower levels, the Guggenheim Museum in New York City made significant strides toward its campaign goal of $100 million when, in 1994, it raised two gifts of $10 million each; yet during the same year, the museum reduced its staff by 10%, shortened its hours, and temporarily closed its library "despite successful fund raising" (AAFRC Trust for Philanthropy, 1995, p. 116). The paradox of deficits and the more common disappointing results of campaigns can be explained by analyzing four issues: (a) new versus expected money, (b) featured objectives versus other purposes, (c) planned gifts versus outright gifts, and (d) accounting and reporting abuses related to these and other issues.

Disappointing Results

As J. P. Smith (1981) suggested, announced results tell less than an accurate, entire story about the financial outcomes of campaigns. The first issue in need of analysis is the difference between new and expected money generated through comprehensive campaigns. Most of the dollar goal, often as much as 80%, would have been raised without the campaign. For example, an organization that, on average, raises $1 million a year through its annual giving and major gifts programs would raise $7 million over a 7-year period. Therefore, when it conducts a 7-year capital campaign with a dollar goal of $9 million, only $2 million, or 22% of the goal, will be *new money*, or money that would not have been raised without the campaign.

Illustrating, Hancock (1994) described Harvard's $2.1-billion campaign as "audacious"; the goal is "a huge figure made manageable only because it includes almost every dollar the university would have collected anyway. Still, the campaign is expected to net at least a 25 percent premium" (p. 83). During the 3 years before Harvard began its advance gifts phase, it averaged $205 million per year in private support (Council for Aid to Education, 1991, 1992, 1993). Multiplying that average by the 7.4 years allotted for the campaign (and not adjusting for inflation), Harvard was expected to raise more than $1.5 billion, or 72% of the $2.1-billion goal, during the campaign period—without any campaign. Only $0.6 billion represents new money, or funds likely to make a difference, which stakeholders have been told is imperative.

Featured objectives are organizational funding needs specified and featured in the campaign, which constitute the priorities list or case statement. Collectively, they represent the reason the organization is conducting the campaign. Other purposes cover everything else for which gifts may be made during the campaign period. All objectives cumulatively providing the case for a comprehensive campaign rarely are met, a well-known rule in fund-raising circles (Luck, 1990). Although the campaign demands a variety of projects with their own dollar goals to present a viable case and—more importantly—to enlist widespread internal support, 100% of the featured objectives are almost never funded at the conclusion of what most term a *successful* campaign. For example, campaigns for colleges and universities regularly fund endowed chairs in engineering and business, but those in modern languages—which may be equally or more needed—are left unfunded. Some needs are more fundable than others (i.e., they require less effort to obtain), and campaigns, given their rigid schedule and concentration on the overall dollar total, provide neither the time nor the motivation for fund raisers to match gifts with organizational priorities.

Elaborating on the second of their two "disturbing maxims," fund raising is donor driven rather than need driven, Nahm and Zemsky (1993) stated, "In other words, the money that *is* raised is the money that *can be* raised, because alumni, friends, corporations, and foundations are most prepared to support their own priorities" (p. 57; italics in original). The underlying problem, they explained, is that accommodating employee, client, and other stakeholders' needs with donor interests during campaign planning usually means giving in to all and hoping that enough money will turn up to pay for the promises.

Dove (1988) said that although campaigns are preceded by months of discussion about the projects for which it is important to raise money, "the product of that discussion often is a comprehensive wish list rather than a rigorous evaluation" (p. 169). He argued that campaigns rarely force organizational managers to make hard choices, "but instead encourage the optimistic attitude that the longer the laundry list of desirable objectives, the more probable it is that the institution will achieve the vast dollar amount that represents the total objective" (p. 169). The resulting wish lists have minimal impact on campaign outcomes. The dollar amount of gifts, not their purpose, is paramount. A breakdown of major gifts to most campaigns would reveal funded purposes never contemplated, let alone prioritized (e.g., a chapel, a new course in Western civilization, or artwork for the lobby).

CASE underscored the seriousness of the issue by rooting its management and reporting standards in two important convictions: "One is that how well the campaign meets its objectives is far more important than the size of its dollar goal. The other is that success should be measured primarily in terms of how well the institution meets its own needs and fulfills its unique mission" (Peterson, 1994, p. iii). These convictions were the heart of reflective practitioner Joel Smith's (1981, 1982) arguments more than a decade earlier. Capital campaigns, he said, encourage neglect of gift utility, or the degree to which a gift contributes to organizational priorities. Because campaigns emphasize haste and a preoccupation with large-dollar goals, Smith (1981) argued, "fund raisers pursue additional and often cosmetic objectives, rather than the basic institutional needs" (p. 66).

I discussed Smith's ideas and linked them to measuring effectiveness in my earlier book (Kelly, 1991a; see particularly chap. 14). I concluded with him that the success of any fund-raising program should not be judged by a big number on the bottom line. Indiscriminate dollars contribute little to the success and survival of charitable organizations. Furthermore, acceptance of gifts for purposes other than self-determined priorities represents loss of organizational autonomy. As J. P. Smith (1982) simply stated, "Gifts should help accomplish the goals we have set for our institutions" (p. 36).

The difference between planned gifts and outright gifts was explained in chapter 13. Much of the money raised through campaigns, often as great as half the dollar goal, will not benefit the organization in the near future. The larger the campaign, the more likely it will rely on gifts made through planned giving vehicles. The charitable remainder of such gifts generally is not available until the death of donors or others; therefore, the growing reliance on planned gifts is incongruent with the sense of urgency that traditionally has defined campaigns (i.e., gifts that will not materialize for as long as 25 or 50 years are accepted to fund supposedly urgent and important needs). Illustrating, the University of Michigan announced at the beginning of its general public phase in September 1992 that it planned to raise $150 million of its $1-billion goal, or 15%, through just bequest pledges (Stehle, 1992b). In May 1996, 1.3 years before the campaign's set date for completion, Michigan announced it already had raised $1.02 billion; however, promised bequests accounted for $215 million, or 21% of the total ("Univ. of Michigan," 1996). Gifts made through planned giving vehicles other than bequests were grouped with outright gifts so their proportion of the total is unknown, as is the method by which all planned gifts were valued. Students will recall that counting the face value of planned gifts, as opposed to their charitable remainder value, falsely inflates dollar amounts. Be that as it may, Michigan's early proclamation ensured its place in fund-raising history as the first public university to break the billion-dollar ceiling; it increased the goal of its campaign to $1.12 billion and continued toward the official closing date.

Accounting and reporting abuses occurring in many campaigns were listed in an opinion piece by Peterson (1993), who chaired the CASE standards advisory group:

- Including gifts made before the campaign begins.
- Counting gifts twice by counting pledges in one campaign and again as cash gifts in the next.
- Distorting the value of art and real estate.
- Inflating the value of planned gifts, such as bequests, charitable remainder trusts, and life insurance.
- Including government funds in the totals.

Nicklin (1992) provided examples of some of these abuses in higher education. Yale University is counting two $20-million gifts from members of the Bass family of Texas, even though the gifts were pledged before the date the university officially began the advance gifts phase of its current campaign.[8] Yale also has chosen to count toward its goal a $50-million pledge of artwork, stock, and cash from Paul Mellon, even though officials said they did not know how the amount was divided.

In 1990, Wichita State University appeared well on its way to raising $300 million in a 9-year campaign when faculty realized that much of the announced dollars represented planned gifts counted at face value. Faculty charged that the campaign was only raising "headline totals," not money that would help the institution in the near future (Nicklin, 1992, p. A33). The campaign was stopped 4 years early with less than one half the goal raised. Of the $130 million reported, 53% was the face value of planned gifts.

In its campaign that ended in 1992, Stanford University counted at face value a charitable remainder trust that will not benefit the institution until the trust's then 10-year-old beneficiary dies! Virginia Military Institute (VMI), in its last campaign,

---

[8]Yale originally counted three gifts from the Bass family, but—as discussed in chapter 12—$20 million was returned to Lee Bass in 1995.

counted at face value a $100,000 life insurance policy from an alumnus in his 20s, as well as promises of bequests from other young alumni. VMI's campaign lasted 12 years, and the face value of planned gifts accounted for 41% of the $178 million raised. Finally, the University of Vermont counted federal and state grants toward its $100-million campaign goal. About 20% of the institution's dollar totals in 1992 consisted of public money. A Cornell University fund raiser commented: "That's ridiculous. That really compromises integrity" (Nicklin, 1992, p. A35).

The end result of the four issues, from new versus expected money to abuses, is that campaigns raise significantly less than implied by their heralded amounts. Organizations find little budget relief and soon turn to other means for increasing income. In light of the impressive dollar totals, stakeholders, whose high expectations were driven by campaign propaganda, are left feeling frustrated and deceived. Peterson (1993) posed the questions:

> Does the public have a right to be annoyed when colleges and schools report that they are raising millions in private donations—and then raise tuition and fees by more than the rate of inflation while simultaneously cutting their operating budgets? Should donors be irritated by hospitals that aggressively seek more and more private support even while costs keep going through the roof? (p. 42)

Worth (1993) focused on employees, one of charitable organizations' most important stakeholders:

> When they learn that most of the campaign income consists of annual gifts that already have been spent or bequests that will not be received for many years ... disillusionment is the understandable result. This disillusionment is even more severe if the announcement of a successful campaign is combined, as it has been in some institutions, with budgetary problems and cutbacks. (pp. 402-403)

In 1996, a strike by employees at Yale University was countered by officials asserting that the institution could not accede to labor union demands because it had a deficit of $12 million (Anthony, 1996)—even though Yale's campaign had raised $1.3 billion toward its $1.5-billion goal ("Status," 1996).

Concluding this discussion, the effectiveness of capital campaigns, as measured by dollar production and stakeholder evaluation, is low. Yet most of the literature continues to propagate the opposite opinion, represented by Greenfield's (1991) claim that campaigns are "the most productive, most efficient, and most cost-effective method of fund-raising [sic] yet invented" (p. 170). The flawed assessment relies on evidence gathered in the absence of consistent standards and in the proliferation of ambiguous, if not deceptive, reporting. Reform, introduced by CASE, promises to dramatically change how the effectiveness of campaigns is perceived.

CASE Campaign Standards

In April 1994, the CASE Board of Trustees approved new management and reporting standards for campaigns (CASE, 1994). The standards, which went into effect during academic year 1994–1995, were the result of 4 years of intensive effort. Each organization conducting a campaign is asked to file a report annually with CASE, which will publish and disseminate the information. Although the standards apply only to its members, the association seeks universal voluntary compliance.

According to Peterson (P. M. Buchanan et al., 1992), "The impact on campaigns, if these standards are followed, will be to deflate the goals and the announced results of the campaigns." He described the then current work of the advisory group he chaired: "We're trying to do some things that will give us more realistic bases for reporting on our campaigns more honestly." He continued, "I think the era of the mega billion-dollar campaigns could well be over if, in fact, we as a body of development officers nationally adopt these standards and live within them."

The standards depend on three fundamental concepts: (a) campaign reports should separate results by featured objectives and other objectives, (b) they should separate outright gifts and pledges from planned gifts the organization expects to receive after the solicitation and pledge-payment periods end, and (c) they should record planned gifts at both their face value and their discounted present value.

The requirement to report the present value of planned gifts, discussed in chapter 13, will have the greatest impact on decreasing campaign goals and results. Organizations, such as VMI, that previously reported only the face value of planned gifts and raised almost one half their campaign totals through such gifts will have to adjust downward. The simple requirement of separating outright gifts and pledges from planned gifts will provide a more accurate picture of campaign results as measured by funds available for the organization's use.

Similarly, the breakdown of gifts by featured objectives and other purposes provides a measure of accountability sorely missing in past campaign reporting. Gifts in support of those objectives that necessitated the campaign in the first place, as opposed to all gifts received, are the appropriate indicators of this strategy's effectiveness. Although every organization has many ongoing needs for private funding, those specifically featured in the campaign's priorities list constitute the purpose of the campaign and should be given special attention. Featured objectives usually are for capital needs, or endowment and construction; other purposes usually consist of expendable programmatic support and annual giving income. According to CASE (1994), "It is never appropriate to report only one number when announcing campaign results" (p. 5).

Furthermore, the standards state, it is preferable that credit for gifts received in the advance gifts/nucleus fund phase—when pace-setting gifts are sought—be limited to those given for featured objectives. The value of large dollar goals diminishes when gift purposes are weighted appropriately. Goals and results also will be deflated by other standards, which are presented in the following discussion and related to current practice.

The length of a capital campaign, as defined by the time allotted for both the advance gifts phase and the general public phase, can be no more than 7 years. Excessively long campaigns that run for 11 to 12 years do not qualify (e.g., New York University's, VMI's, and Columbia University's), nor do those that exceed the limit by a few months. In addition to Columbia, three organizations currently conducting campaigns for $1 billion or more do not meet the standard: Harvard, Berkeley, and Michigan (7.4, 7.4, and 7.2 years, respectively). The new time parameters prohibit organizations, such as Yale, from counting gifts made before the campaign begins.

The maximum time allotted for payment of pledges is 5 years. This standard clashes with the University of Michigan's decision to count the entire amount of a 20-year pledge toward its current campaign. According to Nicklin (1992), the university made a "rare exception" (p. A35) to its 5-year payoff policy when it counted a $30-million pledge at full value even though the gift will be spread out in $1.5-million annual payments over 20 years. Under the new standard, only $7.5 million, or 25% of the total amount, can be counted. CASE also advocates not reporting oral pledges. Pledges of cash should be written and should commit to a specific dollar amount with a fixed time schedule. A pledge received even on the last day of a campaign is counted toward the goal, but the subsequent payment period must not exceed 5 years. The value of any canceled or unfulfilled pledges must be subtracted from totals when it is determined they will not be realized.

The standard is congruent with the new accounting rule on pledges from FASB. Introduced in chapter 7, one of the 1995 changes made by FASB requires charitable organizations to record written pledges as income at the time they are made and to discount the full amount to present value (Larkin, 1995). The pledge must be more than an intention to give and its payment dependent only on the passage of time (i.e., unconditional). FASB also requires donors, including businesses, to record the full amount of an unconditional pledge as an expense for the year it was made—although, as pointed out in chapter 11, unpaid pledges are not deductible from taxable income. Most recipient organizations previously counted pledges as income only when they received cash. On the other hand, the same organizations usually counted the full amount of unconditional and conditional pledges toward capital-campaign goals regardless of when the money was received. The two treatments resulted in significant discrepancies between financial statements and fund-raising reports. Even though organizations rarely sue donors for nonpayment (although court action has increased in recent years), recording legally enforceable pledges as income provides a more accurate picture of the organization's financial status. It also inhibits those who inflate campaign totals because financial officers will be reluctant to add income unless pledges are expressed as explicitly binding in a written document (i.e., more than just an oral promise).

Excluded from campaign reports are gifts counted in previous campaigns, investment earnings, earned income, surplus income transferred from ticket-based operations (except for the amount permitted as a charitable deduction), contract revenues, contributed services, and government funds. In contrast to the University of Vermont's practice, CASE (1994) explicitly stated, "Governmental funds should NOT be reported in campaign totals" (p. 6). Revocable gifts are excluded; however, bequests can be counted if they are verified by irrevocable, legally binding documents and are reported at both face and discounted present value.

Finally, the standards argue that campaigns must be designed to reconcile the needs of the organization "with the interest and capacity of its constituencies to fund them" (p. 1). CASE (1994) explained, "The tendency of institutions to focus their attention on the size of the goal of their proposed campaign rather than what should and can realistically be achieved is probably the greatest cause of dissatisfaction with campaign results" (p. 1). To ensure more symmetrical outcomes, it recommended that a campaign plan contain, at minimum, the seven following elements: financial needs that will be addressed; reporting policies to which the organization will adhere, including the treatment of pledges, planned gifts, and gifts of property; how exceptions to the policies will be handled; the tentative goal for both featured objectives and other purposes; an objective analysis of the organization's fund-raising potential; purpose and duration of the advance gifts/nucleus fund phase; and the duration of the general public phase. CASE added, "High participation—by young as well as more mature [donors], by persons of modest means as well as the wealthy—will be an important factor in gauging the campaign's success" (p. 2).

Two forms, "Campaign Report I: Results by Objective and Sources" and "CASE Voluntary Annual Survey of Cumulative Campaign Activity by Member Institutions," must be submitted each year with a certification of compliance signed by the organization's CEO.

Many fund raisers hope the new standards will help erase "the public's perception of colleges as money-hungry institutions—a view that has grown with the increasing size and frequency of campaigns" (Nicklin, 1992, p. A34). Other practitioners maintain that campaign reporting is nobody's business—that individual organizations should be free to determine the length of the campaign, the types of gifts and pledges that will be accepted, and how they will be counted. It is important to emphasize, as Worth (1993) did, that reform has come from fund raisers, not from external agencies, such as watchdog groups, or from other organizational actors. He stated, "Motivated perhaps by what they see as unrealistic pressures, and concerned by the challenges to campaigns' credibility, development officers and fund-raising consultants have been the first to speak out for change" (p. 409).

Although the standards promise to greatly improve the accountability of organizations conducting campaigns, they are not as strong as originally intended. In addition to the weaknesses pointed out in chapter 13, such as allowing dual reporting of the present and face values of planned gifts, a minimum age requirement for donors of such gifts was removed before the standards were approved. Peterson (P. M. Buchanan et al., 1992) reported that earlier versions included an age criterion of 70, below which planned gifts could not be counted for campaigns. Buchanan (cited in Goss, 1994b), CASE's president at the time, commented on the overall effort: "Thoughtful people across philanthropy felt something had to be done" to help organizations determine the real value of their capital campaigns; but he added, "Self-policing seems to be by its nature a controversial matter" (p. 30).[9]

Be that as it may, the days of smoke-and-mirror accounting for capital campaigns, which emphasized the bottom line and fund raising for its own sake, are over. Once results defined by the new standards are widely disseminated, the media will catch on to deceptive practices and will ask appropriate questions about campaigns for all types of organizations.[10] Publicity will no longer be possible without close scrutiny. Donors and other stakeholders will be better equipped to challenge the purpose, motivations, and effectiveness of campaigns. For the first time, standardized and certified evidence will be available to accurately determine the degree to which campaigns are financially successful.

---

[9]Buchanan's leadership in implementing the 1994 and 1996 standards despite strong resistance is commendable. His impact on ethical fund raising will remain long after his departure from CASE in October 1997.

[10]CASE's first report, consisting of 1994–1995 figures for 187 campaigns, was published in late 1996, and is listed in suggested readings at the end of this chapter.

The situation provides students with excellent opportunities for research. A thesis study on the ratio between featured objectives and other purposes funded through campaigns promises to be enlightening. Another might examine differences between new and expected money by computing yearly gift averages before campaigns are started and comparing them to campaign goals. CASE has pledged to make its compilations of campaign reports and other fund-raising results available via the Internet, which will make empirical analyses of national samples inexpensive and convenient. It is likely the findings from these and other studies will significantly alter the way campaigns are perceived. As Pray (1981) reminded us, too often what is called the "body of knowledge and practice" in fund raising is accorded "almost the acceptance of law when, in fact, some of it may be merely myth" (p. xiv).

REPLACING THE CAMPAIGN

All serious discussions on capital campaigns—even those extolling their virtues—raise questions about their future use and present the alternative of raising major gifts through a continuous program. The two views represent asymmetrical and symmetrical presuppositions about fund raising. The first, supporting campaigns, is based on the premise that the purpose of fund raising is to raise as much money as possible. As the Haas Fund study (Blake, 1994) pointed out, capital campaigns "have the added appeal of being a proven way to maximize donative revenues" (p. 26). The second view, in support of continuous programming, holds that the purpose of fund raising is to build and maintain relationships with donors and that sporadic campaigns contradict this purpose. Its leading proponent J. P. Smith (1981) declared, "Fund raising should be sustained, not episodic" (p. 68).

The literature highlights the division between the two views, as well as the reluctance of practitioner authors to take a stand on the worthiness of one over the other. Worth (1993) stated in a historically inaccurate explanation, "Since the advent of the campaign, there have been those who argued against it, preferring an ongoing major gifts program as the way to raise the most dollars over the long run and to appropriately match philanthropic support with institutional needs" (p. 141). But he concluded, the overwhelming majority of fund raisers think there is simply no better way for an organization to raise large amounts of money for a defined purpose within a limited period of time. Broce (1986) presented a similar analysis:

> For many years questions have been raised about the effectiveness of the capital campaign—whether it is the best means of raising funds for institutions. Critics argue that many donors have become too sophisticated to be motivated by pledge cards, deadlines, and report meetings. Advocates counter that the capital campaign is the only way to increase the sense of urgency that is required to *persuade* donors to contribute sacrificially and promptly. Both views are factually correct. (p. 43; italics added)

Rosso (1991) said raising capital, or asset-building, gifts can take two forms: an "intensive campaign to attain a specified goal within a relatively short period" or "a strategically designed major gift effort directed to the interests of a limited number of donors capable of making large gifts" (p. 288). Although he stopped short of recommending one approach, he presented an "integrated development plan" in the last chapter of his book that "captures all of the organization's financial needs in an overall goal for a slower paced fund raising [sic] program that can be extended over a number of years" (p. 286).

In his book on capital campaigns, Dove (1988) presented the "continuing major gifts program" (p. 13), integrated in planned, ongoing fund raising, as an alternative model to historical, single-purpose and comprehensive campaigns. Calling it the "strategic planning approach," he said the model is based on two premises: The charitable organization is committed to strategic planning, and fund-raising managers participate in the process, resulting in programming "designed in supportive concert with institutional strategies" (p. 13). He concluded, however, "There is no one correct model" (p. 14), and all organizations will "from time to time continue to engage in intensive, time-specific 'capital campaigns'" (p. 13).

Yet the very characteristics of intensity and limited time led the Haas Fund study (Blake, 1994) to its conclusion that campaigns are not in the best long-term interest of charitable organizations. A campaign, the study warned, "can seriously encroach on an agency's ability to accomplish its central mission" (p. 3). Explained by Green-field (1991), campaigns "demand a total effort throughout the organization, which forces everyone to concentrate on campaign objectives and on major gifts" (p. 170). The required concentration redirects organizational attention from program services to fund raising. Systems theory tells us that undue focus on one stakeholder group, in this case donors, increases the vulnerability of organizations to crises. Stanford University provides an illustration of the danger.

Stanford's capital campaign successfully surpassed its $1.1-billion goal at the beginning of the 1991–1992 academic year, a few months before the university's centennial. During what was planned as a year of celebration, Stanford announced its second budget deficit in 3 years, projected at $90 million (Kantrowitz, 1991). The university also was embroiled in a controversy surrounding its excess billing of overhead research costs to the federal government. It agreed to pay back more than $2 million in misused funds and was forced to implement an overhaul of its accounting practices, estimated to cost $10 million. Donald Kennedy, who was president for 12 years, resigned because of the scandal. But those were only the most visible problems. As Kantrowitz described in a Newsweek article on Stanford's centennial, "From the scandal over misuse of federal funds to the emotional debate over multiculturalism to the embarrassing resignation of a female medical-school professor amid allegations of sexual harassment, the university is majoring in controversy (with a minor in bad publicity)" (p. 54). The 5-page article concluded that Stanford had become a symbol of everything wrong in U.S. higher education. The institution's "successful" campaign was never even mentioned.

According to Dove (1988), organizations conducting campaigns find it difficult "to maintain an appropriate focus" on priorities "because there is so much attention directed to the bottom line" (p. 169). "The point of a campaign," he emphasized, "is *to force* as many gifts as possible in a prescribed period of time in order to achieve a goal that is often a terrific stretch" (pp. 168–169; italics added). The Haas Fund study (Blake, 1994) countered, "Nonprofits should not blindly make revenue maximization their fundraising [sic] objective" (p. 26).

Capital campaigns have outlived their usefulness. There are numerous reasons to believe they will not survive in their present form much past the dawn of the third millennium. I recommend they be replaced with continuous efforts to raise major gifts, and I am not alone in my assessment. M. R. Hall (1993), for example, predicted that the cycle of extensive campaigning is over for higher education:

> Donor burnout, administration exhaustion, and the recessionary status of the economy [in the early 1990s] have come together to end this cycle. Over the next decade, universities probably will be less noisy about their development. The mega-campaigns will almost certainly give way to less ambitious projects, to fund raising on a more human scale. The pleasure of working with a group of potential donors to achieve a shared goal will replace the carnival-like kickoff dinners and black-tie extravaganzas of the recent past. Universities, donors, and society will enjoy the respite. (p. 53)

J. P. Smith (1981) also advocated replacing campaigns with continuous efforts to raise major gifts. The new approach, he argued, is inherently more conducive to the two-way symmetrical model, or what he called "professional" and "sophisticated fund raising" that "is patient, subtle, and sustained" (p. 65). He anticipated and answered the question that would be raised by those holding asymmetrical presuppositions about the function: "Will that kind of sustained program yield as many dollars as campaigns? Maybe, maybe not. But the point I wish to make is that we ought to be asking a different question: Which pattern will provide more support year-in, year-out for the most important objectives of the institution?" (p. 68).

Fund-raising managers and their organizations increasingly will choose not to conduct campaigns. J. P. Smith commented: "In the past such a decision has been interpreted as evidence of institutional timidity. In the future it may well be evidence of superior judgement" (p. 68). I agree.

SUGGESTED READINGS

Council for Advancement and Support of Education (CASE). (1994). *CASE campaign standards.* Washington, DC: Author.

Council for Advancement and Support of Education (CASE). (1996). *CASE report of educational fund-raising campaigns 1994–95.* Washington, DC: Author.

Dove, K. E. (1988). *Conducting a successful capital campaign: A comprehensive fundraising guide for nonprofit organizations.* San Francisco, CA: Jossey-Bass.

Gearhart, G. D. (1995). *The capital campaign in higher education: A practical guide for college and university advancement.* Washington, DC: National Association of College and University Business Officers.

15

Donor Publics: Individuals, Corporations, and Foundations

This final chapter examines the three sources of gifts, or donor publics. Addressed in reverse order, the bulk of the chapter is devoted to foundation and corporate donors because individuals, who provide 86% of all gift dollars, rightfully have been the focus of attention until this point in the book. The central thrust of chapter 15 concerns commonalities among the three donor publics, although definitional and operational differences are explained. The issues of interdependence and autonomy are revisited in relation to each gift source.

FOUNDATION DONORS

There are approximately 37,600 active U.S. foundations, which collectively account for 8% of all gift dollars, as of 1993 (Renz et al., 1995).[1] Gifts from these nonprofit organizations typically are referred to as *grants* to differentiate them from the tax-deductible gifts they receive from their donors. The foundations are broken down by four types: (a) independent, (b) corporate, (c) community, and (d) operating. *Independent foundations* are by far the largest group, accounting for 88% of the total number and 78% of the annual dollars. Distinctive characteristics are that their funds come from a single source, either one individual or a small group such as a family, and the funding is endowed to generate income for grants, usually in perpetuity. *Corporate foundations* also are funded by a single source, the sponsoring corporation, but they

---

[1]Chapter 15 relies on statistics from 1993 because of the time lag in detailed reports on giving (i.e., 1993 serves as a common time frame to compare and contrast the three sources of gifts). Statistics from later years are presented when appropriate. For example, in 1995, 44,000 foundations were registered with the IRS (1996). As explained in chapter 2, however, the number of foundations varies by the source's selection criteria. Unless otherwise noted, foundation figures cited in chapter 15 are based on estimates from the Foundation Center (e.g., Renz et al., 1995). Also, students will note discrepancies between estimates provided by the AAFRC Trust for Philanthropy (e.g., 1995) and other sources cited in this chapter because the AAFRC Trust counts grants from corporate foundations as gifts from corporate donors, not foundation donors, and includes gifts *to* foundations in figures for individual and corporate giving. For example, in 1993, $6.3 billion, or 5%, of the estimated dollars attributed to gift sources went to foundations, not directly to charitable organizations.

rely on continuous funding from annual corporate earnings to make grants. Corporate foundations provide about 14% of the foundation dollars, but own less than 4% of the assets.

Community foundations, on the other hand, are funded by multiple donors and are endowed. Smallest in number, their grants represent 7% of foundation dollars. As denoted by their name, they are established to serve a specific community or geographic area. *Operating foundations* also are described by their name in that they operate their own program services. Because they devote most of their income to their own activities (at least 85%), operating foundations—unlike the other three types—make few grants to charitable organizations. They account for 6% of all foundations, but only 1% of the grant dollars. Like independent and corporate foundations, their funds come from a single source. Illustrating this type, the California-based J. Paul Getty Trust, established in 1982 with a $1.2-billion bequest from J. Paul Getty, is concerned primarily with preservation of the Getty art collection (Renz & Lawrence, 1993).

Because they are funded by a single source, independent, corporate, and operating foundations are legally defined as *private foundations*. As such, they must be organized and operated under specific regulations first passed in the Tax Reform Act of 1969 and modified through subsequent legislation. The 1969 law set up a separate category with a more favorable tax status for operating foundations and established the criteria for distinguishing private foundations from *public charities*. Simplified, public charities receive at least one third of their annual income from multiple donors, with consideration also given to government funding and mission of the organization (API, 1990). Community foundations, therefore, differentiate themselves from private foundations by qualifying as public charities, along with charitable organizations. Both can lose their status if they rely too heavily on a few donors. Illustrating, private foundations in the IRS' 1991 database included 8,900 *lapsed* public charities (Bowen et al., 1994). Private foundations, it is important to note, are subject to an excise tax on their investment income, a minimum payout requirement of 5% of the market value of their assets, and lower tax deductibility for donors' gifts. Public charities are exempt from those rules. Representative of their special status, community foundations file the IRS Form 990, whereas private foundations file Form 990-PF.

Differences between private and community foundations were dramatically reinforced at the end of 1994, when a 10-year-old law expired that had allowed full market deductibility for gifts of stock to private foundations (Murawski, 1994b). Starting that same year, donors could claim deductions for the full market value of gifts of appreciated stock to community foundations and charitable organizations. Therefore, stock worth $1 million that originally cost $100,000 reduced donors' taxable income by $1 million or only $100,000, depending on the organization to which the gift was made. Because appreciated stock is the primary form of major gifts, experts predicted that the change would have a damaging impact on independent and corporate foundations (operating foundations were not affected). In contrast, a community foundation fund raiser commented: "It affects us positively. It's a boon for community foundations, but I think it's a negative to philanthropy in general" (Murawski, 1994b, p. 8).

Congress waited almost 2 years to resolve the imbalance and then placed an 11-month limit on renewal of full market deductibility for stock given to private foundations (Murawski & Stehle, 1996). Explaining the short extension, Congress said the law's new expiration date of May 31, 1997 was due to concern about the cost of the full deduction to the Treasury. Left unsaid but likely contributing to its decision is that Congress has a historical mistrust of private foundations, which is explained shortly. A surge in creating and supplementing private foundations was expected as a result of the 1996 reenactment.

By definition, operating foundations are not viable prospects for fund raising; the discussion, then, continues by examining the other three types in more detail. A common theme is that size, as well as foundation type, determines patterns of giving and growth.

Independent Foundations

When we talk about foundations, we usually are talking about independent foundations because their number and financial capacity dominate this gift source. In addition to providing 78% of the grant dollars, they own 86% of all foundation assets (Renz et al., 1995). Wealth, however, is not distributed equally. Just 25% of the independent foundations, or about 8,500, have endowments of $1 million or more and account for 96% of the assets and 90% of the grant dollars. Slightly more than 1%, or roughly the top 400, have endowments of at least $50 million and account for the majority of assets and dollars, 68% and 55%, respectively. In other words, independent foundations consist of three important subtypes based on their capacity, or size: the largest, the large, and the small. The 75% belonging to the last subtype are termed *family foundations*.

Different Sizes.   Consistently ranked first in size among all types, the Ford Foundation is the largest independent foundation, with assets of $7.8 billion (S. G. Greene, 1996). In 1995, 24 independent foundations had assets of $1 billion or more, with at least 3 others positioned to join the elite group the next year (Foundation Center, 1997). Among the leaders are W. K. Kellogg, Lilly Endowment, Robert Wood Johnson, Pew Charitable Trusts, John D. and Catherine T. MacArthur, Rockefeller, Andrew W. Mellon, Robert W. Woodruff, and David and Lucile Packard.[2]

Those foundations constituting the largest 400 scarcely change in membership from one decade to the next, although rankings do change as a result of asset growth and additional gifts to endowment. Illustrating, assets of the Michigan-based Kellogg Foundation increased 761% during the 1980s, moving it from eighth to second place (Renz & Lawrence, 1993). Its grants tripled from $50 million in 1981 to $154 million in 1991. More recently, a booming stock market in the mid-1990s enriched the wealth of many foundations; for example, Ford's assets grew by nearly $1 billion in 1995 (S. G. Greene, 1996). Astute fund raisers pay attention to increases in wealth because they usually signal a forthcoming increase in dollars that must be given away due to the 5% payout requirement.

Each of the largest independent foundations annually gives between $2 million and $282 million (Renz et al., 1995). Not surprisingly, then, they account for most of the paid staff, with Ford employing almost 600.

---

[2]Due to the 1996 death of David Packard, cofounder of the Hewlett-Packard Co., the Packard Foundation's assets increased to $7.2 billion in 1997, making it one of the three largest foundations (Hafner, 1996).

According to Boris (1989), "Most of the estimated 8,000 staff members work for the 500 largest foundations" (p. 200). A survey conducted by the Foundation Center in 1992 showed that whereas 87% of the foundations with assets of $100 million or more have paid staff to review and investigate proposals, only 12% of the foundations with assets of $1 million to $5 million have staff (Renz et al., 1995). Few, if any, of the small foundations have full-time, professional staff.

Family foundations, or 75% of all independent foundations, are managed by the donors who funded them, their families, friends, lawyers, or bank trustees. Most are used to dispense small annual grants of $100 to $5,000 to organizations of interest to the donor, often repeated each year. Unmediated by staff, their giving behavior is personal. In other words, family foundations resemble individual donors, and fund raisers approach them as such. Nielsen (1993) pointed out that problems typically arise after the donor's death:

> In some admirable cases, family involvement remains active for two or three generations. But in many more cases, the foundation becomes little more than a file in the family lawyer's desk drawer, and the dispersed family members consider it increasingly tiresome to travel considerable distances to go through the annual routine of making the same grants to the same standard list of grantees. (p. 63)

Boris (1989) presented four management models of independent foundations that are useful for planning fund-raising strategy. The models progressively follow a common life cycle of foundations based on maturity, increasing size, and distance from the original donor. The first, then, is the *donor model*, which describes family foundations. Grant decisions are made by the donor or are guided by the donor's interests. Although the foundation may employ part-time legal or clerical help, prospect research should focus on the individual who funded the foundation.

The *administrator model* describes the smaller of the large foundations that have staff. Trustees are dominant in the grant-decision process; therefore, relationships with them are important. The foundation employs one or two staff members to help manage paperwork, and a COO who usually has little authority and rarely has the title of president or executive director. Many of these positions, Boris claimed, are filled by women.

Under the *director model*, a CEO has more authority and consults often with trustees. The model describes large foundations that may still have some donor or family participation. Fund raisers should take all actors into account when planning activities, particularly the CEO, who often has high visibility in the community.

The *presidential model* is found in the largest foundations that do not have significant donor or family involvement. Trustees delegate broad authority to the CEO, who is considered a member of the board. The board only concerns itself with very large grant proposals. Program officers review grant applications, investigate applicants' credentials, summarize proposals, and offer funding recommendations to the board. Because employees have almost complete control over grant decisions, fund raisers should take special care in building relationships with them. As Mixer (1993) reminded practitioners, "Like the founders, trustees and managers have values and preferences that seek satisfaction" (p. 83).

The life cycle followed by the models underscores the important point that fund raisers should pay attention to family foundations. Not only is repeat giving one of their characteristics, but some small foundations become large ones. According to Renz and Lawrence (1993), studies have shown that the largest independent foundations received their primary endowments about 18 years after they were created, usually following the death of the founder. Starting relationships early in the life of a foundation can benefit a fund raiser's organization for years to come. Nearly half of the very largest foundations were created in the 1940s and 1950s; about 13,000, or one third, of all foundations were formed since 1980 (Renz et al., 1995).

Historical Perspective.   Independent foundations draw their legal definition from the English Statute of Charitable Uses of 1601, but it was not until the turn of the 20th century that wealthy individuals in the United States created the first modern foundations, including the Russell Sage Foundation (1907), the Carnegie Corporation of New York (1911), and the Rockefeller Foundation (1913). Furthermore, it was only after World War II that foundations experienced "explosive growth" (Renz & Lawrence, 1993, p. 23). Federal and state tax laws, as Ylvisaker (1987) pointed out, "made foundations an attractive shelter for the great personal and corporate affluence of the postwar period" (p. 375). The number of large independent foundations more than doubled during the 1950s, from 1,126 to 2,631 (Renz & Lawrence, 1993). The phenomenal growth went almost unnoticed. There was minimal government oversight; scholars paid little attention to the study of foundations; and there was no general reference work that even listed them until the first edition of *The Foundation Directory* was published in 1960 (P. D. Hall, 1989). Conditions changed dramatically with Representative Wright Patman's Congressional hearings in the late 1960s.

Prompted by charges of subversive behavior, Patman, a Texas Democrat, pressed the Treasury Department to conduct an investigation of 1,300 foundations—some with diversified assets and others with assets consisting primarily of stock in the donor's company (Nielsen, 1993). The investigation and resulting hearings revealed widespread abuses. Many independent foundations were found to be merely holding companies, mechanisms for building dynasties, or methods of tax avoidance (P. D. Hall, 1989). Foundations with diversified assets received more than double the return of those with concentrated assets. Half of the latter received *no* income from their assets. Nielsen (1993) stated: "In plain language, foundations were being widely used simply to gain tax benefits for donors and their families and to maintain control over the family company. Philanthropic purpose was secondary or non-existent" (p. 64).

Illustrating, the Ford Foundation was established by Henry and Edsel Ford in 1936 because they wanted to avoid outsiders controlling the Ford Motor Company and to avoid paying the new estate taxes introduced by the Roosevelt administration (Curti & Nash, 1965). After the deaths of Edsel in 1943 and his father in 1947, the Ford Foundation acquired 90% of the Ford Motor Company stock—essentially making it one of the nation's biggest holding companies. Odendahl (1989) asserted that half of the largest foundations had been created with enough stock to constitute control. According to P. D. Hall (1989), whereas independent foundations "had been used to further enrich the very rich" (p. 195), community foundations were shown to be exceptionally free of abuse. Congress' trust and mistrust were reflected in the 1969 tax act, passed at the conclusion of the Patman hearings.

Among the regulations imposed on independent foundations were rules against *excess business holdings*, a minimum payout requirement, an excise tax on investment income, and stronger provisions against self-dealing (Odendahl, 1989). Furthermore, the discrepancy in tax deductibility between foundations and public charities was increased. Cash gifts from individuals to public charities became deductible up to 50% of the donor's adjusted gross income (AGI), whereas deductibility of gifts to private foundations was first set at 20% of AGI and later increased to 30%. Magat (1989) summarized, "The 1969 act was a heavy blow to foundation formation, not only by limiting deductibility but through the 'excess business holdings' provision that prohibits individuals from using a foundation to maintain a controlling interest in any company" (p. 15).

The Patman hearings had future ramifications. In 1984 when Congress decided to allow full deduction for gifts of appreciated stock to foundations, a 10-year limit was included in the law, discussed earlier. Lingering distrust of independent foundations, engendered in the 1960s, resulted in the law's expiration in 1994 and a limit of just 11 months when it was reenacted in 1996 (Murawski & Stehle, 1996). As a former Treasury expert on tax policy recalled, "There were tremendous abuses in private foundations; they were sort of private pocketbooks" (Murawski, 1994b, p. 8).

According to Renz and Lawrence (1993), creation rate of new foundations "plummeted in the early 1970s following passage of the 1969 Tax Reform Act" (p. 24). They elaborated, "Regulation and the generally hostile climate that surrounded it appear to have had a very chilling effect on new formation, especially of independent or family foundations" (p. 24). By the early 1980s, foundation decline was of paramount concern to the philanthropic community, particularly to the Council on Foundations—the major association for foundation donors and staff. Despite what many believed were excessively punitive regulations, market performance and economic expansion during most of the 1980s spurred "an astonishing resurgence in foundation creation" (Renz & Lawrence, 1993, p. 25). More than 2,500 new, large independent foundations were created, surpassing the milestone decade of the 1950s. A number of the rich, famous, and infamous added their names to foundations, including Sam Walton, Ted Turner, David Geffen, J. Willard Marriott, Jr., Andy Warhol, Liz Claiborne, Barbra Streisand, Henry Kravis, and Michael Milken.

In 1992, foundation grants topped $10 billion for the first time (Renz et al., 1995). Assets, according to Blake (1994), increased more than 22% in inflation-adjusted dollars during the period from 1988 to 1992. San Francisco Bay Area foundations, for example, grew by 43% and increased their total grants by almost the same percentage. The rate of creating new foundations declined after 1992, partly because lower income tax rates reduced incentives for giving. Predictions for the remainder of the 1990s are conservative. Although a surge in giving was expected due to the 1996 reenactment of full deductibility for gifts of stock, Congress has yet to extend the law in 1997, which could dramatically slow growth, as could reduction of the capital-gains tax rate. Be that as it may, independent foundations provide a stream of regulated giving, $8.7 billion in 1993.

Payout Rates.   Before turning to corporate foundations, which are subject to the same regulations as independent foundations, a clarification of the 5% payout rate is necessary. In calculating how much they give away, foundations are permitted to include administrative and operating costs, fees and honoraria for board members, loans made for charitable projects, and the costs of constructing, renovating, and maintaining buildings and equipment.

Some independent foundations, such as Samuel Roberts Noble, operate extensive program services; therefore, they give away much less than 5% of the market value of their assets. Illustrating with grant totals and asset values from the same year, in 1993, the Noble Foundation gave only $5 million in grants, although 5% of its assets totaled $28 million (Renz et al., 1995).[3] Freedom Forum International, which also runs programs but has also been investigated for lavish administrative expenses, gave less than $9 million in 1993, about one fourth of the calculated rate. On the other hand, Lilly Endowment gave $132 million, but 5% of its 1993 assets called for only $126 million. In short, the amount given to charitable organizations cannot be predicted solely from assets.

Salamon (1993) found in his study of foundation investment patterns that, generally, "foundations pay out more than required by law" (p. 247). The median payout rate was 7.7% per year during the 1979 to 1986 period studied, or more than 50% above the minimum. The rate was higher for small foundations than for large ones. Salamon explained:

> Small foundations are more likely to be influenced by the original donors or their immediate families and to be more interested in maximizing current grantmaking than in holding the foundation's assets for the long term. This would lead them to favor low-risk/high-current yield investments and to give away all of their earnings in a given year even if this eats into the asset base over time. By contrast, the larger foundations, run by professional staffs, are more likely to be committed to operating in perpetuity and therefore to selecting investment and payout policies that encourage this. (p. 250)

Among those he studied, Salamon (1993) found that the most common policy, reported by close to 40%, was to set payout equal to investment income. Another 30% reported that payout decisions were shaped by overall investment performance, including endowment growth. Only 14% reported paying out exactly what the law requires. "Strikingly," Salamon said, "a mere 7 percent indicated that the primary determinant of payout levels is programmatic goals" (p. 247). Adding to these findings, Blake (1994) found from his longitudinal study of San Francisco foundations that "the main determinants of overall level of giving are asset base and the 5% spendout requirement" (p. 19). He concluded, therefore, "The level of overall foundation giving is not linked to fundraising [*sic*] activity" (p. 20).

In other words, fund raisers do not affect whether foundations give, but rather what specific organizations they give to, the exact purposes of the grants, and their amounts. Practitioners should further understand that the payouts of large independent foundations usually are limited by investment policies designed to perpetuate the foundation's existence; therefore, once funding limits have been reached, paid staff

---

[3]The 5% payout rate generally is based on the market value of assets at the end of the previous fiscal year. Furthermore, foundations are allowed to average their assets' value over 3 years when determining payout.

will not recommend additional grants—even if a proposal is a near match to the foundation's goals and objectives. Unless otherwise instructed, proposals should be submitted at the beginning of a foundation's fiscal year, as given in its guidelines or various reference sources, discussed later in this section. Family foundations, on the other hand, are likely to pay out an amount equal to or greater than earnings. They are more flexible about reviewing proposals even when spending limits have been reached.

Corporate Foundations

There are some 6 million companies in the United States (U.S. Small Business Administration, 1995), but only about 2,000 have an active corporate foundation (Renz et al., 1995). Although small in number, the foundations' grants annually represent 25% of total corporate giving. The proportion would be even higher, as much as 40%, if just cash gifts were counted. Corporate donors—discussed later in this chapter—make gifts of cash and property, such as products, directly to charitable organizations. Even those with foundations usually have a direct-giving program, separately administered and funded from the company's pretax income, or earnings after paying expenses and before paying taxes. Corporate foundations, then, are only part of corporate giving—but an important part.

The nonprofit entities are funded by tax-deductible gifts from the sponsoring corporation's pretax income. Much like the relationship between family foundations and individuals, corporate foundations act as an extension of their sponsor. They maintain close ties with the company and support its giving objectives. Their boards of trustees and staff usually are composed of employees and directors of the parent company. Based on a study of 48 large U.S. corporations, Knauft (1989) reported, "Where both foundation boards and company contributions committees exist, the same individuals typically serve on both" (p. 266). A few foundations with large endowments, no longer financially dependent on their sponsor, may have more autonomy; however, they are the exception, not the rule. In short, when fund raisers are talking to a corporate foundation, they are—in effect—talking to the corporate sponsor.

Foundations Versus Direct Programs.   Given such close ties, a corporation's reasons for establishing a foundation may not be readily apparent. Indeed, N. J. Webb (1994) found from her research on the subject that using a foundation to make gifts sometimes differs little from using a direct-giving program, and in some cases is more difficult. Restrictive regulations are a disadvantage. Particularly problematic for corporations, according to John Edie (1991), vice president and general counsel of the Council on Foundations, are violations of the *self-dealing* rules, which prohibit the use of charitable funds to benefit donors, trustees, and officers. Purchasing a table at a fund-raising gala can be viewed as self-dealing—a fact practitioners are advised to remember when soliciting gifts through special events. Adding to regulation, foundations have start-up costs, gifts may not be as strongly associated with the company's name, giving is centralized rather than handled through local sites, and the names of gift recipients and amounts must be made public rather than kept private (N. J. Webb, 1994). Knauft (1989) found from his study of corporate giving that the existence of a foundation had no statistically significant impact on total gifts, gifts as a percentage of taxable income, or a subjective rating of the program's quality.

Why then do corporations establish foundations? Of the advantages listed in the literature, four stand out. A company can reduce its tax liability and maximize its profits by giving more to its foundation in higher profit years and years when tax rates are high and conversely contributing less when profits and tax rates are lower (N. J. Webb, 1994). Unlike a direct-giving program, the foundation can serve as a holding tank to "maintain a reserve store of funds to be used for corporate charitable purpose" (p. 46). This provides a second advantage of allowing the company to even out its annual grant levels by divorcing much of its giving from fluctuations in earnings. Regression analysis of historical data by N. J. Webb (1994) provided evidence that corporations do, indeed, use foundations for these first two advantages.

Third, the company can avoid capital-gains taxes on appreciated property by giving the property to its foundation, which can sell it without owing any taxes and distribute the income as grants (N. J. Webb, 1994). Setting aside Congress' fluctuating treatment of appreciated stock, the company's income tax deduction is based on the fair market value of the property rather than original cost. Finally, corporate foundations can give outside the United States, whereas companies cannot deduct gifts made overseas. The advantage is significant given the global economy and increasing reliance on international markets.

Based on data from the Conference Board, one of the leading sources of information on corporate giving, Renz and Lawrence (1993) reported that manufacturing companies are more likely to have foundations than nonmanufacturing companies. Of the nonmanufacturers, telecommunications and finance companies are most likely to form foundations; insurance companies are least likely. Only about 30% of the top 1,000 U.S. firms have corporate foundations (N. J. Webb, 1994), and they do not always play a major role in the company's philanthropy. For example, International Business Machines (IBM) Corporation, currently the sixth largest firm and a leading corporate donor, channels the vast majority of its gift dollars through direct-giving programs. Virtually all contributions made in the United States are handled directly, although the company uses the IBM International Foundation—which was given its new name and an expanded geographical scope in 1992—to address problems in other countries (IBM, personal communication, July 22, 1996).

Wealth and History. The majority of corporate foundations, about 65%, have assets of less than $1 million (Renz et al., 1995). Because they have small endowments, Edie (1991) said they act as "pass-through" entities, whereby corporate earnings are annually or periodically channeled through the foundation. Therefore, size by total grants given in a single year is a more accurate measurement of capacity than assets. The five top corporate foundations in 1993 were AT&T, Amoco, U S West, General Motors, and the Ford Motor Company Fund. The AT&T Foundation, which made grants totaling $35 million in 1993, ranked first in giving. It held the position of largest corporate foundation for 10 consecutive years following its creation; however, another foundation will take its place in 1997. AT&T Corporation's decision in 1996 to split into three companies meant that its foundation would also be broken up into three separate entities ("AT&T Foundation," 1996). Officials refused to predict whether total giving would be affected.

Similar to their independent counterparts, a small minority of corporate foundations are responsible for the majority of gifts. Of the total 2,000, only 360, or less than 20%, give at least $1 million per year and account for 83% of the grant dollars (Renz et al., 1995). A few foundations have accumulated substantial endowments over the years from their corporation's gifts. Five have assets of $100 million or more, the largest being Pennsylvania-based Alcoa Foundation at about $270 million. Only two of the five were among the top givers in 1993, AT&T and General Motors.

Corporate foundations did not exist until the 1900s, and only a handful existed before 1940. The first, according to N. J. Webb (1994), was the Altman Foundation, established in 1913 as a holding company for the Altman department stores. Sears, Roebuck and Co. followed in 1918. The small number was due to the absence of tax advantages: There were no corporate income taxes until 1909, and no deductions were allowed for corporate gifts until 1936. When gifts were granted deductibility through the Tax Reform Act of 1935, Congress attached two important conditions. First, gift deductions could not exceed 5% of the corporation's pretax income (later raised to the current rate of 10% by the Economic Recovery Tax Act of 1981). Second, which is pertinent to discussions about motivation, gifts could qualify for deduction only if they resulted in a *direct benefit* to the corporation.

According to H. W. Smith (1993), the philosophy regarding corporations at the time was that "the business of business was business" (p. 218). All effort, including charitable giving, should be directed at profit maximization. Smith cited the 1953 landmark court case that overturned the direct-benefit precedent, *A. P. Smith Mfg. Co. v. Barlow*, which ruled that an unrestricted gift made by a small New Jersey company was acceptable as an act of good citizenship.

Corporate foundations boomed during the 1950s, with peak years during the Korean War (N. J. Webb, 1994). One reason for the explosive growth was excessively high corporate tax rates, with some companies facing rates exceeding 80% of their taxable income. The number of foundations more than quadrupled (Renz et al., 1995). Creation of new foundations declined until the 1980s when a second expansion took place, although—unlike independent foundations—the 1950s level remained the highest for corporate foundations. A period of zero growth in giving started in 1990.

Equally dismaying, the foundations began paying out significantly more in grants each year than they received in gifts from their companies. The gap between pay-in and payout was $485 million in 1991, or 48% of all grants, compared to only 4% in 1988! Gaps have been most pronounced among the largest foundations. Former giants, such as ARCO, have been drastically reduced in size; others have closed down completely. Shortfalls for the 4 years from 1990 through 1993 totaled about $1.3 billion.

Clearly, corporate foundations are eroding their assets, which likely will mean fewer gift dollars in future years. Renz and Lawrence (1993) similarly predicted after 2 years of shortfalls, "Since most company-sponsored foundations are not fully endowed and cannot live off investment income, continuation of the pay-in/payout imbalance will undoubtedly signal a tightening of the foundation belt" (p. 36). Despite strong business profits in the 2 years preceding 1993, Renz et al. (1995) reported a fourth straight year of zero growth and a shortfall of $248 million. With fewer companies forming new foundations and expectations that corporate philanthropy would remain flat, they declared prospects for giving "highly uncertain" (p. ix).[4]

Community Foundations

Community foundations continue to enjoy steady growth and a surge in popularity. From 1991 to 1993, they increased in number by 12%, in gifts received from donors by 34%, and in grants made by 32% (Renz & Lawrence, 1993; Renz et al., 1995). Translating those percentages, there are about 375 community foundations that raised $857 million in 1993 and gave away $718 million.[5] They are a hybrid. They raise money as public charities and make grants in a geographically limited area as foundations. Gagen-McCarthy (1993) explained: "In simple terms, the community foundation's purpose is to raise money from the public, pool and invest those funds wisely and use the income to fulfill the wishes of the donors and meet local community needs. This mission places community foundations in the unique position of being both fund raiser and grant maker" (p. 24). P. D. Hall (1989) called them the most interesting and least understood creations of American philanthropy.

History and Wealth.   Community foundations, in Nielsen's (1993) words, were "the wonderful invention of a Cleveland Banker named Frederick H. Goff" (p. 64). Cleveland, Ohio was the birthplace of community foundations, as well as today's federated campaigns. Both concepts, it is recalled from chapter 8, were spurred by businessmen's attempts to find a middle ground between socialism and *laissez-faire* capitalism during the first decades of the 1900s (P. D. Hall, 1989). The same year that Cleveland's Chamber of Commerce created the Cleveland Federation for Charity and Philanthropy (1913), Frederick Goff, who was president of the Cleveland Trust Company, developed a plan for a new type of foundation.

P. D. Hall (1989) described the plan: "A foundation would be set up to receive and manage charitable trust funds, which, as under the federation scheme, their donors could either designate for particular purposes or leave to the discretion of the foundation for distribution" (p. 187). Goff (cited in Hall) elaborated, "It is a fund created by the union of many gifts—many different estates or parts of estates. . . . By the combining of many small funds a large income is provided with which work of real significance to the

---

[4]Supporting these expectations, the AAFRC Trust for Philanthropy (1995) reported that corporate giving in 1994 failed to keep pace with inflation. AAFRC's estimate was based on giving by the sample of donors it traditionally used, primarily the 500 largest U.S. corporations—as ranked by *Fortune* magazine—and their foundations. A year later when the AAFRC Trust (1996) added smaller companies to the sample, including firms in rapidly growing service industries, it substantially revised the 1994 estimate, showing a 7% increase in inflation-adjusted dollars rather than a 2% decrease. Based on the augmented donor sample, corporate giving also increased in 1995, by 4.5%. How these changes relate to grants from corporate foundations currently is unclear as AAFRC combines them with companies' direct gifts and separated figures from the Foundation Center lag by 2 years. However, given that only 360 foundations account for 83% of the grant dollars and their sponsors most likely are among the largest corporations, we can hypothesize from the original 1994 estimate that corporate foundation giving is still in a period of zero growth, even though giving by companies of different sizes has increased (i.e., firms unlikely to have a large foundation—if any at all—are responsible for the increases). Providing supportive evidence, a survey by *The Chronicle of Philanthropy* found that giving in 1995 remained flat for corporations ranked in the top third of the Fortune 500, which prompted the conclusion that "small and medium-sized companies increased their giving at a greater rate than did the big corporations" (S. Gray & Moore, 1996, p. 12).

[5]The Columbus Foundation, which conducts annual surveys on its sister foundations, claims there are 600 community foundations but that meager assets keep many out of official reports.

community may be accomplished" (p. 187). Goff's plan called for a board consisting of two directors of his trust company, the mayor of Cleveland, and two judges. According to Hall, contemporary community foundations often have publicly appointed trustees. One of their desirable characteristics, he argued, is that—unlike private foundations—their boards broadly represent the community and are not self-perpetuating.

The Cleveland Foundation was established in 1914 as the nation's first community foundation. By 1924, its assets totaled more than $100 million. This type of foundation remained largely a Midwest phenomenon during the next 40 years. Its appeal to inland cities, P. D. Hall (1989) said, was based on "elite-dominated reformist" (p. 188) cultures that trusted citizens to use charitable resources intelligently. In the 1960s, the concept started to take off and shift geographically, with most growth in the West and South. Today, almost all major cities have a community foundation, and counties and states are represented by multiple entities. Their wealth, however, is not distributed equally.

Only 30% of all community foundations own 92% of the assets and account for 91% of the grants (Renz et al., 1995). These foundations have assets of $10 million or more and span the country from Rhode Island to Oregon. The largest is New York Community Trust, which in 1993 had assets of $1 billion and made grants of $151 million. Representing mid-America, the Cleveland Foundation is in second place with assets of $740 million and grants of $30 million. The Marin Community Foundation in California geographically balances the top three. In contrast to the wealthiest, slightly less than one third of all community foundations have assets of under $1 million; they account for less than 1% of both assets and grants.

The upper two thirds almost always have paid staff, usually about six persons. Unique to this foundation type, some of the staff members are fund raisers (i.e., community foundations are potential employers of practitioners, as well as being prospective donors). Their fund-raising ability is reflected in the increasing dollar amounts given to them each year. Seventeen community foundations were ranked among the top 400 organizations raising the most money in 1995; their collective total was an impressive $683 million ("Philanthropy 400," 1996).

Formation and growth patterns of community foundations have differed substantially from independent and corporate foundations. Whereas the 1950s were peak years for private foundation development, followed by a sharp decline in the 1970s, community foundations expanded rapidly in the 1970s and continue to grow. This is not surprising given their different treatment by Congress, particularly in the Tax Reform Act of 1969. P. D. Hall (1989) speculated, "If federal regulation of foundations continues along the increasingly restrictive path it has followed since the early 1950s, community foundations and other kinds of public charities may well become the distinctive philanthropic vehicle of the next century" (p. 181).

Donor-Advised Funds.

Community foundations raise gifts from individuals, corporations, and private foundations, with a concentration on major gifts for endowment. As with charitable organizations, a donor can name the endowed fund and restrict the purposes for which the fund's income will be used in perpetuity. Restrictions can include limiting grants to specific organizations in the geographic area. Unrestricted funds provide income for grants made at the discretion of the foundation's board and staff.

Unlike endowed gifts to charitable organizations, however, a donor can influence how the income is spent *after* making the gift by establishing what is termed a *donor-advised fund*. Such funds allow the donor to continually advise the foundation as to the organizations and activities to be considered for grants, which can be changed from year to year. In other words, an individual donor can deduct a cash gift up to 50% of his or her AGI and still control its future use, whereas gifts to charitable organizations qualify for tax deduction only if the donor forfeits control beyond the original conditions of the gift. Individual donors who make gifts to independent foundations also influence future use of their gifts, but they can only deduct up to 30% of their AGI.

Community foundations offer individual donors an attractive alternative to establishing family foundations. In addition to greater tax deductibility for gifts, they provide valuable services to donors, such as tax and estate planning assistance, accounting, tax reporting, grant advising, program tracking and evaluation, and investment responsibility (Gagen-McCarthy, 1993). Pooled resources, including staff expertise, are underwritten by fees charged to administer endowed funds. As Gagen-McCarthy explained, donor services and grantmaking are intertwined: "Without appropriate services, the foundation will have difficulty raising the money necessary to make grants" (p. 26).

The fact that their grants are limited almost exclusively to a specific locale is not as much of a deterrent as might be assumed. The overwhelming majority of all types of foundations limit their giving to their local community or state (Renz et al., 1995). Even among foundations with assets of $1 million or more, only 20% give on a national or an international basis and those are usually the largest independent foundations or corporate foundations whose sponsoring companies operate nationally or internationally. Furthermore, most gifts from all three sources—individuals, corporations, and foundations—are made locally. Based on its four decades of estimating U.S. giving, the AAFRC Trust for Philanthropy (1995) stated, "Philanthropic dollars do not generally support international, national, or even regional programs; they are primarily focused on local issues and tend to stay within communities" (p. 66).

As touched on earlier, to qualify as a public charity and maintain that beneficial status, community foundations are required to raise at least one third of their annual gift income from multiple donors who give less than $5,000 a year, or representatives of the so-called general public. Failure to do so may result in reclassification as a private foundation under IRS regulations. Charitable organizations also can lose their status as public charities if they fail to prove they have received ongoing financial support from the general public (Renz & Lawrence, 1993). In other words, concentration on a few major donors is dangerous for many reasons, not the least of which is the possibility of being reclassified as a private foundation subject to more stringent regulation. Fund raisers protect their organization's public charity status by developing a broad and diverse donor base.

Foundation Relations

During the early 1990s, growth in foundation giving outpaced that of corporations and individuals (Renz et al., 1995). Increases were most pronounced from the largest independent foundations and from community foundations. As related to the missions of grant recipients, education traditionally receives the largest share of foundation dollars (24% in 1993), followed by health, human services, arts, culture and humanities, and public/society benefit. Religion receives only 2%. An important point for students to understand is that whereas religion traditionally receives almost half of all gift dollars, almost all those gifts come from individuals; foundations and corporations make few gifts to religious organizations. When religion is excluded from analysis, the combined proportion of U.S. giving provided by foundations and corporations nearly doubles, 20% versus the 12% reported when accounting for religion (AAFRC Trust for Philanthropy, 1996).

Because much of the scholarly work for all types of charitable organizations is carried out at colleges and universities (e.g., research on diseases), 40% of the grant dollars actually go to education and educational support agencies (Renz et al., 1995). The largest foundations allocate 41% of their dollars to educational institutions. Nielsen (1985) declared, "The emphasis on education is so heavy in many cases that big philanthropy can to a considerable extent be described as a financial adjunct to higher education, particularly the private portion of it" (p. 418). In 1993, 30 of the 50 organizations that received the most foundation money were colleges or universities (McLaughlin, 1995). Harvard, for example, was given $45 million through 311 grants. It received almost twice as much foundation support 2 years later, $89 million (Council for Aid to Education, 1996). Clearly, fund raisers who work in education have an advantage when it comes to attracting foundation support. So do those who work for mainstream organizations.

Foundations, as is true of all major donors, are basically conservative in their giving. Jenkins (1989) stated, "Foundation support goes overwhelmingly to established charities and nonprofit institutions" (p. 294). Social movements, or organizations dealing with societal problems that only recently have been recognized, receive a small fraction of grant dollars (e.g., quality of life for people of color). Contrary to conventional rhetoric, foundations are not at the vanguard of social issues; their aggregate giving supports the *status quo* from which their wealth was acquired. Most are adverse to taking risks or funding unknown organizations. As Jenkins pointed out, "Personal contacts and a past track record are often essential" for obtaining grants (p. 299).

Close to one third of both grants and dollars represent continuing support; that is, they are gifts renewed from the previous year or payments on a multiyear pledge (Renz et al., 1995). The proportion is greater when the time frame for gift renewal is expanded. Illustrating, the majority (54%) of grants made by the Kresge Foundation in 1995 went to organizations that the foundation had funded before (Marshall, 1996). As with corporations and individuals, repeat gifts from foundations demonstrate ongoing relationships with charitable organizations that are closely linked to the interests and needs of the foundations' donors, trustees, and staff. Stated another way, the best prospects for grants are foundations that are previous donors. In 1993, 88% of all grant dollars were made for restricted purposes; only 12% were for general support. The percentage of unrestricted foundation dollars has been decreasing in recent years.

The northeast section of the United States historically has held a disproportionate share of foundations and their resources (Renz et al., 1995). A geographic redistribution has been underway since 1975. New York, which is home to 6,000 foundations, is the top-ranked state by grantmaking; California is the second highest. Just eight states—New York, New Jersey, Pennsylvania, Illinois, Indiana, Michigan, Ohio, and Wisconsin—account for the majority of foundation assets and gift dollars, 54% and 53%, respectively. This is good news for fund raisers employed by organizations based in those states as—it is recalled—most foundation giving is local.

Interdependence and Autonomy.   Relationships with foundations, as with all donor publics, are best understood in the context of social exchange theory. Mixer (1993) explained, "Foundation grants are provided to nonprofit agencies in *exchange* for activities that satisfy the interests of founders, trustees, and managers" (p. 83; italics added). In other words, both parties in the relationship are dependent on each other, and fund raisers should never apologize for approaching well-researched prospects. Nor should practitioners be "ingratiating," which Boris (1989) claimed is how they often are perceived by foundation staff who exhibit "a curious mix of altruism and arrogance" (p. 207). Misconceptions about one-sided dependency and the power of wealth contribute to arrogance and loss of autonomy.

Foundations other than those classified as operating depend on all types of charitable organizations to carry out program services that will meet the foundations' goals and objectives. M. R. Hall (1993) simply stated, "They *seek* grant recipients who can help them achieve their goals" (p. 10; italics added). More generally, foundations are dependent on the charitable subsector because their very existence requires them to make gifts (Sheldon, 1991). If all organizations refused to accept their grants, foundations would cease to exist—an unlikely but insightful possibility. More specifically, universities, which receive the largest share of grant money, illustrate the interdependency between foundations and their recipients. Foundations recruit a majority of their officers and staff from universities; they depend on universities for projects and programs essential to meeting their objectives; they rely on universities for their research needs; and they use university faculty as program assessors (Whitaker, 1974).

Foundations differ little from corporate and individual donors in that mixed motives direct their giving to specific interests that may or may not coincide with those of an organization. As Mixer (1993) stated, "Foundations come into existence for the fundamental reason of enacting the donors' values and preferences, which include both idealistic influences and pragmatic concerns" (p. 81). Addressing the issue of autonomy, Levy (1994) pointed out that "the development office is charged with raising money to support the institution," whereas "the interest and responsibility of the grantmakers are to fund projects that advance *their* missions" (p. 42; italics added). She urged a symmetrical approach to resolving differences in the legitimate claims of self-interest on both sides: "We should also discuss with our funding sources the tension we feel between the availability of funding and our programming goals. Through dialogue, we might be able to raise awareness of the enormous influence funders wield over programs" (p. 43).

Foundations historically have received the greatest amount of criticism for their infringement on autonomy.[6] The criticism stems primarily from the characteristics that the vast majority of grant dollars are restricted and that foundations, particularly

---

[6]A historical analysis of autonomy and the three donor publics can be found in my earlier book (Kelly, 1991a; see particularly chap. 8).

the largest independent foundations, perceive their societal role as change agents. Mixer (1993) addressed the latter: "Foundations are notorious for their desire to be the first wave on the beach and to develop new practices and innovative programs, sometimes at the expense of the new projects, which may be left high and dry after the initial grants subside because the foundation has finite funds and other innovations are now the attraction" (p. 87). Many foundation grants are made for new projects with the expectation that other funding sources—the government, unidentified donors, or the organizational recipient through reallocation of resources—will maintain or expand the original projects. This does not happen often and likely will occur less in the future as federal and state governments implement funding cutbacks. To protect their organizations, fund raisers carefully analyze the ramifications of short-term funding for new initiatives.

The restricted nature of most grant dollars mandates that practitioners pay special attention to matching their organization's interests and needs with those of foundation prospects. The larger the foundation, the more likely it will have formal and rigid giving objectives. Identifying overlaps in objectives, therefore, is critical. Greenfield (1991) advised, "Only foundations and corporations that can participate in the organization's priorities of need should be solicited" (p. 123). Howe (1991) quoted a former foundation president's warning, "Look for a fit; don't try to create one where it doesn't exist" (p. 44). As with all gifts, the purpose of foundation grants is of greater importance than their dollar amount.

Process.   Foundations are the easiest of the three donor publics on which to begin prospect research because they are required by law to annually file IRS Form 990-PF (Form 990 for community foundations) and to make the forms available to the public. The forms provide information on trustees and managers, assets, grants made, names of recipients, and dollar amounts. Specific forms can be obtained from the public affairs office of regional IRS Centers, such state regulators as Attorney General offices where the forms also must be filed, and the foundations themselves.[7]

The Foundation Center offers a more convenient and productive course of discovery through its 5 libraries and 200 cooperating regional collections. Its two major libraries in New York City and Washington, DC house complete sets of the IRS forms on microfiche, whereas the libraries in Cleveland, San Francisco, and Atlanta contain records for foundations in their respective regions (Renz, 1991). Two thirds of the center's cooperating collections, from Alaska to Puerto Rico, have IRS forms for their area, and can be located by calling the center at (800) 424-9836.

That same toll-free number can be used to order catalogs of the center's publications, arguably the finest secondary sources of information on foundations. In addition to reference works listed earlier, the center publishes the *National Data Book of Foundations*, the *Foundation Grants Index*, and *The Foundation 1000*, which provides comprehensive profiles of the 1,000 largest foundations. The center also produces customized computer printouts of grants in 72 fields of interest, called COMSEARCH (Renz, 1991). It offers an Associates Program for an annual fee of about $500, which provides telephone reference, photocopying, database searching,

---

[7]Students will recall from chapter 7 that a new law went into effect in 1996 that requires all 501(c)(3) organizations, including foundations, to mail copies of their forms to people requesting them.

and other services for add-on fees. Valuable secondary sources also are available from regional associations of foundations and from such publishers as the Taft Group and Oryx Press.

Unfortunately, prospect research gets more difficult after the preliminary stage. The richest source of information on specific foundations is publications produced and disseminated by the foundations themselves, particularly their grantmaking guidelines and annual reports. Yet only about 25% of all foundations publish guidelines, and only 10% publish an annual or biennial report (Renz et al., 1995). Almost all come from large foundations; little information is known about those with assets of less than $1 million or annual grants totaling less than $100,000. Frankly, many foundations—large and small—treat their giving as a private matter, and some are quite secretive about their operations.

The Harry and Jeanette Weinberg Foundation in Baltimore, Maryland, for example, does not publish guidelines, an annual report, or its telephone number (E. Greene & Moore, 1992). One of the country's 30 wealthiest foundations with assets approaching $1 billion (Foundation Center, 1997), it strongly discourages *unsolicited* grant proposals. According to E. Greene and Moore (1992), "The trustees say they prefer to learn about non-profit projects through newspapers, the radio, and advice from trusted friends, rather than wade through proposals filled with volumes of 'charts and gobbledygook'" (p. 10), as one trustee put it. Other very wealthy foundations that do not publish annual reports are Robert W. Woodruff and Annenberg. The percentage of foundations publishing guidelines and annual reports actually has declined since 1981 when the number of private foundations greatly increased (Renz et al., 1995). Such behavior not only makes fund raising more difficult, but it demonstrates an absence of accountability and a disregard for the society that subsidized the tax benefits received by foundation donors.

In contrast, a number of leading foundations have made information about themselves more accessible through the Internet—and their number multiples each month. The Charles A. Dana Foundation and the Rockefeller Brothers Fund were among the first to establish World Wide Web sites ("Foundations," 1995). Dana's site, for example, provides a copy of its annual report, general guidelines about its grantmaking, and specific information on applying for grants in its interest areas of health and education. Rockefeller's site includes a list of recent grants organized by program area. Addresses for the two sites, respectively, are: *http://www.*, followed by *dana.org* and *rbf.org/rbf*.

The Council on Foundations, which is located in Washington, DC and has 1,400 foundation members, also has a Web site of value to fund raisers ("Foundations," 1995). The site offers highlights from its respected magazine *Foundation News & Commentary*, links to the home pages of more than 50 of its members (e.g., Robert Wood Johnson Foundation), and a list of regional associations of grantmakers. To get there, type *http://www.picnet.com/cof*. Sarah Lutman (cited in J. Moore, 1995), a staff member of the Bush Foundation in St. Paul, Minnesota, commented on the new interactive technology during a recent council meeting: "One of the best things foundations can do is to be active in this environment as users and to listen to what people are saying and to speak back. I think that talking with applicants and listening is one of the most effective communications strategies foundations could adopt" (p. 14).

Members of the Council on Foundations adhere to standards for responsible and responsive practices as outlined in the council's Statement of Principles and Practices for Effective Grant Making, which was adopted in 1980 (Boris, 1989). James A. Joseph, author and renowned leader in philanthropy, served as president and CEO of the council from 1982 to 1995, when he was appointed U.S. ambassador to South Africa (Radelat, 1995). An African American native of Louisiana, Joseph is credited with much of the council's foresight and innovation, particularly its advances in diversification. The council's new president is Dorothy Ridings, a former journalist and newspaper publisher who, when named in 1996, declared that her top priority would be informing the public about what grantmakers do (S. Gray, 1996).

The research step in the fund-raising process largely determines how specific foundations should be approached. Grantmaking guidelines from the 25% that publish them should be requested and carefully followed. Stated restrictions on geographic areas and funding purposes are inviolable. If guidelines limit solicitations to a 2-page letter, then fund raisers follow those directions. This procedural requirement cannot be stressed enough. Philip Havens (cited in Walker, 1995), executive director of the Edward E. Ford Foundation in Providence, Rhode Island, voiced a common complaint:

> Proposals too often come in with a request for $125,000 when we limit grants to $50,000, single-spaced when we stipulate double-spacing, eight pages when we request six, with improper financial data, and so on. . . . Our annual report spell[s] out our requirements. But approximately 40 percent of the proposals we get need rewriting because fund raisers don't read carefully and don't follow instructions. (p. 39)

Generally, foundation solicitations involve interpersonal techniques implemented in four progressive activities: (a) letter of inquiry, (b) initial interview, (c) proposal, and (d) project interview, or on-site visit. After qualifying a prospect through thorough research, a 1- or 2-page letter of inquiry briefly describing the fund-raising opportunity is sent to the most appropriate person at the foundation (e.g., a staff member responsible for a particular area of interest, such as the arts). A follow-up telephone call determines the degree of shared interest. If the response is negative, a thank-you letter is sent to maintain relationships for future opportunities. A positive response prompts a letter requesting an initial interview, during which the fund raiser and other organizational representatives explore how their request for funds can most closely match the foundation's goals and objectives. The interview is most productive when it is based on collaborative negotiation. Agreed-on conditions are restated in a letter thanking the person for the interview and are then incorporated in a personalized proposal.

Harvard University's corporate and foundation relations director, Bayley Mason (cited in Walker, 1995), advised, "Adjust your proposal to their objectives without compromising your institution's integrity" (p. 39). He claimed that by the time the formal proposal is submitted, it should be 80% close to being funded. "If you've gone through the visits and your conversations are fruitful, they will point you toward what the final proposal should contain" (p. 39).

The proposal generally consists of 10 components in the following order:

1. Table of contents
2. Executive summary
3. Problem statement
4. Objectives
5. Project description
6. Evaluation
7. Organizational expertise
8. Future plans
9. Budget
10. Appendix

The executive summary of about three paragraphs succinctly presents the proposed project and states how it matches the foundation's interests. The amount of the request is included in the first sentence or paragraph. In his essay on characteristics of effective grant proposals, Koperek (1993) instructed, "Good proposals are simple and direct" (p. 49).

The problem statement outlines the substantiated needs the project will address and who will benefit. Koperek (1993) elaborated, "A winning proposal clearly defines the problem to be solved and the urgency of its solution" (p. 49). Specific, realistic, and measurable objectives are given, which provide the means by which the project will be evaluated. The project description tells what methods or procedures will be used to accomplish the objectives and includes a time table. The proposed solution must match the identified problem.

Increasingly, foundations require—or at least desire—evaluation of funded projects to determine the degree to which stated objectives were met. Whereas fewer than 100 foundations seriously evaluated their own programs or grantee projects before 1990, evaluation is now one of the most prominent trends in grantmaking (Doermann, 1993). Fund-raising managers who set objectives for and evaluate their own programming through the ROPES process will have little difficulty offering evaluation to all donor publics. Accountability, demonstrated during the stewardship step, is of growing importance in effective relationship management.

The proposal's section on organizational expertise explains the organization's unique ability to carry out the project. Whereas the problem statement deals with why a particular problem should be addressed, this section answers the question, "Why at this organization?" Relevant aspects of the mission, established program services, qualified line managers and staff, and available technology are discussed. Koperek (1993) emphasized, "Credibility is the single most important factor in reviewing grant applications" (p. 49). Future plans focus on what happens to the project after the grant ends. Given the unlikelihood of continued funding by government or other donors, the plans must be well thought out and practical.

The budget, encompassing all direct and indirect expenses, also must be realistic and as precise as possible. Koperek (1993) warned, "Questionable numbers will sink a proposal faster than any other flaw" (p. 47). Internal allocations and funding from other sources are displayed. According to Koperek, "In general, foundations dislike being the sole source of project funding" (p. 47). They are attracted to projects that already have some financial backing. He explained, "Broad sponsorship spreads risk and greatly increases the chances of a successful project" (p. 49). Jenkins (1989) agreed that potential for success is important: "The clearer the likelihood of victory, the greater the probability of funding" (p. 302).

Finally, the appendix includes required or critical information in support of the proposal, such as a copy of the organization's IRS letter of tax exemption, its latest annual report, and personnel résumés. It is not a catch-all for indiscriminant documents that simply add to the proposal's bulk.

The proposal usually is mailed to the foundation with a cover letter from the CEO, who attests to the project's importance in relation to the organization's goals and strategies. He or she also emphasizes its match with the foundation's objectives. Overall, the proposal package is framed in terms of how outcomes from the grant will help the foundation fulfill its mission, rather than how the organization will be helped. Koperek (1993) concluded, "There is no magic to writing winning grant proposals" (p. 49).

Approximately 2 weeks after the proposal is sent, the fund raiser requests—usually by letter—a project interview, preferably at the organization's facilities. This meeting allows such foundation representatives as trustees, managers, and staff to investigate the organization in light of the specific proposal. Individuals representing the organization must be prepared to describe the proposed project accurately and concisely. Mary Bringegar (cited in H. Hall, 1993c), with the Dallas Opera, administers what she calls the "elevator test" (p. 60) in preparation for such meetings. Organizational representatives pretend they have stepped onto an elevator with a foundation officer, who demands that they explain immediately why the opera should get the grant. They must answer in the time it takes to travel two or three floors. A thank-you letter is sent following the meeting, after which the organization waits for the foundation's decision, which—depending on its grantmaking cycle—may take up to 9 months. Cultivation activities in the form of informational mailings or special events continue.

The two interview activities are not always possible; some foundations' guidelines prohibit or limit meetings with prospective recipients. Demonstrating the opposite viewpoint held by many foundations, John Marshall, III (1996), president of the Kresge Foundation, reported that in 1995, "Anyone who requested an office appointment or conference call was given one, as did 539 organizations that year" (p. 48). Practitioners agree that such forms of communication are vital. The head of the Oregon-based environmental group Pacific Rivers Council declared, "We rarely get a grant without a personal meeting first" (H. Hall, 1993c, p. 59). However, the director of foundation relations at the University of Miami claimed, "It's more and more difficult to get an appointment with top foundation program people" (Walker, 1995, p. 37).

In the second situation, cultivation activities—largely bypassed in this discussion—become even more important to the fund-raising process. Steele and Elder (1992) advised, "It is essential to understand that gifts from foundations and corporations rarely come about as the result of an impersonal application process. In fact, they come from individuals in those organizations, and these individuals should be identified and cultivated just as you would any other individual major-gift prospect" (p. 6). Siegfried Herrmann (cited in Walker, 1995), director of institutional advancement at Miami-Dade Community College, confirmed this course of action: "Our success in raising foundation funds comes from our unceasing attempts to develop new friends" (p. 39).

Furthermore, communication does not always begin with the organization. A second prominent trend in grantmaking is that foundations increasingly are directing more money to projects developed by trustees or staff members, instead of simply responding to submitted proposals (Millar & Moore, 1994). Requests for proposals (RFPs) that outline a foundation's own ideas for projects are sent to selected organizations, thereby starting the fund-raising process. In other words, requests for funding are *solicited* by prospective donors. As Mixer (1993) explained, the largest foundations, such as Ford, Kellogg, and Lilly, "not only react to proposals from nonprofit organizations but also frequently stimulate requests from nonprofit agencies that function in the areas of the foundations' interests" (p. 85). Of all grants made by the John S. and James L. Knight Foundation in 1993, which totaled $42 million, almost one half went to projects that started as board or staff ideas rather than as proposals from charitable organizations (Millar & Moore, 1994). Fund raisers practicing the two-way symmetrical model are alert to situations in which foundations begin communications; however, they are cautious about pursuing grants that may contribute little to organizational goals or even end up costing money.

Whether the grant request is funded or not, a timely thank-you letter is sent to the foundation. When the request is denied, fund raisers follow up by asking how they can improve future solicitations. When it is approved, they seek clarification of the foundation's requirements on stewardship. Unpleasant surprises can be avoided before accepting the grant. For example, the Harry and Jeanette Weinberg Foundation *requires* that any building constructed with more than $250,000 from the foundation must bear the names Harry and Jeanette Weinberg (E. Greene & Moore, 1992).

New fund raisers, according to Jon Pratt (cited in H. Hall, 1993c), think of foundation relations as "the art of well-crafted sentences and a detailed budget, when most of it is timing, relationships, and credibility" (p. 59). I would add that research on the organization, opportunity, and publics is key to success.

Concluding this discussion, Jenkins (1989) reported that conservative critics view foundations as "financiers of revolution" (p. 293). Liberal critics challenge the motives and cooptative impact of foundations, which are tainted by wealth. Moderates criticize foundations for being too timid and avoiding risk. In contrast, fund-raising managers recognize foundations as somewhat complicated but essential partners in America's philanthropic tradition. They understand that the behavior of foundations differs little from the behavior of the other two donor publics.

CORPORATE DONORS

According to Galaskiewicz (1989), critics on the right argue that businesses have no business giving away profits rightfully belonging to their owners, whereas critics on the left argue that gifts from corporate donors are nothing more than strategies to coopt those opposed to the ways of corporate America. A middle stance, adopted by most observers, is that corporate giving—more so than giving by foundations or individuals—is motivated by self-interest. H. W. Smith (1993) declared, "The very term *corporate philanthropy* is not only inappropriate, it is an oxymoron" (p. 216; italics in original). To emphasize this supposedly unique characteristic, gifts from corporate donors commonly are referred to as *contributions*. Shannon (1991), for example, alerted readers of his edited handbook: "Most of the authors (and this book's title) do not speak of corporate philanthropy but of corporate contributions. This usage on our part is deliberate" (p. 353).

The theory of donor relations presented in this text prescribes a different viewpoint: Corporations, in aggregate, hold a mixture of self-interest and altruism similar to that of foundations and individuals. Like their counterparts, they do not give just for the sake of giving. They are more likely to contribute if they are offered fund-raising opportunities that clearly are consistent with their own interests and have potential for successfully addressing societal problems they deem critical.

Continuum of Motivation

The Tax Reform Act of 1935, which held that corporate gifts were deductible only if they resulted in direct benefits, and the 1953 New Jersey Supreme Court Case (*A. P. Smith Mgf. Co. v. Barlow*), which ruled that all corporate giving was an act of good citizenship, form the opposite ends of a continuum of motivation. Prior to World War II, a widely shared philosophy was that it simply was not appropriate for businesses to get involved in social action, including charitable giving (H. W. Smith, 1993). Advancing public and common goods was the function of government, churches, and individuals—including business leaders. The mission of for-profit companies was to make money for their owners; therefore, the only rationale for charitable giving was to generate benefits that directly affected corporate profits.

The philosophy waned in the decades following World War II and was replaced in the 1970s by the concept of social responsibility (H. W. Smith, 1993). According to the newer view, corporations have obligations to society; good corporate citizenship requires a certain amount of responsible social action. Cutlip (1965/1990) quoted a significant passage from the New Jersey Supreme Court's decision: "Modern conditions require that corporations acknowledge and discharge social as well as private responsibilities as members of the communities within which they operate. . . . Indeed, the matter may be viewed strictly in terms of actual survival of the corporation in a free enterprise system" (p. 514).

At one end of the continuum, then, are direct benefits, which represent motives weighted toward self-interest, and at the other end is social responsibility, which represents motives weighted toward altruism—keeping in mind from earlier discussions that self-interest and altruism are not mutually exclusive. Points along the continuum are encompassed under the rubric of *enlightened self-interest*, although the term generally refers to a balanced, or center, position. J. A. Joseph (1991) explained that whereas unmitigated self-interest begins and ends with the corporate interest, enlightened self-interest "seeks a congruence between public and private interest" (p. 10). Lord (1983) quoted one CEO's rationale for a balanced approach, which is grounded in systems theory: "The underlying philosophy of corporate philanthropy is that it is good business to be an enlightened corporate citizen. It doesn't make sense to talk about successful corporations in a society whose schools, hospitals, churches, symphonies, or libraries are deteriorating or closing" (p. 114).

In other words, corporations—unlike foundations—do not exist to give money away to charitable organizations; their mission is to sell goods and services at a profit for their owners—stockholders in cases of publicly owned corporations. Yet, when their foundations' grants are included, they give an estimated $8.5 billion annually, accounting for almost 6% of all gift dollars (AAFRC Trust for Philanthropy, 1997b). As pointed out earlier, their proportional contribution is even greater when religion is removed from analyses. H. W. Smith (1993) described their motives as "the desire to be a good corporate citizen and *simultaneously* to enhance the corporate interest" (p. 220; italics added). Corporate donors' emphasis on the benefits they expect in exchange for their gifts shifts their position along the continuum, with apparent differences over time and among specific companies.

Benefits Categorized.   Through an extensive review of the literature, Galaskiewicz (1989) identified five ways corporations use contributions, which are presented here in slightly revised form as five categories of benefits: (a) marketing, (b) tax savings, (c) social currency, (d) public relations, and (e) social responsibility. Gifts are used, Galaskiewicz said, to meet marketing and tax objectives (economic strategies), as social currency (social strategy), and for purposes of public relations and social responsibility (political strategies). Companies seek benefits of all types to varying degrees.

Marketing is broken down into short- and long-term benefits. As broadly conceived, according to Galaskiewicz (1989), "Marketing strategists view contributions as a way to coopt or win the good will of prospective customers" (p. 247). A short-term emphasis results in immediate sales and is represented by joint ventures, such as cause-related marketing and corporate sponsorships. The long-term approach holds that all forms of socially responsible behavior help attract and retain customers. Galaskiewicz explained, "To the extent that firms are living up to the expectations of various social interest groups, they ensure their legitimacy that in turn should have some bottom-line payoff" (p. 247). Studies have shown that contributions are positively related to a company's dependence on individual, as opposed to organizational, consumers and to advertising expenditures. Relationships between increased sales and social responsibility have not been substantiated.

Corporations seek tax savings through their contributions and analyses of IRS data consistently show that tax rates have a positive relationship with corporate giving. As the rate goes up, contributions increase because the cost of giving declines. On the other hand, Galaskiewicz (1989) reported, "The ceiling on the amount of charitable contributions that firms can deduct from their taxable income has a very limited effect on company giving" (p. 251). Corporations, it is recalled, collectively give about 2% of their taxable income, although they are allowed to deduct 10% and to carry forward excess contributions up to 5 years (Hodgkinson et al., 1992). A few—primarily smaller companies with average total giving of less than $10,000 per year—give 5% or more. Scholars have noted little variation in the past 50 years even though the ceiling was increased from 5% to 10% in 1981. The highest collective percentage ever recorded was 2.35% in 1986 (Bailey, 1994), when managers knew the cost of giving would significantly increase starting in 1987 due to new laws cutting the corporate income tax rate from 46% to 34%.

Galaskiewicz's (1989) theory of contributions as social currency was described in chapter 2. Basically, a norm of giving exists in business subcultures, and executives make corporate gifts to adhere to the norm. Galaskiewicz elaborated, "Through the institution of peer pressure, executives learn the expectations of their peers, are solicited, and are awarded certain *status benefits*" (p. 252; italics added). He found from his studies conducted in the Twin Cities of Minneapolis and St. Paul, Minnesota that companies give more money if their managers and directors are in the networks of locally prominent business persons active in philanthropy. The effect, he found, is independent of pretax income, percentage of sales to individual consumers, and variables related to the other categories of benefits. Galaskiewicz concluded, "Executives' social positions influenced the specific allocations that their companies made, as well as the overall amount" (p. 253).

Public relations benefits are closely associated with social responsibility (i.e., recognition of the company as a good corporate citizen). Contributions are not aimed at increasing sales, and benefits are related to publics other than consumers, such as community residents and government officials. The ultimate benefit is autonomy of the company from external formal controls. Galaskiewicz (1989) explained, "It is a political strategy to win the good will of local influentials, who sooner or later will deliberate over zoning ordinances, property taxes, environmental regulations, disclosure, affirmative action, and other matters affecting business in the community" (p. 248). In this light, then, public relations benefits also can be viewed as economic in that they *save* the corporation money by avoiding laws and regulations that impose higher costs. The importance of the category is supported by consistent evidence that "companies donate a large proportion of their contributions budget in the communities where their headquarters are located" (A. White & Bartolomeo, 1982, p. 41). As Galaskiewicz (1989) pointed out, however, research on corporate giving and public relations benefits is "scanty and inconclusive" (p. 248).

Dwight Burlingame (1994), professor of philanthropic studies and director of academic programs and research at Indiana University's Center on Philanthropy, also identified public relations as a category of benefits through his review of the literature. Recent studies, he said, have focused on how Japanese companies operating in the United States have used philanthropy for public relations purposes. For example, one study found that contributions helped Toyota, Nissan, and Hitachi gain trust and support from government and community leaders in locations where they operate.

Social responsibility, which Galaskiewicz (1989) and others equate with the encompassing concept of enlightened self-interest, provides long-term benefits to corporations. This category is based on the premise that a better society produces a better environment for business, and that companies build supportive communities in which to operate by responding to the needs of their communities through contributions. Chief among the benefits is legitimation of our capitalistic economy—common to all types of major donors. Many of the people controlling corporations believe that capitalism, or the free enterprise system, is protected by returning to society some of the monetary gains derived from the system. "Such returns," Mixer (1993) said, "are felt to offset complaints about exploitation, and at the same time make society more humane" (p. 83).

Social responsibility explicitly recognizes the corporation's dependency on other organizations and groups for its success and survival. Robert Haas (cited in J. A. Joseph, 1991), CEO of Levi Strauss & Company, explained:

> However small or large our enterprise, we cannot isolate our business from the society around us. Nor can we function without its goodwill. We may need the goodwill of a neighborhood to enlarge a corner store. We may need well-funded institutions of higher learning to turn out the skilled technical employees we require. We may need adequate community health care to curb absenteeism in our plants. Or we may need fair tax treatment for an industry to be able to compete in the world economy. (pp. 4–5)

"Haas," Joseph reported, "is convinced that if a corporation ignores the needs of its communities, it may actually be ignoring its own needs in the long run" (p. 5). Stated another way, the long-term welfare of corporations requires them to sacrifice some of their short-term profits in the form of contributions. H. W. Smith (1993) simply said corporate giving is a cost of doing business. The subject of interdependency is returned to later in this section.

Few studies have examined the relationship between social responsibility and the attainment of political goals, and scholars have had difficulty measuring the concept's impact on financial performance (Galaskiewicz, 1991). Aupperle, Carroll, and Hatfield (1985), for example, found neither a positive nor a negative relationship between corporate social responsibility and profitability. Regardless, studies have shown that managers' *belief in* social responsibility has a significant effect on a company's level of giving. Galaskiewicz (1989) reported, "Rationalizing contributions on the grounds that they help to protect the long-term interests of the company or the free enterprise system appears to have led some companies to give more money to charities" (p. 254). He identified two problems inherent in long-term benefits: Managers, directors, and owners will not be around to see or get credit for them, and the *free rider principle* explains that—as with all donor publics—some corporations will leave the cost of giving to others while gaining much of the contributions' benefits.

Finally, Burlingame (1994) identified employee issues, such as morale, loyalty, and workforce productivity, in a separate category of benefits. Two studies sponsored by IBM in 1989 and 1992, he reported, found that employee morale was higher in companies that were actively involved in the community, and higher community involvement translated into better financial performance. He concluded: "Corporate image appears to be as important internally as it is externally" (p. 477). This book holds that benefits associated with employee publics are more appropriately incorporated in the category of public relations.

Empirical research on the benefits obtained from contributions, as Burlingame asserted, has been handicapped by an absence of comparable data among different types of companies. The problem is twofold: Much of the research consists of proprietary studies with restricted access to their findings, and studies have suffered from inconsistent measurement of key variables. The concept of philanthropy, for example, is operationalized as dollar amounts in some studies and as percentage of pretax income in others. Corporate social responsibility is measured by multiple variables that sometimes do not even include contributions. Dependent variables measuring the bottom-line impact of gifts range from increased sales to changes in stock prices. Agreement on common measures and greater dissemination of findings are needed in future studies. Research advancement is imperative in light of the recent emphasis on short-term marketing benefits.

Continuum Shift.   According to Stendardi (1992), enlightened self-interest has been redefined for the 1990s. As originally conceptualized, benefits included the corporation being perceived as a good citizen, employees becoming more motivated to work for the firm, customers becoming more inclined to buy the firm's products and services, communities being more hospitable to the firm, and government at all levels being less inclined to regulate the firm. The common theme, Stendardi said, was that the corporation would receive a benefit, but the benefit was not immediate, certain, or measurable. Corporate America, he argued, is no longer content to justify its giving on such a basis. Companies now view their contributions as *social investments* and require returns that affect the current bottom line—most often by increasing sales.

The redefinition, which Stenardi and others erroneously generalize to all corporate donors, is driven by major changes in the U.S. economy. Companies face multiple problems in today's competitive global environment—an environment characterized by decreased profit margins and market share. Rising production costs, coupled with barriers to raising prices, make it difficult to increase or even maintain levels of giving. Managers are forced to explain why they give away money while laying off hundreds or thousands of employees. "Downsizing," proclaimed Craig Smith (1994), founding editor and publisher of the newsletter *Corporate Philanthropy Report*, "has transformed the management of corporate philanthropy in the United States" (p. 105).

Although corporate profits jumped by 18% in 1992 and 14% in 1993, corporate giving in 1993 failed to keep pace with inflation for the sixth consecutive year (Bailey, 1994). Philanthropy did not follow profits, experts explained, because companies achieved their higher net income by cutting expenses more than by increasing revenues. In inflation-adjusted dollars, corporate contributions totaled the same amount in 1993 as they did a decade earlier—$6.8 billion in 1984 and 1993 (AAFRC Trust for Philanthropy, 1997b).[8]

Blaming their array of problems, many—but not all—corporations shifted on the continuum of motivation toward marketing benefits that are short-term and direct. They have to some extent reverted back to the pre-1950 philosophy that the business of business is business, and all effort, including charitable giving, should be concentrated on profit maximization. Indeed, Stendardi (1992) described the redefinition of enlightened self-interest in terms reflective of the earlier position:

> Contemporary CEOs are compelled to use all of the firm's assets at their command to maximize their firm's earnings, and boards of directors are demanding a more market-driven, bottom-line approach to philanthropy. Philanthropy is viewed as another method

---

[8]As previously noted, the AAFRC Trust for Philanthropy (1996) estimated from an expanded donor sample that corporate giving, adjusted for inflation, increased a total of 11.5% during the 2 years following 1993; however, contributions from the largest corporations—which, as discussed shortly, account for most corporate giving—did not increase. Yet large U.S. corporations have enjoyed strong profit gains since 1992. In 1996, profits for Fortune 500 companies surged 23.3%, far greater than other measures of economic health ("Profits up," 1997). As in the past, however, increased sales were not responsible for the growth: The companies "restructured, reengineered, refinanced, downsized, laid off, split up, and merged their way to prosperity" (p. 1-D).

to achieve business objectives, and these social investments must have a discernible payback for the firm. (p. 25)

Cause-related marketing, Stenardi said, exemplifies social investments.

C. Smith (1994), in an article for the *Harvard Business Review*, argued that more than a redefinition occurred at the beginning of the 1990s, a new paradigm of corporate philanthropy emerged—one that mixes traditional contributions with *quid pro quo* arrangements. The fastest growing ties between charitable organizations and companies, he reported, are "business-to-business" relationships. Counter to no-growth statistics, Smith asserted that when all the budgets indirectly supporting charitable organizations, such as marketing, are added up, the total level of corporate funding is rising steadily. He concluded, "The strategic use of philanthropy has begun to give companies a powerful competitive edge" (p. 105).

Before discussing the continuum shift further, it is important for students to remember that laws governing gifts do not preclude returning benefits, including economic ones, to donors, but the benefits cannot be fully captured as they are in a marketing exchange. The degree of *quid pro quo* a company expects determines whether the money transferred qualifies as a gift or as a business expense.

Contrary to popular belief, companies are not free to choose how their contributions are deducted from taxable income. If the payment is a charitable gift, it cannot be deducted as a business expense (Arthur Andersen & Company, 1992). Payment can be deducted as an expense only when it bears a direct relationship to the business and is made with a reasonable expectation of financial return *commensurate* with the amount of the payment. In other words, when companies define their contributions to charitable organizations as business expenses, they view the exchange as commercial, not philanthropic. Technically then, such payments represent nongift income.

This is a contorted and controversial area of our tax laws, with rulings applied almost on a case-by-case basis. It has created confusion for both businesses and those who study philanthropy. White and Bartolomeo (1982), for example, found that 38% of the companies they studied chose to declare some of their contributions as business expenses. Hodgkinson et al. (1992) maintained that corporate giving is understated because many companies deduct contributions as business expenses, rather than report them as charitable contributions. Without acknowledging the issue of commensurate financial return, the IS researchers urged scholars to go beyond contributions reported on tax returns to better estimate the scope of corporate philanthropy. This area warrants scholarly attention; legal and definitional clarification is badly needed.

Relating to the paradigm presented by C. Smith (1994), Eisenberg (1995) rightfully argued that corporations have always used philanthropy to affect their bottom-line goals, but the emphasis on short-term benefits is new. "Not that long ago, many companies viewed their charitable contributions as a means of stabilizing and strengthening the communities in which they would operate for many years to come. It was a long-term approach, motivated by enlightened self-interest" (p. 38). The new paradigm, he declared, "is often not compatible with good citizenship" (p. 38).

Symmetry between private and public needs has given way in some corporations to greater weight on self-interest. The result has been increased reliance on joint ventures, which many—including myself—consider *pseudo philanthropy*. In defense of this assessment, funding for such joint ventures as cause-related marketing cannot come from corporate foundations because of IRS rules on self-dealing (Shannon, 1991). Instead, funds come directly from advertising or marketing budgets. The AAFRC Trust for Philanthropy (1995) described the increase in nontraditional forms of support as positive, yet, at the end of its discussion proclaimed, "Corporate social investment, as the practice has been called, is not, strictly speaking, 'philanthropy' and is not included in *Giving USA*'s estimate of corporation contributions" (p. 77).

As argued in chapter 8, joint ventures may be profitable for companies, but their use represents a dangerous trend for fund raising. The more charitable organizations act like businesses, the more likely Congress will decide to treat them like businesses—eroding or eliminating the privileged status they now enjoy. The proper balance between self-interest and social responsibility must be maintained if the subsector is to be preserved. Similarly, the shift to short-term marketing benefits is detrimental to corporate donors, who are dependent on multiple stakeholders for their success and survival (Kelly, 1991a; see chap. 12). Based on systems theory, a corporation puts itself at risk when it contributions program ignores the expectations and interests of important constituencies, such as government officials. A balanced approach to philanthropy is necessary to satisfy all who have a stake in the company. I agree with Eisenberg (1995), who warned, "Both corporations and non-profit groups must be vigilant in protecting the equilibrium between community and corporate interests" (p. 38).

Autonomy and Interdependence. In 1994, two federal agencies investigated allegations that Genentech, a leading pharmaceutical company, was improperly using a northern Virginia charitable organization as a marketing arm to recruit customers for one of its prescription drugs (Millar, 1994a). The organization, Human Growth Foundation (HGF), screened schoolchildren for growth abnormalities using equipment provided by Genentech. When children unusually short for their age were discovered, school officials sent letters on HGF's letterhead to the children's parents suggesting they seek help. Parents who then called HGF for information were routinely provided with the telephone number for Genentech, which manufactures a growth hormone for children that costs $20,000 to $30,000 for a yearly dosage. A number also was given for the other manufacturer of the hormone, Eli Lilly, but that company was not accused of acting improperly.

Of central concern was the fact that Genentech's contributions to HGF accounted for more than 50% of the organization's annual income; furthermore, HGF managers were defensive about releasing gift information (Millar, 1994a). Although alliances built on mutual interests are common (and symmetrically desirable), nonprofit leaders said they were surprised to hear of an organization getting such a large percentage of its budget from a single company. An official at the Center for the Study of Commercialism commented, "From Genentech's point of view, it may be done in all innocence, but it certainly looks sleazy and looks like they are trying to co-opt a non-profit and use it as a marketing arm" (Millar, 1994a, p. 18). Both the company and HGF denied any wrongdoing.

Lombardo (1991) addressed such situations in her essay on conflicts of interest with corporate donors. Risks, she said, can be mitigated by taking two measures, which were endorsed earlier in this book:

First, to the greatest extent possible a nonprofit should seek a wide range of funding sources. This protects it from being excessively dependent on or controlled by any one funding source, and it further protects against the perception of such dependence or control, which can be damaging in itself. Second, open disclosure of funding sources is a proactive way of avoiding the adverse publicity that can result when the media or another watchdog group discovers what can be perceived as excessive control or conflictive relations. (pp. 97–98)

Summarizing the issue of autonomy, Lombardo stated, "Conflicts can arise due to the degree of control that the corporation requests as a stipulation of the grant (p. 93). Pratt (1991) advised, "Grantseekers need to assert, and corporate supporters to respect, nonprofit autonomy as an essential ingredient of the nonprofit sector" (p. 225).

Corporations, like foundations, are dependent on America's charitable organizations. Dayton Hudson, the Minneapolis-based conglomerate that owns more than 1,000 department and discount stores, including Marshall Field's and Target, provides a dramatic illustration of businesses' dependence and the benefits they derive from philanthropy. An acknowledged leader in social responsibility, Dayton Hudson is one of the few very large corporations that annually contributes 5% of its pretax income—a policy it adopted in 1946 (S. Gray & Moore, 1996). During the last 50 years, it has given more than $350 million, or roughly $19,000 a day, to charitable organizations in the various communities in which it operates. The investment paid off royally in 1987 when community organizations rallied to the corporation's aid and helped it survive a hostile takeover attempt by the Dart Group of Landover, Maryland.

According to Ann Barkelew (1993), then Dayton Hudson's vice president of corporate public relations, in June 1987, the corporation confronted "the very real possibility of being taken over by people we knew would 'bust up' the corporation and sell off its assets to finance the takeover" (p. 8). The CEO asked Minnesota's governor to call a special session of the legislature to tighten the state's antitakeover laws, thereby providing greater protection for the company. Legislators took action just 7 days later, largely because of a groundswell of support from the media, other businesses, government officials, and, as stated in the *Minneapolis-St. Paul Star Tribune*, "'groups that have received millions of dollars of contributions'" (Barkelew, 1993, p. 8). Barkelew presented Dayton Hudson's philosophy: "We know that the health of a community directly affects the health of our business. Conversely, healthy businesses make for a strong and vibrant community. . . . So, strengthening communities has been and is a part of our business strategy—as much a part as operations, distribution or human resources" (pp. 11–12).

Interdependence can be further addressed on three levels: society, community, and organizational type. H. W. Smith (1993) stated, "The fact that [corporations] make charitable gifts is… a reflection of their realization that they are integral parts of society and that their long-run prosperity as business enterprises is very much *dependent* on the health of that society" (p. 225; italics added). As already touched on, capitalism is fundamental to corporate America. Foresighted managers, directors, and owners recognize and have an interest in "the long-term social investment necessary to perpetuate the legitimacy of the free enterprise system" (Galaskiewicz, 1989, p.

256). A healthy nonprofit sector protects the business sector from big government, of which it traditionally has been wary (Lombardo, 1995). Without the services provided by charitable organizations, government would be forced to add programs—to increase in size and power. Through gifts, Lombardo said, business expresses "its preference for this alternative to big government" (p. 299).

On the community level, nonprofits, including charitable organizations, are critical partners in building local economies on which businesses are dependent. Charles Heying, a faculty member in the Department of Urban Studies and Planning at Portland State University, stressed this point in a message on Internet's ARNOVA forum (December 21, 1994). Nonprofits, he said, are important in terms of employment, services, and quality of life. Companies with "land-based interests and regional market dependencies" look to their nonprofit partners to protect and enhance profits. Illustrating, banks are heavily invested in local real estate, and regional utilities are dependent on a local customer base. The relationship, Heying argued, is symbiotic, not parasitic (i.e., it is based on interdependence, not one-way dependence of recipients on donors). Although often overlooked, charitable organizations also are important consumers for businesses. They collectively spend $458 billion annually in operating expenses and have assets worth $686 billion (Hodgkinson et al., 1996).

Corporate donors are dependent on different types of organizations to carry out their philanthropic objectives. Their interests and needs vary, although—as with foundations—education is the leading recipient of corporate dollars, 42%, or $2.5 billion, in 1993 (Bailey, 1994). And higher education gets the majority of those funds. Not surprisingly, then, corporations' dependency is exemplified by their relationships with universities, which provide them with future employees, research, technology, consultants, and sales. Milton Eisenhower (cited in Meuth, 1991), the late president of Johns Hopkins University, stated: "Higher education and business are basically interdependent. One needs money to produce educated people, and the other needs educated people to produce money" (p. 27).

In short, corporations make contributions not because fund raisers persuade them to become donors, but because interdependence prescribes a giving behavior. Or as Karl (1991) simply stated, "Corporations give because they believe that it is in their interest to do so" (p. 24). As with foundations, fund raisers have no need to apologize when approaching well-researched corporate prospects. They must understand, however, that recent changes in the economy and the resulting problems faced by businesses demand greater accountability in corporate relations.

Corporate Relations

Of the 6 million U.S. companies, only about 700,000 report charitable contributions on their tax returns (H. W. Smith, 1993). Following patterns comparable to foundations, less than 1% of the donors, or 5,600 corporations with assets of $250 million or more, contribute most of the dollars (Doty, 1994). Just 325 corporations accounted for one third of the total in 1993 (Bailey, 1994), and 100 of the largest companies gave one of every five dollars in 1995 (S. Gray & Moore, 1996). As Useem (1987) stated, "Virtually all corporate giving is by the nation's major firms" (p. 340).

The names of leading donors reads like a Who's Who of corporate America. Listing just a few with only their cash contributions, in 1993, Exxon gave $54 million, du Pont gave $28 million, J. C. Penny gave $23 million, Coca-Cola gave $20 million, Sara Lee gave $14 million, and Intel gave $11 million (Dundjerski & Moore, 1994). The largest corporate donor in 1993 was IBM, which gave $60 million—even though it lost $8 billion that year (Stehle, 1994a)!

Although the dollar amounts are impressive, a comparison with cash contributions from the same leading donors in subsequent years demonstrates that giving by the largest corporations, in aggregate, is stagnant. Using current dollars for the comparison and excluding IBM for the moment, three of the six Fortune 500 corporations increased their contributions by a total of $6 million in 1994, whereas two decreased theirs by $6 million and one gave the same amount as it gave in 1993 (S. Gray & Moore, 1996). The pattern was repeated in 1995: Three of the corporations gave a total of $5 million less, two gave $4 million more, and one stayed the same—resulting in a net loss of $1 million. These figures do not take into account the impact of inflation, which increased about 4.5% during the 2-year period.

IBM's giving record dramatically affects the pattern. The computer giant held the top position in corporate philanthropy for more than a decade, from the early 1980s to the mid-1990s. The record high for the company—and probably all corporate donors to date—was in 1985 when it ranked first among the Fortune 500 and its cash contributions alone totaled more than $188 million (S. Gray & Moore, 1996). IBM's giving in current dollars has been decreasing ever since. In 1990, it gave $102 million in cash and another $46 million in noncash (Stehle, 1994a). By 1993, when the corporation had dropped from first to fourth place in the Fortune 500, it gave just $60 million in cash and a total of $92 million. Financial losses and the company's declining share of the computer market were the reasons offered by IBM managers for continued decreases. In 1994, the company gave $52 million in cash, which was reduced to only $41 million in 1995, although the amount totaled $66 million when noncash contributions were included (S. Gray & Moore, 1996).

IBM no longer is the top corporate donor. Comparing its record high with the most current figures available, the company's annual cash giving has decreased $147 million in 10 years, and the former leader now gives 22 cents for every dollar it gave in 1985! Its entire giving, including donations of products and other noncash contributions, has fallen $123 million, or 65%. During the same period, IBM dropped just five positions in the Fortune 500 rankings, from being the first to the sixth largest U.S. corporation by income. In other words, reductions in the company's well-being were not comparable to reductions in its giving (i.e., lower contributions could not be fully explained by financial reverses).[9]

Managers recently provided a different reason for the decline in gifts: IBM's strategy is to reduce its contributions budget to more closely match those of its corporate peers. Paula Baker (cited in S. Gray & Moore, 1996), director of IBM's corporate-support programs, said that in rough economic times "you look at what's appropriate; you examine where you are in the ranking" (p. 16). She continued, "When we saw we were so far ahead of everybody else, we realized we didn't have to be" (p. 16). Adoption of this strategy by one of philanthropy's major actors represents a grave concession to the

---

[9]In 1996, IBM had the fifth highest profit of all U.S. corporations, $5.4 billion ("Profits up," 1997).

free rider principle and a loss of critical leadership. If conformity with peers becomes the overriding factor in gift decisions (i.e., keep up, but do not give more), corporate donors will seek the lowest common denominator and giving by the largest corporations will remain stagnant or even lose ground.

The more immediate impact of IBM's intentional reductions is apparent in a review of the giving levels of its peers. The five corporations ranked above IBM in the Fortune 500 for 1995 are unlikely to replace lost dollars. Four of the five—Ford (2), Exxon (3), Wal-Mart (4), and AT&T (5)—gave less than IBM in total contributions in 1995, and the first-place holder, General Motors, gave about 40% less in both cash and total contributions in 1995 than IBM gave in 1990 (S. Gray & Moore, 1996). Whereas the five largest corporations, together, increased their cash contributions by $7.5 million from 1994 to 1995, IBM's decrease was $11 million, representing a net loss of $3.5 million for charitable organizations! IBM is used as a touchstone in later discussions on trends in corporate relations.

Studies have documented variation in giving among different industries. Doty (1994), for example, analyzed corporate tax returns from 1980 to 1991 to identify those industries that deduct the largest dollar amounts as charitable contributions. Of 14 groups with deductions of $100 million or more, manufacturers of chemicals, drugs, and allied products give the most, $500 million in 1991. Banks are second, and manufacturers of foods and beverages are third. Other high-ranked industries are computer manufacturers, utilities, petroleum refiners, and publishers and printers. By percentage of pretax income, which often is used as a measure of generosity, the securities industry is first, giving away seven times the percentage of petroleum refiners, for example.

The recipients of corporate dollars after education are—in descending order—health and human services, culture and art, and civic and community organizations (AAFRC Trust for Philanthropy, 1997b). Like all major donors, corporations are basically conservative in their giving, preferring well-known organizations with whom they have long-standing ties. For example, only about 40 elite research universities out of the more than 3,000 U.S. colleges and universities receive one half of all corporate dollars given to higher education (Council for Aid to Education, 1996). As Useem (1987) stated, "Companies prefer recipients that are prestigious, large, and located near headquarters or plants with large staffs" (p. 342). Innovation and risk taking are rarely found in corporate giving; instead, "preservation of the basic social-political status quo" is the underlying purpose (Preston, 1981, p. 10).

Although conservative in their selection, corporations—like foundations—view their contributions as catalysts for change. Their support of primary and secondary public schools illustrates this characteristic. Known as school reform, most of the philanthropy assumes radical restructuring and even dismantling the current system (Jehl & Payzant, 1992). School reform is returned to later in this section.

Because they dominate gifts from businesses, when we talk about corporate philanthropy we usually are talking about large corporations, primarily those that are publicly owned. Referring to this public as corporate donors is not a misnomer. Similar to foundations, large corporations account for most of the staff, called *contributions officers*. Small companies, particularly proprietorships, handle their gifts as an extension of their owner's philanthropy. Fund raisers approach them as individuals, as they do family foundations. Midsize firms and closely held corporations generally are also less structured in their giving. The discussion that follows, then, concentrates on large public corporations.

Strategic Philanthropy.   Until the 1970s, giving was an informal, almost casual activity for businesses, on the outer margin of corporate concerns (H. W. Smith, 1993). Contributions were made without any plan, with minimal review, and with little expectation of measured or even reported results. Smith explained, "Contributions were often no more than the pet projects of senior management" (p. 222). Duties for distributing funds were assigned arbitrarily, usually to elderly employees as a final position before retirement. Smith described the haphazard nature of earlier efforts:

> It was not uncommon for companies to make contributions without any clear under-
> standing of why they did so, without any clear vision of what they were trying to
> accomplish, without any clear notion of what difference their contributions made in the
> scheme of things, and without any clear understanding of how the corporate interests
> would be served. (p. 221)

The surge in activism during the 1970s spurred the development of corporate philanthropy (Useem, 1987). Demonstrations, boycotts, and riots made businesses more aware of the need to improve the climate in which they operated (i.e., to enhance a sociopolitical environment supportive of the capitalistic system). Social responsibility grew in favor, and corporate contributions more than doubled during the latter part of the 1970s.

According to Shannon (1991), a study sponsored by the Council on Foundations in 1982 found that CEOs believed corporate contributions programs still were not as well managed as the rest of their company's operations. When the study was repeated in 1988, CEOs reported that their programs had improved markedly, "were more effective in reaching desirable targets set by the company, and were comparable to other departments of the company in the quality of their management" (p. 344).

Today, most major corporations practice strategic philanthropy. The activity has matured into a formal, institutionalized, and somewhat professionalized function, well embedded in the corporate structure (H. W. Smith, 1993). Corporations determine what they hope to accomplish with their contributions and how those contributions should be distributed in order to attain the desired outcomes. Contributions officers prepare budgets with explicit objectives for each area of giving, based on articulated philosophies and policies. Corporate interests are spelled out, and connections are drawn between those interests and the budget. The process typically begins 6 months or more prior to the start of the company's fiscal year, and the budget is set at a total dollar figure appropriate to the firm's financial outlook.

Once set, the amount rarely is changed. Top management reviews and approves the budget, which then directs the contributions staff's implementation of the program. Printed guidelines are available to those seeking contributions, and requests are evaluated by how well they fit the self-determined plans. Progress toward objectives is periodically reviewed. Some corporations use cost–benefit analyses to measure the long-term returns of their philanthropy (Burlingame, 1994).

The maturity reached in corporate giving, H. W. Smith (1993) asserted, imposes rigorous requirements on charitable organizations hoping to establish relationships with corporations or their foundations. As with all donor publics, a close match in interests and needs is imperative. Smith warned:

> No relationship between a charity and a corporation is likely to develop and succeed without a clear connection between the charity's purpose and its programmatic activities on the one hand and the corporation's business interests on the other. If—and only if—the charity's program and the corporation's interests are demonstrably and identifiably in concordance is there any potential for a long-lasting relationship. (p. 226)

Whereas the redefinition of enlightened self-interest described earlier concentrates on short-term marketing benefits, strategic philanthropy deals with all categories of benefits that will help the corporation succeed and survive. An overriding factor, however, is that contributions must generate outcomes in support of the corporation's objectives and the outcomes must be specific and measurable—requirements not unlike those imposed by foundations.

Measurable Benefits.   Although "firms are under pressure to tie their giving more directly to company operations and to measure the payoff of their charitable investments" (Magat, 1989, p. 18), benefits returned to donors need not be limited to only those that are immediate and economic. Most corporations welcome fund-raising opportunities aimed at nonmarketing objectives. According to Burlingame (1994), a 1992 study found that "nearly 80 percent of U.S. business people would like to see better results from their giving programs in terms of meeting the companies' philanthropic goals for society, community, employees, and themselves" (p. 473). A survey of 463 leading corporate donors by the Conference Board (1995) found that image enhancement and increased employee loyalty are among the valued benefits the companies say they receive from their contributions.

The demand for measurable benefits requires greater accountability by charitable organizations; specifically, more attention to stewardship is needed. A frequent complaint by corporate donors is that they do not receive enough credit for their contributions ("What's new," 1994). Organizational recipients, they claim, spend little time or effort on appropriate recognition. Such charges are serious given that benefits categorized as social currency, public relations, and social responsibility are dependent on awareness of the gift by members of society and strategic publics. Publicity, in other words, plays a critical role in returning desired benefits to corporate donors. Galaskiewicz (1989) advised fund raisers to include assurances in their solicitations that contributions will be publicized. Rather than rely on the traditional grip-and-grin photograph of a check ceremony, however, publicity should focus on the purpose of the gift, or what it will achieve. As Paul Ostergaard (cited in "What's new," 1994), president of the Citicorp Foundation and an authority on corporate philanthropy, explained: "Handing over a check is not news, but solving a problem is. Public relations efforts need to concentrate on the results of the donation rather than on the donation itself" (p. 24).

In an exploratory study of fund raisers' perceptions of the benefits expected by corporate donors, Duhé (1994) found that the new business environment has heightened expectations for publicity. She also found that practitioners perceive reporting as a benefit provided to donors, not as an obligation or necessary element of the fund-raising process. Supporting this finding, H. W. Smith (1993) implied that stewardship generally is unsatisfactory and commanded, "Progress reports, modifications of programs and projects, and other similar information must be communicated to corporate donors on a continuing basis" (p. 227). Duhé (1994) quoted the director of development for a health organization: "Thank-you notes no longer suffice. Fund raising is moving to a new spectrum—there are fewer donors and those that do contribute have a higher interest in where their money goes" (p. 21). Drawing from the literature and her own perspective as a contributions officer for an international oil corporation, Duhé asserted, "Corporate contributors demand nonprofit accountability and want to know where their dollars are going and if those dollars are making a difference" (p. 21).

Fund raisers are responsible for telling corporate prospects what they can expect to achieve from their gifts and how the outcomes will be documented. The popularity of joint ventures, I suspect, can be attributed in part to practitioners who lack the managerial skills to propose measurable benefits other than those dealing with marketing. Senior managers' preferences for unrestricted gifts also promote the use of joint ventures over more worthy partnerships based on mutual interest and interdependence. In the meantime, corporate giving remains stagnant and criticism about businesses' self-interest increases. Curt Weeden (1995), vice president of corporate contributions at Johnson & Johnson, argued, "Part of the problem rests with businesses as they try to define the 'right' level of giving in newly re-engineered organizations. But part of the problem also rests with some fund raisers who haven't adjusted their thinking and approach to motivating corporations to be more generous donors" (p. 54).

Fundamental to such charges is that some practitioners do not understand the concept of mixed motives. Illustrating, two of the seven fund raisers interviewed by Duhé (1994) said changed conditions for businesses have not affected giving because corporate philanthropy is mostly altruistic. One of the two, a female practitioner with a local chapter of the American Heart Association, said corporations do not expect any benefits in return for giving!

Duhé's study prompts questions for further research. In particular, how accurate are charitable organizations' views about the benefits corporations expect? How well do those views match the expectations of corporate donors?[10] To what extent do fund raisers perceive agreement between the views of dominant coalition members and

---

[10]Duhé (1996) conducted her thesis study on the benefits corporate donors get and want from giving to a local United Way. Utilizing survey methodology, she tested 13 benefits drawn from this chapter's discussion and her own work. She also operationalized and tested Galaskiewicz's (1989) five ways corporations use contributions, which Duhé (1996) defined as giving philosophies. She found that the 181 corporate donors in her study predominantly hold the public relations philosophy, which correlation analysis showed is statistically related to the following benefits at the .01 level of probability: "enhanced company reputation" (.67), "company publicity" (.45), "improved employee morale" (.44), and "volunteer opportunities for employees" (.41). Of importance for future research, her study documented that all five philosophies are theoretically and empirically related to benefits valued by corporate donors. For example, of the 13 benefits measured, the marketing philosophy had the strongest significant relationship with "increased sales and/or profits" ($.66, p .01$), whereas the social currency philosophy was most closely related to "approval from other UW contributors" ($.68, p .01$). There was no relationship between any of the philosophies and "satisfaction of doing a good thing." Because this altruistic benefit typically was ranked highest of the 13, the absence of variation means that although the philosophies differ by the self-interested benefits expected from giving, altruism is common to all five.

estimates of corporate donors' views? Studies employing coorientation theory could provide answers to these questions. Case study methodology would allow researchers to focus on one charitable organization's relationships with multiple corporate donors. Survey research using random samples of organizations and donors might identify incongruencies between what organizations offer and what corporations expect. The typology of benefits described earlier could be used to design such studies. Benefits represent an important problem suitable for theses or dissertations. Indeed, information presented in this section strongly suggests that fund raisers cannot manage corporate relations effectively until they gain a better understanding about the measurable benefits corporations desire.

Trends.   In addition to the call for accountability, fund raisers and their organizations must adjust to other trends in the turbulent business environment of the late 1990s.

Corporations are redirecting their dollars to recently emereging societal problems, which is altering traditional patterns of support. School reform illustrates the trend. After the 1983 publication of *A Nation At Risk*, the book that first drew attention to public schools' poor performance, many companies started reallocating contributions from higher to elementary and secondary education ("What's new," 1994). From 1983 to 1993, public schools increased their share of the dollars given to education from 5% to 15%, and the proportion continues to grow (Bailey, 1994).

In 1994, IBM announced it was going to contribute more to schools and less to colleges and universities, which typically had received half of the corporation's contributions (Stehle, 1994a). CEO Louis Gerstner, who took over in 1993, had long been active in school reform. He originally hired Stanley Litow, a former New York City school official, to head IBM's corporate-support programs. Litow (cited in Stehle, 1994a) explained the company's new philanthropic interest: "There is not a more important issue to the future of business than the quality of our public schools. If we don't have functioning, excellent schools that prepare young people well for higher education and jobs, it's going to be very difficult to compete in the global economy" (p. 6).

If schools have been the leading beneficiaries of redirected dollars, major losers during the first half of the 1990s were arts, culture, and humanities organizations. Milton Rhodes (cited in "What's new," 1994), president of the American Council for the Arts, proclaimed: "Corporate America is withdrawing from the arts in droves. When it comes to fighting the problems of society, corporations don't see us as a problem" (p. 24). Any organization overly dependent on corporate contributions is vulnerable to shifts in interests; balance among gift sources is necessary.

Corporations also are giving less at the local level as their scope of operations expands. According to C. Smith (1994), companies now spend about 60% of their contributions budgets in the cities where they are headquartered and most of the rest in local communities where they operate, but in the near future only about 40% of all corporate dollars will go to charitable organizations located in headquarter cities. The trend is driven by two forces: internationalization and delocalization.

As U.S. businesses expand into global markets, corporate contributions increasingly are being targeted abroad. Illustrating, Digital Equipment, which receives 60% of its income from foreign countries, currently sends 40% of its contributions overseas and is moving to a percentage equal to income (S. Gray & Moore, 1996). Such gifts, students will recall, must flow through a corporate foundation to be tax deductible.

Ostergaard (cited in S. Gray & Moore, 1996) reported that, in 1995, grants from Citicorp Foundation to organizations outside the United States totaled $6.5 million and represented 25% of the contributions from his company, which does business in 100 countries. Plans called for increasing the proportion to 28% in 1996. International activities generally are funded by reallocation rather than by additional money; therefore, local giving is decreased in corresponding amounts.

Heying addressed the "pattern of delocalization", in his message on Internet's ARNOVA forum (December 21, 1994). Because their profitability is rooted in local economies, home-growncompanies such as banks, utilities, insurance firms, and real-estate developers traditionally have been stalwart corporate donors for local charitable organizations. The interdependent relationship is weakening as business ownership becomes more concentrated. Illustrating, the deregulation of banking has brought about mergers that result in national and international corporations replacing hundreds of locally owned banks. Due to interstate banking, prosperity is less dependent on one geographic area. Heying, who researched business elites' involvement as trustees, said the same pattern is occurring in other types of companies. In the utility industry, for example, power now is bought and sold on a national and international market and deregulation is coming fast. Eroding local support requires greater effort by fund raisers to maintain longstanding ties with the business community.

Corporations are giving more gifts of property. Until recently, contributions over-whelmingly were in the form of cash: 85% cash, 15% property (10% company products and 5% other property and equipment), and 1% securities (Hodgkinson et al., 1992). C. Smith (1994) claimed the proportion of cash to noncash contributions is rapidly changing from roughly 80/20 to 60/40. His prediction may be too conservative. For example, at the same time it announced its new focus on school reform, IBM also announced that its contributions of products would rise and cash would fall (Stehle, 1994a). The company said 50% of its gift dollars would be in the form of computer equipment by 1997, as compared to only 27% in 1993. Taking into account noncash gifts other than products, the change indicated that IBM is moving toward a 40/60 ratio in its future giving. Since the announcement, IBM has decreased its cash contributions and increased noncash gifts each year, and, in 1995, its ratio of cash to noncash was 62/38 (S. Gray & Moore, 1996), a close match to Smith's prediction. Whether or when IBM will reach a 40/60 ratio is not clear; however, products will continue to represent a substantial portion of its contributions in the foreseeable future.

One reason for this assurance is that a number of top corporations, including competitors of IBM, already rely on products for 40% or more of their contributions. In 1995, for example, Apple Computer and Hewlett-Packard gave 80% and 79% of their gifts, respectively, in the form of computer and other equipment (S. Gray & Moore, 1996). Medical, printing, and cleaning supplies constituted 60% of total contributions from Minnesota Mining & Manufacturing, popularly known as 3M. Johnson & Johnson gave away medical supplies and pharmaceuticals valued at $31 million, which represented 40% of its 1995 contributions. Corporate donors believe that gifts of products build brand loyalty among the users of their gifts (e.g., college students using donated computers will buy that brand when purchasing their own computers).

Illustrating gifts of property other than products, BankAmerica contributed $2 million worth of computers, desks, and other items after it merged with Security

Pacific Corporation in 1993 (Dundjerski & Moore, 1994). General Electric gave a building valued at $39 million to Columbia University the same year (Bailey, 1994). As companies continue to merge and downsize, furniture and equipment in unoccupied offices—and sometimes entire buildings—become surplus property that can be converted to tax-deductible contributions.

Fund raisers may be unprepared for this trend. Cash has been the preferred form of gifts from corporations, yet cash is always at a premium, perhaps now more so then ever. Companies have fewer restraints on giving away products and other property. Practitioners, unfortunately, show little ingenuity in identifying matches between their organization's needs and what corporations have to offer.

I must admit that during my fund-raising career I shared a common prejudice against gifts of property. The bias largely stemmed from unsolicited "gifts-in-kind" that had little value and were periodically offered by small companies, but more often by individuals (e.g., cars that no longer were salable). Prospective donors seemed to think that just because they wanted a tax deduction, charitable organizations should be willing to accept what usually were white elephants—or sometimes turtles. When I was the director of development at the University of Maryland, the owner of a regional shopping mall tried to donate a 30-foot metal statue of a turtle that had to be removed from the mall due to renovation. The owner was sure I would take the turtle off his hands because the university's mascot was a terrapin! He wanted the university to pay for the cost of relocating the statue, was not interested in the donation's usefulness, and still was surprised when I turned his offer down.

Such contributions should always be declined; however, prejudice against noncash gifts can no longer be tolerated. Gifts of property can help an organization reach its goals when the interests of the donor and recipient are carefully matched. Fund raisers need to proactively solicit company products and other property, which requires an understanding of their tax deductibility.

Special rules govern businesses' contributions of property—termed *inventory*. The Tax Reform Act of 1969 changed the deductibility for inventory gifts from fair market value to cost basis only, except when they are made for certain purposes (Galaskiewicz, 1989). The Tax Reform Act of 1976 provided a special incentive for inventory gifts made to assist infants, the infirm, or the needy. The amount eligible for deduction is equal to the cost of the donated property plus 50% of the difference between cost and fair market value. The Economic Recovery Tax Act of 1981 added the same incentive for inventory gifts to colleges and universities for research purposes. A corporation's tax savings, therefore, increase significantly when its products are solicited and used for a purpose congruent with the sanctioned incentives, which astute fund raisers keep in mind when conducting research. Illustrating, a program of a hypothetical human services organization in Detroit, Michigan involves delivering medicine to homebound elderly residents. Transportation is a major expense. General Motors, headquartered in Detroit, regularly gives away cars, trucks, and other vehicles—$25 million worth in 1995 (S. Gray & Moore, 1996). The overlaps suggest a match between opportunity and prospect, and probability for noncash support is high.

Companies selling services rather than products cannot deduct their services as gifts of inventory. Services, it is recalled from chapter 7, are not deductible as charitable contributions, although companies deduct contributed services as business expenses.

The output of entire industries, such as telecommunications, finance, entertainment, hotels, and airlines, do not qualify as gifts. This does not mean, however, that fund raisers should restrict service companies to requests for cash only.

For example, a university could ask an airline company servicing its community to contribute up to $10,000 in tickets during 1 year for the purpose of sending junior faculty to academic meetings at which they will present research papers. The company rightfully would be credited with advancing educational excellence in the community it serves, and the university would free up its operating budget. Opportunities for stewardship would be plentiful. For example, faculty members could be asked to recognize the airline in any published articles resulting from their presented papers, much as they already do with grants. The free travel would not be deductible as a gift, and the fixed costs of scheduled flights would already be deducted as business expenses by the airline. Be that as it may, service companies appreciate fund raisers who show them ways they can help a charitable organization achieve its goals without contributing cash.

Corporations are making fewer unrestricted gifts, a trend also observed among foundation and individual donors. C. Smith (1994) said that whereas about 60% of corporate contributions in the past were for general operating support, such gifts now comprise only 20% of all corporate dollars. The days of routinely soliciting $5,000 from businesses to buy a table at the organization's annual dinner may well be over. Gifts that supply unrestricted income almost always result in vague feedback on what the gift accomplished or a complete absence of reporting, neither of which provides corporations with measurable returns. As argued in earlier chapters, less concentration on unrestricted giving and more emphasis on purposes to which donors can restrict their gifts is called for.

Finally, more corporations are empowering employees to participate in philanthropic decisions. Whereas senior managers historically have volunteered as trustees and directed corporate contributions to their chosen charitable organizations, *volunteer incentive programs* involving all levels of employees have become a visible force only in the last decade (Burlingame, 1994). Drawing from a survey by the Points of Light Foundation (1993) in cosponsorship with the Conference Board, 90% of all U.S. companies have formal programs to encourage employees to volunteer and 68% provide release time from work. Senior managers overwhelmingly (90%) believe that volunteer programs help attract better employees.

Volunteer incentive programs increasingly are linked to corporate contributions. Illustrating, San Francisco-based Chevron matched employees' gifts and those they raised from others for participating in a 1993 walk for AIDS in San Francisco (Bailey, 1994). Chevron also has decentralized its gift decisions by pushing them as far down the line as possible. Although staff at headquarters provides policy guidance, each gift must be sponsored by a company manager. Skip Rhodes (cited in Bailey, 1994), head of corporate contributions, explained the intended effect: "Managers ask not only how a grant will meet community needs, but also how it will help them meet their own departmental objectives" (p. 7).

Empowering employee volunteers emulates to some degree the older practice of basing corporate giving on senior managers' pet projects (i.e., personal whim is substituted for strategic objectives). Dayton Hudson, which turned over almost two thirds of its giving to employee committees at its stores, for example, found that conflicts of interest were a problem (S. Gray & Moore, 1996). The company now prohibits employees from voting on contributions to organizations at which they volunteer. My major criticism of the trend is that it places undue emphasis on one corporate stakeholder at the probable expense of others. Regardless, opportunities that tap a corporation's human resources, as well as its cash and inventory, likely will have the highest probability for future funding. As Chevron's Rhodes (cited in Bailey, 1994) declared, "Cash may have been the single denominator in the past, but now other resources, such as volunteers, are moving into the picture" (p. 7).

Process. Effective management of corporate relations requires commitment to the research step in ROPES. Secondary resources are plentiful. Touching on just one, a popular reference work is the *Corporate Giving Directory*, which is annually updated and published by the Taft Group. The directory profiles 1,000 U.S. corporate foundations and direct programs that contribute at least $250,000 per year. Entries include financial data, giving and geographic priorities, recent gifts awarded, contact and application information, and names of company and foundation officials.

It is not enough, however, to simply search through published directories; corporate prospects must be studied in depth through the business media and individual sources if insight is to be gained about how contributions can be useful to the company. As a practitioner, I found it helpful to purchase one share of stock in any publicly owned corporation that was a qualified prospect or a major donor. The information provided to shareholders was valuable for keeping up with corporate activities, such as elections of directors and acquisitions of new businesses that signaled possible new interests. Owning one share of stock also entitled me to attend the corporation's annual meeting, which sometimes provided opportunities for in-person cultivation. The research tool also is useful for individual prospects who are CEOs or directors.

Similar to foundations, the larger the corporation, the more likely it will have formal objectives and guidelines outlining its contributions program. Fund raisers request copies of guidelines and follow them carefully when qualifying prospects and soliciting gifts. Pratt (1991) presented 10 common complaints corporate donors have about practitioners, of which 5 relate to the research step: failing to read guidelines, submitting boilerplate proposals, asking to be exempted from the guidelines, failing to appreciate funding limitations, and failing to take advantage of resources other than cash, such as volunteers and products.

Research increases in difficulty as the size of the company decreases. Furthermore, many companies—both large and small—treat their contributions as a private matter. For example, when *The Chronicle of Philanthropy* conducted its 1996 survey of the top 150 corporations, one third of those contacted declined to provide information on their giving (S. Gray & Moore, 1996). Among the well-known companies choosing not to participate were Walt Disney, Federal Express, Goodyear, McDonald's, Philip Morris, and Xerox.

Programming differs little from that for all major donors (Sheldon, 1991), although cultivation and solicitation usually must be targeted at multiple actors in the corporation. The more decentralized the contributions program, the more actors there are involved in the gift-decision process. Cases in which contributions are closely tied to employee giving and volunteering are best approached as a combination of raising annual gifts from individuals and major gifts from the corporate employer.

Of particular interest to this discussion is the role of the contributions officer. C. Smith (1994) claimed that whereas fund raisers focused their cultivation activities on senior managers and directors in the past, they now treat contributions officers as their "customers." Similarly, Galaskiewicz (1989) viewed the contributions officer as a key functionary who enacts a gatekeeper role for corporate dollars. In other words, experts on corporate philanthropy assume that contributions officers have considerable influence over gifts.

My experience as a fund raiser contradicts their assumption. In almost all cases, relationships with individuals other than the contributions officer, such as the CEO, were in place before contributions were sought. Requests, therefore, logically were channeled through those individuals. Furthermore, contributions officers I encountered usually were low-paid employees with limited access to their corporation's dominant coalition. Some were technicians who merely handled the administration of gift giving according to others' directions. Most frequently, I found that companies had levels of sign-off by the amount of the gift requested. Contributions officers were empowered to deal with requests for about $5,000 or less, which limited their contact to charitable organizations that did not employ fund raisers and to annual giving requests from those that did. Larger gifts generally were decided by contributions committees composed of vice presidents, and the corporation's board of directors had to approve anything greater than $100,000. Communications, then, most often flowed directly to senior managers and directors.

Corporate downsizing during the 1990s has resulted in fewer contributions officers. For example, from 1991 to 1996, Chevron reduced the size of its contributions staff from 15 to 10, Digital Equipment went from 14 to 4, and IBM eliminated 53 positions, or about three fourths of its staff. (S. Gray & Moore, 1996). In short, the number of contributions officers is decreasing as the number of fund raisers continues to increase. How this change has affected corporate relations currently is unknown. I strongly endorse Galaskiewicz's (1989) recommendation for studies on the relationship between fund raisers and contributions officers—many of whom are public relations practitioners assigned to community relations.

Solicitation generally follwos the progressive activities and interpersonal techniques already presented for foundations, with an emphasis on the initial interview. Probability of success is greater when corporate prospects have preliminary input on the proposal, and the resulting relationship is more likely to be mutually beneficial. Because gift decisions are influenced by multiple actors, requests must be in writing. Broce (1986) explained, "The corporate officer almost always needs a written request for review and consideration by others" (p. 147). He provided samples of letters and a proposal directed at foundations that can be adapted for corporations.

There is some disagreement among practitioners about the format of the final request. Sheldon (1991), for example, argued:

> Most companies discourage lengthy proposals. Nothing more than a two-page letter from the not-for-profit's executive director or board president to the company's CEO may be needed. The proposal will specify the project for which support is being sought, the specific amount being requested, and how the company will benefit from making such a gift. (p. 239)

Broce (1986), on the other hand, recommended a comprehensive proposal: "I believe that all major prospects (individuals, corporations, and foundations) that are being asked for substantial gifts deserve detailed proposals" (p. 122). Fund raisers are advised to inquire about the preferences of each prospect.

Stewardship has already been discussed, although it bears repeating that improvement is needed. Four of the 10 common complaints Pratt (1991) presented coincide with the four areas of stewardship: not sending thank-you letters (reciprocity), failing to disclose major facts or changes during the funding period (responsible gift use), failing to submit progress and financial reports (reporting), and only calling when money is needed (relationship nurturing). The remaining 10th complaint, he said, was "grantseekers who have a smug, self-righteous certainty that their own cause is the most important and that they act out of ideals while others act out of self-interest" (p. 224).

Concluding this section, making contributions is a permanent, annual activity for businesses. As H. W. Smith (1993) affirmed, "The nonprofit world can confidently look to corporations for continued support" (p. 225). Smith added advice to those who raise gifts, which provides a transition to the last donor public, "Soliciting corporate support is a time-consuming process somewhat similar to that involved in the cultivation of wealthy individual donors" (p. 226).

INDIVIDUAL DONORS

Individuals are the most important donor public because they provide 86% of all gift dollars—$130 billion in 1996, consisting of gifts from living individuals and bequests (AAFRC Trust for Philanthropy, 1997b).[11] Although proportions vary by missions and specific organizations, cases in which individuals do not provide the plurality of private funding are rare. Religion, as stated earlier, receives virtually all its gifts from individuals, whereas higher education, which is the favored recipient of foundations and corporations, receives one half of its gift dollars from individuals—consistently half from alumni and half from nonalumni. Of the $13 billion given to colleges and universities in 1994–1995, individuals accounted for 51%, foundations for 19%, and corporations for 20% (religious, community, and other organizations gave about 9%, primarily to affiliated institutions; Council for Aid to Education, 1996).

Because individual donors were the focus of attention in preceding chapters, the book's final section limits its discussion to the commonalities individuals share with corporate and foundation donors.

Mixed Motives

Individuals have objectives they wish to accomplish with their giving. They make gifts to causes, or the societal problems represented by organizational missions, that are important to them. Odendahl (1989) confirmed, "Personal interest, involvement, and satisfaction are important motivations" (p. 172). Individuals give not only to advance

---

[11]A portion of these dollars, not broken down by the AAFRC Trust, does not go directly to charitable organizations but to foundations.

a common good, but also to receive private goods, or benefits that are internal, intangible, and tangible (Steinberg, 1989).

Benefits and Interdependence.   Benefits and reciprocity are related. Whereas previous discussions focused on the obligations of recipients after a gift is made, reciprocity also embodies motives for making a gift. M. W. Martin (1994) presented three types of reciprocity that affect individual giving: (a) gratitude, (b) fairness in cooperative ventures, and (c) fairness in passing on inherited goods. Starting with the first type, people perceive obligations to pay back services rendered to them in the past. For example, gratitude often is an underlying factor in alumni giving to colleges and universities. Prince, File, and Gillespie (1993) categorized 10% of the major donors in their study on motivation—discussed shortly—as "Repayers," or individuals who typically have benefited from charitable organizations they support.

People also perceive obligations to contribute a fair share to cooperative ventures from which they currently receive benefits worth more than their costs, the second type of reciprocity. M. W. Martin (1994) used lower level gifts to public television as an example: "People who voluntarily enjoy substantial amounts of public television have a responsibility to pay their share of expenses, assuming they have the resources to do so" (p. 72). Explaining the third type, which others term *serial reciprocity*, Martin said, "Each of us is a steward charged with conserving and (if possible) advancing public goods which we have received from our predecessors" (pp. 72–73). Examples of public and common goods to which Martin referred are community libraries, public education, and the environment. Individuals benefit from inheriting such goods, which creates obligations to give so that future generations will continue to enjoy the same advantages. Martin added: "We did not ask for these benefits, nor did we voluntarily accept them. They represent a vast heritage of public goods generated largely through the beneficence of thousands of people and transferred to us through the stewardship of millions of other people" (p. 73).

Connecting benefits to interdependence, making gifts to charitable organizations provides individuals with a way to put their beliefs into action, beyond what they can express through the ballot box and the marketplace. As M. W. Martin (1994) stated, "Philanthropic giving transforms lip service into commitment by enabling us to put our money and time where our mouth is. That is essential for personal integrity in the sense of consistency between conviction and conduct" (p. 153).

Wealthy individuals, like their major donor counterparts, depend on the charitable subsector to protect our capitalistic economy and avoid big government. Odendahl (1989) concluded from her interviews, "Many wealthy people believe that the private nonprofit sector is essential to the American way of life" (p. 171). Respondents generally held strong antiwelfare state ideologies and endorsed *individual social responsibility*, or behavior as good citizens. A woman from New York stated: "If there were not a nonprofit community out there . . . . I do not think we would still be a democratic country. This may be exaggerated, but the public demand for the government to do this, that, and the other. . . . We would probably be a huge big government doing all these things, socialistic" (p. 171).

Although this chapter purposely segments the three donor publics, individual major donors are intertwined with foundations and corporations. The philanthropy of James Buchanan Duke illustrates how the three intersect and how mixed motives reinforce interdependence.

In 1924, Duke, who founded the American Tobacco Company, created the Duke Endowment—one of today's 15 wealthiest independent foundations ("Foundation annual," 1995; Foundation Center, 1997). Duke stipulated that his foundation's grantmaking be limited to North and South Carolina, where he made most of his millions, and to only four very specific purposes, including grants to nonprofit hospitals. A unique aspect of the health care directive—still carried out today—is the $1-a-day program, whereby the foundation pays qualifying hospitals $1 for each day of charity care provided to indigent patients. In 1994, the program accounted for $3 million of the $18 million the foundation gave to health ("Foundation annual," 1995). According to Panas (1984), Duke probably has been responsible for more financial support to health care institutions than any other single person, but Panas also quoted Duke on his proclaimed reasons for this giving: "People ought to be healthy. If they ain't healthy, they can't work, and if they don't work, they ain't healthy, and if they can't work there ain't no profit in them" (p. 52).

Based on principles of marketing, Prince et al. (1993) identified seven philanthropic styles of individual major donors by their primary motivation. Cluster analysis of responses from 218 individuals, nonrandomly selected, yielded 16 benefit-oriented items that defined the seven styles. The styles, percentage of donors represented by each, and the item rated highest by each group are as follows:

Communitarians (26%)	I donate to reinforce business ties I have.
the Devout (21%)	I support nonprofits for spiritual or religious reasons.
Investors (15%)	I donate at the specific suggestion of my financial advisers.
Socialites (11%)	Nonprofit-related social events let me enjoy myself for a good cause.
Repayers (10%)	I or someone close to me has benefited directly from the services of nonprofits, so I give.
Altruists (9%)	I support nonprofits because their goals are consistent with my values.
Dynasts (8%)	It is expected of me to support nonprofits.

Other than documenting assorted reasons for giving, the study's findings have limited use. They are based on the flawed assumption that a single cross-situational motivation determines philanthropic behavior (findings also are not generalizable). Of a half-dozen or more overlapping motives a person may have for making a gift, any one may be prominent at a given time (M. W. Martin, 1994). Martin asserted, "Usually present is a shifting mixture of altruistic and self-interested motives that function in tandem and with varying degrees of motivational strength and significance" (p. 127).

Prince et al.'s (1993) findings are useful, however, for emphasizing two important points about individual donors. First, those who make major gifts usually derive their wealth from business. The authors found that, except for dynasts, or those who inherit their wealth, between 70% and 82% of the donors classified in the other six philanthropic styles gained their wealth from owning a business. Similarly, File et al. (1994) found that 89% of the 476 donors who had created a $1-million-plus charitable remainder trust funded the trust with money acquired from business ownership. Furthermore, Prince et al.'s (1993) communitarian style of individual giving—their largest group—is closely associated with business. Illustrating, the authors quoted the founder of a local bank to describe communitarians' motivations: "In this area, all the big shots are involved with the symphony. A whole lot of business deals get cut at symphony board meetings" (p. 261). Fund raisers are advised to pay attention to business owners when researching individual prospects for major gifts.

Second, Prince et al.'s (1993) findings support this book's thesis that fund raisers do not make people give. The authors quoted a businessman who said: "It's not a question of whether to give or not. It's a question of how to do it so that you're doing something that means something" (p. 262). Another respondent stated: "It was not a matter of giving. I was certainly going to give. It was really a matter of how much to give, what is the best way to give, and to whom" (p. 262).

Touching on annual giving donors, IS (1994) found that the primary motive for giving by people who contributed at least $100 in total in 1993 was "to insure the continuation of activities that they and their family benefitted from" (pp. 85–86). Other distinguishing characteristics were income ($55,000 or more was the primary discriminator for three of four groups), itemizing on income tax returns, having more education (some college), and being older. Itemizing on income tax returns is discussed in more detail shortly; for now, it is important to point out that regardless of tax savings, it always is cheaper for individuals *not* to make a gift.

All three donor publics, then, have mixed motives for giving. They receive benefits from and are interdependent with organizations constituting the charitable subsector. Through philanthropic exchanges, donors and recipients advance their self-interest, as well as common goods, which—collectively—enrich our society. Fund raisers, therefore, have no reason to apologize when requesting support from well-researched prospects. As Rosso (1991) argued, fund raising "is justified when it is used as a responsible invitation, guiding contributors to make the kind of gift that will meet their own special needs and add greater meaning to their lives" (p. 7).

   Autonomy and Accountability.   Individuals' excessive concern for benefits "distorts commitments to the internal goods of philanthropy in ways that cause harm" (M. W. Martin, 1994, p. 18). Martin, unlike other authorities, approached autonomy from perspectives of both recipient organization and donor. In addition, he linked donors' infringement on organizational autonomy to mixed motives for giving. Illustrating the latter, he presented two conflicting views about the philanthropy of the late Armand Hammer, the Occidental Oil magnate. Hammer, according to Martin, portrayed himself as wanting to help others even more than wanting money and influence. He gave away hundreds of millions of dollars. Yet, Martin reported, Hammer is portrayed differently by critics, who see him as "domineering, shrewd, egotistical, selfish, [and] scheming" (p. 129). They charge that Hammer spent $100 million of his corporation's money to create the Armand Hammer Museum of Art and Cultural Center, which houses Hammer's collection of art. The collection had been publicly promised for 17 years to the Los Angeles County Museum of Art, but Hammer "peevishly broke his pledge when he could not secure a guarantee for a separate wing of the museum to bear only his name, rather than to include the name of one other donor" (pp. 129–130). Martin said the truth about Hammer's philanthropy lies somewhere between the rosy self-portrait and his critics' denigration.

The other side of autonomy is infringement on what M. W. Martin (1994) called donors' individual autonomy—people's rights and efforts for self-determination. When fund raisers manipulate donors, they violate autonomy. The manipulation may be unintentional or it may constitute cynical exploitation using coercion, duress, fraud, or deception. Nevertheless, Martin said, "Either may occur as fundraisers [sic] fall into the habit of viewing people as moneybags, as mere means for promoting their ends (even when those ends are desirable)" (p. 49). Adoption of the two-way symmetrical model ensures that both the interests of donors and the recipient organization are balanced. Advocating such an approach, Martin concluded, "Respect for autonomy is crucial if philanthropy is to be a source of caring relationships rather than of exploitation" (p. 49).

Individuals, like foundations and corporations, are demanding greater accountability. People do not give for the sake of giving; they expect that their gifts will make a difference and that the impact will be communicated to them in demonstrated results. Improved stewardship is not only ethically desirable, but also pragmatically sound.

Based on findings from its biennial survey, IS (1994) reported that lower giving and volunteering were statistically related to the following beliefs about charitable organizations: (a) are not honest and ethical in their use of gifts, (b) are wasteful, (c) do not do a good job in helping those who need help, and (d) do not play an important role in making communities better places to live. In contrast, "Respondents who had positive attitudes about the role and effectiveness of charitable organizations gave and volunteered at higher rates than the national average" (p. 98).

In addition to responsible gift use and reporting, the other two elements of stewardship require attention. Effective fund raising depends on repeat donor behavior, which—in turn—is dependent on reciprocity and relationship nurturing. M. W. Martin (1994) explained, "Altruism usually is conditional, with tacit conditions and expectations in the background. We care for one another genuinely and deeply, but if that care is spurned or never returned, despite ample opportunity for reciprocation, we have reason to limit or withdraw caring" (pp. 138–139).

The discussion turns now to the familiar pattern of a relatively few in number dominating the philanthropic arena.

Upper Income Donors

A minority of individuals provide the majority of gift dollars. Only about one fourth of all U.S. households itemize deductions on their federal income tax returns and deduct charitable contributions, yet they give two thirds of all dollars from living individuals (i.e., gifts other than bequests). In 1993, for example, roughly 30 million of 114.5 million individual tax returns (26%)—representing single or dual taxpayers—claimed $67.2 billion of the $101.2 billion contributed by living individuals (66%;

AAFRC Trust for Philanthropy, 1995; IRS, 1995).[12] Taxpayers with incomes of $200,000 or more constituted only 3% of the 30 million itemizers, but accounted for 22% of the total dollars deducted. The top 0.2% of the itemizers, or about 60,000 households that earned $1 million or more, accounted for 10% of the dollars deducted. Transposing the figures to all people that filed tax returns, just 1% of the taxpayers gave 15% of all gift dollars from individuals, and 0.05% gave 6% of the dollars.

The average contributions deduction for all itemizers in 1993 was $2,260, whereas those with incomes of $200,000-plus gave about $17,000, and those in the $1-million-plus group gave about $109,000, on average (IRS, 1995). In contrast, IS' (1994) survey, which did not include households with annual incomes over $200,000, found that the average contribution in 1993 for all taxpayers—itemizers and nonitemizers—was only $650. IS' studies and other research have shown that tax deductibility influences the amount people give and has a positive relationship with income. Illustrating with IS' findings from 1993, people who said they intended to file nonitemized returns—and, therefore, could not deduct contributions—gave an average of $330 and 1.2% of their household income, whereas people who said they would file itemized returns and deduct contributions gave 350% more, $1,490, and 2.6% of their household income, on average. Itemizers who intended to deduct gifts had an average household income 80% higher than nonitemizers ($53,100 vs. $29,500).[13]

As with foundations and corporations, gifts to religion camouflage the actual impact of upper income individuals on philanthropy. The AAFRC Trust for Philanthropy (1995), which accounts for wealthy individuals—in addition to foundations and corporations—in its estimates of giving, reported that 45% of all gift dollars in 1993 went to religion. IS (1994), which draws its statistics from samples of individuals who earn $200,000 or less, found that religion received 62% of the gift dollars in 1993. Other organizational types distantly followed: education (11%); human services (9%); health (6%); youth development, public/society benefit, and other (3% each); arts, culture, and humanities (2%); and the environment (1%). The difference of 17% between IS' and AAFRC's (1995) figures for gift dollars to religion cannot be explained by different methods, definitions, or rules on foundation and corporate donors; rather, the difference is attributable to the giving behavior of individuals in upper income brackets. Providing supportive evidence, reanalysis of 1993 data by Independent Sector (1995) showed that religious organizations receive the biggest share of their gifts from individuals who make less than $40,000 per year.

Students will recall from earlier chapters that the poor tend to support religion more than the middle class or the wealthy. Studies utilizing IRS data have concluded that gifts to churches claim a declining percentage of income as income rises, and as income rises, people give an increased percentage of their income to educational

---

[12]Figures for giving in 1993 are taken from the AAFRC Trust's 1995 report rather than from its report a year earlier because original estimates were revised.

[13]As given in chapter 2, differences were more pronounced 2 years later. For example, in 1995, nonitemizers gave an average of only 0.9% of their income, whereas itemizers who deduct contributions gave 2.9% of what they earned (IS, 1996). Attesting to the widening gap in U.S. wealth, which is discussed shortly, the average household income for itemizers who claim gifts increased by $7,900 (15%) between 1993 and 1995, whereas the average income for nonitemizers increased by only $1,000 (3%).

organizations and hospitals (e.g., Jencks, 1987). In other words, giving to religion is characterized by lower level gifts and religion dominates individual giving, thereby skewing donor patterns.

Removing religion from the amount given by living individuals in 1993—as reported by the AAFRC Trust for Philanthropy (1995)—reduces the total from $101.2 billion to $55.7 billion. Based on the revised figure, itemizers with $1-million-plus incomes accounted for 12% of the dollar total, itemizers with $200,000-plus incomes—1% of the 114.5 million individual tax returns filed in 1993—accounted for 27%, and 3.7 million itemizers who earned $100,000 or more—3% of all taxpayers—provided 44%, or almost half, of all gift dollars.

Obviously, fund raisers should pay attention to individual prospects who earn at least $100,000 and file itemized tax returns. The group of taxpayers most likely to itemize are homeowners, who can take a deduction for interest payments on their mortgage (IS, 1994). Even for religious organizations, such as a Catholic parish, a minority of individuals account for most of the contributions (AAFRC Trust for Philanthropy, 1995). Maintaining a broad base of donors, however, should not be ignored.

The percentage of individual returns that include charitable deductions has stayed at about 26% since 1990 (IRS, 1995). This group's share of total giving remained steady between 1991 and 1993 (IS, 1994). On the other hand, nonitemizers, who have not been allowed to deduct gifts from their taxes since 1987, are giving less each year. IS (1994) found that the percentage of household income given by donors who did not intend to itemize declined from 1991 to 1993 (as previously noted, the percentage declined again from 1993 to 1995). Contributing nonitemizing households that gave 1% or more of their income, for example, dropped by 7% in 1993. The average amount given was $19 less than in 1991, which represented a reduction of 8% after inflation. IS reported, "These findings suggest that a smaller group of itemizers who take a charitable deduction maintain the same proportion of total contributions, while the growing percentage of the population who do not itemize their charitable deductions are showing a relative decline in their contributions" (p. 50).

Concentration of Wealth.   Fewer charitable dollars from nonitemizers cannot be separated from the growing economic inequality in the United States. According to IS (1994), between 1991 and 1993, average household income increased by 2% in current dollars, but declined in real terms by 4%. Breaking down such statistics, U.S. Census Bureau figures showed that in 1993, personal incomes rose for the most affluent 40% of households, whereas the earnings of the less affluent 60% fell after adjusting for inflation (Vermeulen, 1995).

Unequal distribution of wealth is a characteristic of our capitalistic economy, but the gap between the affluent and the majority of citizens began widening in the 1980s. As a result, Rosenman (1995) proclaimed, "The U.S. is now experiencing the greatest disparity in the distribution of wealth since it began to track such data in the 1940s" (p. 56). During Ronald Reagan's presidency, the wealthiest 1% of taxpayers saw their after-tax income rise by 80% compared with a 4.2% rise in real median family income (Rockefeller, 1992). From 1982 to 1988, the number of billionaires in the United States almost quadrupled, the number of centimillionaires tripled, and the number of decamillionaires rose 157% (McNamee, 1993).

The assets of the 400 wealthiest Americans are greater than the combined assets of all U.S. foundations. Whereas 37,600 foundations had combined assets of $189 billion in 1993 (Renz et al., 1995), the estimated net worth of *Forbes* magazine's 1995 list of the 400 richest people in America was $395 billion—twice as much (P. Newcomb, 1995). The minimum amount required to make the top 400 in 1995 was $325 million, and the list included 94 billionaires, up from 83 in 1994 and 13 in 1982—an increase of 623% in 13 years. Students should remember that only 24 foundations had assets of $1 billion or more in 1995 (Foundation Center, 1997).

Leading the Forbes 400 list—as they have since 1992—were William H. "Bill" Gates, III, and Warren E. Buffett, who, in 1995, also were named the two wealthiest people in the world, excluding royalty (Button, 1995). Bill Gates, 39 years old in 1995, is the cofounder and chairman of Microsoft Corp. outside Seattle, Washington, the world's largest computer software company and manufacturer of such products as MS-DOS and Windows. His wealth, which consists primarily of Microsoft stock, was estimated at $14.8 billion (P. Newcomb, 1995). It increased $5.4 billion between 1994 and 1995, or an average of $450 million per month! Warren Buffett, 65 years old in 1995, acquired his wealth in the stock market as owner of the investment company Berkshire Hathaway, which is a big shareholder in such companies as Coca-Cola, Gillette, Geico, and The Washington Post Company. A resident of Omaha, Nebraska, Buffett's estimated net worth was $11.8 billion (P. Newcomb, 1995). It increased about $2.6 billion from 1994 to 1995, in part because the Walt Disney Co. purchased Capital Cities/ABC—one of Berkshire's longtime holdings.

Gates' and Buffett's placement at the top of the global list in 1995 marked the first time that U.S. citizens held that distinction since *Forbes* began tracking the world's megarich in 1987 (Button, 1995). American billionaires comprised more than one third of the list. They included members of the Walton family, owners of Wal-Mart stores; the Mars family, makers of such candy products as Snickers; the du Pont family, chemical and plastic manufacturers; Donald and Samuel Newhouse, Jr., representing the media industry; and the Bass brothers—Sid, Edward, Robert, and Lee. Commenting on Gates' and Buffett's achievement, Button (1995) stated, "This is one more symbol of America's improved economic standing, a recovery made possible by the tax cuts and economic restructuring of the 1980s" (p. 110).

At the other end of the economic spectrum, poverty soared in the mid-1980s when federal spending for social services programs decreased significantly under the Reagan administration (Wulff, 1995). Gaining control of Congress in 1994, Republicans proposed to slash $60 billion from welfare programs. Rosenman (1995) warned that tax-cutting plans called for in the Republicans' Contract with America "would further polarize the nation along stark economic lines" (p. 56). Bill Clinton, representing the growing faction of fiscal conservatives in the Democratic party, had promised during his 1992 campaign for president "to end welfare as we know it" (Adler, 1996, p. 43). In August 1996, the two political forces came together when Clinton, who was running for reelection, signed a Republican bill that abolished the 60-year-old welfare system guaranteeing payments to the poor and shifted responsibility for 13 million needy people from federal to state government. Charitable organizations were expected to assume most of the burden.

Described by Adler (1996) as "radical" and "the most profound change in social policy" since the Depression (p. 43), the new law, called the Personal Responsibility and Work Opportunity Reconciliation Act, will cut welfare costs by $55 billion over the next 6 years—including $27 billion in food stamps. Whereas many taxpayers applauded its cost-saving provisions, such as a lifetime benefit limit of 5 years, the Urban Institute estimated that the law will push 2.6 million people—1.1 million of them children—below the federal poverty line. Conditions for the poor, then, are likely to worsen under recent legislation. In contrast, tax-reform proposals pending in Congress, such as lowering the capital-gains rate and exempting investment earnings from income taxes, would result in the rich getting richer. Rosenman (1995) argued, "It really is Robin Hood in reverse" (p. 56).

The widening gap in wealth in the United States is a factor of concern for fund raisers. If giving predominantly becomes the prerogative of a few, it is doubtful that the charitable tax deduction will survive. Practitioners have little control over the distribution of wealth; however, they can take measures to ensure that their organization's donors are inclusive of people from all economic levels. The fact that fund raising increasingly is moving from an 80/20 proportion (i.e., 80% of the dollars provided by 20% of the donors) to one of 95/5 or less demonstrates a reckless disregard for the widespread support necessary for protecting the charitable subsector. Less bragging about multimillion-dollar gifts and more concern about broad-based philanthropy is called for.

Philanthropists.   The current situation is not without optimism. Although threatened, America's tradition of philanthropy is alive and active. Shortly before the holidays in December 1995, St. Jude's Children's Research Hospital, a Memphis, Tennessee-based organization that treats catastrophic childhood diseases, regardless of patients' ability to pay, received a plain white envelope with no return address, postmarked Dallas, Texas ("St. Jude's," 1995). Inside the envelope was a peel-off game ticket worth $1 million! An anonymous donor had sent the ticket after first discovering its monetary value. The ticket was part of a game sponsored by McDonald's, which agreed to make good on the payoff although rules legally barred the transfer. The odds of getting one of the only three $1-million tickets distributed nationwide were 200 million to 1. The odds of a winner sending it to a charitable organization were unknown. St. Jude's chief fund raiser, Richard Shadyac (cited in "St. Jude's, 1995"), called the gift "a holiday miracle" (p. A-7). He importantly added, however: "We consider all the gifts we receive, large or small, as special. Clearly, this donor believed in our cause. For that reason, we think of this gift as a holiday miracle" (p. A-7).

As described in previous chapters, wealthy Americans are held and often hold themselves to a philanthropic standard that is unusual in the modern world. The individual assets of Bill Gates and Warren Buffett are substantially greater than the assets of the largest foundation, Ford. Both men are capable of dwarfing the legacies of the Fords and philanthropy giants John D. Rockefeller, Sr. and Andrew Carnegie, and have promised to do so in the future—one at the time of his death and the other when he is in his 50s.[15]

---

[15]Still leading the Forbes 400, Gates' estimated net worth was $36 billion in mid-1997 and Buffet's was $23 billion. Rockefeller and Carnegie, students will recall from chapter 2, gave away $5.4 billion and $3.5 billion, respectively, in dollars adjusted to 1996.

Buffett has announced that he will leave most of his estate to the Omaha-based Buffett Foundation, which had assets of only $22 million in 1992 (Seneker, 1993). *Forbes* estimated that if Buffett lives until 2013 and his investments grow by 15% each year, the foundation will get $100 billion when he dies! His investments have grown at an average annual rate of 29% since 1970. Buffett, who said he wants his foundation to concentrate on ways to reduce population growth, has been criticized for giving away little money to date.

Gates also has been the target of such criticism, although he recently established a foundation with a $200-million gift and gave another $70 million to various organizations (Hafner, 1996). Representative of his philanthropy, he made two major gifts to the University of Washington in honor of this parents: $12 million in 1996 for a new law school building named for his father, a law school alumnus; and $10 million in 1995 for an endowed scholarship fund named for his late mother, an alumna and a regent for 18 years until her death in 1994 ("3 universities," 1996). Gates has announced in several media interviews (e.g., "Bill Gates plans," 1994) that he will give away 95% of his fortune, but not until he retires from Microsoft—which he said will occur sometime in his 50s (he will turn age 50 in 2006). The interests he specified were research, human services, education, and—like Buffett—population control.

In Summer 1996, media mogul Ted Turner accused Gates and Buffett of doing too little to benefit charity—and placed much of the blame on the press, which he charged does not do enough to honor wealthy individuals who give away their money ("Press clippings," 1996). Specifically, Turner attacked *Forbes'* annual publication of the 400 richest Americans, saying that the prestige of being on the list made too many people unwilling to give. Using himself as an example, he described how in 1994 he had been "shaken up" when he gave $200 million to his foundation and realized that because of the gift, he would not have a chance of making the top echelon on the next year's list. (Turner's assets totaled $1.9 billion in 1995, placing him in the third highest category; P. Newcomb, 1995.) He challenged the press to provide greater recognition of gererous individuals and urged the creation of a Forbes 400-like list of philanthropists.

Turner's stand has had positive results. Within months, five major magazines had published rankings or articles featuring many of the individuals mentioned here and in chapter 12 ("Press clippings," 1996). For example, Hungarian-born billionaire George Soros was praised in three of the magazines as an imaginative philanthropist who comes closest to historical giants. Even *Forbes* included an article on Turner's accusations in its 1996 listing of the richest people. The publicity has focused attention on America's tradition of philanthropy. It also has generated numerous recommendations about what Bill Gates should do with his fortune, which range from he should keep it and concentrate on Microsoft, thereby creating more jobs and expanding computer use, to he should contribute it all to improving the nation's public schools and—ironically—finding a way to close the gap between rich and poor.

Anticipating this fascination with his wealth and our expectations for his philanthropy, Gates (cited in "'The New Yorker,'" 1994) explained his delay in an e-mail response to a 1994 magazine query:

I think that giving money away takes a lot of effort. Not as much effort as making it, but still a lot to do it properly. Therefore, when I am old and have time I will put some effort into that. Assuming I still have a lot of money by the time I retire, which is certainly no certain thing, I will give away well over 90 per cent of it since I don't believe in kids having too much money. (p. 37)

Concluding Remarks

Gates' reasoning is not unfamiliar. According to Cutlip (1965/1990), the first executive to be assigned full time to the duties of a corporate contributions officer, Claude Alexander, executive secretary of the Contribution and Membership Committee of the Standard Oil Company of New Jersey, wrote in 1950, "'Many corporations have discovered that it is frequently harder to give money wisely than it is to make it'" (p. 509). Providing a much earlier perspective, Lord (1983) quoted Aristotle: "To give away money is an easy matter and in any man's [*sic*] power. But to decide to whom to give it, and how large and when, and for what purpose and how, is neither in every man's power—nor an easy matter. Hence it is that such excellence is rare, praiseworthy and noble" (p. 112).

Interacting with donors—individuals, corporations, and foundations—makes fund raising a unique occupation. A practitioner interviewed by Duronio (1994a) put it this way: "In fund raising you meet people at the highest level of being human and kind. This is a marvelous career working with good people who want to do good things" (p. 16). Another focused on prospects for major gifts: "I get paid to meet some of the most important people in the world" (p. 17). Students should note that if Bill Gates were to keep his money under the same conditions applied earlier to Warren Buffett, he would possess somewhere around $1 trillion when he reaches his mid-80s!

Looping back to the beginning of this book, philanthropy is necessary in a democratic society, and fund raising is necessary to philanthropy; therefore, fund raising is essential to our democratic society (Payton et al., 1991). I agree with M. W. Martin (1994), who concluded, "With all its ambiguities and perils, philanthropy provides a forum for moral creativity, for putting our vision of a good society into practice, and for fostering caring relationships that enrich individuals and communities alike" (p. 172).

Effective fund-raising management goes beyond raising dollars. Its greatest contribution is protecting the charitable subsector so vital to our way of life. Those choosing a career in this exciting and rewarding field are to be congratulated. The pride they derive from their work will be in direct correlation to how well they carry out their larger responsibilities.

SUGGESTED READINGS

Burlingame, D. F. (Ed.). (1992). *The responsibilities of wealth*. Bloomington: Indiana University Press.

Geever, J. C., & McNeill, P. (1997). *The Foundation Center's guide to proposal writing* (2nd ed.). Cambridge, MA: Harvard University Press.

Murray, V. (1991). *Improving corporate donations: New strategies for grantmakers and grantseekers*. San Francisco, CA: Jossey-Bass.

Ostrower, F. (1996). *Why the wealthy give: The culture of elite philanthropy*. Princeton, NJ: Princeton University Press.

Schervish, P. G., Coutsoukis, P. E., & Lewis, E. (1994). *Gospels of wealth: How the rich portray their lives*. Westport, CT: Praeger.

Shaw, S. C., & Taylor, M. A. (1995). *Reinventing fundraising: Realizing the potential of women's philanthropy*. San Francisco, CA: Jossey-Bass.

References

Abbott, A. (1988). *The system of professions*. Chicago: University of Chicago Press.

Abrams, D. B., & Foster, J. S. (1995, March). Solving the planned giving puzzle. CASE *Currents*, pp. 26–32.

Accord reached in dispute over $100-million gift. (1993, November 2). *The Chronicle of Philanthropy*, p. 11.

Accountants for the Public Interest (API). (1990). *What a difference nonprofits make: A guide to accounting procedures*. (Available from Author, 1012 14th Street, N.W., Suite 1103, Washington, DC 20005.)

Adams, M. F. (1993). How to solicit a major gift. In M. J. Worth (Ed.), *Educational fund raising: Principles and practice* (pp. 131–140). Phoenix, AZ: American Council on Education and Oryx Press.

Adler, J. (1995, March 27). The fall of Western civ. *Newsweek*, p. 59.

Adler, J. (1996, August 12). Washington washes its hands. *Newsweek*, pp. 42–44.

Aid to "Great Performances" withdrawn by Texaco. (1992, April 21). *The Chronicle of Philanthropy*, p. 13.

Ala. charities face disclosure rule. (1995, September 7). *The Chronicle of Philanthropy*, p. 32.

Aldrich, D. G., III. (1994, March). A boom in baby-boom marketing: A close-up look at one planned giving strategy for 30- and 40-somethings. CASE *Currents*, pp. 26–29.

Alexander, G. D. (1990, January 23). Unrealistic goals for major capital campaigns are leading to dangerous accounting abuses. *The Chronicle of Philanthropy*, p. 27.

Allen, P. A. (1991). How to research and analyze individual donors. In H. A. Rosso & Associates, *Achieving excellence in fund raising: A comprehensive guide to principles, strategies, and methods* (pp. 217–228). San Francisco, CA: Jossey-Bass.

Almanac issue. (1993, August 25). *The Chronicle of Higher Education*, pp. 1–120.

Altizer, A. W. (1992). *Seeking major gifts: How 57 institutions do it*. Washington, DC: Council for Advancement and Support of Education.

American Association of Fund-Raising Counsel (AAFRC) Trust for Philanthropy. (1987). *Giving USA: Estimates of philanthropic giving in 1986 and the trends they show*. New York: Author.

American Association of Fund-Raising Counsel (AAFRC) Trust for Philanthropy. (1989). *Giving USA: The annual report on philanthropy for the year 1988*. New York: Author.

American Association of Fund-Raising Counsel (AAFRC) Trust for Philanthropy. (1995). *Giving USA: The annual report on philanthropy for the year 1994*. New York: Author.

American Association of Fund-Raising Counsel (AAFRC) Trust for Philanthropy. (1996). *Giving USA: The annual report on philanthropy for the year 1995*. New York: Author.

American Association of Fund-Raising Counsel (AAFRC) Trust for Philanthropy. (1997a). Annual survey of state laws regulating charitable solicitations. *Giving USA Update*, Issue 1, pp. 1–7.

American Association of Fund-Raising Counsel (AAFRC) Trust for Philanthropy. (1997b). *Giving USA: The annual report on philanthropy for the year 1996*. New York: Author.

American Institute of Certified Public Accountants (AICPA). (1993, September 10). *Proposed statement of position: Accounting for costs of materials and activities of not-for-profit organizations and state and local governmental entities that include a fund-raising appeal*. (Available from Author, 1211 Avenue of the Americas, New York, NY 10036-8775.)

America's poor showing. (1993, October 18). *Newsweek*, p. 44.

Anderson, C. (1992, November–December). Cash on the barrelhead. CASE *Currents*, pp. 26–28, 30, 32.

Anderson, R., Ericson, F., Thee, B., & Williams, W. (1991, Summer). IRS regulations: A quiz. NSFRE *The Journal*, pp. 40–42.

Annenberg gives $7.8-million to private school; other new gifts. (1993, April 6). *The Chronicle of Philanthropy*, p. 12.

Anthony, R. N. (1996, July 11). New tax form for charities is useless. *The Chronicle of Philanthropy*, pp. 46–47.

Ark. company charged with charity fraud. (1994, July 12). *The Chronicle of Philanthropy*, p. 31.

Armstrong, R. (1995, Fall). The route to effective fund-raising letters. NSFRE *Advancing Philanthropy*, pp. 42–43.

Arthur Andersen & Company. (1992, Fall). What is a charitable gift—and what is not? The Grantsmanship Center *Whole Nonprofit Catalog*, pp. 5–9.

Assertions. (1991, November 18). IEG *Special Events Report*, p. 2.

Association of Alumni Secretaries. (1913). *Report of the first conference of the Association of Alumni Secretaries.* Ann Arbor, MI: Association Office of the Secretary.

Association of Direct Response Fundraising Counsel. (1992, March). *Rules of business ethics and practice.* (Available from Author, 1319 F Street, N.W., Suite 300, Washington, DC 20004-1106.)

Association of Philanthropic Counsel (APC). (1996). *Your invitation to become an APC charter member.* (Available from Clover B. Apelian, APC Chair, 1400 East Hillsboro Boulevard, Suite 201, Deerfield Beach, FL 33441.)

Association for Research on Nonprofit Organizations and Voluntary Action (ARNOVA). (1997). *Membership directory.* (Available from ARNOVA Executive Office, Center on Philanthropy, Indiana University, 550 West North Street, Suite 301, Indianapolis, IN 46202-3162.)

AT&T Foundation may be split. (1996, March 21). *The Chronicle of Philanthropy*, p. 17.

Attorney General of the State of California. (1994, December). *Attorney General's report on charitable solicitation by commercial fundraisers.* (Available from Author, Public Inquiry Unit, P.O. Box 944255, Sacramento, CA 94244-2550.)

Aupperle, K. E., Carroll, A. B., & Hatfield, J. D. (1985). An empirical examination of the relationship between corporate social responsibility and profitability. *Academy of Management Journal, 28*(2), 446–463.

Auten, G., & Rudney, G. (1989). The variability of the charitable giving by the wealthy. In R. Magat (Ed.), *Philanthropic giving: Studies in varieties and goals* (pp. 72–91). New York: Oxford University Press.

Bailey, A. L. (1987, March 18). Professors taking on important roles in raising funds for their institutions. *The Chronicle of Higher Education*, pp. 34–35.

Bailey, A. L. (1988a, October 25). Reagan years: Profound changes for philanthropy. *The Chronicle of Philanthropy*, pp. 1, 19–20, 22–23.

Bailey, A. L. (1988b, December 20). Texas medical center given $104.6-million in 13 months, $60-million of it in past 3 weeks. *The Chronicle of Philanthropy*, pp. 4, 9.

Bailey, A. L. (1990a, October 2). Indiana U. Center on Philanthropy gets $15.1-million. *The Chronicle of Philanthropy*, p. 7.

Bailey, A. L. (1990b, October 16). Major domo of Penn's billion-dollar campaign. *The Chronicle of Philanthropy*, pp. 7, 20–21.

Bailey, A. L. (1992, July 14). College fund raisers' group aims to improve training and hiring. *The Chronicle of Philanthropy*, p. 26.

Bailey, A. L. (1993, June 29). Annenberg gives $365-million for education—and says he plans to donate millions more. *The Chronicle of Philanthropy*, pp. 7, 10.

Bailey, A. L. (1994, September 20). Corporate giving loses ground to inflation despite an increase in pre-tax profits. *The Chronicle of Philanthropy*, pp. 7, 10.

Barber, P. (1996, September 19). A big chance to regain the public's trust [Letter to the editor]. *The Chronicle of Philanthropy*, pp. 56, 58.

Barkelew, A. H. (1993). *Building bridges: The public relations challenge in the public and private sector.* Vernon C. Schranz Distinguished Lectureship Monograph. (Available from Department of Journalism, Ball State University, Muncie, IN 47306-0485.)

Bauer, H. (1993, September). Be prepared. CASE *Currents*, p. 43.

Becken, T. (1993, May). One cloud's silver lining [Letter to the editor]. *Fund Raising Management*, p. 16.

Becker, L. C. (1986). *Reciprocity.* New York: Routledge & Kegan Paul.

Beddingfield, K. T. (1995, December 4). Sizing up the biggest: Stories and stats of 50 favorite American charities. *U.S. News & World Report*, pp. 88–95.

Benjamin, E. (1989, July–August). Let faculty be faculty. CASE *Currents*, pp. 8–11.

Berdahl, R. O., & Altbach, P. G. (1981). Higher education in American society: An introduction. In P. G. Altbach & R. O. Berdahl (Eds.), *Higher education in American society* (pp. 1–9). Buffalo, NY: Prometheus Books.

Bergan, H. (1992). *Where the money is: A fund raiser's guide to the rich* (2nd ed.). Alexandria, VA: BioGuide Press.

Bergan, H. (1996). *Where the information is: A guide to electronic research for nonprofit organizations.* Alexandria, VA: BioGuide Press.

Berger, C. R. (1996, April). Hyperbole, deceit, and just causes. *ICA Newsletter*, pp. 2–3.

Berton, L. (1994, December 14). Roll call: Towns fight for right to tax some property of nonprofit groups; Struggles sometimes end with agreement to make "in lieu of" payments; Gift to charity hits snag. *The Wall Street Journal*, pp. 1, 8.

Big charity coalition to give tax court advice in controversial case. (1993, May 4). *The Chronicle of Philanthropy*, p. 34.

Big G swims with sharks to stir up snack sales. (1991, November 18). IEG *Special Events Report*, pp. 7–8.

Bigelow, B. E., & Lumpkin, S. R. (1993). *Planned giving in the United States: A survey of donors*. (Available from the National Committee on Planned Giving, 310 North Alabama, Suite 210, Indianapolis, IN 46204-2103.)

Bill Gates plans to give to charity. (1994, June 3). Lafayette, LA, *The Advertiser*, p. D-6.

Bintzer, H. R. (1981). The many uses of professional counsel. In F. C. Pray (Ed.), *Handbook for educational fund raising: A guide to successful principles and practices for colleges, universities, and schools* (pp. 216–223). San Francisco, CA: Jossey-Bass.

Blades, S. D., & Milofsky, C. (1992, November). *Watchdogs and government agencies: Who's evaluating our national charities?* Paper presented to the Association for Research on Nonprofit Organizations and Voluntary Action Annual Conference, New Haven, CT.

Blake, M. (1994, June 15). *A study of capital giving to San Francisco nonprofits, 1988-1992.* (Available from Walter and Elise Haas Fund, One Lombard Street, Suite 305, San Francisco, CA 94111.)

Blanchette, R. (1993, Summer). Predicting giving behavior. APRA *Connections*, pp. 1, 13–14, 17. (Available from the American Prospect Research Association, 414 Plaza Drive, Suite 209, Westmont, IL 60559.)

Blau, P. M. (1986). *Exchange and power in social life*. New Brunswick, NJ: Transaction Publishers. (Original work published 1964)

Blau, P. M. (1987). Microprocesses and macrostructure. In K. Cook (Ed.), *Social exchange theory* (pp. 83–100). Thousand Oaks, CA: Sage.

Bloland, H. G., & Bornstein, R. (1991). Fund raising in transition: Strategies for professionalization. In D. F. Burlingame & L. J. Hulse (Eds.), *Taking fund raising seriously: Advancing the profession and practice of raising money* (pp. 103–123). San Francisco, CA: Jossey-Bass.

Blum, D. E. (1996, December 12). Shepherding Christian charities. *The Chronicle of Philanthropy*, pp. 39, 41–45.

Blum, D. E. (1997, January 9). State studies deal involving March of Dimes. *The Chronicle of Philanthropy*, p. 33.

Blum, D. E., Demko, P., Gray, S., & Hall, H. (1996, September 19). Top dollar for charities' top leaders. *The Chronicle of Philanthropy*, pp. 1, 42–49.

Blumenstyk, G. (1992, July 15). N.J. public college gets $100-million and a new name. *The Chronicle of Higher Education*, pp. A27–A28.

Boardman, R. B. (1993). Measuring fund-raising costs and results. In M. J. Worth (Ed.), *Educational fund raising: Principles and practice* (pp. 265–274). Phoenix, AZ: American Council on Education and Oryx Press.

Boaz, D. E. (1991, September). Robin Hood and the double agent. *Fund Raising Management*, pp. 44, 46–47.

Boorstin, D. (1962). *The image*. New York: Atheneum.

Boris, E. T. (1989). Working in philanthropic foundations. In R. Magat (Ed.), *Philanthropic giving: Studies in varieties and goals* (pp. 200–218). New York: Oxford University Press.

Boris, E. T. (1992). The nonprofit sector research fund. *Nonprofit Management & Leadership, 3*(1), 105–110.

Boris, E. T., Daniels, A. K., & Odendahl, T. J. (1985). *Working in foundations: Career patterns of men and women*. New York: The Foundation Center.

Boris, E., Fox, D. M., & Hall, P. D. (1993). Usable knowledge: A symposium. *Nonprofit and Voluntary Sector Quarterly, 22*(3), 219–239.

Boris, E. T., & Odendahl, T. J. (1990). Ethical issues in fund raising and philanthropy. In J. Van Til & Associates, *Critical issues in American philanthropy: Strengthening theory and practice* (pp. 188–203). San Francisco, CA: Jossey-Bass.

Borum, R. A. (1991). *A comparative profile of African-American and caucasian institutional advancement professionals in selected influential colleges and universities in the United States*. Unpublished doctoral dissertation, Union Institute, Cincinnati, OH.

Bothwell, R. O. (1993, July 27). Welcome to the 90's, United Way [Letter to the editor]. *The Chronicle of Philanthropy*, p. 40.

Bovet, S. F. (1993, November). Sexual harassment: What's happening and how to deal with it. *Public Relations Journal*, pp. 26–29.

Bowen, W. G., Nygren, T. I., Turner, S. E., & Duffy, E. A. (1994). *The charitable nonprofits: An analysis of institutional dynamics and characteristics*. San Francisco, CA: Jossey-Bass.

Brain, P. S., Jr. (1991). Establishing a planned giving program. In H. A. Rosso & Associates, *Achieving excellence in fund raising: A comprehensive guide to principles, strategies, and methods* (pp. 96–116). San Francisco, CA: Jossey-Bass.

Brakeley, G. A., III. (1993). The use of fund-raising counsel from counsel's perspective. In M. J. Worth (Ed.), *Educational fund raising: Principles and practice* (pp. 157–166). Phoenix, AZ: American Council on Education and Oryx Press.

Brakeley Recruiting. (1988). *The Brakeley compensation report*. Stamford, CT: Brakeley, John Price Jones.

Brasseux, S. G., Grayson, N. A., Parker, M., Shields, A., & Sutley, J. W. (1996). *The practices of fund raising and public relations*. Unpublished paper, University of Southwestern Louisiana, Lafayette.

Bremner, R. H. (1988). *American philanthropy*. Chicago: University of Chicago Press. (Original work published 1960)

Bremner, R. H. (1989). Giving for children and youth. In R. Magat (Ed.), *Philanthropic giving: Studies in varieties and goals* (pp. 315–333). New York: Oxford University Press.

Bremner, R. H. (1990). Foreword. In J. Van Til & Associates, *Critical issues in American philanthropy: Strengthening theory and practice* (pp. xiii–xiv). San Francisco, CA: Jossey-Bass.

Brewster, K. (1989). Series foreword. In R. Magat (Ed.), *Philanthropic giving: Studies in varieties and goals* (pp. v–viii). New York: Oxford University Press.

Brilliant, E. L. (1990). *The United Way: Dilemmas of organized charity*. New York: Columbia University Press.

Briscoe, M. G. (1994a). Ethics and fundraising management. In M. G. Briscoe (Ed.), *Ethics in fundraising: Putting values into practice (New directions for philanthropic fundraising*, No. 6, pp. 105–120). San Francisco, CA: Jossey-Bass.

Briscoe, M. G. (1994b, March). Is an endowment justified? *The NonProfit Times*, pp. 10–11.

Brittingham, B. E., & Pezzullo, T. R. (1990). *The campus green: Fund raising in higher education* (ASHE–ERIC Higher Education Report No. 1). Washington, DC: George Washington University, School of Education and Human Development.

Broce, T. E. (1986). *Fund raising: The guide to raising money from private sources* (2nd ed.). Norman: University of Oklahoma Press.

Brody, E. W. (1988). *Public relations programming and production*. New York: Praeger.

Broom, G. M. (1982). A comparison of sex roles in public relations. *Public Relations Review, 8*(3), 17–22.

Broom, G. M., & Dozier, D. M. (1986). Advancement for public relations role models. *Public Relations Review, 12*(1), 37–56.

Broom, G. M., & Dozier, D. M. (1990). *Using research in public relations: Applications to program management*. Englewood Cliffs, NJ: Prentice-Hall.

Broom, G. M., & Smith, G. D. (1979). Testing the practitioner's impact on clients. *Public Relations Review, 5*(3), 47–59.

Brown, J. J., Jr., & Feagin, S. K. (1994, March). *Planned giving in the '90s: The golden age of fund raising*. Presentation to the National Society of Fund Raising Executives, International Conference, Boston, MA.

Brudney, J. L., & Durden, T. K. (1993). Twenty years of the *Journal of Voluntary Action Research/Nonprofit and Voluntary Sector Quarterly*: An assessment of past trends and future directions. *Nonprofit and Voluntary Sector Quarterly, 22*(3), 207–218.

Buchanan, A. E. (1993, August). *Talking philanthropically*. Speech presented at the Indiana University Center on Philanthropy Sixth Annual Symposium on Taking Fund Raising Seriously, Indianapolis, IN.

Buchanan, P. M. (1993). Educational fund raising as a profession. In M. J. Worth (Ed.), *Educational fund raising: Principles and practice* (pp. 368–379). Phoenix, AZ: American Council on Education and Oryx Press.

Buchanan, P. M., Peterson, V. T., & Welter, L. A. (1992, July). *Capital campaigns—What do we really get from them?* Presentation to the Council for Advancement and Support of Education (CASE), Annual Assembly, Atlanta, GA. (Tape available from CASE, 11 Dupont Circle, Suite 400, Washington, DC 20036-1207.)

Buchholz, R. A., Evans, W. D., & Wagley, R. A. (1989). *Management response to public issues: Concepts and cases in strategy formulation* (2nd ed.). Englewood Cliffs, NJ: Prentice-Hall.

Bumgarner, S., Georges, A., & Luna, E. (1987, Spring). Women on women. *National Association of Hospital Development Journal*, pp. 15–17.

Burlingame, D. F. (1994). Empirical research on corporate social responsibility: What does it tell us? *Nonprofit Management & Leadership, 4*(4), 473–480.

Burlingame, D. F., & Hulse, L. J. (1991). Preface. In D. F. Burlingame & L. J. Hulse (Eds.), *Taking fund raising seriously: Advancing the profession and practice of raising money* (pp. xxi–xxvii). San Francisco, CA: Jossey-Bass.

Burns, J. (1993, November 1). Hospitals made to justify marketing's worth. *Modern Healthcare*, p. 52.

Bush, B. H. (1991). What fund raisers should know about the law. In D. F. Burlingame & L. J. Hulse (Eds.), *Taking fund raising seriously: Advancing the profession and practice of raising money* (pp. 200–218). San Francisco, CA: Jossey-Bass.

Bush, B. H. (1994, Summer). The new reality: Life after regulation. NSFRE *Advancing Philanthropy*, pp. 28–33.

Bush, B. H. (1996, May–June). Registration: Is your organization in compliance? *NSFRE News*, p. 4.

Button, G. (Ed.). (1995, July 17). The billionaires. *Forbes*, pp. 110–226.

Cal. limit on fees loses in court. (1995, April 20). *The Chronicle of Philanthropy*, p. 29.

Cal. suit alleging fraud settled out of court. (1994, January 11). *The Chronicle of Philanthropy*, p. 29.

Carbone, R. F. (1986). *Agenda for research on fund raising* (Monograph No. 1). College Park: University of Maryland, Clearinghouse for Research on Fund Raising.

Carbone, R. F. (1987). *Fund raisers of academe* (Monograph No. 2). College Park: University of Maryland, Clearinghouse for Research on Fund Raising.

Carbone, R. F. (1989). *Fund raising as a profession* (Monograph No. 3). College Park: University of Maryland, Clearinghouse for Research on Fund Raising.

Careers can thrive in recession: Magazine lists hot jobs. (1991, June 18). *USA Today*, p. 2B.

Carnegie, A. (1983). The gospel of wealth. In B. O'Connell (Ed.), *America's voluntary spirit* (pp. 97–108). New York: The Foundation Center. (Original work published 1889)

Carson, E. D. (1989). The evolution of black philanthropy: Patterns of giving and voluntarism. In R. Magat (Ed.), *Philanthropic giving: Studies in varieties and goals* (pp. 92–102). New York: Oxford University Press.

Carson, E. D. (1991). Contemporary trends in black philanthropy: Challenging the myths. In D. F. Burlingame & L. J. Hulse (Eds.), *Taking fund raising seriously: Advancing the profession and practice of raising money* (pp. 219–238). San Francisco, CA: Jossey-Bass.

Carter, L. K. (1988, February). Diamond jubilee: Advancement's founding field looks back on 75 eventful years. *CASE Currents*, pp. 17–20.

Carver, J. (1990). *Boards that make a difference: A new design for leadership in nonprofit and public organizations*. San Francisco, CA: Jossey-Bass.

Cash compensation of executives of non-profit organizations. (1989, October 17). *The Chronicle of Philanthropy*, p. 28.

Charity chiefs face a new question: How much do you make? (1992, March 10). *The Chronicle of Philanthropy*, pp. 31, 35.

Charity coalitions take sides in controversial court case. (1994, January 25). *The Chronicle of Philanthropy*, p. 35.

Charity federation saw 42% gain last year. (1992, September 8). *The Chronicle of Philanthropy*, p. 22.

Charity gambling and pay come under IRS scrutiny. (1995, October 19). *The Chronicle of Philanthropy*, p. 41.

Charity gambling on the way out? (1993, May). *Fund Raising Management*, p. 8.

Charity told to pay taxes on telephone sales venture. (1995, January 26). *The Chronicle of Philanthropy*, p. 28.

Clotfelter, C. T. (1989). Federal tax policy and charitable giving. In R. Magat (Ed.), *Philanthropic giving: Studies in varieties and goals* (pp. 105–127). New York: Oxford University Press.

Clotfelter, C. T. (Ed.). (1992). *Who benefits from the nonprofit sector?* Chicago: University of Chicago Press.

Cloud, S., Jr. (1993, Winter). The new philanthropists. *NSFRE Advancing Philanthropy*, pp. 51–52.

Clymer, J. M. (1993, May). To each his own. *Fund Raising Management*, pp. 42–43.

Cnaan, R. A. (1993). Reviews [Book review of *Who benefits from the nonprofit sector?*]. *Nonprofit and Voluntary Sector Quarterly, 22*(2), 184–188.

College and University Personnel Association (CUPA). (1996). *1995–96 administrative compensation survey*. (Available from Author, 1233 20th Street, N.W., Suite 301, Washington, DC 20036-1250.)

Colton, K. (1992, November). Hospitals upbeat despite new concerns. *The Nonprofit Times*, pp. 1, 51.

Columbia University seeks $2.2 billion. (1995, December 14). *The Chronicle of Philanthropy*, p. 29.

Commission on Undergraduate Public Relations Education. (1993). *Design for undergraduate public relations education*. New York: Public Relations Society of America, Educational Affairs Committee. (Original work published 1987)

Commodities suit is settled. (1995, November 2). *The Chronicle of Philanthropy*, p. 64.

Conference Board. (1995). *Corporate giving strategies that add business value*. (Available from Author, Customer Service, 845 Third Avenue, New York, NY 10022-6601.)

Connell, J. E. (1993, Fall). Demographics and the charitable estate planning marketplace: Part 2—Targeting the mature market. *AHP Journal*, pp. 21–29.

Conry, J. C. (1991). The feminization of fund raising. In D. F. Burlingame & L. J. Hulse (Eds.), *Taking fund raising seriously: Advancing the profession and practice of raising money* (pp. 144–169). San Francisco, CA: Jossey-Bass.

Constantine, H. C. (1994). *Gender bias in fund raising: Perspectives on the past, present and future of female practitioners*. Unpublished paper, University of Southwestern Louisiana, Lafayette.

Cook, W. B. (1993, December 18). *Selected comments from interviews* [Unpublished data].

Cook, W. B. (1994a). *Courting philanthropy: The role of university presidents and chancellors in fund raising*. Unpublished doctoral dissertation, University of Texas, Austin.

Cook, W. B. (1994b, October). *Toward a theory of fund raising in higher education: The role of presidents and chancellors in fund raising*. Paper presented to the Association for Research on Nonprofit Organizations and Voluntary Action Annual Conference, Berkeley, CA.

Copeland, J., & Rudney, G. (1993, April 6). End tax breaks for non-profit hospitals. *The Chronicle of Philanthropy*, pp. 40–41.

Council for Advancement and Support of Education (CASE). (1994). *CASE campaign standards: Management and reporting standards for educational fund-raising campaigns*. Washington, DC: Author.

Council for Advancement and Support of Education (CASE). (1995). *Matching gift details 1995–96*. Washington, DC: Author.

Council for Advancement and Support of Education (CASE). (1996). *CASE management reporting standards: Standards for annual giving and campaigns in educational fund raising*. Washington, DC: Author.

Council for Advancement and Support of Education (CASE) and National Association of College University Business Officers (NACUBO). (1982). *Management reporting standards for educational institutions: Fund raising and related activities*. Washington, DC: CASE.

Council for Aid to Education (CFAE). (1991). *Voluntary support of education 1989–1990*. New York: Author.

Council for Aid to Education (CFAE). (1992). *Voluntary support of education 1990–1991*. New York: Author.

Council for Aid to Education (CFAE). (1993). *Voluntary support of education 1991–1992*. New York: Author.

Council for Aid to Education (CFAE). (1994). *Voluntary support of education 1993*. New York: Author.

Council for Aid to Education (CFAE). (1995). *Voluntary support of education 1994*. New York: Author.

Council for Aid to Education (CFAE). (1996). *Voluntary support of education 1995*. New York: Author.

Craig, J. (1997a, February 6). Judge strikes down key parts of Los Angeles's tough rules for charities. *The Chronicle of Philanthropy*, p. 25.

Craig, J. (1997b, February 6). 20 states will allow charities to use common form to register to solicit gifts. *The Chronicle of Philanthropy*, p. 24.

Craver, R. M. (1991). The power of mail to acquire, renew, and upgrade the gift. In H. A. Rosso & Associates, *Achieving excellence in fund raising: A comprehensive guide to principles, strategies, and methods* (pp. 65–79). San Francisco, CA: Jossey-Bass.

Critz, D. W. (1981). Women as senior development officers. In F. C. Pray (Ed.), *Handbook for educational fund raising: A guide to successful principles and practices for colleges, universities, and schools* (pp. 285–289). San Francisco, CA: Jossey-Bass.

Crowder, N. L., & Hodgkinson, V. A. (Eds.). (1991a). *Compendium of resources for teaching about the nonprofit sector, voluntarism and philanthropy* (2nd ed.). Washington, DC: Independent Sector.

Crowder, N. L., & Hodgkinson, V. A. (1991b). An overview of teaching about philanthropy, voluntarism and the nonprofit sector: Responses from faculty. In N. L. Crowder & V. A. Hodgkinson (Eds.), *Compendium of resources for teaching about the nonprofit sector, voluntarism and philanthropy* (2nd ed., pp. 1–11). Washington, DC: Independent Sector.

Culbertson H. M. (1992). Linking beliefs: What are the links? *Public Relations Review, 18*(4), 335–347.

Culbertson, H. M., Jeffers, D. W., Stone, D. B., & Terrell, M. (1993). *Social, political, and economic contexts in public relations: Theory and cases*. Hillsdale, NJ: Lawrence Erlbaum Associates.

Curti, M., & Nash, R. (1965). *Philanthropy in the shaping of American higher education*. New Brunswick, NJ: Rutgers University Press.

Cutlip, S. M. (1990). *Fund raising in the United States: Its role in America's philanthropy*. New Brunswick, NJ: Transaction Publishers. (Original work published 1965)

Cutlip, S. M. (1994). *The unseen power: Public relations. A history*. Hillsdale, NJ: Lawrence Erlbaum Associates.

Cutlip, S. M. (1995). *Public relations history: From the 17th to the 20th century. The antecedents*. Hillsdale, NJ: Lawrence Erlbaum Associates.

Cutlip, S. M., & Center, A. H. (1952). *Effective public relations*. Englewood Cliffs, NJ: Prentice-Hall.

Cutlip, S. M., Center, A. H., & Broom, G. M. (1985). *Effective public relations* (6th ed.). Englewood Cliffs, NJ: Prentice-Hall.

Cutlip, S. M., Center, A. H., & Broom, G. M. (1994). *Effective public relations* (7th ed.). Englewood Cliffs, NJ: Prentice-Hall.

Dannelley, P. (1986). *Fund raising and public relations: A critical guide to literature and resources*. Norman: University of Oklahoma Press.

Davis, H. T., Jr., & Thomas, M. A. (1996, August 8). New penalties unlikely to cut abuse at charities. *The Chronicle of Philanthropy*, pp. 52–53.

Davis, M. (1994, February 12). Q&A: Talking with Vincent Pellegrino. *The Chattanooga Times*, p. A12.

DeFleur, M. L. (1993). *The forthcoming shortage of communications Ph.D.s: Trends that will influence recruiting*. New York: Columbia University, The Freedom Forum Media Studies Center.

Delhomme, R. (1992, April 19). Misconceptions dog local United Way. Opelousas, LA, *Daily World*, pp. 1C–2C.

Demko, P. (1996a, October 17). Financier Soros invests $50-million to help legal immigrants. *The Chronicle of Philanthropy*, p. 13.

Demko, P. (1996b, September 5). Soros goes west. *The Chronicle of Philanthropy*, pp. 9–10, 12.

Demko, P. (1996c, June 27). Turning a campaign around. *The Chronicle of Philanthropy*, pp. 23–24.

Demko, P., & Dundjerski, M. (1996, April 4). UCLA attacked for donors' role in admissions. *The Chronicle of Philanthropy*, p. 27.

Demko, P., & Gray, S. (1996, December 12). When public agencies seek private funds. *The Chronicle of Philanthropy*, pp. 1, 12–17.

Dessoff, A. L. (1994, November–December). Moving pictures. CASE *Currents*, pp. 30–34.

Detmold, J. H. (1981). The distinguished record of women in fund raising. In F. C. Pray (Ed.), *Handbook for educational fund raising: A guide to successful principles and practices for colleges, universities, and schools* (pp. 154–157). San Francisco, CA: Jossey-Bass.

Development Resource Group. (1990). *Trends in hiring development professionals.* Unpublished survey summary. (Available from Author, 36 West 44th Street, Suite 1416, New York, NY 10036.)

Devillier, C. R. (1996). *A national study of state regulators' reports on solicitation firms.* Unpublished paper, University of Southwestern Louisiana, Lafayette.

Diabetes charity gets $10-million; other gifts. (1994, February 8). *The Chronicle of Philanthropy*, p. 16.

Direct Marketing Association. (1995). *The voice of the donor: 1995—Who gives and why.* (Available from Author, 1101 17th Street, N.W., Washington, DC 20036.)

Dittman, D. A. (1981). Criteria for judging staff size and functions. In F. C. Pray (Ed.), *Handbook for educational fund raising: A guide to successful principles and practices for colleges, universities, and schools* (pp. 226–231). San Francisco, CA: Jossey-Bass.

Doermann, H. (1993). Preface. In Council on Foundations, *Evaluation for foundations: Concepts, cases, guidelines, and resources* (pp. xiii–xvii). San Francisco, CA: Jossey-Bass.

Donovan, A. (1993, May). Consultative gift planning. *Fund Raising Management*, pp. 25–26, 28.

Dorich, D. (1991, April). The making of a president. CASE *Currents*, pp. 6–11.

Dorsey, E. (1991). Foreword. In D. F. Burlingame & L. J. Hulse (Eds.), *Taking fund raising seriously: Advancing the profession and practice of raising money* (pp. xiii–xx). San Francisco, CA: Jossey-Bass.

Doty, G. (1994, Summer). America's best corporate donors: An analysis. NSFRE *Advancing Philanthropy*, pp. 41–44.

Douglas, J. (1983). *Why charity? The case for a third sector.* Thousand Oaks, CA: Sage.

Dove, K. E. (1988). *Conducting a successful capital campaign: A comprehensive fundraising guide for nonprofit organizations.* San Francisco, CA: Jossey-Bass.

Dozier, D. M. (1983, November). *Toward a reconciliation of "role conflict" in public relations research.* Paper presented to the Western Communication Educators Conference, Fullerton, CA.

Dozier, D. M. (1984). Program evaluation and roles of practitioners. *Public Relations Review, 10*(2), 13–21.

Dozier, D. M. (1992). The organizational roles of communications and public relations practitioners. In J. E. Grunig (Ed.), *Excellence in public relations and communication management: Contributions to effective organizations* (pp. 327–355). Hillsdale, NJ: Lawrence Erlbaum Associates.

Dozier, D. M., & Broom, G. M. (1995). Evolution of the manager role in public relations practice. *Journal of Public Relations Research, 7*(1), 3–26.

Dozier, D. M., Chapo, S., & Sullivan, B. (1983, August). *Sex and the bottom line: Income differences among women and men in public relations.* Paper presented to the Public Relations Division, Association for Education in Journalism and Mass Communication Annual Convention, Corvallis, OR.

Dozier, D. M., & Ehling, W. P. (1992). Evaluation of public relations programs: What the literature tells us about their effects. In J. Grunig (Ed.), *Excellence in public relations and communication management: Contributions to effective organizations* (pp. 159–184). Hillsdale, NJ: Lawrence Erlbaum Associates.

Dozier, D. M., Grunig, L. A., & Grunig, J. E. (1995). *Manager's guide to excellence in public relations and communication management.* Mahwah, NJ: Lawrence Erlbaum Associates.

Dressel, P. L. (1980). *The autonomy of public colleges.* San Francisco, CA: Jossey-Bass.

Duhé, S. C. (1994). *Benefits of corporate philanthropy: An exploratory study of selected nonprofits and the self-perceived benefits they provide to corporate donors.* Unpublished paper, University of Southwestern Louisiana, Lafayette.

Duhé, S. C. (1996). *Benefits of giving the United Way: A study of the fund-raising relationship between United Ways and their corporate donors.* Unpublished master's thesis, University of Southwestern Louisiana, Lafayette.

Duhé, S. C., Tyler, L. M., Constantine, H. C., Devillier, C. R., Hollems, M. D., Deranger, W. A., & Mouton-Allen, D. (1994). *Exploratory study of fund raising.* Unpublished paper, University of Southwestern Louisiana, Lafayette.

Dundjerski, M. (1994, October 18). Carnegie Mellon's fund-raising shake-up. *The Chronicle of Philanthropy*, pp. 22–25.

Dundjerski, M. (1995, September 7). United Way: 1% increase in gifts. *The Chronicle of Philanthropy*, pp. 27–29.

Dundjerski, M. (1996, June 13). Watchdog case settled out of court. *The Chronicle of Philanthropy*, p. 37.

Dundjerski, M., & Moore, J. (1994, September 6). A rebound ahead for corporate donations? *The Chronicle of Philanthropy*, pp. 1, 6–7, 11–18.

Dunlop, D. R. (1987, May). The ultimate gift. CASE *Currents*, pp. 8–13.

Dunlop, D. R. (1993). Major gift programs. In M. J. Worth (Ed.), *Educational fund raising: Principles and practice* (pp. 97–116). Phoenix, AZ: American Council on Education and Oryx Press.

Dunn, J. A. (Ed.). (1986). *Enhancing the management of fund raising*. San Francisco, CA: Jossey-Bass.

Duronio, M. A. (1993, December). *Summary of selected survey items* (Professionals in philanthropy: Fund raisers at work, Working Paper No. 1). Alexandria, VA: NSFRE and Indiana University Center on Philanthropy.

Duronio, M. A. (1994a, January). *Summary of interviews* (Professionals in philanthropy: Fund raisers at work, Working Paper No. 2). Alexandria, VA: NSFRE and Indiana University Center on Philanthropy.

Duronio, M. A. (1994b, February). *Summary of male/female differences* (Professionals in philanthropy: Fund raisers at work, Working Paper No. 3. Alexandria, VA: NSFRE and Indiana University Center on Philanthropy.

Duronio, M. A. (1996, Spring). Fund raising: A portrait of the profession. NSFRE *Advancing Philanthropy*, pp. 11–22.

Duronio, M. A., & Loessin, B. A. (1991). *Effective fund raising in higher education: Ten success stories*. San Francisco, CA: Jossey-Bass.

Easter Seal telethon sets record. (1993, May). *Fund Raising Management*, pp. 14, 16.

Edie, J. A. (1991). Legal standards for corporate foundations and contribu-tions programs. In J. P. Shannon (Ed.), *The corporate contributions handbook: Devoting private means to public needs* (pp. 201–212). San Francisco, CA: Jossey-Bass.

Edwards, A. H. (1989, April). Go for the gold. CASE *Currents*, p. 72.

Effort to honor donor leads to court fight. (1992, September 8). *The Chronicle of Philanthropy*, p. 11.

Eisenberg, P. (1992, March 10). Corporate values could poison non-profits. *The Chronicle of Philanthropy*, pp. 41–42.

Eisenberg, P. (1994, May 3). Charities' response to criticism: Business as usual. *The Chronicle of Philanthropy*, pp. 45–46.

Eisenberg, P. (1995, January 26). Today's corporate philanthropy: More "self-interest" than "enlightened." *The Chronicle of Philanthropy*, pp. 37–38.

Eisenberg, P. (1996, August 8). Will charities learn from United Way mess? *The Chronicle of Philanthropy*, pp. 53–54.

Eldridge-Karr, C. (1991). *An investigative study of predictive characteristics associated with alumni planned giving*. Unpublished doctoral dissertation, University of Tennessee, Knoxville.

Endorsement controversy. (1996, August 19). *USA Today*, p. 5B.

Endowments over $35-million. (1993, August 25). Almanac issue. *The Chronicle of Higher Education*, p. 40.

Esman, M. J. (1972). The elements of institution building. In J. W. Eaton (Ed.), *Institution building and development* (pp. 19–40). Thousand Oaks, CA: Sage.

Estey, G. P., & Wilkerson, S. (1994, June). Harmonious arrangements. CASE *Currents*, pp. 22–26.

Ethics Resource Center. (1990). *Creating a workable company code of ethics*. Washington, DC: Author.

Evans, G. A. (1993). Organizing the development program. In M. J. Worth (Ed.), *Educational fund raising: Principles and practice* (pp. 275–285). Phoenix, AZ: American Council on Education and Oryx Press.

Expanded, revised Code released at press conference. (1993, April). *NSFRE News*, p. 6.

Experienced tastes. (1993, February). *NSFRE News*, pp. 1, 3.

File, K. M., Prince, R. A., & Cermak, D. S. P. (1994). Creating trust with major donors: The service encounter model. *Nonprofit Management & Leadership*, 4(3), 269–283.

Filer, J. H. (1993, Fall). Terra incognita: Charting the third sector. NSFRE *Advancing Philanthropy*, pp. 51, 53.

Fink, J. (1990). Philanthropy and the community. In J. Van Til & Associates, *Critical issues in American philanthropy: Strengthening theory and practice* (pp. 133–164). San Francisco, CA: Jossey-Bass.

Fink, N. S. (1993). Legal trends affecting philanthropy. In M. J. Worth (Ed.), *Educational fund raising: Principles and practice* (pp. 389–399). Phoenix, AZ: American Council on Education and Oryx Press.

Fischer, L. R., & Schaffer, K. B. (1993). *Older volunteers: A guide to research and practice*. Thousand Oaks, CA: Sage.

Fischer, M. (1994, Spring). Ethical fund raising: Deciding what's right. NSFRE *Advancing Philanthropy*, pp. 29–33.

Fisher, J. L. (1985, September). Keeping our place at the academic table. CASE *Currents*, pp. 11–14.

Fisher, J. L. (1989). Establishing a successful fund-raising program. In J. L. Fisher & G. H. Quehl (Eds.), *The president and fund raising* (pp. 18–32). New York: Macmillan.

Fisher, M. A. (1993, November–December). Seasoned CEOs. CASE *Currents*, pp. 38–40, 42.

Fisher, R., Ury, W., & Patton, B. (1991). *Getting to yes: Negotiating agreement without giving in* (2nd ed.). New York: Penguin.

Fleishman, J. (1995, Fall). Putting our houses in order. NSFRE *Advancing Philanthropy*, pp. 32–36.

Florida Department of Agriculture and Consumer Services. (1993). *Gift giver\$ guide: A guide to contributing to charities in Florida.* (Available from Author, 407 South Calhoun Street, Tallahassee, FL 32399-0800.)

Fogal, R. E. (1991). Standards and ethics in fund raising. In H. A. Rosso & Associates, *Achieving excellence in fund raising: A comprehensive guide to principles, strategies, and methods* (pp. 263–275). San Francisco, CA: Jossey-Bass.

For your information. (1949, May–June). ACPRA *College Public Relations*, p. 22.

Form 990 inaccuracies damage not-for-profits. (1992, September). *NSFRE News*, p. 8.

Forum: The donor perspective on regulation. (1995, Fall). NSFRE *Advancing Philanthropy*, pp. 16–20.

Forum: Recruiters reveal what's hot and what's not. (1996, Spring). NSFRE *Advancing Philanthropy*, pp. 23–29.

Foundation annual reports. (1995, September 7). *The Chronicle of Philanthropy*, pp. 25–26.

The Foundation Center. (1997). *The foundation directory* (19th ed.). New York: Author.

Foundations and charities add World-Wide Web sites. (1995, July 27). *The Chronicle of Philanthropy*, p. 33.

Franz, P. J. (1981). Trustees must lead by example. In F. C. Pray (Ed.), *Handbook for educational fund raising: A guide to successful principles and practices for colleges, universities, and schools* (pp. 161–166). San Francisco, CA: Jossey-Bass.

Freeman, R. E. (1984). *Strategic management: A stakeholder approach.* Boston, MA: Pitman.

FTC cracking down on fraudulent telemarketers. (1997, April 14). Lafayette, LA, *The Advertiser*, p. C-1.

Fund-raisers integral to America's social contract. (1993, April). *NSFRE News*, p. 8.

Gagen-McCarthy, M. (1993, January). A case for strategic planning for community foundations. NSFRE *The Journal*, pp. 24–29.

Galaskiewicz, J. (1989). Corporate contributions to charity: Nothing more than a marketing strategy? In R. Magat (Ed.), *Philanthropic giving: Studies in varieties and goals* (pp. 246–260). New York: Oxford University Press.

Galaskiewicz, J. (1991). Making corporate actors accountable: Institution building in Minneapolis-St. Paul. In W. W. Powell & P. J. DiMaggio (Eds.), *The new institutionalism in organizational analysis* (pp. 293–310). Chicago: University of Chicago Press.

Gallup Organization. (1993, August). *Americans' attitudes regarding regulation of charitable organizations.* (Available from the Council of Better Business Bureaus, Philanthropy Advisory Service, 4200 Wilson Boulevard, Arlington, VA 22203.)

Gaul, G. M., & Borowski, N. A. (1993). *Free ride: The tax-exempt economy.* Kansas City, MO: Andrews & McMeel.

Gearhart, G. D., & Bezilla, M. (1991, March). Fund-raising success takes teamwork. *Fund Raising Management*, pp. 42–44, 46.

Geever, J. C. (1991). How to select and use fund raising consultants. In H. A. Rosso & Associates, *Achieving excellence in fund raising: A comprehensive guide to principles, strategies, and methods* (pp. 203–214). San Francisco, CA: Jossey-Bass.

Gilley, J. W., Fulmer, K. A., & Reithlingshoefer, S. J. (1986). *Searching for academic excellence: Twenty colleges and universities on the move and their leaders.* New York: American Council on Education and Macmillan.

Give & take. (1992, September 23). *The Chronicle of Higher Education*, p. A31.

Goldstein, H. (1994, January 11). When charities swap donor lists, does anyone really object? *The Chronicle of Philanthropy*, p. 40.

Gonzalez-Campoy, R. (1996, Spring). Answering the call for help. NSFRE *Advancing Philanthropy*, pp. 36–40.

Goss, K. A. (1989, March 21). Influx of women into fund raising poses paradox: They're effective, but pay and prestige could suffer. *The Chronicle of Philanthropy*, pp. 1, 10–11.

Goss, K. A. (1990, June 26). Public's perception worries fund raisers. *The Chronicle of Philanthropy*, pp. 19–21.

Goss, K. A. (1992, June 16). Ross Perot's philanthropy: He demands results. *The Chronicle of Philanthropy*, pp. 6–7, 10–11.

Goss, K. A. (1993a, August 10). Coming: A bill to curb charity abuses. *The Chronicle of Philanthropy*, pp. 39–40.

Goss, K. A. (1993b, June 15). A crisis of credibility for America's non-profits. *The Chronicle of Philanthropy*, pp. 1, 38–39, 41.

Goss, K. A. (1993c, November 30). A flawed system for stopping charity fraud. *The Chronicle of Philanthropy*, pp. 1, 26–27, 30–31.

Goss, K. A. (1993d, August 10). In planned giving, the banks are coming. *The Chronicle of Philanthropy*, pp. 31–33.

Goss, K. A. (1993e, November 16). New charity watchdog vows to tell donors what they really want to know. *The Chronicle of Philanthropy*, p. 31.

Goss, K. A. (1994a, February 8). Boys Town sues watchdog group over failing grade in new guide. *The Chronicle of Philanthropy*, p. 34.

Goss, K. A. (1994b, May 3). Counting campaign gifts. *The Chronicle of Philanthropy*, pp. 27, 30.

Goss, K. A. (1994c, February 22). Finances of Toys for Tots Foundation scrutinized. *The Chronicle of Philanthropy*, p. 39.

Goss, K. A., & Moore, J. (1994, May 17). More scrutiny for charity salaries. *The Chronicle of Philanthropy*, pp. 1, 29–34.

Goss, K. A., & Williams, G. (1993, April 20). Widespread mistakes found in effort to classify nation's non-profit groups. *The Chronicle of Philanthropy*, pp. 33–41.

Goss, K. A., & Williams, G. (1994, March 22). 4 charities under investigation for direct-mail claims. *The Chronicle of Philanthropy*, p. 27.

Gottlieb, M., & Healy, W. J. (1990). *Making deals: The business of negotiating.* New York: New York Institute of Finance.

Gouldner, A. W. (1960). The norm of reciprocity: A preliminary statement. *American Sociological Review*, 25(2), 161–178.

Grace, J. D. (1993). Trends in fund-raising research. In M. J. Worth (Ed.), *Educational fund raising: Principles and practice* (pp. 380–388). Phoenix, AZ: American Council on Education and Oryx Press.

Grace, K. S. (1991a). Can we throw away the tin cup? In D. F. Burlingame & L. J. Hulse (Eds.), *Taking fund raising seriously: Advancing the profession and practice of raising money* (pp. 184–199). San Francisco, CA: Jossey-Bass.

Grace, K. S. (1991b). Managing for results; Leadership and team building. In H. A. Rosso & Associates, *Achieving excellence in fund raising: A comprehensive guide to principles, strategies, and methods* (pp. 140–173). San Francisco, CA: Jossey-Bass.

Graham, C. (1992). *Keep the money coming: A step-by-step strategic guide to annual fundraising.* Sarasota, FL: Pineapple Press.

Gray, J. W. (1993). Raising funds for athletics. In M. J. Worth (Ed.), *Educational fund raising: Principles and practice* (pp. 219–228). Phoenix, AZ: American Council on Education and Oryx Press.

Gray, S. (1995, October 19). United Way's controversial makeover. *The Chronicle of Philanthropy*, pp. 1, 22–23, 30.

Gray, S. (1996, February 22). Council on Foundations names Fla. publisher to be its new president. *The Chronicle of Philanthropy*, p. 15.

Gray, S. (1997, May 1). Harvard will use $10-million gift for new center for non-profit study. *The Chronicle of Philanthropy*, p. 10.

Gray, S., & Moore, J. (1996, July 11). Big gifts from big business. *The Chronicle of Philanthropy*, pp. 1, 12–20.

Greene, E. (1990, June 26). Women fund raisers for hospitals found to earn less than their male counterparts. *The Chronicle of Philanthropy*, pp. 19, 22.

Greene, E. (1992, July 14). Could Jews be giving more? *The Chronicle of Philanthropy*, p. 12.

Greene, E. (1994a, August 9). A surge in planned giving. *The Chronicle of Philanthropy*, pp. 24–25, 29.

Greene, E. (1994b, January 11). Walter Annenberg's aim: Give it all away. *The Chronicle of Philanthropy*, pp. 1, 10–11.

Greene, E. (1995, September 21). Charities may sue over rules. *The Chronicle of Philanthropy*, pp. 27, 29.

Greene, E., Greene, S. G., & Moore, J. (1993, November 16). A generation prepares to transfer its trillions. *The Chronicle of Philanthropy*, pp. 1, 8, 11–12.

Greene, E., & Moore, J. (1992, August 11). Weinberg's "contrarian" philanthropy. *The Chronicle of Philanthropy*, pp. 6–7, 10–11.

Greene, E., & Moore, J. (1993, July 13). Charities' pop-music connection. *The Chronicle of Philanthropy*, pp. 1, 7–8, 10–14.

Greene, E., & Murawski, J. (1995, April 20). The verdict on Aramony: Guilty on 25 counts. *The Chronicle of Philanthropy*, pp. 30–34.

Greene, S. G. (1992, December 1). Product donations confuse charity ledgers, tempt some to cook the books. *The Chronicle of Philanthropy*, pp. 28–29.

Greene, S. G. (1993, March 9). Accounting proposals under fire. *The Chronicle of Philanthropy*, pp. 29, 31.

Greene, S. G. (1994a, September 6). Court rules that Sierra Club's credit-card program revenue is tax-exempt. *The Chronicle of Philanthropy*, p. 33.

Greene, S. G. (1994b, July 12). 2 panels approve bills to regulate health charities. *The Chronicle of Philanthropy*, p. 36.

Greene, S. G. (1995, March 23). Yale's decision to return $20-million gift may harm capital campaign. *The Chronicle of Philanthropy*, p. 13.

Greene, S. G. (1996, March 7). Ford speaks up for itself. *The Chronicle of Philanthropy*, pp. 10, 15.

Greene, S. G., & Millar, B. (1994, September 20). The Aramony indictment. *The Chronicle of Philanthropy*, p. 31.

Greene, S. G., & Murawski, J. (1996, March 21). New faces in fund raising. *The Chronicle of Philanthropy*, pp. 37–38.

Greene, S. G., Moore, J., & Williams, G. (1997, February 6). A donor's obsession with secrecy. *The Chronicle of Philanthropy*, pp. 1, 12–14.

Greene, S. G., & Williams, G. (1992a, December 1). The battle of the balance sheet. *The Chronicle of Philanthropy*, pp. 1, 29, 31.

Greene, S. G., & Williams, G. (1992b, December 15). Truckloads of books tie relief group to charities sued by 2 states. *The Chronicle of Philanthropy*, pp. 23, 25.

Greene, S. G., & Williams, G. (1993, May 18). Charities' big gamble. *The Chronicle of Philanthropy*, pp. 1, 26–29, 31.

Greene, S. G., & Williams, G. (1996, April 18). A question of saving or spending. *The Chronicle of Philanthropy*, pp. 1, 25–27.

Greenfield, J. M. (1991). *Fund-raising: Evaluating and managing the fund development process*. New York: Wiley.

Grønbjerg, K. A. (1993). *Understanding nonprofit funding: Managing revenues in social services and community development organizations*. San Francisco, CA: Jossey-Bass.

Gross, S. J., & Niman, C. M. (1975). Attitude-behavior consistency: A review. *Public Opinion Quarterly*, *39*(3), 358–368.

Grunig, J. E. (1989a). Sierra club study shows who become activists. *Public Relations Review, 15*(3), 3–24.

Grunig, J. E. (1989b). Symmetrical presuppositions as a framework for public relations theory. In C. Botan & V. Hazelton (Eds.), *Public relations theory* (pp. 17–44). Hillsdale, NJ: Lawrence Erlbaum Associates.

Grunig, J. E. (1992). Communication, public relations, and effective organizations: An overview of the book; What is excellence in management? In J. E. Grunig (Ed.), *Excellence in public relations and communication management: Contributions to effective organizations* (pp. 1–28, 219–250). Hillsdale, NJ: Lawrence Erlbaum Associates.

Grunig, J. E. (1993). Foreword. In H. M. Culbertson, D. W. Jeffers, D. B. Stone, & M. Terrell, *Social, political, and economic contexts in public relations: Theory and cases* (pp. vii–ix). Hillsdale, NJ: Lawrence Erlbaum Associates.

Grunig, J. E., & Grunig, L. A. (1989). Toward a theory of the public relations behavior of organizations: Review of a program of research. In J. E. Grunig & L. A. Grunig (Eds.), *Public relations research annual* (Vol. 1, pp. 27–63). Hillsdale, NJ: Lawrence Erlbaum Associates.

Grunig, J. E., & Grunig, L. A. (1991). Conceptual differences in public relations and marketing: The case of health-care organizations. *Public Relations Review, 17*(3), 257–278.

Grunig, J. E., & Grunig, L. A. (1992). Models of public relations and communication. In J. E. Grunig (Ed.), *Excellence in public relations and communication management: Contributions to effective organizations* (pp. 285–325). Hillsdale, NJ: Lawrence Erlbaum Associates.

Grunig, J. E., Grunig, L. A., Dozier, D. M., Ehling, W. P., Repper, F. C., & White, J. (1991). *Excellence in public relations and communication management: Initial data report*. San Francisco, CA: International Association of Business Communicators (IABC) Research Foundation.

Grunig, J. E., & Hunt, T. (1984). *Managing public relations*. New York: Holt, Rinehart & Winston.

Grunig J. E., & Repper, F. C. (1992). Strategic management, publics, and issues. In J. E. Grunig (Ed.), *Excellence in public relations and communication management: Contributions to effective organizations* (pp. 117–157). Hillsdale, NJ: Lawrence Erlbaum Associates.

Grunig, J. E., & White, J. (1992). The effect of worldviews on public relations. In J. E. Grunig (Ed.), *Excellence in public relations and communication management: Contributions to effective organizations* (pp. 31–64). Hillsdale, NJ: Lawrence Erlbaum Associates.

Grunig, L. A. (1990). Focus group research in public relations. *Public Relations Review, 16*(3), 36–49.

Grunig, L. A., Grunig, J. E., & Ehling, W. P. (1992). What is an effective organization? In J. Grunig (Ed.), *Excellence in public relations and communication management: Contributions to effective organizations* (pp. 65–90). Hillsdale, NJ: Lawrence Erlbaum Associates.

Gurin, M. G. (1985). *Confessions of a fund raiser: Lessons of an instructive career*. Washington, DC: Taft Group.

Gurin, M. G. (1987, January). Is marketing dangerous for fund raising? *Fund Raising Management*, pp. 72–76.

Gurin, M. G. (1991). *Advancing beyond the techniques in fund raising*. Rockville, MD: Fund Raising Institute.

Gurin, M. G., & Van Til, J. (1990). Philanthropy in its historical context. In J. Van Til & Associates, *Critical issues in American philanthropy: Strengthening theory and practice* (pp. 3–18). San Francisco, CA: Jossey-Bass.

Haberman, D. A., & Dolphin, H. A. (1988). *Public relations: The necessary art*. Ames: Iowa State University Press.

Hafner, K. (1996, December 30). The wealth and avarice of the cyber rich. *Newsweek*, pp. 48–51.

Hage, J. (1980). *Theories of organizations: Form, process, and transformation*. New York: Wiley.

Hall, C. (1993, February). Demystifying marketing. CASE *Currents*, pp. 30–31.

Hall, H. (1992, July 28). Head of college fund raisers' group calls for end to protracted capital campaigns with huge goals. *The Chronicle of Philanthropy*, p. 20.

Hall, H. (1993a, May 4). How to avoid pitfalls in raising money with special events. *The Chronicle of Philanthropy*, pp. 35–36.

Hall, H. (1993b, March 9). Many boards are said to be unhappy over fund-raising costs. *The Chronicle of Philanthropy*, pp. 24–25.

Hall, H. (1993c, November 2). Winning a grant takes a lot more than a good proposal. *The Chronicle of Philanthropy*, pp. 59–60.

Hall, H. (1994a, January 25). Dividing up donors can lead to benefits in fund raising. *The Chronicle of Philanthropy*, pp. 28, 30.

Hall, H. (1994b), December 13). Postage set to increase for charities. *The Chronicle of Philanthropy*, pp. 25–27.

Hall, H. (1994c, May 17). Postal service issues rules barring some advertisements from charity mailings. *The Chronicle of Philanthropy*, p. 27.

Hall, H. (1995a, October 5). Fund raising goes to college. *The Chronicle of Philanthropy*, pp. 30, 39–42.

Hall, H. (1995b, January 26). The struggle to raise operating funds. *The Chronicle of Philanthropy*, pp. 33, 35.

Hall, H. (1996a, June 13). Charity leaders split over ethics of goodbye gift to United Way chief. *The Chronicle of Philanthropy*, p. 36.

Hall, H. (1996b, September 5). Many charities will see decrease in postage costs under new rate system. *The Chronicle of Philanthropy*, p. 35.

Hall, H. (1996c, October 3). New York United Way leader is named to head national organization. *The Chronicle of Philanthropy*, p. 34.

Hall, H. (1996d, June 27). United Way chief declines controversial goodbye gift. *The Chronicle of Philanthropy*, p. 32.

Hall, M. R. (1992). The decentralization of development: Impact on power, priorities, faculty perceptions. *Teachers College Record*, *93*(3), 569–582.

Hall, M. R. (1993). *The dean's role in fund raising*. Baltimore, MD: Johns Hopkins University Press.

Hall, P. D. (1987). A historical overview of the private nonprofit sector. In W. W. Powell (Ed.), *The nonprofit sector: A research handbook* (pp. 3–26). New Haven, CT: Yale University Press.

Hall, P. D. (1989). The community foundation in America, 1914–1987; Business giving and social investment in the United States. In R. Magat (Ed.), *Philanthropic giving: Studies in varieties and goals* (pp. 180–245). New York: Oxford University Press.

Hall, P. D. (1990). The dilemmas of research on philanthropy. In J. Van Til & Associates, *Critical issues in American philanthropy: Strengthening theory and practice* (pp. 242–262). San Francisco, CA: Jossey-Bass.

Hall, P. D. (1992a). *Inventing the nonprofit sector and other essays on philanthropy, voluntarism, and nonprofit organizations*. Baltimore, MD: Johns Hopkins University Press.

Hall, P. D. (1992b). Teaching and research on philanthropy, voluntarism, and nonprofit organizations: A case study of academic innovation. *Teachers College Record*, *93*(3), 403–435.

Hall, P. D. (1993a). A call to reflection. *Nonprofit and Voluntary Sector Quarterly*, *22*(4), 277–280.

Hall, P. D. (1993b). Reviews [Review of *Architecture and the after-life*, *The last great necessity: Cemeteries in American history*, and *Variations on a theme park: The new American city and the end of public space*]. *Nonprofit and Voluntary Sector Quarterly*, *22*(2), 167–183.

Hanchette, C. Q., & Williams, G. (1995, October 19). Claims against New Era Foundation total more than $350-million. *The Chronicle of Philanthropy*, pp. 34–37.

Hancock, L. (1994, December 12). Sick and tired at Harvard. *Newsweek*, p. 83.

Hancock, L. (1995, March 6). Breaking point. *Newsweek*, pp. 56–61.

Hansmann, H. B. (1980). The role of nonprofit enterprise. *Yale Law Journal*, *89*, 835–898.

Hansmann, H. B. (1987). Economic theories of nonprofit organization. In W. W. Powell (Ed.), *The nonprofit sector: A research handbook* (pp. 27–42). New Haven, CT: Yale University Press.

Harrah-Conforth, J., & Borsos, J. (1991). The evolution of professional fund raising: 1890 to 1990. In D. F. Burlingame & L. J. Hulse (Eds.), *Taking fund raising seriously: Advancing the profession and practice of raising money* (pp. 18–36). San Francisco, CA: Jossey-Bass.

Hartsook, R. F. (1993, May). Nurturing deferred gifts. *Fund Raising Management*, pp. 47–48, 63.

Harvey, J. W., & McCrohan, K. F. (1990). Changing conditions for fund raising and philanthropy. In J. Van Til & Associates, *Critical issues in American philanthropy: Strengthening theory and practice* (pp. 39–64). San Francisco, CA: Jossey-Bass.

Hawthorne, E. L. (1950). *Fund-raising for the small college*. New York: Bureau of Publications, Teachers College, Columbia University.

Heath, R. L., Liao, S., & Douglas, W. (1995). Effects of perceived economic harms and benefits on issue involvement, use of information sources, and actions: A study in risk communication. *Journal of Public Relations Research*, *7*(2), 89–109.

Heath, R. L., & Nelson, R. A. (1986). *Issues management: Corporate public policymaking in an information society.* Thousand Oaks, CA: Sage.

Hedgepeth, R. C. (1993). The institutionally related foundation. In M. J. Worth (Ed.), *Educational fund raising: Principles and practice* (pp. 323–336). Phoenix, AZ: American Council on Education and Oryx Press.

Hedgepeth, R. C. (1994, January 10). *Results of the NSFRE survey on developing educational offerings for the executive leadership of not-for-profit organizations* [Unpublished data].

Heetland, D. L. (1993, January). Identifying, evaluating and cultivating prospective donors. NSFRE *The Journal,* pp. 10–13.

Hendrix, J. A. (1995). *Public relations cases* (3rd ed.). Belmont, CA: Wadsworth.

Herman, R. D., & Block, S. R. (1990). The board's critical role in fund raising. In J. Van Til & Associates, *Critical issues in American philanthropy: Strengthening theory and practice* (pp. 222–241). San Francisco, CA: Jossey-Bass.

Herman, R. D., & Heimovics, R. D. (1990). The effective nonprofit executive: Leader of the board. *Nonprofit Management & Leadership, 1*(2), 167–180.

Hiebert, R. E. (1966). *Courtier to the crowd.* Ames: Iowa State University Press.

Hocker, J. L., & Wilmot, W. W. (1995). *Interpersonal conflict* (4th ed.). Dubuque, IA: Brown & Benchmark.

Hodgkinson, V. A. (1990). Mapping the nonprofit sector in the United States: Implications for research. *Voluntas, 1*(2), 6–36.

Hodgkinson, V. A., & Toppe, C. (1991). A new research and planning tool for managers: The national taxonomy of exempt entities. *Nonprofit Management & Leadership, 1*(4), 403–414.

Hodgkinson, V. A., & Weitzman, M. S. (1986). *Dimensions of the independent sector.* San Francisco, CA: Independent Sector and Jossey-Bass.

Hodgkinson, V. A., Weitzman, M. S., Abrahams, J. A., Crutchfield, E. A., & Stevenson, D. R. (1996). *Nonprofit almanac 1996–1997: Dimensions of the independent sector.* San Francisco, CA: Independent Sector and Jossey-Bass.

Hodgkinson, V. A., Weitzman, M. S., Toppe, C. M., & Noga, S. M. (1992). *Nonprofit almanac 1992–1993: Dimensions of the independent sector.* San Francisco, CA: Jossey-Bass.

Holt, L. (1993, October). To hell with strategic planning. CASE *Currents,* p. 72.

Hopkins, B. R. (1990). Legal issues in fund raising and philanthropy. In J. Van Til & Associates, *Critical issues in American philanthropy: Strengthening theory and practice* (pp. 204–221). San Francisco, CA: Jossey-Bass.

Hopkins, B. R. (1995, Fall). A struggle for balance. NSFRE *Advancing Philanthropy,* pp. 26–31.

Hopkins, B. R. (1996). *The legal answer book for nonprofit organizations.* New York: Wiley.

Horton, A. J. (1981). Acknowledgement of gifts and volunteer efforts. In F. C. Pray (Ed.), *Handbook for educational fund raising: A guide to successful principles and practices for colleges, universities, and schools* (pp. 265–268). San Francisco, CA: Jossey-Bass.

Hotaling, D. H., & Sabo, S. R. (1993, September). Postal partners. CASE *Currents,* pp. 54–58, 60.

Houle, C. O. (1989). *Governing boards: Their nature and nurture.* San Francisco, CA: Jossey-Bass.

House panel to suggest new laws on charity regulation early next year. (1993, November 30). *The Chronicle of Philanthropy,* p. 30.

Howe, F. (1985). What you need to know about fund raising. *Harvard Business Review, 63*(2), 18–21.

Howe, F. (1991). *The board member's guide to fund raising: What every trustee needs to know about raising money.* San Francisco, CA: Jossey-Bass.

Howes, R. (1994, January 23). Backer pushes MSU to go after the "best." *The Detroit News,* pp. 1D, 4D.

Hunt, M. (1990). *The compassionate beast.* New York: William Morrow.

Hunt, T., & Grunig, J. E. (1994). *Public relations techniques.* Fort Worth, TX: Harcourt Brace.

Huntsinger, J. (1994, March). What do you mean, "deregulation"? *The NonProfit Times,* pp. 56–57.

Hyman, H. H., & Sheatsley, P. B. (1947). Some reasons why information campaigns fail. *Public Opinion Quarterly, 11*(3), 412–423.

IEG's ninth: March sponsorship seminar to address impact. (1991, November 18). IEG *Special Events Report,* pp. 1–3.

Independent Charities of America (ICA). (1992, November 3). Get listed in workplace fund drives. Now! [Advertisement]. *The Chronicle of Philanthropy,* p. 17.

Independent Sector (IS). (1991). *Ethics and the nation's voluntary and philanthropic community: Obedience to the unenforceable.* Washington, DC: Author.

Independent Sector (IS). (1993). *Academic centers and programs focusing on the study of philanthropy, voluntarism, and not-for-profit activity* (3rd ed.). Washington, DC: Author.

Independent Sector (IS). (1994). *Giving & volunteering in the United States: Findings from a national survey* (1994 ed., Vol. I). Washington, DC: Author.

Independent Sector (IS). (1995). *Giving & volunteering in the United States: Findings from a national survey* (1994 ed., Vol. II). Washington, DC: Author.

Independent Sector (IS). (1996). *Giving & volunteering in the United States: Findings from a national survey* (1996 ed.). Washington, DC: Author.

Institute for Public Policy and Administration. (1988). *Part of the solution: Innovative approaches to nonprofit funding.* Washington, DC: Union for Experimenting Colleges and Universities.

Internal Revenue Service (IRS). (1995). *Statistics of income bulletin, 14*(4). Washington, DC: Department of the Treasury.

Internal Revenue Service (IRS). (1996). *1995 annual report.* Washington, DC: Department of the Treasury.

International Events Group (IEG). (1996). *1996 IEG sponsorship sourcebook.* (Available from Author, 640 North LaSalle, Suite 600, Chicago, IL 60610-3777.)

IRS revokes tax exemption of evangelist Falwell's ministry. (1993, April 20). *The Chronicle of Philanthropy,* p. 40.

Jacobson, H. K. (1986). Toward a network: Problems and opportunities in fund raising research. In R. F. Carbone, *An agenda for research on fund raising* (pp. 37–40). College Park, MD: Clearinghouse for Research on Fund Raising.

Jacobson, H. K. (1990). Research on institutional advancement: A review of progress and a guide to the literature. *The Review of Higher Education, 13*(4), 433–488

Jeavons, T. H. (1991). A historical and moral analysis of religious fund raising. In D. F. Burlingame & L. J. Hulse (Eds.), *Taking fund raising seriously: Advancing the profession and practice of raising money* (pp. 53–72). San Francisco, CA: Jossey-Bass.

Jeavons, T. H. (1994). Stewardship revisited: Secular and sacred views of governance and management. *Nonprofit and Voluntary Sector Quarterly, 23*(2), 107–122.

Jehl, J., & Payzant, T. W. (1992). Philanthropy and public school reform: A view from San Diego. *Teachers College Record, 93*(3), 472–487.

Jencks, C. (1987). Who gives to what? In W. W. Powell (Ed.), *The nonprofit sector: A research handbook* (pp. 321–339). New Haven, CT: Yale University Press.

Jenkins, J. C. (1989). Social movement philanthropy and American democracy. In R. Magat (Ed.), *Philanthropic giving: Studies in varieties and goals* (pp. 292–314). New York: Oxford University Press.

Jerry Lewis: Points of spite. (1992, March 23). *Newsweek,* p. 6.

Johnston, D. (1993a, November 16). A look at what the public gets for letting non-profits go untaxed [Review of *Free ride: The tax-exempt economy*]. *The Chronicle of Philanthropy,* p. 35.

Johnston, D. (1993b, March 9). The next scandal: Charity gambling. *The Chronicle of Philanthropy,* pp. 38–39.

Johnston, D. (1994, August 9). Trouble ahead for the poor man's gift annuity. *The Chronicle of Philanthropy,* pp. 45–46.

Jones, J. P. (Ed.). (1946). *The yearbook of philanthropy 1945–46.* New York: Inter-River Press.

Jones, J. P. (Ed.). (1949). *Philanthropy today.* New York: Inter-River Press.

Jordan, R. R., & Quynn, K. L. (1994, March). The new planned giving officer. *CASE Currents,* pp. 20–24.

Jordan, R. R., & Quynn, K. L. (1995). *Planned giving: Management, marketing, and law.* New York: Wiley.

Joseph, D. (1992, July 14). Pay for hospital fund raisers grew by 8.2%. *The Chronicle of Philanthropy,* p. 37.

Joseph, J. A. (1991). The corporate stake in community involvement: Has business lost its social conscience? In J. P. Shannon (Ed.), *The corporate contributions handbook: Devoting private means to public needs* (pp. 3–19). San Francisco, CA: Jossey-Bass.

Kalson, S. (1992, March 2). Contributing a fair share of lost faith. *Pittsburgh Post-Gazette Magazine,* p. 21.

Kanter, R. M. (1983). *The change masters: Innovation and entrepreneurship in the American corporation.* New York: Simon & Schuster.

Kanter, R. M., & Summers, D. V. (1987). Doing well while doing good: Dilemmas of performance measurement in nonprofit organizations and the need for a multiple-constituency approach. In W. W. Powell (Ed.), *The nonprofit sector: A research handbook* (pp. 154–166). New Haven, CT: Yale University Press.

Kantrowitz, B. (1991, October 7). Showing its age. *Newsweek,* pp. 54–58.

Kaplan, D. A. (1993, November 22). Take down the girlie calendars. *Newsweek,* p. 34.

Karl, B. D. (1991). The evolution of corporate grantmaking in America. In J. P. Shannon (Ed.), *The corporate contributions handbook: Devoting private means to public needs* (pp. 20–34). San Francisco, CA: Jossey-Bass.

Katz, D., & Kahn, R. L. (1978). *The social psychology of organizations* (2nd ed.). New York: Wiley.

Kay, R. (1994). The artistry of leadership: An exploration of the leadership process in voluntary not-for-profit organizations. *Nonprofit Management & Leadership, 4*(3), 285–300.

Kearns, K. P. (1992). From comparative advantage to damage control: Clarifying strategic issues using SWOT analysis. *Nonprofit Management & Leadership, 3*(1), 3–22.

Kelley, K. (1978). *Jackie Oh!* New York: Ballantine Books.

Kelly, K. S. (1979). *Predicting alumni giving: A study of donors and nondonors at the College of Journalism at the University of Maryland.* Unpublished master's thesis, University of Maryland, College Park.

Kelly, K. S. (1991a). *Fund raising and public relations: A critical analysis.* Hillsdale, NJ: Lawrence Erlbaum Associates.

Kelly, K. S. (1991b, Summer). Marketing: A flawed and dangerous approach to fund raising. NSFRE *The Journal,* pp. 28–34.

Kelly, K. S. (1991c). Public relations education incorporates fund raising: A report on a program of research. In N. L. Crowder & V. A. Hodgkinson (Eds.), *Compendium of resources for teaching about the nonprofit sector, voluntarism and philanthropy* (2nd ed., pp. 55–71). Washington, DC: Independent Sector.

Kelly, K. S. (1992). Fund raising: Functional element in public relations education. *Journalism Educator, 47*(2), 19–25.

Kelly, K. S. (1993a). Fund-raising encroachment on public relations: A clear and present danger to effective trustee leadership. *Nonprofit Management & Leadership, 4*(1), 47–68.

Kelly, K. S. (1993b, November). *Practitioner perceptions of public relations as a support function: Fund-raising encroachment revisited and informed.* Paper presented to the Educators Section, Public Relations Society of America National Conference, Orlando, FL.

Kelly, K. S. (1993c). Public relations and fund-raising encroachment: Losing control in the nonprofit sector. *Public Relations Review, 19*(4), 349–365.

Kelly, K. S. (1994a). Building fund-raising theory: An empirical test of four models of practice. *Essays on Philanthropy, 12.* Indianapolis: Indiana University, Center on Philanthropy.

Kelly, K. S. (1994b). Fund-raising encroachment and potential of the public relations department in the nonprofit sector. *Journal of Public Relations Research, 6*(1), 1–22.

Kelly, K. S. (1995a). The fund-raising behavior of U.S. charitable organizations. *Journal of Public Relations Research, 7*(2), 111–137.

Kelly, K. S. (1995b). Utilizing public relations theory to conceptualize and test models of fund raising. *Journalism & Mass Communication Quarterly, 72*(1), 106–127.

Kelly, K. S. (1996, Summer). NSFRE research agenda and policy. NSFRE *Advancing Philanthropy,* pp. 47–49.

Kelly, K. S. (1997a, February). The $500,000 penalty. CASE *Currents,* p. 56.

Kelly, K. S. (1997b). From motivation to mutual understanding: Shifting the domain of donor research. In D. F. Burlingame (Ed.), *Major issues facing fund raising* (pp. 139–162). New York: Wiley.

Kennedy, G. (1983). *Everything is negotiable: How to get a better deal.* Englewood Cliffs, NJ: Prentice-Hall.

Kerr, C. (1991, May–June). The new race to be Harvard or Berkeley or Stanford. *Change,* pp. 10, 15.

Killoran, R., & Estey, G. P. (1993, May). Planned gifts, major gifts: They belong together. *Fund Raising Management,* pp. 18–21, 63.

Kleid Company. (1996). *Seasonality study, update 20.* (Available from Author, 530 Fifth Avenue, 17th Floor, New York, NY 10036-5198.)

Klein, E. (1988, November 22). Survey finds women outnumber men among fund raisers; pay rises rapidly. *The Chronicle of Philanthropy,* pp. 1, 18.

Knauft, E. B. (1989). The management of corporate giving programs. In R. Magat (Ed.), *Philanthropic giving: Studies in varieties and goals* (pp. 261–276). New York: Oxford University Press.

Knott, R. A. (1992). *The makings of a philanthropic fundraiser: The instructive example of Milton Murray.* San Francisco, CA: Jossey-Bass.

Koperek, E. (1993, Winter). Writing winning grant proposals. NSFRE *Advancing Philanthropy,* pp. 47, 49.

Korten, D. (1989). *The U.S. voluntary sector and global realities: Issues for the 1990s.* Boston, MA: Institute for Development Research.

Lafer, M. (1996, July 29). *1995 CASE survey of institutional advancement: Male–female salary comparison* [Unpublished data].

Landers, A. (1993a, February 25). Landers apologizes for adding conclusions. Baton Rouge, LA, *The Advocate,* p. 9A.

Landers, A. (1993b, February 4). Questionable fund-raising company has changed its name. Lafayette, LA, *The Advertiser,* p. B-3.

Larkin, R. F. (1993, Fall). Making the case—by the numbers. NSFRE *Advancing Philanthropy,* pp. 47–49.

Larkin, R. F. (1995, Fall). Accounting for the charitable sector. NSFRE *Advancing Philanthropy,* pp. 21–25.

Layton, D. N. (1987). *Philanthropy and voluntarism: An annotated bibliography.* New York: The Foundation Center.

LDDS Communications. (1993, Fall). Lower long distance rates with your Ragin' Cajuns connection [Advertisement]. University of Southwestern Louisiana *La Louisiane,* p. 37.

Leatherman, C. (1994, September 7). Stanford's shift in direction. *The Chronicle of Higher Education,* pp. A29–A30.

Ledingham, J. A. (1993). The kindness of strangers: Predictor variables in a public information campaign. *Public Relations Review, 19*(4), 367–384.

Lenkowsky, L. (1995, April 6). A tale from Yale with lessons for fund raisers. *The Chronicle of Philanthropy,* pp. 43, 46.

Leonard, M. (1992). The response of the private sector: Foundations and entrepreneurs. *Teachers College Record, 93*(3), 376–381.

Less than half of Americans rate fundraisers trustworthy. (1990, March). *The NonProfit Times*, pp. 1, 17.

Levis, W. C. (1991). Investing more money in fund raising—wisely. In D. F. Burlingame & L. J. Hulse (Eds.), *Taking fund raising seriously: Advancing the profession and practice of raising money* (pp. 257–271). San Francisco, CA: Jossey-Bass.

Levner, N. (1993, Winter). Developing powerful campaign communications. NSFRE *Advancing Philanthropy*, pp. 39–41.

Levy, B. R. (1994, Spring). Any grant is a good grant. Not! NSFRE *Advancing Philanthropy*, pp. 41–43.

Lewin, K. (1975). *Field theory in social science*. Westport, CT: Greenwood Press. (Original work published 1951)

Lewis, P. F. (1993a, Winter). Leadership: Our opportunity. NSFRE *Advancing Philanthropy*, p. 9.

Lewis, P. F. (1993b, Fall). Toward a definition of profession. NSFRE *Advancing Philanthropy*, pp. 9–10.

Lewis, P. F. (1996, Spring). Expressing our profession. NSFRE *Advancing Philanthropy*, p. 3.

Lexus accelerates music ties. (1991, November 18). IEG *Special Events Report*, pp. 1–3.

Lies, V. S. (1994, Spring). Forum: Straight talk from donors. NSFRE *Advancing Philanthropy*, pp. 18–22.

Lindahl, W. E. (1992). *Strategic planning for fund raising: How to bring in more money using strategic resource allocation*. San Francisco, CA: Jossey-Bass.

Lindahl, W. E. (1994, Spring). Major league gifts: Keeping score. NSFRE *Advancing Philanthropy*, pp. 44–47.

Lindahl, W. E., & Winship, C. (1992a, October). *Interactive CHAID models for predicting donor giving behavior*. Paper presented to the Association for Research on Nonprofit Organizations and Voluntary Action Conference, New Haven, CT.

Lindahl, W. E., & Winship, C. (1992b). Predictive models for annual fundraising and major gift fundraising. *Nonprofit Management & Leadership, 3*(1), 43–64.

Linehan, J. D. (1961). *Some aspects of educational fund raising*. Washington, DC: American College Public Relations Association and American Alumni Council.

Loessin, B. A., & Duronio, M. A. (1989, May). *A model for fund raising effectiveness*. Paper presented to the Association for Institutional Research Annual Forum, Baltimore, MD.

Loessin, B. A., & Duronio, M. A. (1993). Characteristics of successful fund-raising programs. In M. J. Worth (Ed.), *Educational fund raising: Principles and practice* (pp. 39–50). Phoenix, AZ: American Council on Education and Oryx Press.

Lohmann, R. A. (1992a). The commons: A multidisciplinary approach to nonprofit organization, voluntary action, and philanthropy. *Nonprofit and Voluntary Sector Quarterly, 21*(3), 309–324.

Lohmann, R. A. (1992b). *The commons: New perspectives on nonprofit organizations and voluntary action*. San Francisco, CA: Jossey-Bass.

Lombardo, B. J. (1991). Conflicts of interest between nonprofits and corporate donors. In D. F. Burlingame & L. J. Hulse (Eds.), *Taking fund raising seriously: Advancing the profession and practice of raising money* (pp. 83–99). San Francisco, CA: Jossey-Bass.

Lombardo, B. J. (1995). Corporate philanthropy: Gift or business transaction? *Nonprofit Management & Leadership, 5*(3), 291–301.

Lord, J. G. (1983). *The raising of money: Thirty-five essentials every trustee should know*. Cleveland, OH: Third Sector Press.

Lowenberg, F. M. (Ed.). (1975). *Professional components in education for fund raising*. New York: Council on Social Work Education.

Lowery, S. A., & DeFleur, M. L. (1995). *Milestones in mass communication research: Media effects* (3rd ed.). White Plains, NY: Longman.

Luck, M. F. (1990, Summer). A new twist on old fund-raising maxims. NSFRE *The Journal*, pp. 30–33.

Luck, M. F., & Evans, G. A. (1993, February). All you really need to know about major gifts. *NSFRE News*, p. 12.

Lyddon, I. W. (1994, January). Paying attention—at all levels. *NSFRE News*, p. 9.

MacKeith, J. (1994). Interdepartmental relations and voluntary organizations: An exploration of tensions and why they arise. *Nonprofit Management & Leadership, 4*(4), 431–446.

Magat, R. (1989). Introduction. In R. Magat (Ed.), *Philanthropic giving: Studies in varieties and goals* (pp. 3–25). New York: Oxford University Press.

Magat, R. (1991). Publishing about philanthropy. *Essays on Philanthropy, 2*. Indianapolis: Indiana University, Center on Philanthropy.

Mantese, G. (1994, Summer). Winning negotiations. NSFRE *Advancing Philanthropy*, pp. 49–51.

Marchetti, D. (1995, November 2). Red Cross struggles with first deficit in 111-year history. *The Chronicle of Philanthropy*, pp. 50–51).

Marion, B. H. (1994). Decision making in ethics. In M. G. Briscoe (Ed.), *Ethics in fundraising: Putting values into practice (New directions for philanthropic fundraising*, No. 6, pp. 49–61). San Francisco, CA: Jossey-Bass.

Marlowe & Company. (1996, July–August). NSFRE educates legislators. *NSFRE News*, p. 3.

Marlowe, H. (1993, April). To advocate or not to advocate: NOT the question. *NSFRE News*, p. 5.

Marlowe, H. (1994a, March). Not-for-profits and the big chill. *NSFRE News*, pp. 4, 7.

Marlowe, H. (1994b, January). The tax-law changes are upon us. *NSFRE News*, pp. 3, 8.

Marshall, J. E., III. (1996, July 11). Foundations are not closed to new ideas [Letter to the editor]. *The Chronicle of Philanthropy*, p. 48.

Martin, M. W. (1994). *Virtuous giving: Philanthropy, voluntary service, and caring*. Bloomington: Indiana University Press.

Martin, P. (1996, Spring). In the company of sponsors. NSFRE *Advancing Philanthropy*, pp. 30–33.

Marts, A. C. (1953). *Philanthropy's role in civilization*. New York: Harper & Brothers.

Marts, A. C. (1961). *Man's concern for his fellow man*. Geneva, NY: W. F. Humphrey Press.

Maryland v. Joseph H. Munson Co., 467 U.S. 947 (1984).

Matching gifts go high-tech. (1996, June). CASE *Currents*, p. 5.

Mauss, M. (1954). *The gift: Forms and functions of exchange in archaic societies*. Glencoe, IL: The Free Press. (Original work published 1925)

McCarthy, K. D. (1992). *Women's culture: American philanthropy and art, 1830–1930*. Chicago: University of Chicago Press.

McCombs, M. E., & Shaw, D. L. (1972). The agenda-setting function of the mass media. *Public Opinion Quarterly, 36*(2), 176–187.

McCombs, M. E., & Shaw, D. L. (1993). The evolution of agenda-setting research: Twenty-five years in the marketplace of ideas. *Journal of Communication, 43*(2), 58–67.

McConnell, T. R. (1981). Autonomy and accountability: Some fundamental issues. In P. G. Altbach & R. O. Berdahl (Eds.), *Higher education in American society* (pp. 35–53). Buffalo, NY: Prometheus Books.

McElreath, M. P. (1997). *Managing systematic and ethical public relations* (2nd ed.). Dubuque, IA: Brown & Benchmark.

McGoldrick, W. P. (1993). Campaigning in the nineties. In M. J. Worth (Ed.), *Educational fund raising: Principles and practice* (pp. 143–158). Phoenix, AZ: American Council on Education and Oryx Press.

McIlquham, J. D. (1978, March–April). Developing women: Their attitudes, ambitions, growth. *Fund Raising Management*, pp. 19–28.

McIlquham, J. D. (1995, March). Rebuilding from a pillar's fall. *The NonProfit Times*, pp. 15–16.

McLaughlin, B. (Ed.). (1995). *Who gets grants/Who gives grants: Nonprofit organizations and the foundation grants they received* (3rd ed.). New York: The Foundation Center.

McLeod, J. M., & Chaffee, S. H. (1973). Interpersonal approaches to communication research. *American Behavioral Scientist, 16*(4), 469–500.

McNamee, M. (1993, February). The transforming gift; Can there be a transforming gift in your future? CASE *Currents*, pp. 6–8, 18–24.

McNamee, M. (1994, March). Such a deal! CASE *Currents*, pp. 30–33.

Meckstroth, A. (1994). Nonprofit organizations and charitable giving, 1986–1992: A compendium of statistical information and analyses. *Nonprofit Management & Leadership, 4*(3), 359–364.

Median salaries of administrators, 1986–87. (1987, April 22). *The Chronicle of Higher Education*, p. 18.

Median salaries of college and university administrators, 1990–91. (1991, January 23). *The Chronicle of Higher Education*, p. A15.

Mehegan, S., Bush, B., & Nacson, S. (1994, March). Charity regulation today: How the states see it. *The NonProfit Times*, pp. 1, 12–19.

Melillo, W. (1989, March 21). Lawsuit charges man was fired for refusal to give to United Way. *The Chronicle of Philanthropy*, pp. 5, 11.

Meuth, E. F. (1991). *Corporate philanthropy in American higher education: An investigation of attitudes towards giving*. Unpublished doctoral dissertation, University of Akron, Akron, OH.

Middleton, M. (1987). Nonprofit boards of directors: Beyond the governance function. In W. W. Powell (Ed.), *The nonprofit sector: A research handbook* (pp. 141–153). New Haven, CT: Yale University Press.

Millar, B. (1990, July 24). Lax rules for counting gifts seen harming fund raising's image. *The Chronicle of Philanthropy*, pp. 8–9.

Millar, B. (1992a, December 15). Easing the pressure to contribute. *The Chronicle of Philanthropy*, pp. 19–20.

Millar, B. (1992b, September 8). Peace Corps chief to head United Way. *The Chronicle of Philanthropy*, pp. 19–20.

Millar, B. (1992c, April 7). United Way of America: "A story of excess." *The Chronicle of Philanthropy*, pp. 1, 33.

Millar, B. (1993a, August 10). Giving to United Way falls 4.1%, worst decline since World War II. *The Chronicle of Philanthropy*, p. 33.

Millar, B. (1993b, March 9). Nation's oldest United Way faces the fight of its life. *The Chronicle of Philanthropy*, pp. 23, 26.

Millar, B. (1994a, September 6). Investigators explore whether a health charity serves as a drug company's marketing arm. *The Chronicle of Philanthropy*, pp. 7, 18.

Millar, B. (1994b, March 8). More United Way donors said to earmark gifts. *The Chronicle of Philanthropy*, p. 35.

Millar, B. (1994c, January 25). Red Cross's ambitious fund-raising goal. *The Chronicle of Philanthropy*, pp. 22–25.

Millar, B. (1994d, August 9). United Way campaigns raise $3.05-billion, only a small increase over previous year. *The Chronicle of Philanthropy*, pp. 25, 28.

Millar, B. (1994e, April 5). A warning for United Way leaders. *The Chronicle of Philanthropy*, pp. 27–28.

Millar, B., & Moore, J. (1993, March 9). United Way: A year later, controversy lingers. *The Chronicle of Philanthropy*, pp. 1, 26–28.

Millar, B., & Moore, J. (1994, February 8). Foundation giving: Slow growth ahead. *The Chronicle of Philanthropy*, pp. 6–7, 12–15.

Milofsky, C., & Blades, S. D. (1991). Issues of accountability in health charities: A case study of accountability problems among nonprofit organizations. *Nonprofit and Voluntary Sector Quarterly, 20*(4), 371–393.

Miltner, J. R. (1990). *A study of the characteristics of successful chief development officers in selected public colleges and universities.* Unpublished doctoral dissertation, Union Institute, Cincinnati, OH.

Minnesota charges charity with deceptive fund raising. (1997, January 23). *The Chronicle of Philanthropy*, p. 23.

Mixer, J. R. (1993). *Principles of professional fundraising: Useful foundations for successful practice.* San Francisco, CA: Jossey-Bass.

Mongon, G. J., Jr. (1992). *NSFRE profile: 1992 membership survey.* Alexandria, VA: National Society of Fund Raising Executives.

Mongon, G. J., Jr. (1996). *NSFRE profile: 1995 membership survey.* Alexandria, VA: National Society of Fund Raising Executives.

Montague, W. (1990), January 9). Proliferating "look-alikes" cause headaches for many charities. *The Chronicle of Philanthropy*, pp. 25–26.

Moore, J. (1992, August 11). Congress weighs major tax changes. *The Chronicle of Philanthropy*, pp. 21–22.

Moore, J. (1993, December 14). A joint bid to find ecologists at the office. *The Chronicle of Philanthropy*, pp. 26, 28–30.

Moore, J. (1994, July 26). Pills to carry name, hopes of arthritis fund. *The Chronicle of Philanthropy*, p. 28.

Moore, J. (1995, May 18). Foundations urged to catch the wave of information technology. *The Chronicle of Philanthropy*, p. 14.

Moore, J. (1996a, October 31). Drug manufacturer kills controversial "Arthritis Foundation" pain relievers. *The Chronicle of Philanthropy*, p. 64.

Moore, J. (1996b, April 18). Education group issues guide for reporting gifts. *The Chronicle of Philanthropy*, pp. 28–30.

Moore, J., & Williams, G. (1996a, September 5). Dole scales back planned tax credits for people who give to help the poor. *The Chronicle of Philanthropy*, pp. 27–28.

Moore, J., & Williams, G. (1996b, October 17). Taxing times for the tax agency. *The Chronicle of Philanthropy*, pp. 1, 29–31.

Moore, J. E. (1993, July 13). I already gave, so why do charities keep asking? *The Chronicle of Philanthropy*, pp. 40–41.

Moran, W. J. (1991, July). Where the real money is in planned giving. *Fund Raising Management*, pp. 38, 40, 42, 54.

Mundy, L. (1993, March–April). The dirty dozen: Academia's skankiest funders. *Lingua Franca*, p. 1, 24–31.

Murawski, J. (1994a, October 18). Rising interest rates and an IRS action lure donors to pooled-income funds. *The Chronicle of Philanthropy*, p. 27.

Murawski, J. (1994b, November 1). A rush to donate to foundations. *The Chronicle of Philanthropy*, pp. 7–8.

Murawski, J. (1995a, December 14). Congress votes to exempt gift annuities from antitrust and securities laws. *The Chronicle of Philanthropy*, pp. 27, 29.

Murawski, J. (1995b, July 13). Former United Way Chief gets 7 years in jail; sentence praised by charities. *The Chronicle of Philanthropy*, p. 37.

Murawski, J. (1995c, September 7). House votes to place new limits on lobbying by non-profit groups. *The Chronicle of Philanthropy*, p. 47.

Murawski, J. (1995d, October 5). New public-interest law firm to challenge regulations on fund raising. *The Chronicle of Philanthropy*, p. 32.

Murawski, J. (1996, September 19). Law penalizing lavish non-profit salaries causes uncertainty. *The Chronicle of Philanthropy*, pp. 37, 39, 42.

Murawski, J., & Moore, J. (1995, March 23). Capital-gains cut may hurt charitable remainder trusts. *The Chronicle of Philanthropy*, pp. 32–33.

Murawski, J., & Stehle, V. (1996, September 5). Donors get new tax breaks for stock gifts. *The Chronicle of Philanthropy*, p. 51.

Murawski, J., & Williams, G. (1996, August 8). Tax watch. *The Chronicle of Philanthropy*, p. 51.

Murray, D. J. (1995, Spring). The CEO's role in fund raising. NSFRE *Advancing Philanthropy*, pp. 19–23.

Muscular-Dystrophy group cuts staff by 5%. (1992, January 28). *The Chronicle of Philanthropy*, p. 32.

Mutz, J. M. (1993, August). *Keynote address*. Speech presented at the Indiana University Center on Philanthropy Sixth Annual Symposium on Taking Fund Raising Seriously, Indianapolis, IN.

Myers, D. G. (1993, March). Major gift marching orders. CASE *Currents*, p. 16–19.

Nahm, R., & Zemsky, R. M. (1993). The role of institutional planning in fund raising. In M. J. Worth (Ed.), *Educational fund raising: Principles and practice* (pp. 57–66). Phoenix, AZ: American Council on Education and Oryx Press.

National Association of Fundraising Ticket Manufacturers (NAFTM). (1996). *Charity gaming in North America: 1995 report*. (Available from Author, 810 Lumber Exchange Building, 10 South Fifth Street, Minneapolis MN 55402.)

National Commission on Graduate Study in Public Relations. (1985). *Advancing public relations education: Recommended curriculum for graduate public relations education*. New York: Foundation for Public Relations Research and Education.

National Commission on Private Philanthropy and Public Needs. (1977). *Giving in America: Toward a stronger voluntary sector*. Washington, DC: U.S. Treasury Department.

National Committee on Planned Giving. (1994). *A guide to starting a planned giving program*. (Available from Author, 310 North Alabama, Suite 210, Indianapolis, IN 46204-2103.)

National Federation of Nonprofits. (1994). *Analysis of comments received by the American Institute of Certified Public Accountants*. (Available from Author, 815 15th Street, N.W., Suite 822, Washington, DC 20005-2201.)

National Society of Fund Raising Executives (NSFRE). (1996, June 28). *Summary report of 1996 membership: NSFRE demographic information* [Unpublished data].

National Society of Fund Raising Executives (NSFRE). (1997). *Payments in lieu of taxes: A position paper*. (Available from Author, 1101 King Street, Suite 700, Alexandria, VA 22314-2967).

National Society of Fund Raising Executives (NSFRE) Institute. (1986). *Glossary of fund-raising terms*. Alexandria, VA: NSFRE.

Netherton, R. (1994, March). New twists on old technology. CASE *Currents*, pp. 38–42.

New drive to spur gifts to charity. (1995, April 20). *The Chronicle of Philanthropy*, p. 16.

New England Association of Catholic Development Officers (NEACDO). (1993, September 1). *Together, we advance: Report of the 1993 survey of development programs in Catholic elementary and secondary schools in 11 New England Dioceses*. (Available from Author, c/o Development Office, Ste. Jeanne d'Arc School, 69 Dracut Street, Lowell, MA 01854.)

New ruling explains standards for pooled-income funds. (1994, July 12). *The Chronicle of Philanthropy*, p. 36.

New School for Social Research. (1996, March). A master of science degree in nonprofit management [Advertisement]. *The NonProfit Times*, p. 40.

"New York": History museum faces criticism over spending. (1992, April 7). *The Chronicle of Philanthropy*, p. 37.

"The New Yorker": Bill Gates and his future philanthropy. (1994, January 25). *The Chronicle of Philanthropy*, p. 37.

Newcomb, P. (1995, October 16). The Forbes four hundred. *Forbes*, pp. 106–368.

Newcomb, T. M. (1953). An approach to the study of communicative acts. *Psychological Review, 60*(6), 393–404.

Newman, J. (1992, May). Thinking of a career switch? Try PR! *Cosmopolitan*, pp. 96–98.

Nichols, J. E. (1992). *Targeted fund raising: Defining and refining your development strategy*. Chicago: Precept Press.

Nicklin, J. L. (1992, October 21). Fund drives flourish, but how much do they really raise? *The Chronicle of Higher Education*, pp. A33–A35.

Nielsen, W. A. (1985). *The golden donors: A new anatomy of the great foundations*. New York: Dutton.

Nielsen, W. A. (1992, October 6). A reason to have fund raisers: Stingy rich people. *The Chronicle of Philanthropy*, pp. 41–42.

Nielsen, W. A. (1993, November 2). Why some foundations are too small. *The Chronicle of Philanthropy*, pp. 63–64.

$90-million gift causes rift among Christian Scientists. (1991, October 8). *The Chronicle of Philanthropy*, p. 16.

Novak, M. (1988). An essay on "public" and "private." In R. L. Payton, M. Novak, B. O'Connell, & P. D. Hall, *Philanthropy: Four views* (pp. 11–26). New Brunswick, NJ: Transaction Books.

NPT 100 Directory. (1992, November). *The NonProfit Times*, p. 28.

NSFRE chapters, members on rise. (1993, May). *Fund Raising Management*, pp. 52, 54.

Nudd, S. P. (1991). Thinking strategically about information. In H. A. Rosso & Associates, *Achieving excellence in fund raising: A comprehensive guide to principles, strategies, and methods* (pp. 174–189). San Francisco, CA: Jossey-Bass.

O'Connell, B. (1991). The strategic links between business and the nonprofit sector. In J. P. Shannon (Ed.), *The corporate contributions handbook: Devoting private means to public needs* (pp. 35–49). San Francisco, CA: Jossey-Bass.

O'Connell, B. (1993). *The board member's book: Making a difference in voluntary organizations* (2nd ed.). New York: The Foundation Center.

Odendahl, T. J. (1989). Independent foundations and wealthy donors. In R. Magat (Ed.), *Philanthropic giving: Studies in varieties and goals* (pp. 159–179). New York: Oxford University Press.

Odendahl, T. J. (1990). *Charity begins at home: Generosity and self-interest among the philanthropic elite.* New York: Basic Books.

Office of the Attorney General, Commonwealth of Massachusetts. (1992, November). *Attorney General's report on charitable fundraising.* (Available from Author, Division of Public Charities, One Ashburton Place, Boston, MA 02108.)

O'Neill, M. (1989). *The third America.* San Francisco, CA: Jossey-Bass.

Opinion, timing—not info—triggers human behavior, says consultant. (1993, November 22). *PR News*, p. 8.

Ormstedt, D. E. (1995, Fall). A regulation primer: What the laws say. NSFRE *Advancing Philanthropy*, pp. 11–15.

The orphanage. (1994, December 12). *Newsweek*, pp. 28–32.

O'Shea, C. L. (1993, November–December). Countdown to success. CASE *Currents*, pp. 30–36.

Osterholt, J. W. (1996, June 13). UCLA fund raiser on why he left [Letter to the editor]. *The Chronicle of Philanthropy*, p. 44.

Ostrander, S. A., & Schervish, P. G. (1990). Giving and getting: Philanthropy as a social relation. In J. Van Til & Associates, *Critical issues in American philanthropy: Strengthening theory and practice* (pp. 67–98). San Francisco, CA: Jossey-Bass.

Ostrower, F. (1989). Donor control and perpetual trusts: Does anything last forever? In R. Magat (Ed.), *Philanthropic giving: Studies in varieties and goals* (pp. 279–291). New York: Oxford University Press.

Other people's money. (1992, March 16). *Newsweek*, pp. 46–47.

Over $45-million raised for muscular dystrophy. (1992, September 22). *The Chronicle of Philanthropy*, p. 30.

The Oxford English Dictionary (2nd ed.). (1989). Oxford: Clarendon Press.

Pa. judge says private college does not deserve tax exemption. (1994, September 6). *The Chronicle of Philanthropy*, p. 47.

Pa. sues police group again for fraud. (1996, May 2). *The Chronicle of Philanthropy*, p. 31.

Pace, R. W. (1983). *Organizational communication: Foundations for human resource development.* Englewood Cliffs, NJ: Prentice-Hall.

Packard, V. (1957). *The hidden persuaders.* New York: David McKay.

Panas, J. (1984). *Megagifts: Who gives them, who gets them.* Chicago: Pluribus Press.

Parsons, M. H. (1993). *Negotiating the planned gift for higher education: A learning organization paradigm.* Unpublished doctoral dissertation, University of Minnesota, Minneapolis.

Pavlik, J. V. (1987). *Public relations: What research tells us.* Thousand Oaks, CA: Sage.

Payton, R. L. (1981). Essential qualities of the development officer. In F. C. Pray (Ed.), *Handbook for educational fund raising: A guide to successful principles and practices for colleges, universities, and schools* (pp. 282–284). San Francisco, CA: Jossey-Bass.

Payton, R. L. (1986). Foreword. In R. F. Carbone, *An agenda for research on fund raising* (pp. 7–13). College Park: University of Maryland, Clearinghouse for Research on Fund Raising.

Payton, R. L. (1987). American values and private philanthropy; Philanthropic values; The philanthropic dialogue. In K. W. Thompson (Ed.), *Philanthropy: Private means, public ends* (pp. 3–46, 123–136). Lanham, MD: University Press of America.

Payton, R. L. (1988a). *Philanthropy: Voluntary action for the public good.* New York: American Council on Education and Macmillan.

Payton, R. L. (1988b). Philanthropy in action. In R. L. Payton, M. Novak, B. O'Connell, & P. D. Hall, *Philanthropy: Four views* (pp. 1–10). New Brunswick, NJ: Transaction Books.

Payton, R. L. (1990). Teaching philanthropy, teaching about philanthropy. In J. Van Til & Associates, *Critical issues in American philanthropy: Strengthening theory and practice* (pp. 167–187). San Francisco, CA: Jossey-Bass.

Payton, R. L. (1991). Foreword. In H. A. Rosso & Associates, *Achieving excellence in fund raising: A comprehensive guide to principles, strategies, and methods* (pp. xiii–xv). San Francisco, CA: Jossey-Bass.

Payton, R. L., Rosso, H. A., & Tempel, E. R. (1991). Toward a philosophy of fund raising; Taking fund raising seriously: An agenda. In D. F. Burlingame & L. J. Hulse (Eds.), *Taking fund raising seriously: Advancing the profession and practice of raising money* (pp. 3–17, 272–281). San Francisco, CA: Jossey-Bass.

Pearsall, F. W. (1943, January). How we do it at Northfield. ACPA/ACPRA *Publicity Problems*, pp. 8–10.

People. (1996, November 28). *The Chronicle of Philanthropy*, pp. 34–35.

Peters, T. J., & Waterman, R. H., Jr. (1982). *In search of excellence.* New York: Warner.

Peterson, V. T. (1993, October 5). Counting campaign gifts. It's time for reform. *The Chronicle of Philanthropy*, pp. 42–43.

Peterson, V. T. (1994). Preface: Why institutions need campaign standards. In *CASE campaign standards: Management and reporting standards for educational fund-raising campaigns* (pp. iii–iv). Washington, DC: Council for Advancement and Support of Education.

Petty, R. E., & Cacioppo, J. T. (1986). *Communication and persua-sion: Central and peripheral routes to attitude change.* New York: Springer-Verlag.

Pfeffer, J., & Salancik, G. R. (1978). *The external control of organizations: A resource dependence perspective.* New York: Harper & Row.

Philadelphia urges charities to pay fees for city services. (1994, July 12). *The Chronicle of Philanthropy*, p. 36.

The philanthropy 400. (1991, November 19). *The Chronicle of Philanthropy*, pp. 1, 20–27, 30–32.

The philanthropy 400. (1993, November 2). *The Chronicle of Philanthropy*, pp. 1, 24–39, 42–44.

The philanthropy 400. (1995, November 2). *The Chronicle of Philanthropy*, pp. 1, 32–48, 51–53.

The philanthropy 400. (1996, October 31). *The Chronicle of Philanthropy*, pp. 1, 40–47, 50–60.

Philanthropy 2000: Talking with Robert Payton. (1993, Winter). NSFRE *Advancing Philanthropy*, pp. 12–17.

Phillips, A., & Taylor, B. (1980). Sex and skill: Notes towards a feminist economics. *Feminist Review*, pp. 5–9.

Podolsky, D. (1995, December 4). Inside the cancer charities: Why they draw more queries than other health groups. *U.S. News & World Report*, pp. 84–85.

Points of Light Foundation. (1993). *Corporate volunteer programs: Benefits to business.* (Available from Author, Corporate Outreach Services, 1737 H Street, N.W., Washington, DC 20006.)

Poll finds public ill-informed about United Way aid. (1992, October 6). *The Chronicle of Philanthropy*, p. 30.

Pollard, J. A. (1958). *Fund-raising for higher education.* New York: Harper & Brothers.

Porter, W. E. (1958). *The advancement of understanding and support of higher education: A conference on organizational principles and patterns of college and university relations.* Washington, DC: American College Public Relations Association.

Powell, W. W. (Ed.). (1987). *The nonprofit sector: A research handbook.* New Haven, CT: Yale University Press.

Pratt, J. (1991). What grantmakers should know about today's grantseekers. In J. P. Shannon (Ed.), *The corporate contributions handbook: Devoting private means to public needs* (pp. 213–226). San Francisco, CA: Jossey-Bass.

Pray, F. C. (Ed.). (1981). *Handbook for educational fund raising: A guide to successful principles and practices for colleges, universities, and schools.* San Francisco, CA: Jossey-Bass.

Press clippings. (1996, October 31). *The Chronicle of Philanthropy*, p. 68.

Preston, L. E. (1981). Corporate power and social performance: Approaches to positive analysis. In L. E. Preston (Ed.), *Research in corporate social performance and policy* (Vol. 3, pp. 1–16). Greenwich, CT: JAI.

Prince, R. A., File, K. M., & Gillespie, J. E. (1993). Philanthropic styles. *Nonprofit Management & Leadership, 3*(3), 255–268.

Professional opportunities. (1992, December 1). *The Chronicle of Philanthropy*, pp. 45–55.

Professional opportunities. (1993, June 29). *The Chronicle of Philanthropy*, pp. 49–55.

Profits up for Fortune 500. (1997, April 8). Lafayette, LA, *The Advertiser*, p. D-1.

Public Relations Society of America (PRSA) Research Committee, Body of Knowledge Task Force. (1988). Public relations body of knowledge task force report. *Public Relations Review, 14*(3), 3–40.

Public TV: "Safely splendid" or "left wing"? (1991, December 17). *The Chronicle of Philanthropy*, p. 33.

Quinn, J. B. (1993, August 16). How to plan ahead for the new tax hit. *Newsweek*, pp. 24–25.

Quinn, J. B. (1994, December 12). The Santa season: Tax-saving charitable gifts; How to do well by doing good. *Newsweek*, p. 61.

Radelat, A. (1995, August 24). Acadiana native picked for key diplomatic job. Lafayette, LA, *The Advertiser*, p. A-6.

Redman, C. (1993, October 14). Bingo's shrinking slice of state gambling pie. Baton Rouge, LA, *The Advocate*, p. 10B.

Reeves, F. (1992, March 13). Casey backs bill to open Pitt books. *Pittsburgh Post-Gazette*, pp. 1, 3.

Reiss, A. H. (1993, May). A winner on the mall. *Fund Raising Management*, pp. 49–51.

Renz, L. (1991). Researching foundations: What we know and how we find out. *Nonprofit Management & Leadership, 1*(3), 293–300.

Renz, L., & Lawrence, S. (1993). *Foundation giving: Yearbook of facts and figures on private, corporate and community foundations* (1993 ed.). New York: The Foundation Center.

Renz, L., Lawrence, S., & Treiber, R. R. (1995). *Foundation giving: Yearbook of facts and figures on private, corporate and community foundations* (1995 ed.). New York: The Foundation Center.

Riddle, C. N. (1990, January 9). Charities risk a loss of public confidence if they don't help fight fund-raising fraud. *The Chronicle of Philanthropy*, pp. 28–29.

Riley v. National Federation of the Blind of North Carolina, 108 S. Ct. 2667 (1988).

Rise in gifts to United Ways fails to keep pace with inflation rate. (1992, June 16). *The Chronicle of Philanthropy*, p. 26.

Robbins, S. P. (1990). *Organization theory: Structure, design, and applications* (3rd ed.). Englewood Cliffs, NJ: Prentice-Hall.

Rockefeller, D., Jr. (1992). America 2000 and philanthropy's education agenda. *Teachers College Record, 93*(3), 370–375.

Rocque, A. (1995). Threat of federal cutbacks helps bring increases in donations to public TV. *The Chronicle of Philanthropy*, p. 27.

Rogers, E. M., Dearning, J. W., & Chang, S. (1991). AIDS in the 1980s: The agenda-setting process for a public issue. *Journalism Monographs, 126*.

Ronald McDonald children's charities receive $50-million gift. (1995, November 2). *The Chronicle of Philanthropy*, p. 11.

Rosenman, M. (1992, June 16). After the United Way scandal: Non-profits must return to their altruistic roots. *The Chronicle of Philanthropy*, pp. 40–41.

Rosenman, M. (1995, Summer). The new Congress: Changing the terms of the social contract? NSFRE *Advancing Philanthropy*, pp. 53–56.

Rosso, H. A. (1991). Preface; A philosophy of fund raising; Understanding the fund raising cycle; Developing a constituency: Where fund raising begins; The annual fund: A building block for fund raising; Asset building through capital fund raising; The trustee's role in fund raising; Putting it all together: The integrated development plan. In H. A. Rosso & Associates, *Achieving excellence in fund raising: A comprehensive guide to principles, strategies, and methods* (pp. xvii–xx, 3–15, 28–38, 51–64, 80–95, 133–139, 286–293). San Francisco, CA: Jossey-Bass.

Rosso, H. A., & Associates. (1991). *Achieving excellence in fund raising: A comprehensive guide to principles, strategies, and methods*. San Francisco, CA: Jossey-Bass.

Rotstein, G. (1992, February 28). Paradoxical O'Connor changes Pitt. *Pittsburgh Post-Gazette*, pp. 1, 5.

Rudney, G. (1987). The scope and dimensions of nonprofit activity. In W. W. Powell (Ed.), *The nonprofit sector: A research handbook* (pp. 55–64). New Haven, CT: Yale University Press.

Ruge, R. B., & Speizman, R. A. (1993, November 1). Substantiation and disclosure of charitable contributions: Congress asks for more. *Tax Notes*, pp. 609–615.

Ryan, E. (1992, November–December). Many paths to endowment. CASE *Currents*, pp. 40–42, 44.

Ryan, E. (1993, July–August). Sticky wickets. CASE *Currents*, pp. 58–62.

Ryan, E. (1994a, January). Happy anniversary, matching gifts. CASE *Currents*, pp. 26–30.

Ryan, E. (1994b, June). Too many hooks. CASE *Currents*, pp. 34–37, 39.

Ryan, E. (1996, June). Making the most of the World Wide Web. CASE *Currents*, pp. 50–51.

Ryan, J. P. (1994, March). Thanks a million: You need strong recognition programs to foster healthy donor relations. CASE *Currents*, p. 64.

Sabo, S. R. (1994a, June). Hybrids in bloom. CASE *Currents*, pp. 28–29, 32–33.

Sabo, S. R. (1994b, April). Power plays. CASE *Currents*, pp. 10–15.

Salamon, L. M. (1993). Foundations as investment managers, Part II: The performance. *Nonprofit Management & Leadership, 3*(3), 239–253.

A sampling of charities' holiday mailings. (1993, December 14). *The Chronicle of Philanthropy*, pp. 32–34.

San Diego museum rejects Philip Morris. (1996, May 16). *The Chronicle of Philanthropy*, p. 15.

Sapp, R. E. (1993). Fundamentals of planned giving. In M. J. Worth (Ed.), *Educational fund raising: Principles and practice* (pp. 117–130). Phoenix, AZ: American Council on Education and Oryx Press.

Schervish, P. G. (1993, Fall). Does generosity run in the family? NSFRE *Advancing Philanthropy*, pp. 26–29.

Schervish, P. G., & Havens, J. J. (1994, August). *Wherewithal and beneficence: Charitable giving by income and wealth*. Paper presented at the Indiana University Center on Philanthropy Seventh Annual Symposium on Taking Fund Raising Seriously, Indianapolis, IN.

Schervish, P. G., & Havens, J. J. (1995). Do the poor pay more? Is the U-shaped curve correct? *Nonprofit and Voluntary Sector Quarterly, 24*(1), 79–90.

Schervish, P. G., & Havens, J. J. (1997). Social participation and charitable giving: A multivariate analysis. *Nonprofit and Voluntary Sector Quarterly, 26*(3).

Schervish, P. G., & Herman, A. (1988). *The study on wealth and philanthropy final report*. Chestnut Hill, MA: Social Welfare Research Institute, Boston College.

Schiff, J. (1989). Tax policy, charitable giving, and the nonprofit sector: What do we really know. In R. Magat (Ed.), *Philanthropic giving: Studies in varieties and goals* (pp. 128–142). New York: Oxford University Press.

Schmeling, D. G. (1990). *Planned giving for the one person develop-ment office: Taking the first steps* (2nd ed.). Wheaton, IL: Deferred Giving Services.

Schreiber, W. (1993, October). All roads lead to research. CASE *Currents*, pp. 24–28.

Schrum, J. B. (1993). Ethical issues in fund raising. In M. J. Worth (Ed.), *Educational fund raising: Principles and practice* (pp. 359–367). Phoenix, AZ: American Council on Education and Oryx Press.

Schuster, J. M. D. (1985). *Supporting the arts: An international comparative study.* Washington, DC: National Endowment for the Arts.

Schwartz, J. J. (1990). Introduction to the Transaction edition. In S. M. Cutlip, *Fund raising in the United States: Its role in America's philanthropy* (pp. xix–xxx). New Brunswick, NJ: Transaction.

Scripps Institute to get $100-million; other gifts. (1996, May 30). *The Chronicle of Philanthropy*, p. 16.

Sebastian, P. (1992, October 30). Nonprofit groups seek to set standard for ethics in aftermath of scandals. *The Wall Street Journal*, p. A7C.

Seltzer, M. (1987). *Securing your organization's future: A complete guide to fundraising strategies.* New York: The Foundation Center.

Seneker, H. (Ed.). (1993, October 18). The Forbes four hundred. *Forbes*, pp. 110–313.

Sennott, C. M. (1992). *Broken covenant.* New York: Simon & Schuster.

Seymour, H. J. (1947). *Designs for giving.* New York: Harper & Brothers.

Seymour, H. J. (1988). *Designs for fund-raising: Principles, patterns, techniques.* Rockville, MD: The Fund-Raising Institute. (Original work published 1966)

Shannon, J. P. (1991). Successful corporate grantmaking: Lessons to build on. In J. P. Shannon (Ed.), *The corporate contributions handbook: Devoting private means to public needs* (pp. 343–358). San Francisco, CA: Jossey-Bass.

Shapiro, J. P. (1993). *No pity: People with disabilities forging a new civil rights movement.* New York: Times Books.

Sharpe, R. F. (1989, September 19). An invasion of greedy tax-shelter promoters is threatening to harm charitable giving. *The Chronicle of Philanthropy*, p. 40.

Sharpe, R. F. (1993a, Winter). How to encourage gifts of life insurance to nonprofit institutions. NSFRE *The Journal*, pp. 16–17.

Sharpe, R. F. (1993b, Winter). Philanthropy in uncertain times. NSFRE *Advancing Philanthropy*, pp. 28–32.

Sheldon, K. S. (1991). Corporations as a gift market; Foundations as a source of support. In H. A. Rosso & Associates, *Achieving excellence in fund raising: A comprehensive guide to principles, strategies, and methods* (pp. 229–260). San Francisco, CA: Jossey-Bass.

Shell, A. (1989, July). Cause-related marketing: Big risks, big potential. *Public Relations Journal*, pp. 8, 13.

Shoemaker, D. (1992, November–December). The good ship endowment. CASE *Currents*, pp. 34–38.

Siegel, E. (1993). Operating a donor research office. In M. J. Worth (Ed.), *Educational fund raising: Principles and practice* (pp. 251–274). Phoenix, AZ: American Council on Education and Oryx Press.

Simmons, R. E. (1990). *Communication campaign management: A systems approach.* White Plains, NY: Longman.

Simon, J. G. (1987). Research on philanthropy. In K. W. Thompson (Ed.), *Philanthropy: Private means, public ends* (pp. 67–87). Lanham, MD: University Press of America.

Skolnik, R. (1993, September). Rebuilding trust: Nonprofits act to boost reputations. *Public Relations Journal*, pp. 29–32.

Small-business lobbyists complain of competition from charities. (1994, June 28). *The Chronicle of Philanthropy*, p. 32.

Smith, C. (1990, August–September). Cable cowboys come of age. *Corporate Philanthropy Report*, pp. 1, 14–15.

Smith, C. (1994, May–June). The new corporate philanthropy. *Harvard Business Review*, 72(3), 105–116.

Smith, C. F. (1992). *Lenny, Lefty, and the chancellor: The Len Bias tragedy and the search for reform in big-time college basketball.* Baltimore, MD: Bancroft Press.

Smith, D. H. (1993). The field of nonprofit and voluntary action research: Then and now. *Nonprofit and Voluntary Sector Quarterly*, 22(3), 197–200.

Smith, G. T. (1977). The development program. In A. W. Rowland (Ed.), *Handbook of institutional advancement* (pp. 142–151). San Francisco, CA: Jossey-Bass.

Smith, H. W. (1993). The maturity of corporate giving and its long-term consequences. *Nonprofit Management & Leadership*, 4(2), 215–228.

Smith, J. P. (1981). Rethinking the traditional capital campaign. In F. C. Pray (Ed.), *Handbook for educational fund raising: A guide to successful principles and practices for colleges, universities, and schools* (pp. 60–68). San Francisco, CA: Jossey-Bass.

Smith, J. P. (1982, September). Setting fund-raising priorities. CASE *Currents*, pp. 34–37.

Smucker, B. (1991). *The nonprofit lobbying guide: Advocating your cause—and getting results.* Washington, DC: Independent Sector.

Smurl, J. F. (1991). Three religious views about the responsibilities of wealth. *Essays on Philanthropy, 4.* Indianapolis: Indiana University, Center on Philanthropy.

Spinner, J. H. (1994, Winter). Reviews [Book review of *Fund raising and public relations: A critical analysis*]. NSFRE *Advancing Philanthropy*, pp. 56–57.

Squires, C. (1992, June). Don't let your donors go without a fight. *Fund Raising Management*, pp. 55–56.

St. Jude's given "holiday miracle." (1995, December 8). Lafayette, LA, *The Advertiser*, p. A-7.

Staley/Robeson/Ryan/St. Lawrence. (1988, August). Increased competition in the philanthropic environment. *Fund-Raising Institute Monthly Portfolio*, p. 1.

State of Minnesota Office of the Attorney General. (1994, November). *Million$ on the line: Professional fund-raising report*. (Available from Author, Charities Division, Suite 1200, NCL Tower, 445 Minnesota Street, St. Paul, MN 55101-2130.)

Status of billion-dollar campaigns. (1996, May 30). *The Chronicle of Philanthropy*, p. 32.

Steele, V., & Elder, S. D. (1992). *Becoming a fundraiser: The principles and practice of library development*. Chicago: American Library Association.

Stehle, V. (1989, July 25). Non-profit hospitals step up campaigns, hire more fund raisers. *The Chronicle of Philanthropy*, p. 5.

Stehle, V. (1990, January 9). 2 Oregon YMCA's stripped of property-tax exemptions. *The Chronicle of Philanthropy*, p. 25.

Stehle, V. (1992a, December 15). The Met's controversial Mr. Hoving. *The Chronicle of Philanthropy*, pp. 26–28.

Stehle, V. (1992b, October 6). University of Michigan joins ranks of institutions seeking $1-billion. *The Chronicle of Philanthropy*, pp. 31–32.

Stehle, V. (1993, May 4). Ronald McDonald Houses' $60-million surprise. *The Chronicle of Philanthropy*, p. 8.

Stehle, V. (1994a, July 12). Corporate giving: Big changes at big blue. *The Chronicle of Philanthropy*, pp. 6–9.

Stehle, V. (1994b, November 29). N.Y. Jewish federation's advertising controversy. *The Chronicle of Philanthropy*, pp. 23–26.

Stehle, V. (1994c, February 8). Soaring interest in annuities. *The Chronicle of Philanthropy*, pp. 27–29.

Stehle, V. (1995, February 23). Ketchum fund-raising company to close. *The Chronicle of Philanthropy*, p. 35.

Stehle, V. (1996a, December 12). Conflicts at the top threaten the existence of Independent Charities Federation. *The Chronicle of Philanthropy*, p. 35.

Stehle, V. (1996b, August 8). 2.3% increase for United Way. *The Chronicle of Philanthropy*, pp. 31–33.

Stehle, V., & Williams, G. (1994, May 31). Coping with a new law. *The Chronicle of Philanthropy*, pp. 22–23, 27–30.

Steinberg, R. (1987). Nonprofit organizations and the market. In W. W. Powell (Ed.), *The nonprofit sector: A research handbook* (pp. 118–138). New Haven, CT: Yale University Press.

Steinberg, R. (1989). The theory of crowding out: Donations, local government spending, and the "New Federalism." In R. Magat (Ed.), *Philanthropic giving: Studies in varieties and goals* (pp. 143–156). New York: Oxford University Press.

Steinberg, R. (1993a). Public policy and the performance of nonprofit organizations: A general framework. *Nonprofit and Voluntary Sector Quarterly, 22*(1), 13–31.

Steinberg, R. (1993b, June). *United Cancer Council v. Commission of the IRS and the indirect regulation of fundraising*. Paper presented to the Central Regional Tax Institute on Exempt Organizations Conference, Indianapolis, IN.

Steinberg, R., & Gray, B. H. (1994). "The role of nonprofit enterprise" in 1993: Hansmann revisited. *Nonprofit and Voluntary Sector Quarterly, 22*(4), 297–316.

Stendardi, E. J., Jr. (1992). Corporate philanthropy: The redefinition of enlightened self-interest. *Social Science Journal, 29*(1), 21–30.

Stephens, C. R. (1995, March). Why not licensing for fundraisers? *The NonProfit Times*, p. 70.

Stern, J., & Stern, M. (1991). *The encyclopedia of bad taste*. New York: HarperCollins.

Steuerle, E. (1987). The charitable giving patterns of the wealthy. In T. J. Odendahl (Ed.), *America's wealthy and the future of foundations* (pp. 203–221). New York: The Foundation Center.

Strand, B. J. (1996, June). Getting a payback from online services. CASE *Currents*, pp. 52–54.

Struck, R. (1993, May). Confirming the major gift. *Fund Raising Management*, pp. 37–39.

Synodinos, J. (1992, November–December). An endowment philosophy. CASE *Currents*, pp. 22–25.

Tata, J. (1993). The structure and phenomenon of sexual harassment: Impact of category of sexually harassing behavior, gender, and hierarchical level. *Journal of Applied Social Psychology, 23*(3), 199–211.

Tax watch. (1997, May 15). *The Chronicle of Philanthropy*, p. 47.

Tempel, E. R. (1991). Assessing organizational strengths and vulnerabilities. In H. A. Rosso & Associates, *Achieving excellence in fund raising: A comprehensive guide to principles, strategies, and methods* (pp. 19–27). San Francisco, CA: Jossey-Bass.

Texas hospitals would have to meet new charity-care rules under bill. (1993, June 15). *The Chronicle of Philanthropy*, p. 43.

Text of the report on United Way of America. (1992, April 7). *The Chronicle of Philanthropy*, pp. 22–33.

Thaves, B. (1995, June 15). Frank & Ernest. Lafayette, LA, *The Advertiser*, p. B-4.

Thieblot, B. A. (1992, October). Tracking the trends. CASE *Currents*, pp. 8–14.

Thinesen, S. A. (1992). *University public relations: An analysis of the relationship between university presidents and university public relations directors.* Unpublished master's thesis, St. Cloud State University, St. Cloud, MN.

Thompson, J. D. (1967). *Organizations in action: Social science bases of administrative theory.* New York: McGraw-Hill.

Thorsen, J. (1993, February). Spies are (not) everywhere. CASE *Currents*, p. 64.

3 universities get large donations; other recent gifts. (1996, May 16). *The Chronicle of Philanthropy*, p. 11.

Tidwell, G. L. (1993, May). The anatomy of a fraud. *Fund Raising Management*, pp. 58–62.

Titmus, R. M. (1970). *The gift relationship: From human blood to social policy.* London: Allen & Unwin.

Top Clinton adviser calls for end to mail subsidies for non-profits. (1992, December 15). *The Chronicle of Philanthropy*, p. 10.

Trachtenberg, S. J. (1993, November–December). What I expect of my CDO. CASE *Currents*, pp. 18–22.

Tuleja, T. (1985). *Beyond the bottom line.* New York: Facts on File.

Turk, J. V. (1986, June). The changing face of CASE. CASE *Currents*, pp. 18–20.

Turner, R. (1991). Metaphors fund raisers live by: Language and reality in fund raising. In D. F. Burlingame & L. J. Hulse (Eds.), *Taking fund raising seriously: Advancing the profession and practice of raising money* (pp. 37–50). San Francisco, CA: Jossey-Bass.

$12-million for college in Oregon; other recent gifts. (1993, June 15). *The Chronicle of Philanthropy*, p. 14.

2 charities sue company over promised donations. (1991, November 19). *The Chronicle of Philanthropy*, p. 8.

U. of Cal. at Berkeley receives $50-million; other recent gifts. (1995, January 26). *The Chronicle of Philanthropy*, p. 10.

United Negro College Fund extends capital campaign. (1993, December 13). *The Chronicle of Philanthropy*, p. 31.

United Way after Chao: Readers' advice on setting a new course. (1996, August 8). *The Chronicle of Philanthropy*, p. 55.

Univ. of Michigan raises $1-billion. (1996, May 30). *The Chronicle of Philanthropy*, p. 32.

Unkefer, J. M., & Chewning, P. B. (Eds.). (1992). *Institutional advancement professional area guide.* Washington, DC: Council for Advancement and Support of Education.

U.S. Bureau of the Census. (1993). *Statistical abstract of the United States: 1993* (113th ed.). Washington, DC: U.S. Government Printing Office.

U.S. Department of Labor, Employment and Training Administration. (1991). *Dictionary of occupational titles, Vol. I* (4th ed.). Washington, DC: U.S. Government Printing Office.

U.S. Small Business Administration. (1995). *The state of small business: A report of the President.* Washington, DC: U.S. Government Printing Office.

Useem, M. (1987). Corporate philanthropy. In W. W. Powell (Ed.), *The nonprofit sector: A research handbook* (pp. 340–359). New Haven, CT: Yale University Press.

Vandeventer, D. J. (1993). *The phenomenon of American philanthropy: A parallel to the theories of the Chicago school of social thought.* Unpublished master's thesis, University of Northern Iowa, Cedar Falls.

Van Til, J. (1988). *Mapping the third sector: Voluntarism in a changing social economy.* New York: The Foundation Center.

Van Til, J. (1990). Introduction; Defining philanthropy; Toward guidelines for effective philanthropic practice. In J. Van Til & Associates, *Critical issues in American philanthropy: Strengthening theory and practice* (pp. xix–xxiv, 19–38, 276–281). San Francisco, CA: Jossey-Bass.

Van Til, J. (1992). Foreword. In R. A. Lohmann, *The com-mons: New perspectives on nonprofit organizations and voluntary action* (pp. xi–xiii). San Francisco, CA: Jossey-Bass.

Van Til, J., & Associates. (1990). *Critical issues in American philanthropy: Strengthening theory and practice.* San Francisco, CA: Jossey-Bass.

Vermeulen, M. (1995, June 18). What people earn. *Parade Magazine*, pp. 4–7.

Village of Schaumburg v. Citizens for a Better Environment, 444 U.S. 620 (1980).

Von Schlegell, A., & Hickey, K. E. (1993, Winter). Women as donors: The hidden constituency. NSFRE *Advancing Philanthropy*, pp. 24–27.

Walker, M. M. (1995, February). Command performance. CASE *Currents*, pp. 37–39.

Walters, J. (1983, October). Uphold a code of ethics in the eighties? *Association Management*, pp. 63–107.

Warner, I. (1992a, March 16). If they drop the tax deduction, I won't mourn. *The Chronicle of Philanthropy*, pp. 35–36.

Warner, I. (1992b, April 21). Let's increase tax breaks for gifts to the truly needy. *The Chronicle of Philanthropy*, pp. 41–42.

Warner, I. (1994, March 8). Here's the secret of Jewish fund raising. *The Chronicle of Philanthropy*, pp. 53–54.

Warner, I. (1995, November 2). Fund raisers need to find a 2% solution. *The Chronicle of Philanthropy*, pp. 67–68.

Warwick, M. (1995, March). How much choice do donors want? *The NonProfit Times*, pp. 20, 22.

"The Washington Post": Small share of vending profits go to charity. (1993, October 19). *The Chronicle of Philanthropy*, p. 37.

Watchdog watch. (1992, November 17). *The Chronicle of Philanthropy*, p. 33.

Watchdog watch. (1995, November 2). *The Chronicle of Philanthropy*, p. 64.

Watchdog watch. (1996, May 30). *The Chronicle of Philanthropy*, p. 41.

Waterman, R. H., Jr. (1987). *The renewal factor*. New York: Bantam.

Webb, C. H. (1982). *A policy-relevant study of development programs at representative institutions within the State University of New York*. Unpublished doctoral dissertation, Michigan State University, East Lansing.

Webb, N. J. (1994). Tax and government policy implications for corporate foundation giving. *Nonprofit and Voluntary Sector Quarterly, 23*(1), 41–67.

Weeden, C. (1995, September 7). Companies won't give for the sake of giving [Letter to the editor]. *The Chronicle of Philanthropy*, p. 54.

Weick, K. E. (1979). *The social psychology of organizing* (2nd ed.). Reading, MA: Addison-Wesley.

Weisbrod, B. A. (1988). *The nonprofit economy*. Cambridge, MA: Harvard University Press.

Wetherell, B. L. (1989). *The effect of gender, masculinity, and femininity on the practice of and preference for the models of public relations*. Unpublished master's thesis, University of Maryland, College Park.

What's new in corporate philanthropy: It's a gift, or is it? (1994, February). *Inside PR*, pp. 23–25.

Whitaker, B. (1974). *The philanthropoids: Foundations and society*. New York: Morrow.

White, A., & Bartolomeo, J. (1982). *Corporate giving: The views of chief executive officers of major American corporations*. Washington DC: Council on Foundations.

White, J., & Dozier, D. M. (1992). Public relations and management decision making. In J. E. Grunig (Ed.), *Excellence in public relations and communication management: Contributions to effective organizations* (pp. 91–108). Hillsdale, NJ: Lawrence Erlbaum Associates.

Wilkerson, G. S., & Schuette, A. W. (1981). Elements of the annual giving program. In F. C. Pray (Ed.), *Handbook for educational fund raising: A guide to successful principles and practices for colleges, universities, and schools* (pp. 26–34). San Francisco, CA: Jossey-Bass.

Willard, T. J. (1984). *A study of the characteristics of successful chief development officers in selected private colleges and universities*. Unpublished doctoral dissertation, University of Colorado, Boulder.

Williams, G. (1991, October 8). Charity fraud: States intensify the battle. *The Chronicle of Philanthropy*, pp. 30, 34.

Williams, G. (1992a, November 3). Charities must prepare to confront greater scrutiny of their affairs, leaders say. *The Chronicle of Philanthropy*, p. 8.

Williams, G. (1992b, December 1). Do accounting rules help charities exaggerate their good works? *The Chronicle of Philanthropy*, pp. 30–31.

Williams, G. (1992c, September 8). Tax trial offers clues on how IRS plans to crack down on charity misconduct. *The Chronicle of Philanthropy*, pp. 21–22.

Williams, G. (1993a, March 9). Landers apologizes for altering letter from watchdog group. *The Chronicle of Philanthropy*, p. 32.

Williams, G. (1993b, October 5). Regulators' new strategy: Comparing charities' claims to their accomplishments. *The Chronicle of Philanthropy*, pp. 33–34.

Williams, G. (1994a, September 6). Congress considers measures to stem abuses by charities. *The Chronicle of Philanthropy*, p. 37.

Williams, G. (1994b, June 14). Deductions claimed for contributions continue to rise, IRS says. *The Chronicle of Philanthropy*, p. 40.

Williams, G. (1994c, March 22). IRS changes non-profit tax form to obtain more data on non-cash donations. *The Chronicle of Philanthropy*, pp. 32–33.

Williams, G. (1994d, May 31). IRS mulls change in little-known rules on charity auctions. *The Chronicle of Philanthropy*, pp. 23, 30.

Williams, G. (1994e, November 15). States, IRS announce moves to simplify registration and reporting by charities. *The Chronicle of Philanthropy*, pp. 29, 32–33.

Williams, G. (1994f, March 8). Watchdog group asks for new disclosure in charity mailings. *The Chronicle of Philanthropy*, pp. 33, 36.

Williams, G. (1994g, September 6, 1994). Watchdog to postpone new policy. *The Chronicle of Philanthropy*, p. 32.

Williams, G. (1995, November 30). Budget bill could have big effect on charities. *The Chronicle of Philanthropy*, p. 31.

Williams, G. (1996a, January 11). Charities asked to surrender earnings from fund-raising scheme. *The Chronicle of Philanthropy*, pp. 28–35.

Williams, G. (1996b, October 17). Charities plan lawsuits to fight government regulations they consider excessive. *The Chronicle of Philanthropy*, p. 31.

Williams, G. (1996c, August 8). A holy war against tax exemptions. *The Chronicle of Philanthropy*, pp. 1, 42–44.

Williams, G. (1996d, May 30). Philanthropy can't make up for federal cuts, study says. *The Chronicle of Philanthropy*, p. 38.

Williams, R. L. (1991, July–August). Presidential perceptions. CASE *Currents*, pp. 52–56.

Williams, R. L. (1993). The role of public relations in fund raising. In M. J. Worth (Ed.), *Educational fund raising: Principles and practice* (pp. 289–302). Phoenix, AZ: American Council on Education and Oryx Press.

Williams, R. L. (1996, February). Survey of advancement: Advancement's steady advance, salaries on the upswing, CASE's special cases. CASE *Currents*, pp. 8–22.

Willmer, W. K. (1993, October). Blueprint for a small college: Ten building blocks for strong advancement in challenging times. CASE *Currents*, pp. 36–40.

Winfree, W. (1992, November). *In pursuit of the major gift: Effective utilization of the president, trustees, private citizens and staff/faculty in the solicitation of major gifts.* Paper presented at the Indiana University Center on Philanthropy Fifth Annual Symposium on Taking Fund Raising Seriously, Indianapolis, IN.

Winship, A. L., II. (1984). *The quest for major gifts: A survey of 68 institutions.* Washington, DC: Council for Advancement and Support of Education.

Wise, C. B. (1994, November–December). Ready or not? CASE *Currents*, pp. 19–22.

Wolfenden, J. (1968). British university grants and government relations. In C. G. Dobbins & C. B. T. Lee (Eds.), *Whose goals for American higher education?* (pp. 206–215). Washington, DC: American Council on Education.

Wood, E. W. (1989). The four r's of major gift solicitation. *reid report* (141), 1, 6. (Available from Russ Reid Company, 2 North Lake Avenue, Pasadena, CA 91101.)

Wood, J. R., & Hougland, J. G., Jr. (1990). The role of religion in philanthropy. In J. Van Til & Associates, *Critical issues in American philanthropy: Strengthening theory and practice* (pp. 99–132). San Francisco, CA: Jossey-Bass.

Wood, J. T. (1992). Telling our stories: Narratives as a basis for theorizing sexual harassment. *Journal of Applied Communication Research, 20*(4), 349–362.

Worth, M. J. (Ed.). (1993). *Educational fund raising: Principles and practice.* Phoenix, AZ: American Council on Education and Oryx Press.

Wulff, J. (1995, Summer). A street-level view of the contract with America. NSFRE *Advancing Philanthropy*, pp. 11–14.

The years in review: Highlights of alumni administration's history. (1988, February). CASE *Currents*, pp. 22–24.

Ylvisaker, P. N. (1987). Foundations and nonprofit organizations. In W. W. Powell (Ed.), *The nonprofit sector: A research handbook* (pp. 360–379). New Haven, CT: Yale University Press.

Young, D. R. (1993). An interview with Brian O'Connell. *Nonprofit Management & Leadership, 3*(3), 313–320.

Zapler, M. (1994, September 7). Tax court rules that revenue from "affinity" cards is tax-free. *The Chronicle of Higher Education*, p. A52.

Author Index

A

Abbott, A., 105
Abrahams, J. A., 40, 68, 73, 328, 329, 599
Abrams, D. B., 513, 525, 532, 535
Adams, M. F., 87, 427, 475
Adler, J., 67, 479, 480, 618, 619
Aldrich, D. G., III, 464, 528, 540
Alexander, G. D., 10, 546, 548
Allen, P. A., 406, 411, 412
Altbach, P. G., 341
Altizer, A. W., 447, 484, 501
American Association of Fund-Raising Counsel
    (AAFRC) Trust for Philanthropy, 39, 40,
    61, 72, 73, 75, 76, 120 136, 145, 146, 150,
    152, 154, 179, 188, 189, 221, 230, 239, 259,
    260, 328, 329, 454, 476, 477, 478, 479, 508,
    546, 560, 570, 580, 582, 583, 592, 595, 597,
    601, 611, 616, 617
Anderson, A., 323
Anderson, C., 460, 482, 483
Anderson, R., 59, 265, 266, 267
Andrews, F. E., 173
Anthony, R. N., 257, 563
Armstrong, R., 470
Arthur Andersen & Company, 47, 262, 268, 596
Association of Alumni Secretaries, 140
Association of Direct Response Fundraising
    Counsel, 281
Attorney General of the State of California, 283,
    284, 290
Aupperle, K. E., 594
Auten, G., 46

B

Bailey, A. L., 6, 42, 69, 75, 80, 108, 119, 295, 329,
    477, 559, 592, 595, 599, 605, 607, 608, 609
Barber, P., 253
Barkelew, A. H., 598

Baroudi, C., 474
Bartolomeo, J., 47, 51, 593
Bauer, H., 449
Becken, T., 39
Becker, L. C., 434, 435
Beddingfield, K. T., 256, 257
Benjamin, E., 490
Berdahl, R. O., 341
Bergan, H., 28, 410, 443
Berger, C. R., 176
Berton, L., 221, 247, 258
Bezilla, M., 209
Bigelow, B. E., 507, 509, 513, 515, 519, 521, 523,
    524, 525, 526, 531, 536, 539, 540, 542
Bintzer, H. R., 145, 147, 152, 158, 208
Birnbaum, R., 218
Blades, S. D., 186, 227, 228, 232, 242, 256, 257,
    259, 304
Blake, M., 548, 549, 552, 559, 567, 568, 575, 576
Blanchette, R., 364, 368, 408
Blau, P. M., 44, 326, 334, 357
Blazek, J., 270
Block, S. R., 80, 137, 202, 203, 206, 448, 449
Bloland, H. G., 80, 81, 86, 104, 105, 112, 115, 116,
    124, 128, 129, 192
Blum, D. E., 243, 252, 301
Blumenstyk, G., 477, 478
Boardman, R. B., 207, 208
Boaz, D. E., 172
Boorstin, D., 160
Boris, E. T., 4, 89, 102, 108, 232, 257, 273, 304,
    343, 573, 584, 587
Bornstein, R., 80, 81, 86, 104, 105, 112, 115, 116,
    124, 128, 129, 192
Borowski, N. A., 224, 225, 270
Borsos, J., 130, 142, 144, 146, 151, 158, 159, 170,
    196
Borum, R. A., 85
Botan, C. H., 387
Bothwell, R. O., 313, 315

Bovet, S. F., 497, 498, 499
Bowen, W. G., 53, 59, 60, 61, 62, 64, 68, 81, 571
Brain, P. S., Jr., 503, 505, 510, 517, 519, 530, 537, 540
Brakeley, G. A., III, 547
Brakeley Recruiting, 96
Brasseux, S. G., 131
Brehmer, D. A., 50Bremner, R. H., 14, 43, 63, 64, 106, 144, 175, 254
Brewster, K., 35, 154
Brilliant, E. L., 136, 309, 310, 311, 312, 313, 315
Briscoe, M. G., 57, 248, 249, 253, 258, 271, 272, 323
Brittingham, B. E., 109, 151, 262, 328, 338, 340, 348, 350, 351, 428, 487, 488
Broce, T. E., 3, 6, 12, 36, 130, 138, 139, 147, 198, 203, 206, 207, 324, 336, 351, 358, 363, 369, 396, 407, 421, 422, 426, 493, 494, 495, 506, 509, 516, 545, 550, 551, 552, 553, 555, 556, 557, 567, 610, 611
Brody, E. W., 336
Broom, G. M., 10, 24, 36, 98, 99, 102, 103, 105, 126, 175, 192, 193, 194, 195, 197, 198, 199, 200, 201, 206, 227, 310, 311, 325, 335, 353, 358, 359, 361, 371, 374, 376, 377, 387, 396, 403, 405, 412, 419, 420, 432
Brown, J. J., Jr., 454, 509, 514, 529, 534, 541
Brudney, J. L., 108
Bryson, J. M., 443
Buchanan, A. E., 305, 306
Buchanan, P. M., 114, 119, 127, 204, 548, 554, 557, 559, 564, 566
Buchholz, R. A., 394
Bumgarner, S., 89, 102
Burkhart, P. J., 443
Burlingame, D. F., 36, 105, 125, 340, 593, 594, 602, 603, 608, 621
Burns, J., 221, 248
Bush, B. H., 219, 220, 221, 222, 236, 239, 240, 241, 242, 244, 280, 285, 287, 291, 308
Button, G., 618

C

Cacioppo, J. T., 365
Carbone, R. F., 4, 6, 74, 76, 77, 80, 81, 82, 86, 87, 102, 103, 104, 106, 109, 111, 112, 115, 116, 119, 121, 122, 123, 124, 131, 169, 196, 197, 200
Carnegie, A., 15, 42, 57
Carrell, B., 387
Carroll, A. B., 594
Carson, E. D., 34
Carter, L. K., 141, 149
Carver, J., 203, 218
Center, A. H., 10, 24, 36, 99, 103, 105, 125, 126, 175, 194, 198, 199, 201, 206, 227, 310, 311, 325, 335, 353, 374, 376, 377, 403, 419, 420, 432

Cermak, D. S. P., 363, 422, 423, 508, 509, 516, 542, 614
Chaffee, S. H., 358, 370
Chang, S., 353
Chapo, S., 99
Chewning, P. B., 81, 117
Cline, C., 102
Clotfelter, C. T., 48, 49, 51, 63, 64, 68, 224
Cloud, S., Jr., 86
Clymer, J. M., 518, 519
Cnaan, R. A., 65, 476
College and University Personnel Association(CUPA), 83
Colton, K., 506, 516, 523, 524
Commission on Undergraduate Public Relations Education, 112, 127, 128
Conference Board, 603
Connell, J. E., 504, 515, 535
Conry, J. C., 69, 89, 94, 96, 97, 98, 99, 100, 101, 128, 196
Constantine, H. C., 442, 496
Cook, W. B., 11, 153, 191, 204, 205, 206, 208, 332, 343, 347, 445, 456
Copeland, J., 79, 220
Council for Advancement and Support of Education (CASE), 30, 31, 66, 92, 100, 178, 440, 443, 460, 461, 462, 475, 537, 538, 554, 557, 563, 564, 565, 569
Council for Aid to Education (CFAE), 61, 76, 256, 476, 483, 508, 524, 550, 560, 583, 601, 611
Coutsoukis, P. E., 621
Covington, S., 270
Craig, J., 239, 293
Craver, R. M., 378, 457, 468, 470
Creedon, P. J., 102
Critz, D. W., 95, 100
Crowder, N. L., 3, 36, 81
Crutchfield, E. A., 40, 68, 73, 328, 329, 599
Culbertson H. M., 332, 335, 336, 360, 365, 366, 367, 377, 387, 401, 403, 404, 422
Curti, M., 61, 115, 137, 165, 173, 345, 574
Cutlip, S. M., 10, 14, 24, 36, 99, 103, 105, 125, 126, 130, 135, 137, 139, 140, 141, 142, 143, 144, 145, 146, 147, 148, 150, 158, 159, 160, 161, 162, 163, 164, 165, 166, 170, 173, 174, 175, 194, 198, 199, 201, 206, 210, 224, 227, 233, 257, 310, 311, 325, 335, 353, 374, 376, 377, 403, 405, 419, 420, 432, 591, 621

D

Daniels, A. K., 89, 102
Dannelley, P., 3, 295
Davis, H. T., Jr., 292
Davis, M., 339
Dearning, J. W., 353
DeFleur, M. L., 115, 116, 352, 483

Delhomme, R., 310, 316
Demko, P., 61, 75, 252, 343, 478, 559
Deranger, W. A., 442
Dessoff, A. L., 379
Detmold, J. H., 97
Development Resource Group, 120
Devillier, C. R., 284, 294, 442
Direct Marketing Association, 540, 542
Dittman, D. A., 152
Doermann, H., 588
Dolphin, H. A., 209
Donovan, A., 506
Dorich, D., 171, 539
Dorsey, E., 2, 35, 53, 54
Doty, G., 33, 599, 601
Douglas, J., 7, 53, 332
Douglas, W., 366
Dove, K. E., 198, 450, 458, 544, 550, 551, 561, 568, 569
Dozier, D. M., 98, 99, 102, 126, 183, 192, 193, 194, 195, 197, 199, 200, 218, 332, 338, 339, 352, 353, 354, 355, 358, 359, 361, 370, 371, 387, 396, 403, 405, 412
Dressel, P. L., 226, 227, 228, 340, 341, 350, 387
Duffy, E. A., 53, 59, 60, 61, 62, 64, 68, 81, 571
Duhé, S. C., 51, 52, 320, 442, 603, 604
Dundjerski, M., 34, 255, 315, 317, 318, 319, 321, 322, 343, 430, 436, 437, 440, 441, 459, 600, 607
Dunlop, D. R., 170, 171, 190, 356, 412, 421, 423, 431, 536
Dunn, J. A., 11
Durden, T. K., 108
Duronio, M. A., 75, 76, 77, 81, 82, 87, 88, 96, 102, 112, 119, 128, 130, 154, 179, 193, 195, 208, 271, 272, 279, 343, 405, 621

E

Edie, J. A., 577, 578
Edwards, A. H., 95
Ehling, W. P., 183, 332, 341, 347, 352, 353, 354, 355, 370, 451
Eisenberg, P., 227, 244, 259, 271, 275, 320, 596, 597
Elder, S. D., 5, 306, 328, 347, 351, 356, 362, 363, 370, 386, 387, 393, 395, 411, 421, 425, 426, 427, 442, 452, 494, 589
Eldridge-Karr, C., 542
Ericson, F., 59, 265, 266, 267
Esman, M. J., 337
Estey, G. P., 214, 217, 541
Ethics Resource Center, 272
Evans, G. A., 214, 215, 216, 492, 493
Evans, W. D., 394

F

Feagin, S. K., 454, 509, 514, 529, 534, 541

File, K. M., 363, 422, 423, 508, 509, 516, 542, 612, 613, 614
Filer, J. H., 153
Fink, J., 39, 56, 314
Fink, N. S., 18, 20, 22, 49, 220, 228, 239, 248, 259, 269
Fischer, L. R., 448, 474
Fischer, M., 335
Fisher, J. L., 75, 192
Fisher, M. A., 205
Fisher, R., 28
Fleishman, J., 69, 222, 239, 274, 275, 292, 294, 479
Florida Department of Agriculture and Consumer Services, 285
Fogal, R. E., 128, 272, 462
Foster, J. S., 513, 525, 532, 535
The Foundation Center, 42, 68, 572, 586, 613, 618
Fox, D. M., 4
Franz, P. J., 346, 446
Freeman, H. E., 443
Freeman, R. E., 336, 337, 385
Frey, L. R., 387
Friedman, P. G., 387
Fuerst, R. A., 270
Fulmer, K. A., 193, 401

G

Gagen-McCarthy, M., 396, 580, 582
Galaskiewicz, J., 42, 51, 52, 590, 592, 593, 594, 599, 603, 604, 607, 610
Gallup Organization, 250, 274
Gaul, G. M., 224, 225, 270
Gayley, H. T., 474
Gearhart, G. D., 209, 569
Gee, A. D., 474
Geever, J. C., 145, 621
Georges, A., 89, 102
Gillespie, J. E., 612, 613, 614
Gilley, J. W., 193, 401
Glaser, J. S., 323
Goldstein, H., 240
Gonzalez-Campoy, R., 77, 154, 155, 334
Goss, K. A., 20, 72, 92, 93, 122, 251, 252, 253, 254, 255, 256, 275, 290, 291, 292, 342, 551, 512, 538, 539, 566
Gottlieb, M., 340, 451, 487, 489, 490, 491
Gouldner, A. W., 44, 45, 333, 434
Grace, J. D., 109, 111
Grace, K. S., 196, 200, 207, 327, 331, 334, 335, 356, 363, 377, 414, 417, 441
Graham, C., 452, 457, 463, 474
Gray, B. H., 168
Gray, J. W., 262, 472
Gray, S., 61, 75, 107, 252, 309, 314, 315, 316, 321, 322, 323, 580, 587, 598, 600, 601, 605, 606, 607, 608, 609, 610
Grayson, N. A., 131

Greene, E., 29, 41, 42, 100, 176, 293, 316, 319, 424, 504, 505, 511, 513, 517, 524, 526, 586, 590
Greene, S. G., 29, 58, 74, 97, 100, 221, 229, 232, 233, 234, 244, 245, 246, 255, 256, 297, 303, 304, 316, 479, 480, 504, 505, 517, 572
Greenfield, J. M., 9, 32, 226, 230, 231, 249, 270, 276, 282, 296, 297, 426, 432, 433, 436, 437, 452, 453, 454, 456, 472, 473, 474, 510, 512, 536, 537, 549, 550, 563, 568, 585
Griffith, J., 501
Grønbjerg, K. A., 312, 316, 319, 325, 339, 340, 345, 346, 471, 472
Gross, S. J., 356
Grunig, J. E., 9, 10, 12, 24, 36, 45, 86, 88, 103, 105, 112, 116, 122, 124, 127, 129, 131, 155, 156, 157, 163, 165, 172, 183, 184, 185, 190, 191, 192, 193, 217, 218, 227, 326, 331, 334, 336, 337, 338, 341, 347, 350, 352, 353, 354, 355, 356, 357, 364, 365, 366, 367, 368, 369, 370, 371, 373, 374, 376, 381, 386, 387, 394, 405, 407, 415, 418, 419, 434, 451, 489
Grunig, L. A., 157, 183, 191, 192, 193, 218, 336, 341, 347, 404, 451, 489
Gurin, M. G., 12, 14, 40, 105, 130, 137, 146, 149, 151, 173, 195, 326, 506, 541, 547

H

Haberman, D. A., 209
Hafner, K, 42, 572, 620
Hage, J., 184, 213, 214
Hall, C., 13
Hall, H., 81, 114, 150, 173, 189, 246, 247, 252, 319, 320, 329, 378, 408, 409, 463, 464, 469, 470, 471, 472, 504, 505, 532, 544, 547, 548, 551, 554, 557, 558, 589, 590
Hall, M. R., 111, 214, 215, 216, 218, 336, 344, 345, 347, 391, 424, 487, 488, 569, 584
Hall, P. D., 4, 13, 42, 54, 68, 107, 137, 138, 153, 154, 173, 225, 313, 574, 580, 581
Hammack, D., 68
Hanchette, C. Q., 276
Hancock, L., 556, 558, 560
Hansmann, H. B., 168, 211
Harrah-Conforth, J., 130, 142, 144, 146, 151, 158, 159, 170, 196
Harris, A. L., 474
Hartsook, R. F., 505, 510, 515, 516, 520, 522, 536, 537
Harvey, J. W., 12, 64, 402
Hatfield, J. D., 594
Havens, J. J., 328, 329, 330, 332, 367
Hawthorne, E. L., 150
Healy, W. J., 340, 451, 487, 489, 490, 491
Heath, R. L., 366, 397
Hedgepeth, R. C., 151, 206, 211, 212, 216, 546
Heetland, D. L., 475, 476, 492, 493
Hendrix, J. A., 377, 391, 404, 413, 414, 415, 416

Heimovics, R. D., 203, 218
Herman, A., 351, 362
Herman, R. D., 80, 137, 202, 203, 206, 218, 448, 449
Heying, C., 599, 606
Hickey, K. E., 411
Hiebert, R. E., 142, 165
Hill, F. R., 270
Hocker, J. L., 489
Hodgkinson, V. A., 3, 36, 40, 52, 53, 54, 59, 60, 61, 62, 64, 68, 72, 73, 81, 328, 329, 592, 596, 599, 606
Hollems, M. D., 442
Holt, L., 401
Hopkins, B. R., 2, 20, 48, 49, 50, 220, 231, 239, 246, 257, 259, 268, 270, 288, 289, 299, 300
Horton, A. J., 107, 433
Hotaling, D. H., 469
Hougland, J. G., Jr., 13, 175, 242
Houle, C. O., 202
Howe, F., 29, 31, 194, 197, 203, 330, 334, 335, 342, 343, 356, 369, 373, 374, 425, 426, 436, 446, 470, 585
Howes, D., 342, 343
Huettner, J. S., 110
Hulse, L. J., 36, 105, 125, 340
Hunt, M., 43
Hunt, T., 10, 12, 103, 105, 112, 116, 122, 127, 129, 131, 155, 156, 163, 165, 172, 184, 190, 227, 326, 331, 337, 352, 353, 354, 355, 356, 364, 365, 366, 368, 369, 370, 371, 376, 386, 387, 415, 418, 419
Huntsinger, J., 288
Hyman, H. H., 352

I

Independent Sector (IS), 26, 33, 40, 48, 49, 266, 271, 273, 323, 328, 367, 368, 372, 378, 425, 439, 445, 457, 458, 614, 615, 616, 617
Institute for Public Policy and Administration, 2, 35
Internal Revenue Service (IRS), 43, 48, 49, 53, 54, 59, 60, 259, 292, 309, 570, 616, 617

J

Jacobson, H. K., 169, 324, 333, 381
Jeavons, T. H., 44, 52, 55, 307, 434
Jeffers, D. W., 332, 335, 336, 360, 365, 366, 367, 377, 387, 401, 403, 404, 422
Jehl, J., 601
Jencks, C., 58, 476, 617
Jenkins, J. C., 46, 47, 48, 583, 589, 590
Johnston, D., 225, 227, 303, 304, 528, 529, 530
Jones, J. P., 148, 149, 440
Jordan, R. R., 505, 509, 541, 542
Joseph, D., 82, 89, 94
Joseph, J. A., 385, 591, 594

Josephson, M., 323

K

Kachorek, J., 474
Kahn, R. L., 192, 325
Kalson, S., 251
Kanter, R. M., 217, 226, 430
Kantrowitz, B., 568
Kaplan, D. A., 498
Karl, B. D., 599
Katz, D., 192, 325
Kay, R., 305
Kearns, K. P., 270, 396, 397, 398, 400
Kelley, K., 41
Kelly, K. S., 3, 4, 5, 9, 11, 12, 36, 52, 58, 65, 70, 84,
    91, 102, 106, 117, 123, 125, 127, 131, 139,
    141, 151, 155, 173, 177, 179, 184, 193, 196,
    209, 210, 215, 231, 273, 325, 328, 341, 348,
    349, 368, 380, 381, 383, 384, 396, 408, 429,
    450, 492, 542, 561, 584, 597
Kennedy, G., 490, 491
Kerr, C., 549
Killoran, R., 541
Kirschten, B. L., 270
Kleid Company, 468
Klein, E., 152, 378, 505
Knauft, E. B., 577
Knott, R. A., 6, 130, 173, 421
Koperek, E., 588, 589
Korten, D., 176
Kreps, G. L., 387

L

Lafer, M., 85, 92
Landers, A., 287, 288
Larkin, R. F., 228, 231, 233, 236, 268, 322, 440,
    538, 565
Lawrence, S., 32, 43, 51, 60, 570, 571, 572, 573,
    574, 575, 576, 577, 578, 579, 580, 581, 582,
    583, 586, 618
Layton, D. N., 106, 136
LDDS Communications, 296
Leatherman, C., 560
Ledingham, J. A., 199, 312, 379
Lenkowsky, L., 480, 481
Leonard, M., 353
Levine, J., 474
Levis, W. C., 230, 231, 232, 372
Levner, N., 420, 552
Levy, B. R., 344, 584
Lewin, K., 25
Lewis, E., 621
Lewis, P. F., 8, 105, 108, 135, 221, 237, 276, 279
Liao, S., 366
Lies, V. S., 435, 437, 457

Lindahl, W. E., 372, 415, 419, 425, 429, 432, 450,
    452, 493, 512, 517, 542
Linehan, J. D., 149
Lochray, P. J., 542
Loessin, B. A., 96, 179, 193, 195, 405
Lohmann, R. A., 8, 11, 14, 15, 16, 36, 55, 56, 57,
    65, 224, 280, 331, 332, 335, 362
Lombardo, B. J., 273, 434, 435, 598, 599
Lord, J. G., 45, 57, 147, 179, 194, 204, 326, 328,
    333, 336, 341, 357, 362, 365, 369, 371, 373,
    376, 387, 395, 406, 412, 417, 419, 422, 423,
    437, 441, 448, 458, 591, 621
Lowenberg, F. M., 45
Lowery, S. A., 352
Luck, M. F., 29, 31, 446, 448, 492, 493, 560
Lumpkin, S. R., 507, 509, 513, 515, 519, 521, 523,
    524, 525, 526, 531, 538, 539, 540, 542
Luna, E., 89, 102
Lyddon, I. W., 249

M

MacKeith, J., 400
Magat, R., 36, 49, 137, 153, 575, 603
Mantese, G., 489
Marchetti, D., 318
Marion, B. H., 306, 307
Marlowe & Company, 50, 51
Marlowe, H., 52, 226, 269, 518
Marshall, J. E., III, 583, 589
Martin, M. W., 45, 333, 334, 346, 360, 362, 434,
    439, 612, 613, 614, 615, 621
Martin, P., 299
Marts, A. C., 159, 162, 409
Matheny, R., 501
Mauss, M., 44
May, J., 501
McCarthy, K. D., 34
McCombs, M. E., 353, 354
McConnell, T. R., 227, 228
McCrohan, K. F., 12, 64, 402
McElreath, M. P., 272, 273
McGoldrick, W. P., 555, 557
McIlquham, J. D., 99, 547
McLaughlin, B., 583
McLeod, J. M., 358, 370
McNamee, M., 43, 360, 395, 459, 477, 496, 618
McNeill, P., 621
Meckstroth, A., 238
Mehegan, S., 285
Melillo, W., 311
Meuth, E. F., 599
Middleton, M., 203
Millar, B., 69, 275, 310, 311, 314, 315, 316, 317,
    318, 321, 590, 597
Milofsky, C., 186, 227, 228, 232, 242, 256, 257,
    259, 304
Miltner, J. R., 88, 109, 111, 113

Miner, L. E., 501

Mixer, J. R., 62, 135, 152, 198, 210, 212, 213, 215, 218, 226, 278, 333, 367, 372, 377, 378, 379, 395, 418, 424, 427, 435, 445, 452, 453, 458, 471, 488, 549, 554, 557, 558, 573, 584, 585, 590, 593

Mongon, G. J., Jr., 16, 17, 73, 74, 76, 77, 79, 80, 81, 82, 84, 85, 86, 87, 89, 90, 91, 94, 97, 99, 115, 154, 180, 190, 195, 230, 546

Montague, W., 291

Moore, J., 29, 41, 67, 211, 251, 252, 292, 295, 297, 298, 299, 316, 479, 504, 505, 517, 528, 580, 586, 590, 598, 600, 601, 605, 606, 607, 608, 609, 610

Moore, J. E., 457

Moran, W. J., 30, 507, 522, 523, 524, 536

Mouton-Allen, D., 442

Muir, R., 501

Mundy, L., 480

Murawski, J., 67, 74, 97, 100, 221, 238, 252, 253, 260, 293, 316, 319, 454, 528, 529, 531, 571, 572, 575

Murray, D. J., 427, 431, 432, 443, 446, 447

Murray, V., 621

Mutz, J. M., 57

Myers, D. G., 476, 492, 493

N

Nacson, S., 285

Nahm, R., 557, 559, 561

Nash, R., 61, 115, 137, 165, 173, 345, 574

National Association of College University Business Officers (NACUBO), 270, 462

National Association of Fundraising Ticket Manufacturers (NAFTM), 22, 302, 303

National Commission on Graduate Study in Public Relations, 129

National Society of Fund Raising Executives (NSFRE), 74, 76, 77, 80, 84, 154, 249

NSFRE Institute, 5, 7, 277, 422

Nelson, R. A., 397

Netherton, R., 513, 537, 541

New England Association of Catholic Development Officers (NEACDO), 302, 392

Newcomb, P., 43, 480, 618, 620

Newcomb, T. M., 358

Newman, J., 104

Newsom, D., 387

Nichols, J. E., 372, 387, 501

Nicklin, J. L., 556, 557, 562, 563, 565, 566

Nielsen, W. A., 105, 573, 574, 580, 583

Niman, C. M., 356

Noga, S. M., 53, 54, 60, 62, 64, 329, 592, 596, 606

Nolte, L. W., 387

Novak, M., 43

Nudd, S. P., 8, 407, 411, 412, 423, 424, 492

Nygren, T. I., 53, 59, 60, 61, 62, 64, 68, 81, 571

O

O'Connell, B., 53, 56, 202, 203, 204, 207, 218, 282, 331

Odendahl, T. J., 14, 43, 47, 89, 102, 221, 232, 257, 273, 304, 343, 476, 574, 575, 612

Office of the Attorney General, Commonwealth of Massachusetts, 277, 278, 282, 283, 284, 285, 301

O'Neill, M., 40, 68, 102, 323

Ormstedt, D. E., 236, 240, 281, 292

O'Shea, C. L., 425

Osterholt, J. W., 546, 558

Ostrander, S. A., 106, 169, 177, 178, 332, 333, 340

Ostrower, F., 438, 540, 621

P

Pace, R. W., 201

Packard, V., 138

Panas, J., 12, 43, 44, 97, 98, 139, 177, 178, 344, 363, 424, 425, 447, 613

Parker, M., 131

Parsons, M. H., 542

Patton, B., 28

Pavlik, J. V., 10

Payton, R. L., 2, 3, 6, 7, 8, 9, 13, 14, 16, 36, 40, 44, 45, 73, 105, 106, 127, 135, 168, 172, 174, 197, 304, 330, 340, 366, 428, 621

Payzant, T. W., 601

Pearsall, F. W., 148

Peirce, S. P., 474

Peters, T. J., 217, 416

Peterson, V. T., 538, 539, 548, 549, 550, 554, 557, 559, 561, 562, 563, 564, 566

Petty, R. E., 365

Pezzullo, T. R., 109, 151, 262, 328, 338, 340, 348, 350, 351, 428, 487, 488

Pfeffer, J., 325, 345, 346, 347, 380, 387, 429

Phillips, A., 96

Podolsky, D., 281, 290

Points of Light Foundation, 608

Pollard, J. A., 149

Porter, W. E., 149, 381

Powell, W. W., 68, 153, 169, 173

Pratt, J., 227, 293, 334, 341, 344, 350, 590, 598, 609, 611

Pray, F. C., 128, 148, 149, 152, 197, 198, 381, 463, 475, 545, 567

Preston, L. E., 601

Prince, R. A., 363, 422, 423, 508, 509, 516, 542, 612, 613, 614

Q

Quinn, J. B., 49, 517, 518

Quynn, K. L., 505, 509, 541, 542

R

Radelat, A., 587
Redman, C., 302
Reeves, F., 252
Reiss, A. H., 79
Reithlingshoefer, S. J., 193, 401
Renz, L., 32, 43, 51, 60, 570, 571, 572, 573, 574, 575, 576, 577, 578, 579, 580, 581, 582, 583, 585, 586, 618
Repper, F. C., 24, 183, 192, 331, 336, 338, 350, 357, 364, 365, 366, 367, 368, 369, 374, 407
Reuss, S., 443
Riddle, C. N., 279, 292
Robbins, S. P., 210, 213, 218, 325
Rockefeller, D., Jr., 617
Rocque, A., 354
Rogers, E. M., 353
Rosenman, M., 50, 66, 304, 617, 618, 619
Rossi, P. H., 443
Rosso, H. A., 2, 3, 6, 7, 8, 11, 13, 36, 45, 105, 106, 112, 127, 135, 155, 168, 172, 178, 179, 183, 304, 324, 328, 336, 345, 351, 356, 357, 363, 366, 373, 379, 380, 394, 412, 418, 427, 428, 434, 444, 447, 449, 450, 451, 452, 455, 465, 503, 551, 555, 567, 614, 621
Rotstein, G., 251
Rudney, G., 46, 64, 79, 220
Ruge, R. B., 20, 263
Ryan, E., 214, 215, 216, 410, 421, 460, 461, 462, 484, 496
Ryan, J. P., 422, 436, 437, 441

S

Sabo, S. R., 215, 216, 217, 469, 496, 497, 498, 499
Salamon, L. M., 68, 576
Salancik, G. R., 325, 345, 346, 347, 380, 387, 429
Sapp, R. E., 454, 455, 506, 513, 516, 521, 525, 527, 528, 530, 532, 533
Schaffer, K. B., 448, 474
Schervish, P. G., 106, 169, 177, 178, 328, 329, 330, 332, 333, 340, 351, 362, 367, 504, 621
Schiff, J., 46, 48
Schmeling, D. G., 512, 516, 540
Schreiber, W., 406
Schrum, J. B., 171
Schuette, A. W., 446
Schuster, J. M. D., 43
Schwartz, J. J., 135, 137, 159, 168, 173, 225, 296
Sebastian, P., 250
Seltzer, M., 441, 513, 514, 522, 529, 533, 534
Seneker, H., 620
Sennott, C. M., 275, 323
Seymour, H. J., 147, 334, 369, 450, 545
Shannon, J. P., 65, 591, 597, 602
Shapiro, J. P., 305
Sharpe, R. F., 18, 149, 419, 504, 508, 510, 512, 520, 533, 534

Shaw, D. L., 353, 354
Shaw, S. C., 621
Sheatsley, P. B., 352
Sheldon, K. S., 43, 584, 610
Shell, A., 296
Shields, A., 131
Shoemaker, D., 484, 485, 487
Siegel, E., 409, 410
Simmons, R. E., 352, 395, 419, 451
Simon, J. G., 14, 15, 48, 54, 55
Skolnik, R., 213, 237, 250, 317, 319
Smith, C., 295, 595, 596, 605, 606, 608, 610
Smith, C. F., 262
Smith, D. H., 107, 323
Smith, G. D., 193, 195
Smith, G. T., 356, 423
Smith, H. W., 26, 33, 43, 579, 590, 591, 592, 594, 598, 599, 602, 603, 611
Smith, J. P., 147, 170, 347, 412, 425, 428, 429, 544, 550, 557, 558, 559, 560, 561, 567, 569
Smucker, B., 260
Smurl, J. F., 175, 304
Speizman, R. A., 20, 263
Spinner, J. H., 129
Squires, C., 26, 458
State of Minnesota Office of the Attorney General, 284, 285, 289
Steele, V., 5, 306, 328, 347, 351, 356, 362, 363, 370, 386, 387, 393, 395, 411, 421, 425, 426, 427, 442, 452, 494, 589
Stehle, V., 81, 151, 152, 258, 265, 314, 317, 318, 454, 478, 520, 528, 529, 547, 557, 562, 572, 575, 600, 605, 606
Steinberg, R., 8, 46, 63, 168, 177, 250, 281, 282, 283, 330, 333, 612
Stendardi, E. J., Jr., 595
Stephens, C. R., 119, 121
Stern, J., 175
Stern, M, 175
Steuerle, E., 523, 542
Stevenson, D. R., 40, 68, 73, 328, 329, 599
Stone, D. B., 332, 335, 336, 360, 365, 366, 367, 377, 387, 401, 403, 404, 422
Strand, B. J., 409
Street, W. D., 173
Struck, R., 485, 486
Sullivan, B., 99
Summers, D. V., 226, 430
Sutley, J. W., 131
Synodinos, J., 482, 483

T

Tata, J., 496, 497
Taylor, B., 96
Taylor, M. A., 621
Tempel, E. R., 2, 3, 7, 8, 13, 45, 102, 105, 106, 127, 168, 172, 304, 326, 357, 380, 393, 427, 428, 621

Terrell, M., 332, 335, 336, 360, 365, 366, 367, 377, 387, 401, 403, 404, 422
Thaves, B., 402
Thee, B., 59, 265, 266, 267
Thieblot, B. A., 546, 550, 553, 555
Thinesen, S. A., 381, 384
Thomas, M. A., 292
Thompson, J. D., 184
Thorsen, J., 411, 412
Tidwell, G. L., 243, 274, 323
Titmus, R. M., 44
Toppe, C., 53, 54, 59, 60, 61, 62, 64, 72, 329, 592, 596, 606
Toth, E. L., 102
Trachtenberg, S. J., 205, 382
Treiber, R. R., 32, 43, 60, 570, 572, 573, 574, 575, 576, 577, 578, 579, 580, 581, 582, 583, 586, 618
Tueller, A. B., 543
Tuleja, T., 45
Turk, J. V., 91, 207
Turner, R., 138, 305, 306
Turner, S. E., 53, 59, 60, 61, 62, 64, 66, 81, 571
Tyler, L. M., 442

U

Unkefer, J. M., 81, 117
Ury, W., 28
U.S. Bureau of the Census, 69
U.S. Department of Labor, Employment and Training Administration, 69
U.S. Small Business Administration, 33, 577
Useem, M., 600, 601, 602

V

Vandeventer, D. J., 331, 332
Van Til, J., 3, 8, 14, 36, 40, 44, 47, 52, 55, 120, 137, 173, 175, 250
Vermeulen, M., 450, 617
Von Schlegell, A., 411

W

Wagley, R. A., 394
Walker, M. M., 587, 589
Walters, J., 273
Warner, I., 50, 176, 221, 329
Warwick, M., 464, 470
Waterman, R. H., Jr., 217, 401, 416
Webb, C. H., 179

Webb, N. J., 577, 578, 579
Weeden, C., 604
Weick, K. E., 448
Weisbrod, B. A., 48, 68
Weitzman, M. S., 40, 52, 53, 54, 60, 62, 64, 68, 73, 328, 329, 592, 596, 599, 606
Welter, L. A., 548, 554, 557, 559, 564, 566
Wetherell, B. L., 99, 193
Whitaker, B., 9, 176, 359, 584
White, A., 47, 51, 593, 596
White, D. E., 543
White, J., 9, 45, 88, 183, 192, 334, 338, 339, 350, 381, 434
Wilcox, D. L., 387
Wilkerson, G. S., 446
Wilkerson, S., 214, 217
Willard, T. J., 88, 111
Williams, G., 21, 58, 59, 66, 67, 72, 221, 229, 234, 239, 240, 241, 242, 243, 244, 245, 246, 249, 252, 255, 256, 261, 265, 267, 274, 276, 281, 282, 286, 290, 292, 293, 300, 303, 303, 479
Williams, R. L., 16, 73, 80, 84, 85, 91, 92, 93, 94, 100, 178, 324, 382, 493, 546, 556
Williams, W., 59, 265, 266, 267
Willmer, W. K., 386
Wilmot, W. W., 489
Winfree, W., 196, 206
Winship, A. L., II, 196, 484
Winship, C., 372, 415, 419
Wise, C. B., 377, 547, 555
Wolfenden, J., 347
Wood, E. W., 351, 393
Wood, J. R., 13, 175, 242
Wood, J. T., 497, 500
Worth, M. J., 75, 138, 139, 145, 150, 151, 170, 422, 433, 443, 444, 455, 475, 481, 523, 545, 549, 555, 563, 566, 567
Wulff, J., 63, 65, 618
Wuthnow, R., 68

Y

Ylvisaker, P. N., 51, 57, 574
Young, D. R., 36, 68

Z

Zapler, M., 296, 297
Zeff, R., 474
Zemsky, R. M., 557, 559, 561

Subject Index

A

Abuses as regulatory force, 20, 168, 226, 239, 241, 247, 252, *see also* Overvaluing gifts of property
Academic centers, 106–107
  Case Western Reserve University Mandel Center, 106, 108, 114
  Indiana University Center on Philanthropy, 14, 35, 86, 107–110, 113–114, 125, 279, 393, 542, 593
  New School for Social Research Nonprofit Management Program, 53, 106
  University of San Francisco Institute for Nonprofit Organization Management, 81–82, 106–107, 113
  Yale University PONPO, 106–108, 154, 169
Accountability, 20, 186, 226–228, 250, 325, 340–341, 347–350, 360, 396, 438, 440, 566, 586, 588, 603–604, 614
  financial measures of, *see* Cost ratios
  fund raisers as agents of, 222, 306–307, 434
  low accountability as regulatory force, *see* Endowments, excessive; Salaries, excessive; and Unfair competition
Accounting basics, 228–229
Accounting groups and guidelines
  Accountants for the Public Interest (API), 236–238, 260, 270, 428, 571
  American Institute of Certified Public Accountants (AICPA), 232, 236, 538, *see also* Joint costs
  Financial Accounting Standards Board (FASB), 232, 236, 268, 270, 322, 429, 440, 538, 565, *see also* Endowments, FASB standards
Affinity credit cards, *see* Cause-related marketing
Agenda-setting theory, 353–354
American Association of Fund-Raising Counsel (AAFRC), 108, 117, 120–122, 145, 147, 150–151, 154, 240, 277, 307, 547, 553, *see also* Author Index
American Cancer Society, 78, 137, 141, 207, 280–281, 291, 298, 312
American Council on Gift Annuities (ACGA), 120, 511, 520, 529
American Heart Association, 22, 78, 280, 298, 301, 604
American Red Cross, 39, 59, 67, 70, 78–79, 143, 147–148, 161–162, 164, 213, 311, 317–318
  Elizabeth Dole, 21, 39, 251, 318, 453
Annenberg, Walter, 41–43, 477, 558, 586
Arthritis Foundation, 297–298
Association for Healthcare Philanthropy (AHP), 6, 62, 72–74, 76, 80–82, 87, 89, 93–94, 100, 102, 107, 116–122, 150–151, 230, 307
Association of Philanthropic Counsel (APC), 120–121
Association of Professional Researchers for Advancement (APRA), 107, 120, 405, 410–412
Association for Research on Nonprofit Organizations and Voluntary Action (ARNOVA), 107, 111, 223
Autonomy
  donors' individual, 360, 362, 494, 615
  organizational, 12, 227–228, 325, 340–350, 360, 396, 399, 423, 435–437, 452, 487, 561, 584–585, 593, 597–598, 614

B

Billion-dollar capital campaigns, 546
Brown University, 140, 483, 537
Body of knowledge
  fund raising, 105–112, 114, 124, 169
  public relations, 10–11, 124–125
Boundary-spanning role, 338–340
Boys and Girls Clubs of America, 79, 361, 472–473
Boy Scouts of America, 78, 141, 251, 311, 445

Boys Town, 254–256, 258
Broce's nine cardinal principles, 198, 206, 324, 336, 369, 407, 422, 426
Budget replacement
annual gifts, 438–439, 463–465
endowed gifts, 483, 485
noncash gifts, 607–608
Budgeting for fund raising, 206–207, 416, 420, 439, 441, 493, 555–556, *see also* Cost ratios
Buffett, Warren, 618–620

C

CARE, 211, 251–252, 445
Carnegie, Andrew, 15, 42, 57, 61, 142, 574, 619
Carnegie Mellon University, 141, 430, 436–437, 440–441, 458
Case statement, 324, 326–327, 556, 560
Cause-related marketing, 13, 295–298, 592, 596–597
Challenge grants, 459–460, 484
Charitable contributions deduction, importance of, 48–52
Classification of nonprofits
Internal Revenue Code, 53–54
Classification of charitable organizations
Internal Revenue Code, 59–61
NTEE and other systems, 72–73
system adopted by text, 73
Collection canisters, *see* Honor boxes
Columbia University, 546, 548, 554, 564, 607
Commons and common goods, theory of, 15–16, 55–58, 280, 331–332, 335, 362
Computer software, 407, 461, 541–542
Consultants
dependence on capital campaigns, 30–31, 146–147, 151–153, 544, 547, 553
nonsolicitor role, 18, 144–146, 445
Consulting firms and founders
Brakeley, John Price Jones, 120, 144, 147, 150, 164, 405, 440, 452
George Brakeley, Jr., 144
John Price Jones, 143–146, 148–150, 15 6–157, 165–166, 178, 440
Ketchum, 143–144, 547
Carlton and George Ketchum, 142–143, 159–160
Marts & Lundy, 120, 144, 148, 161, 215
Arnaud Marts, 142–143, 158–162, 409
Staley/Robeson/Ryan/St. Lawrence, 117, 146, 279
J. Patrick Ryan, 146, 422, 436–437, 441
Ward, Dreshman & Reinhardt, 143–144
Charles Sumner Ward, 142–146, 156, 158–162, 164–166, 174–175, 544, 551, 554
Contract failure, theory of, 168
Coorientation theory, 24, 357–362, 370, 373, 406, 416, 604

model for identifying gift prospects, 359
Cornell University, 150, 170–171, 251, 423, 431, 546, 559
Corporate contributions officers, 601–602, 610, 621
Corporate matching gifts, 460–462
Corporate relations process, 609–611
Corporate sponsorships, 298–300
International Events Group (IEG), 299
Corporations
A. P. Smith Mgf. Co. v. Barlow, 579, 591
benefits received from giving, 592–595
continuum of motivation, 591–597
contributions vs. business expenses, 596
Dayton Hudson, 598
General Motors, 579, 601, 607
IBM, 578, 594, 600–601, 605–606, 610
Johnson & Johnson, 297, 478, 604, 606
trends in giving
demand for measurable benefits, 603–605, *see also* Accountability
dollars redirected, 605
emphasis on short-term marketing benefits, 595–597
employee participation, 608–609
fewer unrestricted gifts, 608
less local giving, 605–606
more gifts of property, 606–608
Cost ratios, 20, 207, 229–232, 234, 276, 284, 290, 322, 366, 378, 420, 428, 432, 512
Council for Advancement and Support of Education (CASE), 6, 62, 67, 69, 72–76, 80–82, 84–87, 89–94, 107, 109, 113, 116–123, 136, 150, 152, 154, 192, 207, 214, 223, 230, 272, 294, 307, 386, 421, 484, 488, 498–499, 539, 541, 544
history, 140–141, 148–150, 152, 381
management and reporting standards, 66–67, 440, 460, 462, 475, 537–539, 549, 561, 563–567
Peter McE. Buchanan, 67, 544, 546–547, 551, 558, 566, *see also* Author Index
Council on Foundations, 353, 575, 577, 586–587, 602
Cross-training, 385–387
Cultivation's centrality to fund-raising process, 369, 373, 391, 393–394, 421–425
Cy pres doctrine, 540

D

Decentralization of the function, 213–217
component fund raisers, 214
Definitions
charitable gift, 8, 20
charitable organizations, 14–15, 59
donor publics, 327–328
fund raisers, 7, 336

vs. paid solicitors, 7, 278–279
vs. volunteers, 7
fund raising, 7–9
vs. marketing, 12–13
fund-raising programs, 26, 27
philanthropy and charity, 13–15
public relations, 10, 336
purpose of fund raising, 9
typology of gifts, 328
Development, 6, 72, 150
Direct mail, 163–164, 176–177, 230, 235, 241–243,
264, 363, 374, 378, 404, 408, 414, 419, 426,
429, 431, 457–458, 468–471
USPS rates and regulations, 246–247, 468–470
Direct Response Consulting Services, *see* Watson
and Hughey
Dominant coalitions and power-control theory,
184–188, 191–192
Donor Bill of Rights, 307–308
Dual character theory of gifts, 46–47

E

Education and training
fund raising, 80–82, 112–116
public relations, 127–129
Effects of fund raising
conceptualization, 369–373
hierarchy of, table, 371
Electronic fund transfers, 453
Electronic screening, 409
Employers of fund raisers
diverse missions and opportunities, 78–79
estimated number, 60–62
nontraditional, 79
types employing the most, 73–76
where NSFRE members work, table, 77
Encroachment by fund raising, 24, 70, 187, 209,
382–385
Endowments, 228–229, 482–487
excessive, 253–258
FASB standards, 232–233, 257–258
Enlightened self-interest, *see* Corporations, continuum of motivation
Environmental blinders, 382
Environmental linkages, 337
Ethics, codes of
fund-raising associations, 120–122, 412
organizational employers, 272–274
Evaluation by objectives, 430–432
delay factors, 429, 512, 532
gift utility, 170, 428, 561
Events sponsorships, *see* Corporate sponsorships

F

Feasibility studies, 31, 152, 360–361, 404, 406,
552–553

Federal Trade Commission (FTC), 236, 274, 285,
292
Federations, 141, 160–161, 210–211, 314, *see also*
United Way
Combined Federal Campaign, 211, 244, 314
Independent Charities of America, 244, 314
Filer Commission, 54, 153–154, 168
Ford, Henry and Edsel, 574, 619
The Foundation Center, 60, 72, 410–411, 477, 570,
573, 585
Foundation relations process, 585–590
Foundations
affiliated, 75, 79, 117, 210–212, 260, 296
community, 571, 574, 580–582
Cleveland Foundation, 581
donor-advised funds, 581–582
corporate, 570–571, 577–580
AT&T Foundation, 578–579
vs. direct-giving programs, 577–578
independent, 570, 572–577
family foundations, 572–574, 577
Ford Foundation, 108, 514, 572, 590, 619
management models, 573
payout rates, 43, 571–572, 576–577
operating, 571–572
Free rider principle, 594, 601
The Fund Raising School, 6, 113–115, 152, 393,
449, 488

G

Gambling, 22, 267, 302–304
Gates, Bill, 618–621
Gender discrimination
backlash against female majority, 93–94
gender gap in salaries, 89–92, 97, 100
two-tier hierarchy of positions, 94–97
undervaluing women, 97–98
women in technician roles, 98–99
Gift clubs, 436–437, 458–459, 465, 539
Gift-range charts, 451
Gifts as proportion of GDP, 40, 150, 189–190,
329–330
Girl Scouts of the USA, 41, 141, 213
Goodwill Industries International, 64, 311, 455
Government's need for revenue as regulatory
force, 50, 226, 246–250, 259

H

Hammer, Armand, 614–615
Harvard University, 78, 107, 138, 142–143, 164,
166, 479–481, 546–547, 550, 554–558, 560,
564, 583
Hierarchy of fund-raising positions, table, 95
Historical evolution of the function
era of consultants, 143–147
era of nonspecialists, 140–143

era of staff fund raisers, 151–155
era of transition, 147–150
table, 140
Honor boxes, 300–301

I

Independent Sector (IS), 2–3, 36, 54, 56, 60, 62,
72, 83, 107, 121–122, 150, 154, 252, 260,
269, 280, 329, 332, 337, 479, 596, *see also*
Author Index
Institutional advancement, 6, 70, 117, *see also*
CASE
Interdependence with donor publics, 9, 325, 340,
346, 350, 441, 490
corporations, 33, 594, 597–599, 606
foundations, 32, 584–585
individuals, 33, 612–614
Internal Revenue Service (IRS), 7, 20, 47, 53–54,
59–60, 78, 153, 226, 236–239, 246, 250,
270, 292, 296–300, 303, 454, 459, 505, 522,
525, 530, 538, 582, 585, 589, *see also*
Author Index
IRS commensurate test, *see* United Cancer Council
cil
IRS Form 990, 59–60, 72, 237–239, 246, 252–253,
405, 571, 585
IRS intermediate sanctions, 252–253
IRS nondistribution constraint (NDC), 63, 168,
224, 250–251
IRS regulations
appreciated property, 269, 454–455, 518, 571,
578
capital-gains tax, xvi, 269–270, 518, 527–528
electoral campaigns, 259–260
gift and estate tax rates, xvi, 269, 518
income tax rates, 49, 269, 455
3% floor, 261
lobbying, 260–261
noncash gifts of property, 265, 455
corporate inventory, 607
Forms 8282 and 8283, 265, 455
nondeductible "gifts," 266–268
services, 268, 607–608
"fund raisers," 266–267
quid pro quo, 261–265, 436, 459, 474, 485
low-cost items, 264
substantiation, 261, 263
IRS and unrelated business income tax (UBIT),
238–239, 258, 266–267, 295–297, 299–301,
454, 470
International Society for Third-Sector Research
(ISTR), 107–108
Internet, 113, 223, 379, 403, 410, 453, 474, 567, 586
table of listservs, 223
table of web sites, 107

J

Job mobility, 101–102
Job satisfaction and turnover, 86–88
Joint costs, 233–236, 242–243, 286, 292

K

Kroc, Joan, 478–479

M

Magic bullet theory, 352–354, 357
Domino model, 354–357
Magic buttons, theory of, 350–352, 357
March of Dimes Birth Defects Foundation, 22,
137, 147, 213, 298, 301, 377, 517
Memorandum of Understanding (MOU), 485–486
Metaphors as indicators of presuppositions,
305–306, 551
Metropolitan Museum of Art, 34, 42, 78, 152
Minorities in fund raising, 84–86
Misconceptions about the charitable subsector,
14–15, 32, 58, 63–67, 279–280, 333–334,
463
sources of income, table, 64
Mixed-motive model of giving, 9, 44–47, 333, 366,
460–461, 489, 520, 604, 611–615, *see also*
Social exchange theory
Models of fund raising, *see also* Presuppositions
empirical studies, 179–192
press agentry, 158–162, 174–176, 291, 307, 326,
335, 349, 356–357, 442–443, 446, 464,
470, 504, 551–554, 559, *see also* United
Way
public information, 162–165, 176–178, 326, 335,
442–443
table of characteristics, 156
theory of, 155–157
two-way asymmetrical, 165–167, 178–179, 326,
335, 339, 406, 442–443, 551–554
two-way symmetrical, 167–172, 200, 231, 326,
335–336, 339, 346, 349–350, 358, 373,
380, 396–397, 402, 442–443, 464, 489,
492, 542, 556, 590, 615
Mount Vernon College, 240, 466, 472
Moves management system, 423–424, 431, 492–493
Muscular Dystrophy Association (MDA), 175,
304–305

N

National Associations of Attorneys General
(NAAG) and State Charity Officials
(NASCO), 241, 291, 294
National Catholic Development Conference
(NCDC), 120–121
National Commission on Private Philanthropy
and Public Needs, *see* Filer Commission

National Committee on Planned Giving (NCPG), 120–121, 507, 511–512, 541, 543

National Committee for Responsive Philanthropy, 227, 275, 313, 315

National Federation of Nonprofits, 235–236, 243, 280–281, 290, 293–294

National Society of Fund Raising Executives (NSFRE), 5–6, 35, 45, 50, 62, 69–70, 72–74, 76–77, 79–82, 84–87, 89–94, 96–97, 107–108, 115–122, 125, 130–131, 135–136, 150, 152, 154, 195, 203, 206, 208, 219, 225–226, 230–231, 249, 252, 273, 279, 287, 306–307, 327, 348–349, 357–358, 378, 442, 449, 457–458, 471, 479, 488, 505, 509, 523, 540–541, 546, 553, *see also* Models of fund raising, empirical studies

    Patricia F. Lewis, 8, 100, 122, *see also* Author Index

New York University, 113, 127, 477, 546, 554, 564

Nonprofit Sector Research Fund, 4, 107–108

Number of fund raisers, 69

O

Objectives
    formulating, 413–414
    impact and output, 414–416

Organizational chart, figure, 202

Overvaluing gifts of property, 244–246

P

Payments in lieu of taxes (PILOT), 247–250

Personality traits, required, 88

Philanthropic tradition, 39–43, 328–330

Philanthropy 400, 75, 78–79, 207, 256, 290, 334, 581

Planned giving vehicles, 29–30, 502–503
    charitable bequests, 505–509, 513, 521–524
        sample codicil, 522
    charitable gift annuity, 528–530
    charitable lead trust, 532
    charitable remainder trusts, 526–528
    life insurance, 533–535
    pooled income fund, 530–531
    remainder interest in home/farm, 532–533
    table of, 521

Planning and management tools
    budgets, 420
    decimal system, 417–418
    Gantt charts, 418
    message platform, 420

Pledges, 440, 453, 455, 562, 564–565

Police and firefighters organizations, 285–286

Predictors of giving
    practitioner, 363–364
    theoretical, *see* Situational theory of publics

Present value discounting, 30, 537, 53

Presuppositions about fund raising, 9–10, 18–19, 29, 164–165, 185, 191, 231, 279, 304–308, 319, 393, 505, 510, 520–521, 551–552, 567, 569

Principle of proportionate giving, 159, 328, 450–452, 476, 555

Principle of sequential giving, 363, 452–453, 555

Privileged status of charitable organizations, 48, 145, 167, 224–225, 261, 272, 371, 445, 452
    threatened, 49–50, 65, 220–222, 225–226, 239, 247, 276, 520, 597, 619

Professional allegiance and autonomy, 122–123, 126, 213, 217

Property, gifts of, 438, 454–455, 519, 525–526, 530–531, 533, 606–607

Proposals, writing, 587–589

Prospect rating sessions, 411, 447

Prospect research, *see* Research on the publics

Publication subscriptions, table, 223

Public charities vs. private foundations, 571, 575, 582

Public Relations Society of America (PRSA), 70, 107, 125–127, 131, 194, 383–384, 553
    Body of Knowledge Task Force, 11

Pyramid of donors, 451–452

R

Reciprocity
    as an element of stewardship, 434–438
    norm of, 45, 333–334, 350, 434–435
    serial reciprocity, 612

Research on fund raising, 1, 3–4, 125, 351–352, *see also* Body of knowledge
    grants and awards for, 108, 117
    suggestions for theses and dissertations, 34–36, 52, 94, 97, 131, 136, 184, 191, 200, 230, 243–244, 272–273, 294, 354, 380, 415, 442–443, 449, 496, 539, 542, 567, 604–605, 610

Research methods, 403–404

Research on the opportunity, 406

Research on the organization, 405

Research on the publics, 406, 407
    group analysis, 407–409, 465
    single-unit analysis, 409–412
        reference materials, 409–411

Resource dependence theory, 325, 345–346, 423

Rockefeller, John D., Sr.; John D., Jr.; and John D., III, 42, 142, 154, 163, 574, 619

Roles, theory of, 98–99, 191–192, 199
    four fund-raising roles, 193–200

Rule of thirds, *see* Principle of proportionate giving

S

Salaries,
    excessive, 250–253

of fund raisers, 80, 82, *see also* Gender discrimi-
    nation and Minorities
    vs. public relations practitioners, 83–84
Salary negotiation, 99–101
    commonsense advice, figure, 101
Salvation Army, 67, 78, 311, 318, 366
Scandals, headline-making, 274–276
Sexual harassment, 98, 495–500
Seymour, Harold, 117, 137, 144, 159–160, 170,
    326, *see also* Author Index
Shriners Hospitals for Children, 58, 64, 256–258
Situational theory of publics, 364–369
Social exchange theory, 44, 169, 332–336, 341, 357,
    359, 419, 584
Solicitation's placement in fund-raising process,
    421, 425–427
    unwarranted fears of rejection, 426–427
Soros, George, 478, 620
Special events, 182, 230, 268, 378, 422–423, 446,
    448, 468, 471–474, 577
    sample *quid pro quo* statement, 474
Staff vs. line functions, 201–202
Stakeholders, 336–338, 380–382, 385, 399, 445,
    448, 561, 563, 597
    mapping, 337–338
    segmenting into donor publics, 369
Stanford University, 58, 327, 342, 360, 377, 447,
    546, 548, 556, 559–560, 562, 568
State regulators and regulations, 220–221, 236,
    239–241, 244, 276, 292, 301
    registration laws, 145–146, 221, 239–240
    publicizing and prosecuting paid solicitors,
    282–287, 289
Stewardship, 26, 228, 230, 321, 422, 432–442, 459,
    462, 486–487, 491–493, 495, 539–540, 588,
    590, 603, 611, 615
Stock, gifts of, 454–455, 525–526, 528
Strategic planning and fund raising, 394–396
    SWOT analysis, 396–400
Strategic thinking, 401–402
Students' perspective of philanthropy, 40–41
Systems theory, 10, 23, 157, 209, 323–327, 333,
    336–337, 341, 372, 380, 382, 395, 429, 448,
    451, 483, 568, 591, 597

T

Tax credits vs. deductions, 49–50
Techniques of fund raising, 12, 23, 161, 208, 231,
    386, 394, 418–420, 422–423, 465, 468, 556,
    587, 610, *see also* Direct mail and Special
    events
    by communication levels and programs, figure,
    375
    conceptualization, 373–380
    in-person solicitation, 493–495
    letter and follow-up phone call, 465–468
    new technologies, 379, 474, *see also* Internet

phonathons, 378, 418, 429, 453
Turner, Ted, 575, 620

U

Unfair competition, 258–259, 520
United Cancer Council (UCC), 280–283
United Jewish Appeal (UJA), 78, 176, 424
United Jewish Appeal—Federation of Jewish Phi-
    lanthropies (UJA—FJP) of New York,
    520–521, 529, 546, 554
United Way, 22, 51, 64, 75, 175, 213, 264, 271,
    281, 308–323, 379, 383, 446, 461, 464, 512,
    604
    William Aramony, 250, 275, 308, 316, 319
University of California, 152
    Berkeley, 478, 546, 564
    Los Angeles (UCLA), 343, 546, 558
    Santa Cruz, 464, 540
University of Maryland, 93, 262, 267, 397,
    401–402, 424, 427, 435–436, 473, 553, 556,
    607
University of Michigan, 140, 152, 546, 557, 562,
    564–565
University of Pennsylvania, 75, 115, 216, 477, 492,
    529, 546, 556
University of Pittsburgh, 160, 251–252
University of Southern California (USC), 477,
    484–485
University of Southwestern Louisiana, 127, 129,
    442
Upgrading annual gifts, 458–465
U.S. Congress
    House Ways and Means Oversight Subcommit-
    tee, 20, 67, 225–226, 252
    legislation passed and proposed since 1994, xvi,
    50, 65–67, 220–221, 226, 252, 257, 260,
    269–270, 292, 354, 527, 529–530,
    571–572, 575, 618–619
U.S. Olympic Committee, 78, 296, 298
U.S. Supreme Court landmark cases, 167, 241,
    278, 291
    Maryland v. Joseph H. Munson Co., 225, 232,
    240, 277
    *Riley v. National Federation of the Blind of North
    Carolina*, 225, 234, 240, 277, 293
    *Village of Schaumburg v. Citizens for a Better
    Environment*, 224, 277

V

Vending machines, *see* Honor boxes

W

Watchdog groups
    Evangelical Council for Financial Account-
    ability (ECFA), 243

National Charities Information Bureau (NCIB), 229, 242–243, 255, 287, 290
Philanthropic Advisory Service (PAS), 242–243, 250, 257, 290, 295, 297
Watson and Hughey, 21, 122, 234, 240–241, 244, 274, 280–282, 284, 286–290, 309
Wealth
    American perspective of, 41–43, 619–621
    concentration of, 450, 617–619
    upper income individuals, 615–617

Working with the board, 202–204, 446–449
Working with the CEO, 204–207, 445, 446

Y

Yale University, 327, 479–483, 487, 546, 548, 550, 562–563
YMCA, 130, 137, 142–143, 156, 158–160, 175, 249, 258, 311, 321, 361, 459, 544
YWCA, 78, 159, 314, 361